ENFANT TERRIBLE:

THE TIMES AND SCHEMES OF GENERAL ELLIOTT ROOSEVELT

Chris Hansen

August 2012

ENFANT TERRIBLE:
The Times and Schemes of General Elliott Roosevelt

For inquiries, comments, and requests contact
Able Baker Press,
5250 N. Mt. Lemmon Short Rd.
Tucson, AZ 85749
Email ablebakerpress.com

Front cover photograph is an AP Wirephoto of Lt. Col. Elliott Roosevelt unloading a reconnaissance camera from an aircraft, taken January 1943 in Algeria. Original purchased from Historic Images, 2012. Cover design by author.

Library of Congress Catalog Number: 2012914881
ISBN: 0-615668925
ISBN-13: 978-0-615-66892-5

Contents

PREFACE

Although it follows the thread of one man's life, this book is not about one single subject. Instead, it links together a number of seemingly unrelated issues and events by examining the career of a now mostly forgotten Air Force officer – who just happened to be the son of the president.

Following this highly twisted track, we can travel from the rum-running days of Prohibition to the sand seas of the Sahara; from the hot embrace of Howard Hughes's starlets to Greenland's ice fields; from Texas oil tycoons battling federal taxes to inebriated world leaders carving up Europe. We end with a remarkable profusion of swindlers, gangsters and dictators settling their scores.

There's a lot of dubious entertainment along the way – fast women and faster airplanes, booze, dirty politics, dirtier money; even an unsettling number of very large dogs. At times the reader is likely to be shocked and appalled. The writer was.

But we will also see how the United States learned how to map the world and conquer the oceans by air, and with its closest ally create the new science of air reconnaissance, the definitive tool of world domination. We will watch America's brief romance with Marshal Stalin flourish and then founder. We will uncover more than the proverbial iceberg-tip of the corrupt and volatile mix of politics, the defense industry, and organized crime.

All along, we shall have a front-row seat to the furious but now dimly remembered battle over the Roosevelt legacy; with luck we can rip open some wounds that have, even after seventy years, by no means healed.

This is emphatically not a political book, but inevitably some will think so because of its revelations of criminal conduct in the Roosevelt family, including some directly attributable to the president. However overwhelming the amount of shady deals described herein, there were numerous additional alleged schemes whose pursuit seemed unlikely to lead anywhere, and most evidence has at any rate probably evaporated by now. These are not political issues. On the contrary, it is striking just how politically flexible, even chameleonic the Roosevelts actually were. As always, Eleanor, the first lady, provided the exception.

Eight Elliott Roosevelt scandals required some level of Congressional investigation, and some of them implicated the president. A much greater number did not rise to that level; and many more potential controversies managed to fly under the radar until now. Like him or not, there is no question that had the political correlation of forces differed, President Roosevelt could have been impeached for several of these.

However controversial FDR's political and economic legacy remains today, the scandals are a separate issue from the immense and bitterly contested changes the United States underwent from 1933 to 1945. Without FDR and his flamboyant family in charge, history might well have followed a somewhat similar path, but it would probably have been much less entertaining.

Elliott Roosevelt was the quintessential Kilroy. He was at home in not only the White House, but the Kremlin, Chequers, and innumerable lesser headquarters. He was the fly on the wall at five world-shaping summits. Afterwards he was determined to tell all, and then some. Always on his trail, criminal and congressional investigators had no need of thumbscrews; Elliott talked, wrote, and gestured with relish. Yet he skated from every scandal, every time.

Along with his almost equally controversial brothers, Elliott was long a mainstay of "gossip news." In the 1930s and 1940s, everyone knew his name. Its mention might provoke laughter, gagging, head-shaking, or spitting fury. But his zig-zag track through history yields insights hard to obtain otherwise, even if we have to lift a great number of rocks in the process, and trip over critters whose existence we never suspected.

I became interested in the subject because Elliott Roosevelt had been instrumental in locating and founding Arctic air bases, at some of which I had once served. Veterans of these unique installations find their historical origins a matter of great fascination, comparable perhaps to the continuing love of the land-taking sagas that inform the northern peoples of their beginnings.

Initially, I was entirely focused on Elliott's aviation work. I certainly did not set out to write his biography. If it turned out thus, it was the result of increasingly startling revelations that simply could not be ignored. He made me do it.

Still, the emphasis is not on the rogue Elliott, but on the troubles he got into. Not that there is a single great career or extraordinary adventure defining his life's work. On the contrary, Elliott's trajectory forms a twisted, intermittent smoke trail like one left by a defective rocket. The only common theme is his incredible ability to pop up where history was made, good and bad.

My goal has been to tunnel under the official history, or at least throw a sideways light at it. Few are alive today who remember the controversies of the 1930s and 1940s. The rest of us, as consumers of second-hand history, often fall victim to orthodoxy and panegyrics. The critical inflection point occurs when the last people who remember the events die, and history is handed off to a professional class. Context and contemporary chaos is lost; false inevitability and rote formulae are substituted. The Roosevelt era exemplifies the vast divergence of "received" history – what most people now "think" it was all about – from the contemporary assessment.

A sideways look, rather than a top-down one, can help restore the balance. The utility of this approach was confirmed when Elliott's FBI file yielded deeply incriminating material on the president himself.

My emphasis has been on the aviation aspects, not simply because they are interesting to me, but also because Elliott – at the age of 23 already given to grandiose declarations – called aviation his life's work. Despite the postwar era's ceaseless and highly repetitive retelling of the FDR years, little has been said about how the Roosevelts affected the aviation issues they involved themselves in.

Most professionals have overlooked Elliott's crucial role in developing the art and science of air reconnaissance. If all that his enemies said of him were true, that accomplishment would still secure his place in aviation history. For this reason, aviation historians should find this book of particular interest.

Both Roosevelts, father and son, played crucial roles in the development of civilian and military aviation. Since these initiatives left their imprints in mostly forgotten archives, there is much new to be said about them. Some of Elliott's military operations were very important, but his role in them (if not always the operations themselves) has been utterly neglected.

For example, the Soviet-American shuttle-bombing project has gained little attention compared to its lasting significance, perhaps because it left few people looking good. Likewise, the coup-like, wholesale transformation of American aviation in 1934 has gained only cursory attention from FDR's political chroniclers. At first the subject seems arcane, and people have forgotten how life-changing the New Deal was to aviation; certainly young Elliott's shadowy but significant role has been wrongly allowed to fade from the pages of history.

Although the wartime summits Elliott Roosevelt attended were of unsurpassed historical importance, there is no need here to reiterate the diplomatic details of them. The emphasis is on what they looked like to Elliott and his friends, among whom General Arnold, chief of the Air Corps, and General Eisenhower, supreme Allied commander in Europe, were the most important.

This subject leads inevitably to the controversy over whether Elliott was, in the jargon of the day, a communist fellow-traveler, and to the vicious settling of scores after his father's death. About these matters people tend to have strong opinions, but few new facts. Again, Elliott's fast-falling star provides insight into the real climate of that short but crucial post-war phase.

Elliott's post-war career was increasingly tragicomical. Yet again, it's not the booze, women, and squandered fortunes that are of primary interest; it's the way he got involved with important events and people. That many of these people were dictators and criminals heighten the interest, if not the sympathy.

Because Elliott Roosevelt was a public person who simply could not stay out of trouble, it has been fairly straightforward to track his progress and setbacks. Also, the Roosevelt family is one of the most studied and written-about in history. Elliott's own voluminous writings, maddening as they might be in their repetitions as well as their omissions, ensured that the man need not go unheard.

There was no danger of that in his own time, and it will not happen here.

The serious reader or researcher will profit from first reading the section "Sources and Methods," which follows the Illustrations. It describes the source material and methodology used for this work. The endnotes (last section) document sources; footnotes are used only to convey additional information.

The main text concludes with a condensed version of some of the documents and interviews critical to the subject, including Elliott's own words. They should be of special interest to aviation historians.

Reference maps follow sections II, III, IV, and V.

I. BEFORE THE WAR

THE IMMACULATE COMMISSION

July 1941 found the second son of the President of the United States slogging through the mapless tundra of Baffin Island, looking for a big flat place.

The Arctic has attracted more than its share of colorful characters. In the case of Elliott Roosevelt, though, this brief dabble in arctic exploration usually fades into the background, obscured by the scandals that trailed him like wake turbulence throughout his life. Still, this highly specialized undertaking was a cornerstone of a short but high-flying career that almost magically intersected with some of the most critical turns in aviation, in military history, and in great power rivalry.

Elliott was the fourth child, third son, and second surviving son of President Franklin D. Roosevelt and Eleanor Roosevelt. His illustrious surname opened many doors for him. It also earned him more than his share of public scorn. One cannot survey his career without constantly puzzling over who was right, those who despised him or those who found in him an American hero. For example, his wartime work may have saved countless lives, yet he has been accused of at least two murders (one merely attempted). And that's not counting the numerous murders he made up as a writer.

This persistent ambiguity is a faint echo of the receding, but by no means settled dispute over FDR's own legacy. Only at a great remove, and with sufficient indulgence, does the Roosevelt era seem a time of selfless heroes saving the world. Viewed with a contemporary eye, both the New Deal and the subsequent intervention in Europe transcended ordinary political controversy and caused a bitter domestic schism. Even today, that wound persists.

The young Elliott Roosevelt had a truly meteoric career in the military. He walked in as a captain in 1940, and left as a brigadier general less than five years later. Was nepotism a factor in this startling ascent? Many thought so; more precisely, they were damned sure of it. Yet it is indisputable that the man did make important, even unique contributions, and that – when kept on a short enough leash – he served his president, both the father and the commander-in-chief, ably and bravely.

When the United States reluctantly adopted conscription in September 1940, Elliott was in a quandary similar to that faced by many young men in troubled times (a few later presidents surely come to mind). Then, as later, it was a common device, if morally ambiguous, to seek a commission in the Reserves or National Guard. But, as we shall soon see, Elliott had other reasons for this preemptive strike. For one thing, he urgently needed to escape his creditors.

Although he was subject to the just enacted and still contentious draft registration, most likely Elliott would not have been conscripted anyway. The initial modest measure excluded him both on grounds of age and family dependents. But not serving when his father – as his enemies claimed – was relentlessly scheming to send others to war would have looked bad. And the election was six weeks away.

Eleanor Roosevelt spoke out about the draft days before her son signed up. She thought that her four sons should all be conscripted – in preference to younger men whose families depended on them. Whether that helped make up Elliott's mind is not clear, but Eleanor was certainly right that it would set an awful example if her progeny shirked their patriotic duties. Eleanor's ideological instincts were revealed by her interpreting the draft as only the precursor to universal national service by all. She hoped for "permanent legislation for 'service training' as distinct from military training. Such service would include old and young, men and women." [1]

Her well-intentioned belief in sending everyone to forced labor camps for a period was oft repeated.[2] If she realized that such statements stoked fears of an emerging new fascist America, she was tone-deaf to the concern.

Unlike his wife, Franklin Roosevelt was a realist. Getting conscription passed in peacetime was enough of a struggle. Whether his sons served was up to them.

In his first memoir, *As He Saw It* (1946), Elliott freely admits discussing the issue with his father in the White House. It does appear that Elliott thought this preemptive step could save him from future trouble. He was pretty sure he'd soon be in uniform anyway, so why not get a head start?

Since he already had an aviation background, his natural choice was the U.S. Army Air Corps. He wanted to be a pilot, although he knew his defective eyesight precluded that.[i] Finally, starting as a captain seemed eminently fair to him; besides the relevance of his civilian experience, he turned thirty on 23 September 1940, the same day he took the oath of military service. [3]

On that solemn occasion, Elliott could not resist issuing an unctuous statement: "No matter what the sacrifice it is important for all young people to join up and take part in the defense program." [4]

He completely misjudged public reaction.

By a family yardstick, Elliott had ironically picked the shorter straw. In 1936, his elder brother James had been made a Marine Corps lieutenant colonel fresh off the street so that he could serve his father as an "assistant" in Washington. James got to go with the president on his South American cruise, looking most majestic in his Marine uniform. At home, not everyone appreciated this touch of royalty; as a result of searing criticism, especially in the military, he voluntarily retreated to captain rank. [5]

Throughout the 1930s, Jimmy had enthusiastically and aggressively used his numerous positions and offices to profit from his father's name and influence. The negative publicity had gotten so bad that he decided to rejoin at a lower rank, and earn his way up – which he did. [6]

FDR was not lacking in ability to secure appropriate positions for his friends and acquaintances, especially in the military. For example, during the Great War, when he was Assistant Secretary of the Navy, he had made his favorite female, Lucy Mercer, enlist in the Navy, and then arranged for her to work as his assistant.[ii]

When the next war came, Lucy's four stepsons (the Rutherfurds) also secured their preferred military assignments via Oval Office intervention. [7]

In yet another example of presidential favor, famous broadcaster and friend Arthur Godfrey was given a commission and became a naval aviator although he couldn't pass

---

[i] The USAAC became the USAAF in June 1941 and the USAF in September 1947. It was a dvision of the Army until then. Regardless, "Air Force" suffices in common usage.

[ii] Collier: 220. Lucy Mercer's long relationship with FDR was a rather well-known secret even at the time. It should be viewed in context of the pulchritudinally challenged Eleanor's coldness, Lucy's charms, and later the president's illness. Many now believe it was not polio, but Guillain-Barré that crippled him. According to both James and Elliott, the president's penis was not paralyzed. The sexual antics, probably exaggerated, of both Franklin and Eleanor have gained enormous and hardly justifiable historical attention.

the physical with his injured legs. FDR asked if he could walk. This being affirmed, he retorted, "I'm commander-in-chief and I can't walk, so give it to him." [8]

It may sound charming, but it was a hell of way to run a Navy.

Elliott clearly acted of his own volition, though. A catalyst for his sudden fit of patriotism – not that he mentioned it – was his failed broadcasting business and the several hundred thousand dollars he owed and couldn't repay. The loans, some of which were obtained through the considerable persuasive powers of the president, would become a toxic issue five years later when Congress investigated his financial affairs.

During an entire week in 1945, General Roosevelt endured the well-earned indignity of a grueling interrogation by Bureau of Internal Revenue (BIR) investigators. In that context, he was pressed to recall that his debts to several high-profile creditors would be suspended while he was in the Army. He said:

> ER: Up until the middle of 1941 I anticipated that I would probably be coming out of the Army very quickly but then as the war became more and more imminent, I became discouraged.
>
> BIR: Did any of your other creditors bother you during 1940 and 1941?
>
> ER: Numerous contacts were made by the other creditors to endeavor to secure payment of interest and principal mostly by phone with my representatives in Texas. [9]

Whatever the real reason, by the fall of 1940 Junior was clearly ready for a change.

To join up, Elliott did not shuffle into his local Fort Worth recruitment office. His first step was to look up an acquaintance, Major General Henry "Hap" Arnold, who happened to be commander of the Army Air Corps and in practice directly subordinate to General George Marshall, Army Chief of Staff.[i] Elliott wrote later:

> I'd known Hap Arnold when he was a lieutenant colonel, stationed out at March Field in California, years before. Father had a high regard for Hap's ability and his ideas; by 1940 Arnold was a major general and commander of the Army Air Forces. It was logical for me to drop in to say hello to him, and find out from some officer on his staff what I could do about joining up. As a pilot, I hoped. [10]

Hap Arnold is today viewed as the father of the Air Force. His career spanned the entire period in which the Air Force was subordinate to the Army. Hap had learned to fly at the Wright Brothers' school at Huffman Prairie, Dayton, in 1911. [11]

Brash young Elliott had long been impressed with the highly seasoned Arnold's abilities. On 18 April 1934, he took it upon himself to tell his father to promote Arnold to brigadier general. Arnold was indeed promoted in March 1935. Elliott's telegram confidently stated:

> Col. Arnold – in charge March Field and Western Division Army Air Mail – Would like to see Col. Arnold get appointment as Brigadier General. [12]

This presumptuous advice neatly bookends with Arnold's own recommendation of Elliott to the same rank ten years later.

---

[i] In 1940, Arnold was chief of the Air Corps, which became the Army Air Forces next year. With the creation of the independent Air Force in 1947, he became the only-ever General of the Air Force (5-star).

The importance of Elliott's impromptu telegram can easily be overestimated, but the next decade's friendship between Elliott and Hap truly was important. Arnold had enemies in the White House and held a precarious position with the president, at least until 1941. Despite his enormous achievements in the air, his intellectual deficiencies and naïvety were more noticeable in the company of Generals Marshall and Eisenhower, not to speak of the British top brass. Hap's careful management of the Elliott account was important to his survival.[13]

Although Arnold's promotion was well-earned, and there is no evidence Elliott actually caused it, the episode is an example of the irregular ways in which decisions that are supposed to be highly structured may actually come about. Elliott had every right to write approvingly of public servants to his father, and to register his opinions of all and sundry. He had no business interfering with promotions, nor should he have messed with laws and regulations, or – even worse – contract awards and licensing grants. But as long as "Pops" was in office, "Bunny" would have a hard time understanding that.

By 1940, when Elliott asked him for a job, Arnold knew him well, though possibly "not well enough." The two would continue to help each other out; Hap maintained to his dying day that he was very impressed with Elliott's contributions to the Air Force.

About his difficult military debut, Elliott continued in his memoirs:

> But as a pilot, it was no go. The physical they gave me was enough: they told me I was definitely unfit for combat service, that I'd have to sign waivers even to get an administrative job. I grabbed at that chance; the officers I talked to thought my experience as a radio network executive would be valuable in the procurement division; and my age at the time qualified me for a reserve commission as captain – that part of it was routine. [14]

Though it was soon disputed, in this case Elliott's version was the truth. His eyesight was poor, his height was 6'3", and his weight and age already excessive for new pilots. He was lucky to get a desk job. Yet he had always known that his eyesight was a problem; and when he was finally separated from the Air Forces in 1945, a well-connected gossip columnist revealed the hilarious tidbit that General Elliott Roosevelt had spent his entire military career classified 4-F, the draft category for defectives unacceptable for military duty.[15]

On the face of it, joining up was both shrewd and commendable at a time when war clouds loomed on both eastern and western horizons. His father was proud of him. That hadn't happened much lately. Elliott happily said that the president, with his assembled family, drank a toast to him. He claimed to have won a new and lasting closeness with his father.[16]

Elliott was at the White House from 19-21 September, celebrating his birthday, and he remembered his father's proud toast to his old age.[17]

He did not mention that his brothers promptly held an "indignation meeting" to ridicule him. James, the eldest, was actually already in the Marine Corps Reserve; he was called to active duty, also in September 1940. Franklin Jr. and the youngest, John, would follow in due course, both in the Navy, as family tradition preferred.[18]

Interestingly, Jimmy was already a civilian pilot; he had learned to fly during his brief Hollywood career, along with Jimmy Stewart, the already-famous actor. Stewart later said that the one movie James Roosevelt produced was the worst he'd ever played in.[i] Jimmy admitted it might be the worst movie ever made.[19] Stewart, however, became as successful in the air as he already was in cinema; he commanded a bomber wing and retired as an Air Force brigadier general. James Roosevelt also eventually became a brigadier, but in the Marine Corps Reserve.

Captain Elliott Roosevelt was given a painfully dull assignment as a procurement officer in the Air Corps (Specialist Reserve) at Wright Field, near Dayton, Ohio – the nerve center of Air Corps research, development, and materiél. With his background in aviation and radio, that seemed perfectly reasonable. General Arnold said he personally selected the procurement assignment for his new captain – a job so civilian in nature it required no uniform.[20]

The posting was probably a bit more important than Elliott thought. Dayton (technically Springfield, now home to Wright-Patterson AFB) was the site of the Wright Brothers' first airfield. Then and now the city was a technological nexus for both civil and military aviation. Wright Field would play a critical role in the development of the Air Force, especially before flight testing was moved to sunny but lonesome corners of the Mojave Desert.

Elliott testified later that "the purpose of my commission was to have me work on radio matters, with which I was familiar…," but:

> However, as often has happened in the Army, they evidently lost my qualifications file, and the purpose for which I was commissioned, because when I went to Wright Field I had everything to do with every other subject but radio. [21]

That's typical of the military, of course, but it is surprising that it should happen to the president's son. It is the more startling since the Army paper-pushers must have been the only people in the country who didn't know of Elliott's controversial career in radio. For years, his broadcast opinions had been nearly inescapable.

I Want to be a Captain, Too!

The new captain was stunned by the outrage his unexpected rank triggered. It was only six weeks before the general election, and the already agitated public immediately went on a rampage against him. Elliott wrote later that he received about 35,000 letters and postcards expressing opinions which, he claimed, mostly seemed to require anonymity. He even triggered a popular movement expressed in "I wanna be a captain too" clubs, ballads, and buttons, although this profound cultural phenomenon was clearly manipulated by the Republican Party.[22]

The lyrics of the catchy song are indicative of what many people felt about not only Elliott, but about his father's ominous and unprecedented third term as president:

> *A Captain's bars are burnished, and they glitter in the sun.*
> *Their wearers are the wise ones, who have all their duties done.*
> *I haven't passed the courses, and I haven't done "squads rights,"*
> *But I guess I'd be a Captain, if by Dad was big and bright.*

---

[i] JR: My Parents, 254-6; The film was *Pot O' Gold* (1941). He was quoted 15 MAR 57 by AP (Indiana Evening Gazette), but also mentioned four other "worst" films.

I want to be a Captain – a Captain in the U.S. Army Corps;
I had my CC training – while Elliott spouted radio and I'm sore.
I have no friends in Washington, ain't got no party pull;
But when it comes to common sense, you bet I'm no darn fool;
Chorus: OOH, I want to be a Captain, a Captain in the U.S. Army Corps!

Fuhrer Hitler made his Captains, from his secret chosen few;
Il Duce followed Hitler, and he made his Captains too.
They've wrecked the whole of Europe, and brought misery and tears;
Now King Franklin makes his Captains, and he asks for four more years.

I haven't had the courses, and I haven't made the grade;
I can't shoot a pistol, I can't pass on parade.
But Father was the Chief, and he knew his stuff.
He just whispered to "my friends" and my friends ran the bluff.

I haven't been to Hyde Park, and I'm not known up there;
I have no pull in Washington, and I'm not treated fair.
My Congressman's not friendly; King Franklin doesn't care.
So I'll have to be a private, and the burden I must bear.[i]

The "captain, too" movement is one of those frivolous but intense political episodes that is now mercifully forgotten, yet at the time it clearly riled millions. One fellow who noticed this in his own home was none other than General Arnold:

> The sons of famous people are always targets for criticism. When I commissioned Elliott Roosevelt as a Captain in the Air Corps I was severely taken to task and all kinds of stories were circulated. One evening as I sat down at my own dinner table, I saw that my own son, David, aged fourteen, had a button in his lapel. It read, "Papa, I want to be a Captain too!" [23]

A prime reason for the outrage was that peacetime conscription went into effect at this same time, so the issue was acutely personal for many young men. Those between 19 and 36 years of age – 16½ million in all – had to register for selective service beginning on 15 October, although that didn't mean they would necessarily be drafted. To the nation's families, the draft was an ill omen as well as a highly publicized bureaucratic exercise. It was vitally important that it was administered with fairness and universality – and perceived to be so.[24]

It was the first peacetime draft in U.S. history. As a form of involuntary servitude, the draft was and remains a tender point in the American constitutional and ideological corpus. But after the fall of France, most Americans could see where things were headed. Grudgingly, a majority went along with FDR's registration drive; but they keenly patrolled its fairness.

That's why so many people flew into a rage when Elliott's seemingly cushy new job was revealed. It didn't help that the kid already had a purple reputation for self-seeking shenanigans. Veterans were as much enraged as those preparing to register; officers of

---

[i] ER File, John Boettiger papers, FDR Lib. In a letter of 8 October 41 to Boettiger, L.A. Casey, Chairman of the "Southern Conference of No Third Term Democrats," in Tennessee, took credit for instigating the song and associated campaign. Casey offered $10 for each additional appropriate verse accepted and used.

the American Legion wrote scathing diatribes against the nepotism and cronyism that seemed so obviously involved.[25]

Apparently, the tone of public debate was no more elevated then than it is now. It seemed perfectly fair to kick not only the president, but also his children. The kids had already become scarecrows of the New Deal. For example, it is quite likely that Wendell Willkie, the rather genteel Republican challenger in 1940, got more votes out of the Elliott scandal than he earned from his own initiatives, especially considering that he was not a neutralist and thus could not exploit anti-war sentiment.

Willkie was considered by many to be a fake candidate, a mugwump, because he had recently switched parties and was a committed internationalist. After his defeat, he would go on to serve President Roosevelt in a diplomatic function. As a nice guy, he did not hit too hard on the admittedly phony Captain Elliott issue. At one meeting, he was interrupted by a young man yelling, "I wanna be a captain, too" and Willkie deftly answered, "You don't belong to the right family." [26]

"Did you get to be a captain?" shouted another supporter at a rally when Willkie recounted his own hard time in the Army. "Yes, but I was recommended for it only after two years of hard work." [27]

One of Elliott's chief accusers was the retired general and influential columnist Hugh S. Johnson, who had been a prominent administrator in the early stages of the New Deal. After a few years he had turned on President Roosevelt, and indeed noted in September 1940 that "if he is not beaten, we have seen the last of American democracy as we have known it and loved it." He was "uncertain that we haven't got a pretty good imitation of Hitler in the White House right now." [28]

General Johnson's views were particularly germane because he had been the administrator of President Woodrow Wilson's conscription program, but by now he was a prominent neutralist and America Firster. Coming from a New Deal apostate, his newspaper column mattered to many.

General Johnson's tirade against Elliott ran in the papers on 30 Sep 1940:

> While President Roosevelt was declaring the selective service act is deadly serious business and that nobody must be allowed to put over any "clever little schemes" to get one boy out of the draft while another, with no more reason not to serve, is taken, his own son, Elliott, was commissioned and called to service as a captain in the air corps.
>
> As a flier? Oh, deah, no. A young man has to work and train for that. Elliott goes in as what airmen call derisively a "kee-wee" – a bird without wings.
>
> He didn't apply to any recruiting office. The head of the Army air corps, General Arnold, himself, assigned him from the "specialists reserve" to a job in "procurement" – which means something to do with buying supplies. When asked what kind of a specialist Elliott claimed to be, the official said that was "confidential." As a captain, he will draw $200 a month, plus allowances that may be as high as $116 a month.
>
> At his age of 30, he would have been in the selective draft pool. There he would have been subject to serve, as Woodrow Wilson said, "not in that place that will most pleasure him but where it shall best serve the common good."
>
> He might have served in some "specialty" – but that would have been decided not by him but by his qualifications in fair competition with all other boys – as also would the place and condition of his service. His compensation would have been $30 and not $200 a month. He would have been honored by having to wear the uniform and not "privileged" as is reported in the press of this new captain to wear civilian clothes.
>
> "No matter what the sacrifices," Captain Roosevelt is quoted as saying, "it is important for all young people to join up and take part in the defense program."

> Okeh, but could your boy "join up" in this soft fashion? "Try and do so" or "It's nice work if you can get it."
>
> Now the president's second son will not even have to register for the draft or take his place on a footing of equality with all other young Americans of his age. Without any discernible military training, preparation or qualifications, and without any known preparation in "procurement," he is made a "captain" by the scratch of a pen and an officer and a gentleman by act of congress.
>
> There might be a worse way to lead off this great democratic and equalitarian crusade in decency called the draft, but I can't for the moment think what it is. It looks like hateful nepotism, favoritism and unfairness at the very head of the system. It is so raw that I am very sure of one thing – the president either did not know about it, or else didn't give any thought to the implications. I doubt that Elliott did, either.
>
> The only real trouble with that kid is that he has no inferiority complex. Guiltless as I believe this act was of heart, it ought to be undone just as quickly as it was performed. Otherwise it will remain a stench to Heaven.[29]

The row gave Elliott Roosevelt an opportunity to engage in one of his endlessly recurring tasks: composing indignant, angry, wounded denials. To the "disgusting old man" Johnson, who had "never occupied any position except at a desk, far from the dangers of dropping shell fragments," Captain Roosevelt had this message:

> If he had had the decency to check into the true facts, he would have discovered that I volunteered for any service and asked no special assignment. He would have discovered that under terms of the act I would not be subject to call now under the draft, because I have a wife and two children.
>
> Furthermore, the gentleman states that I will draw a salary of $200 a month plus allowances that may be as high as $116. I would like to point out that at present I enjoy an income a great many times in excess of this amount, all of which must be sacrificed as a result of my going into government service.
>
> I would like to state definitely… that I did not ask for any special assignment of any type and did not ask for any designation as an officer or make any request as to salary. I merely volunteered for service.
>
> If, on the basis of my past record, I have been assigned to procurement, all I can say is that I am sorry, because I would much rather have been assigned to active flying duty, and hope that the opportunity will arise in the future where I may be transferred to this division.[30]

Amid the cries of "tin soldier," "draft dodger," and "shyster" Elliott fought back gallantly, but his mother noted that he was "extremely bitter." [31]

His father was bitter as well. The president came close to delivering an angry nationwide address defending his son. We know this because a primitive and purely experimental tape-recording system had just been installed in the Oval Office, and for 1940 we have a few badly muffled recordings of the president's verbalized contemplations. Sometime in September, FDR delivered a histrionic soliloquy to his aide Lowell Mellett, intending it to be the germ of a speech: [32]

> Now, these are the facts. You've got a boy, you've got a boy who's 30 years old. Tried to get into the Naval Academy *12 years ago*. They took one look at his eyes and said, "Why, heavens above, he could no more qualify than [fly]!" Thereupon, *without* going to college – mind you, a lot of the editorials said he went to college – Harvard! – he went into the airplane business, and he obtained a very great familiarity with the construction of

> planes…this is *your* boy. He goes in to serve. He has his eyes checked. One eye can see 2/20th, *2/20th*s. The left eye can see 3/20ths. He is told that going into the Army or the Navy, either one, he would be put in the home guard…they couldn't possibly…put him in any active service in the Army or the Navy, and they wouldn't do it…
>
> He says, "All right, *Love* to do it. Put me to work. What can you put me in as – a private?" – "No." "Well, I'm not asking to be an *officer*." "Well," I say, "we're awfully sorry but the only way we can take you in is as an *officer*." He says, "Alright, put me in as the lowest *kind* of officer." They say, "We can't do it. We have to put you in as a captain." He said, "I don't rate a captain." "Well, if you were 35, we'd put you in as a *major*!" <recording ends>.

The furious private reaction revealed here closely mirrored the one FDR had five years later, when he ordered the Air Force to make Elliott a pilot and a general. But in 1940, fortunately he thought better of speaking out in public. Instead, he cunningly allowed the Republicans to overdo it with their unfair accusations.

Withal the uproar made enough of an impression that Elliott, a serious liability to his father in this election as in several others, attempted to prove his courage in more obvious ways.

As an instant captain, Elliott did not need to worry about boot camp and its attendant indignities. He didn't even have to wear a uniform. Before joining the service, Elliott was allowed a couple of weeks to disentangle himself from his exceedingly complicated business matters back in Texas.

He and his wife Ruth had a 1,330 acre ranch in Benbrook, twelve miles southwest of Fort Worth. It was, according to frequent visitor Eleanor Roosevelt, a delightfully serene and secluded place. Quiet and serene was not, however, Elliott's style.[33]

Though busy as a radio executive, Elliott had taken to raising Great Danes and Arabian horses, reveling in the manners and style of a Texas rancher and gentleman – although that overlap seemed tenuous at times. It must not have been an easy life to leave, yet he never could stay in one place for long. His five years in Texas was a record for him. But by 1940, Elliott was flat broke and in deep trouble with his creditors.[34]

When Elliott finally did get to Wright Field – he was initially supposed to show up on Monday, 7 October – his military career immediately took a highly unusual turn.[35]

It must have been a unique experience to join the colors under the microscope of relentless, hostile national attention. As the Roosevelt family was motoring from Texas, a new poem circulated among the politically engaged:

> *I am a dashing captain*
> *In the good old U.S.A.,*
> *For Papa is the President*
> *and always has his way.*
> *He thinks his sons are just too good*
> *to carry gun and pack;*
> *To march and train and drill with boys*
> *from down across the track.*
> *So while those boobs are slaving hard*
> *for just one buck a day,*
> *I'll cock my feet upon a desk*
> *and draw a captain's pay.*[36]

Elliott and Ruth had driven from Fort Worth to Dayton and arrived on Wednesday. He reported for duty at the gate, and was resolutely refused entry until he finally convinced the skeptical sentry of his identity and business. There was no room at the base, so the Roosevelts, with their two young children, had to take hotel quarters in Dayton. They were subjected to catcalls on the street.[37]

Next day, Thursday, Elliott finally got to serve in the Army. On Saturday, he resigned. On that same day, 12 October, President Franklin D. Roosevelt stopped by on an inspection trip of Ohio military installations. He left again on Sunday, having visited for a few minutes with Elliott, who got squeezed into an intense schedule that included an important nationwide foreign policy address.

Son told father about his troubles and his decision to resign.

Monday, Elliott again submitted his resignation, and again it was turned down.[38]

The president's Ohio visit was, of course, a poorly camouflaged campaign trip. He toured a number of bases and received a 21-gun salute as he entered the enormous Wright Field installation. The Materiel Division commander, Brigadier General Oliver Echols, gave FDR the grand tour of the base, although the paralyzed guest remained seated in his convertible automobile. Echols was also Elliott's commander.[39]

On his Ohio visit, President Roosevelt was accompanied by his air force chief, General Hap Arnold. When Elliott dropped by the president's train car, Hap stuck around. Elliott pleaded his case to the commander-in-chief. He remembered the encounter this way:

> When General Arnold came back to the lounge, Father told him what I'd asked. "I'm going to leave this one up to you, Hap," he said. "It's your problem. Do with it what you want." And he turned away, to the window. [40]

Elliott's story had changed slightly by 1975:

> I saw Father alone for five or ten minutes on his train to talk about "Poppa, I Wanta Be a Captain, Too" and the damage it might bring on election day.
>
> "I'd like to resign," I said. – "You're talking to me now as Commander in Chief?" This with a twinkle in his eyes. Yes, I was. He had General Arnold come into the lounge car. "I'm going to leave this one up to you, Hap," he said, turning to look out the window.
>
> "What do you want to do?" my commanding officer said. "Reenlist as a private?"
>
> If I couldn't do that, I replied, I was thinking about the Royal Canadian Air Force.
>
> "Put your request for resignation through official channels. Give all your reasons. It'll be acted on." [41]

General Echols acted on it by very publicly refusing it.

After Elliott's second resignation on the Monday following FDR's visit, General Echols released an explanatory statement to the media. Its content illustrates the tough corner he was in: trying to expand his division of the Air Corps by an order of magnitude, yet having to juggle the hot political potato General Arnold had thrown him. Echols was forthright but unyielding:

> The publicity given to him by the press as the result of his having accepted a captaincy in the U.S. Army air corps special reserve, and his opinion that it might have an injurious effect on the selective service program, has caused Captain Elliott Roosevelt to

> submit his resignation to Brig. Gen. O. P. Echols, his commanding officer at Wright Field, with the intention of registering for the draft.
>
> General Echols has refused to accept his resignation on the grounds that Capt. Roosevelt's physical examination shows that his eyesight is such that it renders him unfit for either combat or flying duty. Due to the large amount of work resulting from the Air corps expansion program, it has become necessary for the air corps to commission a large number of non-flying reserves for duty in connection with the administrative, supply, inspection, procurement and engineering functions of the air corps materiel division at Wright Field, the air corps depots and field inspection units.
>
> Instructions from the chief of the Air Corps provide that these reserve officers will be commissioned from personnel not physically fit for flying and will be trained in administrative supply and procurement activities with the view of using them to replace physically fit flying officers now on this duty.
>
> There are now 25 non-flying officers on duty at Wright Field and additional officers of this class are being commissioned daily for duty at Wright Field and other air corps activities. Present instructions are to commission 400 additional specialist reserves in the grades of major and captain for duty with the materiel division. The regulations require that the officers commissioned will be in conformity with the age group. Specialists between the ages of 30 and 40 years of age will become captains and those above 40 years of age majors.
>
> With Captain Roosevelt's background in radio, he is perfectly capable of carrying on the duties to be required of him in regard to liaison work between the air corps and signal corps in connection with the procurement of aircraft equipment. His services are needed. He is signed up for one year for duty at Wright Field and his resignation will not be accepted. [42]

Elliott's physical defects – primarily, his eyesight – seemingly precluded his ever serving in combat, much less as a pilot. His mother Eleanor stated that he couldn't see ten feet without his glasses, an assertion that was quoted publicly.[43] But she wrote to friend Lorena Hickok that General Arnold himself had told her that Elliott:

> …couldn't be accepted in the draft or in the army as a private because, without his glasses, he can't see more than 10 ft. He can only get in on a commission on account of experience as a specialist of some kind, so resigning would do no good & he might as well stay put. Of course in case of war many of these regulations will go & then he could change. I am sorry for him…[44]

"Ten feet" is a misguided figure of speech; vision is limited by acuity, not distance. However, at some point thereabouts, Elliott "triumphantly told me that a new kind of lens which he had just acquired enabled him to take off and land an airplane, and he had his civilian-pilot's license." [45]

This seems to have been an exaggeration. He had a student certificate with a solo endorsement. He reportedly only held it for two years.[46] According to the FAA, Elliott did not get a private pilot certificate until 1955.[47]

It is true that civilian vision criteria allow for optical correction. The military is rarely so accommodating. One informed wag noted that: "Elliott Roosevelt has 2/20 of normal vision in one eye, 3/20 in the other, and he can't see why people make a fuss over his being a captain." [48] The quip agrees with flight surgeon records showing his visual acuity at 20/200, but *correctable* to 20/20.[49]

Elliott was also 6'3" and rather "bulky." Without some miracle Elliott would never have his wish to face the enemy.[50]

As was his by then already finely honed custom, Elliott did not take no for an answer. He demanded that his resignation request be forwarded immediately to Washington. On his own responsibility, General Echols refused to do so. This was treatment Elliott was definitely not accustomed to, and he still did not give up.[51]

It was only the first of the fights these two officers would have.

The captain now started a campaign of complaint that he described as a "systematic nagging of superior officers." The president's son was not happy, and evidently a lot of important people needed to know it.[52] Amusingly, this fight was in full public view, with laymen as well as experts taking sides, as was the drill whenever Elliott was in the news.[53]

Elliott was many things, but he was not a coward – on the contrary, he cherished physical danger to the point of recklessness. The threat to join the RCAF – utterly idle, since that esteemed outfit also required the gift of sight – is interesting because it became a pattern for Elliott, whenever he was under criticism, to demand a transfer to some more glamorous or dangerous position.

In the service, being a pain in the butt can often earn you a change of view, but not necessarily the one you had in mind.

A few months after his rebellion and the onset of his bureaucratic guerilla campaign, Elliott was sent to Bolling Field in the District of Columbia for training as an "air intelligence officer" – i.e., a reconnaissance expert – under the able direction of the young, dynamic Captain Lauris Norstad.[i] Technically, this was a transfer in-grade to the Air Reserve (from the Specialist Reserve), effective 21 February 1941. The course took the rest of the winter, the last one America was at peace.[54]

After training, Captain Roosevelt received a field assignment that brings to mind the proverb about being careful what you wish for. Elliott would be among the first Americans sent to Newfoundland to establish a U.S. presence on the "Rock" under the terms of the destroyers-for-bases deal with the United Kingdom, signed in August 1940.

Elliott Roosevelt was now even more unhappy. He noted:

> I hopefully applied for service somewhere in the sunshine – the Philippines, Hawaii, Panama, Bermuda. There was no trace of nepotism in the posting I ultimately received – as an air intelligence officer assigned to the 21st Reconnaissance Squadron in the woebegone wastes of Newfoundland.[55]

Captain Roosevelt's service record shows that he was not officially transferred from Wright Field to the 21st Recon Squadron until 24 April 1941. White House records show that Colonel Stratemeyer advised the president on 30 May that the squadron had landed in Newfoundland on 26 May.[56] In other words, Elliott was only up north for three months in summer, and about half that time he was on travel status.

Elliott would later maintain that he spent much longer in the Arctic. However, he had evidently finished with Materiel Command and General Echols months earlier. Correspondence shows that over the winter, he spent much time taking care of his own business matters, apparently from his ranch in Texas.[57] As is usually the case, the president's fingerprints are missing from Elliott's odd military assignments that winter.

---

[i] Lauris Norstad was then Assistant Chief of Staff for Intelligence, Air Force, at Langley, Virginia. He would rise to Supreme Commander Europe (SACEUR) by 1956. His papers are in the Dwight D. Eisenhower Presidential Library, Abilene, KS (DDE Lib).

An Auspicious Meeting

Although his couple of months at Wright Field had not been happy for Captain Roosevelt, much that happened there would help determine his next five years in the military. An unexpected dividend involved another highly controversial Air Force officer who got to meet both Roosevelts, father and son, on the base.

President Roosevelt's October 1940 visit to Wright Field had been the culmination of a triumphant campaign swing, during which the president visited not only the Columbus memorial in the state capital on Columbus Day, but also the Wright Flight memorial in Dayton, accompanied by no less than the surviving Orville Wright himself.[58]

The visit was a major Air Force occasion. Having brought General Arnold with him, FDR met also with Major General George Brett, the commander of the field, as well as Brig. Gen. Oliver Echols, chief of the Materiel Division. He enjoyed a modest air show of new aircraft, and toured the expansive facilities on the famous base.

As he drove past the exhibits in his open limousine – he did not dismount – FDR made the acquaintance of a somewhat notorious major, George W. Goddard. He was an expert – *the* expert – on aerial photography and reconnaissance, then a badly neglected field. Cunningly, Goddard had prepared for his allotted five minutes of fame by flying over the Roosevelt's Hyde Park compound and snapping some pictures.

When he showed the photographs to the president, the five minutes turned into half an hour of excited conversation. FDR acquired an interest in reconnaissance, Goddard's superiors were incensed, the president ordered numerous copies of the photos – and quite possibly thereafter associated his son Elliott, Major Goddard, and Wright Field with the intriguing new discipline of aerial photography. At the very least, President Roosevelt ordered Goddard to once more fly over Hyde Park to obtain color photographs, of which he obtained 200 prints, less the one Goddard kept for himself.[59]

Elliott Roosevelt and George Goddard, two of the founding fathers of Air Force reconnaissance, would later become friends and accomplices. Again, the Hyde Park picture did the trick. Goddard wrote:

> [Elliott] stopped by my lab one day and I presented him with the famous aerial color picture of Hyde Park. He was delighted to receive it, and we had a long session on aerial photography both generally and specifically. I took an immediate liking to him not just because of his curiosity but because of his straight-forward manner. Whether our conversation planted a seed that stirred his interest, I never knew, but soon afterward he transferred from Procurement to Aerial Reconnaissance.[60]

And though of short duration, that *would* actually be Elliott's life's work – at least if measured by its importance. But he was already thirty. By what long, winding trail had the son of the president arrived at this critical crossroads?

OIL, TEQUILA, AND AIRPLANES

In an unusual fit of modesty, Elliott said merely that he chose the Air Corps because "some years before I'd been a private pilot." [61]

In truth, during FDR's first two terms (1933-41) the young man had been a prominent participant in aviation's swift rise. In the estimation of his numerous enemies, he had left a slime trail of corruption. In his own mind, he was one of aviation's bigshots – or, at the very least, hung out with a good many of them. Always, ambiguity followed Elliott like two shadows.

It is necessary to take a step back to see why FDR's son was such an issue, whether inside or outside the military. Although Elliott is little remembered today, during the New Deal he and his brothers were known to just about everyone, and usually not in a nice way. Elliott's media attention brings to mind some of the overpublicized antics of royal offspring, but this controversy was certainly lacking in any respect for majesty.

Privilege and Entitlement

Love them or hate them, the Roosevelts of history were larger than life. Park rangers at their Hyde Park estate enjoy telling the story that Franklin Delano Roosevelt was an only son because he weighed in at ten pounds at birth, and Sara, his barely surviving mother, swore that there would be no more.

But out of the more stoic Eleanor, Franklin's third son Elliott emerged as a colossal baby of almost twelve pounds; and his fourth wife testified that he was the "shrimp" of the litter of five.[i] And in all respects Elliott lived large; he was the most uncontrollable, aggressive, and reckless of a rambunctious lot. As pilots say, he lived his life full-throttle.[62]

Those who see genetics behind everything might nod knowingly. Broken-hearted after the loss of baby Franklin Jr. ten months earlier, Eleanor named Elliott after her father, whom she utterly adored. Unfortunately, Elliott the elder, President Theodore Roosevelt's kid brother, was an insane alcoholic whose short but epically dissolute life ended with a botched suicide – the details are disputed.[63] It was his boundless charm and self-confidence the shy and deprived Eleanor preferred to remember.

An evocative account of Elliott senior's last days states:

> During the summer of 1894, Elliott completed his self-destruction. Two weeks after his drunken carriage wreck, a fatal attack of delirium tremens set in. He thrashed about and tried to hurl himself out of a window in a mad attempt to flee the monsters that had him at last. Finally he collapsed in a convulsive fit and expired.[64]

While Eleanor detested her mother, who seems to have been a narcissistic snake, she worshipped her father, whose love for her was effusive but unfortunately also elusive. Even more tellingly, her son Elliott, whose life exhibited striking parallels with his grandfather's, had a sunny and apologetic assessment of him that conflicts with all other sources.

---

[i] Oral History Interview (OHI) with Minnewa Bell, Elliott File, 63, FDR Lib. For the giant John, nr. 5, Eleanor had a special bed built by her Val-Kill furniture shop (Parks: Family in Turmoil, 146)

Elliott took great exception to the common depiction of his namesake. He said that Elliott senior actually died of a brain tumor. His drinking was an act of self-medication, and the madness was caused by the tumor: "He didn't die of drink at all!" He could possibly be right, but the remark does illustrate how the impression of a person can be spun a plumb 180 degrees when it serves one's needs.[65]

The account brother James left of the elder Elliott is much more negative, and is but one portrait in a rogue's gallery he painted in his memoirs. We are conditioned by history to associate the Roosevelts with great public accomplishments and a drive for public service. The almost supernatural energy that Eleanor's uncle Theodore Roosevelt put into his career was a distinct family trait, but it is easy to see how it could, with a slight nudge, be derailed into something cosmically destructive. Many of Elliott's relatives went insane or died of drink. James particularly remembered "Uncle Vallie" whose habit was to sit in the upstairs window of his property and shoot at people at random.[i] Eleanor said she escaped death only because Vallie was so drunk he couldn't hit anything.[66]

The bizarre American practice of copying full names down through the generations – seemingly defeating the purpose of first names – makes it a chore to keep track of all the Franklins and Theodores and Jameses and Elliotts. Eleanor's brother, who died in infancy, was Elliott Junior. Her son, our Elliott, begat another Elliott Junior with Ruth Googins in 1936, and he in turn produced Elliott III.

We need not get into all the Jameses and Franklins, but note dutifully that Elliott Roosevelt had two brothers named Franklin Junior, one being a replacement for an older sibling who died after a sickly few months the year before Elliott was born. This made Elliott nr. 2 after James (Jimmy), with whom we shall also become considerably acquainted hereinwith. Headstrong Anna was the first-born; the *ersatz* Franklin and the comparatively well-tempered John brought up the rear.

The older children thought that Eleanor "favored" or "coddled" her son Elliott, called "Bunny" by his father. Elder siblings usually think this, but in this case it was only a reflection of Eleanor's instinctual understanding that Elliott had special needs. She openly said: "Elliott was a sick and lonely child, and needed more tenderness than the others." [67]

Everyone noticed this. Without resentment, James wrote that Elliott received the most attention:

> You might say mother always liked Elliott best... She used to sigh and say he seemed to have inherited many of her father's traits: He was unreliable and always in trouble; he just seemed to demand her attention. I don't think father really had a favorite.[68]
>
> She did more for Elliott than for the rest of us. She always felt closest to Elliott, and it was no secret that she always felt he needed the most from her, that he was the one least able to manage on his own. The rest of us felt that way, too, and understood.[69]

For some reason, when James in old age reminisced about Elliott, he demanded that his remarks be kept secret until his brother was safely dead. He said:

> Oh, I think that mother worried about Elliott much more than she did about the rest of us, because she felt he was perhaps less stable, less sure of how and what he wanted to do. I think the fact that he was named after her father whom she associated certain

---

[i] JR: My Parents, 10. He was referring to Eleanor's maternal Uncle Valentine, a terrifying drunk.

> problems with and was afraid they might develop in Elliott, and saw in Elliott some of the characteristics that she had felt brought about the downfall of her father. And I think because of this, and the fact that he was sort of in the middle, it was Franklin and John as a team on one side and Anna and I as a team on the other side, and there was nobody for Elliott to team up with sort of made it a natural thing for her to feel, well, she would fill in the void in Elliott's life which wasn't there in Franklin and John's or in Anna's or mine. And I think also that Elliott's problems started early enough so that she began to have to worry about them earlier. You know, Anna and I got along, and neither of us were too much of a problem; we didn't make any real problems or have any real crises in our lives. [sic!] But Elliott had them from the time he was at Groton, and very deep problems. So I think all of these things added up together resulted in her feeling a feeling of responsibility for him that she wanted to try to see if she could help him overcome them. Elliott was, for instance, the only one of us who never went to college. And in mother's mind this had to indicate something. When he would disappear, as he did once out West, nobody knew where he was, just the way we don't know where he is now. [Laughter] Right this very minute. Just talked to brothers Franklin and John this morning; we don't know where he is. We've put some things in motion to find out.[70]

That opinion was colored by the enmity between the two brothers, a hatred (mostly on Elliott's side) which flared from time to time and deepened towards the end. Since James certainly wasn't without his own problems, it is likely that Elliott would have made some choice remarks, too; in his books he certainly set some barbs.

Eleanor and her children agreed that she had not been a good mother. She might have been good as a person, but she was clueless at child-rearing; her own tragic childhood provided no guidance. It certainly didn't help that father Franklin, another charming rogue, seemed not merely indulgent but an active co-conspirator with the rowdy bunch. The indulgence reached extraordinary heights when backed up by grandmother Sara Delano, who ran circles around Eleanor. Sara controlled the whole lot with her money, and she seems to have barely tolerated Eleanor as hired help with extra breeding duties.

Among many others, grandson Curtis noticed the peculiar paradox that Eleanor's formidable, undying reputation rests on her empathy for others and her never-flagging compulsion to serve noble causes. But as a mother and grandmother, she was cold and rigid, programmed and scheduled. She was the opposite of her husband.[71]

Despite that assessment, Eleanor's family correspondence was sappily florid, gushing in declarations of love. It might have been only a Victorian affectation, but that style has caused some raised eyebrows, especially when found in letters to her friends both male and female. But there is no question that she did love her children, and that she went out of her way to assist and please both them and her grandchildren.

It is no secret that Franklin D. Roosevelt was a Mama's boy. That his children were also his Mama's boys – rather than Eleanor's – may be news. But James remembered Sara declaring: "Your mother only bore you. I am more your mother than your mother is." The White House help quietly seconded that opinion.[72]

The little ones could do no wrong. They were accustomed to getting what they wanted, especially in the financial sense. They'd wreck their toys, and then their cars, and swiftly be given new ones; if their parents objected, they were overruled.[73] As James wrote, the kids were fortunate to have a grandmother who would do for them, when they had a mother who couldn't and a father who wouldn't.[74] Or maybe not: Elliott said

Sara showed "tremendous affection and a great deal of generosity," deliberately and triumphantly sabotaging Eleanor's attempts at child-rearing.[75]

We know from Elliott's 1945 tax investigation that his grandmother gave him numerous large cash gifts until and even after her death in 1941; that year he received a $19,000 inheritance, supplementing about "$20,000 to $35,000" received in earlier gifts. In other words, although Elliott was virtually always broke, he didn't suffer much.[76]

Eleanor's grandson through Anna, Curtis, tells an interesting anecdote that illuminates the financial *modus operandi* of the Roosevelts. "Granny" Sara had given James $1,000 for a trip to Europe. Certain he could strike it rich in the stock market, Jimmy gambled the money instead, and lost it all. Since the boy had asked advice of a very reluctant Curtis Dall, Anna's stockbroker husband, a grim family meeting was held in which Curtis was forced to repay Jimmy the money.[77]

Curtis was generally loathed by the Roosevelts. Anna got rid of him in 1934, after Elliott's first divorce. He later became a prominent right-wing conspiracy theorist.

For the children, Eleanor was the ogre trying to instill a semblance of responsibility. In a much retold story, Elliott reminisced that upon some grievous transgression his mother sent him to be beaten by Franklin, who conspiratorially urged him to make some suitable screams while he whacked the desk.[i]

In the complex calculus of family relations, Franklin and Eleanor were "fifth cousins, once removed." The awkward issue of inbreeding probably mattered little at that stage. The "Roosevelts" descended from an adventurer from the Netherlands, Claes van Rosenvelt (v spoken as f), who had come to Nieuw Amsterdam (New York) in the mid 17th century. The family, generally prosperous and prominent, split into two branches, known from their lairs as "Oyster Bay" on Long Island and "Hyde Park" on the Hudson River.

By the time Franklin met Eleanor five generations had elapsed, and even their "Dutchness" was more figure-of-speech than genetic fact. For those who kept track, FDR was only 3% Dutch and mainly English, but one interviewer claimed that Elliott inherited only the ornery 3%.[ii] Apparently, there was then such a popular concept as "Dutch stubbornness" or combativeness. This appears to be one stereotype that has faded into oblivion, but the Roosevelts took pride in it.[78]

By the time Franklin was born, the family was living off accumulated wealth. Franklin was no tycoon. He didn't have to be. But the family was slipping, if not in social prestige, then in financial rank. After the five surviving children took over the inheritance, the empire unraveled fast; what remains of the once baronial Roosevelt property is now in part a National Historic Site, and there is no single recognizable Roosevelt fortune.[iii]

A hundred years ago it was a privileged and pleasant existence on the rolling, wooded estate on which Franklin lived all his life, excepting official postings. His children, too, had every opportunity to flourish. Without the bitter struggle for survival, a certain cheerful lightness of being, often degenerating into exuberant recklessness, characterized Franklin and the children. Only mother Eleanor stood out as the serious, suffering type, a condition aggravated by her squirming under the firm thumb of her

---

[i] Told with slight variations in virtually all Roosevelt books. James said FDR only hit his children once, the convicted being James and the judge Eleanor, and it unnerved FDR enough to abstain therefrom ever after.

[ii] John T. Flynn: Country Squire, 5; has FDR's father 6% Dutch, 6% German, and 12% Swedish.

[iii] The sylvan, idyllic Eleanor Roosevelt National Historic Site is two miles east of the Hyde Park mansion, which is the center of the Home of Franklin D. Roosevelt National Historic Site.

mother-in-law, Sara Delano. With a bit of artistic exaggeration one might say she lived in a hell, surrounded by hellions.

Anyone who has seen Franklin's cherished library in the Hyde Park mansion realizes that he loved books. Elliott later claimed: "He was able to read a 300 or 400 page book and recite any paragraph from any page that you questioned him about months and months later. He recited verbatim, because he could read that book in an hour and a half. He had a photographic mind." It was Elliottian hyperbole, but he made his point.[79] (Others claim that the adult FDR read few serious books.)

Add the vitrines of stuffed birds, ship-models, and the famed stamp collection, and it is clear that FDR was intellectually curious all his life. That was true for most of the children as well. Elliott collected books, a problematic affliction for someone who could not remain in one place for long. He was highly gregarious and had to be around people, but when he wasn't, he did read and write prodigiously. Although much of his voluminous oeuvre turns out not to be his own work, Elliott did publish thirty books under his name.

It is the more surprising that the Hyde Park Roosevelts can hardly be called the intellectual or academic type. Franklin senior was a rotten student, but Elliott was worse. This wasn't merely a matter of rebellion or mismatched academics; the term "shallow" almost inevitably arises in assessing much of their writings. They were definitely intelligent, but they had no interest in ideas or abstraction. There are certain fields of life where this is a tremendous advantage. Politics is one. Advertising is another, and that would be Elliott's first brief career.

In Elliott's case, the insincerity required of politicians was not faked. Although he was rebellious in person, he was not so in theory. Much later, his strident defense of his friend Joseph Stalin did stand out as a serious miscue; but it was not ideological in nature. He had no ideology and apparently wouldn't have recognized one if he had been staring right at it – which he often did.

Rooseveltologists have long puzzled over how two such diametrically opposite personalities as Eleanor and Franklin ever could have gotten together. In two aspects, however, they were very much alike. Both were supersocial: Eleanor had a sincere, consuming interest in people everywhere, individually and collectively; her life revolved around people and what she could do for them. Her bonds to people were painfully sentimental. In Franklin's world, entranced people orbited around him, as his pathological mother had done, while he contemplated how he could use them. When they were no longer useful, he could discard them without the slightest hesitation regardless of how long or devoted their service. Observing this once too often, Interior Secretary Harold Ickes remarked "he is as cold as ice inside." [80]

The other common trait was "Roosevelt energy" – both parents had the strength and stamina of a whole team of Clydesdales. Whether at work or play, their productivity, even when crippled by disease or old age, was almost supernatural. An often noticed aspect of this trait was that they could fall fast asleep, almost on command, regardless of circumstances: in an airplane seat, or in the bottom of a bucking motorboat. That was immensely helpful given their constant, strenuous traveling.

These qualities were definitely passed on to the children.

"A traitor to his class" has Franklin Roosevelt been called, due to his pursuit of wealth redistribution, or "social justice" as the euphemism goes. That was actually much truer for Eleanor. In Franklin's case, the empathy was an affectation appropriate to his *noblesse oblige*-oriented upbringing. Unlike his wife, who even in her youth volunteered in the tenements, Franklin did not intend to get dirt under his fingernails; in his free time, he preferred the company of other idle rich.[81]

In the case of his sons, all doubt evaporates. None of Eleanor's deep-felt compassion carried over to them. Although far from an incapable man, Elliott became famous for wanton profligacy in every sphere of life. His sense of entitlement and belief in wealth redistribution applied mostly to the fortunes of others, and especially to those of wealthy women. Only John, the last sibling, earned a reputation for honest work.[i]

Not everyone viewed this trait the same way. Patricia, Elliott's wife nr. 5, offered an interesting anecdote. Elliott, without a dollar to his name but appalled that she proceeded to iron clothes in a hotel room, made her call valet service. Patty said:

> This was one of my practical lessons in adopting the ways of the man I was engaged to marry. It brought home to me the fact that Elliott Roosevelt lived life with certain services and prerogatives, things he had always been accustomed to and would remain so, regardless of his financial condition. This was one of the sharp distinctions between him and others I had known, and a characteristic which endeared him to me.[82]

Often one hears of the suave, confident impostor who, under pretense of being a temporarily inconvenienced Rockefeller or Vanderbilt, secures access to the lives and money of sympathetic rich widows or others of similarly brief utility. This stereotype might apply to Elliott except that he needed not fake his identity. To balance this rakish image, it is necessary to assert that he also accomplished much on his own; far more, it can be safely said, than the average person. But even in his most admired wartime accomplishments, closer examination reveals a vexing ambiguity.

In his financial promiscuity, again a genetic component undeniably looms in the background. The prewar Franklin D. Roosevelt was always cooking up some new money-making scheme with his friends; they usually failed, and he lost several minor fortunes. James recalled, "Father and Howe lost money in all sorts of schemes to make a fast million in bonds, oil wells, shipping, lobsters, almost anything you can think of." [83]

It was always his mother Sara's money that saw him through. Incidentally, "Howe" was Louis Howe, the political brain behind FDR's meteoric rise, a Rasputinesque, leach-like gnome who masterminded Franklin Roosevelt's career until his death in 1936. He was far more than a strategist; like Harry Hopkins after him, he was a live-in adviser in all manners, including financial. The rest of the family didn't care for "the dirty little man." [84] Elliott said, with emphasis, that Eleanor "hated" Howe, but she mellowed with time, and the two ugly ducklings came to appreciate each other.[85]

Neither Eleanor nor Franklin had a smidgeon of financial savvy, but FDR's ill-fated ventures did not cause him significant legal trouble, only financial losses. As an example of his judgment, one might mention his idea to buy live lobsters and keep them alive in tanks in order to sell them at some future time of higher prices. But the lobsters were too expensive to keep alive.[86]

Another example, referred to by Elliott with deceptive superficiality, was FDR's directorship in the International Germanic Trust. This major financial company was investigated for multiple levels of criminality associated with its demise after the 1929 stock market crash. Elliott said that his father's law partner, the much wiser Basil

---

[i] To be sure, sister Anna's short and problem-plagued newspaper career was not marked by corruption.

O'Connor, demanded that FDR resign from it, or from the law firm. Unfortunately, the IGTC was deeply embedded with Democratic interests, yet Governor Roosevelt had to call for the state's investigation of the bank. Whatever else might have been lurking under the surface in this regard, FDR managed to avoid public taint.[87]

This and many similarly dubious schemes pursued by the father will be important later in assessing the ceaseless financial plotting of his sons. Evidently, it was in the blood. From a historical standpoint, perhaps the more interesting angle was the overlap between Democratic Party kingpins and moneyed interests. The Republicans did not have a lock on corporate largesse. Regional differences mattered greatly. The corrupt Tammany machine in New York was a major factor. So was legitimate money. Perhaps the most fateful intervention was that of John J. Raskob, one of America's richest men, who had been chosen as Democratic National Committee Chairman. He sent FDR a check for $250,000 to get him to run for governor in 1928. Although that story has multiple, financially complex versions, it is clear that big money was the persuader, and FDR took care to protect his financial back before he plunged into politics again.[i]

Elliott said his father hated aeroplanes, ostensibly due to his frightening early trips in naval seaplanes. FDR strongly favored dirigibles (zeppelins), but his attempt to make a fortune on a commercial airship passenger line in the early 1920s failed spectacularly.[88]

That company was the General Air Service (GAS), undertaken with other prominent businessmen (such as chewing-gum boss William Wrigley). It proposed to run a helium-zeppelin service between Chicago and New York. That this mode of transportation would have been slower and less reliable than train travel somehow didn't register; at the time, the promoters thought that the combination of captured German technology and American helium would be the wave of the future.[89]

The idea deflated even before the spectacular crashes of several dirigibles in the 1930s. It is interesting, though, that young Elliott was then also fascinated with the idea of lighter-than-air flight. He wrote about it in *Murder in the Rose Garden*: "'My son Elliott', said the President, 'is thinking of taking a trans-Atlantic flight on this new German airship. The Hindenburg. Always had an interest in aviation, you know.'" But for political and other reasons, it would have been a bad idea for Elliott to get aboard that ill-fated zeppelin.[90]

Although he never served (directly) in it, Franklin D. Roosevelt always retained a soft spot for the Navy. But Elliott, unlike his maritime-minded siblings, chose airplanes and, eventually, the Air Corps.[91]

Born in 1910, Elliott grew up with the certain knowledge of his father being an important warfighter. Franklin served as Assistant Secretary of the Navy throughout the Wilson administration. To the Republicans, of course, he was merely another swivel-chair wanna-be admiral. Franklin, who (like many then) glorified manly, patriotic combat, made a desultory effort to sign up during the Great War. President Wilson advised him to remain in his office, where he was deemed the most useful. At any rate Franklin saw this post as the traditional Roosevelt road to the presidency.[ii] He later

---

[i] ER: An Untold Story, 265; Josephson, chapter XI, has another interesting though venomous investigation of the money behind the Roosevelt candidacy. Jesse Jones, 460, believed FDR's attempt to have the RFC buy the Empire State Building was an effort to repay Raskob and Al Smith.

[ii] ER: An Untold Story, 89. Numerous Roosevelts have served in this post. FDR's actions during his Navy tenure were extremely controversial.

counted himself a "combatant" because he visited the battlefield in France on an inspection trip.

Although a junior cabinet member, Franklin had maintained an exceptionally high profile, further boosted by war. Young Elliott saw his father enter politics and serve as state senator (1911-13), governor (1929-32), and vice-presidential candidate (1920). He would have been unaware of FDR's early reputation as an affable lightweight ("Feather Duster Roosevelt") propelled by his cultivation of friends and connections, as well as by his famous name.[i]

Elliott wanted to be his own man, though within limits that would become painfully obvious. Highly physical, he constantly got in trouble, caught ill, or suffered injuries. In 1928, he pulled off perhaps his most spectacular feat of self-liberation. After physically assisting his paralyzed father at the Democratic National Convention in Houston, he went to Arizona, where he had family links, and then bummed around incommunicado for about two months. The police eventually found him on a ranch in Idaho, where he was subsisting as a cowhand and algebra tutor. When he did write his father, it was to ask: "Do you think I could have a little money to come home on…" [92]

Later, Elliott said that Governor Roosevelt had an all-points police bulletin out, and someone recognized him in the hospital in Wilson, Wyoming (near Victor, Idaho). Eleanor took the train out there and found him recovering from gangrene in his foot. He'd suffered a deep cut after a fall from a horse, and had refused to take care of it.[93]

Elder brother James later wrote about that trip:

> He was feared kidnaped until he wrote home for money, having not only spent what he had but run up considerable debts. Father, admiring his adventurous spirit, sent the money. Mother, relieved, did not reprimand father.[94]

James got some details from Elliott's long rambling letter home, preserved in the archives; but parts of it just don't ring true. People not attuned to aviation might skip right along with Elliott, but there was more to this youthful lark than cowboy fantasies.

So how did he get this unusual idea to begin with? The local newspaper had a clue. On 2 July 1928, the Prescott paper noted "another rather interesting event in aviation:"

> …the trip which Mr. Fred Harvey [the famous hotelier and restaurateur of the Western railroads] and G. Hall Roosevelt [Eleanor's brother] are making at the present time. They left here Wednesday noon, piloted by LaMar Nelson, in the Scenic Airways Ryan Brougham, flew over Havasupai Canyon, Bryce Canyon, and many of the interesting sights in southern Utah, arriving in Salt Lake City three hours and fifty-five minutes from the time they left the canyon…[95]

Taking a cue from Uncle Hall, Elliott said his father had given him $70 for airfare from Arizona to Utah, across the Grand Canyon. Elliott did indeed fly over the big hole with a local outfit led by a pilot named "Vanzandt." This fellow "apologized profusely" for not being in Phoenix where he was supposed to be to meet Elliott. Then "Vanzandt" said it would cost $240 dollars for four hours, sorry Dad. And Elliott had no choice but to accept. There was no suitable ground transportation. And so he flew across the great gap up to Salt Lake City, where he got on the train to Idaho.[96]

---

[i] "Feather Duster Roosevelt" seems to have originated with the snake-tongued Alice Roosevelt, Ted's daughter. "She further called him 'Miss Nancy" because he pranced and fluttered." (Persico, 39).

That flight would be $1200 per hour in today's money. It turns out that Elliott was referring to J. Parker Van Zandt, then president of Scenic Airways, Inc., today's renamed Grand Canyon Airlines. A former Army pilot who had survived the world war, he was one of the really big names in early aviation. Van Zandt held the 17th American pilot's license, and he founded Phoenix's Sky Harbor airport. It is likely that Elliott knew him through his uncle Hall, and possibly personally from New York.[97]

Van Zandt was at that time operating a famous touristic passenger service at the Grand Canyon, using Ford Trimotors. President Roosevelt would hire him into the CAA (Civil Aviation Administration) in 1939. Van Zandt obtained a physics doctorate from UC Berkeley and served as assistant deputy Secretary of the Air Force during the Truman administration. He died the same year as Elliott, 1990.

Van Zandt's airline still operates at Valle Airport; it claims to be the oldest continually operating airline in the world. Moreover, the Ryan in which the Roosevelts flew remains in pristine flying condition. And to top it off, the airline still flies passengers over the canyon in a Ford Trimotor, eighty years after the debut of that notable service.

Perhaps Elliott told a tall tale about the cost of his ticket; it is not likely that Van Zandt ripped him off. However, Mr. Jack Frye, another pioneering Arizona pilot, Elliott would most certainly hear more of. Frye was then head of the Aero Corporation of California, another early airline. At any rate, Elliott's attraction to flying was already evident; but it was merely an aspect of his love of adventure and risk.

An interesting vignette showing Elliott's uncertain judgment and interest in flying survives in the president's personal file. In November 1930, when Governor Roosevelt was increasingly concerned with the plight of the newly destitute, Elliott proposed that he mobilize the Air Guard to fly surplus farm produce to New York City for distribution to unemployed families.

To his great credit, the governor responded respectfully:

> I have thought about that plan of flying provisions from upstate farms to N.Y.C., but I am convinced it is not practicable because of the great weight of things like apples or other fruits and vegetables…the cost of getting it there would be approximately 500 times as much as if it came on a freight car or even in a motor truck. Also the state has no possible fund for paying any of the expense…[98]

Elliott's noble idea should have pleased a father with a first-class temperament, especially if it had come from a ten-year old. But Elliott was twenty.

Early Career

Elliott's career as the president's son – and he did make a career of it until the day he died, *and well after* – began inauspiciously. He took six highly delinquent years to get through Groton, the Massachusetts high school for the super-rich.[99] Elliott hated the place. Eleanor said her son was kept at Groton because anywhere he went he would resent discipline, but this famous school would provide at least some – yet Elliott refused college precisely because he disliked his years at Groton so much.[100]

It was worse than that. Elliott played hooky. Days at a time he disappeared from sight. He was in constant academic trouble, and also acquired a reputation as a dangerous brute on the playing fields. There is a surviving correspondence with his father in which the principal fretted about Elliott's casual brutality, but FDR stood up for his son.[101]

"It is a fact that he gets overexcited and allows himself to go on blindly, so that in a way he was responsible for the offense," wrote the rector after Elliott sent a kid to the hospital. FDR answered, "I am not making an excuse for a quick temper, which at times he shows & and which we have recognized for many years," - then excused his son:

> He is extremely sensitive to praise or blame. The first four years he struggled at or near the bottom of his form. This year he has done really better in his scholastic work – but apparently no one has given him an encouraging word…an inferiority complex at Elliott's age is an unfortunate and dangerous thing for after-life. Even at a cost of an occasional bit of over-praise it is worth it if it shall bring back a degree of self-confidence with which to face life.[102]

An "inferiority complex" is not usually associated with the Roosevelts, but Elliott was in trouble. Still, the teachers at Groton thought Elliott "had an excellent mind," and that "his thought was original and exceptional." Eleanor reported this while trying to develop a salvage plan that would place Elliott in a tutoring school to make up for his academic deficits before college.[103]

Elliott clearly was not stupid, but he completely lacked focus and discipline. He thought college an intolerable, stuffy delay on his expected path to fortune and greatness. Eleanor said he had "failed some of his college entrance examinations and quite frankly admitted that he had failed them on purpose." [104]

His brother James said that Elliott mooted the issue by "turning in a blank college exam book." But Eleanor asserted that, by way of compromise, after leaving Groton in 1929 he was sent to Princeton's preparatory Hun School, "where he did extremely well, both in scholarship and in athletics."

> He not only passed his college board examinations with flying colors, but also was offered a sports scholarship in two of the major universities. He was outraged by this and it fixed his determination not to go to college. Since we could not persuade him to change his mind, he started at once to earn a living.[105]

Back then it was not grades, but pedigree that got you into the Ivy League. Academic achievement was for the low-born. But it was only reasonable for Franklin père to suggest that Elliott didn't have the discipline or attention span required for college. Eleanor was far more worried, but all she got for her remonstrations was the silent treatment. She said Elliott didn't speak to her for three months. "At the end of that time he was ill and had to come home and then he deigned to make up with me."[106]

This was also before a college degree was a requirement for holding a military commission, but considering Elliott's aristocratic provenance, the omission was notorious to the edge of scandalousness. He might have been right that not everyone need strive for a university education, but the other children went to college – although they didn't all graduate. Franklin himself had done well at Harvard, but he failed to graduate from Columbia Law School – he passed the bar on his own.

Elliott went to jail instead. Roosevelt family biographer Peter Collier wrote:

> ...He finally agreed to college only because he wanted to play football. He spent a semester raising his grades and then went West for a vacation with a friend, which was highlighted by a night in a Juarez jail after a drunken brawl in a Mexican cantina.[107]

Forced to attend Princeton University, he never completed any work. Instead he tried, on his own (though hardly unassisted) initiative, to break into the advertisement business. It was promptly reported in the gossip pages:

> Elliott Roosevelt, 20-year old son of Governor Roosevelt, has become associated with the advertising firm of Albert Frank & Co., 165 Broadway, with the idea of learning advertising and making it his life work. Mr. Roosevelt was admitted to Princeton last Spring but decided in favor of a business career during the Summer vacation period. He was graduated from Groton School with the class of 1929, after playing two years on the football team and rowing in the school crew for three years. He stroked the crew and was a member of the swimming team at Hun School, from which he was graduated last Spring. Mr. Roosevelt took up his work yesterday morning. He will be assigned to each department of the organization in turn, thus making a thorough study of every detail of the advertising business.[i]

How did Elliott break into this cut-throat field? It turns out that having successfully evaded college, Elliott demanded that his parents instead provide him with a well-paying job. To their credit they refused to do so, causing the young man to do what he always did in that case: go to Grandma. Sara then went to Bernard Baruch, the Wall Street plutocrat who, as a hobby, ingratiated himself with presidents and did various assignments for them. Baruch got Elliott in with Albert Frank & Co.:

> Elliott was put into a job as a sort of semi-partner...He knew absolutely nothing about the business and was only there because of Mr. Baruch. Little by little it dawned on him that he did not know anything about the business and was able to do very little of real value." [108]

Nevertheless, advertising seemed a perfect fit for the loud, brash, and none-too-scrupled Roosevelt. What he did seemed of little importance; what mattered was whom he met. Advertising lasted him only a couple of years, but it gave him insights into the aviation business, and in particular, got him acquainted with the powerful industrialist Errett Lobban Cord. Cord was engaged in a fierce battle to take over the airline industry, something that apparently planted a seed in young Elliott's mind.[109]

This *modus operandi* was common to the Roosevelt children. As James wrote much later, "Because of who we were, not what we were, Elliott and I, and Franklin and John, and Anna, too, were handed positions we could not handle and did not deserve. We never set goals and grew into them." [110]

But then, why should they? Elliott always made much of the tragic burden of being the president's son. The expectations! But many are the offspring of high office who have become solid if unremarkable citizens. Had FDR lost in 1932, would Elliott have joined their ranks? More likely, in time the ice breaking behind him would have caught up with his skating. As it was, he always stayed just one skate-length ahead.

---

[i] NYT, 30 SEP 30. Note the emphasis on sports and the slighting of academics.

Impulsive and impatient, Elliott soon branched off on his own and helped form the Kelly, Nason & Roosevelt Advertising Company in September 1931.[111] He appears to have overestimated the magic of his name while Dad was still merely governor. Trading off his political connections, he brought in some accounts, but he stated afterwards that the company was not earning enough to support three men and their families.[112] One observer noted: "They sat at desks month after month, getting no business, and finally to ease the strain Elliott got out and went with the Paul Cornell agency in 1932." [113]

As was often the case, there was also a darker side to Elliott's advertising career. It was generally assumed that the agency used Elliott to extract business from politically exposed companies, much as his brother James clearly was bait for big insurance accounts. But it was difficult to prove; who would have an interest in blowing the whistle? And how could you prove anything when threats or enticements were assumed but never explicitly stated?

An anonymous letter sent to a newspaper columnist illustrated this phenomenon, and its pitfalls. Apparently from an insider familiar with the W.R. Grace Line steamship company, the writer, still fearful for his job, bitterly recalled:

> The Grace advertising account had, for years, been handled by an old line advertising agency. Word was passed around to Mr. Iglehart and to Mr. Daulton Mann [president and CEO] of the Grace Line that all their troubles and persecutions would come to an end if they were smart enough to take their large and lucrative advertising account away from their present agents and hand it over to a new advertising agency who most certainly had all the aforementioned back-stairs-pipe-line to the white house. The name of this new agency was Kelly, Nason & Roosevelt. (Yes, it was little Elliott again). The change was made and then began an almost continuous series of treks from New York to Washington [--] the guidance of Jack Kelly, (Elliott's pardner) and presently the subsidy was restored and huge government loans were made available to the Grace Line for building new mail and passenger liners.
>
> Of course Elliott, being too damned dumb to be an advertising executive, was merely the bait used by this agency in garnering accounts of clients that were out on the *persona non grata* limb of the new deal comrades. After the young prodigy had served his purpose as a "front man" and "fixer upper" he severed his connection with the agency (no doubt at the insistence of Kelly who hated his guts anyhow) and went to Texas ...[114]

The story might sound persuasive, but most of it is overblown. The columnist, the renowned Westbrook Pegler, conscientiously checked out the story, and to his regret found it to be misleading. Elliott had left the agency by the time of his father's inauguration, and it was Jack Kelly who had hijacked the advertising account. He was apparently "something of a Tammany power, with influence with the Port of New York Authority." And switching the accounts did get W.R. Grace favorable treatment.[115]

Thus the letter was simply emblematic of the many rumors that never made it into print. In this case the agency (which retained the Roosevelt name after he left) actually used the name without Elliott's efforts behind it.

Not a rumor was the fact that Elliott went to Louis Howe and got him to award the agency the account of the Democratic National Committee.[116] It was also not a rumor that as soon as his father had been elected, the governor of a Mexican state asked Elliott to do publicity for a project. Raymond Moley, then a close FDR adviser, told Elliott to be extremely careful about such things.[117]

Wife nr. 1: Betty Donner

A few other things helped change Elliott's priorities and scuttle his advertising career. He said his father's election to the White House made his advertising business political, but getting unhappily married may have played a greater role.[118]

After an indecent interval of partying, as a twenty-one year old Elliott married rich, beautiful Elizabeth (Betty) Donner, heiress to Donner Steel of Philadelphia. She was twenty. The engagement was announced on 30 October 1931, with a marriage to follow on 16 January. It was a curious merger; the bride's father, William H. Donner, a major philanthropist and cancer research funder, later hated the Roosevelts and federal taxes so vehemently that he renounced his citizenship and spent the rest of his life abroad.[i]

People who don't think there is aristocracy in America should read the press reports of this royal wedding, attended by 900 guests, including top government and Democratic Party officials.

> Mr. Roosevelt is related to many prominent New York families. He is a grandson and namesake of the late Elliott Roosevelt, the only brother of the late President Theodore Roosevelt, and of Mrs. James Roosevelt and the late James Roosevelt, who was vice president of the Delaware & Hudson Railroad. Through Mrs. James Roosevelt, who is the former Miss Sara Delano, he is a great-grandson of Warren Delano of Fairhaven, Mass., who was head of Russell & Co., a large American mercantile and tea house in China. The Delano family for many years lived in Lafayette Place and had a country home in Newburgh, N.Y. On the side of the Delano family young Mr. Roosevelt is related to the Astor family, through his ancestor, Franklin Delano, who married Laura Astor, a daughter of William Backhouse Astor and granddaughter of the original John Jacob Astor... [etc. ad nauseam] [119]

Those who do realize there is aristocracy in America may be relieved to hear that such families often seem to self-destruct. It was not obvious in 1931, but the Roosevelts of Hyde Park were in the middle of a long process of spectacular self-destruction, a flamboyant decay that Elliott Roosevelt would come to personify to the nation.

At that particular time, Franklin Roosevelt was governor of New York and definitely a member of the upperest crust of the state. But his finances had not kept up with his social standing. Franklin was an enthusiastic but inept investor and a somewhat dissolute worker who accepted sinecures for his keep. *Time* summed it up nicely: "Franklin Roosevelt was at that time a not particularly hard-working lawyer, with no personal fortune but an amazing ability to make friends." [120]

As the third surviving progeny of this most charming but financially declining second-tier land baron, Elliott Roosevelt was accustomed to high living, but he had not the means to match his self-image. Although he was paid a small monthly sum from his family fortune and could cadge funds from relatives, he was merely living rich without money of his own. He intended to fix that in no time. Marrying the demure and beautiful Donner Steel heiress seemed to provide an excellent head start.

Despite the enormous financial and professional benefits associated with the Donner-Roosevelt alliance, the marriage seems to have ruptured within days. Eleanor

---

[i] NYT, 2 OCT 38, 13 SEP 39, etc.; the Internal Revenue Bureau pursued Donner during the FDR years, but Betty got along well with Eleanor and her mother.

said it was a "quick disillusionment. He had found no community of interests with his wife and realized rather soon that he had mistaken a feeling of sympathy for love." [121]

Peter Collier, who wrote about the Roosevelts decades later, had been told that the disillusionment was of a sexual nature.[i] Elliott muttered something about Betty's one hundred pairs of shoes and other expensive tastes. Others noticed that the young lady was shy and inexperienced, rather unlike her husband. In most photographs, she looks as if her cat had just died. The circumstantial evidence suggests that Betty required more attention than her husband could muster.[122]

Eleanor was despondent at the failure of his son to appreciate Betty. As early as May 1932, she wrote to her husband the governor: "I wish I knew what to do for Elliott and Betty. He is so utterly inconsiderate – and lacking in care and gentleness. I am writing to him today to try to make him understand certain things but I can't say that I feel very hopeful.[123]

Legally, the marriage lasted over a year. On 17 November, it produced one son, William.

It wasn't the first failed marriage in the family, even excepting that of Eleanor and Franklin themselves. Stranded with her two children, elder sister Anna was also living in the White House. She loathed Curtis Dall, the man she had originally married to get away from there. But Elliott would be the first to make it formal.[ii]

Four days after President Roosevelt's inauguration, on a Wednesday morning, 8 March 1933, Elliott dumped both mother and son in the White House and took to the road. [124] A worried Eleanor, informed of the caper, saw him off in a Plymouth convertible stacked so high Elliott and his traveling companion couldn't close the top.[iii]

She recalled later that as she saw "Elliott and another young man who had attached himself to Elliott start off on this trip, my heart was heavy. I did not doubt that he would find a job, but I had a feeling of separation and uncertainty about his future." [125]

"What a gamble it is. I wish I felt surer about Elliott," she wrote Lorena Hickok.[126] Her anxiety would turn out to be well-founded.

The staff noticed, too. Always warning that "nothing is at is seems," maid Lillian Parks remembered: "The only secrets she seemed anxious to keep from the public, those early days at the White House, concerned son Elliott's marriage, which was on the rocks. She had told people Elliott's wife, Betty, and his son, Billy, were just staying with her a little while and were going to follow Elliott as soon as he found a place for them to live. But we knew differently. We knew Elliott and a buddy were having fun roaming around out West, and the chances of finding Elliott and Betty living together again were about as good as finding an icicle in Hades." [127]

The occasion was extra memorable because Elliott interrupted his father's first press conference to shake hands and say goodbye. This conference marked a new era of affable approachability of the U.S. president; previously, written questions had to be submitted in advance, and were dourly answered only if it should please the chief executive to do so. It also marked the beginning of FDR's highly successful charm offensive with reporters. And the levity was egged on by the spectacle of Eleanor watching uncertainly for a few minutes, then sending her son in to bid farewell.[128]

---

[i] Collier, 371. He heard this from Kermit Roosevelt's wife.

[ii] Curtis R.: Too Close to the Sun, describes in pitiful detail how much the Roosevelts hated his father.

[iii] Streitmatter: Empty Without You, 20; in Elliott's memory, it was a yellow Plymouth coupé. (Collier, 371)

For one year the second son had lived high on the Donner family's money, and the twenty-one-year-old had been made a vice president of Donner Steel. Now he firmly declared that he had no use for the East and never intended to live there again.[129] True to his word, he set a heading for Tucson, Arizona, taking along an equally adventurous buddy, Ralph Hitchcock.[130] Ralph was a former classmate who had been with the advertising company Elliott quit two days before the inauguration.[131]

They drove hard and fast. A day later, in Arkansas, the two were nearly broke – but hardly despairing. As always, Pop would fix it!

Today it boggles the mind that a presidential son, especially one with a bride and newborn baby, would take off cross-country with no particular plan, and without a busload of Secret Service agents in trail. Those were simpler times – perhaps the last of the simpler times – before White House family members were imprisoned by their own office. At least we must give Elliott credit for insisting on his freedom, and his parents for granting it, regardless of considerations of public propriety. It was in character.

Instant gratification was Elliott's objective in all matters. This became especially easy after his father became president, but neither was it apparently difficult for him beforehand. He had a way of ingratiating himself with important people, and most remarkably he effortlessly attracted women. His public womanizing, whether under marital cover or otherwise, would become a subject of constant snickering in the press.

Elliott maintained that he was merely his father's apprentice in this matter. Of his trip to Europe in 1929, he wrote:

> It was my first trip outside the United States, and I had only one complaint to make: Father was even more flirtatious than I was. My shipboard romance was with a girl not yet twenty who had danced in the chorus of Charles Cochran's London revues, then gone into Fleet Street newspaper reporting. Sheilah Graham was due to be a leading Hollywood columnist, but right now she was the sudden object of my affection, and Father's, too. He was, I decided, about the most flirtatious character I had ever known. I was used as a kind of understudy in his flirting with another charming passenger, Rosa Ponselle, the buxom opera singer. [Ponselle, then 34 and one of the greatest voices ever, was on her way to her European debut at the Covent Gardens.] The one thing Father could not do was dance with her, so I was brought in as his deputy…[132]

He was then beginning a long career of inspecting female fuselages. Certainly, the fun he had with this particular chorus girl would turn out to be useful years later.

If Elliott's conquests aroused lurid interest (his father's were suppressed), his financial affairs would bring him endless scorn and ridicule. During his long life, he started one business after another, usually with the funds of others, and they failed in progression; but for him there was always a new project, bound to make him rich once and for all.

One of these projects was flying airplanes. During high school, when his father was governor, he hung around Roosevelt Field on Long Island, and indeed met Charles Lindbergh there before his epic flight.[133] Elliott said that he cadged flying lessons from the then ubiquitous "barnstormers" – surplus pilots from the Great War making an uncertain living with their equally surplus (and uncertain) biplanes.

Incidentally, Roosevelt Field at Mineola on Long Island was named for Quentin Roosevelt, the son of Theodore, who died in air combat in France in 1918. In the inter-war years, it was one of the nation's leading airports. It no longer exists.

Elliott got enough snippets of dual instruction to acquire a basic CAA student license, and although he apparently did not exercise its privileges much, the skill would stand him in good stead later. Certainly more so than his competitive rodeo skills, which he had picked up as a vacationing ranch hand in the West, or the extreme driving skills that earned him a thick stack of tickets – for speeding and worse – throughout his life.[i]

Elliott recalled that E.L. Cord, the industrialist, let him drive his Duesenberg (Cord owned the company). The kid promptly got a speeding ticket in it (in 1929) – but when the motorcycle cop realized that Elliott was the governor's son, he provided him with an escort to his destination. If this was his first ticket, it was certainly not his last. Nor was he the black sheep in this regard; his brothers also attained extra fame as road demons.[134]

Elliott's wife nr. 4, Minnewa, remembered an especially egregious case involving young Franklin Jr. .:

> He smacked up his La Salle car that his grandmother had given him, and his mother and father chided him and said, "No more car for you, young man." Three or four days later Franklin was driving in a new La Salle, and his mother was just furious. Granny had given it to him.[135]

Some years later Franklin Jr. got in legal trouble for nearly killing someone on the road, and Elliott himself beat off an otherwise iron-clad drunk driving charge. But in their youth, often "traffic officials let them off free when they got a ticket" because of their father's position.[136]

John and Franklin Jr. "used to go out and swipe" police motorcycles. The new president told a complaining officer: "If you're damn fool enough to leave your keys in it then you deserve to have your motorcycle stolen." [137]

The equine connection would also stay with Elliott his entire life. He said that as a toddler, he had been forced to wear hip-high braces because his parents thought he was knock-kneed. It seems the parents had been talked into believing that the infant was bowlegged and needed braces. This was quite common back then, and probably helped cause the condition ostensibly to be corrected. But it also reflected the fear that the child was "so wan and sickly that there was grave family concern whether he would survive." [138]

Elliott later wrote that he walked with a rolling, bowlegged gait from the day he got rid of his braces, and it turned his mind in the direction of wanting to be an honest-to-goodness cowboy when he grew up.[139]

While his riding skills only served him in his youth, whenever he had money later, he would have horses. As it was, he said he was gored by a bull in the 1929 Madison Square Garden Rodeo, which his parents coincidentally attended; but they did not recognize the young Robinson/Robertson who was carried to the hospital! In old age, Elliott told that story with some variations. It should have left traces both in the news and family remembrances, but none could be found. (Another cowboy really did suffer that fate.)[140]

All his adult life, Elliott sported a screaming eagle tattooed on his forearm. He got it in a drunken haze in the summer of 1928, the night before he shipped out as a seaman

---

[i] Ibid, 367; TIME, 8 JUL 46, 1 NOV 48; ChigTrib, 18 JUL 48, 28 DEC 49. There are numerous mentions of the Roosevelt kids as road terrors. One is in JR: My Parents, 48. Franklin Jr.'s rap sheet is in Morgan, 457.

on a tanker bound for the Pacific. It was hard work and he deserted in the Gulf. "Granny" Sara was appalled when she discovered this emblem of rebellion.[141]

A pattern of thrill-seeking was emerging. The cross-country escapade in March 1933 was right in character. On this trip, his rodeo skills would suddenly be especially handy.

Striking Oil in Texas

After abandoning his wife and baby and emerging broke in Arkansas, a call to Dad set Elliott up with local friends of President Roosevelt. "Broke" was $32, actually a handsome sum back then; and it seems that the travelers had managed to go "broke" in less than 48 hours. FDR quietly arranged for his son's rescue without informing him:

> We took a southerly route through Little Rock, Arkansas. Despite scrimping on funds, our cash balance had sagged below the danger line. The banks remained closed. In our hotel room, I picked up the telephone and asked the operator to put in a call to the White House, National 1414. Very shortly, Father was on the line.
>
> "How are you, Bunny? How's the trip going?" – "Just fine, Pop. Only I have a problem." – "What's that?" – "I've gotten this far, but now we've only $32 left between us. I don't think we can stretch it to get all the way to Arizona. You've got the banks shut tight. There's no place around to cash a check."
>
> "That's too bad, Bunny, but I can't send you any money. You'll just have to use your ingenuity and do the best thing you can. Find a place along the way and stay there until things clear up. I'm sorry for you, but all I've got is eight dollars."
>
> I fervently wished him the best of luck in getting the banks breathing again and hung up, wondering how much closer to our destination $32 would take us. As it turned out, there was no need for concern and no call for ingenuity. The next 24 hours provided a foretaste of the lures and enticements that surround the children of the Presidency.[142]

Word got out quickly. The press reported the two in Little Rock on 9 March. It was a simple matter to plot their route. The White House must have alerted the Texas high and mighty to Elliott's planned transit. Whoever made the connection, it was a fateful call that would determine much of Elliott's life thereafter, and a good part of the country's.[i]

In the meantime, back East poor Betty was becoming distraught. She showed up at the White House with baby William and complained to Eleanor:

> [Eleanor to Hickok] Elliott telephoned her [Anna] today that Betty was angry at the job he had taken [none yet] & wanted a divorce. She [Betty] phoned me this a.m. & is coming here tomorrow with Bill. If she is willing to go down, I think he should let her go & talk it out, but far from me to settle anyone else's lives! [143]

Eleanor would be caught in the middle of all Elliott's tempestuous marriages.

On his way from Little Rock to Dallas, Elliott and Ralph were pulled over by Texas motorcycle police (who had been looking for the car) and given an unexpected escort into Dallas, where they were told some important people wanted to see the son of the president.[144] Elliott remembered he was escorted to the Baker Hotel, whose

---

[i] NYT, 10 MAR 33. A logical call would have gone to major FDR-backer Amon G. Carter in Fort Worth.

owner was waiting for him. "Oh, I've got connections," he explained to the curious guests.[145]

On Friday, 10 March, the *Fort Worth Star-Telegram* carried the following unusual front page invitation underneath a picture of the second son:

> *You are invited, Elliott Roosevelt, to visit the Southwestern Exposition and Fat Stock Show tonight and meet the cattlemen of Texas who are gathered here for the occasion.*[146]

Now powerful Democrats allied with the Fort Worth elite and the Dallas oil industry took Elliott under their wings. The man designated as host was Walter R. Scott, who took him to the rodeo and the Texas Hotel to meet the moneyed interests.

That Friday night, Elliott inaugurated the much-awaited rodeo. He made a spectacle:

> After he had cantered slowly around the arena in a maze of gaily-clad riders in the grand entry, young Roosevelt was introduced by Bob Calen, world's second best roper. A splendid figure at ease in the saddle, Roosevelt wheeled the high-stepping cow pony around and waved a ten-gallon white hat, a souvenir of his visit.[147]

To general applause, the second son made another rodeo appearance Saturday afternoon. In the meantime, he had been invited to pick out suitable footwear: He toured a Western boot factory and announced that he needed "at least three-inch heels" to go with his 6'2" frame. He had to settle on black 2½ inch cowboy boots, still ensuring instant visibility, especially with the hat.[148] Then, the Fort Worth notables presented him with "a beautiful, pearl-handled revolver." [149]

That weekend the real networking took place at the fanciest local watering holes: the Texas Hotel in Fort Worth and the Baker Hotel in Dallas. At the latter, the two travelers were luncheon guests of owner Fenton Baker and manager Bob Pool, these having been responsible for arranging the Dallas part of the stopover.[150]

When Elliott met with the editors of the *Star-Telegram,* he let everyone know how much he enjoyed the rodeo, which he pronounced the best he'd seen. He knew all about "roping and bronc-riding and steer-bulldogging," having been on the rodeo circuit as a teenager – although he admitted he'd never won any prizes.[151] (Yet in his old age, Elliott claimed that in his teenage years he won "a wad of prize money" every summer when he toured the rodeos as "Robinson.")[152]

The most valuable of many eagerly accepted gifts turned out to be a wealthy young thing of estimable intelligence, expensive education, and approved breeding. This beauty was Ruth Googins. Elliott met Ruth at a Dallas party given by a certain young airline manager, C.R. (Cyrus Rowlett) Smith. His was definitely a name to remember, but it was universally shortened to "C.R." Alerted to the arrival of the tired and dusty Elliott and Ralph, Smith spotted his chance and invited them, and a number of local "debutantes," to a dinner-dance at the Baker Hotel. One among the dangled-but-disappointed bait was Elizabeth Samuell, who recalled:

> 'It was quite a trial for the rest of us…We couldn't dance, for someone recognized Elliott. The only ones who didn't mind were Ruth and Elliott. They talked to each other the entire evening, ignoring everything else. They contributed absolutely nothing to the

> party. Ruth was my guest that night. I asked her how she liked the president's son. She said, 'He seems to be a very attractive man.'[i]

Fenton Baker had installed the travelers in the Presidential Suite. As Elliott remembered, "The refreshments set out on a table there gave no sign that repeal of Prohibition lay in the future." [153]

The party lasted late. Reportedly, the mesmerized Elliott was entrusted with driving Ruth home – a risky but evidently profitable idea. Ruth was the daughter of John B. Googins, manager of Swift & Co., a meat packing plant enterprise. She had graduated from Wellesley and, at 23, was prime bait in Dallas-Fort Worth society.[154] Locals said her "debut" in 1929 was "one of the most brilliant in years." [155]

Ruth went along to Fort Worth next afternoon – it was obvious that the two were already an "item." She was apparently much more fun than Betty. After eventually replacing the latter, she turned out to be a good match insofar as she was resourceful and seems to have been able to keep Elliott's already legendary profligacy somewhat in check. In her 1945 testimony about Elliott's finances to the Internal Revenue agents, Ruth comes across as a clueless nitwit who had no inkling of her husband's business affairs. That was clearly a coached stance; in fact she took an active part in running the business, and was locally known for her acumen.[156]

In Texas, there was seemingly no end to the hospitality. Once again, C.R. struck a swift blow for aviation. American Airways flew the two back to Dallas, then took them on the midnight flight to El Paso. Elliott's host, Walter Scott, directed his chauffeur to drive the Plymouth there, where it was waiting with a full tank of gas after the two travelers had flown across to Ciudad Juarez to sample the local specialties (Mexico having a special recreational role during Prohibition).[157] As Elliott wrote later:

> The highlight of El Paso hospitality was a plane trip across the border into Mexico. The feasting there included an escorted visit to a huge distillery which was busily producing Kentucky bourbon by the barrel load.[158]

Although everything Elliott said or wrote has to be checked out, this version corresponds well to the press coverage of the day. He was feted wherever he went, and he left a slightly amusing trail for local newspaper readers to follow.[159] In El Paso, Elliott (6'3") was pictured shaking hands with local giant Jake Erlich (8'6"). After his Mexican trip, he posed for news photographers with his huge hat, pistol, and a serape over his shoulder.[160]

> At Juarez, he was met by officials and businessmen, and after a short drive about the city was taken to a distillery where he was shown through the plant and given samples of the product, which he tasted. "It's legal over here," he explained. He was guest at a luncheon in Juarez and at a dinner dance there tonight.[161]

None of this cost the two kids a nickel.

Having arrived at El Paso, Elliott politely wired his host back in Fort Worth: "Arrived safely under beautiful Texas moon. Regret you are not here because we are still under the spell of your splendid hospitality. It will be a real effort to cross the state line, thanks to your thoughtfulness and kindness. This goes for Ralph too. Regards...[162]

---

[i] UP, 23 JUL 33, in the Miami News. ER & Ruth attended Ms. Samuell's wedding that Christmas in Dallas.

Then he shot off an ecstatic letter to "Ma:"

> Gosh but this is what I should have done three years ago! Nothing could pay me to go back East again. The people, the spirit of hospitality and friendliness is marvelous and so different from New York. At Dallas we were stopped on our way through town and invited to stay over for the rodeo in Fort Worth – of course I could not resist and we stayed....The whole trip is a revelation to Ralph and he says he wouldn't live in any other section of the United States than the Southwest – he just can't believe that people are built to be so hospitable – We've both been offered every kind of conceivable job and if Arizona proves not to have room for us we're going to come back to Texas to live.[163]

He also made some disparaging remarks about his "poor" wife back home. Writing from Tucson's Arizona Inn a few days later, he sneered:

> I don't know what all the fuss was about last night about Betty being down there [DC], but if it was just another crazy notion, I'm sorry. Lord, I know Betty has just made up her mind she'll hate it out here. So there isn't much to be done about it. I know I won't try anymore to get her out of herself, it's too much trouble when you have to do it over regularly every two weeks.[164]

Although Betty Donner might well have been "high maintenance," there was another reason for Elliott to stick it to her. He now had a replacement in mind.

Interestingly, aboard that American Airways flight to El Paso was another important person: Frank Harris Hitchcock, the publisher of the *Tucson Daily Citizen* and an effective booster of that city during its rapid growth. Hitchcock had been boss of the Republican National Committee, for which he was rewarded with the post of Postmaster General, as was then the custom in political patronage. Hitchcock was also an "airplane nut" and history credits him with creating the first air mail service – really just an experiment – in 1911. Though a Republican, the still influential "General" Hitchcock was a good man to know.[i]

All along, Elliott spoke freely to reporters about his ambitions. He would like to have a ranch, but he had no money; he liked to work with animals, be they cattle or sheep. He needed to find a job and would see about that in Arizona. His casual remarks resulted in a flood of letters from those offering him land or work. But Elliott was "disillusioned by the devious ways of big business." He professed great disdain for the East; now he was fixin' to "make a living on his own merits rather than on his name."

Elliott said he had a $40,000 a year offer after Pop was elected. But, "the advertising business seems to be closer to activities that are interwoven with the operations of government than any other branch of government...I got tired of explaining."

> I've talked things over in a vague way with Mrs. Greenway [in Tucson], but I haven't reached any decision on exactly what I'm going to do. Of course, I'm not going west just to punch cows and have a good time. I expect to look the situation over and then go into shares with someone on a ranch. I can't tell until I've looked into things whether it will be a cattle, sheep or dude ranch.[165]

No mention of Betty or the baby.

---

[i] Fort Worth Star-Telegram, 14 MAR 33; NYT, 6 AUG 35 (obituary). True air mail service began in 1918.

From El Paso, the two travelers drove on through the magnificent, empty desert to the stage-coach stop and motel town of Lordsburg, New Mexico. There, Elliott spoke to the Lion's Club and the student assembly.[166] The prairie newspapers were impressed:

> Young Elliott has shown himself a young man of sound good sense and considerable delicacy of feeling by cutting loose from Washington and New York and heading for the Far West to establish himself on a cattle ranch. The President's son had been an advertising man in New York. But he found it almost impossible to solicit business which does not have some connection with Washington. He was offered a host of new jobs, but in almost every case his would-be employer quietly assumed that he would serve as a close-to-the-throne lobbyist at the capital. So he decided to go West, to the ranges where the fact that his father is President will make no difference to anyone.[167]

It was a good story, well told. That newspaper, the *Lubbock Avalanche*, closed by offering him a local job: "If Mr. Roosevelt has a penchant for politics he may find New Mexico a good proving ground."

It seems the two travelers had to go pretty far to find a place where Elliott's father's position would "make no difference to anyone." They had no real rest until they were safely under "Aunt" Isabella Greenway's gracious protection in Tucson.

The Hidden Meaning of Texas Hospitality

Why would so many prominent Texans so enthusiastically go out of their way to show a 22-year-old virtual runaway a rollicking good time, beginning with a police motorcycle escort and ending with jaunts on the "corporate jets" of the age?

One clue might lie in the impending changes in regulation of the oil industry. Having barely assumed office, President Roosevelt and Interior Secretary Harold Ickes were already planning a major "oil stabilization conference" which would set limits of production, importation, and oil allocation, and would curtail the dreaded "competitive drilling." The initiative reflected the characteristic fears of "overproduction" of that time, however bizarre that would appear to economists of today.[168]

Oil was the life-blood of Texas, and thus the local luminaries had ample reason to curry favor with the new president's family. After he "struck oil" in Texas, Elliott had a solid line of friendly credit and a very comfortable life – for quite a while, at least. And his new friends had a key to the White House – almost literally.

On that first fateful Texas sojourn, Elliott made friends with some crucially important entrepreneurs. In his own words:

> A number of genial people were introduced during that stay in Texas. C.R. Smith became a close friend as time went by. He was an intimate of the big operators of the oil industry, which at that moment of its history was dying on its feet. The greatest natural resource of Texas could not command enough of a market price to make it worth pumping from the wells. The producers were going broke and looking to the federal government to save them.
>
> I met Charles Roesser [Roeser], whose wells were earning him some money, and Sid Richardson, who had none, since the holes he was drilling seemed fated to be dry. Both men, along with another, Clint Murchison, whom I met later, were to show a certain

> interest in my career while Father was in the White House. I was vaguely aware that I was being sized up as a prospect. A real courtship was due to follow.[169]

"While Father was in the White House" was an accurate delimitation, but "a certain interest in my career" turned out to be a gross understatement.

The names matter. C.R. Smith, the young local airline executive, became president of American Airlines next year, and he was determined to cultivate Elliott.[i] He was the one who had invited the president's son to the Dallas dance, taking care to include all the most eligible local debutantes. He claimed credit for introducing Elliott to Ruth Googins.[170]

When the war came, General Arnold made "C.R." a colonel, and he soon rose to major general, chief of staff of the Air Transport Command. Arnold had total confidence in Elliott's buddy; he said "once I had George [General Harold George] and Smith running our military air lines, I did not have to worry about that problem any longer. No matter what mission I gave them, I could count on its being carried out 100%." [171]

After the war, C.R. Smith returned to American Airlines, which he ran until 1968, when he joined his old friend Lyndon B. Johnson in Washington D.C. as Secretary of Transportation. Along with Jack Frye, Eddie Rickenbacker and Juan Trippe, Smith is considered one of the great airline men of American history. Throughout his life he maintained the connection with the Roosevelts.

C.R.'s friendship with the family – in particular, Elliott and Eleanor – was far-reaching in time and space. Not only did C.R. have the run of Hyde Park, but Eleanor and her family would stay overnight at his place in Washington when convenient.[172] As late as the 1960s, Patricia Roosevelt – wife nr. 5 – remembered encountering C.R. on a troubled overseas flight, and swiftly finding herself with a private jet at her disposal.[173] Similar assistance occurred from time to time, and as we shall frequently see, the White House would call on "C.R." rather than the Air Force when it needed something involving air transportation. The president even approvingly noted Smith's timely and efficient assistance at the Casablanca summit.[ii]

That the C.R. – Eleanor link was not mere strategic ingratiation is evidenced by Smith's own recollection: "She was one of the most unusual women I ever met, in intelligence, in energy. She was always interested in doing for someone else instead of someone doing for her. A generous woman and a prodigious worker." [174]

The connection with the Richardson – Murchison – Roeser crowd was of an equally fundamental nature. What they did for Elliott Roosevelt is quite well documented. What Roosevelt senior did for big oil is a much murkier matter. Nonetheless it is clear from preserved bits of Elliott's correspondence with his father that he repeatedly secured the oil barons' access to the president. It seems to have been little appreciated, however, that this connection was the opening chapter of what we might fairly call a "Texas Cabal" controlling much of the Democratic Party, and with it, often White House policy.

At that time the rough Texas *nouveau riche* were virtually unknown nationally. The sudden visit of Elliott Roosevelt ignited a generational political influence racket fueled

---

[i] E.L. Cord appointed C.R. Smith president on 26 October 1934, after his successful operation of the southern operations and FDR's abolition of the old airlines. (Serling: Eagle, 73).

[ii] ER: FDR, His Personal Letters II, 1393. C.R. visited the White House 12 times 1933-45. (FDR Lib).

by seemingly unlimited Texas oil money. In those days, Texas was a one-party state. Democratic bigwigs could arrange amongst themselves who should have which office, which perk, which license; and they unapologetically did so.

The two "good ol' boys" made rich as Croesus by a quirk of geology, Sid Richardson and Clint Murchison, were just starting out as plutocrats when Elliott met them, but they would be central figures in understanding the hidden side of American politics for the next generation-and-a-half. Richardson was the founder of the Bass Brothers megafortune, a goldmine for the increasingly right-wing politicians who found favor. Clint Murchison was later closely associated with Mob interests and also funded right-wingers. The two together hosted their favorites at their posh Hotel del Charro in La Jolla (north of San Diego); these included many people we shall meet later. They also used their friendship with J. Edgar Hoover, FBI Director, to obtain the nearby Del Mar racetrack from mob-affiliated interests.[i]

Not only "oiligarchs" were members of the Cabal. Publishers were equally important: Amon G. Carter, Sr., the tireless promoter of Fort Worth and publisher of the *Fort Worth Star-Telegram*, was one. Some suggested that Carter exploited his friendship with Elliott: "camping outside the Oval Office so frequently there was a story among reporters that an exasperated FDR told an aide: 'That man Carter is always wanting me to do something nice for Fort Worth, and if possible, to the detriment of Dallas.'"[175]

That was backwards. Amon was rich, and FDR curried his favor; and Amon had funded the Democrats well before he captured Elliott. Amon founded the first radio and television stations in the area, and American's first airport hub south of present-day Dallas-Fort Worth (DFW) was, officially, Amon Carter Field.

In 1936, Carter provided FDR with his "lucky hat." Secret Service boss Mike Reilly said it was so lucky that the president "wore it throughout the next three campaigns. When he ran in 1944, he had to get it back from a Hollywood movie star who had purchased it in a war bond auction."[176]

Of Amon's interest in aviation, his eponymous museum in Fort Worth has stated:

> In 1911, he headed a committee that brought the first mail plane to the area. In 1917 he was responsible for three World War I flying fields being located in Fort Worth. By 1928 he was a director and part owner of the Aviation Corporation [AVCO, a complex holding company], later a component of American Airlines.[177]

Thus, Carter and C.R. Smith were like peas in the pod. Whatever one might think of their machinations, they were extraordinarily accomplished achievers. They belonged to a business generation more focused on giving than taking, more interested in building the future than stripping existing wealth. The term "cabal" does not in itself imply criminality. If these people bent or broke the laws, it was a reflection of their robust, results-oriented mentality – something that would serve especially C.R. extremely well during the war.

Another Cabal member was Jesse Jones, who played a similar but even more influential role in Houston as the publisher of the *Houston Chronicle*. When FDR took over in Washington, Jones became the head of the RFC (Reconstruction Finance

---

[i] What happened at del Charro is a subject to itself (see an amazing exposé in San Diego Reader: Oil and Politics in La Jolla, 5 and 12 JAN 11.) Visitors included Hoover, Nixon, Connally, and famous mobsters.

Corporation), and thus effectively the world's biggest banker. Jesse Jones had been one of the main contributors to FDR's campaign. Though he was in the inner circle initially, Jones, reputedly an honest man, grew to dislike FDR's character. However, in Texas, Jones's brother John became quite close with Elliott Roosevelt. The Joneses, being Houstonians, were also friends of native son Howard Hughes.[178]

Politicians were important facilitators in this game. Texas's own John Nance "Cactus Jack" Garner was Vice President of the United States and, FDR thought, unseemly eager for promotion from that maligned office. Texas governor James Allred and his family were part of the favor mill. Allred, who served as governor from 1935-39, was a fierce supporter of FDR, and the White House was generous to him in turn.

Raymond E. Buck, a Fort Worth attorney prominent in Democratic politics, was also chummy with C.R. Smith and Lyndon B. Johnson. LBJ and his understudy, John Connally, were new but rapidly rising stars, promoted especially by Sam Rayburn, the long-serving Texas representative and Washington power-broker. Even in 1937 they, youngsters then, played important roles in the emerging Texas Cabal.

Elliott would work with them all. Or, perhaps more accurately, he would become their eager pawn.[i]

Running Gilpin Air Lines

While the unplanned 1933 sojourn in Texas would determine much of Elliott's path in life, at the time it was merely a highly memorable stopover on his celebrated cross-country escapade.

Elliott continued over to Tucson, Arizona. He knew a very important lady there. Her name was Isabella Greenway, and she was his mother's very close friend. Eleanor and "Aunt Isabella" had met in their teens because of Uncle Theodore's extensive connections. Isabella's parents were rancher friends of Teddy's, and both Isabella's future husbands had served in the Rough Riders.[ii]

As a sideline among her many adventures in the Wild West, Isabella Greenway founded that garden of desertly delights, the world-renowned Arizona Inn of Tucson. It came modestly into being during the Depression because Isabella took to employing desperate veterans as artisans and furniture-makers, and the inn served as a place in which to put their products to use. In so doing, she anchored the upscale neighborhood of Blenman-Elm, soon a refuge for affluent Easterners in need of sunshine and rest. That's where Elliott headed.[179]

Rooseveltiana connoisseurs probably remember that Eleanor did a very similar thing – at almost the same time – when she founded Val-Kill Industries, a small producer of fine colonial revival furniture in Hyde Park.[180] Unlike the Val-Kill business, the Arizona Inn is still in existence, and its private, peaceful cottages surrounding a Spanish-Moorish garden still attract wealthy people of good taste; if they are the former, they can exercise the latter in the resort's elegant old restaurant. The Roosevelt children were among the earliest guests.

---

[i] Approximately what here is labeled the Texas Cabal has been referred to as the "8-F Club" after the Houston hotel room where the principals convened over many years to discuss their initiatives.

[ii] 1st U.S. Volunteer Cavalry Regiment in the liberation of Cuba, 1898. Isabella Selmes married first Robert Munro-Ferguson, then John Greenway, and was widowed for the second time in 1926.

Isabella was elected Arizona's Congresswoman in a special election on 3 October 1933. She had to travel to Washington D.C. then, but in the meantime she had straightened out Elliott just enough to land him a fixed address and a job. Eleanor was immensely grateful to her friend.

Eleanor and Isabella exchanged a flurry of letters and telegrams in 1933 when the Elliott crisis was foremost on their minds. The focus of their concern, however, was having the time of his life.[i]

Elliott and Ralph Hitchcock motored into Tucson on 15 March, announcing that they would rest at the Arizona Inn.[181] Aunt Isabella seems to have kept them on a low profile for a while, but Elliott did get hauled to various social and political functions. It was a time of momentous events: the banks reopened, and President Roosevelt cut veteran's benefits to save money. The Disabled Veterans of the World War held a protest meeting, to which Isabella and Elliott showed up. The boy was invited to speak, and he made some inane remarks about the president trying his best in the unparalleled crisis that was unfolding: "Roosevelt received warm applause at the conclusion of his short talk. The veterans felt an obvious sense of relief at hearing words direct from the son of the man who had such powers over their future." [182]

Isabella Greenway, already revered, was the star. She was the one to whom Arizonans in general and veterans in particular appealed when in need of help from Washington. The Roosevelt kid was merely a curiosity at that time.

On 22 March Elliott wrote his mother: "Have decided to develop Indian Hot Springs with Aunt Isabella. Feel it would be a great mistake for Betty to bring baby out until next fall if she intends to rough it with us. Springs are 150 miles from Tucson facilities very primitive not having heard from Betty since start of trip do not feel that I should write or wire to her. Love. Elliott." [183]

There is a scribble in Isabella's archives, apparently from grandmother Sara, which casts light on Elliott's unceremonious dumping of his wife:

> I am happy to hear from Eleanor that you & Elliott are to develop the Hot Springs, it seems to me a great chance for dear Elliott to do <u>anything</u> with you. Personally I did not want him to have a ranch. Also I am fond of Betty & I did <u>not</u> like the way I heard her spoken of in Washington as "his wife."
>
> She is very young & inexperienced, & very shy, but <u>I</u> consider she is very like her father, & will show many fine qualities. She adores Elliott & their beautiful baby, but she <u>needs</u> love & affection, & <u>consideration</u>. Please be good to her dear Isabella…[184]

Indian Hot Springs, then co-owned by Mrs. Greenway, is near the upper Gila River northwest of Safford. Though remote, it was once a popular recreation spot, famed for its "curative and recuperative powers." Elliott's plans soon were rumored to the press. Probably he was inspired by his father's spa project in Warm Springs, Georgia.[185]

In those prewar days, hot springs were thought to convey magical healing powers on the infirm. President Roosevelt was a fervent believer, which is why he spent so much time at Warm Springs. The water did nothing of the sort; but it was surely pleasant. It is amusing to note that today FDR's extravagant claims for his spa resort,

---

[i] The Greenway – Eleanor correspondence and supporting documents are kept at the Arizona Historical Society (AHS) , Tucson.

despite their attracting thousands of lame and ailing customers, might have gotten him accused of quackery by his own alphabet soup regulators.

Indian Hot Springs, however, may have been just a tad too far out in the Arizona wilderness for most people. Had Elliott and Mrs. Greenway built an airstrip there – there's plenty of room – perhaps the springs would have had a better future. They thought of it, but left it at the thought.

Elliott went out to I.H.S. to arrange for a survey and get plans for a decent hotel drawn up. But Isabella later wrote her regrets to a disappointed subcontractor, a Bisbee engineer: "I am very sorry that it was necessary for Mr. Elliott Roosevelt to change his plans, which resulted in the inconvenience to you of a wasted trip to the Hot Springs. Mr. Roosevelt has taken charge of an airline in California, and for the present, at least, will not be active in the development of the Hot Springs." [186]

The engineer had made blueprints for the resort on an earlier trip, and now wanted to get paid. Isabella again wrote him: "I was exceedingly sorry that a number of confusing problems met Elliott Roosevelt at the time he was to meet you there, and we were both rude and unfortunate in failing to let you know. Please accept my sincere apologies." [187]

By 21 April, Isabella had given up on the resort plans. For whatever reason she decided not to develop I.H.S. after all, and in time handed the property off to other investors. Elliott had gone out there to make some tentative plans. In fact he had a large shipment of "Moose Head" delivered to Safford, the closest railhead, where he apparently forgot it. A year later the railway dunned Mrs. Greenway, saying charges were accreting at six cents a day. Aunt Isabella paid the bill.[188]

Perhaps Elliott had intended to celebrate his father's legalization of beer.

Instead, by early May Elliott was given the job as manager of Greenway's boutique airline, a curious little outfit known as G&G Gilpin Air Lines. It was based in Glendale, near Hollywood. The airline's business records are preserved down to the ticket stubs in the archives of the Arizona Historical Society. Unfortunately, somehow Elliott Roosevelt's brief tenure left no explicit trace in them.

Elliott was then 22, and not a licensed pilot. His flying experience at that time was as haphazard as his formal education. He let it be known that his first flight was in a naval aircraft back in 1918, when his father was Assistant Secretary of the Navy. Since then he had had "scattered instruction and a number of hours of dual control." He also told a story about having taken dual instruction in a homemade flying contraption built by some of his friends at school.[189]

He had never been able to settle long enough to get a license, which even in 1933 required considerable book and practical knowledge. However, in Los Angeles he took out a student certificate. Even in those days a student pilot license allowed for solo flight; there was also an initial certificate known as an "amateur license." Within a year, Elliott managed to rack up 75 hours of solo time, but he was still aiming for his private pilot license by the summer of 1934.[190]

Interestingly, Elliott noted that mother Eleanor was as air-minded as anyone, and that she would enjoy nothing more than to fly her own plane. Eleanor was indeed always eager to take to the skies, and she admired and encouraged those women who did – notably her friend Amelia Earhart.[191]

The small and unprofitable Gilpin Airlines consisted by then of one single route, which ran from Glendale (Los Angeles Co.) over Lindbergh Field (San Diego) to the Agua Caliente resort in "Old Mexico." Agua Caliente was an airport for Tijuana as well as the site of a famous racetrack especially favored by Hollywood's rich wastrels. That was before horse racing and betting, not to mention intoxicating spirits, were legalized north of the border.[192]

Just before Elliott took the job, Gilpin terminated a daily service to Palm Springs due to lack of business. It was clear, though, that the airline specialized in a niche market: recreation trips for the well-heeled.

Truth be told, Gilpin Air Lines was a ragtag outfit. In May 1933, it had five aircraft. One was a single-engine, six-seat Fairchild Model 71. Another was a similarly small San Diego-built Ryan Model B-5, a relative of Lindbergh's *Spirit of St. Louis*. The other three were eight-seat trimotors of the Bach marque. They were numbers 5, 9, and 11 off the Santa Monica line. Only about 30 Bach trimotors were built. They were not very successful. Their main claim to fame was their propulsion by a motley collection of dissimilar engines mounted on the same airframe.[193]

The Mexican route was flown by Bach 3-CT-6 and -8 "Air Yachts." The airline brochure stated that they would land in other airfields enroute if requested. Although Glendale, San Diego, and Tijuana were the scheduled stops, landings were also made at Long Beach, Santa Ana, and Ensenada, B.C.N. The pesky coastal fog made operations difficult, but no fatal accidents occurred on the route.

For our purposes, it is not irrelevant that the airline boasted a mapping and aerial photography capability on request.[194]

Why would people pay good money ($7.50) for an air ticket to Mexico if they could drive the distance in a few hours? Well, during Prohibition, travel and trade with Mexican border towns flourished. Tijuana's bars, casinos, race tracks, and bordellos were teeming with American party animals, and some were in enough of a hurry to flutter along at 125 miles per hour in something that looked like a homebuilt Ford Trimotor.

"Gilpin" was Charles William "Bill" Gilpin, who had been Mrs. Greenway's associate in Tucson. He had learned to fly during the war and then became her husband's chauffeur and fixer. The long distances in Arizona persuaded the Greenways that aircraft were the solution to southwestern travel.[195]

Gilpin Air Lines had its origin in a small outfit called Pickwick Airways, bought by Gilpin in 1929. Pickwick had flown the same aircraft, chiefly in California and Mexico, and Gilpin had been one of its pilots. After the market crash, the airline became unprofitable, and by 1932, Gilpin owed Isabella Greenway $40,000. That January, Greenway reorganized the line as G&G Air Lines Company. At that time it had about thirty employees, of whom G.L. Slaybaugh was the general manager. Mrs. Greenway used the airline much as a personal travel agency, especially in her political campaign in the thinly populated state.[196]

Greenway is widely recognized as one of the titans of Arizona history, but Gilpin is little remembered. Yet it is one indicator of this team's bequest to the state's aviation heritage that for many years Tucson had a "Gilpin Airport" (also called Freeway Airport) near downtown; it ran a flight school, but the operator kept the Gilpin Airlines name. The Davis-Monthan Airport Register (at Tucson's original city airport, now site of the Air Force's famous "boneyard") reveals that Mr. Gilpin often landed there, and that U.S. Customs took an unusual interest in his travels and cargo.[197]

Flying a Fairchild monoplane, Bill Gilpin was killed in a weather-related accident near Toluca, Mexico in July 1932, on a flight from San Diego to Mexico City. The accident also seriously hurt James Crofton, the millionaire president of the Agua Caliente Resort, and a mystery woman who turned out to be his secret new wife Mona Rico, a stunning Mexican film actress.[198] Crofton was one of the "border barons" who had made a vast fortune off Mexican vice. Along with a representative of the Baja governor, he had been on his way to meet President Ortiz Rubio in the capital.[199]

The horrific accident was, in a sense, fate's warning shot across the bow; within two years the United States gave up on Prohibition, and in Mexico, the reformist regime of Lazaro Cardenas closed down the casinos.

Without its chief pilot and driving force, Gilpin Airlines was clearly floundering. Greenway thought she would give the similarly floundering Elliott an opportunity to look into it. The business records suggest that Elliott's posting was little more than a charade. It was G.L. Slaybaugh, the "acting" (but real) manager who signed the paperwork and kept the line running.

In May 1933, there were only four pilots and nineteen employees left. That month the line reported 172 hours flown, 482 passengers carried, and 155 trips completed.[200]

Although Elliott Roosevelt was eminently unqualified, his name brought some free publicity to the airline. The Eleanor-Isabella correspondence shows that the two were trying to "fix" the Elliott situation. They agreed that Eleanor should come out for a visit. Now gainfully employed – at least his gain – Elliott also agreed to the family conference:

> Elliott did telephone me saying he would let me know whether he and girl would be willing to see me Stop He asked me not to see mother till afterwards but I insisted if I did not see her I would write just what I had said to him Stop Will abide by your decision as to whether it is better to have mother in Tucson or not Stop I have had no wires from Elliott yet Stop I shall go to Tucson in any case and if you let them know that I will be there I will feel that I have done my share Stop Am seeing Martha and Charles this afternoon Much love to you.[201]

The "girl" was probably Ruth Googins, who would be wife nr. 2. Elliott had telephoned home, but as late as 1 June Eleanor had no address for him. Interestingly, references to the "girl" and to Eleanor's friends were redacted in the book *A Volume of Friendship* about Isabella and Eleanor's correspondence.

Few could have been fooled that the Gilpin Airlines job was anything but a family favor, but at least initially, Elliott made a good impression. He was also politically attuned enough to foreswear any government subsidy: "I want it understood right now that the Gilpin Line doesn't want or seek any air mail contract," he trumpeted. The national air mail controversy was already heating up.[202]

That was a lie, for there is a record of Elliott submitting a bid for an air mail contract. Historian Ted Morgan found that "Steve Early opened the bid and was horrified that it came from the president's son and turned down Elliott's low bid and gave the contract to Pan American." [203]

That makes no sense since Steve Early was FDR's press secretary, but possibly Elliott had tried to bypass the bureaucracy through him. If Pan Am got the contract, it was probably a Mexican mail route. Many years later, Elliott did refer to this incident when he said bidding on a mail run was the only way Gilpin could raise necessary capital. But he said Postmaster General Jim Farley told FDR, and "Pop" told him "Sorry Bunny…it would look like nepotism." [204]

That Elliott was known as a party-boy and a boozer might actually have been an asset at this particular airline. Prohibition had been good business for many people. So when his father persuaded the states to repeal the constitutional ban on alcohol, effective by December 1933, a lot of enterprising folks were left high and uncharacteristically dry.

Gilpin Airlines folded along with the 18th Amendment, but Elliott Roosevelt actually abandoned his job seven months before that. So how effective had Elliott really been in his short stint as general manager?

Surviving accounts paint a familiar picture of high enthusiasm, limitless optimism, and hard work followed soon by a change of interests.

Elliott assumed the airline position on 11 May 1933.[205] On the occasion of Eleanor Roosevelt's visit on 7 June, a local writer adept at subtlety, Erskine Johnson of the *Evening Independent*, wrote:

> Mrs. Franklin D. Roosevelt found out one thing as soon as she arrived here on her cross-country hop to "see how her son Elliott was getting along." [Eleanor had flown to Los Angeles to talk Elliott out of his looming divorce.]
>
> That was that Elliott Roosevelt isn't afraid of work..."I've got a new job to do," said young Roosevelt, looking up from his paper-littered desk in his office at Grand Central [Glendale] Airport, "and I'm going to do it well or know the reason why. It's taking me 15 to 18 hours a day to get the hang of this business, but it's great fun…"
>
> "I have been interested in aviation for the last six years, and have done some publicity work and aviation surveys in the east. I have flown some, too, and taken dual-control instruction, and perhaps I'll get a chance here after a while to go through with my flying training."
>
> As soon as possible, probably in July, young Roosevelt plans to buy a home here for his wife and six-month-old son, who are living in New York. While embarking on his new career, Elliott is living with friends here.
>
> The business of an airline is new to him, but he has had business experience. At 20, he determined not to go to college and joined an advertising concern. Six months later he was vice president of his own agency. At 21 he had gone broke, and accepted a job with an old, established firm.
>
> He likes his fun, this Roosevelt, it seems, because he got into all sorts of scrapes while a student at Groton school, where any infractions are quickly noted. But all that is forgotten now. He's at his office and in the hangar from dawn until midnight, and there is no loafing. [He] has made a hit with his fellow-workers. He calls them by their first names, and he's just plain Elliott to them. In the office he studies operating methods and ways to increase business. Out in the shop he spends hours with Harold Wolcott, chief mechanic. "Elliott has been over every ship with a fine-tooth comb," said Wolcott.
>
> Veteran pilots of the company, which operates planes between Los Angeles, San Diego and Agua Caliente, and maintains a charter service, like him.
>
> "What I'm trying particularly to do is to build up the charter end of our business," Elliott explained. "I want to keep a fleet of planes and a corps of pilots ready to go anywhere in North America at any time." [206]

Obviously a lot went between the lines. What the "veteran pilots" really thought did not make it into the papers, at least not at first. Elliott, prudently, announced that he would have to get settled down in his new job before announcing any expansion plans or changes of policy. Staying with friends, he supposed that "every real estate man in

Southern California" would try to sell him a house the next day, but he admonished them that he was not yet in the market.[207]

Airlines and Politics

Elliott's brief mention of an aviation survey he had done refers to a peculiar task the then 21-year old advertising agent completed for his friend E.L. Cord, who was plotting to take over much of the nascent airline industry. The industrialist Cord was associated with the beginnings of Stinson, Vultee, AVCO Lycoming, Duesenberg, Auburn, Cord, and many other hallowed names in aircraft and automobiles.[i]

The syndicated columnist Drew Pearson had some contacts in the airline industry through which he appears to have acquired a "funny feeling" about what Elliott had been up to in terms of airline contracts. Pearson also was a "buddy" of Harold Ickes, the Interior Secretary, through whom he learned much of what happened in the Cabinet.[208]

Pearson knew about Elliott's project for E.L. Cord, and his notes suggest he must have heard about another favor involving Northwest Airways. To Drew Pearson, Elliott explained when queried on 8 July 1936:

> In the summer of 1932 the Paul Cornell Advertising Agency was employed by E. L. Cord to make a survey of the management and operations of Transamerican Airlines of Detroit a recent acquisition of his. The fee paid for this service was $5,000 of which as the employee assigned to make the survey I received 15% commission. The Cornell Agency employed Eugene Vidal to aid me as a technical expert. He received $500. I knew nothing concerning any subsequent PWA allotments or mail contracts granted to the above company or American Airways as the report submitted was sufficiently uncomplimentary to Mr. Cord's managers that my employment ceased several months before my father became president.[209]

The long-forgotten Transamerican Airlines served Cleveland, Detroit, Chicago, and Buffalo. Cord wanted TAA in order to secure American Airways a transcontinental route network.[210] (PWA was the Public Works Administration.)

It was then noted that Elliott got the survey job through E.L. Cord's stock market ally, the prominent banker and Roosevelt backer Frank A. Vanderlip. It so happens that Vanderlip was one of Cord's collaborators, along with a certain Amon G. Carter, in wresting control of AVCO, American Airways' owner, away from W. Averell Harriman. And they were all massive contributors to the Roosevelt campaign.[211]

Although Elliott's report was apparently critical, the task already revealed the contours of collaboration between stakeholders who would become important to both Roosevelts, father and son, when FDR became president.[212]

The commentariat naturally assumed that the survey had been thrown to Elliott for political reasons, but he asserted that if so, his report was unwelcome in its conclusions.

It was an odd introduction to aviation.[213]

Drew Pearson, however, was interested in hearing more about the Northwest Airways "job." He had been pursuing a line of inquiry leading to the conclusion that

---

[i] For a survey of Cord's machinations in the airline industy, see Airlines and air mail: the post office and the birth of the commercial aviation industry, by F. Robert van der Linden.

influence-peddling had something to do with Northwest's air mail contracts. In his column, Pearson noted that Elliott's then brother-in-law, Robert Donner, was a director of Northwest Airlines. It needed to light its new St. Paul – Seattle route, and that would reportedly cost $1,200,000. After Elliott's friend Eugene Vidal was appointed head of the Bureau of Aeronautics, the government installed the beacons and radio ranges.[i]

Pearson may have been barking up the wrong tree. At the time the government was beginning to take over the national airspace system, including the then private navigation aids, something people take for granted today. But Pearson's sources, which cannot be identified from his notes, caused him to poke Elliott about the matter. He answered:

> At no time have I ever served Croil Hunter or NWA or contacted any governmental official or agency in their behalf nor have I ever contacted Mr. Farley on behalf of American Airways. I trust that this is a sufficiently clear answer to your questions. I would appreciate a wire if there are any further matters concerning my past with which you might be interested. Sincerely Elliott Roosevelt.[214]

Whatever it was Pearson had – and his scribblings on the matter are voluminous and mention a great many important aviation names – he did not pursue this matter further. Croil Hunter was the president and long-time driving force in Northwest Orient Airlines, known as Northwest Airways before 1934. "Mr. Farley" was James Farley, a close Roosevelt friend and the political strategist behind FDR's victories. He was appointed Postmaster General and thus in charge of awarding the air mail contracts.

These little airline "favors" place in perspective a report of another transportation survey Elliott allegedly completed. One of columnist Westbrook Pegler's informers wrote him that one time after FDR took office, Elliott showed up in Nashville and asked the regional railroad company (Nashville Chattanooga & St. Louis RR) for a job. Informed politely that none was available requiring his skills, he asked instead for a railroad pass since he was going to be in the area for a while. Put on the spot, the railroad president agreed to slip him a contractor's pass. Sometime later, Elliott again showed up with a "rather lengthy report of things he had seen on the railroad that could be improved." This "gift" having been accepted, he then sent a bill for a rumored $20,000, which the railroad eventually found it necessary to pay. [215]

Whatever the actual truth of this story, it does seem to fit with numerous other similar accounts of Elliott's entrepreneurial triumphs, published or not. Only the amount sounds unreal, and it was indeed common to exaggerate the amounts the Roosevelt children finagled from others.

Back at Gilpin Airlines, Roosevelt was – initially – proud of "his" airline. He noted that in 2½ years of operation, the line had flown 25,000 passengers nearly 2,500,000 miles without even a minor accident – at least on its scheduled routes. The fatal Gilpin accident in Mexico was a different story.[216]

Rickety as the trimotors appeared, they were nonetheless the key to safety during that era. Engine failures were common, but with two out of three running you'd be OK. "Bimotor" aircraft were dangerous; they did not have the excess power to survive on one engine, and the asymmetries induced could easily make the plane keel over into a

---

[i] Misc. file, 21 JUN 45, ER file, Pegler/HH; also ER file, Pearson/LBJ. In those days, visual (light) beacons marked air routes for night traffic.

death spiral. Not until Donald Douglas sold his sleek new airplane, the DC-1 and its descendants, would twins become the standard. Then they ruled until the four-engined transports conquered the world in the 1940s.

After a couple of weeks as boss, Roosevelt took a "purely social" trip to Ensenada, the then-quiet fishing village about an hour south of the border. There he met with General Plutarco Elias Calles, the de facto dictator of Mexico, who had formally resigned as president in 1928 in favor of a string of puppets. On that same airplane trip, he also met the recently resigned President Pascual Ortiz Rubio. "There was no discussion of a possibility of establishing an airline from Los Angeles to Mexico City," clarified Elliott.[217]

His denials can never be taken at face value, but what exactly the Mexican semi-fascist rulers and the son of Franklin D. Roosevelt needed to discuss remains unknown. The combustible mixture of casinos, dictators, and gangsters ought to clue us in, however. General Calles, from the border state of Sonora, was cozily in bed with the organized crime figures who herded Americans to Tijuana to separate them from their dollars. But the whole of Mexico was then essentially a Mafia state, and those who could offer the *caudillos* the best deals came out ahead.[218]

At the time of Elliott's visit, Mexico's nominal president was Abelardo Rodriguez, a warlord who had become governor of Baja California Norte before Calles installed him in the presidential palace. Rodriguez was, in fact, one of the "Border Barons" – a motley crew of American entrepreneurs and Mexican enablers who controlled the "sin" business along the border. Another of these superrich oligarchs was James Crofton, the man who had nearly died in Gilpin's crash in Toluca.

There is another clue emerging from Gilpin Airlines' work for the Border Barons. One of the barons was Wirt Bowman, who had made a fortune thanks to the right combination of bribes on both sides of the border. Unfortunately, now the Treasury Department was after his ill-gotten gains. A researcher found that "In Nogales it is still rumored that Bowman donated $25,000 to the Roosevelt presidential campaign to have the tax charges against him dropped. While the contribution cannot be verified, it would have been in character." [219]

His troubles continued, though, and "The Bureau sought criminal charges against Wirt, who was by then Arizona's Democratic National Committeeman, but prosecutors declined 'for the reason that they were considered inadequate.'"

Bowman was a close friend of Jim Farley, FDR's patronage boss. He said himself he had given over $30,000 to the Democratic Party, and he did provably give $10,000 to Roosevelt's campaign. He therefore felt that he was entitled to the ambassadorship in Mexico, D.F., and his *compañero* President Rodriguez seconded the claim; but FDR never followed through. Perhaps Bowman's criminal connections were too obvious.[220]

Back in Arizona, Bowman's self-interested activism was a problem for a furious Isabella Greenway; she was forced to acquiesce to his uninvited cochairmanship of the Roosevelt campaign in that state.[221]

Although he kept interesting company, there is no evidence that Elliott Roosevelt got anything out of the Mexican angle. [222] It is nonetheless startling that Elliott would repeat this pattern many times throughout his life. He seemed to be drawn to dictators, viewing them as lucrative business opportunities. His need for easy money caused him to consort with swindlers and gangsters everywhere he went. While there are many such people, Elliott's last name gave him access to the royalty of that class – tyrants.

Before striking it rich, however, he had some personal business to attend to.

New Deal for Matrimony

Although Eleanor Roosevelt's western expedition had been highly advertised, it is not clear how much reporters suspected of the underlying family dissension. By this time it must have seemed odd that Elliott's wife and baby were languishing back east. Publicly it was still held that Eleanor was simply coming to visit her son and perhaps help him choose a home so his wife and child could follow him to California.[223]

To the last moment, Elliott maintained that the gossip about a new girlfriend was utter rubbish. Tain't so, he protested: "I am not in love with any woman. I am going to devote all my energy to making good in my life work – aviation." [224]

And as he would so many times later, he ridiculed the reporters' suspicions even as he knew them to be accurate: "It's a wonder that they haven't got me in a romance with Helene Madison, the swimmer. We posed for a picture together down at Palm Springs, you know." [225]

Indeed he did; the swimming pool picture was all over the papers. (Ms. Madison was a then famous world-record swimmer turned actress.) Of course there is no reason that dalliance couldn't also have been true. The most persistent rumors, though, seemed to have an epicenter in Fort Worth, Texas.

"Ridiculous," said Eleanor when confronted with the Googins story. "There will be reports of his intending to marry ten different girls at a time like this. You must remember he still is married." [226]

His mother knew that Elliott was demanding a divorce, and she had come to talk him out of it. When she arrived, the cat finally got out of the bag. It was revealed that Elliott had established residency on the Nevada side of Lake Tahoe on 27 May. Under Nevada law, this enabled the absent Elizabeth Donner to file for divorce after six weeks.[227]

This meant in practice that the Gilpin Airlines manager had absconded to the pine forests of Nevada, and had to briefly come back south to meet with mother Eleanor.

Mother and son and Aunt Isabella met up in the border town of Douglas, Arizona, on 5 June. It was a meeting of the trimotors: Elliott flew in on a Gilpin Bach, and Eleanor arrived on a special extra flight of an American Airways Ford Trimotor from Dallas via El Paso. The local newspaper reported that Elliott, who had arrived early, "took up many of the waiting throng for brief rides in the air. While young Roosevelt handled the controls, the regular pilot of the ship, Ben Catlin, sat by his side to watch his chief's ability as a pilot." Apparently, the unlicensed Elliott was already well-versed in airmanship, what with three weeks of experience.[228]

Aboard Eleanor's flight was no less than C.R. Smith of American Airways. From then on he was always ready when the Roosevelts needed him. Also aboard was Amon Carter, the wealthy backer of FDR and influential associate of Smith's and his airline.[229] Carter was already a close friend of Ruth and Elliott's, and he was later instrumental in pushing Elliott to seek Texas elective office, although these plans foundered.[230]

C.R. Smith had gone to painstaking lengths to impress the Roosevelts. He had managed to fly the "First Lady," both coming and going, in a special Trimotor, using two of American Airways' "best-known pilots," Paul Vance and Theron Wilbank. On the return trip, Smith even secured special dispensation from the Commerce Department to get beacon lights turned on between Memphis and Nashville. Evidently such largesse was not common.[231]

C.R. noticed that Eleanor flew without staff or Secret Service protection. At the numerous stops, it was hard for her to protect herself from clamorous well-wishers and people who wanted to be seen with her. So the next time, C.R. told her:

> "Look, you're not going to get by with this traveling by yourself for very long. It's going to run you nuts. You really should have somebody to fend off some of these people that want to fit in what they want to do with what you want to do. And this is a really presumptuous suggestion, but any time you travel on American Airlines I think I'll run along and see that you're well taken care of. And I'll see that people don't bother you unduly, and I think it might save you some headaches." [232]

And so C.R. became Eleanor's steadfast traveling companion. He'd remain a family friend, spending the weekend at Hyde Park often, even after the president's death. It was a nice gesture, and probably also good for business. The hospitality extended to staff and friends: in 1937 Eleanor wrote: "Elliott said he could get Earl a pass on the American Airlines to the coast and back...," for a joyride to visit family.[233]

In those days airline travel was regarded as a novelty and an adventure – and so was the new president's wife, already referred to as "America's flying first lady." Crowds and official delegations greeted Eleanor everywhere. On her way west to talk sense into Elliott, she managed to find twenty minutes to dedicate the new international airport at Douglas, Arizona before a throng of appreciative locals.[234]

Although Eleanor maintained that her trip was entirely private and non-political, the Arizona Historical Society has a striking photo of Eleanor speaking from a platform in Douglas, campaigning for Isabella Greenway, whose primary election was on 7 August.[235] Whether the first lady appreciated it or not, she was inherently political everywhere she went. And naïve as she was, she seemed unfazed about the practice of accepting major favors from the rich and powerful. After all, they were just Elliott's friends!

After landing in Tucson, Eleanor and Elliott motored to Greenway's Arizona Inn, a few miles north. In the peaceful surroundings there, Eleanor finally had the chance to recuperate from her bouncing transcontinental trip. Elliott did not help her rest, however. His insistence on a divorce deeply disturbed his mother.

The next day Eleanor had a busy official schedule, meeting with delegations from the copper mines and the veterans associations. She was already adept at the incessant people-greeting and delivery of pleasant vapidities to delight congratulators. But, as local press coverage showed, she offered more than that, emphasizing social consciousness and the need for global action. She was already an activist. Not so her son.[236]

After spending the night in Tucson, the combined party made a brief stop in Phoenix before heading for Los Angeles. The Ford was flown not by its regular crew, but by Eddie Martin, a Southern California aviation pioneer. When the "giant skyliner" arrived on the evening of 6 June at United Airport (i.e. Burbank), a crowd of 10,000 welcomed the flying circus: Eleanor, Elliott, Hitchcock, Smith, Carter, Martin and a few others. Will Rogers, the ubiquitous humorist and aviation promoter, was among the well-wishers; he told Eleanor that her trip was a big boost for aviation.[237]

During her whirlwind trip, the president's wife didn't have much time alone with her son. For lunch, Elliott brought along a new friend, Robert Gross, the treasurer and leading investor of the new Lockheed Aircraft Corporation. Gross would be Lockheed's president during the following epic decades. Elliott's liaison with Gross would become of interest a couple of years later, but it took Bob Gross less than a year to decide not to have anything more to do with Elliott Roosevelt.

The first lady took time to visit the little Mexican shops on Olvera Street to buy trinkets. Then for dinner, she and Elliott were joined by C.R. Smith and Amon Carter.[238]

In private, Eleanor did her ablest to dissuade Elliott from divorcing Betty. Yet as an unhappy woman trapped in a fake marriage, she failed to convince; especially a headstrong, impulsive boy like her second son. Despite the maternal recriminations, Elliott was able to present Eleanor with a marital *fait-accompli*. His divorce plan was already well along, and the official denials had become stale.

The *Los Angeles Times* managed to corner the Roosevelts and force them to own up to the truth. Here is how the *Times* reported the ambush:

> …he [Elliott] denied having been in Nevada or that there was any marital rift. The President's wife likewise denied on Wednesday that she came West in a final effort to bring about a reconciliation between her son and daughter-in-law.
>
> "We have planned this meeting for some time," was the answer made by Elliott for his mother. But as they were leaving the Biltmore before dawn yesterday Mrs. Roosevelt and Elliott were shown the exclusive story regarding the divorce plans in The Times.
>
> Mrs. Roosevelt then admitted that the story was correct. Asked to explain the technical phase of Elliott's establishing a Nevada residence, she turned to Elliott, who pointed out the means by which his wife could obtain a divorce when he fulfills residence requirements. [239]

Thus on 8 June, the papers reported that Elliott and Betty were getting a divorce, with the husband having already established residence in Nevada.[240]

After only 36 hours in town, Eleanor Roosevelt started back early on the morning of the 9th. C.R. Smith's Trimotor had been flown up to Saugus Field (Santa Clarita) from Burbank in order to beat the "June Gloom" fog that is the bane of the California coast. Smith and Carter still came along; Aunt Isabella left the plane at her Tucson home.[241]

Elliott and Ralph Hitchcock stayed behind and then left for Reno. Down at the historic Grand Central Air Terminal in Glendale, this was of some interest to Gilpin Airlines. Reporters noted:

> That his six weeks' residence in Reno will not effect his position with the airline was declared by those in touch with his affairs. He expects to carry on his duties via telephone and mail. Stacks of letters yesterday awaited his attention at the Gilpin offices, but he did not call there to read them.
>
> A suite of rooms is in readiness for Roosevelt and Hitchcock in a Glendale hotel, but it is expected he will not occupy them until his six weeks are put in at Lake Tahoe. He moved out of his former South Kingsley Drive residence two weeks ago.[242]

Quite apart from running an airline, Elliott Roosevelt stayed immensely active during that very short period in the spring of 1933. That would remain a hallmark of his persona; he was in that special category of "hypersocial" people who operate constantly through a vast store of personal connections, and who find sticking to one task (or one spouse) for any length of time insufferable.

It is recorded that Elliott managed to fly to Memphis and meet his scorned first wife in April, before he took the Gilpin job; that apparently was the last time he saw her.[i] As Eleanor told Lorena Hickok: "Elliott is meeting Betty in Memphis on Wednesday. Franklin talked to him & then he called her. I dread it for her, & yet I see how she may annoy him. Oh, dear, I am an old woman!" [243]

And slightly later: "Betty just came in to tell me she had telephoned Elliott, & he wanted her to go ahead & didn't seem to care. She looks so white, but she's very self-controlled, & my heart aches!" [244]

Entreaties were to no avail. During the same period Elliott made occasional visits to Fort Worth, where the replacement, Ruth Googins, was waiting in the wings.[245] During May Ruth actually came out to stay with Elliott in Glendale. She was seen with him at the office and around town; people just didn't know who she was until the news from Fort Worth broke.[246]

In sum, Elliott seemed to have had an extraordinarily busy social life as an airline manager. He made speeches; he hung out with friends; he met movie stars and foreign dignitaries; he plotted his spousal transplant. All along he flew with the airline throughout the southwestern states and Baja California. In a curiously appropriate remark, given his own situation, he said:

> "Another thing I'm trying for," he added with a twinkle, "is complete cooperation with Cupid. We'll specialize in flying matrimonially minded couples to Yuma, Ariz., (where most of the movie couples elope). And, of course, we'll be willing to fly them to Reno later." [247]

His own complex uxorial exchange would be launched ten days later when Elliott went back to Nevada. By the time his mother returned to the White House, the nation was abuzz with talk of the first White House divorce ever. Elliott had begun to attract the unfavorable attention that would follow him all his life.

One writer provided an insightful snapshot:

> He was the most pleasure loving of the five children of Franklin Roosevelt, and yet the least conscious of his inherent social position. He liked to pick his own friends, to mingle unrecognized with the crowd at theaters and prize fights, to spend weekends with gay young crowds at country resorts, and to rough it in the west during summer vacations, working his way like any ordinary youngster.
>
> As had his brother, James, and their father before them, Elliott attended Groton school … It is so exclusive that the children of old families are registered for enrolment when they are born – an Episcopal institution of monastic simplicity and discipline.
>
> Elliott Roosevelt didn't take very kindly to this environment. He never became a senior prefect as his brother had done. He detested Latin and Greek, skimmed through these courses by a slim margin, but delighted chiefly in schoolboy pranks and in athletics.[248]

The writer noted that Elliott had been introduced to the pretty and, better yet, rich Elizabeth Donner at a dance in Northeast Harbor (Mt. Desert Island), Maine, and that a lightning campaign of courtship, engagement, marriage, and progeny followed. Just as fast, the arrangement collapsed. Elliott would not be pinned down:

> But with the political triumph of his father, Elliott found his life covered with reflected glory and worst of all – with patronage. He felt that much of the business he

---

[i] NYT, 9 JUN 33. White House records show Betty leaving for Memphis on 10 April, returning 13 April.

> brought the firm was tainted with politics. And so, still bent on personal independence, he gave up his position and went to California as manager of an airline.[249]

In those days obtaining a divorce required considerable planning and legal assistance. In Nevada, either Roosevelt could sue for divorce if one of them resided there a total of six weeks. So by the beginning of June, Elliott lived in the home of one Samuel Platt, located at the wooded Elk Point on breathtakingly beautiful Lake Tahoe.[250]

Samuel Platt was no randomly picked landlord. Although both Republican and Jewish, he was very prominent in Nevada politics, business, and society, and as a lawyer and former U.S. Attorney he was specifically selected to handle some of the nation's most prominent divorce cases, including those of both Anna and Elliott Roosevelt.[251]

Oddly, the youngster who had accompanied Elliott across country, Ralph Hitchcock, was still with him. Elliott said he and Ralph intended to live a rugged outdoor life, swimming, fishing, and hiking in the mountains.[252]

By 15 July everything was ready for the wife transplant. In Elliott's own words:

> While I was in Arizona, Betty and I agreed that we had come to a parting of the ways. I became the first White House child in history to seek a divorce. A shock wave of righteous indignation rolled across the land. Father showed great understanding...he sent Mother off on her first transcontinental flight to meet me in Los Angeles. With every member of the family regarded as "hot copy" by the city desks, that trip itself made news headlines. My new friend, C.R. Smith, flew with her from Texas to California...
>
> The divorce was granted in Nevada. From there, I went to Chicago, where Anna joined me, again on the instruction of Father. He wished her to accompany me to my 2nd wedding, which took place in Iowa in July, a matter of days after I left Reno. There was no question yet of Father making difficulties for any one of his children in a domestic upheaval. [253]

On 17 July, the divorce was granted in a secret hearing. Elliott and Betty mutually claimed extreme cruelty. It merely confirmed that the two absolutely could not get along. It barely needs a mention that Betty obtained custody of one-year old William. Elliott had never shown any interest in him. On a visit a year later, Eleanor showed him his child.[254] Maid Lillian Parks recalled: "...it broke our hearts because we didn't see Elliott paying attention to his little child, Billy. They met on the stairs and Elliott didn't pick up or hug or kiss him. The word got to Eleanor and she was heard dictating a note to Tommy [her secretary] to remind herself to tell Elliott he should spend more time with his son." [255]

Yet William, who became an investment banker and pilot, would later assist his frequently broke father financially.[256]

Back at the White House, Eleanor had to tell Betty about Elliott's new belle. She took it like "a brick" – meaning stoically. "There is good stuff there & she'll make some man happy in the future." [257]

Jilted Betty Donner was far from in the White House doghouse. Eleanor invited her and her son along to Campobello Island that summer. It was characteristic of Eleanor that she showed no animosity, and tried her hardest to get everyone to get along. She would show the same generosity and support to (almost) all Elliott's discarded wives, and she tried to do the same with the similar crop produced by the four other siblings.[258]

Betty Donner did get back at the Roosevelts by donating $4,000, a minor fortune, to the Wendell Willkie campaign in 1940.[259] But unlike her father, she did not renounce her citizenship.

Wife Nr. 2: Ruth Googins

Excepting debt service, Elliott Roosevelt was never the dilatory sort. The moment he was a free man, he took a United Airways flight to Chicago, via Salt Lake City, Cheyenne, and Omaha. It is remarkable how accepted and regular cross-country air travel had already become, despite its undeniable cost, hardships, and dangers.[260]

Elliott said he had three reasons to go to Chicago. First, to meet his sister Anna, who was next in line for the Reno procedure; second, to visit the World's Fair, and finally, to discuss the possibility of a job with one of the large aviation companies. He said that the legalization of horse racing in California would cripple Gilpin Air Lines, so he was looking for another job. At that time, he said, he had 70 hours of flying time in the logbook and he was going to "stick to it." [261]

However, reporters knew perfectly well what was going on. Curiously, Ruth Googins also decided to visit the Chicago World's Fair. As is often the case, just before the climax the families indignantly proclaimed their denials of romance to all sides:

> I regret that the newspapers, in their effort to make something out of nothing, have seen fit to drag into this present situation the name of my daughter. It is true that Miss Googins knows Elliott Roosevelt and has seen him several times on his visits to Fort Worth. She regards him highly as a friend and she, too, regrets the attempt to magnify the whole affair.[262]

Similar more or less smirking claims of innocence came from the two principals, whom the Dallas newspaper was nevertheless quick and inordinately proud to first expose to the American public.[263] It wrote that despite the denials, every newspaper in the country except one carried the news of the romance on the first page, giving credit to *The Dallas News.*

Thus, having "coincidentally" met in Chicago, Ruth and Elliott proceeded immediately to Iowa, meeting up again at the home of Ruth's grandparents. Sister Anna came along; at the time, she was "favorite sibling", possibly because she agreed to let Elliott's divorce take priority.[264]

On 22 July 1933, five days after the first White House divorce, Elliott married Ruth Googins in Burlington, Iowa. There were few guests. It was a decidedly low-key affair, marred only by a large crowd of unruly gawkers.[265] Among the select attendees was of course, C.R. Smith, who served as best man.[266] When C.R. himself got married in Dallas in December 1934, Elliott was an usher at the wedding.[i]

There was some difficulty finding clergymen willing to officiate for the freshly divorced father. The Episcopalians were not fond of his antics, and he was ostentatiously dropped from the then highly important New York social register. A willing local official was found. However, the Iowa state law prohibiting the marriage of recently divorced persons was conveniently overlooked, although it was acknowledged that its disregard made Mr. Roosevelt technically guilty of a misdemeanor.[267]

[i] NYT, 30 DEC 34. It didn't last (the bride gave up on being "married to an airline"); C.R. never remarried.

"Elliott says Granny has tried Ruth to the breaking point because she always talks about Betty!" So wrote Eleanor in 1937. Persistent family taunting about the ex-wives would become a ritual at Hyde Park, but Ruth held up better than her successors.[268]

Ruth was a good catch. The journalist Lorena Hickok later stopped by the Roosevelts' Fort Worth ranch and wrote her intimate friend Eleanor back:

> As for Ruth – she really is a vast improvement over Betty, I should say. She's the neatest sort of person and darned attractive – even when pregnant. There certainly is nothing sloppy about her, mentally or physically...we discussed aviation, politics, and various phases of the recovery program. She certainly held up her end. I doubt if Betty could have...you get the impression of capability and steadiness.[269]

As late as 1939, Anna thought Ruth would straighten out Elliott. Unlike him, she had determination and perseverance. She was also more actively involved than usually acknowledged. Anna wrote to Eleanor:

> I am hoping that that same determination which made Ruth so anxious to marry Elliott without delay will now come to her aid in helping her stiffen Elliott's backbone. I know, because I was with Elliott at the time, that both Ruth and her mother were terribly insistent that the marriage should go through without delay and that they worked on him constantly for this. I am only afraid of one thing and that is that Ruth is so ambitious that she may keep on pushing Elliott to too great an extent with this business of his...[270]

It seems like there wasn't much time for airline management any more.[271] By mid-July, Roosevelt's absence at Gilpin had caused the chief pilot, Jack Slaybaugh, to no longer sign as "acting" manager. The company had not heard from its general manager.[272]

Apparently there was some grumbling; it was noted that the absent chief had publicly dismissed his airline:

> If Elliott Roosevelt returns as manager of Gilpin Airlines it'll probably surprise most of the boys at Grand Central Air Terminal...some of them out there understand the President's son referred to the line in a press interview as being "dinky," – which did not sit so well.[273]

He told *Aero Digest* later that after studying the failing airline, he advised Mrs. Greenway to close it, "which she did with a sigh of relief" – but Gilpin didn't actually cease scheduled operations until half a year later, on 5 January 1934. Of course, it is likely that Greenway had been looking for a way out for some time.[274]

Correspondence suggests that Elliott had been involved in attempts to sell the airline both to Bob Gross of Lockheed and possibly to E.L. Cord. In August, Mrs. Greenway's lawyer was investigating these leads, which, of course, came to nothing.[275]

On 18 July, Roosevelt had already let slip that he was again looking for a job, and Anna said that he "doesn't know where he and his wife will live and he has no plans about his work at the present time." [276] Amidst this uncertainty, the newlyweds stayed for a few days in Fort Worth at Ruth's mother's house, with a disconnected telephone. Her father, he of the meat-packing fortune, had died, leaving her well taken care of.[277]

By the end of July, Ruth and Elliott drove back to California, stopping for a visit in Arizona.[278] On the 4th, they checked into the Miramar Hotel in Santa Monica, where they were soon recognized and cajoled into explaining themselves. Elliott complained:

> I came out here last time as general manager for Gilpin Airlines. The line, I know, doesn't need me and besides that I just can't be connected with any airline because of the air mail contract angle between the Federal government and the companies.
>
> I want to go to work; I must go to work. We want to settle down here while I get in something that holds a future for me. My experience so far has been largely in advertising and publicity fields. I would like to continue along this line.
>
> We want to lead our own lives in Southern California. We want to live here, but I do not intend to take any position offered me merely because I am the son of the President or one in which I would have to be made the center of personal publicity.[279]

During the summer of 1933, Mr. Roosevelt was hardly the only young fellow looking for work. He did not, however, have to sell apples on the sidewalks or surf the roofs of freight trains. He went to auto races, toyed with the idea of a movie career, and posed for photographs with Ruth. Not exactly shunning personal publicity, he pursued his numerous celebrity connections in the town he had called home for only three months – and that was counting two months in Nevada and the Midwest.

The unlicensed pilot even found time to be inducted into the Los Angeles Police Department's "Aero Squad." He carried Badge Nr. 22. What, if anything, he did for the LAPD was apparently not recorded.[280]

A Crack at the Movies

In August, Elliott considered offers from three major Hollywood studios. What he was supposed to do for them, other than bring publicity, is unclear. The *Washington Herald*, however, had one clue:

> Young Roosevelt has been lunching daily with Merian Cooper, head man at Radio [20th Century], and indications are that he'll tie up with that studio. Only thing that's holding up the deal is the grease paint angle. The President's son is more than willing to turn actor, but has been advised against it.[281]

Perhaps posterity lost a great movie actor there. But one of the Hollywood bigshots, Frank W. Vincent, kept – said an insider – a souvenir under the glass on his desk: Elliott's personal check for $500, which bounced.[282]

The bad loans fit with Eleanor's worried lament to her husband, noting that Elliott sounded "a trifle discouraged." "I can't believe he's getting married for he has no job but I'm writing Anna to find out if he actually needs money. I think it is better to let him fend for himself but I don't want him to borrow from others or to give the impression to others that we won't give him anything." [283]

Ominously, another correspondent alerted readers as follows:

> Rob Wagner suggested in the *Beverly Hills Script* that it would be a good idea for some member of the Roosevelt clan to come out and get the young chap before he wore out the carpets in the studio reception rooms, not to mention the damage he might be doing to the reputation of the Roosevelt family, the Administration, and the Democratic Party.[284]

Script was a local film magazine put out by the socialist Rob Wagner, who was a fierce defender of FDR.

Elliott just couldn't stop peddling influence, even within the new movie industry. Correspondence suggests that he was instrumental in getting two very heavy hitters, Eddie Cantor (president of the Screen Actors Guild) and Joseph Schenck (president of United Artists and then 20th Century Fox), to visit the president in Warm Springs in November. At the very same time, the new administration was working on a new code to govern compensation in the film industry. On 11 November, the White House wired Elliott back that FDR would not be able to "discuss code questions of any industry." But the two moguls did visit the president in Georgia, and the newspapers duly told the public that they dwelled entirely on innocent topics.[285]

Then on the 27th, in Warm Springs, President Roosevelt announced the new industrial code for the motion picture industry. In effect, it brought the sector under tight federal supervision, although it avoided introducing government censorship. The president suspended the most objectionable clauses of the regulation, and installed Eddie Cantor on the authority overseeing the industry.[286]

We are not quite done with Joe Schenck, who was a strong supporter of the administration and the Democratic Party; for FDR's sons often crossed tracks, including those of major contributors.

As already mentioned, brother James also later tried his hand at movie making. In this he worked with two other friendly Joes, his "foster father" Joseph P. Kennedy, and Joe Schenck. While Jimmy admitted that the film he produced with Jimmy Stewart was bad, as usual columnist Westbrook Pegler had a more complete version. He wrote that Sam Goldwyn gave James Roosevelt a job "at $35,000 in recognition of latent talents" that however, remained latent:

> This was the time that he borrowed a young star named Jimmy Stewart, a property of great price, and moreover, borrowed $50,000 from a magnate who shall be nameless here because he later had to go to jail for trying to gyp the Treasury….Jimmy borrowed Stewart, produced a turkey which laid an egg and went short the $50,000 on due day.[287]

Pegler wrote that the un-nameable movie magnate later claimed that Jimmy ultimately did pay the debt, and the lender, after his jail term, was then pardoned by President Truman.

Indeed, James Roosevelt later revealed that he borrowed half a million to finance his only film, *Pot o' Gold.* The law-troubled contributor was, in fact, Joe Schenck, and Jimmy admitted trying to keep him out of jail by interceding with President Roosevelt and many others – thereby causing Treasury Secretary Henry Morgenthau to threaten to resign, as he often did when he smelled a rat. Jimmy mentioned no missing fifty grand, though.[i]

Strong dissuasion by "friends" caused Jimmy to resign from Schenck's organization in September 1939.[288] Jimmy and Joe Schenck stayed at the White House on 12 December 1939, but despite Jimmy's persistent and ultimately highly obnoxious efforts with his father and Morgenthau, he was unable to keep Schenck out of jail.[289]

---

[i] JR: My Parents, 254-6. JR may have adjusted the sum for inflation in his memoirs, getting half a million. "As I remember it, I came out of it with a small profit." Others obviously didn't remember it that way.

The Schenck-Jimmy alliance must be seen in wider context. Schenck was with the Mob. Part of his job was to funnel Mafia money to the Democratic Party; "half a million to Roosevelt's campaign for the syndicate" was reportedly mentioned by top mobster Sam Giancana himself. Schenck was the prime investor in Agua Caliente, which Elliott's airline serviced.[290]

Thus it seems likely that the persistent bonds between the two eldest brothers and organized crime were first forged in pre-war Hollywood.[291] However, when Elliott ingratiated himself with Schenck in 1933, the Mob's takeover of Hollywood was only beginning, and the large Mob contributions to the Democratic Party came in later years.

Elliott soon fell in with wealthy schemers outside the movie industry as well. In Los Angeles, he connected with a mysterious entrepreneur who sometimes answered to Grenville Stratton, other times to George W. Stratton. He was best known as a Los Angeles horse breeder and racing entrepreneur; but he was also involved with Donald Douglas in running not only the aircraft business, but a special outfit, Douglas Oil at Santa Monica. Douglas Oil is mostly remembered for having built a brand-new petroleum refinery which Stratton then, in an inscrutable transaction, dismantled and sold to the government for delivery to the Soviet Union in 1942.[i]

In September 1933, in the earliest recorded venture of the two, Elliott and Stratton performed a reconnaissance of new oil fields in the Bakersfield area. Nothing came of that project, but Stratton and Roosevelt were soon working on others.[292]

A correspondent later noted that Elliott engaged a contractor to remodel the house he was renting in Beverly Hills: "It took my friend quite some time to get paid for the work and when he did get paid it was with a check signed by Stratton." [293]

Back in Tucson, the highly esteemed Isabella Greenway concentrated on her political career; she went to Washington as Arizona's only representative in October. She had done enough favors for Eleanor's son, but perhaps surprisingly, they still got along. On 27 September, she wired Eleanor back at the White House: "Lovely visit with Elliott who seems happy full of plans and much work." [294]

In 1947, General Roosevelt was asked by the United States Senate about his experience as an airline manager. His memory was already spotty:

> Mr. ROOSEVELT. I headed an airline company that operated between Los Angeles, San Diego, Caliento, and Ensinato, Mexico, and it operated with no Government subsidy.
>
> Senator FERGUSON [R-Mich]... How long did you remain with that company?
>
> Mr. ROOSEVELT: Sir, I think that I remained with that company from the summer of 1932 until it closed; I think it was about 6½ months.
>
> Senator FERGUSON. Then what did you do, General, in the line of aircraft?
>
> Mr. ROOSEVELT. In line of aircraft, I flew privately, and I learned to fly at that same period of time, and then I went to work for William Randolph Hearst...[295]

It was rather less than 6½ months. The evidence shows that Elliott was actively on his airline job for two weeks, from 11 May 1933 to 27 May, when he moved to Nevada. By the time he came back, Gilpin had no use for him, but the budding airline mogul was

---

[i] LAT, 22 NOV 42, 23 NOV 42. There are "snitch" letters in the Westbrook Pegler papers insisting that Elliott was involved in this affair, e.g.: "A fellow by name Stratton, as President of Douglas Aircraft, asked Elliott how the deal could be managed and Elliott said 'his old man would take care of that.'" This was hearsay, but was dated 17 DEC 42, when the matter was fresh and Elliott was not in the news. (Letter, Greenwood to Pegler.) Three years later, "Douglas Oil at Santa Monica was always a come-on proposition with the understanding that the Administration was behind it through Elliott."

now nonetheless inordinately eager to share his aviation expertise with an insufficiently grateful world.

Hearst's Roosevelts

Elliott Roosevelt had found another important friend. So important, in fact, that some credit him with making and breaking presidents, and starting wars at will. He was William Randolph Hearst, the aging newspaper magnate who controlled much of public opinion in the United States. Hearst's machinations had helped secure Roosevelt's nomination in 1932, and he had made a large investment in his campaign. Hearst allowed FDR to become president in part because he thought he would honor his promise to avoid international involvements.[296]

Hearst was in deep financial trouble owing to the Depression. When FDR devalued the dollar, Hearst gold investments recovered. But he wanted additional control of the new administration, and FDR's children needed jobs. Nevertheless, the new president would soon slip his strings, and by 1936 the two titans were enemies.

After FDR's inauguration, Elliott and his elder sister Anna (and her second husband, John Boettiger) soon had strangely high paying jobs with the Hearst chain. Elliott became aviation editor of the *Los Angeles Examiner* on 26 August 1933.[i] His syndicated columns were printed in other Hearst papers, including the *Rochester Evening Journal* back home in New York.

Elliott must have been deeply gratified that he had obtained the new position entirely on his own merits.[297] He also found that it provided an immense amount of free flying – he said 150,000 miles by air in one year, which would have been about 1000 hours and probably a substantial exaggeration. That is hard to come by even for professional pilots.[298] But it is true that Elliott began his job by touring the routes of all the major airlines, so that he could write about them.

The hostile *Chicago Tribune* sniped that Elliott's "starting salary as a cub reporter was $200 a week, above that of many a star reporter." That was just to begin, though. Worse yet to that rival paper, his elder sister Anna and her husband also got Hearst sinecures: "In 1937, Boettiger was made publisher of the *Seattle Post-Intelligencer*, a Hearst newspaper. His salary was reported to be $40,000 a year. Anna went along as women's editor at a salary understood to be $10,000 a year." [ii]

Whatever Hearst's calculations, it is not good to get on the hate-list of the nation's journalists.

In his old age, Elliott publicly boasted that he had also been W.R. Hearst's personal pilot. That makes no sense, but it is true that he was friendly with WRH Junior, who was also a pilot. The way Elliott remembered it in 1989 was that he had been entrusted with flying guests to the San Simeon castle, which is probably true in a collaborative sense, for he often went there. But it was his newspaper job he was paid for.[299]

In those days, "aviation editor" was an important post, duplicated at many respected newspapers. Today civil aviation is a common and much-cursed commodity, and it can be difficult to appreciate the glamor and excitement it held between the world

---

[i] The Los Angeles Herald Examiner / Express was a major, now defunct, Hearst newspaper.

[ii] ChigTrib, 20 JUN 48. One source has Hearst paying Elliott $30,000 as editor in 1933 and $50,000 as radio chief in 1935 (J.E. Smith, 405)

wars. Admittedly, today air travel is fraught with indignity, irritation, and disgust. It is also safe almost beyond imagination – years go by without a major hull loss, and when it does happen, a hell of recrimination and complaint breaks lose.

By contrast, in the 1930s, flying was exceedingly dangerous, uncomfortable, and unreliable. Yet pilots and aviation entrepreneurs were viewed as heroes and saints (often of the martyred kind), somewhat like astronauts a generation later. The perception was that they were boldly changing the world, as the computer and Internet masters would do two generations later. National and personal pride was bound up in each new aircraft design, each new pioneering flight, each new speed and altitude record. That aviation was only a tiny percentage of the economy (or even of national power) was easily missed. It was the direction that counted. It was up, and fast.

Into this feted atmosphere of promise and hope waded the young Elliott Roosevelt. His oracular epistles fell into a predictable category, that of aviation boosterism. A rising technology always has its fervent cheerleaders, and boosterism is the easy and safe approach. Skeptics and naysayers were unpopular; they represented the massive inertia of the past. Yet they had important points to make, not least because they had vested interests to protect. This was especially the case for the U.S. Navy, and also for the land Army, not yet divested of its rebellious air arm.

In late August, 1933, Elliott launched his first broadside in the Hearst press:

> I hope that those who read what I have to say regarding aviation as an industry, and as a national and social necessity, will not be those who are today taking part in its advancement, or who are today taking advantage and accepting its undoubted service. I aim to reach the average man and woman, who have a vague idea that the industry is growing in importance in their own community, but do not know how it actually affects their lives.
>
> This country has one man to thank for an object lesson. I refer to that great Italian flier, Balbo. – 24 ships flew with ease from Italy to Chicago, and returned. Those 24 ships are fighting craft – instruments of war capable of annihilating the whole populations of cities the size of New York, Chicago, Los Angeles and San Francisco.
>
> The U.S. is no more an isolated nation. Our boundaries, with two vast bodies of water to the east and west, and two friendly nations to the north and south, have made us practically impregnable from a military viewpoint in the past.
>
> Today all that is changed. When 24 ships can fly with ease from Rome to Chicago, 2,400 can likewise accomplish the task. Is this nation prepared to meet attack and launch a counter-attack in case of war? "No," is the sad but unmistakable answer.
>
> Well, let's get around to facing the facts. Our army and navy air equipment is so far behind the rest of the world that today we rank fourth among the nations of the world in number of airplanes in active military service.
>
> England, France and Italy far surpass us in military strength in the air. Nobody in this country seems to realize that Japan and Soviet Russia are concentrating on increasing their strength in the air so that shortly they, too, will surpass us. As far as sheer numbers, then, we seem to be outclassed. How does our equipment stand up by comparison?
>
> I believe our navy could not at the present time duplicate the Italian seaplanes' feat. Navy officials may challenge my statement. The average equipment used by the army air corps, from my observation, is not what might be expected of a powerful nation such as ours. I have actually been in a commercial transport plane that flew circles around a regular army pursuit ship!
>
> That took place only last Spring. How about personnel?
>
> We have a fine group of men in the service in both branches. BUT, they are helpless and would be out-classed against the aviators of the leading nations in battle.

> I do not criticize economy. We have had need for just that in our government for years. But, today, we are striving to keep our defenses impregnable. For that reason we are spending millions on a navy program. I do not blame our government for wanting to increase that arm of our defenses.
>
> In 1917, when Germany had destroyed 155 British ships, we had over 100 cruisers and 350 destroyers. Today we have only 50 of the first type and 150 of the second type. The government has awarded contracts for 37 new ships. These ships will cost $238,000,000. Fine, but all 37 of those ships would be helpless against a similar number of Japanese ships supplemented by their modern airplanes.
>
> The Pacific Coast, with its great pride in advancement and achievement, is asleep. The most powerful industry on earth, in years to come, has made California its cradle. Vast fortunes were founded and built in railroading from its birth through the long years of growth. Railroads became the backbone of our land. Aviation and air transportation stand where railroads stood 50 or more years ago. The same vast fortunes will be built by the same type of pioneering men in this still now infant industry during the next fifty years.[300]

Although he seemed to lose his train of thought, Elliott's arguments were generally well-stated and reasoned; of course, he had plenty of editorial help at Hearst. Everyone was "for" aviation and national defense – in that sense his views were not controversial. But on closer inspection, Elliott's points were airy, perhaps even flatulent.

It was plainly ridiculous to suggest that Mussolini's air force had the power to eradicate all of America's major cities. The idea that a nation's self-respect was tied up in the number of aircraft it commanded was dangerous. In 1933, the alarmism about other powers' might was misplaced. For people of a slightly later generation, the assertion immediately brings to mind the self-interested cries of "bomber gap" and "missile gap."

By 1933, the United States had, under the commercially minded Republican administrations, presented the world an image of peaceful development and of leadership in international disarmament. On the world stage, the Republic stood as an admonition that soft power might be far stronger than the massed divisions of the Old World. The naval arms control treaties of the 1920s were notable triumphs, and they were American-led.

Unfortunately, events slowly began to move in Elliott's direction. Still, it would be nearly eight years before the United States began seriously modernizing and expanding its puny Air Force. That the generals of the "bomber mafia" would then be acclaimed as prophets should not obscure the fact that rearmament in the early 1930s would in many respects have been a waste of money – especially considering the worsening Depression.

Aviation jingoism was popular, but not helpful at home or abroad. To some extent it supplanted and indeed ran afoul of the more accustomed naval jingoism. Yet the era called for wise, skeptical, modest, prudent, careful leadership. The era did not get this – but undeniably Americans got rather more of it than did Europeans. And although Elliott's father was not a neutralist, budget pressures forced FDR to fairly starve the military until the much anticipated European war of revanche finally became a reality.

Still based in Los Angeles, the second son stormed ahead in the papers. His opinions, he modestly protested, were entirely his own. They certainly soon flew in the face of his father's aviation policy. His 31 August column defended the airlines and their air mail subsidies against encroachment and budget-cutting.[301] But air mail had already become a political football, and Elliott was heading for severe turbulence.

He was proving himself useful to the industry. Not only that, he shortly began hatching a scheme that, had it become known or, worse yet, been successful, might have tainted the administration beyond repair. While publicly defending the airlines, he secretly plotted to take them over.

Consistently, Elliott promoted a large, even imperial, government role in aviation. His logic was that of all lobbyists: "My industry good. Market not enough to support it. Government must step in." But unlike many self-interested cynics, Elliott was perfectly sincere about this. And after all, he wrote at a time when people had, at least temporarily, lost their aversion to imperial government. He was not ideological per se.

Elliott was more effective as a cheerleader for aviation than as a lobbyist. On 12 September 1933, he went up in Donald Douglas's new and revolutionary DC-1 at Santa Monica's Clover Field. Eddie Allen, Douglas's test pilot, flew. Among many celebrities, along went George Hearst, the son of WRH. He was also a pilot, and in a prudent move, he made friends with Elliott.[i]

The single DC-1 was built for TWA, but it soon wound up in the hands of the glory-seeker Howard Hughes, who contemplated using it for setting new records. It would be the much improved (but still ornery) DC-2 that TWA brought into service, and the larger and much more docile DC-3 that would conquer the world.

Jack Frye of TWA might be considered the father, or driving force, of the DC-2. But it is necessary to bear in mind that the DC-3 was C.R. Smith's baby. He insisted on it for American Airways, and he noted that "the DC-3 freed the airlines from complete dependency upon government mail pay. It was the first airplane which could make money by just handling passengers." [302]

We may also note in passing that American, as usual, had no money to buy the new planes. C.R. went to Texas friend Jesse Jones, now FDR's head of the Reconstruction Finance Corporation (RFC), and asked for a loan. He got $4.5 million. But it *was* a good investment.[303]

The *Nourmahal* Incident

Elliott Roosevelt was now free to criticize his father's aviation policies in the papers. This did not help his popularity at home in Hyde Park. It all added up: the Texas escapade, the divorce, the failed jobs, and now the criticism of the president, obviously instigated by his Hearst and airline connections.

One incident was seemingly quite amusing, and so it was presented. Few grasped the dark machinations that lay behind it. On 30 March 1934, Elliott telephoned the White House and said that he and Hearst wanted to talk with the president as soon as possible. He said they planned to fly out in the next couple of days. Marvin McIntyre, the secretary, telegraphed the president (who was at sea) "May I wire him OK?" There is no record of the answer, but it seems the kid was coming anyway.[304]

On 2 April 1934, Elliott and George Hearst flew by private plane from Fort Worth to Miami via Shreveport. Hearst junior remained in Miami, although at first it seemed that Elliott intended to take him along to visit the president.[305]

The next day Elliott transferred to a naval seaplane making the presidential mail run, and set out to meet up with FDR aboard Vincent Astor's gigantic yacht *Nourmahal.*

---

[i] Rochester Evening Journal, 12 SEP 33. GH, like Elliott a serial monogamist, was then married to the Western aviation pioneer Blanche W. Hill.

Brother James was also flown out to the ship. It was deep in the Bahamian archipelago, anchored off Guncay Island, constantly escorted by U.S. Navy vessels.[306]

Astor was a close friend and major financial supporter of President Roosevelt. His 263-foot ship *Nourmahal* was a favorite rest-and-relaxation vehicle for FDR. Son James said, "In public life he was the champion of the little man, but in private life he befriended big men," maybe because the super-rich wanted nothing from him. That might not always have been true, though.[307]

For the Navy, supporting the president on the high seas for two weeks was not a minor undertaking. Naval aviator E. E. Elliott made two long trips transporting White House mail, and also passengers, first James, then Elliott. He was officially commended for doing a particularly good job taking off from a rough sea with heavy swells.[308]

The encounter with Elliott aboard the *Nourmahal* was far more important than has been generally assumed. This will become clearer as we unravel the other plots and controversies that Elliott was simultaneously involved in.

It is odd that the president chose to go fishing for two weeks during the Depression, especially considering that the then raging air mail crisis was by no means over. But FDR liked to get out of town, and his "fishing trips" were often in pursuit of more than the finned variety. At any rate, the story that was released to the public was of good-natured sparring between father and sons, and it spawned a tiresome array of silly fish stories. Fed by the president's staff, the *New York Times* reported that "Mr. Roosevelt greeted his sons with hearty handshakes which entirely belied the rumors of ill health, and joined them this afternoon when the yachting company took to small boats to fish among the shoals of Elbow Key, southeast of here." [309]

That was a lie. Later it was leaked that FDR refused to see Elliott, who was publicly undermining his aviation policies.

Collier said that Elliott had "inveigled" his way onto the seaplane, and that FDR told Astor not to let his son – who arrived drunk – on board the ship. This episode was the origin of Elliott's snide remark that "George Hearst had only limited capacity for handling his liquor." [310]

James, who was there, has told the most complete story of the incident, but without realizing its portent. But we may get a clue in one remark:

> The trip was memorable because it was one of the few times I recall that Pa lost his temper completely with one of his children – in this case, Elliott – and the only time I ever knew him to display anger over a family matter in front of an outsider.[311]

Jimmy said that the Navy seaplane carrying mail arrived with Elliott, who was uninvited, unwanted, and badly hung over:

> Father told Vincent, "Do not let him come aboard!" and went off fishing in a small boat so he would not be there to receive him…Vincent was in a dilemma: he was loath to disobey the President, but he just couldn't leave Elliott to swelter in the bouncing seaplane anchored off the yacht. He took Elliott aboard, and hustled him into a shower.
>
> When Pa returned, he was exceedingly annoyed that his instructions had been disobeyed. "He is to go back with the plane, and he is not to have lunch with us!" Father told Vincent. He sent for Elliott and read him a lecture in a voice that carried through the thick doors and walls of his cabin. Then Elliott was sent back on the amphibian.[312]

Jimmy later recalled that "if the irrepressible Elliott felt disgraced he certainly didn't show it. On landing he hunted up the newspaper correspondents, who were unhappily sequestered in a temporary White House headquarters at Miami, and told them a fantastic yarn about the results of a fishing contest in which Pa's luck was not so good." [313]

This, too, was not the whole story, although Elliott's calumny was all over the papers. The well-informed trade journal *Aero Digest* soon wrote: "He [Elliott] went to Hearst and said, 'I don't think that father has had the right advice on this matter. If you'll charter a plane I'll fly to Miami and see what I can do.'" [314]

The article's author spoke with Elliott, so his is likely to be a truer version. In other words, abetted by the aviation-minded Hearsts, Elliott was trying to change his father's policies. FDR refused to see him, well knowing the "advice" that was coming.

The snarky *Aero Digest* article intimated:

> So Elliott and George Hearst took off for Miami, where Elliott met his father, who was cruising around on a fishing and loafing trip with Vincent Astor – which was a lot cheaper for the taxpayers than having to steam up one of the Navy's cruisers for him, just so he could catch himself a sea bass and a couple of flounders. Well, Elliott didn't get much change out of the President, who, like all fathers, didn't take a lot of stock in his own son's ideas. He just said that Elliott should go see some Cabinet officers and tell his story to them. "Now, if you'll excuse me," said his father, "I'm busy with this fish."
>
> He saw the Cabinet officers and spoke right up to them, too. Perhaps this intervention hadn't much effect on the ultimate outcome, but it serves to show the stuff he's made off.[315]

For two years the rest of the story lurked in the shadows, until a disillusioned *Aero Digest* launched a full-scale attack on President Roosevelt. By then, the evidence showed that Elliott had been involved in an exceedingly nefarious scheme to take over the airline industry, and that his mission to the ship was undertaken in a last-ditch attempt to talk his father into supporting the plot. For the details of this caper we must await a following chapter, but for now it provides a clue to "Pa's" explosive fury at "Bunny," and the ice age that followed between the two.

At any rate, back in Miami, Elliott retaliated by announcing that his father was a "rotten" fisherman, which led to a further flurry of light entertainment originating from the *Nourmahal.* Elliott's "gross libel" made an opening for the president to amuse the reporters with a series of increasingly outrageous fish stories. These occupied much of the White House press corps' dispatches from Miami during the next few days. The episode provides an example of how easily the president was able to manipulate the reporters, and the extent to which they – or most of them – preferred light fare and were eager to please the president.

But after the failure of the aeronautical schemes Elliott tried to sell to the president, it was leaked that Elliott would only be welcome at the White House if he didn't mention aviation: "Elliott may come to the White House whenever he chooses and stay as long as he likes and he may talk with his father about any subject in the world – except aviation. That subject is taboo." [316]

After the abortive yacht visit, Elliott went to Washington for a last ditch attempt to work his contacts. He showed up at the White House on the 4th and operated out of there for ten days. He took along an air mail pilot, Ted Kincannon of American Airways. Friends Isabella Greenway and Amon Carter had already been visiting. Elliott had mobilized all his connections, and still he met a stone wall in the cabinet. After a while he returned to Fort Worth.[317] He had put a brave face on it with his fish stories, but the fact was that he was cowed and dispirited. To find out why, we shall first have to examine the famous Air Mail Fiasco of 1934.

Family strife calmed down in June. Elliott and Ruth produced a daughter, Ruth Chandler, who required an introduction to her grandparents; Ruth finally got to see her in-laws; sister Anna went to Reno to duplicate Elliott's feat with the six-week express divorce; and Elliott himself unexpectedly got a new job. He would now be vice president of the Aeronautical Chamber of Commerce of America (ACCA) in Washington – in other words, a lobbyist.

That did not by any means imply that his connection with the Hearsts was over. After a brief pause, Elliott's role in the media empire would continue until the late 1930s, when the inevitable parting occurred. Hearst broke with FDR early (and violently), but Elliott would take his time severing his ties. Elliott said his father sicced the federal tax agents on Hearst, though they found nothing actionable.[318]

Although W.R. Hearst started out as an important backer of Franklin Roosevelt, he soon became a fierce enemy of the New Deal, and he may have deliberately used Elliott to taunt FDR. It certainly worked that way. By 1936, Elliott Roosevelt was appointed a vice president of Hearst Radio, in charge of four radio stations in Texas and Oklahoma.

Of course, Elliott had no money of his own, so his ascent as a radio mogul occurred with considerable assistance. As we shall see, the Texas "oiligarchs" got Elliott into the radio business as an owner, but it was Hearst who started him out running radio stations. The *Tribune's* Walter Trohan, always hot on his trail, later reported:

> From 1935 to 1937 Elliott was back with Hearst as manager of a chain of Texas radio stations. The stations were originally owned by a Texas business man, who gave Elliott a vice presidency at $30,000 a year. Four of the stations were sold to William Randolph Hearst. The FCC was debating the deal and was about to rule against Hearst. Elliott visited the White House and applied to the FCC for approval of the transfer as the representative of Hearst. The transfer was approved by a surprise vote of two Democratic members of the commission, when the protesting Republican member was out of Washington.[319]

Franklin Roosevelt's contemporary critic John T. Flynn had access to more details, and made the case that influence-peddling secured Elliott's place among the media moguls. He said Elliott Roosevelt applied to the FCC for the deal in May 1936:

> One Commission member objected but the two Democratic members were for instant approval without a hearing. The objecting member didn't like the idea of the President's son appearing before the Commission which his father had appointed. Then in a month or two the summer arrived and the objecting member left on vacation. As soon as he was out of town and on only an hour's notice the remaining two called a snap meeting and approved the transfer. A member of the President's family called from the White House to urge to transfer "because it meant so much to Elliott." It did indeed. He got a large sum for each of the stations transferred and was engaged as vice-president of the operating company at a large salary.[320]

Flynn's accusations were usually more factual and temperate than those of the knee-jerk Roosevelt-haters. The question is what they mean, even if true. If it was indeed the case that Elliott obtained the licenses due to White House pressure, it seems that a criminal investigation would be justified. But what if he would have prevailed in any case? It is not easy to prove anything about other people's motives.

Quite possibly this way of doing business was considered par for the course then, and may be so in some venues even today. Certainly, the doctrine of avoiding even the appearance of malfeasance was not yet well-established before the war.

A few years later, when the tax agents grilled him, Elliott did say that Hearst paid him a commission of $25,000 or $30,000 (he could not remember which) for selling the four stations – not bad for standing in for the boss with the FCC.[321]

Elliott also maintained other radio interests in Texas, some in his wife's name.[322] By the end of 1937, Hearst made him president of the ten-station nationwide Hearst chain.[323] One result of this radio empire-building as well as his initial "aviation editor" position was that Elliott, for better or worse, never lacked an outlet for his opinions.

Hearst was sneakier than Elliott suspected. After making the president's son president and manager, the hard-pressed media mogul began selling the stations out from under him. Meanwhile, the breach between Hearst and FDR degenerated into open warfare, and the son was in the middle. He was bitter. He thought brother James, then "assistant president" in the White House, was plotting against him; and Eleanor confessed that "no one is being entirely truthful with Elliott." [324]

As Hearst Radio declined to four stations, Elliott attempted to buy up the Texas stations. By April 1939 he finally quit Hearst entirely.[325]

Hearst and FDR, both Democratic politicians, had a complex relationship of long, wobbly standing. From California, Hearst had been instrumental in helping FDR obtain the Democratic nomination at the Chicago convention in 1932. Elliott described this episode on the eve of the decisive final vote as follows:

> Telephone calls went out to Hearst at San Simeon, California. The newspaper tycoon was no friend of Father's, though he had softened his antagonism when, four months earlier, Father spoke out against America's joining the League of Nations – and thereby infuriated Mother and most of her friends. But Hearst nurtured an irrational hatred of [Al] Smith after a series of feuds with him in New York. Between the two candidates, Hearst preferred Father. If [John Nance] Garner would swing California, which was pledged to him, into supporting Father, the Lord of San Simeon would not stand in the way.
>
> Garner proved willing. "All right," he said, "release my delegates and see what you can do. Hell, I'll do anything to see the Democrats win one more national election." But the Texas delegation struck a bargain before they would go along with California: Cactus Jack [Garner] must be nominated as Father's running mate. That was agreed. [326]

That is the generally accepted though simplistic version, but there are many supplementary narratives illuminating this complex operation. One of them asserts persuasively that Tucson's Isabella Greenway, who led the Arizona delegation, was at least as effective in swinging California over. The wealthy widow's determined and effective campaigning for FDR gained the party's admiration even before she ran for office herself. And, she proceeded to champion the vice presidential slot for Garner, withdrawing her own name.[i]

---

[i] Mrs. Greenway's role at the 1932 Democratic National Convention is detailed in Miller, 170-80. The 1932 convention was an epic political event, and many claimed to have swung the nomination to FDR. Jim Farley wrote that "Joseph P. Kennedy, who was closely associated with Hearst, called the publisher" to urge him to switch California to FDR (Farley, 24).

When Elliott settled in Texas three years later, Vice President Garner became an important ally. Incidentally, Jack Garner is the fellow known far and wide for rating the vice presidency "not worth a bucket of warm piss." He would know, for although increasingly anti-New Deal, he served in the office until 1941, when Henry Wallace eagerly picked up the steaming pail.

William Randolph Hearst was in his seventies, and his press empire was on the downslope. The Depression crippled it. At the same time, Hearst, despite his talk of "Stalin Delano Roosevelt," was never part of the right-wing ideological opposition to the Roosevelt Administration exemplified by Robert McCormick's *Chicago Tribune*. This made it possible for Elliott Roosevelt to continue his affiliation with Hearst, and his friendship with Hearst vice president George Hearst helped him further. WRH Junior, also a pilot, resumed the connection with Elliott when he met him in England in 1944. When Elliott was in big trouble again in 1947, the Hearst press allowed him to present his side to the public, while others fell upon him gleefully.

THE AIR MAIL FIASCO

On 9 February 1934, a day that lives in infamy in American aviation history, President Roosevelt launched a sneak attack against the entire aviation sector, annihilating in one swift strike America's airlines and many of the careers associated with them.

That much has long been known. What has been hidden is the role his son played in the debacle, and particularly in twisting it to serve a crazed scheme driven by the lure of lucre beyond measure.

As aviation editor for the Hearsts, a job he held for about eight months, Elliott Roosevelt had continuous access to high sources within the industry. This would quickly lead him astray. He had made many important friends, and some evidently matched his talent and desire for a quick buck.

During 1934, Elliott managed to be involved in no less than three major scandals simultaneously. These three interlaced controversies can be difficult to keep track of. It is necessary to treat of each by itself, but throughout, one must keep in mind that they ran concurrently and affected each other.

The public would not hear of the two most damning Elliott scandals until two years later, but one, subsequently known to all as the Air Mail Fiasco, was headline material for months in the spring of 1934, and it humiliated the new president. Although now mostly forgotten, it was one of the signal crises of the first FDR term, considered in a league with the Supreme Court packing plan. Its continuing importance is that it wound up redefining the entire landscape of American civilian aviation.

At first it seemed that Elliott's involvement was merely tangential, as a commentator and a go-between. It is necessary, however, to pay close attention to the timing of the air mail issue in view of the shenanigans that were later revealed to have taken place in the shadows.

It is odd that Elliott's involvement has been insufficiently examined. Had the details been known at the time, the administration would have teetered at the abyss; even when the contours of the plot became known, there was probably sufficient dirt to warrant the impeachment of the President of the United States. But Roosevelt historians have routinely reported the crisis as a political event, and have usually had no patience for examining its meaning to aviation, or the covert machinations behind it.

In a following section we shall probe Elliott's own aviation schemes. In this one, we shall first explain those of his father.

Government and Industry, in Bed

Today the public would find it confusing, if not amusing, to hear that federal air mail contracts could be so fiercely controversial. Not so before the war. Air routes and the air mail were a bit like the railroads had been fifty years earlier – the means by which distant cities could prosper or decline. They were subject to furious battles over control, both on the commercial and the regulatory side.

During the interwar years, American commercial aviation advanced dramatically. It soon far surpassed that of Europe, which had been the recognized center of aeronautics at the end of the Great War. In America, this time between the wars is now wistfully referred to as the "Golden Age of Flight."

For better or worse, the rise of the American aviation industry occurred within a peculiar ideological regime: that of increasing federal micromanagement. The New Deal only extended this approach. Like much of the rest of the New Deal, it had – in substance if not in name – begun during the Coolidge and Hoover administrations. In 1926, to reign in "anarchy" in the skies, the Commerce Department created the Aeronautics Branch, the ancestor of the FAA (Federal Aviation Administration). Its regulatory reach reflected the progressivist attitudes of the age.[327]

As a result, unlike many other industries, aviation slowly took on a slightly Soviet tint, led by a federal bureaucracy exercising central planning and control. The airspace was federalized and policed by federal air traffic controllers. Gradually, Civil Air Regulations (CARs, later FARs) grew to a fearsome complexity exceeding even that of the tax code. Certification and regulation ballooned to a level of detail beyond the comprehension of any one person today. The flip side of this corporatist policy was reflected in a massive indirect and sometimes open and direct federal subsidy to the aviation sector.

Whatever the aggravations of this ideological regime, its firm but judicious application did eventually result in today's almost supernaturally safe commercial aviation sector. It is also true that the United States remains, far and away, the premier aviation nation – no other country even comes close. But the effects of the centralized-command approach on innovation, entrepreneurship, costs, and popular access have not been nearly so positive.

The shadow of overbearing government caused a curious give-and-take relationship: the nascent airlines were heavily subsidized in return for federal route management. Aircraft manufacturers depended critically on favorable regulation and contracts as well as on military orders. Pilots, who were already becoming fiercely unionized, alternately favored and recoiled at the effect of intrusive new civil air regulations.

This universe was lobbyist heaven. In the 1930s, the Aeronautical Chamber of Commerce of America (ACCA) became an important trade group, representing about 95% of the industry. It published an annual status of aviation in a thick yearbook that served as a bible for the trade. In 1934, there were already 14,000 pilot licenses outstanding, but only about 500 commercial aircraft in operation. It was still a small sector, but growth – from essentially zero a decade earlier – was phenomenal.[328]

As the new administration settled in, an uneasy, mutually dependent relationship developed between the aviation industry and Roosevelt's energetic and charming new aviation czar, Eugene Vidal.

The record supports the suspicion that Elliott Roosevelt was instrumental in getting Vidal appointed Director of Aeronautics. In January 1933, the two went to Warm Springs, Georgia – which would become the "Southern White House" – to talk things over with the president-elect. After three days of chumminess, FDR hired Elliott's (and Eleanor's) friend over several more qualified candidates.[329]

Vidal was a politically well-connected aviator, former airline operator, and Air Corps veteran. He was also a son-in-law of Senator Thomas Gore of Oklahoma. He maintained a close connection with the Roosevelts.[330] As these things are wont to go, he is now probably better remembered as Amelia Earhart's lover and author Gore Vidal's father.[331]

"This guy is good," wrote Amelia's husband, George Putnam, about his wife's lover. "He knows his stuff. He is honest; he is not tied up with any interests, and he is able to see ahead. You will not regret any help you can give him." The letter was for FDR.[332]

Both Amelia and Gene Vidal were good friends of Eleanor Roosevelt. Amelia went flying with Mrs. Roosevelt in a Curtiss Condor shortly after the inauguration.[333] (Brother Hall came along; so did George Putnam, and Eleanor said she left the flying to the regular pilot.) It is yet another sad commentary on Eleanor's marriage that she wanted badly to fly, passed the physical, and even took lessons from Amelia Earhart. But her husband forbade her from proceeding. And, "Eleanor Roosevelt always regretted not becoming a pilot, because, she said, she liked to be in control of her own mobility." [334]

On the way to the Democratic convention in Chicago in 1940, Eleanor's powerful friend C.R. Smith magically provided her with a small plane to go from New Hackensack to New York City, and:

> …I must record the thrilling experience of actually being allowed to fly the little ship for part of the trip down while in the air. It was so smooth that there was no difficulty in keeping it on an even keel. I watched the river below to keep it on the right course. I have always wanted to learn to fly a plane and even this small experience was exciting.[335]

In the wake of Eleanor's visit to Elliott in Los Angeles, Vidal told the press that her penchant for air travel had produced a boom for the airlines. He said, "Each trip the first lady makes by air is followed by amazing jumps in traffic, in many cases as eight times the former business." [336] This is astonishing; but other factors, such as the incipient economic recovery and the dramatic technical improvements in air traffic probably helped too.

Drew Pearson's notes trace at least some of the lines of communication from the White House and Elliott through Vidal and Amelia Earhart, to Amelia's legal husband and financial sugar daddy G.W. Putnam, and then to Northwest Airlines' redoubtable

Croil Hunter. For example, Drew noted a letter from Putnam to Hunter stating, "Now that Amelia has landed Vidal his job, is there anything else she can do for you?"

The allusions in the notes were far more ominous for Elliott. Drew observed that he "expects to coast along without doing any work" on his jobs. "Intentions are of the best but uses very poor judgment." [337]

Of the liaisons between the airlines and the Commerce Department, Pearson said: "All play politics… Whenever Vidal sees camera he breaks a leg getting in front of it…" Of E.L. Cord, he noted that he got Elliott to intercede with Postmaster General Farley and the result was a lucrative contract for American Airways – '9c a pound on the southern line." Cord was to erect his own navigation aids, but then "now Vidal has appropriation in for buying these aids." [i]

Perhaps C.R. Smith's lifelong friendship and assistance to Elliott Roosevelt has to be seen in this light, too. E.L. Cord hired C.R. to run the nationwide American Airways, which was in deep financial trouble at the time. This was logical, since C.R. had very effectively run American Airways' southern operations. Possibly, C.R. owed a crucial stage of his later so illustrious career to Elliott's timely advocacy in return for the favors he had done the young man during his impromptu stopover in Texas in March 1933.[338]

Someone told Pearson that Cord had already bought 25 Curtiss Condors and therefore needed the government to allocate the southern mail route with extensions to American Airlines. Then Pearson, in an oblique reference to the *Nourmahal* incident, noted that "Elliott visited father on yacht off Florida, then came to Washington and invited Vidal to lunch at White House. Saw Farley on same afternoon when the contract was given to American Airlines." [339]

In other words, the circumstantial but obviously unprovable evidence was that Elliott got C.R. the southern route on favorable terms. Subsequently, the rates would go up dramatically.

The American Airlines southern route was just one suspected example of Elliott's influence. Another – possibly – involved Croil Hunter's Northwest Airlines. Drew Pearson heard that Elliott had worked for Hunter to lobby for Northwest's route extension from Minneapolis to Seattle: "He wanted to get lights (navigational aids) from St. Paul to Seattle. These now being blt by govt…" Also, Hunter was close enough to the family to write Anna Roosevelt Boettiger in Seattle: "hoping she impress on father importance of aviation." [340]

This was the background for Pearson's asking Elliott what he had been up to with Northwest. Elliott denied everything, and for whatever reasons – possibly to protect sources – Drew did not go nearly as far in print as his own hoarded evidence would suggest. Muckrakers have a difficult task; they usually know much more than they can responsibly publish. One misstep can wreck their credibility.

The social network that lay hidden behind the formulation of aviation policy in the 1930s illustrates how both Elliott and his father operated. To a greater extent than most presidents, Franklin D. Roosevelt governed through an extended network of favored friends and acquaintances. "Cronyism" is an admittedly loaded word for this practice. Throughout his administration, FDR preferred to bypass the bureaucracy, most notoriously the State Department, where poor old Cordell Hull served as a kind of hood ornament through most of the war.

---

[i] Notes, ER file, Drew Pearson collection, LBJ Lib. American Airways became American Airlines after the 1934 upheaval.

FDR used instead his special friends, like Howe and Hopkins and Baruch and Harriman. James Roosevelt said of W. Averell Harriman that he would have been a good Secretary of State, "but perhaps father didn't want one that good." [341] Some of the "cronies" held regular offices: Henry Morgenthau at Treasury and Jim Farley at the Post Office. In aviation, it was family friend Eugene Vidal who called the shots until his resignation in 1937. He was assisted there by many other friends and acquaintances.

At the apex of the crony network was, effectively, a secret American prime minister. Louis Howe had been FDR's first. During the second term, Tommy Corcoran, by far the smartest and most dangerous of the lot, played this role. Harry Hopkins followed him.

Elliott operated the same way. His entire life was about who knows whom, who owes whom. The churning of the favor mill and the disregard of the official hierarchy lent a certain randomness and unpredictability to the administration. Everyone recognized that FDR ruled by instinct and intuition, not by deliberation.

In aviation, the choice of Vidal was nonetheless a good one. The president's use of Postmaster Farley and especially Senator Hugo Black was more problematic for aviation.

The limits of acceptable government intervention had yet to be defined. For example, Vidal championed a soon defunct program to mass-produce a safe, $700 personal airplane.[342] It gained a lot of attention, but no market. The point is that such an initiative would be considered government overreach today.

The airlines and the municipal airports still operated most of what today would be called the air traffic control and navigation system, but that too was about to be taken over by the federal government. Finally, the most important payload in commercial aviation was not passengers, who were still few, rich, and often justifiably terrified. At that time, less than ½ per cent of the population had even been inside an airplane.

Instead, what kept fledgling airlines aloft was revenue from mail – and mail was a constitutional prerogative of the United States government.

Crucially and decisively, the U.S. Post Office deliberately subsidized the new industry through a vast, nationwide network of contract air mail. This unhealthy codependency, barely a decade old, would become the occasion for a massive, lasting upheaval directed by President Roosevelt himself.

One Swift Coup against Aviation

Thus on 9 February 1934, President Roosevelt made one of his single most tragic, mistaken, and reviled decisions. He decreed that from now on the Army Air Corps would fly the mail. Until then, this had been a keenly cherished and ruthlessly exploited privilege of private airline contractors. Against even the advice of his own staff, FDR imperiously and arbitrarily "annulled" almost all the air mail contracts and directed Air Corps pilots to become postmen, starting on 19 February.[343]

The legality of this move was immediately challenged, and right away we should point out that the courts eventually ruled against the government and awarded restitution to the wronged airlines. But that happened long after the political and economic battle had see-sawed across the nation. Thus, the case resembled those obviously illegal wartime measures which are condemned many years after they have done their damage.

We get a first hint of Elliott Roosevelt's presence in the debacle by the curious phenomenon that airline stocks fell precipitously in the days just prior to FDR's fateful announcement on 9 February. Historian James Duffy notes about these inside traders and their suspected malfeasance: "Although none were found, many suspected that an administration insider had tipped the big houses off to what was coming." [344]

Heeding the public uproar, the New York Stock Exchange investigated air industry stock trades from 26 January to 9 February. When the results were released to the Senate Banking and Currency Committee on 5 March, they showed overwhelming stock dumping and short-selling by insiders.[345] The damage was already done by 31 January. Somebody had obviously talked, yet nothing eventually came of the probe.

That Elliott and his aviation friends stayed at the White House at the appropriate times would turn out to be important. January 26th happened to be a day when Elliott and his friends Donald Douglas and Franklin Lane had stayed overnight at the White House; that same day, Postmaster Farley and Senator Black met with the president, who had dinner with friend Isabella Greenway that same evening. Thus Elliott and some of his business associates were not only privy to FDR's bombshell decision; they also had some nifty schemes ready in an attempt to turn a profit off the calamity.[346]

Nonetheless, Elliott would soon go on record as opposing his father's aviation policy. In this he spoke for the industry. But as we shall find out, that was not his true objective in the matter. Profit was.

The publicly trumpeted reason for FDR's "annulment" of the airline contracts was that they had been corruptly awarded in a racket organized by the previous postmaster general, Walter Brown, to placate moneyed interests allied to the previous Republican administration. The phrase universally bandied about was "Fraud and Collusion."

The so-called "spoils conference" of 1930 did indeed allocate the lucrative contracts in a somewhat dictatorial way. But the conference and its route decisions were by no means secret; they were reported at the time, and then generally regarded as a prudent exercise of government leadership in cooperation with industry, which was an ideological keystone of the Hoover administration. Furthermore, Hoover's reset of air mail contracts constituted a dramatic improvement over past practices.[347]

Yet federal subsidy of a nascent but powerful industry inherently caused dissension and vituperation. The real problem thus lay in making of the air mail a political football; that it was kicked from one side of the field to the other as each team gained ahold of it might be expected. In this case, however, the teams were especially formidable.

Effectively, there now emerged on one side a supremely confident new president who thought he could arrange the mails, the economy, and indeed the whole world better than anyone else. On the other side arose an ad-hoc coalition of skeptics, businessmen, and technical people informally led by a young, former air mail pilot of impeccable reputation and (almost) inexhaustible prestige: Colonel Charles Augustus Lindbergh.

The U.S. Post Office itself was the logical air mail carrier, and indeed had begun this activity during the Wilson administration. Contracting had taken over explicitly to nurture the air industry. If not scrupulously monitored, contracting out was easily tainted with waste, fraud, and abuse. There had indeed been egregious cases of this during the 1920s.

The later so maligned June 1930 "spoils conference" dramatically reduced the outrages and attempted to form a rational and sustainable route structure and corporate framework. But the arrangement also pitted the three large airlines, which won the long-haul contracts, against the numerous small and "fly-by-night" (literally) outfits which had depended on air mail. These jilted smaller fry now had the ear of FDR's new administration.

As an example, a small company named the Ludington Line had been the low bidder – 25 cents per mile – on a mail contract in the northeast, but the award was given to the much larger and better equipped Eastern Air. The Ludington Line operated an hourly shuttle with Stinson trimotors between New York and Washington. The airline had good press and was reported to be profitable, but closer examination shows that this was not true, and the airline was swept up in the mergers and acquisitions the 1930 conference touched off. Though small, the airline was an important innovator and its demise caused its owners to rage against Postmaster Brown and the larger companies he favored.[348]

And who had been the operator of the Ludington Line? Eugene Vidal.

Another vice president of the line had been Vidal's girlfriend Amelia Earhart, in charge of promotions.[349]

While we are dwelling on coincidences, it was Vidal's Ludington Line that lit the fuse of the Air Mail fiasco.[i] Another Hearst reporter, young Fulton Lewis, Jr., happened to talk with the airline about its failed bid. Lewis found out that Eastern had been selected despite a much higher bid – 89 cents per mile – and from there he began unraveling the story of how Postmaster Brown had assigned contracts based on his own ideas of industrial restructuring, and not simply to the lowest bidder.[350]

But Lewis had more zeal than insight. He didn't understand that in the greater scheme, it was unwise for Brown to simply award the contract to the lowest bidder, however small, inexperienced, and unsafe; nor did he understand Brown's underlying logic of promoting transcontinental route networks rather than haphazard fractional routes. For example, Ludington had bid only on its New York – Washington shuttle route; Eastern's bid was part of a Florida to New England trunk line.

Worst of all, Lewis assumed the matter was secret and scandalous; he did not realize that the decisions of the 1930 "spoils conference" were openly promulgated and publicly justified, and indeed that Brown's edicts had been fiercely opposed by much of the industry at the time.

So Fulton Lewis went to W.R. Hearst, who better understood aviation's larger picture, and chose not to promote Lewis's stories. Next Lewis went to Senator Hugo Black. To zealous Alabama New Dealer Black, it was a gift from the heavens: a chance to smear a big "Republican" industry and, as well, the Hoover administration, while making his otherwise pedestrian post office committee into a platform for political fireworks.[ii]

Hugo Black was the driving force behind the attack on the aviation industry. President Roosevelt, of course, was the man who solely made the catastrophic decision on 9 February. But in the next few months, he was primarily concerned with deflecting blame.

Many would eventually be assigned more than their fair share of guilt. Postmaster General James Aloysius Farley was in on the plot from the start, and he fared the worst.

Farley was no mailman. One of the titans of mid-century politics, "Big Jim" had been FDR's campaign manager and chairman of the Democratic National Committee.

---

[i] To be sure, Vidal later opposed the Army's flying mail; he'd been an Army pilot himself. NYT, 7 MAR 37

[ii] Hugo Black was appointed to the Supreme Court in 1937 and served until 1971.

As was the custom, he received the postal job as a lucrative reward. Farley remained in Roosevelt's inner circle until he broke with the president in 1940. With presidential hopes of his own, he felt that FDR betrayed him by seeking an originally unthinkable third term. But during the first two terms, Farley worked closely with the Roosevelt boys when they needed help.

Upon becoming top mailman in 1933, Farley thought he saw evidence of mischief in the previous administration's air mail contracts. When the simmering controversy came to a head in February 1934, Farley accused the airlines of bilking the federal government of a total of $47 million in "excess payments" during the Hoover administration.[351] However, even he had asked the president that the U.S. Post Office be allowed several months to recompete the contracts.[352] Farley was secretly a moderate in the matter.

That episode began "Big Jim's" long process of FDR-disillusionment. In his memoirs, he was apologetic about the Air Mail fiasco; it was "one of the saddest experiences in my public life." But he also said he "resented" being crucified for a decision that was not his own, and indeed one in which he had been a voice of caution.[353]

> The wrath of an aroused public descended on my head as the author of the order canceling the contracts. I had learned in the past to take abuse and criticism, but when I was called a murderer, I began to look around frantically for help. I looked to the White House. No help came. I was hurt that the President had not seen fit to divert the wrath. Later I realized it was part of my job to take as many blows for him as I could. Nonetheless, a kind word would have been a great help when the lashes were falling.[354]

But to the public, Farley was a new Attila, the scourge of the airlines. It was he who signed for the purple-hued charges the new administration hurled against the industry.

The larger aviation companies were then rapidly becoming laterally integrated. Aircraft manufacturers joined with airlines in exclusionary alliances in a classical attempt at industrial empire-building. This cartelizing tendency caused Congress and White House alarm, especially since there was hardly a Democrat among the new aviation moguls. However, as we have seen, some Democrats, including Averell Harriman, Eugene Vidal, and the prominent Senator William McAdoo in California were associated with bets on the promising industry. But they tended to be out-competed by bigger financial operators and it would be naïve to think they didn't hold grudges.

Thus, the barely concealed reason for the debacle was political. The incoming administration used the purported "fraud and collusion" to embarrass its Republican opposition. Tellingly, the primary instigators of the investigation and the subsequent cancellations were FDR's closest political collaborators – not the regulatory or judicial machinery.

Hugo Black (D-AL), a fervent New Dealer, had initiated the inquisition in his Senate committee, the previously obscure Special Committee on Investigation of the Air Mail and Ocean Mail Contracts. In session from September 1933, the Black committee had patiently prepared the ground for Roosevelt's coup. Senator Black also co-introduced the new Air Mail Bill of June 1934 (known as the Black-McKellar Act) to accommodate FDR's wishes for the total reorganization of the American aviation industry.

The senator and future Supreme Court justice emitted this populist rant in 1933: "The control of American aviation has been ruthlessly taken away from men who could fly and bestowed upon bankers, brokers, promoters and politicians, sitting in their inner offices, allotting to themselves the taxpayer's money." [355]

When Black's inquisition began, Elliott Roosevelt had already abandoned his airline job; but in his new position with Hearst, he hobnobbed with aviation leaders, and would soon plot with some of them to pick up the pieces of the industry.

Postmaster Farley issued a detailed justification of the contract cancellations on 14 February. Unfortunately, his accusations would soon unravel as the victims spoke up. But by then, the administration had circled the wagons.

Speaking for the president, Farley said:

> I do not believe Congress intended that the air mail appropriation should be expended for the benefit of a few favored corporations, which could use the funds as the basis of wild stock promotions resulting in profits of tens of millions of dollars to promoters who invested little or no capital. Nor was it intended to be used by great corporations as a club to force competitors out of business and into bankruptcy. Nor should appropriations and contracts be given to a few favored corporations by connivance and agreement.[356]
>
> ...I am convinced that before any of the air mail contracts were awarded, those interested held meetings for the purpose of dividing territory and contracts among themselves...These meetings resulted in a division of all air mail contracts of the United States and the practical elimination of competitive bidding.

To Farley, the cooperative, government-led assignment of routes was "conspiracy" and "collusion." The practice of not necessarily awarding contracts to the lowest bidder was corruption, not prudence.

To critics, this raised two fundamental questions. Had the Hoover administration "rigged" the process for gain? And if so, what would be the most responsible remedy? In other words, was President Roosevelt's thunderbolt, hurled on 9 February to strike dead an entire industry, truly justified?

One fervent admirer of FDR's action wrote this alarming analysis of the Hoover administration's air mail policy:

> Effected by Postmaster General Walter F. Brown, this policy would prove shocking to the general public when, in 1933, it was fully exposed to the public gaze. Involved was the use of air-mail contracts, which made the difference between the financial success and failure of an airline, to insure that certain big and therefore favored companies survived and grew while their smaller competitors were either crushed or forced into mergers whereby they lost their identity...
>
> Three big aviation holding companies the North American – General Motors group, United Aircraft, and Aviation Corporation walked off with all but two of twenty air-mail contracts. Brown also presided very actively over the shotgun wedding of TWA and Western Air Express from which TWA emerged as "The Lindbergh Line." And Brown could reply to critics by pointing to an undoubted over-all effect of his activities, namely the establishment by July 4, 1931, of a co-ordinated passenger-carrying transcontinental airline system in place of a precarious air mail "carried in an open-cockpit ship with a young lad of 25 years of age sitting on a parachute." [357]

The suddenly reviled former postmaster Walter F. Brown had been a prominent and effective Hoover lieutenant. When Hoover had been Secretary of Commerce under Coolidge, Brown had been one of his assistant secretaries. As with Farley after him, Hoover had made him Postmaster General as a reward for his work as a political strategist, thus completing the symmetry of the tit-for-tat game. Brown had accurately and conscientiously carried out the president's philosophy of voluntary industry-government cooperation, known then as American corporatism. Yet it was not possible to conduct such a policy without picking winners and losers.

Right or wrong, Postmaster Brown's award of the 1930 contracts had been made to salvage the struggling industry and help it build a competent, effective nationwide air network. In this, he had succeeded; but that others were angry was understandable. It may be recalled that in 2001, the federal government made a similar calculation when it gave the airline industry, instantly comatose after 9-11, five billion dollars to get back in the air. That this enraged those smaller fry who did not qualify for the compensation, but bore also the full brunt of the nationwide calamity, was then as before overlooked.

A powerful rejoinder to Farley's letter was issued publicly by Richard Robbins, the president of Transcontinental & Western Air – the airline which, after FDR's coup, was resurrected as TWA. Speaking for the industry, Robbins argued:

> We feel that both President Roosevelt and Postmaster General Farley have been misled in this air mail matter and that if hearings had been held by the Post Office Department and all the facts developed, this wholesale annulment order would never have been issued.
>
> ...An accurate account of the proceedings at the first meeting was published in the New York Times of May 20, 1930, and the Post Office Department itself issued an official press release describing the proceedings. Photostats of both of those have been sent by our Company to Mr. Farley. It is absurd to characterize such a meeting as clandestine or secret.

Robbins proceeded to document that the 1930 awards, whether agreeable or not, had been made in compliance with the authority vested in the Post Office by the Watres Act.[i] To boot, he noted that that same act gave the administration the authority to make changes in contracts as it deemed necessary:

> Could there have been a fairer arrangement from the Government's standpoint? How does Mr. Farley expect to get a better bargain for the carriage of airmail?
>
> ...Mr. Farley quotes many figures. All these figures prove is that there was some subsidy in the air mail payments. Mr. Farley, through the use of arbitrary percentages reaches the conclusion that $46,800,000 might have been saved to the Post Office Department over a period of years, but he does not state what adverse effect this saving would have had on the progress of aviation and what kind of an air mail service the nation would have had for the lesser amount....If the present air transportation system is destroyed, then progress in air transportation in this country will cease...all we ask is fair play and an opportunity to present our cause before an impartial tribunal.[358]

In his apologia, Robbins expressed the views of not only the industry, but of virtually all who had knowledge of how aviation operated in America. But he did not address the fundamental issue of whether the government subsidy was justified; it had simply been taken for granted. The Roosevelt administration obviously was not

---

[i] The McNary-Watres Act of 29 APR 1930 gave Postmaster Brown the authority for his route allocation.

opposed to subsidies or corporatism in general – but it found that the issue could be manipulated to its advantage when the "winners" were not Democrats.

Specialist historians have held that Walter Brown's prodding of the airlines was an important, even visionary initiative in creating the flourishing American airline industry.[359] An aviation historian offered a balanced account:

> Senator Black's committee overlooked the issue of how much growth and progress took place during Walter Brown's handling of airmail contracts. Little time was spent on how United Aircraft and Transport Corporation, Eastern Air Transport, and American Airways had improved passenger service, safety, and aircraft development.
>
> The airlines were not entirely without fault. Expense account favors were utilized in entertaining government officials. Jobs and loans to postal officials were offered. Relatives of senators and congressmen were hired as consultants. However…Walter Brown acted as he felt was best for the United States. If a small carrier's contract was awarded to a large carrier, Brown made it a condition that the large carrier would buy the small carrier at a fair price.[360]

One convincing metric of air mail efficiency was the cost per mile. During the Hoover administration, this cost fell from $1.10 to $0.54, and it was projected to fall to $0.38 in 1934. When the Army was told to carry the air mail, the cost rose to $2.21 – not counting the human costs.[361]

These numbers were well known during the time of the crisis. But then as now, people lined up according to political allegiance; to most of them, it seemed, facts were irrelevant. Soon both sides would have the strongest possible emotions to fan.

The New Dealers' fierce charges of "fraud and collusion" against former Postmaster General Walter Brown were decisively settled by the U.S. Court of Claims on 14 July 1941. The issue had landed there after the airlines had won the right to claim restitution for the government's breach of contract and unconstitutional taking of property without due process.[362] As a standard textbook of U.S. air transportation notes:

> It wasn't until 1941 that Brown was vindicated when the United States Court said that the charges of collusion against him were untrue. Therefore, the cancellation of the airmail contracts, the deaths of the pilots, the property damage, and the high expense were all unnecessary – except as a period in the historical development of United States air transportation. This action of the court made it possible for the airlines, whose airmail contracts had been cancelled by Farley, to claim and receive about $2.5 million in damages.[363]

Army Air Mail

Whatever the controversy over the past, in February 1934, almost without warning, the Army was in the postal business. The president made this decision after long premeditation and inconclusive advice from experts, among whom his son now counted himself. Still, it was a shock to the nation. Roosevelt relied on a rather casually uttered assurance of such an Army capability, interpreted as consent, from the Air Corps commander General Benjamin Foulois.[i] Foulois's boss, Army Chief of Staff General Douglas MacArthur, seemed positively eager to take on the new challenge.[364]

Unfortunately, in those days, the Air Corps was more like a fair-weather flying club than a warfighting outfit, much less a scheduled airline. In trying to transport mail on a regular schedule, the strain on pilots, mechanics, and all others involved was enormous. The new task immediately revealed several weaknesses in Air Corps operations. Elliott Roosevelt thought that his exhortations about stronger air power were vindicated during the debacle that ensued.

At that distant time, Army officers thought air power consisted almost entirely of pursuit and bombardment aircraft. Transport? Why, they have trains for that, and ships. Reconnaissance? Yes, we have observation planes to sneak over and take pictures of the enemy's trenches. Night flying? Why would you do that – you can't see anything! Instrument flight ("blind flying")? Rarely done, too risky. Radios and gyros? Airlines already used them – but for most of the Air Corps, they were still science fiction.[365]

In short, the Army did not have a cargo airline, and did not know how to operate one. But now it had been given ten days to do so.

It was worse than that. Much of the necessary infrastructure – airfields, weather and communications services, even office space – was actually owned by non-federal actors, including the cashiered airlines. They were not necessarily eager to help. To top it off, Congress dilated in funding the operation; at times, the valiant Air Corps pilots were stranded, broke, homeless and hungry.[366]

Amazingly, the officer in charge of the western zone of the air mail effort was a certain Lt. Col. Hap Arnold, who had the ear of Elliott Roosevelt.[367] But clearly the main influence on Elliott was the airline crowd – chief among them his friend and mentor at American Airways, C.R. Smith. We shall soon see that the aircraft manufacturers, chiefly Douglas and Lockheed, had also gotten their piece of Elliott Roosevelt.

Elliott had been keenly aware of the air mail crisis brewing even during his short stint with Gilpin Airlines. Now he was in the thick of it, commenting on the crisis, and conferring constantly with the top leaders of the aviation industry. And he was still working for Hearst. The press prince and Elliott were of one mind in the air mail crisis. This is where Elliott's and George Hearst's abortive mission to FDR's yacht *Nourmahal* becomes of greater interest.

The second son played a dangerous double game. In public, he attacked his father's action. In private, he sought to profit from it.

Four days after the cancellations, on 13 February, Elliott sent a detailed telegram to President Roosevelt. It was the public Elliott speaking:

> After extensive study and inquiry may I respectfully suggest that before the Army Air Corps attempts carrying the mail, more consideration be given to the following incontrovertible facts:
>
> 1. Army pilots are expected to fly blind over territory with which they are unfamiliar, at best, a suicidal move, as is well known to those with the air transport business.
> 2. Army radio equipment is inadequate to the point of absurdity when efficiency in flying a beam is taken into consideration it is well known that Army radio equipment has a useful radius of 40 miles, while commercial radio equipment is useful up to 300 miles.

---

[i] Benjamin Foulois had been the Army's "one-man air force"in 1910, after instruction from the Wrights.

3. Pilots trained to fly pursuit planes will be forced to fly heavy bomber types. At best it takes considerable time to accustom men to change.
4. Army equipment in ships is such that if they fly air routes in all kinds of weather, the loss to life and equipment will be tremendous.
5. The Army has been told to fly the northernmost of the three transcontinental routes. This route has been demonstrated in the past to be extremely hazardous in the winter months.
6. What is to become of thousands of mechanics, field workers, and pilots who do not belong to the Reserve Corps?
7. What will happen to manufacturers who have spent hundreds to thousands of dollars to develop and perfect fast air Pullmans designed to carry passengers, express, and especially mail, and are now employing thousands of men to build quantities of these ships ordered by the lines under fire.

> The above information does in no way come from officials of air lines, but from the rank and file of the skilled workers in the industry and from my own personal knowledge of that industry, gained while aviation editor for the Hearst newspapers.
>
> At this point I wish to take exception to an editorial appearing in those papers of a viciously libelous and unpatriotic, and above all, uncalled for nature. This editorial, appearing the morning of February 14th, is such as to make my position with the newspapers untenable, in view of our personal relationship. I will resign as of this date upon your confirmation of this telegram, with every wish that my suggestions may prove of value, with full permission for you to use any or all of the contents of this wire for any purpose you may see fit. I remain, affectionately yours, Elliott Roosevelt.[368]

This telegram is preserved in Franklin D. Roosevelt's personal file, Elliott correspondence, Hyde Park. So is the answer.

President Roosevelt was apparently not particularly happy to get such "help" from his son – particularly since he was engaged in discussions with others over how to reorganize the industry. But he had the level presence of mind to answer Elliott politely:

> WE ARE DOING EVERYTHING POSSIBLE TO RETAIN AS MANY OF THE PILOTS AND OTHER TRAINED WORKERS AS WE CAN. I AM DELIGHTED TO HAVE YOUR SUGGESTIONS. FRANKLY I SEE NO REASON FOR YOUR RESIGNATION FROM THE PAPERS. THE POINT IS THAT THIS ACTION WILL IN THE LONG RUN DO MORE FOR AVIATION THAN IF WE HAD CONTINUED THE OLD METHODS WHICH LIMITED COMPETITION AND EMPLOYED NO MORE PEOPLE THAN A RECONSTITUTED MAIL SERVICE WILL DO. LOVE TO YOU AND RUTH. (Signed Father)[369]

This brief response is significant because, unlike the snide answers the administration flung to its opponents (like Colonel Lindbergh), it suggested that the president, at least in his own mind, was attempting to restore broader competition in a reorganized aviation industry. This was not necessarily what Elliott had in mind.

While criticizing his father, Elliott also tried to help his friends. Some of it was innocent, some not. For example, in March he plaintively wired the White House:

> Have five pilots not in the Reserve Corps each of whom has three to five dependents who are faced with eviction from their homes within ten days due to cancellation of mail contracts. All are world war veterans of different branches and have from three to seven

> thousand hours in the air. Can the western division of the Army Air Corps take them on. Please answer immediately.[370]

Colonel McIntyre, the president's personal secretary, answered that he would take the matter up with the Army "first thing tomorrow."[i] Clearly, it was smart to be friends with Elliott Roosevelt.

During that spring, Elliott engaged with an enormous number of people interested in the aviation crisis. One of them was Isabella Greenway, now the Congresswoman from Arizona, and one of the very few Democrats who opposed the president in this matter. She in turn endeavored to influence the new legislation in order to secure the airline industry's interests, responding, for example, to the fevered entreaties of the likes of C.R. Smith and Amon Carter. At the end, she wrote to Carter about her meetings with, among others, President Roosevelt: "I have worked so constantly behind the scenes on this problem that it is too long a story to attempt to put in a letter." [371]

Yet her logic, and Elliott's, were totally ineffective against the president's set mind.

It is not clear whether Greenway was informed about Elliott's more ambitious schemes, but she did stay in touch with him. She also worked closely with his Texas friends, Carter and Smith. In that respect she was mainly concerned with saving American Airways' transcontinental route going through her state. In that, at least, she would ultimately be successful.

Greenway made a very deep impression upon Capitol-watchers. One lyricized:

> The other speech made in the House last week which will outlive its every member, was made by a woman, a widow of a veteran of the war with Spain and of the Great War. This speech also was made with deep feeling and in turn left upon the House a profound impression. This was the speech of Mrs. Isabella Greenway, Representative in Congress from Arizona. Republicans united with Democrats in that State to elect her to Congress. She was an intimate friend of Theodore Roosevelt and his family. She is the most intimate friend in public life of the Roosevelt family now in the White House.
>
> Before coming to Congress Mrs. Greenway operated an air line left by her husband. And here is what she said in support of her vote against the bill to abolish the Federal Airmail service, which has become the eighth wonder of the world, and to compel the Army to operate it for a year:
>
> 'I voted against the passage of this bill because I think the last week has proved, without reflecting on either the pilots or the Army, that the Army planes as such are not equipped to carry mail at this time, and I think that might be better to suspend the air mail until the equipment is adequate rather than run a hazardous service.'
>
> For concise and logical argument and for effective eloquence this brief speech of Mrs. Greenway has not been equaled in either House of Congress at this session. The reason it has not been refuted is because it is irrefutable.[372]

Mrs. Greenway was widely hailed for her courage in speaking truth to power. It made no difference. Amid cries of "Murder!" the House passed the president's emergency authority by 248 to 81 on 24 February 1934. This "Brunner Bill"[ii] allowed the Army to carry the mail for one year, but more immediately, it finally enabled

---

[i] McIntyre was a colonel in the Kentucky Guard. He, Steve Early and Louis Howe, the "secretariat," were all journalists by trade.

[ii] Named after William Brunner, D-NY.

General Foulois to pay his starving pilots' expenses and per diem. Greenway's was the only Democratic Nay.[373]

Elliott remained in the loop with the president. As late as a month later, after Elliott's plans had been shot down and his father had secured the passage of the new Black-McKellar bill, we have evidence that Elliott was working on his father in private:

> The Post Office Dept. is interested in the subsequent passage of a joint resolution, on which Sen. McKellar and Rep. Mead are working, the purpose of which is to correct Section 15 of the air mail bill, which prohibits any one airplane company from flying more than three air mail routes. Mr. Early says that this is the matter in which Elliott Roosevelt is particularly interested, -- and the President has discussed it with Elliott and Mr. McIntyre.[374]

That was just two weeks after the *Nourmahal* incident. Elliott was still desperately trying to salvage the remainder of a grand plan he had been working on with friends.

"Legalized Murder"

When the Army pilots began dying, many called it murder. Some said FDR was guilty of "lynching" American aviation.[i]

After a hectic preparation, the Air Corps began flying mail on 19 February, straight into the teeth of one of the worst winters on record. The crashes and deaths began immediately. During the first week, five airmen died, six were badly wounded, and eight planes were lost.[375]

During the entire operation twelve airmen were killed in 66 accidents. The Army planes, though slow and unsafe, were fortunately relatively survivable when crashed.[376] General Foulois protested that the mortality was not statistically large, but he was gradually forced to reduce the operations to a fraction of what the civilians had flown.

Nevertheless, the public uproar was immense. It wasn't merely the Army's troubles that riled; it was the president's dictatorial conviction of the airlines without "trial and jury." If FDR had thought he would score a quick populist victory with his coup, he turned out to be greatly mistaken.

By mid-March, after only one month, it was clear that the intervention had backfired completely. The Air Corps was suffering, the public was livid, and President Roosevelt looked like a fool. Even Elliott was on public record disagreeing with his father.

So, in a classical example of his *modus operandi*, FDR blamed General Foulois for the fiasco. Foulois was forced to retire under humiliating circumstances.[377] Foulois and MacArthur were called to the White House on 10 March, when the disaster had become obvious. Foulois, feeling like a condemned man taken on his last walk, was received in the president's bedroom:

> The familiar smile was gone. In its place was a deep scowl which was fixed directly on me. Without a word of greeting the voice everyone had come to know so well boomed, "General, when are these air-mail killings going to stop?" [378]

---

[i] "Legalized Murder" was a common epithet (NYT 25 FEB 34); "Air Lynching" referred to, for instance, in editorial letter in the New York Tribune, 24 FEB 34.

Foulois said, "Only when airplanes stop flying."

To the general's surprise, the president thought some of the accidents must have been due to sabotage by his political enemies. He said:

> 'Well, believe it or not, General, I want you to investigate those rumors and put a stop to these killings.'
>
> For the next 10 minutes, MacArthur and I received a tongue-lashing which I put down in my book as the worst I ever received in all my military service. There was no doubt that what bothered Roosevelt the most was the severe criticism his Administration was getting over the contract cancellation. He did not seem genuinely concerned or even interested in the difficulties the Air Corps was having.
>
> ...The fact that three brave men had just died trying to do his bidding in the wrong equipment and under the worst possible weather conditions did not seem to concern him. That was my fault, he said. What was worse, and also my fault, was that my personal shortcomings were misdirected at him and Farley, and this he highly resented.

It is worth paying attention to Foulois's memoir, because it reflects a deep loathing of President Roosevelt that would become common in the military. Foulois went on:

> MacArthur said nothing all this time, and for the first time in my military life I sensed the wide gulf that exists between the man in uniform and the transient politician who is suddenly placed in a position of the highest authority. The military man trains all his adult life to attain the next higher rank and position. The politician may be a small-town banker or lawyer, yet by the mere accident of making friends with the "right" people or garnering enough votes can be catapulted into a position in our government, where, with a snap of his fingers, he can send a military man to his death or end his career. Here was one of those politicians who did not understand air power, airplanes, or any of the problems of flying and apparently did not want to learn. From the tone of his voice and his derision of the Air Corps I was, to him just another of those crazy, undisciplined fly-boys who had progressed in rank far beyond my capabilities.

Yet military officers are trained to stand at attention and take these kinds of showers, and these two officers did. Nonetheless, it got worse for Douglas MacArthur. In a sordid episode, President Roosevelt ordered MacArthur to lie, saying the general had telephoned him and recommended the air mail decision. MacArthur refused, causing an unresolved stand-off between the two.[379] In that light, the five-star general's tart comment upon the death of FDR eleven years later makes more sense. He said Roosevelt "never told the truth if a lie would suffice." [380]

Unexpectedly, the air mail crisis later became of additional interest because it marked the first public dogfight between Charles Lindbergh and President Roosevelt. Lindbergh knew from experience that making Army fliers carry the mail was dumb, dangerous, and of doubtful legality. He had the nerve to state these views in a message to the president. His telegram was carried throughout the news media, causing a sensation:

> ...Your present action does not discriminate between innocence and guilt and places no premium on honest business. Americans have spent their lives in building in this country the finest commercial air lines in the world. The United States today is far in the lead in almost every branch of commercial aviation. In America, we have commercial

aircraft, engines, equipment and air lines superior to those of any other country. The greatest part of this progress has been brought about through the air mail. Certainly most individuals in the industry believe that this development has been carried on in cooperation with existing government and according to law, if this is not the case it seems the right of the industry and in keeping with American tradition that facts to the contrary be definitely established. Unless these facts leave no alternative, the condemnation of commercial aviation by cancellation of all air mail contracts and the use of the army on commercial air lines will unnecessarily and greatly damage all American aviation.[381]

Colonel Lindbergh further stated to the Secretary of War:

> I believe that the use of the Army Air Corps to carry the air mail was unwarranted and contrary to American principles. The action was unjust to the airlines whose contracts were cancelled without trial. It was unfair to the personnel of the Army Air Corps, who had neither equipment designed for the purpose nor adequate time for training in a new field. It has unnecessarily greatly damaged all American aviation.[382]

Franklin D. Roosevelt's reaction was very characteristic. "We will get that fair-haired boy," he said. He did not answer Lindbergh directly; nor did he address any of the legitimate concerns raised by his critics. Instead, he had his men launch *ad hominem* counterattacks. Through his staff – Harold Ickes particularly – he accused Lindbergh of being a publicity-seeking profiteer. A glitch that delayed delivery of the telegram until after it was public was offered as proof that the flier was devious and underhanded.[383]

This merely amused the public, which had long considered him the antithesis of this. For example, Walter Lippman, who seems to have created the "Fiasco" label, wrote that it was shocking how "overzealous partisans of the Administration" had tried to discredit the aviation hero; "to investigate his earnings, to make out that he was a vulgar profiteer who was disqualified and had no right to be heard." [384]

Most informed people sided with Lindbergh. Famous aviators, including Eddie Rickenbacker, Clarence Chamberlin, and Amelia Earhart backed him. Even the humorist Will Rogers, an aviation buff and usually a Roosevelt fan, piped up for him.[385]

The *Los Angeles Times* probably spoke for the majority of the public when it editorialized:

> Assuming that the charges are true, they affected three companies. 34 companies have paid the penalty. Even the ferocious Mexican bandit, Pancho Villa, was accustomed to shoot only every tenth man. The administration order massacres all the mail-carrying lines.
>
> What must leave every American appalled was not only the monstrous injustice, but the evident impetuosity and recklessness of the assault. The prosperity, the hopes, the very lives of the people of America have been placed in the trust of such governmental agencies as the NRA and the CWA. It does not add to the feeling of security. Will those agencies also fly at problems with the unthinking emotion of a little boy kicking a chair that has barked his shin?[386]

The Roosevelt sons often said their father laughed at criticism and was utterly unfazed by the vitriol hurled at him. He didn't believe in getting angry, but in getting even. In this case that was not true. Charles Lindbergh earned FDR's life-long hatred.[i]

---

[i] Jim Farley later provided a snapshot: "At heart the President was a boy, sometimes a spoiled boy. Although he had tremendous charm and vitality, he had a few petty attributes which were continually

In the court of public opinion, the Eagle had defeated the Weasel. But further rounds were ahead. In time, the president would indeed "get that fair-haired boy."

Elliott Roosevelt, though hardly as respected, had also signed up for the concerted effort to reverse his father's rash move. This was, at least in part, because Hearst "deputized" him as a lobbyist:

> I had my first experience of being used as an entrée to the White House on a mission that was far from radical and, in my opinion, just. [WRH] deputized me in my capacity as aviation editor to go with his son George from Los Angeles to Washington to lobby for a reversal of Administration policy. I had been writing articles about the need to expand American air power. I had contacts with aircraft manufacturers like Donald W. Douglas and, in the Army Air Corps, with the lieutenant colonel in charge of March Field, whose name was "Hap" Arnold.
>
> As an economy measure, Father canceled the government contracts that paid commercial airlines to carry mail. The army's planes would take over that job, he ruled. These aircraft were little changed from the outdated models that existed at the end of the war. The crews sat in open cockpits. Radio communication facilities were primitive. These machines lagged far behind commercial planes in their ability to fly safely with the help of up-to-the-minute weather briefings for their pilots.[387]

He misremembered certain details; cost-cutting had not been the president's errand in this matter. Elliott wrote in an opinion piece after the deaths began:

> Quite apart from the merits of the mail-contract cancellation…The Army failed to "deliver the goods" as a commercial aviation organization because the Army Air Corps was undertrained, poorly equipped and hamstrung with obsolete regulations and ancient red tape. It failed because for years Congress has been starving it in appropriations for gasoline and other necessary expenses to keep Army pilot flying after they were trained...And it failed because it was plunged into commercial flying operations without the necessary safety devices essential to badweather flying but heretofore not included in military ships… training courses include ten hours blind flying minimum and twenty hours minimum night flying. During the last fiscal year only 7% of the Army's flying was done at night.[388]

Elliott was a little ahead of himself in blaming the Army's planes. The largest factor in the debacle was undoubtedly the lack of training in all-weather, night-time cross-country operations. To boot, it began in the middle of an unusually severe winter.

Elliott knew little, but he knew people who knew:

> "Father's cost-cutting backfired. The price of delivering letters was heavy losses in planes and pilots who were not trained for making transcontinental flights in every kind of weather. At all levels of command in the Army Air Corps, the decision was recognized as a mistake. Its effect on the passenger-flying companies was financially crippling. I knew that much from C.R. Smith, promoted now as president of the renamed American Airlines by his chief, E.L. Cord, who wrested control from its principal shareholder, Averell Harriman. Smith had served as best man at my wedding to Ruth.
>
> Not for the first time I got embroiled in a fierce one-sided argument with Father. "It's probably as great a mistake as you've ever made," I lectured him, "to just outright cancel

---

getting him into trouble. One of these was that he was forever trying to get even with someone for some slight, real or fancied. Another was that he was motivated on decisions, large or small, by his heart rather than his mind, all too frequently, and by hunches rather than by reason." (Farley, 183-4)

> those contracts. If you weren't satisfied with the commercial carrier's performance, why not put in a federal overseer and allow the airlines to do the job that they're equipped for? Then you'd avoid this needless cost in lives."
>
> He heard me out, but he was not to be budged. As an apprentice lobbyist, I had to judge myself a failure. The immediate net result of the mission was my learning that George Hearst had only limited capacity for holding his liquor. But, as happened so often, Father digested what I had told him, together with less vehement opinions from all sides. Eventually [FDR] produced a program to allocate individual routes to the air carriers and so end cutthroat competition between them. He gave the mail contracts back to them, too.[389]

This allusion to the *Nourmahal* incident tells us many things, but unfortunately not all that we need to know about the second son's involvement. Elliott was being used, and would later acknowledge it; yet he was also speaking for the aviation community, and indeed giving voice to the Air Corps, which was allowed none of its own. Hap Arnold must have long remembered the support the Hearst aviation editor gave to the cause. Nevertheless the nation would later find that Elliott's interest in the matter reflected anything but detached, selfless analysis.

Elliott had far greater ambition than just to snipe from the sidelines. Some of the signs of his appetite for empire-building were already noticeable as the air mail controversy dominated the headlines. Senator Thomas Schall (R-MN) noted this when he warned the country on 30 March 1934:

> The latest news in the air mail racket is that it is reported that Elliott Roosevelt, son of our well-known president, is in Washington with a plan to take over the service. Whom he represents has not been made public. It may be E.L. Cord or it may not, but it seems certain he does not appear for the companies whose contracts were cancelled without a hearing. The fact that his father is the President of the United States, and the further fact that his father in such official capacity canceled the contracts of the others, will, it is supposed, not militate against young Roosevelt in his quest for this highly profitable undertaking.[390]

Then Senator Schall, who obviously had his ear to the ground, quoted Elliott from the *Cincinnati Enquirer*, in which he seemed to advocate a socialized aviation sector:

> ...Elliott Roosevelt, son of the President, believes the aviation industry must be subsidized by the Government if it is to take its proper place in national defense...Commercial aviation must be considered in connection with national defense and must have Government aid if it is to play the role in national defense to which it is properly entitled. Not only should airlines be subsidized, he contended, but the entire industry given financial help, even to part payment of pilots by the Government, with Government insurance and retirement rating.[391]

Things never got that bad, but the thinking followed the direction of the New Deal. The quote reveals a mentality that was not explicitly ideological, but activist, statist, and quite without any healthy skepticism as to its own effectiveness or propriety.

The Black-McKellar bill, which the president signed on 12 June, black-listed the old air mail contractors. The entire industry was reorganized, and the old airlines resurrected in modified form. During May, airline contractors again began flying mail on temporary contracts, and by 1 June, the last of the military air mail operations came to an end.[392]

Although the storm was over, the president looked very bad. But his attempts to blame the military and its pilots rankled far more.

The air mail crisis was merely the dramatic leading edge of an immense reorganization of American aviation undertaken under the aegis of the New Deal. The prescription for aviation that FDR finally settled on included the infamous Civil Aeronautics Board (CAB) that allocated routes and regulated ticket prices until 1978, when President Carter's economists deregulated the skies. It seemed like the CAB did very much what Postmaster Brown had done in 1930 – and then some.

In 1938, FDR created the CAA (Civil Aviation Authority) from the Bureau of Air Commerce (BAC), and two years later he also split CAB off from the BAC. The bureau, the progenitor of the Federal Aviation Administration (FAA), had been created from the Commerce Department's Aeronautics Branch in the regulatory upheaval of 1934. Thus BAC/CAA and CAB became the aviation components of the New Deal alphabet soup.

Because the United States was by far the dominant aviation nation in 1944 when the Chicago Convention created the ICAO (International Civil Aviation Organization), American practices, procedures, terminology and technology essentially prototyped the aviation environment worldwide. It is almost pointless to debate the merits of this model; because, like a human language, it changes only glacially, and forever retains its original imprint. Those who were "present at the creation" of aviation regulation from 1926 to 1944 probably could not have foreseen how enduring, even ossified, their awkward compromises and well-meant attempts at order would become.[393]

The president stacked the BAC with his friends. It was originally led by the energetic Gene Vidal, who had befriended the Roosevelt family before the new administration took office. The bureau assumed police authority in the sky (air traffic control) in 1936.

Vidal's controversial departure on 28 February 1937, after a series of high-profile air crashes, got the family involved: "Amelia Earhart was furious and threatened to abandon her promise to Eleanor to campaign. She wrote Eleanor, who appealed to FDR, and Vidal was temporarily restored. After that Earhart made 28 speeches for FDR throughout the country."[i]

After Vidal's final departure later that year, he was out of favor and accepted positions in the private airline industry.

Hostility between the administration and aviation continued through the Roosevelt years. Like the rest of the business community, aviation tended towards the Republicans; but it could not operate without maintaining contacts and cutting deals with those in power. Airlines and manufacturers had to "play ball" to survive. We shall see that many did so with cynical enthusiasm. Yet there remained one odd fellow who would not "play ball" whether in aviation or in foreign policy.

President Roosevelt was confident that he knew how to "handle" people, but he was flummoxed when he ran up against Charles Lindbergh, widely reputed to be the straightest arrow that ever pierced the sky. With the start of the European war in September 1939, the president attempted to bribe the "Lone Eagle" with a cabinet post (devoted to aviation), if he would cease and desist from criticizing FDR's foreign policy.

---

[i] Cook: Eleanor Roosevelt, II/36; Vidal's tenure was contentious and he first resigned at the end of 1936.

It was a sordid offer, the more so because the "hapless" General Arnold was ordered to function as FDR's go-between.[394]

Despite the animosity, the colonel continued to serve the Air Corps in many important capacities. General Arnold was a good friend who used him for important tasks, including the infamous German visit that was actually undertaken to gather intelligence on the German air power build-up. As late as 1939 Lindbergh was on active duty working on Arnold's special projects, and he always remained a strong advocate of American air power.

While the Air Mail Fiasco gradually left the front pages during the summer of 1934, the struggle between the aviation industry, the White House and Congress continued. Critical legislation was to be passed; the Black-McKellar Act would be the basis for numerous modifications and additions in the coming years. The industry needed the best avenue to political access that it could possibly buy.

Fortunately, one was for sale.

The Aeronautical Chamber of Commerce

Elliott Roosevelt seemingly went through his entire life wearing a giant FOR SALE sign. There was a lot going on in aviation during FDR's first term, and Elliott, callow youth or not, was on the inside of it, always looking to trade access for money. This resulted in a mysterious change of employment in the spring of 1934.

Sometime around 1 May, after the collapse of Elliott's aviation schemes and while the air mail crisis was transitioning to a legislative phase, the "powers that be" decided that the 23-year old with a solo endorsement on his student certificate should be made Vice President of the Aeronautical Chamber of Commerce of America (ACCA).[395]

The president of this powerful lobby, Thomas Morgan, took his time in making the odd choice public. Although insiders knew of the appointment, the public announcement did not come until 14 June:

> Mr. Roosevelt is a trained aviator, and a thorough student of aviation and will devote his full time and attention to all the problems that relate to every phase of the industry. His election was unanimous and highly approved in all directions.[396]

Coming on the heels of the air mail crisis, few could have been fooled about what was really going on. Rumors took flight about Elliott's excessive remuneration and what lobbying the boy wonder might have been tasked to perform for the industry group.

The influential Washington journalists Drew Pearson and Robert Allen wrote in an exposé that Elliott had asked O. Max Gardner, former North Carolina governor and then attorney and Washington lobbyist for the chamber, for the job, saying he was "not happy" with the increasingly anti-New Deal Hearst chain. Thomas Morgan then hired Elliott at a reported $15,000 a year salary. For this he was repaid by Elliott with a telegram suggesting he resign:

> When the air mail scandals broke Elliott sent a somewhat peremptory cablegram to Tom Morgan, president of the chamber, who was abroad, advising him to resign – advice which Mr. Morgan resented and did not follow. Elliott also acted in a similarly peremptory and youthful manner with other members of the aeronautical chamber, including Douglas

> Brown, president of United Aircraft, to whom he sent a note asking him to come and see him, receiving the reply that he, Elliott, could come and see Brown since the latter was paying his salary.[397]

Aero Digest ran an impish profile of Elliott entitled "We've captured a Democrat." The slightly exaggerated premise was that Democrats in aviation were as rare as snowballs in hell. This was precisely the reason, the journal assumed, that Elliott was necessary. The industry was fighting for its survival, squeezed by the pincers of the Depression and Roosevelt's assault. Hiring the president's son was a tactical move. The article's author, the prominent pilot and writer Cy Caldwell, said that "young Roosevelt could gain admittance to the White House at any time of day or night without danger of being hurled in jail for collusion, which was more than any one else in aviation could do." [398]

Interviewing Elliott, Caldwell noted: "He has as many ideas as his father has college professors on the public payroll. Some of those ideas are of the rosy variety common to optimistic and somewhat idealistic young men of 23, while others are soundly practical." At least Caldwell thought Elliott was no rubber-stamp for others.

After this cautious endorsement, the industry organ concluded:

> The air mail mess was the one really bad political move that the President has made, for it has shown the people how rapidly we are drifting into a form of government that is throwing aside legal processes and is resorting to bureaucratic bludgeoning and an iron-clad control exercised by one numerically insignificant group of men. There is no essential difference between the policy that can deprive men of their financial contracts without legal processes in open court, and the policy of Hitler, that can deprive political enemies of their lives without a fair and open trial.[399]

It was downhill from there. Two years later *Aero Digest* writers, along with many others, were openly referring to President Roosevelt as "der Führer."

Elliott did keep his ACCA job for over a year. In that time he managed to get excoriated both for being a lobbyist with a highly unfair genetic advantage, as well as for not lobbying. If he didn't do anything, he was nevertheless still a piñata for the administration's enemies. The Republicans in Congress fumed about the aviation legislation passed by the Democrats in 1934-36, but they could do nothing.

Defeated repeatedly, the Republicans accused Elliott. The charge was led by Rep. Melvin Maas (R-MN) who had been a marine aviator in the Great War.[i] Despite entering politics he remained widely respected:

> Mr. Taber. [R-NY] What organization is supposed to be back of this bill?
>
> Mr. Maas. The Aeronautical Chamber of Commerce, representing all of these air transport companies, or practically all of them, is the one now telling us that unless we pass this bill it is going to bankrupt the industry.
>
> Mr. Taber. Who is the chief representative for that organization?
>
> Mr. Maas. Oh, various officers, but at present the most active is Elliott Roosevelt, the vice president of the Aeronautical Chamber.
>
> Mr. Taber. It is rumored around the Capitol that he draws a salary of $25,000.

---

[i] Melvin Maas retired from the USMC Reserve a Major General, in 1952. While remaining in Congress, he served in the South Pacific during WW2.

> Mr. Maas. I believe it is $15,000. I understand he has just been raised from $10,000 for his good work. I believe, as a matter of fact, that if the administration was right when it canceled these contracts because they said the rates were too high and were obtained fraudulently, it is wrong now if it attempts to increase these rates without a searching audit and investigation to determine the actual operating cost of these air mail lines.[400]

Maas, who called the president a murderer due to the air mail cancelation, got his summation of the Air Mail Fiasco into the record: [401]

> The Administration has turned the contracts back to the same people whose rates were called too high and whose contracts were called fraudulent, only they are operating under different names. They were turned back after absolute murder for the sake of political expediency.[402]

Roosevelt's enemies expressed not only resentment that the contract cancellations had been a disaster, but they suggested that the nefarious influence of Elliott Roosevelt was behind the restoration of airline subsidies and increased rates. That the Mead Amendment of 1935, which increased rates, was viewed as an "American Airlines Relief Act" was perhaps inevitable, but all the airlines were thankful for the change.

American Airlines did come out of the entire air mail debacle markedly better than its competitors.

It is true that American was losing enormous amounts on its Fort Worth-centered network.[403] The Mead amendment bill saved it. But despite the bitter Congressional recriminations, there is no evidence that Elliott Roosevelt was behind it. His influence in aviation was waning. Ironically, though, now that Congress had essentially been forced to redress the worst consequences of President Roosevelt's rash act of the previous year, Republicans found the president's son to be a useful scarecrow. Rep. Francis Culkin (R – NY) summarized:

> I am not suggesting any financial impropriety; I am merely expressing curiosity as to whether this pseudotechnical relation of the aviation industry with a member of the family of the distinguished President has any influence on the present attitude, the present reverential attitude of the committee toward these aviation companies which were formally held in so low esteem.
>
> I well, remember, Mr. Chairman, when these contracts were canceled that that distinguished American citizen, Colonel Lindbergh, gave out a message to the country that this cancelation would wreck the aviation industry, and industry which he had done much to foster; and then it was given out to the American people by the White House that Lindbergh was seeking notoriety and publicity. Lindbergh since, of course, has been justified in his attitude; and the introduction of this bill writes the John Hancock of the administration upon his disapproval and his protest. This bill puts us back where we were when the cancelation occurred.[404]

The public's obsession with just how much money Elliott made in his various jobs and deals was already evident. It was at that time complemented by an equal and perhaps even more malevolent interest in the financial doings of his brother James, who, as an instant insurance executive, was much better at selling the family name. Jimmy's activities would at times become an even greater headache for the president than Elliott's. In one case FDR told Treasury's Henry Morgenthau to "pick and choose" evidence released to a Senate investigation in order to get Jimmy off the hook. Henry refused.[405]

There is common story, originating with then SEC Chairman William O. Douglas, that President Roosevelt "cried like a child" when confronted with one of Jimmy's fast ones. James swore this was complete baloney, and it certainly sounds bizarre. He never saw his father "shed a single tear."[i] On the other hand, FDR claimed to be America's best actor, so maybe Douglas did see something.

The attention to James's insurance activities culminated in a very damaging article "Jimmy's Got It" in the *Saturday Evening Post* on 2 July 1938. Investigative reporter Alva Johnston documented in painful detail how Jimmy methodically hijacked, in the "eleventh hour," the biggest and most lucrative accounts in the country with the unspoken promise of favorable attention in Washington. We shall return much later to something Jimmy was then rigging up with Joseph P. Kennedy, but here we need only focus on an aviation case:

> Aviation insurance is a highly specialized type of insurance. Obviously, the problem of keeping down the fire risk and general risk on airplanes is a matter for the expert. Much of this insurance has been in the hands of a few firms which have been in the business for many years. Jimmy succeeded in crashing it last year. He got the Transcontinental & Western Airways, Inc., business away from one of the old-established air-insurance firms, and split it with Fred Roper. Fred is the son of Daniel C. Roper, Secretary of Commerce. Secretary Roper is the Cabinet officer in charge of the regulation of aeronautics.[406]

Johnson's explosive article caused great controversy, and parts of it were contested. Two years later, on 18 May 1940, the *Post* followed up with another article about Jimmy's continued extortionate insurance practices, this one involving a government-controlled shipping line.[407]

Jimmy, who "made no secret of his ambition to become governor of Massachusetts and then President of the United States," was thought – erroneously – to be well on his way to become one of America's richest men. But a major unreported scandal appears to rest in Jimmy's four-month, highly lucrative presidency of a very curious New Jersey outfit named National Grain and Yeast. Alluding to Jimmy's close relationship with Joe Kennedy, one writer said that "Joe wangled Jimmy a sinecure as the president of the National Grain Yeast Corporation…producer of the important ingredient in the production of whiskey, under investigation at the time for bootlegging." [408]

The account James Roosevelt gave in his memoirs, although contrite, poorly matches the public record. Jimmy admitted the company was a criminal enterprise, and that Treasury Secretary Morgenthau got FDR to extract him from it in November 1935 on threat of resignation. But press reports, amplified by archive evidence, suggest Jimmy tried to double-cross the boss, Frank Hale, in order to take over the company, and was in turn thrown out by the professionals. At any rate, the lawsuits associated with the company reverberated for five years.[ii]

---

[i] JR: My Parents, 245; Morgan, 463. Douglas was associated with the circle around Tommy Corcoran and Lyndon Johnson, and served on the Supreme Court from 1939-1975.

[ii] JR: My Parents, 231; NYT, numerous accounts in 1935; also see Flynn, 240-1; also see Pegler collection on James Roosevelt. Pegler received a signed letter stating that "Hale made Jimmie Roosevelt president of his company, briefly, to front on a Wall Street deal. Jimmie R. was dropped by Hale when the latter discovered

As Westbrook Pegler's research would later show, Frank Hale was a very curious character indeed. He had been a vaudeville performer and then a Prohibition agent before getting into the yeast trade. Apparently, Hale was not his real name, but it was the one he used when he retired to Palm Beach as an admired philanthropist.[i]

The significance of Jimmy's forays in the whisky trade will become apparent later.

Not yet as "successful" as his elder brother, apprentice lobbyist Elliott took an estate in Leesburgh, Virginia, whence he could participate in Washington meetings and in suitable upper-crust activities. He did not mind public attention, but he furiously resisted it for his wife and baby. The Lindbergh kidnapping was still on everyone's mind.

Like his brothers, Elliott had a habit of getting physical with people he didn't like. Repeatedly he beat up photographers and smashed their plates. When visiting C.R. Smith in Chicago in December, he roughed up one camera man. Visiting Hyde Park, he had lurking reporters seized and their equipment broken. At his Iowa wedding, he had the police arrest a photographer, breaking his plates. Such tactics probably only spurred on the hounds, but unlike most others, Elliott could call for help from the Secret Service.[409]

Media management is a difficult art. But physical altercations always backfire, because reporters stick up for each other. A writer editorialized:

> Whatever the sons of President Roosevelt learned from their father, gracious manners were not included. If one Roosevelt boy isn't fighting a newspaper photographer, it's another…the Roosevelt sons are not at all loath to command the privileges that go with the prestige of the Presidential family circus. I happened to be in Rome when one of them arrived and the Embassy was all but turned upside down for the royal arrival.[ii]

In other words, they couldn't have it both ways.

When it came to fisticuffs, evidently Elliott brought much of it upon himself. A Santa Fe informer wrote to Westbrook Pegler that "Elliott was practically kicked out of Valley Ranch, a dude ranch about 30 miles from Santa Fe about 1937, for insulting a woman at a Rodeo Dance, by insisting on dancing with her while he was beastly drunk. He left next morning by airplane with a black eye and swollen nose." [410]

The correspondent retold that affair with more details in 1945. He wrote:

> In 36 or 37, Elliott was at the Brush Ranch, up the Pecos, and as I was told, under the care of a guard as he was a dipsomaniac. At a party given for the Ceilo--- (I've forgotten the name, but they were the heads of the Aviation Companies) at Valley Ranch, another Dude Ranch further down the Pecos, Elliott while drunk insulted the wife of another guest and was given the Western Treatment by the wronged husband. A relative who saw the affair said that Elliott was flown out the next day pretty badly bunged up.[411]

The significance of this account is that "Ceilo" refers to the "Conquistadores del Cielo," a legendary but secretive "club" of the true bigshots of American aviation. The

---

Jimmie, in the true tradition of his tribe, was about to knife him in the back with a business double-cross." (Ford to Pegler, 28 JUN 45, Pegler/HH.)

[i] Numerous postwar Pegler columns deal with Jimmy's relationship with Hale. Jimmy also hired brother Franklin for the company. Incidentally, Hale used Jimmy to lobby the German government, which was causing patent problems because of the Jewish names in control of National Grain & Yeast.

[ii] Harry Carr in LAT, 7 DEC 34. The other sons' antics in Europe attracted a lot of attention at the time.

association was formed by Jack Frye of TWA in 1937 and held yearly revels in Arizona. That Elliott managed to get beaten up during one of these manly trysts is quite an accomplishment, and it must have been quietly talked about throughout the industry.

A somewhat similar story centered on Lordsburg, N.M., which happens to be about halfway between Fort Worth and Los Angeles. When Jimmy was working as a movie director in Hollywood, and Elliott had the Texas ranch, they would reportedly meet in Lordsburg for "whoopee" for which purpose numbers of women other than their wives were procured: "Sometimes they would bring their own women. Other times they would pick them up locally from the bars, cafes or just hustlers. The complaint the women had was that they were fed on hambergers in return for the priveliges of being able to associate with the illustrious." [412]

Another informer, an oilman, said that Elliott, after marrying Ruth, "kept a harem with John Jones at the Worth Hotel suite 1506." The significance of that statement is that John Jones could refer to either Jesse Jones's brother or to John Tilford Jones, Jr., his nephew (who was then in his twenties). Others also linked John Jones with Elliott in connection with dubious business deals, but at this remove it is difficult to determine the veracity of the accusations.[413]

Still, aviation promotion remained Elliott's trade. Prior to the anniversary of powered flight on 17 December, Elliott and Gene Vidal led a committee to decide a fitting tribute to the Wright Brothers. The idea was that all airplanes in the nation should take to the air, circle their communities – counterclockwise, specifically – for half an hour and then land, to be admired by the public up close. Elliott would lead one such aerial parade in Dallas.[414]

This grand exercise has fortunately not become an annual tradition, but it does illustrate the central role of aviation promotion during the "golden age." The conquest of the sky was a national project that captured everyone's attention. It made for grand speeches and spectacles. Elliott Roosevelt excelled at this.

By the end of 1934, the air mail crisis had been settled. President Roosevelt had largely gotten his way, but he had been severely bloodied in the process. While Elliott minimized his own role, there were people who decided to dig deeper and find out if there was more skulduggery in his activities than at first met the eye.

There was. Elliott had had two secret plots simmering as he entered 1934. They would ripen during 1935, and become public the year after.

BOMBERS FOR STALIN

In February 1934, just when the air mail storm blew up, Elliott Roosevelt became the kingpin in a secret and probably illegal scheme to sell fifty "civilian" Lockheed Electras to the USSR. The details of this caper became publicly known two years later when the Senate committee that investigated it was forced to reveal its knowledge.

Documentation of the scandal in the contemporary press was then quite extensive. However, the best sources, including copies of the correspondence, contracts, and other details are found in the preserved papers of Senator Gerald Nye, now at the Hoover Library in West Branch, Iowa. They leave no doubt that Elliott thought he had hit the jackpot with the Lockheed Electra sale. As so often, they do leave out details of how much involvement President Roosevelt had in the proposed trade.

Bankrupted by the Depression, Lockheed badly needed to sell new airplanes. The company was just out of receivership and had been taken over by new investors led by Robert Gross. The new Lockheed Corporation gambled its existence on a sleek new twin-engine long-range aircraft. The Model 10 Electra prototype first flew on 23 February 1934. It incorporated modern features such as retractable landing gear, canti-levered wings, and a monococque fuselage in an all-metal airframe.

The Electra and especially its numerous descendants would become a great commercial success. The basic design (Models 10, 12, and 14) was a favorite of many prominent aviators in the 1930s. The Army adopted it first as the C-36, followed by a flurry of variants. The design matured into the Hudson/Ventura/Lodestar light bombers common during the ensuing war. Amelia Earhart flew an Electra; so did Howard Hughes on his round-the-world flight in 1938. It was thus no wonder that the Soviet Union was interested in the aircraft.

If Lockheed needed to sell, the Bolsheviks needed to buy. They were coming out of a long drought in trade with the capitalist world they had sworn to overthrow. On 16 November 1933 the Roosevelt administration offered diplomatic recognition to the Soviet regime, anticipating increased exports to Russia. At the same time, President Roosevelt was working to establish a framework for government credit to facilitate Soviet trade. FDR established the Export-Import Bank by executive order on 2 February 1934. Although this New Deal organization is still very much alive, its original, limited purpose was to extend trade credit to regimes that could not otherwise qualify for it.

Since the Bolsheviks had repudiated Imperial Russia's debts, the big sticking point in US-Soviet relations was a settlement of the defunct loans. Roosevelt had promised that diplomatic recognition of the USSR would lead to debt reconciliation, followed by much expanded trade. Hopes were high during these months; they would soon be dashed.

An immense Soviet purchasing commission, Amtorg, already operated in the United States. It functioned effectively as a shadow embassy, with all which that entails. Citing his aviation connections, Elliott Roosevelt made friends with its top commissars. The Russians were eager for new technology and sent engineering crews to the American aircraft manufacturers. Even during the Hoover administration the Soviets had been able to legally obtain U.S. aeronautical products, most notably the Wright Cyclone engine. They built fine aircraft themselves, but they also needed the products of advanced American engineering to copy and mass-produce.[415]

The term "Amtorg" (American *Torgovaya* (Trade) Company) probably rings few alarm bells today. Not so in the interwar years. Trade was only its top cover. It was, in fact, a gigantic intelligence and propaganda operation with about 500 operatives in the United States. Amtorg was also the conduit of funds, instructions, and recruitment activities preparing the way for the world revolution in America.

Considering Elliott's later activities, the Amtorg connection is significant. However, at that time, Elliott was only interested in selling aircraft to the Communists; they in turn were also interested in checking out the president's son.[i] The Soviets considered Elliott important enough that he attended the Soviet embassy's farewell

---

[i] Morgan: Reds, 124-8; lists activities of Bogdanov, Amtorg, inc. attempts to obtain aeronautical technology.

dinner for Pyotr Bogdanov, the Amtorg head, when he departed for Moscow in November 1934.[416]

In attempting to exploit the new trading opportunities with the USSR his father had suddenly made possible, Elliott established contact with Bob Gross at Lockheed, with Donald Douglas in Santa Monica, with Anthony Fokker, who had come to America to deal with U.S. aircraft manufacturers, and with a handful of opportunistic entrepreneurs he had met in Los Angeles.

Fokker wanted to export the aircraft of other companies as well as his own famed transports, reasoning that it was faster and cheaper to license an existing design than to reinvent it. He talked to Donald Douglas about selling aircraft, both Douglas's and those of Lockheed in nearby Burbank, to the Soviet Union. On 15 January, Fokker signed a contract with Douglas to sell Douglas aircraft in Europe.[417]

Douglas told Fokker that the license to sell Lockheeds to Russia had just been given to a group headed by Elliott Roosevelt, who had befriended both Gross and Douglas while living in Los Angeles. He thought Fokker should try to work out a deal with Elliott.

Elliott must already have been talking to the Russians, because when he connected with Fokker and an entrepreneur by the name of Herbert A. Reed, he stated that the USSR was only interested in military planes, but he thought it unlikely that American authorities would approve such a sale: "He said it would be all right if we sold Russia planes ostensibly for commercial use but into which had been built the structural changes necessary for an easy and inexpensive conversion into military craft." [418]

Reed made this statement in 1936 after he had turned on Elliott.

Thus, in early February 1934, Fokker, Douglas, and Roosevelt met with Lockheed and contrived a scheme to sell the fast new twin-engine aircraft to the Soviet Union, disguised as civilian transports. Fokker built a mock-up with the military conversions in place in order to demonstrate military options to visiting engineers from Amtorg.

Reed's later affidavit to the Senate further stated that on 21 February, Elliott's (and Douglas's) business partner, the Los Angeles industrialist Grenville Stratton, drove Fokker and Reed to Elliott Roosevelt's home in Beverly Hills. After a prolonged discussion of "a proposed plan to reorganize the nation's air lines" in response to the air mail contract cancellations, the three men then plotted how to impress the Soviets with the Lockheed Electra.[419]

According to Reed, Fokker's mockup had three proposed conversions: light bomber, ground attack, and reconnaissance. The Russians would see the mock-up with military conversions, including bomb racks and machine guns. It was particularly auspicious that the Electra prototype was just then ready for its first flight.

Reed said the mockup "was safely hidden in the padlocked room next to the Lockheed plant. Fokker and Elliott Roosevelt got into an argument about 'who shot the bear' – which was entitled to the most credit, Roosevelt for his contract with the Russians or Fokker for his engineering skill." [420]

Despite the argument, only three days later, on 24 February, a Soviet delegation of five aeronautical engineers, headed by a man named Schumanov, met with Stratton in Los Angeles. Stratton took them to Lockheed-Burbank, where they met Elliott Roosevelt, who introduced them to the militarized Electra mockup.[421] According to the trade journal *Aero Digest*, this was merely the first of several Soviet visits. The deal was to be financed by the new Export-Import Bank. This institution, however, could not finance military exports; and at the same time, strict American neutrality laws made exports of war materiel difficult altogether.[422]

Although various parties nosed around in the matter during 1934, the details did not become known until October 1936, when a prominent aviation publisher outed Elliott, and the Senate Munitions committee felt compelled to reveal its already completed investigation. The result was an immediate scandal, not merely because of the illicit scheme, but because of the ugly picture it revealed of Elliott's boundless avarice.

It is from the first exposé in *Aero Digest* in October 1936 that we have the copies of the documents that Elliott thought had been destroyed. The journal had obtained them from the Senate investigation. They included a letter dated 5 February 1934 in which Elliott informed Herbert Reed that the deal was on:

> My Dear Mr. Reed,
>
> Following my conversation with Mr. Stratton the agreement to be formed between your selling organization for Lockheed Electra transport planes and a corporation to be formed by myself for the purposed of aiding in the sale of these planes to the Soviet Union is entirely agreeable to me.
>
> The terms of this agreement, as I understand them, are that this corporation will receive from your organization 15% of the net selling price of each ship, or parts thereto, or any other items pertaining thereto, for delivery to the Soviet Union. In addition it is further understood that my corporation will in no way participate in the sale of the license in so far as commission is concerned, but will at all times further the sale thereof. It is my understanding that a retainer-fee of $25,000 for the services of this corporation will be paid for the year 1934, payable as follows: $5000 dollars to be paid immediately, and the balance as desered [sic]. Pending the drawing up of such a contract I will proceed immediately to negotiate.
>
> I will send this note to you with Mr. Stratton, and the hope that he will arrive safely.
>
> Sincerely yours, Elliott Roosevelt.[423]

On 6 February, on the stationery of the Hollywood Roosevelt Hotel, Elliott hand-wrote a receipt for the first $5,000 and gave it to Herbert Reed. That document would become an inconvenient exhibit when Elliott later denied ever receiving the money.

The contract spelled out the details of the now expanded arrangement. Fokker's intention was clear:

> You are to incorporate a company to be known as Elliott Roosevelt, Inc., which is to be organized for the purpose of conducting, among other things, sales negotiations. The N.V. Nederlandsche Vliegtuigen Fabriek has entered into a contract with the Lockheed Aircraft Corporation, giving the Holland Company the European sales rights, and in addition, the right to manufacture under the license the 'Electra' model airplane in Europe and Russia...
>
> Your corporation is hereby appointed sales representative for the Lockheed Sales & Export Corporation on the following terms and conditions: On any sales of airplanes similar to the 'Electra' model airplane to the Soviet Union, a commission shall be paid to your corporation, provided the order is secured within one year from date. This commission shall be arrived at by deducting from the sales price agreed upon with the Soviet Union the cost price, which, at the moment, is estimated to be approximately $47,000,000. The difference between the sales price and the cost price is understood to be the profit on each airplane. One-half of this amount shall be paid to you when determined,

> and after the actual receipt of the money by the Lockheed Sales & Export Corporation, and is the commission above referred to.
>
> Contingent with the placing of an order by the Soviet Union for fifty (50) airplanes under the agreement, the Soviet Union will purchase from the Lockheed Sales & Export Corporation the license rights to manufacture this model airplane in Russia. For this license, the Holland Company will receive the sum of $250,000.00. Your corporation is to receive no commission for negotiating the sale of this license.
>
> Your corporation shall be paid by the Lockheed Sales & Export Corporation a retainer fee amounting to $25,000. Of this sum the receipt of $5,000 is hereby acknowledged by you on behalf of your corporation, which sum was paid on February 6, 1934. The balance of $20,000 is due and payable to your corporation in three equal payments, which are due on May 6, 1934; August 6, 1934, and November 6, 1934, respectively, providing an order for a substantial number of airplanes is placed by the Soviet Union with the Lockheed Sales & Export Corporation prior to May 6, 1934, or shortly thereafter...[424]

Fokker, Elliott Roosevelt, and Stratton signed this contract on 28 February 1934.

It was all supposed to be a closely held secret because of several awkward little blemishes. Firstly, the aircraft would leave Lockheed-Burbank as civilian aircraft and be converted to bombers by Fokker before the Red Army received them. At that time, the munitions trade was very unpopular in the neutral and mostly disarmed United States – in fact, a very hostile Congress was investigating the arms trade at the time. The issue had become a populist rallying point. The campaign against "merchants of death" was led by Senator Gerald Nye (R – N.D.), who headed the Special Committee on Investigation of the Munitions Industry.

Secondly, the Fokker deal was to be financed by the president's new Export-Import Bank, a device set up to facilitate trade with governments to whom no reasonable bank would otherwise extend credit. The reason Elliott was even in the game was that, with his connections, he promised he could arrange the government credit.

A third major problem was that the president's son was blatantly being used to secure access and influence with foreign governments. Initially, Elliott was supposed to travel abroad and flog the airplanes to foreign buyers who could not, of course, disregard a Roosevelt.

Finally, the deal was, in the vernacular, a major rip-off.

Both Fokker and Roosevelt stood to clear $500,000 dollars on the deal. That's a profit of $20,000 per aircraft. The planes would sell for about 58,000 each, which was far too much, but the 23-year old Elliott assured everyone that he had so much pull with both the U.S. and Soviet governments that he could close the deal nonetheless.

Elliott devised some infantile secret codes for communicating about the matter, but as often happens with this kind of secret, everyone in the aviation trade soon knew something about it. There was also fairly early official interest. A few months later, internal revenue agents became concerned about the $5,000 that seemed to have magically disappeared between Fokker's records and Elliott's tax return. At the same time, Senator Nye's Munitions Committee quietly began investigating the deal. Finally, with the October 1936 issue of *Aero Digest*, the dam burst, and the sensation splattered across the nation's front pages.

The publisher of that influential journal was a "Roosevelt-hater" by the name of Frank Tichenor. He had already ripped into the president over the air mail fiasco. Now he had the goods on Elliott: copies of letters, details, and most of all, Herbert Reed, who no longer was interested in protecting the president or his son.[425]

This revelation forced the Nye committee, which had recommended no further action, to come clean as well. Gerald Nye was an unusual politician. He was a La Follette populist, i.e. prone to left-wing or "progressive" views typical of the prairies at the time. He held neutralist, anti-war, and anti-big business views.

"God! What a Family They Turned out to Be!"

One of Nye's populist beliefs, widely shared at the time, was that the war profiteers, the weapons manufacturers, the evil bankers, and the European imperialists had conspired to lure America into the Great War in 1917. That war had cost the United States much in lives and treasure, but the real annoyance was that afterwards, the Europeans carried on as before, obtusely sowing the seeds of yet another war, and – to top it off – trying to hand the reparations bill to the United States. America had been duped, and it wasn't going to happen again if Senator Nye and his friends could help it.

So why did Nye not unprompted reveal this scandal, seemingly red meat to his ilk?

The senator said he finally released the Fokker affidavit describing the deal with Elliott because his committee had been accused in the *Aero Digest* article of partisanship in suppressing the scandal. He said:

> Obviously, when an attack is made on the committee charging it with concealing files every member wants to resent it. At no time has there been any partisanship on the committee. Obviously, a good many ends were not run down. The Roosevelt-Fokker case was one to which the committee gave a great deal of consideration. The whole purpose in making the affidavit available yesterday was to afford a demonstration of the fact that, after all, nothing had come of the tie-up. Absolutely no pressure was brought to bear to prevent development of any part of this story.[426]

This seems to have succeeded only in making everyone look bad. With the election four weeks away, the New Dealers were furious that the story came out – clearly, the timing seemed intended to harm the president, and that's exactly what Mr. Tichenor had in mind.

The anti-FDR crowd was angry that the case had seemingly been suppressed while Mr. Nye tried to keep his committee afloat without incurring more wrath from the administration than it had already earned. Nye was out on a fiscal limb and his committee was indeed closed down; it issued its final report on 24 February 1936. The October surprise was thus, in a sense, a last sensational twitch of the Nye committee, although Nye had no intention of influencing the election with it.[427]

The senator said that the transaction would have been illegal if it had proceeded; that is, if Elliott had succeeded in selling bombers to Stalin. It seems likely, though, that a court would have had to decide this, at least if the trade had become publicly known – something the conspirators did what they could to prevent.

Many people were puzzled. A representative editorial wondered:

> Senator Nye says that the committee gave the matter careful consideration but that the information was "limited" and they did not have the money to investigate and develop it. They had, however, money enough to investigate, develop, and make public plenty of

> matter regarding the activities of the Du Ponts, of Wall Street financiers and sundry other "economic royalists" who are aligned against the administration…It seems strange that at that point the inquiry should have stopped short for lack of the few dollars and few hours it would have cost to summon Elliott Roosevelt and ask him about it. Much more, both in time and money, was spent by the committee on matters of much less public interest.[428]

The simplest explanation is probably the rightest: Congress did not have the stomach for going after the Roosevelts. Still, Nye lamented in private: "God, what a family they turned out to be!" [429]

Through the fury, Tony Fokker kept his practical Dutch head. He issued a release stating that he had simply been trying to sell airplanes, and he had no intention of getting caught up in a politically motivated row.

Beyond the secret codes, Elliott Roosevelt had taken careful steps to hide evidence of the deal, and especially to avoid implicating the president. His associate, Stratton, had intervened to get the documents destroyed: "Herbert Reed, an associate of Fokker, declared that Stratton had approached him to recover the receipt given by Elliott Roosevelt saying "I have personally assured the President that all papers involving Elliott have been destroyed." [430]

As soon as the story broke, Elliott went into his customary denial mode. His first statement denied that he received any money. He said Stratton got the $5000 to cover his expense account. He complained:

> The $5,000 which he says I received was an expense account allowed G.W. Stratton, now with Douglas airplanes at Los Angeles. At one time we contemplated a three way contract between Fokker, Stratton, and myself under which we would sell transport planes in Europe for which Fokker held the license. I deemed it unwise to sell American manufactured planes abroad and withdrew. Later Stratton withdrew also, but he had an expense account which he was paid for.[431]

Elliott's lie might have gone unchallenged. But he hadn't counted on Fokker's record keeping.

Fokker made a sworn affidavit, dated 18 September 1935, detailing the scheme to Congressional investigators. It is of great interest not only for its account of the Elliott caper, but for the cynical assessment Fokker provided of the aviation industry. A copy of the Fokker testimony survives in the Nye collection at the Hoover Presidential Library, along with further papers of the investigation.

Clearly, the documents had not all been destroyed as Elliott had demanded. Senator Gerald Nye now made copies, some of them with Elliott's signature, available to the public. The cache included some tart references by Mr. Fokker to the character of his temporary business partner.

> Mr. Fokker explained that in the early part of 1934 he had entered negotiations with the Douglas Aircraft Company for a sales and licensing agreement, and later discovered that he could not procure an exclusive sales agency for Russia because it had been given to Mr. Elliott Roosevelt and certain partners in business with him.
>
> He signed an agreement with the Douglas company dated 15 January 1934, in which he is given the right to sell and license certain Douglas planes 'whether used for civilian or military purposes in any country in Europe, with the exception of Russia.'
>
> For the license he paid $100,000. Having discovered that Douglas had made arrangements with Mr. Elliott Roosevelt and his associates to sell Douglas planes to Russia,

> Mr. Fokker then approached Mr. Roosevelt who had been introduced to him by Mr. Douglas and made a contract with Mr. Roosevelt for the sale of military Lockheed planes.
>
> Mr. Fokker states that he met Mr. Elliott Roosevelt in Mr. Douglas' office at the California plant of the Douglas Aircraft Co. in early 1934 and that Mr. Stratton, Mr. Douglas and Mr. Roosevelt were present. At this and other times Mr. Douglas conveyed to Mr. Fokker his impression that Mr. Roosevelt could swing the Russian business...
>
> Mr. Fokker already had signed an agreement to be sales agent for the Lockheed Electra type plane in Europe, including Russia. The agreement signed with Elliott Roosevelt was a special arrangement for the sale of these planes in Russia.[432]

The deal that Elliott talked Fokker into involved vastly inflated commissions:

> Questioned concerning why he had signed an agreement which provided for such a large commission, that is, $500,000 to Mr. Roosevelt and $500,000 to himself upon the completion of the sale Mr. Fokker explained that he had not felt that the prices which it was proposed to charge the Russians for these 50 military planes were at all reasonable; in fact, he had thought them notably excessive, but that he had been persuaded by Mr. Roosevelt and...Mr Stratton, that Mr. Roosevelt had enough influence with the Import and Export Bank and the Russian purchasing commission then in the country to swing the deal at that excessive price...
>
> He relied upon the attitude taken by Mr. Douglas ... concerning the expected influence of Mr. Elliott Roosevelt on the Import and Export Bank and on the Russian commission, coupled with the general expectation that Russian debt negotiations then taking place would result in Russian purchases of very considerable amounts in this country.
>
> Mr. Fokker stated that before the agreement with Mr. Elliott Roosevelt had been signed, he had desired [him] to make a trip abroad with Mr. Fokker to attempt to sell airplanes to various governments, counting on the willingness of high foreign officials to receive Mr. Roosevelt as the son of the American President.[433]

The most worrisome revelation was that the President of the United States was aware of the deal. Apparently he had restrained Elliott from the worst influence-peddling excesses, including a trip to Moscow, but he had approved the arrangement in general:

> When, in the course of taking the deposition, Mr. Carter Tiffany, in Mr. Fokker's presence, stated that Mr. H.A. Reed had reported to Mr. Tiffany that before the contract was signed with Mr. Fokker Mr. Elliott Roosevelt had telephoned the President of the United States from California concerning the arrangement to travel abroad as Mr. Fokker's agent, and gave the President the main details of his proposed contract with Mr. Fokker, and had been told by the President that he had objection to Mr. Elliott Roosevelt's traveling abroad in this connection, but had approved the contract with Mr. Fokker. Mr. Fokker stated that he had not been told the details himself, but had gathered the impression that Mr. Elliott Roosevelt had found it impossible to travel abroad as his representative. This matter of a trip abroad was never entered in any of the drafts of the contract with Elliott Roosevelt, but was in the form of a gentlemen's agreement until vetoed.[434]

Carter Tiffany was a close friend and associate of Tony Fokker.

There were various theories as to why the Soviets eventually walked away from the deal. Fokker said they knew they were getting ripped off. But it is equally true that, in

April 1934, Congress passed the Johnson Act (named for California Senator Hiram Johnson) which placed an embargo on lending to states in default on sovereign debt. The debt negotiations with the USSR had broken down.

> Mr. Fokker stated that the price calculated by Mr. Roosevelt and his associates and offered to the Russians was so high the Russians would have nothing to do with the whole business and had not bought any of the planes.
>
> Mr. Fokker was questioned concerning the correspondence between Mr. Tiffany and himself, in the course of which Mr. Tiffany stated: "I feel that Elliott, Stratton, and Reed have done nothing but chisel in on your affairs under pretenses." Mr. Fokker replied that he had not had that impression originally, because of the confidence expressed by Mr. Elliott Roosevelt and Mr. Stratton of their ability to swing the deal at the high price.
>
> He then was questioned concerning a letter which Mr. H.A. Reed wrote to Mr. Tiffany on 20 June 1934, in the course of which Mr. Reed stated, 'Mr. Stratton resents very much a letter which Tony wrote to Douglas after his trip to Russia. In this letter he tried to get Douglas to handle the sale of planes to Russia and called Stratton and Elliott Roosevelt "chiselers."[435]

By then, Fokker had taken the measure of Elliott. He told how Elliott's people tried to shake him down even after the failure of the deal, threatening to "turn on the heat:"

> Mr. Fokker explained that apparently by this time he had come to that conclusion, since no action had been taken towards the successful sale of Lockheed planes by Mr. Roosevelt and his associates…
>
> When in the course of the deposition Mr. Tiffany was questioned further and stated in Mr. Fokker's presence that he [Tiffany] had complained to Mr. Stratton that he did not like the contract because it was one-sided against Mr. Fokker and entirely in favor or Mr. Roosevelt.…Mr. Stratton had informed him that he had better go through with the contract, and that they had contracts with other people who had also not liked those contracts but had gone through with them after Mr. Stratton had turned on the heat.
>
> Mr. Fokker stated his satisfaction with Mr. Tiffany's method of concluding the contract in the way he did, involving a cash payment of $5,000 for Mr. Roosevelt, and the payment of a further check of $6,666 through a brokerage house which it was difficult for Mr. Roosevelt to accept, in view of the president's dispute with Wall Street at the time…Mr. Tiffany and Mr. Fokker both stated that the check had never been cashed or returned, but that Mr. Tiffany finally had stopped payment on it.[436]
>
> Questioned concerning the sale of the Douglas license, he, Mr. Fokker, stated that his Dutch company had sold it together with his Dutch type license to Airspeed, a British company, for 40,000 pounds and that he had attempted to sell the Lockheed license to the French government, but that the Lockheed plane had not lived up to its claim and that the French government under pressure of its own aviation companies, had declined to go through with the transaction after the failure of Lockheed to meet its performance.[437]

Tony Fokker made this sworn, disillusioned deposition to Senate investigators over a year before the story became public.

Inspired by the whole sordid tale, the Nye report felt entitled to add a timeless truth:

> The munitions industry is a dirty business, partly because it is so big and so much is at stake on the decision of one or two governmental officials who have a responsibility of

> deciding transactions involving millions of dollars and whose personal fortunes may be made by an advantageous commission to themselves or through the certainty of later on securing a position with the private company seeking to make the sale. [438]

Fokker might be in a dirty business, but it didn't trouble him. Though he was a neutral, he had kept the Kaiser's *Luftstreitkräfte* in the air, so it is unlikely that he had qualms about doing business with Stalin. He was, however, considerably upset about the behavior of Elliott Roosevelt. It looked to the world as if Fokker had been taken by a con man. He protested to investigators that he wasn't "generally" corrupt:

> Mr. Fokker, through his plant in Holland, known as the N.V. Nederlandsche Vliegtuigenfabriek of Amsterdam, Holland, has engaged in the sale of licenses to countries throughout the world and airplanes of his own make and the make of others. He states that he has probably sold more airplanes than any other individual throughout Europe. He states that his reputation as an airplane man is sufficient guarantee of his success in selling those planes he is promoting and that he has, generally speaking, not needed to resort to corruption of government officials.[439]

So, the Bolsheviks wised up and didn't buy, Fokker was out $5,000, and Elliott moved on. He did not report the income on his taxes, which would become a matter of interest later, but he was able to deflect the tax men.[440]

As we have seen, initially Elliott categorically denied the allegations. That approach unraveled when the documents were released. But he still tried to protect the president:

> With regard to all conversations and reported conversations which had reference to my father, I desire to state that they are false in their entirety and that at no time did the question of my father's participation or knowledge of the transaction enter into my discussion with Mr. Fokker.[441]

That kind of one-size-fits-all denial was not too impressive considering Mr. Reed's testimony about the president's involvement, cautious as it was. Nonetheless, Elliott threatened to sue, asserting that his rights had been infringed. Then Elliott said that the affair was all a political smear campaign anyway. This coming a month before the election, many voters undoubtedly agreed. Then he went after Fokker:

> Fokker apparently has tried to create a false impression because of personal feeling against me for not continuing in his employ and for ending the agreement…I have my legal rights for recovery for damage to my personal and business reputation by Fokker's statements.[442]

It seems unlikely that Elliott Roosevelt was popular among aircraft manufacturers after this episode.

Stratton had unsuccessfully conspired with Fokker to ensure that all documents involving Elliott would have been destroyed, and now he was willing to lay claim to the suddenly radioactive check. He could not explain why Reed held Elliott's receipt for it, nor explain the next, stopped check to Elliott. But the arcana of the scandal probably had little influence on the election. The real question was the president's role, and except for Mr. Tichenor, most commentators avoided implicating him.[443]

This incident occurred at an odd time in American history when a great public sanctimony was raging against "merchants of death" – i.e. arms exporters – small though they were at the time. Historically, the significance of the Nye Committee is that it fueled neutralist sentiment in the United States by presenting the case that weapons manufacturers and international moneymen had conspired in tricking the United States into joining the Great War, and probably would try to do so again. This viewpoint led directly to the Neutrality Acts which would so hamstring FDR a few years later. It is very interesting, but almost completely overlooked, that this opinion built on the anti-war, anti-big-business populism of the previous neutrality debate in 1914-17 – an angry firebrand of which had been Representative Charles A. Lindbergh of Minnesota.[i]

The Elliott – Fokker case was perfect grist for this mill.[444]

Gerald Nye was in a quandary. He was generally supportive of the New Deal and now stood to incur the wrath of FDR. He now seemed to try to stuff the affair back in the bottle:

> My whole purpose in making the Fokker affidavit available was to demonstrate the fact that, after all, nothing ever came of the tie-up and that there was no pressure on the committee from any source to prevent the development of any part of the story…Since no sales were made, it is obvious that the President's son did nothing illegal, and so far as the Munitions Committee is concerned the incident is closed.[445]

Likewise, Elliott Roosevelt continued to claim perfect innocence, but by 1936 his facts had become scrambled indeed:

> Three years ago when Fokker came out with a new DC-2 type of transport, I was given a contract to sell planes in Europe. By no stretch of the imagination could those planes be construed as war planes…[446] I have never denied that I discussed with Fokker arrangements for selling planes to the Soviet Government, or that I even entered into a contract with Fokker. But the contract was cancelled and returned to me. I never received a penny from Fokker for myself. I never acted for Fokker in any such sales. The contract, which subsequently was canceled, had provided specifically that I should not be requested by Fokker or any of his representatives to contact any representative of a European government or of the United States government. It is obvious that my father never had any part in my dealings with Fokker and I can see no reason why all of this should be brought out at this time, except a desire on the part of someone to besmirch the name of the President of the United States.[447]

Although the scandal broke and then soon dissipated under the pressure of later events, it did illuminate a distinctly sleazy deal – after all, the code words and the document destruction were undertaken for good reason. It also highlighted Elliott's consistent business *modus operandi* – he traded on his name, talked up a storm, but did not deliver in the end.

In that perspective, Senator Nye's offhand comment makes some sense:

> "God, what a family they turned out to be! 100 percent." [448]

---

[i] CAL served until 1917. He wrote the populist rant *Why is your country at war*, seized and suppressed by the Wilson Administration but finally released in 1934.

Behind the Scenes of the Aircraft Industry

In October 1936, the Fokker deal was the worst Elliott scandal yet. But as it was told then, the debacle was missing several important parts. Today, thanks to the documents Gerald Nye saved but didn't publish, it is possible to know the whole story. The investigators subpoenaed the internal letters and telegrams that flew between the principals. That collection is now kept in the modest but delightful Hoover Presidential Library in West Branch, Iowa. The following account is based on Nye's saved documents, which consist mostly of copies of Tony Fokker's business correspondence.[449]

Things were worse than first reported. It turned out that Elliott and a couple of adventurers he knew had talked themselves into a serious business affecting serious people, and those people – Bob Gross of Lockheed, Anthony Fokker, the Soviet leaders, and the President of the United States – now found themselves with a serious problem on their hands. Its first name was Elliott.

The son of the president was good with words, especially after a few drinks. That must have been how Hearst's newly commissioned aviation editor got Fokker to sign the recklessly one-sided contract during those heady days in Los Angeles in January and February 1934. It was said (by Stratton) that Fokker signed the document on the wing of the airplane he was leaving on. By April, everyone except Elliott and his buddies Stratton and Reed were trying to find a way out of it.

That included the Bolsheviks. When Tony Fokker traveled to Moscow in May, he found out that they had decided not to do business with Elliott. Furthermore, they knew perfectly well what Lockheed Electras were supposed to cost, and they had no intention of paying the capitalists nearly 50% more.

Clearly, the Soviets had done their homework.

Elliott did nothing. He didn't even form the agreed corporation. He appears to have thought he was entitled to half the profits simply for the use of his name. But when he was persuaded to take the Aeronautical Chamber of Commerce job in May, he had to get out of the contract due to conflict-of-interest clauses. He attempted to pass the contract on to his co-conspirator Stratton. This caused another crisis, since Fokker and Lockheed's Bob Gross wanted nothing to do with either Stratton or Reed, and moved quietly to eliminate these "chiselers."

The correspondence between Carter Tiffany and Fokker, who was back in Europe, reveals the struggle to get rid of Elliott and then of his partners. On 9 May, Tiffany composed a status report for his boss:

> When I arrived in California and saw Robert Gross I found that he had already placed your contract in the hands of his attorney to find some means of cancelling it. This was because he had learned just enough of the conditions surrounding the possible Russian order from prices that had been quoted to make him afraid of the political consequences, and also the fear that the high prices might not only endanger this particular contract, but even if it went through because of political pressure it would ruin any future chance of doing business with Russia.
>
> I explained to him that you were not responsible for the prices quoted Amtorg and that to the best of my knowledge you did not even know what figures had been quoted. I explained that the reason for the contract between you and Roosevelt was that Roosevelt had claimed he could arrange the financing on more favorable terms than anyone else. After considerable talking they finally agreed to stop any action and to allow you and me to

> handle the Russian contract in any way we saw fit, but they refused absolutely to have any further dealings with Roosevelt, Stratton or Reed. I persuaded them not to appear to Roosevelt, Stratton or Reed, as though there was any change in their feelings at all, and to treat them as always, but to keep me informed on every action they took.
>
> Before I left New York Reed left with me a copy of the signed agreement between yourself and Elliott Roosevelt. After reading it over I was genuinely shocked because in that agreement Roosevelt does not agree to do anything. He does not agree to sell airplanes or to arrange for the financing of any Russian order, does not agree to assist you in any way, while you in turn agree to pay him half the profits resulting from the sale of airplanes to Russia, no matter who sells them. The contract was so one-sided against you that I asked [counsel] to give me an opinion of it. He only had a short time to study it because I was leaving immediately, but he said at that time because of the lack of consideration on the part of Roosevelt he felt that unless Roosevelt actually was responsible for selling airplanes to the Russian the contract would be invalid. While I was in California I worked on this basis.

Mr. Tiffany proceeded to reveal that he had excellent sources within Amtorg and knew exactly what the Russians were thinking:

> ...the Russians were very much upset over the high prices quoted them on both Douglas and Lockheeds, and if it had not been for political expedience they were prepared to go to the President and demand that his son not interfere by raising prices with their purchase of airplanes.
>
> While I was in California word was sent to me by Mr. Schuckman that the Russians had finally decided definitely not to deal with Roosevelt, but to deal directly with you or me as your agent. They have not yet notified Roosevelt of this decision.
>
> The situation briefly while I was in California was: first, the straightening out of the Lockheed contract; second, my belief that your contract with Elliott would be invalid; and third, both Lockheed and the Russians were refusing to deal with Elliott.

As far as is known, the Soviets never did go to President Roosevelt and tell him to slap down his son. But as we have seen, that was exactly what FDR did in the *Nourmahal* incident and subsequent thereto. And it was at this precise time that Elliott found it useful to take the ACCA job in Washington. There he could be watched closely, and he had to disentangle himself from aircraft sales.

Soviet-American relations were hitting a rough spot after the initial euphoria. The Bolsheviks still refused to pay Russia's debts. Congress demanded that no trade favors should be extended until they did. This is where the Hiram Johnson bill became a problem for the airplane sellers.

> During this time the Johnson bill was passed which prohibits any financing by the Government or any member of the Federal Reserve banking system from financing the foreign governments by loans or discounts, if that Government is in default on their previous loans from this country. For some time it was considered that the Soviets were exempt from this ruling because the defaulted indebtedness had been created by the Czarists and Kerinskys Governments, and therefore had no connection with the present Soviet Government. Yesterday Attorney General Cummings ruled that the present Soviet Government is in default, and consequently their purchases cannot be financed until some settlement is reached. This is the result largely of the well formed and active opinion in Washington on the part of many Senators and Congressmen that the recognition of Russia was a mistake.

Clearly, Tony Fokker had an exceptionally capable American representative in Carter Tiffany. Like the Soviets, he was ready to go straight to President Roosevelt to solve the Elliott problem:

> ...The way it now rests is that unless the Russians can obtain financing in Europe they probably will not buy any airplanes. If they do obtain financing elsewhere and are ready to place an order I have arranged for them to ask me to quote them, in which case I will say that I have no power to quote them, and that they must obtain their prices from Elliott. They then will say that it is impossible for them to deal through a middleman due to the regulations of the Soviet Government, and I will then say that if they will write Elliott a letter saying that it is impossible for them to deal with him and then give me a copy of the letter I will arrange to quote them directly within one week.
>
> During that time I will take the contract you have with Elliott and a copy of the letter from Amtorg to Elliott directly to the President and tell him that while we have all sympathy with Elliott's desires to be of assistance we feel that it is impossible for him to furnish any material help, and that further we find it impossible for us to continue business with Elliott's associates. Consequently we are willing to pay the balance of $25,000 due Elliott as a retainer fee, but we must have a cancellation of the contract. Both Zachry and I feel confident that the President cannot possibly know the terms of this contract and that when he reads it he will be very anxious to see it cancelled, because if it should come into the hands of certain politicians it would cause a great deal of embarrassment to the administration.

As it happened, Tiffany did not need to go to the President. FDR took steps to neutralize his son. Had he heard what was going on? The clues suggest so. Having originally encouraged Elliott, now he could not afford to have him wreck relations with the USSR, much less run the risk that Republicans would get hold of the story. Plus, at the time this was only one of Elliott's brainstorms requiring presidential damage control.

Tiffany left a last salvo against Elliott:

> Incidentally neither Elliott nor Stratton had anything to do with influencing the Russians toward Lockheed. Amtorg was in touch with Lockheed through Courtland Gross [brother] even before you arrived in California....I feel that they have acted with fairness and justification all the way through, but I feel that Elliott, Stratton and Reed have done nothing but chisel in on your affairs under false pretenses.

So there. A week later, Tiffany was still trying to get rid of Elliott. He wrote Fokker that his Soviet sources had told him that Moscow had forbidden any further negotiations "because of the political consequences of dealing with Elliott." He said the Russians would like to deal with Fokker but not until Elliott was out. The next day, 16 May, Fokker answered with a telegram instructing to cancel payments due to Elliott's misrepresentations, and "telephone threat father will work." Presumably he meant that President Roosevelt would reign in his son.

At about that time, FDR apparently "suggested" that Elliott take the ACCA job. Herbert Reed said so in a letter to Tiffany. Reed now said that "Mr. Roosevelt wishes to be entirely free from the agreement, as his new duties makes this obligatory to him." Tiffany volunteered to Fokker: "I have heard that Elliott will not be appointed to his new job until after Congress adjoins [sic], so that Congress will have no chance to kick up a fuss over his appointment."

But co-chiselers Reed and Stratton were eager to continue the plan, noting that Douglas had made a deal with Stratton to the same effect already. Here we must keep in mind that a few days earlier in Washington, Elliott had – seemingly inexplicably – dropped Reed like a hot potato. What Reed knew he learned through Stratton. And Stratton was still trying to work through Amtorg; he didn't realize he'd been blackballed.

This placed Fokker in a difficult position. On 25 May, he wired Tiffany to cancel the contract regardless of protests or threats. With both Lockheed and the USSR refusing to have anything to do with the Elliott gang, he knew he had to do this.

Tiffany stopped payment on Elliott's next check, the one for $6,666. Elliott couldn't cash it earlier because it would have revealed his involvement. The trouble was that now Stratton wanted it instead.

On 1 June, Tiffany again statused Fokker in Amsterdam. He said:

> From the information I can gather both Franklin [Jr.] and Elliott Roosevelts activities have been halted by the President, as they have both proved very embarrassing to their father. In addition to that, the check I sent Elliott…I felt sure that he could not accept it because of the fight the Wall Street houses were making against the Stock Exchange Bill. A check from a large brokerage house to the President's son might be very difficult to explain a couple of years from now. Elliott also could not return this check and ask for a personal one since by doing so he would have to admit that the contract was not all that it should be.

The trouble with Franklin Jr. evidently referred to traffic cases that were much reported; that month the president had to pay $4,500 to settle his son's accident, in which a woman was injured.[450]

Tiffany also told Fokker that Stratton was "dangerous" and to avoid a lawsuit Fokker might have to stay away from America for a year. He had a source in Amtorg that let him know of any developments hours after they occurred, and he wrote Lockheed's Bob Gross that "Because of all the chiselors who have been trying to horn in on this business they [Amtorg] have rigid instructions not to deal with any person except company officials."

The chiselers were very upset. Long after Elliott dropped him, on 20 June Reed wrote to Tiffany: "Mr. Stratton resents very much a letter which Tony wrote to Douglas after his trip to Russia. In this letter he tried to get Douglas to let him handle the sale of planes to Russia and called Stratton and E. R. "chiselers.""

Tiffany wrote back that any oral understanding Stratton was relying on was superseded by the contract, and that it contained no clause about transferring rights after Elliott cancelled his interest.

That was the end of the scheme. Fokker managed to get rid of Stratton and Reed without incurring a lawsuit. But it is significant that Stratton's relationship with Donald Douglas continued. The Communists didn't get Electras, but they did get Douglas transports galore. It is a common mistake to assume that the Soviet C-47s were all just lend-lease gifts. The USSR purchased its first DC-2 in 1935, and obtained the license for mass-production the next year. Somehow the Douglas-Stratton relationship worked out in this case, and it would play a renewed role in the subsequent U.S. alliance with Stalin.

The Soviets showed astute negotiating skills. They did not need to beg; their contemporary medium bomber, the SB-2, was probably superior to Lockheed's design. And their selection of Douglas transports turned out to be wise.

What must the Soviets have concluded about Elliott Roosevelt? They unquestionably kept a file on him, and it couldn't have been full of admiration. When Elliott took up with Joseph Stalin ten years later, most likely the dictator knew exactly how to handle him.

With this piece of the puzzle in place, it is easier to understand President Roosevelt's behavior towards his son in 1934. Perhaps the most significant conclusion is that the president was, if not exactly innocent, at least aware enough of the danger to his administration to throttle Elliott before real damage was done. When the scandal broke publicly two years later, it was Elliott who bore the brunt of it, and if the president was damaged, it was only by accident of being Elliott's father.

Nevertheless, Elliott Roosevelt had been far more ambitious than the USSR bomber deal indicated. There was yet another story behind the story.

A FAILED AVIATION COUP

The "Roosevelt-hater" who originally brought the story to wider knowledge was a prominent media owner named Frank Tichenor. He was the publisher of *Aero Digest*, then the leading trade magazine of the aviation industry. His exposure of the bomber story (in the October 1936 issue) was obviously politically motivated, but his real motive was to indict the Roosevelt administration for another, far more sinister aviation scheme.

Invoking the ghosts of the dead airmail pilots, Tichenor stated:

> Unlike the lives of the army aviators sacrificed in 1934 by the New Deal's gambling with the air mail, truth, crushed to earth, may rise again. In rising, after thirty months, it reveals to us that while President Roosevelt was driving the airline operators from the skies, his son was dickering to make a fortune as the silent partner in the promotion of a corporation designed to consolidate and swallow all the airline companies the moment Job Master Jim Farley cancelled their contracts.[451]

Tichenor sprung open to the public a plot so vast, so ambitious, so infamous in its skulduggery that, in view of the accompanying air mail disaster, common sense suggests that the nation would have called into question the president's fitness for office. The charges were true and provable. Still, an understandable lack of White House records left President Roosevelt's role somewhat open to interpretation. About his son, there was no doubt.

The significance of the Tichenor article in indicting FDR was enormous. That was because Tichenor had access to inside sources, some congressional, but perhaps most notably Herbert A. Reed, who was now talking openly about the conspiracy in which he had played a central role. Plus, Tichenor had had a small (liaison) part in the scheme himself. At any rate, in October 1936, *Aero Digest* published chapter and verse about Elliott Roosevelt's plot, complete with documents, telegrams, telephone records, and sworn statements – even the secret code the conspirators had agreed to use.

It is odd that this incontrovertible documentation, along with the Nye committee's archive, was not pursued to the point of criminal charges. Today, the appointment of an independent investigator would surely have followed; impeachment of the president would surely have been proposed, if not necessarily pursued given the overwhelming Democratic majorities of 1936.

Tichenor wrote that, with the active encouragement of President Roosevelt, Elliott Roosevelt and Anthony Fokker had agreed on a plot to form "a great U.S. air transport combine" to replace the airlines that would be wiped out by FDR's cancellation of the air mail contracts. Elliott was to receive 5% of the stock of this quasi-Aeroflot monster. He supposedly told his co-conspirator Herbert Reed at breakfast in the White House:

> Father thinks your plan is the soundest approach to the problem. Mother agrees. I talked the whole thing over with her last night. She remarked that the proper settlement of the air mail problem and full support of the Subsistence Homestead Projects should be the first order of business with the Administration.[452]

Herbert Reed further charged in a telegram to Frank Tichenor:

> Elliott Roosevelt's denial of having planned to sell military aircraft to Russia for Fokker, of having approval of his father, the President, to do so, and of receiving $5000 cash binder on his Fokker contract is not surprising to me. He and his father will probably similarly deny having backed my plan for reorganization of the nation's air lines, of which the air mail contract cancellation on 9 February 1934, was a part and for which Elliott and his associates were to receive an interest estimated at $750,000 per year, because at the time we were dealing I was warned to expect such denials if there was ever any leak concerning our association. But the Fokker-Roosevelt contract signed by Elliott Roosevelt was predicated on the Russian purchase of military planes and one only has to examine and reconcile my private files to see that President Roosevelt and I were working close together for about six weeks, besides which I paid that $5,000 cash to Elliott Roosevelt to initiate our business relations and I still hold his receipt for the money.[453]

If the real objective of the president's sudden and surprising cancellation of the air mail contracts had been to further a secret racket involving his son, resulting in the creation of a government-sponsored airline monopoly, then the deaths of those Army aviators and the closure of the original airlines take on an even more shocking character. Some, but not all, evidence pointed that way. The surviving documentation seems to suggest that the president, very characteristically, altered his approach as he went along, reacting to the political environment as much as shaping it.

With only three weeks to go before the 1936 election, Frank Tichenor, seemingly smelling blood, went in for the kill by sending President Roosevelt this telegram:

> The President of the United States, aboard Democratic campaign special train, Omaha, Nebraska:
>
> Millions of electors whose public servant you are, who have read newspaper accounts of an article appearing in the October issue of *Aero Digest*, entitled 'And Roosevelt and Farley Charged Fraud and Collusion,' wonder at the unusual silence in which you have taken refuge.
>
> Both Elliott and Charles Michelson, publicity director of the Democratic national committee, are quoted in press dispatches as saying one or the other has documents disproving the terms of the Fokker contract seized by the Nye munitions committee, and

held along with all of Fokker's file on dealings with your son, although Nye says the committee decided a year ago this was none of its business.

Your son also denies receipt of $5,000, or any intent to sell military airplanes to soviet Russia. Michelson and Elliott have failed to keep faith with you and with the electorate by not making public whatever they may have in the way of documentary disproof.

Aero Digest's story goes beyond the Russian plane sales deal, and cites a plan promoted by your son and others to reorganize the nation's air lines in connection with your administration's canceling of all domestic air mail contracts, as a direct result of which twelve army pilots ordered to the commercial air lines were killed.

I charge you with having indorsed and approved Elliott's activities in the aeronautical industry. You received delegations of air line operators and aircraft manufacturers brought to the White House by Elliott after they had been denied individual or group interviews. You discussed the sale or barter of planes between American manufacturers and soviet Russia with one of these delegations.

You approved Elliott's employment by Fokker. Moreover, the Nye committee seized Fokker's file, impounding it indefinitely, and the treasury department never pressed Fokker's refusal to change income tax form 1099, as directed by Deputy Internal Revenue Commissioner Russell with regard to that $5,000 which Elliott says some one else got.

Frank A. Tichenor, Publisher of Aero Digest.[454]

The afore-mentioned Charles Michelson was "publicity director" of the Democratic campaign, effectively FDR's propaganda chief under Farley. Why he had custody of Elliott's contract with Fokker is unclear.

At this point an impasse arose. Despite the gravity of the conspiracy charges, FDR's enemies could do nothing further, since they did not control Congress. These and other charges notwithstanding, Roosevelt went on to crush Kansas governor, Republican Alf Landon in a humiliating landslide, and the Democrats attained historic, bullet-proof majorities in Congress. The Roosevelt-haters were left seething; their dark premonitions of a personal dictatorship seemed to be coming true, and to the cheers of a majority of the electorate.

Yet opposition to FDR had always been latent in the Democratic Party as well. Many jumped ship over the next four years, others came aboard, but for most, an uncomfortable accommodation ensued.

One major newspaper went after Elliott Roosevelt uncompromisingly. It was the *Chicago Tribune*, published by the pre-eminent "Roosevelt-hater" Colonel Robert McCormick, who raged against the New Deal for a generation. Elliott complained that 85% of the newspapers were against his father, but that is an exaggeration; as he should know, the Hearst papers were originally for Roosevelt.[i]

Also, while most media owners opposed FDR, this was not the case for individual reporters, and most specifically not for the White House press corps. The president played them like fiddles, although obstreperous exceptions like the *Chicago Tribune's* Walter Trohan stood out. The prime example of White House control of the message is, of course, the conspiracy of silence surrounding FDR's disability and the gradual decline of his health in his last years. One observer noted: "The President is a gentleman of the

[i] ER: Rendez-vous, 132. In 1947 Elliott charged that 90% of the newspapers had been against FDR in his last election: "It is in general very difficult for us to learn the truth from our press, which, following directives from certain circles, colors the news and distorts the facts." ER interview with Ny Dag, Swedish communist daily, 4 NOV 47.

most winning charm. Whatever their opinion of his policies, no correspondent in Washington has ever been able to resist the quality of his personality." [455]

The *Tribune's* Robert McCormick was ambivalent about FDR at first. This reflects the fact that the new administration was initially not ideological, but rather experimental; and that some of the new economic interventions were interpreted as desperation moves in an admittedly desperate situation.

Indeed, during his first presidential campaign, Roosevelt ran on a platform of fiscal prudence, contrasting his common sense with Herbert Hoover's runaway deficit policies. No informed historian holds to the popular caricature of a do-nothing, *laissez-faire* Hoover followed by an activist FDR who ended or blunted the economic downturn with deficit spending. For better or worse, both Hoover and FDR were progressive, activist social engineers; but the former, a brainy technocrat, had not the cheerful, soothing bedside manner of Dr. Roosevelt. Likewise, informed economists agree that neither of the two understood the monetary origins of the Depression, so they both flailed around without gaining traction on the economy. And on election day, in a perceived choice between snake oil and castor oil, a desperate majority preferred the former.

Despite the initial similarity of policies, by 1936 the ideological front was far more clearly defined. Now the *Chicago Tribune* and many other newspapers cast Roosevelt as the fourth horseman of the apocalypse, augmenting the satanic triad of Stalin, Mussolini, and Hitler. So when a juicy scandal involving the president's offspring came within reach, McCormick's venom boiled over during the 1936 election campaign.[456]

James Roosevelt and his dubious self-enrichment in the insurance industry had provided much succor to the Republicans, but Elliott had now trumped him with a scandal that directly implicated the president's aviation policy, already deeply controversial. After all, FDR, by the end of his first year in office, destroyed the airline industry only to revive it in a completely altered form.

We have seen that *Aero Digest* published allegations that Elliott Roosevelt was engaged in a racket to take over the airline industry. McCormick's *Tribune* now picked up the thread and reached a sinister conclusion. One historian summarized:

> McCormick teamed up with investigators from the Republican National Committee who were probing the insurance business run by Roosevelt's son James. Nor was Jimmy the only member of his illustrious family whose taste for wealth exceeded his scruples in obtaining it.
>
> In September [1936], McCormick learned of a potentially explosive story involving Jimmy's brother Elliott. In the last week of January 1934, Elliott and the aircraft manufacturer Donald Douglas had called at the White House. Within days of their visit, FDR moved to cancel existing air mail contracts with American Airways, United Aircraft, and Transcontinental and Western Airlines.
>
> Simultaneously, a friend of Elliott's named Herbert Reed conceived the idea of merging the three into a single company, in a stroke realizing the president's stated objections of wiping out the airmail deficit then plaguing the post office and paying of existing stockholders. Better yet, Reed would enrich his partner to the tune of $750,000 a year (a figure representing Elliott's 5% cut of the new aviation monopoly)....
>
> On 9 February, the same day FDR's cancellation order was made public, Reed was informed of this in a letter, almost certainly typed on Elliott's typewriter. The same message contained a code to be used in all future communications among the participants...

> Herbert Reed was sent to New York in an effort to enlist [former Dem. presidential candidate] Al Smith as chairman of the consolidated airline. Smith, valuing his political independence and probably more than a little suspicious of the deal, spurned Reed's offer.
>
> Then, on 9 March 1934, five army pilots died in an airmail crash, the latest in a series of disasters that spurred criticism of the administration…Elliott's hand, already weakened by the public backlash, was now trumped by none other than Jim Farley. The postmaster general had compelling reasons to look charitably on the disenfranchised American Airlines, a generous contributor to past Democratic campaigns.
>
> At Farley's urging, the aviation lobby employed former North Carolina governor O. Max Gardner, at a salary of $75,000 to press the White House for restoration of the old contractors. The president agreed to reinstate the private carriers pending a permanent solution. This was the end of Reed's monopolistic fantasies. Soon after, the Russian plane deal fell through as well. At the urging of his father, Elliott accepted a $10,000 a year sinecure with the Aeronautical Chamber of Commerce – the same industry group responsible for hiring Gardner.[457]

While this modern account accurately summarizes what became known in 1936, it provides only a few new details. But the analysis was spot on – especially in the realization that the air mail fiasco has to be viewed in the context of party politics, and where the campaign contributions were coming from. Farley's recommendation that the ACCA employ Max Gardner, an able Democrat, was especially significant because it illustrated an attempted rapprochement between the two warring sides, assisted by an increasingly repentant postmaster general.[458]

Elliott was not involved in politics at that time; he was merely out to get rich. Given the air mail debacle, fresh in memory, it is odd that the president was not irreparably harmed by the accusations of his involvement. One reason was that, by early April, he had taken decisive action to reign in his son when he realized the danger he presented.

What did the President know, and when did he know it?

Despite the ardent attempts to cover the tracks, it is now possible to map the contours and track the methodical execution of Elliott Roosevelt's plot to take over the nation's airlines and create a vast government-sponsored monopoly to enrich himself and his friends. The person who had to be protected at all costs, the President of the United States, is seen clearly in the background when all the evidence is put together.

On 16 January 1934, Anthony Fokker, at Donald Douglas's request, met with Elliott Roosevelt and Grenville Stratton. In this meeting the Soviet bomber deal was hatched, but the attempt to take advantage of the then roiling air mail controversy was also begun. This can only have been the result of Elliott's assertions that he knew something of what the president was up to: cancelling the contracts.[459]

On 24 January, Elliott and Donald Douglas flew to Washington, and the next day they showed up at the White House for dining and plotting; Douglas, Elliott, and Ned (Franklin) Lane were listed as "houseguests." That day, the two also managed to confer with the State Department and the Soviet Embassy, and the next day, Elliott and Douglas met with Amtorg executives about the bomber deal.[i]

The significance of this White House conference is that Congressional investigators later determined that this date, 26 January, was the first time the illegal stock market manipulations in expectation of the air mail cancellation could have begun. In the next two weeks, airline and aircraft stocks were badly rattled. Tony Fokker made numerous transactions. Elliott and Douglas flew back to Los Angeles.

On 2 February, Elliott telephoned Washington and presented details of the Fokker / Reed / Elliott / Stratton proposal. Reportedly, Fokker was skeptical of the president's intention to support the deal. When, on 4 February, the White House first threatened that air mail cancellations might become necessary, Fokker took it as evidence that Elliott had his father in tow on the matter.

During the subsequent days, the plan solidified in consultation with the White House, and Elliott secured his $5000 initial payment on the bomber deal. According to Reed and Tichenor's other sources, Elliott kept the conspirators informed about his father's deliberations:

> He said the administration was anxious to oust those who were then operating the air mail, that it would cancel every contract if such action seemed necessary to effect its purpose, but that the President first wanted a substitute plan that would conserve the equities of the innocent stockholders in the airlines.
>
> The Elliott plan would do this by consolidating the three main airlines into one government-led monopoly. The plan also proposed shifting all long-distance mail to this kombinat, thus "assuring capacity loads that would reduce rates and wipe out, he estimated, both the airline and the Post Office deficits.[460]

Reed said that Elliott called the White House and reported back: "The president wants you to do this job. They are wild about your plan."

On 6 February, Reed flew to Washington to meet with Basil O'Connor. This is of acute importance, because O'Connor had been Franklin D. Roosevelt's law partner, and then his personal lawyer. The two looked out for each other. By dealing with O'Connor, the conspirators needed not talk directly with the president.[ii]

At that same time, the four plotters agreed on a secret code in which to communicate details of the plan. That code, although no cryptographic milestone, is important because it outlines who and what was involved. Among the codewords were:

> Franklin D. Roosevelt = Rochelle; Elliott Roosevelt = New Rochelle.
> Douglas = Drive; Lockheed = Brake; Fokker = Chain.
> Baruch = Beta; Moffett = Gamma; Stratton = Spare; Reed = Wheel.[461]

All the airlines and main aviation players, including Vidal of the CAA, and J. J. Raskob, the financial backer of the Democrats, had code-names. Bernard Baruch, the

---

[i] Aero Digest, OCT 36, 19. Except as otherwise stated, the following details are based on the article and reproduced documents therein. Also see FDR Appointments Day-to-Day, FDR Lib. "Ned" was Franklin K. Lane, Jr., a well-connected California Democrat and a friend and pilot Elliott hung out with in Los Angeles. He would serve on FDR's Aviation Commission later that year.

[ii] Jesse Jones wrote that O'Connor's law firm used FDR to extort an exorbitant fee of $200,000 for an RFC deal in 1934. Jones fiercely protested and talked the president down to $135,000. (Jones, 208-210, also see Morgan, 445-6). Whether both FDR and O'Connor were behind the take is not clear.

helpful plutocrat who ingratiated himself with presidents, was considered for assistance; so was James A. Moffett, a Standard Oil executive who had defected to the New Deal and was now head of the Federal Housing Authority. Moffett was a friend of the Roosevelts and Elliott especially; evidently the latter had tried to get a job from him. Jesse Jones later said that Moffett and his Roosevelt ties became problematic for him in keeping the finances of the RFC above reproach.[462]

The plotters knew they could not take an open role in the new airline monopoly, and were thus looking for a well-known national figure to head the undertaking. Al Smith, the former presidential candidate, was also suggested, but that turned out to be a bad idea. Smith loathed Roosevelt.

Elliott seems to have preferred Frank Walker as chairman of the new cartel. Walker was a prominent New Dealer who would succeed Jim Farley as Postmaster General after Farley deserted FDR. But in this case it would be Farley who kept Walker from taking this contemplated post as aviation czar of the United States.

The consultations with Basil O'Connor continued until 9 February. Later on that day, President Roosevelt cancelled the air mail contracts and blacklisted the aviation executives who had been involved with them. He insisted on these drastic interventions even over the protests of his Postmaster General, Farley, who had originally been behind the investigations in order to discredit the Republicans. By this time, Farley was already playing a moderating role.

During the next two weeks, there was an intense flurry of expensive air travel and long hours of long-distance telephone communication as the conspirators fine-tuned their initiative. These contacts involved Elliott Roosevelt, Anthony Fokker, and their agents Stratton and Reed. Basil O'Connor also stayed in the loop. It is interesting to note that Elliott would call from Beverly Hills and always reverse the charges; even Eleanor had complained about this habit of his.

On 24 and 25 February, the Soviet delegation met with the plotters in Los Angeles. They inspected the Lockheed mock-ups and were taken on a flight over the city. Elliott's contract was finalized, and the proposed syndicate plan's profits were divided up. Elliott was to receive 5% of the capitalization of two million dollars, and continue to receive 5% of the profits although he was not to hold office in the syndicate. The expectation was that Elliott would clear $750,000 annually, without holding official posts in the monopoly.[463]

On 3 March, Reed approached Frank Tichenor in order to get to Al Smith, the Democratic kingpin, to get him to chair the proposed syndicate and lend credibility to it. However, as Tichenor reported back, Smith wanted no part of the conspiracy. Smith had been defeated by Hoover in 1928, and then by his former friend Franklin Roosevelt in the 1932 primaries. Smith turned against Roosevelt in revulsion, even to the point of supporting Republicans thereafter.

At this point, the offensive began to unravel. On the one hand, the air mail crisis and the Army's losses had led to severe criticism of President Roosevelt, who refused to back down yet clearly could no longer successfully push his luck. On the other hand, the President now referred to Congress a new aviation plan that incorporated some of the features the Elliott plot had promoted.

On 9 March, four Army mail fliers were killed in accidents. That same day Senator McKellar introduced the bill that reflected the administration's thinking on how to restructure the aviation industry. It only partially reflected Elliott's ideas. At the same time, President Roosevelt announced that things were going so well that he was going on a fishing vacation in a couple of weeks. But things weren't going so well for Elliott, Fokker, Stratton, and Reed.[464]

In mid-March, Elliott Roosevelt attempted to get Walker and Farley to endorse his mega-syndicate. From California, Elliott told Reed to get Walker's acceptance as chairman. At this precise point, Farley killed the plot:

> The next day [17 March] Reed called at Walker's office at Democratic headquarters at the Biltmore. Walkers' secretary said he was going to Walker's house and would transmit the message. While Reed was there Jim Farley came in. Farley and Walker's secretary left the office together. Reed received no word from Walker.[465]

Farley rejected the Elliott plan. Giving directions to the congressional Democrats, he was formulating a different recovery plan that would reconstitute the aviation industry, not as a monopoly, but as separate independent enterprises operating in "managed competition" under government direction.

Tichenor wrote that the plan President Roosevelt presented for reconstitution of the aviation industry incorporated the main tenets of the Elliott-Reed plan. But that seems to have been an exaggeration. While some elements remained, it was really Farley who was driving the new plan. It is likely that the White House used the Elliott proposals as one contributory stream to the general initiative. But disturbingly for the plotters, there was no longer money in it for them.

That was the background for Stratton's concerned missive to Reed on 22 March:

> Politics seem to have gotten into this to such a terrible degree that it is almost impossible to predict what the outcome will be, but you may rest assured that both E. and I are working with you on the matter.[466]

Now the plotters were beginning to run out of rope. In Washington, doors closed to Reed and Elliott. The evidence is that President Roosevelt had made up his mind, and Elliott's shenanigans were no longer in it. And with that out of the way, the president decided to leave town and go fishing in the Bahamas.

But the son was not accustomed to "no" – that simply made him press harder.

Elliott decided on a Hail Mary pass in the form of a direct appeal to his father. To save his plan, he enlisted the aid of George Hearst to fly out to the *Nourmahal* in the Bahamas. Beforehand, he telegraphed Reed to be ready for him in Washington when he came back from the yacht.

Now we can understand President Roosevelt's sudden, unique explosion of rage at seeing his son coming in on the seaplane on 3 April. He knew what he was up to; he knew it had the potential to destroy his presidency. He had resolved to follow the Farley plan and to shut Elliott out of all further decisions on aviation.

Elliott was resilient. When he came back, he did not let on that he had had his empennage whipped. He asserted to Reed that there had been some political complications. Maybe Reed/Fokker would be content to receive the rights to only the northern transcontinental air route? No, said Reed. In that case, Elliott, following the instructions of his father, had to talk to other cabinet members about modified syndicate plans. Elliott would call Reed when he had news.

Then something happened to shut Elliott up. According to Harold Ickes, Elliott was with the president at the White House on 14 April, when a Cabinet meeting was held.[467]

Elliott did not call Reed. On that same day, Reed, after commiserating with "Spare" about "New Rochelle's" silence, went back to Los Angeles empty-handed, still hoping to rescue at least the Fokker deal. Elliott Roosevelt was suddenly incommunicado. On 22 May, Stratton finally told Reed that Elliott had been given the Aeronautical Chamber of Commerce (ACCA) job, thus keeping him employed as an aviation industry lobbyist, yet at the same time having him under strict control.

We know almost exactly when Elliott Roosevelt finally gave up his imperial fantasies. On 7 April, four days after his father had raged against him on the yacht, Elliott sent a disconsolate telegram to Isabella Greenway, who as Arizona's congresswoman had taken an interest in reorganizing aviation. He wrote:

> Father has refused to ammend or delay McKellar Bill and Cabinet powerless Stop Am thoroughly discouraged about the future advance of the industry under the present plans so am going to return to Fort Worth where you may reach me at eleven naught one Penn Street Stop Many Thanks for your interest in attempting to put the industry on a basis where it could have been of great help in the entire recovery program Elliott Roosevelt.[468]

Aunt Isabella immediately responded: "Could I have copy or outline of legislation you proposed for aviation in case we can achieve helpful modification Too disappointed." [469]

It was not to be. During those eleven days of April, from getting kicked off the *Nourmahal* to the Cabinet meeting on the 14th, Elliott's castle-in-the-air evaporated.

Whipped and cowed, at least Elliott still had friends. C.R. Smith was one. He cabled Isabella a week later thanking her for her "splendid support" of commercial aviation. He noted that Elliott and Ruth were now staying with him in Fort Worth.[470]

Another friend in need was Amon G. Carter. He wired Jim Farley a long, infuriated rant, a message we can refer to as the "nigger in the woodpile" telegram, since Amon used that noxious southern expression with alarming frequency. His point was that the airline industry was being unfairly and collectively punished for what appeared to be individual transgressions. Clearly, he was speaking for C.R. in that matter, and he shared the inflammatory wire with Representative Greenway.[471]

Herbert Reed did not see Elliott Roosevelt again until a chance meeting on 4 September 1936. Reed spoke to Elliott; Elliott refused to acknowledge Reed.[472]

The next month, an angry Reed spilled the beans on the whole sordid affair in Frank Tichenor's monthly, *Aero Digest.* In the meantime, Stratton had gone to Reed several times after Elliott became aware that the Nye Committee and the Bureau of Internal Revenue were after him. Their efforts to have Tony Fokker destroy the documents failed.

Fokker was not impressed with this circus. His records, subpoenaed by the Nye Committee, revealed much of the story when Senator Nye was cajoled into making them public. Reed's documented charges and Nye's own records complete the picture for us.[473]

Autopsy on the Aviation Industry

A reasonably detached assessment from decades later must come to the conclusion that it is hardly disputable that Elliott had entertained the notions of which he was accused, because they reflected his megalomania and his half-mad entrepreneurial energy.

But it is unlikely that President Roosevelt was dumb enough to get ensnared openly in the deal. Possibly he cancelled the air mail contracts, against the advice of nearly everyone around him, with the expectation that some monopoly deal would be worked out in the shadows. If so, the whole thing came back to bite him hard, and it helps explain why Elliott was only allowed to come to the White House as long as he shut up about aviation matters.

The stench of this story lingered in the press for only a short while. Since the monopoly plan failed like most of Elliott's projects, the issue may have seemed not worth pursuing – given that the solid new Democratic majority had the real capability and accompanying intention to hurt its enemies.

After eighty years it is still hard to pin down exactly how much blame the president was due. As usual, FDR's fingerprints are missing from the matter, and supplementary archival information has disappeared.[i] Yet it is clear that he first encouraged, then shot down the plans of his son and his son's gang. It is also clear that the break occurred by mid-March when Jim Farley told Frank Walker not to mess with Elliott's scheme.

It amounts to crass conspiracy theory to imagine that FDR abruptly struck down the airline industry in order to allow a cabal involving his son to take it over. The president was aware of Elliott's ideas, thought them partly useful, and kept his son informed of his plans. As Elliott's brazenly self-interested grandiosity became obvious, FDR most likely began to back him out, and became more likely to listen to cooler heads like Farley.

Gerald Nye defended his plan not to pursue the conspiracy investigation further because the plot had not come to fruition. Of course, the air mail fiasco had actually occurred, and the aviation industry was in fact upended. But by late 1936 there was little appetite for overturning the cart once more, much less impeachment over the scandal.

Roosevelt was safe. By 1936, his control of both Houses was crushing.

In the history of American aviation, the bombers-for-Stalin gambit counts for little. Even the air mail fiasco is not as important as the profound and lasting changes that occurred when the New Deal transformed the aviation sector.

This was the revolution that gave the airlines their later so familiar names. American Airways became American Airlines; United Aircraft became United Airlines; Transcontinental and Western Air became Transworld (TWA). That's because FDR, unwilling to admit defeat, refused to permit any airline that had participated in the old, allegedly corrupt deals to win new contracts. So they changed their names.

Postmaster Farley, a comparative moderate, had this in mind early on. It was he who privately showed the airlines the renaming loophole in the Black legislation. Then the "new" airlines bid on their old routes, and mostly got them back.[474] People who bothered to understand what was going on were incredulous at the brazenness of it all. Lindbergh called it "Alice in Wonderland." [475]

---

[i] Press Secr. Steve Early had communications on the Air Mail fiasco, but they cannot be located. (FDR Lib)

The Black-McKellar Act did break up the big holding companies that had attempted to laterally integrate aircraft manufacturers and airlines. President Roosevelt blacklisted the old airline leaders; in fact, the former head of United Airways moved to Canada to start a new airline there. A great shuffling of chairs ensued throughout the industry.[i]

The end result was that the old United Airways spun off parts to Boeing, and other parts to United Technologies (which later, with Sikorsky, conquered the helicopter business).[ii] United Airlines was reconstituted under new management. The old North American Aviation spawned the new TWA, led by Jack Frye, a renowned pilot who would then become associated with Howard Hughes. Eastern Airlines was set up separately and came under the control of the World War ace, Eddie Rickenbacker. American Airlines was split off from General Motors' AVCO. Its new boss was, of course, Elliott Roosevelt's buddy C.R. Smith.[476]

Only Pan American Airways was left alone. Its Democratic flank was well covered, and its monopoly on overseas air travel would continue for another decade. But after the war, the government reaper would come for Juan Trippe's empire as well.

All in all, the complete regulatory, commercial, and industrial reorganization of aviation represented a federal power grab as immense as the American system could conceive, but it fell well short of consolidating everything into an American Aeroflot.

Although the seeds of the debacle had been sown in 1925 by the government's use of air mail contracts to dabble in industrial policy, it is likely that the air mail fiasco and the resulting public uproar had actually prevented President Roosevelt from making even more drastic changes. Prodded by Jim Farley, he had to accept that there would still be competing airlines, and that they would be run by at least some of the same people who had run aviation before. With time, the airlines would become fond of the incestuous relationship with regulators, which would last until deregulation in 1978. Likewise, the aircraft manufacturers would soon become virtual extensions of the War Department.

On the regulatory side, the revolution was equally far-reaching and long-lasting. Until 1934, during the "golden age," the Department of Commerce imposed limited regulation on aviation. Ten years later, the landscape – or airscape – had completely changed. The Bureau of Air Commerce federally regulated American aviation. Civil Air Regulations were first codified in 1937. Next year was created the Civil Aeronautics Authority (CAA), the predecessor of today's FAA and the template for CAAs worldwide. By 1940, the Civil Aeronautics Board (CAB) was formally created to dole out airline routes, set prices, and prevent competition. The Air Safety Board, now the NTSB, was set up to investigate accidents and recommend changes. Finally, by 1944, the Chicago aviation convention essentially spread the American regulatory system worldwide.[477]

It wasn't quite communism, but it wasn't the wild blue yonder anymore, either. Few today think of the aviation regulatory universe as a controversial New Deal imposition, but that's essentially what it is in both spirit and structure. Whether it has impeded or advanced aviation is ferociously debated even today. It is, however, clearly a mistake to assume some innate conflict of interest between government and corporations. Rhetoric aside, historically they have made their accommodation – especially

---

[i] United's president Phil Johnson helped found Trans-Canada Airlines. He later returned to head Boeing.

[ii] Technically, the Boeing-led *kombinat* had been United Aircraft & Transport Co.

during the central planning model for aviation that existed from 1934 to 1978. To this day, many veteran airline pilots think wistfully back on the time when they were high commissars of the sky, answering to the CAB politburo rather than to the fickle, cruel market.

While the repercussions of the New Deal for civil aviation were severe, the maligned Air Corps, paradoxically, seemed to come out ahead in the long run. After all, the debacle had shown just how unprepared and underfunded it actually was.

If the Army fliers couldn't deliver mail, how did they propose to deliver bombs? Why were they this far behind the commercial sector in technology, procedures, and training? These questions started the Air Corps on a path of rehabilitation which would favor its Young Turk movement, the "bomber generals" who would pick up the martyred (or at least court-martialed) General Billy Mitchell's gauntlet and strike out for a modern, strategic Air Force.

General Arnold, who had borne much of the burden, wrote:

> The President probably didn't feel like risking it with a Congressional Committee, so a Military Board was appointed, headed by Major General Hugh A. Drum, and with General Foulois a member. Presently a committee of noted civilians was added, under the chairmanship of former Secretary of War Newton D. Baker. Out of this "Baker Board" the next year, came the formation of the General Headquarters or G.H.Q. Air Force, the first real step ever taken toward an independent United States Air Force.[478]

Even though the air mail crisis did not expand the Air Corps much beyond the small neutrality guard it was in the inter-war years, it thus did propel it towards the Holy Grail of air-minded people: an independent Air Force. While this goal was not reached until 1947, during the Army Air Forces period – 1941 to 1947 – the AAF, under the wartime leadership of General Arnold, effectively operated much like a separate service. Army chief of staff General George Marshall wisely saw to it that his most airpower-hating generals were kept in check, and that Arnold got his say at the table.

Only six years after the air mail fiasco one beneficiary of the new, muscular Air Force with its theology of victory through aerial bombardment would be a young, but definitely not unknown officer, named Elliott Roosevelt.

WASHINGTON LOBBYIST TO TEXAS EXILE

If Elliott Roosevelt failed miserably in his intended mission as an aviation lobbyist, what did he actually do while vice president of the Aeronautical Chamber of Commerce?

As a son of the president, he was in a bind. Even though he resentfully complained that he did not lobby anyone – at least not successfully – many people, including Congressmen, thought that he did. But had he been successful, his victories would have met a wall of derision. This dilemma was quite obvious when he was dragged into the debate over increased payments to the "fake-new" air mail contractors in April 1935.[479]

Instead Elliott did what he was good at: advertising, promotion, being in the public eye. For example, shortly after his appointment he enjoyed a major photo opportunity with then Lt. Col. "Hap" Arnold. On 19 July 1934, Arnold began a month-long Alaskan odyssey, leading ten new Martin B-10 bombers on a mission that included two weeks of mapping interior Alaska. A photographic expert, Captain George Goddard, the officer FDR met at Wright Field, came along to oversee this cartographic project.[480]

Mr. and Mrs. Elliott Roosevelt were at Bolling Field to see the flight off. This is more evidence that Arnold and Roosevelt were, if not good buddies, then certainly friendly, which helps explain Elliott's later career. The ambitious and successful Alaskan operation was seen as an attempt to recoup the dignity and esteem of the Air Corps after the air mail disaster.[481]

As ACCA representative, Elliott Roosevelt also participated in some of the pioneering flights of the age. During the night of 1 August 1934 and the morning of the next day, TWA inaugurated overnight air service from New York to Los Angeles, using a "huge" 14-passenger Douglas DC-2 piloted by Otis Bryan. On board was Elliott, of course. With stops and a plane-change in Kansas City, the trip took under eighteen hours. Elliott took the plane back the next day. It was a powerful vindication of the airline industry, but especially of Douglas's revolutionary new airplane. An enlarged and improved DC-2 would, for the first time, enable airlines to make money flying passengers, freeing them from total reliance on the politically inflamed mail contracts.[482]

During that same period a strange and virtually unreported, but path-breaking aviation initiative gave the lie to Elliott's assurances that he did not lobby. Once again it involved Donald Douglas; once again it irritated a foreign power.

First Transoceanic Foray

Sometime in or around July 1934, Elliott met an accomplished Tasmanian-born navigator, Harold Gatty, who was in the process of forming an airline syndicate for the purpose of running air service across the Pacific to the antipodes. In this project, Donald Douglas joined Gatty because both thought the DC-2, a land plane, might make such a route not only possible but profitable. Douglas was made president of the South Seas Commercial Company, and plans were made to place commercial landing fields on several disputed and uninhabited Pacific atolls and islands. This was three years before Amelia Earhart's disappearance there in July 1937.

When Gatty talked to Elliott in Washington, D.C., Elliott took the detailed proposal to President Roosevelt, who was thrilled by the idea for reasons of his own. He liked for his beloved Navy to stake its claims across the oceans in preparation for what might come. Unfortunately the British Empire controlled the other end of the route, and many of the flyspecks in the middle – in the Line and Phoenix Islands – were claimed by both nations. An American commercial service would be a stalking horse less likely to provoke a diplomatic incident. This sly method would be much used later. The president told the Chief of Naval Operations, Admiral William Harrison Standley, to assist with the plan.

Harold Gatty wrote to Donald Douglas on 1 September 1934:

> ...(Elliott was) all steamed up over the project and apparently has got his father the same way. The father by phone told Elliott to go and explain the whole thing to Admiral

> Standley, the Chief of Naval Operations and see if it fitted in with their wishes. He did this right away and took along all the information I had and which I had fixed up in a presentable manner. As you know I had discussed the matter with Admiral Standley and O.N.I. [Office of Naval Intel.] and they had taken up the matter with Admiral Standley. He was most enthusiastic and offered to arrange the whole thing if the Navy could make use of the fields when they are developed. He also offered to get us Christmas Island, so for good measure I threw in Jarvis, which is also disputed territory, and besides Howland I included Baker. They will not stand for us planning on Marcus and will not permit an airline to run to Japan…The Admiral wanted a letter from us and then he will immediately proceed to get us all the areas mentioned quick as a mouse and as quietly.
>
> I got together the enclosed letter. Elliott included the insert shown which he said father would like. Elliott has taken the letter with all the history, descriptions, photos, charts etc. up to Hyde Park for any further suggestions before turning them over to Admiral Standley on Tuesday morning…
>
> Please go over the enclosed letter to Admiral Standley very carefully and either phone me or wire me immediately any suggestions or objection for Elliott is to take it to him Wednesday morning first thing. Of course he may return from Hyde Park with additions or changes to it, if so I shall wire you…
>
> Elliott is planning, as soon as we have them tied up, to call together Pan Am, Kennedy of Inter-Island, Matson Co and the Dollar Line and make them combine to form one company to operate the line instead of having any race across there. I doubt if Pan Am will be enthusiastic about having anyone else in with them on it but he says that he can force them to it.[i]

There you have it. The president and his son, Gatty and Douglas, had been secretly working to establish an air route to New Zealand, and in that connection annex a large swathe of the Central Pacific. But there's another familiar name involved. Gatty said he and Elliott had been using Stratton as a conduit with Douglas. It was almost a replay of the domestic airline syndicate these principals had been working on six months earlier.

Upon prodding from above, Admiral Standley had requested the official letter Elliott and his father helped compose. It listed the desired islands, and at the end added the paragraph the president had specifically requested. It read:

> Immediately upon acquisition and development of airport facilities the South Seas Commercial Company plans to encourage and stimulate the formation of a Transpacific airline operation governed and patrolled by those parties best equipped to perform such a service and agrees to at no time allow a company whose main purpose is the sale of stock to the public, to use the developments contemplated on these islands.[ii]

It is not clear why the president insisted on this clause, but given past problems it could have to do with restraining Elliott's greed.

The project now included a central Pacific route using Midway, Wake, and Guam to the Philippines, as well as the south Pacific route using the disputed atolls and American Samoa. Kingman Reef and Palmyra as well as Canton and Christmas Islands were proposed for occupation. The Navy was "vitally interested" in this scheme, said Gatty; which is not surprising since the president had been on the phone with Navy

---

[i] Harold Gatty and the Bridging of the Pacific, by Francis Holbrook & John Nikol, in Aerospace Historian, SEP 82, 176-182 discuss this plan in detail. Excerpts here are from National Archives, Gatty Papers, Box19.

[ii] We shall later meet William Harrison Standley as Ambassador to the USSR (1942-43). He played a very important role in diplomacy during the 1930s, and, as seen, he worked closely with both Elliott and FDR.

Secretary Claude Swanson, urging progress on the plan and requesting sovereignty data for the Cocos, Galapagos, Clipperton, Palmyra, Kingman, Fanning, Christmas, Washington, Jarvis, Howland, Baker, and Marcus islands. FDR told the State Department to examine the possibility of obtaining Anglo-American agreements for some of these islands.

All this activity occurred in great confidence because of the need to preclude unseemly competition, but also to avoid triggering a British countermove. As it was, between December 1934 and 1938 President Roosevelt ordered the annexation of numerous Micronesian islands. From the Gilbert and Ellice Islands Colony, Britain countered by taking over Christmas Island and installing "human flagpoles" – Micronesian colonists – on the deserted Phoenix Islands.[i]

In the summer of 1934, refreshed from his long Bahamian fishing trip, President Roosevelt decided to grab a cruiser (*Houston*) and go big-game fishing in the Pacific. En route to Hawaii, he visited the isolated atoll Clipperton, disputed between France and Mexico, and in Honolulu he conferred with top naval officers about the U.S. stance in the Pacific. Indicative of the immense cost of FDR's jaunts was that the zeppelin USS *Macon* flew out to deliver fresh newspapers to the flotilla deep in the Pacific. So, the president was an enthusiastic Pacific booster, and Elliott was probably encouraged to make his boast to the airlines that he could "force them" to heel.

In 1935, President Roosevelt discreetly ordered the colonization of Howland, Baker, and Jarvis. Unlike the extensive Christmas atoll, these were "one-palm-tree islands" with barely enough room for a runway. USCGC *Itasca* was dispatched to carry and resupply the settlers, mostly Hawaiians, who were entrusted with preparing runways and navigation aids as well as reporting weather for the Bureau of Air Commerce.[483]

The British lost out there, but they retained sovereignty over Christmas and Fanning Islands, which are far more substantial. Canton Island became part of one of the few joint-sovereignty areas on the map, the Canton and Enderbury Islands condominium; the UK and the US shared control for forty years. FDR had defiantly asserted the American claim in 1938, backed with occupation, and the atoll and its airfield were of immense strategic value during the war and for many years afterwards. Given that, and the modern emphasis on ocean and seabed areas, the abandonment of U.S. sovereignty over Canton and numerous other Pacific islands to the new microstate of Kiribati in 1979 is of some interest; especially since this almost completely unreported and unremembered move came hard on the heels of the U.S. abandonment of the Panama Canal Zone. One can only wonder what FDR would have thought.

Soon after Gatty's plans triggered the enthusiasm of the president and his son in August 1934, an odd usurpation derailed the Gatty-Douglas interest and ultimately placed Juan Trippe's Pan Am in charge of the route development. Originally, Gatty and Douglas had worked with TWA, but after the airline reorganizations in 1934, TWA lost interest. Trippe, though, apparently became paranoid about the project and muscled in on the route.[ii]

Historian Francis Holbrook has documented Trippe's coup and believes that he had heard through inside sources about the South Seas plan. Trippe contacted the Navy Department and by the end of 1934, the administration decided to work with Pan Am. Gatty instead came to work for Trippe, doing much of the route preparation including

---

[i] Christmas (Kirisimasi) was later used for the British H-bomb tests. It is now part of Kiribati.

[ii] This is the theory of Holbrook & Nikol, op. cit., but Elliott clearly had been in early contact with Trippe.

difficult negotiations with British authorities in Auckland. The British were not about to let Pan Am get this route without appropriate concessions to Imperial Airways. By 1937, Gatty had overcome this obstacle, too, by appealing directly to the New Zealand government.

It is of some interest, then, that on 8 December 1933, Trippe had gone to the White House and was reported to have presented another route report to President Roosevelt. This one was Charles Lindbergh's fresh report on Greenland and the North Atlantic. Lindbergh was Pan Am's consultant, and Trippe took along Cornelius Vanderbilt Whitney, a board member. The Vanderbilts were FDR's neighbors at Hyde Park. Pan Am was thus well connected on the Democratic side. The visit illustrates the president's keen, early, and enduring interest in transoceanic route development.[484]

The thought of flying the Pacific in a DC-2 would make most people apprehensive even today, so maybe it was good that the original plans were changed. Pan Am's giant four-engined clippers – Sikorsky S-42s – only gradually became available in the 1930s. They began flying a central Pacific mail route in 1935 via Midway, Wake, and Guam.

By January 1937, Pan Am's expert oceanic pilot Edwin Musick flew a survey flight across the South Pacific route, using Kingman Reef. With no usable land area there, the lagoon held a supply ship from which the Clippers refueled. Actual scheduled mail service did not begin until January 1938, and then it was immediately canceled because Musick's S-42 exploded after take-off from Pago Pago, Samoa with the loss of the crew (no passengers were carried).[i] Service did not resume until 1940, and then it stopped at newly annexed Canton Island, a far better spot.

Franklin D. Roosevelt followed all these developments with intense interest. The pioneering flights carried presidential gifts and felicitations to and from the Philippine and New Zealand governments. There was another and today much more famous reason for the Roosevelts' attention. On 2 July 1937, Amelia Earhart and her Pan Am navigator, Fred Noonan, disappeared somewhere close to tiny – and incorrectly charted – Howland Island, where USCGC *Itasca* was once again keeping watch. It was a terrible blow to Eleanor, Amelia's friend. The ensuing unsuccessful search increased the public's focus on the route. But it is peculiar, and a bit unfair, that it was Earhart's stunt flight that kept the public transfixed, while Pan Am's simultaneous but far more portentous efforts on the same route (led by Musick and Noonan) have seemingly gone into history's wastebasket – despite the catastrophic loss of Clipper Two and seven crew at Pago Pago.

Elliott's involvement in the development of the Trans-Pacific air route might be considered somewhat peripheral except for one thing. Columnist Westbrook Pegler had heard that Elliott took a bribe for swinging the route award to Juan Trippe: "…one informant said Stratton was once engaged by Juan Trippe and given a hell of a lot of money to split with Elliott to get bases on Guam and Midway for Pan American." [485]

This might have been a vicious rumor except that as we have seen, Harold Gatty involved Elliott and Stratton closely in the route project, and Elliott obtained his father's support for the detailed proposal. Yet, a bit later in 1934, Elliott was trying to involve Pan Am in the project. The enigmatic Stratton, with whom we are already acquainted, worked for and with Douglas and Elliott, and if Elliott took a cut he should by now have learned to let Stratton be the visible go-between. It is quite reasonable to assume that some money changed hands. It was at that moment in October 1934 that

---

[i] NYT, 13 JAN 38. The theory was that dumping fuel with full flaps mixed fuel with exhaust gases.

Douglas moved out of the Pacific picture, and Trippe took over. Technically, Trippe bought out the other interests. Gatty now worked for him, and Douglas had a seat on the board.

That might be legitimate, and the 25-year old Elliott ought to be commended for his role in augmenting the American diplomatic and aviation posture in the Pacific. But it is odd that when, six years later, Elliott would play a similar but even more active role in the North Atlantic, he made no mention of his earlier transoceanic initiative. When the president sent him on his Atlantic quest in 1941, he would have had in the back of his mind the kid's earlier work with the Pacific route. Of course, by late 1935 Elliott was out of the aviation picture and was no longer involved with Juan Trippe. The two would certainly cross tracks again, though.

Lobbyist or Not?

Elliott Roosevelt kept busy making speeches and promotions, but incurred the wrath of a great many people in the process. One of them was ex-General Billy Mitchell, who, among many others, complained about the president's son being used to lobby for self-seeking industrial interests.[486]

Previously, Elliott and Mitchell had been on the same side, arguing for strong air power. Getting in a fight with Mitchell now was not a prudent move. The general was as controversial as Elliott, but in a different sense. Mitchell had been forced out of the military in 1926 due to his highly public and seriously obnoxious advocacy for air power. He offended the establishment, but most famously the Navy, which he viewed as the mortal enemy of air power, indeed of the future itself.

Regardless of the narcissistic histrionics of his aerial evangelism, Billy Mitchell was soon viewed as a martyred saint whose strategic vision formed the basis for the new American air force. To the bomber generals whom Elliott would later work for, Mitchell was a prophet and a role model.

Mitchell inspired what may be fairly called the Anglo-American cult of air power.[i] In less than a decade it would face its first true test, the strategic bombing campaign against the Axis. Although air power enthusiasts admired Mitchell's advocacy, with the benefit of eighty years of hindsight it is easy to see why he was thrown out of the service. Indeed, the then highly publicized Army – Navy rivalry over ships and airplanes has a bit of the character of a carpenters' convention preoccupied with furious arguments over whether hammers are better than saws: The saw will always get through! Every problem is really a nail!

It is the job of the political leadership to prudently select the right tools depending on the situation. Yet then as later the carpenters, not the architects, often seemed to rule the agenda. At any rate, in the 1930s the "bomber mafia" began the great crusade that would lead to the unrestricted aerial reduction of Germany and Japan, and which would reach its logical culmination in the postwar theology of Mutual Assured Destruction.

In December 1935, shortly before his death, General Mitchell testified before the Congressional committee on patent law reform. This sounds obscure, but in this case it wasn't. The chairman of that committee was Dr. William I. Sirovich of New York. He

[i] This doctrine is usually traced to the Italian writer Giulio Douhet, one of the much-quoted war theorists. His analysis was superficial and strident, and if USAF officers read him more they would quote him less.

was friendly with the Roosevelts and would turn out to be most useful indeed. Sirovich, a frequent visitor and fervent admirer of the USSR, was best known for promoting a sort of federal "Ministry of Culture," a concept thought fascistic in America, but perfectly normal in Europe. Because he was an unsuccessful playwright in addition to being a medical doctor, Sirovich also attracted some attention for proposing that theater critics be censored since they had the power to seriously hurt struggling artists.

Interestingly, in 1933, Sirovich began a Congressional investigation of the stock swindles and union racketeering then engulfing the increasingly Mob-dominated movie industry. This gallant effort at justice was reversed in its tracks by "sinister forces" between 7 and 14 April 1933. It might have exposed Joseph P. Kennedy's operation in Hollywood, and perhaps that of Joe's acolyte in the White House, Jimmy Roosevelt.[487]

Since Sirovich's closeness with the president would become crucial in a subsequent Elliott scandal, it is interesting to note Harold Ickes's thumbnail of him:

> He is a Harvard man, a physician and surgeon, and also a Tammany man, who has been in Congress for about ten years. I don't know how influential he is, but he is very active and he thinks he is influential, whether he is or not. It happens that he was in Harvard with President Roosevelt, and I think, knows him quite well. He is progressive, too, in his outlook.[488]

On 27 April 1935, Sirovich came to see Ickes about a scandal he thought he had uncovered in the aviation patents. Sirovich's accusations took flight themselves:

> According to Sirovich, the U.S. government was about to buy the patents of the Wright Bros. and the Curtiss people, about the time of the world war, because both of these outfits were bankrupt. The war came along and a group financed by Wall Street money bought the patents and made the "flaming coffins" that we sent abroad for our aviators. I have forgotten the sum of money that these flaming coffins cost us in royalties to the patentees but it was an enormous sum, in addition to which the American airplanes during the war were not only useless but were really death traps.
>
> As a result of a prior investigation by Congress some of these men were indicted and convicted but not one has served a single day of his sentence. They still control the airplane industry in the country according to Sirovich. He says that Japan has bombing planes of much greater speed than anything we have and capable of sailing so much higher that our defense planes could never even get up to them. They also have a flying radius of 5,000 miles, about twice as far as any American Army or Navy plane. They can carry much heavier loads. They can sail above the clouds, drop their bombs and get away without anyone knowing whence they came or whither they went, or what nation they belonged to.[489]

Talk about bomber gap! Sirovich's link to reality was tenuous at best. Small traces of truth linger in the above, but the episode tells us more of the Congressman's distrust of industry than of the facts of aviation.

Before Sirovich's patent committee, General Mitchell railed against the aviation manufacturers and their political influence. He had managed to convince himself that they were methodically holding back the progress of aviation by squashing new products and initiatives. Yet in this particular case, Sirovich indignantly protested that he "had never been troubled by lobbyists" and he asserted that Elliott Roosevelt should not be singled out for his advocacy.[490]

It was General Mitchell's *modus operandi* to fling outrageous accusations around him roughly in a 360 degree circle, and he didn't disappoint this time. He accused Eugene Vidal of acting in collusion with industry lobbyists to retard the advancement of aviation and secure unfair advantage against competitors. When Sirovich pressed him on these "serious" charges, he named the Manufacturers Aircraft Association as being at the center of the conspiracy:

> The political influence of the MAA goes right into the heart of Washington. The association hires some of the first families...They hired Elliott Roosevelt, and they moved the ACC to Washington. That's the way they do business. But when Elliott Roosevelt found out he was to be a lobbyist he beat a hasty retreat...I am a Democrat, but I don't believe this boy knew what he was doing.[491]

Despite Mitchell's inflammatory rhetoric, he was probably on track with some of the details of his criticism, and it is certain that many people in aviation felt the same way. In truth, throughout the history of American aviation, independent operators have complained about the federal government's retarding of progress, and the undue influence large corporations with armies of lobbyists have on both contract awards and the regulatory environment.

But the details are often harder to prove than the general principle. It did not seem, for example, as if Elliott Roosevelt was effective even if, thanks to his name, he was cast in the role Mitchell described.

To the press, Elliott immediately waved his blanket denial form:

> In the first place, I have never participated in any lobbying activities...I have never contacted any member of Congress or any executive officer in the administrative branch or any army or navy official in any capacity to influence him or them in decisions concerning military or commercial aviation. The statement of ex-General Mitchell is pure libel of the most vicious type and undoubtedly intended to attract unsavory publicity to my efforts to earn a living honestly.[492]

And this leads to a highly illuminating column by a Washington insider, Washington Post's Carlisle Bargeron. It seems that, after a brief honeymoon, Elliott was run out of town by the aviation industry:

> Elliott was employed as the lobbyist here but he would not lobby. The aviation moguls explode every time you mention his name. Just at the time the New Dealers were crucifying them through the cancellation of their mail contracts they employed Elliott as the vice president of their [ACC] at a salary of $12,000 a year. Of course, there is no doubt as to why they employed him but Elliott apparently believed they wanted him for vice president because of some peculiar aeronautical knowledge he possessed.
>
> Anyway, Elliott came here and took an estate at nearby Leesburg, Va., and entertained and insofar as social affairs were concerned acted just like a lobbyist. But he never lobbied. After the aviation interests had had him on the payroll for several months they realized they had been burned, but there was nothing they could do about it. They wouldn't have dared admit they wanted him to use his influence. They were literally boiling over at the matter when this writer finally made the situation public and Elliott went off to Texas to live, subsequently to resign.
>
> Elliott was right when he characterized Mitchell's charge as "libel"... [493]

At any rate, either Elliott wasn't effective as a lobbyist, or he overplayed his cards. His dilemma was unsolvable. Everyone thought he was a shill for the airlines, and the Republicans made hay of that. Elliott refuted it, but when Congress passed the Mead amendment bill increasing air mail payments by 20%, he was still the one to blame. Rep. Mead (D – NY) was acting for the administration. As the *New York Times* reported:

> A denial that he is a lobbyist for aviation concerns was issued here tonight by Elliott Roosevelt, the President's son, in reply to charges made in the House today before passage of the Mead airmail bill. "Those interested in the work that I am doing," Mr. Roosevelt said, "can find out by inquiring. They will learn that I have nothing to do with the legislative program of the aviation companies. I do not even know what the Mead bill contains. As for my having been connected with the legislative program, I have never talked with any one connected with the government or attempted to convert any one's opinion on how he should vote."
>
> He explained that his work as consultant of the Aeronautical Chamber of Commerce is that of organizing and coordinating the various aviation companies to put them on a self-sustaining basis whereby they may survive without government subsidy.[494]

It was a classical Elliott denial, emitted as usual in a highly aggrieved tone. But if this one seemed true, it was not because of Elliott's continence.

Westbrook Pegler later acquired an insider document that described in lurid detail just what Elliott did as soon as he joined the ACCA:

> Hardly had he taken office when firms belonging to the Chamber were approached on a proposition of paying for special services to be rendered by Elliott. The selling talk was that any company having Elliott on its payroll would be sure of getting an edge over competitors in any matter either within or without his duties for the Chamber.
>
> Several fell for the deal – each sucker thinking it had an exclusive. When a few weeks later it leaked out that practically all of the Chamber members had been approached and that Elliott was selling the same special advantages to all of them, hell broke loose and Elliott suddenly found it desirable to take a trip to Texas.[495]

This document appeared to be a draft column based on information from a prominent airline executive. The source was highly knowledgeable:

> Those he had rooked and those he had planned to rook joined unanimously in a demand that his services with the Chamber be terminated; and a committee of four was appointed to dispose of the matter in a way that would avoid any embarrassment either for the industry or for FDR.

The implied source, Paul Brattain, then an executive in Eddie Rickenbacker's Eastern Airlines, was a member of that committee and kept a diary in which he recorded all details of this negotiation. Brattain directly implicated the president. He said that a few days after the special ACCA committee was formed, he received an invitation to dine at the White House, which he did on 20 February 1935. He elaborated:

> He was given to understand that FDR desired to impart to the committee his suggestions as to how it should proceed; and in order to keep the discussion on an intimate and informal basis, the committee was to be dined at the White House in pairs, with their wives on two successive evenings. Brattan, who was deemed least friendly of the four was

> bracketed with Elliott's friend [C.R.] Smith of American Air Lines – a Fort Worth prodigy – for the second of the two suppers.

This was a very strange invitation indeed. It was evidently extremely important for the White House to get the ACCA's Elliott committee reëducated:

> The two couples were ushered into the President's study where he greeted them affably and without any trace of the worries of State...The President told Brattan and Smith how highly he regarded Elliott. Mrs. Roosevelt told them that Elliott was his father's favorite child and that Franklin would do more for Elliott or on Elliott's sayso than he would for the rest of the family. No threats were made. No promises were given. But the committee members could not fail to gather that summary discharge of Elliott might have serious repercussions for the Aviation Industry.

Squeezed by the son and then the father, the ACCA committee eventually arrived at a semi-Solomonic decision:

> When the committee met later, it decided to retain Elliott in his official capacity for one year at a salary of from $10,000 to $15,000, with the proviso that he would remain in Texas, take no part in Chamber affairs, nor in any way trade upon his connection with the Chamber or the Chamber's name.[496]

It was an extraordinary inside account. On the other hand, due to the people involved, the story must have been widespread scuttlebutt in the aviation industry. It is one of the many cases in which the "deep throat" account varies greatly from the more cautious public commentary, and it helps explain why Elliott's reputation, even at this early time, was beyond the pale among many political insiders. Perhaps it even helps explain why the drunk-as-a-skunk Elliott was beaten up at the Conquistadores del Cielo conclave in New Mexico.

Elliott Roosevelt finally resigned his ACCA post on 4 October 1935. He had nominally lasted seventeen months, a new record for him, but he had actually left for Texas in March of that year.[497] While he did pursue some aviation matters during his first year in Texas, he does appear to have become *non grata* in nationwide aviation circles, and he gradually settled into new pursuits, goaded by local powerbrokers.

Although he soon became involved in many new activities in Texas, most publicly he also became embroiled and then embattled in state politics. This was chiefly because the New Deal had become immensely controversial there, and Elliott was viewed as a classical carpetbagger. After a brief tenure, he resigned as first vice president of the Texas Young Democrats in August 1935.[498] "The Young Democrats who do not like him speak of him as The Young Dictator, which may be only malice," said one writer.[499]

As Elliott settled on the ranch, he acquired some hobbies that would become notorious. Perhaps inspired by the racetrack enthusiast Grenville Stratton, Ruth and Elliott began breeding Arabian horses. This was obviously a genteel activity appropriate to the social rank to which they aspired; but it was also a genuine interest of the former rodeo contestant. The horse breeding would pop up from time to time whenever Elliott's peregrinations paused on some suitable acreage.

The "Dutch Branch" ranch property began with 250 acres and grew to 1,330 acres before being sold after Ruth's and Elliott's divorce. Not surprisingly, controversy soon attached to it; locally it was said that Elliott obtained land cheaply by claiming that his father intended to move there after leaving office, and that the property owner then reluctantly agreed to sell on that patriotic basis.

What sounds like a sour local rumor checked out when the House Ways and Means Committee came across the trick in 1945:

> Thirty acres adjoining the ranch were the property of Tom Owens, wealthy Texas oil man. Elliott sought to add these acres to his ranch and asked their price, Owens has acknowledged. Owens told him he valued the land at $1,000 an acre, because the acreage had good oil prospects.
>
> Elliott found the price too high. Some time later he again approached Owens, cautioning the oil man to secrecy. Elliott said he was seeking the additional acreage not for himself but for his father. His father, Elliott continued, desired to live in Texas on leaving the White House in 1940.
>
> Elliott said his father had arrived at this decision on a visit to Dutch ranch. Elliott then produced a check payable to Owens for $9,000, signed by Franklin D. Roosevelt and offered it in payment for the land Owens had valued at $30,000.
>
> Owens said he decided to sell the land at a sacrifice in order to fulfill the reported wish of the President of the United States. Later, Owens discovered Roosevelt not only had no intention of settling in Texas, but he also had no intention of leaving the White House in 1940 or even in 1944. Owens acknowledged that Elliott pulled a fast one with the aid of his father's check.[500]

Other explanations for FDR's check being farfetched, these details imply that the president had consented to play his part in Elliott's negotiation strategy.

At any rate, the ranch and its livestock was soon heavily mortgaged. The U.S. Treasury inquisitors also appeared to believe that Elliott had used the property to shield funds from creditors; it was held in his wife's name.[501] But Elliott said it didn't matter; it was Texas community property.

Ruth sold Dutch Branch Ranch in 1944. Sid Richardson, the oil baron, obtained ownership of it in 1946, just before the land was taken by the federal government for a reservoir project. It is now submerged.[502]

Another persistent predilection first manifested itself when Elliott, fresh from his disaster with the air mails, collared his father in the White House with a request, the most innocent conceivable. Chief Secretary McIntyre received this note:

> Mr. Early, on August 31, 1934, says Elliott came in to remind his father that on Friday a group would call to present him with a Great Dane dog; that the President is to accept this dog, and then, according to his promise, turn same over to Elliott. Elliott says it is important that his father keep this engagement. Will you see to it that he does, please.[503]

The Great Danes would multiply. Wife nr. 5, Patricia, wrote that Elliott lamented that "some years ago in Texas he had owned nine of the huge dogs at one time, a male and female and their seven pups." [504] Gentle as they are, their size worried Eleanor when she visited.

They worried others as well. Some kind soul sent the president a clipping from a local Tennessee paper. Elliott had been driving along in the country in his roadster, and had a minor accident. The local folks were eager to help him out until a lion-sized animal emerged from the car. Even when the "200 pound" Great Dane was properly introduced, the locals, whom we may infer from the caricatured accents were Negroes, were most worried, until Elliott gave them a big tip and evidently won some Democratic votes.[505]

The dog situation deteriorated. Danes, evidently, need close supervision. Elliott later told Patricia about the night all nine escaped: "They all got out on a rampage across the countryside and killed three calves, seven sheep, thirty turkeys and two hundred chickens before being rounded up with the help of a sheriff's posse. 'Once they get the blood taste, they don't stop.'" [506]

Many more giant dog stories would follow Elliott in the years to come. They had a way of not ending happily.

The Crown Prince from the East

The relationship between Texas Governor James V. Allred and Elliott Roosevelt contains some interesting surprises. While these "surprises" tell us something about how Elliott operated financially, they also show how his father operated politically.

Even while Elliott was still living in Washington in early 1935, he and friend Gene Vidal dreamed up a new project: an air race between the United States and Latin America. In those days, intercontinental air races with generous prizes caught the public's imagination and were believed, rightly or wrongly, to promote the future of aviation.[507]

The ambitious concept originally called for the greatest air race ever. Miami was to be the starting point; thence a 20,000 mile closed course would take the planes south to Argentina, across the Andes, north to Vancouver, and back to the East Coast. Elliott promoted this notion while he was still with the ACCA. His original idea was that Hugh S. Johnson would be in charge. The old general apparently still had Elliott's ear at this point. That would not last.[508]

In March 1935, after having been exiled from Washington, Elliott and his wife bought the first 250-acre section of their Texas ranch. From then until he joined the Air Corps five years later, he would be a controversial figure in Texas politics.

At that point Elliott began touting the air race to Texas officials, who were planning the state's centennial celebrations for 1936. He assured them that his father was deeply interested, and that he would surely visit Dallas if his idea of starting and ending the race in that town was adopted. He even suggested that FDR would probably present the prizes. First place was set at $50,000.[509]

In July he got with young, capable Governor Allred to promote the air race idea as a capstone of the Texas Centennial Exposition, whose main venue would be Dallas. Now the race, to begin in April, would run from Dallas to South America and back. It would, naturally, require a significant purse, which would, of course, require a full-time fund raiser. And, said Elliott, he would be glad to pre-fly the route in a large cabin monoplane, provided by the sponsors, in order to secure the necessary permissions and generate maximum interest among Latin American governments. His visibility as the president's son should encourage the foreigners.

On 9 July Elliott got the job to raise at least $100,000 for the race. By 17 August, he could report that he had "completed raising a fund of $150,000 to finance the 19,000 mile air derby scheduled to begin at Dallas, Texas in September 1936."[510] The date had already slipped five months.

Then… nothing happened. The air race vanished. If there was any money, Elliott seems to have been the only one who got any. His salary was understood to have been $1,000 a month. In September, the Texas Centennial Central Exposition dumped Elliott as "aviation adviser," and the race was cancelled.[511]

Columnist Drew Pearson heard something about the trouble. He said Texas staked Elliott to a large salary while he promoted the race - "but the most essential part of the promotion was raising the money; and here Elliott fell down." [512]

Evidently, Governor Allred had set himself the task of providing the president's son with a living. On 5 September, he appointed Elliott to a very unusual post as a "member of an unofficial airport development advising committee" whose task was to seek WPA (Works Progress Administration) funds to improve Texas's airports.[513]

This was a ten-man committee whose chairman was Fort Worth oil man and aviation supporter, William H. Dunning. The committee went to Washington asking for two million dollars. Elliott was a good man to have on board; not only could he bend the president's ear, but Gene Vidal at the Bureau of Air Commerce was his personal friend. It does sound like Elliott had invented a new job for himself, trying to talk the federal government out of money for Texas; and Allred, a strong FDR supporter, thought that was a really good investment.[514]

The governor doubled up on his investment when the kid who had refused to go to college was appointed to the Board of Regents of Texas A&M on 10 December.[i] It was a six year-term. Although not an intellectual powerhouse, Elliott in his new capacity got to travel, talk, and meet important people – even more so than he already did. Local opinion stated: "The Governor's appointment of young Roosevelt recognized a personal and political friendship which has matured…in the past gubernatorial campaign, Roosevelt made some speeches for Allred."[515]

In another, more prosaic coup for Elliott, next year President Roosevelt came to visit and inspect Texas A&M. On that occasion, he was presented with the ultimate Texas gift, a prize Hereford heifer. After a decent interval, the cow was sent to join Elliott's menagerie in Fort Worth.[516]

Governor Allred was very generous but he didn't act entirely out of charity.

"A Dallas Citizen" had a malevolent view of what was going on. He wrote Westbrook Pegler:

> …you might be interested in a donation of the Federal Government of three million dollars to the Texas Centennial. Following which Elliott was made head of the Aviation Department at a salary of $30,000. But at the end of about thirty days that department was discontinued, but Elliott apparently kept his thirty thousand dollars.[517]

Though a probably scurrilous rumor relating to the state aviation job, the letter evidently reflected some of the attitude in Texas. Indeed, the eyes of Texas were upon Elliott, and they were not all as indulgent as Governor Allred's. The trouble hit home when, in June 1935, the president's son was elected to the first vice-presidency of the Young Democrats for Texas in a vote that was widely seen as illegal.[518]

---

[i] Texas Agricultural and Mechanical College at College Station, the state's flagship college.

First Shot at Politics

Perhaps it wasn't really the fault of the Roosevelt children that they often took the political track, and just as often derailed spectacularly. So strong is the dynastic instinct in humans that people constantly encouraged the Roosevelts to seek public office, assuming that this was their natural calling. It would have taken some willpower to resist, and only the kid brother, John, had it.

In Texas, Elliott was immediately involved in a whirlwind of public occasions and social obligations. He proved good at that part: cutting ribbons and cake, making flowery speeches, giving interviews and parties, attending the shindigs of the state's movers and shakers. That his only qualification was his name was no problem; he was articulate in a folksy way, and played the role well.

Then as now, the political circus attracted its share of clowns and mountebanks. That a 25-year old fresh from back east should be considered for high office, Congress or governor, wasn't so odd. But then as now, the real action was beneath the ever-shifting surface chop, and we shall soon see that important forces were clashing in the depths. That's why a seemingly obscure office, president of the Young Democrats of Texas, attracted such an odd fascination even beyond state limits.

There was more at stake than the "carpetbagger" Elliott Roosevelt. The soul of the Democratic Party was beginning to rip apart. The old slave-owners' party could not be expected forever to coexist with the socialistic tendencies of the growing urban North-eastern faction. Although President Roosevelt did little for civil rights in the South, he did move the party away from its identification with white southern interests. He also converted "the Negro vote" from the Republican to the Democratic Party.

When Elliott showed up, "states' rights" Democrats were further incensed. The controversy over restricting oil production to prop up prices had deeply aggravated Texans, and the high, punitive tariffs imposed by the northern industrial interests rejuvenated old Confederate battle cries rooted in its agricultural, free-trading past. [519]

Governor Allred and Elliott Roosevelt had met "politically" in Amarillo in June 1935 before the Texas League of Young Democrats. Although the Democratic governor supported FDR, Allred had blasted the federal government. Elliott then supported the New Deal. He said that the governor was "hot under the collar about something he doesn't have to be worried about."[520]

Responding to Texas sentiments, Allred professed to worry about "states' rights" and "individual liberties." Despite the Supreme Court striking down the NRA, a national price-fixing plan, the New Deal was becoming increasingly totalitarian and unpopular. But the ruckus between the two young politicians seemed stage-managed. Both got their talking points in, without disagreeing on substance. Young Elliott showed himself as an effective speaker and sharp debater. Governor Allred's relationship with Elliott subsequently appears to have been of the mutual backscratching type.

The son defended the president to the extent of blurting out that "many features" of the NRA were unconstitutional, but "there was an emergency and someone had to meet it."[i] At the venue, both sons, James and Elliott, defended the idea of passing new constitutional amendments to defeat the Supreme Court's opposition. That wasn't what most Texans wanted to hear.

---

[i] NYT, 8 JUN 35, 9 JUN 35. Effectively a planned economy, the National Recovery Administration was struck down unanimously by the Supreme Court on 27 MAY 35.

"Young Elliott Roosevelt has volunteered to prevent Texas politics from going wrong and is perfectly willing to explain to us how these things are done up in New York," editorialized the *Dallas Morning News.* He already rubbed many the wrong way.[521]

Powerful forces were promoting Elliott as a candidate for President of the Young Democrats, but unexpectedly stiff opposition made him settle for a vice-presidency. A man named Jack Burroughs, of Dallas, voluntarily stepped aside for Elliott. All this shadowy maneuvering was a problem for some equally powerful people who were determined to throw Elliott out.[522]

The row caused the convention to split into a pro- and an anti-Constitution wing, to a great extent reflecting what delegates thought of Elliott and the New Deal. In the general assembly, the conservative pro-states-rights side won decisively.[523]

Nevertheless, the initial move to oust Elliott failed in the controlling committee. Only select members "in good standing" voted on it, and the result was 16-12 in favor of retaining him. That was only the beginning.[524] In July, another vote was held in the organization's small executive committee. Elliott's opponents claimed that he caused dissension; that he knew nothing of Texas's problems; and that he had been illegally installed as vice president.[525]

The vote in the executive committee was now 14-1 for Elliott. Oddly, the chairman of the committee was Fort Worth attorney Raymond Buck, who, coincidentally, was also the owner of radio station KTAT, which Elliott wanted to acquire. KTAT, inspired by "Texas Air Transport," was, like the airline, a creation of the Fort Worth oilmen. Raymond Buck not only fought to keep Elliott, but to purge his opponents from the Democratic Party. Still, the fury in the ranks gradually rose to fever pitch.[526]

Behold, if Buck wasn't also general counsel of American Airways and one of C.R. Smith's close friends. Raymond Buck was never a household name nationally, but his importance in the Texas Cabal may be gauged by this remark, attributed to a political insider: "Sam Rayburn owned Lyndon Johnson, but Raymond Buck owned Sam Rayburn."[527] Rayburn, of course, was the supremely powerful speaker of the U.S. House of Representatives from 1940 on.[528]

Just to perfect the point: Buck owned the land on which Dallas-Fort Worth airport, American's hub, was eventually built. He lost the land to C.R. in a card game.[529]

"This organization is becoming a rubber stamp," charged the leading Elliott-hater, Joe Humphreys: "We are jumping through the hoop at the command of the man heading the band wagon. Elliott Roosevelt was elevated to this position in the organization because of family connections. The crown prince and the rubber stamp from the East has not merited his position."[530]

Next month, Elliott gave up, or was induced to do so. His resignation was effective on 6 August, but oddly enough, it wasn't announced until 4 September. "I want to make it plain that I wasn't forced out," announced Elliott.[531]

A few people were aware of the real game, and columnist Drew Pearson was one of them. After the plot failed, he revealed to the nation that Fort Worth interests had intended to run Elliott for Congress in 1936:

> The idea was sponsored chiefly by Amon Carter, publisher of the Fort Worth Star-Telegram, intimate friend of the Roosevelt family. He wanted Elliott to oppose Fritz Lanham, congressman from Fort Worth and to that end boosted him first for the presidency of the Young Democrats of Texas. However, Elliott did not go over very well in

> the Lone Star state. He was too good looking, his manner too suave, his attitude just a trifle superior. Also, friends of Fritz Lanham set out to knife him.
>
> So after a knockdown and dragout fight among Texas young democrats, Elliott lost out on the presidency, compromised and got the vice presidency. But with opposition to the elder Roosevelt growing in Texas, Elliott's chances for congress appeared futile. Also his spot in the limelight was not helping his father. There is too much resentment against the Roosevelt family. So Elliott resigned even his vice presidency.[532]

That was not quite the end of Texas talk of a political career for Elliott, but it deepened a schism in the ruling party. Amon Carter and his clique had been stymied for now. Texas was even then a state of many competing powerful factions, and as a pawn, Elliott was not fast enough on his feet to turn up on the winning side. That despite the fact that he now began a long journey to the right, distancing himself more and more substantively from his father's policies.

Amon Carter scored a minor coup that October 1st, when he introduced Eleanor Roosevelt to Fort Worth. She had flown in from Santa Fe, naturally on American Airlines and with its new president, C.R. Smith, by her side. Governor Allred was there to meet her; so was Fritz Lanham. There were no hard feelings, and Elliott would need Lanham again in the future. Eleanor stayed in Benbrook with her son and his family for a few days, and was, as everywhere, in hot demand for speeches and appearances.[533]

The young Roosevelts were building a spacious country home, ideal for entertaining. At that time it was well out in the pleasantly sylvan country southwest of Fort Worth, hilly and with plenty of water. It would turn out to be an ideal spot for the president and his family to visit; there he could have both a measure of privacy and meet with local supplicants and favor-seekers. Of course, Elliott had to turn it into a working cattle ranch; he did not intend to be "all hat and no cattle," as Texans say. But as it turned out, the cows too were soon mortgaged up to their horns, and, according to some, beyond.[i]

In his yearning to become a true Texan and in his need to play with the big boys, Elliott also tried his hand at wildcatting, not on his ranch, but on his wife's land near the New Mexico border. It was a gamble he lost, as most did; but that did not deter him from trying to find oil repeatedly throughout his life. He was drawn to risk, and the romantic Texas pastime of trying to find the next big gusher fit the bill.[534]

The day after Elliott's resignation from office with the Young Democrats was made public, Governor Allred appointed him to the airport commission intended to get federal funds out of the WPA.[535] Next month, his sinecure with the ACCA expired; he had apparently kept his promise not to cause any more trouble for the chamber. Simultaneously, Elliott entered the radio business in Fort Worth.

Raymond Buck's transactions with Elliott regarding KTAT Fort Worth are very curious indeed, but we shall have occasion to look at them in another chapter. For now, it is of interest that on 1 October 1935, Elliott got yet another job, this time as vice president in charge of sales for the Southwest Broadcasting Company, which operated KTAT and some other radio stations owned by millionaire Alva Pearl Barrett.[536]

A.P. Barrett had made his fortune in the Texas-Louisiana Power Company. In 1928 he bought TAT, the airline founded by the local Bowen brothers. Next year he formed Southern Air Transport (SAT), which was the forerunner of American Airways.

---

[i] DallasMN, 13 NOV 35. References to Elliott's finances further discussed in the Hartford Loan chapter.

Barrett had spotted the capable young accountant C.R. Smith and groomed him to run his airline. When AVCO bought SAT from Barrett in 1930, C.R. stayed on board.

Intriguingly, a local Texas broadcast historian lets us know that, "Texas Air Transport (TAT) was a small airline started at Meacham field by A.P. Barrett, a close friend of WBAP owner Amon Carter. Apparently fascinated by Amon's radio station, Barrett purchased KFQB and changed the call letters of its new station to the more appropriate KTAT."[537]

Eventually, Elliott Roosevelt was allowed to buy KTAT, whose license he then replaced with his own KFJZ. Technically, Ruth bought the station, in June 1937.[538]

Thus it looked like C.R. and his Fort Worth clan was as much Elliott's entry into the radio field as were the Texas oiligarchs. Elliott certainly was not seen as a true competitor; instead the North Texas *nomenklatura* played the second son like a fiddle.

From Washington, there would soon be good news for Governor Allred. As Elliott had promised, President Roosevelt made sure to visit the Texas Centennial Exposition in Houston in June 1936, make speeches, and have his picture taken with the governor. FDR spoke in front of more than 50,000 people in the Cotton Bowl Centennial Stadium in Dallas, with Elliott standing next to him. Of course, Elliott was there to hold his father upright, but on his other side, as if glued on, stood Governor James Allred.[i]

Not all presidents get a perfect welcome in Dallas, but in 1936 FDR still seemed to be genuinely popular there. The royal visit was an immense public celebration:

> More than 100,000 eyes were trained on the man who is the third head of the Nation to visit Dallas and the greatest political idol in Texas. Immaculate in a white linen suit, the President radiated health and vitality. A deep suntan over face and hands betokened a familiarity with sun and air which made it certain that he would not be overbothered by the Texas weather….
>
> The thing with which President Roosevelt most impressed Texas was his virility. In 1936 he stood under a boiling sun at the Texas Centennial and made a speech at the Cotton Bowl and for 30 minutes alternately harangued and pleased a packed crowd, part of which was fainting. Ambulances ran in and out during the speech and at that time the President's most enthusiastic followers wondered how a cripple could stand up under such pressure.[539]

It was supremely important for FDR to present this energetic image to the nation, and for this the assistance of his sons, Elliott in this case, was essential.

From the Cotton Bowl, the cortege proceeded down Commerce to Downtown. FDR attended a sumptuous Texas luncheon at the Adolphus; Eleanor one at the Baker Hotel. Afterwards, the party proceeded to Lee Park.

What a coup for Elliott! Even more so for Amon Carter, the "first citizen" of Fort Worth, if not its feudal lord, and a major Roosevelt contributor. Carter stuck to the party as closely as did Allred. So did Jesse Jones. But it was Elliott who got to drive his father past the cheering crowds all the way to Fort Worth and to his home in Benbrook.[540]

The president's 1937 visit to Texas will be discussed later for its permanent imprint on party politics. It gave Allred a further high profile, as well as a settlement of some prominent illegal oil production ("hot oil") cases. Allred's brother Renne Jr. was later implicated in continuing hot oil operations.[541]

---

[i] The president's visit was breathlessly covered, in great detail, by the Dallas News, 13 to 15 June 1936.

In July 1938 came the big payoff. FDR again traveled through Texas, staying overnight with Elliott and Ruth at the ranch. On the train with him were most of the usual suspects: Elliott and family, Lyndon Johnson, Allred, Carter. Father and son were photographed leaving Fort Worth in the cheering company of Allred as well as Representatives Johnson, McFarlane, Maury Maverick, and Fritz Lanham.[542]

Congressman McFarlane would later be quoted as being one who complained to the president about Elliott's Texas business matters and asked that he be indicted: "McFarlane referred to a certain $40,000 Elliott had collected in a Texas radio scandal and declared that several people should be indicted, including your son Elliott."

> Whereupon, the late President laughed heartily…and replied: 'Why, Bill, don't you know there are certain people who just can't be indicted?'[543]

Absent was Vice President Garner, the sage from Uvalde, Texas. He said it was too far to walk. His split with FDR was already in the open. Another man who was there but apparently wished he weren't, was Texas Senator Tom Connally (not to be confused with later Governor John Connally, a distant relation). He had been unreliable, and FDR treated him coldly. 1938 was the "year of the purge," the president's attempt to eliminate anti-New Deal Democrats nationwide.

The climax for Governor Allred came in Wichita Falls, when the president, with Allred at his side and Elliott standing behind, appointed the governor to the post of federal judge for a newly created district in southern Texas. Allred had only two terms as governor – George Washington's example was followed in that state – and in Texas that low-paying and somewhat ineffectual job is viewed mostly as a step to better things, whether in business or in politics.[i]

Allred's appointment caused deep resentment, not only in Texas, but in the federal Senate. Allred wasn't even a resident of his new district; but it seems that most of the worry was caused by the imperious, arbitrary way the selection was made – a bit reminiscent of Latin American dictators touring the countryside and tossing money and jobs to cheering supplicants. It wasn't what the Senate had in mind when it came to selecting federal judges.

At the instigation of irascible Representative Martin Dies (D-TX), a Senate judiciary subcommittee held a public hearing on the controversial appointment. Dies thundered that "If this sort of appointment is allowed to stand, it will be the beginning of carpetbag rule." The *Dallas News* puzzled:

> Washington has not fully understood why President Roosevelt appointed Allred, since neither Texas Senator recommended him. His backer was said to have been Elliott Roosevelt of Fort Worth, whom Allred had named to the board of Texas A & M College.[ii]

The local Texans were not impressed, either. It was quickly rumored that this was an Elliott-FDR plot to pave the way for the son's political career. Speculation again ran rampant about what kind of deal had been made, and what office Elliott had been

---

[i] DallasMN, 12 JUL 38; notes that "Texas comment reaching Washington was that Allred had a better chance to be a third-termer than some people higher up." 13 JUL 38 notes that ER was already proposed for Lieutenant Governor in 1937, but support had not been forthcoming.

[ii] DallasMN, 22 JAN 39. Martin Dies, a South Texan, considered Allred a carpetbagger as he was from North Texas.

promised. But with Allred gone from the political scene, the support for the president's son evaporated. To rumors that he was groomed to take Senator Connally's seat, or the gubernatorial office in 1940, Elliott responded, "I do not plan to run for any political office now, two years from now, or four years hence."[544] Later that year, that decent interval was extended to "at least ten years."

That probably was really how Elliott felt in the summer of 1938. He was getting into deep trouble with his new business, and he had worn out his welcome with many Texans. The appointment of Allred was probably just the president's deft move to reward a crony. But Allred had not been favored by the Texas political class, and the appointment was viewed as something of a snub, and most likely Elliott's work.

Senator Tom Connally, in particular, was steamed. He had not favored Allred.

1938 was a watershed year for President Roosevelt, especially in Texas. Because of his nationwide popularity, he felt strong enough to undertake the controversial "purge" of unreliable elements in the Democratic Party. This did not exactly have Stalinist implications, but his visit to Fort Worth that year, during the campaign, was clearly undertaken to punish "capitalist-roaders" and favor New Deal stalwarts.

In Texas, the gambit failed. FDR's coattails were no longer magic there, and many Texas mavericks gained office. However, the real Maverick, i.e. Representative Maury Maverick, who had stood by FDR, was defeated.

FROM AIRWAYS TO AIRWAVES

Real power operates beneath the surface. Even those who surf merrily on the waves are often unaware how the currents move them. Elliott Roosevelt was always a flamboyant surfer on shifting seas he didn't understand.

At the end of April 1937, President Roosevelt took off on yet another of his famous "fishing" trips. In retrospect, a lot more than fish were caught on that jaunt. After a long train ride, the president was met at Gulfport, Miss. by his son. He was accompanied by Louisiana governor Richard Leche, who would later go to jail for corruption on a biblical scale. But before that, his alliance with FDR opened wide the federal tap, in a gusher known as the "Second Louisiana Purchase."[i]

The party went on to New Orleans and there boarded a new destroyer, the U.S.S. *Moffett*.[545] It's nice to be able to call on a destroyer when you want to go tarpon-fishing, but *Moffett* was intended only to be an escort, along with two other warships. The third functioned as the radio relay for the flotilla.

Somewhere off Port Aransas, the party met up with the presidential "yacht" *Potomac*, which had steamed up from Corpus Christi, and Elliott and his father resumed their journey aboard *Potomac*. This new 165-foot vessel was actually a Coast Guard cutter (USS *Electra*), which the president had appropriated for his own use.

A temporary White House commanded by Marvin McIntyre was established in the Hotel Galvez in Galveston. Jesse Jones, the Houston publisher who was now chairman

---

[i] DallasMN, 2 OCT 40. Pundits appear to have since lost track of the numbering, there having been several "Lousiana Purchases." Drew Pearson wrote about this scandal as late as 23 MAY 68 (column).

of the all-important Reconstruction Finance Corporation (RFC), also met the party, and so did Governor Allred.

On 7 May, the presidential party and Elliott's oil baron friends enjoyed a discreet tryst on a delightfully lonely barrier island. It was apparently not technically on Matagorda, as reported, but on adjacent San Jose Island, which is across the channel from Mustang Island at Port Aransas. The meeting took place in the vacation lodge of Clint Murchison and Dudley Golding, who headed the American Liberty Oil Company and the Channel Transport and Marketing Company. There was an airstrip, and to this day the sandy island holds an exclusive fly-in resort. In fact, President Bush relaxed with fellow Texas oil men there in December 1989.[546] The Eisenhowers also visited with friend Sid Richardson here. John Connally, who was very close to Richardson, said that "at one point, Murchison talked him into buying his own private island, St. Joseph [San Jose]…Clint had one, farther north at Matagorda; it had become a Texas thing to do."[547]

In the May 1937 *rendez-vous,* Sid Richardson, Elliott's other oil friend, was also present. The meeting was not revealed even to the temporary White House; it was reported by the local papers, and the president later confirmed that he had gone ashore to lunch with friends of Elliott's.

Murchison and Golding were under federal indictment for stealing oil – what was then called selling "hot oil" in excess of their quotas under the 1935 Connally Act. They had been indicted by a federal grand jury on 23 April. The U.S. Attorney for Texas, reportedly a zealous type, was about to "nail'em to the wall" in the local idiom. Ten individuals and six companies were facing imminent trial on the hot oil charges.

The next Monday, the whole affair was settled in the Southern Federal District Court in Houston. The "hot oil" indictees were allowed to re-plead *nolo contendere* (no contest) and were given tolerable fines. On the prosecutor's recommendation, Channel Transport paid $17,500.[548]

From then on, the Texas oil barons could call on Elliott when they wanted to arrange a meeting with the president. The association would remain lucrative for all concerned – not least Elliott.

On that same Monday, President Roosevelt's fishing trip ended in port in Galveston. Governor Allred, Lyndon B. Johnson, and Galveston's mayor Adrian Levy greeted the president at the dock. FDR then proceeded to Fort Worth to visit with his son and his family. Elliott had taken color home movies of the fishing trip.[549]

Governor Allred's brother, Renne Allred Jr., was indicted in a "hot oil" case also involving Murchison and Golding; he and several others had conspired to sell hot oil to Channel Transport.[i] That case, in U.S. District Court at Houston, was disposed of in a no-contest settlement in 1939 for a fine of $1,000.[550] There was no openly reported link to Elliott in that case. However, a Texas insider grumbled that the three Allred brothers were so entangled with Elliott that it forced James out of office in 1938:

> They organized a hot oil racket in 1935 when Texas Rangers arrested Rennie Allred and O.H. Allred went to Oklahoma and Elliott denied all knowledge of same to his father… Those who know say that if Amon Carter, O.H. Allred, Sidney Samuels, James

[i] DallasMN, 18 NOV 39, 1 FEB 40. Renne and former Asst. Attorney General Neal Powers were indicted and fined. A jury acquitted Allred of federal perjury charges in 1941. (DallasMN, 15 MAR 41)

Allred, John T. Jones could all be made to testify on Elliott's income tax racket it would reveal queer things.[i]

Hot oil was an explosive issue in Texas from 1935-39. Since the Connally Act was a price-fixing and supply-limitation scheme, many locals were bitterly opposed to it, and that may account for the flagrant defiance of the law throughout Texas and Louisiana.

Even more important to Texas oilmen was the so-called oil depletion allowance, an immense tax break given to producers on the grounds that petroleum reserves were finite. In practice, the write-off was protected by Congress on condition that politicians got kickbacks. This equation would explain much of the future of Democratic politics.

What really happened on that sandy beach? While the superficial chain of events can be reconstructed from press coverage and in particular from reports in the trade journal *National Petroleum News*, the words exchanged cannot be known with certainty. However, the results are known.[551]

The Matagorda Pact

One of the surest sources for the island meeting is a letter that Houston oil man Clifford Mooers wrote to Westbrook Pegler in 1945 in an attempt to ensure that the reporter got his facts straight. Mooers was a friend of the oil barons involved, and his account of the meeting, though unprovable by its nature, is explosive:

> The part about my 'phoning McEntyre, his secretary, from a public telephone and warning him that Elliott Roosevelt and Bob Violet, a Fort Worth lawyer, and their wives were waiting on the island for the President to come ashore and have lunch with Murchison and Golding, who were under federal indictment for stealing oil, probably does not have the right kind of newsvalue for Pegler's articles. Incidentally, McEntyre said to me, "well, I don't think that has been arranged yet." His remark indicated to me that he knew that the meeting was being arranged and knew the reason for it. Sometime previous Clint Murchison is supposed to have said to someone in Houston that he would give $150,000.00 to get out from under the indictment and Emil Hurja, who lived in the same fraternity house that I did in school, told me that Clint Murchison had paid him $50,000.00 as a donation to the democratic campaign fund. I have recently learned that Frank Foster, who also was indicted in this same case, wrote a letter to Jim Lewis, the Chief Federal Investigator on that case, and stated that he had paid $25,000.00 into the democratic campaign fund and that he was a good democrat and that there was no use of trying to stick him…I know where to contact Jim Lewis, who investigated and prepared many of the important hot oil cases in Texas, and who knows as much or more than any one other individual about this case and many others, including the Freeman Burford case. You will recall that Drew Pearson has been after Burford and that General Summerville seems to be protecting him…
>
> P.S. Clint Murchison and Sid Richardson have been lifelong friends, and I believe that Sid arranged the meeting on Matagorda. Sid and Elliott and Charles Roeser (by far the best of the lot and really a high-class business man excepting his connecting with Elliott) were partners in the Texas Quality Network.[552]

---

[i] Letter on Hot Oil, Geologist H.P. Willis of Dallas to Pegler, ER box, Pegler/HH. Samuels was a prominent Fort Worth attorney. John T. Jones was Jesse Jones's brother.

One can easily appreciate Pegler's dilemma in receiving this letter and many like it. He could not go public with unprovable stories, yet he certainly could not get the federal authorities interested in pursuing the matter. However, the broad outline of this story checks out. The famed pollster Emil Hurja was executive director of the Democratic National Committee until 1936 and was widely known as Jim Farley's right hand man.[553]

Burford was a Dallas oil millionaire who was involved in a hot oil case that eventually landed Governor Leche of Louisiana in federal jail. General Somervell appointed Burford a U.S. Lieutenant Colonel. Drew Pearson's column on that particular snakepit of corruption ran on 17 April 1945.[554] Freeman Burford later worked for Sid Richardson.

Politics in America has always been "pay-to-play." Thus it was common practice for businessmen to make "preventive contributions" to the campaigns of powerful politicians, especially when they needed protection of a legal or legislative nature. Then as now, brazenness seems to be the real variable.

The more disturbing rumors associated with the Matagorda pact related to Elliott Roosevelt clearing a massive bribe for arranging the meeting. That, of course, is also unprovable; what is public record, however, is that the oil men financed Elliott's budding radio business and held the mortgage on his Fort Worth ranch. Their "investments" in Elliott appear to have approached half a million dollars during the prewar years, but the Texas contributors (those who controlled Elliott) did get their money back in the end.

Recently one sleuth did get to the crux of the matter. Bryan Burrough, writing as late as 2009, found that historians had overlooked what transpired after Elliott fell into the lap of the oiligarchs. It's ugly, so better let him explain:

> Seven months earlier, in Nov 1936, a federal grand jury had indicted one of Murchison's largest subsidiaries, the pipeline that took East Texas crude down to the ports around Houston, for running hot oil. Murchison himself escaped charges; neither of his biographers even mentions the episode. What Elliott Roosevelt's IRS interrogators suggested, and this was the story that leaked to columnist Westbrook Pegler in November 1945, was that a secret deal had been struck between Roosevelt, Richardson, and Murchison, apparently, the IRS believed, in a late-night meeting following the barbecue. The following week Murchison's subsidiary suddenly changed its plea from not guilty to no contest and paid a nominal fine of $17,500. The mainstream press didn't make the connection, but oil-industry periodicals did. *"Roosevelt's Hosts Company in Texas fined for Hot Oil Law Violations,"* read the National Petroleum News headline. Eight years later an IRS attorney pressed Elliott during a deposition whether he had interceded with the White House to go easy on not only Murchison but on Richardson and Charles Roeser, who the IRS suggested had been under investigation for hot oil violations.
>
> > IRS Attorney: There were rumors, and I don't know whether they are founded on fact, that Richardson and Roeser were both involved in the Hot Oil conspiracy and that you had interceded with the federal officials and a member of the Cabinet in charge of the Government oil lands, in their behalf.
> >
> > Elliott Roosevelt: I don't know anything about these rumors. I never knew that Mr. Richardson and Mr. Roeser were involved and I most emphatically state that I never interceded in their behalf with [anyone].
>
> The inference was that President Roosevelt had persuaded federal prosecutors to go easy on Murchison. If so, the IRS attorneys clearly believed, the favor had been returned by Sid Richardson. Richardson gave two depositions in Elliott's tax case. As he told the IRS,

> he developed a new appreciation for Elliott in the wake of the president's visit to Texas. "Up to the time I had an opportunity to visit with Elliott on the island," he said, "I thought that he was more or less wild in his ideas, and after I had a chance to visit with him there I changed my opinion and thought the boy had something that I hadn't even had a chance to see in him before, and I thought it was worthwhile."[555]

This was merely the beginning. There were numerous unpublished rumors in Texas suggesting that Elliott was not the passive tool he professed to be (at least afterwards), but an active extortionist who went after all the Texas oil men he could lay his hands on, promising White House audiences and favorable treatment in return for "investments." One informer from Houston noted that after Elliott appeared on the scene, "When people of Texas wanted something they called Richardson, not their congressmen or senators as they properly should."[556]

The "investments" had to do with Elliott's sudden but fleeting riches as a radio station magnate in the late 1930s. One of the Roosevelts' most dogged nemeses, Walter Trohan of the *Chicago Tribune*, also dug into the Bureau of Internal Revenue testimony and by November 1945, with FDR gone and Elliott's finances under investigation, was able to report:

> The new evidence on Elliott's financial operations shows that he secured loans and substantial investments in his radio venture after he presented Texas oil men to his father during the fishing trip on which he was a member of the Presidential party. Subsequently Elliott secured White House Invitations for the Texas oil men, Sid W. Richardson and Charles F. Roeser, who invested and lent almost $250,000 to help Elliott in Texas. At the White House the oil men advised the President on oil policy.[557]

Internal Revenue had an 800-page dossier on Elliott Roosevelt, but no action other than investigation was taken against him. Walter Trohan had also tracked FDR's and Elliott's movements in Texas, when the president was on his "fishing trip":

> At New Orleans, Mr. Roosevelt boarded the Presidential yacht Potomac, which was accompanied by three destroyers, the Moffett, Decatur, and Schenk. It was estimated that the fishing jaunt cost the American taxpayers $200,000 thru the operations of the naval craft and other expenses.
>
> On May 1, 1937, Elliott, who accompanied the President, went ashore at Port Aransas, where he met Richardson and J. C. Nelson, a friend of Richardson, according to the *Corpus Christi Caller-Times*. Elliott left Aransas with Richardson for an island named Matagorda, owned by Golding and Murchison, in the "Saltaire," an area off the Texas coast 50-75 miles northeast of Corpus Christi.
>
> On May 7, President Roosevelt left the Potomac to lunch with his son, the latter's wife at that time, now Mrs. Ruth G. Eidson, and their friend on Matagorda, at the clubhouse of the American Oil company, which was owned by Golding and Murchison.
>
> ...On May 11, 1937, the Corpus Christi paper reported that the Channel Transportation and Marketing Company of Houston paid a $17,500 fine on a charge of transporting petroleum products in interstate commerce in violation of federal law. The *National Petroleum News* on May 19, 1937, headlined the fine as "Roosevelt's hosts' company in Texas fined for 'hot oil' law violations."[558]

Cruelly interrogated by the Treasury Department after his father's death, Elliott said there were about sixty guests at his home in Fort Worth the night in 1937 when his father visited. Messrs. Richardson and Roeser were among them. The Treasury auditors wanted, almost desperately, to ascertain if the oil men were ever in private with President Roosevelt. Elliott stubbornly denied it. But the real meeting took place on the island the previous day, so Elliott was in the clear.[559]

At any rate that meeting was only the first; for example, in the period 1939-41 Charles Roeser visited the White House at least five times. The last visit on the Sunday after Pearl Harbor would be critical for Elliott's future.[560] And on the train trip to Washington, Sid Richardson made lasting friends with an accidental travel companion, Colonel Dwight D. Eisenhower, who already knew Elliott.[561]

There is no proof – nor should we expect to find any – that the President of the United States sat down with the oil sheikhs of Texas to strike a deal to settle the "hot oil" case, support each other henceforth, and, in the process, have the oil men take good care of the president's son.

Nonetheless, this was the beginning of a strategic alliance between the White House, Elliott, and the oiligarchs. From then on, the oil men had access to the president on demand. The coalition would continue over the decades, involving Lyndon B. Johnson and large parts of the Democratic Party. Mutating to the Republicans in the 1970s, the Texas oil pact encompassed the era of the two Bushes.

The term "hot oil" probably leaves people puzzled today. In the 1930s, the concept was deeply controversial. There was a glut of oil because of the Depression and many new petroleum discoveries, leading to a government attempt to prop up oil prices by limiting production. This was an aspect of New Deal "corporatism" – a sort of Mussolini-inspired marriage of government and industry that naturally created a hell of corruption and drove to despair those few free-traders that remained. In this case, the "hot oil" was contraband production that almost inevitably seeped into the marketplace through dark and subterranean channels. It is no wonder that Elliott Roosevelt's oil friends were mixed up with it – or that they had few compunctions about it.

The *Chicago Tribune* went on to detail the settlement of the "hot oil" criminal case following the meeting with FDR. If there was an illegal influence-peddling cabal at work here – and the circumstantial evidence points unwaveringly there – then it began paying off for Elliott after the president's visit. It is blatantly obvious that the Dallas-Fort Worth *nomenklatura* nurtured the relationship between big oil and the Roosevelt administration from the day of Elliott's first visit in March 1933.

FBI documents prove that the Department of Justice was looking into Elliott's involvement with the "hot oil" cases from 1933 to 1939. Nothing happened in the matter until the case was resurrected in October 1945, when FDR was dead and Elliott's troubles attracted renewed media attention. The record shows that the FBI looked for its old material to forward to the Department of Justice, but no hot oil reports were in the material released under the FOIA.[562]

For the Treasury Department investigators, the clincher was the radio network that Elliott created at about the same time as FDR's Texas "vacation." They drilled Elliott repeatedly on whether President Roosevelt had told him to create the regional Texas State Network, using funding from the oil men. Elliott denied this explicitly, but he did say that the president's visit led to his decision. He said that after inviting his father to broadcast a speech on Elliott's own few stations, he was markedly encouraged:

> After the speech we got such a fine reaction from all over the State from all of the smaller stations, which had never before been able to broadcast any of the speeches of the president due to the fact that they were small stations operating in small communities and

> had never been able to make a connection with the major net works, that I conceived the idea from that broadcast that it might be possible to organize a regional net work to serve all of the smaller communities in the State of Texas and give them the same service that was made available on a national scale to the very large stations.[563]

The result was the creation of the Texas State Network, incorporated 8 August 1938. Elliott said it was his idea, but the oil men's money, and that he advised his father of his plans in "considerable detail." Sid Richardson's drills had recently hit the Keystone Field, which founded one of history's biggest fortunes. He could afford to indulge Elliott.

Walter Trohan, the *Tribune's* Roosevelt-hunter, offered the following narrative:

> Shortly after the fishing trip, according to Richardson's testimony in the internal revenue investigation of Elliott's operations, Richardson lent Elliott $20,000. This sum went toward the purchase of Elliott's first radio station KFJZ at Fort Worth Sept. 7, 1937, for $57,500. Subsequently Richardson lent another $15,000 to Elliott for radio operations and $5,000 for personal expenses.
>
> Richardson received stock in Elliott's chain in settlement in 1944 for these "poor boy" loans, as he designated them to federal investigators. This stock was valued below the amount of the loans. Richardson also purchased $25,000 of stock in the radio chain on two occasions.
>
> Roeser purchased $125,000 of the stock in 1938 and $25,000 in 1939. The stock now [1945] is earning money and is valued above the purchase price. At Fort Worth last Sept 12, Richardson told internal revenue investigators how White House invitations followed his financial contacts with Elliott. Roeser told a similar story to investigators Sept. 5.
>
> "The first time I was invited to the White House was some months after I made Elliott the loan to buy the radio station with," Richardson said under oath. He explained that he opposed a certain phase of the President's oil policy and Elliott "asked me if I didn't think it was a good idea for me to go up there and discuss it with his father."
>
> "My answer was that I might try to help him [Elliott] on the radio business if he got into trouble but I damn sure was not going up there to tell the President how to run the United States. Then, he asked me would I go if his father sent for me and my answer to this was that any time the President of the United States sent for me I would be glad to go.
>
> "About two weeks after this conversation I was in New York, as well as I remember, and Mr. Elliott Roosevelt called me from Washington and said his father wanted to talk to me and would I be good enough to come to Washington and have lunch with him and his mother on a given date and have a visit and discuss this oil business with his father, which I did.
>
> "Later on I was invited to the White House several times when I was in Washington, but always the invitation came thru Elliott except for the last visit that I had with the President, and that was on the Sunday after Pearl Harbor."[564]

The timing of that last meeting will become extremely interesting later. It was not held for purposes of abstract conversation.[565]

These maneuvers didn't become public knowledge until after FDR's death in 1945, but they were clearly widely known by insiders from 1937 on. They illustrate the difficulty of clearly separating politics from corrupt conduct.

Bryan Burrough's recent work investigating Texas oil money and its political tentacles is important in understanding Democratic politics from FDR to LBJ. Burrough, writing in 2009, based his work on the forgotten accusations of 1945, and additionally discovered the following:

> Two weeks after the president's visit, Richardson lunched with Elliott and listened as he sang the praises of several Texas radio stations he would love to buy – i.e. if he had the money. "He told me one of them was a wonderful buy, not trying to sell me on it, but merely discussing the situation," Richardson said. "[So] a few days after that I called [Elliott] myself and suggested to him that I loan the money and to see if he could buy the station."
>
> ...In July 1938, a year after President Roosevelt's visit, Richardson loaned Elliott $25,000, which Elliott used to buy a Fort Worth station, KFJZ. Several months later came two more loans, totaling $15,000, which Elliott used to buy additional radio stations that soon formed his own network, the Texas State Network. Richardson became a major shareholder in Elliott's business.
>
> Whether or not Richardson's dealings with Elliott Roosevelt had anything to do with Murchison's indictment, the relationship gave Richardson immediate entry to the White House. Just two weeks after agreeing to invest in Elliott's radio network, Richardson was invited to chat with the president in Washington. He used the occasion to complain about a proposal, backed by Treasury Secretary Robert [sic] Morgenthau, to eliminate the oil industry's all-important 27.5% depletion allowance, a tax loophole that allowed oilmen to write off nearly a third of costs associated with dry holes. "Mr. Richardson did ask me on several occasions whether there wasn't something I could do to stop Mr. Morgenthau from trying to ruin every individual oil operator in the country by eliminating the [allowance]," Elliott testified in 1945. "He was always complaining to me during the entire time of our acquaintance about that particular feature."[566]

Interestingly, that reference to Henry Morgenthau's fight against the oil depletion allowance was in the original testimony followed by Elliott's declaration that "If he knew Mr. Morgenthau like I knew him, he wouldn't ask me to go to him because he was the type of individual that such an approach, even on behalf of a friend, would be like waving a red flag in front of a bull."[567]

This matches other reports that Morgenthau was an unusually honest member of FDR's cabinet. He fought a constant rear-guard action against the Roosevelt boys' schemes. In May 1934, Elliott called him and asked that tobacco taxes be reduced; Reynolds Tobacco had put him up to it. That didn't go over well, but Morgenthau's battle against the oil tax loophole proved quixotic.[568]

The oil depletion allowance was an outrageous and unparalleled example of corporate welfare. As long as the Texas Cabal maintained its power in Washington, it was sacrosanct. Its real purpose was to give politicians ready access to the enormous fortunes pumped out of the ground in Texas.[569] The oil depletion allowance remained untouchable until the 1970s, when most Texas oil had been, well, depleted.

Burrough continued:

> Though neither man ever described their meetings, Richardson and the president got along well, for Richardson was invited to the White House several more times. Richardson characterized his advice to the president as a counterpoint to the opinions of major oil companies, whom Roosevelt did not trust. Whatever his counsel, the oil depletion allowance stayed put. Richardson didn't get everything he wanted, however. On the only occasion he mentioned Richardson publicly, in his 1975 book *A Rendezvous with Destiny,* Elliott recounted a 1940 trip Richardson made to the presidential retreat in Warm Springs, Ga. With war looming, the White House was poised to block oil shipments to Italy, one of Richardson's major customers. During a two-day visit, Richardson refused to stop

supplying Italy with oil. It did him no good. Not long after, shipments were indeed blocked. Years later Elliott made clear he felt Richardson had used him. "I became the tool of the oil lobby in Washington," Roosevelt wrote.[570]

There is no official record of this Italy-related meeting, which actually seems to refer to the controversy over the Abyssinian war in 1935. In November of that year, the administration, led by Ickes, urged oil exporters to stop selling to Italy. The new Texas friends ignored him, with reason, since that would have been an empty unilateral gesture.[571] Elliott Roosevelt wrote far more bluntly:

> Up-and-coming American producers such as Sid Richardson, Clint Murchison, and Charles Roesser would not agree to cut back on oil for Italy in any way. The market there was too tempting. This much I knew, because in the mid-1930's, after I left Los Angeles to return to Texas, I became the tool of the oil lobby in Washington.
>
> I introduced my three oilmen to Father and on one occasion arranged for Roesser and Richardson to spend two days at Warm Springs, conferring with him. I watched, not always on the sidelines, the industry's uninterrupted maneuvering to hold onto the fat oil depletion allowance…[572]

This is an unusual case of Elliottian self-insight, but it did come forty years late. To place it in perspective, it must be recalled that almost all the Roosevelt family members were more or less used in similar ways, and also that this was certainly not the only way the "Elliott Roosevelt tool" was deployed by various interests during his heyday.

The LBJ Connection

This was far from the full extent of the Texas connection. Elliott also made it clear that his string-pullers were major financial backers of the Democratic machine during the 1936 election, and they had influenced others in their circle to be equally generous:

> They were sending people out in farm states, cattle-raising areas, and oil-producing areas and were receiving uniformly encouraging reports. They had me pass on these reports to Father. To bolster his courage, each time they told me to pass on the news that their contributions were rolling in from all points of the Middlewest, Southwest, the Rocky Mountain states, and the Far West. Needless to say, these reports from me were looked forward to as an offset to otherwise gloomy predictions.[573]

But it wasn't just reports Elliott collected.

Politics is about money – you pay in a bit and hope to get plenty back. The Texas Cabal understood that better than most. A river of cash soon left the tributaries in the oil wells, joined up in the Democratic Party, and emptied itself in a gusher on favored candidates. Until the far more cunning operator Lyndon Johnson took over, Elliott served as a conduit for cash and checks from Texas to the Democratic National Committee.

Here we see a dropout in his early twenties already on the inside of a curious racket. The New Deal changed the rules and put a premium on political influence. It had always been helpful in business; but under the New Deal it could be a matter of survival. Access to the president was the big price; money was the essential lure and lubricant.

By the 1940 campaign, when Charlie Roeser asked Elliott for a method to get money to national candidates, Lyndon stepped in via Speaker Sam Rayburn and organized the cash flow. As biographer Robert Caro noted, "A new source of political money, potentially vast, had been tapped in America, and Lyndon Johnson had been put in charge of it." But it was not idealism that drove the donors. By now, the rules of the game were becoming clear.[574]

Elliott mentioned, in passing, that FDR set the Bureau of Internal Revenue (BIR, now IRS) on his enemies, specifically William Randolph Hearst and Moses Annenberg. He said: "My father may have been the originator of the concept of employing the IRS as a weapon of political retribution. Each of his successors followed his lead." Elliott probably didn't know that; he read it in books. But he wasn't upset.[575]

President Roosevelt also used the FBI in a Nixonian way, although apparently without much luck. At that time wiretapping was illegal and disreputable; but after FDR's discreet permission, Director J. Edgar Hoover never looked back. At Treasury, Henry Morgenthau protested bitterly, but had not jurisdiction of the FBI; and at the FCC, Chairman Lawrence Fly strenuously opposed the new methods. They were spitting into the wind. When the war came, rules hardly existed anymore.[i]

Westbrook Pegler noted that after he began going after the Roosevelts in his columns, he was audited every year, without result. Even more disturbingly, Eleanor Roosevelt set the FBI on Pegler, but the G-men too could find nothing objectionable.[ii]

In his much-celebrated abuses of power, Richard Nixon thus merely stood on the shoulders of giants. It seemed the brawniest of these was FDR. Curt Gentry needed an entire chapter in his biography of J. Edgar Hoover to catalog President Roosevelt's wire-tapping, secret recording, dirt-collecting and tax-hounding. Contrary to some expectations, along that sordid road J. Edgar and the president got along famously well. It turned out that FDR loved to hear secrets about the escapades of not only his enemies, but especially those of his own minions.[576]

The president also looked out for his friends, and people knew it. The political-business cabal that began with Elliott's Western escapade formed a part of the emerging Democratic power base in Texas, through which the president and Vice President John Nance Garner gained the trust of local powerbrokers. As early as March 1937, a young, gangly, but insanely ambitious, supernaturally energetic, and utterly unscrupulous teacher named Lyndon Johnson triumphantly claimed the support of Elliott Roosevelt during his successful run for a vacancy in the House of Representatives.[577]

Lyndon and the Roosevelts were already acquainted. The Texan schoolteacher had acquired a post in the National Youth Administration (NYA), which, its enemies thought, was a kind of incipient Roosevelt Youth. Eleanor Roosevelt was a strong advocate of the NYA, whose precursor, the American Youth Congress, was later revealed to be a Communist front. At any rate, the NYA was abolished in 1943 when young folks had more important things to do than serve in make-work projects.

The exact nature of the Elliott-Lyndon liaison deserves scrutiny. Robert Dallek, who chronicled Lyndon Johnson's rise to power, heard that Elliott sold his

---

[i] Morgan, 554-560, contrasts the persecution of Annenberg with the spiked investigation of LBJ's election. However, Moe was with the Chicago Mob and, according to Henry Morgenthau, deserved what he got.

[ii] OHI with ER on Eleanor, 35-6, FDR Lib; Pegler column, 24 AUG 54, in Sarasota Herald Tribune discusses tax targeting in detail; James Roosevelt also confirms tax story in My Parents, 190.

endorsement for $5,000, and that LBJ wasn't the only candidate Elliott tried to shake down:

> Subsequently his opponents charged that Johnson carried his determination to win beyond the limits of legality. Johnson campaign workers persuaded federal officials to let Lyndon hand out parity checks to farmers, which, as Emmett Shelton said, "was of course illegal." Moreover, Polk Shelton believed that the Johnson campaign paid Elliott Roosevelt $5,000 to endorse Lyndon. According to Shelton, a man he never saw again approached him during the campaign with an offer to have Elliott Roosevelt endorse him for that sum of money. Shelton said that he declined the offer but he heard later that the man "approached one other candidate who was running for Congress." Since Elliott Roosevelt endorsed Johnson, the implication of Shelton's statement is clear.[i]

Polk Shelton was Lyndon's main opponent out of seven other Democrats. There were no Republicans. The *Dallas News* mused that "neither the state nor the national Democratic administrations took a hand in the campaign. Governor James V. Allred said several times he had no official preference." Elliott was apparently the only nationally known Democrat who urged the election of Johnson.

What Shelton actually said in the oral history interview in 1968 is less clear evidence against Elliott. Shelton became a friend of Johnson after his defeat and had nothing but good to say about him. Either he did not wish to implicate him, or he did not think Johnson paid the bribe:

> During the campaign for Congress, Mr. Shelton, what was the most unusual thing that happened to you?
>
> Shelton: I was in Brenham one night, made a speech down there, and a man came to my room at the hotel and told me that he could have Elliott Roosevelt endorse me if I was willing to pay $5,000. I told him that I wouldn't give $5,000 to any endorsement and I didn't have the money to start with, and that no Roosevelt would endorse me because of my feeling toward the Supreme Court which is set out in my platform [Shelton opposed the court-packing plan]. The last time I saw him was when I told him that I wasn't interested.
>
> Was this a reputable person?
>
> Shelton: I never saw him before and I haven't seen him since. I couldn't vouch for his veracity or anything else.
>
> Do you think he took the same offer to the other candidates?
>
> Shelton: I've been advised that he approached one other candidate who was running for Congress.[578]

That might get us to 90% certainty, but it clearly falls short of a proof. Incidentally, parity payments were a typical new federal subsidy to farmers for not growing crops.

Naturally, Elliott Roosevelt's recollection was quite different. He wrote about the Johnson endorsement at length a few years before he died, in the book in which he called Johnson a crazy lying criminal. Forty-five years of aging seemed only to have burnished Elliott's memory to a fine, verbatim shine:

> One of those who joined the presidential party [train] at San Antonio was a very eager and very young man by the name of Lyndon Johnson. Apparently Johnson was running in

---

[i] Dallek: Lone Star Rising, 153. Caro does not mention a bribe, though he's clear that LBJ, hardly a man of means, had much more campaign money than his rivals.

> a special election to fill a vacated congressional seat in that district, and ardently wanted Father's endorsement.
>
> I was able to arrange a meeting between Johnson and my father, and even then the young man was outspoken and brash. "Mr. President," he said, "I'll be the best man you ever had in Washington, if you choose to help me. Now, if you could just stand with me out on the observation platform of the train as we go through my district, it would help me ever so much. Just stand out there with your arm around my shoulders, and I'll wave as we go through the towns. You can get the engineer to go through these little towns real slow so that the people will have a chance to see us together. Just between San Antonio and Austin, you understand!" [579]

Unfortunately, the president was unable to do that. He had to sit down, but he agreed to wave and point at Lyndon.

Johnson was elected with a plurality of the primary vote. He had glued himself solidly to FDR's policies, even the plan to pack the Supreme Court with New Deal partisans.[580] In Congress, LBJ unerringly toadied for the most powerful men he could find, headed by the president. One of his own disciples was his young aide John Connally. Elliott Roosevelt and Connally would help each other out many years later.

From 1937 on, the Roosevelts and Lyndon Johnson were tight friends. Elliott Roosevelt would go all the way with LBJ, campaigning for him in 1964, but by then the accidental president did not want to be publicly associated with Elliott. His name was no longer worth a hefty bribe. Maybe that helps explain why Elliott turned on Johnson in his memoirs.

Johnson was a political genius whose scheming skills exceeded even those of his protector and "political father." President Roosevelt let it be known that Lyndon was his boy. He assigned Tommy "the Cork" Corcoran, a political cardsharp who was one of FDR's closest advisers in the late 1930s, to look after LBJ and see to it that he got what he wanted in return for his absolute loyalty. Thereafter, in Texas, the friends, relatives, supporters and acquaintances of LBJ grew rich fast.

To use Corcoran's term, with true "operators" like FDR and LBJ, one enters a parallel universe where classical notions of integrity and accountability become meaningless; they are replaced with relativistic measures of relentless manipulation and elastic connectedness. Corcoran himself was a prime example. He was soon recognized as a political gangster; Vice President Garner, who could turn a phrase, said that if he was going to rob a bank, he'd want Corcoran with him.[581]

This was not why he was removed from the inner circle in 1939-40. As an Irish Catholic, he hated the British and the Soviet Union, an increasingly awkward position to espouse by then.[582] But even from outside the White House he exercised vast influence.

Corcoran's total control of the FCC would be very useful for Lyndon B. Johnson.

Like most of his brothers, Elliott Roosevelt aspired mightily to the influence game, but every time he was invited to the table, the pros cleaned his clock. He was always a wannabe among true sharks.[i]

Thus it was that after FDR died, most of the Texas bigshots, notably the oiligarchs, summarily discarded Elliott as no longer useful. But they doubled up on their investments in Lyndon B. Johnson. Friends Sid Richardson, Charlie Roeser, and many others gave large piles of cash to LBJ.[583] Still, in 1940, Lyndon was savvy enough to

[i] Dallek (and Caro) provides a striking portrait of LBJ's political maneuvering throughout. "Operator" was Corcoran's term; he immediately recognized Lyndon's nature.

turn down a potentially lucrative partnership with Sid. He said, "it would kill me politically."[584] The unofficial partnership continued and strengthened until Sid's death in 1959.

Instead, LBJ proved himself valuable by redistributing the contributions he solicited from the newly rich in Texas. He had assumed a post with the Democratic Congressional Campaign Committee and used it to allocate the moneys to congressmen in need. He was already farming politicians.

Radio Mogul

During the remainder of 1935, Elliott Roosevelt concentrated on getting a foothold in another new and rapidly advancing technology: broadcasting, or "wireless" radio. He started as a shill for William Randolph Hearst, but by 1937-38, his oil men friends had helped him purchase a chain of stations of his own. As we have seen, the crucial FDR visit to Texas in 1937 cemented the oiligarchs' alliance with the New Deal administration. As the go-between, Elliott profited handsomely from his connections – at first.

There are striking parallels between the rise of aviation and radio. Both were rapidly developing technologies of a transformative nature. Both were subjected to pervasive federal rather than state regulation during the 1920s and 1930s. Both got caught up in the New Deal, whereby central planning became the governing paradigm. Finally, because of these political and ideological trends, both aviation and radio enterprises placed a high premium on political connections, influence, and horse-trading of dubious ethicality.

It is a common mistake to think that this all started with Franklin D. Roosevelt. In truth, the "New Deal" began under Herbert Hoover, the Progressive Republican, to use the vocabulary of that time. (Hoover referred to his program as the "New Day.") He was an extremely effective and activist administrator when he was Secretary of Commerce in the 1920s, and it was under him that aviation and broadcasting came seriously under the federal regulatory domain. In these as in many other matters, Roosevelt essentially continued Hoover's policies. But he certainly did change the direction of the "spin."

As early as September 1935, Elliott Roosevelt had been helped into the radio business by his Fort Worth connections. C.R. Smith's original boss, the utility mogul A.P. Barrett, hired Elliott into the radio business. Barrett owned five stations and was affiliated with eight more. The kid – he was now 25 – was made vice president in charge of sales.[585]

In early March 1936, Elliott took out options before the Federal Communications Commission on three of the Southwest Broadcasting Company's stations. They were KOMA in Oklahoma City, WACO in Waco, and KTAT in Fort Worth. At the same time, Hearst Radio applied for the stations in San Antonio and Austin (KTHA and KNOW).[586]

By 10 March 1936, Hearst bought four of the five stations and made Elliott vice president, reportedly at $20,000 a year. It was later revealed that Elliott got a commission of $30,000 from Barrett for making the sale. A slightly different fate awaited the fifth station, KTAT Fort Worth.[587]

Raymond Buck, the Democratic insider and attorney, had been instrumental in defending Elliott during his fight with the Young Democrats. Now Buck was evidently designated to buy KTAT for Elliott, because Elliott's ownership would not be approved. Buck had acted as attorney for Barrett in the sale to Hearst.[588]

In the new regulatory environment, these transactions all required approval by the Federal Communications Commission, which was given on 5 May.[589]

It is essentially pointless to debate whether the radio transactions, KTAT in particular, were illegal as it was then rumored. These insiders knew how far they could go. The point is that the radio trades were machinations of the Democratic Party machine in Texas, aided and permitted by President Roosevelt's new agency, the FCC. As we shall see later in the matter of WMCA in New York, honest entrepreneurs deficient in connections were basically shark-bait in this sport.

Who used whom is another unproductive question in such finely tuned crony capitalism. Obviously, the Texas Cabal was using Elliott, but Elliott got his bundles of cash out of the game. Likewise, he was only one cog in the machinery; Lyndon Johnson, Jesse Jones, A.P. Barrett, Amon Carter and the Texas oiligarchs were all involved in running and trading radio stations.

It seems that William Randolph Hearst, an outsider, was at a disadvantage in this Texas game. Clearly, Hearst was using Elliott to get his radio-empire-building through the FCC. But in the long run – about five years – the out-of-staters were left holding the bag, and the Texas Cabal made the money.

Hearst had other Roosevelts: Anna and John Boettiger. They were running the *Seattle Post-Intelligencer*, and they soon plotted expansion plans with Elliott. On 8 February 1937, Elliott wrote to John Boettiger in Seattle:

> I believe the Boss is planning to return to San Simeon very shortly, and I think it would be an excellent idea if you would suggest to him that we should both be called there "for a conference," and that our wives should be there also in order to decide whether we should have a radio station in Seattle or not. I don't know whether Mr. White has told you or not, but he has given me a roving commission in which I dash around all over the United States looking for ways and means of building up Hearst Radio, Inc. to be the outstanding radio organization in the world.[590]

Elliott thought he was close to Mr. Hearst. He said, "I saw a great deal of Mr. Hearst" during the period 1933 through 1938. He said that Hearst "very definitely" dictated the editorial line of the radio stations, which became increasingly anti-Roosevelt. Elliott maintained that he did a good job for Hearst:

> I was hired first of all to run those stations. They were having difficulties in their other operations principally on the West Coast and New York City. I was then given general supervision of all of their operations and during the period that I was with their organization I brought their overall radio operations from a net loss to a net profit.[591]

Nonetheless, the Hearst empire was going downhill fast. Elliott and Hearst would have a falling-out in due course, but from 1935 to 1937 it seemed that things were going good for Elliott. This apparent success led him to risk more, and to think he could operate better on his own.

Perhaps it was Elliott's fast profits dealing radio stations that alarmed the Bureau of Internal Revenue. At any rate, he telephoned the White House in a panic on or about 1 May 1936. McIntyre, the secretary, told the president:

> Elliott says the Bureau of Internal Revenue moved in on them, demanding check for $45,000, which was given with the agreement that the check would be held until Monday and if funds were not then available, the government, would, of course, take over. Elliott wants to know the possibility of the Treasury Dept. here could arrange with the Dallas B.I.R. to extend that "concession" over Monday until they could find out what can be done by the commission here. Elliott wants you to phone him immediately after the reception. He is standing by at [number].[592]

McIntyre said the president would call Elliott. Although this tax problem came just after his lucrative deal with Hearst, there is no other evidence of a financial crisis then; whether FDR ordered the Revenue Bureau off his back or found some other way to save his hide is not clear. But the incident surely illustrates how useful it is to be able to call the president for help in a tax audit.

Ruth and Elliott should have been wealthy, but, pitifully, next spring Eleanor promised to send them a little check once she was done with her taxes, to "make the trip to Franklin Jr.'s wedding easier."[593]

Another fellow who had heard bad things was Interior Secretary Ickes. In early July 1936, he wrote in his secret diary that Jim Farley told him that Elliott and Amon Carter had come to him to try to get him to use his influence to get a certain wave length for "interests that either were Hearst interests or closely allied therewith."

> Elliott told him that there would be a commission of $40,000 in it for himself. Farley refused to have a thing to do with it and said that he not only wouldn't help but that he was opposed to the proposition. He told Elliott to go to Steve Early and have Steve put it up to his father.[594]

At that time, Ickes was planning to lash out at Hearst, but he also committed to his diary how much he loathed Elliott. Commenting on the Fokker scandal, he noted:

> Personally, I haven't any use for Elliott ... I would not put it beyond him to capitalize on his father's position for his own personal advantage. They say that James Roosevelt does the same thing in Massachusetts in his insurance business. Jim Farley intimated to me on our trip into Virginia over July 4th that both of these boys skated on very thin ice.[595]

From 1936 to 1940, Elliott stayed in the news, and not only because of the aviation scandals that broke in October 1936. Elliott made sure of it, for by 1938 he was a nationally broadcast radio commentator, whose regular radio column was monitored carefully for indications of what FDR might be up to, or conversely, whether a rift had opened between him and his son. The latter was more often true.

In the summer of 1937, Elliott and Ruth bought the small stations KFJZ in Fort Worth and KABC in San Antonio, and continued to run the now four Hearst stations. By October, he was president and general manager of Hearst Radio in the Southwest. Acting surreptitiously for Hearst, Elliott also formed a holding company called Frontier Broadcasting in order to assume control of more stations.[596]

On 1 January 1938 Hearst promoted him to vice-president of nationwide Hearst Radio, Inc. Elliott now spoke for Hearst on all his ten radio stations, not merely the ones owned by Elliott and his wife. By August of that year, Elliott had also created the Texas State Network, comprised of widely scattered Texas stations. In an opaque maneuver, he tried to control the municipally owned Dallas station WRR; reportedly, Elliott had made secret attempts to buy the station, but this failed, and he instead was at first allowed to attach the station to his network.[i]

Publicly owned WRR dated to 1925 and became a bitterly fought prize that, through intervention by the courts, eventually eluded Elliott. But by then, his empire controlled 23 stations; although, to be sure, the oil men with the money in turn controlled Elliott.

The network was the first and the largest of its kind in the United States. [ii]

TSN was a separate entity from Elliott's next, nationwide network project. It was affiliated with the Mutual Broadcasting System. Using the Mutual Network, Elliott was now able to offer a regular nationwide commentary on current events.[597] In truth, there was much less to the radio empire than one might think. A reporter noted: "In Elliott's financial deals the collateral was largely TSN stock, the assets of which consisted solely of Elliott's agreement with 23 radio stations to furnish programs, sell advertising, and, in the case of five stations, to act as manager."[598]

It should be obvious that the advertisers held this network by the short hairs. If it lost the confidence of major advertisers, it would collapse instantly. That was where Papa in the White House came in handy.

Adding an extraordinarily lucrative radio commentary contract with Emerson Radio, netting "in the neighborhood of $1,500 a week," Elliott was rolling in dough at the nadir of the Depression:

> I was on three times a week. In addition, I drew some money for lectures in various parts of the country, part of which was under the sponsorship of an organization known as "Town Hall," and the average of these lectures ran between $500 to $1,000 per lecture.[599]

When his nationwide network went bankrupt in 1940, Elliott was making $76,000 a year. He testified to the FCC that TSN lost $100,000 in the first three months of operation, beginning on 25 September 1938. Much more was lost before the card-house tumbled. Everything ran on borrowed money, and by doubling up on debt.[600]

Radio's role was special before television became common in the 1950s. There was a lot of quality programming because there was no other way of instantly addressing the country. Nearly the entire nation (that had electricity) tuned in for specific programs, and the politically active tuned to radio stations catering to their views. President Roosevelt's famous "fireside chats" are a prime example. Elliott enabled his father to make some of these broadcasts from the radio studio he had built on to his ranch house in Texas.

---

[i] DallasMN, 17 MAR 39, 21 MAR 39, and consistent DallasMN coverage. U.S. commercial broadcasting began in 1920. The 3-letter call signs preceded 4-letter call signs.

[ii] NYT, 18 AUG 38; DallasMN, 11 AUG 38, 17 AUG 38. The 23 were KTAT, KFJZ, WRR, WACO, KTEM Tempe, KNOW Austin, KABC San Antonio, KXYZ Houston, KRIS Corpus Christi, KRVG Weslaco, KLUF Galveston, KGNC Amarillo, KFYO Lubbock, KBST Big Spring, KGKL San Angelo, KRBC Abilene, KRRV Denison, KCMC Texarkana, KFRO Longview, KAND Corsicana, KPLT Paris, KGKB Tyler, and a Beaumont station. TSN opened 15 SEP 38 and is still in operation.

It was logical for W.R. Hearst and his strawmen to reach for national influence and profits through the airwaves. After 1936, Hearst was a sworn enemy of Franklin Roosevelt, so this left his relationship with the president's son a curiosity to all.

People were not fooled by Elliott Roosevelt's insistence that he was acting entirely on his own. His relentless nemesis, the syndicated columnist Westbrook Pegler, noted in a diatribe in 1940:

> It is conceded that Elliott Roosevelt participated in negotiations before the [FCC] which yielded him a profit of extraordinary size for a boy of his years at the time, and it has since been said by his own representative that he has been earning an income of $1,000 a week as a broadcaster…
>
> [Vice President] John N. Garner stated the correct position when early in the first term of the New Deal, in rejecting an offer of $1,500 a week for radio work he said that if the sponsor was trying to hire the Vice-President of the United States the price was too little, and if he was trying to hire John Garner, it was too much…[601]

Another indefatigable pit bull, John T. Flynn, wrote a contemporary exposé of how Elliott got his foothold in radio in his book *Country Squire in the White House*. He charged:

> …William Randolph Hearst wanted to have four radio station franchises transferred to him in Texas at a time when he was lambasting the President. He had to get permission of the Communications Commission, appointed by the President. He employed Elliott to get these transfers. Elliott handled the job – and with great success. He was later made general manager of the whole Hearst chain at $25,000 a year.[602]

This was the least of Elliott's remuneration. When he had his wife apply to purchase a station in 1937, she listed as security assets over $89,500, a large ranch, and noted that her husband's income exceeded $20,000.[603] As his radio network went nationwide, a tooth-powder company paid him $1,000 a week for "weekly comment programs."[604]

In Elliott's convoluted financial affairs it is often of critical importance to note the timing of events carefully. Early in 1939, while he was desperate to get funding for his new network, he was still nominally working for Hearst, but Hearst was also struggling financially and trying to get out of radio. Yet at the same time Elliott finally exercised an option to buy KTAT from Raymond Buck for a little over $100,000. That money appears to have come from the later so infamous Hartford loan. The *Chicago Tribune* wrote later that Elliott junked KTAT and transferred its 1,000 watt license to his own KFJZ, a puny 500-watter. Later he received federal permission to upgrade that station to 5,000 watt and made it the keystone of his network.[605]

It was a very odd arrangement indeed. It evidently started a lot of rumors in Texas.

Hearst could not contain Elliott's boundless ambition. In the fall of 1938, the increasingly besieged Hearst network began divesting itself of many stations, and Elliott's Fort Worth-based TSN obtained some of them. On 14 April 1939, Elliott resigned his position in the Hearst System, then down to four radio stations. At the same time he was trying to go nationwide, but on his own terms. His dream was to create a radio network to rival CBS, Mutual, and NBC.[606]

Behind the Scenes of the Radio Racket

All these convoluted transactions had to be approved by the FCC, the Roosevelt-designated overseer of the "public airwaves." In the division of the spoils, a tug-of-war between bureaucratic and business interests inevitably ensued.

The FCC was (and remains) one of the New Deal alphabet soup agencies, created in 1934 to ensure "fairness" on the air. The agency was immediately suspected of being a Rooseveltian patronage racket, and the award of station licenses was subject to political taint or to the ceaseless suspicion thereof. In Elliott's case, hostile politicians demanded an investigation. The congressional majority prevented it.

Already in June 1937, a commentator noted:

> An investigation of radio undoubtedly would run, sooner or later, into what, if anything, went on behind the scenes when Elliott Roosevelt, on behalf of W.R. Hearst, obtained the commission's approval, without a hearing, of the purchase of four Texas radio stations. Two were approved in the spring of 1936 and application for sale of the other two was set for hearing, presumably in the fall, but the commission suddenly called off the hearing and granted approval in August...Elliott Roosevelt was vice president of the Southwest Broadcasting System, of which A.P. Barrett was principal owner. He conducted negotiations for sale of four of the five stations in the system to Mr. Hearst and afterward became vice president of Hearst Radio, Inc. with headquarters at Fort Worth. He is reported to have received a handsome fee for arranging the sale. He was in Washington while the applications were before the FCC.[607]

It might all have been legal, perhaps even perfectly above-board. But to the public, it stank. It stank so much that Rep. Roy Woodruff of Michigan offered the following tart analysis to the House in 1940, after Elliott Roosevelt had been made a captain while lamenting that he was sacrificing an income of $76,000:

> It is because he is the son of the President, and not because he is himself, that he could get $1,000 a week for broadcasting for a tooth-paste advertising program. He got that $1,000 a week by capitalizing commercially on the Presidency of the United States. And there was a time when that sort of thing was looked down on by the people of this country.
>
> But Elliott also got, according to his manager, $20,000 a year salary as president of his broadcasting corporation. And how did he get into the broadcasting business? He was a very young man, indeed, then – scarcely 25 – and with literally no experience or talent to sell to an employer beyond that of other young men who work for $60 a week and consider themselves fortunate.
>
> Well, there were four radio stations in Texas. They belonged to an old oil man [Barrett] who had made a good deal of money out of them. A large-scale publisher [Hearst] wanted to buy those stations. But no one can buy a radio station without the permission of the FCC. The Commission was and is appointed by Franklin D. Roosevelt, President of the United States. The man who wanted to buy these stations was one of those publishers who was an ardent critic of the President and pretty well settled in the dog house so far as the White House was concerned.
>
> In those days the man who wanted to get a radio license transferred was well advised to be represented before the Commission by some lawyer who had the proper pull, or by some person who was on the inside. Well, who was more on the inside than the President's 25-year old son? And so this great publisher hired Elliott to represent him as his agent before the Commission, and Elliott had three of the licenses transferred to his employer by the Commission his father appointed.[608]

By the nature of things it is impossible to prove that the FCC illegally favored the son of the president. To arrive at some probability, one has to sample the opinions of successful FCC applicants. In Texas, those were essentially a roster of the "Cabal" – Jones, Carter, Johnson, Buck, Roeser, Richardson, Connally. There is little doubt where they stood on the issue. They obviously used Elliott because it worked.

Such was the stench around FCC license approvals in general that Congress repeatedly investigated the Commission. Some of the more spectacular cases occurred a bit later, and we shall not neglect them. But even in the 1930s, with a solid Democratic majority, there were constant cries for congressional intervention. Interestingly, one of the cries came from Mr. Elliott Roosevelt, who as usual couldn't keep his opinions to himself, and thus took the opportunity to berate the Commission for various practices destructive of good business – such as the impossibly short six-month station license.

But he could get away it. With the FCC sword of Damocles over them, others dared not speak up.

Today, there are some devious and obscure ways to get an even closer view of what went on behind the scenes. An anonymous informer, clearly from the *sanctum sanctorum* of the Texas Cabal, wrote Westbrook Pegler in 1948. The man had finally decided to play "Deep Throat" to the relentless columnist. The letter was an extraordinarily important summary of the Texas radio racket, and it is worthwhile to keep it in mind as we uncover some of Elliott's other adventures.

The writer's contention was that Elliott was merely used as a tool by the Texas tycoons, who made sure to come out ahead:

> During the last ten years you have made me twist and turn when you should be so near to the facts about the "dealings" of Elliott Roosevelt that I am at last going to give in to the force that makes everyone help set the record straight.
>
> When Elliott came (went) to Ft. Worth, it was to see what he could do for the old S.W. Network, but the pickings looked too poor for him. He had the favor of Amon G. Carter, and only because of that sponsorship, he met quite a few Texans of good character and brains as well as means. His brief efforts brought in Ruth Googins, who is and was a fine person.
>
> Thereafter, Elliott needed to sink his teeth into some part of Texas with an angle that would "produce" when father Roosevelt pushed the button. Radio! That he knew. Carter had a pending application before the FCC to move KGKO from Wichita Falls, Texas to Ft. Worth but two stations had protested and Carter had to buy them to defeat the protests. He had Raymond Buck (atty) to buy KTAT from Rev. J. Frank Norris and Elliott bought KFJZ from others. Ruth put $60,000 of her money into it. Things started slow but Elliott had the "old man's" ideas and went to work. He must have a ranch to bring Pa and the neo-rich to gather and swing the old hatchet. That's where they both made a mistake. They played Texans to be as stupid as the Hudson Valley folk.
>
> Sid Richardson and Clint W. Murchison…were reared as friends in Athens, Texas and remained close friends. Both had quite a large fortune and thought they needed New Deal protection from the amature Commies [sic] in power so were natural targets for Elliott. He produced tax benefits and got loan enough to expand KFJS (250W from 100W) and buy the ranch at Benbrook where Papa had so many visits. Now these men were not in business together, but visited quite a bit. They put out the cash, but took a mortgage on the land and stock in KFJZ Inc. (they now own both.)
>
> Papa had his FCC grant an increase to the radio and Elliott started the Texas State Network on Sid and Clint money. They were generous, but took a mortgage on land and

owned one half of the stock. The FCC was majic [sic] in making stations give Elliott a contract to "operate" it for them until he gathered up all of the small stations in Texas and formed a working network. Carter had KTAT on his hands and Buck wanted to get out – so Sid and Clint put up $80,000 for him to buy it and move to Wichita Falls where the only station there would not deal with him. Elliott's appln. To move KTAT was so fraudulent that he had to forfeit KTAT to keep from having it revalled [sic]. Then KFJZ got its frequency and increased to 5000 watts.

Just as T. S. Network got into the black, Elliott saw larger and better things.

He had been able to get advertising where no other network could enter. He set out to build T.B.A. Transcontinental Broadcasting Asso. In New York he got assistance from all that needed other kinds of assistance and after about six months of hard work and enormous expenditures he found out that he had impoverished Tex. S. N. – destroyed his credit with Sid and Clint and was in a tight spot close to success. Then is when he put the finger on John Hartford. But – all of that money went fast (ask Jack Adams) [of TBN] and he went back to Ft. Worth defeated and busted. He called in all of his creditors and "gave up the ghost." All of us took notes of TSN for our debts. He transferred (in fraud of creditors) all of his and Ruth's stock in TSN to a trustee for his children and turned the network over to Jean Cagle, who has made a big fortune out of it for Sid & Clint and his children but nothing for Ruth. Then he left Ruth and you know the rest.

In the meeting in Ft. Worth, everyone called spades, and when Tilford Jones [nephew and successor of Jesse Jones] asked about the large sum owed to KXYZ and Uncle Jessie [Jones], as well as that owed John Hartford, he openly made a deal to dismiss his then pending application for 50,000 watts in Houston for Uncle Jessie's (KXYZ) promise to satisfy Hartford.

When discussion got around to "the St. Louis money" he said that it was taken care of. What he meant I do not know, but Budweiser did a lot of useless broadcasting in dry parts of Texas, and Grover Cleveland Bergdoll did get to go home [he was a brewery heir who had defected to Germany to escape charges for defying the WW I draft].

When Elliott started over, he undertook the Hudson River Folk ("our kind") because he never got any Texas money without giving up property protection or radio worth well more than he got.

Uncle Jessie got his 50,000 watts (KTRH) and also got protection against outsiders for a long time. Until FDR died. That was worth more than the Hartford note.

Thanks for your ear.[609]

This was an explosive insider letter that Pegler evidently could not reveal. If the term "Uncle Jessie" is to be taken literally, it may have been written by John Tilford Jones, the nephew who would eventually take over as *Houston Chronicle* publisher after Jesse Jones. That the source knew what was really going on is pretty obvious, although unverifiable.

The note clears up why Jesse Jones bailed out Elliott on the Hartford shakedown, which we shall look at in detail later. Jesse was acting far from selflessly. He apparently secured his Houston radio interests for as long as FDR was alive. The Texas Cabal had gotten its way with the administration and the FCC, and Elliott eventually got nothing. But he did stay out of jail and he did get his debts settled by Jones.

The reference to Amon Carter is also critical. Carter, publisher of the *Fort Worth Star-Telegram*, could pull strings all over Texas, and some of them were Elliott's. That would turn out to be useful even during the war, as we shall see.

Finally, "the St. Louis money" is a new issue; evidently the breweries there had also been working with Elliott for favors. The reference dovetails with a tip Pegler received from Texas state senator Joe L. Hill:

> President Roosevelt at one time called Adolphus Busch [probably meaning A.B. III, owner of the Anheuser-Busch brewery empire in St. Louis] and said that they owned him quite a lot for he was instrumental in getting the repeal of the 18th Amendment and so he thought they should take some advertising from Elliott.[610]

The "St. Louis money" also figures in Elliott Roosevelt's grueling 1945 testimony to the Bureau of Internal Revenue; unfortunately he could not remember any names.[611]

One name he couldn't remember might have been Gerald Stanley's:

> A St. Louis New Deal paper had to take a nibble at the developing story of Elliott's operations the other day and reported that Gerald P. Stanley... the son of a rich cigar manufacturer, invested $20,000 in Elliott's network and became a vice president and general manager. It added that this Gerald P. Stanley was now working in the men's wear department of a Chicago store and that he refused to talk.[612]

Other sources revealed that President Roosevelt had advertisers and contributors over for dinner at the White House and discussed with them (singly) how they might "help" Elliott. One of them was Hill Blackett, whose company was then the main purchaser of radio time in the United States.[613] Pegler followed up the story by talking to Blackett, who confirmed the account. Blackett dined with the Roosevelts on 11 October 1939, and said that the Roosevelts were "delicate" about approaching the issue, emphasizing how important their son's welfare was to them. Then they discussed advertising in general. Blackett said, "Like anyone else who wants business, they will entertain you. That's all I could see. After all, they knew I wasn't a tailor."[614]

Blackett not only was not a tailor, he signed up to be the chief advertising contractor for Elliott's ill-fated network in 1939. That was a firm contract for approximately $2.8 million of advertising, to go into effect on 1 January 1940.[615]

But as usual Elliott thought he was the one getting the shaft. Eleanor wrote home from Texas in July 1937 that her son was "dreadfully upset" because he was not getting his applications approved by the FCC in the swift manner he expected. Surely that was discrimination? Eleanor made an ill-advised plea to her husband to get on the FCC's case. She was foolish enough to commit her plea to paper, writing, "couldn't you or James say a word which wld. hurry them? You know Elliott's disposition, he is beginning to think you are both agin' him."[616]

There is no evidence the president acted on it; but there wouldn't be if he did. Elliott got his licenses.[i]

Enthusiastic as he was about everything, Elliott collared the American Society of Broadcasters and "not only wanted to be made a director, but he was boosting a friend for the place of czar." Since President Roosevelt and his wife were not home in Washington, Elliott decided to invite fifty broadcasters to be his guests at the White House. A writer recounted:

> Some of his best friends steered him away from that plan. They pointed out that there were 450 other broadcasters who could not be invited for reasons of space, and would therefore be sore, and that an untrammeled press would rip his innards out if he tried such a trick.[617]

---

[i] JR, Affectionately, 216: "To the best of my recollection, Father and I stayed out of this situation..."

This was a very typical Elliott approach. While in the Army, he would often invite his comrades-in-arms to the White House, or to the Hyde Park estate. For a laugh, he once issued invitations to a tea party at the White House and then left town. Apparently that wasn't funny to everyone.[618]

Practical jokes were in character: another time, after patient, suffering Eleanor had dutifully stood at the head of the reception line for more than an hour, shaking hands and exchanging pleasantries with strangers, Elliott gave a false name and joined the line of well-wishers, betting that his mother wouldn't recognize him. She did.[619]

In Texas, Elliott's antics were also the topic of much scuttlebutt. After the Hartford scandal broke, the *Chicago Tribune* sent a reporter, Guy Gentry, to gage local sentiment. Raymond Buck, the Democratic bigwig, agreed that Elliott was a "salesman of first rank" – but as a businessman, he stank. He said, "Elliott found out you can't practice New Deal spending methods unless you have the U.S. Treasury behind you."

In Fort Worth, Elliott's spending habits were legendary. The *Tribune* wrote:

> Elaborate offices were opened in Rockefeller Center in New York and in the Wrigley building in Chicago. Elliott hired so many vice-presidents that one of the jokes at the Fort Worth club at that time was that every stranger getting off a plane at Meacham Field was a new vice president. A beautiful studio building was constructed for KFJZ in Fort Worth.[620]

The inevitable reckoning would not be long in coming.

A Tightrope on the Air

Although Elliott Roosevelt was a quite adept debater and an effective and occasionally eloquent speaker, he was never accused of being an original thinker. In fact, his thinking seemed often to be a "bent pipe," a conduit from which consistently emerged second-hand thoughts. The question was to whom the first hand belonged.

As one observer said, "People would listen to the son of the President even if he had nothing to say, and Elliott has things to say. He may not be a deep thinker, but he knows on which side of his bread the butter spreads best. In Texas it spreads on the Texas side."[621]

> "I'm not a New Dealer, and I'm not an anti-New Dealer. But I do regard myself as the President's severest friendly critic. I'm looking at governmental affairs in the interest of business. ..It is true that government has all fingers of each hand in business. And that makes it imperative that business be active in government. I'm interested in helping guide government to make things better for business. If business generally improves, Texas will prosper. Then my personal business will be better.[622]

Thus spake Elliott Roosevelt over the Texas State Network in March 1939, when he championed his friend, Vice President John Nance Garner, as his father's replacement in 1940. The statement was a fair encapsulation of his mindset at that time in his life. From his TSN microphone, thrice weekly for fifteen minutes he blessed the nation, including the all-important Boston – Washington corridor, with his views on politics and whatever else caught his fancy.[623]

This enraged the New Dealers, Interior's Harold Ickes in particular, though Ickes was often in that condition. "Elliott Roosevelt is being insufferable again…he said that Garner was in the driver's seat for the Democratic nomination…I think he is little short of disloyal to his own father, and I cannot understand the President's tolerance. He is certainly working against his father's plans." Ickes and Hopkins wanted to "pin his ears back." But President Roosevelt had snapped back: "Leave him alone. They are my children."[624]

A couple of weeks later, on 15 April 1939, Ickes was fuming once more: "Elliott Roosevelt broke out in the press again on the national political situation on Tuesday, this time more offensively than at any time previously. He frankly criticized the New Deal and insisted that it had failed in certain important respects."[625] Ickes was not somebody you wanted for an enemy.

Elliott was definitely no mouthpiece for his father. On the contrary, he was more attuned to the conservative and exclusively Democratic Texas he now called home. Inevitably he would clash with the New Dealers back East.

Texas suited Elliott well. He began speaking with a drawl, to much family mockery; his loud, rowdy braggadocio increased.[626] The ten-gallon hat and the expensive cowboy boots completed the picture. He now spoke of "The War Between the States" instead of the Civil War; he now asserted that "the industrial East, which grabbed the balance of power in this country immediately after the WBTS to impose insufferable burdens on the South and Southwest, still holds that balance of power, and … intend to wield it for their own selfish advantage as long as it is humanly possible to do so."[627]

Charles Hurd of the *New York Times* offered the following Elliott sketch in 1939:

> He has become so aggressively Texan, so aggressively independent of his family, that it does not seem strange that he should be blowing Vice President Garner's horn at a time when Garner is fighting the more radical aims of Franklin D. Roosevelt's New Deal. Taken to task by his brother-in-law, John Boettiger, for espousing the Garner cause, he replied in an open letter: "I am not a politician, not a New Dealer, anti-New Dealer or any other type of supporter of isms."[628]

This referred to a celebrated press incident in which Elliott and John Boettiger exchanged acerbic remarks (mostly for show, since they got along fine). In a mean, sarcastic fit, Elliott had written to John, responding to a light-hearted, chiding editorial of his:

> My Dear John,
>
> Thank you for your open letter. I am glad you like Garner for his fishing ability, chewing of tobacco, drinking of whisky straight, cussing and other human traits. You list him as too 'sot in his ways' and too old-fashioned. You ask whether he has tied into a big King salmon like they have in Puget sound.
>
> Incidentally, the largest kind of King salmon is about the size of the smallest tarpon caught off the Texas coast, so don't boast about your fish like a chamber of commerce official until you ascertain whether you can outdo us in Texas.
>
> You infer by your public letter that I am not as strong in support of the president as you are. I am not a politician. I am not a New Dealer, anti-New Dealer or any other type of supporter of 'isms,' but I am as loyal as you or anyone else in the country to my father.
>
> I do not always agree with his individual programs and I believe he appreciates constructive suggestions and criticisms. My statement regarding Garner was purely my observation and report to the people of Texas via my semi-weekly broadcasts over the

Texas state network of a political trend within the Democratic party according to my own survey of the situation.

I have no way, nor do you, of knowing whether the president would run for a third term or not. When he makes up his mind he will announce it, not through you or me, but to the world at large. What the family thinks or feels has no bearing on his decision and therefore should not be discussed by the family.

Texas would like to see a Texan in the White House and so would I. Texans regard Garner as a progressive who has supported the president's fundamental efforts throughout and has been loyal from the bottom of his heart. He may disagree from time to time, but any man who thinks for himself would.

Get to know Garner sometime when you get a chance to leave Seattle. You'll find him to be much the same kind of humanitarian thinker that the president is.

All this is aside from the point. I am advocating nothing and nobody. I am a reporter reporting the news and political happenings of the day as I find them. I do not allow my personal beliefs to affect my reporting if I can help it.

Very truly yours, Elliott Roosevelt.[629]

In its snide and highly disingenuous posturing, the letter was characteristic. But the public spat was apparently soon forgotten by both epistolary combatants. "I feel soundly spanked!" kidded John back.[630]

The commentary also clues us in to Elliott's worldview. There was a certain parallel with his father's public expressions, not in substance, but in style. The son was voluble and opinionated, but there was no philosophical coherence to his views. Abstraction was not for him. Stirred by some outrage, he would be for censorship one day, yet against it on another, if it threatened to restrain his own editorial reach.[631]

It was ostensibly as a protest against "censorship" that Elliott withdrew his radio stations from the National Association of Broadcasters. The NAB had issued a rule against inflammatory opinions on paid programs. Correct as Elliott might have been, his reasons probably were that he might lose money if rabble-rousers like Father Charles Coughlin were not allowed to buy air time.[i]

This too was a break with his father. The White House had worked assiduously to silence anti-regime voices, leading to Father Coughlin's exile from radio. But Elliott said he was welcome to buy air time from him, provided he didn't foster racial or religious hatred or advocate the overthrow of the government – admittedly a high bar for the priest. (Coughlin's Social Justice movement had initially supported Roosevelt.)

In this context, Elliott made revealing comments in a hearing called before the FCC in March 1939. He complained that the requirement that radio stations renew their licenses every six months created an atmosphere of fear and acted as "a restriction upon free speech." The regulatory uncertainty made it impossible for radio stations to obtain regular bank financing. "As a result, the people who went into radio were those willing to gamble rather large sums of money."[632]

This was at the exact time that he was trying to persuade some people to "gamble large sums of money" on his radio network.

Others had a darker theory. The six-month limit was, in reality, a Damocles-sword dangled above the heads of radio executives. One political miscue and the FCC would let it slip. Those worried about the power now being concentrated in the federal executive had previous cases to ponder. They were not merely the ease with which the

[i] NYT, 29 OCT 39. The notorious priest railed against Sin, Jews, Communism, and helping the British.

president's friends were getting broadcast licenses; when the Chairman of the National Petroleum Council told FDR that the irascible Secretary Ickes should be fired, the New Deal alphabet soup promptly went after him like a cloud of angry bees.[i]

Even when the FCC worked as it was supposed to, Elliott had an excellent point. The notion of the "ether" as a public commons imposed a certain two-faced blandness on radio, and later on television. In a sense, the electronic media became system-preserving. This would not change until cable and other delivery means began to replace broadcasting.

Much of Elliott's relationship with the FCC, twisted or not, is largely beyond the reach of researchers because political or corrupt considerations, if any, seldom left a paper trail. The smoke was thick, though. The FBI investigated the agency in 1936 without finding evidence of corruption, merely hearsay.[633] In 1943, the House of Representatives would set up a special committee to investigate corruption in the FCC.

John Connally, the later Texas governor, said that of course the FCC was politicized, and subject to robust persuasion from the well-connected. He should know, because he served as an aide to Lyndon B. Johnson; and LBJ was in the process of building up a Texas radio empire of his own. This empire, originating in Austin, would include television stations after the war.

The story of how Johnson swindled the owners of KTBC Austin, his first station, by manipulating the FCC and White House staffers is eye-popping. His biographer, Robert Caro, has examined this case in great detail. Here it concerns us only because it reveals how ruthless and connected politicians could use the FCC to get what they wanted.[634] LBJ was able to obtain favorable FCC rulings, including a long monopoly in Austin that drove up advertisement rates for his station. Like Elliott, LBJ also used his wife, Lady Bird, as a front for his broadcast business.[635]

But Elliott was no LBJ. He couldn't resist giving the regulators a piece of his mind, even as he tried to cajole the FCC into granting his wishes. On 7 March 1939, he took the witness stand at the FCC and called it "an aged, decaying, tortoise-like body." He railed against the six-month license and "undue restrictions on the sale of stations." He said that the difficulty of getting bank financing due to the FCC's regulatory straightjacket had caused his network to lose $105,000 by September 1938, "and is only now reducing its indebtedness." Perhaps only he had the courage to tell the FCC the truth.[636] After the public hearings in 1939, an observer noted the following:

> The FCC is one of the pets of his eminent father. It has the power of a silent and quibbling censorship which might conceivably be of great value in a hot campaign. Elliott so definitely called attention to some of the FCC's faults that Chairman McNinch ran to the White House the next day. He would scarcely have done that if he had not believed that the President listens to the problem child on occasion. Elliott has stepped out of the shadow of the White House, but he has not stepped so far that he cannot step back in. When he calls on an advertiser he is the President's son. When he told the FCC that it had not been playing the game quite as nicely as the radio industry would like, he was the President's son. Most men in the business will say that what Elliott told the FCC was true and needed telling but that no other man dared tell it.[637]

---

[i] DallasMN, 9 MAR 39. FDR's systematic persecution of oilman J. Edgar Jones was a serious but now forgotten scandal. It was primarily an SEC issue, not an FCC one. The Supreme Court ruled in his favor. NYT, 31 DEC 37 etc.

Those are interesting words about an agency that had been created in order to allow wise, impartial bureaucrats to allocate radio spectrum fairly to the masses. As usual, it did not work that way in practice. Something similar undoubtedly held true about many other bureaucratic clumps in the New Deal alphabet soup. Perhaps those who thought FDR had created the FCC to secure a friendly ether that would counteract a hostile press had been on to something. It was in part because of this fear that the broadcasters (Elliott excepted) agreed on self-censorship. It preempted FCC political censorship.

When the long-awaited European war finally broke out in September, Elliott Roosevelt went to the FCC with an appeal for control of broadcasts originating abroad. He failed; at this time self-censorship sufficed. But soon the notion of censorship became much less odious than it had been, and would be again after the war.

Nonetheless, viewed in comparison to other countries, the United States had virtual radio "anarchy." Almost everywhere else, radio soon was made a government monopoly in order (at the minimum) to prevent unhealthy opinions or unwholesome entertainment. Americans never would be so easy to control. Even with the best of intentions, the FCC had a difficult task, especially on the cusp of the European war. The agency remained deeply controversial during the FDR years.

When he spoke up on the issues of the day, Elliott Roosevelt was not the mealy-mouthed type; but he was not predictable either.

He spoke forcefully for Texas interests because he lived in Fort Worth. He was for Vice President Garner because he was a friend and a Texan. He was for his father and the Democrats, but not necessarily for the New Deal. He was against FDR's third term until he was for it.

His commentaries tended to the facile, popular, somewhat informed, common-sensical, the kind of analysis you might hear from the more intelligent bar-lizards. If there was a lodestone for him to steer by, it was provided by the talk of his rich and connected friends – whoever they were at any given time. Throughout his life, people commented on how easily influenced he was.

As an example, in June 1939 he railed against illegal immigration, promoting laws against the hiring of the undocumented. He applauded the exclusion of foreigners holding "un-American" views. Then as now this was common populist bluster, but in 1939 it was especially poignant because at that particular time, the "aliens" whom nobody wanted tended to be refugees from Germany.[638]

The nativist slant occasionally veered off into the bizarre. Like many ruling-class Texans, Elliott was worried about Mexico. The Cardenas reform government aggravated American investors by its nationalization program. Elliott thought the "good neighbor" policy went too far if it meant acquiescence to Mexican seizure of oil fields without compensation. This remained a thorny bilateral issue during Cardenas's rule.[639]

But some saw an even greater danger: an actual Mexican attack across the border. That fear sounds ridiculous today, but it had its roots in the embryonic German-Mexican alliance that had precipitated America's entry into the Great War in 1917. Now, with the nationalist-socialist PRI in control, Elliott Roosevelt saw the danger of Mexico joining in cahoots with the Hitler-Stalin pact.

After the European war began, Elliott warned that 200,000 Mexicans were about to invade Texas: "the Nazis were financing and arming a Red militia in Mexico which is to shortly descend upon the helpless United States." He got this idea from reports of the so-called "Red Militia" – the Army of Workers and Peasants – being formed by President Cardenas to combat an insurrection in Monterrey.[640]

The charges were so absurd as to cause great hilarity in Washington D.C. as well as in Mexico D.F. But the operative question is as always to whom Elliott had been listening. It is likely that Texan businessmen, angry with the Mexican government, were feeding him inflammatory tidbits.

Politically Derailed

In Texas, there was considerable talk of Elliott running for either governor or nationwide office. To this there was equally fierce resistance. He had been headed off at the pass during the Young Democrats' brawl in 1935, but his close friendship with Governor Allred and his seeming success with the radio network reawakened the muttering in the back.

Elliott was coy about this, as politicians usually are when they are trying to determine when to jump into the fray. Late in 1936, he responded cagily to the suggestion that he should succeed Governor Allred:

> May I express to you my gratitude for suggesting my name as a possible candidate for Governor of the State of Texas? In view of your interest I believe I had better explain some of the reasons for my desire not to be a candidate for Governor in 1938.
>
> In the first place, the Constitution of Texas requires that the Governor of the State shall be at least 30 years of age, and as I will not have reached that age by that date I am afraid I would be ineligible under the Constitution. In the second place, I have resided in Texas for three years and while I have been fortunate in acquiring the friendship of a great many people during that time, I am afraid the rank and file of the voters of Texas do not have any knowledge of my ability to perform in such a high office…
>
> I feel very strongly that the voters of Texas should not be called on to accept me because of the fact that I am my father's son, but when the time comes they should weigh me as an individual and have an opportunity to decide whether my record in business and in the life of the community entitles me to be their representative.[641]

In other words, "not yet." Still, he managed to keep the interest high. His radio commentaries were obviously political. He became more and more strident in advocating Texas interests.

Elliott began attacking the New Deal. As early as 1937, in advance of his father's controversial "purge," he distanced himself markedly from the president's views. Two years later, like apparently most Texans he deemed the New Deal to be a failure. He pontificated:

> Without specific aid and encouragement from the administration, the South can not be expected to take its place in the economic sun…In constructing their theory the New Deal planners seem to have overlooked the fundamental fact that without healthy competition and adequate returns there can be no healthy trade.[642]

You can't make much sense of his economics, but what is clear is that he supported government intervention if it favored his interests, otherwise not. In that regard he differed little from most voters.

The occasional trouble with his father broke out again in earnest when, in 1939, the issue of a third term for Franklin Roosevelt began to exercise and divide the public. While such a move was then not technically illegal, it fanned the fears of a New Deal dictatorship that had already been ignited by FDR's attempt to neutralize the Supreme Court.

Initially, Elliott himself was strongly against the notion; be repeatedly spoke out in favor of a presidential challenge by Vice President Garner. As early as January of 1939, Elliott proclaimed that "the time soon will come for a Texan to be elected to the presidency of the U.S." In that broadcast, he praised Cactus Jack to the skies, noting that he was "neither a reactionary nor a conservative." In fact, Garner was a conservative, business-friendly populist who had by now clearly parted with FDR's policies.[643]

But Elliott was not just one wayward kid. The entire family was against Franklin's third term. In truth almost everyone of note was against the third term. Garner was against it; Postmaster Farley was against it. Secretary of State Cordell Hull was against it. Of course they were, said James Roosevelt, because they were suspected of wanting the presidency for themselves. Grumpy Harold Ickes was against it; he wanted to be vice-president. Same for Jesse Jones.[644]

FDR could not be dissuaded. To him it was unthinkable that the country should be run by anyone else. "I think I am needed," he told son James. "And maybe I need it."[645]

James said Elliott was in tight with Jesse Jones, and that would become very important later. For now, though, he'd bet on the losing horse:

> He was one of Elliott's Texas gang. After Garner folded at the convention, Elliott switched his support to Jones. When Jones folded, too, Elliott was out in left field. He had opposed father and lost. While they remained father and son, I don't think feelings were ever the same between them. Garner lost his hold on the Texas Democrats to Sam Rayburn. And Elliott's hopes for power in this part of the country caved in.[646]

One wrong choice and it's all over. Rayburn and Lyndon Johnson went with the "third-term, New Deal, even with Wallace-as-vice-president," crowd. Blind loyalty would pay off for them in spades. Elliott tried to correct his mistake, but it was too late. Nonetheless, many still thought he was destined for high Texas office.

After the president's men shot down the Garner insurgency and its threat to the third term, Elliott supported another Texas friend, Jesse Jones, for vice president, in contradistinction to his father's new and highly controversial choice, Henry Wallace. This strange man, who was ambitious well beyond his capabilities, was widely suspected not merely of being a socialist or communist, but of not being right in the head.

At the national convention in Chicago, Jim Farley, who was separating from FDR politically, also championed Jones. He let it be known that he had asked Elliott to approach Jones to accept the nomination – "young Roosevelt was scheduled to second Jones's nomination if this plan to shunt aside Wallace went through." But Jones would not do it without the president's direct request.[647]

As Jim Farley told it, Elliott stopped by on the afternoon of 18 July to complain about Wallace and propose Jones instead. Farley agreed, and moreover talked Eleanor into calling her husband, thus joining the rebellion at least momentarily. But FDR wouldn't budge. Even Franklin Jr. thought his father had made a destructive decision. Farley said: "Mrs. Roosevelt and I went out to the convention together. At the hall we met Elliott, who was determined to see Jones nominated. She urged him not to do anything for Jones, because if he did 'Father would feel very, very badly.'[648]

Farley later said Roosevelt selected his new vice president because "there was less chance of Wallace developing into a presidential candidate than anyone else."[649]

As Jesse Jones told it, he thought Farley was joking when he first mentioned that he ought to be vice president; but a few hours later Elliott came to his hotel room and declared that he would speak for his nomination after Farley had entered the name.

> I told Elliott that under no circumstances would I permit it, that the President had already let it be known that he wanted Henry Wallace for Vice President.
>
> That afternoon Elliott came back to my apartment and reiterated that they were going through with their plan…it was then that Elliott remarked that his father did not know what he was doing in wanting Wallace. I again insisted that under no circumstances did I want my name proposed to the Convention, and immediately issued a statement to the press to that effect.[650]

"We would all have been saved a lot of trouble" if Wallace had not been vice president, wrote Jones afterwards; and he also said he would have gladly taken the job if the president had asked him. He would, in truth, probably have made a solid and competent president. But he was clearly much more loyal than the president's own son.

This was a well-publicized family spat. Eleanor put down her foot and forbade her son to speak against her father. The way he remembered it was blander:

> Jim Farley told her that he thought one of several candidates would be acceptable, mentioning that I was planning to second the nomination of Jesse Jones. As it turned out, Father wanted Henry Wallace to be his vice president, and Mother had to inform me just prior to my making the seconding speech that it would be in opposition to Father's choice. As a result, I made no nominating speech.[651]

Thus the father eventually forced the son to backtrack twice. But if Elliott felt slapped down, so did most of the Democratic elite. Their leader had forced an unwanted and unqualified vice president down their throats; even if the party won in November, the powerbrokers felt abused, yet forced to pray for the president's health for four more years. Although FDR did win, he now ruled through personal cronies more than ever before.

Farley resigned his posts. Jones remained precariously in the cabinet. Elliott was in the doghouse once more.

Nevertheless, just before Elliott Roosevelt left radio for the Air Force, he launched a fierce rhetorical defense of his father at the Texas State Democratic Convention. The reason was that strong elements – the Texas Regulars – of the party were increasingly opposed to a third FDR term as well as to New Deal excesses. That Elliott had previously taken a similar stance did not moderate his outburst:

> His face flushed, and apparently angry, Elliott Roosevelt arose to begin his talk. This was the signal for a "We Want Roosevelt" demonstration, which included parading of district delegations bearing their banners. It was not until 30 minutes later that the President's son was able to continue…
>
> "Who was the man who cleaned up Tammany Hall? Who was the man who cleaned up our next-door state, Louisiana? Who was the man who brought clean government to Kansas City for the first time in history?"[652]

That fiery speech showed the young man as an able demagogue. The inference that FDR brought cleaner government should be viewed in historical context – pundits back then compared the present irregularities to past, even viler corruption. In truth, FDR did not "clean up Tammany" – instead he rather enthusiastically cut deals with the various political machines around the country. But Henry Morgenthau did help liquidate the Pendergast machine in Kansas City, at about the time Elliott was speaking.[i]

At the state convention, Elliott was technically a delegate from Tarrant County (Fort Worth). So, incidentally, was his financial backer Sid Richardson, who had also been at the national convention in Chicago – not as a delegate, but "as a personal friend of President Roosevelt."[653] Elliott was made temporary vice-chairman of the convention, and used the podium for maximum exposure. The youngster who had raised eyebrows by defying his father as a conservative Democrat now declared that "in Texas there is no room for hyphenated Democrats."[654]

In September 1939, neutrality had instantly become the dominant issue in American politics. Americans had been disillusioned and embittered by the Versailles settlement of 1919. This time, virtually everyone was for neutrality, but people didn't agree on what it meant. To the Roosevelts it meant sympathy and assistance to the democracies. To FDR's enemies, it meant "strict" neutrality, that is, an arms embargo on the warring nations and a "porcupine" approach to national defense.

Elliott spoke up. He was for a strong defense. Who wasn't? He warned against Germany taking over the world. But to the horror of leftists, he defended the controversial Dies committee – the later Un-American Activities committee, known as HUAC, which at that time was investigating both communist and fascist subversion. Elliott said that fellow Texan, Representative Martin Dies was the greatest statesman in America; yet Dies was widely seen as an early Joe McCarthy. The outburst was apparently occasioned by union leader John Lewis's campaign against Dies. Reportedly Eleanor countered: "He is much younger than I thought."[655]

His war views were Texas mainstream: Americans should prepare for the worst, but not step into the European mêlée. Only gradually did the pressure of events shift U.S. views toward an Anglo-American alliance. During 1939 and 1940, it looked to Americans as if they would have to stand alone in a world run by dictators. Of course, many FDR-haters thought America was pretty much among the tyrannies already.

Because later convention tends to misrepresent the neutralist sentiment as marginal, it is worth remembering that during the German-Soviet alliance, mainstream opinion in the United States was against all the dictators and firmly in favor of American non-intervention. In view of his later pro-Soviet stand, Elliott's August 1939 tirade against Marshal Joseph Stalin is particularly interesting. He called him the "bloodiest of all the murderous despots that encumber the earth." He said that Adolf Hitler was a "boy scout" by comparison.[656]

Evidently Uncle Joe chose to take it as a compliment – it's not conceivable that the remarks were forgotten in Moscow. But on 22 June 1941, the day Hitler betrayed Stalin, the fierce anti-Soviet campaign (and the harassment of Communists) popular among many in the United States vanished like a fata morgana.

---

[i] DallasMN, 2 OCT 40; This mentioned the Pendergast Machine (Missouri), the Huey Long gang (Louisiana), Boss Hague (Jersey City), Kelly-Nash (Chicago), and Boss Flynn (NY).

A fair representation of Elliott's views on neutrality emerged when he condemned Charles Lindbergh for speaking up. It was a betrayal, he said, since the Colonel was a reserve officer. But Elliott too could see no reason for America to become involved.

> I can't see how we can possibly enter this war...the people are against it and the country has taken a definite stand on the question. I doubt very much if American men will be called upon to fight in Europe.

He paid the so far successful new German chancellor a backhanded compliment:

> A lot of people think he is crazy, but he has done a wonderful job in a short time. The most amazing thing is that he armed Germany to the teeth with the full knowledge of other nations. He had a plan in mind and he followed it through in spite of everyone.[657]

Some people say that Elliott was "isolationist," the pejorative for those who wanted to stay out of the war.[658] Yet it would be plumb wrong to interpret Elliott's occasional outbursts as a preference for Hitler. Adolf and his U.S. supporters were also in for his criticism. In the two years of American neutrality, people tended to view the European events with both overall disgust and a specific ideological bias. For example, the right-wing demagogue Father Coughlin was criticized by Elliott on his radio program. Coughlin's supporters denounced Elliott, in turn, for being soft on communism.[659]

It is likely that Elliott, along with most Roosevelt-aligned Democrats, gradually came to see Germany as the main enemy simply due to the march of events in Europe. In contrast, Republicans and neutralists were much more influenced by the older and more philosophical opposition to worldwide communism. After Hitler was finished, those well-rooted stems of anti-communism remained to blossom anew.

The Ghost-to-Ghost Network

Elliott did not make a new mark on aviation, his "life's work," during this period. Instead he maneuvered to become a true media mogul. In 1939 he abandoned his Hearst posts and began work on the new Transcontinental Broadcasting Company (TBN), a network that was scheduled to open on 1 January 1940 with one hundred radio stations coast to coast. It was intended to be a competitor to the established networks, CBS, NBC, and Mutual. [660]

Thus in 1939 it seemed to the public as if things were going swell for the president's son. We now know the opposite was true. "Your mother tells us you are having a tough time in business," wrote brother-in-law John Boettiger in March."[661]

With enormous operating losses and a bloated overhead, after only a few months Elliott couldn't meet payroll. A desperate search for new financing began. The resulting extortion racket could have ended not just Elliott's career, but his father's. For the secret details we must await the 1945 Congressional hearings; in the meantime there is sufficient entertainment in dwelling on the twisting trail of Elliott's publicly known predicament.[662]

Elliott's fast train to riches and glory finally jumped the track entirely as 1940 rang in. The new network was first delayed to February; then it evaporated entirely. Elliott resigned his post at the end of 1939; then, on 9 January he announced that his own

Texas State Network would be forthwith reduced from 24 to 15 stations to "streamline" operations.[663]

People were puzzled. Creditors were worried. They were especially upset because after the spring of 1940 they couldn't find Elliott; or perhaps more accurately, he didn't respond to inquiries by "telephone, letter, and everything else."[664] That trouble was brewing was also suggested by his being injured in a December crash that demolished his car, and that he stood up twenty Dallas business leaders in an important February meeting, when he was "stricken" by a sudden stomach ailment.[665]

Reports surfaced that the network's financing simply wasn't real. Insiders called it a "ghost-to-ghost" network.[666] Advertisers who had been supposed to support the enterprise backed out. It would take a court case to unravel the convoluted affair, and it would be years before the entire story became known. The core truth of it would await release until 1945.[667]

The industry journal *Advertising Age* revealed in 1945 that the TBN essentially had been a shell, a fiction created in order to shake down funds. Proceeding from bankruptcy court records, the magazine wrote that there was a great deal of confusion concerning the entire project and that one of the officers accused Elliott Roosevelt of "taking a run-out powder" when he resigned his presidency after less than a month. The entire corporation existed only three months.[668]

The aforementioned "president" John Adams, a New York broadcasting executive, had served only 17 days before he resigned in favor of Elliott. "Officers were divided, in their court testimony, as to whether Mr. Roosevelt was president merely in name and did nothing for the firm or whether he 'did a lot of negotiating without the knowledge of the other directors.'"[669]

In his later testimony to the Treasury Department, Adams admitted that he had been taken in by Elliott's enthusiasm, and that he left when the network collapsed with feelings that "weren't very friendly" towards Elliott.[670]

Adams told of the meeting in which Elliott "gave up the ghost":

> He cried. He actually did. He said that he was never so unhappy about anything. He thought, right up to the last minute, that he was going to get the money, even when he knew that it was not coming from the original source, that he thought he had other people who would put it up.[671]

Indicative of the concern is a statement from H.J. Brennan, treasurer, who stated (not quite accurately) that on Nov 17, 1939, "nobody had put a dime into the thing yet. There wasn't a five-cent piece paid into it." Brennan continued that the number of radio stations in the network seemed to be pulled out of the ether:

> We heard…one day 50, the next day it would go to 20; the next day it would go up to 50 and then it would go to a total of 100 and you would never be able to tell what was done. Mr. Adams further testified that on Dec. 21, Mr. Roosevelt just "walked in and resigned." It was at that point that Mr. Adams suggested to Mr. Brennan that he (Mr. Adams) go back to Texas and "see what I could salvage" from TSN.[672]

After Franklin D. Roosevelt's death, a congressional investigation into Elliott's finances revealed a sordid financial conspiracy which netted him hundreds of thousands at the expense of several hapless investors and anglers of influence. Elliott had set up his original Texas chain (TSN) with investments from his Texas oil baron friends, reportedly to the tune of $500,000. The chain netted Elliott $76,000 a year, yet it lost money.[673] The radio stations began making money again after Elliott left.

However, the failure of the Transcontinental Broadcasting System, which was Elliott's moon shot, greatly exacerbated the ruin. Despite the help of his oil friends, Elliott had a hard time securing financing for a gamble this big. But impending financial doom never did crimp his style, then or later.

It seems that his troubles were greater than was let on at the time. James, his brother, later reminisced that Elliott thought of killing himself. He repeated the charge later, writing: "There were times when he'd call up threatening to take his life if he didn't get help. We'd hustle up some help for him, call back and find he was at a party."[674]

It could be true; or it could be payback for Elliott's assertion in one of his books that after Jimmy's political career had reeled under the weight of financial and sexual escapades, Eleanor had sent Elliott to Los Angeles to talk Jimmy out of killing himself.[675]

Before the collapse, through political contacts, Elliott found a number of people for whom it was currently awkward to refuse a presidential request. The most unfortunate of these businessmen was John Hartford of the Great Atlantic & Pacific Tea Company (A&P), the famous chain store that was the Walmart of its day. Oddly enough, Congress had just introduced legislation to impose a special tax on chain stores. The bill was proffered by one Wright Patman, Texas Democrat. Had it not been killed, the tax was estimated to have cost A&P $261 million a year.[676]

Patman, coincidentally, was a Texas Cabal affiliate and friend of Elliott Roosevelt. He was among the few politicians who stuck his neck out and vociferously defended Elliott when he received his captain's commission in 1940.[677] Patman would represent the 1st Texas district (Texarkana) until his death in 1976.

Elliott did not force the $200,000 deal on Hartford; his father did. FDR called the businessman and amiably persuaded him that this would be a really good investment for all involved. Sensing an offer he couldn't realistically refuse, Hartford granted the loan against the TSN stock collateral.

The Patman tax bill was retracted in response to White House pressure. This was in 1939; by 1940 the TSN stock was thought worthless. In late 1941, President Roosevelt told Jesse Jones, the Secretary of Commerce, to take over and settle Elliott's financial affairs. Thus, in March 1942, Jones induced Hartford to settle the loan for $4,000, and the matter was closed. Or so the principals thought.[678]

Jesse Jones was the publisher of the *Houston Chronicle* and one of the richest and most influential men in the Democratic machine. He was also more than a friend of Elliott Roosevelt; he was one of his string-pullers in the Texas radio business. It is not necessary to feel sorry for him being out $4,000 on behalf of little Elliott. After Elliott bankrupted the radio business, the Texas backers took over and brought it back to profitability, and the resurrected stock was put to good use.

That is the short version. We shall reexamine these disturbing but inescapable facts in due course.

Residual Texas Scandalettes

A strange occurrence involved Lyndon B. Johnson's first radio station, KTBC Austin. LBJ knew he could have his way with the FCC. But when he had Lady Bird apply to purchase KTBC in January 1943, he heard via John Connally that Elliott Roosevelt and Sid Richardson were upset about this unwanted competition and intended to retaliate. Johnson responded that he had no intention of being a competitor. To the contrary, he said his purchase thwarted "enemies of the Congressman, enemies of Elliott and enemies of the president."[i]

But by then Colonel Roosevelt wasn't supposed to have been involved with the network, and again the oil men must have been behind the warning shot. In August 1943, Elliott ditched Ruth and took up with starlets provided for him by Howard Hughes. So if he took an active role, it must have been among his last gasps in Texas. Yet, he is recorded as having lunch with John Connally on the 31st, and Connally had told Johnson that an angry Elliott had accused LBJ of "greasing the skids" with the FCC, obtaining not only the marginal KTBC but then immediately being given a favorable new frequency and night-time broadcasting privileges. Two years later the station's licensed signal power was increased five times. This made it many times more valuable than what it had been worth – which was again much more than the FCC had forced the owners to sell it to LBJ for.[679]

This incident seems to indicate that Elliott retained his interest in his wife's radio business even after the president got his debts annulled. Apparently he kept that residual proprietary interest until 1944, when he and Ruth legally split.

Thereafter Elliott personally appeared to have nothing more to do with his old network, but his ex-wife Ruth Googins had received, directly from the hand of FDR, Hartford's stock, in addition to what she already held in the Texas radio business. Ruth remained on friendly terms with papa Roosevelt after her divorce from Elliott and continued to visit the White House. She was given not only the stock, now according to Elliott worth over a million, but reportedly also preferential treatment in the FCC's handling of her company, Alamo Broadcasting of San Antonio.[680]

With the divorce settlement, which Elliott signed in the American embassy in London in March 1944, Ruth Googins (the later Mrs. Eidson) obtained stock in Texas State Network, Fort Worth Broadcasting, Tarrant Broadcasting, and the odd company Alamo Broadcasting. (Incidentally, in that settlement Elliott kept title to three Arabian horses and three colts; they would cause trouble later.)[681]

While FDR was still alive, Alamo was involved in a cross-border controversy that secured the Mexican transmitter XENT in Nuevo Laredo, one of the "border blasters" that hid from U.S. law across the Rio Grande while broadcasting to Americans. XENT was owned by a famous, flamboyant quack, Norman Baker, who had to go away to Leavenworth on account of some cancer cures he had promoted. While he was in jail, allegedly Alamo paid off a XENT employee to obtain the radio station equipment. The FCC gave Alamo the right to use the new super-high-powered station. It was then smuggled to Texas in violation of a Mexican export ban.[682]

On 15 December 1945, Norman Baker filed a petition with the FCC to get his station back. Westbrook Pegler broke the story publicly two weeks later. Baker asserted that Ruth Googins had visited the White House in 1944 to persuade FDR to clear the

---

[i] Dallek, 249. Connally's correspondence was dated 31 AUG 1943, when Elliott was in the country.

path in the FCC. This caper was important to her company because civilian radio equipment was essentially frozen during the war, so the powerful Mexican transmitters would come in handy. However, apparently nothing but unproductive lawsuits came of the matter. Most likely Baker, the well-known super-swindler, could not convince anyone of his own victimization.[683]

While Ruth Eidson, and very probably the president, were somehow mixed up with this matter – at least as far as the FCC application was concerned – it doesn't seem like Elliott could have been involved. He was very busy in Europe. The oilmen remained behind the Texas State Network and determined its direction.

Still, Elliott was done with Ruth, but not quite with radio. He was allowed to keep 250 shares in TSN, although he doesn't appear to have been particularly welcome in Texas after his father's death.

The radio scandal lay dormant. At home and abroad, Elliott Roosevelt saw a lifetime of action in the few short years until that mangy cat was finally let out of the bag. The controversies he got into had a way of simmering on a low boil for a few years before blowing up in a major official investigation.

How Elliott short-circuited the Electric Cooperatives

One of the lesser scandals had to do with the Rural Electrification Administration (REA), a New Deal agency involved in providing electric power to farms and rural homesteads. REA was considered one of FDR's pets, but the agency collided with the interests of local power companies. A long political and legal war then erupted between the administration and the large utilities.[684]

Although this might seem like a local and arcane subject, it certainly wasn't so in the 1930s. For one thing, the electric utilities were usually parts of giant economic combines that could buy politicians by the bushel; for another, the New Deal's laudable attempt at rural electrification threatened to duplicate local commercial services as well as hoard resources needed for the defense program. At the tips of the tentacles of the vast new power grids sat individual homestead families, wondering whether they were getting a fair deal.

As Elliott told it many years later, his own Fort Worth (Benbrook) ranch did not have electricity, and the couple at first ran generators for power. The electric company tried to gouge Elliott for a power line, and he threatened to set up a rural electric cooperative instead. The utility relented and provided somewhat cheaper service.[685]

That version, told parenthetically in 1983, is diametrically opposite to the one supported by public records. During the Depression, Elliott was in fact paid by the local electric company as a lobbyist. Since Elliott ran a radio network, that wasn't a bad move. In 1950, John T. Flynn, another leftist who had turned on Roosevelt and became a rightist, wrote:

> For instance, there was an electric transmission cooperative in Texas on the Brazos River. Harry Slattery, the Rural Electrification Administrator, refused to approve a contract for the sale of power and its operations were held up for three months, resulting in a $180,000 loss. Elliott wrote a letter to Steve Early, his father's secretary, to delay action on the project. That letter is in evidence and is attributed to Elliott's connection with a private electric power company which paid him $12,000 a year as its advertisement agent - a mere side issue.[686]

Again, Elliott cast two shadows. He spoke up on the utility issue on his radio network and let his father know his mind, and it is virtually certain that he was indeed the origin of the costly delay. The people of Texas were apparently not in doubt: "The Brazos River people have been unable to figure out why the contract was held up…They have suspected the hand of Elliott Roosevelt in the delay," testified one angry opponent to the Senate.[687]

Clyde T. Ellis of the National Rural Electric Cooperative Association testified to the Senate committee investigating the REA. He said that Elliott's intervention sabotaged the cooperative:

> The belief was based on the close friendship the President's son is known to have had with officials of the Texas Power & Light Company of Dallas, which was contesting the REA cooperative… the Brazos River project was delayed for more than three months when Harry Slattery, REA Administrator, declined to approve a contract for the sale of power. This resulted in a loss of $180,000 in revenue to the cooperative.[688]

The NRECA wrote to President Roosevelt on 8 May 1943, demanding that Slattery "must go as REA Administrator, and quickly, otherwise we are faced with immediate explosions and investigations in Congress and a scandal of major importance."[689]

Indeed, in normal times it probably would have developed into a major scandal. But these were not normal times, and both Colonel Roosevelt and his Commander-in-Chief evaded getting held to account for this one. Still, there were obviously many grumbling people in the know.

The Rural Electrification Administration was a new agency from the New Deal mold. In the Roosevelt revolution, Harry Slattery was an important player who is perhaps better remembered for his disastrous plan to colonize Alaska with collective farms (kolkhozes) on the Soviet model.

The letter John T. Flynn referred to is in press secretary Stephen Early's files. In it, Elliott made a strong case for the utility company and against local competition. Writing from Fort Worth on 1 March 1941 on Texas State Network letterhead – at a time when he was supposed to be an officer training for the war, and to have washed his hands of the radio business – Elliott argued:

> …my place here is served by the local company by virtue of a rural extension. I personally know that the local companies in this area have at all times cooperated with the Rural Cooperatives in developing and extending service to those not previously receiving services.
>
> …If the local companies had not cooperated with the development of the Rural Electric Cooperatives in this area to the extent which they have, I might possibly take another position, but as shown by the enclosed information and by my personal knowledge, the private companies have made possible the fullest utilization of Federal appropriations for the purpose of extending electric service in west and central Texas. There is therefore no excuse whatever for an attempt on the part of the Federal agencies involved to establish "Experimental plants" or "Yardsticks" in this area.[690]

After discussing the details of rural electrification in general and the Brazos River Project in specific, Elliott got to his purpose in writing the president:

> I am genuinely and personally interested in this thing. I know that it involves a major policy but a policy which has not so far received the sanction of the President…
>
> P.S. Please do everything you can to see to it that nothing is decided definitely until I can see you in Washington – Probably Wednesday evening if you're available. E.R.[691]

Here we have the president's son acting as a high-paid lobbyist for a private company, trying to stall and deflect a national policy by going straight to his father. It is thus not surprising that the press sooner or later smelled a rat. The issue was discovered tangentially in May 1944 after Congress investigated the Brazos River project. Elliott was fingered as someone suspected of holding up rural electrification to boost utility profits, but that was not the main complaint against the REA.[i]

The REA scandal surfaced only because a subcommittee of the Senate Agriculture Committee was investigating the agency for malfeasance and incompetence. Elliott's letter thus was placed on the public record on 14 February 1944, although it took time to attract attention. His efforts to thwart the REA and allocate the Brazos profits to the power company failed, but not until he had held up the matter for a long time.[692]

Drew Pearson discussed Elliott's role in the REA scandal publicly on 21 June 1945. Having seen the letter to Early, he wrote that Elliott urged his father to ensure that the REA (which FDR favored) not be allowed to develop the Brazos River project, but that it be given to Texas Power & Light, which had hired Elliott. But he also noted that:

> Elliott also intervened in the Democratic primary campaigns of two of his father's best Texas supporters, Congressmen Maury Maverick and William McFarlane, whom the big power companies helped defeat.[693]

This reflects Pearson's pro-New Deal view. From the opposite corner, Westbrook Pegler ripped into Elliott as well.

> …in February 1944, it was shown before a Senate committee that Elliott wrote to Steve Early urgently interceding for a private owned Texas power company. 'I am genuinely and personally interested in this,' Elliott said, 'I know these people and they will do anything necessary…If you need any facts, call me --- Please to everything to see that nothing is decided until I can see you in Washington.'

Elliott's 1945 testimony to the Treasury Department reveals that he was, in fact, employed as an agent by the Texas Electric Service Company for one to two years, at a rate he recalled as $12,000 per annum.[ii] His job was to advise the company on its advertising operations. Lobbying his father for relief from laws and regulations could obviously save the utility many times his salary.

On merits, Elliott may or may not have had a valid cause, but with him, the first question always was who paid him. Yet another concern is that, by the time he wrote nonchalantly about this matter in 1983, his memory had evidently turned 180 degrees. He remembered the fight to get his own electric line, but he had forgotten whose side he was publicly on at the time.

---

[i] ChigTrib, 23 MAY 44. Slattery was forced to resign on 11 December 1944.

[ii] Texas Power & Light and Texas Electric Service were both subsidiaries of American Power & Light, again a subsidiary of giant utility company Electric Bond and Share.

The Sacrifice

Elliott still managed to infuriate the public and become a burden to his father in the 1940 election. His application for military service, coming after having lost so much of other people's money on the aborted Transcontinental Broadcasting Network enraged people because it looked like a classical Elliott scheme. It was not.

The evidence actually supports the view that Elliott – like millions of others – sought to combine two noble purposes: serving in the military while safeguarding his own interests.

When Elliott joined the Air Corps – after the failure of his radio network – he lamented that he was "sacrificing" an income of $76,000 a year. That was roughly equivalent to 1.5 million in 2012, and many noticed ruefully that it was 1,000 a month more than his father, the President of the United States, was paid.[694]

Not everyone was impressed by this sacrifice. At first, Elliott merely surrendered his radio presidency to his wife, Ruth Googins, who drew a salary, and he remained the principal stockholder. Ruth was sharp and savvy and had tried to control Elliott's profligacy. Now Elliott terminated his by then triweekly radio commentary. Ruth got a cut of Elliott's military pay.[695]

Drew Pearson noticed that before joining up, Elliott "had to ask those to whom he owes large sums of money." That was partially true in so far as Elliott's backers, primarily Sid Richardson and Charlie Roeser, had little warning but were quick to take advantage. Wife Ruth was taken care of, but professionals were put in charge of the Texas State Network. Another investor, Gene Cagle, was then made president and instituted an economy program.[696]

From then on TSN began climbing back to profitability. By the time Elliott divorced Ruth Googins in 1944, the oil men had made their money back. Another clue to their influence was that the oil barons had been invited to Thanksgiving dinner with President Roosevelt in 1941. Who intended to thank whom (and how) become more clear after the Treasury Department's investigation of Elliott's finances in 1945.

The worsening crisis with Japan preempted that friendly get-together, but Elliott's oil friends did meet with FDR on the Sunday after Pearl Harbor.[697]

The good relations between the Texas oil men and the White House continued. In June 1942, Commerce Secretary Jesse Jones and Harold Ickes, Petroleum Administrator for War, approved the purchase of an obsolete and defunct pipeline to be relaid across the Florida Neck. The sellers were Murchison and Roeser, owners of the lodge FDR had visited in 1937. As reported, "The project was proposed by the American Liberty Pipeline company, Dallas, Texas, to be built with second-hand pipe excavated in Texas."[698] Insiders said the price, $4 million, was drastically inflated for what they called "junk."[i]

So despite the crash of his network and his unpaid debts, Elliott came out of the radio business with considerable funds. A high-profile bankruptcy court case (conducted by the Delaware Court of Chancery) revealed that the liquidation of TBN netted Elliott $33,438 of the remaining funds of $94,448. Other investors were not so lucky.[699]

---

[i] Letter, Woodward to Pegler, Hot Oil file, ER box, Pegler/HH. This pipeline was different from the contemporary Big Inch and Little Big Inch, which went from Texas to the Northeast.

It is important to note the dates: the court appointed the receivers on 29 August 1940, right before Elliott decided to join the military. The residual was distributed in 1941. However, Elliott's portion was then demanded by two lenders who had been hit up for "investments" and had lost most of their money.[700]

It might seem that there was an unusual public interest in Elliott's finances, and that is definitely true. Important to remember, though, is that all of the Roosevelt children were followed with – at the very least – raised eyebrows during this time. Eldest brother Jimmy's considerable income was a source of great consternation (he was forced to reveal his tax returns). As an insurance executive (among various other sidelines) who ruthlessly traded on his name, Jimmy was probably considered even more scandalous by the nation, at least before the war. In the view of many, the war redeemed the brothers.

Anna Roosevelt Boettiger, who worked for Hearst's media empire, was also subject to rumor and scrutiny. Although aggressive and foul-mouthed, she was no financial wizard and struggled all her life. In the case of these three siblings, the media attention was amplified by the ceaseless gossip about their recurrent divorces. But it was all of a piece. Guilty or innocent, all the progeny were now suspects.[701]

Mother Eleanor saw the problem. She noted that:

> ...because of my husband's theory that once a male child of the family was educated he should be on his own, our two older boys, James and Elliott, were not given an allowance after they finished their schooling. They, therefore, had to begin at once to earn a living. That complicated their lives considerably [don't it always?] because instead of being allowed to start at the bottom and work up, they were offered jobs that gave them too high returns. And they were too young and too inexperienced to realize that they were offered those jobs only because of their name and of their father's position.[702]

There, Eleanor sounded almost like the Roosevelt critics. In a contemporary letter to friend Joe Lash, she elaborated, quoting General Arnold:

> I've discovered one thing which makes me feel a bit better about Elliott's situation. Gen. Arnold says he couldn't be accepted in the draft or in the army as a private because, without glasses, he can't see more than ten feet. He can only get in on a commission on account of experience as a specialist of some kind, so resigning would do no good & he might as well stay put. Of course in case of war many of these regulations will go & and then he could change. I am sorry for him & sorry for the effect on the young people but knowing he couldn't get in as a private makes me feel less badly about 'sitting tight.'[703]

On this rich background, Elliott Roosevelt's appointment to captain, USAAC Reserve, in September 1940 does not look so fishy at all. His management, industrial, and aviation background coupled with his physical limitations made him a good choice for the Specialist Reserve, a division intended for civilians with special expertise. Wright Field was no backwater; if Elliott had stayed there, he would have been involved with critical decisions shaping the Air Force for years to come. But with his baggage, of course he might have gotten into trouble there as well.

General Arnold was probably correct in making Elliott a captain. His management experience and technical background might have called for a higher rank, yet his checkered past could well have marked him down. Many civilians of measurable accomplishment found themselves suddenly majors and colonels as the Army expanded by a factor of fifty, from a puny neutrality guard to the sky legions of a global empire.

The uproar over the sudden captaincy was thus clearly political. But the accumulated measure of hatred and bitterness was grotesquely expressed by a war veteran, Rep. John Schafer (R – WI), who only two days after Elliott's service oath stood up in the House of Representatives and snarled a welcome to the "New Deal Führer's" son:

> Mr. Speaker, the millions of men in the country who are under 35 years of age and subject to a year's compulsory peacetime military service at $21 per month under the New Deal-Stalin-Hitler type of "involuntary servitude," which violates the 13th Amendment to the Constitution of the United States, are no doubt wondering why our multimillionaire President's multimillionaire 30-year-old son, Mr. Elliott Roosevelt, can come to Washington on September 23, 1940, and apply direct to Gen. H. H. Arnold, Chief of the Army Air Corps, and walk out of his office on September 24, 1940, with a captain's commission and an assignment to a soft swivel-chair job in the Army Air Corps procurement center at Wright Field, Ohio, and the press of the country furnished with a statement from a War Department spokesman that Mr. Elliott Roosevelt's special talents earned him the commission.[704]

Schafer called for a congressional investigation, but he was spitting into the wind. The Democrats had a solid majority in Congress. Still, with that kind of welcome, you can't blame the new captain for trying to get out of his "swivel-chair" assignment.

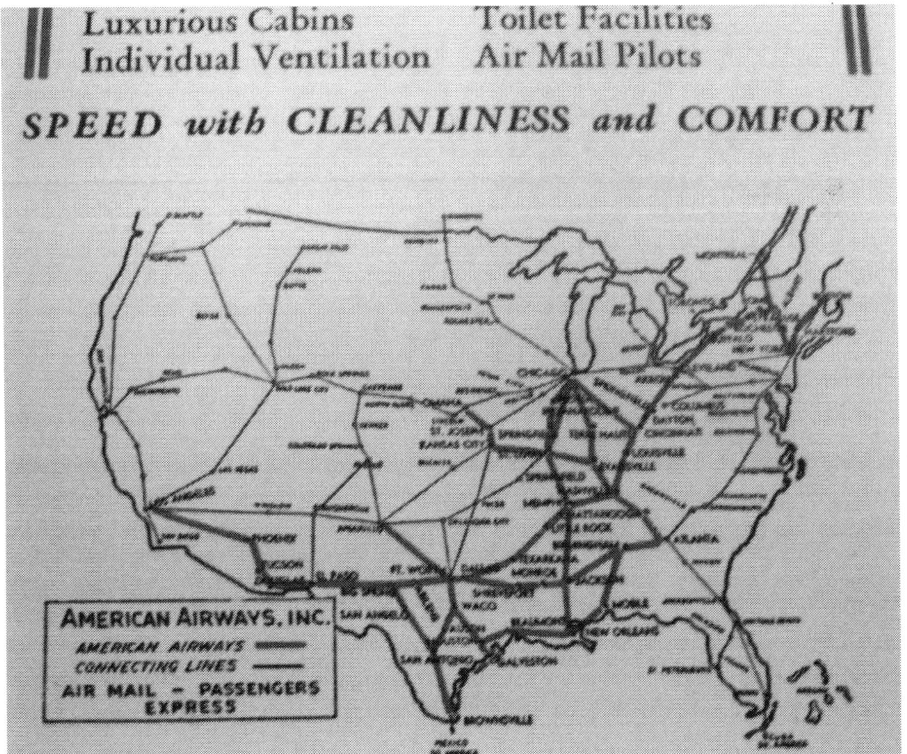

Map of American Airlines and connecting routes, ca. 1933. Greenway Collection, AHS

II. NEITHER WAR NOR PEACE - 1941

A CIRCUS IN THE NORTHLAND

When his finances were investigated in 1945, at the prompting of his lawyer General Roosevelt offered the following summary of his Arctic explorations:

> During the months of May, June, July, August and September, 1941, I was assigned to a special project of exploring Labrador, Baffin Island, Greenland and Iceland for the establishment of airfields which could serve as intermediary fields for the shuttling of fighter and bomber aircraft to England. I conducted this survey and located a site in Southern Labrador at Goose Bay in the early part of June, 1941. I located a site a few miles inland just south of Ungava Bay which if off the Hudson Straights in the Northern part of Quebec. I located three possible sites for airfields on Baffin Island in July and in August and September located two possible sites for airfields in the Eastern Coast of Greenland. This work entailed a very great deal of standard flights over uncharted areas and I was considerably concerned before the completion of this task over the fact that the very nature of the work entailed a considerable opportunity for loss of the aircraft and the personnel involved in the operation. As a result I was considerably exercised over what might be the result to my family in the event of anything happening to me in this type of operation which I knew would be continued in the future.[705]

Faced with accusations of deserting his debts and defrauding investors, Roosevelt was holding up his Air Corps service as an alibi. He was, however, also largely correct about what he had done in the Arctic. About the details we can quibble, and so we shall.

Two years later, when Congress hauled him in for investigation of the Hughes Aircraft scandal, Elliott again provided details of his service to an agitated public:

> Mr. ROOSEVELT. I was at Wright Field, sir, up until March of 1941, and then I was transferred over to Bolling Field for a special intelligence course, under the then Captain Lauris Norstad, who is now one of the high-ranking generals of the Army, to be given special intelligence training to serve as an intelligence officer of the 21st Reconnaissance Squadron, which had been assigned to Newfoundland to do anti-submarine patrol of the North Atlantic waters, and to guard our shipping lanes against German submarine activity. It was before the war, sir.
>
> We arrived in Newfoundland, and I received an additional assignment from Washington, ordering me to take charge of all planning and execution of the survey of the North Atlantic possibilities for establishment of bases across the North Atlantic for the delivery of fighter and bomber aircraft to England.[706]

Elliott Roosevelt would be among the first U.S. troops in Newfoundland. There was, however, a bit of uncertainty about when he got there and how much time he actually spent at his post. Not uncertain is that Dad watched closely.

"Get planes there as soon as any place can be prepared. FDR." So scribbled the president on a War Department memo dated 8 April 1941. For Newfoundland, Henry Stimson had recommended "one half battery of 8" guns and one squadron consisting of three medium and three heavy bombardment airplanes, totaling approximately 57 officers and 575 men," all within ten days. And now Bunny would be one of the 57. [707]

Newfies and Yankees

Newfoundland Base Command would later grow to major proportions, but in the year of transition – 1941 – few facilities were available on the barren, wind-swept rock. The American presence consisted of tent camps and shipborne lodgings at the capital of St. John's and at Gander Lake, where there now was a new airstrip and a seaplane base. Also, the U.S. Navy was developing a base at Argentia (Placentia Bay) in the south of the island. Both Britain and Canada were also rapidly developing bases in these locations, but they had nowhere near the resources the Americans could bring to bear.

The official history of the Air Corps states that the arrival on 9 March 1941 of a weather and communications detachment at Gander Airport preceded the establishment of the first U.S. air units in Newfoundland by two months. The first U.S. Army Air Corps aircraft (light bombers) flew up in early May. However, small U.S. naval contingents had already been active on the island, operating seaplanes out of Argentia, Gander Lake, and other sheltered anchorages. For the time being, the Air Corps would operate out of Gander along with British and Canadian squadrons.[708]

Gander, a storied field which is the present home of the North Atlantic Aviation Museum, is forty miles from the iceberg-strewn coast and has much better flying weather. Being next to Gander Lake and a few miles from the new Pan American seaplane terminus at Botwood, the otherwise isolated settlement (previously known as Hattie's Camp) already had a total transatlantic focus.

Because of Canadian dilation, President Roosevelt asked Britain directly for the right to build an air base detachment at Gander and received permission on 8 April 1941. With sudden alacrity, the Royal Canadian Air Force (RCAF) then moved the 10th Bomber Reconnaissance squadron there. Then it was only a matter of getting the U.S. 21st Recon. Squadron, Elliott Roosevelt's outfit, in place. The unit arrived on and around 9 May. The total garrison now amounted to 1,666 men.[709] But facilities were still primitive and had to be constructed or completed over the summer, causing Captain Roosevelt to complain bitterly to his mother of his misery and suffering there.[710]

The swift American militarization of the British colony of Newfoundland and Labrador would in only two more years include Pepperell and Torbay Air Bases (at St. John's), Stephenville (later Harmon AFB), and Argentia and Botwood naval bases. The investment, peaking at about 6000 men, would completely transform the island – then usually thought to be a remote, backwards, even malnourished bleakville – to the extent that a popular groundswell arose to have Newfoundland join the United States rather than Canada, though she narrowly chose the latter by referendum in 1948.

Viewed in this greater context, Elliott Roosevelt had not been banished to Siberia. His father was keenly aware of that. Elliott was at the cuttingest edge of a sword being hurriedly unsheathed. His job now was to help prepare an air route across the Arctic to Britain. His new playground, reflecting America's extending arm, would be Newfoundland, Labrador, Baffin Island, Greenland, Iceland, and Scotland.

Escaped Countries, Roaming Wild

Biased as we inevitably are by hindsight, it is tempting to view the geopolitical situation in the North Atlantic in 1941 as rather straightforward. Surely, everyone simply joined in to whip the Hun?

Quite the contrary. The still neutral United States found itself faced with a kind of geopolitical circus, complete with the equivalent of escaped animals roaming the streets. This is one of the "most untold" stories of that uncertain time.

Starting at the far end of what would become known as the North Atlantic Route, the Danish colonies of the Faroe Islands and Iceland had been occupied by Britain in April and May 1940, respectively. Iceland wanted no part of the war, protested the occupation, and – said Elliott Roosevelt – her people hated the British and were bound to hate the Americans as well.[i]

Roosevelt overstated his case; the Icelanders were rather more measured and pragmatic. They were happy to be rid of the Danes, but not necessarily pleased with their uninvited replacements. Although for ideological reasons, Germany's National Socialist government was much enamored with the Nordics in general and Iceland in particular, the feelings were not returned by the Icelanders, except for a small cantankerous minority. The Icelandic National Socialists never exceeded a 5% vote share.[711]

After President Roosevelt ordered the American occupation of the island on 1 July 1941, Elliott stated that there were many Nazi sympathizers among the local people, and that the Anglos were not welcome:

> At the present time they are on the fence regarding their attitude toward the U.S. forces. The way the situation is being handled, in another six months the Icelanders will dislike the U.S. as fervently as they do the British.[712]

The "neutral" American forces began relieving the Imperial troops on 7 July 1941, preceding Elliott's tart evaluation by only a few weeks. Both the British and the Americans built airfields in the Reykjavik area as soon as they could. The Dominion of Iceland did manage to declare full independence from Denmark whilst under American protection. The Icelanders made sure to get U.S. recognition of this from the beginning.

The massive sub-continent of Greenland had been under direct Danish rule, but was cut off when the motherland was invaded in April 1940; incidentally, this was due to the British blockade, not any Danish or German action. To ensure its supplies, and to avoid getting sucked into the war, the colonial administration promptly sought trade links with the United States. In a situation analogous to that of some French colonies, Greenland thought American assistance preferable to Canadian occupation. British-prompted Canadian intervention was forestalled by very robust American diplomacy in May 1940, and again early in 1941.[713]

However, the colony got more "aid" than it bargained for. On 9 April 1941, the anniversary of the fall of Denmark, Washington signed a treaty with the defected Danish ambassador, Mr. Henrik de Kauffmann, giving the United States essentially unlimited military rights in Greenland. The treaty's obvious illegality was mitigated by Kauffmann's assurance that he was acting the way his sovereign, King Christian X, would have wanted him to act if he could have spoken his mind.

However, King Christian and the Danish Foreign Ministry, which had been forced to accept a similar German protectorate over the motherland, did soon speak their minds, and quite emphatically so. The rogue ambassador was fired, indicted for high

---

[i] Glines: Bernt Balchen, 135. Glines said this quotation was from an ER report in Balchen's AFHRC collection, but it is not there now, and the report could not be located elsewhere.

treason, and the Greenland treaty declared null and void as far as Denmark was concerned.[714]

Only in the face of Kauffmann's *fait accompli* did the colonial regime in Greenland's tiny capital of Godthaab accept the treaty with the United States. They might as well welcome the Americans, for they would certainly get them anyway.[715]

The Dominion of Newfoundland and Labrador was perhaps the oddest animal in the circus. The sparsely populated colony had been under direct British rule since 1934 due to local mismanagement, corruption, and virtual bankruptcy. It was nonetheless still neglected and impoverished. Britain was now free to offer leases on bases there, and she did so to both Canada and the United States. Importantly, the Dominion also included the Atlantic watershed of the Labrador Peninsula, where Elliott would soon discover the site of a giant future air base.

Oddly, the British Foreign Office technically offered the Newfoundland bases as a gift to the United States, not as a *quid pro quo* for the U.S. warships obtained under the destroyers-for-bases deal of August 1940. The official history notes:

> On 22 August Churchill advised the President that his government wished to offer the base facilities without strings, and not as a trade for the destroyers. Since Roosevelt felt that he had no authority to give the destroyers without compensation, discussions continued for a few days on this point until a formula satisfying both governments was found. The final agreement, embodied in an exchange of notes on 2 September 1940, provided that the base rights in Newfoundland and Bermuda were given "freely and without consideration." The other base rights, in the Caribbean area, were granted in exchange for the fifty over-age American destroyers.[716]

It was a face-saving touch; of course, the trade had been mostly a charade anyway, very much *quid* and very little *quo*. The warships were old and worn; the territorial concessions of enormous and permanent significance.

Completing the North Atlantic portrait, with a sort of thin mustache, the French islands of St. Pierre and Miquelon had remained loyal to Vichy. They were invaded by de Gaulle's forces on Christmas Eve 1941, to the lasting fury of the U.S. State Department. The islands played no significant role in the war, but during Elliott Roosevelt's sojourn in the neighborhood the strange-tongued fishermen did manage to get mistaken for German agents by some overly sensitive Americans! [717]

Nominal or substantive, the destroyers-for-bases deal slid the U.S. camel's nose under the North Atlantic tent. While Churchill was loath to surrender one inch of the Empire, he knew that Britain's very survival depended on getting America into the action. Leased or donated bases in Newfoundland, Bermuda, and the Caribbean would accomplish that. In return, FDR could present the treaty as simply another muscular move to extend and defend America's perimeter. It was another artful tackle of neutrality.

But one year, 1941, made an enormous difference. At the beginning of that year, the American strategic outlook focused on hemisphere defense, particularly in view of the expected fall of Britain, and fears of German activity in Greenland. A few incidents were absurdly overplayed in still-neutral America; the Germans made some reconnaissance flights over the Greenland east coast, and the Coast Guard intercepted a civilian weather station crew from Norway there, although it was operating legally under treaty rights.[718]

By the end of that year of decision, all the animals in the North Atlantic circus had been lined up on the Allied side. From then on, the emphasis was on aid to Britain and on the build-up to the invasion of Europe, optimistically expected in 1942. But the Arctic fringe of the Atlantic had lost none of its importance.

Perhaps Captain Roosevelt, in his miserable Newfoundland backwater, did not need to worry about these immense issues, but he certainly did. His reports from the islands touched upon the political and strategic situation, and he mouthed off in public about the need to aid Britain; he was in liaison with the top leadership of both the United States and Britain; and most of all, he had a first-row seat at the Argentia summit between Churchill and Roosevelt in August 1941. For a captain with less than a year in uniform, he had gained an unusually distinguished audience.

At the Misty Edge of the World

Captain Roosevelt was attached to the 21st Reconnaissance Squadron, commanded by Major Jarred "Jimmy" Crabb. Roosevelt was a worthless drunk who caused him a lot of trouble, Crabb later said, although this seemed to reflect, at least in part, a political revulsion.[i]

The 21st Recon relocated to Gander from Miami in April-May 1941 with eight Douglas B-18 Bolos. If this aircraft is unfamiliar to the reader, think of it as a bomber version of the DC-3. (Technically, it is a DC-2 cousin.) It was obsolete but still good enough for anti-submarine patrol, reconnaissance, and general liaison duties. Not coincidentally, at Gander the RCAF (No. 10 Squadron) already operated the same aircraft in its Canadian incarnation, the Douglas Digby.[719]

Elliott's unit remained at Gander until the end of August, when it was relieved by the 41st Recon with eight of the early straight-tail B-17Bs. During that summer the Newfoundland Base Command also had eleven light transport planes available. Until December, the American aircraft had no combat role, and they wouldn't have been effective had they had one. Nevertheless, the sheer build-up of American forces was in itself a major logistical task.[720]

Although Elliott complained of "inactivity" at the remote post, there must have been quite a bit to interest an alert intelligence officer.[721] German submarines were an increasing threat to all shipping in the area, even neutrals. Shortly after Elliott left the theatre, General Marshall was pleased to advise the president that Gander-based B-17s had begun bombing German submarines, neutrality be damned. Nor was that the only German presence. The cruisers *Gneisenau* and *Scharnhorst* had made a successful foray off Greenland and Canada in early 1941, and in May the German capital ships *Bismarck* and *Prinz Eugen* made their celebrated dash south of Cape Farewell, Greenland.

That audacious expedition worried the Americans. In Washington, Secretary Ickes noted, "It is said that the Bismarck was on its way to Greenland to land troops and supplies there. If it had done so, it would have been very difficult for us to dislodge them, as we would have been under obligation to do."[722]

"Neutral" U.S. Navy PBYs (Catalina flying boats) and U.S. Coast Guard vessels from Newfoundland participated in the hunt for these vessels.[723]

---

[i] AFHRA, OHI Interview w. Maj. Gen. Crabb. Crabb later commanded Newfoundland Base Command.

The 21st Recon had much else to do. In particular, ice and weather reconnaissance were critical in a region that had plenty of both commodities. Airborne weather reconnaissance was a task whose importance Elliott Roosevelt would not forget in the future. Of course, above all the squadron supported the build-up of American troops and bases across the North Atlantic.

There were a lot of cooks in the kitchen. Duplication, or rather quadruplication of effort was rampant in these confused early days. Britain, Canada, the Navy, the Air Corps, even the Coast Guard had important roles to play, and they all fought over turf and surf, as bureaucracies are wont to do.

Roosevelt's unit at Gander was thus only one contributor. The Navy conducted its own surveys for bases using Catalinas from Gander Lake and Reykjavik.[724] The RAF contributed with their big new American LB-30 Liberators, of which six were assigned to the Return Ferry Service.[725] Transatlantic aircrews, after all, had to make their way back to pick up more planes, and they could help out locally along the way. Not to be forgotten, the Coast Guard had assumed a "neutral" protectorate over Greenland, and its activities, seasonally moderated by ice, largely emanated from Newfoundland. This service, too, used crane-hoistable light seaplanes, precariously carried aboard its larger cutters.[i]

Elliott said that "the most ticklish aspect was to keep the Army from rubbing rough against the Navy" and that may be an understatement.[726] As for sharing the task with the later Allies, Roosevelt soon recommended giving the entire aircraft delivery mission to the U.S. Army Air Forces, complete with support units all the way to Scotland. As he pointed out, "if the USAAF operate a ferrying of aircraft for delivery in the British Isles, they must control the weather and communications systems all the way to the British Isles, including the terminal point."[727]

A sustained, intensive air bridge requires your own support staff in place along the route. But Elliott also realized that the RAF simply did not have the resources to cope with what was coming. In this, however, he echoed existing American command thinking. Nonetheless, for political and resource reasons, it wasn't until 1942 that the Americans would essentially take over the North Atlantic air service.[728]

Acting in part on these recommendations, General Arnold and his British counterparts continuously tried to keep the command structure adjusted to the evolving reality. In July 1941, the latter set up RAF Ferry Command to replace the previous quasi-civilian ATFERO (Atlantic Ferry Organization). Still, the line between the civil BOAC (British Overseas Airline) and the RAF remained fluid and indistinct.[729]

Arnold created the U.S. Ferrying Command in May 1941; in July 1942 it became Air Transport Command (ATC). After the war this global behemoth became MATS (Military Air Transport Service), then MAC (Military Airlift Command), and now it is known as Air Mobility Command (AMC). The frequent name changes obscure the fact that the outfit is essentially a cargo airline at the call of all the military services.

In 1941, the notion that the military should run what amounts to an airline was odd and controversial, and there were very few dedicated cargo aircraft. The result was that civilian aircraft were impressed into service, and so were their crews. Major American airlines and their pilots made a pretty penny supplying the remote North Atlantic bases. This was a good thing, for the airline crews were far better prepared for these kinds of long-distance operations than were the military.[730]

---

[i] Initially, Curtiss SOC-4 Seagulls; later Grumman J2F Ducks.

Gander would become the most critical node in this immense but then embryonic transatlantic air traffic. This period of massive growth was oddly referred to by one writer, an ATC officer, as "The Eagle in the Egg." By that curiously evocative analogy, Elliott Roosevelt was pecking hard at the shell, but what kind of bird he would be was still up in the air.[731]

The Wingless Pilot

To be perfectly accurate, Elliott Roosevelt did not fly Arctic reconnaissance missions. He was a passenger aboard planes that did. Of course, we could look at it the way Admiral Byrd did: the aircrew was just an accessory.[i]

After the war, Roosevelt said that he had personally flown every single type of reconnaissance airplane in use, including the single-seaters. This raised many eyebrows. Elliott's piloting career was an object of great controversy and often vicious dispute.[732]

Until 1945, Roosevelt was not a rated (Air Force) pilot, though he had a pre-war civilian (CAA) student license. He could not pass the physical examination for military aviators; his eyesight was far too weak.[733] However, in January 1945, the White House exerted "considerable pressure" to have him made pilot, and upon discharge in 1945 his MOS (Military Occupational Specialty), which had been NAVIGATOR AND BOMBARDIER, was listed as PILOT AND NAVIGATOR.[734]

James Roosevelt wrote that Elliott inveigled himself onto the pilot rolls by signing physical disability waivers.[735] This, of course, was far from normal procedure, but he did a lot that was abnormal, and got away with it. The Air Force values exceptional eyesight; it is a proven advantage. In contrast, the FAA tolerates civilian pilots who can artificially correct their visual acuity to "normal."

Rated or not, Elliott Roosevelt eventually did fly combat missions, although he did not have to. His service record listed over 1100 flight hours, 300+ of which in combat, and 89 combat missions. It was also carefully noted that Elliott, around the time of his promotion to flag rank in January 1945, had performed 30 combat missions in single-seat aircraft. Those are exceptionally high totals, especially for someone who came home alive and unscathed. However, discordant reports from subordinates sharply questioned the accuracy of those numbers, and they are probably inflated.[736]

In 1945, Elliott proclaimed that he had "470 hours combat time" and "to join the Army, had in excess of 2500 hours air time."[737] For comparison, we may refer to General Robert Dixon, then 14th PRS squadron commander, who was reputed to be the highest-time reconnaissance pilot in the theater; he had 235 combat hours in 65 missions before he was shot down. It was generally accepted that a "tour" was 200 hours.[738]

If Elliott's numbers were exaggerated, perhaps the rub lies in the exact definitions of air time, command pilot, combat, and mission. He did fly many important and dangerous sorties, and if he padded the numbers he was not the only one. Glory aside, there was coveted flight pay to claim. We shall have reason to look at this in more detail when we come to the European theater, but in the meantime, it is clear that Elliott was desperate to fly, and to get as close to the action as possible.

---

[i] Admiral Richard Byrd led numerous polar expeditions. In 1926, Floyd Bennett reportedly flew him over the North Pole (investigators do not believe this), and Bernt Balchen flew him over the South Pole in 1929.

Elliott later claimed to have been wounded – four times, his last wife, Patricia, said. His *New York Times* obituarist had heard "twice" – but that is contradicted by military records. His discharge papers state that he was not wounded. It was known that he got roughed up in a few incidents, but not to the extent of requiring medical care.[739]

Critics were most puzzled how a navigator acquired this record – especially later when Elliott was promoted to brigadier general – without pilot's wings. This was thought unique for a non-rated airman. But with his waivers, his proven capabilities, and the approval of his superiors, Brigadier General Roosevelt did indisputably end the war as a *bona fide* veteran combat pilot.

Until 1945, as far as officialdom was concerned, Elliott Roosevelt always had a pilot flying him – right from the beginning in the Arctic. In those hectic days, though, rules were often flagrantly disregarded, and Elliott was not the kind who took no for an answer. General Jimmy Doolittle said that, later in the war, he forbade Elliott from flying combat because he was totally fearless, and Doolittle did not want to have to explain to the president how he had let his son get himself killed. But he added, "I almost broke his heart when I took him off flying." [740]

The units he commanded had larger aircraft assigned as "hacks" or supplemental types. The accounts we have of Elliott in action usually place him in a multi-engined bomber, but he often flew as pilot. In North Africa, he had his own B-25, and in England, his own B-17. He also routinely flew the de Havilland Mosquito, a fighter-bomber flown by a crew of two side-by-side.[741] In his North Atlantic job, though, he was only an eager guest in the cockpit, armed with cameras, film and incorrect maps.[742]

Apart from Elliott's crippling nearsightedness, critics also noted that at 6 foot 3 and 225 pounds, he was far from the best fit for a cockpit. Again, his service certificate in 1945 lists his weight as 199 pounds, and he did later point out to gossip meister Walter Winchell in the Stork Club that he'd lost 43 pounds overseas.[743]

The adjectives "chunky," "strapping," and "husky" seemed to stick with him, even from birth. One account (from North Africa) mentions that Elliott would fly with a very crowded pilot at his side. In fact, the pilot said, Elliott was so large that he could not wear a parachute: "That plane [Mosquito] we fly is just big enough for two of us, and he is a big man – so big he cannot even wear a parachute. You know what that could mean if we got winged. That takes what we politely call fortitude."[744]

It might also have been evidence of the hazy line between courage and idiocy, and perhaps of the "good old days" of Air Force regulations. At any rate, it fits the image of a fearless officer who was keen to demonstrate that he was given no special coddling on account of his family.

The identity of the pilot who made this admiring remark is not irrelevant. He was Major Harry T. Eidson. We shall meet him later, for he'd get to fly more than Elliott's airplane, so to speak.[745]

In Newfoundland, Elliott volunteered to carry out reconnaissance of the Arctic in preparation for further Allied bases and installations in the region. This task having priority and high visibility, Elliott had access not only to the dowdy B-18s, but to other aircraft that could be impressed into duty on an occasional basis. Most importantly, Elliott was able to secure the use of the odd B-24A Liberator. There were very few of these long-range four-motored bombers available in 1941, but a handful was used for special missions, including route-proving operations and VIP transport.

Elliott flew on a Liberator on an extensive East Greenland reconnaissance mission in late August 1941. He crossed the Atlantic to the United Kingdom twice during his route surveys. [746]

Captain Roosevelt did not have a high opinion of his Arctic assignment. To let him describe it:

> I've reached around in my mind for the proper word to describe conditions – weather conditions, living conditions, conditions of terrain or rather lack-of-terrain – up in Newfoundland, in March of 1941. Perhaps "rugged" will serve, if by "rugged" you will understand that I mean miserable, muddy, bleak, and woebegone, all rolled into one. Operating as much as anything on the theory that nothing could be more unpleasant than Newfoundland in March of 1941, I volunteered for a survey job to locate air-force sites in the North Arctic area which could be used as staging points for the delivery of fighter aircraft from the United States to the United Kingdom. ...the job took me from Labrador to Baffin Island to Greenland and Iceland and eventually clear over to England, where I was to compare findings with British fliers and officials of the Air Ministry. I would have preferred, frankly, to have timed my visit to England a bit later: I arrived at the tail-end of the Nazis' May-June blitz of 1941. To be sure, it was only the tail-end, but it was enough...[747]

Elliott's breezy style understated the critical importance of his task. Air Chief Marshal Sir Hugh Dowding and U.S. General Carl "Tooey" Spaatz flew to Ottawa in the spring of 1941 to press the case for the northern air route.[i] Captain Roosevelt followed there in early June and, among other tasks, discussed the surveys he planned to make of the Labrador and Baffin Land coasts.[748]

Another, seemingly insignificant, part of the job was to be friendly with dignitaries who came through Gander Airport. For example, when the president's closest aide and alter ego, Harry Hopkins, stopped over in July 1941, Elliott took a day off and went fishing with him.[749] Hopkins was a former social worker who had risen to be FDR's closest political adviser and fix-it guy – as well as a permanent house guest. He was on his way over to meet Winston Churchill to smooth lend-lease deliveries and discuss ways to get America deeper into the war.

On this trip in late July, Hopkins went ahead to Moscow, where he spent five days preparing the "United Nations" for the top-secret Argentia summit. He then returned to Newfoundland with Churchill aboard HMS *Prince of Wales.*

Elliott and Harry Hopkins would be on friendly terms thereafter. Hopkins was also a close ally of Joseph Stalin. There is an unresolved dispute over whether he was a true Soviet agent, but this is largely irrelevant. During the summits and his shuttle diplomacy across the Atlantic, Hopkins worked as much for Uncle Joe as for FDR. A striking example emerges from Yalta, the summit at which half of Europe was conceded to the Soviet Union. Elliott writes, in regard to the reparations issue, that Hopkins slipped a note to FDR: "The Russians have given in so much at this conference that I don't think we should let them down."[750]

While he was in Newfoundland, Captain Roosevelt's admiration for Stalin was not yet apparent. Prior to the Argentia summit, he apparently held to the anti-dictator view

---

[i] Both were air power legends. Dowding, controversial Fighter Command victor of the Battle of Britain, had been "kicked upstairs." Spaatz would command the U.S. strategic air forces in Europe.

he had broadcast as a civilian. Until 22 June 1941, the USSR was widely viewed as part of the problem, not the solution. But Elliott could turn on a dime, and so could Stalin.

Although Captain Elliott could now claim to be part of the solution too, and not a problem for FDR any more, the Roosevelt-haters were not quite done with him. While he whined about his miserable time on the barren island, his stay – four months, nominally – wasn't nearly as bad as it was for most of his colleagues. That's because he spent most of the time traveling. As he gathered information and briefed superiors on his work, his flights ranged from Washington to London and capitals in between.

At the beginning of May, Elliott was still in Washington.[751] Eleanor wrote on the 14th that Elliott and Ruth were still there.[752] White House records show him departing on the 23rd, which matches Colonel George Stratemeyer's notice to the president that Elliott arrived in Gander on the 26th.

In her memoir, Eleanor elaborated on her son's first leave. As we know, his squadron commander considered him an obnoxious nuisance, which might have been a factor in his trip home:

> It [Gander] was a very unpleasant experience for them. There was no flying field [not true], so they had to start building one. One railroad train a week brought in the necessary oil for the field. There was a small Canadian camp adjoining, but nothing else in the way of civilization. These combined circumstances produced a good deal of unhappiness and considerable illness. I had some depressed letters from Elliott at that time, and he was jubilant when the commanding officer sent him down in early May or June to sit in somebody's office in Washington until he had acquired the necessary medical supplies and recreation equipment. We had a glimpse of him on that trip, and he went back feeling much better, knowing that if the boys could not get away [like him] at least they would have some kind of recreation in camp.[753]

Elliott told her mother that at Gander, it was easy to think that you'd been forgotten by your family and friends as well as your government.[754]

On 5 June, he was in Ottawa, continuing on to London and back. He was at the White House again from 17 to 21 June. On that last day, an alert apartment manager in Washington found Elliott's wallet with his and Ruth's identification on the roof garden of a seemingly entirely unrelated building complex. A resident noticed a young lady, unknown to him, who had just left at the time he found the material, which included airline tickets. The manager very kindly forwarded it to the FBI.[755] Intelligence training apparently hadn't taught Elliott to be careful with his belongings. It wouldn't be the first time he lost important papers.

Obviously this wasn't quite the same drudgery as befell other Arctic assignees; typically, they stayed on post for a year. No extended sleepovers at the White House or Chequers for them. And they were lucky to get a mail drop from an airplane a few times a year. The Roosevelt-haters took note.

Through the Air Corps, the parents kept close tabs on Elliott. Captain Norstad even had to wire Elliott's wife about his movements and any delays on his travels.[756] Eleanor noted that he arrived safely back in Newfoundland on 22 June, and was then preparing for "a mapping trip which should be over in August," which means, in effect, that the president gave or approved his son's orders.[757]

Captain Roosevelt again lodged at the White House from 14 to 21 July. In late July 1941, he showed up in the beach resort town of Swampscott, Mass., along with his wife and children, for a weekend of leisure and recuperation. Although the White House had long planned this diversion, the beach vacation didn't go over too well with the public after the newspapers found out. Soon it was reported that the president's second son had arranged to take weekends off from his military assignments. It did not help that the other Roosevelt boys in uniform also seemed to obtain quite a bit of relaxation stateside.[758]

Not fair, in Elliott's view; but at least he knew he was being watched. Two weeks later Swampscott was rumored to be the location of the Roosevelt-Churchill summit. The yachting town was a favored bolt hole for the nautically inclined Roosevelts, and it wasn't unhelpful for the press to speculate that this was where FDR was headed on his mystery voyage. The president used his son and his family as a decoy, and it worked. The bloodhounds of the press were in Swampscott, panting and circling, while FDR was at sea enroute to Newfoundland.[759]

All this considered it is not so hard to understand why Major Crabb, commander of the 21st Recon, hated Elliott's guts. There is a surviving flurry of dispatches between the White House, Bolling Field, and Gander Lake about Elliott. A handwritten note stated:

> Bolling Field phoned at 935PM and stated as follows: Gen Watson [FDR's military aide] phoned that President wants to know present whereabouts Capt. Elliott Roosevelt and wants him to remain at Gander Lake when he returns from present reconnaissance.[760]

Newfoundland responded to Washington that Elliott had arrived on 30 July and expected to continue to Bolling on 4 August.

The president did not want that. For reasons unfathomable to Major Crabb, he was told to keep Elliott around, and that he might "receive further instructions from higher authority other than this headquarters." Since that signal was from HQ Air Force Combat Command, Crabb may well have thought the White House was jerking his unusual subordinate around at will. He had to tell Captain Roosevelt not to go home to Washington as scheduled.[761]

Instead, the president would come to Elliott.

Beginning on 8 August, Elliott attended the Argentia summit, of which much more later. After that memorable experience, he flew to London for an extensive and highly publicized visit.[762] He continued back to Iceland by 31 August. He submitted his last report (No. 4) on the Iceland situation to the Air Corps on 8 September 1941. Then, by 4 September, he was back with the family at the White House. He attended his grandmother Sara's funeral at Hyde Park on the 9th, and stayed another couple of days until his next assignment in Texas came due.[763]

Captain Roosevelt's Arctic explorations had taken him only a few weeks in total.

AN OLD QUEST

General Arnold cast some surprising light on Elliott's Arctic exploits in his memoir, *Global Mission.* He wrote:

> Elliott Roosevelt was the first man to come to me with a plan for flying over the ice cap. He had selected a crew, had a plane picked out, and all he needed was my authority. Elliott Roosevelt took the first airplane across the Greenland ice cap. When he returned, he brought first-hand information. There were no big mountains, 14,000 feet high. There were a few hills, a few mountains, but they weren't especially tall. In general, he reported, the top of the Greenland ice cap was a big dome, made of solid ice. The wind blew and there was apparently one blizzard after another, but the weather wasn't impossible for flying by any means. In many places it would be possible to land airplanes successfully, Elliott thought, so we might even get airplanes in and out in case of emergency. That picture tore away the veil of mystery in which the Greenland ice cap had been shrouded for centuries.[764]

This is a disconcertingly shallow evaluation of a weighty matter, although it does reaffirm Arnold's high opinion of Elliott's initiative and productivity.

The problem is that by the summer of 1941, the Greenland ice cap was fairly well known; it had been flown over several times, although not crossed by the American military.[i] The ice cap had even been traversed on skis and motorsleds. Was Arnold not aware of all the work his own staff had prepared on Greenland since the German occupation of Denmark on 9 April 1940? More likely, Arnold was simply very busy, and in his recollection his personal relationship with Elliott trumped staff studies.

Elliott's synopsis was also quite superficial. Yes, the wind blew in Greenland. But his overall assessment, which was actually one of many produced by the U.S. military, did not advance the general knowledge very far. At the time he made his reconnaissance flights in August, the main base at Bluie West One (BW-1) was already beginning construction, and the expedition for BW-8 (Sondrestrom) was being organized.[ii] Neither Captain Roosevelt nor General Arnold appeared to have a good grasp of all the studies and surveys that had gone before. Perhaps the president was better informed; he had always followed transatlantic air route developments closely, especially in the Greenland case.

If he did not necessarily discover much that was new, Captain Roosevelt did learn a lot about photographic reconnaissance. He later said:

> Sir, during the survey of the North Atlantic bases through which was established the Goose Bay terminal in Labrador, and the Crystal bases, and Blooey bases in Greenland, I was required to learn by the hardest way, which was experience through the taking of photographs of the terrain and the establishment of whether that terrain would be satisfactory for bases, and after the pictures were developed then we had to go back and go ashore from PBY aircraft and land on these areas, and survey them on foot. That was my first contact with photographic survey work.[765]

---

[i] The Ice Cap was first crossed by air eastbound by Americans Parker Cramer and Oliver Paquette in 1931, followed immediately by Wolfgang von Gronau's flight in the opposite direction (Grierson, 271).

[ii] Nobody knows why American sites in Greenland were named Bluie (it could have been a joke), but they had other codenames as well, which served to confuse not only the enemy. This was also true for the Canadian Arctic stations.

He had joined the pursuit of one of aviation's holiest grails. The search for a Northern Air Route, a modern analogue of the fabled Northwestern Passage, is almost as old as human flight. It takes little genius to look at a globe and realize that Iceland, Greenland, and Labrador are keys to domination of the North Atlantic as well as stepping-stones across it. This was especially true in the days when aircraft were severely range-limited, acutely weather-sensitive, and prone to need emergency fields. The stepping stones can keep the individual legs of a transatlantic flight to around 660 nautical miles and, with doglegs, even less.

While the Atlantic had been flown from Newfoundland directly to Ireland in 1919, the first proof of the stepping stone concept came in 1924, when the U.S. Navy's two remaining Douglas World Cruiser seaplanes transited via Iceland, Greenland, and Labrador in completing the first aerial circumnavigation of the Earth. But the early efforts mostly demonstrated just how treacherous the route was.[i]

The most significant of the prewar route-proving surveys was that of another American officer, Colonel Charles Lindbergh, in 1933. (Reserve Lt. Lindbergh was appointed colonel after his first transatlantic flight in 1927. It was a real rank, although it was used as an honorific in his case.) Pan American Airways had sent him to the North Atlantic, and his sober report on the tough local conditions emphasized the difficulties of operating aircraft in the region. Because Lindbergh was preoccupied with the complicated problem of operating with hull, pontoon, ski, and wheel undercarriage in some reasonable combination, he ultimately thought it was better to wait until long-range seaplanes could operate directly between Newfoundland and the British Isles.[766]

Pan Am would take his advice. In 1939, the airline initiated scheduled flying boat service between Botwood, Nfld. and Foynes by Shannon, Ireland. Events soon overtook the commercial version of this nascent route, but it continued as a crucially important passenger service for official travel during the war.

Lindbergh's unenthusiastic report (which Juan Trippe showed to FDR) must be viewed in the proper context. He was concerned about the safety and regularity of civilian service and did not consider wartime operations. Of course, by the time Elliott Roosevelt got to the Arctic, Lindbergh was *persona non grata*, especially to a Roosevelt!

Until FDR taunted the reserve colonel into resigning his commission, Lindbergh's boss and admirer had been one Henry "Hap" Arnold, for whom the famed flier had carried out some delicate foreign surveys.[767] It is inconceivable that Hap would not also have been aware of Lindbergh's arctic survey. The colonel's report shows that he had already located the sites that later surveyors, including Elliott, would be credited with:

> In laying out a northern air route I believe the coast should be avoided wherever possible...subject to much more detailed study, I suggest laying a tentative northern transatlantic route along the west coast of Newfoundland to the vicinity of Botwood; from Botwood to the vicinity of Northwest River; from Northwest River to a point between Godthaab and the Ice Cap, and from there to Iceland...Dr. Hobbs has located several places where fields could be constructed in the Holsteinsborg vicinity, and Major Logan found a valley where a two-way field a mile or two long could apparently be constructed without too great difficulty.[ii]

---

[i] Glines: The First Flight Around the World; Grierson, Challenge to the Poles. The first transatlantic flight was made by a companion of the Curtiss NC in which FDR took a hop in 1919. NC-4 flew to Portugal via the Azores later that year. A British flight by landplanes from Newfoundland to Ireland soon followed.

[ii] Grierson, 646-55. Refers to RCAF Squadron Leader R.A. Logan, who also wrote reports on the Arctic.

Lindbergh's analysis was supplemented by his own visual scouting:

> ...From the air it seemed that a field location would not be difficult to find at Northwest River...There seemed to be several possible locations east of Holsteinsborg and east of Godthaab. Even these may prove expensive to develop after a ground survey...in contrast to Greenland there are many natural landing areas in Iceland and comparatively little difficulty would be encountered in constructing airports in almost any section.

This would indeed become the geometry of the northern route. Gander (and nearby Botwood), Goose Bay (by Northwest River), and Sondrestrom (Bluie West 8) would be far better suited weather-wise than the Julianehaab area, near Cape Farewell. According to Lindbergh, the area near Angmagssalik (Bluie East 2) would be extremely difficult and should be avoided if possible. Several airfields would be needed for alternates in Iceland. Lindbergh even knew about the approximate future site of BW-1, which would become the headquarters of Greenland Base Command in 1941:

> ...Apparently the country south east of Julianehaab is less subject to fog. Governor Ibsen suggested the lake at Greenland Forest as a fog-free area. Our observations supported this. The lake is large enough, but surrounded by mountains on three sides. In this respect it should be born in mind that there are very few level areas in Greenland, and most of these in places impracticable for a transatlantic air line.

He could not then have anticipated that a world war and almost unlimited American resources would nonetheless soon open up alternative short-hop routes across the Atlantic stepping-stones, anchored in almost exactly the locations he had suggested.

Bases and Stations

The task that Elliott Roosevelt faced should not be underestimated on account of previous surveys. The problem is not merely that the North Atlantic islands suffer with atrocious weather and lack natural airfields. It must also be recalled that half the year, it is mostly dark and very cold. In addition, icing, severe turbulence, and unmapped mountains could make an aircrew's life difficult and short.

Air traffic requires not only airfields; it also depends on navigation beacons, weather stations, fuel depots, and radio communications sites. Suitable locations had to be found for all these. Finally, air traffic, however revolutionary, usually is supported logistically by seaports, roads, and railways. Little of this infrastructure existed in the Arctic, and the anchorages that did exist were likely to be frozen during most of the year.

Against this formidable backdrop arose a desperate need. Since Atlantic shipping was increasingly vulnerable, the search for a northern air route across Greenland and Iceland was reactivated by London as soon as the Danish colonies were left dangling by the German occupation of Norway and Denmark in April 1940.

It wasn't merely a matter of ferrying aircraft. At the very highest level in Canada and the United States it was immediately recognized that Greenland had, at Ivigtut, the world's only operating cryolite mine, being a large quarry right next to tidewater.

Cryolite was then essential for aluminum production, and North American aircraft factories depended absolutely upon it.

The mine as well as its sea traffic had to be protected. A single shell in the right place could have flooded it, and it is curious that the German marine raiders never gave it a try; had they done so, North American aircraft production would have been crippled. Of course, this probably would have provoked the United States into the war.[i]

Secondly, transatlantic convoys desperately needed air cover, and patrol aircraft did not then have sufficient range to effect this from Iceland and Newfoundland. Greenland was earmarked for anti-submarine patrol as soon as the first field there was ready in the spring of 1942. Ancillary to this, ice cover had to be charted, and weather systems tracked; search and rescue capabilities had to be improvised. A considerable amount of air work had to be allocated simply to supplying this infrastructure itself.

Weather reconnaissance was a crucial factor which can be hard to appreciate in the age of computers and satellites. To exacerbate the issue, a prewar theory known as the Greenland Glacial Anticyclone, or popularly, "the North Pole of the Winds," had gained unexpected prominence. This was chiefly due to the efforts of Dr. William Hobbs, whose meteorological expeditions to the Sondrestrom area had coincidentally located a promising landing field during his pursuit of regular upper-air circulation data.[768]

Hobbs's theory held that Greenland was a sort of weather factory for Eurasia. Although it is true that the Greenland ice cap is a factor in the creation and modulation of storms later to hit Europe, by 1941 it was already recognized by meteorologists that the Greenland anti-cyclone concept had been blown way out of proportion.[769]

Nonetheless, the weather issue was still deemed so critical that not only the Allies, but also the Germans – against even more forbidding odds – would set up regularly reporting meteorological observatories in the Arctic Islands from Labrador clear over to the Soviet Union. Both sides also operated weather ships in the North Atlantic, and they regularly flew dedicated weather reconnaissance missions over it.

This was a good education for Elliott Roosevelt. Three years later, in England, he commanded entire squadrons of weather reconnaissance aircraft over the North Atlantic.

So fixed bases, stations, and minor support sites had to be found whether they were possible or not. During the summer of 1940, a joint Army-Navy-Canadian seaborne mission explored for bases in Greenland. At the same time, Britain occupied Iceland and built two small airports at Reykjavik and Kaldadarnes, with smaller strips elsewhere. In November, Britain also began to use Gander airport for direct ferry flights to Scotland.[770]

At first, the British flew small formations of bombers across at a time. As time went on, it was considered more advantageous to proceed singly. The inaugural flight on Armistice Day in 1940 landed at Aldergrove, Northern Ireland, but presently the terminus at Prestwick, Ayrshire, was found to be more reliable. During this period the Irish Free State not only did not interfere with overflights, but allowed Shannon/Foynes to be turned into a major hub for Allied civilian transatlantic operations.

The first aircraft flown across were Lockheed Hudson twin-engine light bombers, a type the RAF found useful for coastal patrol although it could not survive over

[i] This issue was discussed intermittently with great alarm in U.S. and Canadian diplomatic notes. (see Foreign Relations of the United States and the Canadian equivalent.)

Europe. Britain had surprisingly good results with direct ferry; but the immense build-up promised for the future and the need to ferry smaller aircraft with shorter range reinforced the push to obtain Arctic bases.[i]

After Britain ran out of money in March 1941, Lend-Lease replaced Cash-and-Carry as the barely legal framework for dramatically expanded weapons deliveries.[ii] During April 1941, a month before Elliott's debut in the region, General Arnold visited London and conferred with the Air Ministry about the securing of bases in the North Atlantic to support the rapidly increasing aircraft exports. From this point on, the search for bases in the Arctic had the highest possible priority.[771]

During 1941, President Roosevelt always justified the case for intervention with the fear of German invasion. Between the Greenland Treaty of 9 April and the Iceland occupation on 6 July he was very preoccupied with the North Atlantic. On 28 May, he ordered the American development of the ferry route, right on the heels of sending the 21st Recon with his son north to Gander. The night before, the president spoke to the nation, presenting to a worried people a frightening west-bound mirror image of his own east-bound Arctic thrust:

> Most of the supplies for Britain go by a northerly route, which comes close to Greenland and the nearby island of Iceland. Germany's heaviest attack is on that route. Nazi occupation of Iceland or bases in Greenland would bring the war close to our continental shores, because they are stepping stones to Labrador, Newfoundland, Nova Scotia, and the Northern U.S., including the great industrial centers of the north, east, and Middle West.
>
> Equally, the Azores and the Cape Verde islands, if occupied or controlled by Germany, would directly endanger the freedom of the Atlantic and our own physical safety. Under German domination they would become bases for submarines, warships, and airplanes raiding the waters which lie immediately off shipping in the South Atlantic. They would provide a springboard for actual attack against the integrity and independence of Brazil and her neighboring republics.[772]

With this long and ringing speech, President Roosevelt declared a state of "unlimited national emergency."

At about that date, Elliott was tasked with exploring for air bases. Arnold said it was on his own initiative; but since the captain spent many days at the White House at just the right times, it defies credulity that he and his father had not discussed the idea beforehand. At the very least, we know that the 21st Recon's commander thought the whole thing a political imposition.[773]

This was still a few weeks before Elliott flew his Arctic reconnaissance. He wrote afterwards as if he had been the only one to go air base prospecting in the North Atlantic, and it is possible that he simple did not know about the stacks of preparatory work that had been carried out by others.

When the U.S. Coast Guard took over the supply and care of Greenland in the shipping season of 1940, Air Corps Captain Julius K. Lacey, a meteorologist, was sent along to scout the terrain.[774] Flying aboard the cutter *Duane's* SOC-4, he identified some

---

[i] Atlantic Bridge, passim. "Surprisingly good" means 263 of 266 aircraft were successfully delivered.

[ii] "Lend-lease" of course is a euphemism for a give-away of equipment. Due to residual neutrality sentiment, FDR reportedly thought it could get him impeached, but Congress approved the idea in part to evade direct involvement in the war. (J.M. Burns, 43-49)

sites as promising; but by August-September it was too late in the season to do anything more that year.

In February 1941, the Air Corps obtained two reports on air bases in Arctic Canada and in Greenland. They had been prepared by Squadron Leader R.A. Logan, RCAF, who had a good appreciation of the problems involved. Logan had consulted for Pan American Airways in 1932, but his "Notes on Greenland" focused almost entirely on seaplane access.[775]

The first important reconnaissance of the new season took place on 22 April 1941, when Don Bennett of ATFERO, the British ferry organization, commandeered a spanking new LB-30 Liberator at Gander. This was an epochal flight. It appears to have been the first operational use of Liberator bombers, since Bennett took the first of a batch of six, before they were even delivered to Britain. Bennett, an Australian who would rise to Air Vice Marshal, was already an accomplished Atlantic pilot – in fact he had led the first Hudson deliveries over the winter. At any rate, Bennett raved about his first Greenland mission (as indeed most pilots do). He said he had the aircraft full of photographic equipment and a great deal of film:

> We searched in and out the fjords and we hunted as best we could, taking photographs as we went. Wherever we could see the slightest piece of flat, we went and investigated and took photos. We found the ketch successfully, as planned, and dropped our messages...[776]

Perhaps because it was British, this flight has not received the historical attention it deserves. The narrative in the official Air Ministry account *Atlantic Bridge* is an important source to the joint efforts to reconnoiter Greenland, and worth quoting at length:

> ...The USAAF informed the British that South Greenland was being explored for a possible aerodrome site by a Danish ship which was to proceed later up the West Coast. A second expedition was being arranged to survey the East Coast. The ferrying of single-engine fighters, it was agreed, was dependent on the finding of available aerodrome sites at Angmagssalik or Scoresby Sound and at Godthaab or Holsteinsborg. There would also have to be an aerodrome in Labrador at Northwest River and another, if possible, farther north.
>
> It was arranged to send a B-24 Liberator over South-Western Greenland to reconnoiter possible sites, to carry out a general inspection of the South Coast of Greenland from its southern tip (Cape Farewell) to Julianehaab, and to photograph the country. An outline map of the possible sites, as viewed from the air, was to be marked and the marked map dropped in a waterproof container near the ship; the photographs would be developed later, and any information useful to the ship would be wirelessed by the U.S. Army.
>
> On 22 April a survey flight took off from Gander at 0407 GMT and proceeded to carry out a non-stop survey flight to Julianehaab, Greenland, and Hamilton Inlet, Labrador [Goose Bay area]; it returned to St. Hubert [Montreal] at 1851, the airborne flight time being 14 hours and 44 minutes.
>
> The report by Captain D.C.T. Bennett of this survey included these comments: "The landfall was actually made at a point near Aluk, east of Cape Farewell. At this point there was a 50-knot wind from the North, with clouds well down over the mountains, and it was therefore impossible to go up the deep fjords; but the nature of the terrain (hard black rock mountains rising straight out of the sea) made it appear extremely unlikely that any possible sites would exist in this part of the coast. After we

> rounded Cape Farewell, the weather conditions improved considerably, and also the type of country improved slightly. This improvement took the form of a different kind of rock, apparently sandstone, as the basic construction of many of the small islands around the coast and parts of the mainland itself. Whereas the hard black rock of the mountains appeared to be the worst possible kind of country, the sandstone looked as if it might well be worked with pneumatic drills, blasting, etc. The sites which we chose were pinpointed quite independently both by myself and by the First Officer. Unfortunately in the case of the two sites near Julianehaab, the First Officer and myself disagree on the actual fixes on the chart. This unfortunate situation has apparently occurred because of the difficulty of orienting oneself with the compass swinging as badly as it does in that vicinity during manoeuvres. I have therefore marked on the accompanying sketch the position of the two possible sites near Julianehaab both as I found them and as the First Officer found them.
>
> A small motor vessel was then seen to the east of Julianehaab [in the fjord]; when we circled, it stopped and lowered a small boat. We flew over it and dropped one copy of the large-scale chart on which we had marked the possible sites chosen. I wrote on the chart the following: 'To Commander Sinton. I regret that I have not found any place suitable for an aerodrome, but the points marked are bare possibilities. D.C.T. Bennett.'
>
> The course was then set for a direct track to North West River, Hamilton Inlet. On our arrival at that place, however, the weather was so bad that it was impossible to carry out any inspection of photography. The flight was, therefore, continued direct to Montreal."[777]

The areas photographed near Julianehaab probably covered the Narssarssuaq plain, which would become the famous (or infamous) Bluie West One (BW-1).

This British flight required coordination of Canadian, American, and Danish authorities, including the U.S. Coast Guard. In this task, the USCGC *Cayuga* was aided by the tiny Danish naval vessel *Ternen*.[778]

However, this South Greenland Survey Mission had to rely on aerial reconnaissance in those areas where the fjords were still frozen hard. In addition, at this time of year the ground is still snow-covered, so even aerial photographs, whether obtained by the Liberator or *Cayuga's* small J2F Duck, could only provide approximations.

Nonetheless, confidence was high enough to green-light the BW-1 project at the end of April. The construction convoy arrived in June, when the fjord was finally open, and the engineers promptly found that conditions were not as easy as had been promised.[779]

Only the desperate would have selected the BW-1 site. Surrounded by mountains, the fields sits at the far end – plus a final devious dogleg – of a complex fjord system. The topography can be thought of as a giant funnel directing some of the worst weather in the world straight to the base. It was necessary to place auxiliary stations for radio beacons, weather and communications at carefully selected points in the fjord system. The Americans even installed coastal and anti-aircraft artillery in suitable places along the narrow fjord.

Captain Roosevelt came upon the scene too late to take credit for BW-1, although he later did so. In fact, there was a story at his Gander base that they began receiving weather reports from BW-1, but since the location was secret, they were of little help to forecasters![780] But Elliott was instrumental in the establishment of the Goose Bay airfield in Labrador, a similar and equally important base on the North Atlantic route.

Goose Bay, Labrador

At home, General Spaatz was holding meetings with Arctic experts in late May, revealing that the Air Corps was planning a series of expeditions to find airfields in the Canadian Arctic.[781] On 5 June, Captain Roosevelt went to Ottawa on what was described as a "mysterious mission." He spent four days there on an "officially private mission" during which he met with ranking political and military contacts. Elliott then went to England for more talks.[782]

As we have seen, Spaatz and Dowding also went to Ottawa, and the consultations continued in London, where an important discussion of the ferry route at the Air Ministry on 10 July also left a trace in Canadian archives.[783] It seems Captain Roosevelt was extremely well connected in his new endeavor.

By late June, he was finally ready to get out in the field.

In his later imagination, Elliott Roosevelt found and founded the giant Goose Bay airport in Labrador. He knew better, but the facts tended to slip a bit in his favor after a few years. Nonetheless it is true that he was "present at the creation" of that important installation.[784]

The area around Lake Melville had been eyed for an airfield for years. In fact, Don Bennett's epic flight in April attempted to photograph it. But Canadian civilian geodesist Eric Fry found the actual construction site first.[785] In May 1941, he was asked to operate out of Gander in order to find suitable locations in Labrador.[786]

Flying in a Supermarine Stranraer, a large, ugly and very obsolete seaplane, Fry landed at the small settlement at Northwest River, a "Grenfell Mission," i.e. a charitable support point in the northern wilds. From there he explored the Lake Melville area, and on 28 June he surveyed the plateau that would soon be host to Goose Bay airport. Eric Fry had to fly some risky survey flights in horrible weather and later remarked:

> Taking those chances, however, made history and gave Goose Bay Airport to Canada. Colonel Roosevelt of the USAAF flew to Goose Bay on exactly the same mission. He arrived a few days after I had finished staking out the area for the new air base. I had already sent in the report of my preliminary survey when he arrived.[787]

This account illustrates how important it was for Canada to claim priority. However, as we have seen, the general area was already known as a potential airport location. That's why Roosevelt went there, too.

On 19 June, General Marshall requested the Navy's assistance with an airfield reconnaissance project in Labrador. Two days later, the Atlantic Fleet was told to cooperate with the 21st Recon Squadron in Gander, providing two patrol bombers and a tender to assist in finding air base sites: "This detachment was to be assembled in Argentia as soon as possible, and in the meantime, the RCAF was to make aviation gasoline available at Cartwright, Hebron, and Lake Harbor and in Newfoundland."[788]

Thus suddenly Elliott had control of two Navy PBYs. His first target was Goose Bay.

The survey team included Dr. Alexander Forbes, Lt. Cdr., U.S. Naval Reserve, a prominent neurologist who, as a recreational sideline, had completed three aerial photographic surveys of the coast of Labrador in the 1930s. His advice and earlier photographs were helpful in focusing the search. Forbes, bless his heart, was a keen observer who took both notes and pictures, and he published a detailed account of the expedition after the war:

> On the morning of June 30 two flying boats arrived [at Gander] from Argentia to take us on the first lap of our journey. After a final conference we proceeded to Gander Lake, a mile from the field, and boarded. Captain Roosevelt was to be in command; Mr. Preston, a civil engineer with much airport experience gained at Stephenville, in western Newfoundland, was to accompany us as chief expert on airport requirements; two young Army lieutenants, Zienowicz and David, and two Army photographers with surveying cameras were also in the party. My designation was "technical adviser."
>
> The planes took us first to their base at Argentia in the southeast corner of Newfoundland where they would refuel and be ready to start at dawn the next day for Lake Melville. The harbor at Argentia presented the greatest possible contrast to the Gander airport. Here, in a sheltered haven bordered by noble hills with precipitous slopes, lay a substantial detachment of the U.S. Navy – a battleship, a cruiser, destroyers, and a number of flying boats. This included the Task Force under Admiral Le Breton, about to start for the occupation of Iceland, but we didn't know it until our return a few weeks later. We were taken aboard the *Albemarle*, a fine new seaplane tender, where her Commanding Officer and Captain Mullenix welcomed us in the cabin and discussed our project with charts spread out on the table.

FDR gave the final go-ahead for the invasion of Iceland on the next day.

> Next morning we were roused at 3:50, saw the first glow of dawn over the Newfoundland hills, and were soon aboard the flying boats and headed for the Strait of Belle Isle, separating Newfoundland and Labrador. The sea north of Belle Isle presented a strange picture. A vast ice pack, borne southward by the Labrador current against the north shore of the island, extended seaward for many miles....
>
> Soon we were over Cartwright, 100 miles up the Labrador coast, and then over the mouth of the North River, 50 miles further up the coast, where my photographs of 1935 had revealed an area of level ground. Our one objective was to find a flat place big enough for 5,000 foot runways. We circled over this pebbly estuary and examined it for a few minutes before swinging back in our course to Lake Melville, 30 or 40 miles inland. There several areas were studied and photographed before the planes set down on the water and anchored off the tiny settlement of Northwest River situated at the west end of the lake. Old friends from the Hudson's Bay Post and the Grenfell Mission located there came out in motorboats and brought us ashore in good time for lunch at the Grenfell Hospital.

The highly secret expedition discovered that its existence was "common knowledge among the trappers and traders." Eric Fry's Stranraer had arrived a few days earlier and lay at anchor on Little Lake by the village. Fry's team got to the Goose Bay site on 1 July, three days before Elliott.

> We were scheduled to start on our quest for an airport site at 5:30 the next morning, and a motorboat had been engaged for that purpose. Our objective this day was Epinette Point on Lake Melville, 12 miles east of Northwest River, where a large area of swampy but level ground, as seen from the air, appeared to offer possibilities of development. The little cabin motorboat of the Hudson's Bay Company took us across the 10 miles of open water exposed to the full force of the northeaster; she pitched and rolled wildly, but Captain Roosevelt amazed us with his ability to stretch out on the hard floor of the cabin and sleep as soundly as an infant in the cradle! The motorboat trip was followed by an equally

strenuous spell in a heavy open boat that had to be rowed a mile across the bay which at this point was too shallow for the motorboat. Reaching the shore of Epinette Point, we plunged into a dense forest of spruce and fir. For an hour we trudged and struggled in the rain through the meanest kind of tangled, boggy woods till we came to the more open part of the swamp. Examination of the ground led to the conclusion that bulldozers could clear away the swampy top soil and lay bare a foundation of sorts for landing strips, but only in case nothing better could be found.

Captain Roosevelt had warned us to keep together in so dense a forest; as we started back toward the shore, he led the way, striding vigorously through the tangled underbrush, and as I brought up the rear it took some exertion to keep him in sight. I soon noticed that his course kept curving to the left – perhaps because of some hereditary tendency [!!] At frequent intervals I hailed him and asked for a compass check on our course to avoid traveling in a circle. When at last we reached the shore we were only 100 yards or so from where we had left the rowboat.

Epinette Point is across the lake from North West River, and it clearly wasn't the best place for an airfield except for mosquitoes.

Next day we planned to visit a great elevated shoreline terrace on the south shore of Goose Bay, in the southwestern corner of Lake Melville, which I had photographed from the air just two years before. This seemed to be by far the most promising site in the entire region and had already been chosen by the Canadians for intensive study. But when morning came, the wind had backed into the north and was blowing hard. The skipper of the Hudson's Bay Co. motorboat pronounced the going too rough for such an undertaking. By afternoon the weather was still rugged and Captain Roosevelt, who had set out in another boat for Goose Bay, was forced to return and await the morrow.

The following day, July 4th, the weather was clearer, but still the wind blew hard from the northwest. At last we found a man with a motorboat capable of taking an exploring party to Goose Bay. The round trip, including walking over the ground, was estimated to be a matter of nine or ten hours. The radio brought us a better weather report for flying, and while Captain Roosevelt and his party departed on the day's expedition, I was busily occupied superintending the removal of a wounded trapper from Northwest River down to Cartwright.

Forbes left with the trapper aboard the PBY, which was then ordered to proceed to Gander Lake. This left Elliott's party at Goose Bay, where the village of Happy Valley now provides access to the lake. Another seaplane would pick them up the next day.

Captain Roosevelt and the others arrived the next day in the flying boat. They had returned from Goose Bay to Northwest River after midnight, weary but well satisfied that they had found on the great terrace much the best airport site in all that region. All next day and far into the night Cpt. Roosevelt worked on his report of the trip. A darkroom mounted on a trailer arrived, and the photographs were speedily developed, so that they could accompany the report, and on July 7th this report was dispatched by plane to Washington.

The Canadians, as we have seen, were surveying Goose Bay before we arrived. Captain Roosevelt, after studying the problem, became convinced that they were not prepared with equipment and manpower to develop an airport soon enough or on an adequate scale to meet the emergency. He therefore proceeded on the assumption that the task would fall on the U.S. Army Air Corps.[789]

Elliott Roosevelt was wrong to join in this common assessment of Canadian ability and determination. But it would take robust prodding from the Americans to get their northern neighbors out of the starting blocks. Canada was absolutely not interested in having the Americans build Goose Bay airport, so the Air Ministry rose to the challenge and had the field ready in record time, if in a primitive condition.

By next year, it would by some measures be the busiest airport in the world, with sometimes over a hundred aircraft movements a day.[790] In truth, during the war many remote fields could probably claim that distinction from time to time. In Goose Bay's case, paperwork lagged behind construction. Canada's 99-year lease with Britain was not signed until October 1944.[791]

Nonetheless, American resources soon overshadowed the Dominion's effort there. General Arnold recorded an infamous episode in which he, on a 1942 stopover, became infuriated at the meager Canadian rations and ordered decent food flown in. Although he left out the expletives in his own account, it is nonetheless revealing:

> After a stormy Atlantic crossing, our party, including Lord Mountbatten, Air Marshal Slessor, and Mr. Harriman, landed at Goose Bay at midnight where an incredibly bad cold meal was waiting for us. The American mess sergeant said we were having trouble with the Canadians because of our superior rations. They wouldn't let us run our own mess. 'In fact, General,' said the mess sergeant, 'they actually take our good food out and bury it in the woods.' I made up my mind to do something about the setup at Goose the minute I got back to Washington.[792]

These were not random remarks. There were other complaints about Canadian hostility at the base. Captain Norman Vaughn, Admiral Byrd's Antarctic dog driver who had been appointed American control officer at Goose Bay, offered similar opinions in a memorandum dated 27 May 1942.[793]

So much for Allied brotherhood. Arnold did exactly what he said he would do, and with a vengeance.[794] The "American side" soon became much larger than the "Canadian side" on the northeastern field, or for that matter the RAF encampment on base.[795]

Incidentally, Eric Fry also took credit for the new base's name. He thought that with a Gander, there should be a Goose, and the airfield site was located near the Goose Rapids on the Hamilton River.[796]

As Lindbergh had predicted, Goose Bay was a far better site than any of the others discovered; thanks to its northern, inland location it has about twice the annual flying days of Gander.[797] It has seasonal ship access, and the surrounding terrain is topologically benign, though barren. It was for this reason that the base, as the only one of the "Roosevelt sites," became crucial to the war effort. It serves to this very day as an important training field for NATO air forces.

The Crystal Stations

When Elliott returned to Gander, a new team (still including Dr. Forbes) was assembled for another reconnaissance of the area around Ungava Bay, the giant indentation on the north coast of the Labrador peninsula. About 25 miles upstream from the Koksoak river estuary, there was a tiny Hudson's Bay trading post and missionary station ministering to about a hundred local Eskimos. It was therefore already known that a reasonably flat area existed in the vicinity.

Elliott's report on Goose Bay went back to Washington on 7 July. As a measure of how closely the White House followed Elliott's activities, Colonel Walsh advised General "Pa" Watson, FDR's aide, on 8 July that Elliott was to leave for Fort Chimo that day. The expedition did not actually depart for a few days, probably for weather reasons.[798]

On 12 July, the aircraft landed in the river by the Fort Chimo mission. Captain Roosevelt borrowed a small vessel and proceeded upstream to the suspected site. It was on the opposite, western bank of the river, about five miles up, and river access was problematic due to uncharted and shifting banks and reefs. However, there was agreement that five-thousand foot runways could be built in the sandy area, and the team returned to the aircraft with the necessary pictures and diagrams.[799]

On the return flight, Elliott flew across the tip of Labrador and photographed the coast searching for further sites. The coast was so rugged and indented that no suitable field could be located there. The importance of immediately getting the report to General Arnold overshadowed all. Forbes reported:

> Early the next morning [15 July] we landed on the lake at Gander and Captain Roosevelt, without even stopping for breakfast, went right to work on his report of our reconnaissance with its recommendation of the Chimo area. All day and nearly the entire night he was busy, while the photographers developed their pictures and Mr. Preston worked on his drawings. As soon as it was finished the report was flown to Washington. Captain Roosevelt was to accompany it, and I was to go on to Boston…there I bade farewell to Captain Roosevelt, who went on to Washington with the report.[800]

Two good aerodrome sites were now in the bag. On the return to the States, Elliott was giddy enough to ask the pilot to buzz the Roosevelts' Campobello Island retreat. This island, now the site of the Roosevelt-Campobello International Park, is located where New Brunswick meets Maine.[801]

Fort Chimo, codenamed Crystal I, was of little use in future air traffic, but any Arctic airfield is of automatic local importance because of the lack of transportation alternatives. Fort Chimo is now known by the local Inuit name Kuujuaq, and thanks to the airport is has grown from the isolated settlement Roosevelt found in 1941 to a regional hub.

Elliott lodged in the White House from 14-21 July, and then took his controversial beach vacation in Massachusetts.

Returning to Gander in late July, Captain Roosevelt next performed an aerial reconnaissance of southern Baffin Island. In this case, the results were not nearly so promising. One site was selected at Cape Rammelsberg, a promontory in Frobisher Bay. However, when the supply mission tasked to establish a weather station arrived in October, it could not find Roosevelt's promised flat field. Instead, the station was established on a suitable island ten miles farther out, and a wintering crew of eight under the command of Captain John T. Crowell was left there.[802]

The official report of the founding of the temporary camp suggests that great difficulty would be encountered at Frobisher due to high tides, shoals, and hostile topography, although at that time it was still thought that Roosevelt's site might be rediscovered next year.

When the survey ship (Captain Bob Bartlett's arctic veteran *Morrisey*) and the resupply convoy arrived in July 1942, it was decided to discard Roosevelt's recommendation and look for a better location. The Cape Rammelsberg site appears from satellite imagery to offer barely 4000 feet of runway, although the approaches are clear. Dr. Forbes said that it lacked safe access from the sea.[803]

The team, headed by Forbes, Crowell, and Bartlett, finally found a "beautiful patch of green turf" close to Sylvia Grinnell River on mainland Baffin. This site, about twenty miles from the original designated site, became Crystal II; after the war, it was renamed Frobisher Air Base, and then, when the Eskimo territory of Nunavut was created in 1999, it was made the capital under the name Iqaluit.[i]

The aerial reconnaissance of the eastern tip of Baffin Island also turned out to be problematic. The logical position for an airstrip would be near Cape Dyer, the closest approach to Greenland. Unfortunately, the topography there seemed at first truly forbidding, with deep fjords cutting through steep mountains.

Roosevelt instead recommended an area on the southern edge of Padloping Island, which is about fifty miles northwest. But Padloping is by no means flat, and the slightly less rugged terrain there, swampy and mountain-crowded, could not realistically support an airstrip. Instead, the sea ice would be used for landings, such as the one made by a ski-equipped Norseman that visited next spring as the site's first aircraft movement.[804]

This outpost became Crystal III, the most isolated and least used of the stations. By the winter of 1943, an improvised airstrip was available: "The ice runway which is on the lee side of Padloping Island is 6000' X 250' marked with flags and is smooth with about 1½" of snow on it."[805] This runway was usable from December to June.

Oddly, a natural shelf near the Cape Dyer site about 40 miles southeast of Padloping was later found to be much better. In the 1950s, a DEW line (Distant Early Warning) radar station was placed on a mountain top there, connected to a coastal airstrip and an important communications relay facility. But in 1941, this site was either overlooked or for unknown reasons discarded.[ii]

In building these sites, time was of the essence. Elliott submitted four reports to Arnold, two of them on the Labrador sites on 6 and 15 July 1941, and the third on Baffin Island on 3 August. The fourth was a summary. The Air Staff worked on the report during August, filed them, and ordered construction to begin on 3 September. Elliott said the Crystal stations had to be built before the beginning of November due to ice; he admitted it would not be possible to construct airstrips until the next shipping season.[806]

It was decided to combine five expeditions, three for the Crystal stations and two more for BW-8 and BE-2 in Greenland, neither of which were in the Roosevelt report. On 20 September, the main vessel, USAT *Sicilien* left New York. It arrived at the tip of Labrador on 7 October, in an anxious race against the winter.

Fort Chimo, Crystal I, was founded on 10 October. The ground team there was led by Lt. Cdr. Isaac Schlossbach, a veteran of Antarctica and already a well-known explorer.

---

[i] Martin Frobisher first explored here in 1576, but the only maps available in 1942 were from Charles Hall's 1861 expedition. Hall named the river Sylvia Grinnell after an acquaintance. Iqaluit means "lots of fish here."

[ii] The DEW Line was a continent-spanning "trip-wire" of radar stations that began in Alaska, proceeded across Canada, and with extensions tied into European air defense systems.

Trawlers reached Frobisher Bay, Crystal II, three days later, but after five days could still not find Elliott's site. Instead the weather station was offloaded on a nearby island. On the 16th, *Sicilien* reached Padloping, Crystal III. All ships barely escaped before the ice froze them in. They returned to the east coast of the United States in mid-November.[807]

Lt. Cdr. Charles Hubbard's report of 11 November summarized the situation at each Crystal site. Of Crystal III he said:

> It was possible to establish this base exactly at the site chosen by the Elliott Roosevelt survey. The island of Padloping forms the northwestern side of an excellent harbor. Between the bluff at the southwest end of the island and the rising ground behind the proposed landing field site, the shore is indented forming a cove with good anchorage for ships. The rise of tide is about four feet. The shoreline is a beach, in some places smooth sand, affording good landing facilities. A camp site was chosen about one mile along this shore from the high bluff, and one hundred yards back from a stretch of good beach. The principal advantage of this site was that it was away from the shadow of the southwesterly bluff and obtained a southern exposure with maximum of winter light. Although it is not adjacent to the fresh water ponds which exist on the island, it is close to a stream bed which will bear water in summer. For the winter, the camp will depend on melted snow for water supply…
>
> The site was chosen with the advice of the Eskimo "Vee-vee" who had lived in that area many years. There is some shelter from the north, which is the prevailing storm direction. Snow drift will accumulate due to this lee, but should not reach excessive depth and will serve to bank the buildings. Immediately above the camp and a few hundred yards distant is the stretch of level ground proposed as a landing field. This is too exposed to collect a snow cover to form a snow landing field and it is strewn with boulders. Immediately below the camp is the harbor which should freeze to form an excellent landing area.

Eleven men led by Captain J. Glenn Dyer, a surveyor also with Antarctic experience, were left to face a hard and lonely winter at this site.

The Bluie West 8 expedition to Greenland was much bigger, with 31 men led by the famous polar aviator Bernt Balchen. It split from the main group early, along with the eleven men for BE-2. The latter were led by Navy Lieutenant (j.g.) Frederick Crockett, who, as an Antarctic veteran, had been given special orders by the Secretary of War to join the Air Corps expedition.[808]

Elliott's Crystals stations – Chimo, Frobisher, and Padloping – turned out to be nearly irrelevant to the war, but the first two later keystoned the Canadian presence in the North. And the value of the synoptic meteorological reports from these sites should not be dismissed – whether for the forecasters of that time or for the climatologists of today.

On 23 February 1942, a flight of two Norsemen and one Hudson set out from Montreal to find the Crystals again after the winter darkness, and scout the sites for future runways. During the fall shipping season all three sites were reinforced, although the last one, Padloping, could not support a land airfield. The Crystal sites were turned over to Canada in 1944, but American personnel continued to operate there for years.[809]

Greenland Bases

It is important to keep in mind that the "Roosevelt sites" formed the backbone of an alternate northern route, not the main artery which ran from Gander or Goose Bay via BW-1 to Iceland. From Baffin Island, the alternate route continues across the narrowest section of Davis Strait to Søndrestrømfjord (BW-8) in Greenland, and it then jumps across the icecap to Ikateq (Bluie East 2) near Angmagssalik in Greenland. Elliott Roosevelt claimed BE-2, but not BW-8.

"Sondrestrom" had been well known since the 1920s, when Professor William Hobbs had used the site for meteorological research and had prepared there a landing strip, Camp Lloyd. It has excellent weather – for Greenland – and it is accessible by ship during a brief period in autumn.[810]

The final survey of the BW-8 site had already been performed by the USCGC *Cayuga* in October 1940, when the ice allowed it. That ship, so essential to the initial Greenland build-up, was among the small vessels given to Britain the next year. Colonel Balchen's team began construction in October 1941. BW-8 (named Sondrestrom Air Base after the war) now carries the decolonized name Kangerdlugssuaq, and it has long been Greenland's main airport.[811]

The hardest task was finding a suitable location in East Greenland. In 1941, the president was almost obsessed with Greenland; he demanded and got frequent updates on the military situation there. On 18 April, just after the Greenland treaty, FDR wrote:

> I am principally concerned over possible German operations in Scoresby Sound, Northeast Greenland. That's seemed to be where the Germans are headed. Please let me have recommendations to counteract any possible establishment of military, naval or weather base even if it be for the summer months only.[812]

The war cabinet was highly dubious about that. But the president shot back:

> I cannot agree that Germany will not attempt to establish a military base in Northeast Greenland this year. I think Germany will probably seek to get a definite foothold even if this foothold can only defend its own location. Therefore, our own expedition should be fitted out with sufficient guns to hold the Scoresby Sound area until early September, leaving just before the ice closes in.[813]

By "cannot agree," the president rejected the assessment of most of his advisers that the Germans had neither the intention nor the capability to invade Greenland. He had to cloak his advances in the North Atlantic in a defensive sheen. He did not actually get guns to Scoresby Sound, and the Germans would not oblige him with their own modest weather stations in East Greenland until the fall of 1942.

By the time FDR focused on the North Atlantic, the U.S. Navy was just surveying Argentia, Newfoundland for permanent use, and now was told to fly over Greenland. By May, the Atlantic Fleet met the president's challenge.

The Navy sent a seaplane tender to Reykjavik, and in the period 26 May to 6 June four PBYs from patrol squadron VP-52 were dispatched in teams of two to look both for airport sites and the rumored wayward Germans. They found neither. One pilot reported:

> Except for the area in the immediate vicinity of Angmagssalik, there was absolutely no sign of any kind of habitation. There was no place where a possible landing site for airplanes could be imagined. Tremendous glaciers and mountains are all that formed the shoreline for at least two hundred miles…This entire section is by far the most barren, desolate and uninhabitable area that can be imagined.[814]

This detachment operated out of Argentia and returned there after its brief Icelandic deployment.[815] Yet both Iceland and Greenland remained foremost on the president's mind. Since he approved the various expeditions, it is amusing to note that he would have known that his son's flights were only a small part of a much larger picture, especially considering the British efforts. Not only did President Roosevelt pull the strings of the surveys, but he had major operations in mind: the invasion of Iceland in July, followed by the Argentia summit in August.

Elliott did not realize that. When the Navy gave up, he was asked to take another look, which immediately followed the Argentia summit. In August General Arnold, who was there along with the top Navy admirals, must have been aware of the various surveys. They were "prolix" but "repetitive" to quote the official history. Still, by August nothing usable had been found in East Greenland.[816]

Because Elliott was busy keeping Churchill and other dignitaries company in August, he did not personally participate in all the Greenland flights. Instead, he supervised some B-24 flights out of Reykjavik, carried out by Captain James H. Rothrock. The report on the "Arctic Survey Flight, 13 August to 4 September, 1941" to Air Corps Ferrying Command, authored by Rothrock, was dated 6 September.[817]

Elliott himself left Argentia on 12 August and arrived in London on the 19th. By the 27th, he left England and was reported in Reykjavik on the 30th. His Iceland summary report to the Air Corps was dated 8 September. By then he was at Hyde Park, his grandmother having died there the preceding day.[818] His mother said Elliott had to fly back from the funeral to Washington to deliver his report.[819]

Thus Elliott's own participation in the Greenland flights was concomitant to his travel to London and back.

General Arnold received another report from Iceland in early September:

> A B-24 airplane of the Air Corps Ferrying Command, on a special mission, landed at Reykjavik, Iceland, on August 28, 1941. On August 29th, this airplane completed a reconnaissance flight of the east coast, Greenland. On August 30th, when preparations were started for another reconnaissance flight it was found that the airplane had broken through the runway, where it had been parked over night, forcing cancellation of the mission.[820]

This illustrated the difficulty of operating from the improvised RAF airfield, now Reykjavik city airport. In their haste, the British had poured concrete over a soggy peat bog. The Americans were now even more concerned with constructing usable facilities in Iceland than with finding a site in East Greenland.

When Elliott was there, the American build-up on the island had just begun, and the first echelon was experiencing a logistical breakdown. By the end of the year, the Air Corps directed a massive program of construction to begin as soon as feasible: a giant airbase at Keflavik, sufficient for 68 heavy bombers, and fighter bases at Akureyri (RAF Melgerdhi), Höfn, and Oddi.[821] Captain Roosevelt had a characteristically low opinion of the British in Iceland. He wrote:

> The airports could be placed out of commission with the greatest of ease...Because the British used Iceland as a rest camp for infantry troops after Dunkirk, a plan of defense has grown up which is extremely vulnerable and which leaves open the question as to whether too much reliance can be placed on Iceland as a ferry base of operation.[822]

It is true that the hasty British occupation by a defeated and largely disarmed army left much to be desired. However, their first line of defense was the Royal Navy, which was quite a different story. Perhaps the Germans could have taken Iceland, but lacking sea power, they could not have held it.

The Mysterious Origin of Bluie East Two

The east coast of Greenland is far more ragged and ferocious than is the west, and also much harder to access due to the southward-drifting polar ice pack.[i] There is only one important Eskimo village, Angmagssalik, populated by a unique tribe of Eskimos that had been unknown to the world until the late 19th century. Smaller settlements later radiated from it.

Although Elliott later said he had found two sites of interest in East Greenland, the Rothrock – Roosevelt flights of late August 1941 failed to locate a suitable place for an airport. Instead, we know that Rothrock's B-24 circled Angmagssalik on 29 August, and, like the naval aviators beforehand, found no hope for a serious airport.[823] The village already supported a Danish radio station. Under the oversight of the US Coast Guard, that station then reported weather using the codename Bluie East Two (BE-2) .

That Elliott did not discover the final BE-2 site was confirmed by Professor William Carlson, who was familiar with the station's origin.[824] So urgent was the need, Carlson wrote, that serious thought was given to constructing a floating airport in Boston and towing it to East Greenland. That probably would not have worked due to the grinding brutality of the sea ice.

Carlson also noted that the "real" BE-2, the airstrip at distant Ikateq, was finally discovered by Major Frederick Crockett, commander of the Angmagssalik station, during November 1941. Crockett was no hapless weather observer posted to a frozen backwater, but a polar explorer who had been a dog driver for Admiral Byrd in the Antarctic in 1927. In East Greenland, which is sled-dog country, he and his team were able to reconnoiter for airfield sites and also to participate in the epic rescue missions that would unfold on the icecap later in 1942 and 1943.[825]

Air Corps records also show that Colonel Balchen, commander of BW-8, was asked to do an aerial survey of the east coast in early 1942, and identified no less than 46 sites of interest. But there's a big difference between a Cub strip and a B-24 base. The conventional view was that a serious field needed 5,000 feet of runway with reasonably clear approaches, and that was what Roosevelt had been looking for.[826]

It is no wonder that it took close examination to find BE-2. The "field" is a notch in a fnord surrounded by steep mountains. It compares to an airport approximately as a narrow window-sill does to a patio. In terms of wind, snow, darkness, and terrain it was among the worst in the world. Perhaps most aggravating, the field is hidden away about 40 miles north of the native settlement. It was clearly another desperation choice.

---

[i] South of Scoresby Sound. NE Greenland, where the Germans landed, has many natural landing fields.

Interestingly, the Air Corps history of the North Atlantic route attributes the Ikateq site to Navy Lt. Atterbury, who participated in the supply-and-survey operations in June 1942. Lt. Cmdr. Hubbard's report of 9 July 1942 then cleared the path for airfield construction.[827] On 26 July, USCGC *Comanche* led a supply flotilla to Ikateq, and construction of the airfield began.

Thus it came to be that the four-man weather detachment at "Optimist," as Ikateq was referred to, arrived on 17 October 1942, "after several months at Angmagssalik and a month and a half at "Onoto" (BW-1)." The station began reporting weather on 1 November.[828]

The original American detachment at Angmagssalik had reported weather from February 1942 to October 1943. The station at Cape Dan, which is thirty miles east near Kulusuk, reported from October 1943 to September 1945, and then Kulusuk (DYE-4) reported from January 1961.[i]

"Optimist Field" did come in extremely handy as soon as it was available. Not only did some aircraft use it in emergencies, but next spring (1943), Colonel Balchen flew in with a couple of B-17s in an attempt to bomb a German weather station that had been discovered about 600 miles north of there. (The raid failed due to weather, and Balchen completed the job from Iceland a few weeks later.)[829]

Still, BE-2 was never an important traffic node, and it was abandoned after the war. Kulusuk is now Angmagssalik's airport. Although it is a far more convenient and safer site, it is likely that the extensive blasting needed to build it would have deterred the 1942 surveyors. Interestingly, the abandoned field at Ikateq came in handy for civilian support of the DYE-4 construction at Kulusuk.[ii]

The Roosevelt Sites in Retrospect

Captain Roosevelt thought he had discovered all these sites, but now we know that he had in fact not found usable air base sites in Greenland or in Baffin Island. That leaves Fort Chimo and Goose Bay; but of course these sites were known beforehand, so some skepticism has to apply to the importance of Elliott's reconnaissance. To be extra cruel, consider that Chimo actually was a poor location because of its atrocious marine access, past the forty-foot tides and thirty miles down a shallow and shifting river. Chimo never had more than a local development role.[830]

Elliott's project only took a few weeks during the high summer, when snow cover is least. For the Canadian surveys, the first Roosevelt flight was on 24 June, and the last on 31 July. Had he not carried out his flights, it is likely that the outcome would have been little different; others would have done similar work. But that conclusion fails to consider the high visibility the president's son brought to the project.[831]

Carlson noted that Elliott, in flying over the Scoresby Sound area of East Greenland, asserted that he had found a 25,000 foot mountain inland from there. This would certainly have been a startling geographic discovery. Carlson, a Greenland veteran, knew this could not be true; he attributed the observation to a "mirage."[832] Perhaps Elliott was the source of Air Corps rumors of giant 17,000-20,000 foot monster

---

[i] WBAN records (weather reports), National Climatic Data Center (NCDC), Asheville, N. Carolina. Four DYE stations formed the continuation of the DEW-line across Greenland.

[ii] A fourth natural airstrip, named Teague Field after its first and very lucky user (in a lost B-17) was accidentally dicovered in west Greenland, June 1942. It is on the coast midways between BW-1 and BW-8.

mountains in central Greenland. The 1942 route-proving flights discovered that these rumors were false, since they crossed southern Greenland at 8-9,000 feet.[i]

Carlson said Elliott was "pessimistic" about the entire route – which was perfectly understandable, but surprising in view of his trademark enthusiasm. In fact, Elliott was hard at work selling his project to the Air Corps.

Eleanor also stated that her son claimed to have found a previously unknown range of mountains in Greenland. She was grateful for his stunning photographs; they "were some of the best I have ever seen of that part of the world."[833]

Interestingly, when Elliott flew over the Torngats in northern Labrador, Dr. Forbes remembered that he (Elliott) insisted the mountains were 10,000 feet high, and they apparently rather unsettled both Elliott and his pilot.[834] In fact, as the Labrador expert Forbes well knew, they only reach 5,000 feet, and he seems to have been rather disappointed that the aircrew was not interested in a closer reconnaissance.

One more story may assist in characterizing Elliott's judgment. An intimate friend and close confidante of FDR, Margaret Suckley, kept a diary which casts light on family matters in the White House. On 7 November 1942, over a year after Elliott's return from his Arctic job, she recorded:

> About 8:30, we left the dining room table [at Shangri La, now called Camp David] after a delicious dinner of which the main course was musk-ox – (Elliott Roosevelt was sent on a detail to find air bases for the U.S. in the north. As he was flying over the 5,000 feet deep ice-cap of Greenland he saw a black mass on the ice. He flew lower, to see that the black mass was moving. He flew down to perhaps 400 ft & found the black mass was a herd of musk-ox, frightened at the airplane & running at the most amazing speed. The plane slowed to the least speed they could go, without coming down. This was around 60 mph. & the musk-ox almost kept up with them. They estimated the number to be somewhere between 15-20 thousand! They brought back photographs to prove it. This was a scientific discovery, as the musk-ox is supposed to be practically extinct.) It was like the most tender beef but with a tiny difference in taste which can not be called "gaminess."[835]

You don't have to be an Arctic expert to know that none of this makes any sense at all. Perhaps a lot got "lost in translation." Possibly, Elliott had observed herds of caribou in Arctic Canada – although even they are not known to cruise at 60 knots. As for the musk oxen, he might have obtained some such meat from Greenland; but the incident does illustrate his knack for telling a good story.

The other odd aspect of that account is that at that time – and Ms. Suckley recorded it specifically because after the dinner, FDR broke the news of the invasion of North Africa – Elliott was in command of a Britain-based reconnaissance group engaged in these very landings. The musk ox must have been pretty stale by then.

Like most soldiers, Elliott did pick up souvenirs everywhere he went. On a visit to the ranch, his mother noted that "the summer spent flying with the Army in Iceland, Greenland and Newfoundland has produced little white bear rugs, which are in front of Chandler's bed and scattered through the house."[836]

---

[i] NADHIST, AFHRA. ER probably saw Gunnbjörn's Peak, Greenland's highest at 12,139 feet. It was climbed in 1935 and is not much higher than the ice cap, which reaches near 11,000 in the central north.

The Crimson Project

If Elliott Roosevelt's actual accomplishment in determining the Northern Air Route can easily be overestimated, one cannot exaggerate the visibility he brought to the project. After all, it is a rare captain who gets to sit down with the President and the Prime Minister, explain that he has found the bases they need, and so now they can go ahead and win the war.

This is only a slight caricature. Captain Roosevelt was now aware that his work was part of a massive infrastructure project aimed at bringing American aircraft and equipment to Europe via the great circle route. The Canadian side of that monumental undertaking would come to be called the Crimson Route.

On 3 August, Elliott submitted his collective report on the Crystal stations. After a summary of the sites he had found, and a rather elementary description of the flight routes between them, he wrote:

> Sites 1, 2, and 3 enjoy good weather the year round being practically completely free of fog, and having but a small percentage of days during the year when contact flying is not completely practical. Site 4 being close to the sea will experience higher wind velocities and more fog during the summer months, In winter all four sites should be entirely practical for flying as clearer weather will be experienced and snow can be cleared or compacted with proper equipment. All lakes and bays along the route freeze smoothly during the winter to enable the plane to have many emergency landing fields if some should prove necessary. All routes can be flown during daylight hours the year round. Radio reception is practically as good as that experienced throughout the United States. Contact flying is recommended, and single plane flights recommended against. The latter is order to keep closer contact with the place that any plane might be forced to come down.
>
> Sites 1 and 2 will require grading equipment, and will have to be surfaced inasmuch as ground is sandy. Site 3 has very fine type of alluvial soil which packs hard. Main problem here will be one of the filling in one wash which will require the moving of about 500,000 cubic yards of dirt. Site 4 will require the use of caterpillar trucks and tractors as ground is composed of small boulders about a foot to a foot and a half in diameter. The landing of equipment at the sites will be comparatively easy. Docks will have to be constructed at all four sites. Barges will have to be used to lighter the equipment ashore at the first two sites, but the third and fourth sites can have docks constructed in deep water to enable the docking of a large vessel. All labor will have to be imported for all sites. Boats can gain access to the waters adjacent to each site as follows:
>
> - Site 1 – June 10th to November 10th
> - Site 2 – July 1st to October 20th
> - Site 3 – July 10th to November 1st
> - Site 4 – July 10th to November 1st.
>
> It is recommended that if the areas should be developed for airplane landing fields, that consideration be given to the following suggestions:
>
> a. It is now too late in the year to install an airport at any of the sites.
>
> b. Therefore it is suggested that a complete weather staff and radio equipment with adequate personnel be sent to each one of the four sites before October 1st. These men should be equipped in addition to the technical equipment with prefabricated houses, provisions for a year, clothing and other equipment suitable to the country.
>
> c. This would serve a double purpose: 1) Enable the War Department to gain valuable information concerning flying conditions during the year. 2) Enable the Weather

Bureau to obtain a great deal more information concerning weather in order to more accurately forecast weather over the Atlantic and along the Eastern Seaboard.

d. It is further suggested that flights similar to those just completed be made this coming winter during the months of February and March to the same areas to ascertain at first hand what flight conditions at that time of year are like. It is recommended that ski-equipped planes be used. Personnel familiar with the country should be used.

e. If construction is started next year as soon as water routes become ice free, plans for ships, supplies and equipment should be initiated immediately.

f. If personnel should be sent to these areas for the winter, it is suggested that married men be accompanied by their families in as much as there is no contact with other people outside of a handful of widely scattered Whites, some Indians and Eskimos.

ELLIOTT ROOSEVELT,
Captain, 21st Recon. Sq.,
Newfoundland Air Base

These excellent recommendations, including the early winter airborne inspection, would be followed. Except, that is, for his closing idea of conjugal relief on the remote sites. The Army doesn't work that way. But he was right; an unvarnished account by an officer sent to Crystal III in 1944 noted that most of the crew had abandoned their duties and taken to living with Eskimo ladies.[837]

In his report on Frobisher Bay, Elliott said that Baffin Island:

> …offers a power desiring to attack the Western Hemisphere an isolated, but at the same time not too remote vantage point from which to launch air attacks against cities as far south as Detroit and Chicago. It also offers numerous hidden harbours from which surface and subsurface craft may pray on Western hemisphere shipping.[838]

That level of geostrategic thinking was a bit over his paygrade. Perhaps General Arnold reasoned that Elliott was severely under-employed as an obscure captain in a frozen backwater. But as a long-standing friend, Hap would listen to him and take care that he received special tasks appropriate to his talents.

Captain Roosevelt's argument to the top brass in the summer of 1941 was, in the aggregate, quite reasonable. He realized that the southern branch – Goose – BW-1 – Reykjavik – would be traffic-saturated as well as subject to horrible weather conditions. By going inland, via Frobisher – BW8 – BE2 – Iceland, far better weather conditions could be obtained. In addition, the two routes would serve as alternates for each other; pilots need to file alternate destinations when the forecast is not ironclad ahead. And smaller, short-range aircraft would not be so far out on a limb on the northern branch.

Unfortunately, there were also serious problems with Elliott's argument. The northern "Crimson" route ran approximately along the Arctic Circle; it could not be safely used in winter on account of darkness and difficulty keeping the airstrips lighted and plowed. Also, it was sufficiently remote that resupply was highly problematic. Fuel and other supplies would have to be moved in during a few brief ice-free weeks in the fall. And the route ran far to the north of the great circle route to Britain.[i]

Still, during this brief heyday of Lend-Lease, planners called not only for this route, but several feeder branches. From the aircraft factories on the west coast of the United States, it was expected that thousands of new planes would proceed over Edmonton,

---

[i] For all but the aircraft deliveries from Seattle factories.

the Pas, Churchill on Hudson Bay, and Coral Harbor on Southampton Island, thence pick up the transatlantic route at Crystal 2. From the middle continent, planes would proceed up the east side of Hudson Bay via Moosoonee and Fort Chimo to Crystal 2. As before, ferry flights would continue in the south using Gander and Goose Bay nodes.[i]

It was an incredibly ambitious idea, yet only a small part of the worldwide air ferry network planned and built during 1941-2. The route along the Alaska Highway to Siberia was another critical lifeline; the South American route a third. In total, the network represented an immense expenditure of manpower and funds. When the emergency was over, these airfields opened up the far corners of the world.

In retrospect it is easy to question this effort. In the North Atlantic, only the Newfoundland – Iceland axis turned out to be essential. Even the main base in Greenland played a rather marginal role in the following events. As for the Crystals and the minor Arctic bases, their chief importance lay in supporting their own existence, reporting weather, and in assisting in rescues of the wrecks, air and sea, that occurred to some degree because of the bases themselves. The Arctic bases were slowly eclipsed by the 1943 victory over the U-boats, and by the increasing range and safety of aircraft.

But in 1941 and 1942 nobody knew this. The United States would not be able to play a role in Europe until a year after Pearl Harbor. Building infrastructure worldwide was actually a wise use of the immense resources available to the Americans during a time when the country was nowhere near ready for combat.

In Argentia on 8 August, General Arnold noted in his diary that Captain Roosevelt had indicated that "perhaps the President would like to have the AAF take over the trans-Atlantic ferry system [from Britain]. Then what?" The next day he also recalled a "Conference relative to change in route of ferry service to Montreal, Holsteinsborg, Glasgow, with alternate fields at Baffin Land, Fort Chimo and Northwest River." Clearly Roosevelt had made a persuasive case and his views would be listened to.[839]

After Elliott left Newfoundland in September 1941, his father and General Arnold did not by any means lose interest in the project. The building of the Crimson route continued in 1942 under intense American pressure; neither the British nor the Canadians, nor certainly the overwhelmed Danes in Greenland, could at first believe the vastness of the whole project.

There was a grim and very little acknowledged additional reason for the American emphasis on the far northern route. Planners had to consider not only a west-to-east traffic of men and materiel. Expecting an invasion of Europe in 1943, they had to anticipate a returning flow of wounded and dying soldiers. For this reason, large and well-equipped base hospitals were located at many of the sites.

Indeed, the Crimson moniker has been thought by many to refer to this sanguinary expectation. The Arctic dog driver and rescue specialist Willie Knutsen was called in to Arnold's office in 1942 and quoted the general thusly:

> Have you heard of the Crimson Route? It's the route used by planes loaded with men and cargo, bound for the European theater of war. That is, up to Labrador, across to Greenland, Iceland, and then Scotland.
>
> The 'crimson' part was apparently dreamed up by Churchill – because of the dead and wounded being brought back, you see. We are losing planes and crews, particularly over

[i] Thomas: Metmen in Wartime, 107. Moosonee, at the bottom of Hudson Bay, had rail access.

> Labrador. Your knowledge of arctic survival would help Allied flight crews. We've got an Arctic Survival School started in Maine. I'm going to send you there, if that's all right with you.[840]

That does sound like a rather fictionalized quotation, and it doesn't help that "Crimson" was actually selected because it was an early code name for Canada.[841]

Whatever the fears, in practice only the large 200-bed hospital at BW-1 would play a role in air evacuation. The hospital on uninhabited Southampton Island (Coral Harbour) was never used and became a symbol of the mad waste of war when inspectors visited it in 1944.[842]

The code words were a pestilence. When the airfields were substantially finished in late 1943, "Crimson East" referred to the Crystals, known now as Bookie, Chaplet, and Delight. The "A" was awarded to Goose Bay, named "Alkali."

"Crimson West" was made up of Le Pas, Churchill, and Coral Harbour. They became Appelation, Ermine, and Suspicion. An extra airport the Americans had insisted on (over Canadian objections), at Mingan on the St. Lawrence estuary, was "Spongebay."

In Greenland, which was not part of the Crimson network, the main station at BW-1 was Onoto; BW-8 was Bodkin, and BE-2 was given the "Curio" codename to supplement "Optimist Field." Iceland was commonly referred to as Indigo, and the airport there as Pewter.

In addition to the airports, numerous supporting remote stations were also given obscure names. It's no wonder the first aircraft movements across the route in 1942 were badly messed up.

In 1943, second thoughts intruded even as construction on Crimson reached its peak. On 19 April, Brig. Gen. C.R. Smith recommended to Arnold that construction be stopped at Le Pas, Churchill, and Southampton Island, as these airstrips were not worth maintaining even for emergencies. That was the beginning of the end for the Crimson project.

The U-boat menace was broken in May 1943, and the southern branch of the air route was built up to higher capacity and safety. Whatever its advantages, the northern branch, especially the Crystals, would see little use during the war. The Western Crimson saw no use at all. Pilots ferrying aircraft from California were not inclined to fly across Arctic Canada, even if it was a tad shorter on the map.

This should not disparage the high utilization the southern branch would receive. But the pillars of the air bridge were Gander, Goose Bay, and the Iceland bases. What the ATC called the Northeast Ferry Route was, incidentally, known to the British as the Arnold line; but not, as one might expect, for the Air Corps chief.

ATC colonel Milton Arnold had been ordered to carry out a route proving flight – a sort of inauguration – which he did from 8-29 April 1942. His damning report on the total unpreparedness of the stations along the trail ended with an eminently sensible recommendation: a high-ranking, un-ignorable officer should be assigned to fly the route continuously in a C-54 in order to identify the problems and ensure that they were corrected. For this, Colonel Arnold proposed Bernt Balchen. But, as often happens, the man with the idea got the task. From then on Arnold and his crew flew back and forth across the Atlantic, along the way whipping the radiomen, the weather people, the fuelers, the base operations staff, and so on into compliance. It worked, but not until several high-profile air crashes had focused the minds along the route.[843]

On less-used Greenland and Baffin Island bases, tactical activities – mainly sub-hunting – were winding down by 1944. Only one attempt at ferrying single-engine fighters was made, although that had been the route's original *raison d'être.*[i] Four-engined aircraft mostly skipped the small fields and used Iceland, or flew directly to Scotland. The expected vast stream of small aircraft went by sea after the 1943 victory over the U-boats.

In *As He Saw It*, Captain Roosevelt summarized his Arctic achievements rather offhandedly:

> By midsummer of 1941, my squadron had located five sites for stations in the Arctic Circle [sic]. We gave them names familiar probably only to the fliers that were to use them in the next four years. Goose Bay in Labrador, Bluie East on Greenland, and Crystal One in Quebec, Crystal Two and Crystal Three on Baffin Island were our contributions to the ferry system that enabled so many fighters and bomber planes to get over to England in the summers of '42 and '43.[844]

Still, Elliott's project had the personal attention of the president and the prime minister. Perhaps it is not insignificant, then, that the captain, during a turnover in London after an exploratory flight along the proposed route, found himself invited to stay overnight with Mr. Churchill at his Chequers estate. It would be far from his only acquaintance with the great man, but perhaps the most agreeable one.

The archives prove, however, that this was no mere courtesy visit. Elliott was eagerly suggesting new bases to everyone, and not only in the Arctic. At the same time, Averell Harriman was sent to the Middle East to assess the ferrying situation there, and to investigate the possibility of U.S. assistance with the southern route that would go via Brazil and West Africa to Cairo. Elliott, Ambassador Harriman, and the prime minister already contemplated American bases in Africa. It is interesting that in tracing the entire ferry route across Africa from Bathurst in the Gambia to Basra in Mesopotamia, Harriman also met up with Captain James Roosevelt (in Bathurst), who was on a similar fact-finding trip. Jimmy traveled around the world westwards, carrying his father's secret assurances that the United States would soon be in the war and eager to help. Obviously, the president was using his two eldest sons as unofficial ambassadors and secret agents.[845]

According to Churchill, it was Elliott who proposed American occupation of the Bathurst airport. As well, he had the idea that Port Sudan (on the Red Sea) should be developed as an air base, not just a port. Churchill was enthusiastic about this; he suggested also Monrovia, Liberia and Freetown, Sierra Leone, knowing that one landfall from Brazil would be insufficient. On 11 June he wired President Roosevelt:

> Personal and Most Secret for the President from Former Naval Person.
>
> I am looking forward to welcoming your son here. I have been told that he has a plan to take over, equip and defend an air base at Bathurst in Gambia as a staging and servicing point for heavy U.S. bombers to be flown across the Atlantic to the Middle East. His idea is that USA should lease base and install naval, military and air defenses. Bombers would be flown from USA via Pernambuco to be serviced Bathurst, then flown on by American ferry pilot organization to Egypt. Bathurst base all American. We are whole-heartedly in favor of this proposal and would be prepared to give you a lease at Bathurst on similar terms to

---

[i] A squadron of P-47s. Lt. Barry Goldwater participated in that delivery through BW-1 and Reykjavik.

> those already given for bases in the Western Atlantic. I had intended to postpone putting this proposal to you until I had talked it over with your son, but he has been delayed and the matter is so urgent that I wanted to put it to you at once. If the proposal commends itself to you in principle, our staffs here could work out the details.[846]

Elliott's idea was in tune with Harriman's recommendation that the United States should take over the African ferry route. For political reasons, this was utterly premature for the president, but it is remarkable that Elliott was already pushing a route he would be personally involved with next year. And for the British, who were conducting a full-spectrum campaign to persuade (or trick, as neutralists said) the U.S. into the war, Elliott was welcome new leverage to use on the president.

Name recognition was obviously not Elliott's only advantage. He worked extremely hard when kept from temptations. He was bright enough, could write well, knew already the geostrategic situation and was personally acquainted with many of its highest actors. Gifted with his father's enthusiasm and optimism, he moved with suave confidence among them. These qualities impressed his superiors, though not always his subordinates. Regardless of the rows over his legacy otherwise, Elliott's North Atlantic airfields will always stand as monuments to his work.

THE ATLANTIC SUMMIT

Thus it came to pass that when President Roosevelt and Prime Minister Churchill met for their great "Atlantic Charter" conference on board warships in Placentia Bay, Newfoundland, the president had General Arnold summon his son. As we have seen, he had earlier ordered him to stay in the area. Now Elliott found himself swiftly conveyed from a freezing outpost to the seat of the very highest decision-making of the war – or half-war, for the United States.[i]

General Arnold made sure to have him bring Army photographers, as he sensed that the British were about to present a one-sided view of the historic proceedings. He also found time to confer with Elliott about his recent work and the proposed realignment of the ferry route further north.[847]

Was Elliott Roosevelt a mere errand boy and drink mixer for the high and mighty? He said that FDR liked to have family around when engaged in the stressful foreign summits, so as to allow him to relax and feel more at home. Another obvious advantage is that FDR much preferred to have his sons around to hold him upright, a constant issue for the crippled president. Certainly, Winston Churchill mentioned in passing that Elliott came along to hold up his father.[848]

Elliott wasn't the only son FDR had summoned for help. Ensign Franklin Jr. was detached from his regular sea duties and assigned to the summit. Young Franklin then

---

[i] The "Atlantic Charter" is a journalistic invention for the joint communiqué. How much these noble values guided the later war effort is disputed; their disappearance at later summits opened President Roosevelt to criticism at home.

accompanied Churchill to Iceland. The prime minister had him stand beside him for photographs when he stopped in Reykjavik a few days after the summit.[849]

Inevitably, Elliott's accounts from the field found eager listeners at Argentia. He wrote of his sudden entry into top Allied strategy-making:

> By early August I was back at Baffin Island, slogging through knee-deep tundra, surveying a possible airport site at the head of Cumberland Sound, when an order was radioed through that I should return at once to my base at Newfoundland. Routine, I figured. At my base at Gander Lake I was assigned an OA-10 Grumman [sic] and a pilot. We were told we were to pick up the general commanding American forces on Newfoundland at St. John's on Friday, August 8th, and then proceed direct to the naval base at Argentia[850]...

Elliott told a quite different story in 1975:

> At my base, Gander Lake, I received strange secret orders to pick up the British Minister of War Production, bustling Lord Beaverbrook, from an incoming British plane, then take him by train to a transfer point and fly him to Argentia Harbor. I was in the copilot seat of our little OA-10 Grumman when we cleared the mountain spur overlooking the bay. None of us aboard could figure out how the bay had come to be filled with American warships. The puzzle was solved a few minutes later, after we had tied to a mooring post and I had been whisked in a tender to the *Augusta.* Along with Lieutenant (jg) Franklin Jr., who was equally surprised to find himself on the scene, I got to see Father shortly before lunch, which my brother and I shared with him.[851]

Elliott Roosevelt told the same stories, even the same words, over and over in his various books. But here he confused himself. In truth, he took General Harms of Newfoundland Base Command to Argentia; he returned by train with Lord Beaverbrook. Harms whined about his bleak assignment to General Arnold, and was promptly replaced.[852]

Escorting Beaverbrook was important because Churchill had told him to bring the latest reports: "On or about the 10th an aeroplane, possibly carrying Lord Beaverbrook, will come out to meet us. This must bring, apart from letters and urgent papers, an assortment of the most important Foreign Office telegrams...they must be put in a weighted case so that they will sink in the sea if anything happens to the aeroplane."[853]

USS *Augusta* with the president aboard had arrived the preceding day, 7 August. So had General Arnold aboard *Tuscaloosa.* HMS *Prince of Wales* with the prime minister and a very large delegation would arrive on 9 August. All along the press back home had been led to believe FDR had gone fishing. His tendency to drop out of town on prolonged fishing trips had again come in handy.[854]

Captain Roosevelt made full use of his time with General Arnold in particular:

> Marshall came in and said: "Come on, we have an amphibian and the Commander-in-Chief has given us permission to fly to Gander Lake and St. John." So General Marshall, Captain Roosevelt, General Harms, and I took off and flew 2½ hours from Argentia to Gander Lake and St. John, then returned to our mooring...We found new ships in the harbor. There were several corvettes, some new destroyers, a couple of destroyer leaders, cruisers, a battleship, two tankers, an aircraft carrier, and about 18 PBY's and PBYM's. Quite a fleet was being assembled – a good target for a German submarine. Just as we were

> about to get up to the *Tuscaloosa*, in came a four-engine flying boat, and on it were Sumner Welles and Averell Harriman.
>
> The next morning – Saturday, August 9th – we had a long conference with Elliott Roosevelt and General Harms about changing the route of the ferry service to Montreal, Holsteinsborg, Glasgow, with alternate fields at Baffin Land, Fort Chimo, and Northwest River, in order to bypass the absolutely abominable weather that was normal in and around southern Greenland, Iceland, and northern Ireland. However, right in the middle of the conference, we heard a lot of noise, and an orderly came in to announce that the *Prince of Wales* was entering the harbor…[855]

How many captains with ten months of service would be invited to bounce along with a planeload of generals? And who would be bold enough to bend their ears with theories about how they could do better? It was all perfectly natural to Elliott Roosevelt. Perhaps Marshall and Arnold sensed that "Bunny" was wasted on shuffling papers. By direct intervention of the top brass, Bunny would go on to make himself useful.

Given this, it is jarring to find that Elliott's commanding officer, Major Jimmy Crabb, thought that Elliott, was, well, just wasted. He said he caused him more trouble than anyone he ever served with; he said Elliott's Arctic flight were just some political assignment; that although Elliott was attached to him for rating, he did his own work with the Navy which Crabb "officially" didn't know of. So upset was Crabb that he, too, flew down to Argentia on a mission:

> I remember I went down to see them – they were in Argentia Bay and I flew down there in an amphibian and got ashore and went into the ship and talked to the Admiral about Elliott being such a drunkard: he wasn't much good to me; he wasn't much good to the United States either, as far as I was concerned.[856]

Captain Roosevelt's career wasn't hurt in the least.

The rest – quite literally this time – is history. Elliott became one of the most important eyewitnesses to the Roosevelt-Churchill summit that defined the Atlantic Charter, a manifesto of Allied ("United Nations") principles for a post-war settlement.[i] His vignettes of Churchill, in particular, are priceless. Irrelevant but impossible to skip are the descriptions of the fat old man going swimming, and (later in London) Churchill's practice of receiving visitors "clad only in a cigar."[857] (Had Hitler done this the psychologists would have spewed theories about it forever).[858]

Still, historians approach Elliot's memoirs with great caution. He said he had lost his notes, and was writing in 1945 from recollections. This might account for the strong biases – such as the anti-imperialist tirades attributed to FDR – and the odd tendency for these biases to add up to the left-leaning orientation then associated with Eleanor Roosevelt, who helped her son with the book.[859]

This is not the place to analyze the diplomatic results of the Argentia summit – such as they were – but it is the place to remark on how Captain Elliott was involved. One amusing spat concerns the press coverage. The Americans had gone to great lengths to blow the prowling journalists off back in the States, only to find that the British, far better prepared and with a much bigger delegation, showed up with press photographers ostensibly working for the government. This was contrary to agreement, but this deliberate British deception failed. At one point it got to be too much for some

---

[i] The "Atlantic Charter" was formally known as the Joint Anglo-American Declaration of Principles.

of the more status-conscious American brass, who decided to take action – full well knowing they were knee-deep in history:

> General Hap Arnold slipped up in back of me, to whisper in my ear that we'd damn well better get some cameramen and some film aboard in a hurry, and did I know if there were any air-force cameramen available up at Gander Lake? That morning I sent our pilot back up in the Grumman, to get supplies and a couple of Army photographers, so that our press would have at least some service on the conference.[860]

The American photographers came aboard on Sunday, in time to document the perceived grandeur of the summit. Elliott was impressed into service as Arnold's note-taker; the general had not brought his own, and was mortified to find his British counterpart, Air Chief Marshal Wilfrid Freeman, "flanked three-deep with aides."[861]

The photography was another way in which Arnold found Elliott useful. He did indeed note that he met with Elliott and "signed orders re photographs that were taken during session here, letter to Mint Kaye re printing." This is amusing because the then-unsuspecting Elliott would later wind up in a fierce bureaucratic fight with Minton Kaye, then director of Headquarters Map and Chart Section.[862]

As to official photography, this wasn't the whole story. When the newsreel companies received the material back in the United States, they complained bitterly of the "rank amateurism" the military operators had exhibited in producing the historic material – in fact, only 10% of the 2,000 feet was even usable. Perhaps they did not realize that they almost got nothing at all (except British official film). Elliott did not mention anywhere in his memoirs, however, that on his own, he produced an extensive 16 mm color film of the meetings; over 1,000 feet of Kodachrome, reported *Life*.[863]

This incident was reflective of the different attitudes and levels of preparation. To President Roosevelt, it was a "get-to-know-you" meeting; to the British, it was a matter of life and death.

The hard-fought words of the "Atlantic Charter" now belong to the ages, but when Elliott wrote about them in 1945, he was obsessed with their hypocrisy. And he was not referring to what was then going on in Eastern Europe – he complained about the Europeans trying to reestablishes their empires, and in specific about President Truman's policy towards the Soviet Union. A special barb was reserved for Major General Groves, who had run the Manhattan project and was proposing expansion of the nuclear stockpile when Elliott wrote.[864]

When Elliott left for his duty station – by train, due to the weather – he took along Lord Beaverbrook, who was to fly to Washington from Gander:

> The Beaver and I made the trip back to Gander Lake on a train that was a real antique; wooden seats, a potbellied stove in the middle of each car, a 20-minute wait at each tenth-mile stop. Our uncomfortable ride didn't sit well with my astonishing little companion. When an inoffensive trainman made an understandable error, and misdirected us, the Beaver let him have it for nearly three minutes in a wonderfully shrill voice, interlarding his choicer comments with some of the more pungent Anglo-Saxon four-letter words.[865]

Aitken, First Baron Beaverbrook might have gotten away with this because he was originally Canadian. But like many Americans, Elliott was in the process of discovering the "insufferable" British class society, Canadian backwardness and phlegmatism, and their effects on optimistic American notions of fairness and progress. He had a poor opinion of the British and a tendency to take it for granted that the United States had all the answers as well as all the money. The colonial attitude of Lord Beaverbrook, who was otherwise highly regarded, probably didn't help.

Sleep-over at Chequers

When the summit was over on 12 August, FDR made a detailed note of the activities in a letter to Margaret Suckley, his close friend. He noted in passing "Elliott left on a different secret mission, flying over Greenland's ice cap to Ireland."[866]

Elliott showed up in London on 19 August, a few hours after Churchill, who had paused in Iceland on the way home on the ill-fated *Prince of Wales*.[i] He was engaged in his new reconnaissance task, but also in socializing. In London, though registering at the Hotel Dorchester, he would again be Winston Churchill's houseguest at Chequers. He stayed in London until 26 August.[867]

During that week he toured aircraft factories and RAF bases and participated in conferences with high officials, including Baron Brabazon of Tara, the renowned aviator who was then minister for aircraft production. Clearly Elliott was no ordinary captain; the British, from the prime minister on down, had decided they could use this guy.

It is notable that Elliott got away with making a lot of public statements in which he echoed the sentiments of the Roosevelt-Churchill policy: "We shall be with you at the finish." But true to form he also did his share of pub-crawling, attracting crowds.[868]

Obviously, Elliott spoke for FDR in his impromptu declaration of solidarity. But in August 1941, how did he know what "the finish" would be? Remarkably, at that early time, one finds little uncertainty how the war would end, at least on the American side.

The tiebreaker had been Operation Barbarossa on 22 June 1941. Subtracting the USSR from the Axis and adding it to the Allied side seemed to have settled the issue for most. When Japan later brought the USA in full-time, instead of finishing off the USSR – perhaps the greatest strategic blunder in the history of the world – everything was just a matter of time. To be sure, Lindbergh and the America Firsters kept insisting on American neutrality until 7 December, but during their last few months they resembled the classic cartoon character walking obliviously off a cliff.

The gossip journalist Sheilah Graham happened upon Elliott in London. She had been one of the women Elliott flirted with aboard the SS *Aquitaine* in 1931. Now she quoted him at length:

> The British are not getting all the production they need today from America. Why? Because we do not as yet have sufficient material to give them. But it won't be long in coming. We can supply most of their needs in 1942....The British and American effort combined is too powerful for any other combination of nations to defeat. With regard to the aircraft output of both nations, it is wrong to say that the British have the best fighters and Americans the best bombers. Some American fighters, for instance, are as good as the British Spitfires, and that means they are as good as any aircraft built today in their class. The B-24 Liberator is as fine a four-engine bomber as exists. It all comes down to this: Both countries are building the best types of planes in their own line.[869]

---

[i] HMS *Prince of Wales* was sunk by Japanese torpedo planes off Singapore on 10 Dec 1941.

That testimony should be seen in the context of the prevailing British view that they were getting second-rate equipment from America.

Elliott continued:

> Churchill has one of the most forceful personalities of any man I have ever met. He typifies better than anyone in the world the dogged determination of the English people to win through.[870]

At this early time, Elliott clearly knew to say the right things about his host.

By 29 August Elliott Roosevelt was again in Iceland, where the new British airfield at Reykjavik was beginning to see extensive use. The previous month his father had sent U.S. Marines to take over the occupation of Iceland from Britain, and the 33rd Pursuit Squadron's P-40s were setting up shop there. The Americans were intensely interested in building up the aviation infrastructure in Iceland, which for the first time brought them into contact with German patrol flights.

The East Greenland survey flight at the end of August was Captain Roosevelt's last North Atlantic job. By early September Elliott was back in the United States, delivering his report as well as attending his grandmother's funeral.[871]

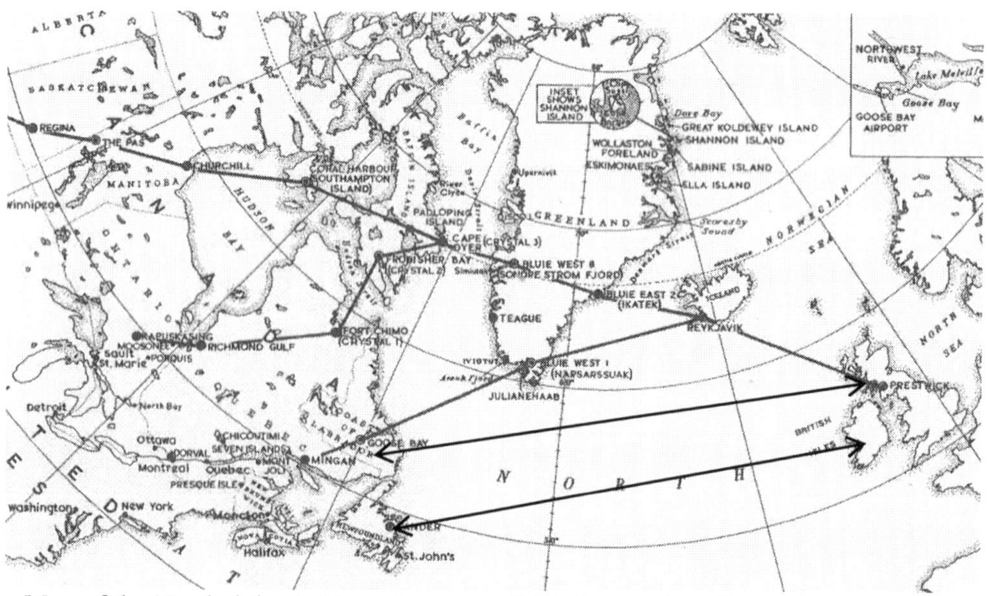

Map of the North Atlantic Ferry Route, modified from a Canadian government map.

III. THE WAR YEARS

FROM COLD TO HOT: PROJECT RUSTY

Project RUSTY, operational from March to May 1942, is also one of the most intriguing untold stories of World War II.

> Senator FERGUSON. When did you first go to the European or the North African theater?
>
> Mr. ROOSEVELT. I was assigned, sir, after my return from Newfoundland in the fall of '41. I went through navigation school at Kelly Field, completed that at the time of Pearl Harbor, and was assigned to the Special Reconnaissance Squadron and the 6th Reconnaissance Squadron at Muroc Dry Lake, California. We were flying B-24's on anti-submarine patrol; they were called reconnaissance squadrons. Actually, they were anti-submarine squadrons, and our job was to guard the shipping lanes to Hawaii and to guard the approaches to the west coast.
>
> I was taken off of that very soon after I started that work, and sent back in February to Bolling Field again, where I was assigned to the 1st Mapping Group, and to a subsidiary special mission known as the "Rusty mission."
>
> The "Rusty mission," I believe it is all right to relate this publicly today, but it was secret then; was assigned the task of surveying the routes across Africa for the delivery of planes to the Chinese theater of operations, and also was to do reconnaissance in North and West Africa for the purpose of deciding on operations in Africa which took place later.[872]

Elliott's unanticipated and unlamented Arctic career had ended as abruptly as it had begun. The 21st Recon Squadron returned to the U.S. in September 1941, and after Sara's funeral (she died on the 7th) Elliott went home to Texas. Conveniently enough, on 10 September he was ordered to attend the Navigation course at Kelly Field, followed by an Aerial Observer course at Brooks Field, both bases being part of the extensive training facilities around San Antonio.[873]

Convenience was not the motivation, though. Elliott said he fiercely hoped his application would be approved, for he wanted to get into airplanes, even though he couldn't be a pilot.[874] He later said that since he had spent his time flying over the "polar ice cap" [sic], "not ever really knowing where the hell I was," his posting to navigation school in San Antonio was intended to not only make him a flight crew member for his own satisfaction, but also to make him more valuable to his squadron. [875]

Navigator was then a very important rating in the air corps. It is difficult for today's spoiled aircrews to appreciate the critical importance of abstruse, time-consuming navigational techniques laboriously indoctrinated in young innocents during those years. Celestial navigation using sextants and reams of almanac tables was a very important technique; dead-reckoning and compass-tracking were honed to a fine edge. The navigator section of the combined navigator-bombardier course normally took fifteen weeks, but Elliott's class was graduated two weeks early because of the Japanese attack in the Pacific.

As an interesting reminder that he was no ordinary student, Elliott invited two of his instructors to spend the night at the White House. Just minutes before Eleanor heard of Pearl Harbor, she noted that "Elliott is supposed to arrive with two other boys this afternoon but no word yet & it is after three."[876] On the day after the attack, Elliott led his last navigation training flight to Washington, D.C., and Elliott showed up at the White House at 16:45 along with Major G. B. Dany and Lt. Gerald Keely. He would make a habit of this hospitality to his buddies as the war ground on. The trio left on the 11th.[877]

Seizing a photo opportunity, Kelly Field's Advanced Flying School commander, General Hubert R. Harmon, saw Roosevelt off in his plane when he left for his first combat post on 20 December. It made a humorous scene when the diminutive general pinned navigator wings on the twice-as-large Elliott. More seriously, Harmon noted that Elliott's course highlighted the difference between democracy and dictatorship: the president's son showed up requesting no special treatment, and got none. This was true except for Elliott being the only captain in a class with fourteen cadets, he was five years older than the normal limit, and he had been sent to a school close to his ranch.[878]

Interlude at Muroc Dry Lake

On 15 December, Elliott was ordered to join the 6th Reconnaissance Squadron at Muroc Dry Lake, California. He participated in long-range Pacific patrols at a time when there was still fear that the Japanese were lurking off-shore, ready to land in California. From the dry lake, the squadron flew the B-18 Bolos, familiar from Gander, but it soon received a few new LB-30s. These were Liberators intended for Britain but hurriedly redirected west due to the Japanese attack. The long flights over the Pacific turned up no "Nips," but they made for excellent navigation training.[879]

The very image of desolation, Muroc Dry Lake had been picked out as the perfect training site by Hap Arnold a few years earlier when he was still at Riverside's March Field. The wind-whipped sand lake was relatively close to the aircraft factories on the coast, and also to the glittering parties of Hollywood and Beverly Hills.

Ruth came out to visit. Also, a certain notorious "public relations" man by the name of Johnny Meyer – who had just gone to work for Howard Hughes – claimed that he first met Captain Roosevelt when he was at Muroc, which would have been an odd encounter for any other junior airman.[880] Meyer reputedly had ties to the underworld, and his specialty was to procure human specimens for the sexual pleasure of rich people in Hollywood. It is likely that James Roosevelt, with his short movie career, had encountered Meyer first. One writer who researched him says Hughes and Meyer first met in 1938 in connection with the extreme-living group of drunken wastrels around Errol Flynn. One of the creatures in this club was another movie star, Bruce Cabot.[i]

It is not known what transpired between Elliott Roosevelt and Johnny Meyer in 1941, but remember these names; they'll pop up again.

War notwithstanding, Elliott had occasion to look after his wrecked finances. From Muroc Lake, on 22 December, he wrote his main creditor that he had no money.

---

[i] Porter: Hell's Angel, 396-402 provides an introduction to Meyer and the crowd he associated with. Meyer's FBI file documents some of this, and notes his earlier association with the Chicago mob.

However, Jesse Jones forwarded paperwork to him for his signature, for use in calling off the hounds.[881]

Officially, Muroc was still a Bombing and Gunnery Range. Although busy after Pearl Harbor, it did not become an Army Air Base with its now legendary flight test role until July 1942. The name Edwards AFB dates from after the war.[882]

Elliott served as senior navigator with the 6th and then the 2nd Recon. Squadrons over the winter. On 25 February he was ordered to Hammer Field near Fresno along with the squadron. The local press noticed the president's son in Fresno, and he rented a house there; but on the 27th, he advised that he had been ordered to Washington, and he left Fort Worth for D.C. on 3 March. It is not clear if Fresno was a decoy. [883]

Captain Roosevelt's superiors had something special in mind for him:

> Until late in January, I served first with the 6th and then the 2nd; then, unexpectedly, secret orders came through directing that I report to the commander of the 1st Mapping Group at Bolling Field in Washington. There was so much secrecy attending my orders, and the nature of my future assignment, that my hopes were really soaring. Must be something big and important. Surely some sort of overseas assignment…[884]

To his bitter disappointment, he was posted to do aerial mapping of Vichy-ruled North Africa. He claimed that he didn't understand the importance of the task or the reason he'd been selected. Contrariwise, General Arnold maintained that after his North Atlantic flights, Captain Roosevelt had come to him and "requested permission to make a photographic exploratory flight over Africa." The discrepancy may simply result from faint and divergent recollections; but it may also be related to Elliott's earlier proposal for an American air base in Bathurst.[885]

Certainly the president kept close tabs on Elliott and may have dreamed up a new assignment together with Arnold, who was frequently at the White House. Eleanor noted that Elliott was "patrolling the Pacific, but apt to leave soon for parts unknown."[886]

There's another possible explanation for Elliott's sudden elevation from humdrum patrol to secret spy flights. It had to do with a most fortunate and highly portentous acquaintance he made while he was training at Kelly Field.

The chief of staff of the Sixth Army in Texas was then a certain balding, slightly trollish but little known colonel by the name of Dwight David Eisenhower. Though a conscientious and hardworking officer, his career had long been stalled. But Eisenhower suspected he'd soon be busier than he had ever been, and he liked to be well-prepared.

When Ike heard that the president's son was training at Kelly, and that he had had some adventures up in the frozen North, he asked Elliott to swing by:

> Ike was full of questions about my just-completed tour of duty in Newfoundland and was fascinated by the aerial surveys we had conducted in the Arctic. His intense interest was in marked contrast with the general air of complacency which pervaded the peacetime Kelly Field of 1941.[887]

Colonel Eisenhower, who actually had just received the temporary rank of Brigadier General, listened with rapt attention to the adventures of Elliott in the North:

> "I don't suppose you brought any of your survey reports with you?" he asked, almost forlornly.

> "Better than that, sir," I responded. Not only do I have complete sets of my reports, but still photos and motion pictures of most of the areas we reconnoitered."
>
> "Splendid! Do you suppose that you could bring them over to my quarters tomorrow night? I'd greatly appreciate seeing what you've been up to."[888]

And thus began an extremely important friendship of sufficient duration to make a big difference to them both. Ike and Elliott spent several evenings together going over the North Atlantic ferry route. The exuberant Elliott was a born salesman, and Ike was a keen listener.

Even back then, the Eisenhower – Roosevelt connection went beyond a chance meeting. Ike wrote to John Boettiger, whom he had met earlier in Seattle, that he'd just encountered John's brother-in-law:

> A couple of days ago Captain Elliot Roosevelt came into our office and chatted with General Krueger and me for quite a while. He's had some intensely interesting experiences – hope you get a chance to talk to him soon about Iceland, England, etc.[889]

Someone in Washington had long recognized Colonel Eisenhower's qualities. He was Army Chief of Staff General George C. Marshall. After the Japanese attack in the Pacific, Ike was hauled up to Washington to be effectively Marshall's deputy. From that moment Ike's previously lackluster career shone like a supernova. And like Marshall, Ike well remembered those whom he could best use.

Until Eisenhower went to North Africa in late 1942, he, in a sense, ran the war for Marshall, making sure that everyone was getting their bullets and beans, and helping with the planning of the offensives to come. Per British insistence, North Africa was tops on the agenda; but Eisenhower was also struggling to find a way to get supplies to China now that the Pacific was largely shut down. He knew someone who could help with scouting the terrain.

Africa's Blue B-17

It is interesting to note that Project RUSTY was, as a strategic reconnaissance initiative, a forerunner of the extreme-altitude U-2 program that would become operational only fourteen years later; and Elliott Roosevelt was a kind of early Francis Gary Powers, except he didn't get taken captive. The parallel is strengthened by the fact that the United States wasn't at war with Vichy France and technically was conducting illegal overflights of her colonies. Perhaps Eisenhower would have occasion to reminisce about such past compromises when, in 1960, he ruefully had to admit that he had ordered Powers's last mission.

However secret, RUSTY was high-profile. The president knew about it; and he knew who he was sending to do the job.

In 1975, Elliott Roosevelt recalled a January 1942 breakfast with his Commander-in-Chief:[i]

> I was due off to North Africa, one of two navigators assigned to the photographic mapping of the terrain as part of something identified as Project Rusty. I couldn't see the

---

[i] This was more likely in the first week of March. (See FDR Appts Day-by-Day, FDR Lib).

> point of taking pictures of desert sand until he spelled out the implications of TORCH. It was essential, he explained, to keep hold of the Mediterranean and the Suez Canal to get aid to China by airlift from India and to ship lend-lease arms to the Soviets across Iran.[890]

Always novelizing and rationalizing, he might have been getting ahead of himself, since operation TORCH was by no means settled at that time. The initial staff study was called GYMNAST and was seen by the Americans as a very poor substitute for dealing with Hitler head-on. On the other hand, both Roosevelt and Churchill were getting worried about maintaining lines of supply across Africa to the Middle East, where they branched off to the Soviet Union and to China.

In this latter view, the attention focused on North Africa was not an excuse for not invading Europe; it was an emergency measure to prevent Axis capture of the Suez Canal and preclude a renewed German thrust into Mesopotamia and Persia. Because of this emphasis, early in 1942 the United States sent to Cairo a small Army unit, the North African Military Mission, a logistics command headed by Major General Russell Maxwell.

Maxwell was responsible for supply and service of American equipment in the Middle East. It was a non-combat operation, but the British urgently needed all the U.S. materiel that could be filtered in. So did the Soviets, and even China. Without access to the Mediterranean and North Africa, it was a herculean, very nearly impossible task.

The Cairo operation was at the limit of American logistical reach at the time. In that context, Elliott Roosevelt's reconnaissance of North Africa was much more important than he thought. From the American perspective in particular, supplying the small force in western China seemed essential, whereas the British endeavored to hold the Persian supply corridor open in order to reach Soviet forces in the Caucasus. It was an enormous amount of geography for such a small, scattered force.

Even today, flying the distance from Liberia or Sierra Leone to Khartoum and Cairo seems a frightening task, especially in single and twin-engine propeller aircraft. From bases in Libya, Germany and Italy had the actual capability to cut the thin lifeline in half. Arnold and Marshall might not have been pleased with the notion of invading non-belligerent French West Africa, which wasn't causing any trouble, but they did have reason to worry about their grasp on the sub-Saharan region.

In the winter and spring of 1942, this became especially important to General Arnold. He had shut down the North Atlantic air route for the winter on 18 October. The South Atlantic route via Brazil and British Africa took its place.

Again, unsung work had preceded the American troops. What would become known as the Takoradi Route, after its terminal airport in the Gold Coast, had been pioneered by Imperial Airways and the RAF. Then, in 1941, President Roosevelt and Prime Minister Churchill had each and jointly persuaded Juan Trippe of Pan American Airways to take over the job of building and supporting airports and running a ferry service from Miami to Cairo via Brazil and innumerable smaller stops. This was a discreet, unacknowledgeable military use of a civilian airline. In 1942, the military took over after Pan Am, but the ferry route (with its various extensions) was already well-established, if primitive.[891]

With Field Marshal Rommel's advance nearly to Alexandria in 1942, the Allies were greatly worried about their tenuous hold in sub-Saharan Africa. Arnold wrote:

> I was most interested because at that time the French had in effect turned over their government to the Germans but were themselves holding a line of airports from Dakar eastward almost to Khartoum. That string of bases paralleled the airway we were using from Accra …It can be understood why I was glad to have a qualified observer go down into that section of Africa and photograph those French air bases. Elliott Roosevelt volunteered to do the job, and, as usual got his pictures. From them we were able to determine just what was going on – what kind of installations the French had there.[892]

In this perspective, Elliott's new job made eminent sense. It was similar to what he had been doing in the Arctic: blaze the trail for supplies and aircraft to be ferried to the Middle East, and lay the groundwork for an actual invasion of French West Africa.

The task – the Special Reconnaissance Mission to Africa – was codenamed RUSTY, and for Elliott Roosevelt it would occupy March, April, and May 1942. In truth, he only spent a few weeks in theater, chiefly in April. He left the White House on 8 March and was back on 7 May.[893]

In 1946 he reminisced:

> *Rusty Project* for me meant Accra, on the Gold Coast, and Bathurst, in British Gambia, and Kano, in British Equatorial Africa, and Fort Lamy, in French Equatorial Africa (always Free French). It meant several months of painstaking work, mapping the whole of northwestern Africa from the air, by photographs, occasionally running into Fascist patrol planes, occasionally under fire, but by and large just getting a hot, dry job over with as expeditiously as possible…[894]

Well, he had complained heart-rendingly about the cold, wet Arctic, so now he received the antidote. He wasn't aware at that time that his new mapping assignment would become essential for TORCH, the Allied conquest of French North Africa. He also didn't know that this would lead to a promotion, a high-level command, and an invitation to attend the Casablanca, Cairo, and Teheran conferences of the great powers.

It is not easy to find documentation for this undertaking. It has languished in the bucket of forgotten epics – projects which, however critical (and secret) they might have been, have been overshadowed by subsequent, bloodier events.

Contrary to Elliott's impression, he was just a participant in a bigger expedition. The 1st Mapping Group organized the project and gave the command to Lieutenant Colonel Paul T. Cullen. He was an excellent choice, having already been a photo reconnaissance instructor at Lowry Field, Colorado, and a military observer to the Middle East and the Far East just before assuming command of this special operation.

Colonel Cullen would return to command the 1st Mapping Group from July 1942. Colonel Minton Kaye, who was later an avowed enemy of Colonels Goddard and Roosevelt, commanded the unit in 1941 and again in 1943, until he was banished to an Asian command following Roosevelt's and Goddard's complaints.[895]

Cullen's and Elliott's assignment to the 1st Mapping Group at Bolling Field indicates the nature of the mission. At that time, the Army was taking on the aeronautical mapping of the world. The size of that task boggles the mind, but there was no way around it if the United States expected to prevail in the global conflict. This extraordinary but much-ignored effort, which continued after 1945, would result in the issuance of the familiar WAC (World Aeronautical Chart) maps in the 1:1 million scale, as well as many other more detailed cartographic products.

The 1st Mapping Group was constituted in January 1942 from the 1st Photographic Group (of June 1941) and comprised four photomapping squadrons: the first, second, third, and fourth reconnaissance, neatly assigned to the northeast, northwest, southeast, and southwest of the American continent. Thus, the 1st Reconnaissance Squadron was now responsible for mapping Greenland, Labrador, and Newfoundland, initially using the obsolete B-18s and Martin B-10s.[896]

The aircraft would typically obtain their results by carefully taking paired stereoscopic photographs of the earth from high altitude. An alternative trimetrogon technique was developed whereby one vertical camera was supplemented by overlapping images from a left and a right oblique camera. Photo-mapping required the pilot to maintain a steady altitude and course. This was considerably more difficult under fire, as Elliott soon found out.

Roosevelt's off-hand, one-paragraph summary about RUSTY covers a lot of ground, figuratively and literally. Military records show him leaving the United States on 3 March 1942 and arriving in theater on 13 March; yet Mr. and Mrs. Elliott Roosevelt were recorded checking out of the White House on the 8th.[897]

That spring there were Elliott-sightings far and wide. On 11 March, he and Ruth stayed in Palm Beach, Florida, attending social functions.[898] West Palm Beach happened to be the U.S. terminus of the new southern ferry route.[899] The press found Elliott in Cairo in April 1942, where he was temporarily attached to the North African Mission under Maj. Gen. Maxwell. It was reported that Elliott spent ten days in that threatened city about the same time that his promotion to major was announced to the press.[900] Another reporter spent an evening with Elliott in Khartoum. He noted, unverifiably, that at one time fully one third of Americans in theater were in hospital with malaria, but Pan Am's capable route management reduced the incidence to 1%. People wore "mosquito-boots" to discourage the ankle-biters, and took preventive quinine.[901]

After spending April in Africa, Elliott caught a Pan Am Clipper (Boeing 314) returning to the Americas.[902] He was reported in a hotel in Belem, in the Amazonas, one of the important staging bases the United States was now using in South America.[903]

Colonel Goddard later described Roosevelt's work at this time as aerial mapping on a scale from the United States to China. This reflects the urgency Washington felt in having to find a way to relieve China now that the Pacific and South East Asia were being rapidly lost to Japan. The expedition was given two specially outfitted B-17s for the task:

> They were stripped down and equipped with the latest navigational aids and three wide angle mapping cameras locked together to form a single tri-lens camera. Under suitable weather conditions, Elliott's expedition could make photographic strips from horizon to horizon for hundreds of miles in a day. And they did just that, although one of the B-17s disappeared on a flight between Puerto Rico and Trinidad and was never found. The other, with Elliott on board, went on down the coast of South America to Natal, Brazil, then across the ocean to Liberia. From there they spanned the African continent heading for Cairo. Beyond Cairo lay the Near East, India, the Himalayas and finally China. They mapped it all, and did a marvelous job in gathering the material out of which our airway charts were made. In the days and years that followed these maps greatly aided our pilots in flying across unknown lands and undoubtedly saved many lives.[904]

Goddard's account is slightly off-tune. The prime objective of RUSTY was not route-proving; it was reconnaissance of denied territory, i.e. French, Italian, and Spanish North Africa. But some of both was done.

The two B-17s were from the batch of 39 B-models, the very first production models of the Fortress. They were much prettier than the later versions, and may have been especially useful in reconnaissance due to their aerodynamic fairings and blisters; the guns were removed from the expedition aircraft.

Cullen's and Roosevelt's B-17B was painted all-blue in an effort to reduce its visible signature when seen from the ground. The lightened airplane was intended to fly so high, approximately 30,000 feet, that it wasn't expected to be viewed from above. Due to this peculiar camouflage, it earned the nickname "Blue Goose."

Despite this B-17B's reported crash in Africa, no accident report could be found in the archives. It is possible that this aircraft was serial 39-5, which is listed cryptically as "crashed outside of USA" and dropped from records in August 1942.[905]

The second B-17B disappeared en route. Tail number 38-223, flying to Trinidad from Borinquen, Puerto Rico, on 9 April 1942, was thought to have missed its destination and continued into the mountains of Venezuela. Its pilot was Captain Lovell S. Stuber; five other crewmembers perished with him and were also never found.[906]

Perhaps the surviving bomber had a better navigator – Elliott – or maybe it was just the luck of the draw. But the trouble was by no means over. That B-17B reached its operating location at Accra in the British Gold Coast (now Ghana), but quickly found rough flying conditions. After all, this was the equatorial region, not the Sahara, although the latter was the photographic objective.

The expedition sent a secret, cryptic dispatch to Arnold through the RAF wireless service on 24 April:

> The operation of Fox 4 aircraft is made hazardous in Rusty project area owing to inaccurate maps, poor weather data, and low visibility. Similar conditions exist Aquilla. Recommend that a minimum of three pilots from the Eidsons squadron are flown at once to this station regardless of decision on Gymnast. Aircraft follow as quickly as possible.[i]

Cullen was referring to Major Harry Eidson's 13th Recon Squadron, which was just forming at Colorado Springs. Unfortunately that unit had neither airplanes nor trained pilots yet.[907]

The objectives of RUSTY were summarized in a resulting Air Staff memorandum for General Arnold on 28 April 1942:

> The object of the Rusty project is photographic reconnaissance of the Cape Verde Islands, Dakar, and the French West African Coast. Its base is at ACCRA and its present aircraft equipment consists of one B-17B' which is not in operational condition. The Director of Photography [Kaye] has suggested to Col. Cullen, Commanding Officer of Rusty, that P-38s be sent to ACCRA for his use. This proposal is replied to unfavorably in the attached cablegram (Tab B), and request is made that three pilots from the 7th Photographic Squadron (Edison [sic]) be flown to ACCRA with planes to follow as soon as possible.

---

[i] Signal, Cullen to Arnold, Arnold File, AFHRA. Aquilla probably referred to South Asia (HQ 10th AF). FORCE AQUILA under Col. Caleb Haynes had flown to Karachi with 12 B-17Es and one B-24, transiting Africa early April.

> The 7th Photographic Squadron is now assigned to OTU [training] at Colorado Springs, Colorado, and no planes are available for allocation to Rusty. Col. Cullen is being advised to this effect by cablegram sent to him, this date (Tab C).
>
> It is understood that Col. Cullen is now en route to the United States and his arrival is expected at any time.[908]

There would be no such help from home. Instead, the RUSTY expedition improvised, roaming far and wide in North Africa, taking pictures as conditions would permit. And that's how, in April 1942, Elliott Roosevelt wound up in Cairo.

By early 1942 only a few American aircraft had reached Cairo, and they could not be brought to bear against Rommel until June, when a small force of B-24s arrived. By that time, Elliott Roosevelt was already finished with his African job. He had, as in the Arctic, been among the pioneers of the Air Force, but not for purposes of combat. If that is why the story of RUSTY has remained largely unrecorded, it is unfortunate. The mission was one of the earliest and most important encounters in which Americans took part.

The German raids on the Suez Canal, the installation of a Nazi-allied regime in Baghdad, and the wavering of Iran made the importance of the African route extra critical in the fall of 1941. By next spring, hundreds of aircraft were flying the new route. In *As He Saw It*, Elliott's brief geographic hints refer in part to this fabled "Takoradi Route" since project RUSTY used the same bases.

Fort Lamy in French Equatorial Africa is the current Ndjamena, now capital of Chad. It is at the southern edge of the Sahara. The distances over absolutely desolate country were enormous, and Elliott's recent navigation training must have been extremely helpful. For example, Fort Lamy is almost twice as far from Algiers than it is from London. Nevertheless, in January 1942, a daring Luftwaffe air raid destroyed the fuel depot that had been so laboriously established at Lamy. The Germans could have interdicted the African route more thoroughly in 1942, but they failed to follow up. Their action, though, did succeed in making the Americans paranoid about losing sub-Saharan Africa as well.[909]

The distance from the Gambia to Cairo along the Takoradi Route is comparable to New York – London; but that was only the last third of the ferry route from American factories to British users. The latter complained that not only were American aircraft inferior, they were already worn out by the time they got them.

Roosevelt soon realized that the photomapping missions over the Sahara seemed a lot like the long flights in the Arctic. At 30,000 feet it was just as cold, but the neighbors were less friendly. His job definitely impressed, for he was promoted to major in April, and awarded the Distinguished Flying Cross (DFC) later that year. The citation specifically praised his arctic, desert, and equatorial photoflights:

> ELLIOTT ROOSEVELT, O-396475, Lieutenant Colonel, 3rd Photographic Group, 12th Air Force, United States Army. For heroism and extraordinary achievement while participating in aerial flights. As a member of parties making aerial surveys of important ferry routes, Lt. Col. Elliott Roosevelt participated in long and dangerous flights over Arctic, sub-Arctic, and Equatorial regions many of them being over water and uninhabited areas. On one expedition, Lt. Col. Roosevelt was the only member who made every operational flight. As a result of his experience and energy, he has been of great assistance in the establishment of ferry routes. As Commanding Officer of a Photographic Group assigned to the American forces in North Africa, Lt. Col. Roosevelt personally participated

> in many flights deep into hostile and heavily defended areas, acting as observer, navigator, photographer, and radio operator. He made these flights voluntarily with complete disregard of his personal safety as he well knew the extremely vulnerable characteristics of his unarmed airplane. The efficiency of his Photographic Group as proven by the valuable information it has obtained, is due in a large degree to the ability, leader ship, and inspiration of Lt. Col. Roosevelt. His courage and skill reflects credit both on himself and on the military service.
>
> By command of Major General Doolittle: HOYT S. VANDENBERG, Brigadier General, USA, Chief of Staff.[910]

General Eisenhower awarded Roosevelt this medal on 23 December 1942, after the invasion of North Africa, but it was Doolittle who pinned it on Elliott's chest.

Interestingly, Elliott did not use his first book (*As He Saw It*) to advertise his own military service; his objective was to document his father's summits with Allied leaders. That might be commendable, except that a second book about his wartime duties was sorely needed. Perhaps, given the fierce controversy about his military career, he thought it better to touch on the subject tangentially. We are left to reconstruct his exploits with the help of more conscientious record-keepers.

Elliott nonetheless was famous for telling tall tales about his exploits. Collier noted:

> One trait Elliott shared with his father was an inclination to fabulate his experiences. All through his postwar life he would embroider on his combat experiences, making them seem ever more dangerous and grandiose than they had actually been. One of the stories he told was of flying into China on board a B-17 outfitted for reconnaissance to do a photographic survey of Chinese supply lines and then being ambushed by Messerschmitt fighters on the way back and being forced to crash land in British West Africa. This experience was not officially confirmed, but it was true that Elliott flew hazardous missions and his unit suffered heavy losses. On one mission one of his gunners was killed and he was the only member of the crew not to suffer a wound of some kind.[911]

For sheer geographical implausibility, the China story above must have raised eyebrows. More careful analysis suggests that a number of separate incidents got scrambled together down the line, because there is archival evidence of the individual elements of this particular war story. Most likely, Elliott's enthusiasm and raconteur instinct rubbed some listeners the wrong way. But it is definitely true that in old age, Elliott wildly exaggerated his wartime adventures.

Eleanor noted in her column on 7 May 1942 that just before noon, an infirm Elliott had shown up at the White House, fresh in from Africa.[912] He told everyone of his exploits. In a further breach of security, Eleanor wrote to an acquaintance:

> Elliott arrived from the Africa trip with 18,000 plates 2 days ago. They photographed every single thing they were sent to get but he brought back a little African bug & has some kind of dysentery from which I hope he soon recovers…Elliott thinks nothing of the British high command in Africa & less of what they have done in sanitation & education through their years of control. He thinks from all he heard that Italy did a far better job of giving rather than taking in Eritrea. Of course don't say this but he says the Colonials all feel the same way.[i]

[i] Lash:, Love, Eleanor, 389. The letter was to her aunt Maude Gray, wife of the U.S. ambassador in Dublin.

She wrote daughter Anna that "Elliott dropped from the sky today just 45 hours from Liberia to Washington…The plane fell to pieces when they made their last landing & and they just got in."

> Africa was a shock to him, he can't get over the disease & filth & how the natives have been exploited. He brought back 18,000 plates and they photographed everything they went after. Almost had to come down in the desert the last day. One engine nearly dropped off 850 miles from base over the desert but it froze & hung by hair & and they limped in with all landing gear gone & and after landing Elliott said the plane practically fell apart. Weren't they lucky?[913]

The sensational war stories told, Major Roosevelt set to work on his reports.

Results of Rusty

Was RUSTY a success or not? Two aircraft and one crew were lost. But the Air Corps needed the photos badly, and in that light the operation was considered a success. Colonel Cullen submitted his first report to Arnold on 22 May. As the expedition's harvest to date, he listed reports on fifteen airdromes and adjacent installations in French West Africa, and furthermore, RAF-prepared reports on nine airfields in Togo and Dahomey, plus maps, photographs, and analysis.

Cullen's intelligence estimate was startling for its seemingly irrational fear of an aggressive French thrust to the south. At this time of dramatic Axis advances, the Anglo-Americans were prone to see France simply as Hitler's accomplice:

> 1. Vichy French forces, French West Africa, have the following capabilities: The Ground, Naval and Air Forces present in the Dakar-Kaolack Tambacounda-Ziguinchor area [Senegal] can seize and hold the British colony of Gambia. Once this colony is occupied by the French, its recapture by the British is extremely difficult because of the lack of air bases within reasonable striking distance. Portuguese Guinea affords the only possible base for British operations.
> 2. The existing French Air Force operating from air bases at Macenta, Kerouane, Kankan, Conakry [Guinea] can neutralize Freetown [Sierra Leone] as a survey watering and assembling point. The French Ground, Naval and Air Forces can occupy simultaneously the British colonies of Gambia and Sierra Leone. [914]

The analysis proceeded to demonstrate how Vichy forces could rout the Allies from Africa, and ended with this clincher:

> 6. The great capability is the use of Vichy French West African Air, Naval and Ground facilities by the Luftwaffe and the German Army as a base of operations against (1) anti-Axis shipping in the South Atlantic, (2) the African Ferry Route, (3) penetration (economic or military) of South America.

As for the British, Cullen noted that there was little hope of resistance, except in Nigeria:

> 4. The British colony of Nigeria has the best road-rail system in any of the British colonies in West Africa. With the troops now present in this colony, it is believed that an

> adequate defense against ground movement can be maintained. However, there are practically no air units in this colony, and a sudden air-ground attack might be successful. This situation is not as serious as in the case of the other British colonies, as air reinforcements could be moved rapidly to this theater from the Middle East in forty-eight hours. There is a limited number of adequate airdromes from which medium and heavy bombardment can operate. There is no natural defensive line between the Maiduguri-Kano area and the French concentrations to the north in the vicinity of Zinder [Niger]. The country is semi-arid, rolling farm land, thickly populated, offering an excellent theater for the operations of mechanized forces. Whereas the bases now used by the American and Royal Air Forces' Ferrying Commands at Maiduguri-Kano may be easily subjected to air attack from the Vichy French bases to the north and west, these bases also provide an excellent springboard for offensive action against the Vichy French forces in the north and west.

The assumption seems to have been that Vichy was simply an extension of the Axis – not a rather harmless residue of French sovereignty. The report wildly overstated both Vichy intentions and capabilities.

A summary of photographic evidence accompanying the RUSTY report emphasized potential Vichy aggression, but also provided a catalog of where the *Blue Goose* had been:

1. The most striking feature which is common to all the airports covered by this mission is their recent construction and/or large scale expansion.
2. Some sites have evidently been prepared for future occupancy. In this group are the airports at St. Louis, Kaolack [Senegal], Conakry, Kerouane, Kankan [Guinea], Abidjan. Other sites have been occupied in strength and are still expanding. These include Dakar, Thies [S], Bamako [Mali], Zinder [Niger], Gao [M], Niamey. The airport at Macenta is still in the first stages of construction. The airports at Tillaberi [N] and Sikasso [M] may be classed as emergency landing fields.
3. By referring to the attached map, it will be seen that the largest installations are located along the 15 degree North latitude line between Dakar and Zinder. Within this belt are located Dakar, Thies, Bamako, Gao, Niamey and Zinder. In the Dakar-Thies area positions of considerable size already exist and tremendous activity is in progress. Bamako is the site of several ground establishments. Niamey gives every appearance of being made ready for large troop installations. Zinder is already the center of several encampments and it is here that tanks are positively located. All this is in addition to the very large scale development of the air position.
4. The landing fields at St. Louis, Kaolack, Conakry, Kerouane, Kankan, and Abidjan are ready for use. Stores and dumps have been installed at these places and it is believed that the existing road net affords easy access to them.
5. The photographs of nine airports in Togo and Dahomey, included in this report, were taken by the Royal Air Force. The airports at Agbeluve [Togo] and Cotonou [Dahomey] have good runways but they are obstructed by logs or hurdles placed on them. The fields at Save [D], Kumina, Lome and Geaa are suitable for landings. Those at Ana [T], Allada and Paouignan [D] can be classed as emergency fields. Little, if any, activity is apparent at any of them.[915]

The emphasis of this report on French West Africa should not be construed to overshadow subsequent reconnaissance activity in all of North Africa. Since Elliott Roosevelt said that he went all the way from Bathurst in the Gambia to China, it bears mentioning that the Air Corps was indeed beginning to fly a few transports across to

Chungking in support of Generalissimo Chiang Kai-Shek's hard-pressed Chinese forces. Elliott's insistence on having been fired upon by "fascist" aircraft is plausible in Egypt as well as in the French territories; the Vichy Air Force was capable there, and as the Americans would soon learn, they meant to fight, at least defensively.

The consistent reference to "fascist" or "Nazi" airplanes and other equipment is part of the jarring vocabulary of the times. (Nobody said the Americans flew "Democrat" aircraft.) At any rate, the mix of Vichy, Free French, Italian, German, and other nationalities in the area, some of them flying planes totally unfamiliar to foreigners, would be a cause of endless confusion. Also, at a distance most planes then looked alike.

Other documents in General Arnold's papers confirm that considerable attention was devoted to how the Allies might react to an Axis advance south. On 30 April, Arnold received an analysis that urged caution but not overreaction. It proposed to prod the Free French into aggressive action against Vichy. The recommendations were:

a. That the completion of the southern ferry route be expedited.
b. That the air bases and potential bases from which action against the ferry route could be initiated be kept under surveillance by photographic reconnaissance and by agencies of the Coordinator of Information. [espionage]
c. That the air defense equipment and installations now scheduled for Liberia be delivered as scheduled and that [adequate] ground protection against attack by low-flying aircraft be provided all principal ferry bases.
d. That the Free French be encouraged to seize territory contiguous to the Slave Coast, including the airdromes at Lome and Cotonou, and the Ivory Coast including the airdrome at Port Louest. To accomplish this, the assistance of the British is essential. In order to obtain the right of transit through and bases in Nigeria and the Gold Coast. Informal discussion with Free French representatives has established their willingness to take this action and their confidence in its success.

> ...That at such time as aircraft are available, one (1) squadron of light bombardment and one (1) squadron of pursuit aircraft be allocated to the Free French for operations by their crews from the Fort Lamy area. It should be noted that the Free French have a force of approximately 14,000 men in French Equatorial Africa and air support would substantially assist their offensive capabilities....
>
> ...It is understood that Colonel Cullen and Major Roosevelt, who have been on reconnaissance duty in this area, are now enroute to Washington. It is recommended that any decision on this subject be delayed until such time as consideration of their reports may be completed.[916]

This course of action would turn out to be unnecessary. Although operation GYMNAST, the early invasion of North Africa, had to be cancelled, its replacement, TORCH, was decided upon in the summer. Afterwards, the French colonies – which had shown no inclination to do anything but mind their own business – were forced to join the Allies.

It is proof of the intense top-level interest in RUSTY that when Elliott came back to the White House on 7 May, General Arnold was there, too; and that on the 13th, the president had lunch with his son, Arnold, Harry Hopkins, and Lt. Col. Cullen. The results of the reconnaissance thus went straight to the top.[917]

Even so, RUSTY was merely one of many African intelligence and reconnaissance operations the Air Forces launched during 1941-42. Another well-documented mission surveyed equatorial Africa for a potential fall-back route to Australia. That flight evidenced the first U.S. interest in the remote Diego Garcia atoll in the Indian Ocean.

Other surveys completed the picture. Thus, before Elliott Roosevelt and Paul Cullen returned home, an aeronautical route guide for the African ferry route was already being completed in Washington. That detailed guide, similar to modern area supplements, seems to have been in large part a result of information collected by Pan Am Africa. It tabulated in great detail the services and pitfalls aircrew could expect all the way from Dakar to Aden. For example, it pointed out that the main operating location in Accra was an extremely well-equipped and well-functioning base, thanks especially to its immediate pre-war development for the passenger service run by Pan Am's giant Clippers.[918]

More curious was the fact that Colonel Cullen – unlike Major Roosevelt – was immediately sent back to Africa. Along with Colonel D.V. Gaffney and Major R.C. Lowe, he commandeered a B-24D and conducted another survey in June, this time for security evaluation purposes. Why this should be necessary so soon after the previous trip is not clear. Perhaps it reflected General Arnold's paranoia about losing the route to a French fascist advance. The Report on Special Mission on Security of the African Ferry Route, dated 10 July 1942, doesn't seem to add much that wasn't already known.[919]

Odder still it is that the very highly respected Paul Cullen remained a colonel during the same period that Elliott Roosevelt advanced from captain to brigadier. Cullen reportedly wouldn't talk about Elliott.[i] He was later instrumental in carrying out the shuttle bombing project in Russia. He rose to Brigadier General, USAF, but was killed in an unexplained C-124 crash in the Atlantic in 1951.

Thus Elliott's brief African opus was but one of many such slightly panicky American initiatives; the British occasionally got tired of answering the same questions to multiple American teams who knew nothing of each other. Secrecy often appeared to be more impediment than asset.

Rusty Secrecy

Project RUSTY was a highly secret operation, but that could not last long. For one thing, the presence of a high-flying blue B-17 all over North Africa was rather conducive to talk. For another, when TORCH settled the African matter in 1943, some American veterans began coming forward with what they knew.

On 19 April 1943, a photographic technician, Aviation Cadet Joseph Condon, gave a rather detailed account of RUSTY to newsmen. He had been head of the photo laboratory on board the *Blue Goose.* He said:

> We were the first American soldiers to land in Nigeria. Our mission was to photograph the West African coast, the central belt across the continent and to photomap the African portion of the air route to India. We used B-17s and B-24s, stripped of all their

[i] "In reference to Col. Paul T. Cullen, I know him personally and he is the officer that normally would have been promoted to Brigadier General if Elliott had not been around. I am not familiar with the background of his story, except that when I first met him I asked him if he knew Elliott. He looked me in the eye and said, "I gave him his star" and then changed the subject." Letter, Benoit to Pegler, 10 AUG 47, ER wartime file, Pegler/HH.

> guns and bomb racks, to carry all our photo equipment and allow for 700 extra gallons of gasoline.[920]

Joe Condon said his Fortress flew over essentially all North Africa, from the Ivory Coast to Cairo. Elliott himself noted that he'd flown the Bathurst – Dakar run and north "three or four times."[921]

Condon noted that the photo-mapping work continued after the return of RUSTY, using local aircraft in preparation for the invasion. He maintained that the *Blue Goose* was never fired on, although other aircraft were attacked by the French. In particular, after the German air attack on Fort Lamy the local French garrison took to firing at all aircraft, friendly or hostile.

Condon related several amusing vignettes. He said that Captain Roosevelt regularly posted his orders on the base bulletin board. Unfortunately his subordinates would pull them down to keep for souvenirs.

Although mainly operating out of Takoradi and Accra, Condon was in Liberia, virtually untouched by development, when the first "Yank Negro" combat engineers arrived.[i] He also had adventures in the Gambia and Nigeria. It is not surprising that the newly promoted Major Roosevelt came back to the United States with several nasty germs.[922]

That the Air Corps considered RUSTY a considerable, even epic success was revealed in a press release a year after the operation's completion, on 5 June 1943. By then, all of Africa was in the Allied bag and it was deemed safe to talk about the project. The disclosure was made at Lowry Field in Colorado, the nerve center of photographic reconnaissance training. Thirty members of the expedition were trained there, and four of them came forward to talk about it.

> The expedition sought out and mapped tactical positions, likely invasion points, concentrations of resistance, topographical conditions and land marks in and about Oran, Algiers, Casablanca, Morocco, Tunis, Bizerte, Rabat, and other vital sections…the mission brought back the first complete photographs of Northern Africa expanses, and was one of the most significant examples of the importance of aerial photography in modern warfare.[923]

The four airmen who spoke were Lt. William H. Teague, Lt. Charles T. Randall, Lt. Benjamin E. Nelson, and Lt. Edgar M. Cohen. Randall said that one of the planes, unarmed, was once attacked by three "Messerschmitts" and barely managed to escape by climbing to an extreme altitude. Randall added that during one attack by German planes, a member of the crew fired his Very [signaling] pistol at the attackers, and Colonel Cullen reprimanded him for the silliness of it.

This supports Elliott's contention that he was attacked by hostile aircraft at least once during the operation.[924] Lt. Teague said:

> We were miles from our objective; our Flying Fortresses had to be specially equipped with cameras and plenty of gas tanks. Each plane had a 3,900 gallon capacity. It was impossible to carry guns of any sort on the bombers. Weight was so carefully allotted that

[i] Liberia had no facilities, and the Americans operated at Roberts Field on the Firestone rubber plantation.

> we weren't even allowed to carry coins in our pockets. In case of enemy attack, our only weapon was altitude – but that was enough.[i]

It would appear from this testimony that RUSTY managed to gain access to other aircraft in the region and completed the North African task by steadily moving north to the Mediterranean coastline. The record does not state which flights Elliott participated in, but he was commended for having completed all the expedition's flights assigned to him, and for having survived air combat and a crash landing.

Understandably the media were especially interested in the role played by the second presidential son. In the Lowry Field press release, Lt. Teague was also quoted in the press as follows:

> Lieutenant William H. Teague, 23, of Weatherford, Texas, a sergeant-photographer on the mission, said a flying photo laboratory named "Blue Goose" dropped one of its four motors during the mission and made a crash landing. Col. Roosevelt, then a major, was aboard the ship as a navigator. He was not injured. "He managed to make his way back to our photo base on foot…as a navigator, the president's son is tops."[925]

Although this sounds like an emergency landing, it was the first of several "crashes" in which Roosevelt was involved.

Before he died, another crewmember quoted, Edgar Cohen, had the good sense to record an oral history interview with the Library of Congress. His recollection, although it took the interviewer some effort to get it out, was that Elliott Roosevelt was for the most part the operational director of the expedition, while Colonel Cullen flew the airplane. Cohen was sent to Africa by boat, but he returned with Elliott and others aboard a Pan Am Clipper, along with malaria and assorted other tropical diseases.[926]

Cohen confirmed that there was one aircraft, an "old" B-17 (three years old) that was painted blue and bore no identification due to the top secret nature of the mission.

Top secret as RUSTY was, nevertheless a sharp observer could put the pieces together. One such was no less than C.L. Sulzberger, the *New York Times*'s star foreign reporter. He was on his way back to the United States from the Soviet Union at the same time Elliott was in Africa, and his route virtually duplicated Elliott's.

From Cairo, where he was in late March, Sulzberger provided a detailed evaluation of the American presence in North Africa and the Middle East. He located the American supply trail from Bathurst to Cairo. He circumspectly described the bases in Eritrea, the Sudan, Chad, and Nigeria, noting that competitors Pan American and BOAC (British Overseas Airways Corporation) were locked in an uneasy, sometimes contentious partnership to provide air transport across the continent. He keenly observed air traffic:

> This correspondent, who recently flew across the principal route, saw on the way not only considerable numbers of DC-3 parachute-troop carriers, which are being used for war transport of personnel and freight, but also Flying Fortresses, Liberators, Bostons attack bombers, Hurricanes and Tomahawks. The fighter planes are flown on short hops in convoy formation after being assembled at recently erected depots.[927]
>
> …It is now being rumored up and down the Gold Coast and Nigeria that considerable new quantities of men and materiel have recently been arriving in Vichy

---

[i] ChigTrib, 6 JUN 43. 3,900 gls = 24,000 lbs, making that B-17B's mass at take-off over half fuel.

> territory. Whether this information is correct cannot be ascertained, but it is no secret that the United Nations are keeping up a steady watch abetted by occasional aerial reconnaissance.[928]

Actually that *was* supposed to be a secret. But since Sulzberger did travel by C-47 via Omdurman, el Fasher, and Maiduguri to Lagos, where he caught the Pan Am Clipper back to Brazil, he could not help but learn what the American reconnaissance mission was up to.

Incidentally, Sulzberger could not mention Maiduguri except by vague description. The reason he alighted there rather than in Fort Lamy was that the German air attack on Lamy had panicked the locals:

> There is a tendency to distrust the many de Gaullists since the desertion several months ago of a handful of Free French pilots who flew bombers up to Vichy territory from Nigeria. Likewise, the administration of Fort Lamy, capital of the Chad Territory, has been exceedingly nervous since that small town was bombed many weeks ago by a lone raider.
>
> This plane, coming from Vichy territory but believed to have been Italian, arrived over Fort Lamy in broad daylight and, meeting with no suspicion, flew over its objectives several times and then proceeded methodically to bomb them, doing considerable damage.

This caused the French anti-aircraft gunners to fire on anything that flew afterwards, and so the Americans tried to avoid Fort Lamy for a while, favoring Maiduguri on the other side of Lake Chad. (Besides, if General Arnold was correct that the loss of the fuel depot there had been a bitter blow, perhaps the aircraft could not refuel.)

The Lamy raid was not the only long-range Axis airstrikes, but it was surprisingly effective. The Italian Air Force had struck as far as Bahrein in October 1940, causing negligible damage. The Suez Canal was repeatedly attacked.[929]

These incidents illustrated General Arnold's tenuous position in tropical Africa. With mere pinprick operations, the Axis could interrupt the trans-African operation. That was why Cullen's and Roosevelt's reconnaissance flights were so important, and why other expeditions were also tasked to survey a fall-back route to the south, through the Congo Basin. There would be a secondary route through Leopoldville, Elizabethville, and Nairobi. One reason for that effort was the uranium mine in the Katanga province, but few understood the significance of that at the time.

Sulzberger noticed the Congo route, too. So much for Top Secret.

Build-Up in England

Elliott Roosevelt said he spent most of the summer in hospital because of the amoebic dysentery and malaria he had contracted in tropical Africa; he did not mention surgeries for an old knee injury, and for piles. For a while, he walked with a cane.[930]

There was time to recuperate in Texas. In June, the president and the first lady came to visit. They stayed at the Benbrook ranch, but although public spectacles were discouraged this time, an estimated half a million Texans turned out to cheer the family on. War does wonders for the leader's popularity, except if he loses.[931]

In mid-July 1942, Major Roosevelt was given command of the 3rd Photographic Group at Colorado Springs AAB, which became Peterson Field later that year. The group comprised four squadrons with photo variants of P-38s and B-17s earmarked for England. Along with Lowry Field in Denver, Peterson was a center of photographic reconnaissance training. Most of the newly formed reconnaissance squadrons were organized and trained there before deployment overseas.[932]

The Secret Service helped move the family to Colorado Springs, where it took up residence at 1st and Elm. This was close by the Broadmoor Golf Course and Hotel, where the rich and powerful gathered. Agents reported: "The Major is the Commanding Officer of the 3rd Photo Group… He works seven days a week, leaving home around 8:30 AM and returns around 6 PM. However, on Sundays, his hours are not quite so stiff." How much help the agents were security-wise is doubtful, but they came in handy as chauffeurs, fixers and gophers, thus freeing the colored servants for other tasks. One of these was the "scarey Negro type," noted the Secret Service. Also troubling, the Roosevelts' family ranch was located in an area of Texas with a large number of settlers of German descent. You can't be too careful. [933]

The temporary posting lasted barely six weeks, and then it was off to war. Elliott checked out of the White House on 11 September. Tagging along with Deputy Prime Minister Clement Attlee and the High Commissioner for Canada, Elliott flew to England.[934] He was to consolidate his units at RAF Steeple Morden, near Cambridge. As usual he spent much of the time socializing with the upper crust:

> I got down to Chequers, Churchill's country home, for one weekend towards the end of September, and took care this time to be slightly better prepared than on my last visit. After dinner he casually mentioned that he planned to talk to Father on the transatlantic phone that night, and would I care to say hello? I'm sure his studied nonchalance was an act; I like to think that it was his thoughtfulness that led him to remember that this day was my birthday…[935]

After much trouble they did get the transatlantic telephone line up, and after the proper felicitations, the president let Elliott know that he might get a visit from a member of the family at his base in England. Next morning, the Prime Minister bade farewell: "He was stalking about the room, clad only in a cigar." Churchill often did this, even when dictating to his (male) secretaries; perhaps it was some kind of domination display.[936]

At that same time, an insolent creditor in Fort Worth, Edelbrock Saddlery, wrote President Roosevelt that his son had not paid his bills for equine paraphernalia for over a year. "Can you please help?" FDR sent Ruth a hundred dollars towards the debt.[937]

Eleanor was in England. At Steeple Morden, she had the chance to see Elliott off for North Africa three weeks before she herself left for the Prestwick-Gander run back to the States on 16 November.[938]

Although the 3rd PRG had only recently arrived in-country, Eleanor met Elliott several times in England. She and her son had dinner with the King, Queen, and Mr. and Mrs. Churchill on 23 October.[939] Both had the run of Buckingham Palace, with its unheated rooms and shattered windows, before the final send-off on 29 October at Elliott's base. Eleanor said some of the units had already cleared out, and Elliott wasn't sure when he himself was going. She wrote home: "He goes soon & not towards home." They both knew the destination at least in outline.[940]

Despite the hectic time, Elliott remembered the Steeple Morden visit well:

> My 1,000 troops had been lined up for four hours in a driving rain to receive her. When she arrived and saw the sodden boys all lined up at attention, she quickly asked that they be dismissed and allowed to return to quarters to change into dry clothes. A great cheer went up at this request.[941]

Eleanor was late because her embassy driver got lost. To confuse the enemy, there were no highway signs. On a historiographical note, Eleanor's biographers ever since tirelessly copied the episode as the "Rover lost her pup" incident, after her callsign and the driver's cryptic call for help. But only Elliott remembered the infuriated troops standing in the rain, presumably catching colds and pneumonia.[i]

Yet Elliott's memory was again fickle. When he wrote of the inspection in 1946, Eleanor was only one hour late, not four. By 1982, it was "more than five hours."[942]

The men remembered, too. They wrote "it was a cold dreary day, but in spite of this Mrs. Roosevelt insisted on reviewing the entire Group, stopping frequently to chat with individual men and officers. Following the review, tea was served at the Officers' Club with Mrs. Roosevelt posing for snaps with various officers and granting an interview with 8-10 British press representatives."[943]

Elliott did not have to go to North Africa; he asked for it, and Generals Doolittle and Spaatz conceded the point. Despite his low rank, Elliott already knew of the plan.[944]

The group would have another two weeks before joining in the hostilities, but the immense logistical challenge caused many of the troops to move by sea, and in small portions. The aircraft, however, flew to North Africa, Elliott in the lead. With the theater commander, General Eisenhower, Elliott set up temporary quarters at Gibraltar. Once again Hitler would rue his neglect in mopping up the Mediterranean.

LIES, DAMN LIES, AND RECONNAISSANCE

Although aerial observation has a history going back to the Montgolfière balloons, in 1939 the U.S. Army Air Corps was essentially devoid of credible means and methods of obtaining aerial intelligence. Nothing illustrates America's unpreparedness better. Had the Americans had effective strategic reconnaissance, Pearl Harbor would not have happened (or would have been quite a different story). Had doctrine, materiel, personnel, training, and standardized procedures been in place for tactical reconnaissance, the first American battles would not have been so disastrous.

This is all the more interesting because the Europeans had already raised the art to a science. For example, in the spring of 1941 when the Americans were just experimenting with cameras in P-38s, the Germans conducted a massive campaign of strategic reconnaissance of the USSR – an ominous activity Stalin chose to ignore, the better to indulge in his fantasy of Russo-German world domination.

[i] Lash: Eleanor and Franklin, 666; Lash did notice that in another such incident, Eleanor said "they weren't any wetter or colder than I was!"

An expert said of the hard birth of Allied air reconnaissance in 1939-41:

> Arnold and his lieutenants were forward thinkers in the realm of air warfare, but their deep thought did not extend to air intelligence. This was nowhere more evident than in their almost complete lack of emphasis on Bomb Damage Assessment (BDA) until a few months before America's entry into the Second World War. What they did have the presence of mind to do – and this proved crucial to the exceptionally close wartime partnership between British BDA and American aerial bombardment – was to send Air Corps officers to Great Britain as observers, not just of British flying operations, but also of their air intelligence activities. It was the latter which impressed them the most, and the recommendations they made based on their findings would play a vital role in the development of an American BDA capability – one that appeared much later than it should have and which was an adjunct to the British capability, but one that worked nonetheless.[945]

Armies cannot fight without intelligence any more than a blind man can win a boxing match. Nor can long-range aircraft operate without accurate charts. Obvious as they were, the twin needs for aerial mapping and reconnaissance were suddenly discovered by the War Department during the brief pre-war build-up.

Reconnaissance was known as "observation" in the pre-war Army, and squadrons of light aircraft were supposed to provide direct support to army units below. Only the Douglas A-20, a medium bomber, was thought useful as a longer-range reconnaissance asset (F-3). Although the large four-engine aircraft slowly coming on line were used for mapping, this was very much an improvised activity.

Observation doctrine was still focused on the first fifty miles beyond the front. Despite the theological devotion to strategic bombing, there was no appreciation of the need for accurate mapping, creation of target catalogs and folders, and bomb damage assessment. Perhaps most debilitating, there was a sharp dispute about how best to provide command and control. The young-Turk Air Corps officers were pushing for centralized control of air assets; the rest of the Army resisted this fiercely.

In other words, most of the Army was still in trench warfare mode.

Allied strategic bombardment has received enormous historical attention, and there remains a perennial fight over its merits and flaws. Here we need not invade this well-trodden ground; but we must remember that the Allied bombing offensive was not a monolithic effort, and cannot be defended or denounced as such. Most of all we must recognize that there is a dumb way to apply air power, and a smart way. The latter depends absolutely on reconnaissance. It is no secret that the U.S. air effort moved, in fits and starts, from tragically dumb to quite smart in the 2½ years the American air war effectively lasted.

Intelligence is the root of power. Equally important, over time this scientific prevalence is rooted in an open society and a free economy. The Allied recognition of this insight is the key to understanding the Anglo-American dominance in world affairs since 1941. No sensible person would argue that the western Allies "outfought" their opponents. It was their development of an intellectual infrastructure in intelligence that made the difference, as much as sheer weight of numbers.

Reconnaissance, as a subset of intelligence, is primarily an intellectual pursuit, and as such it requires the maintenance of intellectual capital devoted to it. Developing this was a slow process, but results in the field – or the lack of them – forced officers to recognize the need for strategic mapping and targeting intelligence, pre-strike surveys, and post-strike battle-damage assessment (BDA).

Even after the uneasy peace of 1945, strategic reconnaissance vastly expanded in importance, because it was the only way to find out what was going on behind the Iron Curtain and to prepare target catalogs for the Doomsday strikes that might become necessary. People understood that next time there would be no learning curve.

It is impossible to overestimate the importance of the seamless Anglo-American cooperation in intelligence. This developed under British tutelage over the years 1939-45, and culminated in the most finely-tuned, scientific reconnaissance infrastructure the world had ever seen. Our present subject provides strong evidence for the theory that intelligence won the war. It also supports the idea that the Anglo embrace of a science-based mode of warfare secured the victory both in 1945 and, ultimately, in 1991. That is a widely held view today, and is, for example, supported by the profound study of reconnaissance published by Dr. Robert Ehlers in 2005.

Remarkable, but little appreciated, is that British leadership continued in this field at least until the Corona reconnaissance satellites in the early 1960s. For example, the redoubtable Mosquito was replaced by the equally superb Canberra, which the USAF put in production as the B-57. The accompanying advances in cameras and interpretation procedures also are to some extent British in origin. Many of the now famous overflights of the USSR were conducted by the RAF, although by then Anglo-American cooperation was so close it was hardly noticed. Colonel Elliott Roosevelt, as we shall see, never much liked "the limeys," but he certainly benefited immensely from their help, and his command was an expression of Anglo-American unity.

Supremely important was that reconnaissance caused a slow but continuous correction of the kinetic war. Early on, British air reconnaissance revealed that aerial bombing was an absolute, unmitigated disaster, at least if the goal was to hit something. When the Americans joined the game, further photographic intelligence proved that even the U.S. daylight "precision" bombing was nearly as bad – i.e. a throwing away of lives and aircraft for little gain. (By then, few cared about the civilian costs.) Only by the end of the war was there a dawning understanding of how to effectively use air power in accordance with the strategic doctrine it purported to execute.

For this reason, reconnaissance evidence was not always welcome. Data showing the failure of the initial strategic bombing campaign tends to remain among the experts, since it sounds off-key in the propaganda which still characterizes the popular history of the war. Likewise, reconnaissance gets short shrift in most historical accounts. Apparently, people prefer bang-bang to click-click, at least when reading about it.

Awkwardly, reconnaissance shows you how wrong you are. Both British and American air officers were often infuriated by it, but in time they learned to adjust their operations. The U-2 and Corona programs were later examples. They brought news that the Western opinion of Soviet strength had been vastly inflated, and resulted in a sharp correction of American military posture.

Air reconnaissance caused a paradigm shift in the application of air power. The Allies went into the war with a "Somme-in-the-sky" mentality that appears in retrospect to be as tragically criminal as the battle of the Somme itself. They exited the war with an understanding of how to use precision airstrikes – a tactical improvement that has now culminated in the ability to send one aerial vehicle to reduce-to-order several targets with surgical precision, near-impunity, and minimum disruption to unrelated people.

This lesson was obtained at the cost of about 100,000 Allied lives – not counting the lives of close to a million hapless civilians of various nationalities.

Today, after two generations of almost fanatic and certainly immensely costly emphasis on reconnaissance, the French term itself has been somewhat eclipsed; it now lives mostly as a part of ISR (intelligence, surveillance, and reconnaissance) and that again is attached as a suffix in C4ISR (command, control, communications, computers, and ISR). While this reflects a hideous jargon, it also underscores the modern understanding that the "kinetic" elements are often the smallest aspects of warfare.

Dr. Ehlers, who has studied the history of reconnaissance intensively, has the following comment on American preparedness in that domain:

> In an inexplicable oversight, America's senior airmen, including Hap Arnold and Carl Spaatz, seem not to have grasped the importance of a high-performance reconnaissance aircraft until they came to recognize the vital role of the Spitfire and Mosquito in the RAF, and by then it was too late. Consequently, they had to rely on converted P-38 fighters (renamed the F-5) in the photoreconnaissance role. These aircraft lacked the combat ceilings of the Spitfire and Mosquito and were therefore vulnerable to German fighters. The results were more failed missions, more aircraft shot down, and more pilots killed. In fact, the 325th Reconnaissance Wing [Elliott Roosevelt's command] had a higher percentage of its pilots killed than any other Army Air Forces unit in the Second World War, a dubious distinction and the moniker of one of the very few abject failures of vision, technical achievement, and leadership in the interwar and wartime air force. Fortunately, the same was not true of the British effort to develop high-performance photoreconnaissance aircraft, or of the cameras they ultimately carried….[946]

Claims for loss rates are subject to some dispute, but leave that for now. By 1945, everything had changed:

> This Allied advantage (scientific, technical, and organizational) was nowhere clearer than in the intelligence effort. In fact, the agencies responsible for producing BDA reports took full advantage of the best human talent and employed it in ways that were highly efficient and effective. Once again, the Allied advantage in this arena was substantial and proved vital to the success of their war effort, just as poor German intelligence capabilities and indeed the shocking lack of interest most German commanders showed in operational and strategic intelligence helped to undermine the Axis war effort. German air intelligence failures, of which there were many, stand in stark contrast to Allied successes, which are finally receiving attention in a growing body of scholarship.[947]

In 1941, the Americans took the first clumsy steps on a steep learning curve. On this background, Elliott Roosevelt's meteoric rise makes quite a bit more sense. The first to happen onto a new science often become its leaders for years to come. Elliott may not have been an expert on much of anything; but by January 1942, when most of the Air Forces' reconnaissance units were being formed, he was among the few who knew a bit about how mapping, aerial photography, piloting, and navigation came together. That is how he ended up as a wing commander within 2½ years of joining the military.

Elliott's mapping job in the Sahara had been a prelude to the first serious U.S. action on that side of the Atlantic. Now he would move on to the reconnaissance task in direct support of ground forces. It would be a failure.

And whose Side are *You* on?

Little attention – and less of it sympathetic – has been given, at least in the English-speaking world, to the odd situation that prevailed in French Africa in the interval between the creation of the Vichy state and the Anglo-American conquest three years later. That may be because it is hard to fit the actors into neat categories. It is even hard to determine whose side anyone was on. Africa was a more dramatic case of the previous circus in the North Atlantic.

The Americans were in a particular quandary because, like most nations, they recognized the Petain-Laval regime as the legal French state. From 11 December 1941, the United States was at war with Germany, but not with France. In a strictly legal sense, the Anglo-American invasion of North Africa was therefore a war of aggression. This made "managing the French account" one of the most confounding headaches of American commanders, particularly since they considered the African adventure unnecessary to begin with. The British, as exemplified by their raw treatment of French colonies, seemed to have no such qualms.

The Protectorate of Morocco, Algeria, and Tunisia stuck with Vichy France because that seemed the least bad course of action. By allowing Vichy to continue to exercise French sovereignty in the unoccupied southern half of France, Hitler essentially gave the colonies a fig leaf of legitimacy that dissuaded them from joining de Gaulle's Free French forces. But the consequences for the French residents in North Africa were eventually dire.

To begin with, shortly after the French surrender, the new Prime Minister Winston Churchill ordered the sinking of the French fleet in Oran, Algeria, to prevent its theoretical later use in support of Germany. It was a Pearl Harbor in reverse; 1,300 sailors died – or were murdered, in the French estimation. The fury against the English burned brightly after this coldblooded assault.

Then Erwin Rommel won tremendous victories in Italian Libya and seemed poised to take the Suez Canal. To the doubters it must have seemed like the fascist horse was the one to bet on.

The Spanish part of Morocco added to the confusion. The Allied planners had to assume that forces there might well intervene to assist the Axis. This never happened; General Franco was too cautious for that, and it didn't hurt that Hitler's expert for that region, Admiral Canaris, subtly urged Franco to stay out of the war.

As for the Italians, it was never quite easy to tell whose side they served except that of their own personal well-being. One of the more admirable activities of their air force was to stage elegant displays of aerobatics at a safe distance when meeting the Americans.[948] Still, other Italian troops did fight hard in Libya and Tunisia, and Italian units had the distinction of defeating Americans in the Battle of the Kasserine Pass (February 1943), which led to the British calling the Americans "our Italians."[949]

An extraordinary example of the interconnectedness of people, however distant, occurred right there at Djebel Lessouda on 14 February 1943. Strong German forces surrounded American positions and forced them to surrender. One of the captives was 2nd Lt. Amon G. Carter Jr., the son of Elliott's friend and backer Amon Carter of Fort Worth. Carter didn't know what had become of his son, but he corresponded with top Eisenhower aide, Navy Captain Harry Butcher at Ike's headquarters about the matter. This was a time when his "Elliott card" turned out to be very valuable.[950]

Carter sent Butcher a trove of cigars, the regular supply of which seems to have been Butcher's main preoccupation. Butcher occasionally saw both Elliott and John Boettiger, then on "secret operations" in North Africa, and he reported to the White House and others that they were both doing "a superb job."[951]

Stepson Curtis demolished Major Boettiger's "heroic" war record in his recent memoir. It turned out that John, a "mere" journalist, had been jealous to see Elliott and Franklin Jr. attending to FDR at Casablanca, and asked the president what he should do to get in on the action. John then enlisted and was dissatisfied to be appointed "a captain, too." He was sent to North Africa, where apparently he had nothing useful to do: 'His superiors concerned themselves more with making sure the president's son-in-law didn't create problems than with trying to make the best use of his talents.'

The highlight of his career was to go to the Teheran summit, and he did bequeath historians important notes therefrom. After that, the bitter and dejected journalist got a transfer stateside. John Boettiger was a talented reporter, but apparently he did not know how to play the game for glory.[i]

At Kasserine Pass, Eisenhower's aide Lt. Craig Campbell was also captured and sent to Germany. Amon Carter Jr. was later located in captivity in Germany. By 5 October 1943, Carter knew his son's fate when, having seen Elliott off from his "special mission" to Hollywood, he reported to Butcher:

> Dear Harry:
>
> Elliott is taking a little package along to General Eisenhower, General Spaatz and General Doolittle and I am enclosing a couple boxes of smokes for you as Elliott tells me that you are on the wagon. We are all tickled pink with the job the Boss is doing and envy you (as tough as it is) the privilege of taking a part in the show. So, hurry up, give 'em hell as we have a lot of American Prisoners of War in Germany, Poland and Italy that we are anxious to see back with their divisions – not overlooking one in particular, Amon Junior, who is a prisoner of war of Germany and interned at Oflag 64, in Poland about 100 miles south of Danzig, with about 152 American officers and 11 doctors, including Jesse Jones' nephew and Senator Herring's son and seven altogether from Texas.[952]

This letter illustrates just how personal the war was for Elliott's stateside friends and protectors. After his liberation from captivity, John T. Jones, the nephew, would later take Jesse's post as publisher and Houston city father. The Senator whose son was also captive was Clyde Herring of Iowa. Not to belabor the point, but even General Arnold noted with great personal relief that his son Hank had barely escaped Rommel's embrace at Kasserine; father and son soon met at the Casablanca summit.[ii]

To general relief, Amon Jr. wrote back from captivity that his team hadn't exactly been captured; they were robbed and knocked out by Arabs who then turned them over to the Germans, who fortunately treated them very well.[953]

Thus there were quite a few who got to see the war from both sides.

The inability to trust those caught "in between" persisted until the Allied victory was certain. In one much-lamented case, Free French pilots, having been given American P-40Fs, promptly defected to France with them.[954] Another memorable event occurred when one of the "free" but homesick Italian pilots assigned to Colonel Roosevelt took one of his F-4 Lightnings and flew home to Italy.[955] When the king

---

[i] Curtis Roosevelt: Too Close to the Sun, 217. Boettiger killed himself in 1950.

[ii] Arnold: Global, 393. It may be a mere memory slip that the Kasserine Pass battle occurred a month later.

dismissed Mussolini in September 1943, Italy henceforth fought on both sides simultaneously, although it often seemed that most Italians sensibly didn't want to fight at all.

In North Africa, it was hoped that the French administration would quickly rally to the Allied side. The military headaches of the invasion seemed to be nothing compared to the political snakepit the Americans had blundered into. To widespread dismay at home, General Eisenhower cut a deal with Admiral of the Fleet François Darlan, the *de facto* executive of Vichy France. He happened to be in Algeria at the time of the invasion. Ike thought this was better than more fighting, and Marshall backed him up in Washington.

It took a while for the French to switch sides, though, and during that interval of about four days, many Americans lost their lives to determined Vichyiste resistance. Some of the American reactions to "the Frogs" have to be considered on this bitter background.

There is no way around it: the regular American soldier often viewed his French counterparts as devious cowards. Veteran Bob Thompson spouted a particularly damning anti-Gallic rant in his war memoir.[956] But Elliott Roosevelt was not immune, nor were – privately – the high and mighty at the summit in Casablanca. Interestingly, Churchill seems to have been more understanding of the difficult French situation than the Roosevelts. Franklin was fluent in the French language (as he was in German), but he detested the French (and the Germans). Admittedly, crude ethnic stereotypes were far more commonly expressed in that age.

Much of the animus was directed against General Charles de Gaulle, and several pages of *As He Saw It* are devoted to sneering at the pomposity and defiance of this seemingly ridiculous pocket-Napoleon. Nor, for that matter, were the Allies the least bit impressed by his rival General Henri Giraud. "We're leaning on a very slender reed," said FDR after his first meeting with him.[957] Giraud had been picked up in France by submarine in order to lend legitimacy to the Anglo-American invasion. He refused to do so unless he was given overall command, and he made himself a pest overall.

But the biggest problem was Admiral Darlan, who commanded the allegiance of overseas France in the name of Marshal Philippe Pètain. In Algiers, Darlan was overthrown by insurgents, and then reluctantly ordered the French surrender. He was also willing to join the Allies if he was made commander in chief, or at least High Commissioner. Eisenhower's brief agreement to this made General de Gaulle's head explode, or so it seemed to the Anglos. Darlan soon outlived his usefulness. He was assassinated on 24 December 1942; it is widely believed Britain's MI-6 was responsible.[i]

Eisenhower's temporary accommodation with Vichy's Darlan, however tactical in nature, is one of the furious but largely forgotten rows of the war. President Roosevelt came under withering criticism for it, but he rode it out. It is interesting that the short

---

[i] Waller: The Unseen War in Europe, 267. Incidentally, Rabbi Isserman provided an extraordinary twist to the coup story: State Department's Robert Murphy had enlisted 400 Jewish leaders in Algeria to overthrow the government on the eve of the invasion. Because of Darlan and a timing problem, they were overcome and the U.S. had to work with the fascist French for a while. Jews from the then substantial local community were the only ones reliably in the Allied camp, said the rabbi. The local French were mostly Vichyiste, and the Arabs rooted for the Axis but could be bought. (Isserman, 72-73) There were 300,000 Jews in North Africa, most anxious to serve in the war, but due to the explosive Jewish-Arab question, the Allies made little use of them. See Memo, Gen. Handy to Undersec of War, 13 DEC 42, in PSF, Arnold/82, FDR Lib.

use of an ambiguous leader like Darlan should cause such accusations of dealing with the Devil; the pact with Stalin seemed above criticism.

In all this drama Elliott was more than a lackey, less than a participant. Ironically his most important role came when he wrote his tell-all book shortly after the war. It contained a suspiciously detailed, day-for-day description of "SYMBOL" – the Casablanca summit. Since Elliott was more interested in telling a good story than in diplomatic propriety, his testimony evoked considerable hostility. One cannot read his breezy gossip without wondering what de Gaulle, Churchill, or other top leaders thought of it. Unlike FDR – and Harry Hopkins, who died in 1946 – they could defend themselves. They would be back in power, and they had been known to bear grudges.

An unfortunate consequence of TORCH was that in response, Germany and Italy occupied all of France including Corsica. The French were left stumbling around like a rooster without its head. The upshot was that not only could the French not be relied on, they couldn't rely on each other. Which faction was legitimate? More to the point, which would prevail? Some French joined the Germans, some the Americans, some did not choose; and many, like Admiral Darlan, chose several times.

The invasion of North Africa was an Allied compromise. After a year of doing nothing offensively, it gave the Americans a certain alibi in Europe. The operation was undertaken because going up against the Germans was premature; but it also weakened that very capability from the British Isles it was supposed to supplement. It should have been easy, but wasn't. Originally intended for May, it was delayed to November. Then it took six months instead of the expected six weeks. Whether these Allied choices were justified remains a matter of great controversy. But the endeavor did allow Roosevelt's reconnaissance pilots to get their act together in time for the big test. Had they gone into France the way they went into Algeria, they would have been slaughtered.

Operation TORCH: Down to our Last Plane

There is good reason American generals are so fond of attributing their victories to divine intervention; there is simply no other plausible explanation. This phenomenon seemed to be demonstrated with startling clarity during the American invasion of North Africa, which began on 7 November 1942.

The godless chaos that ensued proved to all, but especially the British and the Germans, that the United States Army wasn't ready for combat. It is on this sorry background that Colonel Elliott Roosevelt's contribution has to be assessed. As a commander of reconnaissance units, it was easy for him to explain why his results were so meager. When you have a fine mess on your hands, you can loudly proclaim how valiantly you are striving to fix it, or you can assume the responsibility which others are only too happy to surrender. Roosevelt was definitely in the first category; but he also did a lot to fix the trouble.

French North Africa was roughly the size of Western Europe. The small Anglo-American forces had no chance of actually occupying it; the whole strategy was to invade at key points and then leapfrog to hold the positions necessary to prepare further action to the north. But this required a French surrender. In the end, all the Allies got was a sullen, reluctant cessation of fire. Managing the factionalized French would become a painful sideline for Allied commanders throughout 1942 and 1943. Elliott was in the thick of it; he got to fight the French, command French air units, and observe French rivalries at the Casablanca summit.

As a result of the feeble Allied compromises, the initial landings on 7-8 November were concentrated in Casablanca, Port Lyautey (Kenitra), Oran, and Algiers. Colonel Lauris Norstad was the first Air Force officer ashore in Africa, in Algiers.[958] Colonel Roosevelt's units would first operate out of La Sénia (es-Senia) at Oran, then Maison Blanche (now Houari Boumedienne Airport) outside Algiers. With the defeat of the Germans in May they moved to La Marsa near Carthage in Tunisia.

It is an amusing coincidence that this child of the White House would, in this theater, be associated mostly with Maison Blanche and with Casablanca, where the Allied summit was held in January 1943.

All in all, North Africa was a vast, rugged, poorly mapped, little known region inhabited by unpredictable tribes. Even the weather was scant improvement from the Arctic; the sand ruined engines and cameras faster than anything the enemy could do. From Elliott Roosevelt's viewpoint, the theater was a reconnaissance hell. In his view, the failures of his command occurred because he did not have sufficient resources. But that's generally the case; you go to war with the army you've got.

Elliott's squadrons entered Algeria days after the invasion on 8 November. The ground and air echelons of the 5th Photographic Reconnaissance Squadron arrived in Oran on the 12th and 18th of November, respectively, just after French resistance ceased. The actual combat reconnaissance supporting the invasion was flown by RAF 682 Squadron at Gibraltar; this unit moved to Algiers when that city was cleared, and it eventually joined Elliott's North African Photographic Reconnaissance Wing (NAPRW) in February 1943.[959]

The group's deployment was a component of Operation BOLERO, the build-up in Britain for which purpose Elliott's North Atlantic bases had been built during the preceding year. But the objective had now changed; as the 12th Air Force in North Africa was stood up, the 8th Air Force in England was depleted. Although TORCH was widely viewed as a distracting sideshow, after completing RUSTY, Elliott must have been one of the few commanders already familiar with this new theater of operations. Somehow, he'd wound up at the sharp end again.

The 5th PRS flew the early, ill-tempered F-4s (modified P-38Es), and the 15th Photographic Mapping Squadron (only "A" flight went across) flew B-17Fs. They were augmented by a single Mosquito Mark IV that Elliott Roosevelt and Harry Eidson (serving as pilot) borrowed from the RAF in Gibraltar on the way.[960] There were three on the peninsula, and it seems remarkable that Elliott was able to finagle one without worrying excessively about transition training or other fine points.

Elliott and Eidson used that Mosquito to fly the first three operational missions over hostile territory – the Lightnings were having trouble getting established. Roosevelt said later that Eidson was the first pilot to survive five missions, and the sortie list suggests most of those were flown with Roosevelt in the borrowed Mosquito during November and December.[i] The Mosquito "proved itself wonderful for the work it was to do," and so began Roosevelt's long quest for more.

The 12th PRS lagged and flew into Algier's Maison Blanche field on 8 December with 11 F-4As, via Oran. After an engine failure enroute, one Lightning smashed into the water, somehow got back out, and returned to England as a flying wreck.[961] The

[i] NAPRWHIST, AFHRA. Others say Eidson and ER together flew the first five sorties.

others made it, and at the destination Elliott welcomed the badly needed replacement aircraft.

The 3rd PRG's equipment was "eclectic." A July 1943 roster listed four B-17s operational, four B-25s, 23 F-5As, two F-4s and one F-4A. Most of the aircraft lost in action were F-4s and F-4As. One trainer, a humble BT-14, was on hand.[962]

The first headquarters of Elliott's 3rd Group in the hectic, confused days of November and December was at Oran's La Sénia airfield. Between Thanksgiving and Christmas, the group moved to Maison Blanche, where it would settle down for several months as the Allied advance into Tunisia stalled. Here it was joined by the 12th PRS.[963]

It was General Chaos who had the overall command in those days. Although the 3rd Group had been set up with three photo squadrons and one mapping squadron (the 15th), the normal squadron structure broke down completely in Algeria, and in a frenzied case of "ad-hocism" all elements were consolidated. Up to four "units" were detached to operating locations as the need arose. Not until summer did the group restore the squadron structure.[964]

Two reconnaissance B-17Fs (F-9s) had been flown across the Atlantic to England in 1942, since it was thought this would become the primary long-range reconnaissance aircraft. Reality soon vetoed this plan.

On the morning of 19 November 1942, Lt. Col. James W. Anderson piloted the first B-17 operational sortie. Elliott had met Anderson at Muroc, and Elliott twice took him home to the White House as a houseguest in September, just before leaving for England. That first epic flight, all over Algeria and Tunisia, took 7½ hours and strangely encountered no opposition. The problem then was what to do with the exposed plates in the unfolding chaos on the ground, but in time a photo-shop was found, and General Doolittle got to look over the first photographs with Anderson offering a running commentary in lieu of formal interpretation and reports.[965]

That was a deceptively easy beginning. Soon after, another B-17 made "a miraculous escape" into the clouds after being methodically perforated by a squadron of Bf-109s. The plane made it home with four wounded crewmembers. That story matches several accounts that place an unscathed Elliott Roosevelt aboard the bomber.[966]

One of the group's B-17s (41-24440) was named *I Got Spurs* after a popular song and Roosevelt's Texas background. That may have been the aircraft his crew got shot up in. In March, three of Elliott's B-17Fs were tail numbers 41-24433, -34, and -40. After the first shock, it is not likely that any of them tried out the German air defenses again.

In Algeria, two B-17s of the 15th were now relegated to flying freight to and from England, and Anderson returned there in December. The remainder was used for courier duties, while a segment of the crews was reassigned to the single-engine operations.[967] Three B-17Fs were detached to Flight A, 1st Mapping Squadron, which used them in Accra, Kano, and other distant locations. In April, Elliott ordered them back to Algiers.[968]

In addition, the American airfields were subjected to relentless nightly air attacks:

> Heavy enemy bombing raids were carried out against Algiers and the aerodrome, Maison Blanche, with the loss of several more B-17 aircraft (of the 15th PS) and damage to some of the F-4s of the 5th PS. These episodes dispelled any ideas of the use of four-motored planes for reconnaissance mapping, and necessitated the use of F-4s for all reconnaissance work.

> Operations during the winter months were hampered by the extremely muddy fields and the very difficult flying weather, and many aircraft were lost to these factors. ... It was soon discovered that the older F-4s were not suitable for operations, and only the new F-4s [A models based on P-38F] were used from the 1st of January, 1943.[969]

Even the F-4 Lightnings were now reduced to flying courier; only the newest F-4As were allowed into combat. At some point in early February, the group reportedly ceased operating with F-4s and awaited delivery of newer F-5s (based on the P-38G), which arrived about 10 March. Still, the new planes had to have carburetor settings adjusted to operate at high altitudes, but they were much better than the F-4s.[970]

This troubled beginning was reflected in a statistic noting that during the first three months, the group's 36 pilots flew 120 missions, of which 75 combat, for a total of only 435 hours. This supports a complaint that Elliott gave a few favored pilots the few missions available, while most were left to sit around. But that might have been inevitable if the unit couldn't generate more sorties because of a lack of resources.[i]

On paper, the 3rd PG looked fearsome. In the air and on the ground, it soon looked wretched. Operations depleted the group almost immediately.

> Mr. ROOSEVELT. ...We utilized these aircraft in combat, and we lost over 90% of them, and as a matter of fact, I think we were reduced to one aircraft at the end of 2½ months. We started with, if I remember correctly, about 92. We were faced with a very serious situation. We were called upon to provide the ground forces with intelligence information of the terrain over which they were passing, both of a geographical nature, and of the position of the enemy units...
>
> The experience that we had with the P-38's, which were known as F-4's at that time – later models became F-5's, A, B, C, and D, and so forth – was that we were able to operate only to a ceiling of 17,000 feet with these airplanes. Above that they started having engine trouble, and the major trouble was in throwing rods. This rendered the airplane completely uncontrollable, and we lost many pilots from mechanical failure alone.[971]

Elliott really had it in for Lockheed's Lightning. Many years later he complained that "...P-38s airplanes (a type of aircraft in which I flew many hundreds of hours) were coming off the assembly lines with defective Allison engines. After only a few hours of flight, these engines threw connecting rods with distressing regularity." Appalling waste! And in one of his murder mysteries, he even has himself explaining to a visiting Eleanor that no, the invasion won't be in Norway, for his P-38 superchargers would blow up "in the Arctic climate." All agreed that the Allison superchargers were the plane's Achilles heel.[972]

Colonel George C. McDonald, destined to become an intelligence luminary, had operational control of the intelligence tasking in North Africa. He later stated just how bad things looked for Roosevelt's unit:

> In the early part of 1943 the limited facilities of the RAF PRU in North Africa had been almost obliterated by bombing. The USAF photo reconnaissance business, under command of Elliott Roosevelt, was exceptionally hard put due to a series of combat losses of PR planes and other aircraft grounded for lack of essential spare parts and insufficient numbers of special PRU aircraft...

---

[i] One of Westbrook Pegler's correspondents made this accusation after the war. Pegler/HH

> We were so hard put that at one time we were down to our last plane and rather than jeopardize it on other than a vital mission that airplane was grounded. Reconnaissance of the first Ploesti bombing was made possible only through the use of a British Mosquito (South African crew) because no U.S. aircraft had the necessary range. This Mosquito ran out of gas on the return from Ploesti and made a deadstick landing at its African base.[973]

One scholar, USAF Major David Dengler, has investigated the rude awakening of Elliott Roosevelt's reconnaissance group:

> Aircraft difficulties immediately came to the forefront as units quickly found themselves outmatched. The 15th Photo Mapping Squadron employed B-17s for mapping, or at least attempted to do so. Flying as single aircraft, B-17s met near disaster. One crew faced seven Me-109 fighters and suffered four wounded crewmembers before escaping into the clouds. Combined with German raids on the 15th's airfield that damaged other B-17s, the unit quickly discarded them in favor of F-4s. German fighters also outclassed the 154th's P-39s and P-40s performing visual reconnaissance. In fact, they frequently required escort packages as large as twelve fighters.
>
> Squadrons flying F-4s had their own obstacles. After a short time in operation, they sidelined older F-4s due to problems at higher altitudes and resorted to using only newer versions; yet even these variants had issues that required troubleshooting. This further delayed support to theater units until January 1943. With the collective loss of older F-4s and the B-17s, the group had only ten newer F-4As, of which 50% were non-operational. The situation worsened in February with only two operational aircrafts when the group should have had 39 F-4 variants between its three squadrons. With pilot losses of 25% during the same period, the 3rd PG's operations ground to a virtual halt until F-5As began arriving in mid-March…The F-5A provided the solution, but only after units solved its engine problems to permit operation at high altitudes.
>
> A great deal of operational experimentation occurred in the field to improve the capabilities of the F-4 and F-5 variants. Foremost was a significant increase in range. At the campaign's start, they had a 150-mile range, but then increased to 400 miles in May 1943 and to 750 miles by September.[974]

The range problem illustrated the shock the Army received upon confronting reality in the form of the Wehrmacht and the Luftwaffe. American observation doctrine focused on the space fifty miles beyond the front; in fact, the first ten miles were considered crucial. But in North Africa, with its long distances and mechanized movements, hundreds of miles were a minimal range requirement. The issue became even more critical when Elliott's 3rd PG had to map and reconnoiter the Italian peninsula from its main base in Tunis (La Marsa).

A study of reconnaissance during the North African invasion prepared by the Air Force after the war paints an unhappy picture of unworkable command structures, failed logistics, inadequate equipment, and inability to meet warfighter needs. In this view it was a very good thing that there was no serious enemy on the ground (after the first few days of Vichy's halfhearted opposition) until February of 1943, when Rommel finally met the Americans and chased them temporarily out of Tunisia.

The interlude allowed Elliott time to completely reconstitute his command, unify the previously scattered operations, introduce new procedures, and accept better aircraft. The very high level decisions unifying Allied air reconnaissance under Elliott's command were taken at the Casablanca conference, at which the Combined Chiefs were available. From then on things rapidly became much better. Nonetheless, 1943 became the year of the Air Force's "reconnaissance crisis," and Elliott was at its epicenter.[975]

Reclaiming the Sky

After Casablanca, Lt. Col. Roosevelt began improvising in order to meet the increasing demands of his customers, these being primarily Eisenhower's army and Doolittle's strategic bombers.

The squadron structure having broken down, Roosevelt deployed "units" to forward operating locations. On 22 January, Unit 1 went to Telergma/Constantine, where it provided support for the strategic bombers; its 11 officers and 17 enlisted men were moved in two C-47s and a rumbling old Potez 540, of which more later. After a respite at Algiers, the unit was reorganized and reestablished at Telergma on 5 March; then it moved to Le Khroub/Constantine on 15 April. This outfit had 6 F-5As and was reported to have flown 138 missions in support of the strategic air forces.[976]

For cooperation with the 1st Army, on 5 March Unit 2 went all the way forward to Souk el-Khemis in Tunisia, 25 miles behind the front. Here it was strafed like clockwork every day, reflecting the road's nickname, Messerschmitt Alley. Yet Unit 2 played an important role in the next two months as the Germans were driven out of Tunisia. In that period, it flew 103 missions and produced 18,000 negatives and 85,000 prints. The unit was the same size as Unit 1, but it joined with RAF photo technicians and interpreters at the field.

Unit 3 was a detachment on the besieged island of Malta. On 20 March, 6 officers and 28 enlistees arrived in four C-47s. Malta is far from Algiers, and the flight stopped overnight in Tripoli. On the island, the unit mixed with RAF 683 Squadron, and its history noted that Wing Commander Adrian Warburton, one of the most famous reconnaissance pilots of the war, was of inestimable help in carrying out the flights over Italy. One local Warburton story (which was true) told of how he crashed and burned an F-5 during take-off, but before anyone could find him, he got out, snatched another Lightning, and completed his mission.

For a short while, the 3rd PRG had a Unit 4, but it was an unusual Franco-American arrangement based at Oujda, just across the border with Morocco. Apart from training the new Free French pilots of II/33 group, its purpose was to work with Army parachutists in providing imagery of training areas. Unit 4 was active there in May, and reportedly flew only 18 missions. A veteran French reconnaissance pilot just returned to North Africa, Captain Antoine de Saint-Exupéry, trained on F-5s at Oujda.

Centralization of command and control was always an imperative for the air forces. If the Army had its way, each division would have fiercely hung on to its own aircraft, ensuring their availability at any time. This wasteful allocation had to be overridden, but that would only be allowed if the group or wing was immediately responsive to field requests as they came in.

Because of the outdated, trench-warfare-centric concept of operations, there was little notion of strategic reconnaissance; instead light observation aircraft operating closely with ground forces were thought to be sufficient help. That is why so many second-rate aircraft were loaded up with cameras and pressed into service in that role.

Elliott Roosevelt's units began with a mixture of aircraft that were no match for the Messerschmitts and Focke-Wulfs they soon encountered. But higher blame for the early losses must be assigned to poor tactics, maintenance, logistics, weather, and even navigation. For example, during the move to North Africa quite a few aircraft landed in Spain and Portugal, and were duly interned.

The considerable professional interest these reconnaissance woes have attracted among American specialists is curious in one respect: it does not consider the equal and greater trouble the Germans were having. Colonel Roosevelt, if anything, overstated Luftwaffe capabilities:

> The enemy were operating with 109 aircraft, and one or two other types of aircraft, and they laid great stress on their photographic reconnaissance work. We found in North Africa that they were way, a great deal more advanced than we were, in many phases of reconnaissance aviation. They used water injection, for instance, first on their engines to give them short bursts of speed, way ahead of the time that we developed it, and they used it first on reconnaissance planes before even the fighters had it.[977]

Elliott also consistently maintained that the Luftwaffe pilots were credited with two kills for each Allied reconnaissance aircraft destroyed. This evidently was a common rumor, but German kill criteria were actually quite stringent. Whether the story helped or hurt morale is not clear.[978]

In truth, the Germans had much the same difficulty with reconnaissance as did the Allies. Modified fighters didn't cut it, and the Ju-88s and similar types were too slow. The Luftwaffe did use a special extreme-altitude reconnaissance aircraft, the pressurized Ju-86P. But by summer of 1942 certain modified Spitfires were able to reach these aircraft over Egypt, so they had to be withdrawn. By 1943, the Germans were losing air superiority in the West. They retained it in the East, but there the battle was nonetheless like trying to hold back the tide.

Ironically, by the end of the war, Germany fielded by far the best reconnaissance aircraft of all: the twin-jet Arado Ar-234. No one could catch it. For all Elliott Roosevelt's shrill clamoring for the ideal reconnaissance platform, by late 1944 he could see them overhead in England; but they were German.

The maligned F-9 (recon B-17), interestingly proved itself an excellent cartographic aircraft after the war. The RAF cashiered the Fortress after trying to use it as a bomber. General Arnold, who staked his entire doctrine on the B-17, said that the British never gave it a chance; but he was happy, because the RAF was eager to take B-24s instead, and he thought them inferior.[979]

Doctrinally orthodox and unwilling to admit error, the Americans insisted on sending ever larger fleets of B-17s (and B-24s) against the Luftwaffe, with tragic results. Unlike the RAF, they could do so because their factories and training facilities could replenish the line faster than the enemy could attrit it. The outcome was a sort of Somme-in-the-air, reflected in horrific losses for little advantage.

The intelligence director, Colonel McDonald, reflected on the prohibitive losses that led to the withdrawal of the F-9s: "As a make-shift, a limited number of P-38s were modified at our Casablanca depot… The British planes had slightly better performance than ours, but the Mosquito, being largely of veneer construction and wing cover, warped rather quickly in that climate, which naturally reduced its overall speed."[980]

Later, McDonald's little aside about the Mosquito's environmental sensitivity would become evidence against Elliott Roosevelt's judgment.

Losses, real and imagined

In war, everyone apparently wants the honor of having had it worst. The reconnaissance squadrons, Elliott always maintained, suffered the highest casualties of all. But that was true only at very specific times. Later, losses became remarkably low.[981]

For example, during the first three months in North Africa, the 3rd PRG lost 14 out of 51 officers originally assigned to the unit as KIA or MIA. Losses then dropped dramatically, but returned when Elliott's better prepared 325th P.R. Wing operated out of England, because the opposition was stronger there as well. Elliott claimed it was the highest loss rate of any AAF unit, but this is an exaggeration.

It is worth analyzing the exact numbers. Captain George Humbrecht provided a detailed summary of losses to his boss, Colonel Roosevelt, on 12 July 1943, just before Elliott's return to Washington.

Humbrecht stated that nine pilots had been lost as MIA/KIA. Also, three died on courier missions, and one was accidentally killed. Of aircraft, thirteen were lost to enemy action, and seven crashed or were wrecked during the period from the invasion to the 10 July reporting date.[982]

Compared to the small number of original officers, this is a high fraction, but compared to the missions flown it was not. The 3rd PRG flew 796 missions in that period and lost 0.012 pilot per mission, about one percent. Humbrecht listed eight of nine lost pilots as MIA. Since the reconnaissance pilots flew alone, it was usually not possible to verify their fates.

One of the pilots shot down was Humbrecht himself; on 18 April 1943 he was jumped by eight FW-190s. He crash-landed on a forward airstrip, crawled out and returned to duty. And Colonel Roosevelt himself smashed up one Mosquito along with several parked aircraft during that same period.[983]

The group's operational results are what really mattered. In a summary to Elliott, dated 12 July 1943, the operations officer, Captain Henry Bodendieck, noted that of 796 missions flown, 75% were at least partially successful. Of those that weren't, over half failed due to weather, 29% due to engine trouble, and only 9% due to camera failure. In Washington later that month, Roosevelt would complain that 9% of missions were aborted due to camera trouble; that was actually 9% of the 25% failed missions.[984]

Finally, a dramatic pattern revealed itself in the month-to-month summary of operations. Through weather and attrition, the group degraded so far as to fly only 32 missions in March. But next month that jumped to 201. Reinforcements had arrived, the weather cleared, the mud dried up, and heavy demand arose from the renewed American offensive against Tunis. From that time, the 3rd PRG as the main component of the NAPRW sustained a very high tempo of operations, and its losses paradoxically declined dramatically. The balance had shifted fundamentally.[985]

The operational summaries prepared daily by General Norstad's staff also point to a more comfortable situation than Roosevelt let on. During the crucial month of May, when the Germans were cleared out of Africa, the NAPRW fairly consistently had only about 40 aircraft. They were usually 6 F-4s and 15 F-5As, about 8 Spitfires, 1 to 3 Mosquitoes, 3 or 4 B-17s, the BT-14 "hack" and a lumbering war prize, a Potez 540. Of these, about 25 were in condition to fly combat sorties.[986]

With these aircraft the entire wing generated about 5 to 10 sorties per day, most of them by 682 Squadron's Spitfires. That was only about 2-4% of the total Allied air effort in Northwest Africa. Obviously, there was a lot of sitting around, especially on the American side; there were usually six times as many American flight crews as British on the tote boards. Things got much more hectic during Operation HUSKY in late summer, but by then the wing was getting its act together.

An immediate result of the poor start was that the RAF had to do the rough work in North African skies. The British also had to teach U.S. personnel how to effectively operate reconnaissance aircraft, for after three years of war they had become good at it. They were also now using better equipment, late model Spitfires and the new Mosquitoes. An RAF Spitfire photo squadron (Nr. 682) was placed in Algiers at Maison Blanche field on 1 February 1943 and was put under Elliott Roosevelt's NAPRW; a sister squadron (Nr. 683) operated from Malta under British command.

In one example of the British tutelage, the USAAF had brought no trained photo interpreters and thus had to learn from their ally. It is striking that General Doolittle had to spend hours going over images carried to him directly by reconnaissance pilots. Of course, this deficiency too was gradually rectified.

In effect, the poor American results in North Africa were mitigated by the fact that at this time the British were still senior partners in the war. The American reconnaissance crisis was no secret, except perhaps to the home front. But reconnaissance was not unique in failing its first test.

The TORCH plan had been to jump all the way to Tunis within the month. With distance, the American forces simply ran out of steam, whereas the countervailing German invasion of Tunisia took hold. After one month, checked outside of Tunis, Eisenhower had to call retreat. The American army mired down in the winter weather, and was unable to resume the offensive until April 1943. The winter weather and harassment by the Luftwaffe took a similar toll on the air forces. By jumping in immediately, Hitler had effectively gained six months. Whether that was worth the depletion and ultimate loss of his African forces is another question.[987]

Elliott Roosevelt was not relieved of duty, as was for example the American ground commander General Lloyd Fredendall, defeated at Kasserine. Instead he gained an appreciative audience for his demand that he should have better aircraft and more resources. It was not mere carping, for he made sure to go on dangerous missions himself, and his able reorganization of his command countered much criticism. He also became known for creative ways of overcoming the shortage of useful air intelligence.

Since he was not himself a rated pilot, Elliott flew aboard the medium bombers when going on missions ranging over Sardinia, Sicilia, southern Italy, as well as Tunisia. His B-25 obviously was easy pickings for the Luftwaffe in daylight. In time, it earned its keep in night missions. The two initial Mosquitoes loaned to his unit by the RAF also gave Elliott the chance to engage in combat. One factor in his strong advocacy of the Mosquito was simply that he was personally familiar with it, whereas he did not fly the single-seaters that were the mainstay of his group.

The brass knew intellectually that reconnaissance was as important, if not more so, than bombing, but it took a while for this fact to be reflected in the apportionment and allocation of resources. Elliott argued for performance: the reconnaissance aircraft needed speed, range, and payload. He needed to send these aircraft, one at a time, on pre-strike target identification and post-strike damage assessment runs. Why couldn't America build a dedicated reconnaissance aircraft that could survive?

The Lightning: Eagle or Dodo?

Elliott thought that the Lockheed P-38 was inadequate, almost useless. That was the origin of his ill-fated two-year campaign for a dedicated reconnaissance aircraft.

At first glance, the argument was reasonable enough. When you pick at the details, questions emerge. *Everyone* desperately wanted speed, range, and payload. In that respect there was no need for specialized aircraft. Minton Kaye's idea of replacing the P-38E's guns with cameras was therefore perfectly reasonable – especially since the lighter weight made the plane fly faster and higher. With some specialized exceptions, fighter conversion has always been the standard method for producing reconnaissance aircraft – until today, when unmanned aircraft have mostly taken over this role.

But whereas the early P-38s had their flaws, they were not poor performers. They had, in fact, better speed, range, and payload than other American reconnaissance aircraft of the period, such as the P-39s used in the tactical role. They lacked maneuverability, but recon pilots were supposed to flee combat. With time, the Lightnings only got better, while many other fighters were stuck at their maximal potential.

Other advantages held by the P-38 were a tricycle undercarriage, greatly facilitating ground handling, and counterrotating propellers (i.e. "handed" engines). This was highly unusual. Allison built left and right handed engines for the P-38. The result was a much safer twin-engined aircraft in low-speed handling. If both engines turn the same way, flight characteristics are "lop-sided" and fatal loss of control can easily result below a certain critical airspeed.[i]

Lt. Col. Roosevelt was aware of the version differences even before going to Africa. In conference with General Spaatz on 5 October 1942, he pointed out that the F-4s were underpowered and should be relegated to operational training. Even before going to Africa, he wanted them replaced with F-5As (P-38Gs).[988]

That pilots did not sneer at the later model Lightnings is shown by a memorandum from the 3rd PRG, dated 8 September 1943, ironically when its chief Elliott Roosevelt was home hectoring the Air Corps for a replacement:

> Colonel Dunn and I [Lt. Col. Alan Eldridge] are in accord on the following:
>
> 1. The F-5A has proven itself in this theatre in mapping as well as in reconnaissance. Its range approaches that of the Mosquito, and its chances of surviving interception are superior to the Mosquito.
> 2. The Mosquito with low or medium-altitude engines is useless for our purposes. With the Merlin 6100 engine its usability has yet to be proven.
> 3. It seems waste of manpower and machines to order in two complete squadrons of Mosquitos before their performance is proven.... [989]

It was an interesting letter not only because it contradicted Elliott's arguments, but because Colonel Eldridge was court-martialed by Elliott when he returned. The point about the Lightning, though, was hotly disputed, especially by foreign pilots. Roosevelt's South African pilots had quite a different opinion:

---

[i] Vmc, the speed below which the aircraft becomes uncontrollable if the most critical engine fails. Even more unusually, the Lightning's engines turned *outwards*, which unfortunately did not help on Vmc.

> When it was based at San Severo in August [43], No 60 Sq (SAAF) was placed in the awkward position of having more than enough pilots but few aircraft. More Mosquito Mk IXs were then anxiously awaited to bring the unit's complement to seven aircraft by September. On the other hand, Lt. Col. James Setchell's 3rd PRG [immediately under Elliott Roosevelt] had a surplus of aircraft and the South Africans were offered three F-5s. While they appreciated the gesture, by all accounts the pilots were not exactly impressed by the PR Lightning. Apart from missing the services of a navigator, which made life a great deal easier when flying the Mosquito, the F-5 compared unfavorably on a number of other counts. Pilots felt that it was a heavier aircraft to maneuver, particularly at the kind of altitudes – around 32-35 thousand feet – they adopted for the best PR results. Adverse comments were made about some of the "quaint" controls including the roll-down car-door-type- cockpit panels. The Lightnings were handed back as soon as possible.[990]

Usually it was the Americans who complained about "quaint" foreign aircraft. But the P-38 had oddities, like a steering wheel instead of a stick. That wheel was actually a center extension on a side-mounted control column, making the control-feel rather strange compared to most fighters.

The P-38 was also famous for becoming uncontrollable in steep dives due to compressibility (high Mach) effects on the wings and tail. Lockheed did not fix this deadly problem until late in the war. The sharper pilots found out that they could escape death-dives by using the elevator trim.

A big issue was visibility. A P-38 pilot cannot see what he is flying over, which makes photographic runs tricky. In contrast, the Mosquito had a glass nose for observation, as well as a second crewmember to keep track. The Americans had to be extremely meticulous, exacting pilots to produce usable imagery.

Colonel Minton Kaye, Air Corps director of photography, took credit for adapting the Lightning for reconnaissance. He said Arnold gave him 100 for that purpose after Pearl Harbor, and he maintained that the lighter F-5A was the fastest airplane in the world – 40-60 mph faster than the P-38:

> The F-5 is superior to the Mosquito with the 6100 engine. It is faster, will climb faster, and is more maneuverable than the Mosquito. The latter, however, has greater range and carries a navigator; it can penetrate up to 1,000 miles, whereas the F-5 will go only 500 to 600.[991]

Colonel Kaye visited Elliott's African headquarters in 1943. At that time they were "on very poor terms." Elliott alluded partly to Kaye when he wrote his mother that the staff at home was incompetent and unable to get the planes he wanted: "The aircraft is 80 mph too slow, has difficulty getting to the necessary altitude, and all because of incompetent people in charge of Photo-Reconnaissance in the United States dealing with the Air Ministry in London."[992]

In his August report to General Arnold on reconnaissance aircraft, Elliott bluntly said, "All of these problems can be traced directly to the lack of organizational responsibility centered in one man in HQ AAF, Washington." He basically meant, "Minton Kaye is an idiot." We shall hear more about that.[993]

In July, one of Elliott's squadron leaders, Colonel Frank Dunn, wrote an assessment for him to take to Washington:

> During the first two months of operations, the pilots of this Group demonstrated a lack of confidence in the F-4 and the F4A airplanes…due to…mechanical failures, camera failures, poor performance above 20,000 feet due to electrical trouble, pilot inexperience, and pilot losses. However, as the pilots gained experience, they gained confidence in the airplane until at the present time each pilot is accomplishing 15-25 pinpoints per mission over the most highly defended areas.[994]

Dunn went on to say that the F-5A had comparable if not superior performance to the Spitfire XI. Clearly, the American pilots had made their peace with the Lightning now. But Elliott, the non-pilot who flew the Mosquito but not the single-seat F-5, went back to Washington harping to everyone about getting more Mosquitoes.

Dunn knew how to man-handle a Mosquito. We know this from John Connally's memoirs: he hitched a ride to Tunis with Dunn and was treated to a wild ride including a dive *inside* a Roman theatre-ruin near Sousse. This stunt was not unique; the Wing's picture book (preserved in Elliott's file at the FDR Library) has an F-5 oblique photo of the el Djem amphitheater, looking *up* at the galleries. [995]

Since the Lightning has its proponents as well as detractors, it is worth listening to an expert *par excellence*, Captain Eric Brown, a Royal Navy test pilot known for having flown more types of aircraft than any other person (and somehow living to old age). Brown's evaluation came after General Doolittle went out to RAF Farnborough and requested an impartial opinion:

> We had found out that the BF 109 and the FW 190 could fight up to a Mach of 0.75…we checked the Lightning and it couldn't fly in combat faster than 0.68. So it was useless. We told Doolittle that all it was good for was photo-reconnaissance and had to be withdrawn from escort duties. And the funny thing is that the Americans had great difficulty understanding this because the Lightning had the two top aces in the Far East.[996]

Another concerned view was held by Col. Homer Saunders, who succeeded James Hall as 7th PRG commander. After nearly killing himself in a P-38, he told his pilots: "Boys, we're going to get ourselves some Spitfires!" He got one squadron thus equipped, but when Elliott Roosevelt came back to England from Washington, he said that American pilots were going to fly American planes, so they went back to the Lightnings. This quote is attributed to Major Robert R. Smith, 13th PRS commander.[997] Others corroborate it: by 1944, Roosevelt's unit was trying to extract itself from the kind embrace of the RAF, and he now insisted on American equipment.

And this is why the P-38, after a protracted and difficult pregnancy at Lockheed, was largely rejected by combat crews in Europe, and also why it lived on as a reasonably successful reconnaissance type. It explains why the RAF refused to take delivery of the Lightnings ordered from Lockheed. And finally it explains why the USAF scrapped its P-38s in 1945, while its tasks were taken over by the F-6 (recon P-51s), a small fighter that remained in American use until 1957.

Finally, while everyone always wants better equipment, the proof lay in comparison to the opposition. For reconnaissance, the Germans largely relied on the Ju-88, a sturdy and ubiquitous workhorse. But by the time Rommel fought his last stand in Carthage, the Luftwaffe had lost air superiority and the Ju-88s were mostly relegated to nocturnal missions. Despite their whining, the Americans were by then far ahead.

The air force's analysis points to the fact that the "reconnaissance crisis" was more one of command, control, and communications than of aircraft. Certainly there were horror stories to go around; thousands of photos rotting away for lack of equipment, or with no one to interpret them, or due to failure of initiative at some link in the chain.

One of Elliott's best reconnaissance pilots, George Humbrecht, remarked:

> I flew reconnaissance for the British First Army, and every day I photographed the front. I would take the pictures, land, drive the film to the processing lab and wait for it to be developed, and then take the photographs directly to the commanding officer in a big old touring car we had scrounged for that purpose. I even helped them interpret the photos. Yet, even with this service, not nearly all the pictures were used. Once, when I was requested to get some photos of an area which I knew had been covered many times I drove to the British First Army HQ and began looking around. I not only found those pictures but a barn filled nearly to the haymow with photos which had to be stored to await someone who could interpret them. It was a frustrating situation.[998]

At that time the Americans had no reconnaissance experts in the theater. When they finally trickled in, they were ill-trained and inexperienced, and the overworked RAF photo interpreters had to teach them the ropes. The interviews Elliott Roosevelt gave to Air Corps and Navy officers in Washington after his return from Europe in July 1943 clearly and succinctly describe the shortcomings – and achievements – of all elements of the growing American photo reconnaissance capability.

Family Summits

Unlike most American servicemen overseas, Elliott Roosevelt was rarely deprived of family contact for long periods of time. Not only did he come home frequently, his family came to him. When he was given his first command in England at Steeple Morden, Eleanor visited him. And not long after the problematic invasion of North Africa, Dad himself dropped by. Of course, in all cases the family reunions were parenthetical to the official purpose of the conferences.

It is understandable that the crippled president wanted the company of his husky sons. But it turns out that the children were also feverishly eager to partake of the glory and excitement of the summits. From 1941-43, the honor fell to Elliott and Franklin Jr., on account of proximity, but towards the end, strangely enough it was Anna, the eldest, who took charge. As her father declined precipitously in his last year, she increasingly held up the family end at the White House, having found this calling after her long exile in Seattle with John Boettiger.

The family seems to have thought of the epochal conferences as adventurous cruise-ship vacations. When Eleanor heard that Stalin had finally deigned to meet his Allies, she desperately wanted to join her husband. The president sensibly turned her down. "Eleanor was crushed, not simply by the decision itself but by the insensitivity of her husband's attitude," wrote one historian. But what help she expected to offer on Allied strategy was not obvious.[999] At least she gave up graciously.

Not Anna; she threw tantrums. Why did the sons have all the fun and glamor, but not her? Besides, she would then be able to see her husband John, who was suffering badly in his posting to North Africa. But again, FDR wanted no females on board. When Anna saw that Sarah Churchill went with her father – not to speak of Madame Chiang kai-Shek in Cairo – she flew into a kind of proto-feminist rage against her father.

> Pa seems to take for granted that all females should be quite content to keep the home fires burning, and that their efforts outside of this are merely rather amusing and to be added by a patronizing male world only as a last resort to keep some individually troublesome female momentarily appeased.[1000]

John Boettiger came along to Teheran in December 1943. It was the highlight of his brief military career; while he otherwise left little mark on history, he fortunately did leave his notes to historians. In January 1945, when the Yalta meeting was being planned, it was again Anna who insisted on coming along. Since Elliott was in the dog house at the time, she had her way. Again we see that sibling rivalry among the Roosevelts amounted almost to civil war.

Curtis Roosevelt, in his recent fetching but revealing memoir, shows us that his mother was hardly above these battles:

> Watching her father summon her brothers to join him as he traveled to meet Churchill, and later Stalin, roused in Mummy the sort of sibling rivalry I'd often seen my uncles exhibit but had thought her immune from. She was even keeping score – her letters to [John] make this clear – when it came to Churchill's own children, noting when and where his daughters Sara and Mary or son Randolph had accompanied him to high-level meetings. In one angry missive, my mother gave full vent to her sense of grievance: '*Why in hell should I be forced to miss all of the actual excitement and interest, and be forced to live the kind of life I now lead?*' In the end, we all suffered from our attraction to the president's world and our longing to be part of it.[1001]

Anna's triumphant relief from "the life she was now leading" was Elliott's bitter disappointment. He didn't get to Yalta, as he thought was his birthright.

Across the Atlantic, similar family scenes played out. The aristocratic Churchills were also a political family with long-standing notions of entitlement. The prime minister took the hint from FDR and invited his daughters and son along to the summits. In Captain Randolph Churchill, the voluble Elliott finally discovered a fellow who could completely silence him with his imperious soliloquys.[1002]

Though Elliott's acquaintance with the Churchills was brief, it is full of stunning parallels. Randolph was, like Elliott, a spoiled drunkard and wastrel, though more pompous. He was already a Member of Parliament and evidently a courageous asset to the Special Air Service. His wartime career intersected Elliott's numerous times: he was in Cairo when Elliott was there; in Northwest Africa for TORCH; and he attended the same summits. Both men capitalized on their names, and had memoirs of their fathers written for them. They could have had some epic parties, but clearly Elliott disliked Randolph.[i]

Even odder is the sexual component of the Anglo-American alliance. The newspapers tried to link Elliott with the Churchill daughters, Mary and Sarah, apparently in vain. But President Roosevelt also did so. Mary Churchill reminisced that FDR remarked that it would be "grand" if Sarah and Elliott got something going together, to which the shocked mother, Clementine, responded that both of them were already married "to other people."[1003] Perhaps it didn't help that FDR called her "Clemmie."

If previous arrangements seemed an obstacle to Clementine, her children didn't agree. Sarah, a professional actress married to another actor, went to bed with the

[i] For a similar startling comparison with General Vasilii Stalin, see the Teheran chapter.

American ambassador, John Winant, in an affair that ended badly after the war and may have resulted in Winant's suicide in 1947. Randolph Churchill's wife Pamela countered by bedding Ambassador Harriman, which enraged Randolph but not his father, the prime minister. For Pamela, Averell Harriman was merely another notch in a dizzyingly tall totem-pole of super-rich conquests; but, in 1971 when they were both old, the two actually married and Pamela, by virtue of money and contacts, became a highly esteemed Democratic Party powerbroker.

We are clearly not talking about ordinary folks here.

The coincidences don't end there. Like all the Roosevelt sons, the Churchill children served in the war. Sarah was in the WAAF – Women's Auxiliary Air Force – and she was assigned to the interpretation of reconnaissance photographs. She served with Flight Officer Constance Babington Smith, an early postwar chronicler of photo-interpretation, at the Central Interpretation Unit at RAF Medmenham, and she must have run into Elliott on occasion, not merely at the summits. Constance tells the story of how Sarah, off duty on the eve of the TORCH landings, went to spend the night at Chequers. Her father proudly told her of the ongoing operation. She responded, that yes, as a matter of fact she'd been working on that for months, but it was secret, so she couldn't tell him![1004]

Sarah was not at Casablanca, but at Teheran, Cairo, and Yalta. She danced with Elliott and with young Robert Hopkins, but that was probably as far as it went.

The president and the prime minister clearly shared a dynastic, monarchical worldview that was reflected in their treating their offspring as deputies. It is difficult to imagine others doing this – Reagan and Thatcher, for example. It's just not modern. FDR had the excuse of infirmity for this preference; but he also treated Anna, James, and Elliott as advisers, emissaries, and confidantes.

The friendship between the Churchills and the Roosevelts has been much feted, but the personalization of international relations is a treacherous and fundamentally unprofessional approach. General de Gaulle hit it on the nail when he said nations do not have friends; they have interests. During the last sixteen months of the Churchill-Roosevelt alliance, matters veered dangerously off course due to the personal peculiarities of both these titans. One can wonder if less colorful but more level-headed – dare one say normal – people might have managed better. As it was, Churchill bequeathed to all subsequent prime ministers a fundamental rule: Never lose the Americans.

Casablanca

Punsters can appreciate the fact that Franklin D. Roosevelt traveled from the White House to Casablanca, where he summoned his son Elliott from Maison Blanche. The latter was the airfield outside Algiers that served as a temporary headquarters for Elliott's 3rd Photographic Group. And when FDR went to Tunis later that year, he stayed at the Casa Blanca. The coincidences actually confused German intelligence.

On 11 January 1943, Elliott was ordered to fly to Casablanca, taking a passenger, Admiral Royal Ingersoll, who was then U.S. CINCLANT (Atlantic commander). He knew he would be playing approximately the same roles he had fulfilled so ably at Argentia: office boy, drink mixer, suave conversationalist, and upholder of the infirm.[1005] This time he would also be the designated purchaser of Moroccan souvenirs, fine woven carpets especially.

Casablanca was one of the three main landing areas that had been secured on 8 November 1942. The hulk of the battleship *Jean Bart* lay in the harbor – its pointless resistance, and that of its sisters, had cost a thousand French casualties.[i] The ship was a useful source of armor plate for an improvised bomb-shelter next to FDR's bedroom. The Germans had recently bombed Casablanca and might do so again.[ii]

But despite two days of fierce American-French fighting, the city remained charming and largely intact. In fact, Elliott said: "It was bright, it was warm, it was gay. It was the antithesis of Argentia."[1006] Winston Churchill and Franklin Roosevelt would be staying in requisitioned luxurious villas within a compound centered on the Anfa Hotel, along with their accompanying top brass.

For the president, it was a major expedition, via train, ship, Boeing Clipper, and finally the C-54 from Bathurst to Casablanca. Elliott wrote that General Arnold himself flew the Pan Am seaplane part of the way.[1007] That was not true; Arnold flew one of the two C-54s that accompanied the expedition. Captained by Otis Bryan, that aircraft carried Marshall and several other generals.[1008]

FDR took an interest in the fact that Elliott's airline friend C.R. Smith, who was checking the president's route out, was now a Brigadier General and Chief of Staff of the Transport Command.[1009] So close were Smith and Elliott that it was Smith who told FDR that his son was fine and would be meeting him in Casablanca.[1010] Smith also told Arnold that the big dark summit secret was common scuttlebutt all over Africa.[1011]

Though appalled at the poverty in that "awful, pestiferous hole," the British Gambia, the president noted that the American facility at Bathurst was "incredibly up to date" and had a 6,000 foot steel-mesh runway already in heavy use by transport planes.[iii] At Medouina Airport outside Casablanca, Elliott recalled that he and Mike Reilly of the Secret Service finally welcomed the president on 12 January, a little after 6 PM, after having Reilly vouch for him![1012] FDR said his son was "looking very fit & mighty proud of his DFC."[1013]

Again, Elliott's details were shaky. The President's Log showed him arriving at Medouina at 1820 on Thursday the 14th. He immediately proceeded by automobile to the Anfa Hotel. Churchill had already arrived. At the president's villa, Elliott and Franklin Junior were also installed. The official record states that the "first five" WACs (Womens' Army Corps), including Elliott's new mistress Ruth Briggs, were also present at the summit; indeed they had dinner with Elliott and the president on the 16th.[iv]

For the next ten days, Elliott was probably the closest to immense power that he would ever be. He not only served as his father's constant aide, but actively participated in many high-level meetings. Unlike Teheran, Casablanca was a prolonged conference heavy on military decisions. Unfortunately, the participants either kept poor records, or did not reveal them. For this reason, Elliott's gossipy accounts are a fall-back, if dubious, even for the official Foreign Relations of the United States (FRUS), which

---

[i] Churchill: The Second World War, IV/620. Only a small proportion of casualties were on the battleship.

[ii] Reilly: Reilly of the White House, 150. 8 FW-200s of KG 40 at Bordeaux struck on 30 December 1942.

[iii] The Gambia made a deep impression on FDR, and he mentioned the horrible conditions there to numerous correspondents. He blamed the British for the rampant poverty and disease.

[iv] FRUS, The Conferences at Washington and Casablanca, III The Casablanca Conference, 485-849. The Women's Army Corps sent their first detachment to North Africa. Dinner: FDR Day-by-Day, FDR Lib.

attempted to recreate the proceedings in meticulous detail. In retrospect, the president should have told his son, or someone reliable, to keep minutes – of every minute. And to secure the document afterwards. Elliott later asserted that he had had a diary, but he lost it.

Among FDR's companions were Harry Hopkins, Generals Marshall and Arnold, and Averell Harriman. Of the Allies, only Churchill and his extensive staff were present. Joseph Stalin had refused the trip; he couldn't leave his empire. Chiang wasn't invited. But the big issue was how to get some sort of French representation.

About Generals Charles de Gaulle and Henri Giraud, Elliott recalled: "'You've got to get your problem child down here,' said Father [to Churchill]. It was his nickname; from then on, throughout the conference, de Gaulle was the PM's "problem child"; Giraud was the President's."[1014]

So followed a long diatribe about the silliness, deviousness, and pompous arrogance of General de Gaulle specifically and the French in general. Elliott wrote this in 1946, putting the words in the mouths of Churchill and FDR – probably not realizing that the Anglos would have to deal with President de Gaulle for twenty-five more years. Harriman said "it was a pity that no other Frenchman appeared who had the courage of de Gaulle but who was something less of an egotist." There seemed to be no recognition of the legitimate grievances of the French, who had now suffered the ignominy of having been defeated and occupied by both sides in the world war.[1015]

For Elliott, the hostility held up over the years. In his old age, he remembered the French general as "opinionated, bullheaded and irascible to the point of complete rudeness."[1016]

The ill treatment of General de Gaulle and, by extension, France, was one of the less glorious legacies of the Allied cause. Virtually everyone agrees that Churchill and Roosevelt provided great, almost god-like leadership during the war. But we forget that they were great leaders because they won. They did not win because they were great leaders. Had they lost, the pages of history would be overflowing with ridicule of such megalomaniacal clowns and buffoons. That is always the loser's fate. And had, somehow, France been victorious and the Anglos laid low, then perhaps Churchill and FDR would have come as supplicants, hat-in-hand to the French leader for aid, moaning all the while about the lack of respect they received.

Elliott somehow developed the theory that Churchill wasn't interested in bringing de Gaulle to the summit. This later was hotly disputed. Elliott claimed to recall:

> "Was I just imagining things," I began, "or isn't the PM really worried by de Gaulle's pouting?"
>
> Father laughed. "I don't know. I hope to find out, in the next few days. But I have a strong sneaking suspicion" – and he accented those words – "that our friend de Gaulle hasn't come to Africa yet because our friend Winston hasn't chosen to bid him to come yet. I am more than partially sure that de Gaulle will do just about anything, at this point, that the Prime Minister and the Foreign Office ask him to do."[1017]

This is only one example of Elliott's consistent attempt to show that Churchill was playing games with the president at Casablanca. Possibly he got this impression due to the simplistic American notion that de Gaulle was in Britain's bag and could be produced as necessary.

This assertion sufficiently annoyed Winston Churchill that he took several pages to refute it in his memoirs, published in 1950. He made it abundantly clear that he had had to wring de Gaulle's arm almost out of its socket – i.e. threatened to derecognize him and his organization – to get him to attend the conference. A very irked PM wrote:

> It is very odd to see the account which the President's son, Elliott Roosevelt, gives of this in his book which he hastened to write about the confidential talks he heard at the meals to which he was brought by his father. He seems to suggest that the President suspected me of trying to stop de Gaulle coming, and objecting to his being brought there, whereas I was putting the utmost pressure possible to get him to come. This rubbish has had a wide and long currency. The telegrams dismiss it for ever.[1018]

And then Churchill proceeded to quote at length from his threats to the infuriated, embittered, and humiliated French general. We need not go into the details of Anglo-French relations, but Elliott's divergent memory on this occasion was far from the only one an angry Churchill would later protest.

Equally confounding, Elliott's novelized and highly suspect account had FDR – repeatedly and *ad nauseam* – launching into long anti-colonial tirades, at the end of one of which he asked: "How is it where you are? How is it in Algeria?"

> I told him it was the same story. Rich country, rich resources, natives desperately poor, a few white colonials that lived very well, a few native princes that lived very well, otherwise poverty, disease, ignorance. He nodded.[1019]

That is merely a brief sample. Most of Elliott's book reads almost as if President Roosevelt were waging war on the British and French Empires instead of the Axis.

Elliott's cartoon caricature of imperialism was not so unusual at the time, particularly in America. It was the bedrock of Leninist ideology, but it was also a considerable component of the general American critique of the imperial powers. It is likely that Elliott was parroting what he heard in Eleanor's circle. The discovery that things weren't quite so simple would await the decolonization process itself. While Elliott might be trusted to report overall matters from the summit, it would be absurd to suggest that every conversation unfolded as he so glibly retold it. In particular one has to question the incessant anti-British emphasis – other sources to the summits do not confirm such persistent vehemence in the talks.

Unconditional Surrender!

Endless controversy attaches to the origin of the term "unconditional surrender" as it applied to World War II. Elliott firmly contended that his father came up with it over lunch on 23 January:

> At lunch that afternoon there was just Harry, the P.M., Father, and I. And it was at that lunch table that the phrase "unconditional surrender" was born. For what it is worth, it can be recorded that it was Father's phrase, that Harry took an immediate and strong liking to it, and that Churchill, while he slowly munched a mouthful of food, thought, frowned, thought, finally grinned, and at length announced, "Perfect! And I can just see how Goebbels and the rest of 'em will squeal!"...

> Father, once his phrase had been approved by the others, speculated about its effect in another direction. "Of course, it's just the thing for the Russians. They couldn't want anything better. Unconditional surrender," he repeated, thoughtfully sucking a tooth. "Uncle Joe might have made it up himself."
>
> And Harry said, "We'll get to work drawing up a draft of the statement right after lunch."[1020]

Elliott told the exact same story, words slightly rearranged, tooth still sucked, in *A Rendezvous with Destiny*, published in 1975.[1021] Or, more likely, his ghost looked up the passage to copy.

It is one thing that this light-hearted lunch banter seems an inappropriate origin of famous terms that might have cost millions their lives. It's quite another that it cannot be true. Again, the other high-functioning alcoholic at the table, Winston Churchill, who also had a way with words, fired back in his memoirs:

> ...it will be well to state the facts as my records reveal them. Elliott Roosevelt asserts in his book that the words were used by the President at one of our dinners. I am reported by him to have "thought, frowned, thought, finally grinned, and at length announced "Perfect," and also that "the nightcap toast proposed by Mr. Churchill that evening was 'Unconditional Surrender.'" I have no recollection of these private and informal interchanges where conversation was free and unguarded. The matter must certainly however have cropped up in my official talks with the President. Hence paragraph 6....[1022]

Churchill was here referring to his report to the War Cabinet of 20 January 1943 – three days earlier - wherein item 6 stated:

> I should be glad to know what the War Cabinet would think of our including in this statement a declaration of the firm intention of the United States and the British Empire to continue the war relentlessly until we have brought about the "unconditional surrender" of Germany and Japan. The omission of Italy would be to encourage a break-up there. The President liked this idea, and it would stimulate our friends in every country.[1023]

Clearly, Elliott must have made something up. But Churchill also quotes from Franklin Roosevelt's own account to Harry Hopkins. In that exchange, FDR claims to have had the sudden inspiration for the expression on the last day of the summit. It arose from his trouble getting de Gaulle and Giraud together, which reminded him of Lee and Grant. General Grant's initials were widely joked to stand for "Unconditional Surrender." "And the next thing I knew, I had said it."[1024] This was at the 24 January final news conference.

Enigmatically, Churchill added: "I do not feel that this frank statement is in any way weakened by the fact that the phrase occurs in the notes from which he spoke."[1025] Churchill knew that FDR was embroidering, which he often did. We know today that "Unconditional Surrender" had been brought up at staff level long before Casablanca.[1026]

Churchill was also being disingenuous. Averell Harriman remembered him as being in "high dudgeon" over FDR's unannounced use of the term: "I had seen him unhappy with Roosevelt more than once, but this time he was more deeply offended than before. I also had the impression that he feared it might make the Germans fight all the harder."[1027]

Whether Elliott was right that the two had talked about "unconditional surrender" beforehand, it does seem that publicly, the president went off half-cocked with the term. The prime minister felt compelled to agree, again publicly.

The spat over ownership is rather trivial compared to the controversy over whether the phrase dramatically prolonged the war – a subject that has occupied many historians ever since. In a spirited defense, Churchill said it did not, chiefly because the terms the Allies expected to impose on the Axis were then so extreme that publishing them would certainly have ensured a fight to the death. "Unconditional Surrender" at least left room for mercy.[1028] But whether it hurt or helped, this slogan, so treasured by Allied jingoists, seems like it should have had a more dignified origin, or have been balanced by some other program – consider, for example, the role Wilson's 14 Points played in the Armistice of 1918.

Without regurgitating the intensive scholarship on the issue of "Unconditional Surrender" we may safely conclude that the principals were already familiar with the phrase and some of its implications – but it clearly was the first time that Elliott Roosevelt had heard it.

Overhearing the War Plans

At Casablanca the Allies agreed on operation HUSKY, the invasion of Sicily that would follow the capture of Tunisia. It was again, a foul compromise: the British wanted baby steps in the Mediterranean, the Americans were itching to go ashore in France. However foolish the Italian campaign looks in retrospect, it would be the center of American attention, and Elliott's work, during 1943.

Ominously, Churchill and Hitler shared in the belief that they were military geniuses of the first rank. The Briton was always coming up with dubious military schemes, of which Gallipoli is the most infamous. At Casablanca he drove the Americans to distraction with his emphasis on Mediterranean action in lieu of a decisive invasion of France. After North Africa, Sicily (HUSKY) rather than Sardinia (BRIMSTONE) was his favorite goal, and he even attempted to talk the Americans into invading the Dodecanese (Rhodos specifically) which finally infuriated General Marshall to the point of loud blasphemy. At Teheran, Elliott quoted FDR as saying "Marshall has got to the point where he just looks at the PM as though he can't believe his ears."[1029]

Colonel Roosevelt was allowed to view one element of Churchill's *modus operandi:* his traveling war room, complete with giant maps and moving ship symbols and associated military paraphernalia. As a boy, Winston had massed his tin-soldiers for battle – now he had the real thing. Every day, the PM and his top military men would huddle in the war room and decide the next move – "there was a sense of mighty suspense about it." The visiting Churchill even set up his own war room in the White House.[1030]

Elliott was mesmerized. His father didn't pretend to be a general; FDR's role was mostly to arbitrate the disputes of his officers. He did have a "war room" – the Map Room in the White House; but at least he didn't prance around in uniform, which the other leaders on both sides liked to do.

Generalissimo Josef Stalin was one uniformed leader who was definitely not impressed by the Anglo-American decisions at Casablanca. His demand for a real second front, it is true, was entirely selfish, but what of the strategic point he made?

The decision on HUSKY, forced by Churchill, meant a delay of a year in the real war. The Allied decision to attack neutral French colonies had temporarily strengthened the Axis. Had the Allies landed in Tunisia instead of irrelevant Morocco, Rommel would have been cut off in Libya. Instead, Rommel beat the Americans to Tunis and held them up for six months. Had the Allies taken ill-defended Sardinia, naval and air superiority over southern Europe would have been theirs at low cost, and a path cleared for a twin-pronged invasion of France in 1943. There was a reason Hitler thought the TORCH force was headed for the Italian islands; that would have actually made sense.[1031]

Perhaps too much can be made of it; after all, Allied industrial supremacy was such that victory was assured one way or another. But struggling up the Italian gantlet for two full years did not seem the best use of resources to the Americans. Ironically, Stalin eventually profited more than anyone from this decision.

One evening, General Patton held forth at dinner about the absolute supremacy of armored warfare in the modern age. The episode permits us a glimpse of Elliott's role:

> "Armor!" Patton exploded. "Modern warfare has developed to the point where most if not all the fighting will be done by tanks and armored mobile vehicles. Infantry? What's it got to do, beyond mopping up, and securing the ground captured by the tanks?"
>
> I imagine it was I who put in a word about aircraft.
>
> Patton was politely disparaging. "Of course, it has its role. I would be the last to say that the air forces were worthless. There's no question in my mind but that airplanes can be helpful in supporting the armored ground operation…"
>
> Beyond that one oar, loyally stuck in on behalf of the air forces, I maintained a discreet silence. For his part, Father ate and relaxed and enjoyed himself. He was certainly not going to allow himself to get involved in any intra-military imbroglio. So General Patton held the floor at his will. (And a month or so later, when he took command of the southern front in Tunisia, I would be amused to recall this conversation, while listening to the two-way radio at our African headquarters pour out frantic requests from Patton's command for more air reconnaissance, more tactical air support – *in advance of his armor.*)[1032]

Ha ha ha. Apparently, Lt. Franklin Jr., who was also at the summit, failed to chime in to assert that ships and a sea blockade were all that really sufficed to win the war.

It wasn't the only chance Elliott had to stand up for the air force. As at Argentia, he was again vexed that the British seemed to have two officers present for each American. Eyeing Air Vice Marshal Arthur Tedder, commander of the Allied air effort in the area, he whispered in his father's ear: "They've got Tedder. Why isn't Spaatz here?" FDR promptly told General Spaatz, who was between Elliott and Tedder in the line-of-command, to fly to Casablanca.[1033]

On a purely professional level, Elliott Roosevelt lucked out unexpectedly in his modest role as an assistant. Like many bartenders and butlers, he learned of top secret matters. His Senate testimony brought it out:

> For instance, if my memory serves me rightly, it required approximately 7½ million pictures to prepare for the invasion of Sicily; pictures that the Ground Forces required. The only reason that that job was accomplished in time for the Ground Forces to properly prepare for that invasion, and I might add it is the first invasion by ground troops, the War Department records will show, where they had complete terrain and military information; the only reason that that was accomplished on time was that I happened to be present on detached duty at the time of the Casablanca Conference, and I was told by General Arnold

> and General Marshall and others of the final decision to make the invasion of Sicily, and as a result we laid aside the few supplies that we had for a long period of time before our orders came down from General Eisenhower, a certain amount of equipment and supplies, and started flying the missions to have the information ready when it was needed. As it was, we just got it prepared in time. If we had not done that, we would have been completely in the soup on that invasion.[1034]

Roosevelt overstated his genius. In January there was no guarantee that the next high-tempo operations would definitely be in Sicily, and indeed HUSKY was not executed until six months later. It stands to reason that as reconnaissance commander, Roosevelt should hold back reserves for any future operations, but he would need them in Tunisia. Still, his secret knowledge must have reduced his uncertainty and given a slight advantage.

Managing the security for President Roosevelt was usually an issue for the Secret Service, but in Morocco the task also gave the military anguish. The president badly wanted to see some real war. So did Churchill, who at least was ambulatory. In the view of the military, the idea would have involved long flights, considerable inconvenience, and totally unnecessary danger. After much argument, FDR finally said: "You, Sir Charles Portal, Hap Arnold, and Bunny make up the plan, but Bunny, you have no say in fixing the places where we go; you are merely Secretary."[1035]

The result was that the president got to meet some American troops at Rabat – hardly a war zone.

When General Charles de Gaulle finally did show up, he was in a foul mood. Elliott's account of de Gaulle's first meeting with the president is disdainful enough. More disturbing is Mike Reilly's account. He was the chief of the Secret Service detachment and a friend of Elliott's. Reilly drew his weapon on de Gaulle during a heated exchange with FDR, although he kept it concealed.[1036] The Frenchman obviously had his peculiarities, but with so many people mocking him it's hard not to sympathize with the exiled leader.

The Casablanca summit concluded with a tenuous cease-fire between de Gaulle and Giraud. "Like two dogs, the two Frenchmen started almost to circle each other, and then exchanged a brief, reluctant handshake."[1037] To Mike Reilly, the two Frenchmen rather resembled a mongoose and a cobra.[1038]

The truce was for the satisfaction of the Anglos. In the long run, de Gaulle would gain full control on the French side. Admiral Darlan had been assassinated on Christmas Eve 1942, and General Giraud would be shunted aside later in 1943. De Gaulle tolerated no competitors.

That Elliott had much fun and made many friends in Casablanca is exemplified in a curious encounter with Mohammed V, the Sultan of Morocco. The president honored the sultan, then still *de facto* a French puppet, with a state dinner.[i] Churchill didn't like treating colonials as equals, and he sulked at FDR's provocation, though Harold MacMillan noted that this was in part because no alcohol of any kind was served. Still, this was a case where Elliott rightly noticed that his father deliberately tweaked imperialist noses, both British and French.[1039]

---

[i] Recklessly, the Allies had informed Mohammed of the North African invasion details in advance. The sultan told the notorious Grand Mufti of Jerusalem, who told German intelligence chief Admiral Canaris. But his report was disbelieved in Berlin. (Waller, 251-2)

Many years later, Elliott went to Morocco again, accompanying his mother Eleanor. Appropriately, they stayed at the Anfa Hotel, which had been host to the Casablanca summit. Strangely enough, Elliott wrote later that when he and Eleanor again met the sultan, now king of independent Morocco, he recalled:

> Father and I had both told her of our meeting him as a nine-year old when his grand vizier, aged 90, brought him to dinner on the same night as Churchill during the Casablanca Conference. I took the boy up in a P-38, struggling to talk with him in French.[1040]

There are all kinds of problems with that story. One is that Elliott wasn't flying single-seat fighters at the time, much less with kids sitting in his lap. The second is that Sultan Mohammed V was 33 at the time. His two sons were in the right age range, though. Perhaps Elliott took Prince Abdallah, then seven, or Crown Prince Hassan, then thirteen, for a ride in a B-25? Or perhaps he got the kid mixed up with the young Shah of Iran, whom he met in Teheran? But most likely of all, Elliott's writer James Brough reconstructed the scene from Eleanor's *My Day* column of 2 April 1957, which has some of the same language, and then Elliott added some misremembered details.[i]

In *As He Saw It*, Elliott made much of Roosevelt's promises of aid to the ever-after grateful Mohammed V, but he mentions no joy rides. The confusion is a pity, for the Roosevelts were highly regarded in Morocco, and Elliott was one of the few American holders of the Moroccan royal order of Alaouite.[1041]

To settle the matter, the official record has the Sultan, "his early 'teen son, the Heir Apparent," meaning Moulay Hassan, and the Grand Vizier Mohammed al-Mokhri attending dinner with the Allied leaders during the Casablanca conference.[1042]

Elliott and Franklin Jr. had a grand ten days in Morocco. They hit whatever night life Casablanca had left to offer, and the elder brother commented that Franklin Jr. was in "rollicking form…I do hope that after this war he can settle down to some kind of work, because if he doesn't I fear that he may waste a brilliant mind like Hall did."[1043]

On 24 January, Elliott Roosevelt flew back to Algiers, and his father began the long journey home to Washington (though after a pleasant tour of Marrakech with Winston).

For the next six months, the son would be buried in reconnaissance work as Rommel struck back from Tunisia, and as the preparations for HUSKY necessitated increased aerial mapping and surveillance of Sicily, Sardinia, and the Italian mainland.

A Trap Snaps on the Hill

James Roosevelt later wrote: "I remember my father's rage when he was accused of seeing his sons safely through a war in which we all faced fire. I remember my brother Elliott saying it would be best if one of us was killed in action in order to clear his record."[1044]

Politics is a sport for cowards. This was as true in the 1940s as it is now. Congressman William P. Lambertson, Republican from Kansas, had never heard of "swiftboating," but in Congress he repeatedly sliced into Elliott and his sibling Roosevelts for being coddled and jerked from dangerous assignments.

---

[i] See the Teheran chapter for Elliott's friendship with the shah.

Lambertson made quite a name for himself criticizing the Roosevelts' war service in colorful terms. As late as 4 March 1943 he rose in the House and declared that, as others were dying, Franklin Roosevelt Jr. "and his du Pont wife" were "doing the night clubs of New York." "When Rommel started west, so did Franklin, Jr." he stated.[i]

In view of the Roosevelt kids' playboy image, what Lambertson said was probably common bar-talk in the heartland, especially after the "I want to be a captain too" smear campaign only two years earlier. By now, the only valid point in the criticism was that the Roosevelt sons got a lot of travel time and interesting official duties because of White House interest. Perhaps Lambertson meant to attack this only, but he seemed to be accusing the Roosevelts of cowardice.

Well-known facts had made the criticism obsolete and then obnoxious. Even considering the source, an anti-FDR and previously anti-war politician, the harangues got to be too much for Lambertson's colleagues, Democrats and Republicans. Colonel Roosevelt would be the hero selected to extinguish that Kansas boy's political career.

During the Casablanca conference, said Elliott, his father had been kind enough to bring him American newspapers, the first he'd seen since he left the United States in September – an odd claim since he'd spent much of that time in London![1045] Stranger still was that the Lambertson attack Elliott claimed to be responding to landed in the newspapers at home during the middle of the conference.[1046]

At any rate, FDR made the accusations of cowardice available to his son. According to the official narrative, the outrage Elliott felt at the charges then prompted him to write a searing rejoinder via his own congressman, Fritz Lanham of Texas.

Brother Jimmy said FDR himself then brought Elliott's letter back with him from Casablanca – but it seems not to have been the letter that was later released. The president was uncharacteristically "white, and shaking with anger," when one day he showed Eleanor a letter from Elliott saying: "Pops, sometimes I really hope that one of us gets killed so that maybe they will stop picking on the rest of the family…"[1047]

Six weeks later, Elliott's exceptionally well-written letter to Representative Lanham became an instant classic when Lanham read it in the House on 5 March. It read:

> Dear Fritz,
>
> I am writing you this note because, first of all, you are my Congressman, and, secondly, you have known me for a long time, and can speak for me as a citizen of the State of Texas.
>
> I have just had an opportunity of seeing my father over here, and he gave me the first American newspapers I have seen since I left the states last September.
>
> In the papers I read something that deeply disturbs me. A fellow Congressman of yours has undertaken to criticize some of my brothers and their war records by stating that two of them were pulled out of combat zones so that they would not be exposed to danger. In as much as I know the Congressman could not be referring to me, because I am here with the troops in North Africa, and because I know that my brother Franklin has been on a destroyer in the north Atlantic and still is, there can be only two brothers to whom the gentleman in question refers, my brothers James and John.
>
> I happen to know that James has insisted on carrying on, on active duty, even though he is not physically up to the strain of combat. He could easily sit back and not be exposed to actual combat, because if he were anybody else's son he would be exempted from such duty. He is a hell of a fine officer and has plenty of guts. Ask any man who has served with

---

[i] AP, 4 MAR 43, in Milwaukee Journal. FDR Jr.'s ill-fated first marriage was to Ethel du Pont.

> him – that is the test. John, my younger brother is in the Naval Supply Corps. He's been fighting like hell ever since he got in to go on foreign service, and I know that my father or anyone else isn't going to stop him before this show is over.
>
> The fact that my brother James has won the Navy Cross for gallantry in action speaks for itself.
>
> Such criticism aimed at men who are fighting for their country strikes me as sort of unfair. They can't answer back. We feel we are fighting for all America. We are not in politics. In the forces there is a unity of purpose – the continuation of American freedom and American ideals.
>
> Please explain this fact to your colleague, and try to explain to him that we, as soldiers, don't care whether or how much he disagrees with the president, but for God's sake let us fight without getting stabbed in the back for the sake of politics.
>
> If I ever get home and am out of the Army I'll be glad to stand up for my own honor, but in the meantime see if he won't lay off until such time as a fair fight can be made of it.
>
> I don't care whether a man is a Republican or a Democrat. Let's get together and get this damn war won. I'm tired and I want to go home and live in peace on my ranch with my family. The sooner the better, too.
>
> If the Congressman questions my service, you might tell him that I have spent over two-thirds of my service in the past 2 years on foreign duty. I have been in every lousy spot the Air Corps can think of to send its men. It's not much fun I can tell you, especially the butterflies that fly around in your stomach when the German gets the range and lets loose everything he's got at your plane.
>
> Thank you, sir, for passing on these personal sentiments to your honored colleague in the House.
>
> Sincerely your friend, Elliott Roosevelt [1048]

That one hit home. Both sides of the aisle had to rise and applaud.[1049] Lambertson was shamed before the entire nation. On 9 March, President Roosevelt wrote a thank-you note to Fritz Lanham.[1050]

When Elliott sampled his father's correspondence for his work *FDR: His Personal Letters* after the war, he was careful to include the above exchange, but he excluded a preceding correspondence that proves it was President Roosevelt himself who engineered the downfall of Congressman Lambertson.

James Roosevelt said Elliott gave the letter to FDR at the Casablanca summit, which he left on 24 January. This is quite possible since Fritz Lanham showed the letter to Steve Early, FDR's press secretary, weeks before the showdown in Congress. Early and Lanham then proceeded to plan the ambush together.

On 6 March 1943, the day after Lambertson had again accused the family, Early wrote to the president:

> I have been conniving with Fritz Lanham for some time, waiting for Lambertson or some of his ilk to renew the attack. Lambertson did this in the House late Thursday. Fritz Lanham was not on the floor at the time. I saw him Friday and we arranged with Sam Rayburn for Fritz Lanham to get recognition of the Chair yesterday and tell the story to the House – how he had received Elliott's letter, had gone to see Lambertson, and how Lambertson, in the face of the appeal, had renewed the attack. Then Fritz read Elliott's letter and supplemented the story with data I prepared for him. When Fritz Lanham concluded, the Democrats and Republicans rose en masse in applause.
>
> Fritz Lanham did a magnificent job and did it so effectively that even Lambertson should be silenced from now on…Fritz told me weeks ago of Elliott's letter. In fact, he

brought it to my office. I thought it was a great letter – a soldier's letter, and it was at my request that Fritz used it as he did together with the other data.

I hope we acted as you would have. I said nothing to you about this because I thought it best that we act independently, without your knowledge. --- S.T.E. [1051]

Early need not have worried. It seems incontrovertible that the entire sequence was carefully planned by President Roosevelt himself. Was the letter even written by Elliott, or was he merely asked to sign it? Elliott's letter was dated 22 January, just before the Casablanca summit ended. One week before, on 14 January, when FDR was busy at the conference, Lambertson had charged in the House that James and Franklin Jr. had been temporarily "jerked" from the front on pretenses.

The timing suggests that father and son agreed on a course of action during the conference. Thereafter, for over a month, Early worked carefully with Lanham to set the trap Lambertson blundered into.[1052]

The *coup de grace* landed when the popular columnist of political gossip, Walter Winchell, revealed that Congressman Lambertson's own son had refused to join up – he claimed conscientious objector status! After that, the congressman kept the peace, at least until he lost the next election in 1944.[1053]

Yet here again, FDR's hand hovered behind the scenes. Winchell worshipped the president, who soon learned to use him as a mouthpiece. FDR had shown Elliott's letter to Winchell beforehand, but forbidden him from printing the story early. After Lanham sprang the trap in Congress, Winchell revealed the Lambertson conscientious objector story in his column, and next morning the president called him from New York to the Oval Office to thank him for his role in the ambush.

Walter Winchell was Roosevelt's most fanatical devotee in the media. He sat in the Stork Club night after night, eavesdropping on the more or less confidential conversations between the powerful, well-connected carousers who hung out there. After the war, General Roosevelt showed up in the Club to seek out Winchell. He saluted and proclaimed: "Mr. Winchell, I am wearing this uniform for the last time tonight. Before I take it off, I want to salute you for what you have done for our country, and for being a loyal and brave friend to my father."[1054]

With expert plotters like this it is not surprising that Roosevelt could not be dislodged from office by normal means, and that his enemies were left to rage incoherently from the "ash-heap of history."

The Multinational Reconnaissance Wing

The Casablanca conference resulted in an air command shake-up. Although only a small component of the burgeoning North African Air Force (NAAF), the Northwest Africa Photo Reconnaissance Wing (NAPRW) reflected a major step up for Elliott Roosevelt. Effective 18 February 1943, he would now head a true Allied command, reporting to NAAF's General Spaatz, who reported to Air Vice Marshal Sir Arthur Tedder, head of Mediterranean Air Command (MAC), who reported to General Eisenhower.[1055]

Formally, this structure superseded the 12th Air Force, although the name remained in currency. General Doolittle was now head of the NASAF, the strategic air force, good training for his later command of the 8th Air Force in England.

NAPRW added the 5th Photographic Group with the 23rd PRS to Elliott's 3rd PRG. But more importantly, RAF 682 Squadron (formed from 4 PRU at Gibraltar) and SAAF 60 Squadron were assigned to the wing. The South Africans had come from Cairo with Martin Marylands and Baltimores, and in February began receiving the Mosquito PR IV, partly assuaging Colonel Roosevelt's clamor for them. Months later the Free French Group II/33 with hand-me-down F-4s came under Elliott's command. So did all the appropriate engineer, intelligence, service, weather and communications detachments. By October 1943, Elliott commanded 2,922 troops, of whom 393 were officers.

1,824 of these were Americans, 821 British, 214 South Africans, and only 63 French. However, the French squadron included the already world-acclaimed author Antoine, Comte de Saint-Exupéry. He worked hard to get Colonel Roosevelt to arrange the full transfer to NAPRW of the French unit with twenty pilots and the few Lightnings the Americans could spare.[i] For diplomatic reasons Elliott tolerated the volatile St.-Ex, and indeed gave him a commendation for his work with the Wing's Unit 4 at Oujda.[1056]

Originally the Malta PRU flight, RAF 683 Squadron under Adrian Warburton was attached to the wing in the summer. This small unit supported the ill-starred Salerno campaign. Other RAF detachments were under Wing command from time to time.

NAPRW was still not nearly as strong as on paper. The squadron structure wasn't reinstated until after the Tunisian victory. But by the summer, Allied air superiority was beginning to take hold. Perhaps NAPRW's greatest single job was to complete a large photo-mosaic of the entire island of Sicily. In some of the unit's photographs, one sees a copy of that mosaic carefully stuck to an entire wall of the headquarters; it was the biggest reconnaissance job ever completed up until that time, and it was of great assistance to the invasion of Sicily in July.

At the same time, wing aircraft ranged across the sea all the way to France, Albania, and Greece, indeed claiming photos of Barcelona and Budapest. A close watch was kept on shipping, on airports, and other infrastructure. By the end of 1943, all important facilities were routinely covered at regular intervals, sometimes twice a day.

The operational tempo increased exponentially. In November 1942, the groups flew a rather symbolic 14 missions and lost three aircraft to enemy action. By September 1943, NAPRW reached 572 monthly missions, of which 492 were successful, but only one aircraft was lost to the enemy. Over that nearly year-long period, 29 aircraft were lost to enemy action, and 21 to accidents. The losses per month remained in the low single digits, representing a vastly smaller fraction of total sorties.

The paycheck, however, came from the imagery. Over the December-September period, the wing produced 765,035 negatives and 3,401,805 prints. These enormous numbers were necessarily somewhat inaccurate, but they make the point.

Being a non-pilot, Elliott flew in the B-25 and the Mosquitoes, and indeed participated in the development of new techniques, especially in night flash-bomb photography. Reportedly, he participated in the first three missions of that type, earning him a DFC oak-leaf cluster. Nonetheless, experts said the results were disappointing, due to "malfunctioning flash bombs, expired film, and operational inexperience."[1057] It was the effort that counted, and results would improve in due course.

---

[i] St.-Exupery: Wartime Writings. After ferocious string-pulling, St.-Ex was restored to flight duty in 1944. On his ninth mission on 31 JUL 44, he was killed in an F-5B crash off Toulon.

Top commanders thought well of Colonel Roosevelt's management of his wing. By the time he turned over his command to Colonel Karl Polifka in December 1943, the wing was a powerful and effective air force, based in Italy and renamed the Mediterranean Area Photo Reconnaissance Wing (MAPRW).

Mosquito Envy

As we have seen, the experience with the F-4 and F-5 Photo-Lightnings in Africa had been disappointing. The grumbling was all the more pronounced because the Americans, who were working next to the RAF's Spitfires and Mosquitoes, knew that better alternatives existed.

The British began the modern era of aerial reconnaissance. This priority can be attributed not to the RAF's stolid bureaucracy, but to the clandestine work of the Secret Intelligence Service (SIS). Sidney Cotton's prewar "spy" flights using four Lockheed 12As have justly gained fame. These aircraft pioneered vitally important techniques, notably heating of the cameras to prevent icing and fogging, as well as the use of trimetrogon-like installations of three cameras covering a wide strip of land below.[1058]

A highly unorthodox Australian, Cotton was told to take over the critical RAF reconnaissance unit (1 PRU) soon after the outbreak of war, because the RAF was unable to obtain usable reconnaissance results until new technology, tactics, and procedures were introduced. From this odd beginning grew the modern concepts of photo reconnaissance that would play such a decisive if mostly unsung role in both the Hot and the Cold Wars.

Using their best aircraft, the RAF had already established the division between tactical and strategic reconnaissance, which in practice usually comes down to short and long range. Stung by initial losses, British pilots were acutely aware of the need for premium performance as well as specialized camera equipment. Furthermore, this technology was a moving target – new equipment might only have the edge for a year or even less.

Even the celebrated Spitfire was only popular because new marks came out constantly; older ones, if they survived, were swiftly relegated to less hazardous duties. Indeed, by 1943 the RAF found the Spitfire PR.IV to be inferior to the opposition, and in North Africa pilots demanded new PR.XIs that restored the balance for a while. These again yielded to the bigger Griffon-powered PR. XIXs by the end of the war.

By 1945, highly optimized Spitfire PR marks still trumped all but the jets. The old slow reconnaissance standbys – Blenheims, Marylands, Bostons, and others – had been put out to pasture in less dangerous skies.

The Mosquito was something else again. When General Arnold had visited England in April 1941, he had been given the honor of watching Geoffrey de Havilland, Jr., put that sleek new twin through its paces. He was hooked. When TORCH rolled ashore in North Africa, early Mosquitoes were already being used by the RAF for reconnaissance in the Mediterranean. On urgent American request, Geoffrey repeated the aerial exhibition in Washington D.C. in December 1942, using the first production Mosquito.[1059]

An Air Corps report revealed how Elliott Roosevelt acquired a taste for Mosquitoes:

> Some of the first sorties of the 3rd PG over enemy-held territory are reported to have been flown in a Mosquito loaned to the group by the RAF and picked up at Gibraltar by Lt. Col. Elliott Roosevelt, Commander of the 3rd Group, and Major Harry Eidson, Commanding Officer of the 5th Photographic Squadron, on their way to North Africa.[1060]

This corroborates Roosevelt's statement to the Senate that he "also succeeded in borrowing from the British a Mosquito for experimental purposes, and we picked that up at Gibraltar two days after the invasion started," i.e., on 9 November 1942.[1061]

Gibraltar was the original command post for TORCH. General Eisenhower's headquarters was there, and Roosevelt's planes staged through the short runway along the Spanish border. Evaluating the Mosquito B.IV, Elliott found that it was faster and had five times the range of his F-4s (an exaggeration). He probably also liked it because he could fly it – a two-seater.[1062]

RAF 544 squadron loaned Elliott the first two Mosquitoes. Then in February two more from RAF 540 squadron were loaned and never returned despite British pleas. These were Elliott's first combat steeds, flown by Major Eidson in the left seat.

When Colonel Roosevelt had the chance to bend the ears of Arnold and Spaatz at the Casablanca conference, his enthusiasm for the Mosquito resulted in Arnold's directive of 25 January 1943 to the effect that the Air Corps obtain them as soon as possible, and also develop a dedicated PR aircraft of similar performance.[1063]

Later, one Canadian-built F-8 Mosquito, tail nr. 43-34926, nicknamed *The Spook*, was associated with Elliott's use. Originally B.VII KB 315, it was the third Mosquito delivered to the Americans. If the numbers are correct, this was the same plane Elliott and Karl Polifka had a bad experience with at Bolling Field. It was apparently one of only two B-VIIs to see extended combat use with the USAAF. However, according to the pilot's son, *The Spook* was Major Jim Setchell's aircraft and Elliott only flew it on occasion. Setchell, who would command 3rd PRG, and Captain J.C. Alexander took delivery in Toronto in August, flew the North Atlantic route, and delivered this much-photographed aircraft to La Marsa on 18 October. Evidently Setchell and Elliott took it to Algiers on 10 November 1943. *The Spook* went to San Severo on 7 December and crashed on landing in August 1944.[1064]

In November, via the South Atlantic, Colonel Polifka flew the other F-8 to arrive safely in Africa. It was named *Faintin' Floozie III*; F'F-II had been an F-4 he had flown in New Guinea. Ten more Canadian-built F-8s were delivered to combat units in 1944.[1065]

We shall find that the story of the Canadian Mosquitoes was quite entertaining, in a highly calamitous sort of way.

In 1944, when Roosevelt lost hope of getting the Hughes F-11 in time, he again turned to the Mosquito. This is how he remembered his advocacy to the Senate when grilled on the F-11 program:

> Mr. ROOSEVELT. It did happen, sir, and the recommendation was made by me for the acquisition of Mosquitoes because of the fact that the Materiel Command insisted on violent changes in design and in changing to an all-metal ship, and I maintained that we had to have airplanes, and the next best thing was the Mosquito, and I recommended through channels that they go ahead and get us Mosquito aircraft.
>
> General Arnold and his Procurement Division proceeded, and they secured Mosquito aircraft, which had a magnificent record with the USAAF pilots operating them. All-weather reconnaissance in the European theater during the European campaign was carried on by a group of Mosquito aircraft, and if the committee desires testimony as to the

> efficiency of that airplane as a stop-gap, because of the fact that the Hughes airplane never did come through to us, and in spite of the fact that the Materiel Division said that a wooden airplane was not any good for combat, by golly, this Mosquito airplane did a magnificent job, and there is an officer in the American AAF, a full colonel, who can testify, Leon Gray, to the efficiency of that plane, because he commanded that group.[1066]

Thus, when Elliott was commanded home in late July 1943, one of his goals was to obtain the first Canadian Mosquitoes, which would turn into a splitting headache for the procurement officers at Wright Field. Colonel McDonald, the intelligence director in theater, wrote:

> It was even proposed that while Elliott Roosevelt was in the U.S. he should try to acquire a minimum of twelve (12) Canadian made RAF Mosquitoes. It was recognized that there was an acute shortage of high-powered Rolls Royce engines required for these Mosquitoes at that time. However, it seemed possible that the necessary airframes could be made available to be powered by two each Allison liquid-cooled engines which were obligated to our P-51 program. This was just one of the various stopgap ideas proposed to remedy our situation while hoping that a superior performing airplane might be developed and produced.[1067]

That plan would not only fail; it would cause much gnashing of teeth. But for early 1943, it was interesting to see that the pilots didn't worry about the plane's wooden wings rotting or warping. They would give anything for an extra knot of airspeed *right now*. In six months, the plane would probably not be around anyway.

Because of his early acquaintance with the aircraft, and his subsequent advocacy for it, Elliott Roosevelt would wind up in the middle of a transformation of air tactics brought about in large part by the Mosquito. Unfortunately for him, he would not become known for his work with that plane, but for his steamy affair with its ambitious American challenger, the sexy but difficult Hughes F-11.

Sometime around 1938, Geoffrey de Havilland had an epiphany that would change the face of aerial warfare fundamentally. He realized that in the air, victory came from technology: i.e., from performance alone, not from massed attack or ostentatious displays of courageous self-sacrifice. To lukewarm official interest, he set out to build an aircraft that would fly faster, higher, and farther than any other.

To that end he sacrificed all the seemingly necessary paraphernalia of bombardment aircraft: the ten-plus man crews, the gun turrets stuck like leeches to the fuselage, everything that could possibly slow him down. What he wound up with was something like a double Spitfire: a very high performance, two-seat wooden aircraft powered by twin Rolls-Royce Merlin engines.

Until jets came along, Mosquitoes were the fastest operational aircraft in the world. The aviation writer J.W.R. Taylor said of it:

> The Mosquito proved too fast to be intercepted, and towards the end of the war, flying at altitudes between 30,000 and 40,000 feet, it suffered a loss rate of only one per 2,000 sorties, the lowest by far of any type used by Bomber Command. It was particularly effective against pin-point targets. Thus, Mosquito bomber squadrons destroyed one V-1 … site for each 40 tons of bombs dropped compared with 219 tons from Mitchells, 182 tons from Marauders, and 165 tons from Fortresses. Mosquito fighters shot down 600 V-1s… in two months.[1068]

The two Mosquitoes the RAF lent to Elliott's 3rd PR Group did not work out well for the Americans. This may have been because they had the single-stage turbochargers, and an inadequate camera suite. Arnold, Eisenhower, and Roosevelt kept bugging the British for new Mosquitoes, but the British were adamant about keeping theirs.

In principle, lend-lease worked both ways. In practice, most of the "lending" was a give-away from American factories to British and Soviet units. Of course, the British thought they had the better equipment, as well as the most urgent need. And there was obviously no Soviet "lending" to America.

General Arnold touched on this issue repeatedly. In *Global Mission* he wrote that while he needed "something like the Mosquito" he was leery of having it placed in production in the United States, because of the start-up difficulties with knowledge transfer, woodworking techniques, different units of measure, etc.[i]

On Arnold's request, Mosquito airplane drawings and data were forwarded to Wright Field as early as June and July 1941. Unfortunately, it turned out that General Echols' Materiel Division was markedly unimpressed, even at times horrified. In November, the Division stated that there was significant question whether the plane would fulfill American needs. The toned-down message to Arnold stated:

> Further, the attached report on the Mosquito indicates that its structural strength is quite likely less than that for standard American practice. It would appear desirable, therefore, that a complete Mosquito aircraft be obtained from the British for evaluation and test of the actual article prior to rendering final decision on whether or not such aircraft is suitable for the Army Air Forces.[1069]

The battle lines were thus drawn up early. They would zig and zag for years before the public denouement in the Senate in 1947.

To relieve both British and American needs, de Havilland Canada placed the unusual aircraft into an urgent production scheme, and by late 1943 the USAAF began to receive 40 of an order of 120 of them. They were 5 B.VIIs and 35 B.XXs, designated as F-8s by the Americans. Interestingly, many such aircraft flew across to Europe via Elliott Roosevelt's old route. Many didn't make it and were lost in Greenland waters. It is thought that icing and engine defects might have contributed to these problems. Very likely though, D.H. Canada, which had only built simple trainers before, had little idea how to construct the very complex wooden aircraft; the "crash program" was too much crash and too little program.

Wright Field obtained a handful of early production Canadian Mosquitoes for evaluation. The Materiel Command guys well and truly hated them. Two test pilots, later high-ranking, crashed Mosquitoes there. Most of the others were wrecked in accidents on the ground. At one point Materiel Command said that the planes were so dangerous military pilots refused to fly them, and civilians had to take them back to Canada.[1070]

Refusing an order in wartime is not looked upon kindly except when there are good reasons. When the 3rd Ferrying Group did so on 17 August 1944, the reasons quoted were unsatisfactory engine operations and powerplant failure on take-off; coolant failures; and aerodynamic instability, notably "extreme tail heaviness." By September and October, the USAAF handed all its Mosquitoes back to the British, and the painful and costly debacle came to an end.[1071]

---

[i] Arnold: Global, 377-8. The latter is odd since British units were mostly the same as American.

Clearly these Canadian versions were not ready for prime time when they reached North Africa. Not only did they fly worse than the RAF models, they stank: the Canadian glues were different. Elliott Roosevelt had close calls at least three times in Mosquitoes. He continued his campaign for an American aircraft capable of matching the loaners. Except for one, the early models were eventually sent to England to be used for training.[1072]

On 11 April 1943, in a hand-underlined message, the RAF (apparently Air Marshal Portal) responded to Arnold's request for new Mosquitoes in North Africa:

> Very much regret that it is impossible for us to hand over to American Forces either in North Africa or in this country the 24 Mosquitos that you ask for [10 April]. We have here a total of 13 serviceable PR Mosquitos only and this is inadequate for the many urgent commitments for which they are required...we have to make do with Spitfires for many tasks for which Mosquitos would be more suitable. <u>It is airframes rather than Merlin 61 engines which are short so that I am afraid the suggestion you made in you paragraph 2 would not help</u>...I understand that your pilots over here have found the F-5 most satisfactory for PR work and that it is at least as good as the Spitfire. Tasks requiring deeper penetration than the F-5 is capable of must continue to be carried <u>out by our Mosquitos which are of course available to meet your needs as well as our own.</u>
>
> With regard to North Africa I understand that the PR wing has 25 F-4s which have similar performance to F-5. I presume that there are droptanks for these and range should therefore be adequate for all tasks in that theater. As so many of the targets are located on the coast and as weather conditions are dependable in Mediterranean Area navigation does not present the difficulty that it does in Central Europe and there seems no reason why single seater aircraft should not reach any target. I hope therefore that the F-4 working with our Spitfires can cover all normal requirements.
>
> I do not however forget the special circumstances in North Africa... I am afraid it is impossible for me to allot 4 Mosquitos <u>but I will make every effort to send out in the near future 2 Mosquitos for the PR Wing and maintain them in that theater.</u>[1073]

Reading this, perhaps General Arnold rued the times he had given the RAF thousands of aircraft he desperately needed himself; but the British had a point. Weren't they in the same war?

The RAF response was quite an earful, but Arnold did not give up, and simultaneously he joined the American advocates for obtaining a domestically produced equivalent. There is no question that Elliott Roosevelt was the driving force behind the requirement – the Americans specifically wanted the unarmed reconnaissance version.

By July, the RAF was able to offer Arnold 15 Mosquitoes a month during 1944, "and even this allocation represents a considerable sacrifice."[1074] At that time, the RAF agreed to furnish 120 Mosquitoes to the USAAF, but allocated them as 40 unarmed bombers from Canadian production and 80 night fighters from U.K. production – including the trickle already "placed at the disposal of the USAAF by the RAF Mediterranean Air Command."[1075]

The USAAF eventually received over a hundred advanced PR.XVIs from British production. These worked much better, primarily because they were powered by the new two-stage supercharged Merlins. Also, by this time, pressurized cockpits were being used, which made a huge difference for the crews now operating at stratospheric altitudes.

By 1943, the engineering commands responsible for preparing maps and "tourist guides" demanded a new, dedicated aircraft when they found out that they could not get the crews to fly the suicide missions they apparently required.[i] During the first half of 1943, General Arnold was thus squeezed by the demand for Mosquitoes, a new American type, or modification of existing aircraft. The answer would become a bit of each, a bit too late. Better Lightning models came to the squadrons, and the British slowly loaned new Mosquitoes.

Robert A. Lovett, then Assistant Secretary of War for Air, visited North Africa in June-July 1943 and conferred with Colonel Roosevelt, among others. Lovett was a former naval aviator who had, interestingly, been in charge of the naval air station FDR visited in France in 1918.[1076] Lovett was effective and competent. He would become Secretary of Defense during the Korean conflict, and he was intimately responsible for the buildup of American air power during World War II. Most everyone had the highest opinion of him.

As a result of Lovett's and Elliott's deliberations, Arnold decided to call some of his best reconnaissance pilots back to the United States to analyze what the aircraft manufacturers could offer on short notice. Elliott reported to Arnold in the Pentagon on 1 August 1943.

The quest for an American Mosquito-like reconnaissance aircraft had roots reaching back to before the war, but until the shooting started, these advocates were largely ignored. However, Major Goddard, head of the Air Corps's Aerial Photography Laboratory at Wright Field, had made the recommendation in a comprehensive report released in October 1940.[1077]

The report from this special board on future reconnaissance requirements reads like clairvoyance – which is a useful talent for intelligence types. Goddard's wish list included an American optics capability similar to that of Zeiss-Jena in Germany; trimetrogon camera installations; infrared and color film; flash bombs and electric arc flash equipment; and various ground-based paraphernalia to rapidly process, interpret, and mark up the imagery recovered.[1078]

Perhaps the most important request was for a dedicated high-performance reconnaissance aircraft. This aircraft would need to cruise to at least 35,000 feet, requiring a pressurized cabin and an automatic pilot. It would also need remote-controlled automatic camera equipment.[1079]

The design that initially came out of this request, seconded by General Arnold, was the North American B-28, which was based on the famous but limited B-25 Mitchell. This airplane might have relieved the reconnaissance crisis by 1943. But it would probably not have performed like the Mosquito, which was unknown to the Americans until 1941. As it was, the B-28 project failed and was cancelled in 1943.[1080]

By then, Elliott Roosevelt, George Goddard, the Army Engineers, and many others were hammering Arnold for a top-performing reconnaissance aircraft. This would lead to much acrimony and immense wasted effort, but not to a usable aircraft beyond the modified combat types.

After Elliott's persistent advocacy, on 26 May 1943 General Arnold renewed the requirements for a reconnaissance aircraft. This time they called for a pressurized, heated aircraft capable of reaching 60,000' and ranging out to 3,000 miles. It was

[i] The conflict between the operational commands & the Corps of Engineers is told in a following chapter.

completely unrealistic to get such an aircraft before the whistle blew, and Materiel Command made no secret of it.[1081]

The quest for a survivable, dedicated reconnaissance aircraft would not be crowned with success until the 1950s. By then technology had advanced so dramatically that the old debates from 1943 seemed irrelevant. Actually the 1940 and 1943 requirements were, in principle, right on the money.

Reconnaissance Expert

In Africa, things gradually improved for the NAPRW. After the German surrender in Tunisia the squadron structure was reinstated, the three main units becoming the 12th, the 5th, and the 15th PR squadrons respectively. Then these squadrons began deploying to bases in Sicily, Corsica, and the mainland.

Colonel Roosevelt's headquarters moved from Maison Blanche, Algiers to La Marsa, Tunis in June 1943. Late in 1943, it moved on to San Severo (near Bari) in Italy. The sheer weight of Allied air power was now able to provide regular, even routine coverage of the Italian peninsula. Losses now were minimal.

In Algiers, Roosevelt had an occasion to explain aerial reconnaissance to a jam-packed, Red Cross-organized "Town Hall" meeting. Always a superb speaker, he enthralled the audience with a detailed and captivating description of his work in reconnaissance and the importance of the discipline: "He spoke with confidence and fluency and without notes." Unfortunately, the show had been too good; for security reasons, Elliott was banned from making any further such speeches.[1082]

After the presentation, said Rabbi Isserman, organizer of the program, Elliott was besieged by hundreds of autograph-seekers, as seemed to be his fate most anywhere. The rabbi said that he'd heard that Colonel Roosevelt had one of the most luxurious apartments in Algiers, and also a "good cellar."

Despite his preference for easy living, Elliott led from the front, and he was publicly credited with the early flights over Rome as well as other important targets.[1083]

Many names important to the history of reconnaissance emerged in the Mediterranean in 1943. Besides Elliott Roosevelt, the most well-known was Lt. Col. Karl Polifka, who had engaged in the same trade in the Pacific before being posted as vice commander of the NAPRW in November 1943.

The two met stateside during Elliott's special mission, and that led to a little show for the press. In November 1943, *Reader's Digest* ran a crude article about reconnaissance pilots, "Fliers who fight without guns." It caused quite a bit of snickering:

> The Army censored it, pursuant to the President's wish that his son's exploits remain anonymous. The article finally was submitted to the White House, where one change was made before permission for publication was granted. The article ended with a quote: "He would have had the DSM [Distinguished Service Medal] long ago, if his old man weren't the President of the United States." The White House changed that to "if his dad didn't happen to be just who and what he is."[1084]

That was pure FDR-orchestrated coyness.

Reader's Digest had actually reprinted a short piece by William White in the *American Mercury*, and no reader could have been dumb enough not to realize who "the Nameless

Colonel" was. The article was based on interviews with Polifka and Elliott. It was a propaganda-puff piece of the kind common in wartime. White said the Army told him that sitting next to Karl would be "another colonel you are sure to recognize from his pictures. Just back from Africa, he's one of the best officers we've got. But remember this: you can't use his name."

> Why not? -- Because of who he is, they said. If we told you only half of what he's done, they'd say we were bragging him up. So if you quote him he's got to be nameless.[1085]

The lurid article was full of incredible braggadocio, such as when Polifka said he got into a typical P-38 death dive, and recovered pulling so many G's his intestines came out of his "behind" and had to be repackaged by medics when he landed.

"Nameless Colonel" let out a similar one about Leon Gray being chased by two Macchis on either side, suddenly pulling up and thus making the two Italians shoot each other down. "Gray laughed about it all the way home!"

White trumpeted the heroism of both men. Polifka was already widely known as a hyper-aggressive reconnaissance pilot, and of Elliott he said:

> There's a fine officer. You heard him tell about how some of his boys like to go out on those dicing missions skimming along the beaches through the ack-ack fire? What he'd never tell you is that they are also a specialty of his. That's why his boys are nuts about their Old Man, as they call him. He doesn't order them out, he *leads* them. They know he will never send a man on a mission he wouldn't fly himself. In combat he has all the guts in the world and his boys will tell you he would have had the DSM long ago if his dad didn't happen to be just who and what he is.[1086]

Now how did he know that, considering that he had just met Elliott and had yet to go to Europe? Well, perhaps he knew it because twice in two months he'd gone with Elliott to the White House to meet the family and recount his war stories.[1087]

The Roosevelt-Polifka team had a few more adventures while still in the States, even apart from those paid for by Howard Hughes. On 13 October 1943, the two flew one of the new Canadian-built F-8 Mosquitoes, 43-34926, from Wright Field to Bolling Field, D.C. The hydraulic fluid drained during flight, and the crew had to crank down the gear manually and make a no-flap landing. Furious, Roosevelt submitted a report that suggested sabotage or negligence at the factory. It was common back then to blame mishaps not on incompetence of friendlies, but on the demonic cunning of the enemy, although the former seemed more likely. The dismal experience with the Canadian F-8s caused a major row in Air Force procurement circles.[i]

Polifka arrived in the Mediterranean theater on 23 November and immediately began flying dicing sorties noted for aggressive audacity.[1088]

> Many of the sorties had a definite tang of the spectacular: The Spitfire executed two sorties at low altitudes down to 19,000 feet; Colonel Polifka breaking all precedents flew a total of four successful missions of the dicing variety skimming over treetops, waving to civilians, and serpentining around hills and thru valleys. One of these four missions just mentioned was rated as the most spectacular feat in the history of the Squadron. In it, Col.

[i] Stanley, 92, 366. A drill had punctured a hydraulic line, and an "amateurish packing" was placed over the hole. (F-8 in AAF Service, AAHS Journal, Spring 2007.)

> Polifka, Lt. Mills, and Lt. DeYoung, with the Colonel in the lead, brushed the treetops in a glorious effort to photograph three strategic dam sites.[1089]

For such dangerous low-altitude sorties, Roosevelt recommended Polifka for the DFC, which General Eisenhower personally presented to him on 22 December 1943.[1090]

"Pop" Polifka was known as a fixer who could get the job done in spite of obstacles, enemy or friendly. One of the stories often told of him is how he faked the name "Jones" on some of his most dangerous sorties to defy orders to not risk them, a ruse that worked until General Mark Clark called in "Jones" for commendations. Polifka would serve as deputy to Roosevelt until the latter moved to England in 1944. Recognized as the Air Force's top reconnaissance pilot, Colonel Polifka was killed in Korea during a characteristically risky RF-51 sortie.

Another prominent reconnaissance pilot was Colonel George Humbrecht, who would later command the 7th Photographic Group in England. He had survived getting shot down in Tunisia. John G. Hoover gained prominence for several missions, including the first long-distance flights to Russia. Clarence Shoop and James G. Hall were other friends of Elliott who would go on to great things, but not without getting caught up in an Elliott scandal. Leon Gray, who had been a ferry pilot, wangled his way into reconnaissance with Elliott. Gray and Shoop quickly became highly regarded reconnaissance pilots.

James G. Hall was a most unusual character. In 1942, he commanded the 13th PRS of the 7th PRG in England; he was made a colonel and given command of the entire group in 1943. Here's what a reconnaissance expert had to say about him:

> He listed his age as 47, although several officers who knew him well vowed that he was 6-8 years older. Jim Hall was half Indian, a handsome well-to-do broker in civilian life who owned a seat on the New York Stock Exchange but never permitted membership in such a staid organization to interfere with his fun. He had been a pilot in World War I and when he returned to civilian life after the armistice, Hall continued his flying. In the thirties he broke several flying records while publicizing an anti-Prohibition group and thus earned the nickname of the "flying broker." When the Japanese bombed Pearl Harbor, Hall immediately applied for active duty and with the help of Elliott Roosevelt he finally got back in the service...On March 28, 1943, Hall became the first pilot of the USAAF to fly a photographic mission in Europe...a forerunner of 1367 missions flown by the 13th PRS from its base at Mount Farm, near Oxford.[1091]

The most famous of Elliott's pilots also gave him the most trouble. He was Antoine, comte de Saint-Exupéry, and the attention he attracted provides more insight into the fractious life in the NAPRW with its inter-Allied resentments. Ironically, St.-Ex could say that he was merely returning to his unit, for his last assignment after the fall of France had indeed been II/33 Escadre at Maison Blanche. You would think this pilot was an immense asset; he had 6,500 hours of the most varied flight experience conceivable. Yet he was a total disaster.

Elliott was attuned to diplomatic and public relations matters, and had welcomed the reconstituted Free French escadre and helped equip its two escadrilles with hand-me-down Lightnings. He allowed St.-Ex to fly combat missions in July 1943, after cursory training. It took some intervention, since he was well over the age limit; but the

Frenchman badgered both Elliott and Robert Murphy, the ranking American diplomat, for permission.

St.-Ex did get to see southern France, sightseeing over family estates, but on his next mission, he cracked up. He'd forgotten to raise the brake pressure before touchdown, so he ran out of runway and wrecked the P-38. Since this was only one of many horror stories, he was grounded.

Much of St.-Ex's dreamy literary *oeuvre* does read as if his oxygen supply had cut out at 30,000 feet. This endeared him to poets and philosophers and Frenchmen. The brutish, semi-literate cretins from America (as one senses they were to the French) were not the least bit impressed. Colonel Leon Gray said "he didn't know St.-Exupéry from a bale of hay" when he met him.[1092]

St.-Ex wrecked a lot of planes in his career, but this habit didn't go over so well with the Americans. Once, he reportedly rolled down his window at 30,000 feet, losing his oxygen mask, and then dove in a panic with the result that the wings were permanently bent. Since he had little English, he misread instruments and misunderstood instructions. He was said to have flown a mission while reading a novel, even aimlessly circling the base while finishing it.

He complained that the Lightning was a "flying torpedo," bereft of the romance and chivalry of the old days. And with all their gauges and numbers, pilots now were mere "accountants." *Oh Tempora, Oh Mores…*St.-Ex was old, ill, gravely depressed, and despairing of the future of mankind.[1093]

When Elliott left at the end of July, Col. Leon Gray was in operational command, and he didn't cut any slack. St.-Ex was forbidden to fly. It pierced his French heart. To ingratiate himself, he gave a banquet for the Wing and melodramatically announced that his goal was to die for France. In the French version, "the American colonel," who drank heavily all night, chewed him out, and St.-Ex went home crushed.[1094] In Leon Gray's version, as told to St.-Ex biographer Stacy Schiff, the Frenchman begged and beseeched, and Gray told him, "I don't give a damn if you die for France, but you're not doing it in one of my planes."[1095]

The grounding probably delayed St.-Ex's demise by a year. In 1944 he was finally able to hound the generals into allowing him to fly again. Reportedly, General Eisenhower said that with luck, "he will bother us less in the air than on the ground." St.-Exupéry disappeared on his ninth mission, on 31 July 1941, off the coast at Toulon.[1096] (The wreck has since been found.)

By 22 November 1943, Colonel Roosevelt was briefly given command of the U.S. 90th Reconnaissance Wing, which included both his old 3rd Group and the sister 5th Group. Initially headquartered in Tunisia, this command moved to Italy to provide support for the entire Italian campaign. In December, the NAPRW was reorganized as the MAPRW, still with a multinational character. However, Roosevelt was not present from mid-July to late October. He had exciting work to take care of back home.

New Reconnaissance Tactics

On Secretary Lovett's urging, Colonel Roosevelt returned to the States and showed up at the White House on 22 July.[1097] Two days later he spoke to the press, mentioning that he had recently flown a mission over Rome.[1098] That mission was significant because the city had been bombed for the first time on 19 July – by no less than 500 aircraft – and the bomb damage assessment had indicated a great success.

We have a lurid propaganda account of that raid in Quentin Reynolds's 1944 book *The Curtain Rises.* Reynolds wrote from Tunisia that Elliott's photo planes had cased the eternal city for two weeks, and Doolittle's bomber pilots were meticulously trained in avoiding damage to cultural and civilian areas. After the attack, the reporter described the elation at headquarters as almost all bombers returned:

> Back at General Spaatz's headquarters the pictures were coming in. First there were the pictures taken by the bombers as they dropped their eggs. There were dozens of pictures taken of each target, and in no case could you see a burst... outside the target area. Then Colonel Roosevelt walked in with his pictures, taken by high-flying photo-reconnaissance planes two hours after the bombing. The smoke had cleared and the damage done could be ascertained and weighed by Spaatz and his staff. These pictures were amazingly clear even without the aid of the magnifying stereopticon glass. Roosevelt had done a great job here from the beginning, but this was his masterpiece. Late that night the reports were all in. We had lost five aircraft out of the more than 500 that had participated in the raid. The bombers had completely destroyed the targets assigned to them.[1099]

In fact, the bombers hit not only the rail yards, but also the University Medical Center next door, killing a thousand civilians there. San Lorenzo district was hardest hit. The Italians later counted 2,800 dead and 11,000 wounded, although the numbers may be inflated. The raid was successful, but as was often the case, the human cost had been immense while the military damage was quickly repaired. Yet the attack contributed to the king's ouster of Mussolini a week later, followed by Italian surrender. The Germans were ready to abandon Italy at a line north of Rome, but surprised at the lack of Allied follow-up on the ground, they then occupied the city and the rest of Italy. Despite all the self-satisfied propaganda bluster, the outcome was thus a calamity for the Allies, and Rome wouldn't fall until a year later.[1100]

Although the real results of the raid were not fully publicized until after the war, the immense gap between the initial Allied BDA (damage assessment) and the actual results would be a continuing handicap; perhaps it is so to this day. Skeptics soon learned to divide own reports by some suitable correction factor.

After accounting for his role in the bombing of Rome, Elliott provided detailed debriefings of his operations in the Mediterranean to his superiors in Washington. Although technical in nature, the recorded discussions provide fascinating insight into the initial failure of American reconnaissance and the slow but sure recovery that followed.

When the war broke out, the USAAF still had ideas of sending charting aircraft on straight flight paths at constant altitudes. This was dictated by the focal length of the cameras used and the scale requested by commanders. There were several cameras in use with differing focal lengths, but the most commonly used camera was the Fairchild K-17, which could accept many lens options. In the F-5B, the front "hole" could take a 6" charting K-17; the middle could take two of these, or one 12 or 24 incher; and the aft compartment accommodated two 24" K-17s or one 24" K-18.[1101]

The standard arrangement resulted in a preferred altitude at mid-levels, ten to twenty thousand feet. Unfortunately that was also where hostile fighters and anti-aircraft artillery (AAA) were most effective. It was quickly discovered that altitude saved lives.

For example, most flak could not reach above 26,000 feet, and with a fast enough penetration, opposing fighters could not climb that high soon enough to engage. This explains the disappointment with the altitude performance of the early F-4s and Mosquitoes. That, however, was not the aircraft's fault, but a limitation of the powerplant, and was in time rectified.

While flying at 30,000 feet provided some safety, it degraded the image quality unless longer focal lengths and better cameras were used. That's where the more tactical aircraft, such as Spitfires and Mustangs, fell short. There wasn't room enough in them. The twin-engined aircraft were modified to carry bigger cameras, and there was a continuing race to develop better optics and longer focus lengths. Still, with barely heated and unpressurized cockpits as well as unreliable oxygen, high-altitude flight was dangerous and difficult, and most of all unpleasant.

The mapmakers insisted that the aircraft fly straight and level for long distances at high altitude, covering a strip of land with their cameras. Then the plane was supposed to do the same coming back, at a reciprocal course offset by something like 25 miles. That simply wasn't going to happen in disputed airspace.[1102]

For safety, the reconnaissance pilots wanted to climb above 30,000 feet, and the missions took several hours. Some of the pilots who didn't return probably fell prey not to enemy action, but to hypoxia or other incapacitation. Unpressurized flight at those altitudes is definitely not healthy, particularly with rapid ascents and descents and repeated missions. The unit's medical personnel wrote worried memos about altitude sickness, and warned pilots that their blood might boil over 40,000. Calls went out for warmer gear and better heaters.[i]

Another new problem was the contrail level, often at 27-30,000 feet. A contrail was a giant "here I come" sign to the enemy. Pilots learned to duck under it, thus assuring themselves that they would be able to see anything above them while remaining largely invisible to the ground. The contrail level became a staple of forecasts and briefings.

High-altitude imagery was excellent for certain purposes, such as keeping track of ships and counting trucks and airplanes. But there were other tasks which required close-ups. Sometimes commanders wanted to determine the models and markings of equipment, or catch humans in their activities on the ground. For this, a new and dangerous low-altitude tactic was developed. It was called dicing.

The term "dicing" reputedly originated in the RAF. Their reconnaissance pilots would allegedly "play dice" about who had to fly these risky sorties, or else they referred to the activity as "dicing with the devil." The term was one of many Briticisms the Americans quickly adopted. Already in North Africa, pilots would talk about dicing runs against Axis installations, and by the middle of 1943 the term was in common use, as was the tactic. Flying at minimum altitude offered the advantage of remaining below radar coverage, using terrain for cover, maximizing surprise, and minimizing time over target.

Unfortunately, flying flat-out at fifty feet is absolutely terrifying and requires all the concentration the pilot can muster. That made it difficult to obtain good photographs, since for that, timing was essential. Often, pilots came back with blurry images of the wrong things simply because the synchronization of film and triggering failed. The Mosquito turned out to be a better choice for dicing because the second crewmember

---

[i] This phenomenon, ebullism, doesn't actually happen until about 60,000 feet, but why take a chance? At any rate, even at 40K, even 100% demand oxygen could not make up for the lack of pressure to the lungs.

could assist the pilot, set the camera controls according to speed and altitude, and capture images at the right moment.

In contrast, the single-seat Lightnings required the pilot to set an "intervalometer" according to a table that correlated speed, altitude, and film speed. The pilot could trigger the camera from the control column like he would have his (removed) guns, but whether the results were useable could not be known until after landing.

Now think about doing all this at fifty feet, 250 knots, with people shooting at you.

Of course, many aircraft flew into the water, the ground, or obstacles such as wires, poles, and trees during dicing runs. You balance the equations of risk the best you can. Many extremely important photographs came back from such operations, such as those identifying radar antennas, V-1 sites, etc.

After a while, it was discovered that night imagery could be essential in determining what was really happening on the other side – especially after the Axis decided that travel at night was far safer than during daylight. This was an experimental activity in which Elliott Roosevelt would take a leading role, both in the Mediterranean and in France, and it would earn him his Oak Leaf Cluster to the DFC. The Wing Commander participated in the first three experimental night photography missions over Sicily.[1103] Spaatz's commendation read:

> …to meet emergency requirements, you were directed to organize and operate night photographic facilities for the Sicilian battle. In spite of the short time available, necessary training and organization was accomplished and you are now successfully operating over hostile territory at night. I feel that this accomplishment is typical of the spirit and skill of the NAPRW. It adds to your fine record of achievements.[1104]

Back then there was neither infrared imagery nor low-light optical equipment. If you wanted to take pictures in the dark, you had to set off a "flash bulb." At 20,000 feet you needed one gigantic flash bulb to illuminate the ground below. For this purpose, flash bombs were developed, and later, Dr. Harold Edgerton of MIT brought out the so-called Edgerton flash system, a device which would electrically generate enough light to expose film by discharging capacitors in a xenon tube. Then the exposure had to be timed just right to make use of that illumination.

This procedure was obviously rather incompatible with the principle of stealth. A reconnaissance aircraft dropping flash bombs ran the risk of having every searchlight within line-of-sight trained on it. A bad case happened to Colonel Roosevelt himself.

Roosevelt led in the development of reconnaissance tactics. His night missions began in July 1943 in preparation for the landings in Sicily. Here is an account of one of his first night operations:

> …Col. Lauris Norstad, Director of Operations, HQ, North African Theater of Operations, called Roosevelt's airbase and told him that he suspected the Germans were moving supplies into Sicily at night. Recon photos taken during the day didn't show any such enemy action but Norstad wanted to know what was happening on the island after dark. He had to know since the Allies were already planning to invade Sicily. Roosevelt took the problem to Humbrecht, who decided that they would need a B-25 to accomplish the mission. Norstad got them the B-25 but there was not enough time to transfer a crew to the 3rd Rec. Group to fly the aircraft. Consequently, Humbrecht checked himself out in the B-25, loaded the bomb bay with flash bombs for night photography, and the belly of

> the plane with three K-17 cameras. Roosevelt, the CO who had not attended USAAF flight school, went along as co-pilot.
>
> They took off on a pitch-black runway since the Tunisian airfield at La Marsa had no lights, and once the B-25 was airborne Humbrecht headed for Palermo. He maintained an altitude of 12,000 feet, and as he neared the city he motioned for Roosevelt to turn on the cameras. Everything went smoothly until the first flash bomb was dropped. Preset to explode at 5,000 feet and light the target below so that the cameras could record the scene on film, the flash bomb alerted the defenses of Sicily. Within minutes every searchlight in Palermo was centered on the lone B-25. Humbrecht, nearly blinded by the glare, had to resort to his instruments in order to maintain level flight. With flak bursts rocking the B-25 and threatening to ignite the remainder of the dangerous flash bombs inside the bomb bay and blow the aircraft to pieces, Humbrecht jettisoned the flash bombs. Forty flash bombs dropped together, and when they all exploded simultaneously at 5,000 feet the concussion was so great it blew the searchlights out and Humbrecht and Roosevelt slipped away in the darkness. They had obtained only a few frames of photographs, but they were enough to prove that the Nazis were moving supplies into the island at night. The bombers began night sorties afterward in an attempt to stop the incoming supplies.[1105]

This complements an account by the war correspondent Richard Tregaskis, who flew on a B-25 piloted by Humbrecht and copiloted by Roosevelt on the night of 15 July, observing the progress of the Sicilian operation. The preceding day, Elliott's unit had flown no less than 24 sorties over Sicily, and Elliott had been aboard an A-20 on a night flight. On the 15th, the objective was Palermo, but in the darkness interrupted only by scattered fires and searchlights, the crew could not find it. Before the night's safety expired, the B-25 returned to La Marsa, still with its complement of flash bombs. It was rather boring; still, Tregaskis was impressed and noted the colonel's willingness to share risks with his pilots.[1106]

Roosevelt himself touched on his night operations in a remark he attributed to a talk with his Father in the fall of 1943:

> He wanted to know about how night reconnaissance had worked out: I had flown the initial, experimental missions over Sicily, and I told him about the dodges we had worked out for getting a good look at Nazi night-time troop movements; how we had used flash bombs, dropped thirty seconds apart, which went off two-thirds of the way down, and lighted up a square mile around, affording us magnificent opportunities for getting pictures of the enemy on the move.[1107]

Despite the reportedly poor initial results and Elliott's departure for the States days later, techniques for night reconnaissance would indeed become one of the signal developments for which Elliott Roosevelt was remembered in the Air Force.

Gradually, the NAPRW also greatly expanded the range of its aircraft. This was critical to the pursuit of the air war as it developed over Germany in 1944. The P-38 was not designed for long range, and it became critically important for the reconnaissance squadrons to extend the paltry 150 mile range the aircraft was initially thought to offer.

There are two ways to get better range: carry more fuel, or burn less. Both were done. By mid-1943, large jettisonable tanks were available for the P-38s. They were carried under the wings between the fuselage and the engines. But more interestingly, pilots learned to economize. The first example of how a range of over 700 miles could be achieved was noted by the wing in a commendation letter on 29 July 1943:

> ...On 5 June 1943, one hour after the bombing of Spezia by Flying Fortresses, Major Gray [Leon Gray, CO 3rd Group] covered the target area with excellent results in the face of determined enemy opposition. He was intercepted by 3 enemy aircraft over his first target, but he completed two runs, then flew out to sea for 5 minutes. After he eluded the pursuing aircraft, he proceeded to his second target, Leghorn [Livorno], where he again encountered enemy aircraft at his altitude. He took evasive action again after making an additional run over the harbor, completing his mission. Heavy intense, accurate flak burst at his altitude of 28,000 feet as he approached both targets. Although this was the first flight attempted at this extreme range with this type of aircraft, the pilot covered shipping and several other pinpoints on his return trip to base [La Marsa]. In spite of the hazardous conditions confronting him, not only were the photographic results excellent, but he so adjusted his fuel settings in the face of enemy flak and fighters that he returned to base after 5½ hours of flight with an ample supply of gasoline, thus pioneering in establishing a safe combat range of the F-5A of 700 miles.[1108]

This range work would pay big dividends next year when flights from England to the Ukraine were begun. It also facilitated fighter escorts over occupied Europe, although the twin-engined P-38 did not work out in that role as well as the drop-tank equipped P-51, which gained air superiority over Germany beginning in early 1944.

As many aviators are aware, Colonel Lindbergh gained considerable attention for his work in extending the range of the Lightning in the Pacific, but this actually occurred almost a year after the problem was worked through in the Mediterranean. The reality is that no one man – Gray, Roosevelt, or Lindbergh – deserves all the credit. Conditions forced the issue, and a combination of experience and theoretical knowledge gradually pushed the range out. Lindbergh, as a factory consultant unofficially flying combat on the side, obviously had both. Similarly, the work done in the Mediterranean was trial-and-error; after all, some aircraft did indeed run out of gas.

The key to the problem was twofold. First, an airplane inherently has a "most efficient" speed; a point at which the excess of lift over drag is highest for the distance traversed. This speed is much, much lower than most pilots can stand. However, with the long, relatively safe over-water legs in both theatres, the maximum economy speed was a logical, if tedious, choice.

The second key was power and propeller settings. Pilots are taught some variant of "props-on-top" – the notion that propeller speed should be high relative to engine power (boosted manifold pressure) in order to avoid overstressing the engine. But as Lindbergh pointed out, that matters only at high power. For the low speeds yielding best range, it was perfectly fine to set low propeller RPMs, which yields the most efficient propulsion. There were other factors to juggle – winds, fuel mixture, cowl flaps, etc. – but that was the essence.

At any rate, few aircraft lasted long in wartime; to baby the engines made no sense if the Hun was on your tail. Pilots would use the highest possible power when in combat. In other words, these "warbirds" weren't flown the way they are today. Some of them even had sealed "emergency war" throttle settings that could be forced if necessary, but might require an engine tear-down if you made it back.

That's how the term "war-weary aircraft" came into use – after surviving many hard missions, many aircraft got "tired" and were relegated to secondary duties. They were often called "Weary Willies." We'll meet some of them in operation APHRODITE, but they were scattered around the fields of North Africa within months of the invasion.[1109]

The Wackiest Ship in the Air Force

Among the reasons Colonel Roosevelt's creativity and resourcefulness were admired by his superiors was a certain old and, in pilot-speak, "butt-ugly" French bomber. Officers must have done a double-take when they saw that entry in the daily totals of aircraft for the NAPRW, along with the usual Spitfires and Lightnings. What the hell is a Potez 540?

Roosevelt found it soon after the invasion, hidden away in the rear of a hangar. The aircraft was the result of an interwar French design philosophy that favored straight lines, right angles, and lots of struts. The result looked like farm machinery interpreted by Picasso. It was a twin-engine, high-wing monoplane, although it had some extra stubwings to help out. The boxy fuselage came with numerous glassed "corner offices" for observers, gunners, and other helpful bystanders. That's why France used the plane for cartographic missions in the colonies. It was obsolete when it was new, in 1933.

When Roosevelt found out that a certain French pilot, Adjutant-Chef Arnould, and a surviving mechanic wouldn't mind helping out with the war in return for sundry considerations, he formulated a remarkable plan. Promptly the plane was hauled out, received an overhaul, a "new coat of many colars fresh from the camoufleur's brush," culminating on both sides of the fuselage with a Tricolore and Old Glory collegially crossed.[1110]

The Group ripped out the insides and replaced it with printers, developers, and other photo lab equipment. And *voila*, Elliott now had a self-propelled, air-mobile photo trailer to offer his customers. He could make house-calls!

A photograph in the unit's files shows the Potez as it was being readied for the trial flight on 15 January 1943. The file states:

> This old bus flew equipment and laboratory personnel to the Group's first Forward Unit near Constantine and was used as a Field Laboratory. The time and distance saved by this method marked a new era in Photo Reconnaissance work in North Africa and was hailed as an innovation. Hours were saved in the delivery of prints to General Headquarters. From this time on, the Forward Unit system marked the operational success of NAPRW.[1111]

Obviously, as an "*objet trouvé*" the Potez was not necessarily the best choice for its new task, but it was available. The attachment of Free French to Elliott's wing assisted him in the use of French equipment. However, the French squadron, Groupe II/33 "Savoie" allocated to the 3rd PRG would be equipped with American Lightnings, and was not operational until much later in 1943. The Potez was an entirely improvised initiative, and is listed as having been grounded on 12 July 1943.[1112]

The Potez operated with Unit 1, providing "instant photoshop" for the bombers:

> Colonel Roosevelt descended upon us for a flying visit. He was highly pleased, and after a visit to the bomber command, more than pleased. For they were boundlessly enthusiastic. Until now they had had to plan missions on the basis of a terse, condensed photo interpreter's report made at the base several hundred miles away. Now they were receiving pictures of the day's work in time to plan the work for tomorrow. They couldn't be getting hotter coverage from a winged tabloid photographer. One general had been particularly delighted with a certain print, and was carrying it about with him everywhere.

And he had left word that he was to be called at whatever time of the day or night fresh pictures came in. The idea was proven an unqualified success.[1113]

Not only that: from accounts in the files it seems that this crew was particularly elated that the collaboration with Monsieur Arnould resulted in the organization of delightful French cuisine from the neighboring villages in return for American staples. (Maybe that's why they called him "Chef.")

You will not find the Potez on the register of American aircraft that participated in World War II. But, in its unique way, this one did, and it struck a subtle blow for Franco-American collaboration.

EXTRACURRICULAR ACTIVITIES

Elliott Roosevelt made a big impression everywhere he went, but it was not always the same kind of impression.

A combat camera man, Tech Sergeant Robert Thompson, wrote a stark memoir of his wartime service fifty years after the events. He offered several illuminating vignettes of conditions in North Africa. A few of them presented a most undignified, even repugnant image of Colonel Roosevelt.

The worst first: in Biskra, Algeria, Thompson's unit had a highly valued air-conditioned photo-processing trailer, brought along as original equipment from the United States. This trailer was important due to the environmental control that photo development required. Up in Algiers, the Colonel heard about this prize, and through channels demanded it be turned over to him. As this would cripple his unit's work, Thompson would not voluntarily surrender it until his commanding General so ordered him.[1114]

The men were so enraged they stuffed a vile, rotted cheese into the air conditioning system for the trailer's two photo laboratories. Then it was carted off to Elliott Roosevelt's Maison Blanche headquarters, and Thompson was given a few days off until he calmed down.

The trailer travails left a trace in the archives. After a confrontation, on 2 February 1943, Lt. Col. Roosevelt wrote an enraged letter to his commander:

> In a telephone conversation this date, Colonel Peter Rask, Chief of Staff of the 12th Air Support Command accused the undersigned directly of lying about a photographic trailer, which had been ordered to the 3rd PRG without the knowledge of the undersigned. He further directly accused the undersigned of lying regarding reasons given why an advance unit of this organization, now at Telergma, had not been attached to the 12th Air Support Command….it is requested that Colonel Rask be called upon to prove the truth of his accusations, including the statement that the undersigned deliberately lied to him, or withdraw them.[1115]

That was an early example of "classical Elliottese." In response, Colonel Rask, a supply officer, collected statements from a number of witnesses backing up his charges. For example, Colonel Paul Williams stated:

> I was present in my office when the telephone conversation in question was being carried on between Colonel Rask and Lt. Col. Roosevelt. Colonel Rask was irritated because of the continued delay in the movement of this equipment. He said words substantially as follows: 'I know it is a good trailer and you would like to have it but it is ordered here and you have no business keeping it.' At no time, however, did he indicate that Colonel Roosevelt was deliberately lying to him, or in any words indicate this.[1116]

It seems that under cover of rank, Elliott stole, or "organized," equipment for his unit. That wasn't uncommon in those chaotic days. Colonel Rask was trying to put a stop to it. But in the end it was he who was reassigned, and Elliott who prospered. Sergeant Thompson's account differed somewhat:

> 'Sergeant, you've got to let Captain Wallace take the trailer with him.' – 'Excuse me, general, but you know better than anybody that we can't support your groups without it.' – 'Colonel Roosevelt and I discussed it on the phone and as of *now* it's *his*.'[1117]

The incident might have had something to do with the unit's attempts to protect and retain its equipment in general. It turns out that Army units, hard pressed at the front and always in need of something or other, made a habit of absconding with such goodies as panel trucks or other major items. In war, as in prison, people are admired on the basis of what they can scrounge through dark and mysterious ways. The group eventually posted highway checkpoints to thwart such daring enterprises.

In this case the caper apparently wasn't admired by too many. Of course we only have the tech sergeant's version of this row, but next time Thompson was in Algiers, he visited Roosevelt's headquarters:

> The trailer was still there, all right, parked between two trees. I drove up to it wondering if I was about to have a confrontation with the President's son. He wasn't there, but four fellows were busy stripping everything out of it. I said, "Hey, what are you guys doing?"
>
> "We are throwing all of this junk out of here so we can convert it into an air-conditioned villa for Colonel Roosevelt."
>
> Converting it into a villa? I couldn't believe it. Here was a piece of equipment that had been serving the war effort in a very important way and then some big shot came along and grabbed it to satisfy his own personal comfort! Everybody sacrifices a few personal needs during wartime, but not the President's son!
>
> My thoughts at that moment were, "I'd like to punch him. I'd like to punch that SOP – that Son of a President!"[1118]

One reason Sergeant Thompson was so furious that he saw stars – at least his commanding general's star – was that this wasn't his first run-in with the "SOP." During his initial assignment at 8th Air Force HQ in High Wycombe, England, before TORCH, Thompson met Roosevelt for the first time:

> It usually happens that a "rotten egg" shows up in every group. The rotten egg sitting in one corner was Lieutenant Colonel Elliott Roosevelt. It soon occurred to me that he had

> not achieved that lofty rank because of a knowledge of photography, but because he was the son of the president of the United States.
>
> I wasn't sure why Captain van Cleave was so interested in finding out what kind of rings Colonel Roosevelt wore, but I was able to report that he wore *no* rings. [the captain was a freemason and they apparently wear special rings]
>
> Roosevelt had a habit of disappearing for three or four days, and then returning for long enough to put his feet up on his desk, lean back, lace his fingers behind his head and relate the details of his conquests in London. I knew that rank had its privileges, but I was not impressed.[1119]

The freemason remark is curious. Shortly after his father was elected president, FDR had Elliott initiated as a "third degree mason" – the master mason level – in a very elaborate ritual at the New York Masonic Lodge. It was noted that Franklin D. Roosevelt, attending the ceremony, was "Grand Representative of the Grand Lodge of Georgia near New York" – whatever that meant.[1120] Later reports held that it was public knowledge that FDR belonged to Holland Lodge nr. 8 in Manhattan. Press photos of this event were dug up later when it suited certain ill-tempered people.[1121]

It must have meant a lot to the president, who loved ritual and ceremony, especially as long as he was the center of attention. Two years later he took pains to get James and Franklin Jr. elevated to master masons. It was reported that the president himself had attained the 32nd degree; but since masons keep their secrets, the public was left to fantasize about what this meant.[1122]

As is well-known, some people believe "the Jews" are behind "everything" in the world. Others reserve this honor for the Freemasons, or for even more obscure groups. The Nazis, however, thought these all were behind everything together, and when the war came they made hay out of the Roosevelt's "masonry." The Berlin press went amok when the Germans received a photograph of Roosevelt and his sons engaged in this ancient, monstrous conspiracy:

> Without exception, morning newspapers published on their front pages a picture of President Roosevelt with his sons, James, Franklin, and Elliott, at a Masonic lodge session. According to Nazi tenets, being a Mason is almost a cardinal sin and the picture is supposed to be particularly damning evidence.[i]

Further on in his war memoir, Sergeant Thompson went on to recount an episode in England in which he had disassembled a K-20 aerial camera into its 109 pieces, laid out in strict order on his desk. When he later returned to his desk to reassemble the camera for his practice, suddenly nothing fit. It turned out that Colonel Roosevelt had scrambled the order while the poor sergeant was out. After watching the confusion, Elliott left the room laughing his head off. Thompson did not find it funny at all.[1123]

Thompson was then told that the president's son was a practical joker. He probably didn't know that this was an inherited trait. Among his staff, President Roosevelt was well-known for his pranks, many of which unfortunately involved the humiliation of his underlings. Harriman said the president always enjoyed the discomfort of others.[1124]

---

[i] 23 JUL 41, reported by AP from Berlin to numerous newspapers. The item was taken from *Völkischer Beobachter*, headlined: "Roosevelt is the main tool of Jewish world freemasonry." The accompanying photo had been found in Oslo Masonic HQ. Nazis also referred to President "Rosenfeld" and his "Jew Deal."

James Roosevelt wrote of several elaborate cases where the president taunted and fooled his advisers at dinner – Henry Morgenthau, for example, was cheated at poker via an elaborate ruse. We shall see this trait again at the Teheran and Yalta summits.

Inevitably, commanders are liked or disliked depending on the extent to which their personal characteristics fit with those whom they command – not so much on whether they are capable officers. Popularity is, however, rarely uniform, and resentment can be triggered by trivia – such as being of the wrong political party. While many sneered at Elliott, many others admired him. One officer, Major Albert Weaver, wrote the president in 1943: "Am looking forward to serving again with Col. Elliott anywhere he might go and that is the sentiment of every man in the whole [3rd] group."[1125]

In contrast, superiors should and must evaluate commanders on the results they produce. It seems that Elliott, popular or not, produced impressive results.

Elliott's superiors, Generals Spaatz, Doolittle, Arnold, and Eisenhower, thought well enough of him to entrust him with progressively higher duties. At Casablanca, Elliott was elevated to command the joint Allied reconnaissance unit, the NAPRW. Much of the success in hammering together an effective joint command must be attributed to the enthusiasm, energy, and determination of Elliott Roosevelt.

Busy as he must have been, it seems extraordinary that Elliott could find time for some of the other exploits that would reach public attention. Sometimes, he had no choice. In January 1943, when he attended the Casablanca conference, the newspapers made note of his recent accomplishments.

Later that year, Elliott would also attend the Cairo conference, where Chiang kai-Shek joined Churchill and Roosevelt, and then Teheran, where he met and was won over by Marshal Joseph Stalin. His recollections, though highly questionable, are essential for understanding the dynamics of these critical summits, and they provide us with gossipy snapshots of Stalin, Churchill, Giraud, de Gaulle, Chiang, and the planeloads of top generals, admirals, and marshals who milled around at the summits.

Throughout *As He Saw It* Elliott maintained an almost cartoonish anti-British, pro-Stalin attitude, but how much did he really hate the British? Enough that he repeatedly found it necessary to deny it. Perhaps the best answer was given by his mother. Eleanor revealed that when she visited England in 1942, she was concerned about Elliott's anglophobia. She found that Elliott's posting there had evidently softened his views: "Eleanor had a long talk with Elliott, and was pleased to note that his hostility towards the English was changing to admiration."[1126] Nonetheless, Elliott's later writings showed that he had a way to go in liking the Limeys; the Frogs and the Krauts fared no better.

In fairness, this kind of sniping occurred on both sides. It's a human characteristic; but it should not be tolerated at high level. Eisenhower had to emit stern reminders that the Allies were not supposed to be fighting each other, but the enemy. In fact, he thought his Yanks didn't hate the Germans enough![1127] Doolittle quoted one of his officers that "getting along with the British was almost as hard as winning the war… I had to keep an iron hand to prevent all-out combat."[1128]

Elliott's relationship with Winston Churchill, having started off with at least well-feigned admiration, foundered completely at the Teheran summit in December 1943 and turned to mutual detestation, an unfortunate turn of events considering the importance of personal relationships at this level. But Elliott seemed to get along well with British air commanders; often the air folks stick together, regardless of nationality, a phenomenon that was even more impressively demonstrated in the later operation in the Soviet Union.

We may also gingerly note that for some time in 1944, Elliott was romantically linked – at least in the media – with Mary Churchill, the PM's youngest daughter, who often served her father as *aide-de-camp*. How this came about is unknown; he claimed not to have met her. What we do know is that Elliott was a notorious womanizer whose extracurricular activities kept the rumor mills turning back home.[i]

A Ruth Here and a Ruth there…

As we have seen, being posted overseas did not restrain Elliott in the mating department. And in the sands of the Sahara he carried on a most public affair with a top staff assistant, Captain Ruth Briggs. He had met her in Algiers, playing cards with the top generals at headquarters. Journalists knew of the romance, but since Elliott was generally popular with reporters, and other top officers acted likewise, there was no commotion. But the rumors filtered back.[1129]

Briggs was one of the initial five WAACs (Women's Army Auxiliary Corps) sent to Algeria at the explicit request of General Eisenhower, who needed French-speaking secretaries. Early in the morning on 21 December 1942 their ship, the troopship *Strathallan*, was torpedoed a few hours short of Oran, and the survivors took to the lifeboats.

Due to favorable conditions, almost all of the thousands aboard were saved – including the five WAACs. Along with them survived Eisenhower's comely driver Kay Summersby, and, fortuitously, the renowned photo journalist Margaret Bourke-White, who described the harrowing episode to readers back home. The ladies of Eisenhower's staff formed a strong bond, and most stayed with the general through the war. In military history, these "first five" have attained legendary status.[ii] "We came to know each other as sisters," said Kay Summersby.[1130]

Elliott Roosevelt came to know them better than that. Accounts of his escapades differ. One remarkably positive version was provided in the unpublished recollections of Mattie Pinette, one of the five:

> I know a lot of bad things happened to him after he got out of the Army, and I know they were bad, at the same time he was a very good friend to all of us five WACs. If his mother sent us some coffee, he'd always share it with us and of course that abominable coffee that they had in the Army, we were very happy to have a good cup of coffee now and then. He used to come over and eat with us; he said our mess was a heck of a lot better than his mess. So we'd just set up an extra plate and he'd eat with us. If he ever had anything, he always shared it.
>
> Not only that, we had lost all our kit at sea, you know, and here was this beautiful Mediterranean and these nice beaches and on our half day off we wanted to go swimming but we didn't have any bathing suits so when he goes to Cairo, he picks up 3 or 4 bathing suits and brings them to us so we'd have something to go swimming in. Then, I didn't have a bag to put any clothes in, after I acquired some clothes, one of his aviators got

---

[i] TIME, 27 MAR 44, 17 JUL 44. The press also linked ER to Princess Marina, the Duchess of Kent.

[ii] LIFE, 22 FEB 43. WAAC became WAC later in 1943.

killed, Lt. Hessler. He says, "He doesn't need that bag any more, but you could use it. I'll bring it!"

He was also married several times. He was attractive to women and women chased him and he didn't run away. And most of the Roosevelts are that way. So you can't just blame the boys for everything that's happened to their marriages. But Elliott could come into your bedroom, even though you were just in pajamas, he wouldn't even notice anything. …

He was like a brother to all of us. Except Ruth, of course. [1131]

Elliott Roosevelt zeroed in on Captain Ruth, a 36-year old former social worker. She was intelligent and competent. Their liaison was so generally acknowledged that word filtered back to the United States. This so distressed the other Ruth (Googins), back home on the ranch in Texas, that she complained to the president, who could only offer that "these things happen" in wartime.[1132]

Indeed they do. FDR's own dalliances are by now well known, thanks in part to Elliott, but the president was also highly entertained to discover that Elliott's boss, General Eisenhower, was a bit close with the Irish-born model Kay Summersby, his driver. A historian noted:

FDR delighted in gossip and, having met Kay in Algiers in 1943, was convinced she and Eisenhower were having an affair. "Roosevelt had come to the conclusion, he confided in his daughter Anna, that this attractive young British woman was sleeping with General Eisenhower! What made the subject even more titillating was that Anna's brother, FDR, Jr., had fallen hard for Kay Summersby but nevertheless regarded her as unstable and "a bit of a psychopathic case." [1133]

Overstated as the unconsummated Ike-Kay liaison has been, this odd endorsement suggests that Elliott's own affair was well known and tolerated. That's because Kay and Ruth were tight friends, and they and their bosses socialized together.

The WACs were in a difficult situation. They were often viewed as sluts back home, and the pressures of war and the hardly enlightened attitudes of the day exacted their toll. It was a smart WAC who attached herself to an important officer and obtained the benefits and protection he could extend.

Now it happened that Elliott Roosevelt's deputy commanding officer and frequent pilot, the able Lt. Col. Harry T. Eidson, was going back to the States to see if he could scare up some help for the reconnaissance squadrons. Elliott asked him to drop by the White House as well as Ruth's ranch in Texas to try to mollify the infuriated wife.[1134] The mollification succeeded above all expectations.

The loss of Eidson (and Ruth Googins's proportional gain) occurred in a curiously roundabout manner. In January 1943, when the reconnaissance group had been depleted in Africa, Headquarters asked for experienced personnel to assist in solving the problems that had now become too obvious to ignore. As Elliott testified:

Mr. ROOSEVELT. The next thing … was that they asked for personnel from our theater in January 1942 [sic], that had combat experience. Well, actually, we had very few pilots that were able to give very many combat missions before they got lost. We managed to get one man through five missions. His name was Col. Harry Eidson, whose name I have mentioned here. He was sent back by me. He was one of the squadron commanders, and sent back to Washington D.C., to give them advice on what could be done to reorganize and speed up the reconnaissance, the overall reconnaissance program, in the United States.

Senator FERGUSON. When did he return to the United States?

Mr. ROOSEVELT. January 1943. He remained over here for the remainder of the war, and I believe he did start back over to the European theater, but he got in a plane accident at Ascension Island, and cracked up permanently.

Senator FERGUSON. What was that?

Mr. ROOSEVELT. I think that was in – late; about December of 1943, I believe; November or December of 1943, and I know that he was in and out of hospitals, because at the end of the war, when I saw him last, he was still very much confined in hospitals. That was in 1945.[1135]

Colonel Roosevelt was so generous as to give Harry Eidson a letter of introduction to the White House, so he could tell the president and the family of their adventures in North Africa. This Eidson did on his visit there on 3 February 1943.[1136] The president was on his way home from Casablanca, but, apparently, Grace Tully, the White House secretary, thought she was fatefully responsible for introducing Eidson to the visiting Ruth Googins, telling her:

> Oh, he seems like a very nice young man, although he didn't impress me particularly one way or another. He's short and not very attractive but I thought perhaps you would like to ask him to tea and hear about what Elliott is doing in North Africa.[1137]

Actually Ruth knew Harry perfectly well, because he and Elliott had gone through training together and were close friends. Grace Tully was blameless in what followed.

While Eidson apparently did not succeed in straightening out the reconnaissance crisis with the Air Force, he made far more progress on his home-front morale task. When Elliott himself came home in August 1943, he complained that his young son David greeted him with "Harry!" – and Ruth was now no longer so interested in remaining married to him. To the distress of his parents, Elliott talked flippantly about another divorce. He was not lacking for female company at home or abroad.[1138]

Preserved correspondence between Ruth and Eleanor Roosevelt indicate that the ladies were far more upset about the breakup than was Elliott. Eleanor thought Ruth should at least wait to demand a divorce until the war was over. But by January 1944, Ruth had had enough, and she initiated the process to replace her philandering husband. She filed for divorce on 16 March, reported the Secret Service detachment at her ranch, and it was granted on 17 April. The family immediately sold the ranch and left the three agents to seek new postings. Eleanor was "sick at heart and grieving for the children." She thought the president's health was declining in part because of this new marital setback – "though he has said nothing."[1139] Friend and biographer Joe Lash wrote:

> At the moment it was Elliott who wrote her from overseas about his troubles with his wife Ruth. She is "upset, more upset than I have seen her," Trude [Mrs. Lash] wrote me. "Ruth wants a divorce right away and Elliott told Jimmy he hoped he would crash. She's upset because she feels she did not start Elliott out in life right. Has [Trude's son] if he should go wrong a right to reproach me as Elliott reproaches Mrs. R? What a shortsighted,

> tormented and pitiful person he must be! She seems the only one who can help because he can never seriously doubt her love.[i]

Shortsighted, perhaps. Tormented and pitiful? Hardly. And Eleanor did not yet know that Ruth had usurped the affections of Elliott's pilot.

On 27 November 1943, during the long flight back to Italy, Harry Eidson crashed F-8 Mosquito 43-34929 in a severe landing accident at Wideawake Field on Ascension Island in the middle of the Atlantic. This was one of twenty Canadian Mosquitoes originally intended for the Mediterranean. One source says the plane was sabotaged, but that was a commonly used alibi in those days; in fact, Eidson had undershot the sloping island runway while returning with one feathered propeller.[1140]

With a smashed leg, Eidson returned to Texas an invalid, to retire at the rank of colonel. Ruth visited him at the hospital and helped nurse him back to health. He then got the run of the ranch, though on crutches.

Elliott was eager to get matters over with and did not contest the divorce. In the London Embassy he signed over most of his community property to the couple's then three small children. Ruth got custody, of course, but Elliott kept the horses and eventually gave them to a generous friend of FDR's, Walter Kirschner. Faye Emerson, Ruth's replacement, later said that Elliott gave up without a fight because Ruth "would go to tremendous lengths to get what she wanted," and he could not afford the discredit to the president's family resulting from a long, bitter legal fight. But, reporters thought, a disputed split would also have brought out some extra names that the new wife, Faye, didn't know of.[1141]

Ruth married Harry Eidson shortly after divorcing Elliott in March 1944. As the newspapers reported on 23 June:

> Convalescing from a leg fracture and other injuries, he laid aside a cane after entering the church with the bride, and walked up the center aisle without it. [They] met at Colorado Springs in the summer of 1942 during organization of the photo reconnaissance group to which both he and Colonel Roosevelt were attached.[1142]

Maritally, both Ruth and Elliott claimed to have been severely wronged. As the Bureau of Internal Revenue and Congress found out later, Ruth did quite well financially. Colonel Eidson seems to have been a wise catch indeed. With a DFC and a Purple Heart, he was a genuine war hero, married to a radio-station executive, and with the leisure to pursue an esteemed career in the actuarial and pension management business. Despite the indignity of having to beg the President of the United States to tell his son to keep his pecker in his pants, the Texas-based Ruth ended up way ahead in comparison.

Of course, Elliott said Ruth divorced him. In private, he was more contrite. He wrote his mother: "If she has decided to go ahead now, I can't blame her. After all, she is perfectly right, as I am the one who failed in our marriage. I'm afraid I just won't make a fittin' husband for anybody…I'm sorry, because if I couldn't succeed with Ruth I will never be able to do so for anyone." [1143]

Yet Ruth claimed "unkind, harsh, and tyrannical conduct" and that her husband had said he no longer cared about her.[1144]

---

[i] Lash: A World of Love, in reference to 10 DEC 43 entry; "Elliott's letter disturbs and depresses me greatly," wrote Eleanor to Lash.

About the first thing the newly-wed Eidsons did was to move closer to town and sell the Benbrook ranch to an Oklahoma oilman. The Roosevelt family wouldn't have anything to return to.[1145]

The other, African-based Ruth now might have thought herself the winner in the battle for Elliott's affections. She was no mere pretty young "girl soldier," as the expression went in those days, but General Eisenhower's and then General Walter Bedell Smith's most formidable secretary.[1146] She was so good she stayed in top company, rising to Lieutenant Colonel.

From Ike's driver and companion, Kay Summersby, we know that Ruth, Kay, Elliott, the generals, and assorted staff did some memorable sightseeing and socializing in Africa during 1943.[1147] But Ruth did not become Mrs. Elliott Roosevelt Nr. 3. Some matters of great importance intervened. To find them out, we first have to make a detour to meet Mr. Howard R. Hughes.

THE HUGHES-ROOSEVELT CAPER

The striking new genre in modern painting known as Air Force "nose art" suggests that most airmen, in their dreams, would prefer to see themselves suddenly transported from the flak-shredded skies of Europe to some Southern California swimming pool, surrounded by naked movie stars. The dream would come true for very few, but Colonel Elliott Roosevelt was among them.

For him, it had been a stunning rise from suspected draft dodger to General Arnold's reconnaissance guru only three years later. By July 1943, Elliott's complaints about American aircraft and his insistence on getting "something like" the Mosquito had reached Washington, where they gave aid and comfort to an already existing but embattled school of thought.

As Roosevelt later testified to Congress, in early summer the Assistant Secretary of War for Air, Robert Lovett, came to Tunisia to discuss the problem. Lovett suggested that Elliott go back to the States to be placed in charge of all photo-reconnaissance. At that time, the AAF director of photography was Colonel Minton Kaye.

> Mr. ROOSEVELT…He told me that he and General Arnold had been getting a great many complaints from all theaters, and he told me that the Ground Forces in particular were so disgusted with the lack of intelligence material from reconnaissance aviation provided by the AAF, that they were agitating to take over and separate reconnaissance aviation from the Air Forces and control it themselves.
>
> …And then Mr. Lovett said: You have performed a terrific job here…and you seem to have satisfied at least partially the Ground Force commanders and General Eisenhower, and the Air Force Bomber Commands – who equally were very dissatisfied, in all theaters with the reconnaissance materiel that they were getting, and who were blaming reconnaissance aviation for the poor showing made by the bombers.
>
> So he said: I am going to order you back to Washington to the Pentagon Building, and put you in charge of the Reconnaissance Branch.

> I begged him very, very forcefully not to do that. I said:
>
> You can't do that, sir, because of the fact of who I am. While I have had considerable overseas experience, I am the son of the President of the United States, and you will open him to a great criticism if you bring me back and have me sit out the war in the Pentagon Building, and you will give the Members of Congress who don't like Franklin Roosevelt a wonderful opportunity to get up and smear him.
>
> ...Mr. Lovett said: I agree with you, that it would be wrong, but I am going to talk it over with Hap Arnold. He called him that to me, sir. I call him General Arnold. And then he told me that he was going to talk to General Arnold and request my return on temporary duty to Washington, D.C...
>
> As soon as he returned, practically overnight a cable arrived ordering me to return to Washington.[1148]

After ten months overseas, Colonel Roosevelt arrived in the White House on 22 July, twelve days after the invasion of Sicily began. Ruth was already there, and apparently there were some "issues." At least Eleanor wrote shortly thereafter that "I loved seeing Elliott but I felt Ruth was entitled to him as much alone as she could have him & you know fundamentally we think so little alike on many things that tho' I love him, I have to be careful when with him & that means that short visits are better than long ones!"

Elliott was getting ready for some reconnaissance in California, and he didn't take his wife with him.

Off to Hollywood

Elliott's new assignment was to survey potential reconnaissance aircraft in general, and in particular to evaluate a new aircraft promoted by the Hughes Aircraft Company in Culver City, California (just north of the present KLAX international airport). This innocent undertaking lit the fuse of another scandal, though it wouldn't detonate until FDR was out of office.

Here it is necessary to split the narrative. The procurement saga occurred in secret at the height of the war, but the circumstances in which it was conducted exploded upon the national stage during the 1947 Senate investigation. For chronological consistency, the revelations, though startling, of those Senate hearings must be mainly dealt with in due course. However, the aeronautically significant details were very carefully recorded in the Air Materiel Command's secret *Case History of the Hughes D-2, D-5, and F-11 Project*, issued to selected recipients in August 1946.

Writing in 1946, Elliott was publicly a bit elliptical about the assignment, perhaps realizing there would be more explaining to come:

> Our troops were in the process of cleaning up the last Nazis in Sicily when, late in July, from the War Department to my commanding general came a request that I be sent back to the States, to consult on questions of reorganization of reconnaissance operations. At the same time, from the Pacific theater was coming Colonel Karl Polifka, who had been doing work similar to mine. The request meant two months' assignment in Washington, August and September; and while I regretted leaving my command still I looked forward to seeing Father and Mother and the rest of the family – those of them who were not overseas on duty.

> The work I had in the Pentagon was absorbing and bore importantly on our future reconnaissance operations but, fortunately for me, it was not so exacting but what I had several opportunities to chat with Father.
>
> He was not looking as well as I would have liked to find him: he had aged perceptibly, even since Casablanca, six months before…A very few days later, Father and a group of his advisers took a train north for another meeting with the British Prime Minister and their chiefs of staff, at Quebec. This was the conference which was code-named QUADRANT, and I was unable to attend it in any capacity, by reason of my air forces assignment, which took me, during the month of August, out to California – to various manufacturing plants and the airfield at Muroc Dry Lake – three or four times, working on special reconnaissance problems.[1149]

When Elliott reported to General Arnold in the Pentagon on 1 August, he was given rather explicit instructions. Because of the furious complaints Arnold had received about reconnaissance in every theater, Elliott was to "look into the whole problem of the reconnaissance program of the USAAF, and figure out a way whereby we can overcome the objections and not be forced to turn over reconnaissance units to the control of the ground forces" – a fate worse than death from the Air Force's standpoint – "and at the same time rectify it so that both the Air Force and the ground force in all theaters will get proper service."[1150] But not only that:

> Mr. ROOSEVELT. General Arnold told me and Mr. Lovett that reconnaissance was very poor, but that under no circumstances was I to come in there and pull apart the whole fighter program, because he knew that I would recommend it if I had my way; I would pick off all of the best fighters and take the guns out and put cameras in and lighten them up…He said, "Don't you dare do that."[1151]

That ban on interference did not extend to Howard Hughes's other big project, the giant Hercules flying boat. The military services would have loved to see that expensive project cancelled, but politics overruled them.

Hughes Aircraft Company: It is going to blow up right in your face!

Elliott assembled a team of five experts to travel to California and investigate new candidate aircraft. He himself focused on the Hughes design number two (D-2) and a proposed modified version known as the D-5. The D-2 looked a bit like a larger, sleeker P-38. As usual, the engines were the key to the projected performance, but the proposed Wright Tornado engines never materialized.

Hughes had been trying to interest the Air Corps in his project for a long time without success. In March 1940, Wright Field had paid a nominal $50 to be kept informed about the plane, but the procurement czar, General Oliver P. Echols, had no faith in Hughes Aircraft's ability to deliver.[1152]

Although Howard R. Hughes was at that time already intermittently insane, he was able to function well enough to impress visitors, and he still basked in the breathless adoration of the media. He especially kept the public's attention during the controversy surrounding his new movie, *The Outlaw,* a Western devoted primarily to displaying young actress Jane Russell's allegedly extraordinary breasts.

But Hughes's heart was still in aviation. He was obsessed with breaking into the military market with his aircraft, which he thought were far ahead of all others. In June 1943 he test-flew the then R-2800 powered D-2 at Harper Dry Lake, near Barstow, California. For only two short hops, the results were awful. The military later said the airplane proved to "have a lift somewhat less than expected" in addition to unstable airflow over the ailerons.[i]

It was clear that major changes were needed. As the Air Staff recorded on 13 August, at the very time Colonel Roosevelt was formulating his gushing recommendation:

> The DX-2 made its first flight on June 20, 1943. After 35 minutes, it was landed and returned to the shop for modification. Subsequent flight have brought the total time on the airplane to over 9 hours, but the changes found necessary became so numerous and so drastic that the DX-2 design eventually was abandoned and a new design, the D 5, evolved. As far as the AAF is concerned, the DX-2 project must now be considered closed.[1153]

Hughes Aircraft Co. (HAC) was then a quite small outfit. Although it had some war subcontracts, it still served essentially as a hobby shop for its famous owner. The Hughes Tool Company, which made madly profitable petroleum drilling equipment, subsidized it. HAC reportedly lacked direction, effective management, and the disciplines of cost and schedule that otherwise ride defense contractors like demons. Some people would later refer to it as a "country club," which is in accord with the reputation HAC maintained for years after the war.

In 1943, when Elliott Roosevelt twice visited Hughes Aircraft, the outfit was still able to put on a good show to those of less skeptical bent. We have, however, a rather terrifying snapshot of what was really going on in a telephone conversation recorded for posterity and entered as evidence in the Senate hearings four years later. This transcript was recorded between the two Air Corps evaluation visits in the summer of 1943:

> Memorandum.
>
> On Friday, August 27, Mr. Ed Bern, General Manager, Hughes Aircraft Corp., called Mr. Nelson [Chairman, War Production Board] and the conversation went in general as follows:
>
> BERN. We have got a terribly chaotic situation out here. It is going to blow right up in your face. I was put in as General Manager of this company 58 (?) days ago, and I took 30 days to study it and sent a report to Howard on the 12th that I thought the job was being sabotaged, retarded, held up by a clique that wanted to do the building of it. Howard studied it by remote control from his home (he is making his decisions from his home). The newspapers have been tipped off that there is a bad deal out here. I have been with American Airlines for so long. They called me (meaning the newspapers). I have not gone to the plant for two days. They are running it like a bunch of school kids would do business. I tried to get hold of Grover [Loening] before I called you, and when he was out here I could not even see him. I still have to work for a living, and I do not want to be tied up with anything that is a lie or anything that involves our Government funds. I sent through this report, and every report is a lie. Even when I was in Washington they sent me reports that were not the truth. I have tried to clean up the place. I have so much opposition, and yet I am the responsible party. Now Howard is making his decision today to turn four or five departments over to the Engineering Department to operate. The CAA

---

[i] SBC Hearings, 1947, PART 40, 24482. The Pratt & Whitney R-2800 was common and highly rated.

> men here will not approve it. The boy who is the Chief Engineer [Kenneth Ridley] on the project was a $135 man until about four months ago, now is $165, with four years' experience. I have been in the business for 26 years and I am trying to clean things up and they will not let me.
>
> NELSON. Who will not let you?
>
> BERN. Howard interferes -...Howard owns the company. The only time we see him is at his home late at night – at 10, 11, 12, or 1 or 2 in the morning...We have got a Kaiser-Hughes deal here that has a $400,000 a year payroll, padded up with ex-Hollywood people, and I am trying to clean out the thing so that the little reputation I have is not ruined. The CAA is out here and know the picture and DPC know the picture, and I would recommend that you get a report from them and them only. See my point? We are to deliver this plane in November, and there are about 170 pieces made and 9½ million of the money gone. I am brought in at a late stage trying to clean it up, and I cannot do it. I cannot get availability and go back where I feel I am doing something. So help me God, it is going to blow up in your face. I do not want to be a part of it...[1154]

That was HAC's manager talking – although he quit that day. And that testimony was by no means the only screams of shock and horror emanating from the company. Thus there was good reason for the Air Force to be worried. The quoted conversation confirms the picture of managerial if not technical incompetence bordering on insanity when it comes to Howard Hughes, and the suspicion that early days in the Hughes Aircraft Co. had more to do with some people "in the loop" exploiting the old man for their own enrichment and entertainment.

This counterbalances the shallow but prevalent interpretation, favored by his fawning fans, that Hughes was a man of genius persecuted by mediocrities in Congress and by devious competitors. It would be a long time before Hughes Aircraft became a respected company in the industry, and when it did, it was because Howard decided to essentially let the Air Force and its trusted people – read retired officers – run it. Although it never produced successful airplanes, HAC's glory days came when it pioneered defense electronics in the 1950s and 1960s.

However, from the beginning Hughes insisted on leading edge technology, and he was not particularly concerned about costs. HAC could get away with this, first because of the Hughes Tool subsidy, and, after 1947, because it concentrated on electronics, where profit margins were higher and more certain than in the airframe business.

The company's rehabilitation was largely the work of Lawrence "Pat" Hyland, who ran it for four decades. Hyland, a radar expert who came from the Bendix Corporation, assumed his post in November 1954, and said later: "Looking back, I realize that at the time I had the 'rose-colored glasses' public view of Howard Hughes. I didn't understand the total intertwining of his diverse operations. They were out of control."[1155] HAC was rescued by Pat Hyland and a number of retired Air Force generals, among whom Ira Eaker and Harold George were perhaps the best known.

Prior to the war, HAC had built the H-1 Racer, which for all the glory it earned Howard had no military application; it was not designed with ruggedness and survivability in mind, and it nearly killed Hughes when he mishandled a test flight. It is absurd to maintain, as Hughes did, that later fighter planes, foreign and domestic, were copied from the H-1. Likewise, neither the D-2 nor the F-11 was derived from the Hughes H-1.

When war broke out and the aircraft industry was stretched beyond its wildest earlier imaginations, Hughes wanted in on the action, but he refused to follow the rules.

He pursued glory over profit, for the drum-tight labor market during the war would have easily enabled HAC to prosper as a subcontractor; but Howard wanted to build his own airplanes, and to force the Air Corps to buy them. The resulting prolonged squabble gave rise to some of the great legends of aviation – but no usable aircraft.

The Hughes D-2, DX-2, DX-2A, D-3, D-5, DX-5, XA-37, XP-73 and…F-11

From a 30 June 1942 Air Force memorandum:

> Hughes Model DX-2A. Has been submitted as a convoy protector, convoy destroyer, pursuit airplane, fighter, and light bombardment type. Its longest life has been as a convoy protector, but the latest specification which will be used in the negotiations calls it a fighter. If the present airplane is completed as a military weapon, it will have armament substantially as on the XP-58. Its sole claim to being a bomber is the fact that it is equipped with bomb bay doors. Since it is to be purchased in its commercial form…it is considered advisable to call it the XP-73 for the sake of administering the contract.[1156]

This designation soup shows that the Air Corps was struggling to find a use for this unsolicited offering from Hughes. Interestingly, a reconnaissance role wasn't even thought of at first. Since the aircraft ended its short life as the XF-11, we shall default to that moniker. (The X stood for the two flying prototypes.)

By a remarkable coincidence, at the outbreak of war two great names set out on the same quest: to build the fastest aircraft in the world, one the air force would simply have to buy even though it had been privately developed. One of these two men was Geoffrey de Havilland, and we have seen what became of his Mosquito. The other was Howard Hughes. His plane would be an utter disaster, aeronautical, financial, and political.

Both men chose an unorthodox manufacturing technique in order to get the sleekest design, and to circumvent any impending aluminum shortage. De Havilland went for wood. It was new only in its application to high speed aircraft, but in his hands it turned out to be surprisingly successful. Not everyone was convinced of its durability and strength, though.

Hughes had become infatuated with a variant of plywood called Duramold, a wood-and-resin glued sandwich material that showed great promise in principle, but turned out to be difficult to use in practice. When finished, it made for a smooth, slippery surface. Hughes used it in the D-2 and the HK-1 Hercules. However, as the Air Force held, no two pieces of wood are alike, and no one piece of wood is alike on two different days or two different places.[1157]

The Hughes-Kaiser HK-1 (later, H-4), was ridiculed as the "Spruce Goose" by the media. Only one was completed, but the original idea was to build five hundred of the monsters. This was a project of the War Production Board (WPB), headed by civilians Donald Nelson and (from 1944) Julius Krug. The Army and Navy considered this project a terrible waste, and of course they strongly opposed others' waste.

Hughes's original intention with the D-2 is unclear, but it is obvious that he was thinking more in terms of a private racer than a military aircraft, which requires a sturdy and maintainable construction. This initial discrepancy would be the font of the Materiel Division's long, rancorous struggle against Hughes's airplanes.

As early as October 1941, Wright Field complained about the plywood. The USAAF's top officers much preferred aluminum. They knew it worked, and it facilitated manufacturing and maintenance. In August 1943, the Air Force canceled its biggest wooden airplane project, the Curtiss C-76 transport. It had been a deadly disaster.

Materiel Command's secret case history of the F-11 is the best guide to the saga, and the following account is based on it and the Senate investigation of 1947.

By late 1943 the fears of an aluminum shortage had been convincingly put to rest. Contrariwise, in Germany, manufacturers were increasingly forced to use wood, even in jets. For the F-11, this issue became a major sticking point, but Hughes assured Elliott Roosevelt that it would be easy to convert the plane to an aluminum airframe.[1158]

At that very same time, the AAF finally dismissed wooden airplanes, as recorded in this Air Staff memorandum of 13 August 1943:

> ...Quite apart from the failure of the DX-2 to fly with any reasonable degree of success; and the estimated performance, which is considered optimistic, the materiel command continues to entertain grave doubts as to the advisability of building a high-performance airplane out of duramold plywood as employed in the Hughes designs. These doubts are based upon the varying physical responses of the combined wood and steel structure when subjected to expected operational variations in humidity and temperature. It is also becoming increasingly apparent that American airplane craftsmen, unlike the British, are essentially metal workers and that superior craftsmanship is to be expected only in the medium with which they are the most familiar. That is to say, if the ultimate is to be expected in engineering, fabrication, and speed in production, the airplane must be made of metal.
>
> This office recommends against any further action tending to encourage the development of, and diverting facilities to, a project which has not progressed favorably to date and which shows so little promise in the future.[1159]

The Hughes design did not become "political" until 1942, and only because the normal, legitimate channels had turned thumbs down on the project. In January, Materiel Division surveyed the Hughes plant and rendered the following pitiless verdict:

> ...The present DX-2 is being redesignated as the D-3. It is a Duramold duplicate of the [Lockheed] P-58. It is not quite as well armed, weighs about the same and has more range than the P-58; however, the P-58 will be flying in approximately nine months, whereas this airplane is about two years away. By the time this is built and flown, the XP-58 could be put in production, with the same range. It is estimated by Mr. Bell of the Hughes Company that they can produce ten airplanes a month with the present facilities, whereas it is believed that the Lockheed Corporation can produce four times that number without increasing facilities.
>
> It is the opinion of this office that this plant is a hobby of the management and that the present project now being engineered is a waste of time and that the facilities, both in engineering personnel and equipment, are not being used to the full advantage in this emergency. The gentlemen contacted during this visit gave the impression of being capable, energetic, and more than willing to play a more active part in National Defense.
>
> It is the recommendation of this office that the Air Corps should discontinue any further aircraft projects with this organization. This plant cannot produce enough airplanes in time to be of any material aid; however, it can be of great aid in producing Duramold parts necessary in the fabrication of other military aircraft and gliders.
>
> Signed F.O. Carroll, Colonel, Air Corps, Chief, Experimental Engineering Section.[1160]

But Hughes knew important people in Washington, D.C., and he was not going to be flipped off by Wright Field. General Arnold repeatedly inquired about progress and by June he directed procurement of one DX-2 "in its present commercial form as a prototype for possible future bomber development."

This advanced the project only slightly. Now the aircraft was redesignated XP-73, and then in July, it became the XA-37. Evidently nobody quite knew what kind of mission the aircraft would, could, or even should meet.

Now the Commander-in-Chief himself got on the case. On 8 July 1942, General Arnold wrote to the president that "the AAF had been in close touch with Mr. Hughes during development of his twin-motored bomber. Mr. Hughes had volunteered to build the airplane at his own expense, and claimed it would make 430 mph fully loaded. Negotiations for the sale of the airplane to the AAF were then under way."

Arnold was being squeezed between the Hughes lobby in Washington and the skeptics in the Materiel Division. On 17 July, Arnold again reported to the president that he had spoken with Hughes and agreed to absorb the cost of the DX-2 if the resulting aircraft was satisfactory. At this point, the program went forward only very slowly, and the AAF awaited the results of flight testing.

By next year, the reconnaissance crisis was beginning to trouble Arnold so much that he made a renewed effort to get the Hughes project out of the doldrums. Now he requested that the DX-2 be flown to Bolling Field so that his staff could look it over. That was far too ambitious an idea; the plane had not even flown yet, except for two short hops. Hughes replied on 1 July 1943 that the plane had to be reworked and it wasn't going anywhere for a while.[1161]

Hughes then requested substantial additional funds because he had to completely redesign the aircraft. On 1 July, the AAF Western Procurement District visited Harper Dry Lake, and "Mr. Hughes personally supplied the data obtained." The conclusion was that a new wing, including flaps and ailerons, was needed. The ailerons were ineffective, and Hughes's early flight tests found the plane almost unflyable.

General Echols noted on 13 August that "changes necessary to make the DX-2 a flyable article became so numerous and drastic that this design was abandoned and a new design, the D-5, was evolved. Hence the AAF considered the DX-2 to be a closed project. Materiel Command doubted advisability of building a high performance airplane out of Duramold plywood." The recommendation against the aircraft was approved by the Chief of Air Staff (Giles) on 21 August – virtually contemporaneously with a wholly new evaluation by a completely different team.

The new team was Elliott Roosevelt's. General Arnold, prodded by the War Department, needed some operational eyes on the design. Perhaps real reconnaissance pilots would have an opinion different from that of the naysayers at Wright Field.

> Senator FERGUSON. Did you know at that time, generally, that as far as the D-5 was concerned, the Army, the engineers, those that were in the "know" wanted no part of it?
>
> Mr. ROOSEVELT. Sir, I had been told in no uncertain terms by the Procurement Division and by Gen. Bennett Meyers and General Echols, why they were against it… they told me that they were against it for the same reason that they had been against another recommendation of mine which had come back from the theater. They were against, for instance, our building Mosquito aircraft in this country, which was a British-designed airplane, and they maintained that wood or plywood aircraft would not be suitable in many or most of the theaters of operations. I maintained that they did not know much about the

war, for the simple reason that the British were using at that time in India, Burma, north Africa, eastern Mediterranean, England, and in every theater in which the British operated, they were using Mosquito aircraft and using them successfully….

Senator PEPPER. [D-FL] And it was made out of plywood, or some kind of plastic?

Mr. ROOSEVELT. Yes, sir; and their operational efficiency was higher than any of our aircraft, at that time, and in my theater and in the British theater, and their rate of loss was less than half our rate of loss.

Senator PEPPER. Did you have any personal knowledge of the performance of this Mosquito plane?

Mr. ROOSEVELT. Certainly; I flew a lot of missions in it.[1162]

Colonel Roosevelt had a couple of weeks back east before tackling his new task. His team arrived at the Ambassador Hotel, Los Angeles, on 8 August 1943.

Elliott Rescues the D-2

Howard Hughes knew this was his last chance. What happened next should be viewed in that troubled context – a failed airplane just rejected by the Air Forces.

On his August 1943 trip west, Colonel Roosevelt was accompanied by operational reconnaissance pilots Colonel Harry T. Eidson, RAF Wing Commander D.W. Steventon, Major W.R. Boyd III, and Lt. Col. Karl Polifka. It appears that other experts not named to the committee also participated. The entire mission was to look at Southern California aircraft manufacturers Boeing, Douglas, Lockheed, and Vultee, but also at Air Corps reconnaissance facilities. Elliott said the team visited six or seven aircraft factories in all.

Wing Commander D.W. Steventon, DFC, DSO, was by then already renowned for his flights, operating mainly from the British reconnaissance hub at RAF Benson. Elliott later testified that he was regarded as the top Allied reconnaissance pilot, although several have claimed that title.

Mr. MEYER [HAC]. Could I say this? One of the first days after Colonel Roosevelt's mission arriving, we went to Harbor Lake, where the plane was being built, or rather tested up there. It was a dry lake in the interior of California. I will say about 100 miles from Los Angeles. While we were up there, in Colonel Roosevelt's mission was a Royal Air Force boy that had been quite well decorated. I think his name was Commander Stevenson, or squadron leader, or something.

This chap, when he saw the plane inside the hangar, just about fainted. He said, "I have never seen anything more magnificent that would do a better job." This young kid and Colonel Hoover, who was also associated with Elliott Roosevelt, just went into ecstacies about what a terrific plane it was. So it was obvious that the other planes they had seen did not compare with this plane, and that is the truth.

Johnny Hoover, although not officially on this survey team, was a young Elliott protégé who often traveled with him. He flew some of the most exciting reconnaissance missions of the war, but he also got caught up in Elliott's stateside controversies.

Senator O'CONOR [D-MD]. Did he seem to know what he was talking about?

Mr. MEYER. Certainly, because this kid, John Hoover, and Elliott Roosevelt were the first fellows to come back from the war with actual combat experience and knew what

> they were talking about, and the men sitting at Wright Field do not know a plane until they see one, until it has gone through the war. And this kid, Squadron Leader Stevenson, this chap was just overenthusiastic about the plane. He had gone through the war since the very start, when the Germans attacked England.[1163]

At the hearings, Roosevelt was asked to characterize the qualifications of his team:

> He [Steventon] had been under my command, sir, in north Africa, and he is a very outstanding flying officer, reconnaissance flying officer of all services. He served throughout the Malta campaign and was flying from the first day of the war in the Battle of Britain, and was transferred right after the Battle of Britain to Malta and went through all of their flying when they were reduced to flying one airplane, and he has one of the greatest records of any flying officer in the war.
>
> Lt. Col. Karl Polifka was the officer who commanded the first reconnaissance squadron which went to the Southwest Pacific. He afterward became the group commander in the Southwest Pacific, and returned approximately within a week or so the same time that I did. He was called back from the Pacific theater. He had one of the finest records, also, of any officer that you will see in the war.
>
> ...Maj. W.R. Boyd III was an officer of the Reconnaissance Section in the headquarters of the Pentagon Building, and he was sent along by the Reconnaissance Division, I believe it was called, ... to keep tabs on just exactly what we saw and what new recommendations that we would have and offer any assistance in view of his experience in their over-all procurement program in the problems that they had, with which he was more familiar.
>
> ...Lt. Col. Harry Eidson I have already told you about. He was the first of the officers under my command to achieve five missions without getting knocked off. [1164]

If Roosevelt had any ill feeling toward Harry Eidson for stealing his wife, it was not obvious here. In general, he later spoke glowingly about the pilots he served with. On this trip, Elliott did manage to squeeze in a visit to his wife at the ranch in Fort Worth. It was not a joyful reunion. Having just indulged in some intense hanky-panky in Hollywood, Elliott thought the bloom was off the marriage to Ruth. And she, too, had kept up with the rumors.[1165] By October, they were separated.[1166]

Hughes Aircraft test pilot George Marrett later wrote that Col. Clarence A. Shoop ("Shoopy") accompanied Elliott on the D-2 inspection, but he was not officially on the team. Shoop would later command the 7th Reconnaissance Group in England, directly under Elliott. Interestingly enough, after the war, Shoop would come to work for the Hughes Aircraft Company in charge of flight operations. Marrett said that Hughes planned to use Shoop to support his efforts to complete and sell the F-11.[1167]

At Harper Dry Lake, Elliott's survey team spent only a little over an hour physically going over the ill-fated D-2. Roosevelt later said:

> It was in a hangar, one engine was out, and had been lifted from the nacelle and they were working on an overhaul of that engine. He [Howard Hughes] had been flying it, he told us, about two days prior to that, on a test operation...[1168]

Questioned how he could make definitive claims after such a short visit to a disassembled airframe, Roosevelt protested:

> That is the wrong impression to create. We spent hours and hours at the Hughes plant in going over the details of the construction of the airplane from the blueprints stage

> to the lamination of the wood, the methods by which the whole aircraft was assembled, and everything else, but to look at a finished airplane, it does not take a very long time to be able to tell what the finished product can do.[1169]

In the Senate hearings, Elliott would indignantly maintain that Wright Field had sabotaged the acquisition by demanding the aircraft be built of metal. In his view, only minor modifications were required to the D-2:

> The principal changes were that they had to put on more gas capacity, in order to provide more range, and that it had to have more space for ... cameras, and that the camera installation could not interfere with the use of drop tanks and a very careful study was made to determine whether it could carry out what we considered were the major requirements of speed, distance, and altitude, carrying all of the equipment which we desired.[1170]

Roosevelt thought the metal redesign shifted the schedule 18 months to the right. But he also failed to account for the immense difficulty of hand-building the complex aircraft out of wood and composites – much less producing 100 of them in a hurry. The Canadian Mosquito experience showed the pitfalls of such an approach. Yet Roosevelt bought Hughes's pie-in-the-sky promise of getting the first D-5 in six months.

It is true that the competing aircraft manufacturers did not have suitable aircraft ready for review at the time, and relied on promises of how they could enhance the performance of existing aircraft. But that, of course, was also the situation at Hughes's plant; apparently his promises counted more. At any rate, the AAF team did not realize that the aircraft they were shown, the D-2, was already an evolutionary dead end.

As carried on Hughes's expense account, the initial California tour lasted from 8 to 10 August, but there were follow-up consultations in New York and Washington during the week of 20 to 28 August. Sometime in mid-September, Roosevelt took the high brass on a new visit to see the D-2. This trip included no less that Lt. Gen. Barney Giles, who as Chief of Staff was second only to General Arnold, and Maj. Gen. Bennett Meyers, a then highly regarded go-getter in the procurement branch.[1171]

Although General Giles said the desert excursion was incidental to a visit to Lockheed-Burbank, this trip was highly significant because it marked the operational crowd's conversion to the Hughes cause. Giles had one important suggestion, strongly seconded by Colonel Roosevelt:

> I would like to say this: After I had looked over the wooden airplane, I came back to Mr. Hughes' aircraft factory and spent a couple or three hours going through it. I found at the time he had three large flying boats under construction and a mock-up fairly well completed on one. – I was of the opinion that if the three large airplanes were moved out of the plant, moved to some other place or even cancelled, we would have a much better chance to complete the wooden aircraft there, where he had so many people to work with wood. So, upon my return to Washington, I reported to General Arnold about this particular aircraft and made a verbal recommendation to make the wooden airplane out at the west-coast plant, and asked if he could use his influence to have the large boats canceled or moved out of the plant, because it would seriously interfere, in my opinion, with our photographic aircraft.[1172]

Thus, when Elliott submitted his recommendation on 20 August 1943, he was speaking not merely for himself, but for a team of top-notch operational veterans. In later testimony, Elliott maintained that all team members "concurred completely."[1173]

Nevertheless, Elliott's report, included in the Appendix, is a strange mix of opinions, denunciations, jeremiads, and recommendations. Most importantly, it was full of starry-eyed admiration for Howard Hughes and an uncritical acceptance of obviously unrealistic promises relating to the D-2.

Still, Elliott's searing criticism of USAAF reconnaissance programs was probably mostly justified, and it was certainly supported by his combat colleagues. It is one thing, however, to curse the darkness; another to find a candle that will shine true light and not just blow smoke. For General Arnold to verbally order the Hughes aircraft on the strength of Elliott's opinions largely unsupported by proven numbers and sober expectations was extremely unusual.

Are we to think then, that Arnold was gullible? General Lauris Norstad thought so. In his oral history interview, he noted how he had tried to convince Arnold that his, Norstad's numbers, were correct, and that another officer, Bennett Meyers, was trying to pull one over on him. We'll soon deal with Meyers, but in this case Norstad noticed that Arnold seemed to trust those who told him what he wanted to hear. That dovetails with the general impression of the chief of the Air Corps as a capable, honest, but insufficiently skeptical officer.[i]

As reported, on 21 August 1943, the Air Force initially rejected the Hughes F-11. Colonel Roosevelt did not like that. During those last ten days of August, "things" must have happened between the White House, Elliott, and Arnold. The exact nature of these "things" is untraceable, but we know that during that period Arnold came on board with the president and his son. We also know that after Elliott submitted his recommendation, he was in and out of the White House; and that on 30 August, Mr. and Mrs. Elliott Roosevelt, Generals Arnold and Marshall, and the president had dinner together.[1174]

On 1 September, Elliott got his way. Arnold verbally told General Echols to order a hundred F-11s. Now it was the Materiel Division's turn to rant and rave.

The next day, Echols protested:

> And while it is not within the province of this office to determine the requirements for specific tactical aircraft nor to "talk down" the need of this airplane as a type, nevertheless, and all things considered, the previous recommendations made by this office and approved by the chief of air staff should remain unchanged.[1175]

Echols was driving at the fact that while his office did not set requirements, he found it highly irregular that those who did had preemptively decreed that a wooden aircraft could meet requirements.

On 11 September 1943, after some back-and-forth, Materiel Command acceded to headquarters's demands for action and priority on the F-11 project with the following, later so controversial words:

> Following a recommendation from Col. Elliott Roosevelt to Gen. Arnold to the effect that the Hughes D-5 is the only airplane designed which is suitable for photographic

[i] OHI with Lauris Norstad, Norstad collection, DDE Lib. The "numbers" related to aircraft deliveries.

> purposes, Gen. Arnold issued verbal instructions to this office that steps would be taken to contract with Hughes for photographic airplanes.[1176]

General Echols later testified that this preamble was justified by the need to explain to the entire procurement chain why its earnest and persistent advice on the matter had been bluntly overridden.

The furious flap between Wright Field and the Pentagon brought Elliott back into the fray. He met Arnold again on 3 September. At which exact point he went to the president and worked him over is not obvious, but he definitely squealed to Dad. Despite his denials, we know this because Margaret Suckley, FDR's confidante, noted in her diary on Tuesday, 14 September 1943, that:

> Ruth & Elliott, the P. & I had dinner in the P.'s study – Elliott was telling the P. about his difficulties in persuading Gen. Arnold about this new reconnaissance plane which he wants to have made by a man called Hughes – It goes faster than any other, a necessity for reconnaissance, as they are unarmed & rely on speed alone – Elliott says he has accomplished what he came for, & has the approval of Gen. Arnold, etc., but Gen. A. has given him no help whatsoever & has rather grudgingly allowed the thing to go through. Elliott is an example of a great many men in his position. He has been on "duty" for 3 years, is sick of it all, longs to get home and has only one present thought; to get the war over – Anything which retards that goal is distracting – I could feel how he felt - … Another thing Elliott said, which is important, is that a story is going the rounds that the reason this Hughes plane is to be made is only because of pressure by the President, because his son, Elliott, is trying to get it done – This is completely untrue – Elliott was ordered home from North Africa to "sell" the plane to Gen. Arnold.[1177]

Clearly it was smart of General Arnold to watch his back when Elliott was in town.

On 17 September 1943, the Engineering Division – the "Hate Hughes Club" in Howard's estimation[1178] – "expressed disapproval of the contemplated production of the DX-5 and presented engineering and production difficulties involved to substantiate the statement… Wright Field stated that the XP-58 modified as a photographic reconnaissance airplane would fly higher, faster and farther than the DX-5 and made a recommendation that further consideration be given to this modification of the XP-58."

Soon after, Elliott returned to California accompanied by General Giles, Arnold's deputy, who wanted to see for himself what Elliott was raving about. Hughes's expenses on him continued through 18 September. On the last two days there was yet another "business-related" tour of the nightclubs of New York City for him and his team. Per the ledger, on the 17th he had dinner at Chasen's restaurant with Howard himself. He was clearly making up for the months of lean living. He was also encountered at the Stork Club. Complimented on his decorations, he protested that he hadn't received the Purple Heart. It bugged him:

> "You are thinner in the face," said a newspaperman, and then pointing to his ribbons, added: "but a lot heavier across the chest." "The only decoration that really counts," was the reply, "is the Purple Heart Medal, which I wish I had."[1179]

Elliott had a clear understanding that he was in a fight with the Air Forces to get the F-11 approved. Precisely as Wright Field suspected, the Senate investigation later revealed that General Arnold, in finally ordering a hundred F-11s in defiance of his own procurement staff, had given in to pressure from the Hughes-friendly White House. That lobby included Harry Hopkins and Jesse Jones, as they were assumed to communicate the president's view of the matter.[1180]

Howard Hughes took another trip to Harper Dry Lake on 22 September with Grover Loening, an aeronautical expert who was detailed by the War Production Board to evaluate the HK-1 seaplane. Loening's exceptionally well-informed but damning report makes clear that the wooden construction was still taboo in polite company:

> This was rather a useless trip, because it was discovered that the plane in question is housed almost immediately after any flight in a hangar that is considerably air conditioned by desert coolers and humidifiers, which are of course necessary in this hangar in order to make conditions bearable for the men to work in. So, any conclusions from the experience with this plane in the desert as to weathering properties of the Hughes type of wooden construction, cannot be arrived at one way or the other.[1181]

Then, on 29 September, Wright Field Commander Maj. Gen. Charles E. Bradshaw intervened with Arnold to attempt to kill the contract, calling attention to "certain storm warnings" in dealing with HAC. In addition, the chief of air staff, Maj. Gen. Barney Giles issued a directive "stating in the most final terms that the Hughes project must be cast aside and 'regarded as closed' so far at the Army was concerned."

Presciently, it stated:

> In view of the above, it is the considered opinion of this command that to rush into production with such an undeveloped and unstable article is an invitation to later severe criticism. It is concluded that in view of the amount of money involved, and many uncertainties connected with it, that this project will probably, at a later date, draw congressional attention and possibly public criticism upon the Army Air Forces.[1182]

Colonel Roosevelt kept up the campaign for the Hughes airplane, even as he careened from night club to night club during his stateside tour. On 8 October 1943 he reasserted his claim that the F-11 would win the war in a meeting in Washington in the ill-fated General Bennett Meyers's office. Attending this meeting were Jack Frye of TWA, who represented Hughes, and Colonel Hall, now the reconnaissance chief. Hughes himself was consulted via telephone.[1183]

Wright Field was outgunned, but did not give up. (The USAAF's case history for the F-11 project is the main source for the following account.)

On 9 October, General Meyers went directly to Arnold and protested: "Hughes's facilities considered insufficient to produce aircraft under proposed schedule and substantial subcontracting would be necessary. Again pointed out that the many uncertainties and amount of money involved in this project might draw Congressional attention and public criticism upon the Army Air Forces."

Now Arnold was really in the middle, catching it hard from both sides. He decided to stick with his decision, perhaps choosing future Congressional outrage over current presidential disfavor. His mind had been made up for him. On 11 October, the preliminary cost-plus-fixed-fee contract – a letter of intent for 100 F-11s, costing $48,500,000 – was signed.[1184]

On 21 October, Assistant Secretary Lovett spoke with Maj. Gen. Bennett Meyers, General Echols's deputy commander and executive officer. Meyers opposed the plane, but Lovett informed him that there was immense political pressure in favor of it.

From this recorded conversation we have the famous quote that "there is going to be an awful smell" when the story became public.[1185] Meyers mentioned Commerce Secretary Jesse Jones and the president as being in on the deal, in addition to Colonel Roosevelt. The Senate committee later found a confidential memorandum from Jesse Jones to the president, dated 27 June 1942:

> Howard Hughes, airplane designer, builder and holder of most of the world's speed records, will send into the sky at an early date his twin-motored plastic bomber, which will fly faster than any pursuit ship in the world. (handwritten): 485 miles an hour.
>
> Mr. Hughes has put $6 million of his private funds and several years of intensive work and study into the development of this plane, the Hughes Design nr. 2. Hughes Design Nr. 1, which inspired his fast bomber, was the plane in which seven years ago he flew non-stop from Los Angeles to New York in 7 hours 29 minutes. This record still stands and is by far the fastest long cross country flight ever made. Nowhere in the world has anyone yet approached Hughes' record of 2500 miles at a sustained speed of 333 mph. [1186]

But there's more; it was a coordinated Hughes attack. Russell Birdwell, whom Press Secretary Early identified as a "high-powered Hollywood press agent" wrote the White House shortly thereafter with extraordinary claims for the Hughes plane and a plea for a few minutes in private:

> During all of this time we have kept the project most quiet but now on the eve of the ship being ready for flight Mr. Jones recommended to the President that he might possibly want to make an announcement to the press concerning Mr. Hughes' plane, which will, no doubt, revolutionize all war time fighting.[1187]

Mr. Birdwell had intended for Jesse Jones's hyperbole to become the basis of presidential press release trumpeting the plane that would revolutionize war. A more level-headed Steve Early told McIntyre, the recipient, that "I see no reason whatever to drag the President into it except to publicize Hughes' plane. And that isn't the President's job." Thus, FDR resisted the temptation to become Hughes' propagandist.

Obviously, from the start Hughes used political connections to get around the skeptics at Wright Field. Lovett said the problem with these pressured contracts was that "you can never bring up the outside pressure in your defense" afterwards.[1188]

Elliott was briefly reported in London on 9 September 1943, apparently to confer with reconnaissance commanders there, including Colonel James Hall.[1189] But he did not return to his command in the Mediterranean until late October. He had the satisfaction of receiving a glowing written appreciation from General Arnold for all his work stateside during the preceding three months.[1190] Arnold knew to "watch his six."

Arnold's Dilemma

Elliott's F-11 report to General Arnold stated that "the Hughes airplane was the only airplane, already designed, suitable for photographic purposes." As usual, he went much further verbally: He firmly declared in an October meeting that "procurement of 16 airplanes in 16 months would shorten the war by six to eight months."[i]

---

[i] Elliott's words are preserved in the Case History, apparently deliberately to absolve Materiel Command.

We cannot tell for sure if the AAF historian rolled his eyes when he recorded this, but this imperious edict was repeatedly quoted in the case history in 1946. Had Elliott taken leave of his senses? Did he think Hughes's troubled design was more decisive than anything else in the war? Sixteen months later Allied troops were rushing the gates of Berlin. Would a squadron of F-11s then stop the war cold? Elliott was nothing if not sure of himself. Even when he was utterly, absurdly wrong.

And yet, despite the protests he encountered from his materiel officers, there was good reason for General Arnold to listen to Colonel Roosevelt. In North Africa, Elliott had made a respectable call when he demanded British Mosquitoes. Oddly enough, both the Germans and the Americans were scratching their heads and asking why they couldn't build something like that. Neither ever did, but not for lack of trying.

As if to emphasize the point, high hopes for the reconnaissance-optimized North American XB-28A had just been dashed. This much enhanced, pressurized Mitchell crashed on 3 August 1943, and the Air Force gave up on it.

Arnold had to assume that the war would be over in a year or two. There was no way that a new design would make it into the field by then. Of course, the war could take longer, and even if not, there would surely still be a need for a high-performance reconnaissance aircraft. But, the perfect being the enemy of the good, the project might also hog badly needed resources.

Arnold was also dealing with a moving target. When the new aircraft was fielded, the enemy was likely to have much faster and higher-flying interceptors, probably jets, in which case any propeller aircraft was going to become target practice.

The research, engineering, and procurement staff, led by Elliott's old nemesis General Oliver Echols, insisted that Hughes Aircraft did not have the competence or discipline to provide a useful product, certainly not in time. Even though hard pressed, most of the other aircraft manufacturers had by now demonstrated that they could deliver on their promises, but not Hughes.

Wright Field said the novel Duramold construction was a reckless stab in the dark despite Hughes's glib assertion that the F-11 could easily be converted to aluminum. Hughes had tinkered with the D-2 for years without results. It was well-known to procurement professionals that both the D-2 and Hughes Aircraft Company itself were troubled entities. To top it off, General Echols confessed to a deep personal dislike for Howard Hughes.[1191]

Materiel Command engineers also had been involved with evaluating the wooden Mosquito. They had obtained 13 from the new Canadian line, and they truly hated them. The senior civilian engineer, Ralph Graichen, would later testify that after some scares in the air, the pilots refused to fly them. That was odd given the plane's popularity in Europe, but apparently the first Canadian copies were simply not up to snuff.[1192]

This epic procurement debacle, which would make a deep imprint in Air Force history, represented a classic confrontation between the engineers and the users – the "ops guys." Each understood some of the puzzle; each failed to see the remainder. Elliott and his pilots were impressed with the promised F-11 because on paper, it delivered exactly what they needed: speed, altitude, range, payload. They were comparing to the Lightnings they had to fly, and to the Mosquitoes they coveted and tended to overestimate.

But the pilots did not know, and could not be told, of other important developments. Many other contenders were being discussed at Wright Field. The most obvious rival was the sleek, beautiful Republic F-12 Rainbow, a fast four-engined reconnaissance aircraft which appeared to have obvious postwar civilian application.

Perhaps most critical of all, the research and development officers knew by late 1943 that turbojets would rule the future. The British were already flying the first Gloster Meteor at that time, concurrently with the troubled but exceptional German Messerschmitt Me-262.

Using British engines, the Americans were trying to catch up in jets. The Bell P-59 had turned out to be a total dog, but Lockheed's P-80 showed promise, and it would be in the field by 1945. A reconnaissance version, the F-14, would soon follow. So why spend a lot of money on a half-designed, unbuilt aircraft that was almost guaranteed to be obsolete by the time of its IOC (initial operational capability)?

Finally, there was the F-11 itself. For a twin-engined piston aircraft, it was enormous. It was eventually projected to have a gross take-off mass in excess of 50,000 pounds. That's comparable to the F4H Phantom fifteen years later, but that was powered by two large turbojets. Hughes proposed the 3,000 hp Pratt & Whitneys with contra-rotating propellers, an arrangement virtually guaranteed to cause trouble. This would give the F-11 a power/mass ratio around 0.10, compared to the P-38's 0.16. How did Hughes think this would be the fastest thing in the sky, if it ever got up there?

In the public mind the Hughes Hercules flying boat, the so-called Spruce Goose, has tended to overshadow the XF-11. In truth, HAC, a small aircraft plant, could not effectively work on both. Ironically, Elliott Roosevelt later claimed that he had been firmly against the flying boat, asserting that it would cripple Hughes's ability to deliver on the reconnaissance plane – but he was not able to get that across to his father, who threw good money after bad on the Hercules.[1193]

Was Colonel Roosevelt a qualified investigator of this issue, or merely a political meddler? This would become a contentious issue later. Predictably, the engineering and procurement staff said Roosevelt had no clue what he was doing. But the operational types defended him. General Barney Giles, the chief of air staff, protested that Elliott was fully qualified to make an assessment. If you count merely the operational performance aspects, he was. But this is a classical case where that is only one piece of the puzzle.[1194]

Of course, this is all presuming that Colonel Roosevelt's report was not swayed by the booze, bimbos, and lavish accommodations Hughes offered him. Considering the revelations that would be made to the Senate investigators after the war, Elliott looked ridiculous when he insisted that he was completely impartial. But he had a good case when he pointed out that his operational colleagues backed him up.[1195]

The next three years of the Hughes contract inevitably brings to mind the army expression "FUBAR." The tortured and eventually tragic story of the F-11 will be revisited when we arrive at the famous Senate investigation, conducted in 1947.

In retrospect, General Arnold should have stuck with his first inclination to cancel the F-11. We know this because that is indeed what he said he should have done when asked four years later. However, it is quite likely that he thought that the aircraft would "hang itself" and that there would be an opportunity to cancel it later. This theory is supported by the fact that he went ahead and ordered the promising F-12 Rainbow anyway – right after meeting with the Roosevelts, father and son, in the White House.[1196]

Ironically, neither the F-11 nor the F-12 Rainbow would ever go into service. They belonged to a whole generation of aircraft which might be called the absolute pinnacle of piston-to-propeller technology. In December 1947, the Boeing B-47 Stratojet took to the air for the first time. By the time of the Korean conflict, "prop-jobs" were largely obsolete no matter how good they were. The RB-47 would perform critical strategic reconnaissance for the Air Force in the 1950s. The F-14 jet (which soon was renamed the RF-80) would do the same for tactical reconnaissance.

General Goddard later said that "it was through the combined efforts of Elliott Roosevelt and key intelligence officers that the standard for the separate production of reconnaissance aircraft was finally established."[1197] Evidently, even if Roosevelt wasn't always right in his recommendations, his emphasis was correct and it would never be disregarded again as it had been until 1943.

The search for an adequate strategic reconnaissance platform was by no means over. It had just begun, and would evolve into a national obsession. The shiny Hughes F-11 was simply deadwood on the tree of evolution.[i] Remarkably, only eight years separated the first flights of the F-11 and the famous Lockheed U-2. Six years more and the Corona project (cover name *Discoverer*) would be launching photo-reconnaissance satellites. If Hughes was disappointed, he should have considered that numerous other projects, some far more promising, simply found themselves overtaken by events.

A mere combat pilot couldn't see these things coming. That's why they pay generals "the big bucks." For the time being, though, Colonel Roosevelt had been narrowly successful. He was at his peak. Yet he had made many enemies, and they were not going away.

FEMALE RECONNAISSANCE

The August 1943 "survey expedition" became famous later, but for reasons other than reconnaissance arcana. Howard Hughes well knew that Colonel Roosevelt shared his own consuming interest in fuselages of the female kind. He procured all the best for his guests. Along with madly expensive wining and dining came agreeable company otherwise only seen in the movies.

Howard Hughes has attracted an immense literature, but the more salacious revelations are by their nature virtually impossible to verify. In such cases, it is best to allow those writers who seem to know every last sordid detail to speak for themselves. For example, the story was vividly told in *Hughes: the private diaries, memos and letters*:

> Hughes was aware that Roosevelt was unmarried and available [not true], and while all the other aircraft plants were attempting to impress the President's son with their expertise by extensive tours of facilities and lunches with scientists and engineers, Hughes told Meyer [his social handyman] to wait until Roosevelt returned to his hotel and pay a visit with what

---

[i] The Republic F-12 Rainbow, eagerly awaited also as an airliner, failed because of its troubled engines – the same ones that powered the B-29, an aircraft the Air Force saw no choice but to accept.

> he labeled "a boob buffet" – one redhead, one blonde, and one brunette. If Roosevelt was embarrassed by Hughes' approach, he covered himself nicely by cancelling appointments during the day to make himself available for Meyer.
>
> While the other members of his committee handled Lockheed, Boeing, and Douglas, Roosevelt concentrated on Hughes Aircraft. Instead of planes, what he saw was the inside of MGM, RKO, Paramount, and Warner Bros. studios. Each day, Meyer made certain that there was always a "boob buffet" waiting for Roosevelt's arrival. Meyer hit pay dirt when he moved Roosevelt through the executive dining room at Warner Bros. and introduced him to Cary Grant, who was then shooting *DestinationTokyo* at the studio. They joined Grant and actress Faye Emerson for lunch, with Faye recommending the day's special, Mulligan Stew. As it turned out, Roosevelt was far more interested in Faye than the stew, and began to monopolize the conversation with the actress.
>
> Faye Emerson was not one of the "boob buffet" although Hughes would later take credit for the introduction. Clearly smitten, Roosevelt asked Faye to join him for dinner at the Beverly Hills Hotel, and she accepted, fawning over the President's son and allowing her hands to linger on his shoulders as she rose to return to work. The following day, Hughes gave Roosevelt a personal tour of his plant, after hearing about Faye Emerson's charms, and he personally flew all five members of the Air Corps team to Lake Helen [Harper Dry Lake] to inspect the secret D-2, still unfinished after four years of development…[1198]

It may be of interest that the ambitious climber Faye Emerson had recently played in the hit movie "*Air Force,*" which starred a B-17C bomber named *Mary-Ann.* It was released in early 1943. Hughes had picked Emerson for Elliott's company because she was an intelligent conversationalist as well as a vocal Democrat and supporter of FDR. A journalist who interviewed her years later noted that she differed from the usual Hollywood bimbo: "she was 26, older than the average starlet, a spunky, witty woman who could discuss politics and the war eloquently and with passion, her lovely breasts swelling and falling as the conversation quickened."[1199] With such artillery trained on him, Elliott found resistance to be futile.

Howard Hughes also had just the right man to reel in Elliott: Johnny Meyer. He had picked up Meyer after Warner Bros. fired him, paying him $200 a week plus unlimited expenses. Hughes reportedly also got Meyer his draft deferments due to his "essential" war work: premium pimping. Meyer picked up Elliott and his team at the Town House in Los Angeles, and he would take care of his considerable needs for the next two years.[1200]

Factual details differ a bit in the various accounts. An independent explanation by Collier, who had access to Elliott Roosevelt's unpublished recollections as well as Charles Higham's gossip (below), focused on other peak experiences:

> Knowing of Elliott's appetite for a good time, Hughes had him met on his arrival by an employee named Johnny Meyer. Meyer, whom some called Hughes's "official pimp," took him to the Hughes home in the Hollywood Hills, where a bevy of starlets were tanning themselves around the pool. Hughes introduced Elliott around. When he came to Jane Russell he spent several minutes describing the special bra he had designed for her. Finally he gestured for her to pull off her blouse. "Jane, show Elliott those amazing breasts of yours."
>
> One of the women at Hughes's house was Faye Emerson, a $500 a week starlet appearing in B movies at Warner Bros. Coolly intelligent, with style and ambition, she allowed Hughes to put her together with Elliott. John Meyer paid their hotel bills over the

> next few days and financed a holiday to Catalina Island. On August 1 [sic], Hughes himself took Elliott to his aircraft plant and testing grounds…[1201]

Whatever the reconnaissance team may have thought of Ms. Russell, Hughes was obsessed with her twin peaks – indeed, so much so that he had engineered a special brassiere for their most advantageous exhibition (Jane didn't use it). In turn, the public was obsessed with Hughes and his fixations. This would be a major factor in the enormous publicity the scandal attracted when it finally broke open four years later.

In film history, Ms. Russell's breasts have attained mythical proportions. This was due to their single-minded promotion by Howard Hughes in the then just completed and (for that reason) highly controversial film *The Outlaw*, as well as subsequent gigs. However, just as for the equally double-barreled F-11, it may be that the numbers don't live up to the hype. Her measurements were 38D-24-36. Experts consider this well-endowed but not extreme. The then-happily married Ms. Russell, who is also renowned for having successfully resisted Mr. Hughes's coital requests, died on 28 February 2011, aged 89, and she was kind enough to publish her memoirs beforehand.[1202]

As Jane Russell told it, she, Elliott, Howard, and Johnny Meyer, along with Faye Emerson and Ava Gardner, had been having an all-night party. Also at the party was millionaire Jorge Guinle, a world-class playboy described as "the Brazilian Howard Hughes," and incidentally someone whom the Roosevelts had established friendly contact with before the war.[1203]

After the revelers finally left, Jane demurely stayed for the night, only to have Meyer attempt to rape her, getting "rescued" by Hughes, who then got too friendly and had to be pushed off in turn. Apparently Elliott got the better of that party; the two others had already test-flown Faye for him.[1204]

Although Hughes's promotion of Ms. Russell's curvature was probably mostly a publicity gimmick, the link between the F-11 and *The Outlaw* is far from trivial. It turned out that Hughes had important connections to two other high-ranking Air Force officers via these famous breasts. To expose them we shall have to wait for the 1947 Senate hearings.

Concerning Elliott's entertainment, reports differ in the details, such as dates and places, but the essence remains the same. In his intensely hostile book, *Howard Hughes: The Secret Life,* Charles Higham wrote:

> Meyer knew an actress who would be an ideal ally for him in his negotiations: the coolly intelligent Warner Bros. player, Faye Emerson. After bedding her several times to check out her sexual performance, he found her expert at fellatio and introduced her to Roosevelt, who was looking for a wife, and, as he and Hughes planned, he proved to be exactly what Roosevelt wanted. She had the looks, the poise, the presence, and the elegance to entertain his wealthy and important friends in Washington. Meyer offered Roosevelt a house to live in, one of Hughes's several properties in Beverly Hills. But Roosevelt felt that would be too obvious and instead rashly allowed Hughes to pick up his hotel bills – a dangerously corrupt move. Hughes also set about bribing high-level military officials.
>
> Meyer never paid the various dignitaries in cash, but instead arranged for their bills at the Town House in Los Angeles to be met through a fictitious organization called Howard Hughes Productions. He arranged for gifts of hard-to-obtain black market nylon stockings, or handbags, to be given to the wives; Meyer obtained the stockings through a network of hotel bellhops who would trade the stockings for liquor. He made gifts to Major General Bennett E. Meyers, who was a crucial figure in Air Corps procurements. Hughes

> entertained Meyers lavishly at Hollywood restaurants, including the currently popular Romanoff's, and gave him a $40 a day suite at the Town House.
>
> More funds were expended on a trip to Catalina in which Hughes acted as a host to Faye Emerson and others, including some very high-ranking military officers in the procurement division in Washington, D.C. Hughes basically controlled the War Department. The list went on and on. Hughes even had Meyer deduct the cost of certain available girls he was supplying to individual Army Air Corps figures on his taxes.
>
> On August 11, 1943, Hughes did the unthinkable: he personally took Elliott Roosevelt around his plant, then flew him to the D-2 testing ground at Lake Harper. Roosevelt, as Hughes expected, went back to Washington glowing with praise, and Meyer followed him with a gift of a parcel of TWA shares. By now, Roosevelt was Hughes's property: Hughes told Meyer to spare no expense in paying for Roosevelt's and Emerson's nightly jaunts in Washington and New York…[1205]

Unlike Elliott Roosevelt, Howard Hughes has long attracted writers and biographers, many of whom are of mixed credibility. In those cases where they don't copy or rewrite from each other, you have to wonder about their sources. Undoubtedly much Hughesiana remains apocryphal. However, in this case it is necessary to pay attention to Higham, for he had done his homework. He tracked down and interrogated the still exuberantly "amoral" Johnny Meyer at "his favorite watering hole" in New York, so the graphic details of how Hughes and Meyer set the trap for Elliott Roosevelt came from the original source.[1206]

Yet, in the passage above, it was certainly false that Hughes "controlled" the War Department. And the writer made up that Elliott was looking for a wife; he had one. He was only looking for nookie.

In general, for the Hughes-Roosevelt relationship, which lasted until Elliott left the Air Force, the painstaking Senate investigation of 1947 remains the foundation. Although Hughes was very powerful and claimed he could buy any man in the world, he was already in the aeronautical doghouse. The intense resistance he met in the USAAF – and then the hostility of the new Republican Congress – contradicted Higham's accusations.

Faye later said that she had come to know Johnny Meyer in 1941, because she and he frequently flew back and forth from Los Angeles to San Diego. Though married, she already was in with a daring crowd: "Johnny or Errol – Errol was such a darling man – would ask me to come out to the boat for a party. I knew all I had to do was bring my husband out there once to those parties and the next day I'd be out of a marriage."[1207]

Hughes knew he could use Faye: "I got the big rush from Howard. I know he liked me very much, became very interested, because he and Johnny decided I could talk, I was presentable. Not all actresses are."

Soon the day came when Johnny knew just whom to call: "Faysie, we're having a little party at Chasen's tonight for Colonel Elliott Roosevelt – you know, the president's son – and we'd love to have you come."

After a lot of much-appreciated whining and pleading, Meyer got Faye to agree to come along:

> I knew most of the people there. Meyer had rounded up everybody in Hollywood who really counted. The only ones I didn't know were the Army officers, Elliott's staff…and this very tall man in suntans turned around and Johnny said, "This is Miss Emerson, Colonel Roosevelt," and I looked up and he was, oh, so very tall, very tanned,

> and with those great blue eyes and that Roosevelt grin. I took one look at him and he took one look at me and I said, "How do you do," and we shook hands and I turned to walk on. "Wait a minute," said Elliott Roosevelt, "what are you drinking?" "Straight Scotch, please, and water on the side," I said.
>
> ...I never did get to the other half of the room. I had a drink with him, we began to talk, we started laughing. We not only sat next to each other at dinner, we held hands. We went dancing later at the Mocambo. I remember dancing with my shoes off. He was so tall we must have looked pretty ridiculous. It was one of those things that happen at first sight. I never really believed in it before, but it must be true – it happened to me that night.

And so the colonel came home with Faysie that night, and they talked "until daylight." Next night they went to Howard Hughes's place in the Hollywood Hills. Elliott and Faye were at one end of the table, Howard at the other. In between were the Air Force's procurement team and their social facilitators:

> ...and there was Elliott's staff and with them the most beautiful girls I've ever seen in my life. I don't know who they were, a couple looked familiar, but if they were call girls, well, I'd never seen call girls like that. Everyone was drinking and laughing and the doorbell wood ring and in would come another dame or maybe two dames together. Elliott and I got hysterical, we were laughing so much and Howard kept shouting "What are you saying down there? What's so funny?"[1208]

That night they took off, went to the Mocambo restaurant, and Elliott proposed. Faye said no. But she agreed to come along with him to New York; he had to tour Republic's Long Island factory, which was building the F-12.

Elliott spent only three highly entertaining days in Los Angeles before he returned to New York. As it later became known, Johnny Meyer accompanied him there and put him up at the Waldorf-Astoria at Hughes's expense, and had Faye Emerson installed in an adjoining room. Still, the colonel somehow found time to write his F-11 report there.

According to his FBI file, Mr. Meyer was a loathsome pimp. He first ingratiated himself with Errol Flynn, flooding the Warner Bros. studio with under- and overage males and females to keep Flynn and his extreme crowd in style. Meyer, according to the FBI, may also have blackmailed some rich people, sharing the proceeds with the bait. Meyer was considered an ugly toad, but he made up for this with charm, confidence and hundred-dollar bills, enabling him to test the goods beforehand. As a "public relations man," Meyer was a shoo-in for Howard Hughes, who needed a procurer as much as Flynn. The FBI reported that Meyer was the man closest to Hughes during the war years. It is interesting to consider that Elliott Roosevelt seems almost a spiritual twin of Errol Flynn, and so Flynn's pimp was the ideal guy to reel in Elliott.[1209]

On 20 August 1943, the very day Colonel Roosevelt completed his F-11 report, Mr. Meyer entertained him and Faye Emerson at the Stork Club, the 21 Club, and Club el Morocco to the tune of $106.50. That didn't include the $115 he spent on liquor at the Ritz Towers where he had put Elliott and Faye. This was only the beginning of a whole week of boozing and partying.[1210]

Columnist Walter Winchell also sat nightly in the Stork Club, his antenna-ears tuned to maximum gain. He wrote that Faye Emerson was going to be married soon, to a war hero. But that famous fellow couldn't be named yet, for he was not yet "unwound." The public at large did not learn of the Faye-Elliott liaison until over a year later.[1211]

That Elliott, in true Roosevelt style, could run at full throttle for days on end without sleep is suggested by Faye's memory that she had tree "glorious" days in New York: "I remember we had tickets four times in a row for *Oklahoma* at a time when you couldn't get tickets, and we never got to the theatre."[1212]

Remarkable all the same is that Elliott managed to put together a 3,000 word report which contained an urgent recommendation to purchase the F-11, along with accusations of grave incompetence against the materiel officers who had denigrated it. From an engineering standpoint the report seemed boisterous and unprofessional enough that Elliott must have been the main author, but his team-members backed its conclusions.

Although he snuck in a few more fun-filled days in California, during September and early October Colonel Roosevelt was mostly busy at the Pentagon reorganizing reconnaissance and applying the lessons learned in combat to planning, procurement, and training. General Arnold pronounced himself impressed with his work.

Faye remembered that Elliott came back out to California to restate and reinforce his wedding proposal: "Yes, she said to him during a quick visit to Palm Springs. Yes, she said as they danced at the Mocambo, Yes, she reiterated the following day, as they lunched at Romanoff's in Beverly Hills."[i]

Then trouble intervened. Trouble this time, as often before and after, was James Roosevelt. He met them at Romanoff's, and the two brothers caught up on war and family news. Apparently the conversation was not to Faye's liking, for after that she dropped Elliott like a snake. Of course, the Roosevelts did have a habit of exchanging loud stories about their past sexual exploits, but Faye appeared to be more upset that she was thought to be just another passing conquest, of no particular interest to the family.

At Hughes's house that night, Faye told Elliott she wouldn't marry him if he was the last man on Earth.

Howard Hughes panicked; he had only hours to get Faye in line before Elliott went back to war. "Faye, for Christ's sake you've got to talk to Elliott. He's dying. His heart's broken. What have you done to him?"

Faye later said she'd been in Hollywood long enough, "had gone through enough to get where she was," to know that Hughes had to be obeyed. And so she agreed to talk with Elliott by telephone, and she promised not to marry anyone else in the meantime.

Hughes had saved the F-11 again.

Shortly thereafter, Elliott was on his way back to his Mediterranean command. He could not keep up the connection with Hughes overseas, and it would be another year before he came back to the Zone of the Interior (ZI). But neither Hughes nor Elliott had forgotten the good times they had together, and they were set to resume.

The fuse that was lit in August 1943 fizzed and sputtered in the background for some time. It finally reached the F-11 in 1947, when the Senate began probing Hughes's contracts during its ongoing investigation of war profiteering. In that August, the explosion cleared the nation's front pages.

---

[i] The story of the courtship is Faye's own, as told to Leonard Slater (San Diego Mag., JAN 76).

Today this scandal is popularly remembered for Hughes's ferocious defense of the Hercules flying boat, but at the time Elliott's extravagant adventures with the F-11 were more entertaining. The explosive combination of Roosevelt, Hughes, movie stars, free-flowing money, and fast aircraft was simply irresistible.

In the meantime, however, Colonel Roosevelt had numerous other adventures.

CLOSE CALLS IN THE SKY

"I'm tired and I want to go home" was perhaps the most striking part of Elliott's diatribe against his tormentors. That he was not a born warrior and military man had been obvious from the beginning. We get more insight from the diary of Roosevelt's dear confidante, Margaret Suckley: "He has been on 'duty' for three years, is sick of it all, longs to get home and has only one present thought: to get the war over – anything which retards that goal is distracting – I could feel how he felt –"

Ominously, she continued: "Little Ruth Googins was feeling it in a very personal way, and suddenly turned to me, smiling, with tears in her eyes. "He's a nice boy, isn't he, Margaret, I'm so happy to have him here." [1213]

This entry was made on 14 September 1943, when Elliott was back in the United States on his "secret" mission. It was right between his two trips to California to see the D-2 and Faye Emerson. Ruth knew the score, and her tears were not from happiness. She initiated the divorce shortly afterwards.

She almost needn't have bothered.

It's a bad sign when the pilot comes back to the cabin and asks if anyone knows anything about navigation. It is extra odd that this happened on a flight that almost lost Elliott his life, since he was a freshly educated navigator. But as John Connally told it, the B-24 that returned them both to the U.S. in December 1943 did indeed get lost in atrocious weather, and everyone aboard prepared for death:

> An hour or two over the North Atlantic, I was invited into the cockpit. The pilot asked if I knew anything about navigation. Startled by the question, I replied that I knew very little. "Well," said the captain, "our radio is out and our instruments are down and we're uncertain where we are." --- I said, "If you need help from me, we're in even worse shape than you think."[1214]

As we have seen, for both business and political reasons, John Connally and Elliott Roosevelt were well acquainted. Connally had been Lyndon Johnson's most able aide and later became Sid Richardson's attorney, confidant, and estate executor. The shrewd lawyer would rise to become governor of Texas, take a bullet meant for JFK in Dallas, become a Republican, serve Richard Nixon, become super-rich, and go bankrupt.

In 1943, the young Connally served in Algiers as a lend-lease officer. When Elliott went back home he asked if John wanted to come along. He did. The account he gave of the harrowing trip across the ocean reveals a cool, fatalistic Elliott and an impressed Connally. Lost, the bomber was running with two engines shut down to conserve fuel.

When the pilot gave the option to jump or ditch, Colonel Roosevelt explained that he had already parachuted twice from airplanes – the second time merely to see if he would be as terrified again – and he had no intention of doing it a third time. But about that time of decision, the pilot gleaned through the mist the light from a beacon at St. John's, and the B-24 landed in the Newfoundland capital without any more excitement than press reports that the president's son was five hours overdue into Gander.

The details of Connally's account don't necessarily make much aeronautical sense, and his dates may have been off, but the point of his war story was that the two Texans thought they were going to die; only "blind luck" saved them.

Connally and Elliott "bonded" on that harrowing trip, which the latter didn't find notable enough to mention. But elsewhere he did admit to having twice abandoned an airplane – the second time evidently to try out a new egress technique from the P-38, whose tailplane was reputedly prone to slice jumpers in twain. (Lockheed claimed that other aircraft had equally ill-mannered tails.)[1215]

When you survey Elliott Roosevelt's flying career, it is astonishing that he came home in one piece, much less two.

Papa hated flying – Bunny loved it

Elliott considered himself a man of the air just as his father fancied himself a man of the sea. The president was famously averse to flying, but the journey in the giant Pan Am Clipper to Casablanca was far from his first flight. Although many think so, neither was his celebrated Ford Trimotor victory lap with his family from Albany to Chicago to accept the Democratic nomination on 2 July 1932.

On that long, brutal ride through violent weather, Elliott and the president-to-be were the only two passengers who did not get sick.[1216] The Ford was chartered from American Airways for a nominal price of $300; the airline had wisely decided against offering it for free.[1217] The trip was a highly successful publicity stunt, but it did not make FDR any fonder of flying.

Ominously, two years later that triumphant flight would be emulated by the new German chancellor when he so famously flew to the Nuremberg party convention in another trimotor, a Ju-52. But the story is darker than that; most likely FDR emulated Hitler, because the latter had been given a Ju-52 for his 1932 presidential campaign against Paul von Hindenburg. The flights (3-24 April) made a stir even in America, exemplifying a vigorous, modern demagogue campaigning against a staid and stiff old order. Since FDR hated flying, he must have found the publicity worthwhile.[1218]

It is understandable that many scholars think the Chicago flight was FDR's first. But Elliott recalled that as Assistant Secretary of the Navy FDR had gone up in a Curtiss NC-4 seaplane at Campobello Island, and the experience, left him with a deep "dislike and distrust" of winged aircraft.[1219] It would have been an adventure: the NCs were large, multi-engined seaplanes, and the NC-4 was the first airplane to cross the Atlantic (via the Azores) in May 1919.

Here again we can improve on Elliott's memory: His father actually flew in the sister ship NC-2 for ten minutes, along with eight other passengers, on 13 April 1919. And it was not at Campobello Island, but at the naval air station at Rockaway Point, Long Island.[1220]

But Assistant Secretary Roosevelt had been aloft before, in France during the war. These were short rides, not "active submarine patrol," as Elliott let on. In August 1918 FDR toured naval installations, including the flying boat bases. On 14 August he flew on a Curtiss HS seaplane out of Pauillac, near Bordeaux: "I went up for a hop in one of the seaplanes, flying up and down the Gironde, and getting an excellent idea of the geography of the region."[1221]

Pauillac was a major American base built of seaplane packing crates; all the naval aircraft arriving in France came ashore there. FDR noted that equipment was in bad shape; there were over 100 seaplanes in France but only two self-starters. He, a French-speaker, met with many family friends in the area.

Three days later he went aloft in the French-built airship AT-1 at Paimboeuf, near Nantes. He called the new American naval base there "Point Boeuf," and wrote:

> They brought out one of the dirigibles for me, the ropes being manned by about 400 of our bluejackets. I climbed into the forward car with the two pilots, the ropes were let go and we rose to about 500 or a 1000 feet and made a trip of about one half an hour. I tried my hand at running the lateral steering gear and also the elevating and depressing gear. The sensation is distinctly curious, less noise than an aero. and far more feeling of drifting at the mercy of the wind.[1222]

If these had been his very first trips through the skies, he would surely have mentioned it. He told a reporter that he often flew during his Navy Dept. days, and occasionally used a plane during the 1920 campaign[1223].

FDR thus had a certain personal familiarity with both heavier and lighter-than-air aeronautics.[1224] It was these, undoubtedly dangerous, adventures that FDR alluded to when he told Elliott at Casablanca that "there were some flights – you were just a baby – when I was with the Navy. In naval airplanes. Inspection trips. The kind of flying *you'll* never know."[1225]

Despite his personal aversions, Franklin Roosevelt was a strong advocate of air power in general and naval aviation in specific. But that fierce naval advocacy carried over into a raging hostility to a "Unified Air Service," i.e. the concept of a separate air force.[1226] That deep philosophical argument occupied the minds of strategists for much of the time between the creation of the Royal Air Force in 1918 and the U.S. Air Force in 1947. FDR was contemptuous of the idea of an air force, and he advanced cogent and persuasive arguments for his view. In retrospect, contemplating the excesses as well as the tactical neglects to which the cult of air power eventually led, it is easier to sympathize with FDR's view. But Elliott, who parroted the air-supremacist views of General Arnold and the "bomber mafia," parted ways with his father over that.

In 1943, Elliott wrote to his mother:

> Our Air Force is wonderful. The only thing holding it down is the fact that we are not a separate air force. I know father doesn't like the idea, but he's wrong. The RAF and the British Army have a closer cooperation as separate entities than we do as one force. General Spaatz has done a wonderful job, in spite of rather than because of the help of the ground supreme commanders. He is really and truly a great tactical general.[1227]

A week later, he drove the nail in further:

> I guess we can never get a break, though, as long as Father keeps the Air Force under the Army, where it is forced to compromise in its efforts to help its component units, because development is held down by Ground generals who spend their careers fighting against the rise of Air Power.[1228]

Unlike his father, who vetoed Eleanor's pilot's license, Elliott was in the air camp from the beginning. He had hung around Roosevelt Field on Long Island as a kid, and had welcomed the risks and ostentatious daring associated with both pre-war flying and combat duty. General Doolittle called him completely fearless.[1229] Of course, by the time he saw combat, he was 32 years old, which made him virtually senile compared to some of the wild teenagers who often wound up in the cockpits. Although not a cautious and methodical pilot, the judgment that comes with age may well have kept him alive. Finally, as far as the Air Force knew, until 1945 he always had a "real" pilot with him.

Still, he had close calls. On 16 May 1943 (by one account) in Algiers, he and his pilot wrecked a Mosquito during a tricky crosswind landing.[i] They careened into a large cargo plane, and both crew crawled out "not injured enough" to require medical care: "I took quite a bump on the base of my spine – it doesn't hamper my movements any, but is uncomfortable. I thought it was just a bruise, but it doesn't get any better, so I'm having an X-ray to see what's wrong."[1230]

On board the cargo plane, however, two war correspondents, George Tucker of AP and George Palmer of UP, were badly hurt.[1231] Tucker in particular suffered a severe concussion, then a stroke, and was medevaced to New York for brain surgery.[1232]

Elliott commented: "there's not much left of the plane."[1233] Tucker had been reporting on the Axis surrender in Tunisia a few days earlier, and on the continued nightly German air attacks on Roosevelt's base in Algiers.

Eleanor Roosevelt referred to this incident when she quoted to the media from a 23 May letter from Elliott. The letter, reproduced in her memoirs, threads a rather squiggly line between horror and reassurance:

> …I know you worry about us children in different parts of the world. Don't worry about me. I lead a charmed life. I had a crack-up the other day and escaped with a sore tail although my ship was demolished. The tail fell of another airplane that I flew to England five minutes after we landed. Anyway, if anything should happen remember no one could ask for a better exit line…[1234]

In feeble old age, Elliott maintained that "I was shot down three times in Africa." Records do not bear this out, and he probably embroidered on the incidents he was in. "The Germans reported me captured for one week; they thought they had me, and they were broadcasting that they had me. But then some Arab nomads took me up in the mountains and all the way around the front, and I got back to a British unit. It took a week. They took me on a burro."[1235] Italian reports in November 1943 said Elliott had been shot down and had parachuted into captivity; but they confused him with John G. Winant, the London ambassador's son. The family did not take the rumor seriously.[1236] This was well after North Africa, and the official sources do not show any Elliott crashes.

---

[i] An untitled narrative in the Group History says Roosevelt and a Col. Plothinger crash-landed a Mosquito at Maison Blanche on 21 May 43, without injuries (to them). It may have referred to visiting Col. Pottinger.

Oddly enough, in an interview with General Goddard after the war (reproduced in the appendix) Elliott told the same story, burro and all, about one of his pilots:

> That is, until we got this one kid – a second lieutenant. He was shot up by an ME-109, to the east of the German lines, and he lost both engines. He eased the nose up and stepped out on the wing and dove over the leading edge of the wing – between the wing and the windmilling prop – he dropped and opened his chute. He was rescued by some Arabs – he'd been shot pretty bad and had a lot of shrapnel – but they brought him back through the German lines on a burro and delivered him to the Allies. I interviewed him in a field hospital about six hours later.[1237]

On another flight with Lt. Col. Eidson flying the Mosquito, Roosevelt was in the nose taking pictures. Then Eidson noticed his own oxygen tube lying in his lap, but failed to summon the strength to grasp it. This alerted Elliott, who returned to fly the aircraft while also securing his pilot's oxygen mask: "Aside from this curious temporary incapacity, Eidson felt no effects until they landed, and his legs began buckling under him. It was then that Col. Roosevelt told him that he had been out of his head for five minutes."[1238]

There were apparently two B-17 incidents in which Elliott barely escaped with his life. The *Blue Goose* was shot at and made an emergency landing; the other, possibly *I Got Spurs*, seems to have been the one in which everyone was wounded except Elliott. The Mosquito incidents appear to have been accidental, but no less dangerous. The accident in which he smashed into a transport on landing grew into a "mid-air collision" in some retellings. He also told one reporter that "he escaped by a matter of three feet from being hit by Axis fire when his motor was smashed by the explosive." [1239]

Well after the war, Roosevelt claimed to have been repeatedly wounded, although Army records deny this. He did spend a lot of time in hospital for other reasons.

In late May 1942, when Elliott was in Fort Worth after his first African trip, he checked into Cook Memorial for a minor operation.[1240] The first family would not release its nature. But Eleanor wrote to Maude Gray, her aunt, stating that "Elliott is still laid up but should soon be well. Africa seems to give them all dysentery & then he had the operation for piles which was very painful & they found him very anemic." [1241]

During leave, he also had a small operation on his knee. The injury was not sustained in action.[1242]

They don't give Purple Hearts for hemorrhoids, but sympathy is maximized if you don't mention the exact nature of this injury. This turned out to be the case when Congressman Lanham mentioned Elliott's suffering during his ringing defense of him in the winter of 1943:

> When it was necessary for him to go to a hospital for an operation, he brought the African films back to the United States. On his mission to Africa he was taken ill, but he completed his mission and returned home before he reported to the Army doctors or was treated for the illness which finally led to the operation in Fort Worth.[1243]

Given all the accidents and incidents in which he was involved, it was pure luck that Elliott came home from the war with merely inconvenient medical issues. His superiors recognized this and tried to restrain him from the most dangerous missions.

That the chief of the Air Corps valued Colonel Roosevelt's service highly is evident in a peculiar exchange between Arnold, the president, and Ruth Googins Roosevelt. At

Casablanca, FDR had decided to send Arnold to Chungking to work on the matter of increasing supplies to Generalissimo Chiang Kai-shek, a perennial sore point during the war. FDR asked that Elliott accompany Arnold on the two-week mission because the Chinese were thought to be particularly sensitive to family and filial responsibility.

At any rate, on 1 February 1943, a thoughtful Franklin D. Roosevelt personally wrote to Ruth Googins, enclosing a copy of Arnold's refusal to detach her husband from his duties. Arnold wrote:

> I have conferred with General Spaatz, AAF Commander in North Africa, concerning procuring detached service for Lt. Col. Elliott Roosevelt for such time as might be required to cover the proposed trip to China. – I regret to advise that General Spaatz has reported that it does not appear possible to spare Col. Roosevelt's services during this critical period of operations in Tunisia. He states that the position occupied by Col. Roosevelt is one of high responsibility and his presence is, in fact, indispensable at the present time to the adequate functioning of his organization.[1244]

That rings true. It would be five months before Elliott could be spared. That's how long it took to clear the Axis out of Africa. And Hap Arnold went on to China from Casablanca without Elliott.

The significance of this exchange is, however, not Elliott's indispensability. It is that the president would take it upon himself to demand that his son be assigned to tasks as the White House wished. While the request was perfectly legitimate, obviously this was not something that happened to just any junior officer. Likewise, while FDR was talked out of it this time, any sensible officer would normally accede to a "request" from the commander-in-chief.

This was an inherently awkward situation, and it does explain how Elliott's career could be both fully legitimate and, at the same time, saturated with opportunity and visibility that simply would not accrue to anyone else.

CAIRO – TEHERAN – CAIRO

Colonel Roosevelt returned to his command on 22 October 1943 and immediately began planning for the move of the wing to new bases in southern Italy. Some units were already operating from Italian bases, but the transfer of the whole wing was a big job, and Elliott spent several weeks exploring for suitable locations.

Shortly after selecting his headquarters at the newly liberated San Severo field near the "spur" of the Italian boot, on 19 November Elliott was ordered to fly back to Oran to meet a very important person. This turned out, again, to be his father, who had arrived there on the new battleship *Iowa*.[1245] With General Eisenhower and Franklin Jr., Elliott welcomed his father ashore at Mers-el-Kebir at 0830, on 20 November.

The ensuing weeks were extraordinarily strenuous yet productive for the crippled president. He would participate in three high level summits, meet with innumerable civilian and military dignitaries, and travel by air across deserts and mountains his son had mapped and photographed. The president flew in a standard Douglas C-54; this was not the unique, wheel-chair accessible VC-54C the president would fly to Yalta in 1945. Nonetheless, Elliott already called it the *Sacred Cow*, and noted:

> Over his protests about needless expense, the plane had been remodeled to his use with a galley, leg rests, room for a worktable, and two berths, one of them reserved for Hopkins on this trip. A knockdown ramp had been built in, again contrary to Father's wishes, since the standard thirty-foot model which had to be pushed across the tarmac was conspicuous notice that the wheelchair President was due to land.[1246]

As at Casablanca, the Skymaster was flown by Otis Bryan. He was TWA's chief pilot, directly under Jack Frye, and was only temporarily given military rank.

Only 25 years earlier, the notion of the president leaving the country had been beyond the pale, as President Wilson had discovered when he went to Paris.[i] The pattern was being set for future presidential travels, with their immense, costly logistics; but at least back then the effort was defensible, considering the difficulty of communications and the need for prolonged periods of critical deliberations with allies. Still, with the battleship and the fleet of transports and fighter escorts, the operation consumed military resources comparable to that of a significant battle.

Oran was merely a transit stop. After loading his father aboard the first of the four allocated C-54s at La Sénia airfield, bound for Tunisia, Elliott followed behind in the Mitchell bomber he had appropriated. He said:

> I had my own plane at La Sénia, a B-25 night photographic reconnaissance plane; and one of my squadron commanders, Major Leon Gray, was there to accompany me. We had a few minutes of anxiety when one of the engines would not act properly, but finally, thirty minutes after the official plane had taken off, we were airborne; we set our engines a little higher than usual, and beat them to El Aouina after all.[1247]

The president stayed at Villa Casa Blanca in Tunis. El Aouina was close to La Marsa/Carthage, the seaside resort where many of Elliott's units were still operating – 250 planes, on paper at least.[1248] He took the opportunity to persuade his father to inspect the field:

> At that time, I commanded the Northwest African Photo Reconnaissance Wing, which was made up of some 6,000 Allied troops – about 2,800 of them stationed here, the rest in southern Italy. Leon Gray, Frank Dunn (my second-in-command), and I hustled everything into as apple-pie order as we could…by five-thirty my men were drawn up, looking pretty elegant, we had to admit. Father, from a jeep, reviewed the entire complement.
>
> "See the uniforms, Pop? We've got a regular United Nations, right here." – "Americans, of course. French, British, Canadians…what's that uniform?" – "South African. And there are New Zealanders and Australians, too." – "Looks like a fine outfit, Elliott. You should be proud." – "Don't worry. I am."[1249]

Mike Reilly, head of the Secret Service detail, had another view:

---

[i] Theodore Roosevelt visited the Panama Canal Zone, which was not a foreign destination.

> Elliott and young Franklin were waiting for their Dad on an apron off in a distant corner of El Aouina Field near Tunis. The President greeted them like any father meeting warrior sons so far from home. He looked in great awe at the remains of countless German six-motor transport planes [Me-363s] that were strewn along the runways, charred reminders of the recent Battle of Tunis. He had another reminder of the bloody days that were not long departed when he arrived at his villa, the White House [yes, again], in ancient Carthage. Only a few months before it had been the home of the crack Nazi general, Rommel [not a Nazi]. FDR could see Cape Bon, the last stronghold of the once terrifying Rommel legions. That afternoon, Elliott Roosevelt was a proud youngster who looked like he'd burst his buttons any minute as his old man inspected the [NAPRW], which was Elliott's command.[1250]

Writing Eleanor from Tunis on 21 November, President Roosevelt noted that he reviewed Elliott's outfit, all 5,000 men and 250 planes. "He flies to Italy tomorrow and joins me in Cairo. By the way all this is secret."[1251]

Despite an agenda of local sightseeing, Carthage was only yet another rest stop. With a fighter escort, the presidential party proceeded by night to RAF Cairo West Field. Elliott would land at Payne Field to the east of Cairo the next day. This was a new American airfield built to serve Air Transport Command, and it would later become Cairo's international airport.

Evidently, the president's staff had not yet learned the fine art of shooing away ordinary flying folks. Elliott said a biplane ignored the red warning flare and landed right in front of the C-54, waiting in position to take off at Tunis. Then at Cairo, three escort fighters had to chase away a French aircraft that was coming "uncomfortably close."[1252]

Cairo I

Elliott followed his father to Egypt a day later, not in his own plane, but as Eisenhower's guest aboard the general's C-54.[1253]

In Cairo, at the Mena Hotel and adjoining villas, Winston Churchill and Chiang Kai-shek came to meet with the president. These discussions are generally known as Cairo I; then, after the return from the Teheran meeting with Stalin, a Cairo II summit primarily discussed Anglo-American war plans.

Again, Elliott expected to fulfill his by now accustomed role as helper, gopher, and office boy, but he found that this time the Navy had already sent such people along; Filipinos, in good cruise-ship fashion. Elliott also wasn't privy to the formal conferences. He gleaned his insights indirectly from conversations with the participants.[1254]

The discussions focused more on the China-Burma-India (CBI) theater this time, an otherwise mostly neglected area. Elliott was able to tell his father about the troubles ATC pilots experienced in supplying China, although this could hardly have been a surprise. In return, FDR confided that Churchill was yet again trying to wiggle out of OVERLORD, the invasion of France. Now the prime minister instead wanted to slip up through the Balkans, but the Americans would have none of it, and this time they were strong enough not to be shouted down.[1255]

It is not explicitly recorded that Elliott took a direct personal part in the discussion of how to advance the Soviet shuttle bombing concept at the upcoming Teheran summit. However, the combined chiefs of staff were carefully preparing their requests during Cairo I, and on 26 November they settled on a need for ten Soviet air bases and all necessary support functions.[i]

Socially, Elliott was particularly fascinated by Madame Chiang, the polished, perfect-English speaking wife of the Generalissimo. But he was wary:

> Madame Chiang was at my side and leading me to two chairs almost at once. She struck me as quite a performer. For more than thirty minutes she talked animatedly, interestedly, intensely – and she always contrived to keep *me* the center of our conversation. It was as expert a job of flattery and charm as anybody had troubled to exert on me in years. She talked of her country, but only within the context of urging me to come out to China and settle there, after the war. I was interested in ranching? Then Northwest China was the place for me. As she painted a golden picture of the wealth an able and determined man could amass for himself, out of the toil of the Chinese coolies, she leaned forward, looking at me brightly, agreeing with everything I said, resting her hand firmly on my knee.[1256]

For a while, Elliott was entranced by the idea of making it rich in China after the war. Madame, refined yet terrifying, made an indelible impression on Elliott, and he would often return to it, even in the murder mysteries he published in old age. Language difficulties prevented a similar acquaintance with her husband, but Elliott shared the low opinion of the Chinese leader expressed by General Stillwell and many others American officers. Like Stalin, Chiang unceasingly demanded "more stuff," but got much less.[1257]

Before flying to Teheran, Elliott and Leon Gray took the B-25 down to Luxor, joining the Eisenhower party for a day of sightseeing – General Marshall had ordered Ike to relax.[1258]

Luxor was Air Vice Marshal Tedder's idea, and Kay Summersby says she, Ruth Briggs, Louise Anderson, Tex (Captain Earnest Lee), and Elliott accepted the general's invitation to come along. They had a grand time. In the Valley of the Kings, Kay noticed that even the "irrepressible" Elliott was awed into silence.[1259]

After this excursion, the president prepared for his much-dreaded flight to Teheran. He was not worried about meeting Joseph Stalin, though. The crippled president had traveled across the ocean, the deserts, and the mountains to meet a man who would not be budged from a location where he knew he was 100% in control. And Roosevelt came there without briefing books, policy plans, without his Secretary of State, without Russian experts save his interpreter, Bohlen, and his buddy, Hopkins, who admired their host so much. FDR was sure he could wing it. It was a bit like a bunny rabbit hopping into the open jaws of a crocodile, confident that his winning ways would charm the beast. Had his instincts ever failed him before?

EUREKA – The Teheran Summit

Leonard Lyons, the columnist, wrote shortly afterwards that President Roosevelt directed the Army to send his sons and friends to Teheran via a missive to the Army Pictorial Service: "The message included the suggestion that one of the men desired was to be of the type of Col. Elliott Roosevelt, and that a second be of the type of Sergeant Robert Hopkins."[1260]

---

[i] FRUS, US-USSR Relations 1943, 428. "Combined:" U.S.-U.K. "Joint" (U.S) also came in use in WW2.

That was typical FDR coyness, probably very amusing to him.

The B-25 was again delayed by engine trouble, but on the evening of 28 November Elliott and Leon Gray departed for RAF Habbaniya in Mesopotamia, flying across the vast, empty Arabian Desert by night. It was good to have a well-trained crew – Elliott's navigator wings must have come in handy.[1261]

Habbaniya, near Fallujah, was, along with Basra, one of the two original RAF bases in Iraq. Only two years earlier it had been nearly lost to the Nazi-allied partisans of the Rashid Ali government in Baghdad. Obsolete RAF biplanes beat them off in an epic air-to-ground battle. Luftwaffe aircraft had made it as far as Baghdad before a British relief expedition forced them to evacuate.[1262] Churchill had suggested the now secure RAF Habbaniya for EUREKA; but Stalin was adamant that only Teheran would do.[1263]

Refueling there, Elliott flew to Teheran, over the high mountain passes that had so worried FDR's doctor when his C-54 flew the same route two days earlier. The president's plane had managed to stay below 8,000 feet on the 6½ hour, 1,310 mile flight from Cairo to Teheran's Russian-occupied Ghale Morghi Field.[i] Two other U.S. aircraft had accompanied it, the trio carrying a delegation of 77 Americans. Elliott's brother-in-law, Major John Boettiger, was among them.[1264]

The Americans already in Persia had been worried about Elliott's daylong delay, having heard bad stories about what happened to airmen forced down in the Arabian Desert. But to the president's relief, Elliott's plane made it in at 9:30 AM on the 29th.[1265]

Upon arrival, Elliott had a bit of trouble finding his father. Waiting to get picked up, he looked over the airfield, "with rows of Lend-Lease P-39s," and then headed for the American legation. But FDR was not there. He had moved to the Soviet embassy.[1266]

Today it defies credulity that the American president would be staying at the Soviet embassy during a summit. The Soviets had urgently recommended this action, citing security concerns. A crisis involving no less than 38 German paratroopers who had ostensibly been dropped nearby was used to help FDR make up his mind. In recent years, analysts have cited this summit, and Yalta, as American intelligence catastrophes. That is probably a mistake; for FDR and his team deliberately shared everything with the Reds anyway. It probably made no difference where he stayed, or that Stalin read the transcripts of his private conversations every morning.[1267]

A rather chilling description of the activities surrounding the conference has been provided by Gary Kerns in a paper posted by the CIA's Center for the Study of Intelligence. But however compromised Teheran was, it was merely a prelude to the complete Soviet control at Yalta, and to a much lesser extent, Potsdam. Of course, Elliott Roosevelt did not make it to Yalta, though his sister Anna did; and, interestingly, his father's adviser from the State Department, Alger Hiss, also came along.[ii]

Incidentally, Kern said he investigated the Soviet reports of German assassins and found the story was "complete baloney." But Mike Reilly, the Secret Service chief, who was paid to be paranoid, believed the Soviet ruse.[1268]

Both were wrong, but in a convoluted way. There has been a lot of disinformation about this, partly from the Americans who are inclined to think (in retrospect) that the plot was utter rubbish, and partly from the Russians, who seem determined to make the matter into a great Soviet intelligence victory.

---

[i] This airfield (OIIG), five miles south of downtown, is no longer used. Mehrabad airport replaced it.

[ii] Alger Hiss was already known by many as a Soviet agent, but nothing would be done about it until 1948.

As it turns out, there was indeed a German assassination plan, known as Operation Longjump, originally intended for Otto von Skorzeny, the fearless liberator of Mussolini. Skorzeny turned it down as it had no chance of success; but German intelligence nonetheless inserted dozens of special operations agents via nightly parachute drops from Ju-290s operating from the Crimea. These agents landed in German-friendly areas in Qum and in Qazvin. The Soviets knew of the plan almost as soon as it was formulated and immediately rounded up the Qazvin team, along with many more innocents just to be safe. (This would also be the fate of Allied agents dropped behind the Iron Curtain later.) The Qum team, initially safe among Kashgai tribesmen, was located by British counterintelligence in Teheran on the eve of launching a virtual suicide operation against the departing motorcades on 2 December. There was minimal bloodshed. Again, Allied intelligence had run circles around the Germans.

Although hotly disputed, the fascinating story of these events was recounted by Laslo Havas (and his team) in a 1967 book that is a major *tour-de-force* of the spy genre. But it seems like everyone has his own preferred version of the German plot.[1269]

While historians have been skeptical of the German raid, what matters, of course, is what the actors thought at the time. The Soviets weren't lying in principle about it. And perhaps, even with 3,000 troops, they weren't sure they had everything under control. Molotov was also correct in asserting that the Soviet Embassy was by far the most secure of the three embassies. But the Allies turned down the shah's neutral offer, Golistan Palace, which would have been a superb setting. And if secrecy and security had been the objective, a remote location would have been better, as indeed Churchill had ardently proposed. After all was said and done, Stalin got exactly what he wanted.[i]

The president's trip kept him out of Washington for a full five weeks. It is further food for thought that the entire FDR expedition had crossed over areas of questionable allegiances as well as thousands of miles of dangerous, unforgiving terrain. Whether from the defeated Vichyistes in Northwest Africa, the Germans in the Mediterranean, or the Nazi sympathizers in Egypt and Iraq, there was ample opportunity for mayhem along the route. Now, temporarily safe in Teheran, FDR and his staff finally met with Marshal Stalin, who had unyieldingly asserted that he could not risk traveling any further from Moscow. Unlike his Allied interlocutors, he was worried about leaving home.

The British historian Nikolai Tolstoy wrote of Stalin's trip: "He was also frightened of flying and travelled in an aeroplane only once, to attend the Teheran Conference in 1943. There was no rail line between Baku and Teheran, so he had no choice, but his apprehension was plain to all."[1270]

Stalin's concerns were justified; inexplicable fatal air crashes had occurred to some of his enemies, such as Poland's leader General Sikorski. But he took precautions, as further explained by Paul D. Mayle:

> Previously, he had refused to entrust his life to the skill of a pilot, but, at Baku, he transferred to an airplane for his first flight. Original plans called for Stalin's plane to be piloted by a lieutenant general, while the "lesser mortals would go with a mere colonel at the controls," but Stalin chose to go with the colonel because lieutenant generals did not get much flying practice. Three fighter squadrons escorted his plane to Gale Morghe airport on the outskirts of Teheran.[1271]

---

[i] Mayle, Ch. 3, discussed the venues in detail. Harriman, 264-5, "never believed" in the plot, but he nevertheless supported the move for practical reasons. It appears that Kern (quoted) overstated the Soviet trickery. The real trick lay in forcing FDR and Churchill to go to Teheran, which they had strongly resisted.

Perhaps it wasn't the flying that troubled Comrade Stalin. The DC-3 he switched to at the last moment in Baku was that reserved for Lavrentii Beria, the NKVD chief who attended the summit incognito.[1272]

When Stalin first met the American president in his bedroom in the embassy, he looked quizzically at the invalid's thin, stunted legs. He later told him he finally realized the trouble FDR had to endure to meet him, and promised that next time he would come to him. Yet, contrariwise, the next summit would take place in the Crimea.[1273]

From Elliott Roosevelt's professional point of view, the most important subject of discussion at the summit was the shuttle bombing plan (BASEBALL, later FRANTIC). It had already been formally proposed in Moscow in October; now was the opportunity to press Stalin for action on the stalled project. Elliott apparently personally pushed the project from a reconnaissance perspective only, and his father explicitly pleaded his son's case with Stalin. Fortunately, Uncle Joe agreed to help.[1274]

There is no reason here to recapitulate the crucial, world-changing decisions made by The Three at Teheran. Suffice to mention that Stalin got what he wanted; and, of course, by this time, there was not a lot the British could do about it. The American delegation was firmly in the Soviet corner. Even had it not been, it is hard to see how Stalin could not have got his way; his armies were now victorious, and besides he knew exactly what his guests were thinking.

In his memoir, Elliott makes a big deal of Churchill's insistence on a Mediterranean or Balkan approach, the better to intercept the Red Army's advance in the East. Elliott's anti-British hang-up later came to full flower when he furiously denounced the British intervention to stop the Communist take-over in Athens – although by then he put his words into the mouth of his ailing father.[1275]

But Churchill did circle back to a Balkan invasion like a dog after a buried bone. He wanted Turkey in the war, Rhodos invaded, and the Dardanelles opened up. He had to be almost forcibly restrained from this gambit, and Stalin's hypnotic insistence on OVERLORD by 1 May 1944 eventually carried the day.

Uncle Joe deliberately and obviously targeted FDR's son in a major charm offensive. The first encounter, a courtesy visit, went like this:

> In spite of the fact that I had been told that Stalin was shorter than average, I was surprised. I was also feeling pretty good, for I had received a very friendly greeting, together with a twinkle in the eye which invited me to smile. As he spoke – first offering Father and me each a Russian cigarette, two or three puffs of strong, black tobacco at the end of a two-inch cardboard holder – I realized something else about him: that his quiet, deep, measured voice and his short stature notwithstanding, he had a tremendously dynamic quality; inside him there seemed to be great reserves of patience and of assurance. Beside him, his Foreign Commissar, Molotov, was gray and colorless, a sort of carbon copy of my Uncle Theodore Roosevelt as I remember him. Listening to Stalin's quiet words, watching his quick, flashing smile, I sensed the determination that is in his name: Steel.[1276]

Elliott did not formally attend the meetings, but he hovered around, and eagerly joined in the rampant dining, drinking and socializing at the summit. He noticed Captain Randolph Churchill, and WAAF'ie Sarah Churchill doing the same. His most famous contribution came when Marshal Stalin yanked him into a meeting that was already getting a bit rowdy and didn't really need any extra help from the president's son.

50,000 Germans must be Shot!

The celebrated incident at Teheran is, of course, the "50,000 Germans must be shot" episode. Elliott has by far the most entertaining account:

> The dinner that night took place in a dining room which opened off the board room. Marshal Stalin had invited, besides Father and the P.M., Anthony Eden, Molotov, Harriman, Harry Hopkins, Clark Kerr, and, as interpreters, Bohlen, Berezhkov, and Major Birse. I had not been invited, but during the first course one of the Russian secret service men standing in the back of Stalin noticed me at a side entrance, and he leaned over and whispered to Stalin. I could see the Marshal look up and over in my direction, and I started to beat a hasty and embarrassed retreat; but he was on his feet at once, and came over to fetch me. With gestures, he made it quite clear that he wanted me to join the party; an interpreter doubled his invitation in English, explaining that the Marshal said graciously that he had not realized his secretary had not invited me. Insistently he took me by the arm and pulled me back into the room, and a place was made for me between Eden and Harriman.[1277]

Like most diplomatic shindigs with the Soviets, it was a vodka-drenched occasion, a competition to see who would remain standing at the end. "If your staying power is good, you find that it develops in to quite a lot of fun," said Elliott. Stalin himself came around to fill the kid's glass with vodka. As the guests gradually lost their minds, Stalin offered a toast to justice, and to the goal of shooting at least 50,000 Germans after the war was over.[i]

Churchill shot up like a troll out of a box and swore that Britain would never stand for such an act of mass murder. This merely amused Stalin and Roosevelt. The drunken discussion proceeded around the table, centering on how many Germans, exactly, should be shot. Churchill fulminated. Finally, Uncle Joe inquired what Elliott Roosevelt thought of the matter:

> "Well," I said, and took a deep breath, trying to think fast through the champagne bubbles [he was trying to evade the vodka]. "Isn't the whole thing pretty academic? Look: when our armies start rolling in from the west, and your armies are still coming on from the east, we'll be solving the whole thing, won't we? Russian, American, and British soldiers will settle the issue for most of those 50,000, in battle, and I hope that not only those 50,000 war criminals will be taken care of, but many hundreds of thousands more Nazis as well." And I started to sit down again.
>
> But Stalin was beaming with pleasure. Around the table he came, flung an arm around my shoulders. An excellent answer! A toast to my health! I flushed with pleasure, and was about to drink, for it is the Russian custom for one to drink even when it is his own health that is proposed, when all of a sudden an angry finger was being waved right in my face.
>
> Are you interested in damaging relations between the Allies? Do you know what you are saying? How can you dare say such a thing?" It was Churchill – and he was furious, and no fooling. Somewhat shaken to find the Prime Minister and the Marshal squabbling right over my head and feeling a little like Alice–in-Wonderland being crowded by the Hatter and the March Hare at the celebrated Tea Party, I regained my chair, and sat quiet, worried stiff…

---

[i] This famous episode is recounted with slight variations in virtually all conference summaries.

> ...I don't think he ever did forget it. All the months I was to be stationed in England, later on, I was never again invited to spend the night at Chequers. Apparently Mr. Churchill never forgets.[1278]

This, Elliott's first account, is likely to be fairly accurate. It was a rather indelible memory, even if it was preserved in alcohol. True: Elliott Roosevelt no longer was a friend of Winston Churchill. From now on, Elliott's heart belonged to yellow-eyed Iosif Dzhugashvili, the stumpy, pallid Georgian mass murderer.

According to John Boettiger, Churchill raged that "much as I love you, Elliott, I cannot forgive you for making such a dastardly statement," and stomped out – only to be intercepted by the grinning Stalin.[1279]

The much later account in *Rendez-vous* is essentially identical; Elliott noted that his father "roared with laughter" when he tried to apologize to him: "Forget it. Why, Winston will have forgotten all about it when he wakes up."[1280]

Rubbish. Elephant-memoried Churchill noted in his memoirs that he was not at all convinced Stalin was joking. By that time he knew of the grisly discoveries of thousands of murdered Polish officers in the Katyn Forest, and of Stalin's practice of exterminating the intellectual flower of conquered nations.

Churchill wrote nothing about snarling in Elliott's face, but he did say that Elliott played up to Stalin: "But now, Elliott rose in his place at the end of the table and made a speech saying how cordially he agreed with Marshal Stalin's plans, and how sure he was that the U.S. Army would support it." The PM believed that Stalin had earnestly demanded the liquidation of the German General Staff and about 50,000 officers and technicians that enabled Germany to fight. So after Elliott published his light-hearted memoir, Churchill bitterly commented: "He even intervened in the conversation, and has since given a highly colored and exceedingly misleading account of what he heard."[1281]

People hear different things. Take your pick.

Elliott's vivid account left certain clues that strongly suggest that Stalin's courting of him was deliberate and planned: the whisper that Elliott was lurking outside; the sudden apology for not inviting him; the highly charming greetings and the arm around the shoulder; the effusive, cheering praise of Elliott's extraordinary intellect. Others present did not quite grasp this because they did not know that the two already had a history.

As we have seen, in 1934 Elliott was closely involved with Amtorg and the new Soviet embassy in Washington, and he almost managed to wreck bilateral relations before the USSR forced him out of the bomber deal. Ten years later there must have been a hefty file on Stalin's desk, subject Elliott. It was undoubtedly supplemented with the bugging transcripts. In other words, Stalin knew precisely how to flatter the kid. The theory does presume that Stalin considered that recruiting Elliott was worthwhile; but of course it was. At least as long as Dad was in the White House.

Elliott's meetings with Marshal Stalin (and Foreign Commissar Molotov) sounded a number of such odd undertones. One would be heard when Elliott and Molotov met again in Moscow five months later. Another was revealed when Elliott was given an almost unprecedented interview with Stalin in 1946.

Stalin's recent biographer, S.S. Montefiore, captured a striking, even scary parallel that might well relate to Stalin's approach to Elliott. The dictator's son, Vasilii, although ten years younger than Elliott, had already had a similar, meteoric career in the air forces. Montefiore summed it up in a footnote:

> Stalin had specially invited Elliott to the dinner. Perhaps he sensed the similarity with his own scapegrace son, Vasily. Both were pilots, inadequate yet arrogant drunks who were intimidated and dominated by brilliant fathers. Both exploited the family name and embarrassed their fathers. Both failed in multiple marriages and abandoned their wives. Perhaps there is no sadder curse that the gift of a titanic father.[1282]

However tempting (even delicious), that analogy seems a bit overstated. For one thing, the Roosevelt kids were definitely not intimidated by their father. The horrifying career of General Vasilii Dzugashvili, with its criminality and debauchery, reminds one more of Uday Hussain than of Elliott Roosevelt. Vasilii did fly, although he should apparently never have been let near an airplane. After Stalin's death, he was sent to the Gulag; after his release he finally succeeded in drinking himself to death, in 1962.

Most accounts from Teheran, like Churchill's, are more staid than Elliott's, and some omit the incident entirely. It is undoubtedly mostly Elliott's fault that this sordid little episode has gained its notoriety. "Fifty thousand Germans must be shot" obviously required no further staff study. But for our purposes, the story illuminates a number of interesting personalities: Stalin, whom you could never be quite sure of; Churchill, who would fiercely defend his values no matter how drunk he was; Roosevelt Senior, whose giddy lightheartedness about mass executions were right in character; and Elliott, who tried to avoid offending but wound up doing so.

Much more serious matters were decided at Teheran, and these decisions would cost the lives of not 50,000 innocents, but closer to five million. As the principals staggered from toast to toast, there were nations to deport, dismember, and betray; there were borders to draw with an uncertain finger, and even with three matches on the table; there were spheres of influence to define. British foreign minister Anthony Eden thought that to FDR, nations were like toys: he "seemed to see himself disposing of the fate of many lands, allied no less than enemy. He did all this with so much grace that it was not easy to dissent. Yet it was too like a conjurer skillfully juggling with balls of dynamite, whose nature he failed to understand."[1283]

Had German propagandists obtained the minutes, they would have been ecstatic. In outcome, the show resembled nothing so much as the 1939 Molotov-Ribbentrop proceedings, but didn't rise to the grim dignity of that gruesome deal. (How would historians handle "50,000 Poles must be shot!" Nein, 49,500! Harharharhar! Toast!").

An amusing anecdote they are, the 50,000. But they are far more than that. FDR had not forgotten them. At Yalta, when he again spurned Churchill and played up to Stalin, he suggested to the dictator that he should again offer a toast to the 50,000 dead Germans![1284]

At Teheran, when Churchill exploded at Elliott, there was more at stake than a sick joke. Roosevelt and Stalin had joined in taunting and needling the Prime Minister all day, and that rotund human volcano had remained ominously quiescent. Churchill could not blow up at FDR; the Americans were his sole hope. But he could erupt in the face of Elliott, and he did. FDR clearly enjoyed the spectacle. For the first time, Churchill realized how small his country suddenly was, and that the president had found a new best friend.[i]

Churchill had had a very bad day, and it didn't help that when he and Eden staggered home on foot, the gate guard at the British embassy cussed this tipsy Laurel & Hardy act out and told them to get lost. The couple had sent the limousine on ahead, electing to walk home to get some fresh air.[1285]

Many noticed that Stalin and Roosevelt had toyed with Churchill. Bohlen and Harriman, for example:

> 'I did not like the attitude of the President, who not only backed Stalin but seemed to enjoy the Churchill-Stalin exchanges,' Bohlen recalled. 'Roosevelt should have come to the defense of a close friend and ally, who was really being put upon by Stalin.' Harriman noticed the same unattractive streak in Roosevelt's character: 'He always enjoyed other people's discomfort.'[1286]

The British left Teheran dejected, even disgusted: "It was a pity, [ambassador] Clark-Kerr later regretted, that their words were not recorded, 'that people might know what piffle great men sometimes say.'"[ii]

Field Marshal Alan Brooke elaborated:

> After listening to the arguments put forward during the last two days I feel more like entering a lunatic asylum, or nursing home, than continuing my present job. I am absolutely disgusted with the politicians' methods of waging war. Why will they imagine they are experts at a job they know nothing about![1287]

But here we see the summit with Elliott's eyes, and he was absolutely enthralled. On one night, his father had said, it seemed 365 toasts were drunk, one for each day of the year! Elliott remembered: "…I am afraid that accurate count was lost. I do remember that a good part of the dinner was spent standing up; I do remember Stalin's cheerful habit of touching the glass of everyone in whose name we were drinking."[1288]

It's no wonder Air Marshal Portal said, "What a waste of time this is." He wanted to go back to Cairo since "no useful purpose is served by our being here."[1289] But he may have been referring to the Big Two ganging up on Nr. 3, as much as to the frivolity.

During the prolonged neutrality debate, President Roosevelt famously trumpeted, "I HATE WAH!" That he had to do so is a clue to how untrue it was. He was exhilarated by his short visit to the front in 1918. After being allowed to fire a cannon, he mused, "I'll never know how many Huns, if any, I killed."[1290] As the summits illustrated, the great world leaders (obviously including the Axis) passionately loved war and suffered cruelly without it. As Jesse Jones wrote in his memoir, by the end Roosevelt had come to think of himself as a new Caesar or Alexander.[1291]

As the 50,000-Germans argument illustrated, Churchill was the moral superior of them: he was at least a hypocrite. Confronted with the results of the air campaign, he asked: "Are we beasts?"[iii] As the war degenerated into a frenzied competition to see who

---

[i] Jon Meacham is among those who realized that FDR deliberately betrayed Churchill at Teheran (and Yalta), and placed Elliott's anecdote in that context.

[ii] Mayle, 97. Archibald Clark-Kerr was the British ambassador in Moscow.

[iii] Christopher Harmon, Are We Beasts? Monograph (Newport Paper #1), Naval War College, DEC 91. WC said this in June 1943 (not after Dresden), so he had two years to contemplate the answer.

could kill the most people before the whistle blew, the prime minister's peers had no such qualms. The awkward fact remains, though, that with decent and humanitarian leaders like the tragedy-fated Hoover and Chamberlain, it is doubtful that the war could have been so effectively prosecuted – or even won.

At Teheran, as everywhere, Elliott networked furiously. He met with the young shah of the Persians, Reza Pahlevi, though he had no idea of his later importance. The 24-year old had been installed on the throne by the British, who thought that his father had been much too nice to the Germans – which he had been because of his country's historically tight embrace by the Russian and British empires.

This turned out to be an important connection for the shah and the Roosevelts. After the defeat of Germany, the Soviet Union declared an independent republic in northern Iran – an attempt at division which the shah was able to quash. Again in 1953, during persistent unrest that remains controversial, an American secret agent, Kermit Roosevelt, Theodore's grandson, was instrumental in returning the shah to power.

After the shah's dramatic, humiliating fall in 1979, Elliott snidely reminisced that the young Reza had been more interested in flying "my" airplanes than in serious matters.[1292] Here we have a striking illustration of how adjustable and suspect Elliott's memory was, especially for someone who made a living regurgitating it. In 1946 he had written that the shah was "earnest, serious, and intent."[1293] And when the shah visited the United States in 1949, he visited with Elliott for Thanksgiving dinner.[1294] During that trip, the shah flew a B-25 at Dayton; he said he owned a B-17, and Eleanor chided him for being a "skillful but reckless pilot." Elliott may have gotten the "my" airplane story from that visit.[i]

Then consider that in 1977, with the shah still riding high, Elliott wrote of a post-war meeting with Reza:

> ...the young, hawk-eyed shah of Iran was full of the time he met Father in Teheran. He remembered listening enthralled as FDR predicted that irrigation dams and hydroelectric power would transform a country of sand and dust into an oasis of industry serving as a buffer to Soviet expansion in the Near East. The shah was following the course outlined for him by FDR, he explained, and Mother glowed with pleasure.[1295]

It seems that just two years before the fall, Elliott thought Shah Reza Pahlevi to be the FDR of Iran. For sure, the shah did retain his love of modern warplanes of American manufacture; and he became an accomplished pilot himself.

At noon on 1 December, Elliott and Leon Gray took the B-25 on the long trip back to Tunis, via Cairo. They had spent only two days in the Soviet-occupied city; and it is remarkable how much verbatim memory Elliott retained from the trip, as demonstrated in his book three years later. EUREKA closed at the end of that day.[ii]

The president conducted some courtesy visits to troops in Camp Amirabad, the large American headquarters in the outskirts of the Persian capital. Then later on the morning of 2 December, he also flew, by C-54, to Cairo, via Baghdad.

---

[i] Eleanor, My Day, 29 NOV 49. On the 27th, the Shah flew in to Wright-Patterson AFB on the Sacred Cow and flew a B-25 for 25 minutes. (NYT, 28 NOV 49)

[ii] Technically, Teheran was in a neutral zone, with the rest of defeated Iran divided between Britain and the USSR. By this time both the Americans and the Soviets were all over the city and its environs.

Cairo II

When Colonel Roosevelt came back to Tunis, he was preoccupied with moving his remaining units up to Italy, where the Allied advance was hopelessly but not surprisingly stalled. However, he was not done with family business:

> Early on Sunday, December 5th, I took off for Cairo, again with Leon Gray, and by late afternoon we were settling down at the ATC field (Payne) once more. I went directly to the Kirk villa, where I knew Father would again be staying.[i]

Cairo II, codenamed SEXTANT, had already been going on for four days when Elliott arrived. The Anglo-American military commanders had occasion to refine their plans for the invasion of France, but the two leaders were also interested in patching up relations with Turkey.

It was a short visit, although Elliott seems to have found out from his father everything that happened in the meantime. Stalin had agreed to attack Japan six months after VE-day. The Allies had given up on having Turkey join the war; it would be more trouble than it was worth. Churchill had been singularly eager for Turkey's participation, reflecting his Balkan fetish; the two others saw through that.

Suffering John Boettiger got to be abnormally useful by escorting President Inönu on a flight to Cairo to consult with Churchill and Roosevelt; he thus preempted a British flight for the same purpose.

Elliott was excused when the Turkish leader and the Soviet ambassador to Ankara met with the Big Two. The pasha wasn't worried about the Axis, but about the Soviet Union. Turkey would join the Allies just before the German capitulation, mostly to secure a place in the United Nations. Notably, at this meeting the great air base at Incirlik was agreed on; it would become critically important to the Western Allies in the coming decades.

That Monday, Elliott lunched with his father, Churchill, and Hopkins. He again talked with his father before leaving to fly back to Tunis that night. The president let him know of the appointment of General Eisenhower to command operation OVERLORD, something Ike was absolutely not to know about yet.

President Roosevelt left Cairo on 7 December, but not until he had observed tradition and gone sightseeing with Winston, at the pyramids.

Eisenhower's new Assignment

Elliott was keenly attuned to Eisenhower's constant fretting over who would get the OVERLORD job. Despite the crushing burden of the Mediterranean command, the disappointingly slow progress up the Italian boot, and the fatigue and anxiety reflected in the smoking of three packs of cigarettes a day, Eisenhower desperately wanted the invasion command – the greatest field command in American history. Yet it was widely assumed that his boss, General Marshall, wanted the job and would get it.

In the months prior to the announcement, young Colonel Roosevelt functioned as a sounding board for his commander's discreet inquiries. Elliott was eager to help his

---

[i] ER: As He Saw It, 201. Refers to U.S. Ambassador Kirk's house close to the Mena Hotel.

friend, but he too assumed Marshall would get the job. In fact, Elliott's father thought so too, until he changed his mind at the last moment – not for a lack of confidence in Marshall, but on the contrary because he simply couldn't imagine running the war without him back in Washington. There are several variant versions of the story, though.

Elliott reminisced about the choice a couple of years later. He said Churchill wanted Field Marshal Sir Alan Brooke to have command of the invasion, and the Americans wanted Marshall, "but my father had an awful lot of trouble in selling the Prime Minister anything with regard to General Marshall, because the PM and Marshall tangled many, many times. And in the course of the tangling, the PM had quite an aversion to General Marshall." Furthermore, "and as a result, my Father told me that he was unable to sell the PM on the choice of General Marshall." Scholars disagree. [1296]

In *Crusade in Europe*, Eisenhower touched on the matter in a rather formal way, stating that obviously neither he nor Marshall would stoop to any campaigning for the command – rumors to the contrary were vile and false. But in his diaries he left no doubt that the matter troubled him greatly. On 6 December 1943, he wrote:

> I have seen quite a bit of Colonel Elliott Roosevelt, who is apparently quite close to the president in family councils. He feels that the president is quite undecided as to what is the best thing to do, especially since the meeting at Teheran, where it is understood that Stalin insisted both upon OVERLORD in the spring and upon the utmost pressing of the Italian campaign during the winter.
>
> Colonel Roosevelt has had many conferences with his father and has evolved a formula which he hopes his father will accept. He believes that the things actually troubling the president are that (1) General Marshall's great contributions to the cause of the United Nations (which are recognized and acknowledged by all) entitle him to a field command on the theory that a chief of staff will never be remembered in history, while every independent field commander will be given place possibly far out of proportion to his contributions; and (2) there should be a single mind directing the coordination between OVERLORD and operations in the Mediterranean theater. This means an over-all command for the European theater in some form or other.
>
> Elliott Roosevelt's theory is that General Marshall's place is different from that of any previous chief of staff in the American army and that his position in history is already fixed. He contends, moreover, that the European campaign from England, no matter how important, will be only a phase of the war and that the contemplated change will deprive the president of General Marshall's great abilities during the stages against Japan.
>
> His next point is that the president could secure the needed coordination between OVERLORD and operations in the Mediterranean theater, which coordination is functionally a responsibility of the combined chiefs of staff, by merely appointing General Marshall as the executive of the combined chiefs of staff during the critical stages of the operation. This plan would not remove General Marshall from his present position, would give him a virtual field command during the most critical stage of the operations, and would secure the rapid coordination envisioned by the president in a single command.
>
> Under Colonel Roosevelt's scheme, General [Sir Alan] Brooke would be the actual field commander in England, while I would remain here.[1297]

Elliott's analysis was quite sensible, but the result wasn't exactly what he expected.

The next day President Roosevelt flew to Tunis and told General Eisenhower that he would command OVERLORD. In truth, FDR had sworn his son to secrecy about the appointment, saying it must come from Marshall.[1298] But Eisenhower claimed

Marshall's telegram was garbled, and he didn't know of the decision until FDR got into the car with him that afternoon, 7 December, and said, "Well, Ike, you are going to command OVERLORD."[1299]

Ike planted that version firmly in the history books, but Elliott didn't tell it this way thirty years later. He wrote that FDR told Eisenhower: "Well, Ike, you'd better start packing," which the general interpreted to mean he was going to a desk job in Washington. Not until next morning's flight to Malta was Ike briefed on his new command.[1300]

So was Elliott Roosevelt secretly the scheming architect of the Allied command structure? Ike seems to have thought Elliott had a strong hand in the matter; he raised the subject repeatedly with Elliott beforehand. Elliott downplayed his own role. But it is inconceivable that father and son would not have had words about Eisenhower's and Marshall's roles. It is just as probable that Elliott spoke in favor of his bridge partner. Ike inspired loyalty; in Elliott's case so much that he, leftist Democratic icon as he was, would declare for Ike in 1948 and1952.

However, the romance had ended when Elliott wrote of it in 1975: "Yet Eisenhower gradually became carried away with his own importance. He became an obliging tool in the clasp of manipulators who worked to make him rich and President of the United States…" He continued with a long denunciation of Ike and his administration.[1301]

Elliott failed to mention a cardinal trait of Eisenhower's: abundant caution. It was precisely this risk-avoidant agreeableness that made him an acceptable choice as commander in chief. But many have held that this usually advantageous inclination also prolonged the war, gave the Soviets Central Europe, and, to mention only one later example, sacrificed the people of Hungary in 1956. It also made the president more tolerant of corrupt or undesirable party hacks, his vice president being the most obvious example. Elliott resented this since it benefited Republican influence-peddlers, bypassing himself.

Opinions change; facts don't. Nearly everyone, regardless of party, thought highly of Eisenhower in the 1940s. In the 1960s, he was dismissed as a golf-playing do-nothing who had presided over a stale era. Yet today most historians see him as one of the finest leaders the country has ever produced. Perhaps only Marshall would have been greater! At least that's how Elliott remembered Ike in 1983. Once more he was "a man of great vision and honor, compassion and modesty. I was enriched by having known him."[1302]

Back to OVERLORD: When FDR explained Ike's appointment to Elliott back in Cairo, he said the main reason was that Marshall would stand up to Churchill, but Eisenhower was more pliable:

> It's not absolutely settled yet, Elliott. But it seems pretty clear that Winston will refuse absolutely to let Marshall take over. Marshall…it's not that he's argued too often with the PM on military matters, it's just that he's won too often. It's a disappointment for him, too, I'm sure. [1303]

Churchill's antipathy towards Marshall was mostly a figment of Elliott's imagination. Winston appreciated "jaw-jaw" at the summits. FDR told his son that Marshall was the only American general able to stare down the prime minister in the heated debates over strategy.[1304] Marshall might not have seen it that way – he'd lost the battle for a 1943 invasion, and much of the U.S. war effort had been dissipated in the Mediterranean.

It is disconcerting to witness great men so acutely concerned about "their place in history." But without ambition, they wouldn't have been great to begin with. As for Elliott, he too fretted about his advancement. He wanted to know from his father if Ike's appointment meant that Spaatz would go to England, taking Elliott with him, and putting him in charge of reconnaissance for the invasion. FDR said that matter was too far down the chain for his attention. Still, just weeks later, that is exactly what happened.[1305]

Back at El Aouina Field in Tunisia, father and son and General Eisenhower reconnected. After an overnight stay in Carthage, FDR and Ike went on to Malta and Sicily to meet with the troops.

The paraplegic president might be accused of much, but not of sparing himself. Presidential travel was a lot more strenuous in those days, even for healthy people, and FDR was noticeably flagging. The volume of complex and varied business FDR managed to oversee during his month away from home is mind-boggling, and several similar trips were in the near future. Whether this hectic pace shortened his life is not so clear – at times it seemed to rejuvenate him. His smoking and drinking probably had more to do with his rapid decline and early death.

After Tunis, the president went on to Dakar in a twelve-hour flight which he again resented; unpressurized, the aircraft cruised at 8,000 feet.[1306] At Dakar he caught the USS *Iowa*, aboard which he returned to the United States. Safely home, Anna regaled him with the latest details she knew of Elliott's sex tourism; his torrid affair with Faye Emerson; and what she knew about Franklin Jr. having the hots for Kay Summersby. The president loved it; he'd seen Kay with General Eisenhower and felt sure there was hanky-panky going on.[1307]

At about the same time, Colonel Roosevelt boarded the last transport plane carrying the remainder of his headquarters from La Marsa to San Severo. He would not stay in Italy long. On 19 January 1944, he wrote, his "outfit" arrived in England.[1308] His reconnaissance wing actually continued in the Mediterranean under Colonel Polifka; Roosevelt was given a new task in Britain, directly under General Spaatz.

To celebrate the move, friend Eisenhower gave Elliott Roosevelt a Christmas gift. On 25 December, Elliott received the Legion of Merit. The citation stated:

> ELLIOTT ROOSEVELT, O-398475, Colonel, Air Corps, for exceptionally meritorious conduct in the performance of outstanding services from 7 November 1942 to 30 October 1943. By his dynamic energy and inspiring zeal, he built the small photographic and reconnaissance group which he commanded, into a photo reconnaissance wing which controlled the preparation of photographic intelligence for all planning staffs and operations in the theater. His keen insight into the invaluable aid of aerial photography, and the knowledge of its practical application, enabled him to make an outstanding contribution to the success of the Tunisian and Sicilian Campaigns, and of the initial operations in Italy.[1309]

Arnold and Eisenhower were keen to compliment the president's son. But both of them also realized the value of his trade. In particular, Ike is remembered for being one of the few who already understood that G-2, intelligence, should not be a dumping ground for less capable officers. His appreciation of aerial reconnaissance would move with him to the White House ten years later.[1310]

THE SORCERER'S APPRENTICE

Thus by January 1944, Colonel Roosevelt was detached from the nearly stalemated Mediterranean sideshow and assigned to the new "sharp end" – the preparation for the invasion of France. He was working as General Carl Spaatz's reconnaissance advisor while a new allied air intelligence infrastructure was devised. Indeed, Eisenhower had taken Spaatz and Roosevelt with him to England because he needed them there.

As we have seen, almost everything the Americans knew about air reconnaissance they had first learned from the British. A case in point was that American photographic interpreters were initially assigned to British units, and USAAF aircraft were tasked by British commanders. The RAF had already gained over four years of experience working out the procedures, trying out tactics, and training up the considerable intellectual infrastructure necessary to support reconnaissance operations.[1311]

While RAF Benson in Oxfordshire was the base from which the British reconnaissance aircraft originated, the headquarters of the Allied air offensive was at High Wycombe, Buckinghamshire, a suburb northwest of London without an airfield. Both RAF Bomber Command and the American 8th Air Force were centered on this location, although they commanded a multitude of bases throughout the "unsinkable aircraft carrier" that Britain had become.

High Wycombe was usually referred to by its codename *Pinetree.* In contrast, the headquarters of U.S. Strategic Air Forces (USSTAF) at Bushey Park, Teddington in southwestern London was referred to as *Widewing.* USSTAF was, by 1944, a new level of command above the 8th Air Force (England) and 15th Air Force (Italy). Spaatz commanded USSTAF, Doolittle the 8th and Eaker the 15th.

Photointerpretation had quickly developed into an art and a science, but it was still under the aegis of the Allied Central Interpretation Unit (ACIU) at Medmenham, not far from High Wycombe. Here new U.S. intelligence specialists learned the ropes from practiced British personnel, many of them women from the RAF auxiliary, the WAAF.

But there always comes a time when the apprentice thinks he has learned enough to strike out on his own. It was inevitable that cracks would begin to show in the Allied brotherhood, not because of ill will (although that is usually in plentiful supply in bureaucracies), but because the Americans necessarily had a different long-term agenda.

General Spaatz realized that the American air forces had to be able to fight on their own, since they would sooner or later be redeployed, probably to the Pacific. And, U.S. forces had to look ahead to peacetime operations. Finally, USAAF and RAF strategic bombing followed two different paradigms, with the Americans focused on precision daylight bombing while the British preferred to burn entire cities by night. Naturally the former placed by far the heaviest demands on reconnaissance.

As late as October 1944 General Fred Anderson, who was Spaatz's deputy, bluntly said, "if it would become necessary for us to break off from British sources of intelligence at short notice we would be lost."[1312]

Thus the pressure mounted to develop a capability separate from the RAF reconnaissance organization, and there are indications that Colonel Roosevelt was one of the most eager instigators of the split.

Elliott was known for having anti-British feelings, in some respects parroting the anti-imperialist rhetoric of his parents. But whether this antipathy extended to rank prejudice is difficult to gauge, and obviously easy to deny: he, after all, had commanded multinational units with considerable success before.

The colonel was well aware of the issue. That's why he elaborated in *As He Saw It*:

> …on arrival [High Wycombe] I was told my duties [by Spaatz]: to reorganize all the American Reconnaissance Air Forces units of both the Eighth (bombardment, strategic) and Ninth (light bombardment, tactical) Air Forces, and to supervise their operations so as to obtain all information necessary to the invasion of Europe. ..My outfit joined the swelling ranks of American soldiers in Britain on January 19th, and we promptly went to work beside our British opposites of the RAF. In view of the criticisms which I have expressed in regard to some of the British warmakers, I am anxious to set it down that these RAF officers with whom I worked from mid-January up until D-day and thereafter until the final Nazi capitulation were a group of consummately knowledgeable officers, thoroughly familiar with their job and individually and severally as hardworking and as anxious to win the war as quickly as possible as any group of men it would have been possible to find. Not only were they a constant credit to their country, but they were in large part responsible for the small percentage of losses suffered in the invasion itself. I know I speak for all the American officers who worked with RAF reconnaissance experts in according them a considerable amount of the credit for the success of our arms in Europe.[1313]

This recollection corresponds to the 8th Air Force directive that established the 8th Provisional Reconnaissance Wing. In it, Colonel Roosevelt was tasked with all its operations, including radar, electronic countermeasures, and weather flights; also, preparation of target charts, maps and folders, mosaics, enlargement and models; and processing film, producing prints, and preparing interpretation reports.[1314]

In carrying out these new American tasks, Roosevelt was directed to coordinate with his RAF counterparts, avoiding unnecessary duplication, and ensuring maximum combined efficiency. In addition, Roosevelt's new wing had to take on some of these tasks for the 9th (tactical) Air Force, and assume responsibility for maintaining photo libraries and meet the mapping requirements of the Corps of Engineers "insofar as it was operationally and technically possible."

General Doolittle's order concluded by stating that the new wing "must be self-contained and sufficiently independent to permit movement, at some future time, to another theatre with all essential services intact."[1315]

Clearly, this was an American declaration of independence. Like King George III in his day, the RAF was most unhappy with this and fought the separation bureaucratically but fiercely. Many Americans also felt that they benefitted immensely from the RAF's expertise and experience, and in particular that flying British aircraft and using British cameras was an improvement over American equipment.

Not everyone saw it that way. When Colonel Roosevelt took command he asserted that American pilots should fly American aircraft. One expert noted:

> Despite improvements made in later versions of the F-5, they remained less capable than the British Mosquito or Spitfire IX and XII, the latter being the premier recon. craft of this theater. Although American airmen considered using the Mosquito and actually operated Spitfire IXs in 1943, in early 1944 the commander of the 8th PRW (provisional), Col. Elliott Roosevelt…decided to stick with American-made F-5s supplemented by F-6s (P-51s).[1316]

The Spitfires went back, and the U.S. squadrons flew F-6 Mustangs and F-5 Lightnings.[1317] Lend-Lease worked both ways, so effectively the two allies pooled their aircraft, but still they fought over them from time to time. In particular, the RAF rebuffed constant American demands for more Mosquitoes with the perfectly reasonable rejoinder that they knew best how to operate them, and of course the photographic results were shared for the benefit of both Allies anyway.[1318]

When the Americans finally did get their long-awaited 120 British Mosquitoes, some of them were no longer interested. Almost shockingly, Colonel Roosevelt did finally turn sour on the Mosquito as well. On 27 July, he declined to receive more. General Doolittle disagreed and ordered 23 to 8th Air Force units for Roosevelt's wing to maintain. This caused some trouble:

> Col. Roosevelt protested and refused to accept their assignment. He bypassed Doolittle and dispatched a cable directly to General Spaatz halting further deliveries, stating "No requirement exists in the 8th AF for the F-8." This action upset Doolittle and created irreconcilable differences between the two officers, resulting later in Doolittle's attempt to expel Col. Roosevelt from the ETO.[1319]

This is the first indication we have of a serious spat between the two, and Doolittle later praised Elliott's work. But Elliott's rash action was outrageous, even if his standpoint might have been reasonable. And it does seem that his new preference for American aircraft was practical rather than nationalistic in rationale.

It is well known that both Colonel Roosevelt and Colonel McDonald, a colleague in commanding intelligence units, pressed for a completely American capability organized under USSTAF headquarters. An intelligence historian has described it thus:

> The initial outcome of this American effort – which the British vehemently opposed – was the creation in February 1944 of the 8th PRW (Provisional) to ensure continued reconnaissance support for strategic air operations preceding and subsequent to Operation OVERLORD. After months of memoranda, proposals, counterproposals, and meetings (incl. at least one chaired by Spaatz), first and second phase photo interpretation for daylight bombing missions were shifted in May 1944 to USSTAF. British and American interpreters at Medmenham, redesignated as the Allied Central Interpretation Unit, continued to perform third phase interpretation. For more effective coordination and to reduce duplication of effort, the Allies established a Joint Photo Recon Committee with American and British Army, Air Force, and Navy representatives. In August 1944, the 8th PRW (P) was redesignated the 325th PRW. Roosevelt retained his dual responsibilities as commander of the 325th and photo reconnaissance advisor to Spaatz.[1320]

The phases of interpretation refer to the urgency with which photographs were analyzed and acted on. First phase required immediate action, second within hours, and third being reserved for matters requiring some contemplation. Thus one image could often serve both tactical and strategic needs.

Colonel Roosevelt retained command when the provisional wing became the 325th Photographic Reconnaissance Wing after D-day. By then he had already proved the concept of independent American operation, and his superiors were well pleased.

The 325th Photographic Reconnaissance Wing

It was as commander of the 325th PRW, almost an air force to itself, that Elliott Roosevelt would earn his star. He was already eligible for promotion to flag rank by then, although it would be a few more months before that was allowed to happen. The wing was comprised of two reconnaissance groups, the 7th PRG at RAF Mount Farm and the 25th Bombardment Group (Reconnaissance) at RAF Watton. [1321]

The first of these groups, the 7th, was a traditional reconnaissance outfit flying Spitfire PR XI, Mustangs, Lightnings, and Stinson L-5 light observation aircraft. It was organized into a fluctuating number of squadrons, including photoreconnaissance squadrons 13, 14, 22, 27, 28, 29, and 30. The 7th PRG had moved from Colorado to its English bases without participating in the Mediterranean operations. It was therefore late in seeing action, but that did not mean all its pilots and commanders were green.[1322]

Before Colonel Paul Cullen went to Russia, he had command of the 7th PRG – ironically he was thus subordinate to the young navigator he had taken along on Project RUSTY less than two years earlier. The group, commanded at various times by Elliott buddies Cols. James G. Hall, Clarence Shoop and George Humbrecht, would provide essential coverage of France and the Low Countries as the Allied offensive in Europe proceeded.

Many of Roosevelt's aircraft flew from Mount Farm near RAF Benson, the main British reconnaissance base. Conveniently, Medmenham – the central interpretation unit – and High Wycombe (Pinetree), the 8th Air Force headquarters, were relatively close.

The other group, the 25th Bomb Group (Recon.), was known until August as the 802nd Photographic Reconnaissance Group. It was quite unusual. It has probably received far too little attention given that its missions were of a highly specialized nature. It was organized into the 652nd Bomb Squadron (Heavy), the 653rd BS (Light), and the 654th BS (Special), all operating out of RAF Watton.[1323] In common parlance, they were the heavy, the light, and the special squadron.

The 652nd primarily flew B-17Gs and B-24Js on long-range Atlantic weather reconnaissance missions. This is where Colonel Roosevelt's earlier Atlantic experience was helpful. The unit began weather flights from St. Eval near the tip of Cornwall in September 1943, but moved to RAF Bovingdon near London in November before finally winding up at Watton in 1944. Watton is located in East Anglia.[1324]

By 1944, aircraft were available to patrol the Atlantic Ocean from Iceland to the Azores, reporting back synoptic observations of the vast ocean area where European weather originated. The weather flights, carrying the code name *Epicure*, averaged over twelve hours in duration. The 652nd usually had at least one, often two, aircraft over the Atlantic at any given time. It was quite a contrast to the shortage of men and planes only three years earlier when Captain Roosevelt first scouted the North Atlantic route.

The Azores run was referred to as *Sharon* missions, and the regular Atlantic flights as *Allah*. In the summer, the squadron converted to the better performing B-24; but then it was found that the B-17 was easier to fly in weather and icing, and a back-conversion followed. These B-17Gs were stripped versions with substantially better performance; they were said to pick up 40 mph from the change, which left only the rear turret functional.[1325]

The light squadron, the 653rd, flew the new Mosquito PR XVIs, finally a version that met the expectations the Americans had long harbored. These aircraft would range throughout Europe on diverse tasks such as target weather recon, day and night photography, and ECM (electronic counter-measures) missions. The meteorological missions were code-named *Bluestocking*, while the pathfinder or scouting missions were labeled *Scout.* 653rd squadron also participated in the FRANTIC shuttle missions to the Ukraine, described in a following chapter.

Seaweed missions were coastline reconnaissance. Radar intelligence with scope photography was referred to as *Mickey* flights. In the fall of 1944, *Scouts* were discontinued, *Seaweeds* declined, and *Mickeys* came to be increasingly important.

The special squadron, the 654th, was the strangest of all the units. It had a motley complement of aircraft for use in special operations. These included B-26G Invaders, the new American twin bomber that would become popular in the post-war era, but Mosquitoes, Mitchells, and Lightnings were also used. The B-26s were favored for flash-bomb photography. This squadron was used for regular day and night photo reconnaissance (codenamed *Pru* and *Joker* respectively) as well as ECM activities, including laying chaff (*Green Pea* missions), and some special operations involving communication with agents within occupied countries. The latter, run on behalf of the Office of Strategic Services (OSS), were code-named *Redstocking*, and they were not begun until late in the year. The squadron historian mused: "November also witnessed the advent of another mission, the Redstocking, but as yet no information as to the nature or purpose of the mission has been released." [i]

It is possible that the *Redstocking* code name was selected to associate these extremely sensitive operations with the more innocuous weather flights. In the OSS, the *Redstocking* flights were referred to as *Joan-Eleanor* missions. That code name referred to a new VHF portable radio system used by agents in occupied Europe. Their radio transmissions were recorded in the aircraft for later evaluation at home.

The Americans were also bringing on line a new navigational system similar to British Decca. It was known as LORAN, and Mosquitoes of the 25th BG were specially fitted to perform signal calibration on flights over Europe under the code name *Sky Wave.* Other highly specialized electronic and photographic missions were also given to the 25th BG, including the Mosquito escorts flown for operation ANVIL, the ill-fated drone program.

The obscure and technical nature of some of these flights is undoubtedly the origin of James Roosevelt's contention that Elliott participated in super-secret and highly dangerous flights over Europe. Obviously, the OSS agent insertion flights would be the most sensitive, but during the last year of the war the Allies were able to conduct such operations at night with near impunity.

One month's operational summary of the 325th PRW gives a flavor of the operations Elliott oversaw. Particularly significant is its obsessive emphasis on weather:

> From D-day -7 until D-day +11, reconnaissance and photographic work was carried on in all kinds of weather, and at all hours of the day and night. Vital areas and installations of the German West Wall were photographed completely; enemy activity in all enemy defense zones was photographed; and complete oblique coverage of the entire coast from Antwerp to Bordeaux accomplished. However, the important work of damage assessment, and mapping of German and occupied territory was not curtailed, but was carried out even more extensively. At the same time, more weather information was necessary, and the

[i] For details refer to the 325th PRW History at AFHRA. ECM = Electronic Counter-Measures; Chaff = Cut Tinfoil to defeat Radar; see 654 PRS History, November 1944, AFHRA

> scheduling of more weather flights became mandatory. Many *epicure* flights (weather recon over the ocean), *allah* flights (weather recon over the U.K.), and *bluestocking* flights (weather recon over the continent) were carried out in all kinds of weather. Scout weather planes, a new phase in tactical air warfare, were also dispatched to precede the heavy bombers, and to radio the weather conditions existing over the scheduled targets. This stupendous amount of work was accomplished with a daily effective strength of but 55 aircraft and crews for combined operations (7th PRG and the 802nd Recon Group). There were 335 sorties accomplished, of which 77% were successful flights in which the pilot brought back satisfactory pictures of one or more targets. Of the missions flown, 60% were over the "Invasion Area" of Western and Central France; the remainder over Eastern France, Belgium, Holland, Germany, and Poland. Many of the flights ran into intense enemy opposition, and seven of the planes failed to return.[1326]

This summary indicates a loss rate of 2% during the heavy fighting of June 1944. While surely distasteful to those within that fraction, it was an eminently sustainable rate for the Allied air forces.

The large number of aircraft and personnel under Elliott Roosevelt's command inevitably raises the question of when enough is enough. In war, the answer is almost always: Never. Despite serious worries about idleness of his wing, as the German-held area contracted and winter weather grounded most flying, Elliott wanted more:

> As late as January 1945, at the HQ USSTAF-hosted American air intelligence officers' conference, Elliott Roosevelt noted that requests for reconnaissance support continued to exceed resources despite the presence of 29 American and 15 RAF squadrons in western Europe and Italy.[1327]

By then, the Allies had an immense reconnaissance capability, compared to which the Luftwaffe could barely mount a few successful photographic sorties (such as with the new Arado 234 jet). Allied air superiority had become absolutely crushing.

Of course, although Roosevelt might have chalked in numerous PR squadrons on the boards, the number of available, operational aircraft was always far less than the nominal standard. But the 325th PRW was only one of several wings, American and British, that now covered the quickly shrinking Axis territory. Was enough enough? One consideration was that in principle, reconnaissance should create better economies of bomber force utilization. Despite this, the bomber force also swelled to the point where wanton genocidal bombing became the preferred method of warfare, particularly towards the end in Japan. It was not some tortured strategic decision; it was simply the result of finally having the resources to do so.

Obviously, Colonel Roosevelt was no longer a forlorn captain trying to prove his worth – quite the contrary. At some point, General Doolittle pulled him off combat duty, and that created the impression among a few malcontented subordinates that he was not pulling his load. But he was a wing commander, and in truth could be most effective at his headquarters. Still, his flying record shows that he did get many sorties in.[1328] Although opinions of him were sharply divided, he produced results.

A couple of strange incidents warrant mention. Sometime in early 1944, John Kennedy, an RCAF pilot, wrote a letter mentioning that he had, if not saved Elliott's life, at least gotten him out of a very tight spot. Evidently a Fortress he and "General Smith" were flying got lost in bad weather over England. Kennedy was scrambled to intercept the aircraft and guide it down, which he did. When the story was published,

Colonel Roosevelt issued a denial, which as usual in his case didn't actually deny anything but stated that "there was nothing to it." That it was a "routine emergency" seems clear, but evidently it impressed Mr. Kennedy enough to write home about it.

The newspapers speculated that "Smith" might have been General Walter Bedell Smith, but C.R. seems a far more logical candidate in this case.[1329]

It is not clear whether this incident is related to the rumors that navigator Elliott lost his way in a B-17 and was forced to land in the Irish Free State, a diplomatic inconvenience. That one circulated among servicemen, but detailed records of Irish landings do not support it.[1330] Very likely Roosevelt-haters had heard that Elliott had landed in Northern Ireland, and managed to confuse themselves over it. Elliott also did make an emergency landing on Man at one time.[1331]

Such little snafus were common among the good and the wicked alike. They did not hurt Elliott's reputation among his superiors. His other skills shone brightly enough.

A talent for wheeling and dealing was quite helpful during the period when Allied reconnaissance had to be reorganized. Throughout the war, Elliott's prominent qualities of energy, enthusiasm, optimism, and confidence, all especially prized by Americans, got him a long ways down that road. Indeed, phony or not, these are the traits that allowed his father to win four national elections. It would take closer inspection for many to detect the commensurate characteristics of shallowness, inconstancy, and economy with the truth (though not with anything else). However the balance came out, Elliott Roosevelt was impressive enough to cause General Arnold to approve his promotion to brigadier general at the end of 1944.

Advances in Reconnaissance

In the Air Corps, Colonel Roosevelt was recognized not merely for the (hardly routine) task of running a photo-reconnaissance wing, but for some notable innovations in technology and tactics that greatly improved the amount and usability of information Allied aircraft could bring back.

When he took over as commander of the 8th Provisional PRW in February 1944, Roosevelt was faced with the task of obtaining extra difficult intelligence on German coastal fortifications in France, so as to be better able to plan and execute operation OVERLORD. Unexpectedly, he would get some critical help from an old friend.

Back at the photographic laboratory at Wright Field, Colonel George Goddard had shared Roosevelt's passion to acquire a dedicated reconnaissance aircraft. Both men had so far failed in this endeavor. But Goddard had also been ignominiously kicked out of reconnaissance because of his singleminded pursuit of a new camera technology, the shutterless strip camera, which he promoted to distraction. The camera had an open slit and the film was rolled backwards at the speed of the aircraft, yielding a stationary exposure several feet long. The instrument was operationally controversial because it required careful matching of the speed, altitude, and focal length to the speed with which the film was advanced. Reconnaissance expert Roy Stanley wrote that these cameras were seldom used operationally, but when the aircraft was correctly flown, they were able to capture sharp images at high speeds and ultralow altitudes.[1332]

Ironically, the Navy liked the technology because it promised to provide information about beaches, such as water depth, tidal ranges, and the small-scale barriers like barbed wire and stakes the enemy erected to prevent landings. That's how the "exiled" Goddard eventually got the idea to a very important and exceptionally competent person, Robert Lovett, the Secretary of War for Air, who was already intimately familiar with Colonel Roosevelt's challenges and needs.

At the Pentagon, Lovett promptly released Goddard from his Navy purgatory and sent him across the Atlantic to report to Elliott Roosevelt, carrying a letter from Lovett to Elliott. He arrived on 1 February 1944.[1333]

Unfortunately, Elliott Roosevelt at first seemed to have bought into the "Goddard-is-a-nut" scuttlebutt. As Goddard recounted it:

> "George," he said bluntly, "I wish you'd stop trying to sell this thing. Our people over here have no use for it." – "How can they know how much use they have for it when they've never had a chance to try it?" I was tired. I had been buoyed up, and now the old cold water was hitting me in the face again. – "I've heard a helluva lot about it," he snapped. "A pilot would have to fly so low he'd be mincemeat." – "Well I'd sure like to have you give it one test." "I leave these things to my pilots, and they just don't go for the idea."[1334]

Elliott's dismissal of the new camera on the grounds of his crews' caution sounds odd. The pilots were making dangerous flights already in preparation for the landings in north and south France. Whatever the truth behind it, some officers in the RAF picked up on his attitude and decided that the Americans again didn't quite have what it took. They wanted the new camera. [1335]

Before Goddard left for home infuriated, Elliott persuaded him to help him with some other projects he was struggling with. One was the conversion of a flight of eight Mosquitoes at RAF Alconbury to radar photography, a new but critical technique. Airborne radar sets were large, crude, and unreliable, but the ability to bring back high-resolution radar imagery of selected targets was considered very important, especially since weather in Europe often impeded visual observations.

Unfortunately, the planes so equipped blew up. Three Mosquitoes were lost until it was discovered that when the new camera equipment was turned on, it ignited vapors that had migrated from the fuel system into the fuselage. Once this was fixed, radar photography proceeded successfully to hold its place as one of the primary methods of obtaining airborne radar intelligence.[1336]

Another of Roosevelt's tasks for Goddard involved the conversion of twelve Mosquitoes to night photography, which required complex synchronized illumination equipment. Roosevelt had already pioneered this in the Mediterranean. Now Goddard supervised the conversion at Langford Lodge, near Belfast. In connection with this, Goddard wrote a highly illuminating vignette about Elliott Roosevelt's flying style:

> When our first night photo Mosquito was ready for test at the Irish depot, Elliott Roosevelt invited me to fly with him to witness it. Climbing on board his B-25 the next morning I was amazed to see him sitting in the pilot's seat. He wore no wings, and I had never known he could fly. I wondered if he thought he was going to do so on the basis of being the President's son, but lo and behold, he fired up the engines like an old pro, taxied out to take-off. By the time we were airborne in one piece I began to relax.
>
> The flight to Langford Lodge was smooth and uneventful, and Elliott made a nice landing. We watched the tests and then climbed back on board the B-25 for the return

flight to London. It suddenly dawned on me that the aircraft had no life preservers or a raft, and we had a fair patch of water to cross.

As we were approaching the Isle of Man, I noticed a piece of metal cowling flapping in the breeze on top of the left engine and oil spewing out of it. I quickly went forward to the step behind the cockpit and called to Elliott: "You've got something wrong with your left engine!"

After a moment of glancing out at the engine and studying the instrument panel he called back, "Everything's okay from up here."

"You can't see it from where you're sitting, but you're losing oil. She's thrown a rod or something!" I insisted.

"No sweat, George. Relax, I'll get you back to London."

I went back and had another look at the engine, and I figured it was the wrong time of year for swimming. We were just leaving the Isle of Man when I tapped Elliott on the shoulder and said, "Listen, I'm the command pilot on this plane, and I want to get on the ground and see what the trouble is right now!"

He did not say anything but wracked the plane up in a tight turn and down we went to land at the Royal Navy Field near the town of Douglas.

We had no sooner touched the ground when the left engine let go with a bang. Elliott shut it down and we taxied in with a feathered prop. When he got down out of the plane, he was grinning from ear to ear. He thrust his hand out and said, "Well George old boy, now I know why you've lived so long in the aviation business."

"When I see oil running where it shouldn't, I know enough to run, too," I replied.

That night the pub in Douglas rocked to our happy landing and the fact that the son of the President of the United States was standing drinks at the bar.[1337]

That sounds like classical Elliott. It also makes clear that, rated pilot or not, by then he flew whatever he wanted. Oral history interviews indicate that Elliott obtained his multi-engine proficiency in the Cessna Bobcat, a small twin used for liaison.[1338]

But Colonel Roosevelt had another abrupt one-eighty to execute. The wily Goddard had by now managed to get the RAF interested in his strip camera. The Britons converted some of their own cameras to the continuous shutterless operation and soon provided excellent, continuous detail of the beaches of Normandy. Word soon got back to Roosevelt to adopt the RAF's techniques.

In reconnaissance history, this moment represents the vindication of the strip camera and its creator, George Goddard. Now back in the Air Corps's good graces, he worked hard to get Elliott's aircraft equipped accordingly. Elliott put him up for the Distinguished Service Medal. Goddard then got to work modifying a select subset of the F-5 Lightnings with a new "droop snoot" that would accommodate larger cameras, as well as, on occasion, a human observer.

In summary, Colonel Roosevelt was instrumental in developing new techniques and principles of photographic reconnaissance and interpretation. That this was no mere case of self-promotion is attested by a confidential letter from no less than OSS Chief William "Wild Bill" Donovan to President Roosevelt on 27 March 1944:

> I think you will be interested in work we have done which promises to be of value in photo interpretation. This work was carried on by Lt. N.H. Juran, USNR, of our Field Photographic Branch. Some of it was carried on in the field with your son Elliott's North African Photo Reconnaissance Wing. The bulk of the work was done in England with the Central Photo Interpretation Unit, which is the British photo interpretation center.

> The principles have other uses than photo interpretation. For example, they provide a new method of underwater depth determination, a means for enabling pilots to make accurate estimates of the sizes of ships they sight...[1339]

Considering the importance of these and related advances, which set the stage for the Cold War heyday of reconnaissance, and the prominence of the president's son, it is odd that so little has been made of Elliott Roosevelt's contributions in later years.

Part of the problem is that reconnaissance gets no respect. But blame must also attach to Elliott himself. When he left the Air Force, his military past was just war stories to him. While that is perhaps the most common retrospective taken by veterans, one would have hoped that he, especially, would have taken the time to provide an accurate and detailed account of his wartime activities and their technical and strategic significance for the future. But he chose to focus his writing career on being a Roosevelt, and we are left with the scattered testimony of others for his work in reconnaissance.

Promoting the Constellation

Colonel Roosevelt seemed to still have some issues with the RAF. Not only had the British vehemently opposed the creation of a separate American photo-interpretation infrastructure, they also noted that Roosevelt was opposed to American pilots flying British aircraft. This is odd, since Elliott had been a chief proponent of the Mosquito and the Spitfire in the Mediterranean theatre. Most likely the newer model F-5 Lightnings, with most of their problems fixed, were finally recognized as fine steeds. In the Mediterranean, the units canceled their demand for Mosquitoes in the spring of 1944.[1340]

Likewise, the longer-ranged F-6 Mustangs with drop tanks were now deemed as capable as their Spitfire counterparts. The Mustang was really a British aircraft built in America, and with the Merlin engine it truly hit its stride. In addition, these Mustangs retained their guns; this was highly appreciated by many reconnaissance pilots. The F-6s were cheaper and easier to operate and would soon supplant the much heavier twin-engine F-5s in service. By the spring of 1944, the small, single-engine Mustangs with drop tanks turned out, amazingly, to have the 1,200 mile range needed to fly all the way from England to Russia. Their welcome there would be a thornier matter.

Colonel Roosevelt did get caught up again in Pentagon infighting. One of the worst rows involved Elliott's old nemesis, Major General Echols back at Materiel Command at Wright Field.

On 17 June 1944, Roosevelt wrote a detailed memorandum to his boss, General Doolittle, entitled *Methods of Obtaining Photo Reconnaissance for Target Preparation of Charts and Bomb Damage Assessment Reports on B-29 Operation.* Elliott said he was responding to a verbal request from the Assistant Secretary of War for Air, Robert Lovett, whose attentive ear he had had since North Africa.[1341]

His real purpose emerges later in his detailed and ambitious proposal:

> The B-29 itself is not considered a satisfactory reconnaissance [plane], inasmuch as it contains much more intricate equipment than is needed to do this work, i.e. turrets, guns, bomb-bay for heavy bombs, which all adds up to considerable maintenance problems.

Here Elliott touched a raw nerve, and it was General Arnold's. The Superfortress was a highly troubled project, expensive, complex, and far more advanced than the bombers it replaced. It was also deemed essential for the war against Japan – and for one particular task Elliott did not know about (evidently Arnold was the only air officer who knew of the Manhattan project).[1342] As Elliott was writing, the first B-29s were just beginning some rather ineffective first raids on Japan using bases in Chengdu, China.

Since January 1944, when he found Boeing was producing unusable B-29s, Arnold had been hard on the case. He sent a top officer, General Bennett Meyers (and we shall certainly meet him again) to Boeing's Wichita plant to instigate a herculean, 7/24 effort later known as the Battle of Kansas. It did produce operational aircraft by June. Arnold later wrote that whatever else might be said about Meyers (he lied and stole), he was a "go-getter" who did a superb job in getting the B-29 ready.[1343]

So attached was Arnold to the plane that on his Wichita visit, he went down the line, wrote his name on one Superfortress, and said he wanted it this month (and all the ones ahead of it). He got it; but the "Arnold Special" (42-6365) is mostly remembered for making an emergency landing in Vladivostok. To the chief's distress, the Soviets not only kept it, but copied and mass-produced it as the Tupolev Tu-4 "Bull." [1344]

In his memo, Elliott finally got to the point:

> The only aircraft now in production in the United States having an equal or greater range to that of the B-29, according to information available to the Eighth Air Force, is the Lockheed "Constellation" transport. There is, at the present time, an officer on duty with the 8th Reconnaissance wing, Lt. Col. Clarence A. Shoop, who has flown this aircraft and is familiar with its performance.

By now the reader's alarm lights should be flashing red. The Constellation was Howard Hughes's baby, the airliner upon which he staked the postwar future of TWA. Hughes, with his accustomed megalomania, claimed to have personally designed it – presumably thereby making hundreds of engineers redundant.[1345]

"Shoopy" Shoop was a renowned test and reconnaissance pilot who had been along on the scandalous caper in August 1943 that resulted in the recommendation to buy the Hughes F-11. He had also made the first Constellation flight in April 1944. He would later get a top job at Hughes Aircraft.[1346]

Elliott continued:

> He states that the aircraft in question has as great or greater range than the B-29; that between 20-25 thousand feet altitude it will out-perform the B-29 by approximately 30 miles per hour, he states that this aircraft does not have sealed tanks, but it is believed that this modification can be readily made. He further states that he is familiar with the construction of the aircraft and that modification of the existing transport model can be made for the carrying of flash bombs of the K-46 type without radical redesign of the aircraft to include a suitable standard type bomb-bay capable of carrying above mentioned flash bombs. … Experienced personnel are available within the 8th Air Force to undertake this task, and in addition Colonel George Goddard, who is considered to be the best officer within the USAAF in camera installations and uses, will be available to head this experimental project.

So here we have the Goddard-Roosevelt axis rearing its hairy head again. They were the two biggest names in American air reconnaissance. They teamed up on this one, as they did on many other initiatives. Elliott went on:

> It is believed that the prototyping and modifying of the first squadron of these aircraft, could be accomplished by October 1st, if two aircraft were delivered to the 8th AF by July 19th and the remaining ten aircraft were delivered by September 10th. If during that period, between now and September 10th, the crews for the aircraft together with ground crews [ ] squadron personnel were placed in intensive training, all personnel of the squadron should be fully operational with all flight crews having had operational experience over Germany.

The top brass may well have continued the thought: *...and if pigs could fly...* Only two "Connie" prototypes even existed then.

Elliott then discussed equipment and tactics in detail, admitting that neither the Boeing B-29 nor the Constellation could survive in daytime without fighter escort. He did think that:

> ...the speed of the Lockheed Constellation would be sufficient to expect a rather low rate of loss to night fighter opposition, inasmuch as the speed of the aircraft is comparable to that of the Mosquito, which in the ETO experiences no difficulties from night fighters. It is believed that the operating altitude of the [L.C.], if satisfactory performance can be had from the aircraft, should be around 30,000 feet, and that good photographic results can be expected. In the event that the aircraft has its best operational altitude between 20-25,000 feet, it can be successfully operated between those altitudes with, however, an accompanying higher loss rate from heavy anti-aircraft fire.

His language was passive bureaucratese, with much *"in the event that"* for "if," and *"it is believed"* for "I think." But his game was clear. He'd heard about the "Connie" from Shoop (and probably from Howard Hughes, too), and now "it is believed that" he could have a squadron of them in action within three months. What would Doolittle, Spaatz and Arnold think of this?

Consider that this was less than a year since the furious row over Elliott's recommendation of the jinxed Hughes F-11. In the meantime, that aircraft had proceeded by painful inches. Now Elliott was proposing that another Hughes aircraft (built by Lockheed) be adopted for reconnaissance. While this gambit seems to have been completely overlooked by the Senate investigators, it helps place the F-11 in perspective.

Two interpretations come immediately to mind. One is that Colonel Roosevelt and Lt. Col. Shoop were both working on the "Hughes retirement plan." This is, after all, a common approach for officers who know they will soon be out of uniform. But that is only one elaboration of the factional infighting characteristic of defense bureaucracies. Cliques support one line of thought, one family of systems, other cliques oppose them.

The other interpretation is more palatable. It is simply that Elliott was right about the B-29 and the Connie – even if he did get carried away in his proposal. There is powerful evidence for this. Boeing's Superfortress was a supremely troubled program, similar to many defense projects that would follow in the decades to come. In contrast, Lockheed's Model 049 looked like a real winner: fast, roomy, pressurized, and reliable enough for successful airline service. Best of all, Hughes had been flying the prototypes for over a year with good results.

Both the B-29 and the Connie would see civilian and military service. The troubled B-29 became the progenitor of Boeing's civilian Model 377 Stratocruiser and several military variants. They did have frequent engine trouble and they were not as popular or long-lasting as the triple-tailed Connie. The latter was used as a luxurious airliner, a fast transport, and crucially, as an electronic intelligence aircraft. But perhaps most amusingly, the VC-121 Super Constellations *Columbine II* and *Columbine III* served as President Eisenhower's "Air Force One" from 1954 on. No bouncing around in a Boeing Stratocruiser for him! [1347]

So superficially, it seems like Colonel Roosevelt had good reason to try this "Hail Mary" end-run around the procurement bureaucracy. But then, once again, crusty General Echols lowered the boom on him.

On 1 July 1944, Echols sent a highly unusual letter to Lt. Gen. Barney Giles, then deputy commander Air Forces, and by implication, to General Arnold. Ominously, it was titled *Photographic reconnaissance by Colonel Elliott Roosevelt and Colonel George Goddard.* It stated:

> Attached hereto for your personal and confidential information is copy of a letter from Colonel Elliott Roosevelt to the Commanding General, Eighth Air Force. Please do not ask me how I obtained this copy of this letter, but understand that very probably it soon will be forwarded through channels.
>
> I have had a quick check made in regard to the statements made with reference to the comparative values of the Constellation (C-69) and B-29 for the purpose suggested. It is my belief that the proposal to use the Constellation for this purpose is rather farfetched. Attached hereto is a chart giving a rough comparison of the relative merits of the two airplanes from the viewpoint of high altitude operation and range. While it is difficult to compare the performance of various airplanes unless the exact weights and installations are known, it is believed that this chart gives a fair comparison. The B-29 is a faster airplane, particularly at altitude. The C-69 is equipped with two-speed superchargers which do not begin to give the performance at high altitude which the turbo-superchargers give the B-29. The figures pertaining to range for both airplanes is, of course, based on carrying the minimum amount of cargo load (this is the weight of the photographic equipment now being installed in the F-12) plus the crew and other essentials, and also provides for as much additional gas as we believe would be installed in additional fuselage tanks.
>
> In other words, quick figures indicate that as a photographic airplane, the B-29 can fly higher, faster and farther than the Constellation, with the additional advantage of having guns and leakproof tanks installed therein.[1348]

This memorandum initiated exchanges between the top Air Force brass about Roosevelt's proposal. Very quickly the unsolicited initiative was scrapped. Echols had lost the battle against the F-11, but he won against the Constellation.

To use a popular expression, Echols was up to his eyeballs in alligators at that time. The Hughes F-11 he had been forced to buy was constantly delayed. The Republic F-12 Rainbow, upon which reconnaissance hopes were now focused, was promising and a hot performer. But it wouldn't fly for two years, and then the jet age killed it, along with the F-11. The B-29 program was a nightmare to manage – it had been designed, built, and tested seemingly simultaneously, and now the bill for this precocity was coming due.

The C-69 Constellation still looked good. But at the time Elliott airily requested a squadron, there were only two prototypes, and they would take at least two more months to get through testing. Production was only slowly ramping up – after all, Lockheed was busy with many other high priority tasks.

On that background, Elliott was out of his flying mind when he thought he could get a squadron in three months. The Air Corps only managed to get a handful of C-69s, the transport version, in the air before the war ended. The Air Force finally selected the much improved C-121 version, and that did provide excellent service in the 1950s.

Was Elliott also wrong about the plane's performance? No. Echols was. When the Constellation hit its stride, it did outperform the B-29. Yet high-altitude performance was, purely for engine reasons, an initial problem for the Connie. The B-29 was already operating in the stratosphere over Japan, and the RB-29 reconnaissance variant would soon snap a lot of pictures of the Soviet Union.

In perspective, the flap over the Connie, much as that over the Hughes F-11, illustrates the difficulties procurement officials inherently face, and the facile criticisms they constantly have to weather. The operational folks often have heard of something that would solve all their problems, and why can't they have it? But the procurement officers have to make their selection based on many factors unknown to outsiders: that a great product might not be easily manufactured; that it might delay another desperately needed product; that it might be obsolete when ready; that, during a short war, a bird in the hand is worth more than all the fancy ones that "could" or "should" be available in the future.

A Civil War in Reconnaissance

Somewhat similar issues arose in another bitter feud in which Colonel Roosevelt got entangled. This one also featured Colonel Goddard, but the "enemy" this time was Colonel Minton Kaye, a photo-mapping specialist who had commanded the 1st Mapping Group and remained in charge of many photo-reconnaissance decisions until the Goddard-Roosevelt team had him sent to Siberia – actually, the Asian theater.

Depending on whom you consult, this conflict had its origin in legitimate professional differences of opinion, or in a mad personal vendetta. To be precise, Colonel Goddard wrote in his memoirs that Kaye was expressly and publicly out to get him from the moment in 1941 that he (Kaye) got command of aerial mapping back in Washington.[1349] But Kaye offered persuasive technical and tactical arguments that at least initially convinced General Arnold and a good portion of the air staff that the photo-recon experts (except Kaye) had not performed as needed.

The fight was initially related to the Army Corps of Engineers's insistent demand for accurate photographs from which to make maps. The engineers had very specific requirements. They needed high-altitude vertical photography taken at close intervals from a straight track and constant altitude. For this they standardized on the T-5 wide-angle camera, preferably carried by a large, specially modified aircraft like the B-17. Thus, obtaining the 9½ inch plates and producing maps from them amounted to a slow and meticulous process.[1350]

When war loomed in 1940 and 1941, there was an acute shortage of just about everything, and the Corps was completely buried in charting requests. The Americans had little global coverage, but the British had quite a bit. One of the unsung but crucial instances of close Anglo-American technical cooperation was the Loper-Hotine agreement of 12 May 1942, which provided for sharing of geographical databases. This was very much a one-way street, since the Americans gained access to a wealth of British data, whereas the Americans were still getting up to speed. Even before the agreement, the Americans were getting critical British cartography – for example, in August 1941, maps of Iceland, where "neutral" American Marines had just relieved the British.

At the very same time, the 1st Mapping Group was frantically trying to carry out its own photomapping program. Major Minton Kaye commanded it from June 1941, and he was sent to Alaska to try out new methods. To speed up matters, Kaye's unit invented a form of trimetrogon mount – one vertical and two oblique cameras mounted together. This arrangement let pilots space their tracks not 4, but 25 miles apart. It also gave them some flexibility in speed and altitude as long as camera orientation was recorded. Thus it was almost tailor-made for single-seater operation.

The Corps of Engineers had already complained that Air Corps cameras (Col. Goddard's domain) were junk. Now, with the trimetrogon, they were faced with an almost existential threat:

> The Engineers feared that the trimetrogon mount, with its obvious advantages to the AAF, would deprive them of means for compiling precise, large-scale maps. Trimetrogon photography could not be applied to all mapping needs of the ground forces because this type of photography produced some distortions which no known instrument could correct. Reduction in scale outward from the center of any picture makes it progressively difficult to determine the position and to identify certain features of the terrain. These difficulties were multiplied in the oblique photographs because features relatively close to the camera tend to mask those farther away.[1351]

Whatever the pros and cons of the trimetrogon mount, from now on Colonel Kaye was a burr under the saddle for not only the Engineers, but some of the photo-reconnaissance establishment. In particular, Wright Field's Colonel Goddard feuded with Kaye in Washington to the point that Goddard was banished to absurd postings – including one to combat venereal disease at a remote base. This is why Goddard called Kaye "Colonel Nemesis" in his memoir. [1352]

Goddard had then just sent one of his lieutenants, Harry Trimble, to La Marsa, Tunisia to have Elliott Roosevelt try out the new continuous-exposure strip camera Wright Field had produced. Elliott was on leave, and Trimble said the unit apparently had been forewarned, so it immediately got rid of the camera and impressed both plane and pilot into regular reconnaissance duties.

To top it off, Goddard had revealed his strip camera and much else of his work in a remarkably extensive photo reportage in *Life* magazine.[i] This self-promotion infuriated Kaye, and the hammer fell not long after. Goddard said:

> …the problem was, I really didn't know why I had been thrown out. I hoped to learn the reason in Washington and to have a chance to face Hap Arnold. I did not succeed in either aim and it was not until years later that I learned it had been a complaint submitted

---

[i] LIFE, 10 MAY 43. Both Goddard (and his continuous-strip camera) and Kaye (and his trimetrogon mapping camera mount) were discussed in this pictorial story.

> by the Corps of Engineers on my fa*ilure to take the proper attitude toward aerial mapping!* which the young man [Kaye] had used as the weapon to shoot me down.[1353]

In retrospect it appears that factional infighting and personal vendettas were exacerbated rather than reduced as the war proceeded. This one, however, would end with Kaye exiled, Goddard restored to the throne, Elliott Roosevelt impressed and appearing impressive, and the Engineers gradually mollified.

Apart from the quality of cameras and the usefulness of their mounts, an even bigger bureaucratic fight arose when the United States formally joined the war. Elliott Roosevelt had amply demonstrated that flying straight and level for a long time was tantamount to giving the enemy target-practice. But that's not want the Corps of Engineers wanted to hear.

That's how the specialized B-17Es that were sent to England in the fall of 1942 got diverted to North Africa, and then relegated to courier duty. Their original purpose had been to assist the British with the "Benson Project," the plan to map all of coastal France in minute detail. That wasn't going to happen – planes that went there by themselves were dead ducks.

From then on, the USAAF mapped hostile territory primarily with Lightnings with trimetrogon mounts. Colonel Kaye had to rub salt into the wound. In 1942, he suggested that there was really not that much need for the accurate, large-scale maps the Corps was screaming for:

> Modern offensive warfare, utilizing closely coordinated operations of aircraft with fast moving mechanized ground units and the striking power of aircraft on vital objectives far within enemy territory has completely revolutionized tactical map and chart requirements…Trimetrogon photography and compilation is not the answer to all mapping problems, but, while developed primarily for small scale charts, the method has certain advantages which should not be overlooked when photography must be accomplished in combat areas and maps prepared rapidly for offensive operations.[1354]

That was a convenient argument from an Air Force perspective, especially for those who didn't want to die. But in no way did it satisfy the ground troops, the charting engineers, and, at length, the high staff.

For this reason, and stung by the reverses in North Africa, the PR community began to campaign for a new, dedicated photo-reconnaissance aircraft with the ability to survive over enemy territory. On 25 January 1943, the War Department made it official, ordering the AAF to develop such a plane. This was the quest Elliott Roosevelt was on in the fall of 1943, with such calamitous if entertaining results.

The Corps of Engineers found that the AAF Materiel Division opposed the new plane concept in part because its development would take longer than the war was projected to last. Procurement wanted to stick with modifying existing aircraft. The issue came to a head when Colonel Kaye, the Director of Photography, wrote General Eaker on 8 May 1943. He advocated strongly against the dangerous missions for mapping reconnaissance, said that the Army could not use the data efficiently anyway, and generally repudiated the Engineers' arguments.

By now, however, his line was becoming less appreciated throughout the AAF, and a complaint by the Corps of Engineers seemed to finally reel him in:

> ...taken as a whole Kaye's ideas were no longer deemed sound around AAF headquarters. The poor performance of all types of reconnaissance units in North Africa, the growing recognition of the importance of photography in strategic bombing, no less than outside pressure, convinced AAF policy makers that a major change was in order.[1355]

The Director of Photography who had been opposed to his own mission finally had run out of rope. Whether his highly personal feud with Colonel Goddard had anything to do with it is not recorded, but Goddard rose as Kaye fell. Kaye was replaced by the more sympathetic veteran reconnaissance pilot Colonel James G. Hall.

By 1 June 1943, the AAF reaffirmed the decision to develop a reconnaissance plane. On 22 June, F-5s were dispatched to fly the first mapping missions in the ETO:

> To deliver acceptable photography with F-5 airplanes demanded more skill on the part of the pilot than if there had been room for a photo-navigator. The AAF assured the requisite skill by following through in its plans to improve the training of reconnaissance units, including those assigned to mapping photography. In the end everything hung on this. Mosquito planes were not transferred in any numbers. The special photographic airplane never got into production. Most photographic missions were flown by a small group of dedicated Air Force officers, among whom Col. Karl L. Polifka rendered outstanding service.[1356]

So did Colonel Roosevelt. That he was back in the United States during the critical period in the summer of 1943, talking to Arnold, Lovett, and others who mattered, helped move the cause along. The hammer would not fall on Colonel Kaye, though, until Goddard and Roosevelt got their conniving heads together in England.

Colonel Goddard's arrival in Elliott's headquarters with the recommendation from Secretary Lovett spelled the end of Minton Kaye's reign as photo-reconnaissance boss back in Washington. Goddard may have been a self-promoter and certainly a promoter of his work, but Kaye seems to have been a negativist and obstructionist who made many enemies. But it took Elliott Roosevelt to fell him. As Goddard told it, Elliott wanted to repay him for his work and apologize for having doubted him. He said:

> "I told you in Washington who was behind all my trouble. He's been a roadblock to progress for a long time. How about booting his fanny [sic] out to the Pacific?" – "You know," Elliott rubbed his chin thoughtfully, "you're absolutely right. He's a lousy director of aerial photography. He's not only snafued the war effort on the strip camera, he's failed me, too, a number of times. Where shall we send him?" – "Let's get out a map."
>
> That night a courier took Elliott's letter to Washington, and a short while later, amidst a great gnashing of teeth and caterwauling in high places – but not high enough – young Colonel Nemesis, in a state of profound shock, was on his way to a post in India. The word trickled over that had he remained in Washington a few more weeks, he would have been promoted to brigadier general. As it was, he remained in India for the duration.
>
> Later I learned it had not been Elliott's letter alone that had brought the sudden fall of the young man, but also a complaint to the Chief of the Air Force by the Corps of Engineers, the very service that he, no doubt, had used to discredit me.[1357]

In his oral history interview with Elliott Roosevelt, Goddard made some even more ominous remarks about the Roosevelt-Kaye relationship:

GG: I remember you told me one time, when I first met you, I asked you how you ever got into the photo business, you said, "Well, you know, Minton Kaye got me in for the politics in the thing, and I think I'm going to show him some politics now," and you sat down and wrote that letter to your father.

ER: That's right.

GG: It was one of the finest things you ever did.[1358]

This implies that Elliott told the president to please send Colonel Kaye to Hell, or at least India. But what was meant by "for the politics in the thing?" Did Kaye initially try to use Roosevelt for political advantage? Murky things seemed to go on beneath the level of the written record. Bluntly: When President Roosevelt made a discreet, extraofficial move on behalf of someone who had his favor, the official evidence is almost always missing.

This unseemly squabble is a reminder that within the system, winning the war is often a nebulous abstraction far overshadowed by the real motivators: personal ambition, sympathies and antipathies if not grudges, territoriality, clique loyalties, and fixed ideas. Personal networks and alliances, ambushes and disinformation are the tools of the trade in the battle for bureaucratic survival. The only comfort is that presumably the enemy has the same problem.

OPERATION FRANTIC, or BOMBERS FOR STALIN II

In 1944, Colonel Roosevelt repeatedly demonstrated his extraordinary talent for popping up where history was made. The "FRANTIC" program has, however, received little attention, probably because its results were highly controversial, even at times disastrous, much like Elliott himself. Nonetheless, FRANTIC is absolutely crucial to understanding the origins of the Cold War, and historians ignore it at their peril.

Incidentally, the codename had first been the rather more palatable "BASEBALL," but the uncertain and unsettled implementation of the project caused a change to "FRANTIC," which moniker one general called "a masterpiece of understatement." "JOE" was the suffix commonly used for the first shuttle-bombing operation; later deployments in the USSR were given a sequence number, e.g. FRANTIC-6.[i] Operation "TITANIC" was the code for the 8th Air Force component. It lent its name to an interesting USAAF film on the subject, shot by the 8th Combat Camera Unit.

On a very curious side note indeed, on 8 March 1944, the St. Louis office of the FBI sent a worried report to the Director in Washington. It seemed their agents had located Colonel Elliott Roosevelt's briefcase in a truck. That briefcase, which had been accidentally "torn" when the truck driver discovered it, contained "what appears to be

---

[i] Deane: Strange Alliance, 107. This is one of three books covering FRANTIC. The others are Infield and Conversino (see bibliography). However, the ground truth is Air Force records, in particular a secret history of the project prepared at HQ AF for high level access at the close of 1944. This ("ESCOMHIST") is the primary source used herein. Also, the General Anderson papers at the Hoover Institution, declassified 1989, provide crucial detail.

highly secret and confidential papers, pertaining, among other things, to the location and physical lay-out of airfields and bomber bases in England."[1359]

Most officers would have gotten in deep trouble for a grave security breach like that.

It seems that Elliott had been visiting a friend, Hugh B. Ernst, known as Bud Ernst, in California. Ernst was a well-known radio producer and *bon-vivant*, and also, at that time, a pilot in the Air Corps. When Ernst's car broke down, he had it towed, but he forgot that he had left within it Elliott's briefcase, which the latter had forgotten. Having been notified, the FBI got the briefcase in record time, and saw to it that it was delivered to the White House, where Major General Edwin "Pa" Watson, FDR's military aide, received it.

"Very truly yours, John Edgar Hoover" must have been pleased by this opportunity to demonstrate his discreet effectiveness to the president.

Colonel Roosevelt was at that time working on the super-sensitive project to establish American bomber bases in the Soviet Union, so it is likely that the contents related to that matter. He was supposed to be busy with this in England, not casually running around Hollywood with top secret papers in his briefcase. Significantly, Bud Ernst was one of the small circle of Hollywood hell-raisers around Errol Flynn; Bruce Cabot was another, and Johnny Meyer was their hard-working but well-paid pimp.[i]

What Elliott was doing in California at that time, other than visiting Bud Ernst, is lost to history. The bomber bases, fortunately, are not.

The Shuttle Bombing Project

After Pearl Harbor, the American "bomber mafia" looked at the map of Europe and soon realized that the strategic bombing offensive against Germany could best be conducted from three sides at once. At first, proposals were drawn up for defensive air cooperation in the Arctic and the Caucasus, but while Joe Stalin wanted all the equipment and supplies he could get, he wanted absolutely no foreign troops in the USSR.[1360]

The Americans envisaged a new kind of triangular trade. By conducting "shuttle bombing" operations from England, the Mediterranean, and remaining Soviet territory, the strategic bombers would be able to attack previously unreachable parts of Eastern Europe, keep German air defenses off balance, and assist the Red Army in its titanic struggle. To General Arnold and his staff, it was a "no-brainer."

It also made enormous sense to the politicians. FDR wanted to demonstrate American support to the Red Army, win the trust and confidence of the Soviets, and improve Allied cooperation. It was also extremely important to set a precedent so as to later obtain air bases in the Soviet Far East in order to bomb the Japanese home islands.

Marshal Stalin's motives – and only his motives mattered in Moscow – for eventually agreeing to the project are much more difficult to assess. Certainly, he always realized that the capitalist West was the real enemy, and that the anti-fascist alliance was a mere tactical arrangement. There was no theology of strategic bombing in the USSR, and the Soviets probably saw no significant benefit to themselves in the American air

---

[i] For several descriptions of this circle, see McNulty: Errol Flynn. Ernst was Elliott's type, but erratic. He shot himself in 1950 (AP, 11 APR 50).

operations. It is likely that Stalin thought that he would gain an intelligence benefit, but it also appears that he changed his mind as soon as he had obtained what he wanted.

In the fall of 1944, when the active phase of FRANTIC had ended, the Air Forces commissioned an extremely detailed, secret history of the project, and forwarded it to the top leadership including the State Department. From this report it is possible to reconstruct both the diplomatic and military history of the program, and, equally important, view it through the relatively innocent eyes of a time when the USSR was still an ally. On the other hand, the report, History of Eastern Command, clearly papers over conflicts, even those internal to the American side.[1361]

The shuttle-bombing idea is so obvious that it is silly to ask who thought of it first. Even before Pearl Harbor, American planners realized the potential of Russian bases. It is more productive to trace how one of the many ideas that were kicked around actually came to fruition. Yet since the USAAF had no real capability in Europe until 1943, at first the issue remained in the theoretical stage.[1362]

There had been unsuccessful efforts to talk Stalin into joint air operations before. He declined a British offer of air assistance via Persia during the Battle of Stalingrad. Stalin had barely permitted a cursory American survey of the trans-Siberian route (ALSIB Route), which was to be used for deliveries of lend-lease aircraft, but which American planners really wanted to vet for later operations against Japan.[1363]

After this rudimentary 1942 expedition, known as the Follett Bradley survey for the American general entrusted with it, the Soviets permitted no more Americans to operate in Siberia. This rebuff badly upset American officers, who constantly compared their treatment in the Soviet Union to their own "bending-over-backwards" for the Russians who came to pick up their thousands of gift planes in North America.[1364]

During the critical autumn of 1941, a small RAF detachment of Hurricanes had been allowed to operate in the Murmansk area, although the aircraft were soon given to the Soviets. Yet in 1942, air assistance on the Caucasus front was denied even as the flow of American aircraft to the USSR grew to a flood.

By the fall of 1943, the Red Army had regained the initiative and pushed back the Germans, while at the same time German air defenses inflicted unsustainable losses on American bombers operating from England. With the 8th Air Force nearly defeated over Germany, the Americans, though not the British, felt the time was right to raise the issue with the Russians in its full extent. Soviet airfields were badly needed. A September 1943 mission to Moscow headed by WPB Chairman Donald Nelson and accompanied by USAAF Colonel Alfred Kessler brought up the issue in a tentative way.[1365]

During the foreign ministers' conference in Moscow in October 1943, the Americans set up the first permanent, separate military representation in the USSR. The tasks previously handled by military attachés and the lend-lease office had become too large. Major General John Deane, a diplomatic fellow with a subtle sense of humor, was carefully selected to head this office.[1366]

The detailed USAAF initiative was radioed to General Deane on 26 October 1943. In his first meeting with Foreign Affairs Commissar Vyacheslav Molotov, Deane then offered three related proposals: American use of air bases in western Russia, coordination of weather and communication services beginning with the exchange of ciphers, and increased air transport links between the Allies.[1367]

Deane later wrote that Molotov looked like he'd been hit by a bolt from the blue. This may be true in a strictly tactical sense, but it defies credulity that the Soviets would not have known of the American proposal beforehand. After all, Soviet intelligence usually knew what their Allies were up to before they could even formulate it officially. Most likely, Molotov, acting for Stalin, had already prepared his counterproposals, but he may have been uncomfortable with being put on the spot. Like other high-ranking Soviets, Molotov could do nothing on his own.[1368]

At any rate, that was when Molotov's response "agreement in principle" became a dirty phrase to the Americans.[1369] The Soviets were seemingly not interested in air cooperation at all – they just wanted first dibs on all American war production. Persuading the Soviets to cooperate became the biggest hurdle in getting Operation BASEBALL/FRANTIC up and running. Oddly, Colonel Elliott Roosevelt would soon come to the rescue of the stymied generals.

A clue to the Soviet awareness was Molotov's corresponding demand that the Western Allies force Sweden to give up air bases to the Allies. Deane didn't think it realistic to make Sweden abandon her "neutrality" although Molotov clearly had a point. Molotov already had a bad attitude toward the Swedes, resulting in the recall of the Swedish ambassador.[1370] At that time Sweden was still supporting the German war effort – ironically, to a much greater extent than was Franco's Spain. Sweden's about-face would be slow and late. As it was, Sweden would continue to serve as an emergency landing field; internment was better than captivity.[1371]

Agreement "in principle"

One concern of Stalin's that attracted no attention in the West was that the Soviets had long experience with military cooperation with a foreign power – namely, Germany. During the years when a German air force was effectively prohibited, a joint Soviet-German air base was established at Litebsk, 400 miles south of Moscow, for the purpose of training fighter pilots and exchanging aeronautical knowledge and experience with air tactics. While the Soviet-German military cooperation was successful and apparently well thought of by both sides, the subsequent German doublecross must have weighed on Stalin's mind. At any rate, the German presence had been much smaller than the one now proposed by the Americans. Since, for ideological reasons, Stalin considered war with the West inevitable, it would have required tremendous circumspection to accede to the American requests.

The result of this wariness was that, paradoxically, Stalin wanted no foreign bases when the survival of the USSR hung in the balance; but by the end of 1943, when the outcome was assured, he suddenly became more amenable.

Thus nothing constructive happened until the Teheran conference in late November 1943. There, as we saw, Marshal Stalin took great pains to make a new, devoted American friend: Colonel Elliott Roosevelt, who had direct access to the top Anglo-American stakeholders in the matter. Elliott said that he extracted a promise from the generalissimo to make airfields available for the Americans, which is confirmed by the USAAF's secret history of Eastern Command. You can see how Hap's recon guy could be extremely and unexpectedly helpful – to both sides![1372]

During the day after Elliott had flown into Teheran, President Roosevelt turned down a preparatory meeting with Churchill in order to meet with Stalin – in the view of the British, another indication of FDR and Stalin ganging up on them. According to Elliott, FDR justified this approach by remarking that "the biggest thing was in making clear to Stalin that the United States and Great Britain were not allied in one common block against the Soviet Union."[1373]

Immediately afterwards, the president met with the Soviet delegation and offered Stalin written reports on major issues. One of them was the shuttle-bombing plan. Stalin said he needed time to review the idea. The Soviets were very keen on getting American heavy bombers provided they could operate them themselves, and astonishingly, General Arnold suggested that this might be a solution.[1374]

Arnold later said he had offered the Soviets 300-400 B-24s in return for American bases in the Soviet Union. It would require training of large numbers of Soviet airmen in the United States. He could not understand why Stalin never followed up on this offer afterwards.[1375]

The problem was that it is no simple matter to stand up a strategic air force. Just getting the airplanes is the least part of it. Even if the USSR had had the required infrastructure – long, paved runways, high-octane aviation gasoline, secure radio communications, etc., – training the crews would have taken years. Later the standard U.S. riposte was that the Russians would not be able to take advantage of such a gift in time, even if the Americans had been able to spare the heavy aircraft. But only the naïve would assume that these were the only grounds for American military reluctance.

The Soviets were not naïve. They copied the American heavy bombers that made safety landings in Siberia. But their trump was to demand from the American political leadership what the military would not surrender on its own, such as the highly secret Norden bombsight. And, as the saga of the atomic bomb later showed, there were yet other means to obtain the goods.

On 1 December 1943, after President Roosevelt had softened up "Uncle Joe" by mocking Winston Churchill in front of the British Prime Minister, he let on that his son needed a favor:[i]

> Roosevelt quickly tested Stalin's good mood. Informing the marshal that his son commanded 250 scouting and observation aircraft, Roosevelt asked if Elliott could have permission to fly through from Italy, photograph the Danube Basin, and land in the Soviet Union. Thus, Roosevelt subtly raised what was actually the shuttle bombing question. Stalin, agreeably, proposed to refer exact details to the military mission in Moscow. Also, he agreed to make fields available in northern Russia for flights from England to Russia. This seemed to settle the issue in some minds.[1376]

This promising beginning was slightly offset by Stalin's parting assurance that he would work out the details with Ambassador Harriman in Moscow. He clearly was not going to be rushed, even if he did "favor" the American proposal.

The official account for 1 December noted that the president and Ambassador Harriman both worked on Stalin on behalf of Elliott. Harriman told the dictator that Colonel Roosevelt was "very anxious" to obtain these permissions. But there is no indication that Elliott was allowed to pitch the matter himself. Possibly he did not even know of the detailed plans yet; he was, after all, only a colonel.[1377] Most likely, Elliott mentioned the matter in the limited context of his own reconnaissance operations.

---

[i] FDR: "Winston is cranky this morning. He got up on the wrong side of bed." Stalin: "???" Told in many versions. See for example Robert Nisbet: Roosevelt and Stalin, which provides an effective but chilling summary of the relationship. www.mmisi.org/ma/30_02/nisbet.pdf, retr. 8 FEB 12.

The internal USAAF history asserts that Ambassador Averell Harriman and Colonel Roosevelt together obtained Stalin's approval, although obviously this was a collaborative effort led by the president himself. The history, compiled in late 1944, pointed out:

> From the American point of view, the joint mission required the early addition of photographic reconnaissance. This part of the AAF mission was mentioned by Harriman in discussions with Stalin at Teheran, where it was also brought up by Colonel Elliott Roosevelt, who was in charge of Allied photo reconnaissance operations in the Mediterranean. From that point on, it was continually pressed on the Soviets... [1378]

During that initial phase, to the Soviets the Americans tended to prioritize reconnaissance even higher than the shuttle bombing itself.

However, after the Teheran summit, again nothing happened. It is likely that Stalin, the sole decision-maker on his side, was all along calculating what advantages he stood to obtain from going ahead with the American plan. Interestingly, the British did not take part in the initiative; they saw little to be gained from this complex and logistically monstrous operation.

Like Germany, the USSR had no strategic air force and no bombing doctrine to go with it. These two continental powers viewed air power largely as an adjunct to ground operations. The Soviets saw no particular benefit in the American bombing campaign, but it is likely that Stalin was already considering the need to study American strategic technology and procedures. One Soviet pilot remembered being told: "Fly to Poltava; you will take part in a joint flight with the Americans there. Watch them work, share experiences, and we will make use of everything you learn."[1379] Although this might have been to use this knowledge against the West later, it is more realistic to assume that Stalin was wondering how he could defend against American bombers in the future.[1380]

Stalin must also have been aware that the U.S. ambitions were characteristically extravagant, so he had to consider the proposed air bases to be proverbial camel-noses under the tent. Momentarily lowering his guard, General Fred Anderson, Spaatz's deputy, revealed in an internal conversation in April 1944:

> We've got it in the back of our minds – wouldn't put it in the cable – didn't put it in the cable – that this is just a step toward establishing an air force over there – if it becomes necessary – if this operation OVERLORD becomes a glorified ANZIO – if it stagnates; to build up a division over there – three to five wings. You've got to visualize that; discuss it with Kessler and Deane. We can't put it in cables; you have it in your thinking. I'd like to have an estimate of the requirements on that... [1381]

The American ambition to place a numbered air force in the USSR was motivated by fear of a stalemate in Europe and the need to open an air front against Japan. Even though the officers could not discuss these dreams with the Soviets, it is certain Stalin would have been aware of it, considering that all American offices in the USSR were penetrated by various means.

And so, on 2 February 1944 in Moscow, Ambassador Harriman suddenly broke through the logjam in a meeting with Marshal Stalin himself. Asked, Stalin reminded Harriman that at Teheran he had already agreed to American reconnaissance flights – to include daily shuttles from Italy and England. He said he would be glad to support two reconnaissance missions, one from England and one from Italy, each day, suggesting they could use the fields at Kotli and Velikiye Luki. He also held out hope for an American air force operating from Siberia after the defeat of Germany.[1382]

He clearly recalled his conversations with the two Roosevelts, and the shuttle bombing project was seen by him as a follow-on phase to the reconnaissance operations he had discussed with them. He kept his word, although to the confused Americans it seemed as if the Soviets were blowing hot and cold in unpredictable succession.[1383]

There swiftly followed a meeting on 5 February with Deane, Harriman, and Molotov, and soon bilateral staff consultations were in full swing. This required another expansion of the American contingent in Moscow. A counterpart, the Soviet Military Commission in London, coordinated activities with the top level commanders in Britain. This mission was headed by Major General Andrei Sharapov.[1384] As Elliott remembered: "A Soviet general arrived at SHAEF, carried on some preparatory conversations, and then returned...[1385] He was referring to a 17 February 1944 Soviet visit to USSTAF headquarters by Sharapov, Lt. Col. Roudoi, and Major Samarian of the Soviet Military Commission. Their task was to become familiar with American strategic bombing techniques.[1386] To be polite, General Spaatz played chess with the Russians; but he said he had to drink so many toasts that soon he couldn't tell black from white.

As soon as Deane radioed news of the breakthrough to Arnold on 2 February, Arnold informed London, noting: "Stalin approves project limited to 200 bombers and six airfields." USSTAF at Widewing in London began a series of high-level meetings to get the project up and running in record time. Colonel Roosevelt was an integral part of this staff work, but he also had a special role.[1387]

On 6 February, Ambassador Harriman radioed the War Department that Roosevelt should be given a direct role in FRANTIC. Harriman, as well as Deane, remembered Elliott's rapport with Stalin in Teheran. Reconnaissance was initially given an equal weight with bombing as an objective of the project. The same day, Colonels Kessler, Cullen, and Griffith dined with General Spaatz and were told to get ready to go to Russia:

> This move is much larger than meets the eye. The establishment of bases in Russia for use in shuttle-bombing and shuttle-reconnaissance is a minor factor. If we are successful in this effort it may be of vital importance when we shift our entire attention to Japan and the Far East.[1388]

Two days later, Spaatz held a conference at which Generals Anderson and Curtis and Colonels McDonald, Roosevelt, Alfred Kessler, John Griffith, and Paul Cullen were present. The latter three were designated to go to Moscow to prepare the way on the ground. Griffith was in charge; Cullen, who had been Elliott's commander in 1942, was now his deputy, and was told to plan the reconnaissance flights. They were thought to be of more immediate benefit to both sides than the subsequent bombing missions.[1389]

Thus, on 8 February, Colonel Cullen, who commanded the 7th Group under Roosevelt's 8th PRW, was given orders to develop the reconnaissance program with the Russians in accordance with the conversations Elliott Roosevelt had had with them in Teheran. He was told that the recon flights were so urgent that they were likely to precede bombing flights by a substantial period, and to be prepared to share all photographs with the Red Army.[1390]

Cullen would belong to the "first echelon" of the American movement into Russia, according to the FRANTIC terminology. Echelons two through five arrived in roughly monthly installments.[1391]

Soviet reactions confused the Americans. For example, the history noted that "even after the Teheran conference and the warm discussions held there between Roosevelt, Harriman and Deane with Stalin, Molotov and [Gen. Alexei] Nikitin, an attempt by Deane to pay a direct and personal visit to Nikitin resulted in a cold reception."[1392] To speed things up, Deane had bypassed his assigned liaison officer, but the Americans didn't grasp how dangerous it was for the Soviet generals to speak to them out of turn.

The Griffith special mission departed on 17 February, flying a fully operational B-17, piloted by a Captain Fisher. While in the USSR, this aircraft was also used for demonstration purposes, including test bombing, and "it did prove a considerable aid to negotiations when the Fortress arrived in Moscow on 25 February with the fitting soubriquet '*Natasha*' painted on its nose." The main impediment – throughout the project – was that the Soviets insisted on having their own navigators and radio operators aboard the U.S. administrative aircraft.[1393]

Colonel Griffith, the original commander in the East, was replaced in early April because he was deemed to lack the tact, patience, and circumspection necessary to deal with his inscrutable, proud, and sensitive Soviet counterparts. Instead, Kessler was made the commander of the American bases in the USSR, which officially came to be known as "Eastern Command" when operations began in late May 1944.[1394] However, to match the rank-obsessed and far from classless Soviets, the especially agreeable Major General Robert Walsh was imported to head the overall project.[1395]

Colonel Cullen now became deputy commander of air operations on the Eastern Front. He was an exceptionally able and well-regarded reconnaissance expert. His presence indicates the critical importance the Americans had learned to place upon reconnaissance. Without pre- and post-strike photos, target folder preparation, weather reconnaissance, and associated services, strategic bombing of the German East would be useless. Eastern Command did not report to General Deane in Moscow; neither did Cullen report to Colonel Roosevelt any longer. The command was straight under Spaatz, but it took some education for Deane to understand that.

After the February break-through, General Deane wrote:

> There followed a period of four months which was the busiest of my stay in Russia. A staff of 11-12 young, virile, and vigorous airmen arrived from General Spaatz's headquarters. They had been used to dealing with the British, who were at least approachable. They had been sent to Russia to do a job and couldn't comprehend the delays and frustrations that beset them on every side. They could not get to the Russians to let off steam – but they could get to me. Much of my time was spent in smoothing their feathers.[1396]

Despite the official frustrations, there is general agreement that Americans and Russians got along well on a personal level. The Americans admired the hardiness of Soviet laborers, who seemed to take incredible punishment from both their work and their commanders. In the beginning phases, the Soviets engaged in the type of fraternization inevitable with 1200 "rich" foreigners suddenly among them.

On the eve of Colonel Roosevelt's visit to the Soviet bases in May, Cullen first reported that Eastern Command had 572 personnel attached, of which 266 were at the main Poltava airfield. The number would increase during the summer operations, then decline drastically in the fall.[1397] At all times the Soviets were anxious to limit the number of foreigners to the minimum possible.

In February, Elliott could not be spared despite the fact that the Moscow embassy requested him, and instead he briefed Colonel Cullen on his preparatory conversations in Teheran. Elliott later said that his week-long May inspection trip was the first of two missions to the USSR; he did not state when his second trip occurred.[1398] However, in recollections assembled for a book in 1989 he said that he often flew in advance of the bomber stream, and on one occasion was laid over in Poltava for a while.[1399]

Despite the February agreement, progress was excruciatingly slow due to incessant bureaucratic obstacles. With characteristic grandiosity, the Americans had initially contemplated ten Soviet bases, five in the north and five in the south. During the February meetings, this narrowed to six in all, with an additional two to serve as reconnaissance bases. The Soviets eventually got the number down to three.[1400]

The reasons for this cannot be attributed solely to obstructionism. Outside the main cities, long, hard-surfaced runways with road and rail access were rare in the Soviet Union. Almost all facilities had been destroyed during the gigantic battles fought in the area. In addition, Mother Nature generally turned airfields into quagmires during winter and spring. The Americans were beginning to know an entirely different world.

Even the true obstructionism seemed to be poorly coordinated. The second echelon of American staff officers arrived in Teheran on 21 March after Soviet visa processing had delayed it almost a month. There they discovered that the Soviet Air Force "...had been waiting for it for two weeks with a special, plush-upholstered Russian C-47, thus giving an early demonstration of the SAF's attitude toward the project as compared with the constant reserve shown by the Soviet Foreign Office."[1401]

On his post-war trip to Moscow, Elliott Roosevelt had the pleasure of flying on one of these tarted-up Dakotas. If he regretted that Donald Douglas's license to build the plane in Russia had escaped his grubby hands back in 1934, he did not say. The Soviets copied the plane (under proper license) as the Lisunov Li-2.

A recurrent theme throughout the project was that the Soviet military was far more helpful than the Commissariat for Foreign Affairs, headed by Molotov – and above them both, Beria's NKVD lurked constantly.[i] In that respect, the Americans only slowly apprehended the surveillance which the Soviets never forgot for one moment. One American report noted "The Red Air Force is extremely friendly and cooperative. They are appreciative of our effort and in sympathy with our objectives...The political control in Russia is neither friendly nor cooperative. They are determined that they [we] shall quit Russia as soon as possible."[1402]

This testimony matches the later accounts of American officers. Deane thought that pilots were "a people apart who fail to conform to the accepted pattern" and much inclined to get along in spite of political obstacles. And after the shooting stopped, Allied pilots also got along famously well with their erstwhile opponents![1403]

Colonel Kessler's Soviet diary has survived and reinforces this general view of a cooperative buildup. By the end of March, he wrote, the Russians had decided on the three bases, regardless of whether the Americans approved them or not. Then, on 31

---

[i] NKVD, People's Commissariat for Internal Affairs, later KGB, i.e. the domestic secret police.

March, Kessler, Cullen and other high-ranking officers were allowed to look the bases over. By mid-April, the American commanders flew into the three airstrips and from then on, construction was rapid, local cooperation being far better than in Moscow.

Incidentally, the Air Force also had the chance to demonstrate B-17 bombing to the Soviets. On 15 March, Kessler demonstrated the aircraft to Marshal Golovanov, who turned out to be far more interested in the Norden bombsight than the plane. On 28 March, a bombing demo revealed some problems, but on the 31st it was noted that: "2nd bombing test made today was highly successful. Apparently the constant error on the first one was due to improper altitude correction."[1404]

The Soviets finally were given the coveted Norden bombsight, a complex analog computer coupled with a gyroscopic autopilot, on 1 April.

By late May 1944, three Ukrainian airfields were ready to accept large numbers of American bombers and escort fighters. They were Poltava, Mirgorod, and Piryatin, all located along the railway from Kharkov to Kiev, in that order. They were given the AAF standard designations 559, 561, and 560. Oddly, these sites were relatively far to the east in the Ukraine; they were not the advance bases the Americans wanted nearer the front.[1405]

At that time Elliott was in charge of reconnaissance for the upcoming invasion of Normandy. Still, he was considered such an asset for this special and highly sensitive task that he was detached to participate in the Soviet airfields inspection in mid-May 1944. This was a major military and diplomatic effort led by General Spaatz's deputy for operations, Major General Frederick Anderson, USSTAF.

A number of high-ranking American officers accompanied them. Brig. Gen. Edward Curtis was the next highest ranking officer. With Colonel Roosevelt came also Colonels Frederick Sutterlin and Lowell P. Weicker, plus a few lower ranking assistants.[i]

Orders were cut on 5 May and the special B-17G (42-102642) departed next evening. A pleasantly surprised General Anderson noted in his diary that the aircraft had been named "*Mary Winn*" after his daughter, and the trip was a reminder that bombers modified as executive transports were important tools for generals, no matter the grumbling of lesser mortals. The expedition would take Colonel Roosevelt over some of his familiar territory: Casablanca, Tripoli, Cairo, Teheran, then north. The delegation arrived in Moscow on 10 May.[1406]

Ambassador Harriman had insisted on Colonel Roosevelt's presence. Not only could Elliott drink with the best of them, he already knew Stalin, and his last name was likely to cause his Soviet interlocutors to be extra cooperative. This hunch turned out to be correct. Elliott conducted some of the negotiations, and was able to secure an agreement on reconnaissance flights with his Soviet counterparts.[1407]

A close reading of the messages relating to this summit suggests that Colonel Roosevelt was along more to secure a good atmosphere, and that it was Colonel Weicker who mostly got down to the nuts and bolts of coordinating reconnaissance flights and sharing intelligence. But that doesn't mean Elliott wasn't busy.

On the 11th, Elliott met with Commissar Molotov, conveying his greetings and appreciations. At that meeting were also Deane, Curtis, and Anderson. The meeting covered, among other things, how to exploit publicity about the shuttle operations. It was keenly recognized that major propaganda advantages could be extracted from the

---

[i] Office documents with diary, 6 MAY 44, Anderson/HI. Colonel Weicker was president of ER Squibb, and father of the prominent senator and Connecticut governor of the same name.

joint project. Moscow was designated to take the lead in releasing information to the public when the time was right.[1408]

Much later Elliott remembered that he had met Stalin during this trip: "When we were negotiating in Moscow, I had to negotiate one-one-one, first of all with Stalin, then I had to negotiate with the air-force commanders…So, after meeting with Stalin, we were taken to Poltava." Possibly Elliott and Stalin had a courtesy meeting, but the official account makes no mention of it; the top-level negotiation session was with Molotov.[1409]

Other sensitive issues included the need for joint inspection of captured German scientific sites. To the Americans, investigation of enemy "experimental stations" was an exceptionally high priority, which shows how worried they were about the rumored German wonder weapons. They even proposed parachuting teams of investigators into the sites immediately upon news of a surrender, to ensure that the coveted material did not disappear. The Western Allies were then especially paranoid about the V-2 test site at Blizna, Poland; but when it was overrun, nothing truly important was found.[1410]

In truth, the British mission to Blizna, led by Colonel T.R.B. Sanders, did not examine the site until 3 September, a month after its capture and after many weeks of Soviet obstruction. The mission left for home on 22 September; by that time, V-2s were already hitting London. Sanders packed rocket components and other evidence for shipment to England, but when they arrived, the crates contained old aircraft parts. [1411]

Yet in May, Molotov was agreeable and the Americans were satisfied with Soviet cooperation:[1412]

> Although Mr. Molotov was non-commital on this new subject, our conversation took place in a very cordial and friendly atmosphere. It terminated with an exchange of pleasantries between Mr. Molotov and Colonel Roosevelt, whom the Foreign Commissar had greeted as "an old acquaintance." I feel that the Russians will cooperate with us on this matter, although a formal reply from them may not appear in the immediate future.[1413]

Next day, Colonels Weicker and Roosevelt sat down with their Soviet counterpart, Major General D.D. Grendal, and hammered out detailed plans for the American reconnaissance flights. It was immediately clear that Soviet reconnaissance capabilities were primitive in comparison, and Grendal asked for Roosevelt's existing and future images of areas of interest; for example, the Skoda Works in Bohemia. Soviet photo aircraft could reach only about 150-300 km ahead of the front. The Americans were now in the position of being able to mentor the Soviets, as they themselves had been mentored by the British. The first result was a steady stream of Colonel Roosevelt's photos of Europe going to Moscow.[1414]

It was agreed that Roosevelt would send Colonel Cullen and another pilot in two F-5s to Poltava from Bari, Italy on the first mission, which would cover Skoda and the rail networks. Cullen and his aircraft would then remain in Poltava and fly missions covering Soviet objectives. Another four F-5s at Bari would then institute a triangular shuttle service using RAF Mount Farm as the third vertex.

Reconnaissance conducted by 325th PRW Lightnings necessitated 24-hour notification of Soviet air defenses, as well as cleared routes and altitudes, current weather, and assigned radio frequencies. This was critical in order to avoid engagement by Soviet air defenses. In the beginning, coordination was severely lacking, but at least the problems were now being worked.

Beginning in April, the Americans had been populating the main Poltava base by air shuttle from Teheran. On 14 May, General Anderson's B-17G landed at Piryatin, recording the first American operation at the base. This historic flight, piloted by Captain J.A. Lauro, also brought Generals Curtis and Deane, and Colonels Sutterlin, Weicker, Thomas, and Gormley, along with Elliott Roosevelt, to inspect the three new bases.[1415]

The bomber promptly sank in up to its axles and had to be towed. This base was then designated as a fighter base, light aircraft being easier on the field. Workers at the other bases were still busy laying the perforated steel mat runways (Marsden matting) imported from the United States.[1416] Nonetheless, the trip was deemed very satisfactory and it was agreed the bases were ready to accept operations.

To support the project, a number of long-range Mosquito courier flights were made between England and Russia. At that very time, Elliott Roosevelt was an extremely busy man. On 24 May, back from Russia, he was again decorated by the British. Air Chief Marshal Sir Trafford Leigh-Mallory, on behalf of the King, made Colonel Roosevelt a Commander of the Order of the British Empire (OBE), a major recognition and a well-disseminated photo opportunity.[1417]

The American delegation left Moscow for Teheran on the 16th, having been satisfied with the progress at Poltava, and having at the last moment received the crucial Soviet permission for fighter escorts for the bombers. The officers retraced their route back to England via Cairo and Casablanca.[1418]

The Anderson mission is generally regarded as a success, since the detailed and highly cooperative proceedings cleared the path for shuttle-bombing operations beginning by 27 May. Some of the credit should go to Elliott. The internal history notes that Colonel Roosevelt extracted encouraging promises of compliance from the Soviets. It appears that he enjoyed the trip immensely, and apparently he was quite oblivious to the simmering irritation between the two allies.[1419]

On the other hand, subsequent events suggest that Elliott was less than successful in conveying to the squadron level the absolute necessity of following the Soviet procedures and directions to the letter. By the time operations began, reconnaissance flights were badly messed up, and the pilots and the Russians shared in the confusion and increasingly, in the resentment.

For example, Colonel Kessler recorded as late as 26 May that "We thought we were getting no place rapidly."[1420] Still, General Anderson's report of 21 May 1944 stated that the Soviets were expected to be most cooperative in the air battle against Germany, and that there was a good possibility of them being equally helpful in Siberia when the time came.[1421]

This was Elliott's first trip to Russia, but it would not be his last. Comrade Stalin made sure that the kid had a good time. The press found him living it up in Moscow, where he dined with "all seven" foreign correspondents at the Moscow Hotel. Elliott told Harry Butcher that the bill for the "plain meal" came to the equivalent of $690, yet included no alcohol. But the reporters wrote:[1422]

> Colonel Elliott Roosevelt, on a recent quick trip to Moscow, was wined and dined by correspondents, who treated him to a $50 a person supper of zakuska and borsch (hors d'oeuvres and vegetable soup), scalloped veal, etc. When a Red Army captain was invited over from another table, Colonel Roosevelt insisted, after a due amount of casual conversation, that the captain be told off the record, the colonel's identity. The captain was

at first incredulous, then convinced and delighted. Toasts to President Roosevelt, Stalin, the Second Front were exchanged; finally the beaming Russian whispered to his friend: "You know, I never thought a President's son could be so democratic."[1423]

Extortionate exchange rates aside, the result of the trip was that the airfields were judged to be adequate for the bombing missions. That Roosevelt had a very positive view of Russian life was an extra bonus. As he recounted the trip:

> ...And then in May I got word that I was to accompany General Fred Anderson and Ted Curtis [General Edward Curtis] and some staff officers of the Eighth Air Force to Russia to have a look at the airfields which had been tentatively assigned us, and to settle all final details before the shuttle operations could begin. It was good news that the Russians were agreeable to the shuttle-bombing plan, that they were figuring on giving our bombers fighter support, and especially that they had announced they would permit air reconnaissance photography. It was this last, of course, that involved me on the trip.
>
> The flight took me through some familiar places: Casablanca, Tunis, Cairo, Teheran (where we took on a Red Army navigator and a Red Army radio operator), and then on to Moscow. This was the first of two wartime trips I made to Russia; we were there only a little over a week, so my impressions are necessarily somewhat sketchy, but nevertheless quite vivid. I remember Moscow's wide, wide avenues; and the banquet tendered us by some high-ranking Red Air Force officers, where I was placed between two Russians, and our conversation was almost exclusively pantomime; I remember the Kremlin, where we went to call on Molotov – a vast building that dwarfs even our Pentagon, and seemed unlike any other office building I had ever seen, what with thick red carpets lining its hallways, and the comfortable furniture of its suites; I remember the magnificent opera house where we saw Rimsky-Korsakov's *The Snow Maiden*, infinitely more beautiful, more handsomely staged, better sung than a performance of the same opera I had once attended in our own Metropolitan Opera in New York City; and I remember the audience at the opera – 90% uniformed, but not without a scattering of elegantly gowned women...
>
> And I remember our flying inspection of the fields assigned for our shuttle operations, especially the one at Poltava, which before the war had been equivalent to our Randolph Field in Texas, and was, at the time we saw it, still little more that the shambles the Nazis had left when they retreated....
>
> A one-track railroad fed supplies to the entire southern Soviet front; when our shuttle operations began we insisted on moving in our own 100-octane aviation gasoline and bombs from the Persian Gulf, and thereby snafued their transport, but they cheerfully granted us the permission....We carried away the impression that the Russians were almost childishly eager to get along with us, cooperate with us...Joe Davies demonstrated how simple the job of cooperation with the Russians is; it is a tragedy that our own Government has not seen fit to assign more men like Davies to the critical job of representing us in the Soviet Union.[i]

This last remark of Elliott's illustrates his attitude superbly. Joe Davies, a fervent and enthusiastic admirer of Stalin, was FDR's ambassador to the Kremlin in 1936-38. He was the author of the popular book *Mission to Moscow*, which, at the president's explicit request, Hollywood turned into a nauseating propaganda film of the same name.

Davies, whom we shall meet again in connection with another dictator, was in Roosevelt's circle of plutocratic, high-living friends. He had made millions lawyering, and then multiplied them by marrying an heiress. He wisely invested much of this

---

[i] ER: As He Saw It, 216-9. Notice that he did not mention meeting Stalin in this account of his trip.

fortune in the Democratic Party, of whose National Committee he was made vice-chairman. Davies was widely viewed as a narcissistic megalomaniac with a highly relativistic concept of truth. His blustering defense of the USSR was as contrived as everything else he did, and his antics nearly made the staff at the Moscow embassy resign *en masse*. That Roosevelt would appoint a rich clown to the Moscow post (as he had appointed Joe Kennedy, a Hitler-apologist, to the London post) was somewhat balanced by his later appointment of the exceptionally respected Averell Harriman to the same job.[1424]

Colonel Roosevelt seems to have been one of the very few Americans who left the USSR in rapture. Operation FRANTIC is usually seen as an ill omen of what was to come. May-June 1944 was the high point of the temporary US-Soviet alliance. At that time, Colonel Kessler wrote, "our men and the Soviets are getting along beautifully."[1425]

This was the excuse, if any was necessary, for Elliott's high spirits. The Red Air Force officers with whom the Americans interacted were indeed generally professional, competent, and helpful in the common purpose. The growing impediments and ultimate breakdown in relations originated from the Communist Party apparatus. Since Comrades Molotov and Stalin intended to impress Elliott, he did not encounter or appreciate this situation, and he did not have the skeptical mindset to pick up on it.

As mentioned, a USAAF "Eastern Command" (ESCOM) under Major General Robert Walsh had been set up in Moscow. This cooperated with the American military mission under General Deane, but its principal job was to coordinate the air strikes with Generals Spaatz in England and Eaker in Italy. The logistics involved were herculean; almost everything had to be brought in via Persia, including high-octane avgas (the Russian kerosene couldn't be used in American engines), bombs and ammunition, and supporting equipment for hospitals, radio stations, and fire and wreck removal services. Trains from Murmansk complemented the logistics, delivering immense amounts of construction material and equipment.

As we saw during Stalin's flight to Teheran, there was no direct railway thither; the supplies were ferried across the Caspian Sea to Baku.

Even the runways had to be brought from America. Local women, working like horses, laid down the perforated steel plank runways. The Russians had never seen anything like these runways, and the Americans had never seen anything like these *babushkas*. However, the hardest task was to bring in the firmly limited number of about 1,300 American servicemen. Obtaining visas was a nightmare. Little did the Americans understand that the NKVD had to clear, monitor and follow all foreigners in the USSR, and was loath to admit that this would be impossible on the Ukrainian bases. Grudging concessions were made for groups of servicemen, and finally, by the end of May, everything was ready.

Early Reconnaissance via the USSR

The bombing missions get all the attention, but the reconnaissance flights were just as important. The first plan was to detach four F-5s to Poltava for three months. Because the Soviet bases never were built up to the contemplated strength, these reconnaissance planes were not allocated to Eastern Command, but operated on temporary assignments.

This small but productive detachment was housed in tents on the base until the German air attacks forced it to operate in an apple orchard about a mile away.[1426] The bulk of the missions were long-distance flights between Italy, England, and the bases in the Ukraine. Because of the high level of improvisation necessary to operate in the USSR, many of these flights were also used for liaison and urgent transport duties. This supplemented the impressment of B-17s as auxiliary cargo aircraft; the bombers would often haul parts and passengers along with their regular bomb loads.

A number of reconnaissance flights preceded the first bombing missions. First, Colonel Paul Cullen and a companion, Captain Franklin Carney, took their F-5s across to Poltava from Italy on 25 May 1944, without incident.[1427] However, on a local flight the next day Cullen was fired at by the Soviet anti-aircraft-artillery. Two days later the Russians again tried to shoot down an incoming gaggle of F-5s from Italy.

American complaints simply caused the Russians to ban the reconnaissance flights for a period. The Red Air Force said that it was their practice to shoot down anything that was not specifically notified and identified; therefore, if the Americans couldn't stick to flight plans and agreed procedures, it was impossible to go forward with further operations. It is likely the Russians were simply being blunt and straightforward, but inevitable some Americans would suspect they were fired upon deliberately.

The messages between Poltava and Widewing illustrate the dilemma. "It is absolutely necessary that Cullen's unit photograph all these targets except Mielec and Galatz air fields and rush photographs by air to San Severo for reproduction in quantity for briefing," radioed the Americans. No photo-recon, no bombing. [1428]

That the fault was not simply on the Russian side was highlighted in a furious memo Colonel Sutterlin produced just before launch of the first large-scale operations. He noted that of all the detailed briefing material painstakingly assembled by headquarters at Widewing, virtually nothing seemed to have filtered down to "Pinetree" level; i.e., crews went on missions without a clue of how to act when reaching Russian airspace. If Colonel Roosevelt was responsible for failing to adequately brief his crews, he was not the only one; bomber crews also apparently knew nothing.[1429]

By 2 June, the Russians agreed to establish five safe passage corridors for recon flights, which then resumed. Slowly, communications and coordination improved.[1430]

Many other incidents occurred. On 24 April, a C-87 Liberator, "*Becky*," was fired on between Teheran and Poltava. On 27 May, an F-5 was nearly shot down at Mirgorod (the Cullen incident, above), but this was just the beginning.[1431]

En route from England, Colonel Roosevelt's close friend Major Johnny Hoover and Lt. Ralph Kendall were forced down on 15 June. Hoover got lost and attracted the attention of both flak and fighters. He landed at Ryechitsa. The after-action report explained:

> Hoover…evaded 3 Yak fighters after a 10 minute chase and landed…after drawing Soviet flak. Interrogation shows that pilot was not briefed on contents of JK579 about radio facilities, also photos and drawings of bases now at Widewing. Kendall…was also subject to Soviet flak. Consider it necessary that mission adhere closely to the time tables submitted. Soviets are confused by invasion markings /"stripes instead of star and bar "/. The Yak attack was apparently prompted by such markings and should be removed before aircraft enter Russia.[i]

[i] ESCOMHIST, 4/27. Americans called all Soviet fighters Yaks; they, MiGs and Lavochkins looked alike.

Further on, Eastern Command complained that Major Hoover was under the impression that he could land anywhere within Soviet territory and that he was under no pressure to follow the flight plan as submitted to the Soviets. This sounds like a blistering criticism of Colonel Roosevelt's briefing procedures.

Kendall, who had preceded Hoover by 15 minutes, also got lost and was fired on. He landed only ten miles from the front at Vinnitsa. This was the site of a prewar Soviet extermination camp, and not a place foreigners should be poking around.[1432]

On 26 June, an F-5 flown by Lt. David Rowe of the Ukrainian Photo Detachment was shot down by Soviet fighters – Airacobras, embarrassingly enough – on a sortie to Bialystok from Poltava. Worse, these supposedly low-level fighters allegedly hit Rowe at 28,000 feet.[1433]

On fire, Rowe parachuted, and being found by Ukrainian peasants, stated that "upon hearing that he was an American, they wept and wrung their hands."[1434] Badly burned, Rowe recovered in a Kiev hospital.[1435]

From the Soviet perspective the mess wasn't their fault, but a result of a lack of American discipline. Reconnaissance flights were denied clearance until 29 June.

On 13 September, Yak-9s shot down a B-17 that force-landed without loss of life. Basically it was a miracle that the Americans operated during the summer without loss of life to Soviet forces. Perhaps for perspective, the AAF noted at the time that this had not been the case in Britain:

> There was one report of a Mustang in Western Europe which attacked a weather Mosquito returning to the UK, and this was reported to be the explanation for the fact that thereafter weather scouts came into Russian bases with distinctively painted red noses. Moreover in spite of the less trigger-happy habits of the RAF there have been incidents. As early as February 1942, a Polish RAF pilot shot down (and killed) Lt. Col. Griffiss, who was at that time returning from a secret mission to Russia.[i]

Admittedly, the Russians did shoot down an American B-24 at Murmansk; all crew but the pilot survived.[1436]

After the initial troubles, reconnaissance flights resumed and during each of June, July, and early August, about forty F-5s made it into the US-Soviet bases. Some American pilots reportedly thought the Russians deliberately tried to shoot them down.[1437] The case for this is that the Lightning is absolutely unmistakable. The case against it is that the British also tried to shoot them down from time to time.

There is yet another such account, unsupported by records. It is Colonel Elliott Roosevelt's:

> When I was flying by myself down the corridor ahead of a group of bombers that were coming in after bombing Warsaw, a Russian pilot flying an American-made P-39 came up and shot me, shot one of my engines out. There was no radio communication; there was no way I could tell him. Although they were supposedly briefed and I had the only twin-boomed and twin-tailed airplane in the whole air force – both enemy and Allies – and they should have known that this was a friendly aircraft, they didn't. The pilot was green, I

---

[i] ESCOMHIST, 4/31. Lt. Col. Townsend Griffiss was on a Lend-Lease mission. On 15 FEB 42 he became the first American airman killed in the European war, unfortunately by "friendly fire." Griffiss AFB, NY, was named for him.

> guess. I force-landed on a Russian air base. The Russian pilot came into the same air base after me. They arrested him, and they treated me like I was liquid gold. They were full of apologies. Anyway, he caught it; he was shot for getting mixed up.[1438]

No official source could be found to substantiate this story, which Elliott told shortly before his death in 1990. It sounds a lot like some of the other incidents told above, but with the added dramatic touch of the execution of the Russian pilot. Perhaps telling this incident to the world was inopportune earlier, or else he made it up.

The prevailing shoot-first, think-later mentality made friendly fire a huge issue in the air war. "If it flies, it dies," seemed to be the mantra of the ground forces of all countries; likewise, angry pilots have been known to resort to resolute attacks on their own forces. As demonstrated in Iraq, that often seems to be the only thing that works.

Furthermore, it appears that the Soviet military was deeply embarrassed by the incidents and tried everything to protect their guests, even when this caused unpalatable restrictions from an American standpoint. One interesting result of the American distrust of the Soviet gunners was that General Eaker insisted that a U.S. observer, trained in aircraft identification, be placed at each anti-aircraft battery during President Roosevelt's flight to Yalta the next February. Unusually, the Americans forced the issue on a "no-observers, no FDR" basis. Stalin then conceded the point.[1439]

Shuttle Bombing Operations

Because the 8th Air Force was too busy supporting OVERLORD, the first shuttle bombing runs were given to the 15th Air Force in Italy. General Eaker wanted badly to use the new bases to hit Riga and assorted other northeastern industrial targets. Stalin would have none of it. Instead, he demanded the Americans hit less exciting targets in the Balkans. In the end, the Americans wound up bombing mostly non-essential targets that could have been reached on return trips from Italy. But that was merely the beginning of the problems.

The first run – FRANTIC-1 – was made on 2 June 1944 and was deemed highly successful, although the hits on Debrecen railyards and Romanian airfields were of limited strategic value. 64 P-51s landed at Piryatin, 65 B-17s reached Mirgorod, and 64 B-17s personally led by General Eaker made it to Poltava. Only one B-17 was shot down.

At the Soviet bases, the welcome was enthusiastic, and the vodka flowed freely. For a while, spirits were high. It is universally acknowledged that the Americans and the Russians got along extremely well on a personal basis, as long as official Soviet supervision could be deflected. The problems were clearly with the political and security oversight, not with the true attitudes of the Russians.

As an example, after FRANTIC-1, Ambassador Harriman awarded the Legion of Merit to the leading Soviet generals who had facilitated the operation. The commander of the Red Air Force, Chief Air Marshal Alexander Novikov, stood out in particular as trying to assist the U.S. while covering his back as best he could. But he wasn't good enough. In March 1946, Stalin sent him to the Gulag, along with many other tainted high officers. To rub it in, Vasilii Stalin was promoted to Major General, and he took Novikov's dacha. [1440]

American pilots learned much about just how crude were Soviet operating conditions and procedures. It blew their minds that the Russians didn't bother with sissy rituals like checklists, taxiing, and run-ups. They climbed aboard, went to full power, and took off seemingly in whatever direction they were pointed. This fits with another observation during the handover of American aircraft to the Red Army: the Soviet pilots had no patience for transition training. They just wanted to know how to start the thing, and off they went.[1441]

At one time, when mother Eleanor innocently remarked on the extraordinary powers of recollection of Soviet diplomats she dealt with at the United Nations, Elliott volunteered that Russians seemed to have evolved a superior memory. He said:

> In the Air Force during the war, they were the only foreigners who could arrive late in the afternoon, be given the book of detailed instructions on how to fly an American bomber, study it during the night and then fly the bomber away early the next morning, without an American flier aboard.[1442]

But most American officers observing the Soviets probably realized that life was cheap in the USSR during the war, and pilots could not be allowed to waste time on niceties. Here's a rifle, there's the front. Here's a plane, go fly.

From the high point of FRANTIC-1, it was all downhill. The bill came due during FRANTIC-2 on 22 June. This was a similar large-scale operation, this time by the 8th Air Force in England, comprised of 163 B-17s and 70 P-51s. It is also recorded, as an aside, that two of Elliott's F-5s participated, one from the 13th and one from the 22nd Photographic Squadron.[1443]

The primary target was the Ruhland synthetic oil plant north of Dresden; secondary was the railyards at nearby Elsterwerda. These targets, however legitimate, could have been reached on a return trip from England. 150 Fortresses and 64 Mustangs made it to the American bases in the Ukraine. Losses and cancellations were slight.

It was a very successful operation and high-spirited inter-Allied euphoria ruled on the warm, solsticial eve of one of the greatest disasters in Air Force history.

Happy hour for the Luftwaffe

The Germans knew "Poltawa" well; the Führer himself had been there. The base had been a regional Luftwaffe headquarters when the Ukraine was under German control. German relations with the Ukrainians were ambivalent, and some of the town had been deliberately left standing by the retreating forces. Nonetheless, the Americans were appalled by the civilian situation in the area, and attempted to ameliorate it as well they could, by purchases, barter, and gifts.

When the Germans left, they buried twelve 500 kg bombs under the incompletely demolished building that would become the joint US-Soviet headquarters. The bombs were connected to a radio-controlled trigger mechanism complete with a very large antenna, all covered under straw and weeds 250 yards distant. The infernal device was discovered before the Germans saw fit to set it off.[1444]

Much worse was soon to come. As a bad omen, the occasional German reconnaissance plane was sighted over the bases during the spring.[1445]

The story is usually told that a German aircraft unobtrusively trailed the bomber stream of FRANTIC-2 to Poltava, and returned to allow the Luftwaffe to mount perhaps its single most effective raid of the war. An eyewitness told this story:

> Shortly after passing WARSAW it was noticed that a German single-engine fighter was keeping pace with the task force, flying just above the low broken clouds, about eleven o'clock. The friendly fighters were contacted and told the position of the enemy fighter but when our fighters came to the head of the column the enemy fighter would duck below the clouds to the deck. Then later would take original position, this airplane kept pace with task force until the bad weather at Russian-German front was reached.[1446]

This alone would not have pinpointed the bases, and closer examination shows that it is far from the whole story.

When FRANTIC-1 had departed for Italy, an American combat photographer tried to take out the official photographic record of the operation. The Russians stopped him and demanded that no photographs leave the USSR. The cunning American reluctantly handed over his unexposed film but took along his 500 images of the operation. This was a bad move, since it could only irritate the Soviets. But it was really bad because the B-17 carrying the film was shot down over Romania. Within a few days the Luftwaffe had a fine photographic record of the US-Soviet operation.[1447]

When FRANTIC-2 arrived two weeks later on the evening of 21 June, the Germans flew a long-range He-177 Greif over the airfields to acquire pre-strike imagery. Eastern Command reported this aircraft over the bases at 1815 (i.e., in bright daylight).[1448]

A massive German bomber force was already assembled at Minsk, ready for its orders. These aircraft were mainly He-111Hs, which could not survive in daytime (and in the West, not at all) but for night attack in Russia they were fine. A smaller number of Ju-88s accompanied them. The units involved were KG 4, KG 53, KG 55, and KG 27.[i]

A U.S. eyewitness vividly recalled how "Jerry" interrupted the post-op celebrations:

> The task force commander together with Generals WALSH, KESSLER, and Russian officers, were guests of General PERMINOV at dinner that night. The dinner began at eleven o'clock. At approximately 2320 hours it was announced that German bombers were headed across the front lines in the general direction of POLTAVA. Air raid alarms were immediately sounded. The dinner was ended immediately and the task force commander checked to see that all task force personnel had adequate bomb shelters and so on available. Eastern Command USSTAF officers gave assurance that adequate facilities were near the tent camp and personnel had been alerted.[1449]
>
> Immediately after air raid warnings were sounded, all personnel took shelter in whatever facilities were available and all defense personnel (all Russian) were alerted. At approximately 0015 hours the Russian Anti-aircraft started firing. This anti-aircraft defense seemed to consist of approximately three batteries of 88 mm guns and several batteries of 37 mm guns.
>
> At approximately 0030 hours first German PFF (pathfinder) airplane dropped flares directly above the field, their accuracy was not strange considering that the sky was almost completely clear and the Russian anti-aircraft guns were all around the field and their fire was coned above the field. About ten minutes after the first flare was dropped the first bombs started falling and then for almost two hours, the bastards bombed hell out of the

---

[i] Infield, 141-2. KG = Kampfgeschwader, the main German air unit, roughly equals a group.

flying field, especially that part where the task force B-17s were dispersed. It was one of the most accurate bombing raids that the task force commander has seen or heard of, many thousands of bombs were dropped and approximately 98% of them fell on the flying field. Very few large bombs were dropped and their accuracy was not as good as that of the smaller bombs. One one-thousand pound bomb struck the center of the steel-mat runway. Others were on the airdrome and others were near the tent camp.

The large majority of bombs were incendiary or anti-personnel types. At least 20-30,000 of these types must have been dropped and without exception, they fell on the airdrome. 37 B-17s were completely destroyed, 9 others were damaged so badly that they had to be salvaged, of 73 B-17s on the field 100% were either destroyed or damaged. Three days after the bombing, only nine were operational. All airplanes destroyed or damaged were the result of direct hits. The German target was undoubtedly the B-17s. At least 50-75 Russian ATC and ESCOM USSTAF airplanes were on the opposite side of the field from the B-17s and only three of these were destroyed although some Task Force airplanes were dispersed on same side of field.

There was hardly a square yard of ground in the Task Force dispersal area that was not hit by some type of bomb. Butterfly bombs were dropped in abundance. On the afternoon following the raid the Task Force Commander was in the flying line and a hard rain shower started falling and at least a hundred or so butterfly bombs were exploded by the rain fall. It sounded like a young war for a few minutes. Also the Russian sapper had a unique way of destroying anti-personnel bombs, one system was to pick the bomb up and throw it as far as possible and either fall flat on their face or else run like hell. It worked, but also kept the medical section and coffin builders busy.

During the air raid the majority of the task force personnel reacted the same as in England. That is, when the alarm first sounded, they merely turned over and cussed because they had been awakened, however, when the bombs started falling they found ditches and shelters in record time.

It was only because of the German bombing accuracy that personnel losses were not higher. If the same saturation of bombs had fallen in the tent camp as on the flying field, personnel losses would have been very high. One pilot was killed and one co-pilot was seriously injured. Several received minor injuries. One large H.E. [high-expl.] fell in the tent area causing all losses.

Russian anti-aircraft was very ineffective, they did a hell of a lot of shooting but do no damage to the Hun. Most of their efforts seemed to be just wild firing. An hour after the last bomb fell, they were still firing as much as ever, as if they wanted to expend a certain quota of ammunition. Losses among Russian anti-aircraft personnel were very high. Search lights were ineffective, only one German bomber was picked up and anti-aircraft fire was not bursting anywhere near this airplane.

After midnight, the German task force assigned to bomb Mirgorod had missed that field and instead augmented the force aimed at Poltava. When the bombers arrived there, they effectively erased the American air wing. The internal history noted officially that every one of 73 B-17s on the field was hit:

43 Fortresses were destroyed or damaged beyond repair; 3 C-47s and 1 F-5 were likewise destroyed. 26 Fortresses, 2 C-47s and 1 C-46, and 25 Russian aircraft (mainly Yak fighters) were heavily damaged but repairable; over 450,000 gallons of gasoline were destroyed and over 500 gallons of aircraft oil; over 3200 bombs, 26,000 bomb fuses, and 1,360,000 cartridges were destroyed. [1450]

Personnel losses the night of the raid were 25 Russians killed and 1 American, Flight Officer Joseph G. Lukacek, a Fortress co-pilot, who thus was the first American killed in action on the Russian Front. [1451]

More people died of wounds later. One was Lukacek's captain, Lt. Raymond Estele. 14 Americans were wounded, 6 of them hospitalized.[1452]

The smaller force at Mirgorod escaped that night, but the hurriedly evacuated airfield was wiped out by a precision attack the next night. Since stores, unlike planes, could not be moved, another critical loss of fuel and ammunition dumps occurred. Only three unflyable B-17s had been left on the field, and they were not damaged. The other bombers had been hurriedly flown to Kirovograd during the daytime.[i]

Likewise, the Germans targeted Piryatin on the 23rd. In that case, however, they missed that more rustic airstrip by three miles.[1453]

The Mustang squadrons at Piryatin were untouched and requested permission to engage the Germans. This was denied. In general, no American aircraft was allowed to operate in the Soviet Union before a cumbersome approval process was completed. This is probably why the P-51s were not launched, although some Americans thought it was a deliberate Soviet act to ensure the success of the German attack.

It is important to note that even though 60 bundles of steel matting were required to repair the Poltava runway, that field was back in operation after three days. This again illustrated how difficult it is to wipe out infrastructure from the air using conventional methods. Thus the German success really lay in making the Americans unwilling to risk heavy bomber operations from the Ukraine for several weeks, and perhaps in markedly cooling the ardor of both Americans and Russians for continuing the missions.

The Soviet losses are also of interest. Of a regiment of about 40 Yakovlevs, only four or five were able to take off.[1454] At Poltava, General Perminov lost his personal DC-3. 15 Yak-9s, 6 Yak-7s, 3 trainers, and one Hurricane were damaged. At Mirgorod, one Airacobra was lost and two damaged; two trainers were lost.[1455]

At Poltava and Mirgorod, the fuel and ammunition so laboriously brought from half a world away went up in flames and in secondary explosions. Human losses were low because military personnel hid in slit trenches during the bombing and strafing, but the Russians sent their people out to fight fires. They were killed as aircraft exploded, and when they stepped on anti-personnel mines dropped by the German aircraft. Eastern Command investigators later reported that there were over 50,000 small anti-personnel or fragmentation bombs, over 9,000 butterfly bombs, and over 6,000 incendiaries dropped. [1456] Bombs were still going off as late as the middle of September.[1457]

The Americans were furious to find that the Soviets offered no effective defense. Reports about Soviet fighters being scrambled are conflicting. Although the local AAA sites opened up, firing their guns frenziedly in the general direction of up, the American assessment was that the AAA fire was "intense," but its effectiveness was "nil."[ii]

In two hours of systematic, illuminated bombing and strafing, the Germans suffered no losses. The Americans knew the attack was over when finally a large flare was dropped over the field; it provided the last German aircraft with accurate bomb damage assessment photographs. One of these photos, annotated *2 Nachtaufklärungstaffel*, was published in 1973 by Major Glenn Infield, who had access to the German archives.[1458]

Infield, in his strongly anti-Soviet 1973 history, stated:

---

[i] A Soviet pilot recounted leading the Mirgorod evacuation in Keyssar: Remembering War, 182.

[ii] ESCOMHIST, 6/20. AAA = Antiaircraft Artillery.

> Pleased with the results of the bombing, Antrup [Oberstleutnant Wilhelm Antrup, CO of KG55] checked the sky for a sign of Russian night fighters. He knew that his bombers had been reported by Russian observers at the front lines since it was impossible to "sneak" 80 Ju-88s and He-111s into enemy territory without being spotted. Antrup anticipated that the Red Air Force would defend their air bases with every resource at their command and he had briefed his crews to be prepared for a violent air battle. Why the Yaks or Airacobras had not yet made an appearance puzzled him...[1459]

General Deane was not quite as angry in his 1946 account:

> The Russian anti-aircraft and fighter defenses failed miserably. Their anti-aircraft batteries fired twenty-eight thousand rounds of medium and heavy shells, assisted by searchlights, without bringing down a single German plane. There were supposed to be forty Yaks on hand as night fighters, but only four or five of them got off the ground. Both their anti-aircraft and night fighters lacked the radar devices which made ours so effective.[1460]

Robert Jackson, probably writing from Soviet sources, had quite another story in *The Red Falcons* (1970):

> The distinctive sound of VK-105 engines was suddenly added to the uneven beat of the German motors [famously unsynchronized RPMs] as a squadron of Pe-2 [Petlyakov light twins] night-fighters arrived on the scene. Soon after their arrival, the bombing ceased abruptly and the German bombers droned away; because of the small formations used by the enemy the Pe-2 crews – lacking any form of AI [air intercept] radar – failed to make contact and returned to base, believing that the raid was over. They were wrong. Fifteen minutes later, as Russian firefighters were beginning a desperate attempt to salvage something from the wreckage, half a dozen Ju-88s swept across the field at low altitude, pouring machine-gun fire into aircraft that were still intact and sending them up in flames too. They were followed by two reconnaissance Heinkels, which circled the area for several minutes taking photographs.[1461]

The Poltava catastrophe raised all kinds of issues. It was the biggest single bomber loss the Eighth Air Force suffered in Europe, on a level with the decimation of the Schweinfurt-Regensburg mission a year earlier.

Many Americans thought Stalin had lured them into the country and then tipped off the Luftwaffe to destroy them. In his detailed 1973 history of FRANTIC, Glenn Infield explicitly issued this indictment. It is likely, however, that this is a libelous charge influenced by subsequent East-West tensions. The simpler answer is that the Germans were perfectly able to conduct the operation on their own initiative. In addition, contemporary sources emphasized that the Soviets were going out of their way to prevent any harm coming to the Americans.[1462]

On the other hand it was obvious that the USSR was unable to protect the American forces. Even if locally based fighters had been scrambled, these basic day-fighters would have been ineffective; same for the American Mustangs at Piryatin. The Soviets did not have an effective radar and night-fighter defense. They did claim that they had conducted retaliatory raids on the German air bases.

After the disaster, the Americans insisted on bringing in an effective air defense capability, including radar-equipped night fighters. This the USSR would absolutely not permit. Nor would the Soviets assent to American radar-guided mobile AAA at the bases. Acutely embarrassed as they were, they could not admit fault, and neither could they accept a greatly expanded American role. Although Poltava and Mirgorod recovered to full strength after about one month, both the Soviets and the Americans had cooled markedly on the entire project by then.

As late as June, the Americans had thought their presence in the USSR would soon grow to the numbered Air Force level, and that the greatest effort would eventually be mounted in the Far East. Now supplies already en route were turned around, and evacuation to the West commenced at a measured pace. The 427th Night Fighter Squadron, which was quickly ordered to assume the air defense role in Russia with twelve new P-61 Black Widows, was redirected en route when the Soviets refused permission for its entry.[1463]

Suddenly operation FRANTIC didn't seem so smart after all. Who got the idea that you could operate effectively out of Russia, with its non-existent air defense, its crude, remote facilities, and its uncooperative officials? This episode was a reminder that strategic air power didn't come on the cheap; it required a vast support infrastructure, from long runways to navigation aids to weathermen to radars to effective command-and-control of it all.

Most of all, it required that the Allies cooperate rather than torment each other. After the Poltava catastrophe, US-Soviet relations swiftly cooled, and air force relations in particular turned to bitterness on the American side, icy hostility on the Soviet one.

A basic problem was that the parties had different goals. For the bomber force (and Colonel Roosevelt's 325th PRW) FRANTIC was simply a means of assisting the strategic bombardment of Germany. For Arnold and Marshall it was also a precursor to securing Siberian bases to be used against Japan. And for President Roosevelt, Harry Hopkins, and their ilk, it was a means of making friends with Comrade Stalin and demonstrating to him how selflessly helpful America could be to him in the coming Nirvana of postwar peace.

But for Stalin, most likely FRANTIC was a dangerous, double-edged sword. He would learn the American methods and technology, but the Americans would also learn how defenseless the USSR was to air attack. The potential for American interference with the Soviet subjugation of Europe was apparent. And for a paranoid regime of this kind, any foreign contingent on its soil was inherently a mortal political threat.

This is why Soviet officers helpful to the Americans were instantly suspect, even though they were following orders. The especially esteemed General Novikov, Arnold's counterpart, was tortured and jailed after the war.[1464]

The shuttle operations continued in a much less ambitious mode until September. FRANTIC-3 and -4 in July and early August consisted entirely of fighters – P-38s and P-51s – since these could at least defend themselves, and required much less fuel. FRANTIC-5 resumed bombing, and on 11 September FRANTIC-6 bombed Chemnitz, Stalin having forbidden its initial objective of reinforcing the struggling Polish rebellion.

A curious aspect of the continued operations was that despite the best efforts of both sides, U.S. planes and pilots soon wound up all over the Eastern Front. It was to be expected in wartime, but it apparently wasn't, and this undoubtedly added to the Soviet unease with the foreign presence.

Following the German attacks, American forces were evacuated to airfields at Kharkov, Zaporozhe, and Chuguev. Later, Osnovia and Dnepropetrovsk were added. For photo reconnaissance aircraft, which operated singly and often got lost, forced landings occurred at Zaporozhe, Ouretchytaty, and Klinkowice. There was an amusing incident with one hapless F-5 pilot:

> ...on return from mission he landed at Chernitov because of bad weather. On 24 July he took off and was led by a B-25 until lost again. Out of gas he then landed at Novgrad Severski. On 25 July he took off again, flew to Konotop and returned to Poltava.
>
> On 22 August this same pilot force landed at Gulyai Polye. One weather ship force landed at Melitopol. Emergency landing of American bombers or fighters took place at Kiev, Demievka, Kirovograd, and others were reported at such places as Karlovka, Buishov, Novacheske, Zhulyam, Buzava, Peryasiasjale, Korzel, some of which could not easily be traced on the map.[1465]

Things got more hectic as the air offensive gained momentum in the summer. On 4 August, Lightnings and Mustangs from Italy were scattered like chaff by lowering ceilings – IFR flight being almost unknown on the Eastern Front:

> Landings were made all over the map. There were 10 aircraft at Kremenchug, 10 at Zielce, 6 were reported at Zhmerinka, others at Kirovograd, Dnepropetrovsk, Kolosovka, Karlovka, Vozmesenk, as well as on the regular dispersal fields....[i]

Obviously, Stalin could not have been pleased with this chaos. He was accustomed to the NKVD knowing where every foreigner was every minute. In their eagerness to help, the Americans had turned into a major headache for him. It had to stop.

As the summer turned into autumn, even the reconnaissance flights were losing their appeal. By the end of August, the Soviets refused permission, and it wasn't until 7 September that Colonel Cullen's routine mission from Italy was approved. On 19 September, the final shuttle reconnaissance sortie, a BDA mission, was flown by Captain Frank Carney. Records show him flying to Italy via objectives at Debrecen on 22 September.[ii]

At the end of summer, the Americans judged that it wasn't worth the effort. The USSR made clear that the U.S. presence was unwanted; and although small advance crews remained in the Ukraine into 1945, large-scale operations ceased in September.

Warsaw Betrayed

There were two special tasks for which the shuttle operation would have been eminently helpful, but the first one was the very one that fully revealed Stalin's true intentions to the horrified Americans. In late July 1944, the 1st Byelorussian Front (Rokossovsky) reached the outskirts of Warsaw, and broadcast instructions to the Polish Home Army there to rise up against the German occupiers. For the next six months, the Red Army ceased fighting on this front and left the Germans to methodically exterminate the Polish resistance and level Warsaw to the ground.

Coming on the heels of the discovery of the Katyn forest mass graves, which German propaganda exploited ruthlessly, the Warsaw matter was an unwelcome wedge not only in Allied relations, but in U.S. politics. The controversy irked many anti-

---

[i] ESCOMHIST 6/31. IFR = Instrument Flight Rules.

[ii] Kean, 369; ESCOMHIST 4/35. The target photographed was Szolnok.

Communists because of the desperate contortions Stalin's apologists in the United States stooped to in order to absolve their ally of guilt and suspicion.[1466] Britain had gone to war for Poland, but now the Poles were the fly in the Allied ointment. The incompletely suppressed matter became political in the United States, where ethnic Poles are not without influence. Yet at the same time it is also clear that the episode shook President Roosevelt's naïve confidence in Uncle Joe. Others, from Ambassador Harriman on down, were stunned and infuriated by it.[i]

To view the tragedy in perspective, we should imagine that Anglo-American troops halted their advance outside Paris for six months, awaiting the city's total obliteration by the SS. We should further imagine that the Allies refused to aid the uprising there, and moreover denied Soviet aircraft the chance to fly 1600 miles to airdrop supplies. We should try to imagine that we allowed de Gaulle's forces to be annihilated while we simultaneously held up a straw-puppet government somewhere in Normandy. And we might try to conceive that Britain, as a price for liberating the whole, asserted the right to annex that province, and Aquitaine and Bretagne and Picardie and what not.

That was the kind of ally President Roosevelt had in World War II. However, for our purposes, the question is what role air power could, or could not, play in the matter.

The Warsaw uprising began on 1 August. On the next day, the Soviet divisions about to enter Warsaw were ordered to disperse. This immediately attracted the attention of the Western allies. The British and Americans formulated plans to provide air support to the trapped Poles. The bases in the Ukraine would have made this possible. Stalin forbade it. The British, who had no stake in FRANTIC, flew their own exceedingly dangerous night missions to Warsaw at the limit of their bombers' radius of action, but the tonnage dropped successfully was very small.

General Spaatz planned to support the Polish uprising using FRANTIC-6 on 16 August. It would have involved 70 bombers and 100 fighters. The Soviet refusal to give permission was appealed all the way to the Stalin-Roosevelt level, without success. As a result, unilateral RAF operations began on 19 August, continuing to 29 September. The RAF lost 28 aircraft and 190 airmen, and these operations had little effect.[1467]

FRANTIC-6 was redirected to targets acceptable to the Soviet Union. It must be recalled that during all this time, the Red Army was within artillery and tactical air support range of Warsaw.

Although his facts varied slightly, General Arnold provided a snapshot of the American dilemma:

> General Marshall and I talked this over at length. For some time it had been apparent that if some help was not given to the Polish patriots in Warsaw they would be exterminated. The last time the RAF had sent supplies to them by air they had lost some 48 planes, or about 35% of the total number involved. Furthermore, refugee Germans, not Polish people, had gathered and collected most of the supplies the RAF had dropped by parachute. Now the British were trying to force the Russians to assist in this enterprise.
>
> To us it looked as if the Russians would just as soon have all the Warsaw Poles exterminated; as if they were interested in the Ukrainian Poles only. [probably a reference to the Lublin puppet government.] As far as I could figure out, the Russians simply stood by and watched this Warsaw debacle, when they might well have expedited their offensive, captured Warsaw, driven the Germans out and put an end to it.[1468]

---

[i] Harriman, 337-41. He wrote in detail about the Warsaw debacle, which changed his mind about the USSR.

On 18 September, when only small pockets of Polish resistance remained in Warsaw, Stalin permitted a FRANTIC-7 operation, consisting of 107 B-17s and 64 P-51s. This mission dropped about 100 tons of equipment, but by then almost all air-dropped supplies fell into German hands. The Russians now argued that the Americans were aiding Hitler. No more massed FRANTIC operations were flown, because a planned FRANTIC-8 was preempted by the capitulation of the Polish Home Army remnants on 2 October.[1469]

It is unlikely that full-scale Western air supply would have done anything but protract the disaster, but both the USAAF and RAF considered it to be an imperative since the Polish forces, if supported by the Red Army, could have added measurably to an early victory. This is yet another case where the military observers thought a sharp confrontation with Marshal Stalin should have been the remedy.

General Deane recorded the ominous change in the Soviet attitude:

> When the Polish dispute occurred, Soviet displeasure was reflected in all branches of government and many restrictions were placed on American activities in Poltava. Our aircraft were unnecessarily grounded, rescue crews were refused permission to service American planes known to have force-landed in Poland, seriously injured American airmen were not allowed to be moved from Poltava to our general hospital at Teheran and Russian women were not allowed to associate with American men. Russian airmen, who were undoubtedly simply carrying out instructions from Moscow in applying restrictions, incurred the resentment of the American soldiers. Morale and friendliness waned rapidly. Russians began to loot American warehouses.[1470]

Although Elliott Roosevelt did not say exactly when he was in Poltava during the operational phase, he did leave an account that suggests that the original exuberance had cooled down dramatically:

> We tried to work very closely with them. But they were very adamant about not allowing us a great deal of freedom to get out into the countryside and talk with the people in that area. They wouldn't let any of the Americans mingle with the local population because of our way of going out and fraternizing.
>
> It was a tough duty being over there. You couldn't go anyplace, and the surroundings weren't very pretty. There wasn't anything to do, except just stay right there on the base. So they tried not to make the tours of duty there too long. Almost everybody I knew that was stationed there was very unhappy; after they'd been there for about thirty days, they'd about had it. But most of them had to stay well over six months.[1471]

Despite his generally rosy view of Soviet cooperation, Elliott also had to admit that it seemed to be a one-way street:

> Soviet soldiers were all around, and we were very open in saying come on in and see how we do things. So they were having hundreds and hundreds of officers and enlisted personnel in there all the time, soaking up all the information that they could get. And it seemed sort of one-way, because they never did open up that way to us.[1472]

The Warsaw catastrophe, which cost about 200,000 Polish lives, left the Western Allies dumbfounded. Few of them realized that since 1920, when the Poles had stopped the Bolshevik world revolution at the gates of Warsaw, one of Stalin's top priorities had been to erase the Polish nation, a task he shared with Adolf Hitler during 1939-41. The reason for this vindictiveness was that Komisar Stalin, defying Red Army chief Leon Trotsky's orders, had failed to come to the aid of Tukhachevsky at Warsaw. He instead tried and failed to take Lemberg (Lvov). Much of Stalin's later polonophobia, and his need to kill Trotsky, seem related to the crucial events of 1920.[i]

The last thing Stalin wanted was American troops on Polish soil. And he was not going to allow the West to assist the Poles in Warsaw any more than he would tolerate the restoration of Poland's borders, an issue already conceded in principle at Teheran.

At Yalta a few months later, President Roosevelt agreed to return to Stalin the half of Poland he'd previously obtained in the Molotov-Ribbentrop protocols of 1939. Roosevelt acquiesced in moving the remainder of Poland onto German soil. President Harry Truman inherited, as a first priority, the unsolvable squabble over the Polish puppet regime.

A Missed Opportunity

In recent years, yet another nagging controversy has arisen about a task the shuttle-bombing program was perfect for, yet was never seriously considered by the Air Force.[ii]

"Should the Americans have bombed Auschwitz?" has become a raw issue among historians. The debate has unfortunately involved more political and moral posturing than air power expertise. While such an operation was obviously morally justified, it was also extremely problematic for reasons of range, timing, and bombing effectiveness. It is absurd to attribute its neglect to ill will, much less anti-Semitism.

Most of the German extermination camps were located close to the Red Army's advance in the summer of 1944. Just by the time FRANTIC got under way in June, the Allies received incontrovertible evidence of the monumental scale of the killings at Auschwitz. By that time some of the other death camps had already been liberated.

About the same time Allied reconnaissance aircraft finally reached the area in the hunt for critical war infrastructure. Dino Brugioni, a veteran reconnaissance specialist, determined that Mosquitoes of SAAF 60 Squadron first photographed Auschwitz-Birkenau on 4 April 1944, and this Italy-based unit monitored the area over the next nine months. Brugioni said the camps were photographed at least thirty times, yet – typically – when political interest arose, the 8th Air Force complained it had no coverage. The reconnaissance emphasis had been not on the camps, but on the nearby industrial complex IG Farben at Monowitz. This facility was bombed in August and September; the camps were ignored but also received some damage. The imagery is available on the Yad Vashem internet site. Both the Farben plant and the camps have a gigantic geographical footprint.[1473]

Quite logically, people have argued that a prime target of Allied air power should have been the remaining camps, the marshaling yards and railways serving them, and whatever other infrastructure whose destruction might have impeded the genocide. This issue arose in the 1970s and 1980s, after the Holocaust itself grew to much greater prominence in historiography than it had initially held.

---

[i] This is now so commonly accepted that even V. Putin asserted it during the Katyn memorial proceedings.

[ii] Many books and articles deal with this, prominently Martin Gilbert: Auschwitz and the Allies (1981); David Wyman: The Abandonment of the Jews (1984), and William Rubinstein: The Myth of Rescue (1997).

Nonetheless, there is no evidence that either Elliott Roosevelt's 325th PRW or any other reconnaissance units took any special targeting interest in the matter, and Elliott never mentioned it. While bombing was discussed, this appears to have happened at the political level rather than at USSTAF.

In June, FRANTIC first made Auschwitz raids by Western air power possible, and after the end of shuttle operations in September, U.S. air power could reach the area autonomously. The Ukrainian Front had halted in August less than 100 miles from Auschwitz, so it was a logical assumption that the Red Army would soon overrun the area. As it was, the camp wasn't liberated until January, but the mass killings there had ended in November. The extermination of Hungarian Jews largely ended in July.

At best, there was thus only a six month window available for such attacks. Realistically, Allied air attacks in July-November would probably have had negligible effect. High-altitude bombing was still notoriously inaccurate and would have killed the people ostensibly to be rescued. There are many cases in which slave labor camps or ships full of camp survivors reached their final solution at the hands of Allied air action. That does not mean, however, that all forms of air power would have been useless.

There are some famous examples of the RAF making pinpoint attacks to free prisoners; but even they usually cost plenty of innocent lives. However, had the Allies been trying to save lives through bombing or any other air action, they would certainly have concentrated on their own prisoner-of-war camps. We know this, for example, from the 325th PRW's unconsummated plan to free POWs at the end of the war.[1474]

This does not consider what Marshal Stalin, who could and did veto targets, would have said about the matter. He didn't even permit help to reach the Poles, and he would turn on the Jews himself after Hitler was done with them. The fact that the Red Army stopped its advance short of Cracow in August, and did not move again until January, tends to be overlooked; it matters because even without ground action, the highly effective Soviet tactical air force could certainly have made the German camps untenable. Pinpoint attacks by RAF Mosquitoes using Ukrainian bases would clearly have been the most effective, but that was completely unacceptable to the Soviets.

Early and persistent interdiction of the main railway north from Budapest was the most realistic option for the Western Allies, but that would have had to happen before or during the Hungarian deportations in the spring. As it was, the unrelated 15th Air Force bombing of Budapest on 2 July paradoxically did halt the transports due to Hungarian intervention. That action against railyards, oil centers, and airfields may well have unexpectedly saved tens of thousands of lives.

The Allies bombed Auschwitz, but they bombed the synthetic fuel refinery there, not the concentration camps. To strategic air power ideologues, that was an obvious and uncontroversial choice. Top priority was quite justifiably given to POL (Petroleum, Oil, and Lubricants) installations.

This issue well illustrates the chasm between 1944 thinking and today's attitudes. If officers back then had suggested this "humanitarian" action during target selection sessions, they would probably have been snickered at. The USSTAF and the RAF were not fighting a humanitarian war. They were trying to end the war as quickly as possible. Saving Jews was just not on the Air Force's radar. Besides, the irrational efforts the Germans were expending on genocide detracted from their war effort.

The War Department gave a policy expression of this approach on 11 February 1944. It stated that no military resources would be diverted to humanitarian objectives, because the goal was to win the war as soon as feasible.[1475] Most military analysts seem to believe that this brutal but expeditious approach reduced net human suffering in the end; but arguments necessarily persist over special cases.

Motives count: compare the publicity given this issue with the Warsaw case, which seems to attract almost no attention today (outside Poland). The Warsaw uprising cost many more lives than any "humanitarian" attacks at Auschwitz possibly could have saved.

President Roosevelt has been accused of anti-Semitism by some who think he didn't do "enough." He did make anti-Semitic remarks, but that was common; it didn't mean much, though he was clearly not as philo-Semitic as were his wife and children. So why did American Jews so fervently and generously support FDR? A combination of his interventionism, the suspicion that his policies were for sale, and the WASPishness of the Republicans seems to have done the trick. But the evidence is that FDR viewed the Jews with the same political pragmatism as he viewed Negroes. The results were odious at times, but it is not realistic to suggest that others would have done better.

Closing the Soviet Bases

When Ambassador Harriman made his passionate plea to use Poltava for assistance to the Polish uprising, Foreign Minister Molotov not only turned him down cold; he also noted that it was time for the Americans to get out of the Ukrainian bases. Harriman protested gallantly, but instructions from Washington emphasized the need to lay off on criticism in order not to endanger the bases. Harriman had changed his view of the Soviet regime, but Hopkins and the president had not.[1476]

From about the middle of August, relations between the U.S. and Soviet contingents at Poltava deteriorated until a kind of undeclared war was in progress. The dispatches from General Deane's Military Mission and from the Embassy took on a quite ominous and disillusioned tone as Soviet cooperation turned into methodical obstructionism.

The American mission found that the Soviet regime demanded everything from the United States but could rarely be cajoled into offering any assistance in return. As General Deane noted, he would question Comrade Molotov's demands for equipment he knew the Russians had to excess and couldn't put to any use. Molotov would coldly answer that if Deane didn't approve, he would obtain the approval directly from Washington. Deane mused, "The hell of it was, when I reflected on the attitude of the President, I was afraid he was right."[1477]

While in favor of the general program, Deane grew increasingly disturbed by the excesses of Lend-Lease. He resented Harry Hopkins's "fanatical" devotion to giving the USSR everything it could think of. He lamented the undercutting of negotiations in D.C.:

> Rather than admit that he could not support his requests with facts and figures, [Trade Commissar Anastas] Mikoyan took the stand that he need not support them at all. In many cases, Averell, Sid, and I would have been prepared to support the Soviet wishes had they been based on nothing more than a sob story, but even this was not forthcoming – only the haughty statement that "the Soviet Union requests 50,000 tons of alcohol; therefore she needs it."[1478]

General Arnold, who had admired Stalin at Teheran, developed a similar anti-Soviet rash when he observed how the USSR demanded to take over the Fairbanks base in Alaska, and "they wanted all the best houses; they wanted everything given to them." And then they upbraided him for the deficiencies of the planes and other help they were getting. Not one squawk would the Red Air Force tolerate.[1479]

The swiftness with which US-Soviet relations unraveled immediately after FDR's death should be seen in context with the frustration and impotent rage lower-ranking Americans accumulated in dealing with Moscow during the war – as well as with the thwarted intelligence work at home.

The change in mood hit the American troops at the three bases hard. In a highly revealing, little known report from October, a special committee analyzed the collapse in morale. It noted that chiefly due to far less operational activity than expected, morale dropped noticeably in July and August:

> Men no longer believed that they were participating in one of the most important and interesting undertakings of the war but began to feel remorse and self-pity at having given up more important and comfortable jobs (jobs which in retrospect had promised more promotions) to take part in a failure and to lead a boring existence.[1480]

As officers know, idle soldiers are bad news. The report also commented on troubles with the locals. It was by then clear that the regime was doing everything possible to prevent social contacts, including beating up local girls seen with Americans. To top it all, an absurdly overvalued ruble infuriated the soldiers; they had to pay 17 of their meager allotment of rubles ($3.20) for a beer. Inevitably this led to a rampant black market, which in turn infuriated the Communists back.

At the Ukrainian bases, the Soviets had limited the American personnel to 1270, but by August, a drawdown occurred, and the ceiling was set again at 300. This time, the Americans – who had begun with ambitious plans of over 10,000 troops in the Soviet Union – did not complain.[1481]

In October, the small photo-reconnaissance detachment at Poltava was withdrawn after its airborne elements had flown out. The ground personnel, relieved to avoid a Russian winter as well as their hosts' new chill, traveled by rail to Persia. One of their strangest observations did not get into the official account:

> The devastation along the route and even the stay in the destroyed city of Poltava did not prepare the men for one sight along the way. Early one morning, when they looked out the train window they saw several hundred naked bodies stacked like cordwood. No one knew who they were or why they were there.[1482]

At that time the USSR was engaged in a comprehensive campaign of "ethnic cleansing" in the Caucasus, but this was then unknown in the West.

In the fall of 1944, Piryatin and Mirgorod were returned to Soviet control. Only about 200 Americans were left at Poltava, which now served in a purely auxiliary role. They were subject to increasing abuse and bureaucratic harassment, even the occasional NKVD-orchestrated thefts and beatings, but reportedly they stood their ground defiantly whenever possible. The behavior of the Soviet Union against the small

American detachment at Poltava in many ways resembled the campaign it would later initiate against the Allied presence in Berlin.

On 22 June 1945, the anniversary of the German attacks both on the USSR and on Poltava, the final American servicemen left Poltava in two C-46s and a blind fury. Beforehand, in a characteristic move, the U.S. commander outfoxed his Soviet shadows, loaded up the contents of a warehouse stocked with special supplies that had been intended for clandestine OSS use in Europe, and dumped it all in the river.[1483]

There was no longer any talk of getting bases in Siberia.

General Deane called it a "strange alliance." It was not merely strange, it was impossible. It is now well known that Stalin would have much rather fought with Hitler than against him. The short-lived, one-sided, and ultimately failed alliance with the USSR opened many American eyes, but the experience and operational data Americans obtained there was also of great value during the early years of the Cold War.

Far from helping solidify the US-USSR alliance, Operation FRANTIC demonstrated that it had been built on quicksand. Stalin had only reluctantly and briefly allowed American forces on his soil. Whatever knowledge he had gained of their operations was probably balanced by the Americans discovering the technological backwardness of the USSR and its abject vulnerability to air attack.

Stalin may have viewed the whole project as a way in which the Americans deliberately demonstrated their immense technological advantage, their irrepressible entrepreneurial energy and resolve, and their ability to destroy the USSR from the air. It is interesting to note that the Americans unwittingly furthered that view. As an example, note that General Spaatz had the Anderson mission deliver a personal gift to the Generalissimo, for which Stalin offered due thanks:

> Dear General Spaatz,
>
> It gives me great pleasure to inform you that Mr. J.V. Stalin has received the book STRATEGIC AIR FORCES OF THE UNITED STATES IN EUROPE, operations from the 20th to the 26th of February, 1944, which you so kindly sent to him through General Anderson.
>
> Mr. J.V. Stalin asked me to thank you for the book and to wish you all success in your work.
>
> Yours sincerely, F Gousev[1484]

Maybe Stalin thought the Americans were trying to send him a message there. But the accumulation of indignities soon had the USAAF much less eager to please.

It is probably fair to say that to the American military, though not the White House, the Cold War began in the summer of 1944. The vast majority of American officers involved with the USSR – with the shining exception of Colonel Elliott Roosevelt – appears to have come out of the experience convinced that hard-nosed brinksmanship was the only productive way to deal with the Soviet Union, in peace or in war.

General Doolittle summed it up: "Operation FRANTIC was not a success as far as I'm concerned…My experience with the Soviets was limited, but this [Warsaw] and other incidents that came to my attention convinced me that we were going to have great difficulty dealing with them after the war."[1485]

The otherwise good-natured General Deane always argued for matching every Soviet restriction with immediate freezing of supplies to the USSR, such as the lend-lease aircraft going through Fairbanks; but he was left dangling by the White House. A consequence of this new Air Force attitude was that by 1946, American air power was already engaged in surveillance of the periphery of the Soviet Union.

Of course, in the doctrinaire Soviet view, there had only been a brief, tactical intermission in the history-ordained communist world revolution. As Deane wrote shortly after his return:

> If the record up until the end of the war was not sufficient to clarify Soviet intentions, certainly all doubt should have been dispelled on February 9, 1946, when Stalin reaffirmed the doctrine of Marx & Lenin and exhorted his people to extraordinary efforts in preparation for the inevitable wars which must be expected so long as the capitalist system exists.[1486]

The FRANTIC operation had been a failure measured against all its proclaimed aims. Perhaps this is why it has seemingly disappeared down history's black hole. That it encompassed a kind of second Pearl Harbor in Europe did not make it any more popular. But the real question – perhaps too terrifying for some to contemplate – was whether the alliance with the USSR was itself a catastrophic mistake. Even today, the potential results of any plausible alternatives cannot be easily apprehended. Still, 45 years of cold war was a high price to pay indeed.

A Clear Winner: Elliott Roosevelt

Of course, there was one high-ranking American officer who did not see it this way at all. But by this time, Colonel Elliott Roosevelt had extracted himself from the matter and was busy commanding the Allied reconnaissance effort from England.

When he returned from his Soviet tour, Elliott found high demand for his stories. Eisenhower and his staff had him over and pumped him thoroughly. "Stalin is a stickler for keeping his word," Ike was told, with particular reference to the promise of a second front. Elliott said his pedigree bought him no particular favor in the USSR. At that time he already estimated Soviet losses at 16 million dead, four times that of the Axis. He said virtually all the Soviet air effort was low-altitude close air support (which is why the Russians loved the P-39); and that the Russians primarily wanted "technology" from the Americans.[1487]

Records do not show Elliott visiting the Soviet Union after May, but since he said he made another wartime visit, he may have flown one mission there.

He did gain an important operational bonus from FRANTIC; 117 photoreconnaissance sorties were flown to and from the Ukraine between 2 June and 19 September 1944. Thirty-three of these came from Italy, and six from England. Forty-nine sorties were local to the Soviet bases. The Eastern Command operated a photographic center at Poltava, and the Soviets required access to all data obtained. Captain Frank Carney, who flew many of the long-distance flights, was commander of the photoreconnaissance detachment there.[1488]

The Americans photographed a total of 172 enemy targets during FRANTIC operations, 46 of them more than once. At least 40 were considered by Eastern Command's Intelligence Section to be targets only made possible by the bases in the Ukraine. The secret history allows us a peek into the utility of this imagery to both Eastern and Western Allies:

> These targets might later have, and some actually did, come within range of the UK or Italian bases because of the rapid developments in drop tanks and engine settings, which were extending the range of the F-5 at the very time the Russian bases were being established. However, these 40 targets were more genuinely and uniquely related to the Russian than the British or Italian bases of the AAF. Moreover, 49 of the 172 targets were on or behind the Rumanian or Southern section of the Eastern Front, which was becoming the most active zone of Russian operations during the latter period of Eastern Command operations. Photographs taken by Eastern Command, including the strike photos and the bomb damage assessment photos by the F-5's following each raid, were immediately turned over to the Russians…The reconnaissance of these targets and the interpretation of all these photographs at the Russian bases was thus part of a single process, intimately and essentially linked with the execution of Eastern Command's bomber and fighter operations.[1489]

The Americans thus shared not only photos, but also annotations and first phase interpretation. In effect, the Americans now were to the Soviets what the British had been to them. In return, Eastern Command obtained "additional minor benefits" including some photographs of Soviet airfields in areas that were otherwise prohibited from Allied overflight. Unfortunately, by July it appeared that "the willing American submission of general intelligence data was not being reciprocated fully." Also galling, the Soviets absolutely refused to allow Americans to observe, much less accompany, Soviet bombing missions.[1490]

Still, the Americans obtained much material covering central Europe and the Byelorussia – Ukraine region. After the German capitulation, this imagery supplemented captured German imagery.[1491] However, the Soviets had been extra careful to deny the Americans access to as much of the USSR's landmass as possible:

> …they were adamant in refusing clearances to places where they felt the Americans had no business. Thus, while they cleared freely to established dispersal bases and emergency landing fields, they refused positively to permit American planes to visit airdromes for general reconnaissance purposes with regard to future planning not yet sanctioned by Moscow. Thus they refused Colonel Cullen's request for clearances to view airdromes at Zhitomir, Berdichev, and Odessa.[1492]

Until the Corona satellite program in the early 1960s, the United States therefore lacked elementary mapping data, essential for effective targeting, for most of the USSR.

Determined not to be caught unprepared again, the Air Force expended considerable resources in the aerial mapping of Europe, the Arctic, and much of the rest of the world during 1945-48. These operations had different code names: for example, Casey Jones in Europe, Nanook in the Arctic. By 1946, U.S. patrol aircraft were already being shot down by the Soviet Union. In five short years the Americans had learned the importance of reconnaissance, and now they would learn the importance of its denial.

MASTER OF RECONNAISSANCE

Dearest Mummy... I have been to Paris a couple of times, once the day after the liberation. It was the most moving thing I have ever experienced. All Americans were mobbed – we were treated like Gods, and there was nothing we couldn't do or have. It is now calming down and the people are getting down to systematically taking our American dollars as fast as they can. The war over here should end, according to my guess, about the end of November. The reconnaissance job in this theatre is just about finished – the Jerry has revealed all of his secrets to us by now, and even if I do say so, the job my boys have done has been the outstanding one ever done by a reconnaissance organization.[1493]

During the rest of 1944, the 325th PRW earned its keep providing reconnaissance support for the continued operations in France and the troubled Market-Garden airborne assault in Holland. Yet at the same time, the end was increasingly in sight. The western Allies reached the German border, but were repulsed by unexpectedly tough resistance, leading as usual to a mess of competitive finger-pointing. In Italy, the slow, bloody crawl up the boot continued.

The Allied air forces were increasingly running short of legitimate targets and, although enjoying air superiority, began fretting about jets and other German wonder weapons. The weather deteriorated and kept airplanes grounded for long stretches, even though radar bombing through clouds was increasingly employed.

Colonel Roosevelt participated in these operations and in some unique missions until 13 November 1944, when he returned stateside. Later accounts intimated that he had been deliberately held back in Europe until the American elections were over, just in case he should trigger another load of unseemly headlines. He arrived in the ZI on the 14th and immediately fell into the arms, and expense accounts, of the waiting Johnny Meyer of Hughes Aircraft. Elliott would not return to Europe until 29 December, and then with a fresh baggage of controversy.[1494]

The wing's operational summary for September tells us that people were getting restless, and that technology was increasingly dominating operations:

> The principal "world shaking" operation ... was the Allied Airborne Landings in Holland. The Cover Section of the Photo Intelligence Department dug out existing photos and mosaics for pre-drop planning, and prints were run off by the lab and distributed to all concerned. The 7th PRG flew many sorties to obtain last minute cover and to watch the bridges; and the 25th Bomb Group (Rcn) at Watton had the tremendous task of keeping tab on the weather over the drop areas in addition to their regular weather reconnaissance. Many Mosquito light weather sorties were flown over the drop area prior to the landings, and several flights just preceding the landings. One of the problems of these flights was to determine the low level of clouds over drop area and to do such the Mosquitos were committed to low flying under the clouds over enemy territory. The weather was not particularly good during the period and losses at both groups (F-5 photo recon and Mossy weather recon) ran very high. Several were dispatched to the Arnhem area and were never heard from. Jet aircraft were reported operating in that area. The losses were such that Brig. Gen. O.A. Anderson of the 8th AF has required a detailed report of all enemy interceptions since that time. It is desired to bring out again that these weather flights and photo flights were unarmed and unescorted.
>
> In the matter of general staff problems one of the major ones was the task of keeping men busy as the weather and perhaps reduced operational commitments would allow the enlisted men more idle time. The problem was given much consideration and the general

> opinion expressed and the official attitude adopted was that to make the soldier do "squads left and right" during his spare time would back fire with serious repercussions.
>
> It was determined that an intelligent military training program linked with educational opportunities and organized athletics and Special Service planning of trips, etc. would best serve the purpose. It was likewise emphasized that each section would use manpower to clean house, check property and equipment and accountable documents, and keep all sections in the best of order…
>
> Extensive files were set up to keep tab on all information concerning Jet Propulsion Aircraft. Information was received during the period that certain Strategic and Tactical target material in France was now obsolete and could be destroyed. A master copy was maintained in the wing.
>
> In the operations section of the wing, two new scheduled weather flights were established. The first of these heavy weather flights is known as "Sharon" and was pioneered a month ago to the Azores. This flight was scheduled daily to Logens [Lages] in the Azores, and consisted of 25 positions to report the weather. The crews remained in the Azores for rest before returning to England. The aircraft was serviced by personnel of the unit who had been flown to Logens for permanent base. The other heavy weather flight established was known as "Allah." This flight was over the sea to the west and slightly north of Lands End. These three over water flights gave relatively complete coverage for accurate forecasting…
>
> A new aircraft was delivered to the wing and modified for use in "Mickey" [radar] flights. This aircraft was a P-38 modified into a two place plane to carry a navigator and a "Mickey." The Mosquitos previously used on Mickey missions had been grounded pending investigation by 8th AF Engineering Officers and technicians from Wright Field. Several "Mickey" Mossys have been dispatched and never heard from, and one was observed to explode on take off. It was believed that perhaps the gas fumes had been ignited by arcing of the "Mickey." At this point new Mosquitos have been ordered and their use was planned in the near future. It was also known that German night fighters had been vectored to our "Mickey" aircraft.
>
> Continued experiments and improvements were conducted in Mossy and B-26 night photography, especially as pertains to high altitude night photography.
>
> The code name of "Skywave" was given to experimental work done by Mossys with "Loran" navigator. Tests were run to determine range and accuracy of this type of navigation to determine the suitability for pin pointing the aircraft for night photography. Several special super "hush-hush" operations were undertaken by Station 376 [Watton] in conjunction with the Navy.[1495]

The reference to "jet propulsion" is particularly illuminating. German technical superiority continued to scare the Americans, and as soon as they captured German territory, they determinedly absconded with technology and scientists alike, especially in the field of aeronautics. That the 325th was keen to pass on any knowledge of jets is illustrated by the fact that two pilots claimed to have been attacked by a Heinkel He-280. This is an unlikely sighting, but it is impressive that the pilots even knew about this cancelled German project.[i]

As one might expect from his past practice, General Roosevelt agitated hard for obtaining American jets. He knew of the Lockheed P-80, which had been flying in the States with British engines for a while. George Goddard said Elliott was a strong voice

---

[i] Kean: Eyes of the Eighth, 261. Ms. Babington Smith identied He-280s in test and word was passed to pilots before it was clear that the Me-262 was chosen instead (Babington Smith, 248).

for getting the F-14, the photo-recon variant, into the field as soon as possible. General Spaatz agreed with him and soon the F-14s and the P-80s were produced together.[1496]

Unfortunately, the American jets were not ready for action. Two YP-80s were sent to England. One of them exploded over RAF Burtonwood, the American air depot, during a demonstration on 28 January 1945. That ended the chances of American jets seeing combat. That YP-80 (44-83026) took the life of Major Frederic Borsodi. [1497]

The experiments with the electronics on board the Mosquitoes and the Lightnings were far more productive, but obviously no safer.

Thus, during this last phase of the war, Anglo-American air power gradually merged onto the electronic battlefield we would come to know so well in the Cold War. All the basic techniques, procedures, even the arcane jargon of ECM and ECCM (Electronic Counter-counter Measures) were fast emerging. Technology was taking over the war.

As for the "super hush-hush" activity with the Navy at Station 376, RAF Watton, the next chapter lifts the veil.

OPERATION ANVIL / APHRODITE

Anyone who has ever worked in a bureaucracy recognizes, explicitly or subconsciously, the phases of a typical project: 1) high hopes; 2) disillusionment and failure; 3) panic and hysteria; 4) hunt for scapegoats; 5) punishment of the innocent; and 6) reward and promotion of the guilty.[i]

Contrary to rumor, not all projects follow this path, but operation APHRODITE provides a classical illustration of the general principle. It can also tell us a lot about intelligence failures, the hysteria which the fear of weapons of mass destruction can engender, and the results of acting on such fears instead of on knowledge.

Colonel Roosevelt was in high demand during the summer of 1944. Hardly returned from Moscow, his squadrons were called on to fly the decisive reconnaissance missions to support operation OVERLORD, the invasion of Normandy. It required tremendous effort of both the heroic and the prosaic kind: sustained weather reconnaissance over the Atlantic was a critical factor in kicking off the operation on 5 June 1944.

But at the same time as OVERLORD was unfolding, and succeeding with agonizing slowness, a new threat turned up that would stretch Colonel Roosevelt's skills and abilities, and – according to him – nearly kill him. His aircraft were increasingly returning with pictures of strange installations in Europe, some of them geometrically pointing at London. Thinking this a bad sign, the photo-interpreters at the ACIU at RAF Medmenham worked themselves into a frenzy of speculation.

This would become a crucial test for aerial reconnaissance, and set the stage for its use ever after. David Irving noted that the secret-weapon search would consume 280,000 photo interpreter hours; produce 1,500,000 printed photographs; and launch

---

[i] In some versions, also "promotion of non-participants," thus justifying the common survival strategy of never becoming associated with a project, except in "fixing" it.

4,000 sorties.[1498] Of course, unlike the case in the Persian Gulf sixty years later, there actually was something to look for. But, also unlike the Gulf, the Allied air forces were estimated to have lost 450 aircraft and 2,900 airmen hunting German V-weapons.[1499]

Wing Commander Steventon, who had been with Elliott on the XF-11 survey, had gained some of his initial kudos as early as 15 May 1942 when he returned from the German Baltic Coast with images of the experimental rocket range at Peenemünde.[1500] After reaching the conclusion that ballistic missiles were being tested there, RAF Bomber Command flew one of its most intense raids of the war against the site in August 1943. Unfortunately, the A4 (popularly called V-2) missile program was set back very modestly, while a great number of civilians as well as RAF aircrew died.

The A4, by modern nomenclature a theater ballistic missile (TBM), could not be intercepted in flight. Despite intense efforts, it also proved almost impossible to hunt down on the ground, as the Germans had combined the transporter, erector, and launcher vehicles into a single truck (*Meillerwagen*) – a clever trick that would be emulated by others for the decades to come.

The RAF instead beamed missile defense radar on the area, trying to pinpoint launch locations well enough to immediately dispatch Mosquitoes against them. It didn't work. The Allied air forces faced exactly the same problem fifty years later in Iraq, and they still couldn't catch the Soviet SS-1 Scuds, much improved A4s.

Still, such weapons provide little military advantage unless coupled with nuclear warheads, so in effect Germany wasted immense resources on the A4 program, and on many other V-weapons. In doing so, however, she forced the Allies to do the same.

Reconnaissance was far more successful when it came to neutering the cruise missile threat, which began with the Fieseler Fi-103 flying bomb, popularly known as the V-1. There were two reasons for the vulnerability of this little cross-shaped devil. It was launched from a fixed, sloping track. These tell-tale "ski" slopes were a photointerpreter's dream: almost impossible to hide, always pointed toward the target. These sites became bomb magnets. Only slowly did the enemy switch to air-launch, the obvious remedy.

The other V-1 vulnerability was speed. The Germans, for various reasons, used a primitive pulse-jet engine to power the apparatus. This ensured that the jet's top speed was only comparable to that of high-speed propeller-driven aircraft. Since the cruise missiles showed up nicely on radar, the attacks during the summer of 1944 turned into a superb test of the now formidable Allied air defense system. Thousands of V-1s were intercepted and shot down by fast Spitfires and Mosquitoes.

However, here the Germans did have a genuine strategic point: the relatively low-cost terror effort absorbed enormous Allied air resources that would otherwise have been allocated to the offense – as much as half of all air reconnaissance by some estimates, a number oddly similar to the Scud-suppression effort during the first Gulf War. The Nazis had discovered the vexing issue of marginal cost in missile defense: if it is far cheaper to build each next terror weapon than to defend against it, you are coming out ahead.

V-targets were assigned NOBALL numbers; the offensive against them was given the CROSSBOW code name.[1501] General Arnold said later that only 9% of 8th Air Force bombing was expended on NOBALL sites.[1502] That is misleading.

David Irving noted that in the crucial week prior to 27 June, fully 40% of the *entire* Allied bomber effort was devoted to CROSSBOW.[1503] A similar toll was inflicted on intelligence and reconnaissance. Clearly, the Germans had managed to create a huge diversion with the V-1.

That was not the end of it. In September 1943, reconnaissance found an inexplicably large concrete site at Mimoyecques in the Pas de Calais area, apparently built on an azimuth aimed at London. The installation was important enough to require significant infrastructure, including railway spurs and barracks for workers.[1504]

Numerous traditional bombing raids were flown against this mystery site from November 1943 to July 1944. Despite the short hop, this campaign became one of the countless examples of how easy it was to hit a lot of stuff you didn't need to hit, while it was almost impossible to hit the target. Site construction continued up to 6 July 1944.

On that day, the famed RAF No. 617 squadron hit the site with special munitions: 12,000 lb. Tallboy "blockbusters." These devices were the first iteration of the gigantic bunker busters which are still being perfected even today, because the logical choice – tactical nuclear munitions – are not politically acceptable.[1505]

Some of the Tallboys apparently managed to go through openings in the concrete and down into the warren of activity below. Most of the facility was beyond repair. But the Allies didn't know that. The bomb damage assessment flown afterwards had no way of determining the operational state, especially since nobody even knew what the site was for – a clear example of the natural limitations of overhead surveillance.

After the invasion itself, CROSSBOW had the most urgent attention among the top brass. Although the V-1 was a major nuisance, the gnawing fear persisted that maybe the Germans did indeed have a wonder weapon, perhaps even the atomic device nobody was allowed to talk about. The photo interpreters felt mounting pressure.[1506]

Colonel Roosevelt's 325th PRW was deeply involved in the hunt for NOBALL sites. These flights were referred to as *Dilly* missions. But now Elliott himself would become witness to history – or, perhaps, to the unmaking of future history.

He was detailed to participate in operation APHRODITE, and its Navy counterpart, ANVIL (not to be confused with the other ANVIL, the invasion of southern France). These special drone operations were intended to eliminate hardened targets like the Mimoyecques mystery site, V-1 launchers, and submarine pens.[i]

Allied work on remote-controlled aircraft had a long history, but the aggravatingly unpredictable V-1 attacks on London truly and rudely got the top commanders' attention. Thus, on 26 June 1944, General Doolittle directed the 8th Air Force, 3rd Bombardment Division, to execute APHRODITE.[1507]

He was acting on Arnold's orders, and it was Arnold who seems to have been most dedicated to the ill-starred project. On 1 July he wrote in a memo to subordinates: "This suggests an effective method of disposing of our great and growing number of war weary aircraft of all types in all theatres." Long after the failure of the program was obvious, Arnold would insist on its continuance, even as a pure terror weapon.[1508]

Several large bombers, many B-17s and some B-24s, were converted to flying bombs and packed with ten tons of Torpex, a new super-explosive 1.7 times as

[i] Operations APHRODITE and ANVIL are covered in Hank Searls: The Forgotten Prince, 1969; and Jack Olsen: Aphrodite, Desperate Mission, 1970. Both are well researched and detailed. David Irving's The Mare's Nest is a superb account of the V-weapons and the attacks upon them. Air Force records at AFHRA provide operational, though not personal, information. In particular, "Final Report Aphrodite Project" dated 1 JAN 45 is used herein, as is the folder on the 12 August mission. Wing and squadron histories for the period provide crucial supporting information.

energetic as TNT.[i] The two-man crew was supposed to parachute out before reaching the target, and the final guidance would be flown by remote control from accompanying aircraft, whose crews received television signals from the drone.

This was a complex, expensive, and difficult mission. It would require a large strike package comprised of fighters for escort, guidance aircraft ("motherships"), air-sea rescue aircraft, pre- and post-strike reconnaissance, and even a Mosquito shadowing the drone in order to photograph the progress of the mission.

Colonel Elliott Roosevelt was supposed to be in the trailing Mosquito.

12 August 1944

APHRODITE has received very considerable attention, probably because one mission killed a Kennedy. It was supposedly top secret for decades, but that is completely untrue.[1509] Unfortunately, considerable disinformation, imperfect copying, and sloppy narratives have characterized much of the popular accounts. Archival research suggests that Elliott also contributed to the confusion.

The whole robot-bombing scheme smacks of the desperation measures taken by the opponent during the last year of the conflict. It was about as close to kamikaze as the Allies ever came. As for the Germans, their *Mistel* (mistletoe) explosives-laden bombers seemed far more sensible. *Mistels* were flown by a "parasite" single-engine fighter mounted on top of the bomber. The fighter would jettison the drone at the target and fly off. This did actually work on some occasions.

APHRODITE most emphatically didn't work. Several missions were flown in the second half of 1944, none of them successful, and many of them catastrophic. The six missions in August used the original, makeshift double-Azon (azimuth only) guidance system. After several failures, this equipment was abandoned and replaced by the television-guided Castor system. These operations began in September.

The most famous disaster of them all befell the Navy's me-too attempt at joining the action. The admirals believed that the APHRODITE-ANVIL program would be of potential later use in the Pacific. At any rate, a Special Air Unit 1 (SAU-1) was set up at RAF Fersfield south of Norwich, whence the Army's converted B-17 drone missions originated. A call for volunteers went out. For the first naval mission an ambitious anti-submarine aviator named Joseph P. Kennedy, Jr., and an electronics expert and aviator named Wilford J. Willy, both lieutenants, were selected.[ii]

Elliott's 325th PRW played a crucial supporting role. On 4 August, the 654th Squadron, 25th Bomb Group, was already intensely involved with the APHRODITE raids. Two Mosquitoes with movie cameras flew alongside, and both encountered flak, with one returning damaged. Two days later, another two Mosquitoes operating in support of the 3rd Bomb Division's special project came back unscathed. All along, the squadron flew *Dilly* missions against the NOBALL target sites, snapping the final pictures before a raid.[1510]

On 11 August, Colonel Roosevelt, riding co-pilot with trusted associate Major Johnny Hoover, launched in a Mosquito XVI on a *Dilly* mission over the French coast. Returning without incident, all was set for the Navy's first robot-bombing attempt on

---

[i] Various explosives and loading schemes were used. Some aircraft only carried glide bombs.

[ii] The U.S. Navy refers to aeronauts as "aviators," not pilots – otherwise they'd be guiding ships into port.

the next day. The weather was promising, and numerous missions were launched by the 325th Wing on the next day.

At six pm on 12 August, the highly eclectic strike package was assembled and directed towards the East Anglia coast at Southwold, prior to taking aim south towards Cap Griz Nez. The drones were two Navy Liberators, coming from VB-110, an anti-submarine squadron based in Cornwall. They were stuffed with 21,500 lbs of Torpex.

For the mission on the 12th, serial 32271 was selected. It was actually a B-24J, built for the Air Force as 42-110007 the year before. The Navy called it a PB4Y-1, but the drone conversion technically made it into a BQ-8. (The B-17s became BQ-7s). The point is, however, that there was little "war-weary" about these almost new aircraft. By now the Americans simply had more planes than they knew what to do with.[1511]

The mother ships were two Lockheed PV-1 Venturas, upgraded Hudsons; the Air Force called them B-34s. Two Mosquitoes from Elliott's 25th Bomb Group were tasked in support. The first Mosquito cleared the weather over the target 45 minutes in advance of the strike force take-off; the second followed the "Baby" (drone), with a cameraman in the nose cupola, shooting film of the show. For the 8th AAF Combat Camera Unit, this show was already getting to be a familiar, though definitely not a routine task.

According to his own account, Colonel Roosevelt was also in a Mosquito. He planned on filming the crew's egress from their doomed drone. He had one of his film crews remain on the ground to film the take-off.[1512] Elliott was the logical choice for this, since his pilots had obtained the photographs of the targets for the operations. Hank Searls, who interviewed Roosevelt on 8 October 1968, explained:

> Colonel Roosevelt's photos were passed around. Now the launch site could be seen: a huge concrete bunker sunk in a grassy hill with the turf replanted above it and steel doors opening thirty feet high opening on short railroad tracks aligned viciously on the precise heading of London…Commander [James] Smith, who had taken one of Elliott Roosevelt's prints and squeezed into Colonel Forrest's Lightning for a quick view of the target, returned at 1700, unscathed and jubilant: the target was there, all right, the weather was good, the flak not excessive. Anvil was ready to drop.[1513]

An interesting technical aside was that Base Commander Roy Forrest's Lightning was modified with the droopsnoot conversion allowing the carriage of an observer in the nose. But in the robot aircraft, Kennedy and Willy were alone. They were needed to fly the bomber as well as to arm the explosives.

The strike package was given the collective callsign "Zootsuit." The "Baby" was Zootsuit Black; the PV-1 "Mothers," 143 and 131, were Red and Pink. The navigation B-17 was Zootsuit Able; a radio relay B-17 orbiting over the Channel was Baker; and the weather Mosquito was Charlie. RAF Fersfield was referred to as Mable. A fighter escort of 4 P-51s was given the call sign Balance Six. A dizzying list of further contrived phrases was used to report the progress, or failure, of the mission.[1514]

Given the number of dissimilar aircraft tasked, this was an immensely complex and expensive operation. Let the operations officer summarize:

1. Two PVY_M Mothers took off on time 1755, 1756, circled the field at 2,000 feet. The Navigation ship took off next at 1757, followed by the Robot at 1807. The Mother ships fell in behind the Robot as it left the field on course, for the first control point. The Mother ships were at 2,200 feet with the Robot slightly ahead at 2,000 feet. Before

reaching the first control point the Mother ship had control of the Robot. The turn at the control point was made by the Mother aircraft. Approximately two minutes after completion of this turn at 1820, the Robot plane disintegrated. Both men were still in the ship.

2. In addition to the above, the following aircraft also participated: -- One Mosquito (516) used to send back weather from the target area. -- One Mosquito (569) Photo Ship covering the Robot. -- One B-17 (696) Relay Ship in mid-Channel during the whole operations. -- One P-38 (207) [F-5B 42-68207] to be used for high-altitude photo work over the target. -- Five P-51s providing close fighter cover.
3. The Mosquito photo ship (569) was approximately 300 feet[i] and slightly to the right when the Robot exploded. The Mosquito photographer was hit by flying pieces of the Robot plane causing minor injuries. The plane itself suffered considerable battle damage.
4. Upon receiving confirmation of this report all planes were recalled.[1515]

Note that there were two Mosquitoes in the package, but one was radioing weather reports from the target area.

There seem to have been several P-38s in the air. One was Roy Forrest's Droopsnoot with the Navy's mission commander in the nose. General Doolittle himself was reported to be flying along somewhere in his P-47. Evidently this mission attracted a lot of rubberneckers.[ii]

The aircraft began departing Fersfield minutes before 1800, aiming for a zero-hour of 1900 over Mimoyecques, yielding the best sun angle. As the formation assembled in the air, the two motherships fell in at 2,200 feet, slightly above and about a mile behind the drone. The "Mothers" took control of the "Baby," and after the first checkpoint, a left bank was commanded and the turn successfully completed.

As the formation approached the second checkpoint, the two lieutenants removed the safety pin on the explosive device, thereby arming it, and radioed the *Spade Flush* code for the completed arming. They now prepared to be mere passengers until the scheduled bail-out over RAF Manston near Dover.

A short time later, at 1820, two minutes after completing the first remote-controlled turn, the Liberator exploded. Two distinct explosions a fraction of a second apart were both heard and felt by the accompanying force. The gigantic, circular fireball was seen to consume the trailing PRU Mosquito.

The cause of the explosion has been a matter of endless speculation. Two theories, not mutually exclusive, seem to predominate: one, that a stray signal inadvertently triggered the detonation; two, that the wiring panel was defective and itself caused the signal or allowed a stray to do its work. A British reporter, Andrew Wilson of the *London Observer*, wrote that "almost certainly" a continuous signal used to jam V-2 launches was responsible. That makes no particular sense, since the required communications management and frequency sweep were duly carried out in advance, and V-2s were not jammable anyway.[1516]

Searls surmised that the 100th Airborne Radio Radar Search Group, which flew P-38s, may have jammed the frequency since it turned out that their pilots knew nothing of ANVIL. Yet Elliott Roosevelt told Searls that the 100th had been notified, and thus someone somewhere must have dropped the ball.[1517] Likewise, Jack Olsen held that

---

[i] Should be 300 yards according to several other reports.

[ii] Olsen, 237. Doolittle observed several Aphrodite missions. Keen, 158, has Gens. Doolittle and Partridge observing this mission – but not Roosevelt.

there was no jamming: "All that turned up was a station in Yorkshire that had heard the strange emissions and had considered jamming them, but had not yet got around to it."[1518]

The alternative conjecture is supported by some of the technicians who worked on the drone. Olsen's account supports the theory that the fuse panel had been so ineptly designed that once the manual pin was removed, it was only a question of time before the panel overheated and emitted a stray signal.[1519] In either case, however, the system design was to blame; it was unsafe and insufficiently tested, and it is abundantly clear that higher-ranking officers could be in deep trouble if they did not succeed in tamping down speculation right away.

A board was convened and already two days later submitted a detailed report to the Navy.[1520] There was a fairly overwhelming consensus that a combination of a faulty arming panel and a stray signal were responsible, and appropriate technical and procedural precautions were recommended. That failure mode did not recur, so the fixes must have worked.

Since the explosion happened at only 2000 feet, there was widespread damage on the ground, though no casualties. The physical damages were mostly shattered glass, collapsed roofs, and minor fires. One report states that the debris field was three miles long and two miles wide. Three square miles of heath caught fire. At least 147 properties, some up to 16 miles away, suffered damage, and hundreds of trees were felled directly below the explosion. Technically, the Navy had just demonstrated to the Air Forces what a 0.01 kiloton airburst looks, sounds, and feels like.[i]

Although the explosion was regarded as one of the greatest ever recorded, another such flying bomb had already impacted elsewhere in England – and the drones that did make it to Europe caused similar detonations, many of them in populated areas. The top brass was not worried about those; but great apprehension arose when a BQ-7 drone landed in Germany without exploding, thus compromising the secrecy of the project.[1521]

In *Desperate Mission*, a somewhat novelized but very well-researched account of APHRODITE, Jack Olsen offers the following exciting narrative:

> "1822. Dead on course. Dead on schedule." [Lt.Col. John] Anderson grasped the metal rod on the control box and eased the robot into a shallow left turn. Suddenly the television picture in front of him flickered and died, and in the same instant, he heard a loud gasp over the intercom. Before he could ask what was going on, he heard two powerful explosions and felt two thumps, as though a giant had pounded on the fuselage of the plane, and then he realized that the PV was falling away, out of control.
>
> Harry Wherry's mother ship was about 400 yards behind the drone and several hundred feet above it, and since Anderson was still controlling from the other plane, several members of Wherry's crew were watching through the pilot's windshield. They saw the drone begin a slow turn to the left, but just as the left wing dipped a few degrees below the horizontal, there was a blinding flash of light, and the bright afternoon sky became incandescent. Where the drone had been there was now a yellow nucleus edged in smoke, with fire and flame going straight up and down from it, like a pair of giant Roman candles. In a split second the nucleus had turned into a greenish-white cylinder of fire, slightly compressed in the middle like an hourglass and flattened out on top.

---

[i] These numbers are more than double the Air Force's, and are quoted from the local Norfolk and Suffolk Aviation Museum, www.aviationmuseum.net/Joe_Kennedy.htm, retr. 26 AUG 11

"My God," Wherry said, and his co-pilot Harry Fitzpatrick, said "Holy Christ!" In that same instant the mother ship was hit by two massive jolts, and Wherry fought to regain control. The column burned brightly, almost as vividly as a welder's torch seen at close range, and just as suddenly, it was gone, leaving black smoke streaming away in the wind and a few small fires in the woods below. The men in Wherry's airplane blinked to restore their spotty eyesight.

"Look at Rosy!" Fitzpatrick shouted after a few seconds, and everyone could see the other mother ship slipping toward the ground at a high rate of speed." "Pull out!" Wherry screamed. "Pull out!" The other PV was almost to the ground when the top wing snapped back to straight and level and the plane flew off over the smoking treetops. "They're OK," Wherry said. "Rosy's got it."

"I'm not sure the Mosquito's gonna make it," Fitzpatrick said. A Mosquito camera ship had flown through the center of fire and gone out the other side trailing smoke, and now it was circling and losing altitude.[1522]

Was Elliott Roosevelt in that ship?

Where was Elliott?

Published accounts, long accepted, have Colonel Roosevelt flying a Mosquito 300 feet behind the BQ-8 drone, flying through the fireball, nearly losing control, and finally landing unscathed. Hank Searls, who interviewed Elliott, wrote that 'Colonel Roosevelt's Mosquito was slammed almost to its back; he remembers barely missing wreckage.'[1523]

It is odd then, that the official accounts of the disaster do not mention Elliott being in that Mosquito, even though they certainly note that its assigned crew barely escaped with their lives. Likewise, two detailed accounts, by Olsen and by Bowman, do not mention Elliott's presence at all.

Once again, there is no recourse but the archives. Fortunately, the 8th AAF Combat Camera Unit typed up a thrilling account:

> Aphrodite again held the spotlight on August 12th. Lt. McCarthy flew as cameraman with Lt. Bob Tunnell of 654th Bomb Squadron as pilot. Although the flight was not considered a complete mission, it was packed with action. 'We were flying over England and decided to close in on the "Baby." I was flying in the nose of the plane so that I could get some good shots of the "Baby" in flight ahead of us. The "Baby" just exploded in mid-air as we neared it and I was knocked halfway back to the cockpit. A few pieces of the "Baby" came through the plexiglass nose and I got hit in the head and caught a lot of fragments in my right arm. I crawled back to the cockpit and lowered the wheels so that Bob could make a quick emergency landing,' Lt. McCarthy reported from his hospital bed.
>
> 'I didn't get a scratch,' Lt. Tunnell added, 'but I was damn near scared to death. As Mac told you we were coming in to take close-ups of the "Baby" which was under control and flying level. We came in on the right side high and then the damned thing exploded in mid-air. The Mosquito went up a few hundred feet and I didn't get any response from the controls. I was getting ready to reach for my parachute but decided to check the controls again. This time they responded and I decided to try to make a landing. One engine was cut and the other was smoking. We were near a field so I headed straight for it. We made a good landing and then the second motor cut out. I had just enough speed to get the "Mousy" off the runway but I couldn't taxi in to a hard stand. I'm sure glad that the

pictures of our previous mission were good because I don't think that we are going to get that close to the "Baby" again,' he ended.[1524]

That fits with Martin Bowman's account that Mosquito PR XVI NS569, crewed by Lt. Robert A. Tunnel and Lt. David J. McCarthy, following behind the drone, gained a few hundred feet after flying through the explosion: "McCarthy was injured but Tunnel was unhurt, and he managed to lower the wheels and land the Mosquito at Halesworth, which was the nearest available field."[1525] Halesworth was five miles from the epicenter.

Lt. Tunnel flew numerous dangerous missions with cameramen aboard. His luck ran out when his Mosquito (NS593) disappeared over Europe on 18 September.

Lt. McCarthy, the cameraman on the Kennedy mission, was luckier, despite his initial misfortune. Having been wounded on the 12th, a different crew was sent on an APHRODITE mission on the 13th. That camera-carrying Mosquito was too close to the robot (a glide bomb that missed the target), and the crew was killed.

After the death of Kennedy and Willy, the immediate official cipher-telegram to headquarters stated:

> A PRU MOSQUITO WAS FLYING 300 FEET ABOVE AND ABOUT 300 YDS TO THE REAR OF THE ROBOT. ENGINEER PHOTOGRAPHER ON THIS SHIP WAS INJURED AND THE SHIP WAS DAMAGED SLIGHTLY BY THE EXPLOSION. A B-17 NAVIGATION SHIP WAS FLYING 3 TO 5 HUNDRED YARDS IN THE REAR OF THE ROBOT AND TO THE RIGHT. ITS LEFT WING WAS LIFTED BY THE EXPLOSION BUT THE SHIP WAS NOT DAMAGED. NONE OF THE B-17 CREW WAS INJURED.[1526]

It is certain that a PRU Mosquito flew through the fireball and only by supreme luck and skill managed to get its perforated self safely landed. The Mosquito XVI carries two crew side-by-side; one of whom can slide down in the glazed nose for observation purposes. These two were Tunnell, who was killed next month, and combat cameraman McCarthy. Nobody mentions Elliott on board. Was he a stowaway? Was there some kind of official conspiracy to not mention the son of the president? Or was he flying yet another Mosquito and, as one might expect, also caught a part of the shock wave?

Elliott's story can be traced to his interview with Hank Searls in 1968. Jack Olsen's well-researched account makes no mention of him at all. When the tragic episode gained an unexpected new exposure in 1986, Elliott's memory was not as definite as Searls had recorded. He now said he was "flying in a reconnaissance aircraft not far from Kennedy's aircraft when he saw it blow up."

Unfortunately, he also added that "evidently when they went to go back and leave the plane by the bomb bay they must have tripped a wire and the plane exploded." This tells us that Elliott either wasn't briefed on the details of the operation, or had forgotten them.[i]

Since he directed the photographic support for many APHRODITE missions, he could have confused the flights, and he might have inadvertently given the impression that he was aboard the damaged Mosquito, which was after all, "one of his." Still, since Elliott was well acquainted with Joe Kennedy and his remarkable children, it seems very odd that he had trouble remembering where he was at the time of Junior's demise.

---

[i] ER interview in Boston Herald, 10 NOV 86. The crew would not exit thru bomb bay and did not trip any wires; besides they were supposed to remain aboard as far as Dover.

Considering the discrepancy between the official record and Elliott's two differing explanations, the best we can do may be to suggest he was in one of the untasked aircraft in the vicinity. But in that case his exposure was minimal and left unmentioned by official sources. And a trained eyewitness on the ground saw only one Mosquito.[1527]

The official report summarized the Navy's first ANVIL attempt:

> Commander J.S. Smith, ten other U.S. Navy officers and 16 Navy specialists were attached to AAF Station 136 for the purpose of conducting tactical tests of the Navy FM control equipment. On 17 July 1944, one robot, a B-24, and two PV-1 control aircraft were brought with them and another B-24 robot was made available to them by 3rd Air Division. After conducting various experimental flights and training in technique and target study, the first mission was scheduled on 12 August 1944. Two PV-1 mother aircraft took off and were followed by the robot. The mother aircraft fell in behind the robot and the task force departed for control point one at 2,000 feet. Before reaching the first control point, the mother had control of the robot and remotely turned it around control point one. Approximately two minutes after the completion of the turn, the robot plane disintegrated from a premature explosion. Both men were still in the plane and were killed.[1528]

Exacerbating the tragedy, it was already clear to at least some of the personnel involved that the operation was bound to fail. Indeed one electronics expert contemplated "fixing" the arming panel, which he demonstrated was faulty and would trigger the fuses after a short period of overheating. Instead he went through channels and got slapped down. Told unofficially of the problem, neither Joe Kennedy nor Wilford Willy would take the responsibility for messing with the defective device.[1529]

Aftershocks

For obvious reasons, the program operated under extreme secrecy.[i] It has since been asserted that the top naval commanders were desperate to prevent any word of the specific malfeasance and the general failure of the entire project to become known – particularly since there was a Kennedy involved.[ii] The Navy did announce the deaths of Willy and Kennedy on 14 August 1944, but did not divulge the nature of their special mission until next year.[1530] The two were awarded the Navy Cross the next February, and as a special favor to Joe Senior, a new destroyer was named the *USS Joseph P. Kennedy, Jr.* The family also set up a major charitable foundation in his name.

The coincidence of the president's son witnessing the explosion that killed the future president's brother naturally attracted great attention later. But at the time, it could only be reported that Joe Kennedy Jr. died heroically while undertaking a secret mission. You get to be a hero if you die, but of course he was merely putting his life on the line like everyone else; he did not know or grasp that sloppiness almost ensured his death.

For decades the conventional wisdom has held that APHRODITE/ANVIL was so secret that even Kennedy Senior was not told the details for many years. The secrecy myth may have originated with Searls's well-researched and Kennedy-authorized

---

[i] The Norfolk & Suffolk Aviation Museum's extensive exhibit on APHRODITE says the mission was secret until 1966, and the crew not revealed until 1970. In fact, the Navy released most details in 1945.

[ii] In particular, Olsen makes this case. It may have been generally suspected, but cannot be corroborated.

account written in 1968 – perhaps because Searls thought it was secret, or perhaps for dramatic effect. Olsen, writing two years later, added to it by asserting that Navy officers would not risk embarrassment by revealing the imperfect management of the operation.

However, both President Roosevelt and Joe Kennedy were briefed on the nature of the flight. The perfectly legitimate secrecy for operational reasons was only upheld until VJ-Day. On 24 October 1945, the Navy revealed the ANVIL project and the demise of Lieutenants Kennedy and Willy in almost excruciating detail. Most all the newspapers reported it, because even then the Kennedy Clan was of public interest for its money, its influence, and the naked (if vicarious) ambition of the sons.[1531]

In the *New York Times's* account, even the television-guided Castor project was mentioned, although the Navy dubiously asserted that later missions were successful. Referring obliquely to Torpex, the news stated that 'only 600 pounds of the load was TNT. The rest of the 21,170 pounds of demolitions consisted of a secret preparation more powerful but less stable than TNT.' About the only error in the release was the nature of the target, then assumed to be a V-2 site, but the route of flight was correct. The Navy did not mention that Elliott Roosevelt participated in the mission. [1532]

The heroic story became a basic staple of the "Kennedy Myth" even as John Fitzgerald rose through Congress in the 1950s. JFK made sure to acknowledge Willy's equal role in the mission. The tragic flight was often referred to during his presidency, and was offered again as evidence of "the curse" the day after the assassination on 22 November 1963. The only thing there seems to have been confusion about was the target; some had it as Heligoland, others as V-2 sites. The V-3 program was still unknown when the Navy released the details of the mission in 1945.[1533]

On 26 October 1944, President Roosevelt did have an awkward meeting with Joe. But it was not Junior's death that soured their relationship; that acrimonious break had already come during the neutrality debate.[1534]

Elliott and his siblings knew Joe Kennedy and his promising family very well indeed. A neat press photo shows Elliott and wife chatting amiably by the water cooler with Joe Jr. at the 1940 Democratic National Convention.[1535] The two were then delegates from Massachusetts and Texas, respectively.

Junior had been especially close to John Roosevelt; they were both "rambunctious" denizens of the Harvard class of 1938.[1536] But Joe Senior had taken a special interest in Jimmy, as a virtual "foster father," he claimed. It was a good match; Joe was the ultimate demonic manipulator, and Jimmy was easily led if the right lures were dangled. Some researchers even hold that Joe Kennedy shared his harem with Jimmy; evidently among these people, the numberless girls, procured or volunteers, were passed around.[i]

> Jimmy was always strapped for money, and Joe played him like a fish on a hook, giving him a consulting fee here, a free meal there. During the winter, Joe turned his Palm Beach home into a luxury resort for Jimmy and his family.[1537]

At any rate, Kennedy money and its link to the Roosevelts are key to understanding what went on behind the scenes in mid-century America. FDR first enlisted Joe Senior's partly ill-gotten fortune for his political campaign in 1930, and (like many others), Joe thought he was responsible for swinging Hearst behind FDR at the Chicago convention. In return he wanted, not surprisingly, the Treasury cabinet post,

---

[i] Kessler, 106. Notes that Morton Downey, JPK's Hyannis neighbor, was then chief procurer of females.

but in a spot of good fortune for the nation, FDR left it to his unusually honest friend Henry Morgenthau. Joe instead became the first head of the Securities and Exchange Commission (SEC).[1538]

There are a great many hints and rumors about Jimmy Roosevelt's schemes with Joe Kennedy, not least in Joe's correspondence and his FBI file, but it is hard to tell how much is true – except that the two worked the far fringes of finance together, and that mentally they were almost twins. With unctuous, slippery gregariousness unswervingly attending the raw pursuit of fast cash and women, Jimmy was far shrewder than his brother Elliott. For that, it seems the latter never forgave him.

Joe and Jimmy sailed to England and Europe in 1934. On that trip, the two tried to corner the market on post-Prohibition whisky imports, which, in part, gave rise decades later to persistent but disputed rumors that Joe made much of his fortune as a bootlegger.[i] Rumors, however many, do not suffice as evidence, and Joe's legal and illicit interests were far-flung. Jimmy always rode his coat-tails.

Joe Kennedy had carefully prepositioned himself for the end of Prohibition. The whisky business was legal, sort of:

> In 1933, Jimmy was of great service to Kennedy in launching Somerset Importers, Ltd., exclusive agents for Haig & Haig and John Dewar whiskies. Joe and Jimmy went to London together, and Kennedy introduced Jimmy to many people, including officials of British Distillers, Ltd., which controls many Scotch-whisky brands. Jimmy was regarded as something like an American Prince of Wales. The close friendship has continued ever since. Jimmy has helped Kennedy to reach the two great positions which he now holds – that of Ambassador to London and that of premier Scotch-whisky salesman in America.[1539]

So far, so good. But:

> Kennedy was enabled to get a flying start in the whisky business with the aid of two enormous permits for the importation of Scotch whisky before repeal. These were brought in under medicinal permits granted in Washington. When America officially turned wet, Kennedy was on the market with one huge shipment of Haig & Haig medicine and another huge shipment of John Dewar medicine.[1540]

And this is where we finally tie in with Jimmy's insurance racket. In the 1930s his wealth was augmented by obtaining the insurance accounts on whisky shipments in particular and maritime cargo in general. The first chairman of the U.S. Maritime Commission (1937) was – no kidding – Joseph P. Kennedy. In 1940, Roosevelt & Sargent also acquired the insurance on American President Lines, owned by the taxpayers through the Maritime Commission. As head of the shipping line, FDR chose William Gibbs McAdoo, the former Democratic presidential candidate.[1541]

It is well documented that Joe reneged on a deal to make Jimmy coowner of the whisky import trade. Historian Michael Beschloss had heard from family sources that Jimmy, believing himself swindled, considered suing Joe, but was dissuaded. At any rate the spat was short, for Joe always had new schemes to entice Jimmy. Long after FDR had rejected Joe Senior, Jimmy stuck to him like a pilot-fish following a shark. [1542]

---

[i] Okrent: Last Call, 367-8. Okrent says JPK's alcohol interests were legal and the bootlegging rumors false. This does not match the accounts of JPK's biographers.

Jimmy worked hard to persuade his father to make Joe Kennedy ambassador to London, something FDR wasn't keen on. Jimmy wrote Joe, "It is almost done. I haven't failed you yet." This relationship makes it easier to understand why Jimmy, into his senior years, had the run of the Kennedys' Palm Beach mansion.[i]

Joe Senior wasn't just friendly with the Roosevelt sons; according to Elliott, he tried to rape Anna: "She eluded his embraces by running around his suite [at the NY Ritz-Carlton], dodging behind the sofas, scuttling around the grand piano, with Joe in amorous pursuit until he lost his breath."[1543]

Joe wasn't accustomed to having anyone, much less girls, deny him. All of these shenanigans probably contributed to Eleanor's intense loathing of Joe Senior, a dislike which, to the regret of her own children, extended to John F. Kennedy.

Although he seems not to have talked much about it, Elliott knew both Joes well. Everyone realized that Joe Sr. had transferred his own thwarted presidential ambitions to his eldest son.[1544] For that reason he persuaded Franklin Jr. to campaign for JFK in the crucial West Virginia primary in 1960. In retrospect, Junior, not an angel himself, characterized the patriarch as "one of the most evil, disgusting men I have ever known." He added: "Oh, I know he was a financial genius, but he was a rotten human being," and then explained how Joe secretly cheated his brother Jimmy, his tireless advocate in the White House.[1545]

This makes it that more odd that Elliott reportedly did not talk about the death of Joe Junior until 1968. There was no secrecy to uphold. Patricia Roosevelt, who missed no chance to drop John F. Kennedy's name in her memoir of socializing, does not mention the story of Joe's death. Perhaps this is simply because it is not true that Elliott flew through Joe Kennedy's aerial funeral pyre in 1944.

The Navy expended the remaining BQ-8 in a raid against the already shattered submarine pens at Heligoland on 3 September 1944. The crew survived that mission, but the drone missed the target. The official report said the operator mistook Dune Island, a mile away, for the main island, and the robot went out of control in the last few seconds due apparently to flak hits.[1546]

There were two more failed Air Force APHRODITE raids on Heligoland; evidently the convenience of that island target outranked its irrelevance. There were more attempts at hitting low-value targets in Germany proper. All missed.

In wartime it is sometimes impossible to tell legitimate operations from madness. General Arnold, besotted with the promise of APHRODITE, demanded large-scale attacks at random against German civilians, as a sort of pay-back for the V-weapons. Only intervention on the Churchill-FDR and Truman level eventually put a stop to it. Churchill argued that it was much more logical for the essentially defeated Germans to convert their remaining aircraft likewise and aim them at London, and he saw no point in encouraging that.[1547]

One of the very first things President Truman did in office was to respond to Churchill's cautionary note with a concurring statement. The absurdity of the Air Force's argument that crippling strikes at Germany's industrial centers would end the war must have been apparent at this time; Allied armies were about to cut the country in two.[ii]

---

[i] Hersh: Bobby & JEH, 57; Kessler 150-1, believes "it is likely Joe paid JR to get him the ambassadorship."

[ii] Truman, I/32-33. Churchill's note was a delayed response to a Roosevelt proposal on use of the bombs.

Elliott Roosevelt waited many years to speak publicly about project ANVIL. But, as fate would have it, he was still alive when a classical alternative-history narrative emerged in 1986. An aging German flak officer by the name of Karl-Heinz Wehn went to the trashy tabloid *Bild am Sonntag* and announced that he had shot down Kennedy's aircraft.

He said that on 14 July 1944, while he commanded a flak battery south of Caen, he engaged twelve B-17s returning from a raid on nearby Soissons. One Fortress caught fire and spun in. Two parachutes emerged, and a nearby SS unit captured the fliers.

They were brought to Wehn for interrogation. They gave their names as Joe Kennedy and "O'Patrick." Kennedy said he was an Air Force lieutenant, a son of the former ambassador to Britain, who was a wealthy man back in the States. He said four other airmen were aboard the aircraft, but all died except for the two captives.

Later that night Wehn heard shots. Next morning he was told that the SS had shot the fliers while they were trying to escape.

The alert reader might have noticed that this event ostensibly occurred a full month before the ANVIL mission, the aircraft was the wrong type, and besides Kennedy was in the Navy, not the Air Force. This also occurred to Elliott Roosevelt when the *Boston Herald* managed to get hold of him. He called it "an absolutely cockamamie story" and noted that "if he says he interrogated Joe Kennedy, Jr., I think he's dreaming."[1548]

It's anybody's guess what makes an elderly enemy come up with a story like that, but it is certainly not uncommon for memories of combat to run together, or to be contaminated by later-heard news. But, in the case of the Kennedys, there is always room for one more conspiracy theory. And there are, naturally, adherents of the idea that Franklin Roosevelt had the Kennedy "crown prince" killed. Joe Senior is supposed to have made intemperate remarks to this effect.

The two patriarchs did not get along after the anti-war ambassador was fired in November 1940. Both Kennedys, Senior and Junior, were strongly opposed to American entry into the war – at least on the side of the British Empire.[1549] Even kid brother John Fitzgerald joined the America First movement. FDR and Joe Sr. had a testy relationship. After 1944, it seems to have degenerated into hatred, both for political and personal reasons. The old Democratic kingpin Kennedy even took up with columnist Westbrook Pegler, writing him: "We are just going into an era in which we will need you to fight for what's left of America before they push it all down the drain. It is much closer than most people think."[1550]

Perhaps the most lurid exchange, recounted by Elliott Roosevelt thirty years later, occurred when FDR asked that Ambassador Kennedy end his unseemly affair with his movie star mistress. Joe said he'd get rid of Gloria Swanson "if you give up Missy LeHand." When the ambassador returned from London, there was no cabinet member or other official to greet him, as custom required. Instead a smiling Missy LeHand, the president's secretary, welcomed Joe Kennedy back to the United States.[1551]

That story is so good that it is quite likely made up. Elliott naturally enjoyed telling it, but it appears to have originated with a journalist who wouldn't say how he got it. Michael Beschloss, in his debut history *Kennedy and Roosevelt* refers to the story obliquely without attribution.[1552]

It's quite a jump from this rivalry to an assassination attempt. But to some, the coincidence of the president's son being a close witness to Joe Kennedy Jr.'s death is irresistible. As an example, a Roosevelt-hater posted the following:

> Joe Kennedy, Sr. always believed that FDR had arranged the death of his son to hurt him - really the only possible explanation. We have the anomolous case of a US President murdering the brother of a future US President. In 1974, after Truman's death, Merle Miller published a 1961 interview with Truman done on tape in front of three witnesses in his best seller entitled *Plain Speaking: An Oral Biography of Harry S. Truman.* Truman, according to Miller, was in Boston in 1944 in the Ritz-Carlton hitting up Joseph Kennedy for campaign funds for FDR's run for fourth term, and "Old man Kennedy started throwing rocks at Roosevelt, saying he'd caused the war and so on. And then he said, 'Harry, what the hell are you doing campaigning for that crippled son of a bitch that killed my son Joe?'"[1553]

Merle Miller's book of interviews with Truman was published after the latter's death and has since been shown to have no integrity. Very possibly the quotes were made up, or tarted up, by Miller. Furthermore, even in that book Kennedy meant that Roosevelt killed Joe "by causing the war."

The obvious rejoinder to the assassination theory, if we should momentarily accord it undeserved attention, is that if you are going to blow up a flying ten-ton bomb, the last place you want to be is in an airplane close by. Unless, of course, your conspiracy is so twisted that you deliberately choose this to make it appear you're not to blame….

So what *really* was the German mystery installation that so preoccupied the Allied air forces? Years of research later, it turned out to be a supergun, a multi-staged explosion within a 450-foot long barrel launching a shell at Mach 5. The device was buried in the chalk layers about five miles from the coast, equidistant between Boulogne and Calais. It was ramped up 45 degrees and aimed at an azimuth of 300 degrees, intersecting London a hundred miles downrange.

It possibly could have worked. Smaller examples did, at least until the barrel sections ruptured. But even if these shells had been lobbed at the British capital, they would have made very little difference. The much larger V-1 and V-2 weapons were mostly annoying terror weapons; the V-3, as the supergun became known, could not nearly match even them; and it was nowhere near completion when the area was overrun in late August.

The supergun keeps coming back in history, but usually it appeals to countries (such as Iraq) without air superiority and looking for a cheap way of striking back. Because the device is necessarily unwieldy, it attracts attention, and the lack of air defenses makes it impossible to protect. From a German standpoint, it could be argued that the dozen extensive air raids against the V-3 site represented Allied air resources that were thus not allocated to striking German cities. As with the other V-weapons, they might very well have reasoned that they came out ahead in that particular exchange of pawns.

From the Allied viewpoint, however, it is virtually impossible to justify a crude, ill-tested, hazardous program like APHRODITE – particularly because, in the later absence of accessible high-value targets, most drones were expended on innocuous objectives carrying a virtual certainty of civilian casualties. It is disturbing to learn that in the final missions, pilots were told to launch the robots against any German town if the primary target could not be reached. Thus on 1 January 1945, 325th Wing reconnaissance pilots covered two drone attacks on Oldenburg. The mission report noted:

> When Robot went over the town [Oldenburg] it blended so well with the terrain that it was impossible to see. Mother aircraft did two 360-degree turns before explosion was observed. Mother aircraft was seven miles Southwest of town at this point. Robot exploded just Northwest of the main part of town. The Photo Recon ship reported that it exploded in a residential area….
>
> Mother aircraft were carrying four clusters of incendiaries to destroy Robot if it failed to explode. These bombs were toggled by the lead Mother aircraft on a small town approximately two miles Northwest of Lathen hitting directly in the middle of town as observed by gunners.[1554]

This may be a useful reminder that something about air power causes the moral compass to swing erratically. If an infantry patrol, having decided to use up its excess ammunition, decided to shoot all the people in the next village, few would think it fair.

WEDDING AT THE ABYSS

In the fall of 1944, Colonel Roosevelt was tired of his job and pining to get home again. He was not above pulling strings to that end, and he had ahold of some big ones:

> As for me, I wish Pa Watson could arrange for me to be called back, if only for a couple of weeks, on some pretext or other – it appears that Arnold and Staff aren't too anxious to have me around, but maybe G-2 of the Ground Forces would like for me to come back, as I probably know more about Air-Ground Cooperation on Reconnaissance than anybody over here. Maybe even compassionate leave to straighten out my personal affairs could be worked. I am not too familiar with what would be possible but I am sure that a word from Pa Watson to even General Arnold would probably get the job done.[1555]

It did work, and quickly. After this and other discreet entreaties, Elliott checked into the White House on 15 November 1944. And he had a plan for his leave.

On 3 December, at the Grand Canyon's Yavapai overlook, Colonel Roosevelt married one of the actresses Johnny Meyer had introduced to him in Hollywood a year earlier. She was Faye Emerson, the girl Elliott had glommed onto and taken with him to New York when he completed his Hughes F-11 recommendation for General Arnold.

It had been a close-run thing, but Howard Hughes had prevailed after 14 months of relentless effort.

The election safely over, Colonel Roosevelt had been delighted to be called back to special duty in the United States in November 1944. He had only six weeks stateside, but he certainly made the most of his time. He headed straight for the Stork Club, where he told Leonard Lyons, that no, he was not, actually, going to California to get married, but asked to borrow the columnist's tie; he was trying to travel incognito. Elliott did briefly stop by the White House, where he stayed 15-17 November.[1556]

Even with his short New York stay, he hit the news. Arriving in a taxi, he forcibly interrupted a fistfight among soldiers outside a bar and sent everyone scurrying for cover: "[He] acted like he was God Almighty," a survivor of the altercation said.[1557] "Keep this quiet. A son of the president is involved!" said Elliott's companion, thus ensuring that it would be all over the newspapers the next day.[1558]

But this was incidental fun. What Elliott really wanted was Faye Emerson's chilled heart, and Howard Hughes was determined that he would get it, despite the awkward detail that Faye had resolved to put Elliott out of her mind. Let her tell the story:

> 'I was kind of a columnists' darling. They were always mentioning me, saying I'd been here or I'd been there with someone.'
>
> She quotes Hughes as saying he didn't 'think that you ought to be seeing all these other people and going out so much. Elliott will read about it and it will upset him and he has the war to fight.'
>
> 'But, Howard,' she says she interjected, 'I'm not engaged to Elliott.'
>
> Hughes continued: 'Even if you won't be engaged to him, you can imagine how when he's over there and he reads these things, how he must feel.' Faye says that Hughes followed up the phone call by sending her a three-page letter handwritten on yellow foolscap in which he reiterated his concern adding 'how he felt about Elliott, that he was a very special man, different from a lot of others.'[1559]

Although that sensational letter is lost, it was remarkable evidence of Howard's incessant, surreptitious string-pulling. And it certainly worked this time, too.

Leaving nothing to chance, Elliott's friends from California took well care of him. He headed for the Beverly Hills Hotel where he stayed while working out some romantic details. Faye said Elliott called as soon as he came back to the States. She had been down in Coronado for a party and didn't come home until 6:30 in the morning, and Elliott said he'd been calling her all night:

> "I've been down in San Diego visiting my mother," she lied. "Oh," he said. "I'll be out there in two or three days. I've got a couple of stops to make." This time she said, "Wonderful. I'd love to see you."
>
> He came directly to her house in North Hollywood and "we barely spoke for 15 minutes….He came back with the ice and set it down on the bar and we looked at each other really for the first time. And we started laughing, and he put his arms around me and gave me a big kiss. Then we knew instantly that we were in love."
>
> …Elliott wanted to get married immediately, while she had other considerations, stardom at Warners being one of them. Although that didn't rule out Elliott immediately. As she says of him: "Elliott has curious morals. He never has long affairs. He just marries."
>
> On a quick trip to Palm Springs, she agreed to marry him, changed her mind completely on the drive back, and gave in to him completely on the dance floor at Mocambo.[1560]

She didn't mention that Howard Hughes and chief social fixer Johnny Meyer were assiduously shadowing the relationship and keeping the wheels greased and turning all-along. The fateful Mocambo dinner, for example, was $38. It was all very costly, but courtesy of the Hughes Tool Co. and the taxpayers. On 30 November, the Associated Press photographed Elliott at Hughes's Culver City factory alongside Johnny Meyer and Charles Perelle, the embattled company manager. There was also the short week at the Racquet Club in Palm Springs, as usual with Mr. Meyer alongside.[1561]

Some people had already heard that Colonel Roosevelt was looking to get married while stateside. Packs of frenzied reporters stalked the likely suspects. Most would be thwarted.

But celebrities don't just marry; they manage the stage show. After "giving in," Faye called her mother and her ex-husband, and she and Elliott together called Walter Winchell and Hedda Hopper, their trusted gossipeers on each coast. On 2 December, a Friday, Faye came out of seclusion to reporters and told them a suitable set of lies about her and Elliott's relationship, and that they would marry, but not where.

Faye then said that since Hughes's introduction of the president's son fourteen months earlier, she had kept the romance aglow: "We wrote each other and I saw him here and in New York whenever he was in the country." Yet later Faye would claim that although Elliott had requested marriage in 1943, the two considered themselves "free agents" and did not keep up the connection during his European intermission. "I never wrote him at all for the 14 months he was overseas." She wasn't the pining type.[1562]

Elliott pined. When, after many devious efforts, he was ordered back in November, his campaign was so persuasive that Faye, greatly encouraged by her handlers, gave in. But Elliott was indeed "on business" visiting Hughes Aircraft. Getting married was strictly on the side.[1563]

In the afternoon preceding the snap wedding, Faye and Elliott had been ushered into Jack Frye's special-use TWA Lockheed twin at Hughes Culver City airfield. By 4:15, defying a developing snow storm, the plane landed at Valle airport south of the Grand Canyon. The Secret Service reported that regular TWA captain Glen Knudsen flew. On board were, along with the happy couple, little Ruth Chandler, Faye's friend Mrs. Joseph Livengood, and Secret Service agent-in-charge Robert Wells.[1564]

Three other planes didn't make it. Helen Vanderbilt, Jack's glamorous wife, Johnny Meyer with a girlfriend, and the new Mrs. Shoop landed at nearby Ash Fork; another plane carrying three colonel friends, Clarence Shoop, Johnny Hoover, and David Brooks, landed at Kingman; and the last one, full of disappointed reporters and photographers, had to let down in desolate Blythe on the Colorado River. [1565]

On Sunday morning, after much confusion, bride and groom and the distinguished party were able to get the festivities taken care of at the rim of the canyon, at the imposing Fred Harvey hotel, el Tovar. Johnny Meyer and Jack Frye were there. Howard Hughes was not, but for his money. No relatives (excepting children) attended.

The wedding was no discreet, low-key production. It was a sensationally secret and extravagantly modest affair. And what better place to tie the knot than that beautiful spot at the edge of the south rim, the Yavapai observation station? This is a stone structure overlooking the abyss, not far from the national park visitor center. It took eight minutes; then the party scrambled out of the freezing wind and hit the champagne at el Tovar. Inauspiciously, during the wedding the magnificent view was obscured by snow and mist. It was 29 degrees (-2°C).

Appropriately enough, Johnny Meyer "gave away" the bride. Jack Frye of TWA was "best man." The "maid of honor" was Elliott's and Ruth Googins's ten-year old daughter Ruth Chandler.[1566]

After socializing, the couple got on the mules and rode down the big hole to the Phantom Ranch by the Colorado River a mile below. "No press was going to follow us down there because it was four hours down and six hours back up. And that's where we spent our honeymoon – which was just lovely."[1567]

The Hollywood crowd fawned and fluttered over the royal wedding. The Roosevelt-haters asked how the couple got ahold of three aircraft with fuel when even folks with urgent business had a hard time getting travel priority. They said Elliott had now gotten his "third term." Would he soon catch up with his father?

Wife Nr. 3: Faye Emerson

Louisiana-born and San Diego-raised Faye Emerson was considered beautiful, and enjoyed a profitable and promising movie career. Only 27, she already had one marriage and a young son in the logbook, and she quickly figured out how to work the ropes in Hollywood. For a Hollywood plaything, Faye was unusually smart and politically aware, though obviously not intellectual. To Eleanor's regret, the male Roosevelts did not attract the cerebral kind, but Elliott said that his mother admired Faye's "intelligence, energy and enormous ambition."[1568]

Nevertheless, whether through her own efforts or those of her promoters, cleavage became her best known asset. Even after dumping Elliott five years later, she continued in "video" – i.e., television, where she was known mainly for the way she dressed.

When Howard Hughes set Faye up with Elliott, she was considered an ambitious B-movie actress:

> She never was and still isn't in the big movie money. Her home, which is Elliott's for the duration, is a small cottage in a canyon, strictly a modest-income affair. In her ménage are, of course, Blaze [dog] and her son, Scoop, otherwise William Crawford Jr., age 4. His father is Miss Emerson's former husband, Ensign William Crawford, a naval aviator. Transportation is a 1941 Chevrolet on a "B" [ration] card....she likes music, attends most of Southern California's concerts, operas and ballets. She is a better than amateur painter.[1569]

After the Grand Canyon extravaganza, the couple spent the next few days at Flagstaff and at the Fryes' ranch in Sedona. They flew out a week later.[1570] Faye had some additional work in Hollywood finishing *Hotel Berlin*. Then the two flew off to Washington D.C., where the somewhat intimidated Faye got to meet the family:

> That's how I met the Roosevelts. They couldn't be warmer, more generous or kinder. They made me feel so welcome. They had every reason to say, 'God, that's all we need, an actress in the family.' Except that Mrs. Roosevelt really loved the theatre. Maybe she was kind of secretly pleased to have an actress in the family. [1571]

It was 18 December 1944. They got the Lincoln bedroom. Next day she met FDR, and "in two minutes he had me right around his little finger." Faye was a big hit. She said she was the only daughter-in-law who cared about politics.

Airline mogul Jack Frye is the connecting character in this saga. Howard Hughes had bought a controlling interest in TWA, and Jack was now effectively a Hughes officer. In 1938, Hughes reportedly wanted to buy a Boeing Model 307, the first pressurized airliner (a civilian B-17 variant), but Boeing wouldn't sell because TWA had priority. So Hughes bought into TWA and got his private 307, which he wanted for another record-setting attempt. (It was cancelled with the outbreak of war.)

Frye and his rich, beautiful wife Helen Vanderbilt had discovered scenic, sleepy Sedona and purchased a ranch-retreat there. Frye had a runway put in – though not the one that now graces the mesa overlooking the town – and thus his desert sanctuary was a favorite for the "prop set" that preceded the "jet set." The Roosevelts honeymooned there.

During that era, the aviation industry was dominated by larger-than-life characters like Hughes and Frye. There was a TWA terminal at the Lindbergh-designed Winslow airport, an important stopover for both trains and planes, and the Fryes often stayed at the luxurious Harvey hotel, the La Posada Inn and Restaurant that anchored Winslow. In this respect, the air route closely followed the trail laid by the railroads two generations earlier.

If this were all there was to the Roosevelts' wedding tour, we might say "Congratulations," and go on. But Hughes Aircraft kept good records in order to safeguard profits and secure tax deductions, and when the Senate subpoenaed the books two years later, they showed beyond a doubt that Colonel Elliott Roosevelt and his party was entirely bought and paid for by Howard Hughes. Almost from the moment he set foot on American soil until the day he left, he was fed, housed, and soused, and very well to boot, by the Hughes Aircraft Company.

> Mr. ROOSEVELT. I was staying out there, and I had my family staying with me, and I had three children with me and maid. We stayed at the hotel, and I was at the desk checking out and had written the check to pay for this bill, and Mr. Meyer rushed up to me at the desk and stated, "You cannot pay that bill." I said, "I can pay the bill, I have already written the check." He said, "That is not right, for Howard called me on the phone and told me that he desired to give you a wedding present of your stay here in California."
>
> Mr. ROOSEVELT. I wish to state for the record that I had nothing whatsoever to do at this time with the Hughes contract; in fact, I was completely discouraged over the fact that we were not getting any airplanes and had washed my hands of any possible hope of ever getting the airplanes, and Mr. Hughes being a long-time friend of my wife's, and my wife-to-be rather, and therefore of mine, had offered to give this to me as a wedding present and he knew that I had come to the country with a relatively small amount of money, and he desired that I should save my money for my honeymoon and my wedding expenses; and maybe sir, I will admit it might be said that it was inadvisable for me to have ever accepted a wedding present of any kind from a man like Howard Hughes or from other people. I must admit that I did not examine into the background of all of the people who did give us wedding presents; but it is true that I received wedding presents from other people...I myself, believe that possibly on a strict interpretation of the law, I might be reprimanded for having accepted a wedding present from Howard Hughes.
>
> Senator FERGUSON. You would think it would be a violation of General Arnold's order?
>
> Mr. ROOSEVELT. That might be so considered.[1572]

Indeed it might. In today's Air Force, he'd be on his way to the stockade. But "accepting a wedding gift" was not the half of it; perhaps not a tenth if you consider accepting an entire wife from Mr. Hughes. The Hughes-Roosevelt caper is a bit reminiscent of "Tanker-gate" – the Boeing Company's outright purchase of the USAF's aircraft procurement director with jobs for her and her family in the 1990s. The difference is that the hammer would not fall on Hughes and Roosevelt – they were Teflon before Teflon existed.

Mr. ROOSEVELT. Jack Frye had been a personal friend, had been a friend of mine over a great number of years. I had asked him to be my best man at the wedding. We had told him that we were going to be married in California. He stated to me that it would be much better if we were to come over to Arizona where he was at that time and be married over there. We told him that we would make the arrangements and travel over there by train and would arrive on such and such day.

He stated that his plane, his own plane, was at the Lockheed plant at that time having an overhaul and that it was going back to his field immediately, and there was no reason why my wife-to-be and myself and my daughter and one Secret Service man who was guarding my daughter – much against my will, I might add, to have the taxpayers' money spent that way, but the Secret Service demanded it – could not fly there. We were the only passengers, the names I gave you, plus my wife's matron of honor, Miss Schumann-Heink. We rode over to Arizona on that airplane.

Mr. ROOSEVELT....I was told that Mr. Hughes had been invited to come to the wedding also, and I was told that he was coming over himself in his own plane and that he was going to bring some other people, and I believe that he stated that he was going to bring Mr. Meyer. The facts are that I did not ride in Mr. Hughes' airplane. I did not ride with Mr. Meyer, and I did not have anything to do with his pilot, Franklin, or whatever his name is; and I never rode back on his airplane. The facts of the matter are that Mr. Frye did give my party their wedding breakfast which he, understand, paid for himself personally, which I think might have been a good policy to be followed by other people.[1573]

Whatever Colonel Roosevelt might have thought about the commendable hospitality of Hughes and his minions, the entire entertainment budget was eventually underwritten by the taxpayers of the United States.

The Senate dug up copies of the bill at el Tovar. From this we know that the three days hotel alone cost $850, and that Mr. Roosevelt "and party" (i.e. children, maid, etc.) occupied six rooms, and the party was billed also for the trip to the Phantom Ranch at the bottom of the Canyon. In addition, Elliott's young reconnaissance protégé, Lt. Col. Johnny Hoover, attended, but he got only one room, costing $3.50. The pilot, Paul Franklin, cost only $3.00 to put up.

Those were the days.

Then there were rooms, meals, drinks, and phone calls for Ms. Emerson, the Fryes, Mr. Meyer, and several others. Nine bottles of champagne and 16 half-bottles added up to $220. [1574]

The continued private hospitality at the Fryes' Sedona Ranch could not be billed to taxpayers. But when the newlyweds returned to the East Coast, Hughes Aircraft's expenses on them again spun out of control. Even when Elliott was away to war, his friends and colleagues were taken care of by Hughes.

Elliott was abroad from 30 December 1944 to 13 April 1945. But when he was rushed home to attend his father's funeral, he truly discovered the value of friends:

Mr. MEYER...The minute I heard this on the radio, of the death of the President, I immediately called Mrs. Elliott Roosevelt, Van Nuys, or West Hollywood, I think it is, and told her that I would hold the plane [Jack Frye's] if she wanted to see if she could reach the other daughters-in-law, and hold the plane and they would come right through non-stop.

I called her back, I think about half an hour or 45 minutes later. She had reached Mrs. James and Mrs. John [Roosevelt], if I am not mistaken, and was in San Diego. In the meantime, I had had the pilot waiting in Burbank, had the plane gassed up to move them here. They went right out to the plane, got on the plane, went to San Diego, and picked up,

> I don't know whether it was Mrs. John or Mrs. James, picked up one of the daughters in San Diego and I think they came through non-stop from San Diego to Washington, arrived here the first thing the next morning.[1575]

And that was how a charge of "Auto Rental and tips to a policeman, $15" in Washington, D.C., got charged to Hughes Aircraft's expense account.

Jack Frye and the Washington Kleptocracy

Like almost everyone else, TWA's Jack Frye eventually fell out with Howard Hughes. He was fired in 1946. This proved to be a blessing, for Frye was exceedingly well connected, and needed not fear. Not only was he tight with Elliott Roosevelt, with whom he shared interests in both aviation and attractive females, but despite being a Republican he had been careful to generously support the Democratic Party. With so much to lose, the big money knew to butter both sides of the bread.

Frye's career now intersected with one of the sleaziest and most underreported scandals of the war and its aftermath. When Germany declared war on the United States, German companies in the United States became war booty and were seized to operate for the benefit of the government. The immense I.G. Farben combine had the biggest plum in the United States: General Aniline and Film, with its sibling General Dyestuffs.

These were highly profitable companies, which, fortuitously, generated most of their income from patents. The American appropriation of IG Farben and its patents caused an enormous transfer of wealth away from Germany. In addition, posts at the two "Generals" became political plums handed out to the well-connected, especially those who had been kind to the Democrats.

Jack Frye now became president of General Aniline to the tune of nearly $100,000 annually. Louis Johnson, who had been Harry Truman's chief fundraiser, was awarded first the control of General Dyestuffs, then the exceedingly lucrative legal contracts for both Generals. Friends and contributors rounded out the party.

There were many similar cases of political predation on the Alien Property Office. As we shall see, some of them involved John Roosevelt. There was apparently nothing illegal or secret about this; columnists like Joseph Alsop and Drew Pearson reported freely on the details. The public shrugged, undoubtedly reasoning that the Republicans would have done the same.[1576]

Referring to Frye, Attorney General Tom Clark, and DNC Chairman Hannegan, the Alsop brothers wrote:

> In the early days of the Truman administration, Tom Clark and Postmaster-General Robert Hannigan had no closer business-man friend than Jack Frye, then president of TWA. Frye was popular at Washington as a generous fellow with his private plane and a generous contributor to the democratic party.[1577]

As was the custom, Robert Hannegan, the long-time Democratic powerbroker, had been appointed Postmaster General (1945-47).

Some hold that the chief target of the Office of Alien Property was the California Nisei, i.e. Japanese-descended Americans, eclipsing German companies. The Federal Reserve later estimated that the federal government stole $400 million in 1942 dollars (by "direct property seizures") from this group, and much of it went to the politically connected. The OAP "confiscated 415 businesses with a total valuation of $290 million in tangible assets alone, and over 6,000 German patents (worth exponentially more than the businesses) that would be given to U.S. businesses…" "They are the biggest plums in the entire Truman administration," a politician was quoted. It must be assumed that it was mere timing that let the plums fall to the Democrats and not the Republicans.[1578]

Frye's luck ran out when the Eisenhower administration sold off the "Alien" assets. Drew Pearson wrote that the new regime determined to "clean all Democratic holdovers out of General Aniline. That was why Jack Frye, a Republican appointed by Truman, was ousted as president…" Pearson said Frye was an old friend of former Attorney General Tom Clark, who got him the Aniline job after Hughes ejected Frye from TWA.[1579]

After losing this cushy sinecure in 1954, Frye flailed around for a few years without gaining traction. He tried to get back in the aircraft business. Having meanwhile divorced his Vanderbilt wife, he married a Las Vegas show girl of extraordinarily colorful repute, and then tried to raise money to bring the Helio aircraft factory from Pittsburg, Kansas, to Tucson, Arizona. He had raised $350,000 and was enjoying strong local support for building and heading the Helio Courier plant there.[1580]

He also promoted the Frye F-1 Safari, a four-engine STOL plane intended for rugged operations. It was more a Ju-52 successor than a DC-3 replacement – perhaps because Kurt Weil of Junkers fame now worked for Frye.[1581]

It all was not to happen. A local historian reported that in February 1959, Frye met with Howard Hughes at the sprawling new Hughes missile plant in Tucson in order to be reconciled and to secure Hughes's interest in producing new aircraft.[1582] Aged 54, Frye was killed on the way home from this alleged meeting by a drunk driver who T-boned him at Ajo Way and Palo Verde. (She was unhurt.)

It was a tragic exit for an aviation legend. Frye had held Arizona's first commercial license and brought the first airline service to the state. Ex-wife Helen kept his famous Sedona ranch.[1583]

Whether Frye and Elliott Roosevelt kept up the connection is not clear, but they were both part-time Arizona residents in the late 1950s.

Everyone wants Married

Why did Elliott agree to have Howard Hughes bankroll his wedding, in addition to providing the wife? Perhaps because Hughes had already pulled off a similar favor for Elliott's 7th PRG commander, Lt. Col. Clarence Shoop. In July 1944, Shoop had married the famous movie actress Julie Bishop in similar fashionable style at Jack Frye's mansion in Virginia. Bishop filled in for Faye Emerson when Faye had to drop one movie role in favor of her new responsibilities.[1584]

We last met Shoop when he talked Elliott into recommending the Constellation as a reconnaissance aircraft. Howard Hughes, Jack Frye, and Clarence Shoop had flown the first Connie when it set a new record transcontinental time (6:58) on 17 April.[1585]

The well-regarded Shoop had been sent back to the States in June to work with Lockheed on the problems still encountered with the F-5s. Despite the traveling and hard work, he managed to marry a celebrity along the way. On Elliott's recommendation, Mr. and Mrs. Shoop stopped off at Hyde Park on 31 October 1944.

Here the colonel picked up a few things Eleanor wanted him to take back to her son in England.[1586]

Now that sounds like a commendable get-together – pilots helping each other out. The trouble was that the trip also wound up on Hughes Aircraft's expense account. That's because not only Shoop, but an entire gaggle of Elliott's friends went to Hyde Park, and they were joined and paid for by the ubiquitous Johnny Meyer.[1587]

Certainly, Eleanor was delighted with the visits from Elliott's buddies. On 4 January 1945, she wrote:

> In the evening young Colonel Hoover, who is one of our son Elliott's pilots, brought his new wife to dine with us. The colonel had not gone back with the rest of the crew because he decided to get married, but he will follow them after a brief leave. Out of the whole crew only one enlisted man and one officer went back unmarried, which shows, I think, the urge that the men who go overseas have to leave someone waiting for them on this side of the ocean.[1588]

There is more to it than that. In part, Elliott had sent "Shoopy" back to persuade headquarters to request him (Elliott) for stateside duty: "He is trying to arrange for my orders, which will enable me to come home at the end of this month. If he succeeds, he will keep you advised. If he doesn't succeed with the War Dept., will you please arrange for him to see Pop, and maybe between them they can figure some angles…"[1589]

Shoopy did as told. Next Elliott sent Lt. Col. Hoover, Lt. Col. David Brooks, and Major Pleasant McNeel home with a letter for Eleanor (the first three officers would attend Elliott's wedding in December). Elliott told her to give "my boys" a meal and a stay-over if they wanted it. In the letter he also asked his mother to get word to General Arnold to call him home.[1590]

All this caused a great deal of consternation when the Senate dug into Hughes Aircraft's expenses, which of course had been deducted from taxes, thus evading the confiscatory wartime rates. Wonderful as she was, what exactly did the "First Lady" have to do with aircraft procurement? Elliott explained:

> Mr. ROOSEVELT. It is a very interesting point, these boys that he [Meyer] is referring to, that he accompanied to Hyde Park, were members of my organization in Europe, who returned on temporary duty or on leave to the United States or on permanent transfers. These officers, as well as all enlisted men who came back to this country, I gave letters of introduction to, to my mother and those men, all of them, used to drop in and tell her about what we were doing overseas. These men called my mother when they got to this country and delivered their letters of introduction. They told her that they were going to New York for the week end, two of them with their wives, and there they met Mr. Meyer, who was not known to me, but they met him through a Colonel Shoop, who had been returned a long time previously and who was known and friendly with Mr. Meyer long before I ever knew Mr. Meyer. And they told Mr. Meyer during that week end that they were going to Hyde Park, and they said, "Look, let us call Hyde Park and find out whether we can bring you. You have known Elliott and I am sure Mrs. Roosevelt would not mind."
>
> That is how Mr. Meyer happened to get on the band wagon to go to Hyde Park…
>
> Senator FERGUSON.. Why did you charge that in as a tax-deductible item?
>
> Mr. ROOSEVELT. That is what I would like to know.
>
> Senator FERGUSON. The committee wants to know.
>
> Mr. MEYER. I considered it good business to be invited to Hyde Park.
>
> Senator FERGUSON. What did it have to do with air production?

> Mr. MEYER. It was another contact.
>
> Mr. ROOSEVELT. Contact with Mrs. Roosevelt? Does she run the air production in the United States? [1591]

Eleanor was only trying to be friendly and help out her son. As usual she didn't apprehend how she was being used.

Who let the Dogs out?

When Colonel Shoop returned to his command at RAF Mount Farm on 8 August, he went to his quarters at a nearby farm house:

> He opened the door and two pony-sized dogs almost knocked him over. With this collision, Shoop met *Blitz and Blaze*. The colonel discovered he no longer had top priority on his own base. His wing commander, Col. Elliott Roosevelt, staff, cook, and English Mastiffs had taken over the farm house. The president's son had taken over his bedroom as well. Eventually, this arrangement became less disrupting, especially when Shoop no longer had to go out in the cold dark mornings for breakfast.[1592]

That does sound like Elliott Roosevelt. According to his next wife, he sent the two giant dogs home, one of them to her and the other to John and Anna Boettiger. Others stayed in England.[1593] One of Elliott's officers recalled that one of his guards shot "Blaze's brother," – perhaps Blitz – one dark night. He feared the monster was part of a German attack on the base.[1594]

Shoop, Elliott, and General Bennett Meyers were by this time firmly in Howard Hughes's orbit. Shoop rose quickly to Major General. In 1946, he commanded Muroc Army Air Base, and then translated the connection with Howard into a test pilot job and a vice presidency at Hughes Aircraft in Culver City. The Shoops – Clarence and actress Julie Bishop – became a high-profile Hollywood celebrity couple. The general commanded the California National Guard in later life. He died in 1968, still a Hughes Aircraft vice president.[1595]

Elliott might have gone that way too, but his job offers evaporated after his father's death and the avalanche of scandals that then embroiled him. His own actress wife did not last long. His dogs even less.

But that would be a couple of years in the future. There was much fun in the meantime. First, the dogs.

Blaze, Terror of the Skies

January 1945 shouldn't have been "silly season" in the American press. The Germans had just struck back vigorously at the Western Allies. Americans were fighting desperately to hold on in Belgium. Each day, the names of the dead and wounded ran to hundreds, sometimes thousands. But don't underestimate journalists and politicians.

It is not easy to keep enormous dogs and fight a war at the same time; but when you are a colonel, help is available. One correspondent wrote:

> The dog Blaze was purchased by Elliott while on a junket to England and was flown to Italy. There a detail of about ten soldiers were assigned to guard the dog and my informant states that Elliott himself "warned" him of the dire consequences which would be visited upon him if anything should happen to this dog, then a puppy, for which Elliott boasted he paid $500.00. After eating GI rations and food, the dog was flown to the United States.[1596]

Elliott had again dreamed up one of his trademark schemes. This time he was going to obtain a new dog breed in England and become its originator in the New World. The dogs he flew across the Atlantic were two bull mastiffs, a gigantic male and a female pup.

This plan, too, would end in utter disaster.

Incidentally, the American Bullmastiff Association notes that the breed was known in America shortly before Elliott's 1944 brainstorm. The dog is a massive, muscular cross of "40% bulldog and 60% mastiff" – however that works – and it most emphatically does not get along with other male canines.[1597]

On 13 November 1944, Colonel Roosevelt and his handpicked crew left England in a "worn" B-17. Aboard were two dogs, the giant bullmastiff Blaze and a female pup later seen at the White House. With their crate, the two weighed an amazing 285 pounds. Two other dogs remained behind in England. The B-17 routed via Iceland, Presque Isle in Maine, and New York.[1598]

The dogs were held up at Presque Isle for ten days. Then a passing B-25 agreed to give them a lift to La Guardia, whence another flight took them to Washington. The White House sent a station wagon for the dogs. Blaze spent some "not altogether happy times of White House society," and then went to board at the nearby military post that also stabled Eleanor's horse Dot.[1599]

Young Curtis Roosevelt was at Hyde Park when Elliott dumped Blaze and Dutchess on the unsuspecting Roosevelts. Anna and Eleanor got to take care of the dogs, since Elliott and Faye had important things to do. Curt said Blaze was a ferocious terror, but little Dutchess played well with his own beloved Labrador.[1600]

The help recalled, "Nobody could handle him…FDR finally put it half-jokingly, "There's room for you, son, or for your dog. Which will it be?" But both had to go.[1601]

The fun really began on 5 January, when Anna Boettiger called ATC from the White House to see about getting the dogs to Faye Emerson out in Hollywood, California. Personalizing the exchange, Elliott said Anna "arranged with an assistant of C.R. Smith, a long-time friend of mine" to get space on a cargo plane. That man was Colonel Ray Ireland, a former United Airlines executive, and he would rue the day.[1602]

On the ninth, the big dog was on his way from sea to sea, sporting an A-1 priority sticker.[1603] Wire Service Report, Antioch, Calif., 18 January 1945:

> A Navy gunner called home by his father's death and an army sergeant hurrying to the side of his sick wife told newsmen they were put off an army transport plane at Memphis, Tenn., last week because a huge dog consigned to Mrs. Elliott Roosevelt, actress-wife of the president's son, had a higher priority.
>
> Both agreed a third service man also was "bumped." The wife of a sailor said her husband wrote he couldn't board the plane at Dallas, Texas, for the same reason.
>
> Mrs. Roosevelt, interviewed yesterday aboard a train at Albuquerque, N.M., said she had received "Blaze," a 130-pound bull mastiff at Hollywood from her husband but "I assure you that my dog travels as freight and awaits his turn."

A war department spokesman said three service men were put off a plane at Memphis Jan 11 to lighten the load while a dog, about which the department had no information, continued its journey by air. The dog was consigned from Washington.

In Antioch, the navy gunner, Leon Leroy, told newsmen he boarded the plane at Newark, N.J., after learning of his father's death and had a "C" priority. He said high priority matter was put aboard at Memphis, requiring that some weight be left behind, that he and two other service men had to get off because the crated dog was rated "A".

Last night at Riverside, Calif., T/Sgt. Dave Aks, veteran of the China-Burma-India war, said he was "bumped off" the plane at Memphis while on his way to visit his wife, who is ill. He said a crated dog occupied "almost all of four seats" and a flight clerk told him it was consigned to Mrs. Roosevelt.

"Like two other service men, whose names I don't know, I was pretty sore to think that we got bumped off a plane on account of a dog, particularly since I was on such a short leave and was en route here to see my sick wife," he said. "Of course, we understood we would be subject to being bumped to make room for war cargo but we couldn't understand how the transportation of a dog was going to help the war effort."

Aks, who boarded the plane at Dayton, Ohio, took a train from Memphis to Dallas and there boarded another army cargo plane for Riverside.

At Granite City, Ill., Mrs. Ola Vee Nix said her husband, Maurice Nix, a navy carpenter's mate, who had been home to visit their four ill children, wrote her from San Francisco his trip back was delayed because he was unable to board a plane at Dallas. He said he had a "D" priority and that the plane carried a dog, with an "A" rating, which belonged to Colonel Roosevelt.

Nix now is believed to be somewhere in the Pacific.

Mrs. Roosevelt said the dog was one of two her husband, an air force officer now in England, has sent back to start a breed. She said "Blaze" was delivered to her in Hollywood "by an army major in a truck." She made no comment when asked if the dog traveled by air.

In New York, Mrs. Eleanor Roosevelt, wife of the president commented: "I can't imagine any plane dispatcher who would be as stupid as that. No army cargo plane would put a seaman off for that reason."

Her comment was made at a time when only Leroy had told his version. At Memphis, 4th Ferrying Group officials referred all questions to the AAF in Washington. Leroy, Mrs. Nix and the war department spokesman all referred to the date as Jan. 11 in their accounts. Sergeant Aks said it was Jan. 10.[1604]

Thus began one of the sorrier chapters in American media history, one that fortunately has been almost entirely forgotten (until now). But Elliott Roosevelt's career was gut-shot by the scandal, especially as it came at the exact time his father boldly submitted his name to the Senate for promotion to brigadier general.

Nonetheless, there is some substance behind the posturing. The scandal reflected a mounting fury against not only the Roosevelts, but especially against the abuse of perquisites among high-ranking officers. The common people had gone without for four years; by 1945, any story about bigshots pulling rank, deservedly or not, hit a raw nerve.

The "priority" scandal released a long pent-up general resentment of the Roosevelt sons, and among Republicans, the poorly suppressed rage against the president himself. The papers were full of snarling letters from readers, and even the president's own mail overflowed with hate.

The "injustice" the dog perpetrated against suffering soldiers must be seen in perspective. Air Transport Command, the successor to Ferrying Command, was created to logistically support the fighting forces worldwide. The domestic flights carried freight; military passengers could only be accommodated on a space-available basis, as continues to be the case. That's how the "bumped" servicemen obtained a "C" priority, which, irate senators ruefully noted, was what they themselves rated aboard cargo aircraft.

"A" priority was reserved for urgent and critical war supplies. The dog obtained this priority because the ATC colonel in charge, Ray Ireland, was contacted by the White House, and like most bureaucrats, he knew whom he most needed to please.[i]

It did not help that the enormous dog in its crate took up three seats and required the flight engineer to monitor its feeding, drinking, and exercising according to its accompanying instructions; or that officers chaperoned it on the ground and delivered it to Mrs. Elliott Roosevelt's doorstep. It especially did not please the public when it heard that, that same month, Colonel Roosevelt shipped his prized Arabian horses – a stallion, four brood mares, and three colts – by rail from Fort Worth to Hollywood.[1605]

When the Senate Military Affairs committee reported on the Blaze affair on 10 February, ATC Chief General Harold George included a little noticed disclaimer. He said that the three irate servicemen were not bumped by the dog, but in favor of B-priority cargo being taken on: "…this would have displaced the three passengers even if the dog had not been on board, but the dog did unquestionably displace an equivalent amount in weight of B priority freight."[1606]

In other words, it wasn't the fault of the dog, Elliott, or the White House. It was a pseudo-scandal.

One indicator of the White House's innocence is the well-known fact that Eleanor, despite her celebritous prominence, endured any travel hardship as a matter of course. She was once bumped off a wartime American Airlines flight. She reacted to apologies with effusive reassurances that she was delighted to give up her seats for soldiers.[1607]

It's hard to imagine such a scenario today.

Most curiously, the loudly trumpeted "Blaze Affair" triggered a sort of logistical chain-reaction in the bumping of passengers. Apparently, only some bumpees went public, but it also seems that some very vocal complainers were not dog-bumped at all.

Thus, three B-29 crewmembers wrote a steaming letter to columnist Drew Pearson, saying that on that night of 10 January, they were kicked off a flight from Newark at Patterson Field, Dayton, because "almost 250# of dog and food for the dog were shipped on an ATC plane to Mrs. Elliott Roosevelt in North Hollywood." That this was to them the straw that broke the camel's back was shown in their further remark: "We remember reading about how Colonel and Mrs. Roosevelt had a couple of airplanes for themselves and their wedding party and some weak explanation being offered when they were called on the fact."[1608]

It was hard not to sympathize with them. Pearson sent the three officers, Edward K. Mullen, John H. Johnson, and Hilmer J. Martens, each $77 for their air tickets.

With dogs and horses galore, obviously Elliott, starting out with a new wife and a new home, was trying to recreate the menagerie he had maintained with Ruth Googins in Texas. He was looking ahead to the end of the war and planning a new life in California. Whether he expected to be offered a lucrative gig with his new friends in the Hughes Aircraft Company can, of course, not be determined with certainty.

---

[i] White House aide Jonathan Daniels thought Ireland was an excellent administrator of the priority system who often had to deny "special requests," and some junior staffer had screwed up instead (Daniels, 150).

As if the dog flap wasn't enough, it was soon after revealed that Colonel James Roosevelt, traveling back to his California duty station after attending the fourth inauguration, had managed to hold up an entire train in Chicago for over an hour in order to make a connection. He had sent a telegram ahead, claiming wartime priority. This caused a commotion when the passengers found out, with much exaggerated saluting of "Crown Prince James" accompanied by bad jokes involving Roosevelts and wildlife.[1609]

Jimmy, as expected, claimed it wasn't his fault the train was held. But in his much franker memoirs, he offers a very revealing account of the episode:

> I recall a time during the war when I was on leave and trying to get from Washington to Los Angeles as fast as possible. A snowstorm delayed my train to Chicago and I was afraid I'd miss my connecting train to L.A. I explained my situation to the conductor and he wired ahead to have the train held in Chicago for the president's son. I remember being escorted by railroad officials down the platform in Chicago while some of the waiting passengers booed me. It didn't bother me. I accepted the power of my position. It did not occur to me then that I had no real right to so inconvenience others. There long ago came a time when I became aware and ashamed of such unjustified and inconsiderate acts. Once I thought about it, I did not consider myself better than anyone else.[1610]

He didn't "think about it" until his old age, though. As Anna's son Curtis wrote:

> Given to speeding, often after too much partying, the Roosevelt boys amassed more than their share of tickets and didn't take kindly to police reminders that, as the sons of the president, they should be setting a better example. My uncles had gotten to the point where they expected instant recognition – and special treatment. Woe to the White House guard who didn't recognize them returning to the fold from their carousing just as the sun was coming up and demanded identification at the front gate.[1611]

Obviously this is indicative of how the Roosevelt kids grew up, or didn't. They had always gotten whatever they wanted; why should they hold back? But it is also descriptive of their father's political career. To him, gaining the presidency was not some epic triumph; he'd always half expected it, on account of his name, background, and social standing. Likewise, it would have seemed just not right to surrender the office to which he felt entitled merely because of some two-term custom intended for lesser people.

Back to Blaze. After the monstrous dog captured the headlines across the country, stories about similar acts of official malfeasance, ordinarily submerged, bubbled to the surface in an orgy of indignation against the numerous and perpetual ways in which rank pulls privileges.

"Hounded" by journalists in London, Colonel Roosevelt complained that they were barking up the wrong tree. Yes, he had a dog, and it came along when he flew his B-17 across the Atlantic in early November. But he knew nothing about Blaze's further adventures, he said on 19 January. This was only the beginning of his troubles, though.[1612]

The Senate decided to investigate the affair – or more particularly, the entire subject of the abuse of transportation priorities, since there was accumulated evidence of bribery and unfairness in the allocation of the coveted A priority especially. The Military Affairs Committee would have to look into it. So would General Harold

George's Air Transport Command, which, in a swift but spectacularly "postemptive" strike, banned pet and domestic animal transportation on ATC planes.[1613]

It's pretty sad that at the peak of World War II General George should take time out to investigate dog travel. Same for Colonel Roosevelt. Still, after the journalists came the government investigators. A congressional inquiry is no laughing matter; Gen. George and other top officers were called in to answer probing and indignant questions about flying dogs. How this would help the war effort is not obvious, but the potential political pay-off should not be underestimated.[1614]

On 10 February 1945 the wire services reported on General George's report to the Senate Military Affairs subcommittee. The designated scapegoat was Colonel Ray Ireland:

> Subcommittee Chairman Tom Stewart, D., Tenn., was asked whether Ireland would be subjected to any disciplinary action. "You can be sure Gen. George talked to him and no more dogs will fly on "A" priorities," he replied.
>
> Ireland, a United Airlines executive before he entered the service, is in charge of the ATC's traffic and priorities division.
>
> George's report put it this way: "Establishing an "A" priority for the dog was unauthorized under regulations relating to air priorities. A serious mistake was made and it cannot be justified."
>
> George's report said Mrs. Boettiger telephoned Ireland, after Col. Roosevelt returned to England and said her brother wanted Blaze shipped to his new wife, Actress Faye Emerson, in Hollywood. There was no mention of priorities in that conversation, George said.

But the real problem, or opportunity, was Elliott's impending promotion:

> Publication of his report is expected to clear the way for confirmation on Monday of President Roosevelt's nomination of his second son to be a brigadier general. Action on it was postponed this week because some Senators wanted to know more about Blaze's ride before they okayed a star for Elliott.
>
> Stewart said his subcommittee will seek Senate adoption of a resolution authorizing a full and continuing investigation of all service air priorities. He said the subcommittee would like to have biweekly reports on all priority cargo and passengers.
>
> George's report told this chronological story of Blaze's travels:
>
> Last Nov. 13, young Roosevelt left England for a home furlough in an "old-type" Flying Fortress under his own command. The bomber carried four other officers, five enlisted men and two dogs – Blaze and a 20-pound Mastiff female pup. Even if the dogs hadn't been aboard, the plane couldn't have carried any additional personnel.
>
> The plane landed at Presque Isle, Me., where Roosevelt declared the dogs to customs inspectors. They were left there temporarily, then were flown to LaGuardia Field on Nov. 30, aboard a bomber making an operational flight. The same day, they were flown from New York to Washington by a Marine pilot.
>
> The Marine – unidentified – telephoned the White House when he arrived there. A station wagon picked up the dogs at the airport. That was the last mention in George's report of the female pup. Apparently, however, it was the dog which has been seen around the White House grounds lately.

From the White House, Anna had coordinated the dog's travels with Elliott and his ATC friends:

> Subsequently, Roosevelt returned to his post in England. Mrs. Boettiger telephoned his post in England. Then Mrs. Boettiger telephoned Ireland. On January 9 "the dog was shipped on a military cargo aircraft which left Washington about noon."
>
> It reached Memphis that evening, where some "B" priority cargo was put aboard and the "C" combat veterans were put off. The veterans would have been put off even if Blaze hadn't been aboard, George said.
>
> "Backlog of "B" priority freight existed at Memphis," he explained, "and this would have displaced the three passengers even if the dog had not been on board, but the dog did unquestionably displace an equivalent amount in weight of "B" priority freight."
>
> Sen. Styles Bridges, R., N.H., said there was just one slight item, in connection with Blaze's travels, about which the subcommittee wanted to know more. That was how come the allegedly-undermanned Army was able to have Blaze delivered to Miss Emerson's Hollywood residence on arrival by a major.[1615]

Anna Boettiger, Elliott's sister, was increasingly taking charge in the White House as the president's evident and mounting frailty began to seriously alarm his staff. The Blaze affair meant that it was Anna who went to Yalta with Dad, not Elliott. After four summits, he felt entitled and was furious when Harry Hopkins brought him the news:

> Late in January Harry Hopkins arrived in France, and he looked me up at SHAEF in Paris. I remember with gratitude the tactful way in which he broke the news to me. Casually he let fall the information that a Big Three meeting had been definitely set for Yalta, in the Crimea; that that was why he was on that side of the ocean. Then he remarked that Father was even at the moment, as he spoke to me, on his way over, aboard the *Quincy*, and accompanied by a task force. Seeing that I was about to pop the crucial question, he speeded up the tempo just a bit. Father had wanted me to act as aide again, he said, but had hesitated to put in a request for my services at the War Department. Father, Harry said, did not want to have the War Department put in that kind of spot, since it seemed fairly clear that the Republicans on the Hill would scream to the skies.[1616]

The giant dog could not prevent Elliott's promotion, but apparently it did prevent his going to Yalta. Whether he would have been helpful enough there to justify pulling him from the war effort is another question. His obvious rapport with Comrade Stalin was perhaps no longer particularly useful. At Yalta, the USSR completely dominated the agenda, and Stalin took what he wanted. His army was already zeroing in on Berlin.

Within a few months, there was more bad news from Blaze. His reign of terror came to an abrupt end. Wire Service Report, Rhinebeck, New York, 30 November 1945:

> Blaze, the big bull mastiff with the priority who belonged to Brig. Gen. Elliott Roosevelt, has been executed because he picked a fight with Fala, pet of the late president, it was revealed today. Mrs. Eleanor Roosevelt was so upset by the inglorious end of Blaze that she seemed to weep while talking about it.
>
> Blaze, who weighed 150 pounds, attacked Fala, Mr. Roosevelt's little Scottie, Saturday. Outweighed and outfought, Fala bit back the best he could, but he came out of the scrape with a deep slash on the back. The state health department, which examined Blaze's head, said "There was no evidence of rabies."
>
> Blaze was destroyed at the order of General Roosevelt, who decided he was vicious.
>
> Besides the cut on his back, Fala's right eye was lacerated, but today he was back in form, strutting about in cocky fashion.[1617]

Aughhhh....

This *was* Elliott's fault. Blaze had already attempted to eat one of his children. He later confessed that Blaze liked to rove in the woods and down the hill while he and Faye were working on Top Cottage, the retreat on the Hyde Park grounds that Franklin had built. That fatal day Blaze found Fala and ripped into the little black Scottie until bystanders could subdue the aggressor, reportedly with a large rock to the head. Fala was between life and death for several days. According to Elliott, for his mother's sake, "Blaze was put away"[1618]

In retrospect, the Blaze affair seems to be a clearcut example of a scandal in which Elliott Roosevelt was entirely innocent, yet it probably triggered the most public outrage yet. There is, however, a more subtle interpretation of the event – one that leaves the question of guilt and innocence a little more nuanced.

It was well known that many conscienceless high-rankers routinely corrupted the priority and rationing system. Worse, there is an account from a Kennedy family friend that a furious Joe Kennedy called the White House and successfully demanded that his vacationing son Jack be put on a passenger flight to Miami, thus bumping soldiers on duty travel. JFK told the story with admiration for his father's power and gall: "He called Roosevelt." Though this and similar events probably involved White House staff only, it nevertheless does not absolve the principals. To the country, the dog story thus seemed to exemplify abuses. And with Blaze, it seems that it was Anna Boettiger herself who lit the conflagration.[1619]

Thus Colonel Ireland, or an office-lackey, had a White House request on hand. And who was Ireland's boss? He was Major General C.R. Smith, and he was as friendly with the Roosevelts as Fala the Scottie himself. In fact, when the Roosevelts and their friends needed anything, they were more likely to give C.R. a friendly call than to engage in the tedium of putting in a request through the new-fangled Air Transport Command. That went back to before the war – all the way back to 1933 and Elliott's sojourn in Texas.

This is also clear from General Eisenhower's assistant, Captain Harry Butcher's correspondence in North Africa. Butcher was no ordinary aide. He was a high-powered radio executive who was close friends with the White House crowd and with numerous other centrally placed characters. He constantly exchanged letters with Steve Early, the president's press secretary; with Victor Emanuel, the Dayton industrialist on the president's friends list; with Amon Carter, the Fort Worth press magnate who was Elliott's friend and protector; and with C.R. Smith.

And what did they write about? Butcher was constantly receiving packages of expensive cigars (500 Robert Burns Panatelas, at one time) and liquor, often originating from Emanuel, always forwarded through the magical powers of C.R. Smith. This is clear from a run-in Butcher had with the Treasury Department. Butcher had had C.R. take back some very expensive rugs he had acquired in North Africa. Somehow Customs found them – it's harder to conceal rugs than cigars – and dunned Butcher for a hefty duty. Although Butcher agreed to pay the amount, he protested that C.R. had always been taking goodies back and forth for the top people and it was the expected procedure that no customs would be paid.[1620]

Now think of Blaze and Colonel Ireland. If Ireland had been a pitiless by-the-book officer, untainted by any hint of personal favoritism, then he might have told Anna Roosevelt Boettiger that Elliott's dog was deemed insufficiently essential to defeat the

Hun and the Nip, so the presidential family would have to find regular ways to ship him, sorry!

Such officers are rare because they don't last long. Colonel Ireland knew full well that if he didn't want to wind up on the Burma front, he'd better get that dog absolute top priority and get it swiftly to Faye Emerson's door happy and unscathed.

When the public's fury exploded in his face, as a good Army officer he also knew exactly what to expect next: his crucifixion, necessary to protect the White House, Elliott, and the chain of command, including C.R. Smith. That's how the system works.

BUNNY MAKES BRIGADIER

Dearest Mummy…just a word to let you know that my plans are still indefinite, and to let you know personally of some action I took yesterday. Last May, General Doolittle told me that he had recommended me for promotion – I knew that for one reason or another it had not been acted upon – then I received word that he had been told to resubmit it on the list to come up immediately after the election. Inasmuch as that meant that my promotion was considered political dynamite by the powers that be, and that it couldn't stand the light of closest bi-partisan scrutiny, I yesterday wrote Gen. Doolittle a letter and requested that my name be withdrawn from his promotion list. He withdrew it, per my request, today, so that my name would not come up to Father to submit to the Senate.[1621]

That was in late October. Three months later:

"*Dear Bunny: It is grand to be able to address you as Brigadier General!*"[1622]

"*He was so thrilled when Eliot's promotion went thro –*"[1623]

Flag officers are promoted via presidential recommendation to the Senate. The Military Affairs Committee (now the Armed Services Committee) votes on the individual names, but they are virtually always approved. In January 1945, President Roosevelt referred 103 promotions this way: three lieutenant generals, 22 major generals, and 78 brigadier generals. On the last list was the name of the President's second son.[1624]

Elliott was 34 years old. He had no college education. He had been in the reserves only five years. He had no boot camp and none of the ticket-punching air staff courses. He did not even have pilot's wings, although in January, he demanded and got a pilot rating despite not meeting the criteria. What he did have, however, was far more important in 1945: proven courage and effectiveness in combat and in command.

The Military Affairs Committee approved the nominations on 30 January. In a superhuman act of professionalism, the Senate on 12 February confirmed Elliott Roosevelt's promotion to Brigadier General despite the national hysteria over his flying dog. The vote was 53-11. Eleven Republicans voted no. All the other 77 colonels were unanimously confirmed, as was the custom.[1625]

It would seem like a straightforward victory for the president and his son. It wasn't; it required intrigue. The subcommittee might have stalled Elliott for some time. As the exceptionally informed columnist Drew Pearson let slip, a little parliamentary maneuver did the trick:

> It didn't leak out of the Senate military affairs committee, but last week its new chairman, Senator Elbert Thomas of Utah, made a deft move probably aimed to facilitate confirmation of Elliott Roosevelt as a Brigadier General. Hitherto, all military promotions sent to the Senate have been sent to a military affairs subcommittee headed by Happy Chandler of Kentucky for scrutiny. This committee has then recommended passing or rejecting the promotions.
>
> However, Chairman Thomas told his colleagues last week that this committee had been rather cumbersome and he believed it should be dispensed with...it was decided for the time being to take military promotions up in full committee. The full committee, therefore, was sitting when young Roosevelt's name was voted out of the committee for confirmation. Had a subcommittee handled the matter it might have been bottled up for considerably longer.[1626]

The Senate confirmation was a given, but the trick was to get the nomination out of committee. Of course, the true question isn't whether Roosevelt was confirmed by sleight-of-hand, or even if this was instigated by the White House. It is whether the second son would have received the rank if his name had been Joe Blow. His commanders said so, but the nation was far from convinced.

General Arnold and his staff had included Elliott on the list because he was, in their estimation, excellent at what he did. We have seen how helpful he had been in some of the historic operations the Air Force executed in 1944. He already claimed about 300 combat flight hours and a stack of medals, foreign and domestic.

As early as June 1944, when Elliott had come back from Russia, Drew Pearson noticed that he technically rated at flag rank:

> Elliott is now in London, and his superior officers say he is in a position where he rates the rank of brigadier general if he wants it. Elliott went into the air forces at Wright Field in 1940 at a time when people sometimes jeered at him on the streets or whistled "I Want to Be a Captain, Too." Since then, he was active in North Africa for a long time, briefly in Italy, and now in England, where he has been popular and respected. However, both his father and mother have turned thumbs down on the idea of his becoming a brigadier general.[1627]

The rank of brigadier – "light general" – was appropriate to that of a wing commander. In the USAAF, as opposed to the RAF, a wing was higher than a group, and was normally commanded by a colonel or a brigadier. While brigadiers were rare in the pre-war Air Corps, by 1945 they were, if not a dime a dozen, certainly very numerous.

In contrast, Arnold had only three full (four-star) generals under him, and thirteen lieutenant generals, who ran the numbered air forces. There was nothing suspect in allowing Colonel Roosevelt to end the war as a lowly brigadier. Of course, in common civilian usage, all the starred ones are "generals."

On the other hand, Roosevelt clearly had some issues. Margaret Suckley overheard that he had rubbed an important person the wrong way, but that is an understatement. Suckley's diary account on 22 January 1945 states:

> He [FDR] was, he said, thoroughly mad about this affair of Elliott Roosevelt having his wings removed, etc. He feels it is obviously "politics" on someone's part. He mentioned some man on whose toes Elliott had stepped, etc. I don't blame him for getting mad, and I get furious myself, that his energy should be wasted on all these small personal things.[1628]

Trouble did indeed follow Elliott like a big faithful dog. The Blaze investigation reached all the way to the 325th PRW, where evidently a minor hell of investigations and inspections ensued. In part on his own initiative, Elliott was relieved of command from 17 to 22 January 1945: "The Inspector General himself came down to my headquarters, expecting to find I do not know what."[1629]

Elliott's promotion had brought out the fact that he had mysteriously received his wings without meeting the physical and educational criteria therefore. And by now he had made his share of enemies in the service.

Elliott had blindsided Hap Arnold directly to FDR in order to get the F-11 funded. In the same connection, he had defied, even defiled, a number of high-ranking officers in the procurement chain. He had gone around General Doolittle to protest his allocation of British aircraft to his unit. And while he might be innocent in the Blaze affair, his actions had had the effect of hanging Major General George, a heavy hitter, out to dry on Capitol Hill. Bureaucrats have elephant memories, and you annoy them at your peril.

Interestingly, in 1944 it did not seem to have hurt his military standing that his family and financial life lurched from one crisis to another, and that he was an admirer of Marshal Stalin. That might have been the last year that would be true.

Having weighed the costs, a defiant FDR signed off on his son's promotion shortly before he left for Yalta on January 22. Faye stayed at the White House. Elliott wrote:

> He [FDR] told my wife that he was convinced I rated the promotion, and that was that. Firmly he signed his approval of the list and sent it on to the Senate, and promptly he wrote me a letter telling me what he had done and explaining that he wanted the Senate to decide whether the confidence of my commanding general was justified. I stuck my fingers in my ears, and waited. Sure enough, another Congressional investigation.[1630]

Popular wisdom held that Elliott's Air Force career had been nepotistically accelerated. In the crudest sense, that is untrue. He earned his way. But things aren't quite as simple as that in the military. The reason Elliott received opportunities, visibility, and acclaim was clearly that he was the president's son. Thousands of other exceptional officers did not receive the same recognition, regardless of their contributions. And there is, unfortunately, incontrovertible evidence that the president intervened for his son.

Senator Ferguson expressed the views of many when he mused to Gen. Roosevelt:

> ...in no other instance had there been a case of one in that situation rising during this war to the rank of brigadier general. There was one other case cited to me of a man who had had considerable civilian flying experience, and he was promoted to a brigadier general, but was killed before the promotion arrived. That did give me pause when I was told that there were 2,000 graduates of West Point of captain or other rank who had not achieved your military preeminence. [1631]

Ferguson was probably referring to Brig. Gen. William H. Eaton, assistant chief of the Mediterranean AAF, who was in the same class of 78 nominated colonels. He was killed in an air crash in France before the Senate confirmed him. A graduate of Harvard Law School, Eaton was an experienced civilian pilot who entered the service as a captain in 1942, thus blazing an even more extraordinary but ultimately tragic trail.[1632]

Another fair comparison is with Colonel Karl Polifka, who after a highly distinguished reconnaissance career in the Pacific was transferred to the Mediterranean to take command after Colonel Roosevelt. Yet Polifka's heroic war record (he was killed in Korea) is probably only remembered by reconnaissance aficionados.

Colonel Paul Cullen, a leader in reconnaissance, also missed out on a star during the war, although he did much of Elliott's heavy lifting. As he said, "I got Elliott his star."[1633]

Jimmy Stewart is a similarly meteoric case. He was an aviation fanatic who flew a Stinson before the war. He entered as a private, and by the end of the war commanded a bomb wing of the 8th Air Force. But he was still only a colonel. (He later made brigadier in the Reserves.)

Questioning Elliott's Roosevelt's career would be to question the judgment of his bosses, Doolittle, Spaatz, and Arnold, leaders with a semi-divine status to this day. The Air Corps expanded by almost two orders of magnitude in those years. There were essentially three kinds of operational air force officers: those who died, those who were cashiered, and those who rose rapidly. In this new world, only raw results counted, while the paper-pushers and heelclickers who thrive in peacetime armies were quickly shunted aside. Arnold's diary summed it up: "I miss Elliott Roosevelt. Must get another photo guy."[1634] Arnold was in England at the time (7 September 1943), while Elliott was in the States.

Elliott's commanders also had to consider the fact that he was personally familiar, even friends, with the Big Three and the Combined Chiefs. Since he was hanging out with the big ones at the summits, and with a word to Dad could cause a lot of trouble, it must have seemed extra reasonable to give him at least the "training" star.

And yet... with Elliott, there is seemingly always a hidden corollary. Forgotten correspondence shows that President Roosevelt did indeed put his thumb on the scales.

"The less said about this the better...."

With FDR's little plots, there is seldom a smoking gun left; but often a lot of smoke. In this case, thick smoke was preserved in General Carl Spaatz's personal correspondence, now in the Library of Congress.

Barely had Colonel Roosevelt returned to his command in January 1945 before word got back to Washington that he was very unhappy. What he was unhappy about was much theorized about. It is clear that Elliott contacted his boss, General Doolittle, and told him he was fed up with the Air Forces, and he would like to take a new assignment, such as with the Office of Strategic Services (OSS). In the highest offices, this touched off an Elliott crisis which predated the Blaze debacle by just a few days.

We shall have to let the principals speak for themselves. It seems that by 15 January, General Arnold had heard – probably both from above and below – that Elliott wanted out, and this caused broad consternation. He wrote to Spaatz for clarification:

> This Elliott Roosevelt matter, as you might surmise, is a very muchly discussed case.
>
> Naturally all are trying to find out what is in back of this change of attitude. You state, "He has done an outstanding job both in the Mediterranean and here. The organization he has established is now functioning smoothly and no longer needs his driving ability," and then you also state, "E.R. has requested that he be relieved from his assignment in command of the Photographic Wing and desires to return to U.S." These things are so much in variance with his attitude when he was over here that naturally people are wondering what is in back of it... [1635]

In other words, Spaatz had indicated that he could do without Elliott now. But Arnold had heard more at home:

> ... information here indicates that he wants to transfer to OSS... Naturally, before this is accepted, people want to know why he wants to go to OSS and I can't answer that – why he wants to get out of photographic work which has been his hobby so long – why he wants to get out of an organization in which he had done so well and made such a record for himself. I can answer none of these things. The question was put to me as to whether he was trying to get out because he had not been promoted. That apparently stuck out as a possible motive more than the fact that he was not made a pilot.
>
> In view of the fact that I am besieged by questions, is it not possible for you to give me a little bit of the low-down on this case so that I will know what to say next and what to do next?
>
> P.S. I have pumped Barney Giles dry. [Arnold's deputy]

In other words, Arnold was aware that Elliott thought he deserved both a star and wings. He probably did not know that Elliott was also angry over not having been allowed to go with his father to Yalta. Arnold had to do something to placate him, or have a disgruntled president's son on his hands. And Arnold had always carefully covered his Elliott flank.

On the 17th, the Blaze affair exploded across the front pages back home. That day Elliott's request was met and he was relieved of his command. As Margaret Suckley confided to her diary, his father was furious. On the 20th, the ailing president presided over his fourth, toned-down inaugural; and Elliott was officially rated a pilot under personnel order #5, issued by U.S. Air Forces in Europe on 20 January 1945. Next day FDR defiantly included his son on the promotion list, and then he left for Yalta. Case closed, as far as FDR was concerned.

There seems to have been near-panic in Air Force headquarters, for on the 21st, General Giles wrote Spaatz in more blunt terms:

> Since my return there has been considerable pressure from very high topside to make Elliott a pilot, which you were ordered to do. FYI, he is on the next list for promotion and I anticipate some trouble in Congress. This too came about as a result of considerable pressure... [1636]

It seems that FDR had reacted to Elliott's tantrum by ordering Arnold to make him a pilot, as well as a brigadier. "Very high topside," when uttered by Giles/Arnold can only mean FDR or God; Marshall did not exert "pressure" for personal reasons. So there is no doubt that the Air Force was pressured by the White House to please Elliott. The more delicate issue was whether the pressure was bureaucratically justified. Giles continued:

> In view of the foregoing, I believe it would be desirable to keep him on his present job as Commander of his reconnaissance wing, at least until such time as the boiling pot simmers down a bit. FYI, the promotion to brigadier general is not out of line since Doolittle, you and General Eisenhower recommended that he be promoted last May and this was concurred in by General Arnold. It was thought at that time by the War Department that it would be unwise to bring up his promotion in view of the coming election. Since election is now over and the inauguration completed, I believe his promotion will go through but with some difficulty…

Since Giles was speaking in confidence to Spaatz, it's clear that despite the public uproar, the top brass thought Elliott's promotion legitimate if not uninfluenced. But that logic did not extend to his wings:

> Insofar as the pilot rating is concerned, this is very much out of line because according to the flight surgeon's records, Elliott has a visual acuity of 20/200 correctable to 20/20 with glasses. I recommend that you place a limited restriction on his flying, requiring that he have at least one extra pair of glasses while perfoming duty as a pilot. This is just in case something happens, you will be covered.
>
> The least said about this whole transaction, the better and I will keep you informed on developments.

Bluntly speaking, the president had forced the Air Force to make his son a rated pilot, and now everyone had to keep it secret. The top knew that Elliott did not meet the requirements – vision being only one of them.

And that settled the matter. On the very next day, Colonel Roosevelt was reinstated in his command. The substitute, General Charles Banfill, had served as 325th wing commander for only six days. Spaatz told Doolittle to keep a close eye on Elliott's administrative performance.

A week later, General Spaatz answered Arnold:

> …as you know he officially requested General Doolittle to release him from his command of his Photographic Wing, and I understand stated privately to a number of his friends that he was fed up with the Air Forces and wanted to do something else. So far as I can determine, this was practically entirely the result of the fact that he had never been rated as a pilot. I think he honestly felt that an injustice had been done him and also the fact that he was not a rated pilot was affecting his standing with his organization. This last feeling, I think, existed mostly in Elliott's mind. The fact that he had not been promoted was very secondary.
>
> In any case, as I told you in my cable, the matter is now settled to everybody's satisfaction. Elliott has his command back, General Banfill is A-2 of the 8th Air Force, and as soon as the dog question is settled, there should be no further Roosevelt trouble. Incidentally, in accordance with Barney's request, we have forwarded him a full report by cable covering all we know about the sad story of the dog.

For the Air Force, there would indeed be no more Roosevelt trouble for a few months.[1637] And when trouble did break out again, the generals smartly covered their butts and denied presidential pressure. That's a classic bureaucratic dilemma: "The boss made me do it" is no defense. An officer has to "take responsibility" for his acts, meaning that if necessary, he has to lie to protect the top.

Elliott had no doubt whatsoever that he always got less, or later, than he was due. In his Senate testimony, new evidence about General Marshall's attitude was introduced:

> Mr. ROOSEVELT. I have been informed by a member of General Marshall's staff that that promotion was turned back twice after it had been sent through, originated by General Doolittle, approved by General Spaatz, and approved by General Eisenhower. It was turned back for the following reasons…
>
> Senator FERGUSON.. You mean that it was turned back twice, as Senator Brewster stated?
>
> Mr. ROOSEVELT. Before it was sent to the Senate, sir. The reason why it was rejected by the War Department was that it was very unusual for a man who to as rapidly rise in rank as myself, and that in view of the fact that I was the son of the President – if it had been anyone else, it would have been perfectly alright – but in view of that fact that I was the son of the President, he felt that it would be embarrassing to the President of the United States to have to forward my name to the United States Senate where it would undoubtedly become the cause of a political campaign against him.

This means that General Marshall delayed the promotion until after the November 1944 election.

> He did it twice, and it was on the insistence, the third time, of General Spaatz to him, that I was in the position that should be occupied by a Brigadier General and that I had occupied that position since 1943, January of 1943, under his command; that he felt that I could do a better job; and I would like to state for the record that I was familiar on several occasions with the fact that action was initiated for my promotion earlier while I was in the theater of operations and that I demanded of General Spaatz, General Doolittle, and General Eisenhower that it should not be sent through. They chose to send it through when I was out of the theater, and it was acted upon against my expressed wishes.[1638]

We know that wasn't true. Spaatz had instead done what "very high topside" had told him to do. This appears to be the last word on Elliott's star. If he received undue advantage, it was not his fault. Mostly.

War Hero or Impostor?

Human courage is a very strange thing. For fear of losing face, untold thousands willingly storm beaches and charge into a hail of lead. But of these, only a tiny fraction is willing to tell the truth if it might hurt their careers. The soldier who will do "the right thing" in the face of threats and pressure is rarer than the deserter on the battlefield.

Likewise, leadership – the ability to make people follow someone else's judgment instead of their own – is often a mystery. Madness is not a prerequisite for it, but it may help, as it did for that quintessential leader, Adolf Hitler. Somehow, the extremely eccentric Winston Churchill had it. And it was almost a genetic marker for the Roosevelts.

But magnetism also has a negative pole. If the human iron filings align themselves ecstatically with the leader's force-field, there will still be many others who are every bit as violently repelled. Who has the truth? In history, that depends on who wins.

The result of this paradox of courage and leadership is that – especially in the military – two parallel versions of "truth" tend to develop. The official reality usually pretends that all is right with the world, especially the chain of command. The other truth is often heard after a few beers at the bar. It is frequently one of vicious rumors, petty vindictiveness, and assumed conspiracies. And it is sometimes a tad closer to reality.

In war, Elliott Roosevelt continued to cast two shadows.

Brother Jimmy, whose heroism in the Pacific nobody doubts, wrote long afterwards:[i]

> Elliott had an outstanding record in the war. The truth of the matter is that my brother Elliott was probably the bravest of all the members of our family. He personally flew unarmed planes over the most dangerous enemy territory in spite of a handicap of very poor eyesight. He was never willing to ask any of the men under his command to do anything he had not done himself, and I have had countless hundreds of people come up to me and tell me what an inspirational leader he was. I have also been told, but he will not talk about it, that Elliott performed some extraordinary heroic feats behind the enemy line in southern Europe. He certainly earned his rank of Brigadier General.[1639]

This must be a good part of the truth, but it is also not the whole truth. Elliott had indeed inherited his father's ability to inspire with enthusiasm and optimism. Although cynics call that bullshit, bullshit is known as leadership when delivered with conviction and energy. One can easily picture Elliott exhorting his pilots: "You have nothing to fear but fear itself!"

C.R. Smith knew Elliott well and offered a diplomatic sketch of him:

> I think really Elliott reached his peak during the war. He was a damn good officer. Very capable man. Ran a good outfit – he had a photographic outfit most of the time. But he learned to fly and he was a pretty good pilot, had lots of courage. Did a lot of good jobs for the Air Force. And I don't think he ever did as well after that as he did in the Army. He was an excellent officer.[1640]

Speaking in 1978, C.R. said he would not have thought that from what he'd seen of him in the 1930s:

> I don't think Elliott took things very seriously in the pre-war period. He took things very seriously in the war period, paid attention to his job and got it done and turned out very well. When he came out of the Army, I don't think he knew what he wanted to do or how he was going to do it. I still think a lot of him. I don't see him very often. His daughter is my god-child [Ruth Chandler] …[1641]

Perhaps Elliott was among those who perform well under pressure when provided with the necessary structure and expectations, but flounder when left to their own devices. But as with the president, the real question is what lay behind the jaunty smile and the confident claims of success. And there, as so often before, opinions of Elliott varied widely.

While the official narrative (backed up by commentaries by Arnold, Spaatz, Doolittle, and Eisenhower) glorified Elliott's extraordinary bravery, competence, effectiveness, and resourcefulness, many of his subordinates fulminated against him

---

[i] Jimmy was a "Carlson's Raider." Despite poor health, in August 1942 JR participated (and performed gallantly) in the bloody but useless Makin Island raid, launched by Marines landing from submarines.

almost to the point of a homicidal rage. This sentiment was seldom published (although after the war a few gripes came out, incidental to the political climate). Most of it seems to have simmered along the veterans' grapevine. When committed to paper, a thick stack of it found its way to Old Nemesis – Westbrook Pegler.[1642]

These poison letters have to be viewed with the utmost caution. Many of them exaggerate known issues, and some can be disproved. However, when the accusations independently corroborate each other, it's time to take notice. Some of Pegler's military correspondents intended to work up to a court-martial of General Roosevelt, but far more begged to remain anonymous out of fear of what the system could do to them, their retirement pay, or their taxes. Nonetheless, they were united in their scorn for Elliott and their certainty that his wartime record was at least partially fraudulent.

Before delving into these accusations let us affirm what this investigation has revealed: Elliott more than paid his dues in the war. Whatever else he was, he was not a coward or a shirker. The trouble seems to arise from what he was doing in his spare time.

Instead, this dispute provides valuable insight into what was really going on in the military, and it reminds us that soldiers often spent as much time trying to "get" each other as the enemy. As a representative example, consider a testimony taken from an informer who said he served with Elliott. The informer's name was stated, but he insisted on anonymity, so let him be X:

> These notes may make it possible to disprove Elliott Roosevelt's contention that he had 470 hours of combat time while he was serving in the Army Air Corps in Europe…
>
> 1. Elliott's appointment as commanding officer of the wing was wrong, in the first place, because Army regulations say a commanding officer must be able to do anything his men can do – and Roosevelt couldn't fly a plane until the war was almost over. The first that the men at the base knew he could fly a P-38 – the type of plane which this particular outfit used for most of its photo work – was in March 1945 when Roosevelt landed one on the field.
> 2. Until then, he had a personal pilot, Col. John Hoover of Cresson, Pa., who piloted Elliott's private plane, a Cessna C-78, sometimes called a Bobcat, the number of which was 332082….
> 3. Elliott did most of his flying in this Cessna and in a Flying Fortress which was assigned to him for his personal use. Elliott used the Flying Fortress for trips back to the United States ostensibly on business, but X said every time Elliott made one of these "business trips" the base heard that he was seeing Faye. "Faye" in this case was Faye Emerson, whom he later married. Elliott had the Flying Fortress "redecorated." For instance, X said, he was assigned to paint the interior blue, an odd color for an army plane. The Flying Fort also had built-in bunk beds and a stove.
> 4. X said that Elliott usually used the Cessna when he flew to Paris – as he did often – and this is one way to refute Elliott's contention that he had that many combat hours. The Cessna was unarmed, slow and it would have been suicide to take it over enemy territory. (X explained that combat time was measured from the minute a plane left its home base for a trip over "dangerous territory" until it returned.) Elliott didn't begin making his weekend excursions to Paris until France was safely in Allied hands, thus he was not flying over "dangerous territory." Incidentally, X said Elliott spent more time in France, after France fell, than he did in England, where he was stationed.

5. X said that Elliott returned from these weekend flying trips to Paris with women and champagne, but, he added, this was not unusual because several officers, including many generals, did the same thing. X said he did not criticize Roosevelt on these two counts.
6. As far as X knows, he said, Elliott was only on one "combat" mission. In that case, he flew as an "observer" on a four hour flight over relatively safe territory. X said he was willing to supply names of people who could corroborate what he says, but he didn't know whether they would. Many of them, he said, are indebted to Roosevelt for "fast" promotion and easy war jobs.[1643]

Some of these "sour grapes" accusations are valid. *Newsweek* magazine looked into some details at the time and found:

> He was rated a pilot under personnel order #5, issued by U.S. Air Forces in Europe on January 20, 1945. This order was signed by Carl Spaatz under authority of a cable from Washington. The pilot rating was given as a result of the training he acquired in Africa and Europe. He piloted his own plane on 30 missions and had to his credit 1,100 flying hours, 300 of them in combat.
>
> N.B. War ended in Europe May 1945. 30 missions in 90 days is more than any single pilot made.[1644]

The notabene does exude skepticism. As we saw, the Spaatz papers indicate that Arnold was under pressure from "very high topside" to "wing" Elliott. As Ms. Suckley noted, the president was livid that his son's wings had been "taken away" during the uproar over his promotion.[1645]

Yet with his long experience in the air in both civilian and military capacities, Elliott was surely the kind of person who was entitled to some bureaucratic leeway. The complaints about his pilot wings are a bit querulous and probably would not have occurred if he had not otherwise attracted hostility.

The complaint that Elliott had no "true" combat experience is false and malicious. He repeatedly sought out combat in North Africa and Italy, where he flew with rated pilots. From England, he flew missions to check out new reconnaissance techniques. General Doolittle tried to keep Elliott from risking his life.

Nevertheless, Elliott was publicly reported to have led one mission over the Rhineland on 24 March.[1646] On that flight, which covered the American airborne landings across the Rhine at Wesel (Operation VARSITY), he was accompanied by Colonel Johnny Hoover and Captain Robert Facer of the 13th PRS.[1647]

On 7 April, five days before he was called back to the States, Colonel Roosevelt led yet another mission deep into Germany, to the Halle and Eisleben area. Hoover was with him again, along with the now obligatory fighter escort. The flight encountered rocket interceptors, the new Me-163s.[1648]

The dilemma was a common one: subordinates will not respect and follow an officer who does not lead from up front. Yet, a general officer in intelligence, surveillance, and reconnaissance – as well as the president's son – is not somebody you can risk repeatedly over enemy territory. (In particular, those few trusted officers who knew the ULTRA secret were banned from exposing themselves to possible capture.)

"470 combat hours" may mean that Elliott padded his account; or it could just be that the long, boring oceanic patrols in 1941-42 gave him a head start. Thirty combat sorties in 90 days would have been extreme for an American pilot. Certainly only a small fraction of that time was spent in contested airspace, but that was true for others as well.

A month before he left for his father's funeral, on a day when he flew over Cologne, he wrote his mother: "I have about 25 more combat hours to do to reach 400 and I will have flown about 75 missions in all at that time." He was keen to rack up his numbers, but for the first time felt a "pit in his stomach" when launching on a sortie. He had a common affliction, "short-termer-itis," with a bride back home and a great reluctance to be the last one to die.[1649]

Yet less than six weeks later he claimed 89 missions and 470 hours, "a figure which two young lieutenants, each of whom was shot down three times, have marveled at since. They insisted that they knew of no PR pilot with that many combat hours and regarded Elliott's figures as phenomenal and incredible."[1650]

Thus we are stuck at some indeterminate point within the probability cloud, between two extremes, inhabited by the haters and the flunkies respectively. That kind of ambiguity wasn't unheard of during the war. Plenty of officers weren't quite on the straight and narrow, and came home as heroes nonetheless.

The ceaseless complaints about Elliott always making sure to live in luxury and debauchery, even at the front, must have some element of truth simply by reason of weight and volume. But many high-ranking officers played that game to the maximum. Elliott's superiors knew that and dismissed the concern. They were asking a lot of their soldiers, and it was hard to tell them not to blow off steam.

After the liberation of Paris, Elliott spent much time there, nominally at SHAEF, the supreme allied headquarters. Less nominally, he was having fun. The Wing recorded that due to the prominence of its commander, many famous and important people transited and often caught flights with the auxiliary aircraft, courtesy of Colonel Roosevelt. On one of these junkets on 26 October, the Wing's B-25, *Miss Nashville,* took Lorelle Hearst, wife of William Randolph Hearst, Jr., to Paris. Bill and Lorelle were both war correspondents; they would soon divorce. Bill said his buddy Elliott entertained Lorelle for two weeks, and that "her war experience was with the good-looking guys of Elliott's unit." The aircraft crashed shortly after delivering her, leading to rumors of Mrs. Hearst's demise.[1651]

Painted jet-black, that aircraft, F-10 tail nr. 42-53357, had flown a number of the night photography missions for which Elliott had been commended. It was reputedly the 8th Air Force's only B-25.

Lorelle Hearst, a former showgirl, dabbled in news reporting for the Hearst chain. This gave her the chance to hang out with professional celebrities and socialite friends. Among them were – by the way – Joe Kennedy, Jr., and Sylvia Ashley, whose party Elliott was at when he was told his father had died.

One letter-writer stated, along with much other hearsay:

> Elliott Roosevelt was quite famous for his parties. These parties were frequent and quite "wet" and of course were not for enlisted men. To provide adequate irrigation for these soirees, Elliott requisitioned a B-25 plane for his use to fly to Cairo for the sole purpose of obtaining liquor. My informant was one of the many American soldiers who were detailed from time to time to go on these missions to load and unload cases of liquor; of course Army gasoline was used, but I am not informed who paid for the liquor.
>
> My informant states that the only time Elliott Roosevelt himself ever flew in his much publicized P-38 photographic plane was one time he flew "piggy-back." My informant stated "Elliott Roosevelt just wasn't in the war." Of course my informant was bitter about a review which was held in honor of FDR when he stopped to visit Elliott…[1652]

The charges about liquor-smuggling fit with many other independent accusations. But the non-combat accusation is manifestly untrue. It is likely that his enemies seized on Elliott's lack of time in the single-seat P-38 until he had his rating in 1945.

When it comes to the criminal charges, General Roosevelt probably deserves less leeway. Several embittered officers complained that Elliott's medals were fraudulently obtained. One (Major J.E. Benoit), who actually wrote the citation, later noted that the DFC was given based on flights in Greenland and Africa in peacetime and for five missions as a passenger after the North African invasion:

> I had a hell of a time writing the citation and had to do it 4 times before 12th AF would take it. They asked me to write one "that would justify the award," on the theory that I was better acquainted with his record than anyone else, - but all that will prove is that the DFC was a Christmas gift. Harry Eidson (now step daddy to Elliott's children and living in Fort Worth), who was pilot on all five missions in Africa got the Air Medal for the same 5 flights.

Ill will embellishes the narrative here. Elliott's North Atlantic flights were in peacetime, but not his African mission. And he wasn't a "passenger," but an essential crewmember. But Benoit continued:

> The fraudulent procurement of the Air Medal for Elliott came by giving, as basis for the Air Medal award, 4 of the same 5 flights I mentioned in the preceding paragraph which already had been used as a basis for the award of the DFC. To prove fraud, testimony will be needed from myself and two others. Two of us protested the action and consequently are sure that he knew the Air Medal was not awardable for flight for which he had already been decorated.

Again, it may seem to the civilian that the writer is splitting hairs; but soldiers take their medals seriously. If they already loathe someone, his wearing of unearned colors may put them over the edge.

> Elliott still no doubt has many friends in the service who think it smart to do him favors and associate themselves with the Roosevelt name. This is one reason many of us are guarded in what we say and who we say it to…I am sorry to say that many of us who were associated with him never did know just why he was decorated in several instances. It might interest you that he was sometimes referred to as "The Demanding Officer of the European Theater," which is about the truth…[i]

Here we are getting closer to the real issue. Subordinates often hated Elliott because he was living it up, getting away with things, and running roughshod over his troops. One highly controversial episode occurred when Elliott court-martialed his own chief of staff and executive officer, Lt. Col. Alan M. Eldridge.

[i] Letter, Joseph E. Benoit to Pegler, 23 OCT 46, ER wartime file, Pegler collection, HH Lib. Benoit was a staff officer who said Elliott "actually ruined my military career." He retired to Tucson as a Lt. Col.

Medals and Ribbons and Wounds

Although medals are easily overstated as an index of merit, during his short service Elliott Roosevelt received not just the Legion of Merit and the DFC with oak leaf, but also the Croix de Guerre and the Legion d'Honneur from France; to boot, he was made a commander of the Order of the British Empire (OBE), a somewhat amusing honor in view of his oft-expressed loathing of that same establishment.

Patricia Roosevelt listed 27 decorations, but that counts assorted bling like oak leaf clusters, campaign ribbons, and add-on stars and palms. Elliott did not need to exaggerate his war record, but given his blustery nature, many thought that he did.[1653]

Of course, some medals are courtesy awards (usually the foreign ones), and some are routine awards for serving. For example, on 23 January 1943, Roosevelt received from the Sultan of Morocco the Order of Ouissam Alaouite – the royal order of al-Alaoui – but so did all the Allied commanders at the Casablanca summit.[1654]

General Eisenhower gave Roosevelt the Legion of Merit on Christmas Day 1943. This was a new medal invented to recognize the superior service of high-ranking officers and certain deserving foreigners. It took precedence over the DFC.[1655]

"With these baubles are men led," said Napoleon. It might seem infantile and demeaning – a cheap reification of your master's opinion – but it's the system. Despite grumbling among his men, Elliott Roosevelt was reported to have been "proud as a peacock" of his decorations, starting with the DFC.[1656]

Nonetheless, fifteen years later when Elliott careened into bankruptcy and lost all he owned, even the medals went. Wife nr. 5, Patricia, explained it thus:

> An old French vitrine cabinet of mahogany and heavily leaded crystal which had been the repository for Elliott's war medals, came [back] to us with six inches slashed from the delicately wrought legs with their bronze inlays, The medals were among the missing. Evidently they had been mislaid or disposed of by some insensitive person…Elliott had been the recipient of the Croix de Guerre, Distinguished Service Cross, Air Medal with twelve oak leaf clusters, Commander of the Order of the British Empire, to name but a few. A Purple Heart with three clusters signified each of the four times he was wounded.[1657]

That's where things get strange. Little of this matches official records.

Roosevelt's 1945 military certificate of service lists the Legion of Merit, DFC w/cluster, Air Medal w/cluster, Commander OBE, Legion d'Honneur, Croix de Guerre with Palm, the Moroccan medal, the pre-war American Defense Ribbon w/Star, and the American Theatre Ribbon: ETO W/11 Stars. Of all this confetti, among pilots it's the American and British DFCs that count. Elliott also noted in his 1945 testimony that he had been recommended for the Distinguished Service Medal, which he thought he was denied for political reasons. [1658] He mentioned no Purple Hearts. He received two Air Medals, normally indicating ten combat missions.[1659]

Despite later claims, there are no Army records supporting the claim that Elliott Roosevelt received the Purple Heart, or that he was wounded as a result of enemy action. In support of this finding, the National Personnel Records Center (NPRC) noted on 16 November 1990, evidently in response to Elliott's widow's request, that surviving documents show no evidence of wounds or of receiving the Purple Heart. His 1945 separation document explicitly states "NONE" for wounds received in action.

This matters in part because Mr. Roosevelt, towards the end of his life, attempted to obtain supplemental disability benefits based on injuries received during his military service. A rather voluminous correspondence survives between his representatives, the Veterans Administration, and Senator Mark Hatfield who was looking after Elliott, although technically the general was no constituent of the Oregon senator.[1660]

Elliott had been a sickly and disaster-prone child, and he put in much sick time in the service. He had a knee operation in 1942, and came back from his African tour with numerous diseases.[1661] Eleanor mentioned this (especially the piles) in several letters, but it was not the heroic war wound intimated by his Congressional defenders.[1662]

The combination of a bad knee and two parachute jumps, plus the crash landings, might have caused Elliott some discomfort, but not recorded wounds. Yet Elliott later created the general impression that he was wounded in combat several times. It is possible that the many episodes of prosaic illnesses registered during his service somehow grew, in his imagination, to become wounds received in action. To qualify for supplemental benefits, he did not need to prove this, however – only that some infirmity he suffered later in life was service-connected. But these efforts failed.

A Bloody Brawl over Purple Hearts

Lt. Col. Eldridge got his job as Elliott's operations officer after his predecessor, Col. Furman Limeburner, "who knows plenty," "couldn't stomach the goings on at Elliott's HQ and found himself another job." Limeburner had indeed filled in as commander of the 3rd PRG in the United States, and served as executive officer in England and North Africa until replaced on 15 December 1942.[1663]

Eldridge's problem was that he earned a Purple Heart while Elliott was fornicating in Hollywood.

It is odd that the Purple Heart should be so coveted. It is the most randomly earned medal. If a drunk earns some stitches in his butt for tripping over a broken bottle on his way to the air raid shelter, he gets to be a hero ever after.

As we have seen, Elliott desperately wanted that medal. By the vicissitudes of war, he was not wounded despite repeatedly running serious risks. Perhaps this explains his fury when he got back from the ZI in October 1943 and discovered his deputy, Eldridge, who was a non-flying administrative officer, wearing the purple ribbon - with one oak leaf cluster, at that. Pressed for an explanation, Eldridge said he had ordered up his medal himself in Elliott's absence. Witnesses confirmed he had received a knee injury during a German air attack on Algiers on 12 March, and a flesh wound during the invasion of Sicily. The fragment was introduced at the trial.[1664]

During Elliott's absence, operational command of the NAPRW fell to RAF Wing Commander Eric Fuller, but administrative control of the American units devolved on Eldridge. It was agreed that he did a fine job, and he earned the Legion of Merit for overseeing the production of the gigantic photo mosaics of Sicily and Calabria that preceded the Allied landings.

Eldridge, already 36, was a serious, nerdy professional who "didn't tolerate undue intimacy." He had been a civilian cartographer and became a specialist in creating maps from aerial photographs. Colonel Minton Kaye had spotted him and placed him in the 1st Mapping Group at Bolling Field. From there he got attached to Elliott's unit, landing in North Africa. He was eager to advance his craft, but he did not get along with the rowdy son of a president. He declined the offer to share Elliott's quarters, instead staying with others at the Bey's palace in Algiers.

Eldridge was asked how well he knew his boss. He testified:

> That is rather difficult to say. I know Colonel Roosevelt very well indeed, although I never became intimate with him…In Algiers [he] had an apartment on Rue Michelet and asked me if I wanted to move in with him. I told him I did not. I didn't feel I could stay in the same place with him and at the same time be an efficient Executive Officer. If he was going on the wrong track, I felt it was my duty to differ with him…for a period of one month I elected to live in the Bey's Palace with the officers of the Wing…After he moved to La Marsa, he said, "You will move up and live with me," which I did.
>
> We were so intimate that he came to my bedroom at 3:00 o'clock in the morning after he had returned from the United States, and he insisted on telling me in great detail the preparations he had made in the United States for his divorce, which I understand has now gone through.[1665]

Elliott came back on 21 October. Hardly anyone outside the family knew he had already decided to ditch Ruth and replace her with Faye. His chief of staff was a captive audience to his escapades, but it doesn't seem that Eldridge was impressed.

Just before Elliott had left in July, he had ordered Eldridge to accompany the Sicilian landings in order to find out how the troops were making use of the hard-won air imagery. Eldridge got ashore on day three and soon found that nobody had any pictures. Somehow everything had been lost. Trying hard to figure out what was going on, Eldridge hitched a jeep ride with a private and drove up the road a bit. They came under artillery fire and the officer took a piece of shrapnel in his left upper arm. After first aid, Eldridge went back to La Marsa to organize delivery of the needed reconnaissance products. He did not say he'd been wounded because he wanted to go back to Sicily to continue his mission, which he did. A few days later he had a doctor remove the fragment from his arm. Apparently shy about beating his own drum, Eldridge months later had orders drawn up for the medal, without obtaining all the supporting paperwork. And that was why Colonel Eldridge, technically a paper-pusher, showed up on base one day with the offending ribbon on his shirt.

Everyone seemed to have a high opinion of the man's work. He had a stack of commendations, and Wing Commander Fuller said he was an excellent officer. To most, the ribbon didn't seem to be an issue.

But not all was as it seemed. Eldridge and others had written up the chain that Elliott's hot pursuit of the Mosquito was unnecessary and that the newer F-5As provided equivalent service. Worse, it was said that Eldridge had suggested that Roosevelt had obtained his DFC and subsequent Air Medal without meeting the criteria therefore.[1666]

It was not smart to make an enemy of Elliott Roosevelt. On 5 November, Eldridge was detained, and on the 11th Elliott preferred charges against his own chief of staff for unlawfully procuring and wearing a medal. Elliott said Eldridge hadn't been wounded at all. Eldridge said Elliott himself had asked him to draw up orders for the Purple Heart after the first injury. One of them lied.

The court-martial took place on 22 January 1944 in Foggia, Italy. Elliott, the accuser, was in England, but Eldridge testified ably and persuasively in his own behalf. He was found guilty of reduced charges. The court reprimanded him and fined him

$600. Clearly the panel didn't want to really hurt him, but the judges had to do something. His injuries were real, but he hadn't filed the right paperwork. Unheard of!

Two years later, columnist Westbrook Pegler began to hear ugly stories about the case. Because of the vicious rumors Pegler collected, there was no alternative for a fair researcher but to obtain the dossier of the case from NPRC, and this section is based on that material as well as the letters to Pegler.[1667]

After returning to the States, Lt. Col. Alan Eldridge in turn plotted to secure Elliott's own court martial. He wrote Pegler:

> The only reason that I want no active part in your action against him is that I am looking forward to meeting him in a General Court Martial – his. Make no mistake about him, though – the man is dangerous. Dangerous because he is just stupid enough to be influenced by a clever person without ever realizing it.[1668]

The lawyer who assisted Eldridge in 1943 said that the latter was arrested at Casablanca and brought back to Tunis "where he was dumped into a military police area on the waterfront along with every common drunk and petty miscreant." With the deputy in jail, Colonel Polifka took over as Elliott's chief of staff. Perhaps Elliott had planned this when he took Polifka with him from Washington.

That Acting Staff Judge Advocate, Lt. Ludvick Zupancic, defended Eldridge. He was convinced he was innocent and was being railroaded for what he knew:

> I immediately found that he was trying to force a confession from the Colonel under promise of immunity. I stopped that. Roosevelt tried to get me to have Eldridge sign a confession. I laughed at him. Word filtered through to me that the "Boss" wanted to talk to me, but I avoided him. Several of his boot lickers, Colonels, of course, talked to me about it. Finally I was sent for. I was offered a return trip home. I had been overseas about a year and a half by then, and I had a lovely bride of five weeks waiting. I was offered a promotion to Captain. It had been held up many months on account of this thing – all if I would withdraw from the case. I refused. Elliott was sitting. I was standing – like the ram rod, you know – he is giving it to me right and left, and I am "sirring" the hell out of him.
>
> He goes something like this: "You know, Lieutenant, you seem to forget who I am. I am not only a Colonel and your Commanding Officer, I am also the son of the President of the United States of America. What I do and don't do is of tremendous interest to the Allied Forces. As CO I have seen fit to court martial a member of this outfit. You, one of my subordinate officers have undertaken to defeat my purpose. That will look very bad to outsiders. I can't afford to be embarrassed."
>
> When I mentioned that the defendant had the right to choose counsel and that he, the CO had already issued orders naming me Defense Counsel, he yelled, "Let's not get technical, are you going to withdraw voluntarily?"
>
> I said, "No-sir," and he hollers, "Then I order you to sever all connections with the case." He was purple.
>
> His order, of course, was illegal. You don't have to obey an illegal order. But woe to the man who willfully disobeys an order of his CO in a combat zone. Punishment is quick. Questions may be asked much later.
>
> I talked to my friends about it. I got no consolation there. I went down to see the Judge Advocate General of the Air Force, an officer I knew well. He told me that the Order was illegal, but that if he were in my place there was no doubt about what he would do. He would withdraw, and he continued, "If you quote me, I will call you a God-damned liar."

> I did withdraw…I turned over all my papers, etc. to a new man appointed by the Air Force….There are a thousand things the swine did which you ought to know about.[1669]

After he conducted the initial defense, Zupancic was reassigned adjutant for 5th PRG on 23 November, and another advocate took over.[1670] If Zupancic's story is true, Roosevelt deliberately destroyed his deputy's career and then issued an illegal order to protect himself. He was successful.

Viewed in that perspective, it seems that Lt. Col. Eldridge had incurred the enmity of his boss and paid for it with his career. While he had failed to comply fully with regulations, thus forcing the Army to find him guilty, it is clear that the real motivating force behind the case was Elliott's determination to remove an officer who had seen through him and could have caused him trouble.

Courts-martials are serious matters that take the time and efforts of many high-ranking officers. They should be avoided except in the last resort. In truth, they are often used to carry out vendettas against designated sacrificial goats; and perhaps even more often, they are *not* used in those cases where an impartial observer unbeholden to the hierarchy would see a clear justification therefore. A number of people evidently believed Colonel Roosevelt to be in the latter category of deservings.

The saga of the Purple Hearts will obtain some added significance when we get to Elliott's old-age claims of wartime wounds.

Mysterious Sidelines

Another embittered correspondent told Westbrook Pegler:

> Elliott Roosevelt held an appointment as an observer when he first ventured to North Africa. In fact he did what is called "student flying" in North Africa. It was at this time while flying a Haviland Mosquito belonging to a South African Boer unit that he crashed into a group of Spitfires parked on the air field…And again, Elliott Roosevelt had a large number of bitter enemies in the commissioned & non-commissioned personnel. Many more than the public is aware of.[1671]

Here we happen to know that two parked Spitfires did get written off in a landing accent, and Roosevelt did lose control of the Mosquito on landing. But such occurrences were not so uncommon.[1672]

The bitterest enemies seemed to focus on Elliott's lifestyle – his appropriation of the most palatial accommodations in the area for himself, evicting others and letting his grunts sleep in tents; his use of his personal aircraft to procure liquor and women; his stealing of another unit's air conditioned trailer for his own comfort; and even the princely treatment his soldiers were ordered to give his dogs.

Probably the most extreme charge fell in the category of racketeering. Allegedly, Elliott frequently sent an accomplice to Cairo to buy gold. The gold was flown back to Algiers in the B-25 and sold in an arbitrage scheme.

> Elliott sent one man to Cairo frequently. Was it Bruce Cabbot? It was said to be an ex movie actor. They had a big deal on in Cairo, where gold was plentiful. It was purchased there, hauled on US planes to Algiers across international boundary lines and there sold for Algerian francs. The frank was low at that time, and a profit was made by exchanging the

> francs at a finance office for British pounds. The pounds then went to Cairo for more gold. This three-way trade continued until they were supposed to have been going to get a million bucks on the next trip, but the CID (Counter-Intelligence) stepped in. Shortly thereafter, Elliott was transferred to a new outfit and was promoted to Col. Cabbot was demoted one or two ranks, but the whole deal was kept quiet.[1673]

This referred to the actor Bruce Cabot, who was indeed the ATC operations officer in Tunis (at the same time Elliott was there) and got into a criminal problem (which was not unusual for him). Having enlisted in December 1942, Lt. Cabot was quietly mustered out and came back to make movies in June 1944. There is no court-martial record for Cabot at NPRC.[i] The omni-sexual boozer Cabot had been Errol Flynn's best friend in California. He was in the Hollywood group Johnny Meyer provided with "dates."[1674]

The smuggling story was only partially confirmed by yet another ATC officer, L. Fletcher Prouty, who wrote that he was one of the pilots who helped apprehend Bruce Cabot for the counterintelligence corps. But he said nothing about Elliott's complicity. Prouty met him at RAF Habbaniya, Mesopotamia during the airlift for the Teheran summit. Flying a Lockheed Lodestar, he was taking the Chinese delegation back to Teheran, and at the fuel stop took the opportunity to meet with Elliott and Leon Gray, an old friend. Elliott told Prouty he was going to Teheran because his father wanted him to meet Marshal Stalin. Prouty did apparently not know anything about Elliott's alleged smuggling activities, though he knew Cabot was involved in the gold racket.[ii]

What can one make of the smuggling accusation, which if true should have landed Elliott in jail? With him, it is difficult to make any single charge stick. It is the accumulation of evidence from many quarters that raises suspicion that they could be closer to the truth than were Elliott's high-ranking protectors.

One well-informed observer who straddled the fence was Constance Babington Smith of the WAAF. She said that Elliott:

> …often behaved in a carefree manner which seemed to ask for adverse comments, and at this time he did in fact jokingly refer to himself as 'the black sheep of the family.' He also blithely ignored opinion and feelings within the service when he wanted to get things done. One of his friends once said about him, 'He didn't know how to use official channels, and he didn't need to;' but the things his enemies have said about him are mostly unprintable.[1675]

Then what explains the praise superiors heaped on General Roosevelt? His technical knowledge and inventiveness in reconnaissance should by no means be dismissed. We have seen how the newly minted General Eisenhower was quite entranced by Elliott's presentation of his Arctic adventures back in 1941 in Texas, and Ike was equally dependent on what Elliott could tell him about Russia or about his father's plans.

But there is another, more disturbing angle that touches on the great problem of having politically connected officers on your team. The generals all knew that Elliott

---

[i] NYT, 19 JUN 44. While some sources claim Cabot ran a gold-smuggling service, and Cabot was a friend of Elliott's, no allegation of Elliott's involvement could be found.

[ii] www.prouty.org, commentaries, publications, retr. 12 SEP 11. Prouty, who rose to high level in the black world, is controversial, not because of the data dots he remembers, but the conspiratorial way he connects them. What he personally saw, though, was the smuggling arrest of Mr. Cabot in Cairo in 1944.

could make or break them with a few words home. They all knew that there was much more to be gained by playing along than by causing trouble. General Arnold, as we have seen, may have been promoted back in 1934 in some small part because of a telegram Elliott sent to the White House. And we have seen how General Eisenhower agonized with Elliott over his chances of commanding OVERLORD, without openly begging.

Whatever one can make of that, it is clear that after FDR's death, suddenly not even General Doolittle could find any more use for Elliott Roosevelt.

So, war hero or impostor? The two are not mutually exclusive. Elliott was both, varying in degrees as time went on. It was his nature.

Winding Down the War

The history of Elliott Roosevelt's 325th PRW takes on a slight restlessness as 1944 turned into 1945. The German counteroffensive had been a shock, but afterwards the going got much easier, on the ground and in the air.

The winter weather significantly reduced reconnaissance activities, but so did the shrinking territory held by the enemy. Little effective opposition was met in the air, although the new German turbojets caused great apprehension. The Allies roamed at will, bombing and strafing increasingly worthless and pointless targets. Restraint was not in style on either side.

Still, it was hard to keep the men occupied. Efforts were made to provide them with recreation and suitable non-combat duties.

Elliott was home at Hyde Park for Christmas, when he took the opportunity to introduce wife nr. 3 to the family. That would be the last time Elliott saw his father alive. He was shocked to see how fast he was fading.

When the Ardennes Offensive broke on 16 December, Elliott was seriously concerned that his reconnaissance wing was "gravely remiss" for not warning of the surprising strength of the German attack. But upon reaching his post again in the new year, he determined that his unit had performed correctly, and that others were to blame for the debacle. Characteristically, he asserted:

> Only when my temporary duty in Washington was over, and I had flown back to the ETO, did I find that in fact our reconnaissance had been perfectly up to snuff, that the information on the massing of enemy troops behind the Ardennes had all been satisfactorily collated and passed on "through channels" – and then held up or ignored by an unthinking G-2 [intelligence] officer.[1676]

Elliott didn't make that up. A joint commission came to the conclusion that while the aircraft had obtained the necessary evidence, interpretation had been too fragmented to raise the warning that something was up. Further centralization of intelligence was – as usual – the proposed remedy.[1677] In retrospect, though, the Germans must have gotten better, too; ULTRA did not pick up the extent of the offensive.

In truth, blame was due everywhere, but perhaps especially on the weather. Without air cover, the Allies were suddenly not so superior to the Germans. And when the weather did improve one morning on 1 January 1945, the Luftwaffe launched its last all-out effort against Allied air bases. Operation *Bodenplatte* was a famous, serious setback for Allied air power; but it depleted the last German reserves, while RAF and USAAF units could barely keep pace with the constant flow of replacement aircraft, pilots, and equipment. After that date, the Allies had air dominance over Germany, and could essentially do whatever they liked in the air.

The winter offered a kind of uncomfortable transition for the Air Forces. Operational planners were thinking of how to handle the liberation of prisoners and the carrying out of occupation duties. Intelligence operatives became obsessed with catching German scientists and their products, preferably before their rivals. Generals were focused on how to shift their resources to the Pacific, but they also began thinking of how to prepare for new enemies. The alliance with the USSR was no longer held in high esteem in the military.

That March, the 325th PRW history recorded:

> Less than two weeks after the beginning of the month the whole Wing was shocked to hear of the tragic death of the Commander in Chief, Franklin D. Roosevelt. General Elliott Roosevelt, the commanding officer, heard the news while listening to the final broadcast of news. He immediately called a staff meeting for 3 A.M. and made preparation to return to the Z I. After making the announcement of his Father's death he appointed Leon W. Gray, commanding officer of the 25th Bomb Group (Rcn) as temporary commanding officer of the Wing. Lt. Col. John R. Hoover, A-3, was named temporary commanding officer of the 25th Bomb Group, and in his place was named Lt. Col. Lawrence S. McBee, Assistant A-3.
>
> The final days of the Nazis brought many operations of the Wing to a close and most action consisted of bringing existing operations to a successful conclusion and few new operations were started.
>
> The final squadrons left at Mt. Farm in the 7th PRG movement to Chalgrove were completed early in the month and a clean-up squad was left behind to put the station at Mt. Farm in perfect shape before it was taken over by the RAF personnel…
>
> The 27th Squadron, a part of the 7th Group, which has been on the continent for several months was visited by Lt. Col. McBee and Capt. Anderson and arrangements were made to move the squadron back to the U.K. where it will join its parent unit. [27th was at Denain/Prouvy in France from November 1944]
>
> A significant move to a large number of persons was the attaching of the 19th Charting Squadron to the Wing. The Squadron was attached to the Wing and located at Watton. Shortly after orders attaching them to this organization were issued, seven B-17's arrived at Watton to be used for this organization.
>
> Because of the sudden turn of events in the Western front the operations to take care of prisoners of War who were to be liberated on Germany's signing of unconditional surrender could not be put into operation as the victorious armies of the Allies overran most of the prisoner of war camps and this operation was not needed. However, photo-reconnaissance pilots and interpreters had done much work in finding all of the camps and the operation would have been one of the most spectacular feats of the war should the Germans have capitulated while they still held a number of Allied prisoners.

The reference to the 19th Charting Squadron shows the great urgency with which the War Department now initiated the mapping of Europe while it was still diplomatically possible to do so.

As mentioned, on 12 April 1945, President Roosevelt, twelve weeks into his fourth term, collapsed of a stroke (a massive cerebral hemorrhage) while sitting for a painting in Warm Springs, Georgia. It was not mentioned at the time that he was with his long-time love, Lucy (Mercer) Rutherfurd, or that the picture was for her.

Like everyone else, Elliott remembered how he first heard the news – or he thought he did. Soon after, he responded to a question this way:

> It was at 8.30 PM and I was having dinner with my staff officers when my driver stepped in and informed me that he had just heard over the radio that Father had died…I simply couldn't believe that it was true. I left immediately to go to my headquarters.[1678]

This cannot be true. Many years later the details had changed, but not the time:

> The time in London was 8:35. I had driven in from Mount Farm, my air base south of Oxford, for a dinner party in a West End restaurant. The hostess was Lady Sylvia Ashley, a future wife of Clark Gable's.[i] I had no sooner been seated when she took me aside and said that an officer from General Doolittle's headquarters in High Wycombe was waiting to see me. When I heard the news, I was too benumbed to realize that it could be true. It seemed impossible, that was all. I left straightaway for Mount Farm.[1679]

Elliott suffered from resurrected memory syndrome. FDR was declared dead at 3:35 local time, which was 4:35 Eastern War Time. At the White House, Eleanor was told about a half hour later, and the news was disseminated at about six o'clock that evening. British war time was also two hours advanced, and the BBC flashed the news at 23:07. Allowing for all of it, it must have been nearly midnight before Elliott heard the news.[1680]

It's not a big deal, except that Elliott wrote he had always been "haunted" by the fact that Winston Churchill said that he didn't hear of it until the early morning.[1681] Winston, a night person, had been taking a nap, to which he was surely entitled.[1682]

Apparently Elliott later heard that his father died at 3:35, added the five hour time difference with D.C., and subsequently thought he was told the news at 8:35, triggering the reconstructed dinner memory and the accusation against the Prime Minister.

Right after the war, his answer to the inevitable question was that he received a cablegram at his headquarters, relayed through SHAPE[1683], saying: "Darling, Pa slept away this afternoon. He did his job to the end as he would have you do. Bless you. All our love, Mother." [1684]

At Headquarters, Elliott and his commander, General Doolittle, his boss Spaatz, and Eisenhower himself all combined their efforts to secure passage home for him on the *Sacred Cow*.[1685] The Cow was the first and only VC-54C. Donald Douglas had personally overseen its conversion, throwing in a nautical painting for extra credit. That plane had brought Bernard Baruch, Edward Flynn, and Judge Samuel Rosenman, ranking FDR friends who were in London to work the issues of the coming peace. They were indicative of the president's preference for using his own people to circumvent the State Department.[1686]

Baruch had been sent on a month long unofficial diplomatic mission to work with his old friend Winston Churchill. The *Sacred Cow* was already set to return, and because of the president's death, Elliott and others were able to catch the ride back on very short notice. In so doing, Elliott got to fly on the airplane that his father had used only once, on his trip to Yalta.[1687]

Elliott wrote much later:

---

[i] Ashley was a chorus girl and "socialite" who, through five marriages, rose to become Princess of Georgia.

> It just so happened that Father's good friend, Bernard Baruch, and his friend and speech writer, Samuel Rosenman, had been in London representing Father in negotiations with Churchill and members of his staff. They had an Air Force C-54 standing at an airport just north of London…I was ordered to return on that plane. I bade a hasty farewell to the members of my personal staff, and at 5:00 the next morning flew my own plane over to the airport where Sam Rosenman and Bernie Baruch were ready to take off.[1688]

The long flight was uneventful, but the two presidential advisers pumped General Roosevelt for information on the war's endgame. They deliberately didn't dwell on the sad news.

Elliott Roosevelt made it back for the funeral. The other sons were too far away in the Pacific. The Boettigers, of course, were there. [1689] On Sunday, 15 April 1945, Franklin D. Roosevelt was interred by the rose garden close to his mother's Hyde Park home.

On the train trip back to Washington, the new president traveled with the Roosevelt family. Elliott used the opportunity to launch an attack on Mrs. Henrietta Nesbitt, the White House housekeeper widely reputed to be "the cook from hell." In this, apparently he spoke for all civilization, save his mother, who had protected her neighbor Mrs. Nesbitt all these years. After a while, Truman did what FDR had never been able to: get rid of the housekeeper.[1690] Truman mentioned this bemusedly in his memoirs, as he was apparently surprised at the lack of solemnity and respect for Eleanor, Mrs. Nesbitt's only defender in Christendom. The more hilarious version in Merle Miller's Truman biography may have been a novelistic invention. (Miller said Elliott and Franklin Jr. told HST to fire Nesbitt because she had starved them; and the new president was fed brussels sprouts days on end after advising her that he hated same.)[1691]

Back in England, there was little left for the Wing to do but wind down affairs. Germany's Dönitz government capitulated on 8 May, although as usual the Allies couldn't agree exactly on when the surrender was final. At any rate, the reconnaissance force was now free to carry out some interesting side tasks.

Barely had President Roosevelt been buried (and Elliott sent home) before the 325th PRW was tasked with a new, delicate operation: preparing maps of basically everything that could be reached in the European theater. As the order delicately revealed:

> The objective of this mapping program is to obtain photo maps of as much of Europe as diplomacy, military and political considerations will permit. The need for immediate action is paramount since it is anticipated that certain obstacles to the project may arise at a later date.[1692]

That certainly sounds like the Air Force realists were back in command. And they weren't fooling around: USSTAF specifically called this project highly urgent and secondary only to remaining combat operations. New specially equipped F-9s were allocated to the task. Furthermore: this operation, later code-named "Casey Jones," was only one segment of an urgent global aerial mapping operation carried out in 1946 and subsequent years. It reached from pole to pole. Within months, the Communists began to shoot down western aircraft.

But that was no longer General Elliott Roosevelt's headache. He had had a great war. Despite the deprivations, he seems to have had a very good time indeed, especially during his London and Paris deployments. He publicly said he wanted to go on fighting in Asia, although he told his mother he did not want to go. But the USAAF let him know that there was no more need for him.

After his father's funeral, Elliott did not do anything remarkable in uniform although the Pentagon assigned him a nominal desk job. His eyes were on business and politics. His separation from the service was effective on VJ-day, 15 August.

He would have little rest. The snake eggs laid during the war were about to hatch.

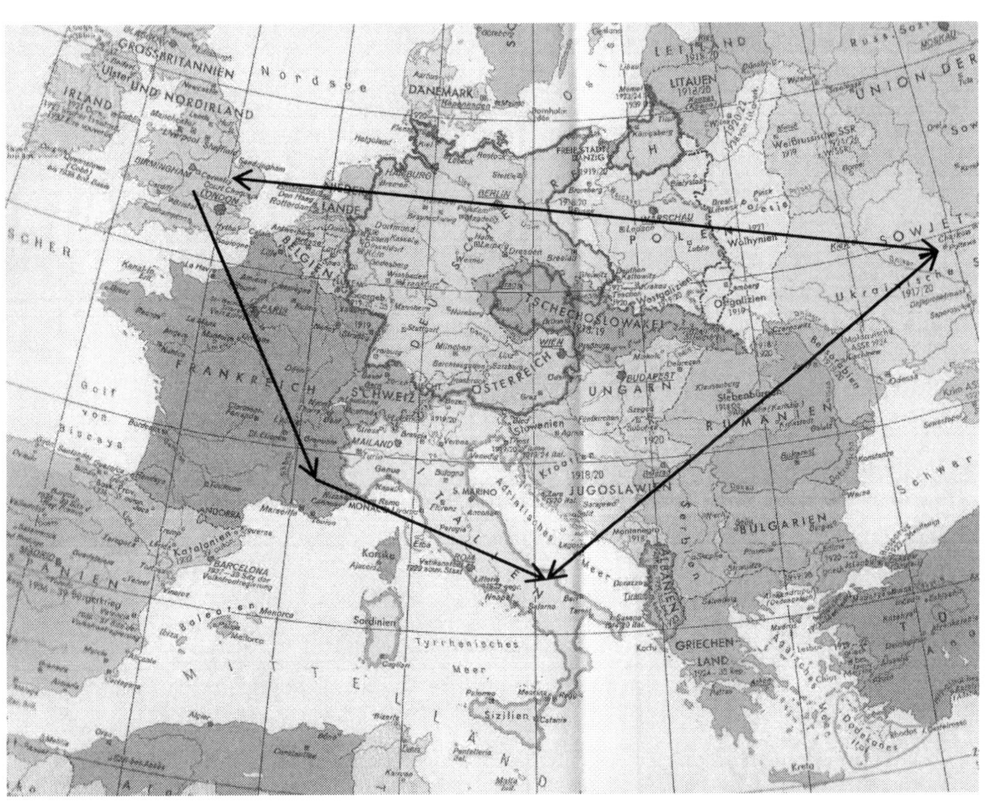

Operation Frantic, the new triangular trade. Note that Berlin is much closer to London than to Poltava. In August 1944, the Eastern front was just short of Warsaw and Cracow.

IV. AFTER THE WAR

TWILIGHT OF THE GENERALS

General Roosevelt did not return to the European theater after rushing home to his father's funeral on 14 April. For the time being, he was assigned a planning job in the Pentagon. Then he was given a sixty-day furlough. Colonel Leon Gray succeeded him as commander of the 325th PRW. By mid-May, organized fighting in Europe was over.[1693]

After the muckraking columnist Westbrook Pegler broke the Hartford loan story publicly on 12 June 1945, Brigadier General Elliott Roosevelt announced his retirement from the Air Forces. Few thought this a coincidence, given the rapt attention his business affairs were suddenly receiving. However, Elliott announced that he had applied for inactive duty on 11 May, after Germany's defeat. The War Department said that it had approved the request before the new scandal broke. In the meantime, Elliott had been told to report to the Air Force Photographic School to brief others on his reconnaissance experience in Europe.[1694]

Elliott's public statement on 31 July was a mix of regret at leaving the battle and fury at the revelations of the loan scandal. He said:

> I have been advised that the Army will place me on inactive duty on Aug. 15. My application for this status was submitted on May 11 – three days after V-E Day – because the Army was unable to give me a combat assignment against the Japs, even though I wished such duty at any rank. I wanted to take part in the fighting against Japan. Above all else, I still want to do so, but the army has no assignment for a reconnaissance officer of my qualifications. I have neither the background nor the training for a non-combat assignment, and I certainly have no desire to finish out the war as an armchair general.[1695]

His real objective in speaking out was to absolve himself and his father of blame in the loan scandal:

> Before the Army took action with respect to my status, it was inappropriate for me to make any statement with respect to the pernicious charges and lies which have been published concerning me by a small segment of the press … I know that any efforts put forth in this hate campaign will have no effect whatsoever on the public judgment of Franklin D. Roosevelt's service to his country.

That was vintage Elliott, as well as a lie. With his political instincts and his frequent practice, he well knew how to conduct at denial campaign to reassure his side.

There is plenty of evidence that this was not all there was to Elliott's mustering out. Before he was out of the service, the *Chicago Tribune* told a quite different story. Because of the discredit his affairs reflected upon the service, the Army had quietly asked Mr. Roosevelt to make himself scarce:

> The *Tribune* has learned that Elliott was urged to take the graceful way out and submit his application for discharge on the grounds that he has served five years and accumulated some 278 points in that service. Elliott debated the advice of his superiors in the family

> home on the Hudson River near Hyde Park, N.Y. It was reported that he encountered difficulty in taking this advice to leave the Army because he had been unable to find a satisfactory post in civilian life. Before the revelations of his "loans" he reportedly had more than a dozen attractive offers from various corporations. Since the congressional investigations have been under way offers have been withdrawn...The air forces have given Elliott no specific assignment since the nation learned seven weeks ago [of the loan scandal]...[1696]

The *Tribune* had this on "unimpeachable authority." And it turns out that during June-July, the War Department and the White House were trying to get Elliott to leave the service as quietly as possible.

Where the *Tribune* got the 278 points from is not clear. The *New York Times* reported him at 233 points, which was one of the highest then heard of. It broke down into 55 for length of service, 42 for overseas service, 36 for dependent children, and 100 for nine decorations and eleven battle stars.

That too would not be the end of the story of how Elliott got out of the Air Force. Like fireworks leading up to a crescendo, the Elliott scandals would climax two years later, and he, never at a loss for words, would then tell the nation his own view of his separation from the service, as well as his opinions about a great many other things.

There is additional evidence that General Roosevelt's separation was carefully programmed. General Fred Anderson, who was in charge of personnel after returning from Europe, exchanged letters with Elliott in July. The matter was referred up to General Eaker, "who now holds the complete file. He directed that a certain course of action be followed." The cryptic references about how the issue was to be handled suggest that the Air Corps wanted to relieve itself of Elliott in a blameless and inconspicuous manner.[1697]

President Truman's file reveals that the delicate operation reached to the top. The War Department responded to Truman's aide, General Vaughan, on 2 July 1945 that the matter had been taken up with Generals Marshall and Doolittle: "It seems that several weeks ago General Roosevelt requested relief from active duty because there was no suitable vacancy for him. At the present time he is on leave preparing to be separated from the services."[1698]

> General Doolittle advises me that when he was originally assigned to the Pacific he told General Roosevelt that he would like to have him there. At that time he intended to use him in command of his photo reconnaissance unit. However, General Doolittle has now found that he has no suitable vacancy for General Roosevelt and consequently has not requested his services. His conversation with General Roosevelt about commanding the photo reconnaissance unit in the Pacific took place prior to General Roosevelt's request for relief from active duty. Under the circumstances I am certain that the action being taken in Gen. Roosevelt's case is entirely agreeable to both Gen. Doolittle and Gen. Roosevelt.[1699]

It thus seems incontrovertible that in view of the scandals that broke in June, the top brass decided to get rid of Elliott, and that his erstwhile friend Jimmy Doolittle either changed his mind or had it changed for him.

On 30 July, the War Department publicly announced Elliott's separation. It noted that he had requested separation on 11 May if there was no need for him in the Pacific, and that the decision to relieve him had been taken:

> ...before the appearance of recent publicity with respect to certain financial transactions...No information regarding these matters was in the possession of the War Department at the time the release was authorized...However, since nothing has come to the attention of the War Department altering the original considerations on which the release of General Roosevelt from active duty was based, action is planned to effect his release on Aug. 15 at the end of his terminal leave.[1700]

General Eaker had no idea the war would end on that date, but he had deftly rid the service of a problematic officer. The Dallas newspaper spoke for many:

> The fact remains that General Roosevelt is getting out of the Army after the disclosures have been made. And that is the 2+2 that the public is putting together in its mind in adding up the reasons for the resignation. If the Army is not accepting Roosevelt's resignation because of conduct not becoming an officer, then it is not doing what it ought to do.[1701]

A news photographer snapped a picture of General and Mrs. Elliott Roosevelt along with a cheering crowd in Broadway on 14 August, when news of the Japanese acceptance of peace terms had just been broadcast. It was probably his last night in uniform.[1702] Elliott completed the demustering formalities at Governor's Island, NY on the 15th.[1703]

During this period Elliott was, by his own admission, out to sea. He asked, "What would the future hold for a retired brigadier general, aged thirty-four?" After his father's demise, he didn't have the constant job offers to mull any more. "I was shaky, and both Mother and I knew it, drifting again as I had before in an uncertain sea."[1704]

How much he was adrift is revealed by his fantasizing, first about again joining the RCAF, then about joining the Jewish insurgency. He tried to get Henry Morgenthau to help him set up a program to train Jewish pilots in the Palestine mandate. Since neither Israel nor its air force technically existed yet, that was quite a career leap. However, many adventurous and idealistic pilots actually did join the ragtag air arm of the Jewish partisans. If nothing else, this was an early indication of Elliott's support for Israel's existential struggle. It also reflected the strong pro-Israel stance of mother Eleanor.[1705]

Before his death, Elliott reminisced about the war. He blamed it for his undeniable instability in the subsequent years. "My balance and evenness were greatly affected by my war experiences, and that lasted until the 1960s."[1706]

Still, an impartial observer cannot help but notice the similarity between the pre-war and the post-war Elliott. The war years stand out as his finest. Whatever people could say about him – a lot – no one could reasonably deny that he had paid his dues in the war. But after that, he was back to his old tricks.

The peace changed everything; it was a revolution in reverse. The troops went home and for a few short years the economy turned again to plowshares. The immense military largely evaporated in chaos and confusion. But to the surprise of many, the Depression did not return. The suppressed fear of the USSR bubbled up immediately, but as with the fascists ten years earlier, it caused no significant rearmament until Soviet-directed coups and attacks began in Europe and Asia.

After Elliott Roosevelt was placed on inactive status, the routine question was whether he should be retained in the status of a permanent reserve officer. General Doolittle was head of the Army Reserve Officers Commissioning Board, and he included Roosevelt on the list of nominations. But when the Truman White House forwarded the nominee list to the Senate for approval, Roosevelt was not on it. Drew Pearson, the columnist, asserted that the omission was political.[1707]

This makes eminent sense, for this decision in early 1947 came after two years of incandescent Elliottian escapades – to his critics tempting treason and corruption charges, to others merely reflecting the poor judgment of the troubled kid. Still, once more he managed to get the last word.

The political fate of general officers should not be understated. For example, Reserve Colonel Lindbergh, who had been *persona non grata* as long as Franklin Roosevelt was president, was suddenly back in good graces, and was called upon to do important armaments evaluation work in Europe. He would have to wait until the Eisenhower administration for his own star; but nobody doubted that his promotion to Brigadier General was a deliberate insult to the Democrats who had cursed him.[1708]

As for General Arnold, Elliott's cautious protector, time was up too. Health failing, he stepped down in February 1946, although he lived to see the creation of the United States Air Force, of which he is today considered the founding father. Professional opinions are mixed about Arnold. His own writings give the impression of a competent in-basket officer. His handling of the Elliott account seems to have been bureaucratically cautious rather than principled.

In 1947, the independent Air Force which President Roosevelt had opposed also was born as a mangled compromise. Yielding the least possible, all the other services maintained their right to have their own private air forces. Ironically, this left the USAF with precisely the core mission the "bomber mafia" worshipped: strategic bombing.

General Spaatz would be the U.S. Air Force's first chief, lasting until retirement in 1948. 8th Air Force commander Jimmy Doolittle was from the Reserves and reverted to inactive status in 1946. The new Air Force would be a different beast, led by a new guard. Almost the entire chain of command above Elliott Roosevelt, from the president on down, would be gone in a very short time, replaced by young officers who had proved their pluck. Generals like LeMay, Vandenberg, Twining, and Norstad knew the second son well enough from work, but they owed him no favors and were not afraid of what he could do to them.

The exception to this rule was, of course, his boss, buddy, and bridge partner, General of the Armies Dwight D. Eisenhower. But when Ike became president in 1953, he did nothing for Elliott, who had self-destructed by then. This despite the fact that the Roosevelt sons had loyally rallied to Ike in 1948 and 1952. Times had utterly changed.

The decade after Elliott mustered out was almost beyond catastrophic for him. He was hardly ever out of the news, whether it was for drunken parties, fistfights, speeding tickets, female trouble, lawsuits, the selling off of FDR's patrimony, or the unending procession of harebrained or ethically questionable business initiatives.

The speeding and other traffic tickets alone threatened to develop into a minor scandalplex, involving many of the brothers independently. Because of repeated failure to appear in court, Faye and Elliott were threatened with arrest in New York.[1709]

But that was the "silly" stuff. The serious problems involved Congress. These scandals were related to his past radio business, and to his friends Joe Stalin and Howard Hughes. There was even a short resumption of his career as an airline president. But first, a disturbing tale from the broadcasting world crawled out from the muck, seemingly parenthetically yet absolutely crucially involving both Elliott and his father.

WMCA New York: An Offer You Cannot Refuse

WMCA was a very important independently owned news station serving New York City.[i] A local entrepreneur named Donald Flamm had owned the station since 1926, making him and his Knickerbocker Broadcasting Company among the very earliest American commercial radio pioneers.[1710] Until Elliott Roosevelt joined the Air Corps, WMCA loyally carried his fifteen-minute commentary on all and sundry matters.[1711] At the time Elliott Roosevelt was trying to get his Transcontinental Broadcasting Network on the air in 1939, he offered Flamm over $1.1 million for his station.

Not that he had the money. It might have been just another fanciful idea.[ii]

Flamm thought it far too little, and wouldn't sell. It turned out, however, that someone else in the White House wanted that station, and he wouldn't take no for an answer.

Candy industrialist Edward J. Noble had been the first head of the Civil Aviation Authority (CAA) and then Undersecretary of Commerce in 1939 to 1940. Noble was a close friend of Thomas Corcoran, President Roosevelt's former political adviser.[1712]

Acting through lawyers without revealing his identity, in November 1940 Noble first offered $500,000 for WMCA, later raising it to $850,000. Finally he made it clear that the offer was of the non-refusable kind. Otherwise Mr. Flamm would lose his FCC license. So said the charges Flamm filed afterwards.

Flamm did not yet know who the buyer was. The offer was handled by law partners Dempsey and Koplovitz, who had been the FCC's lead attorneys until a couple of months earlier. Flamm and his people speculated the prospective buyer might be Elliott Roosevelt, or perhaps Joe Kennedy. But he still wouldn't sell; in fact he offered $25,000 in cash if the buyers would leave him alone and not file to take over his frequency.[1713]

Someone very powerful then saw to it that Flamm signed on the dotted line.

> On the evening of the 29th, just about sundown, the contract was ready to be signed, and Dempsey and Koplovitz had brought with them from Washington a complete set of forms required by the Commission for a transfer of license. Flamm tried to avoid signing the contract by saying that it was after sundown on Friday night, and that he was a religious Jew and doesn't sign contracts on the Sabbath; whereupon Koplovitz became very provoked and abusive of Flamm and said he wasn't going to waste any more time with him, that unless that contract was signed right there and then he was going to drop off negotiations and file an application for the frequency as instructed originally.[1714]

The record suggests that Flamm was not without his faults, and not necessarily to be admired for his victimhood. But he also seems to have been a confused and vacillating man, or at the very least weaker than the forces he was up against. He only slowly found out who they were.

---

[i] WMCA New York still broadcasts, but is not descended from the businesses described herein. The main source for this affair is the final report of the House Select Committee to Investigate the FCC, 2 JAN 45, and the several volumes of hearing transcripts and exhibits supporting it. Contemporary newspaper accounts provide the surface details of the affair. The investigative piece by Alva Johnston in the Saturday Evening Post, 13 OCT 45, is the key to the secret maneuvers behind it. McKean's biography of Tommy Corcoran provides further perspective.

[ii] The offer was from Vallance & Co., of which Elliott was a partner; it expired as TBN did. (FCC 44, I/79)

In the second term, Tommy "the Cork" Corcoran was FDR's most effective adviser and fixer – and thus deserving of the specialized nickname. In fact, said James Roosevelt, "the Cork" and Ben Cohen, known as the "Gold Dust Twins," were the closest to the President, until succeeded by Harry Hopkins – "Harry the Hop." Interestingly, James said FDR had J. Edgar Hoover tap both Hopkins's and Corcoran's telephones, but he didn't say why.[1715] Reportedly, President Truman also considered "the Cork" dangerous enough to have his telephone tapped (illegally of course).[1716]

Possibly, Jimmy confused the facts. The evidence is that Truman's aide General Vaughan asked Hoover to tap Corcoran under terms of strict deniability. When Truman heard of it, he rescinded the tap.[1717]

After Corcoran left the government to become a lobbyist, he retained effective control of many of his earlier appointees and was able to intimidate the rest. This was especially true in regard to the FCC.

Lyndon Johnson's biographer Robert Caro described Corcoran as Johnson's "bluntest tool" in getting his way with the FCC. He also noted that:

> ...both the commission's chairman, James Fly, and its former chief counsel, William J. Dempsey, who was a Corcoran protégé, owed their appointments chiefly to his influence. (Dempsey's predecessor, insufficiently responsive to a telephone call from "Tommy Corcoran at the White House," had found himself dismissed on 24-hours' notice.) And while Dempsey was now in private practice (sharing an office suite with Corcoran, both men representing private clients before a notably accommodating FCC) many officials still at the top of the FCC were indebted to Corcoran for their jobs: the agency had, in the knowing Washington term, been thoroughly "Corcoranized."[i]

"The Cork" was used to getting his way, even after he left the inner circle around the boss in 1940. You might say that now WMCA was about to get Cork-screwed.

Corcoran's friend Ed Noble had made millions selling Lifesavers mints. He was a Republican and not an FDR crony. But when he was Undersecretary of Commerce, his boss was Harry Hopkins. "The Hop" served two years as Secretary before Jesse Jones took the slot in late 1940. In 1939, after Elliott's infamous loan, President Roosevelt told Hopkins and Noble to kill the anti-chain store bill – the Patman bill that would have ruined the A&P Tea Company. Noble submitted a detailed list of objections to Congress on 17 May 1940, and the bill died in the House Ways and Means Committee in June.[1718]

Faced with this massed firepower, Donald Flamm capitulated. He testified that he was told that the deal had been "greased from the White House down."[1719] The man who told him that was Leslie E. Roberts, who pretended to know the president's mind and declared that FDR "was determined that Tommy's friend should have the station."[1720]

When Flamm testified to the House Select Committee in February 1944, he vividly remembered the sale:

> Dempsey lunged at me, and Noble, infuriated, stepped in between us, declaring, 'If this weren't my own apartment I'd like to finish the job right here,'...Mr. Noble's last word

[i] Robert Caro: The Johnson Years: Means of Ascent: Chapter 6. Caro was talking about Corcoran's role in LBJ's take-down of KTBC Austin in 1943.

> to me was 'Flamm, I'll get your station whether you want to sell it or not. The next time we meet will be before the commission.'[1721]

The following day, 2 December 1940, Flamm signed the contract. For once quick as lightning, the FCC approved the transaction on the 17th, and then on 7 January denied Flamm's request for reconsideration. Flamm left for Florida, saying "I was on the verge of a nervous breakdown. I was almost out of my mind. As the witnesses told you, they had been engaged in a terror campaign against me for almost six weeks, and that was the climax of it. I had to get away."[1722]

> Flamm testified that he sold the station to Noble as a result of threats by William J. Dempsey, one-time counsel for the FCC, that refusal would mean loss of its wave band to Noble, whose application for it would be granted by the commission. Mr. Dempsey, according to Flamm, first offered 750,000 and later 850,000 for the station, despite the protests of Mr. Flamm that even if he wished to sell, which he did not, the price was "ridiculously low" for a property for which Elliott Roosevelt, son of President Roosevelt, a short time previously had offered him $1,100,000.
>
> The warning of Mr. Dempsey that a wave length hearing would result in the cancellation of Mr. Flamm's license and reassignment of his wave length was confirmed…by Leslie R. Roberts, vice president of his Knickerbocker Company, headed by Mr. Flamm. Mr. Roberts, formerly in charge of radio programs for the WPA, was engaged by Mr. Flamm on the recommendation of David K. Niles, administrative assistant to President Roosevelt.[1723]

The people mentioned are worth a second look. Very much so.

Corcoran had installed Dempsey at the FCC as general counsel in 1938. Corcoran had called and said the president wanted the existing counsel fired and Dempsey to have the job, which happened the next day. In fall 1940, Dempsey went into private practice, sharing an office suite with Corcoran, who also retired from the government, as he said, "to make a million dollars."[1724] In that office resided also William Koplovitz, who was now Dempsey's law partner. Koplovich had been the assistant FCC counsel.[1725]

Dempsey & Koplovitz was then hired by Ed Noble for the WMCA take-down. Dempsey promptly "called on Donald Flamm, owner of WMCA, and said he was going to file a claim for WMCA's wavelength and that under the law the wavelength could be taken from Flamm without compensation."[1726]

Leslie Roberts was the mid-level bureaucrat whom Flamm had been persuaded to hire as public relations counsel and general manager. Roberts later testified that "promises of a better position under Noble had persuaded him to attempt to stampede Flamm into selling the station."

> Mr. HART. You have testified under oath that you were guilty of the vilest type of treachery and disloyalty to your employer?
> Mr. ROBERTS. Yes, sir.
> Mr. HART. And that your employer charged you with treachery and disloyalty and dismissed you?
> Mr. ROBERTS. Yes, sir.
> Mr. HART. And knowing you to be disloyal, he volunteered to give you a reference so that you might obtain employment elsewhere?
> Mr. ROBERTS. Yes. Am I on trial here?[1727]

Flamm maintained that Roberts had been a stalking horse planted by the White House conspirators. The man who had persuaded Flamm to hire Roberts was David K. Niles, who worked in the White House. David Niles was at that time special assistant to the Commerce Secretary, Hopkins. Sadly, he appears in the Venona decrypts: "Around Niles there is a group of his friends who will arrange anything for a bribe."[1728] As usual the Soviets knew their way around the White House.

But Roberts was a blabbermouth when the matter was investigated:

> Roberts freely termed the deal "a conspiracy" in testimony before the house committee and said that Noble should be given 'the greatest portion of the dubious credit' for success of the scheme. Roberts said Flamm was under the impression that Thomas G. Corcoran, Washington lobbyist and one time intimate of President Roosevelt, and Niles, Mr. Roosevelt's assistant, were behind Noble in the deal and that his station would be taken away from him thru their influence if he did not sell out.[1729]

Leslie Roberts turned out to be the John Dean of this scandal. He had doublecrossed his employer, Flamm, in return for a promise of stocks, bonus, and important duties. But when Noble took over, Roberts, though he did get his raise, was declared *non grata* at the station. Without any duties, he lingered for seven months, then was squeezed out. That alone was not why he turned on Noble. He found out that others in the station had been in cahoots with Noble, and that he had been marked as expendable all along. He admitted to the committee that by now he couldn't get a "dog-catcher" job in the radio business. He was upset enough to spill the beans on the whole conspiracy.[1730] He went to the FCC, which did nothing. Then, despite threats, he went to the House committee. His testimony in 1944 was a sorry, embarrassing affair. But it opened up the can of worms, and in that can, Corcoran was on top.

"The only way you will get to the bottom of this is when one of the boys sings," Flamm's attorney told him. By late 1943, Roberts was ready to sing.[1731]

WMCA: The Cover-Up

Up until that point it seemed reasonable to surmise that WMCA was just another quick Cork-job, one of many favors at the behest of friends and family. But it turned out that there was "an elephant in the room" – an elephant named Elliott. Many on the inside knew of the big creature's presence, but the public was not to know for many years. It would take the release of Hoover's wiretaps to prove the animal's existence.

That was why WMCA turned into a tough, protracted fight three years after the sale. As with Watergate thirty years later, it was not the initial crime, but the cover-up that mattered. In this case, though, the cover-up was successful; to use Richard Nixon's oddly appropriate term, this time the White House was able to "keep the cork on the bottle."

Like many of the really big scandals, this one simmered under the lid for quite some time. Many people knew something, and the pressure was building. The true cover-up began when Congress began investigating the FCC in 1943. In September 1943 Noble sold WMCA to Nathan Straus for $1,255,000, which was about what Flamm thought his station had been worth. Straus had served as head of the U.S.

Housing Authority from 1937 to 1942.[i] Noble sold in order to trade up to the nascent NBC "Blue Network," which the FCC had ordered divested from NBC to prevent broadcasting monopolies. And Noble was no bumbler like Elliott; from the Blue Network he methodically built a media empire that would become known as ABC, the American Broadcasting Network.

Flamm, however, fell on hard times, though he did get a minor government job.

Oddly, despite physical threats, he refused to let the matter go right from the beginning. First he hired a law firm, Handelman and Ives. Colin Ives knew Corcoran and immediately went to see him. He testified later:

> On hearing that Flamm wanted to cancel the sale, Tommy said, according to Ives: 'That's what I thought and that's why I asked Handelman to stay outside. I'm going to tell you something and I'll deny it if you repeat it. If Flamm tries to get out of that deal I'll make him wish he had never been born. I've got the internal-revenue people looking into his income tax, and they have already found out plenty.'
>
> Tommy is said to have denied this at a secret hearing.[1732]

Then Flamm initiated a state court case against the powerful Mr. Noble. That case was ongoing when Noble resold the station. Through a politician friend, Flamm also got word directly to President Roosevelt of what had been done to him in Roosevelt's name. The president told General Pa Watson to call the FCC and ask for an investigation.[1733] A few hours later another White House aide called back and told the commission that "no matter what you may have heard, the White House is not interested in the WMCA case."

Corcoran's secret testimony revealed that he had countermanded Watson's order.[ii]

Flamm interested enough politicians in the case that the House of Representatives asked the Special Committee for Investigation of the FCC to look into the matter. In June 1941, when the Senate Interstate Commerce Committee was also looking into FCC corruption, Senator Charles Tobey (R-NH) asked an FCC witness whether he was aware that Thomas Corcoran had received "a substantial fee" from Mr. Noble, receiving a negative response.

> The Senator then asked if it were not unusual that Mr. Noble, having made application for transfer of the station on December 15, received his permit on December 17. 'It was very quick,' Mr. Craven [FCC minority member] said.[iii]

The matter sat in the House committee for a couple of years while other questionable practices and deals involving the FCC were investigated. The controversial "Cox Committee" had been set up in January 1943. Most observers agreed it was primarily a way for Representative Eugene Cox of Georgia, accused of taking a payoff, to get back at the FCC; and it is a fair guess that Cox thought the kettle blacker than himself. The Cox committee investigation essentially became a proxy war between the White House and anti-New Deal politicians. After a while the House public hearings,

---

[i] NYT, 14 SEP 43. The USHA was an $800 million dollar public housing agency.

[ii] Ibid. On 23 DEC 1940, Corcoran called a White House aide, who called the FCC.

[iii] NYT, 14 JUN 41. Dempsey & Koplovitz billed Noble for $75,000, but was paid only $25,000. The committee could find no evidence that Corcoran received a kick-back (Hearings, Final, 49).

held in 1944, began airing many names of well-known and important people in Washington and New York.

Perhaps for that reason, in February the Committee's majority voted to bury the investigation; i.e. first to suspend and later to conduct further sessions in secret. A second batch of hearings was held after the election, in November; after a while they too were sent to "executive session."

The incensed Republicans reacted:

> The action of the three-man Democratic majority of the select committee to investigate the FCC in squelching the investigation of the strange sale of radio station WMCA and the part played by high officials of the present political Administration makes it perfectly plain that this is a "hush hush" move, pure and simple, to keep unsavory facts from the public. It is part of the whole New Deal scheme to cover up pernicious bureaucratic practices and the graft that is inherent in such a maze as we have in Washington today.[1734]

The committee's opinionated first general counsel, Eugene L. Garey, resigned in fierce protest days after, on 25 February 1944. Saying that he would not be part of a patent fraud, he hurled a parting thunderbolt at the Democratic chairman:

> From the beginning of your chairmanship your hostility to the investigation and its purposes has been clear to me. You have repeatedly ignored the mandate of the House, stymied the investigation to a sheer whitewashing affair wholly responsive to political pressures and dominated entirely by political expediency. To continue as counsel to the committee in these circumstances would serve no useful purpose, would merely produce waste and futility, and would end in shame and dishonor to the Congress.[1735]

Oddly, enough Garey had not intended to resign; he actually wanted to get to the bottom of the matter. Then Corcoran had shown up at his office and had told him to quit; and he still didn't. It had taken much more to change his mind. The story of Garey's prolonged death struggle is instructive.

Garey, though a Wall Street lawyer and anti-New Deal, was "a lifelong organization Democrat and an active Tammany man," so he wasn't expected to cause trouble. But when he did, opinions of him shifted immediately. We know something about how the White House viewed him because Jonathan Daniels, one of the Palace Guard and FDR's last press secretary, left us a curious diary entry on 22 May 1943:[i]

> Lyndon Johnson says that the Cox Committee investigation is a big job which is being ignored as a little thing, that it is headed by E.L. Garey, who has collected a group of Bennett goons (Harry H. Bennett of the Ford Co.) and anti-New Deal lawyers. Johnson says that the lawyer in charge is a member of the anti-New Deal law firm, which, however, at one time included one of the Roosevelt boys, Elliott, I think.

(He meant Franklin Jr., something that would become important later when the records disappeared. Bennett was Henry Ford's union-busting deputy.)

---

[i] Daniels was the son of Josephus Daniels, whom FDR had worked for when Daniels was Navy Secretary.

> The big story they are working on is that one time there was a Jew who owned a radio station in New York who had gotten into trouble for advertising a prophylactic jelly over his radio station, for relationships with Father Coughlin and Mrs. Elizabeth Dilling.

(These were the alleged improprieties that had first caused the FCC to investigate WMCA. As the hearings showed, these were trumped-up to threaten Flamm. Dilling was an anti-communist, anti-Semitic agitator whom the administration prosecuted for sedition in 1944.)

> He was called on the carpet by the FCC; soon thereafter William J. Dempsey… called on him and said that he had better sell his radio station to him quick and if he didn't sell it, it was going to be taken away from him anyway. The Jew is supposed to have gone to Harry Hopkins and asked for his advice about selling and Hopkins supposedly advised him to sell. Also Niles and Noble, who was an Asst. Sec. of Commerce (so Johnson said) gave him the same advice. Also at that time, according to Johnson's story (which he makes clear is not his story but the story the anti-New Dealers are working on), Dempsey and Tom Corcoran had offices together. As I got it from Johnson, the anti-New Deal lawyers who have been put in hope to use this investigation of the FCC as a take-off for smearing the whole Administration or the important people in it.[1736]

This tells us that Lyndon Johnson, who had his way with the FCC that same year, was part of Corcoran's circle and had taken on the task of smearing Garey. Despite the denials, it also shows us that Niles and Hopkins were involved in the plot. Obviously the version LBJ put forward was that the matter was a purely political skirmish, and there seems to have been no sympathy anywhere for "the Jew." For this reason the incidental literature on the FCC investigation reflects a fierce ideological divide, and the partisans neglected to look into the details of what the agency had actually done to people.

The pressure on Garey was now immense. He was offered a multitude of favors, including "anything he wanted" if he would resign.

When that didn't work, the internal revenue agents looked into his taxes. They were in order. Then, the Department of Justice threatened to indict a close friend and business associate of his. That charge had previously been investigated and found to be without merit. But Garey said the attack was serious enough that it would destroy his friend: "Keep on investigating, and this man will be ruined; resign, and the case will be dropped."[1737]

It probably helped in this (and subsequent cases) that the Attorney General was Francis Biddle, who was universally recognized to be Corcoran's installed pawn. At about the same time, the Assistant Attorney General, Norman Littell, protested publicly about the unethical practices of his boss, especially when intervening in cases for Corcoran. President Roosevelt promptly fired Littell.[1738]

Biddle's role is important. As we shall see, he had already been involved in tamping down another very serious Elliott scandal.

The next day, Richard Wigglesworth (R-Mass) and another committee member issued a diatribe to the press. They said that "When the truth is known, whether now, in the weeks and months that lie ahead, or when a new and fearless Congress calls for a complete investigation which cannot now be had because of Administration obstruction, the facts disclosed will not only interest but appall the public."

> It is a contemptible consummation sought, desired and plotted by those whose sordid activities cannot stand the piercing searchlight of an honest investigation. The resignation under pressure of the chief counsel to investigate the FCC is just one more result of the obstruction, intimidation and sabotage resorted to by the White House, the Department of Justice, the FCC and the robed-Richelieus of the Palace Guard, both past and present, to cover up the wrong-doing, and to conceal the pernicious activities of the FCC.[1739]

Even in D.C. you don't often hear that kind of language. But it was all to no avail.

Succeeding Garey, the committee's next counsel was also an honest man who had only agreed to take the job on condition that "he be permitted to go down the line, letting chips fall where they may." Incensed at the shelving of the matter, and certain of the basic truth of Flamm's case, that lawyer also eventually resigned his position.[1740] He would have another spat with the White House years later. His name was John J. Sirica.

The committee cracked apart. Rep. Wigglesworth raged: "Ever since the start of this investigation, this committee and its staff has met with constant obstruction, intimidation and underhand tactics from those in high places."

Some of the ways the inquiry had been obstructed included an edict from the administration that for national security reasons, serving military officers would not be allowed to testify. It is not hard to guess which officer might have been called.[i] It is also notable that FBI chief J. Edgar Hoover had been brought before the committee, but had refused to answer questions under cover of national security.[1741]

After the Hartford loan story broke, a reporter got a "deep-throat" report that the Committee investigating the FCC had been about to crack the Elliott case in July 1943:

> Investigators for the committee had been directed to probe the organization of Elliott's radio network in Texas and the proposed expansion to a transcontinental system...Shortly thereafter, for "security" reasons an executive order was issued forbidding officers of the Army, Navy, and other Governmental agencies from testifying and the investigation began to bog down. The documentary evidence had been secured, however, and was ready for introduction when it was "impounded." It was at this point that Eugene L. Garey, New York attorney, who was special counsel for the investigating committee, resigned and with him practically all of the counsel and investigators. The special committee then under the chairmanship of Representative Cox (D), of Georgia, was "discharged" and the activities turned over to a new committee under Representative Lea (D) of California.[1742]

Representative Edward E. Cox (D-GA) had recently had a row with the FCC over some suspected corrupt move he had made with a Georgia radio station. The evidence does suggest that Cox was paid off. But he was a combative fellow and didn't much care what anybody said – up to a point. One day Cox found it necessary to resign the case: "Cox said that he had been informed on reliable authority that the Department of Justice was warming up the case with the intention of indicting him, unless he resigned."[1743]

Cox got the message. He resigned the committee on 30 September 1943.[1744]

Following Cox, Congressman Clarence F. Lea was tasked with gingerly burying the case. After further threats against another committee member, Edward Hart (D-NJ), the resisters capitulated.[1745] And that was why, on 28 November 1944, the committee voted

---

[i] Other reasons to call military officers about FCC policies were related to suspicions over Pearl Harbor.

3-2 to make all further testimony secret. The subpoenaed but publicity-shy Tommy Corcoran now arrived to testify in secret. He told the newspapers that the committee had authorized him to say that neither he nor anyone in the White House had had anything to do with the WMCA case.[1746]

Lea's staff quit in disgust.

In other words, by the summer and fall of 1943, Congress had received evidence that could have sunk or seriously damaged the president of the United States – and it was buried on the orders of those who could have been hurt. But even then, the public did not realize that the president himself was at stake. Corcoran was the key to that truth, and that was why he had fought so ferociously to sabotage the investigation.

On 3 January 1945, the committee's majority issued a 26,000 word report absolving the administration of blame. The three Democratic members, Lea, Earl, and Priest, signed it. The minority (Wigglesworth and Miller) again protested bitterly. The most damning testimony remained secret.[1747]

It was a very odd final report. The massive body of evidence, even that which was released, was sharply at variance with the conclusions reached. The report said that "Mr. Flamm was under no pressure, coercion, or duress when he finally signed the contract." "That the general allegations to the effect that the White House had anything to do in pressuring Flamm into selling his station to Noble is wholly without foundation of fact." "That the committee finds nothing to censure in the conduct of Mr. Corcoran in the WMCA case. There is no evidence that Mr. Corcoran attempted to, or did use any improper methods or influence in connection with the WMCA case."[1748]

This report was issued two hours before the end of the Congress and the dissolution of the committee. The minority had these two hours to read the report and submit an opinion. Fortunately, the two minority members were prepared, and both attached detailed opinions that might fairly be called a laundry list of damning accusations against the FCC, the Committee, and the Administration. Rep. Wigglesworth led by stating:

> For many years there have been charges of the most serious character leveled at the FCC and its activities. These charges have included inefficiency, political favoritism, illegal action, permitting trafficking in radio frequencies, corruption, and dictatorial domination of the air...These charges have come from within the industry, from outside the industry, and even from within the administration itself.[1749]

The minority opinions were as shocking as the majority report was anodyne. However, there was agreement that the president was not involved in the crime or the cover-up except to the extent that he had asked for the investigation which Corcoran had so swiftly countermanded. Also, there was no mention at that time of the suspected fact that Corcoran had fought so hard to cripple the Committee's investigation because he knew its legal staff had uncovered evidence of Elliott Roosevelt's shakedowns in the broadcasting business.

The name didn't seem to matter much back then, but the commission's second general counsel, the man who left in a fury that November 1944, was a young lawyer, John J. Sirica. Thirty years later the world would hear more from Judge Sirica. He presided over the investigation of the Watergate conspiracy. Obviously, that was a bigger snakepit than WMCA.

Or was it?

Very likely, in 1974 Sirica remembered an earlier case where justice had slipped from his and the nation's fingers, and he wasn't going to let it happen again. When he quit on 28 November 1944, he protested: "I do not want it on my conscience that I submitted to a whitewash. Therefore, I am tendering my resignation, effective at once."[1750]

Sirica had been after more than WMCA when he served as the committee's counsel: he accused the FCC's chairman of having done a similar number on radio station WFTL in Fort Lauderdale. Sirica said that case was a criminal conspiracy engineered by friends of the FCC chairman, James Fly. WFTL had been handed over to friends of the chairman under threats of having its license pulled. Sirica named names and numbers and dates. But apparently the committee didn't appreciate its counsel's good work.[i]

When he resigned, Sirica noted that the White House (i.e., the president) was not involved in the WMCA affair. The White House had been informed all along, but had disavowed interest. Neither had Elliott been involved, except as a clue to the real value of the station. If the FCC was corrupt, it was apparently the work of underlings in the FDR administration.[1751]

But it also mattered that Mr. Sirica informed a number of people, including agents of the Treasury, about the WMCA matter, and the peripheral involvement of Elliott Roosevelt. When a bigger Elliott scandal exploded in 1945, Sirica's files and work would he hauled out, and investigators would find a tenuous vein from the FCC investigation to the mother lode that would become known as the Hartford loan scandal.

That vein had surfaced when General Counsel Garey handed over custody of committee files to John Sirica in Garey's office on 27 September 1944:

> During this conference...Mr. Garey informed Mr. Sirica and the undersigned [counsel Barker] that Elliott Roosevelt had obtained $250,000 from John Hartford and that the consideration for this loan was the killing, in committee, of House Bill No. 1, 76th Congress, introduced by Honorable Wright Patman of Texas, on January 3, 1939, and duly referred to the Committee on Ways and Means, this bill proposing, according to Mr. Garey, a terrific tax on chain stores and would have cost John Hartford & Company several hundred million dollars in taxes.
>
> Mr. Garey talked at length about the matter and in minute detail which lead me to believe that he had all the documentary evidence concerning the transaction.
>
> If there ever was such a file in the Office of the Select Committee, I never saw it. It will be recalled that Franklin Roosevelt, Jr., was one time a member of and associated with Mr. Garey's law firm.
>
> Subsequently, I learned that a New York attorney, David Garrison Berger...was alleged to have been in Washington and offered to sell the entire story concerning Elliott Roosevelt and the Hartford transactions for the sum of $15,000.[ii]

---

[i] Miami News, 7, 8 SEP 44; NYT 6, 8, 9 SEP 44. Chairman Fly's involvement in the WFTL matter is problematic; he was generally thought honest, and is known to history mostly for his long, quixotic battle against wiretapping. The WFTL case was detailed in the Final Report, 2 JAN 45, Fly being censured for his involvement.

[ii] Memo, Robert B. Barker to Commissioner of Internal Revenue, U.S. Treasury, 10 JUL 45, copy in Hartford Loan File, ER Box, Pegler/HH. Chief counsel Barker succeeded Sirica, who resigned 28 NOV 44; Garey had resigned 25 FEB 44.

This letter, a 10 July 1945 memorandum to the U.S. Treasury, was signed by Robert B. Barker, who had been at the Sirica-Garey meeting. Barker was worth listening to, because he had been the committee's chief investigator; and after Sirica quit in anger, Barker took his job. In this post-investigation letter, Barker suggested that Franklin Jr. stole the Elliott files from the committee archive. The "minute detail" Garey had offered suggested that such a file must have existed.

Evidence that slipped into the public portion of the hearings strongly supports this narrative. The committee engaged in an inconclusive discussion about the missing documents: "A search of the files also reveals that quite a number of documents have been removed from the files as they existed in the early months of this year. Some of these papers or documents are essential for the proper investigation…" [1752] Yet no one could find them.

This falls far short of proof that the White House stole the files; instead clouds of suspicion haunted the proceedings.

Barker's reference to attorney Berger is important. We know from a letter Caruthers Ewing, Hartford's attorney, wrote to Westbrook Pegler that this man knew Congressman Sirovich and had the goods on the Elliott-Hartford deal. Three years earlier, he had unsuccessfully shopped the story around to the newspapers. Presumably they recoiled at the lawyer's ethics, his price, or both.[1753]

We are not compelled to use the "allegedly" qualifier in discussing the WMCA case. That's because the courts consistently agreed with Flamm that Noble and his White House connections had ripped him off. After suits and countersuits, in 1946, the New York Supreme Court awarded Flamm $350,000 in damages from Edward Noble. The judge said the only issue was whether Flamm had been "defrauded or coerced."[1754]

That verdict was set aside and a new trial ordered. On 7 October 1949, the parties announced an out-of-court deal. Flamm's attorneys had originally sought $2,925,000, but settled for less. It was part of the agreement not to divulge the amount.[1755]

The WMCA transactions made a sleazy little scandal, in the process revealing a corrupt, politicized FCC and a White House full of thieves. Utterly forgotten today, it had been securely buried by the Committee majority in December 1944. But, even if the vanished Elliott files could not be rediscovered, the Hartford loan landmine lay buried within the recollections of committee staff members.

So, in 1944, young John J. Sirica knew all this. With a little bit more help, it seems that Sirica could have taken down the President of the United States in 1944, thirty years before fate gave him the chance again.

At least that's what Thomas Corcoran thought. On the wiretaps, "the Cork" was heard telling Senator Lister Hill (D-AL) that the first ejected counsel, Eugene Garey, had been about to reveal the corruption of Elliott Roosevelt. "He was gonna burst it in connection with the WMCA thing and that's why Larry [Fly] and I were fighting it so furiously. We were covering the boss…If this had broken during the last election, that's when they were trying to pull it, I tell you it could have thrown the election…I had my own fingers pretty badly mashed, but I did keep it dead for a year."[1756]

Perhaps President Roosevelt had used up the last of his nine political lives just before his physical life expired. A few months after his death, the "elephant in the room" was revealed to the public.

THE GREAT CHAIN STORE ROBBERY

During the summer of 1945, to gradually diminishing acclaim, Westbrook Pegler and others kept up the pressure on the late president and his surviving family with new revelations.

On 12 June 1945, Pegler broke the details of the Hartford loan in the *Washington Times-Herald.* He said that he had received the first tips four months earlier, but it had taken this long to develop and verify the information. We now know that plenty of people within both the executive and legislative branches of government had known of it for a long time. Some knew from the beginning.[1757]

Pegler later wrote that an Irish-descended hater of Britain and Roosevelt, William Griffin, had given him his first leads – and where else but in the Stork Club:

> Our leader was still alive and I will ever regret my inability to stick the proof of his own part in this con-game down his gullet, but it was a long job. The break came when a friend of mine who was close to Hartford told me to walk in on him because John was ready to talk. He was and he did.[1758]

The Hartford loan scandal broke open in an awkward time slot – during the final two months of the war. It received a lot of attention initially, but understandably enough it soon got crowded out to the back pages. That was exactly what the congressional majority wanted. The body of the report released by the House Ways and Means Committee on 1 October 1945 was detailed and damning. But the material was overwhelming in its bulk, and required weeks to digest. The committee majority refused to refer the matter for charges, and even the release of the final report was made as discreetly as possible.

Deliberate, Infamous Lies...

The star witness, General Roosevelt himself, reacted to the initial press accusations in a way that was by now wholly predictable. The charges were a "hate campaign" designed to "smear" his dead father. He said he was completely innocent, that "Franklin D. Roosevelt never promoted or assisted my personal business affairs," and that he was "entitled to a full, public statement of those facts for the sake of my family."[1759]

> Before the Army took action with respect to my status, it was inappropriate for me to make any statement with respect to the pernicious charges and lies which have been published concerning me by a small segment of the press. These falsehoods have not even been confined to me personally. I know that any efforts put forth in this hate campaign will have no effect whatsoever on the public judgment of Franklin D. Roosevelt's service to his country. I believe, though, that those millions who loved and respected him have the right to know that F.D.R. never promoted or assisted my personal business affairs. Any statement that he ever did so is a deliberate, infamous lie. I conducted my own business affairs. The responsibility for them was and still is mine, and mine alone.
>
> False statements have been made as to my willingness to cooperate with the Government in any investigation of my acts. The House Ways and Means Committee and the Senate Finance Committee have charged the Treasury Dept. with making a complete investigation into my business affairs. This investigation is now going on. My cooperation

> with that investigation has been wholehearted. I have asked the Treasury to make public all of the facts, without reservation, at the earliest possible moment.
>
> I have nothing to conceal. The facts will speak for themselves. I am entitled to a full public statement of those facts for the sake of my family. These facts will be their own answer to the falsehoods, half-truths and sly implications of that small, irresponsible section of the press which does not hesitate to violate the truth. Until these facts are disclosed my only request is that any charges concerning my affairs should be confined to me, and that no further attempt be made to smear a man who can't talk back.[1760]

The lion certainly roared. It is wise to keep these words in mind as we examine his affairs. In the history of denials it deserves a hallowed place. Some public figures try to hide when caught in something; others feebly try to fudge or compromise. But Elliott instinctively understood that controlling the message is 90% of "truth." That's why he always counterattacked massively in the headlines; he all but screamed, spat and stomped his feet. Though in a cruder way, in principle he related to "truth" much as his father did.

But this one was a strange denial in that, on close inspection, it did not deny any of the facts released. Elliott knew they were undeniable. Interested observers caught on to this. There was a great concern about the solidity of the evidence and the commensurate absence of a serious defense beyond furious name-calling. The public demand for a congressional investigation could not be ignored.

The House Ways and Means Committee began sessions on the matter on 27 August. In this endeavor it was joined by the U.S. Treasury and independently by the FBI. From all these official sources as well as the sleuthing of reporters it is possible to gain a perfectly clear picture of what had really been going on with Elliott's prewar businesses. There is evidence of President Roosevelt's involvement throughout. What we cannot ever know is "intentions" – i.e. to what extent Elliott, with his father's active assistance, intentionally engaged in apparently criminal activities.

By July 1945, it was painfully clear that President Roosevelt had been closely involved not only with securing the now infamous loans (apart from the Hartford loan, there were several extracted from other businessmen with reason to fear the government), but also with the stunningly devious settlement of them.

Because all the main characters still alive were compelled to testify under oath in the summer of 1945, it gradually became obvious not only why Elliott joined the military, but also why Jesse Jones, a keystone of the Texas Cabal, had agreed to settle Elliott's affairs for the president once the kid had been shipped off to war. The main creditor, Hartford, noted: "Elliott was hiding behind his uniform." And he called him "a few names" as well, but lamented that the way things had been set up, there was no realistic recourse.[1761]

To untangle Elliott's web, President Roosevelt's fabled skills of persuasion had again been much needed. It was Franklin Senior, not Elliott, who directed Jesse Jones, then Commerce Secretary, to pay off the A&P's John Hartford with an insulting token of two cents on the dollar; it was the president who then gave the collateral stock to Elliott's ex-family; and it was he who urged Ruth Googins to pay back Jesse Jones, who was out the $4,000 used to shut up Hartford.

Evidently Ruth did not do so, although the ostensibly worthless stock soon climbed into the millions. Neither did Elliott, who claimed that he could not find his

Houstonian friend Mr. Jones.[i] When the storm blew up, Elliott did eventually pay Jones, who, of course, didn't exactly need the money anyway. In July 1947, having evidently found Jones, Elliott sent him $5,741 to cover the settlements with Hartford and David G. Baird, including 4% interest.[1762]

Malodorous enough as that was, this was just the story that came out of the investigation. There is an alternative, unreported, and far more rancid explanation for Jones's largesse, contained in the supremely well-informed letter to Pegler about "Uncle Jesse." It said, as recorded in an earlier chapter, that Elliott explicitly told Jones he would abandon his radio claims in Houston: "he openly made a deal to dismiss his then pending application for 50,000 watts in Houston for Uncle Jessie's (KXYZ) promise to satisfy Hartford.'"[1763]

Anonymous charges always require independent confirmation. And it turns out that in June 1941, a row had erupted over the FCC's sudden issuance of power increases to Jesse Jones's two Houston stations. One station, KTRH, received an increase to 50 KW on 5 April 1941.[1764]

Mark Ethbridge, former chairman of the National Association of Broadcasters, testified to the Senate Interstate Commerce Committee that "the FCC granted power increases to stations in Houston in which Mr. Jones was believed to hold a financial interest, at a time when it was studying the question of power increases."[1765]

Whatever his true reasons, "Uncle Jesse" did save Elliott's financial skin. In so doing, he also saved his boss in the White House serious embarrassment.

Why would the president intervene to save his son's bacon at that particular time, just before Pearl Harbor? Well, Elliott had become concerned about his mortality. Even though he had been in the military for over a year, his creditors were still after him. He testified:

> ER: In 1941 after Pearl Harbor I became considerably exercised over the fact that in all likelihood I would be ordered into combat operations almost immediately. The condition of my finances was such that in the event of my death, my estate would be in a hopelessly tangled and debt-ridden state. I felt in order to protect my children that my creditors should either take over the collateral which they had or that I should declare bankruptcy and that then, even though I had practically no estate to leave in the event of my death my family would be free and clear of debts which I had contracted. I contacted my father and told him of this situation and he suggested that I should contact Mr. Jesse Jones and get his advice, inasmuch as Mr. Jones was familiar with my operations in Texas and he was personally familiar with the radio business in Texas. I contacted Mr. Jones and explained my situation as I have just outlined it.
>
> U.S. Treasury agent: When did your father suggest that you contact Mr. Jones?
>
> ER: I believe that it was by telephone in December of 1941 after Pearl Harbor and I believe that he stated at that time that he would tell Mr. Jones that the first time that I had an opportunity to see him personally I would contact him and explain the entire matter. This is the part that bothers me. My recollection is that I saw Mr. Jones in Washington the latter part of January 1942 but his records indicate that he had already started to work on this before then...I know what happened. It was before Pearl Harbor. In contacted my father relative to this because I had already served an overseas tour before Pearl Harbor and my uneasiness if anything happened to me and that must have been in September or October 1941.

---

[i] ChigTrib, 14 SEP 45. Jones had resided in the capital for 12 years and maintained an office there.

> U.S. Treasury agent: You contacted your father by telephone?
>
> ER: First by telephone and then he said that if I got up to Washington and I think I was in Washington sometime between that September or October 1941 and the first of December, and I contacted Mr. Jones personally and had several conferences with him on my financial condition and after the final conference with him, I went out to Muroc Lake in December 1941, and Mr. Jones had already told me to leave it in his hands. Before Pearl Harbor I was very much exercised about the whole matter and contacted Mr. Jones again because I felt that I would be sent on foreign duty almost immediately and he told me that he was working on the matter and to leave it in his hands. That he would work it out as fast as he could.[i]

Jesse Jones later confirmed that FDR called him the week after Pearl Harbor – at nine o'clock, Sunday the 14th – and told him to straighten out his son's mess:

> The President said Charlie Roeser and Sid Richardson, of Fort Worth, were then with him at the White House. He asked me to see Sid and Charlie so that they could give me all the facts in the situation.[1766]

In other words, the oilmen did not visit the White House merely to discuss oil business. They were there to offer to save Elliott's butt. But what would they receive in return? Jesse Jones was no fool. He was known to be so cock-sure of his position in the administration that he could defy or correct the president's top men. When Drew Pearson heard of what Jones had done for Elliott, he thought he knew why. "That's the first time I ever heard of Jesse getting trimmed," exclaimed a Congressman. But with Jesse, or "Jesus H. Jones" as FDR called him, there was no quid without a quo.[1767]

Years after, Jones noted bitterly that the president knew that A&P was subject to a federal lawsuit, but did not tell him; otherwise he wouldn't have touched the odious deal. He wrote that he "acted only at the President's behest and would not have acted at all had he known that the company headed by one of Elliott Roosevelt's creditors was then being sued as a monopoly by the Federal Trade Commission."[1768]

Jones also noted that this was merely one item in a pile of dirty laundry: bypassing Congress, President Roosevelt wanted Jones to use his immense RFC funds to buy the Empire State Building skyscraper in order to help out his old benefactors (J. J. Raskob and Al Smith owned it). Jones, for whom it was important to appear honest, would not do that.[1769]

As the tax agents slowly dragged it out of Elliott's mouth, the Jones matter was no parenthetical little sleight of hand. It was a major operation involving many meetings between Elliott, the president, and Jesse Jones over a period of several months. Jones was given a full list of creditors, with the amounts, and told to get to work. Interestingly, after Elliott was forced to perform this financial striptease, which continued through staff members after he went to Africa, Jesse Jones did not fill in Elliott on how he had settled his affairs. Elliott read about it in the papers in 1945.[1770]

In pursuit of this objective, Jesse Jones conscripted the assistance of his Texas friends Sid Richardson and Charlie Roeser. The afternoon after their White House visit, they showed up in Jones's office and began plotting the rescue operation.[1771]

---

[i] ER Testimony, 58-9, Hartford Loan File, ER box, Pegler/HH. ER was at the White House 8-11 DEC, the oil men on 14 DEC (FDR Appts Day-by-Day), FDR Lib.

They each wrote letters asserting to the creditors that Elliott's Texas radio network was broke and the stock worthless. Auditors later became extremely interested in this, because soon after Elliott went to war, the radio stations began posting big profits. Worse, at the same time, Mr. Roeser had, under Elliott's power of attorney, sold TSN stock to others for $17 a share. To the auditors it looked like the out-of-state creditors had been very methodically cheated out of valuable collateral, more than 2,000 shares in the Texas State Network.[1772]

That impression was reinforced by John Hartford's lawyer, Caruthers Ewing's testimony that he had been extremely reluctant to give up the loan notes to Jones, but had finally agreed on the proviso they be torn up, and he be left with the half page with Elliott's and Ruth's signatures – which was promptly done.[1773]

Jesse Jones, whose integrity was questioned over the matter, later explained:

> After I got all the facts I could, I reported them to the President. He then said he would appreciate it very much if I would confer with Elliott's creditors and see what, if anything, they would be willing to do about his debts. He repeated that Elliott was in the Army and had no way of paying his debts.
>
> Helping people in trouble was my business in Washington, and, while I did not particularly like this assignment, I could not very well refuse the request of the President…
>
> Mr. Hartford came to my office on December 30, 1941 …We had a pleasant visit, and he told me a good deal about their business, its growth, etc., which was interesting. When we reached the subject of Elliott's debt Mr. Hartford told me he was willing to do anything the President wanted him to do, that dollars meant very little to him, since from the standpoint of income they were worth about 11 cents as he was in or near the 90% income bracket and at his death taxes would probably take 90% of his estate. He also said that he did not want Elliott's notes in his estate while he was living or after he was dead.[1774]

By the time he wrote in 1951, Jesse Jones roundly detested the president he had served so ably. In this case (as in many others) he accused him of breach of faith:

> At the time Mr. Hartford loaned the money his company was being sued by the FTC under the antimonopoly laws. This was of course known to the President, but not to me. Under that circumstance Mr. Hartford should not have loaned Elliott the money and the President should not have permitted Elliott to borrow it. Certainly, if I had known about the suit, I would not have had anything to do with Elliott's affairs with Mr. Hartford. I did not hear anything about the suit until long after the transaction.[1775]

Jones said the reason he offered Hartford $4,000 to settle the $200,000 debt was simply that this was the maximum amount he could give without triggering gift tax, and he had no expectation of ever seeing the money again. When Hartford's attorney, Ewing, came over with Elliott's four $50,000 notes on 17 March 1942, he carefully cut them up and threw parts of them in the waste paper basket: "I noticed he tried to cut out Mr. Hartford's name."

When Ewing left, the Secretary of Commerce and the world's most powerful banker (via the RFC), dove into the trash and recovered the pieces – you can't be too careful. Then, instead of keeping the TSN stock, he gave it to the president. FDR said he'd get the money back when Elliott got his inheritance from Grandmother Sara.[1776]

President Roosevelt then gave the "worthless" stock to Ruth Googins in the divorce settlement. It made her and the children rich; it was thought then to be worth at least $1.5 million.[1777]

Mr. Jones was very, very careful to document all his moves in this matter. In his book, he published photocopies of the four notes and his scrawled letter to the president. He included a 1947 note to "Uncle Jesse" from Elliott Roosevelt, who then had some money. Elliott wanted to know how much he owed. Jones wrote back, and:

> Two weeks later an envelope arrived in my office in Houston containing Elliott's check to me for $5,741. [inc. 4% interest] There was no covering letter of any other message in the envelope.[1778]

Thus by the end of 1942 the Secretary of Commerce, a solid citizen even at dirty jobs, seemed to have solved the problem. He got the Roosevelts off the hook, and was out only a few thousand of his own ample funds. And that's not counting the power increase granted to his Houston radio stations. His cabinet position was secure.

The non-Texan radio network investors were out of luck, Elliott had run through the money, Ruth and the children prospered after the divorce. Effectively, the Texas oiligarchs – Richardson and Roeser, primarily – had cleaned everyone else's clock. They got back the radio stations they had said were worthless, and ran them very profitably. John Hartford was furious, but on the other hand, the White House quashed the anti-chain store bill, and the other investors who were hit up by Elliott received various considerations.

A loyal lawyer, Charles Harwood, who had loaned Elliott $25,000 in hopes of becoming a federal judge, was instead appointed – or rather disappointed – to become governor of the American Virgin Islands. The president assigned Jesse Jones to settle that loan for $1,000, saying Harwood ought to just take the tax loss; but Harwood sneered at the offer and kept the "worthless" stock, which soon became valuable. John T. Flynn, who wrote in 1950 from published sources, summarized the issue:

> There were three or four other loans which were settled at varying percentages of their face value by Jones at the same time. Altogether, Elliott had some $800,000 of this kind of paper out.[1779]

Harwood was bitter. He said he'd been promised the judgeship for the money, "and, if that was not available, he would take a commission as a general in the Army or in the high brass of the Navy."[1780] Having declined to give up his collateral, he instead was appointed to the little coveted post as Virgin Islands governor until President Truman fired him in January 1946.[1781]

Old Jim Farley had an odd take on the Harwood appointment. On 23 June 1939, the president called the postmaster to the White House, where as usual the two talked stamps at first. Then Farley mentioned that he had a hard time finding a slot for Harwood, who was pestering him for the judgeship he thought he was owed. Farley had not heard that Harwood had paid $25,000 to Elliott for the job, but apparently FDR thought he knew. At any rate, after that meeting, the president was "cold and distant" to Farley. "There was ice in the President's manner toward me."[1782]

According to Westbrook Pegler's unpublished notes and letters, these loans were merely the visible tip of a vast extortion racket. It did come out that a New York banker, David G. Baird, was hit up for $70,000 in November 1939, and a New Jersey manufacturer, Maxwell M. Bilofsky, surrendered $50,000 the preceding August:

> Mr. Jones [Jesse J.] acted as intermediary in these settlements, also, and Mr. Bilofsky says the late William Sirovich, New York New Deal congressman, told him the president knew about the loan. Mr. Baird, however, says that, as far as he knows, the president was not aware of his "investment."[i]

In truth, Internal Revenue agents noted in 1945 that Baird loaned $50,000 and then another $70,000 to Elliott. Of that $120,000, Baird got $40,500 back, partly due to the intervention of Jesse Jones, who again represented to Baird that the collateral stock was worthless.[1783]

While Baird may have thought the president unaware, he did note that Elliott got him an invitation to meet with FDR at Warm Springs, which he did six months after the loan. Baird also said that reports of his company getting "the lion's share" of war plant insurance policies could not be related to him, as he had no knowledge of them.[1784]

President Roosevelt also held up the rich financier Victor Emanuel for money for Elliott. Emanuel was invited to lunch at the White House for the sole purpose of asking him for "financing the purchase of some radio properties in Texas by Elliott." Emanuel declined, telling FDR that it was not a sound investment. Later, Elliott personally made another pass at Emanuel's money, and was again refused. Emanuel was uncomfortable, for he claimed he was getting some "harassment" from the government at the time.[1785]

The *unpublished* portion of the Elliott racket can be triangulated with reasonable precision from the official testimony and the better-informed documents in Pegler's files. One of these letters, backed up in overall substance by others independent of it, states:

> A friend of mine who is in a position to know, has informed me that during Elliott Roosevelt's radio-refinancing operations he compiled a list of prominent and successful or rich independent oil operators in Texas, and determined the amount for which he would "tap" each of them respectively, and proceeded to do so by drawing cash-item sight drafts on them and simultaneously mailing each a letter advising that he was refinancing his radio network and was sure they would want to participate and he was accordingly drawing a cash-item draft for the sum of money and through the bank designated in the letter. As I understood my informant's statements, the letter made no mention of repayment or the delivery of radio network stock or other collateral as security, so that, if true, the scheme was his most brazen effort at extortion, blackmail, or selling political influence.
>
> My informant tells me that as far as he knows, every person in Texas, with the exception of two men at Amarillo, upon whom Elliott Roosevelt drew the drafts, paid the sums and have kept quiet about it; - the exception above noted created this incident:
>
> The two Amarillo partners were on the list; one was out of the state when the letter was received advising that the draft had been drawn. The partner who received the letter before the draft for $50,000 arrived, became excited and called the absent partner by long distance, and first suggested and then urged that the absent partner consent to the payment of the draft, fearing the consequences of retaliation and reprisal. The absent partner

---

[i] Washington Times-Herald clip, 2 JUL 45, Hartford Loan File, ER box, Pegler collection, HH Lib. The Baird-Bilofsky-Harwood transactions were widely publicized; other, more apocryphal, transactions were not.

> declined to stand the charge, and advised the man in Amarillo that if he insisted on paying the draft it should be charged to his own account and that he (the absent partner), not being in the state, was not available for presentation of the draft.
>
> The partner who was on the ground actually, and "on the spot" figuratively speaking, took the tip, and in talking by long distance with the absent partner advised him that if the absent man was not available he, the other partner, would soon be in the same position, and he accordingly left town posthaste, so that when the cash-item draft was received it could not be presented for payment, and of course, being a cash item, had to be paid the day it was received or returned for non-payment.
>
> My informant has not stated the exact number of individuals, nor named any of them, who were "tapped" by the above-described process, but he has definitely stated that, with the exception of the two Amarillo partners all others paid the drafts, either through fear or with the hope of buying favors or otherwise improving their political positions. I think my informant has or can get the names of all the men and the amount of the draft paid by each, and consequently the total amount raised by Elliott in this maneuver…[1786]

Although there were several letters touching on this *modus operandi*, nothing came out publicly. It is not illegal to ask people for money. For the son of the president to demand money from rich people on pain of executive or legislative punishment undoubtedly is. For the president to encourage, or even be aware of the operation is surely grounds for impeachment. But nothing came of it. Why should the marks talk? It would be not only deeply embarrassing; it might bring them in hot water as well.

Only the A&P's John Hartford seemed to have been taken both coming and going, winding up with only two cents on the dollar. Of course, if A&P dodged the chain-store tax because of the "investment," Hartford did very well indeed; but he was an honest man, inclined to give favors without demanding any. At any rate, he made no real effort to protect himself. So he lost on the loan, and then on the stock collateral he was persuaded to surrender to the president.[1787]

All in all, Elliott's *documented* payments from targeted lenders amount to about a half a million dollars. In addition, the federal treasury lost the taxes on the $196,000 Hartford lost to Elliott, and it gained none on Elliott's commensurate profit. That became an issue due to the confiscatory marginal tax rates then in effect. That no one was in any doubt that they were in a game that couldn't stand the light of day was evidenced by Hartford's use of an unusual out-of-town personal check for the $200,000, and the repayment of $4,000 in an anonymous cashier's check.[1788]

More disturbing still was that the $200,000 loan apparently did not go to the radio network. The temporary figurehead president of TBN, John T. Adams, later revealed that as far as he knew the money wasn't used in Transcontinental. However, other well-informed sourced said Elliott paid off prior indebtedness with the new debt.[1789]

Adams also implicated President Roosevelt directly. He testified under oath that Elliott was supposed to get 17½ % of the network stock, but that in the final allocation:

> Elliott Roosevelt personally subscribed for $250,000 which was more than 70% of the total $350,000 issue as planned. I was shocked at the subscription because I knew he did not have any such money but immediately after the meeting, he told me that he had spent the previous evening with his father, and on the advice of his father, he had subscribed to this amount of stock, assuring me that his father had told him that the necessary capital would be forthcoming when necessary.[1790]

Of course, it is possible that Elliott embellished the president's approval.

The summer of 1945 was an awkward moment in American politics. Congress went through the motions, and in August released the report which listed the sordid details but then laid the matter to rest. Congress still had a Democratic majority, so there was a general reluctance to act. In addition, the late president was in the process of being canonized as the savior of the nation, even the world, and fewer critics now wanted to point out the flies in the soup. Besides, there was still Japan to defeat, and a precarious peace to maintain. The Republicans yelled in vain.

On 21 September, the Congressional Republicans were defeated when they attempted to call Elliott to Capitol Hill for questioning, but the House could not agree on what to do next. A reporter heard from some members that they wished they had never agreed to investigate the matter: "It's a bear by the tail."[1791]

The story almost vanished. The way Pegler remembered the report's release was amusing if highly tendentious:

> The subcommittee did not hold any hearings or examine any witnesses. [The agencies, however, did investigate thoroughly.] …Finally they announced that they were going to issue a report tomorrow. So about noon I called on Doughton [chairman Ways and Means] and some secretary handed me a skinny little document which was nothing but the majority report vindicating my leader as a man for the ages and his son as no crook and the minority version that it was a rotten scandal all the way. That was all there was to it.
>
> But where were the questions and answers? Oh, that stuff had not been printed. The Democrats decided to save a little money so they just prepared 12 or 14 sets of photostats for the press. All right, where was my set? Oh, but I was too late. They had dumped them on a table in some room in the Capitol and called in some genial fellows friendly to the Roosevelt family. The photostats were all gone. Snatched up. You know – the early bird.
>
> I was ready to end it all when Bill Hutchinson of the INS [Hearst press agency] told me that the Democrats had not dared withhold it from the press associations.
>
> So Bill let me have his and there, my friends, is a priceless record of the perfidy of a crooked president which is a historic treasure for the Westbrook Pegler Memorial Library, thanks to the martyr Bill Griffin, who went through hell on earth for Ireland.[i]

There indeed are all the testimonies of the involved parties. And they do take your breath away, but their appreciation still requires a lot of time for reading and comprehension. That thief-in-the-night release was quite a contrast to the wild circus that surrounded the Roosevelt-Hughes fracas two years later. The difference was that by then, the Republicans controlled both Houses.

The Roosevelts' "Lend-Lose" Program

The reason for investigating the Great Chain Store Robbery in detail is not that it illuminates yet another of Elliott's shady schemes. It is that it unequivocally implicates the President of the United States in a corrupt, impeachable offense. It might be argued that similar cases could be brought against other presidents, and of course, that other cases of similar merit could be brought against this one. The point is that bringing the chief executive to justice is always a political process, and it fails or succeeds accordingly.

---

[i] Pegler col. 29 MAR 55, Rome News-Tribune. William Griffin: the Anglophobe who first alerted Pegler.

When the 79th Congress released its report declining further investigation of Elliott's finances, the Republican minority issued a scathing dissent. From this diatribe we know some of the details which Congress and the Administration had decided to omit. The congressional report stated:

> On March 31, 1939, Mr. John A. Hartford, president of the Great Atlantic & Pacific Tea Co., advanced $200,000 to Elliott Roosevelt, son of the late President, Franklin D. Roosevelt, in exchange for four promissory notes of $50,000 each, signed by Elliott and his wife, Ruth G. Roosevelt. Three years later, at the request of the President, Mr. Jesse Jones, then Secretary of Commerce, settled the entire indebtedness. Mr. Hartford accepted $4,000 in full payment of all notes, which were destroyed, and returned to Mr. Jones 2,000 shares of the capital stock in the Texas State Network, Inc., which he had held as collateral for Elliott's obligations…[1792]

For context, it is necessary to recall that the Atlantic & Pacific Tea Company chain was then at the height of its nationwide power. It was a kind of pre-war Walmart. John and George Hartford were sons of George Hartford, who had founded the famous and esteemed company to import tea from China in 1857. (The illustrious A&P, after a long decline, finally closed in 2010.)

> The minority is convinced that as a result of this transaction someone is escaping payment of a tax on $196,000 of income – money that the Treasury of the United States, facing a $300,000,000,000 debt, should collect…
>
> How did this debtor-creditor relationship arise, and why? What prompted the parties to act with such speed? Why did Mr. Hartford rely so heavily upon the President's approval of the alleged loan? Why was the obligation settled for 2 cents on a dollar just at the time the network began showing a profit?
>
> In fairness to Mr. Hartford it must be stated that the record clearly shows that he was a reluctant participant in the transaction between himself and Elliott Roosevelt; that the Roosevelts sought out Mr. Hartford, who, until the day before the money passed between Mr. Hartford and the President's son, was a total stranger to both the President and Elliott.
>
> On the other hand, Mr. Hartford and his brother George Hartford were the owners of the Great Atlantic & Pacific Tea Co., operating a nation-wide chain of some 13,300 grocery stores. At the time the transaction took place, in March 1939, a bill was pending before the Ways and Means Committee (H.R.1, 76th Cong., 1st sess.) to provide a special excise tax on such stores. The bill was introduced by Representative Wright Patman, of Texas, about 3 months before Hartford advanced $200,000 to the President's son. After prolonged hearings in 1940, and in the face of vigorous opposition from the administration, the bill died in committee.
>
> At the hearings held in March 1940 Mr. Patman estimated that the Great Atlantic & Pacific Tea Co. would be liable for an annual tax of $6,625,000 if the bill became law…[1793]

Congressman Patman was a New Dealer who would continue to represent his fiefdom in northeast Texas until his death in 1976. His anti-chain store bill would have imposed punitive taxation, although estimates of the size of the burden varied.

The agitation for this bill was very similar to the anti-Walmart sentiment two generations later. The less efficient Mom-and-Pop stores were embittered by the economies of scale of the chain-store competition. The bill was certainly not introduced simply to assist Elliott, but it did make it absolutely imperative for Mr. Hartford to remain in the good graces of the White House. That is why Hartford was about to launch a massive advertising campaign to defeat the Patman bill. Mr. Ewing, Hartford's attorney, issued a probably exaggerated claim that the original Patman bill would have cost A&P $600 million and "would have forced the company out of business."[1794]

After the Hartford loan, the Texas State Network supported the campaign against the chain-store tax, which made investigators extremely interested in whether a hidden quid-pro-quo was struck. Elliott denied having anything to do with killing the bill.[1795]

However, Patman told a snitch that Elliott, after receiving the loan, campaigned and made speeches against Congressman McFarlane of Texas, a strong backer of the anti-chain-store bill. "MacFarland lays his defeat to the presidential son's intervention. Mac won't talk because Papa Roosevelt gave him a fairly decent job with the Smaller War Plants Corporation at Washington."[1796]

The money Elliott shook loose from A&P reportedly stayed the execution of Elliott's struggling radio chain:

> This money, obtained from Mr. Hartford for Elliott, was invested in the Texas State Network, Inc., a chain of 23 or more radio broadcasting stations organized by Elliott in 1938. Within a few years thereafter the corporation acquired ownership in 3 stations, a controlling stock interest in a fourth and service contracts with 19 others. Prior to organization of the network late in 1937, the President spoke over many of these stations in a special hook-up. Thereafter, Elliott organized the corporation. Almost immediately following this event, wealthy individuals were sought out for money with which to capitalize the venture. Among such investors was one man who put in $25,000 and thereafter received a high Federal appointment...[1797]

The minority report's objective went beyond proving the initial shakedown. It now attempted to show that the President of the United States had cleaned out Mr. Hartford both coming and going; and in the process, had also taken his own Secretary of Commerce for a demeaning ride.

> The Texas State Network was a losing proposition until about the time the Hartford transaction was wiped off the books. It was losing money when Mr. Hartford was taken in. Three years later he was given to understand the stock was worthless and that Elliott was impoverished. The record, shows, however, that Elliott and his wife Ruth realized a profit of $16,123 for the year ended April 30, 1942, from his partnership with Mr. Hutchison doing business under the name of Elliott Roosevelt Properties, and that he had other assets.
>
> It is interesting to note that when the Texas State Network did begin to show earnings, in 1942, the President of the United States again stepped into the picture to ask Jesse Jones to settle Elliott's indebtedness and reacquire the stock, even though only half of the indebtedness was then due and payable. As a result of this, Elliott's indebtedness was settled for about 2 cents on the dollar, on or about March 17, 1942...It is significant to note that the Texas State Network has since become a profitable venture; that its principal owners are Sid Richardson, Charles Rosier [sic], Mrs. Ruth Roosevelt Edison [sic], and Elliott's children...
>
> Only a few days ago, on September 27, 1945, Elliott is credited by the United Press with having said:
>
> Beginning in 1942 the corporation began to show a profit and by the end of 1944 was $400,000 in the black before taxes. This year the profits went even higher. In 1944, my stock went to other stockholders, my ex-wife and in trust for my children of that marriage.

> According to that same source, Elliott said he was advised by the network's counsel that at the time the stock was transferred "it should bring from $1.5 -2 million. If I fathered a flop in the Texas State Network," Elliott continued, "I'd like another like it right now."...

The dissenters, unable to open a criminal investigation, attempted to reopen the issue of the tax the Bureau of Internal Revenue had decided not to pursue:

> Elliott indicated that the ranch in Texas was not worth more than the mortgage against it. Since then it has been sold for $150,000 above the indebtedness against it...Clearly, as the case now rests, the Federal Treasury stands to lose the tax on $196,000. That must not be permitted. If John Hartford is entitled to a deduction of $196,000 in his gross income, positive steps should be taken to collect the tax on $196,000 income from Elliott Roosevelt...
>
> We do not concur in the view that these matters should be decided on the basis of political embarrassment.

The minority report concluded by quoting Elliott Roosevelt's testimony to the BIR. It revealed little that was new except that Elliott's memory failed him on precisely those issues that might incriminate him.

Let's get Dad on the Phone!

The victim, Mr. Hartford's, affidavit of 29 June 1945 was substantially more sinister:

> On March 29, 1939, Caruthers Ewing, general counsel of the Great Atlantic & Pacific Tea Co., came into my office located in the Graybar Building, New York City, and advised me that Dr. William I. Sirovich, who at that time was serving in the Congress of the United States, was a friend of his for many years and that the doctor telephoned Mr. Ewing that day, that the President had spoken to him relative to assisting Elliott Roosevelt, his son, in the matter of obtaining a loan of $200,000 for the purpose of purchasing a radio station *** and that it was suggested by the President that probably through Mr. Ewing an approach could be made to the Hartford brothers to obtain from them that loan. Mr. George L. Hartford promptly stated that he was not interested and would neither make nor contribute to the making of the loan. *** I was informed that Dr. Sirovich stated to Mr. Ewing that Elliott Roosevelt had left with him a paper which indicated that the security was worth between 600 and 700 thousand dollars. *** I inquired of Elliott Roosevelt whether his father knew of Elliott's request for the loan and that I certainly would not make such a loan without the President approving it. Elliott Roosevelt stated, "Let's get dad on the telephone," and that there would be no difficulty about obtaining his father's approval. *** When the conversation was made, Elliott said, "Hello, dad," and after some preliminary conversation *** said, "Here's Mr. Hartford," and handed the receiver to me. I inquired of the President whether he was familiar with the matter of the proposed loan requested by his son Elliott, and the President replied that he knew all about it and that he was familiar with all the details and gave assurance to me that it was a sound business proposition and a fine thing and advised me that he appreciated any assistance and consideration that I could give to Elliott in this matter and extended to me an invitation to call on him at the White House.[1798]

Thus it appeared (in 1945) that the shakedown propagated from Elliott via the White House to the New York Congressman and thence to the tax-exposed A&P Company. As we shall see, that Congressman, Dr. William Sirovich, (D., N.Y.), could not testify as he died on 17 December 1939, aged 57, immediately after paying off an individual who threatened to expose the connection between Roosevelt and Hartford.

Indeed, Hartford's lawyer, Caruthers Ewing, who was a "close friend" of Sirovich, testified that "Congressman Sirovich telephoned him and stated that President Roosevelt had requested him to secure an introduction of Elliott Roosevelt to John A. Hartford and George Hartford through Mr. Ewing."[i]

Ewing had been even more explicit in his testimony than press reports suggested. He swore that "Sirovich had told him many times how close he was to the president and that he was assisting Elliott Roosevelt in securing the loan at the direct request of the president, and that this was the only reason for his acting in this matter."[1799]

Ewing said that Dr. Sirovich had a note from the president to call A&P to get money for Elliott. He said that of his two bosses, George Hartford immediately exclaimed that he would not lend the Roosevelts a "plugged nickel" and walked out of the room. And he said that John Hartford reluctantly suggested that if the president asked him to do so personally, he thought he could not reject the loan. And that when he retold this to Hall Roosevelt, he said, "Well, there will be no difficulty about that."[1800]

Gracie Hall Roosevelt ("Hall") was Elliott's uncle; he had been deputized by the president to help Elliott find money.

With respect to the original call from the president, Mr. Hartford testified as follows:

> When I left the office I wanted to get out of making the loan if I could. When I met Elliott I told him that I was not interested in the radio business and I did not want to go into the radio business and I said to him what does your father think about this loan. Elliott, just like that, said let's go upstairs and get Dad on the telephone. He went upstairs to my apartment and went to my private phone and asked for the Little White House in Warm Springs, Georgia, that he was Elliott Roosevelt and he wanted to speak to his father. I don't think it was more than 40-50 seconds before I heard Elliott say hello Dad, he answered some questions, evidently about the children and then Elliott said to him, I am in Mr. Hartford's apartment at the Hotel Plaza, and the next thing Elliott did was to hand me the receiver and said Dad wants to speak with you.
>
> I said "Hello, Mr. President," and I heard a familiar voice, a voice I had heard over the radio many times, say "Hello, John." I then told him that Elliott was in my apartment, and asked him what did he think about this $200,000 loan Elliott wanted to make in connection with the radio business and the President said that he was entirely familiar with it, that it looked good and gave assurance to me that it was a sound business proposition and a fine thing. He said he would appreciate anything I would do for him. I practically committed myself to the loan and he said he wanted me to come down to the White House to see him and then we said good-bye. I then told Elliott, "I am going to make the loan," and that the only reason I was making the loan was that his father practically asked me to make the loan, and I further told Elliott that I was not interested in radio and that I was not asking any favors."
>
> Q. In other words, having spoken to the President and receiving his enthusiastic endorsement, you felt that you had received whatever credit information you needed?

---

[i] Hartford testimony, 7, ER/Broadcast file, Pegler/HH. Dr. Sirovich visited FDR in the White House four times in the seven months before he died. (FDR Appointments Day-to-Day, FDR Lib).

A. I thought that was better than Dun & Bradstreet.

Q. Were any representations made to you by anyone, as to possible benefits that might accrue to you or the A&P if this loan was made?

A. No sir. After the president was so enthusiastic about it, I felt that I was on the spot and I had to make a decision right then and there, and I did not want to do anything to incur the enmity of the President…

Q. Did you feel in your mind, after speaking with the President that you had sort of a moral guaranty?

A. I certainly did…

Q. Now, Mr. Hartford, as long as you knew that the President had turned down Mrs. Roosevelt [this refers to FDR's refusal to permit his wife to broadcast for A&P mentioned in previous testimony], why didn't you turn down Elliott, just as your brother had done?

A. I did not think it was good judgment, being a direct approach from the President, to turn it down.

Q. Mr. Hartford, did you know at that time that Elliott had obtained loans from others?

A. No, I did not know anything about it.

Q. Mr. Hartford, what reason did you have for expecting that this loan would ever be repaid?

A. F. D. R.[1801]

When Elliott testified to Internal Revenue, his recollection of the president's call was magically different. So different, but detailed, that it ought to serve as a clue to the accuracy of his famed recollections of the conversations at the wartime summits. He said that Hartford put down the telephone, and then:

> He said, "The President has told me that if I want to make the loan to you that is between you and me and not to consider him in any way; that he is not connected in any way with what you might do; that he thinks that you should go ahead and stand on your own two feet in business and that the President was very, very agreeable to him on the telephone and that he, Mr. Hartford, was satisfied the President felt that whatever business transactions I would have with Hartford would have absolutely no connection with the Government or the President."[1802]

Elliott also testified that his father knew nothing about his business financing efforts until this call, and that Hartford was enthusiastic about the chance to invest with the President's son. In the grueling Treasury interview, Elliott was advised by his lawyer, Randolph Paul. A strong Roosevelt supporter, Paul had previously been the general counsel for the U.S. Treasury. Obviously Elliott was not taking any chances.

In truth, we know from Mr. Ewing's notes that President Roosevelt's telephone call had been pre-arranged by Ewing, Elliott, and Hall Roosevelt, to "let the President give Mr. Hartford that assurance which I had been told would be most cheerfully given."[1803]

From the transcript, there is little doubt that the Treasury agents believed Elliott was perjuring himself throughout the interview. They drilled and they hammered and they blasted, but the president's son knew his story and stuck to it. Only Hartford could deny it:

> Question: Would it surprise you to know that in the course of this investigation and the talks between representatives of the Treasury Department and Mr. John Hartford that he stated that he called the President in order, among other things, to make sure that the

President would not be embarrassed if Mr. Hartford made this loan to you and that he also stated that he had hoped and secretly expected "to be taken off the hook" and that, when he was asked by a representative of the Treasury Department what he meant by saying that "He hoped to be taken off the hook" he replied that he had hoped that the President would express his disapproval of the loan?

Elliott: It would surprise me very much because at no time did he ever indicate to me in any manner, shape or form that he had any such hopes, or that he ever felt that he was "on the hook."[1804]

In his Treasury testimony, Hartford then accounted for his bitter experience with Jesse Jones, sent by FDR to settle the debt and get back the stock certificates. Mr. Hartford's testimony was almost pitiable. He swore:

[Jones] telephoned me at my New York office on several occasions and told me he wanted to do some horsetrading and from Mr. Jones' conversation, I was led to believe that Mr. Jones was leading up to the past due debt of Elliott Roosevelt....I felt that the reason for the appointment was that I was going to be paid the loan of $200,000 with interest. At that first conference Mr. Jones said in substance that the President was very much worried over Elliott Roosevelt's finances and that the President had put this matter in his hands to see what could be done about it and that Elliott was in the Armed Services and was going overseas, and I replied that the President had worries enough now and did not want to cause him any more and anything that could be done in fairness to me and all concerned, I would go along with.

When I arrived in New York after said conference with Mr. Jones, I received further telephone calls from Mr. Jones in which it was urgently requested and stressed by Mr. Jones that I see him again... Sometime in March 1942 I had occasion to be in Washington on other matters and I had a conference with Mr. Jones and at that conference in Mr. Jones' office in the Reconstruction Finance Corporation Building, Mr. Jones stated that Elliott Roosevelt and his wife were without financial means and could not repay the loan and the collateral was worthless. I wanted to know if any part of the loan would be paid and Mr. Jones mentioned the figure of $4,000. I was very much incensed and disturbed about this, but finally agreed to settle this debt for the amount of $4,000.

...Subsequently and about March 17, 1942, the notes, as well as the 2,000 shares of Texas State Network, Inc. were delivered to Mr. Jesse Jones by Caruthers Ewing, my attorney. Mr. Jones mutilated the notes returning a piece of each note to Mr. Ewing, remarking as he did so I'm going right over and present this stock and mutilated notes to the Boss, so Mr. Ewing informs me.[1805]

This fits with attorney Ewing's testimony that Hartford had expected a much larger amount because he "felt that President Roosevelt was morally responsible to see that the loan was repaid."[1806]

Presumably Mr. Hartford did not know that Elliott and his father had asked Jesse Jones to pay off Hartford with his own funds, and that, however insulting the amount was, the real insult lay in Jones's knowledge that the collateral was gaining in value.

Q. Did you have any basis for feeling that you were going to be paid in full?

A. No.

W. How did you come to feel that way?

A. I thought the President would pay his sons' debts just as any father would pay his sons' debts...

Q. In spite of the lack of real obligation.

A. Don't you think it was a moral obligation?

...I did not check into whether Elliott was lying or telling the truth. Mr. Jones assured me that Elliott was broke and insolvent and the stock was worthless, and being a member of the Cabinet and head of the largest bank in the world [RFC], that was all the assurance I wanted.

...Q. Mr. Hartford, did you make any other large loans to individuals?

A. No sir, that is my first and last.[1807]

Mr. Hartford's indignity seemed to have no end. After his deal with Elliott, some interesting characters emerged from the woodwork to see if they could "help" him.

Hartford testified that the swindler John Kantor (of whom much more later), with former TSN president Jack Adams in tow, had come to him to try to get even with Elliott Roosevelt. Using Hartford's notes and collateral, they proposed taking over the radio network and running it professionally, since Adams was sure it would then be profitable. But despite Hartford's sense of having been raped by the Roosevelts, he wouldn't contemplate such an underhanded move. He had given his word that he would not do anything to embarrass Elliott, he said.[1808]

It would be Mr. Hartford who would be embarrassed, because the tax loss he had taken on the bad loan was problematic. To claim such a loss, one had to perform all possible diligence to recover the amount, and there was also concern that the loss had not been declared in the correct year. Internal Revenue had not initially questioned the tax loss, which at the rates then in effect was enormous, but now that the scandal was out, Treasury announced that it had "never" approved it, and would forthwith examine its validity. But the tax case was eventually dropped.

Hartford got all this trouble because he could not bring himself to inconvenience the President of the United States in the middle of a war for national survival. The surprisingly thorough Treasury investigation made it crystal clear that the President had effectively blackmailed Hartford under cover of his office. But there was, unfortunately, much much more, and it did not make it into the Congressional Record.

The Muckraker Who Got Stuck in the Muck

One who didn't give up was Westbrook Pegler, who wrote the immensely successful but somewhat misnamed "Fair Enough" syndicated column. He had sources inside the administration because he was becoming known as a national clearing-house for information documenting abuses of power. His columns increasingly hunted and haunted the Roosevelts. They continued to do so long after FDR was dead and the public had lost interest. In time, the once highly-regarded Pegler became known as a "stuck whistle" of the editorial pages. By the time of his slow fading out in the 1950s-60s, he was widely seen as a crank.

Before the war, Pegler was one of America's most respected columnists. Today, Pegler is universally remembered as a half-deranged hater, a "guttersnipe" to use Truman's term; but he had a terrific way with words, and it is a supreme irony that in FDR's first term, the young Navy veteran was a fierce New Deal loyalist. It is likely that this was caused by an instinctive, republican hatred of aristocracy and privilege; and it is likely that the break with the Roosevelts fundamentally came because Pegler came to see the family and its hangers-on as a new aristocracy, more devious and hypocritical than the old. At any rate, by the second term he spewed venom cross-country in his column.

Here is an early example of his invective:

> The appointment of a number of a gang of masked, night-riding terrorists to the Supreme Court was an important test in the campaign to corrupt the people, and since then the going has been fairly easy. The dealings of Jimmy and Elliott Roosevelt, the exploitation of office for financial gain, the amazing, bold program of petty larceny nepotism in Washington, the corruption of the ballot by bribery with taxes and borrowed money, the bland repudiation of every promise on which the New Deal was first elected, and the swelling arrogance of the embittered failures named to power in Washington all have combined to soften up the American people for the knockout. Given another mandate in November, the New Deal really will go to town, and the Constitution will be rewritten into Pig Latin and double talk.[1809]

The reader may conclude that they just don't make them like they used to; or that Pegler was a unique blowhard. An alternative explanation is that during FDR's reign, the Republic itself was being torn in two, and the views above accurately reflected the attitudes of that significant minority that believed that America was sliding down the Mussolini-Stalin-Hitler slope.

Pegler was a Tucson, Arizona resident for much of his life, and he did important journalistic work on the local Arizona scene. His investigations reveal the true motivation behind his better-known national opinioneering: he had an innate hatred of corruption and all that smacked of it.

Organized crime has played a significant role in the history of Arizona, perhaps because gangsters like to retire to pleasant climes as much as anyone. The Mob was often in bed with thieving politicians, dubious businesses, and thuggish labor unions. It was this intertwining of organized crime and organized labor that Pegler first exposed in the East, and that was how he earned the first Pulitzer Prize for reporting in 1941. Pegler uncovered the way the Chicago Mob took over the Hollywood movie industry, thus landing the prominent mobster Willie Bioff in jail. Bioff was Joe Schenck's partner in crime, and it is likely that Pegler was aware of Schenck's work with Joe Kennedy and the Roosevelt kids very early.[i]

Thus Pegler made his name as a Mafia-basher before he became a professional Roosevelt-basher, and he clearly thought this a natural progression. When he moved to Arizona, having first become rich and famous on the East Coast, he turned on the crooks in that state, too.

Pegler had no systematic political views; "dissension is his philosophy," as *Time* wrote.[1810] He initially welcomed the Roosevelt Revolution: *"Dear Mr. President...would it be presumptuous of me to say that you are getting along very well in your work?"* he wrote to FDR in July 1934. [1811]

There is preserved an amusing correspondence between the gutsy reporter and the chief executive. It reveals that both had an exquisite way with words, a sly humor, and apparently considerable mutual professional respect at first. In one case, Pegler pointed out that Washington's Hoover Field was hands-down the most unsafe and pestiferous swamp of an airfield in the nation. He columnized that a new ban on flying over

---

[i] Russo: The Outfit, 164-5. Capo Joe Bonanno retired to Tucson. Bioff, who squealed to authorities, resurfaced in Arizona under a new name but was killed in Phoenix in 1955. He had flown in from Vegas on close friend, Rep. Barry Goldwater's personal plane the night before. The Goldwater brothers were deeply embedded with the Las Vegas Mob.

downtown Washington was a safety hazard trivially intended to ensure the president's undisturbed repose. FDR wrote him that by now he should know him well enough to realize he would never jeopardize air safety for the sake of his comfort. (What would Pegler think of today's presidential airspace restrictions?) Two years later FDR built National Airport next to Hoover Field, which in turn became the original site of the Pentagon.

Pegler's slow disillusionment was caused by growing knowledge of the disreputable practices of the Roosevelt family. That may be why Pegler was, after a while, not able to keep a clinical journalistic distance, but slid into a personal hatred of the Roosevelts that would increasingly mar his columns and slowly render him ineffective and ignored. Still, he performed an immense service to history by collecting dirt on not only the Roosevelts, but on all other criminal, twisted, or merely inappropriate schemes he sniffed out.

In other words, Pegler was aggressively honest. It's no wonder he went mad – at least in the journalistic sense of the word.

For another sample of Pegler's gall, consider his 26 August 1947 column, written at a time when Elliott's drunken orgies were on the front pages:

> …Actually, I don't give a damn about Elliott's character. All I care about are facts and I insist that, but for me, posterity's history and literature would have been denied the story of a family without a like from the beginning of time to the date of these presents…Most of our presidents, though, have been mere mooseheads and muskellunge, stuffed with kapok and hay, and, but for my resolute insistence against the idolators, Frank D. would be, also, and his loved ones wax nonentities…
>
> As a historian, day by day I am criticized for delighting in the effronteries of Elliott. But what else, may I ask, has this strange fellow to be remembered for at all? Silence the story of his loans and defaults, his orgies and his invincible gall, and what have you? A sketch for a six-foot male, but not Elliott.

Referring to the recent hearings, Pegler continued:

> Now, during the recent quilting party in Washington, Elliott, in his blundering way, opened a wrong door and revealed a glimpse that posterity will enjoy as another impromptu scene at the fireside.
>
> Elliott said his photo-reconnaissance outfit had sent back to the United States during the war a Col. Harry Eidson, who had come through five missions. "He was the Colonel Eidson who was mentioned so much here," Elliott said.
>
> It seems that Colonel Eidson also had been a guest at some of Johnny Meyer's basket-lunch parties at El Morocco and hay-rack rides to the Waldorf. Eidson accomplished nothing on his assignment to Washington to get new planes, so Elliott, poor devil, tore himself away from the war for a dreary round of sordid relaxation in Washington, New York and Hollywood, mostly on the cuff.
>
> Elliott's second wife, Ruth Googins Roosevelt, married Lieut. Col. Harry T. Eidson on June 23, 1944, about two months after she divorced his commanding officer. Eidson was the pilot of a plane in which Elliott flew in the Tunisian campaign. The record does not state flatly that Elliott ever flew his own plane on actual combat missions, although he came home clanking with medals.

That was manifestly unfair, as we have seen, but Pegler was by now well beyond "fair and balanced:"

> In the official report of the Treasury on the investigation of Elliott's defaulted loans and strange financial practices, Mrs. Eidson swears that on November 9, 1943, President Roosevelt sent her 2,500 shares of Texas State Network, which Elliott had financed largely by gypping suckers.
>
> John Hartford, of the A&P grocery chain, and David G. Baird, a rich insurance man, gave up their stock collateral for two cents on the dollar and were trimmed for roughly $245,000. They were told that the stock was no good. Both said they believed this and turned in their certificates to Jesse Jones, who delivered them to President Roosevelt at the White House. The old man hid them so well that Elliott couldn't find them later, though he tried. Hartford's notes from Elliott were destroyed. Baird turned over to Jones notes made to him by Elliott for a total of $110,000. Baird endorsed them "without recourse." The mere destruction of Hartford's notes and the surrender of Baird's notes to Jones took Elliott out of debt. Without paying a dime he was forgiven debts of about $300,000. But more than that, the old man wheedled back the stock, which he then turned over to Ruth. In two years the stock was worth $250,000, divided between her and her children of Elliott, as alimony. Now Eidson is married to the girl with the fortune and Elliott's notes which Ruth holds are still alive and may be presented for collection at any time Elliott seems to have anything.
>
> About taxes on this fortune, I just don't know. The Treasury handed the Roosevelts special treatment amounting to a great personal gift from the taxpayers. The old man gave the stock and more to Ruth and the giver is supposed to pay the tax on a gift. The giver is dead, but he left a rich estate. So what now? Do the Roosevelt heirs pay a gift tax on Elliott's alimony to the present wife of his former army pilot? And if so, can't you hear the calm and stately accents of the happy circle, especially Sister Anna, as they express their feelings about Elliott and Ruth?
>
> Posterity better clip this little message for historical reference. There never was an outfit like this Roosevelt family.[1812]

Well, consider the message clipped for posterity, then.

The risky value of a stalker like Westbrook Pegler is that he saves every scrap that can be used against his target, and he usually does have the facts on his side; he could not publish half of what he knew because many of his sources wouldn't come forward. Pegler's voluminous poison file on the Roosevelts is now preserved at the Hoover Presidential Library in Iowa.

Part of Pegler's rancor, which in time degenerated into a pitiable rage, had to do with many other buried landmines he knew of in the Roosevelt Administration and the family. For example, he was aware that FDR had asked the industrialist Victor Emanuel, super-rich owner of AVCO, to set up a dummy corporation for the purpose of assuring his sons a comfortable income. Emanuel knew it was illegal and diplomatically told the president to clear the plan with the Department of Justice.[1813]

Like many of FDR's most strident enemies, Pegler had initially been among the president's avid supporters; in fact, he applied for a job in the administration.[1814] But by 1938, Pegler swung violently against FDR, either because of ideological concerns about totalitarian drift, or (as he held it) because of disgust with the never-ending scandals and corruption that characterized the regime.

After about 1950 people got tired of listening to Pegler's "stuck whistle." There were newer villains to argue over; Pegler's repetitive cant about Elliott Roosevelt's misdeeds ceased to entertain. Stale old news is not impressive to readers.

In old age, Elliott described how he and Franklin Jr. once had encountered Pegler in New York's famous Stork Club, practically a second home for Elliott and his roaming pack during the 1940s.[1815] They immediately set out to beat the living crap out of the columnist; however, the management intervened and prevented bloodshed. It was no idle threat; Elliott got into many fistfights over his lifetime.

Of that Pegler-beating story, James Roosevelt published a more detailed variation:

> Elliott came to my house in Washington to discuss Mr. Pegler with me. Things, he thought, had gone too far. I agreed that it was pretty bad.
>
> Then Elliott came up with his proposed remedy. "Jimmy," he said, "there is only one thing to do. You and I have got to waylay the guy and beat the hell out of him. Something humiliating and undignified – maybe with a horsewhip."[1816]

On Jimmy's suggestion, the two went to the White House to discuss the planned assault with their father. The president managed to talk them out of the attack because of the predictable repercussions; but he did agree it was a good idea "in principle."

There is yet another version of the Pegler-beating saga, one told my Elliott's close friend in Seattle, Ben Emerson. Perhaps recalling an elaboration of Elliott's, Emerson reminisced about his recently deceased friend:

> He was aggressive in everything. He was an aggressive bridge player, an aggressive driver, aggressive in everything. He seemed to have an extra measure of energy. He was also aggressive physically. He once beat up his brother Jimmy on the steps at Groton.
>
> One time, he told me about going to the Stork Club with his brother Franklin Jr., whom he called Frankie. They spotted Westbrook Pegler across the room. 'Let's go get him,' Elliott said…so they started over and Pegler hastily left.
>
> They started to chase him out the door, when their way was barred by two big gorillas – Sherman Billingsley's bouncers. Billingsley, of course, owned the Stork Club, and he pleaded with Elliott. 'Don't do it,' he said. 'Please don't do it. If you attack Pegler, all you will do is embarrass your family.'[1817]

Escaping with his life, Pegler continued to harass the Roosevelts and their admirers in a diminishing number of newspapers.

They all had reason to be angry. The press was vicious even then; so cruel was Pegler that Elliott said his mother broke down and cried over his column. Unlike her husband, Eleanor was thin-skinned and worried about criticism. She was not entirely without guile; she asked the FBI to find dirt on Pegler, but the GI-men did not succeed. Neither did the federal tax auditors, who went after him every year after 1934 "in every trifle and detail."[1818]

Yet, despite his relentless pursuit of the Roosevelt progeny, even Pegler did not know the full story in the matter of the loan extortion racket. Another Hoover, J. Edgar, did, and he wasn't talking.

The FBI File

American history might have been quite different if those who really knew had talked. But the one who knew the most talked the least.

Readers of a certain age may well recall that J. Edgar Hoover, the Director of the FBI from 1924 to his death in 1972, was widely believed to be unfirable because of his secret files on all Washington's main players. Another way of saying this was that as long as J. Edgar got what he wanted, he would keep his mouth shut about what he knew. He could even be discreetly helpful to his boss in the White House, earning Hoover the gratitude of no less than nine presidents; he was originally recruited by Wilson to hunt subversives during the Great War.

In effect, the White House had a sort of American Lavrentii Beria on its hands – extremely effective as long as handled with the caution a snake-charmer expends on his cobra.

Despite a presumed ideological divide, Franklin D. Roosevelt got along very well with J. Edgar. That was even the case when the intelligence services spied on the first lady, Eleanor, and accused her of adultery.[i] Hoover also kept files on the kids. The one on Elliott would have blown the lid off the presidency if Hoover had not kept it hidden and maintained a "no comment" stance. Most of the file was released under the Freedom of Information Act for this book.

In 1939-45, there were two cancers growing on the presidency. One was literal: FDR had a melanoma metastasizing from its visible location over his right eye. Recent medical research has strongly suggested that this cancer slowly spread to the president's brain, caused his obvious cognitive impairment in 1945, and eventually probably caused the cerebral hemorrhage that felled him on 12 April. The melanoma theory has been around since an ill-tempered conspiracy theorist, Dr. Emanuel Josephson, promoted it unsuccessfully in 1948, but it has recently been given renewed credit.[1819]

The other cancer was Elliott's troubled radio network. There were no less than three Roosevelts closely involved with this malignancy. Besides Elliott, they were Eleanor's unstable brother Hall, and the president himself. At the urging of Attorney General Frank Murphy, the FBI conducted an investigation of the matter. Afterwards, at Murphy's demand, Elliott's criminal accomplices were paid off, the principals told to keep quiet, and the whole matter consigned to the dark.

When Pegler's stories on the Hartford loan emerged in the summer of 1945, the FBI Director asked for a summary of known information. Because of the shocking material in the file, it is advisable to quote from it at length. It is the main source of this section. Also, as we have seen, the Treasury Department conducted an intense investigation into Elliott's transactions during the summer of 1945. The transcripts of interviews with the principals survive and provide a fascinating insight into not only the facts, but also the answer to the inevitable "What were they thinking?"

J. Edgar Hoover's memo began:

> In accordance with your request, the following summary is set forth for your consideration concerning the activities of Elliott Roosevelt and John M. Kantor in connection with the promotion of the Texas State Networks, Inc., of New York City.[1820]

---

[i] Joseph Lash, Love, Eleanor. The accusation was probably false, but the last chapters provide a horrific account of the alleged Lash-Eleanor liaison: ..."this resulted in a terrific fight between the President and Mrs. Roosevelt. At approximately 5:00 a.m. the next morning the President called for General Arnold, Chief of the Army Air Corps, and upon his arrival at the conference ordered him to have Lash outside the United States and on his way to a combat post within ten hours." (G-2 memo, op.cit., 493)

There followed a summary for John Kantor, a 67-year-old Swedish immigrant. In 1939 Kantor was living in an apartment adjacent to Elliott's New York City residence. According to the building superintendent, Elliott was responsible for obtaining this residence for him.

At that time, Kantor was best known for having witnessed against the criminal enterprise McKesson & Robbins, Inc. in an arms-smuggling case involving 250,000 Lee-Enfield rifles whose intended destination was not revealed (although Kantor told others they were intended for a revolution in Honduras). Kantor was said to be wanted in four states, but had always beaten the rap.[1821] When he was finally sent to jail in 1941, it was noted that he'd been arrested 14 times since 1924 for various offenses, but never convicted until then.[1822]

The FBI noted:

> During the period 1920 to 1939, Kantor was arrested over a dozen times on various charges, including grand larceny, conspiracy, false pretenses, mail fraud, and cemetery fraud. He was also said to be well known to the police agencies in England, Norway, and Sweden for his alleged fraudulent actions in these countries.

The McKesson case attracted a lot of notoriety in its day because the company was run by one of the Musica brothers, famous super-swindlers; in 1938, Philip Musica shot himself when exposed as an impostor.

In Chicago, Kantor was known as a chiseler and swindler going all the way back to 1915.[1823]

However disreputable John Kantor was, he was exceptionally well connected. He seemed to know every businessman who was short on money and scruple, and he had strong contacts in the Jewish community. The balance of the evidence suggests that Kantor was a sort of ambassador between the legitimate and the illegitimate worlds, conversing expertly with both in the common language of money.

Kantor's 1945 testimony to the tax agents reveal an international conniver who habitually and compulsively schemed with Congressmen, legitimate businessmen, and even foreign governments in one convoluted financial initiative after another. Distilled to essence, these chess-games usually came down to siphoning money from the less savvy to the better informed; any actual product involved gave the appearance, in retrospect, of being merely a prop for this trade.

Somehow such people always seem to find each other.

The FBI's New York Field Division had heard rumors in early 1939 from confidential informants that Elliott Roosevelt was involved with Kantor: "...they were to have opened a night club in New York City but now they are involved in a radio chain deal." The FBI observed Kantor meeting with Elliott and decided to pull him in for an interview, which was easily justified since Kantor was at that time involved in a number of other unrelated high-profile scams; in fact, he was out on bail.

So on 16 June, Kantor "incidentally" spilled the beans on Elliott to the FBI:

> Kantor explained during this interview that while he was involved in the McKesson & Robbins difficulty, he received a great many letters from friends. Among them were letters from ... G. Hall Roosevelt, Mrs. Franklin Delano Roosevelt's brother. Kantor stated that about this time he met Hall Roosevelt personally at the latter's office and was advised that Elliott Roosevelt was interested in a network of radio stations in Texas...

Gracie Hall Roosevelt, known as Hall, was Eleanor's younger brother. He was a brilliant engineer and fighter pilot who served as a flight instructor during the Great War. Unfortunately, he was also an alcoholic with severe behavior issues, two failed marriages, and an increasingly bizarre history of crooked business deals. "His mind is pretty foggy," wrote Eleanor, "as he's been drinking an average of at least one quart of gin a day." Hall drank himself to death in 1941, expiring with Eleanor at his side. He lived in a New York apartment one floor from Eleanor's on 11th Street, although Kantor said later that Hall spent most of his time at the Harvard Club.[1824]

When Franklin Roosevelt snapped at his hectoring wife, "It's not my side of the family that has the drinking problem!" he was thinking of Hall and many other Eleanor relatives. And he was right; his side seemed to have developed immunity.[1825]

Hall Roosevelt had a long history of enticing Franklin D. Roosevelt into dubious financial ventures. In the 1920s, he was constantly talking up schemes involving "stock market so-called killings, rice fields in Louisiana, power companies and aviation companies. Nothing ever panned out, though they helped keep Franklin's mind off his ailment."[1826]

Because of his aviation background, Hall also got in trouble using his famous name to sell aircraft overseas. In 1938, he was trying to make an illegal sale of 150 planes to the Spanish republican government. Two years later he was in Cuba trying to build airfields with "underground hangars" to Fulgencio Batista. Although FDR denied official interest, this initiative is important because it illustrates the close links between Batista and the Roosevelts, a subject to which, courtesy of Elliott, we shall return in force.[1827]

Hall's work with Elliott was therefore right in character.

With respect to Hall, President Roosevelt also used Jesse Jones as a fall guy. As head of the Reconstruction Finance Corporation, Jones effectively ran the world's biggest bank:

> Jones was rabid on the subject of Hall Roosevelt. Several times, he claimed, Hall used his relationship to Eleanor to call him about loans. The calls always came from White House phones, said Jones, who admitted to approving two or three loans in which Hall had a personal interest. In one instance, Jones related the story, he approved a "work loan" of $1,250,000 for a gold-mining project in Alaska. It was a "pan-mining" operation, where the gold is found in creek beds. Two days after he had approved the loan, said Jones, one of Franklin's assistants called him. "The President is very anxious for you to make this loan," Jones said Tom Corcoran informed him. "Because if you do it, Hall will get a job with the company as chief engineer, and FDR wants Hall as far as possible from the White House."[1828]

That is a correct rewrite of Jones's memoir, but Jones, ever concerned about his reputation, added that "Neither his efforts nor those of Tom Corcoran on behalf of the President had anything to do with the loan being granted." Regrettably, said Jones, Hall didn't stay in Alaska very long.[1829]

Jesse Jones was in the category of close advisers who came to loathe FDR. He would later write that "in no way did I feel his superiority over other men except that he was President and greatest politician our country ever had known, and ruthless when it suited his purpose."[1830]

In 1939, the boozing rake Hall was barely functional, but obviously still involved with rotten people. Attorney General Frank Murphy, who knew him well from his Detroit days (Murphy had been mayor there and then governor of Michigan), declared that Hall was "no good." Kantor also later testified that he already knew Hall when he held public office in Detroit.[1831]

During 1939, until Elliott was told to call it off, the shadowy moneyman John Kantor and he were very closely allied, even to the point that Elliott and Hall took their meals at Kantor's residence when Elliott was in New York. But Hall was even closer to Kantor and was involved with him in ventures other than the radio fiasco.

The FBI file continued:

> Kantor continued that G. Hall Roosevelt went on to say that President Roosevelt had asked him to breakfast one morning at the White House, and during the course of the conversation, explained Elliott's situation to him. The President is said to have asked Hall to assist Elliott in every way possible and particularly to secure for him the services of an experienced advertising man. Hall is then said to have offered Kantor a position with Elliott's concern, the Texas Network, Inc. Kantor said he accepted this offer and a short time later, in February or March, 1939, met Elliott Roosevelt at the home of his mother in New York City.

In the first Elliott-Kantor meeting, advertising strategies and radio station purchases were discussed in general. For example, Elliott had secured control of a Chicago station by cutting a deal with William Green, then chairman of the AFL-CIO. The union was to get 10% of the profits.

This allegation was in line with other stories about Elliott's radio stations. According to one of Pegler's informers, Elliott had at one time completed a deal for $250,000 to purchase a Washington D.C. station from Hearst. All that was left to do was to sign. But at that point, Elliott demanded a 10% rake-off to complete the deal. The sellers refused to pay the bribe and the deal fell through.[1832]

At about the same time, January 1939, Elliott Roosevelt reportedly ripped off an American expatriate businessman, Samuel Katz, by professing to be able to get the President to pressure the Mexican government to restore some oil wells that had been expropriated by the socialist Cardenas regime. The story's credibility comes from the fact that it was told by Alf Landon, the Republican from Kansas who had lost to FDR in the landslide presidential election of 1936.

Landon said that Katz came to him, claiming that after paying Elliott for his "influence," the president had suggested through Elliott that he, Katz, contact Landon since he had good Mexican connections. But Landon had been warned by oil company contacts that Katz was not the type to get involved with. When Pegler broke that story in January 1947, his correspondence filled up with letters suggesting that Katz and his father, Meyer Katz, were problematic characters of precisely the kind Elliott Roosevelt tended to associate with.

At any rate, Katz flew up from Mexico to Kansas in his private plane and met with Landon, who told him tartly that FDR would need to talk to him, Landon, directly. That was the end of that contact.

Nothing more is known about this incident although it obviously also involved the president directly. The episode is notable because it was an early example of Elliott's influence-peddling with Latin American customers, something that would turn into a main preoccupation years later.[1833]

At the time of the Kantor-Elliott alliance in 1939, Kantor also became aware that Elliott's property in Texas was heavily mortgaged; he evidently owed $110,000 on his radio stations, and more on his ranch. But he had also borrowed money on his livestock – three or four lenders, same cattle. Kantor said he'd heard there was legal action in Texas against Elliott in that regard, but "it was hushed up and straightened out."[1834]

Again, one such story is a rumor; two or more is a probability. Caruthers Ewing, Mr. Hartford's attorney, said he'd heard that Elliott sold mortgaged cattle in Texas without paying off the debt.[1835]

Kantor also said that Elliott told him he had borrowed from his wife's family. In summary, he held that the reason Elliott delayed sending the collateral stock to Hartford, and ignored the letters and telephone calls from Hartford's staff, was that "it took him some time to consummate the different deals with banks and creditors to release the securities whether they were deeds or mortgages or other stock certificates."[1836]

In fact, Elliott had promised Hartford 2,500 shares of TSN as collateral, but even after the struggle to actually get them, Hartford still only received 2,000 shares.[1837]

Despite his troubles or because of them, Elliott had a seemingly inexhaustible number of irons in the fire during the year before he joined the Army. But it was the Kantor liaison that would come back to bite. The FBI account continued:

> In this connection Kantor said it was Elliott's intention to form another company called the Regional Networks, Inc., which would include all of the independent stations through the Midwest from Kansas City to Pittsburgh…
>
> Kantor stated that he was at that time receiving a salary of $10,000 a year and $50 a week as expenses for his connection with Elliott's radio enterprise. He said that when the whole chain became completed he expected to get a 5% interest and they would then be able to offer advertising on a national basis. Kantor advised that President Roosevelt was aware of his connection with Elliott and also of his, Kantor's, past history.
>
> …Kantor mentioned incidentally that Paramount Pictures, Inc., had offered Elliott Roosevelt $100,000 for the Texas Networks, Inc., but that Elliott had refused to accept this because the President did not wish a Roosevelt enterprise to fall into the hands of a chain organization.
>
> …Because of President Roosevelt's attitude at that time towards Wall Street, Kantor stated that Elliott Roosevelt was not in a position to float any stocks or bonds or borrow any money from the general public. He advised very confidentially, however, that John Hartford, of the Atlantic and Pacific Tea Company, was then financing the enterprise.

Recall that in response to the president's telephonic exhortation, Hartford loaned Elliott $200,000 on 31 March.

After pumping Kantor for this information, the FBI went to the Attorney General, Frank Murphy (later a respected Supreme Court Justice). Murphy took immediate action to protect the president:

> The Attorney General, while in New York on June 21, 1939, informed Special Agent in Charge Foxworth that Elliott Roosevelt had stated to him that he had paid Kantor $1500 approximately two weeks ago to release him from all responsibility. The A.G. continued he did not know whether Elliott was telling the truth but believed that he was. The A.G. stated that he told Elliott to get rid of Kantor. Kantor, the A.G. said, had been annoying Mr. Roosevelt during the past few weeks and on that very day had phoned him seven times. The A.G. stated to Mr. Foxworth that he had suggested to Elliott that he call Mr. Foxworth

in the morning, whereupon the latter would come to see him and at which time Elliott would call in Kantor and tell him he did not want anything else to do with him. It was reported that Mr. Roosevelt told the A.G. he would do this.

On 22 June 1939, Elliott and Kantor thus met again in Elliott's office. Special Agent Foxworth attended, but under a fake identity as "Ellsworth," a friend. He said nothing, but he did remain in the meeting despite Kantor's request to be alone with Elliott:

> Mr. Roosevelt told Kantor that while he had severed relations with him several weeks ago, he wanted to have him in for a talk to be sure there was no misunderstanding whatsoever about the matter. Elliott then had Kantor review his entire association with him and Kantor's review of the situation required well over an hour.
>
> In substance, Kantor stated that he knew a Captain Underwood, with whom he had been associated in the Argo Oil Company. He claimed to have met Underwood some time ago at which time he, Kantor, was advised that Elliott Roosevelt was getting a loan of $25,000 from one Becker. Kantor claims he told Underwood that Becker had no money and could not make such a loan as he knew Becker himself was trying to borrow $1500. Underwood is said to have told Kantor to contact his source of information, who was G. Hall Roosevelt, and advise him of this fact and to have him be sure that Becker could raise the money. Kantor states that it was as a result of this that he later met Hall Roosevelt. Kantor related that it appeared at that time that there was an urgent need for money with which to meet Elliott's pay rolls. On the evening before the money was to be made available, Hall Roosevelt ascertained that Becker would not be in a position to put up the money. Hall then apparently proceeded to Washington where he was to make some arrangements to secure the money. As to what arrangements were made there, is not clear but in any event it does not appear that Kantor was concerned in this matter.

In his later 1945 testimony, Kantor still refused to disclose the source of the emergency loan of $25,000 to Elliott, but he made it clear that he was the one who arranged for Hall to pick it up.[1838]

> Thereafter it appears that Kantor endeavored to obtain some financial assistance. In this connection he contacted a Jack Miller, a Joe Fisher, and a man by the name of Segal, who is not otherwise identified. It may be noted at this point that this individual may be identical with Louis Segal, then President of the Segal Lock Company, New York City, hereinafter mentioned. At a later date Kantor said he contacted Congressman Sirovich. Working with Sirovich, Archibald Palmer, whose reputation is none too good, and one Bill Green, who was involved in a New York Investors Company mail fraud case, Kantor eventually secured a loan from Mr. Hartford of the Atlantic and Pacific Tea Company. The amount of the loan was not stated and it appears that no commission was paid on this loan. It then appeared that Roosevelt thereafter paid Kantor the sum of $1500 to cover expenses.

The confidence men associated with Sirovich were well known to the general public. Archibald Palmer was a sharp New York lawyer with some odd clients; he was currently in the news on a couple of matters, one being that a client had shot his wife and himself in Palmer's office. "Becker" could not be identified, although it was later learned that Hall Roosevelt did secure a $25,000 "gratuity" for Elliott from an unknown source.

Kantor later described how he used Congressman Sirovich to get to a number of rich people. He said that Sirovich was associated with him in two enterprises, "Honduras Packing Company" and "an oil situation in Mexico." "Incidentally, the oil situation in Mexico was the proposition in which Mr. Roy Fisher of Detroit, and other men in Detroit, including Governor Grosvenor [sic], were interested and they were friends of Hall Roosevelt." In other words, Sirovich was part of an extensive network of schemers. Fisher was president of the Argo Oil Company.[1839]

In Kantor's words, he was involved in Mexico with a number of other "rich Jews" who were interested in resolving the issue of Cardenas's oil nationalization program. They were also thinking of buying land in Nicaragua to resettle European refugees. They all would have made money, Kantor said, had it not been for Congressman Sirovich.[1840]

Dr. Bill Sirovich, according to Kantor, had lost him a lot of money due to ill-conceived ventures; Kantor said about $55,000.[1841] Kantor claimed "the man never had a dime." In street language, Kantor "owned" the Congressman's hide.

Ominously, the tax investigators were acutely interested in Sirovich's motives, and in whether he introduced or pushed legislation in order to benefit his secret business ventures. Kantor denied this, and said Sirovich agreed to help Elliott in part because he "owed" Kantor. Sirovich gave no sign of wanting in on the deal himself.[1842]

As the FBI knew, by June the Attorney General had taken action to eject Elliott from John Kantor's orbit. Somehow Kantor had been warned that Elliott was going to cut him loose. In 1945, he testified:

> I think it was in July 1939. He [Elliott] said he didn't feel that the company could afford to pay 7½ % commission because they could get all the men they wanted for less money and he wanted me to sign a release. I said to Elliott, why don't you tell me the truth? You know you haven't made any financing and you know you would have a hard time to get any yourself. Isn't it a fact that because of the notoriety that I had in the McKesson & Robbins case, etc., someone might have suggested to your father that it wouldn't be so good if I was acting as your financial agent? I had been told as much by Hall Roosevelt, who had come to see me and sort of tipped me off that that was what Elliott was going to do because someone had said something but that I shouldn't pay any attention to it and that I should work through Jack Adams and go right ahead and arrange for these loans if they could be made.[1843]

In other words Kantor knew perfectly well what was going on. The president, sensing the danger, had decided to throttle his son. While the FBI obviously had gotten word to him, President Roosevelt already knew from Elliott and his own contacts what was up. Oddly, Franklin and Eleanor had had dinner with Kantor's son and his wife during that same period. Nothing can be concluded from this other than that Roosevelt Senior kept his finger on the pulse of the Elliott-Kantor matter.

But brother-in-law Hall was working against the wishes of the president, and kept warm his link with Kantor. Despite being fired, Kantor went right ahead and worked with his Jewish financial contacts to secure more funding. That's when Elliott, urged by Attorney General Murphy, finally cracked down on him. [1844]

Kantor said he admired President Roosevelt's policies, but he quickly came to despise Elliott. He thought about suing him for breach of contract. His contacts thought he had good cause. But through a convoluted exchange involving FDR's law partner, Basil O'Connor, word was passed that it would not be good for Kantor to file a lawsuit. Kantor then went to Sirovich, who also told him to back off. [1845]

To the FBI, Kantor went on to relate the details of his prior employment by Elliott. He thought his employment had been indefinite, but Elliott asserted that he had only hired Kantor for 13 weeks. For his financial machinations, Kantor had already received $4,499.73.

Elliott made it clear that Kantor was fired and that he would have nothing more to do with him:

> Mr. Roosevelt then dictated a letter to Kantor transmitting a check in the sum of $583.33, and advised Kantor that his signature on the letter would constitute acceptance of an agreement that his services with the Texas State Network and/or Elliott Roosevelt were terminated. Elliott further stated that all moneys owed to Kantor for such services would be, by this instrument, fully paid…the original was given to Mr. Foxworth [FBI] with the request that it be transmitted to the Attorney General.
>
> Subsequent to the conference aforementioned, Elliott Roosevelt told Mr. Foxworth that he had no means of knowing with whom he was dealing and when people came to him and told him that they were well known and well connected, he accepted their word for such statements. Elliott continued that about two weeks ago he had received a "rumble" that everything was not well with Kantor, and at that time he decided to terminate his relationship with him. Mr. Roosevelt stated that he had ascertained that Kantor claimed to know people whom he did not know.

Here, Elliott nicely executed the diplomatic maneuver known as "deniability." There is in fact no chance Elliott could not have known who Kantor really was. For one thing, his various scams were all over the papers; for another, Hall Roosevelt had known him for many years. So did the president and his wife.

Attorney General Frank Murphy then informed the FBI that Elliott had told him that Hall was responsible for Elliott's business relationship with Kantor: "Also, Elliott Roosevelt had informed him that Hall Roosevelt and Kantor were interested together in an operation of some type of an airplane project in the State of Kansas several years ago."

> It is to be noted that the New York Office made inquiries respecting this latter relationship but was not able to ascertain any information to verify the allegation. The Attorney General continued that Hall Roosevelt was "no good" and that he had known him in better days when he was more dependable. The A.G. stated that Elliott Roosevelt was a headstrong boy and that the A.G.'s interest in this transaction was to protect the President from any embarrassment.

The FBI document further noted that Kantor did not entirely sever his relationship with the Roosevelts. Eleanor had lunch with Kantor's son and his wife a few weeks later. Then in August, Kantor himself threatened to sue Elliott to obtain more money. What looked like "getting his due" to Kantor looked like blackmail to the Roosevelts. Elliott called the FBI, but said he was "concerned about the publicity that might be given to the filing of such a case."

This again brought in the Attorney General, who realized the political implications of publicity in the matter. Then a unique and almost incredible problem arose: who, exactly, was the New York district attorney?

His name was Thomas E. Dewey, and he was the expected Republican presidential candidate in 1940. Dewey lost the nomination to the kindly Wendell Willkie, the dark horse who came from seemingly nowhere – actually the Democratic Party, in 1939 – to take the Republican nomination.

Dewey ran on an anti-corruption platform and on his tough prosecutorial record of purported honesty and efficiency. Thus, if Dewey had made Kantor sing in 1939, history could have turned out quite differently. As the FBI made clear at the time, Dewey had the bird in his hand:

> By memorandum dated December 13, 1939, Mr. Foxworth advised the Bureau that G. Hall Roosevelt had telephonically contacted him that afternoon and requested assistance inasmuch as he, Mr. Foxworth, knew something concerning the relationship existing between Elliott and Kantor. He then related that D.A. Thomas E. Dewey of New York County had Kantor "on a string" in connection with some cemetery lots that Kantor had sold. The reason Hall gave for calling Mr. Foxworth was that he desired to have Kantor sign a letter of some kind which would prevent Dewey using any information that might be given by Kantor as "campaign material." He related that Louis Segal, President of the Segal Lock Company, could have Kantor sign any kind of a statement or letter and what was desired was to have someone prepare an airtight legal statement for Kantor to sign. Mr. Foxworth reported that he advised that the matter should be taken up with the A.G.'s office in Washington.

Thus it is no surprise the Democrats were terrified what Dewey might do with the Elliott extortion case, since he already knew about Kantor's criminal career. However, Dewey did not bring up the issue. The Administration appeared to have headed Kantor off at the pass, and it managed to keep the story quiet. [i]

Kantor was still in a position to blackmail the Roosevelts. Hall, who was going downhill fast but apparently still able to cause trouble, was operating with Mr. Segal, and the two had something on Kantor they could call in.

This is where Hall's own secret account gets us to the core of the Hartford Loan Scandal. The two met with Special Agent Foxworth on 13 December 1939 at the Biltmore Hotel. To the FBI, Hall recapitulated the saga:

---

[i] However, in 1944, when Dewey did get the nomination, a far more serious matter caused Dewey to clam up. By that time, Dewey knew that the U.S. had been reading the Japanese codes, and he assumed therefore that the common charge against FDR must have been true at least in part: that FDR knew about the Japanese attack in advance and let it happen. Without telling FDR, an extremely alarmed General Marshall sent an emissary with a secret letter to Dewey. (This happened twice in September 1944, because the first time Dewey refused to read the letter, citing its secrecy.) Marshall told Dewey in detail that not only had the United States broken the Japanese codes, but also the German code; and that any more talk about Pearl Harbor or related affairs would seriously harm the war effort, and the American relationship with Britain. After that, a steaming Dewey shut up about the matter. It seems a fantastic breach of secrecy, and Marshall must have been seriously worried to make this play. Dewey and any other Republicans in the know must have been going out of their minds with all they couldn't talk about. It is this episode that made Dewey's demand that FDR should have been impeached, not reelected, current on the right. It is also a reminder that what we often take as a deep dark secret may turn out to have been known much earlier. To his horror, Marshall's letters revealing the ULTRA secret ("we possess other codes, German as well as Japanese") were made public in December 1945 by the Congressional Pearl Harbor commission. He should have known better; but apparently historians paid no attention. Presumably most foreign adversaries were not so dull. See NYT 21 SEP, 22 SEP 45. The two letters are reprinted in NYT, 8 DEC 45.

> Accompanied by Mr. Segal, Mr. Foxworth and G. Hall Roosevelt went to the Harvard Club where Mr. Roosevelt related that some time ago Elliott Roosevelt, while trying to form his two radio companies, found himself in need of finances and that he was unable to meet the payroll.

Later Kantor would explain what Hall meant by that. Hall told him that Elliott had already made out the paychecks and he had 24 hours to cover them, but no money. He needed $25,000 deposited in Fort Worth that afternoon. After that he would need further funds to operate the network.[1846]

> ...[He] stated he had succeeded in getting $25,000 for Elliott Roosevelt, the source of which was immaterial. He stated that in fact the money was a gratuity. In addition, he said that thereafter Elliott needed additional money and that he, G. Hall Roosevelt, had tried to assist him.

In his 1945 testimony, Kantor would still not say where the twenty-five grand came from. He said that his acquaintance with Hall went all the way back to 1916 in Chicago; and "I had some very extensive business deals with some of his friends, and that is how he knew that I might be able to help him."[1847]

The FBI report continued:

> In the meantime, John Kantor had come to Elliott Roosevelt and sold him on the idea that he could be of assistance in securing and financing, as well as obtaining broadcasting contracts from well known manufacturers. Hall said that he went to Congressman Sirovich and told the Congressman about the need of money in the broadcasting enterprise. Hall stated the Congressman suggested that he go to see Mr. John A. Hartford of the Atlantic & Pacific Tea Company. Hall said that Kantor was present when that suggestion was made but that Kantor had nothing to do with later arrangements which were handled entirely by Elliott and G. Hall Roosevelt. As a result of this contact, Elliott obtained a loan of $100,000 from Mr. Hartford.
>
> Subsequent to the Hartford loan, according to Hall Roosevelt, Kantor sold Elliott Roosevelt on the idea of entering into a contract with him which would have made it a life-time proposition. Hall stated, however, that he stepped in and changed the contract, the details of which he said were immaterial.
>
> G. Hall Roosevelt then asked Louis Segal to continue the story from that point. Mr. Segal stated that he knew Kantor was a thoroughly disreputable person to which Mr. Roosevelt agreed. He stated that he was just as dishonest as he could be and he was one of the world's best confidence men. He related that Kantor had been in a number of scrapes but was usually able to get out. He further stated that Kantor was then under indictment in the Federal Court and, in addition, he was in difficulty with the Office of District Attorney Thomas E. Dewey in connection with the sale of some nonexisting cemetery lots.

At this point, the conversation centered on how to buy off Kantor before he talked.

> According to Segal, Kantor had hired two of the outstanding Jewish law firms in New York City to defend him. He related that Kantor was seriously in need of funds and that if he obtained funds he would be able to buy off the original complainant in the state case and pay his lawyers something on account. Mr. Segal related that if Kantor could come into possession of some money he thought he would be controllable.

> Segal then said that he had understood, without stating from what source, that he was afraid Kantor would tell Dewey of his dealings with Elliott. He was of the opinion that Kantor would tell a story to Dewey to make it appear that Mr. Hartford of the Atlantic and Pacific Tea Company had loaned to Elliott the sum of $100,000 at a time when the Patton [sic] Chain Store Bill was pending. Segal stated that this would give the inference that Hartford was anxious to ingratiate himself with the President in order to have him favorably inclined towards Mr. Hartford's position on chain store legislation.
>
> Segal remarked that Dewey was desperate for something to use in the campaign and that while he had made a good D.A., he could not run for President upon that reputation.

As we have seen, the Patman tax bill would have severely clipped A&P. When, on receiving the president's call, Hartford paid the two hundred grand to Elliott, the White House launched a campaign against the Patman bill, and it expired in committee.

Now Segal, speaking for the Roosevelts, came to the crux of the matter – how to neutralize Kantor.

> Mr. Segal went on to say that he was in a position to demand of Kantor one favor and felt that if an airtight, iron-bound release, statement, letter, or document of some kind which would protect the Roosevelt family, were drawn up, he could get Kantor to sign it. Mr. Segal stated that, of course, Elliott Roosevelt would contact private lawyers to draw up such a paper but he wanted to be sure that there was no slip-up whatsoever. He explained that while he could get one favor from Kantor he did not know if he could get two favors.

Mr. Segal was in an apparently honest business and was prominent in the Jewish community. However, he had some involvement, never explored, in the Garsson munitions swindle of 1942 that ended in the downfall of Repr. Andrew May (D-KY). What his "favors" consisted of in regard to Kantor is not known. Now he had in mind going along with Kantor's blackmail.[1848]

> Mr. Foxworth advised that while Mr. Segal did not say how he could secure this favor from Mr. Kantor, there was a strong suggestion that he proposed to do it by paying Kantor a sum of money.
>
> Both G. Hall Roosevelt and Segal stressed the fact that time was of the essence in getting some kind of action from Kantor. Mr. Foxworth informed the two men that he would relay the information to his superior in Washington who in turn would undoubtedly call it to the attention of the Attorney General.

The FBI file does not indicate whether Kantor was, in fact, bought off. Instead, it indicates that J. Edgar Hoover quashed the investigation. Kantor was arrested on 17 August 1939 on the fake cemetery lot charges, and he received a lengthy prison term.

On 4 January 1940, President Roosevelt nominated Attorney General Frank Murphy, who had been so helpful in tamping the cork down on the conspiracy, to the Supreme Court. Francis Biddle, the Solicitor General, would become Attorney General on 26 August 1941. (Robert Jackson served in the post in the interim.)

Biddle had somehow been advised that there was trouble on the Elliott front. Biddle was universally understood to be Tommy Corcoran's man, and whenever Biddle did something it was smart to assume that "the Cork" was behind it.

> On February 16, 1940, Mr. E.A. Tamm [FBI] conferred with Solicitor General Biddle pursuant to the latter's request. Mr. Biddle inquired as to the circumstances and

> background of the situation which involved the dealings of Elliott Roosevelt with one Kantor of New York City. According to Mr. Tamm's memorandum of February 1940, he explained to Mr. Biddle the basic facts in general terms, pointing out that Mr. Hoover was reluctant in matters of this kind to take any action but that acting under instructions of the former Attorney General, Frank Murphy, he had arranged for the Special Agent in Charge of the New York Office to interview Elliott Roosevelt and advised Elliott of Kantor's background.
>
> It does not appear that any further action was taken by the Bureau concerning this matter after this last-mentioned date.

The FBI was not quite the only enlightened party to the case. Old Nemesis Pegler had also heard a few things, but he was unable to develop the line of inquiry until after the president's death. His preserved files cast no light on the cause of the delay. Pegler, who regretted not being free to name his source, had heard something odd about Representative Sirovich's sudden death. In July 1945, he wrote, after informing readers of Kantor's attempt to blackmail the Roosevelts:

> I can't say whether Elliott and Sirovich got wind of this attempt but anyway one night in late 1939 Sirovich and another fellow, whose name I am saving for dessert, called him [Kantor] into a hotel here and, in return for $200, in fist, and a promise of some more money, got him to sign a document releasing Elliott, Sirovich, Hall Roosevelt, who was Elliott's uncle, and Texas State Network from all debts and claims.
>
> The public stenographer who typed and executed the releases was suspicious and reported the incident to the New York district attorney's [Thomas E. Dewey's] office. Sirovich died the next morning and the stenographer now tells me that Kantor, hearing about this, stormed into her office, shook his fist in her face and hollered "That don't go! That don't go!"[i]

There is no evidence that William Sirovich was murdered. He had been in ill health, and was found dead in his bathtub at eleven in the morning after fixing Elliott's trouble with Kantor. He lived alone, and his housekeeper, who lived nearby, had called the police when he didn't show up for breakfast. An autopsy was considered unnecessary, and the official cause of death was given as "heart attack." [1849]

Under interrogation in 1945, Kantor offered a strange opinion of Congressman Sirovich. Asked if he was surprised that Sirovich made him sign the release, he answered:

> No, sir, I was not surprised at anything that anybody in that crowd suggested any more…I never had much confidence in Sirovich as a businessman. I loved and admired the man as an individual, as an artist and as a creator, as a humanitarian, and I was a good deal like the man in Julius Caesar, who said, "I loved him for this and honored him for that, but for his ambition, I killed him." I did not care much about his business ability after having lost $50,000 or $60,000 through him and then having this thing come up…I said, "Where is the money?" He said you sign these releases tonight and I will give you a deposit and we will have your check for you Monday at 1 o'clock….between $8,000 and $9,000.

---

[i] Pegler column, 19 JUL 45, Toledo Blade; also addressed in Pegler, 6 JUL 45, Evening Inpendent. The source "saved for dessert" may have been Gerald Stanley, nr. 3 man in Elliott's network. Stanley hid in Chicago and would not talk. Stanley was fingered in ChigTrib, 18 JUL 45.

At around 8 PM in the lobby of the Roosevelt Hotel, the two finished up. Sirovich said he couldn't pay a big deposit, but he did give Kantor a check, he said, for $400, promising to have the rest in the morning.

> That was the last time I saw Dr. Sirovich alive. That was the last and first and only time I saw those releases. They could not be found at Dr. Sirovich's house, or on his person. Nobody seems to have ever seen them.

Kantor never got the rest of his hush money. He fiercely denied the published claims of any further involvement in the matter; yet he did make unsuccessful efforts to interest Hartford in taking over the radio stations, and he was also forced to give up on suing Elliott for breach of contract. For an old, accomplished swindler of the highest reputation, it must have been infuriating to have been outfoxed by the Roosevelt family.

Like Dr. Sirovich, Kantor lost out in the end – he went to jail for his latest con. Hall Roosevelt died two years later. By 1945, most of the principals were dead, including FDR.

After Pegler's newspaper columns in 1945, J. Edgar Hoover revisited the matter and advised the Attorney General, Thomas Clark, that Pegler's information was "substantially correct." But Hoover wrote to his closest FBI associates, Tolson, Tamm, and Nichols:

> I told the Attorney General that the Times-Herald had called the Bureau yesterday and asked for a statement on this matter. I advised him that we took the position of "no comment" and told them that any statement would have to come from the Press Section of the Attorney General's Office. Mr. Clark indicated that he would take the same position.[1850]

Truman had appointed Tom Clark to succeed Francis Biddle in June 1945.

Thus, in 1940, President Franklin D. Roosevelt dodged a bullet by a fraction of an inch. Had Kantor spilled the beans to Thomas E. Dewey, it is difficult to conceive of a third term for FDR. Had there been a Deep Throat in the highest ranks of the FBI, quite possibly the president would have been dissuaded from running again, even despite the hammerlock the Democrats had on Congress. What Dewey knew we cannot be certain.

On that background, it is easier to understand why the Roosevelt-haters were seemingly foaming at the mouth and chewing carpets during the late FDR era. They had plenty of suspicions, but were powerless to pursue them. Pegler and his once numerous ilk raged against the moon, getting shriller as readers dwindled. Having begun as a Roosevelt New-Dealer, he died as a Bircher in Tucson in 1969, ridiculed by the few who had not forgotten him.[1851] William F. Buckley penned a brilliant, compassionate remembrance of him in *the New Yorker*, years later.[1852]

John Hartford, too, was a disillusioned man. After the president's personal reassurances, he had not expected to lose money, and he had requested regular updates. But things went downhill from the beginning. John Kantor said that Elliott came to him in May 1939, needing more money. Elliott had told Kantor:

> 'Well, I didn't want to tell you before, but I don't stand very well with Mr. Hartford. It seems that Hall Roosevelt promised him certain statements which I didn't know anything about and I haven't been able to send him all of the stock certificates that I owed him because I had them up as collateral for a loan,' I said, 'That doesn't sound so good, does it?'

> He said, 'No.' – He told me that Hartford's office had written a number of letters which he had not answered. Therefore, he wanted me to go if I would do so.[1853]

"Tell the boy to come see me," Hartford had said.[1854] In time, Elliott did, returning apparently encouraged. But about ten days after this, Kantor received a telephone call from Elliott in Washington, "asking me to get real busy [raising money] as he had been told by his father that he could not borrow any further moneys from Mr. Hartford."[1855]

From the shadows, President Roosevelt had watched his son's schemes all along.

From April 1940, Hartford and his staff made numerous attempts to contact Elliott and his broadcasting business. Elliott rarely answered his letters or phone calls. Worse, Elliott did not show up for another appointment with Mr. Hartford. The notes came due, $50,000 each year, and went unpaid.

On 27 September 1940, Elliott Roosevelt entered the Army. His creditors would have to deal with somebody else.[1856]

In effect, Elliott had operated a kind of Ponzi scheme of indebtedness. We get a flavor of it in his answer to the agents' question of how on earth he expected to pay back his loans given the great losses his businesses were incurring:

> At the time I had contracted for all of these loans I anticipated that we would enlarge our operations on a national scale and as you will see by the various loan dates, the last one was that of Baird on the floating of the operation for the Transcontinental Broadcasting System. That, I expected, would be the answer to our financial difficulties, in that Transcontinental would grow and would through the fact that it would start with a guarantee from one agency for 15 hours of business per week across the boards; that this income would be sufficient; that it would grow the company and would be able to purchase the Texas State Network Inc. and put it on a broader financial basis which would allow it to retain a greater amount of net profit after taxes and that on that basis the loans would be paid off the time the Transcontinental purchased the stock of Texas State Network, Inc.[1857]

In simpler terms, Elliott thought he'd be able to keep raising money to pay off his old debts. That's why he needed to expand his operations all the time. It turned out that he didn't skate fast enough; the breaking ice finally caught up with him.

One remaining question is whether he ever expected to run an honest business, or whether the operation was a full-blown confidence racket from the beginning. The fairest guess probably lands somewhere between the two. This is often the case with financial swindlers; they seem to begin with a gamble that they'll get out of the hole, and after a while they simply continue the juggling for as long as they can keep the balls in the air.

In Elliott's case, the underlying business was fundamentally real, and it righted itself after he was out of the picture. Viewed in isolation, one would have to be cautious to attribute nefarious motives (as opposed to incompetence and immaturity) to him in this matter; but seen in the context of an entire lifetime of such machinations, small and large, legal or illegal or somewhere in-between, one must conclude that Elliott Roosevelt was not the kind of man that an honest person should do business with.

The second, historically far more momentous question is this: What was President Roosevelt thinking?

What did the President know and when did he know it? - II

Now we know why Eleanor wrote on 17 July 1939: "Ruth wired me that temporarily their finances were better but Father was to tell me if anything was settled & I haven't heard. I don't feel able to cope with high finance so did not go to Washington to give advice."[1858]

The totality of the evidence proves beyond any doubt that President Roosevelt kept in close touch with what Elliott was doing in the radio business, as he did in everything else the "chicks" did. He raised funds for Elliott from the Oval Office; he met with those marked out to help, and he put the squeeze on the reluctant; he tried to protect Elliott from his worst excesses; he used the FBI and the Attorney General to intervene in the extortion conspiracy, as indeed he used the FBI and Internal Revenue to go after his critics; and he enlisted his staff and his cabinet to disentangle Elliott's business affairs to the benefit of his son and his family.

There is no evidence that the president did any of this for his own financial gain. FDR's game was not mammon, but political power. With Elliott, he was in damage limitation mode most of the time. He did his utmost to make sure that nothing was written down, and that *quids* for *quos* were implied rather than explicit. Yet he also played the game – executive favors in return for contributions – to the hilt.

Franklin D. Roosevelt always had a hard time separating the public from the private. Favors in one sphere carried over into the other. Looking after his friends was his nature. He shook down contributors with the clear implication that they would obtain favorable political treatment. He knew exactly what Elliott (and James) were doing. Again, one such incident may be a trivial matter, a case of an overzealous father trying to assist his screwed-up child. When held up to a background of a lifetime of dubious deals, the conclusion must be different.

Franklin's whole life was one of skating around the rules with a confident grin on his face. That was true both in business and in politics; it was even true in his marriage. It was not illegal to stand for election four times in a row. It was not illegal to try to pack the Supreme Court with six extra judges because the original crew had found most of his program, well, illegal. Until FDR, such things were just not done.

For the public, the great chain store robbery, revealed in the summer of 1945, was a sour corrective to the incipient canonization of President Roosevelt. There is no surer way to sainthood than dying in office during wartime. The bitter split over the president's politics no longer mattered; even Republicans were increasingly content to watch FDR get installed in the American Pantheon.

By late 1945, the newest Elliott scandal reflected only on its perpetrators and no longer on the father. At least that seemed to be the general public view. That the president had clearly been involved in devious, probably criminal activities was a matter of unease and concern to much of the commentariat, however.

A prominent editorialist, Frank Kent of the *Los Angeles Times*, vented this conflicted feeling. In July he noted that Elliott Roosevelt didn't matter; it was the reputation of his father that was at stake: "Either he was this kind of man or he was not." [1859]

And there was something very unsettling about how the scandal was being received; it was as if nobody was willing to deal with the facts, and instead resorted to endless reciprocal mudslinging:

> These are the charges. Mr. Pegler, who makes them, is a reputable and responsible journalist. The hundreds of papers which have printed the charges are all responsible. If they are not true, then Mr. Pegler and these hundreds of newspapers can separately be called to account under the libel law, sued for heavy damages. If they are not true, then the Roosevelt family can recover a very large sum of money. It could, in addition, clear Elliott's reputation; but, what is more important, it could clear that of the late President. Also they could ruin Mr. Pegler not only financially but professionally.
>
> But no move in this direction has come from either family, friends, worshipers, subordinates, sycophants or political allies. There has been some denunciation of Mr. Pegler and others who have referred to the facts as "ghouls," "Roosevelt-haters," "grave desecrators," and "loathsome beasts." But no one has challenged Mr. Pegler's statements or contradicted the charges – literally no one…
>
> In this case, the political opponents of Mr. Roosevelt, still in a minority in Congress, have clamored for the light. But the political friends of Mr. Roosevelt, still in control of all branches of the government, appear determined there shall be no light, apparently hoping the whole business soon will be forgotten. But that is not the attitude one would expect from the family and personal friends of the late President – particularly when it is so easy to establish the truth.[1860]

By the time the truth did come out, most people did not want to hear it. Their political filters were very effective. And then as now, for screening out the truth, Republican filters were just as effective as the Democratic ones.

TROUBLE AT THE CIVIL AERONAUTICS BOARD

As for Elliott Roosevelt, in 1945 he was again without a paycheck. While he was on final leave from the Air Force he lived for a while with Faye in Beverly Hills, for free, in the home of industrialist G.W. Stratton, aka Grenville Stratton. The palatial residence at 528 N. Rodeo Drive would be home until November.[1861]

This Stratton was Donald Douglas's friend and associate, in charge of Douglas's oil interests, and variously described as Douglas's executive assistant or company officer. He was a mysterious character who had several names, and had appeared from the Midwest where he had apparently held various sales jobs. By 1933 he was linked up with Douglas and was known as a "slick, sharp" salesman. At any rate he made it rich.[1862]

Horsethieves

In Los Angeles, Stratton was a well-known race horse owner and aficionado, and owner of the 170-acre Circle S ranch. He reportedly owned eighty thoroughbreds, including a famous winner, Heelfly. A trade journal noted that "the only outsiders as Circle S are two Palominos belonging to Donald Douglas and seven Arabians belonging to Brig. Gen. Elliott Roosevelt."[1863]

It's expensive to board that many horses, so it seems that, through its executive Stratton, the Douglas Aircraft Co. was substantially subsidizing the lifestyle of a USAAF general.

Stratton was having some trouble on the home front; his hospitalized wife sued him for upkeep, complaining furthermore that Mr. Stratton's indulgence of the house-guests was "to the detriment of the community property."[1864]

A lot apparently hides under these laconic legal records. Westbrook Pegler requested information, noting that "Mrs. Stratton was detained for examination of her mental condition – finally there was a rumpus and they were kicked out of Mrs. Stratton's home."[1865]

Evidently nothing came of Cora Stratton's suit for divorce and support, but the Roosevelts did leave. Possibly Mrs. Stratton then regained her sanity, for she was still married to Grenville years later.

Elliott's sojourn appears to have been rather more appreciated by the Roosevelts than by Mr. and Mrs. Stratton. In 1958, the Strattons finally spoke to Old Nemesis, Pegler, who wrote:

> Elliott and Faye Emerson already had encamped in the Strattons' "other" house as their honeymoon cottage. Stratton already had staked the inveterate bridegroom to $300 for pocket-money for the wedding on the Grand Canyon at dawn. Blaze had moved in with the happy couple and so badly defiled the interior of Mrs. Stratton's personal sedan that she hosed it out as best she could and tried to forget about it.[1866]

Where the horses came from was a bit of a mystery. Elliott had kept Arabians at the Texas ranch, but he also seems to have been the vicarious beneficiary of an equine gift of state from the Saudi despot to the American president. In a supremely important meeting founding bilateral relations, FDR met with King Ibn-Saud and his entourage aboard ship in the Suez Canal in 1945. Gifts were exchanged: the king cast covetous eyes on the president's wheel-chair, which he was promptly given (FDR had a spare), with a C-47 thrown in for good measure. Among the reciprocal gifts were apparently a number of Arabian horses, and the president reportedly gave them to his cowboy son. They were trouble:

> Now Elliott phoned Mr. Stratton that he needed grazing and barnroom for five horses. All three mares were with foal and all five horses were weak and scrawny. Two of the foals were born dead.[1867]

The ruler of the herd, the stallion Hatal, made a good impression and was recruited into service to improve equine genetics in California. Eventually, Hatal was given to someone else to keep, and the mares were sold. Blaze the dog was still a problem:

> Elliott and Faye spent eight months in the Stratton's house and Mrs. Stratton is not reticent. Faye wanted to "decorate" some rooms with a wallpaper of "plaid" design. Mrs. Stratton vetoed that, but did consent to some other novelties. When she got her house back, Blaze had committed foul excesses and the lovers, themselves, had been so indifferent to Mrs. Stratton's standards of tidiness that she was shocked and permanently estranged. Elliott also had run up a little chit of $6,600 in casual borrowings.[1868]

Apart from that assistance, at first Elliott lived off of Faye Emerson's earnings, but he had lots of exciting new projects to attend to. If only the newspapers would leave him alone! It was not easy being a Roosevelt, especially after the old man's death. But it would get much, much harder.

Stratton told Pegler that within three months of FDR's death – i.e. while Elliott was still nominally in the Air Corps – Elliott asked him to borrow $80,000 to buy out the other heirs to Hyde Park so that he and his mother could go into the Christmas-tree business together. It seems that Elliott had already taken a hard stare at his father's extensive reforestation project, one of the old man's hobbyhorses. The young spruce trees were starting to look more and more like giant dollar signs.

> Mr. Stratton asked about security. Elliott said that he and his mother would give their personal notes. Mr. Stratton did not have $80,000 available for this purpose. 'Yet,' Mr. Stratton said, 'I think he is the smartest of the bunch.'[1869]

Back to the horses. The Strattons could not find any title to Hatal, although they believed there must have been some kind of deed from the King somewhere. At any rate they gave the stallion to their friend, Eugene Starr, who morosely commented: "Looks as though I might have a stolen horse… I was born in Tucson. I remember what they used to do to horse thieves over there."[i]

When Eleanor and Elliott agreed on their business partnership, Elliott and Faye loaded the notorious Blaze into the Cadillac and drove across the country to Hyde Park. They took a week, enjoying the southern states, but while they didn't mind attention, they wisely wouldn't let the dog be photographed. On the very eve of his swift and unceremonious demise, the ferocious animal was reverently described as weighing 145 pounds.[1870]

Clipping Pan American's Wings

Elliott Roosevelt's last few months in the service were spent mostly on leave, and there was plenty of time to get in trouble. When the Civil Aeronautics Board (CAB) awarded peace-time transatlantic air routes on 5 July 1945, people were shocked to find TWA (then known as Transcontinental and Western Airlines), effectively owned by Elliott's friend Howard Hughes, getting a coveted piece of the action.

American Airlines, also well connected, acquired another important transatlantic route, although at that time in the name of American Export Airlines. Pan American Airlines, previously the sole overseas flag carrier, was left with the remainder.[1871]

The awards were approved, as required, by the president, and they flew in the face of some senators' efforts to recreate the prewar international airline monopoly. After such delays led by Senators Brewster and McCarran, finally Truman lost patience with the opposition and launched the CAB's preemptive strike.[1872]

The CAB award of seven-year licenses to operate foreign air routes is another glimpse into the contentious bureaucratic game that was then associated with federal control of the airlines. The CAB was, like the FCC, supposed to impartially issue its

[i] Tucsonian Eugene Grant Starr was a wealthy oil man and Democrat who owned a good slice of Orange County. There is another report that Walter Kirschner later kept Elliott's horses (San Diego Mag., Faye Emerson Interview, 1975)

quotas, fares, and other directives to the providers according to the "public interest." In reality it was often impossible to prevent political pressure affecting the awards, and it was certainly impossible to prevent the impression of corruption.[1873]

President Truman approved TWA's award of exclusive rights to operate out of Dublin, Paris and Rome, while American got Berlin and Moscow. Pan Am would keep London, Marseilles, and Foynes in Ireland. There were further route extensions through the Middle East to India. From twelve applicant airlines, the CAB had decided to make a triple division of what had been a monopoly, albeit one interrupted by the war. And it had assumed that Pan Am would continue its famed seaplane routes, although it was now clear to most everyone that landplanes would soon rule also the oceanic stretches.

To the innocent observer, this might seem fair enough. But it was a revolution. Not only had Pan Am had its wings clipped, but two specially selected airlines had been given choice routes, while eight other applicants had been shown the door. Immediately rumors and accusations began flying. First, Senator Pat McCarran (D-NV), he of the eponymous Las Vegas airport, noticed that stocks of both TWA and Pan Am moved up dramatically just before the award was made public (they then fell back). Then Pan Am's friends in Congress looked suspiciously at General Elliott Roosevelt's role in the matter. After all, he was considered already to have been bought wholesale by Howard Hughes and Jack Frye. The memories of his lavish Grand Canyon wedding were still fresh.

A day after the award, Representative Paul Shafer (R-Mich.) artfully insinuated: "I make no direct accusation, but I am forced to admit that I am suspicious that some undue influence was brought to bear." He then recapitulated the by now two-year old, well-known association of Hughes, Elliott, TWA's Jack Frye, and the go-between and wheel-greaser, Johnny Meyer.[1874]

"At that time Elliott was back in the States, getting married at TWA's expense to a Hughes-supplied starlet," Shafer said, adding:

> TWA had pending before the CAB an application for an overseas route, and on January 30, the CAB examiner who had conducted hearings recommended that the North African overseas routes be given to Pan American and American Export [which flew the wartime Foynes, Ireland route, with Sikorsky VS-44s]. The examiner recommended that the applications of TWA and eight other companies be denied.
>
> Oral arguments were heard by the board later in which all the companies again presented their requests for routes, with the result that the board tossed aside the examiner's recommendation and granted TWA a share in the international field while otherwise accepting the recommendations.
>
> The board's action has bypassed the Senate Commerce subcommittee which is entrusted with formulating our commercial air policy and which is still undecided whether domestic airlines should be allowed to engage in international business.[1875]

Shafer could not prove his allegations, but they were obviously not drawn out of thin air. On the other hand, White House sources suggest that by 1943 President Roosevelt was already inclined to think that Pan Am's monopoly should not be resumed after the war.[1876]

In 1945, open competition and market pricing in international air travel seemed like total anarchy. Complex bilateral treaties and agreements ponderously decreed how each country's flag carrier would each obtain, preferably, more than half of the benefits of the concession.

In many countries flag carriers were national "Aeroflots" – i.e. government-owned monopoly airlines. At least the New Deal's reorganization of American air travel had not gone that far – it had merely made the airlines supplicants of the federal government. They fought against it, but they soon learned to love being princes of the air, assured of their government sinecures. When Jimmy Carter's economist Alfred Kahn abolished the CAB and deregulated the skies, this era finally came to an end.

World War II had interrupted everything, and contract airlines of many stripes had supplemented the Air Transport Command in flying overseas. As the war in Europe wound down, the airlines waited with baited breath to recover their markets and then some. Everyone knew that postwar oceanic air traffic would far exceed what it had been in the days of giant seaplanes. The aircraft, the infrastructure, and the pilots were now available for this. In 1945, more than ever before or since, it was important to get into the skies on the ground floor.

This was why Juan Trippe exploded in rage when the transatlantic awards were disclosed. The airline filed a complaint with the CAB, noting that the new policy would deprive it of critical routes; that despite its own heroic pioneering of these routes, it would now be cut back to probably less than 25% of the foreign traffic it had hoped to gain; that the award showed "gross favoritism" to TWA and "favoritism" to American, and it urged the Board to reconsider this vile injustice.

The company's petition for redress used some words seldom heard in polite company. It asked whether the board "actually desires to perpetrate the injustice to PAA, the pioneer transatlantic air carrier, and to be guilty of favoritism to American Airlines that would result if the board were to permit this arbitrary decision to become final."[1877]

Saying the award reversed CAB's own experts and flew in the face of recognized legal and regulatory principles, the airline complained:

> In the four countries to which Pan Am was given a permanent certificate in 1939, the board would not only authorize TWA or American to operate in competition with Pan Am but would give them a preferred position by permitting them to operate to all traffic centers while freezing Pan Am to the precise points originally named for technical operating reasons.
>
> After practically throwing Pan Am out of France and Eire for the benefit of TWA and placing it in an inferior position to American in the U.K., the board would exclude Pan Am from all other major traffic areas and confer a monopoly on them on TWA and American.
>
> Although TWA and American would be given monopolies of important traffic areas, Pan Am would be subjected to competition at its single major traffic point, London…[1878]

Trippe had a good point. The government – and Howard Hughes and C.R. Smith – had exploded his monopoly. But it was the right time to do it, just as peacetime air traffic was about to resume in earnest. Whoever made the decision reasoned that international competition was a good thing. If there was influence-peddling involved, it does seem in retrospect to have served a good cause.

But from this moment on, Trippe and Hughes were enemies, and by extension, so were General Roosevelt and Trippe's favorite politician, Senator Owen Brewster.

An expose by Frank Hughes in the *Chicago Tribune* illustrated how important it is to focus, not on the company names, but on the individuals with actual control. The story revealed that while TWA was effectively Howard Hughes's, both Pan Am and American were partly owned by the investor Victor Emanuel, who was a White House insider. Emanuel's Aviation Corporation (AVCO) took over E.L. Cord's aircraft and automobile empire in 1937. Now AVCO controlled Republic Aircraft, Consolidated-Vultee (the later Convair), and many other esteemed names. Thus, the conflict over route awards was very much a personal matter for the new oligarchs of state-regulated capitalism.[1879]

That was merely the shadowy, financial part of the squabble. The bluster would happen in Congress. Representative Paul Shafer openly fingered Elliott Roosevelt, just as Senator McCarran called attention to the obvious stock manipulation. Furthermore, federal records revealed that the CAB examiner who had conducted the hearings on overseas air route permits had indeed recommended that Pan Am continue its monopoly. He was overruled by the Board before the decision was sent to President Truman.[1880]

Elliott, already neck-deep in the revelations of his odious loans, furiously denied the "pernicious lies." He may well have been innocent, but not for lack of trying. His real influence at the CAB vanished quickly in 1945, but it is clear that to interested parties he pretended to have such pull.

The FBI took a keen interest in his airline fabulations with Howard Hughes and TWA. Over the period 1944-45 the agency received reports that Hughes had plans to extend TWA to oceanic routes, and in particular to begin operating in the Soviet Union. It is not hard to see who might be helpful in both respects. However, by late 1945 the agency noted:

> It will be recalled that in the previous report in this case some indication existed that MEYER, together with JACK FRYE, President of TWA, and HOWARD HUGHES might be interested in a trans-Pacific airline to Russia and that this group had hoped that the ELLIOTT ROOSEVELT connection would enable facilitating granting of this contract; however, information most recently developed, which has been set out above, indicates that ROOSEVELT has no intention of entering into any phase of the aviation business.[1881]

The FBI was alluding to several reports relating not only to airlines. The bureau had also noted that a Soviet delegation had visited Hughes Aircraft in September 1944 with the potential plan of purchasing the Hughes Hercules or a similar mammoth aircraft. In May 1945, the bureau heard that Hughes had sold "a quantity of planes to the Russian Army for delivery after the war." That makes no sense, since Hughes never produced an operational airplane; but he probably did try to sell them.[1882]

The rumors about the Hughes-Frye-Elliott initiatives continued during 1944-46. The FBI learned that the Roosevelt-Emerson wedding was engineered by Johnny Meyer "to help TWA obtain lucrative transocean routes in postwar aviation which are currently being bid for by Pan Am."[1883]

The Soviet plans also involved Colonel Clarence Shoop, who was still in the Army as commander at Muroc, but was already working for Hughes unofficially: "As soon as the war is over, it is the intention of these individuals to form a company for the handling of air travel to Russia."

The FBI's Los Angeles division was ordered to furnish everything it could get on the Hughes-Elliott plans. It is obvious in retrospect that Elliott was indeed trying to sell his influence in regard to airline concessions; but it is also clear that the results were meager. The Russian plans came to nothing. Hughes was a fierce anti-communist, but that would never stand in his way of making a buck. While it is unprovable that Elliott helped TWA get its routes, it has some plausibility; but, if so, that was probably the last time the administration listened to him.[1884]

The decision to introduce a managed competition to foreign air travel reflected something much deeper than merely influence-peddling and mutual back-scratching. It was a conscious choice of future policy. However dubious the provenance of this decision, few today would deny that it was a step forward.

Pan Am and its Congressional backers promoted an idea that became known as the "Chosen Instrument." It held that, for inscrutable reasons, foreign air traffic was so important that only one company should be given the job. In return, this company should then selflessly shoulder the burden on behalf of all the domestic airlines, serving them fairly in proportion to their sizes. A more insightful term for "Chosen Instrument" might be "Crony Capitalism."

Not long after the controversial CAB decision, enraged senators introduced legislation to promote this concept. The bill was authored and promoted by the Republican senator from Maine, Ralph Owen Brewster, whom the columnist Drew Pearson called the "kept senator" of Pan Am.[1885] After its defeat by the Democratic majority, it reappeared as the "Community Airline" bill. By "community" was not meant some geographical entity, but rather a coming together of the U.S. airlines to serve overseas destinations under one company – in other words, a blatant attempt to feed Pan Am the business. But nothing much happened until the Republicans regained control of Congress in the fall of 1946. Then a lot happened all at once.

In truth, Pan Am was in a sore spot. Since it only had international routes, it could not build the local self-interested constituency that other airlines used to throw their weight around. In the long run, American Airlines was far better connected. When Lyndon Johnson appointed C.R. Smith his Secretary of Transportation, even the managed, limited competition on international routes ended. American gained again, and Pan American was moribund.

American's mysterious advantage in regulatory intrigues remained even after Elliott was taken out of the equation. After the Republicans took over the White House in 1953, this curious phenomenon survived. One analyst mused:

> …American Airlines' present structure is regarded as a completely Democratic by-product, and yet it walks off with the prize. American's Washington law firm includes as a partner Dean Acheson, Truman's Secretary of State. James Bruce of Baltimore, a key director, banker and industrialist, held important posts under the Wilson, Roosevelt and Truman regimes. Elliott Roosevelt and Franklin D. Lane Jr., a son of a Wilson Cabinet member, have been associated with American.[1886]

The Senate Interstate and Foreign Commerce committee investigated the matter, which reached the headlines when American was handed the New York – Mexico City route after eight minutes' discussion, while five other airlines had been unable to get the route in many years of trying.

Even Texans wondered:

> This is not to say that CAB is corrupt. But it is mysterious. While Democrats were in power, American Airlines had everything to suit, including Elliott Roosevelt. And American did right well. When the Republicans took over CAB, we found that it is

Republican members who hop to the request of American, while the Democratic members of the board dissent. Political-minded people in Congress find this a mystery.[1887]

Perhaps C.R.'s early decision to function as the personal airline of the Roosevelts was not the reason American always came out on top – but it surely didn't hurt either. Incidentally, the Elliott – Franklin Lane connection was of long-standing nature; it was commented upon even during Elliott's early days in California. The point was that even if the CAB were, in some cases, apolitical, no sensible and suitably cynical Washington insider would ever believe it. The Pan Am – Hughes imbroglio of 1945 was the peak of public interest in CAB's alleged corruption.

In the meantime, it might seem petty to pick on Elliott Roosevelt for rumored complicity in corruption of the regulatory process. By Elliottian standards Pan Am was a fairly minor scrape, but it would sit and simmer in the background while other pots worked up to a boil. When this one finally re-erupted two years later, it would be combined with a far more incendiary issue, one that had smoldered since 1943.

In truth, now that the political correlation of forces in the country had changed dramatically, many people who had long been steaming over the behavior of FDR and his brood would burst into full battle. But first there were some lesser controversies that Elliott Roosevelt felt obliged to bequeath to the nation.

Empire Airlines

Gore Vidal was the son of Eugene Vidal, FDR's aviation chief during his first term. Gore later wrote that his father was not pleased that Elliott Roosevelt was going around saying that Gene was *his* man in the Roosevelt administration "and so if you wanted an airline route…"[1888]

Whether Elliott was effective or not, he was clearly known as a "go-to" fellow if you needed favorable attention from the Civil Aeronautics Board. We know this because the 1947 Senate hearings, among many peripheral issues, looked into the tender, inflamed politics of air route allocation.

It turned out that another of Howard Hughes's public relations men, a lobbyist by the name of Russell Birdwell, had been involved with lining up TWA route business as well as Hughes's aircraft contracts. Pan Am made the charges; Elliott, as usual, provided the denials:

> Mr. ROOSEVELT. Charges had been made that I had gotten TWA some contracts and the charges were made by an official of Pan American Airways.
>
> Senator FERGUSON. Did you get them?
>
> The CHAIRMAN [Brewster]. Again, you mean franchises? [route assignments]
>
> Mr. ROOSEVELT. Franchises; yes. I certainly did not. I didn't know anything about it. On top of that, why should Mr. Birdwell be interested in me holding press conferences? I am a private citizen by this time and I certainly have no White House influence.
>
> Senator PEPPER. [D-FL] May I say this; that what you mean to say is that if there had been any politicians that had taken any part in the struggle between TWA and Pan American, you do not happen to be the one that has done it?
>
> Mr. ROOSEVELT. I certainly do not, and I refused to retain Mr. Birdwell or follow any of his advice.[1889]

The committee was unable to get any further with these accusations, and it was much more agitated by the explosive revelations of the TWA – Pan Am duel, whose protagonists were Howard Hughes and Senator Brewster. But Roosevelt certainly was involved with currying favor with the CAB in other respects; for instance, in the matter of the tiny and short-lived Empire Airlines.

As demobilization brought airplanes, pilots, and public travel demand back, Empire Airlines, Inc. was one of many small startup companies reaching for the peacetime skies. It should not be confused with the many other airlines of that name, for it was named after the Empire State, and operated entirely therein.

This fledgling outfit was not led by a mere demobbed pilot looking for a job. Its president was a lawyer named Dean Alfange, an ardent New Dealer and FDR supporter who had been instrumental in creating the communist-dominated American Labor Party and the subsequent non-communist Liberal Party, both of which achieved some success in New York politics. Alfange ran for governor under the ALP banner in 1944 and received an impressive 18% of the vote.

On 26 December 1945, Empire Airlines started out with small feeder-line operations radiating out of La Guardia Field. It had terminals at Watertown, Jamestown, Binghampton, Elmira, Endicott, Schenectady, Glens Falls as well as La Guardia. Buffalo, Rochester, Corning, and Syracuse had also been serviced briefly. The airline maintained offices at Schenectady, close to the capital Albany. At its peak it employed 125 people.[1890]

Cessnas composed the initial fleet, apparently the twin-engine Bobcat type; however, Empire ordered ten Beech Model 18s, almost ubiquitous small twin-engine transports known to the military as C-45s. Indeed, it is odd that the airline purchased expensive new planes with so much surplus on the market.

Like a black bird of death swooping silently down to presage the demise of a company, Elliott Roosevelt stepped in as president of Empire Airlines on 20 September 1946. Dean Alfange remained as chairman of the board and general counsel. Roosevelt offered his full-time services to build up the airline and pronounced plans to offer business air-shuttles throughout the state.[1891]

The first nine-passenger Twin Beeches – D18C Stateliners – were placed in operation by early November. One month later, the airline abruptly ceased operations, citing "drastic precautionary measures" in the interest of "absolute public safety." "Empire's deep sense of public responsibility and high standards of safety made the grounding of the planes unavoidable."

There had been two suspicious incidents. One engine had quit upon landing. Another had to be feathered in flight, reportedly due to oil loss.

These incidents seem utterly trivial. The Model 18 was widely known as one of the most reliable small transports around. Something else must have been going on.

Alfange told the *New York Times* that the airline could only be financially viable if the Civil Aeronautics Board approved it for cross-border operations. Only interstate airlines were eligible for mail contracts, which the tiny airline considered absolutely essential. Consequently, application for routes into Maine, Ohio, and Pennsylvania had been submitted to the CAB.[1892]

In other words, Empire Airlines could not pay its bills without favorable treatment from the CAB.

On 16 October 1946, having been president for less than a month, Elliott submitted his resignation. Alfange said that Roosevelt stated in a letter: "I find that other activities and personal obligations will prevent my devoting of my efforts to Empire Airlines."

That certainly rings true. Roosevelt was busy promoting his controversial bestseller, and getting ready for an even more controversial trip to Moscow. How he proposed to run a struggling new airline is a mystery. But like Gilpin Airlines thirteen years earlier, Elliott's outfit was doomed. After the grounding of its flights in December, it left behind only stacks of equipment and a pile of unpaid debts. The rubble twitched a few times over the winter. A local aviation writer, Larry Murray, quoted Alfange as saying in February 1947: "We most certainly are coming back to Schenectady…" – just before the remaining equipment was advertised for sale.

What role Elliott Roosevelt held in this new and poorly reported debacle is not known today. Obviously he had a political rapport with FDR's disciple Dean Alfange. Since the CAB apportioned air routes, it couldn't hurt to have all the help and name recognition possible. But with FDR gone, Elliott had no clout there. The Schenectady aviation writer Murray stated darkly: "Elliott Roosevelt didn't last long as president of Empire Airlines and the whole story will probably never be known."

Actually we do know that on 27 September 1946, the CAB refused Elliott Roosevelt's application for air service. It denied both reconsideration of a previous case and separate treatment for a pending application. It said that Empire Airlines would have to take its place in line with other applicants for new routes.

Empire had sought to carry passengers, mail and express freight over a series of routes throughout the Northeast. The CAB had just destroyed its business plan. Apparently, the name "Roosevelt" was no longer the Sesame that opened all doors.[1893]

Although "the whole story will probably never be known," yet another cause of the failure of the airline was discussed by insiders. One wrote Westbrook Pegler that "they thought by electing Mr. Elliott Roosevelt president of the Lines it would help them to get in on the air mail – six or eight months ago the Lines went into bankruptcy, due, as to the rumors we learn, that Elliott, now resigned, was throwing parties costing five or six thousand at the Waldorf Astoria."[1894]

However, a pattern had set in. In his long life, Elliott would serve briefly as president for numerous obscure companies. Some thought the name would confer influence, and some were queasy about divulging the names of the real owners.

I AM NOT A COMMUNIST, BUT…

Unlike his imperial predecessor, Harry Truman thought he was "nothing special." Many agreed. It is proof of Truman's plain but native grace that he called on General Elliott Roosevelt after FDR's death and asked his advice. Still, there was much more than courtesy at play. As Eleanor told the new president after her husband's death, "You're the one in trouble now!" [1895]

Indeed he was, for President Roosevelt had quite ignored his deputy. Truman was due to go to Potsdam and meet with world leaders who were likely to wonder why he didn't know what his predecessor had promised them.

Thus, in the first few weeks, Truman tried to find out from Eleanor, Anna and Elliott (and many others) what President Roosevelt's intentions had been.

> The call from the White House came while I was still on leave at Hyde Park. There was a sense of shock at seeing someone else than Father ensconced in the Presidential Office, but Truman couldn't have been more cordial and complimentary about what I had been doing in photoreconnaissance with the USAAF. He was especially interested in what I had learned of Russia and the Russians in the course of setting up a new airfield at Poltava and in my contacts with Stalin and his comrades at the Big Three conference in Teheran. What kind of people were they? How hard or how easy was it to get along with them? I reported that I'd run into few problems.[1896]

President Truman's meeting with Elliott and Anna took place on 16 May 1945.[1897]

It turned out that Eleanor had suggested the meeting, in a "please-be-nice-to-Stalin" letter she sent to the new president on 14 May. She basically told Truman to not trust the State Department and to be wary of Churchill. In an allusion to the 50,000 condemned Germans she noted that the Russians had a rough sense of humor which eluded the British prime minister. Then she offered:

> Sometime when you have time, since my son Elliott is in Washington now and then, you might like to let him tell you about what he learned of the Russians when he was there. He was in Russia quite a good deal and helped establish our air force there and he has an old friend who is the only American who has flown with the Russians from the very beginning. Elliott gets on well with them and understands the peculiar combination that can look upon human life rather cheaply at times and yet strive for an ideal of future well-being for the people and make the people believe in it. He has an understanding of their enjoyment of drama and music and the arts in general and he realizes what few people seem to understand namely that when you telescope into a few years of development in civilization which had taken hundreds of years for the people around you to achieve, the development is very uneven.[1898]

"Uneven" indeed. Unlike Elliott, Harry Truman would run into "a few problems" with the Soviets. Hitler and Tojo had been his predecessor's headache. Stalin would be Truman's.

Although the new president was gracious to the Roosevelts, he already had a well-formed opinion of both Stalin and Elliott Roosevelt. Opinions within the Democratic Party were sharply split about the former, but most had already decided about the latter.

After the death of Franklin D. Roosevelt, U.S. policy towards the USSR executed an abrupt one-eighty. The careerists of the State Department, whom FDR had ridiculed and sidelined, suddenly were taken into the new president's confidence. Military and intelligence officials, who had watched in horror as their work on Soviet espionage was dismissed or even suppressed, and known Soviet agents protected, were now able to act on the information they had collected. Almost immediately, America's communists were in deep trouble.

Only now do we realize the full impact of the debriefings of Soviet defectors along with the beginning trickle of decrypted Venona messages in 1945-47; the un-tellable knowledge of a communist mycelium lying in wait within critical agencies must have made the blood run cold for the few who knew. But at the time it looked as if policy alone drove the switch, and Elliott certainly thought Truman had betrayed his father.

Famous examples of the turnabout were the rise of Russo-skeptics like George Kennan in the State Department; and the sudden clampdown on Soviet spying, contrasted to the case when FDR's loyal Secretary of State Stettinius apologetically returned Soviet codebooks and refused to allow their use in American intelligence.[1899]

Beginning with Truman's administration, far-left New Dealers and open as well as secret communists were gradually purged from the public payroll. Stettinius was immediately replaced with James Byrnes, a respected politician who nearly had become vice president in 1944.

With time, the purge turned into the famous witch-hunt; but by the time of Senator Joseph McCarthy's opportunistic campaign in the early 1950s, most of the damage had been tracked down and the moles exposed. The real purge was part of the undeclared but effective de-Rooseveltization process of 1945-49. It decimated the left-wingers who had controlled much of the federal government in 1941-45. The rest of Stalin's admirers, often highly influential and vociferous cultural and academic figures, felt very hard done by. Their bitter resentment informed an entire generation of American leftism.

After his death, Franklin D. Roosevelt oddly enough acquired his own cult of personality, which to a great extent is still kept alive. Simultaneously, though, bipartisan de-Rooseveltization proceeded in a way that subtly mirrored de-Stalinization a few years later. As the bluntest example, Congress and the States swiftly ratified the 22th Amendment limiting the president to two terms.[i] There would never be another FDR.

Harry Truman had no illusions about his predecessor. He said he was the coldest man he ever met: "He didn't give a damn personally for me or you or anyone else in the world."[1900] As vice-president, Truman had been treated as if he didn't exist. FDR loyalists considered him a nobody. Perhaps FDR could not conceive of a world without him ruling it, or he simply didn't care, but there surely never was a time when a vice-president should have been more "in the loop."

On the other hand, President Truman still tried to cover his flank by appointing Eleanor as a U.S. delegate to the United Nations, an organization she thought was her husband's most important foreign policy legacy. Eleanor became head of the U.N. Human Rights Commission, and chief author of the Declaration of Human Rights. But Truman and the Roosevelts did not see eye to eye on policy, and Eleanor was constantly on the verge of quitting. Through her partnership with her son Elliott, she was able to speak out more openly than in her official role. Elliott was drifting further to the left, at times openly supporting the USSR and denouncing American foreign policy.

Still, the relationship between the Roosevelts and the Communists had become troubled by June 1945. Eleanor wrote an important column in which she disavowed the American communists while maintaining that "it is possible to work with the USSR and the people of that great country," and that "we need have no fear of them." But she accused the American communists of deception, and said "they taught that allegiance to the party and acceptance of orders from party heads, whose interests were not just those of the United States, were paramount."[1901]

This infuriated Communist Party members, who were feeling increasingly exposed after FDR's death. The *Daily Worker* carried some critical, though not hostile, analyses of Mrs. Roosevelt's view. But the paper was more accepting of her son Elliott, who did not criticize the Party.[1902]

---

[i] Harry Truman was "grandfathered in" as eligible to run in 1953, but he chose not to.

By 1947 it was already a bad time to be a "card-carrying" communist or even a "comsymp." But among Stalin's American friends, Elliott Roosevelt had assumed a peculiar, but not entirely unfamiliar role. He was above official persecution, yet certainly not above public contempt.

While Elliott was not accused of being a communist by responsible people, he did find it necessary to assert that he wasn't. It is impossible to separate the unfavorable press attention he received post-war, particularly in connection with the 1947 Hughes hearings, from the rapid shift in the political landscape during this time. Still, he was himself the main author of his destruction.

A perceptive assessment was written by an angry Timothy Turner for the *Los Angeles Times* on 19 April 1947:

> Elliott Roosevelt, who has the family's flair for well-paid amateurism, is now a journalist and author…Mr. Roosevelt has just spoken here at a rally called by the Progressive Citizens for America, which is so Russophile that anti-Communist liberals have formed a rival organization to combat it….Elliott Roosevelt says the press is driving this country into war, but his principal complaint is personal. Some newspaper writers have called him a fellow traveler. After talking with Mr. Roosevelt for nearly an hour I believe this is not true. I do not think he is red, or even pink. I think he is cerise.
>
> The principal complaint of Mr. Roosevelt, and others present who made of the conference a public meeting, is that the press does not publish enough of the statements of Henry Wallace and men like him….The press was invited to interview Elliott Roosevelt, but he refused to answer the one question readers were interested in, "How about Wallace?" [Elliott was expected to endorse the Progressive Party presidential candidate] When a man in public life asks for a press conference it is assumed he will answer any fair question and not hold out to improve his gate at a lecture.
>
> I never encountered this before. Instead, this fledgling man of letters subjected the reporters of the metropolitan newspaper, who indirectly represented the press of the world, to a lecture on journalism. I am sure he would not summon a physician and then tell him he is a quack.
>
> This reporter has interviewed Jo Davidson, the genial Red who acted as advance man for Elliott Roosevelt [Davidson was prominent in the PCA]; on many occasions Norman Thomas, the Socialist, and several times, Earl Browder, the Communist. In my younger days I interviewed Eugene Debs, Emma Goldman, Lincoln Steffens and Oscar Ameringer. All treated me courteously and did not malign my profession.
>
> I never misquoted them, giving their views in some length, and in every case, I learned later, they were pleased with the result. I gave them a break. I was not so disposed to give Elliott Roosevelt a break (though I think I did) because I found that Elliott Roosevelt plays dirty pool.[1903]

There can be little doubt that Turner reflected the views of most of the commentariat of the time. The problem with Elliott was not that he was Red; it was that he was Elliott. Gradually, the newspapers, the radio stations, and even his preferred brand of intellectuals turned away from him. Granted, that was easy to do at a time when Reds had gone from being in charge to being charged.

After 1945, the Communist Party pursued a controversial popular front strategy whose most obvious manifestation was the Progressive Party and its presidential candidate, Henry Wallace. The former vice president was no communist, but he increasingly found himself lumped with them. Elliott stuck with him politically, but did not jump the Democratic ship; in fact, he and Franklin Jr. declared for Eisenhower – if he turned out to be a Democrat![1904] In 1948, Wallace got barely 2% of the vote, most of them in New York City.

We might speculate how the world would be different if FDR had lived longer, or conversely if he had died while Henry Wallace was still vice-president. The thought of one of Uncle Joe's best U.S. buddies as a general in charge of photoreconnaissance after 1945 surely can cause one to sit up straight. After all, Elliott had insisted on sharing the A-bomb with the Soviet dictator![1905]

Instead, Elliott would now begin a long, fitful fading from the scene. Suddenly, there were no more wildly inflated job offers from friends of Dad; no more oddly favorable business deals. His enterprises did not fare well, except for the one he started pushing his mother as a broadcast sage – at least until he depleted the family fortune. Even his relationship with Comrade Stalin had foundered by 1950.

Asking whether Elliott Roosevelt was a Soviet agent is a little like asking whether he was an alcoholic; a fair answer is that he had some of the traits, but no definite diagnosis. Communism was harder to pin on him, simply because he was unable to be faithful to any political direction.

In theory, nobody could have been a more obvious target of the NKVD. Amtorg and the Soviet Embassy had been well acquainted with him in 1934, but evidently thought him unreliable. By the time agents surveilled him in Teheran in November 1943, they already knew that he was for sale; that he was flamboyantly promiscuous; that he had immense debts; and that he was impressed by Soviet communism. But after Marshal Stalin himself put his arm around him and asked him to join the top decision-makers at the table, there would have been no point in running the risks of formally recruiting the son of the president. He was already on the team.

Stalin would use Elliott twice more after Teheran: the next year, when he provided a glowing picture of Soviet cooperation during the doomed shuttle-bombing enterprise, and in the fall of 1946, when he was given the grand tour of the USSR, culminating in a 67th birthday interview with the charming Marshal Stalin himself. However, by the onset of the Cold War Elliott was probably more liability than asset; although *As He Saw It* was swiftly published in Russian, he received no more trips to Moscow, and he was viewed in leading Western circles more as a fool than as a traitor.

When *As He Saw It* came out in late 1946, there was considerable debate about whether Elliott could possibly have been its true author. However, many held that the book was bad enough that this could well have been the case. It was correctly assumed that Eleanor Roosevelt had a significant hand in its preparation. The views expressed in the book, and indiscriminately put into the mouth of Franklin D. Roosevelt, were recognizable as the perspective of the Eleanor – Hopkins – Davies – Wallace wing of the Democratic Party.

While the pundits ridiculed Elliott's pro-Soviet book, he had the last laugh. The book became a runaway bestseller and was translated into numerous languages. To this day, historians return against their better judgment to Elliott's highly entertaining but questionable and tendentious recollections of the summits. And there is no doubt that Elliott's book is interesting, easily read, as well as agreeably short.

The political aspects are beyond our scope, but Elliott's habit of making up FDR quotes was disturbing. For example, he was constantly on his anti-imperialist high horse, and ascribed this same sentiment to his father. It read as if President Roosevelt was really fighting the British Empire, and fascism was only a distraction. The opinions attributed to FDR were certainly not drawn out of the void, but the remaining historical source material – Churchill's in particular – does not support Elliott's steep slant.

When he stated that the French generals "knew to the sou" how much money they could extract from their North African colonies, but gave no thought to how to improve the lot of the natives, he espoused a rather facile, anti-European-imperialist worldview that was commonly held in America at the time.[i] At that time, American attitudes were indeed for swift decolonization. As American hegemony replaced the European empires, slowly things became much more complicated for U.S. decision-makers.

It's safer to trust Elliott as to his own activities. He included details about his flights, meetings, parties, and other activities with the mighty at Casablanca, Oran, Algiers, Tunisia, Cairo, and Teheran. While these asides are not important in a geopolitical context, they do provide texture and support to historians' accounts of these summits. Of course, Elliott did not attend all of them: significantly, Arcadia (Washington), Yalta, and Potsdam evaded the ambitious officer, although this did not deter him from expounding his views of what went on there.

Elliott's pontifications were very carefully monitored abroad. As early as 20 August 1946, the Soviet press began praising his forthcoming book, which was being abridged in *Look* magazine. As the American embassy reported, "Roosevelt reportedly bitterly criticizes reactionaries 'who led American foreign policy to atom bomb and are ready to turn civilization into heap of ruins….and asks why at Washington cocktails there is so much chatter of war with Soviet Union in which it is 'primarily stressed that this war must begin before 1948.'"[1906]

The State Department forwarded that telegram to Elliott's FBI file in December 1946.

Ambush in Moscow

Soon Elliott's success with his first book translated into another visit to Moscow. He said this was Eleanor's idea; she had collared Gardner Cowles, publisher of *Look* at a dinner party, and pushed for her son's trip. Since she worked for the American U.N. delegation, she had no permission to go herself; but, like her late husband, she suffered under the fatal and infantile misapprehension that if one could just sit down and talk heart-to-heart with Uncle Joe, his suspicions about the world could be cleared up, and he would leave convinced of America's good intentions.[1907]

Elliott was deputized to go as a correspondent for *Look*. Faye Emerson rode shotgun as photographer. They left New York just before the election in which they both had campaigned heavily for communist-supported candidates. In New York City at that time, the Democrats, the Liberals, and the American Labor Party formed a "popular front" that was dominated by communist organizations, from unions to cultural groups. Elliott's candidates lost, but it is significant that the popular front dominated the City, whereas Dewey's Republicans swept the State.[1908]

---

[i] "He knew…to the sou how grievously the Moroccans could be exploited" about Gen. Charles Nogues, Resident-General at Rabat. ER: As He Saw It, 87-88.

Elliott was on the losing side in America, but not in the Soviet Union. Arriving in Moscow on 12 November, he declared that the Democratic defeat was the result of not following his father's foreign policy direction.[1909]

Perhaps because he drew in part on Elliott's notes, Peter Collier is misinformed in stating in *The Roosevelts – an American Saga*, that "in the summer of 1946, he and Faye flew to Moscow aboard an Aeroflot jet outfitted for VIPs with a plush red interior that Elliott felt made it look like a turn-of-the-century Pullman car."[1910]

They left in November, for one thing. For another, there were obviously no jetliners back then. Aeroflot operated license-built DC-3s. Some of these were indeed tarted up in clunky fashion, since Soviet tastes seemed to have been frozen in 1917. The Roosevelts flew from the Soviet sector of Berlin to Moscow, having already toured parts of Europe.

The wire services reported on 2 Nov 1946:

> Elliott Roosevelt and his wife, the former Faye Emerson of the movies, left La Guardia Field today aboard an American Overseas Airlines plane for Stockholm en route to Russia. "I hope to study several different subjects and look at things generally," the second son of the late president said, adding that he did not know whether he would see Premier Stalin. Roosevelt said he and his wife had voted by absentee ballot. Roosevelt's publishers, Duell, Sloan and Pierce, said yesterday Roosevelt would gather material in Russia for a magazine series while his wife would take pictures for the articles. The couple plans to spend six weeks in the Soviet Union.[1911]

The Roosevelts visited several countries, freely giving interviews, before getting aboard a flight from Berlin to Moscow. It was the same flight General Walter Bedell Smith, the new American ambassador, happened to be on. This is not insignificant. Elliott and "Beetle" knew each other well from North Africa. They had shared a secretary, although not in the same way. She was Ruth Briggs.

By 13 November, the Roosevelts finally arrived in Moscow, where they were met by a large limousine placed at their disposal by the Soviet international cultural agency VOKS. Among other places, the Roosevelts visited Stalin's birthplace in Gori in Gruzia (Soviet Georgia). It was a very special honor, but not as sublime as the trip's concluding audience with the dictator himself.[1912]

For a couple of weeks, there were no reported Elliott eruptions. That was usually a sign that a big one was brewing. It hit like a thunderclap on 27 November, and it almost lost the general his American passport.

At a reception for a prominent Soviet apparatchik, attended by the Roosevelts as well as American embassy personnel, Elliott – reportedly – went on a drunken tirade against American foreign policy. It was supposed to be confidential, but *Newsweek* had an important – although by no means impartial – source. This person reported:

> Elliott started off by explaining that foreign correspondents have no more freedom in the United States than they have in Russia. Take for instance, he said, the case of Ilya Ehrenburg. Throughout his recent stay in America the Soviet writer was followed by a State Department agent. Moreover, he rightly refused to be registered as a foreign agent. The United States cannot expect the Russians to agree to an exchange of students and writers until the Foreign Agents Registration Act is repealed, said Elliott.
>
> The United States, Elliott continued, has no business meddling in the Danube area. Surely, he pleaded, American boys did not go to war to establish an international regime on

> the Danube. The same goes for the Dardanelles, he said. Obviously, the Russians must have predominant control of the Black Sea straits. They would be foolish to agree to internationalization unless the United States agrees to internationalize the Panama Canal and Britain accepts an international regime over Suez and Gibraltar.
>
> Elliott also thought that the Soviet Union had never broken its word. While the United States and Britain repeatedly violated their pledges at Teheran, Yalta and Potsdam, the Soviets faithfully observed theirs. The Russian failure to withdraw troops on-time from Iran was perfectly justified.
>
> What else could Russia do after Britain, with American connivance, had sent in 7000 so-called oil experts and technicians? The Russians must also build up friendly regimes in neighboring countries as a counterweight to American and British expansionist policies.
>
> Elliott ended the disclosure with a challenge to the audience. "Can anyone here," he demanded, "name one instance in which the United States acted to further the cause of peace?"
>
> After a momentary hush an American reporter suggested: Had not the United States done everything to strengthen the power and prestige of the United Nations? But Elliott was ready for that one. "You know as well as I do," he told the questioner, "that the United States is supporting the U.N. for purely selfish and imperialistic reasons."[1913]

That mouthful came at a time when the USSR was in the process of installing dictatorships throughout Eastern Europe and in any other region it could reach. The USSR made a play for Turkey, Greece and Iran in 1946; the latter could very easily have ended up as another divided country. Elliott's comments came at a time when the Cold War front had not yet frozen; countries were in play all over Eurasia.

It was difficult for Elliott to deny he had said these things, because they sounded so much like him. But over the next week, as he tried to get out of the hole, he only dug himself deeper.

There happens to be a lot more to this little flap than most people were aware of at the time. We shall see that the incident was a classic example of the manipulation of news for purposes other than information. The *Newsweek* story turns out to be a pretty close transcript of a cable the Embassy sent to the State Department on 20 November, a week before the story broke.[i]

The Truman administration and its Moscow ambassador, Bedell Smith, were not amused by Elliott's activities. The State Department was already on the alert, because the Stockholm legation had hurriedly wired a translation of an interview Elliott gave to the communist daily *Ny Dag* on 4 November, just as he began his European trip. It carried much the same views Elliott spouted in Moscow, except that he didn't seem as drunk.[1914]

The Moscow embassy immediately got a copy of the Stockholm report, so staffers there knew what they were in for. But it can't be known whether the Americans deliberately set the trap for Elliott, or they simply waited for him to trip himself up.

Harry Truman's feelings about the USSR had been privately but effectively expressed in a note to Secretary of State Byrnes in early 1946:

---

[i] Cable, Smith to Sec. State, 20 NOV 46, per State Dept. FOIA. Begins: "Following observations by Elliott Roosevelt in conversation with American journalists at reception given November 18 by OIC staff member are reported both because of his relative prominence as son of late President and because his remarks were made in presence of Soviet guest of honor (Khmarski, newly appointed English speaking head American section VOKS), which suggests he may have had no hesitation in making similar statements in talks with Soviet officials."

> There isn't a doubt in my mind that Russia intends an invasion of Turkey and the seizure of the Black Sea Straits to the Mediterranean. Unless Russia is faced with an iron fist and strong language another war is in the making. Only one language do they understand – "how many divisions have you?"…I'm tired of babying the Soviets.[1915]

Ambassador Bedell Smith was also a tough-talking, gruff anti-communist. Since he knew Elliott well, it is likely that he was pleased to get the opportunity to nail him.

The two opposed viewpoints on the USSR could not cohabit within the Democratic Party for long. Henry Wallace was cashiered in September 1946. On 12 March 1947, HST enunciated the "Truman doctrine" of active containment to Congress. In the USSR, the February issue of *Bolshevik* reviewed *As He Saw It* in six pages:

> Most of review is devoted to commending Roosevelt's book which "'is a document of accusations against saboteurs of international cooperation, enemies of democratic peace,'…'unmasks the warmongers' …'evil-wishing careerists' in State Department, reactionaries in camp of both parties in Congress and guardians of 'freedom' of press".[1916]

As late as 2 April 1947, TASS was quoting new remarks by Elliott Roosevelt, fiercely attacking American foreign policy towards the Soviet Union.[1917]

Elliott and the people he spoke for were fighting a rear-guard action. The notion that the Soviet Union was a noble experiment and that Uncle Joe could do no wrong was still held by many. But Elliott's tirade in Moscow does not reveal a thoughtful, reasoned analysis of great power relations. It is the self-righteous rant of an amateur. That is, of course, if he had been quoted reasonably correctly.

When this latest Elliott scandal erupted, there was outrage in Congress. One representative, Lawrence Smith (R-WI) wrote to Secretary of State Byrnes:

> Are his remarks to go unchallenged? Will the State Department remain silent? Should not passport privileges of Mr. Roosevelt be revoked immediately and he be ordered back to the United States? The damage he has done is immeasurable. He openly courted soviet favor at the expense of our standing and prestige abroad. While you are engaged in and honest effort to build good will throughout the world, Elliott Roosevelt has constituted himself an ambassador of ill will. He is outdoing Henry Wallace and he is just as much an amateur. You can silence him by revoking his privileges. Return him to this country, where he can do no harm.[1918]

After the war, the colloquially labeled Dies Committee had morphed into the famous House Unamerican Activities Committee (HUAC), and it was only going after communists now that the fascist threat was considered to be history. But the acting chairman, Rep. John Rankin (D-MS), refused to get involved, because Elliott was still technically an Army officer, though in the inactive reserve. If there was going to be an investigation, it ought to be the province of the Army and the State Department, possibly resulting in a court martial. For that there was plainly no appetite; and Elliott seemed, at any rate, to do more damage to himself than to his country.

Perhaps for that reason, he was allowed to continue on his epic Soviet journey. His enemies in the United States seldom needed to do anything but report his activities. They reasoned he would self-destruct before he could be destroyed.

Hell hath no fury like a…

Caught out, Elliott, true to form, launched a fierce counterattack. Two days after the *Newsweek* story he asserted that he had been ambushed by the U.S. Embassy in Moscow. He said the *Newsweek* story was incomplete, incorrect, and unfair. But he wouldn't tell the full story, because "I refuse to divulge the conversation of others at a private party, just as I expect others to respect my conversation." His wife added the astute observation: "Things like this just happen because he is Elliott Roosevelt – cocktail parties and dogs and things."[1919]

Harry Truman's correspondence files contain numerous enraged letters and cables from "patriotic citizens" who demanded that Truman try or court-martial or expel the errant general. Some wanted to deny him the right to return, others wanted him recalled and his passport seized. This was right at the leading edge of the "third red scare" that would culminate during Truman's second term. But nothing happened to Elliott except acute public embarrassment. He always tolerated that well.

While American public opinion fulminated, and the embassy cabled back its explanations, there would soon be a very special twist on the story to greatly amuse Elliott-followers.

It turned out that the secret source the media had at the reception was no less than Ambassador, General Walter Bedell Smith's secretary, Major Ruth Briggs. She had been so good at her job that Smith had kept her on his staff when he changed into civvies and got the diplomatic post in March 1946.

There was a dispute over whether Briggs attended the infamous occasion – Elliott said she didn't, *Newsweek* that she did – but she was the one who went to Bedell Smith with the story. The Embassy then cabled it to Washington. That the State Department deliberately leaked the story to *Newsweek* seemed obvious, and that's what Elliott charged. And he had good reason to suspect Ruth Briggs.[1920]

While Briggs worked for "Beetle" in North Africa, and again in England, she had been Colonel Roosevelt's highly public consort, so public that poor Ruth Googins back in Texas had complained directly to the president about his son. When the Ruth in Texas divorced Elliott and married his second-in-command, the Ruth in England naturally thought she'd be her replacement.

By 1944, people were already expecting Ike himself to give away the bride. Ruth Briggs was so sure she let her mother tell the newspapers. She didn't know that Elliott was advancing rapidly on the female front in California at the very same time.

Almost everyone else knew that, especially Faye Emerson back in Hollywood. And a London journalist complained in a wire that it was strange that people were confounded, since in England it was assumed that the Briggs-Roosevelt union had merely been delayed until the November election was over; another churn of the marriage machine probably wouldn't help the president. It was definitely safest to keep Elliott out of the country until Thanksgiving – but not because of Ruth Briggs.[1921]

Another of General Eisenhower's staff, Sue Sarafian Jehl, would later recollect in an oral history completed for the Eisenhower Library:

> But anyway, Kay [Summersby] and I were listening to the radio in that room and we heard that Elliott Roosevelt had just married, was in the states, and had just married Faye Emerson. And Kay screamed and I screamed because he was engaged to Ruth Briggs, Beetle Smith's secretary. Given her a lovely ring and then he had to go to Washington on

business and he married Faye Emerson. And we screamed and the General looked up, he was reading. He said, "What's wrong?" And we told him and then Captain Butcher and the General practically screamed too. And poor Ruth Briggs, I really, really felt sorry for her. Because everybody in HQ knew that they were engaged and going to be married, and he came back already married to Faye Emerson.

...Anyway, Kay didn't live with us then, she lived with Ruth Briggs and one other WAAC officer, I don't remember who it was. Elliott bought Ruth an Irish wolfhound as a gift and brought it over. It was the size of a little pony. I had never seen – well, I think it's the biggest dog in the world. I had never seen a bigger dog. And they had their bedrooms upstairs and the first day she had him he followed her upstairs to the bedroom and in the morning he couldn't get down the stairs. So they had to get four GIs to come and carry that dog back the stairs.[1922]

Yes, yet another shaggy dog. This one evaded the media, though. Elliott had known Ruth since before Casablanca; their engagement was told in July 1944 and in December, he wed Faye. Ruth was stateside on leave when the news of Elliott's marriage hit her.[1923]

The "first five" WACs had differing perspectives on Elliott's amorous exploits. Mattie Pinette took a more understanding position:

He became engaged to Ruth, and that was quite a disappointment; to Ruth anyhow. He married Faye Emerson instead. He came back here, engaged to Ruth, had gotten permission from the Chief of Staff. You had to get permission from your boss...her boss was Gen. Smith and he had to get his permission to marry Ruth. Gen. Smith had given his permission and it was all set, it was even announced by Ruth's mother in Washington. He was here a week and married Faye Emerson. So I think that was a lousy trick to play.

But there was also another side. Ruth is a very dominating person and she actually dominated Elliott Roosevelt. It was in her nature to be dominant. Gen. Smith was dominant, and of course she worked for him for the entire war and I think that this increased her dominant trait. I think probably he was afraid to be dominated and decided that this was an easy out. But in any event, I think this was a dirty trick.[1924]

Now, two years later in Moscow, Ms. Briggs – and probably Ambassador Smith – had cruelly evened the score. Scripps-Howard writer, Henry J. Taylor, reminisced:

The story of the famous "leak" of Elliott's Moscow speech in which he is reported to have called Uncle Sam an aggressor does not start in the shadow of the Kremlin. It begins on the third floor of a dingy hotel in Algiers, where sat a WAC. She was Capt. Ruth M. Briggs, later a major, secretary to Lt. Gen. W. Bedell Smith at the 1943 North African HQ in the St. George Hotel.

Whenever he dropped into town, Elliott, then a colonel, would date up Capt. Briggs. In the eyes of many, and in the language of most, they appeared to be "going steady."

That opinion was strengthened by Elliott's practice of skimming his reconnaissance plane low over Capt. Briggs' abode, the WAC barracks, familiarly known as the "Wax Works," and dipping his wings, conking his engines, and in other ways calling attention to the fact that he had arrived....

Miss Briggs, it appears, did not write the report which is said to have quoted Elliott's remarkable words. But she told what he said and the report itself is described as having been written by Ambassador Smith who sent it in code to the State Department – a procedure frequently followed in foreign capitals when American visitors create a local commotion.[1925]

This romantic angle is still not the whole story. A young unknown reporter named Walter Cronkite, who had recently opened UP's office in Moscow, quoted Elliott as saying it was a "put-up job (by the U.S. Embassy) to bait me."[1926]

This caused another furor, to which Elliott protested that he didn't mean it. It was getting to be "a tempest in a teapot." He was now quoted accusing Cronkite:

> …he had not accused the U.S. Embassy … of being implicated in the publication of an off-the-record discussion he had soon after his arrival here. "A correspondent who apparently sent out such a story is the very person who suggested to me that the Embassy was involved," he declared. "I am calling him right now to tell him this. I am also informing the Embassy here."[1927]

Elliott was definitely on the right track. Walter Cronkite had been working with the U.S. Embassy, trying to get his stories out. On 29 November, the embassy sent a wire for him:

> FOLLOWING FROM CRONKITE FOR SALISBURY UNITED PRESS:
> Upon receipt your 25112 I filed first Roosevelt story. It was stopped. Upon receipt 26164 I tried again. Again it was stopped. Thursday morning I scooped all opposition by intercepting Elliott at railway station. He gave me good statement whereon filed six takes – 28112 etseq. It included story surrounding statements. It stopped. I filed service message informing you of difficulties. It stopped. I have written formal complaint to Minister Foreign Affairs but expect no relief…[1928]

While the embassy and Cronkite were trying to heat up the story, the Soviet censors were sabotaging the correspondent's communications.

It so happened that Walter Cronkite claimed to be a "great" personal friend of General Smith's. He already had the inside track. In his memoirs, he recalled the scoop he struck when he intercepted Elliott at the train station as the Roosevelts were coming back from Leningrad. He took them back to their hotel next to the American embassy, pumping them for more outrageous quotes. He thus kept the row going by not only reporting Elliott's absurd foreign policy comments, but then by interviewing him about the "reaction to the reaction:"

> They ranted and they raved, mostly about our government and particularly about our foreign service. At one point Elliott pointed in the direction of the Embassy and delivered a scathing indictment: 'Our State Department is run by people whom my father wouldn't trust to run his messages.' [1929]

And that's the way it was... Franklin had loathed the "striped-pants" men in the State Department – men like Chip Bohlen and George Kennan. And Elliott may well have specifically referred to an outrageous incident in 1943, when FDR sent Stalin's favorite American, Joseph E. Davies, to Moscow with a personal letter to the Marshal. Ambassador Standley wasn't allowed to see the letter; he was even told to leave when Davies delivered it to Uncle Joe. The diplomats were livid at the way the president treated them.[1930]

By 1947, the professionals were back in control at the State Department, with or without striped pants.

Despite the censors, the young upstart Cronkite had a field day. And, having suffered in the Soviet capital long enough, he thought the USSR-enchanted Elliott and Faye were true fools who pontificated that "just a coat of paint and Moscow would be prettier than Paris." But of the visitors "none brought more excitement" to his dreary posting there! [1931]

Elliott's tirades helped him not. He had outed himself as a "traitor" in the eyes of most Americans.

Obviously, as a private citizen Elliott had the right to express his opinions without harassment from his government. He caused a lot of posturing by enraged Congressmen, but nothing happened to him. It was proposed to indict him for violating the hoary 1799 Logan Act, which prohibits Americans from trying to conduct their own private foreign policy. It was unlikely this could have stuck, since he was technically traveling as a private person and merely expressing his opinions.[1932]

But it is worthy of note that others, not protected by name and connections, landed in deep hot water during the anti-communist mania of that time. The infamous HUAC (Un-American Activities Committee) did make noises about stringing up Elliott, too – at least subpoenaing him to testify before Congress. [1933] But in the end it was safer to go after smaller communist-sympathizing fish. For Elliott, the Senate already had something else – and far more spectacular – up its sleave.[1934]

Back home, in February 1947, Elliott was a guest on Mutual's *Meet the Press*, where he was fiercely grilled by several hostile journalists. Elliott launched right back at them. The *Daily Worker*, organ of the Communist Party of the United States, later reported how Elliott had "turned the tables" on his accusers. It said that Henry Taylor of Scripps-Howard admitted that the State Department leaked the highly exaggerated story to the news media, and that there was in fact no story sent from Moscow to the news media, as it had seemed. As the paper said, Elliott had denied the details and submitted a correction to the Embassy:

> The denial and accurate account given by Elliott to the American Embassy were forwarded to the State Department where Elliott saw them later, he said. But this correction of a deliberately leaked and falsified story was not leaked in its turn, Elliott pointed out. Instead, a second story was "planted," falsely accusing him of blaming the Embassy for the original fake.[1935]

Conspiracy theorists take note: the State Department did try to "get," or at least "out" Elliott Roosevelt. Walter Cronkite was in on it, simply in the pursuit of a good story. All because Elliott maintained that "FDR's entire domestic and foreign program has been abandoned and betrayed since the President died."[1936] Well, at least according to the *Daily Worker*. It forgot to mention that Elliott brought it on himself.

That heated exchange on *Meet the Press* was not just for appearances. After the show, a verbal fight broke out that ended with one of Roosevelt's friends (Dick Harrity of Duell, Sloan & Pierce) landing a punch to the jaw of one of the radio men, Fulton Lewis, Jr.[1937] Usually, Elliott himself threw the punches; perhaps he was slowing down.

While they were still touring the Soviet Union in December 1946, Elliott and Faye turned their attention south, to the Georgian Soviet Socialist Republic. Their idol came from there, and they would visit his birthplace, Gori. Then it was onto what was left of Warsaw, via what was left of Rostov. In the Polish capital the Roosevelts stayed at Wilanow Palace – the Polish Versailles, still standing – and "usually reserved for distinguished foreign officials," as the American embassy ruefully reported. They met with party chief Boleslaw Bierut, an NKVD agent installed as ruler of Poland. The Polish press – what was left of it – was already strictly in line and made all the proper noises to celebrate "the valued publicist and disciple of his father's political and social ideals." [1938]

Audience with the Generalissimo

General Roosevelt still had a week of touring behind the rapidly closing Iron Curtain. The climax came on 21 December, when, in a formal interview, Marshal Stalin personally answered twelve questions Elliott submitted on behalf of *Look* magazine. This was an extraordinary honor. Stalin did not give interviews. In fact, his prolonged invisibility in 1946 had caused Kremlinologists to believe he was ill (he was vacationing in the southern republics). Elliott, however, found him very much alive:

> He received Faye and me on his 67th birthday, in the presence of Pavlov, his Russian interpreter. He walked towards us with outstretched arms, and said with a broad smile, 'I remember you very well.' [1939]

Elliott and Faye could be excused for not knowing it, but even the occasion was a lie. Stalin's recorded date of birth was 18 December 1878, and he was over a year older than he said.

In his responses, Stalin managed to sound reasonable and hopeful, expressing his confidence that the current anti-Soviet feeling in America was a passing phase, and that peaceful coexistence would prevail. Importantly, he asserted that his people were tired of war, and that "there are no understandable objectives to justify a new war." Stalin's soothing words stood in contrast to his earlier domestic speech noting that conflict with the capitalist world was inevitable and inherent in the class struggle.[1940]

That was all very predictable and formulaic. It was the unscripted (and unpublished) exchanges that would raise eyebrows later.

Stalin stated that he believed FDR had been poisoned by the "Churchill gang." Ticked off, he had refused to let Eleanor into the USSR, because Ambassador Gromyko had not been allowed to examine FDR's corpse for signs of foul play. Andrei Gromyko had been sent to Warm Springs, Georgia, with specific instructions for that ghoulish task. Elliott said the Soviets made three separate requests to inspect the corpse, but Eleanor, appalled, would not open the casket.[1941]

> The casket was in the East Room of the White House. [Eleanor didn't want FDR to lie in state in the Capitol rotunda] My mother said, "Thank God you're here!" And I said, "Why?" And she said, "Well, the Russian ambassador's been over trying to see me, and I just saw him a few minutes ago. Stalin wanted him and some of his aides to view father in the coffin." I said, "Absolutely not. We're not having anyone see him at all." And she said, "I don't know what their reason is for it." And I said, "Well, let me talk to them." So I talked to them. They said that Stalin believed that Father had been poisoned and that they didn't think that he had had a massive brain hemorrhage. And I said, "You'll just have to take my word for it, because that's what he had. If we open this casket for you and your people to view it, we'll have to do that for the public, and we just don't want the public to see the disfigurement of the results of this massive brain hemorrhage." They said they

would relay it to the generalissimo, and they came back in and said, "We've got to see the body, we've got to have it viewed." And I said, "Well, sorry." [1942]

This account is similar to the one Elliott gave to Peter Collier. He then said the Soviets were obsessed with the need to examine his father's corpse.[1943]

Late in life, Elliott claimed that he had included Stalin's ravings about the poisoning in his *Look* article, but it was edited out. He quoted the dictator: "The Churchill Gang! They poisoned your father, and they continue to try to poison me." [1944]

The reader can only gasp that we are clearly not dealing with normal people here. Joseph Stalin always thought people were trying to poison him, and there is some evidence that Lavrentii Beria finally succeeded therein, in 1953.[1945]

When Elliott revealed this forty years later, it caused quite a stir. A prominent Stalin biographer, Harvard's Adam Ulam, commented: "That sounds like absolute fantasy on Elliott's part. Stalin would never have made such a silly statement." Historians never were much impressed with Elliott, but could he have made up something this shocking? [1946]

If we hazard to disregard Stalin's theory, how did the president die? In 1949, Elliott felt the urge to bless the nation with his opinion of this as well. Prompted by speculation in the press, he published an intemperate but influential article "They're lying about FDR's health!" in *Liberty* magazine. He was absolutely right, but he failed to include himself among the liars. Elliott knew little about his father's medical record. He had seen him only sporadically during the war, and elsewhere he had confessed to being appalled at FDR's deterioration in the fall of 1944.[1947]

The biggest liars were FDR's doctors and some of his close associates, and it is blatantly obvious why. They were engaged in a whitewash in order to justify not only the fourth term, but later to protect the president's reputation. If the truth had been known, there would have been an outcry. This is, of course, an old story when it comes to the health of presidents.

The last and best word on FDR's medical condition came as late as 2009, in *FDR's Deadly Secret*, a book that reflected intense historical and medical research fortified by a consensus of the many medical specialists consulted. The authors document that the president was a wreck during his last year. He had seizures, severe pain, and a dramatic, irreversible weight loss. The authors make a compelling case that FDR had a metastasized cancer that finally resulted in the massive cerebral hemorrhage on 12 April. For good measure they assert that he probably had Guillain-Barré, not polio; and they credit – at long last – the previously mentioned Dr. Joseph Emanuelson for having diagnosed the melanoma over FDR's left eye – an obvious lesion that miraculously disappeared in 1942, leaving a faint scar.[1948]

Domestic politics aside, the president's health raises disturbing questions about the Yalta conference in February 1945. FDR was a living ghost; he was at times incoherent and rambling, and would occasionally sit slack-jawed, mouth hanging open, glassy-eyed, lost to the world. Opinions differ over whether all this gave Marshal Stalin an unfair advantage – his Red Army was really the last word – but it certainly contributed to the perception later central to the "Betrayal at Yalta" argument.

The spectacle should have alerted Stalin, and his advisers, that the president was essentially dying before their eyes. But by 1945 the stumpy, pallid *vozhd* himself was none too healthy, though his mental state was unraveling faster than his physical functions. He was then 66, four years older than FDR.

Later, Elliott wrote that Stalin admitted to knowing English, and said he used this to his advantage during the wartime negotiations. This makes some sense, though it is unlikely that Uncle Joe would have used the American idiomatic expression "Caught me out, didn't you..." attributed to him. But several episodes suggest that Stalin knew a smattering, certainly more than the Allied chiefs knew of Russian. General Arnold thought Stalin understood English, "though he wouldn't admit it." [1949]

Despite the doubts of historians, Elliott further reinforced the notion before he died: "He understood English perfectly, but he wouldn't let on...Stalin was absorbing everything that either Churchill or Franklin Roosevelt said at these meetings and then waiting and listening to the interpretations, and he had all that time when he knew perfectly well what had been said. He had that advantage over both of them, and he never let on to them."[1950]

The contemporary report in *Look*, however, was far more anodyne than Elliott's later recollections. As printed, Comrade Stalin's responses certainly were predictable and harmless. But it turned out that Elliott had managed to slip in two of his own questions, and they tell us more about him than about Stalin:

> Question 7: Sir, I know that you are a student of many other political and social problems existing in other countries. And so I should like to ask whether you feel that the elections in the United States last November indicated a swing away on the part of the people from belief in the policies of Roosevelt and towards the isolationist policies of his political adversaries.
>
> Stalin: I am not so well acquainted with the internal life of the people of the United States, but I would think that the election indicated that the present government is wasting the moral and political capital created by the late President, and thus it facilitated the victory of the Republicans.
>
> Question 12: Does the failure in the American and British zones of occupied Germany of carrying out the de-nazification program give serious cause for alarm in the government of the Soviet Union?
>
> Stalin: No, it hasn't been a cause for serious alarm, but of course it is not pleasant for the Soviet Union that this part of our common program is not being put into effect.[1951]

Neither Elliott nor Faye found occasion to ask about conditions in Eastern Europe.

As they talked, Faye had the presence of mind to note the surroundings in detail. She provided a sketch of the Generalissimo's large but stark office for readers. Evidently, only Stalin, interpreter Pavlov, and the Roosevelts were present in the room.

Elliott had his mind on the money. He had led off by asking Stalin if he would make sure that nobody released anything from the interview until his own story was published. Stalin, perhaps impressed with a true capitalist, reassured Elliott that, yes, "this is your property. Nobody else will get it!"

Stalin smoked one big Russian cigarette after another during the meeting. Elliott, mesmerized, did not. He concluded his article by noting that for those two hours he never thought of lighting a cigarette. He said that was a record for him.

In his own writings, the controversy over his treasonous speech has disappeared. Instead, he debriefed Eleanor after he got back. Of Stalin, Elliott reported:

> Well, he hasn't grown any, of course – he's still inches shorter than anyone in this family. His hair's turning grayer; he still smokes a lot of those Russian cigarettes with cardboard holders on the end; wears a smart uniform.
>
> Who else was there with you?
>
> Just Berezhkov, his interpreter [Valentin B., who defected to the USA the year after Elliott died]. I'd met him before, starting at Teheran. I would question Stalin, and as the meeting went on, more and more he didn't wait for Berezhkov to translate. He'd start answering right away. That told me Stalin understood English, but he didn't realize I knew any Russian.
>
> Could you understand what he was saying?
>
> About 90% of it. Only a few words were unfamiliar. [Elliott had taken an in-depth Russian course in anticipation of the trip.] [1952]

The alert reader will now ask, "So who was interpreting, Pavlov or Berezhkov?" Why, in 1977, had Elliott changed it to Berezhkov? Both interpreters were much used, but Pavlov was Stalin's primary. And in the *Look* article, Faye's sketch shows Stalin sitting across from Elliott, who had Faye to his left, with "Pavlov" between them at the head of the conference table.[i]

The sketch was important because the Roosevelts never received the photos Stalin promised. But Stalin graciously accepted Elliott's gift, a copy of his current bestseller.[1953]

Elliott summarized Stalin's motives:

> I had the feeling that he was trying to pass along a message, something along these lines. He felt he was engaged in a losing battle without Father to explore with him likely avenues of coexistence. Stalin also knows darn well that he's failing to maintain the ongoing Big Three relationship that grew up in the war years….I believe he would go along with U.N. control of atomic weapons and a U.N. police force. If he said as much himself, he'd be afraid of weakening his own position in the USSR.[1954]

In retrospect, this is hardly a convincing analysis – Stalin as a politician concerned about his credibility at home. Eleanor, who also wrote about the Russians for *Look*, was equally naïve. She said: "We can work with Russia as we have with the socialist government in Britain."[1955]

The visit to the Soviet Union would spark a campaign in the Communist media trumpeting Elliott (and others) as the "good" Americans, opposed to the evil warmongers who had usurped the government and trampled on Roosevelt's legacy. In early May 1947, *Pravda* listed the USSR's friends in America. Henry Wallace, Elliott Roosevelt, and Senator Claude Pepper came out tops. Joseph Davies of *Mission to Moscow*, Elliott's hero of Soviet-American friendship, also received prominent mention.[ii]

The *Pravda* article was a kind of catalog of communist and left-wing personalities and organizations still operating in the United States. The Soviet media campaign against Western imperialism had resumed after the Potsdam summit and Stalin's dawning realization that Truman did not yield to bullying. It was equally significant that just two years after FDR's death, the anti-communist campaign was in full steam in the United States, but the left had not yet rolled over or been scared into its holes. With

---

[i] Berezhkov often translated for Molotov, and Elliott may have been familiar with him from that angle.

[ii] Newsweek, 12 MAY 47; Joseph E. Davies was FDR's Moscow Ambassador from 1936-38, and was used as a special emissary to Stalin afterwards. He was an Order of Lenin holder whom Stalin gave millions in stolen art. Claude Pepper worshipped Stalin (then) and secured an interview with him in 1945.

Henry Wallace's presidential candidacy, 1948 was the last year that the pro-Soviet flank could mount major operations on the American political scene.

Of this gallery of strident Soviet friends, Florida's Claude Pepper was especially interesting. Although he was defeated in 1950, in the midst of the witch-hunts, he underwent a sort of lycanthropic metamorphosis and reëmerged as an anti-communist congressman from southern Florida. Still a strong advocate for government remittances, especially to the elderly, he ably served his Jewish and anti-Castro Cuban constituency for decades. Indeed, he would become useful to Elliott again.

After the Soviet visit, Elliott Roosevelt continued to play up his friendship with Joseph Stalin, even as the American political and cultural environment swung into one of its periodic anti-communist panics. Unfortunately, Elliott's own life was simultaneously dissolving in an orgy of booze, babes, and dubious business ventures.

In January 1950, Elliott thought the time was ripe to go on another special mission to interview Stalin, armed with a wire-recorder and a contract with interested American media. The FBI had a source somewhere in the chain and reported that Elliott requested the Moscow trip and interview through Yakov Malik, Soviet U.N. ambassador; and that Elliott met with Ambassador Alexander Panyushkin at the Soviet embassy on 11 January.

It was important enough for Director Hoover to advise the Attorney General.[1956]

Columnist Leonard Lyons was also informed; he said that after Elliott married his then-mistress, he would travel to Moscow. After recording the Stalin interview, he would then receive a Chinese visa, and proceed around the world.[1957]

For some reason, Stalin was not interested. Spring passed, and the visa never came.

By that time the Soviet Union had tested an atomic bomb, had seemingly taken over China, and had given the go-ahead for the attack in Korea. By now USAF officers were beginning to wonder whether a preemptive strike might be the best way to handle the USSR. At home, Marshal Stalin himself was increasingly paranoid and delusional. A new, massive purge was being prepared.

At any rate, the Soviets found no more use for Elliott Roosevelt. Obviously they had used him, as he had used them; but that was all there was to it. For Elliott, all the doors that had been open when FDR was alive were closing, one by one.

He did go to Europe, though, accompanying mother Eleanor on a nine-nation swing through northern Europe. Eleanor was much admired there, and feted almost everywhere. She was especially welcome in Norway, whose royal family had been very close to the late president (some, including son James, thought Crown Princess Märtha had been way too close).[i]

Elliott, with his daughter Chandler and son Elliott Jr., cruised Oslo Fjord with the Norwegian crown prince and his son.[1958] He very undiplomatically asserted that "every Scandinavian we met impressed us with his strength of character, but the Finns, nestled up against the Soviet border, scored the highest of all."[1959]

In Copenhagen, the situation was the opposite. Eleanor stayed at the U.S. embassy, and the King of Denmark would not meet with her. In her early memoir, *This I Remember*, she had written that he, as a young crown prince visiting the White House, seemed most uninterested in serious matters, such as his country's relations with Germany:

---

[i] JR: My Parents, 109. She stayed at the White House during the war while her husband was in London.

> At the time of his visit our impression was that the Danish prince was more interested in his holiday than in the serious questions of the moment, and had perhaps less realization of the menace of Hitler than we had expected of one in his position.[i]

In one of her rare slips of diplomatic propriety, Eleanor had gone on to give an unflattering description of the later King Frederik IX. Unlike his stern father, Christian X, he did have a reputation as an amiable lightweight, but apparently he also had a good memory of affronts.

Back to the Farm

In fall of 1945, the default option for the jobless general was to succeed his father as squire of Hyde Park. Elliott said Eleanor "timidly" asked if he would take over the estate: "I don't think I could live there unless you do. I doubt that I would want to."[1960]

Eleanor was extremely busy. She wrote a daily column, she wrote books, she spoke on the radio and on television, she entertained and went to meetings and talks. Even with her "Roosevelt energy," it's no wonder she needed help. Elliott was the only child sufficiently adrift to consider lending a hand. It would become a famous partnership that would run for five years until Elliott divorced and remarried. By 1951, Eleanor tired of being used as a prop in the radio business and as a source of funds for Elliott's schemes.

Elliott, however, said "those were fun years for me." He marketed his mother to the media, including the new-fangled "television," which he and his father had once dismissed as having no future. It seemed that the public was no longer willing to listen to Elliott's own opinions, but Eleanor's was a different matter. Together, their weekly interview and commentary program on NBC attracted a modest audience.

It should have been a perfectly non-controversial activity. But it was not to be. Probably the best source to the Elliott-Eleanor radio enterprise is Henry Morgenthau III, son of FDR's Treasury Secretary, who helped produce the programs. He reminisced:

> In the radio series Elliott interviewed his mother. It was a commercial series. Elliott wanted the television series to be commercial, too, but it never gained a sponsor. The radio series had a lot of local sponsors. I don't know whether my title was the producer or not; I think Elliott was the producer, and I worked for him. It was his company.
>
> Mrs. Roosevelt was anxious at that time to do things to help Elliott and to make money for him – or allow him to make money. So we did that radio program, and I acted as producer and editor. Then we did the television series, which was called something like, "Tea with Mrs. Roosevelt." Those were done from the Park Sheraton Hotel…Elliott got his mother to move out of her apartment in Washington Square and move into the hotel. The hotel wanted her there. They were able to say that Mrs. Roosevelt was staying there, and then there was some arrangement, I think, that Elliott could live there, too, with his girlfriend of the time. The programs were produced there, and then it was said on the air, "this program originates from the Park Sheraton." And all that, I guess, had some monetary value for Elliott.
>
> As I said, at that time I think Mrs. Roosevelt's main objective was doing something to help Elliott…It was difficult because Mrs. Roosevelt was trying to help Elliott. She didn't.

[i] Eleanor: This I Remember, 183. The Danish Court claimed that the King's absence was unrelated.

> It was difficult for her to accept criticism of him, although I am sure she wasn't pleased with a lot of things that were going on…eventually I resigned because I realized that there were certain things that were going on that she didn't really want to hear about and that were intolerable for me because I knew that she could be persuaded to do things that really were against her better judgment and her taste….
>
> It was a difficult situation to be in. Elliott, of course, was pretty unscrupulous in everything that he did.[1961]

In 1950, WNBC New York transmitted the Eleanor program for 45 minutes daily. Elliott served as the announcer and hawker of products. To some, even in the family, it was all quite embarrassing: "The show proves that a boy's best friend is his mother," opined *Billboard.* But Eleanor was excused in public opinion, and she did have interesting topics and guests on the show. Eventually, she did end the partnership and then proceeded to do television programs on a non-commercial basis.[1962]

But the son's success in hawking his mother to strangers should not be discounted. Proud of his initial entrepreneurial success, Elliott later wrote:

> I was able to help her in negotiating new contracts for her daily column with United Features Syndicate. I negotiated a new contract for her with McCall's magazine to replace her old contract with Ladies Home Journal. I helped her in revising her agency agreements for her literary and lecture efforts. I was instrumental in organizing the syndication of a radio program, and produced for NBC a weekly television program.[1963]

The two did manage to sell a new volume of Eleanor remembrances for $150,000 – sight unseen – to the publisher.[1964] That was particularly savvy, because *This I remember* is not very good; it is long on trivia and short on new information or hard-hitting opinions, both of which Eleanor was well known to possess. Elliott also managed to jack up Eleanor's remuneration for the long-running but insipid "*My Day*" column. Eleanor was perhaps the first successful blogger before blogs; she seemingly wrote like a whirling dervish with a pen in each hand. (She dictated most of it.) But by sticking to "goodwill towards mankind" and harmless quotidian observations she avoided the troubles her more flamboyant and outspoken sons attracted.[1965]

Elliott was justified in pointing out his invaluable assistance to his mother. Eleanor didn't care about money, and gave away what she got. But her children were the opposite way, and they made sure to drive a hard bargain. Unfortunately, in the process, Elliott worked his mother to her limit. A modest success, the NBC radio show had two hundred stations at its peak.[1966] Both the radio and television programs brought in respected and interesting guests, such as Albert Einstein. Winston Churchill, though, declined to appear.

When Elliott retired to Hyde Park, his restless entrepreneurial spirit also focused on the patrimony: about a square mile of rolling woods and farmland on the banks of the Hudson. Franklin had never made much of the agricultural potential, but with his ranching experience, Elliott saw new possibilities.

The mansion and its immediate vicinity had already gone to the National Park Service, although the family retained the rights to use it. Eleanor preferred the secluded, idyllic cottage at Val-Kill (Dutch: valley stream), which was a good distance uphill. Elliott and Faye took over Top Cottage, a rustic retreat FDR had built for his own enjoyment. From there they proceeded to farm.

Elliott, taking a clue from the Bolsheviks, said he was executing a "five-year plan." The goal was to turn the farm into a major producer, supplying hotels, restaurants, and other local enterprises. For a while, things looked up.[1967]

Wife nr. 4, Minnewa Bell's papers contain an unattributed radio script featuring a detailed interview with Elliott Roosevelt, gentleman farmer:

> Faye and Elliott showed me around their magnificent home, the "Dream House," a Dutch field stone Colonial which is officially called "Top Cottage." FDR designed it, and planned it as a hide-away from the "Big House" which had become too much of a public place. Only the President's close friends were invited there. Most of FDR's speeches were written on the desk near the tremendous window which offers a breathtaking view of the Hudson Valley, which he loved so well. This desk is an exact duplicate of George Washington's…I noticed a landscape of Marrakech, a city 120 miles from Casablanca. The painting was signed, W.S.C., which of course, are the initials of Winston Spencer Churchill [*Tower of Katoubia Mosque*]…
>
> Elliott showed me the farm, from the chicken roost to the dairy barn, which is equipped with all the most modern conveniences for cow comfort, including a drinking fountain where the cow only has to nudge a gadget with her nose to get a drink.[1968]

Eleanor would soon find that farming wasn't the best occupation for her son. She said he discovered it was impractical unless you worked the land yourself.[1969]

But the proud farmer explained:

> I happen to have a very warm interest in farming, and I gained a great deal of experience during the time I lived on a ranch in Texas. I bought with Mother the 842 acre Val-Kill property which was added to the 1,000 acre Hudson River estate left by Father.
>
> While Father was alive, Hyde Park had not been exploited on a money-making basis, but I am determined to develop Val-Kill into a prosperous farm. During our first years we have had losses, however I hope that very soon the break will come. 25% of the farm income comes from the dairy. We have 30 Guernseys, all of them giving large quantities of milk. Another 25% is earned from the sale of eggs from a flock of 5,000 white leghorns….
>
> It was father's idea to plant the Christmas trees, which I recently brought to the market. Faye and I became sidewalk salesmen last Christmas in New York. We wanted to bring trees to the public at a reasonable price, and to force the retailers to sell the trees at a fair profit.[1970]

Here Elliott was referring to an unorthodox scheme that caused a few snickers in New York City during the 1947 season. The president's son was hawking Christmas trees on the sidewalk, assisted by a suitable minked-up movie star, namely Faye. He said he was trying to "make Christians out of Christmas Tree dealers." So he sold trees to the public for an even dollar (initially). He figured within a few years he'd be selling 100,000 a year.[1971]

Since Elliott and Eleanor operated together under the aegis of Roosevelt Enterprises, Inc., this too was a family affair. But while the son dreamed of profits, the mother urged charity. She was not "looking to reap any vast profit. We would charge one dollar apiece and put them on sale in the poorest neighborhoods of New York City." But amid local vendor hostility, Elliott had trouble finding good tree-selling spots in Harlem and the Lower East Side. He admitted that, "we hadn't made a nickel on our venture."[1972]

Next year he tried to outdo himself with a new spruce crop from Val-Kill. Again he undercut and infuriated the other dealers. This time Elliott announced plans to create a vast Christmas tree empire, using economies of scale to buy from a regional combine of growers, and still sell the trees cheaper than everyone else. Competitors claimed Elliott's trees were low-quality spruce, quick to drop their needles, and smelled "skunky."[1973]

He defended himself: "We plant 2,500 trees to the acre – two-year old seedlings we buy from the state and commercial nurseries. They have a seven-year growing period…" FDR had been a reforestation enthusiast, both at home and as public policy, and critics said he had obtained his reforestation seedlings free from the government.[1974]

The endeavor received some attention for a while; but FDR's "skunk spruce" soon ran out, and they turned no profit. Hit up again, family benefactors loaned Elliott money to keep the farm going, but he sold off parts of the Hyde Park estate, and mortgaged the rest. And soon, he had other interests to attend to.[i]

It is not clear if Faye's tree-selling on the cold New York sidewalk had anything to do with it, but on Boxing Day 1948, she slit her wrists.

"She accidentally cut herself on some extra razor blades when she reached into a drawer for an aspirin," said her mother, Jean Young of San Diego. "That's exactly what happened," seconded Faye. "That's right, that's what happened," Elliott added.[1975]

The sheriff's deputy initially reported there had been a family altercation and the wound was self-inflicted. Faye had "melancholy" and the doctor said she had to be restrained to prevent further injury.[1976] Elliott conferred with the district attorney for almost an hour. The D.A. then announced that no law was violated and the investigation was ended. [1977]

Perhaps this is a case in which celebrities are entitled to lie in order to defend their privacy. However, the FBI internally archived a different version:

> During the course of the party, there was apparently considerable drinking and FAYE and ELLIOTT ROOSEVELT had a disagreement. FAYE went to the lavatory during the early morning of Dec. 26 and was discovered by FRANKLIN ROOSEVELT JR. with her left wrist and forefinger lacerated. ELLIOTT and FRANKLIN drove her to [doctor] around 4:30 AM Dec. 26, and he applied 7 sutures to the laceration and referred her to the VASSAR BROTHERS HOSPITAL Poughkeepsie, NY. …The ROOSEVELTS informed [the doctor] that FAYE had slashed her wrist with a razor and he also stated that she was in a highly emotional state.
>
> At the VASSAR BROTHERS HOSPITAL it was learned that ELLIOTT and FAYE apparently caused quite a commotion and insisted that the incident receive no publicity. According to hospital employees, both ELLIOTT and FAYE appeared to be under the influence of liquor and were apparently angry with each other. On Dec. 26 around noon FAYE was discharged from the hospital.[1978]

The FBI went on to report that according to New York law, this matter had to go to the sheriff and district attorney for investigation. In other words, the family was able to suppress the investigation.

Faye's relationship with farmer Roosevelt had turned hostile and volatile. James venomously said that Elliott did not like the fact that Faye was making more money than he was, and was the center of attention wherever they went.[1979] To her bitter

---

[i] One benefactor was Walter Kirschner, to whom we shall return. (Anna – Eleanor correspondence).

disappointment, Faye had found Elliott incapable of matching her own ambitions, and those she held for him. Both of them began messing around. Elliott sicced a detective on her and caught her in bed with someone else; he, in turn, hung out with a succession of floozies in New York City. He admitted later that he had been "a poor excuse for a husband."[1980]

The Roosevelt children fought over money; they fought over politics; they fought out of jealousy; and they fought just for the hell of it. A favorite fraternal tactic was to use the media to stab each other in the back. Franklin Jr. leaked dirt on Elliott to the Alsop brothers, influential columnists, during the *As He Saw It* controversy. The enraged Elliott "put that down to Franklin's caginess in making friends in the right places in anticipation of launching himself into politics wearing Father's mantle." [1981]

As often with people of that ilk, the siblings did not simply split apart and mind their own business; they were constantly getting back together on some financial or political scheme. According to many, violence between the strapping brothers did not always remain on the verbal level. It is not recorded that Elliott beat any of his wives; but he did hit his children.

From childhood Elliott was a scrappy, often violent child. The public fistfights he got into as an adult reaffirmed this trait. Joseph Lash recalled one family dinner at which the grown sons ended up in fisticuffs. More ominously, wife nr. 5, Patricia, recounted that Elliott beat her children for bed-wetting – though without anger. She was evidently much impressed. He did say he was far stricter with his children than his father had been with him.[1982]

The habit of beating up people who annoyed him stuck with Elliott. During the war, he got into a major brawl on the street in New York, but escaped charges. In a radio studio in February 1947, during a fierce argument over his Moscow trip, he cursed a fellow radio commentator (the one who had set off the air mail fiasco fifteen years earlier, Fulton Lewis Jr., now considered a right-winger) and Elliott's companion socked Lewis's jaw. An ambiguous remark to his wife, who was present, apparently sent Elliott over the edge. Unperturbed, the Roosevelts "later went night-clubbing." [1983]

Faye wasn't the only Roosevelt who contemplated suicide. Eleanor, who bore the world's sins on her shoulders, was crushed by her childrens' antics. Once, said Joe Lash:

> John and Elliott had nearly come to blows, the former quite drunk and Elliott at his most outrageous. Their scrapping with each other at her dinner table ended with both turning their accusations against her. She talked with David [grandson] afterward about doing away with herself.[1984]

The brothers also believed Eleanor was close to suicide when she was accused of having an affair with her bodyguard Earl Miller (she probably didn't, but her effusive style misled the nosy types). When James went through a catastrophic divorce in 1954, Eleanor sent Elliott off to California to keep Jimmy from killing himself. Later, Elliott would play that incident up when he felt the need to drive the knife in.[1985]

Probably exaggerating his role, Elliott said that Eleanor "used to send me around to comfort, to aid, to assist, and to carry messages and so forth with all the rest of the members of the family." But Eleanor used all of them as best she could, and Elliott was the one most often in trouble.[1986]

The five siblings racked up two suicides among their nineteen spouses, in addition to Faye's attempt. John Boettiger killed himself in 1950, Ethel du Pont, Franklin Jr.'s rich first wife, in 1965. Jimmy's unstable wife Romelle tried to kill herself in April 1948.[i] His next wife in turn tried to kill him, stabbing him eight times.[1987] Some of the surviving ex-spouses recovered to lead happy lives, but not all.

Later, Elliott admitted that his "disturbed personal life" was breaking up his marriage in 1949 - again.[1988]

At the Stork Club, Elliott, despite his carousing, was a prized guest. This would last until 1950, when the liabilities therefrom finally exceeded the benefits of his celebrity. A misunderstanding about an aborted marriage (to singer Gigi Durston) was the straw that broke the Stork's patience. The Club had prematurely announced Elliott's next marriage. For some reason, Elliott didn't want the Stork to bring this babe.

Ex-bootlegger Sherman Billingsley was the owner of the Stork. He had built up the legendary business by luring celebrities and columnists with expensive gifts and free meals. But everyone has his limit:

> 'They are not welcome,' said Billingsley flatly... he barred the couple after he had "words" with them over an engagement announcement party he had arranged in the club's new private dining room. 'When I sent out announcements of the party to the press, they denied that any such party ever had been arranged,' Billingsley said. 'So naturally I called the whole thing off and told them not to come back.'[1989]

Elliott had been "one of the best customers for 15 years, and Gigi sang here for a whole year," and the Stork had planned to pick up the tab for the entire party.

Georgeanne (Gigi) Durston was introduced to Elliott by a "press agent" by the name of Ray Russell Davioni, who later was indicted for pimping: "The D.A. is hanging on his every word, since his every word has to do with the meandering of models around and about the metropolis, in company of gentlemen with high dollars if not high moral standards."[1990]

By late December 1949, Gigi claimed to be Elliott's fiancée, which led to an amusing quote attributed to his wife Faye Emerson. Gigi's mother informed her that Elliott was going to marry Gigi. Faye snapped: "I prefer to announce my divorces myself."

> Faye Emerson shot back that she would take her own divorce at her own convenience. Faye, much annoyed, said it might be two months or two years before she got a divorce.[1991]

Elliott's Gigi trip didn't last long, though: "The engagement ended in the El Morocco, with Gigi sweeping out of the bistro ahead of her mother, a constant companion, and Roosevelt. In the lobby getting their coats, Mrs. Durston is alleged to have informed the former President's son that 'furthermore, you can have your ring back.'"[1992]

The ring was a "star sapphire, reportedly worth several thousand dollars." The spare was a "blue onyx with the Roosevelt crest."[1993] And, "The romance ended with a note from Elliott chiding both Gigi and her mother for joining themselves to him too often in the newspapers."[1994]

---

[i] UP, 16 APR 48, in Pittsburgh Press. "Accidental overdose of sleeping pills" reported police; subsequent family references leave no doubt what happened.

It seems Elliott was annoyed that the two were attempting to profit from the Roosevelt name.

For a few weeks thereafter, a dark-haired Louisiana beauty named Betty Boyd was engaged to Elliott. The two were stalked by the press, to everyone's amusement except theirs. She was a 23-year old model, "quite shapely" – "used to be a blonde." Newspapers said Elliott had telephoned her from Copenhagen, making plans; and they "will wed" July 19. When Elliott and Eleanor came back from Europe on 3 July, Betty Boyd rushed into Elliott's arms before the two waltzed into a car driven by brother Franklin Jr.[1995]

Minnewa Bell (nr. 4) reminisced that she had found a letter from Betty complaining that she had heard he was getting back with Faye (nr. 3); at first, she thought it must have been from Betty Donner (nr. 1), but then realized there was yet another Betty.[1996]

By 14 January 1950 Faye found a more dignified way out of the marriage, obtaining a quickie divorce in Cuernavaca, Mexico. She then had a brief career in television, where she was especially known for her quick wit and provocative dresses. After a short third marriage, she left, apparently shell-shocked, for an unnaturally quiet retirement on the island of Mallorca, Spain, where in 1983 she died, in the artist village of Deya.[1997] James Roosevelt lets us know that Faye and John Roosevelt's equally divorced first wife lived there together in a sort of asylum for recovering Roosevelt spouses.[1998]

Always needing money, Elliott proceeded to sell off bits and pieces of the remaining estate. Minnewa Bell remembered:

> Anyway, the boys were always trying to sell Roosevelt furniture to get money, and they would have auctions, and the Hammer gallery would come and take care of it. Elliott was always trying to get pieces of furniture to sell as Rooseveltiana. It was pathetic. I felt sorry; I really felt very, very sorry. If FDR – and Mrs. Roosevelt – did not seem to see this. She didn't think the Val-Kill or Roosevelt things were all that important, and she wanted the boys to make money.[1999]

This pawning of the patrimony got to be embarrassing, especially when Elliott auctioned off President Roosevelt's private correspondence. In June 1951 there was quite a flap when the Rosenbach Company, a book dealer, announced that several hundred of FDR's letters had been received for sale. "I haven't turned over any letter for sale to anybody," protested Eleanor. Her son Elliott said, "For [Dr. Rosenbach] to say they are for sale is despicable!" It turned out that Elliott had turned over the loot for "cataloguing and evaluation for insurance purposes, but not for sale."[2000]

Elliott had wanted "in the six figures" for the collection, which included books with his father's notes and inscriptions. The idea was that "friends" of FDR would purchase the letters and donate them to the Hyde Park Memorial Library – although it would have been simpler for the family to bequeathe the collection, which was right where it was supposed to be, in Hyde Park.

Next year, Elliott did sell the immensely valuable collection to the Rosenbach Company. The papers included a copy of FDR's first published book, *Whither Bound*, inscribed by him: 'For my son Elliott, this copy of his Dad's first book.'[i]

---

[i] "The prices quoted are about 8 - 10 times what these items would be worth without the magic Roosevelt imprimatur," noted a bibliophile about the book collection. (Neylan to Pegler, 16 JUN 52, ER, Pegler/HH.)

Apparently this evisceration process didn't cause family strain until Elliott sold Top Cottage, his father's retreat above Hyde Park. The Campobello Island estate was sold to the Hammers in 1952. Much of the loot has since been repurchased and restored by the Park Service. Even Campobello Island, which is technically in Canada, has become an "international peace park."

The Hyde Park furniture fared no better. It is disputed how angry Eleanor was:

> One day Eleanor read in the papers that Elliott had sold Top Cottage. It was the final betrayal: getting rid of the place that FDR had designed as a retreat for himself when his days in the White House were over…she terminated Roosevelt Enterprises. She decided to phase out the television and radio programs.[2001]

In his own account, Elliott persuasively (as always) rejected this version. He said his mother was well aware of the sale in advance and took no offense at it; she was not attached to material things. He sold "because of certain internal problems not involving mother or myself." Furthermore, Elliott said his brothers had been spreading the noxious rumor. At any rate, if the Eleanor – Elliott connection was strained from this time, it was not strained enough to keep Elliott from hitting his mother up for money repeatedly.[2002]

Eleanor must have slowly and painfully realized the truth. Yet she was deeply resistant to it. Henry Morgenthau III remembered:

> My father had been concerned when Elliott was doing things with the property in Hyde Park, selling it off….and Mrs. Roosevelt really got quite annoyed at my father and just said, "Well, Elliott is here with me, and he lives here in Hyde Park. This means a lot to me. I'm alone, and if he wants to sell off everything, I'm not going to stop him if he does. He can do it. I'll just move somewhere else if I have to."[2003]

The young Morgenthau caught on to something that most of Eleanor's numberless admirers failed to see: her innate goodness attracted and enabled evil. The principle carried over from her family into her politics. She did not comprehend that endless generosity can cause what it purports to heal. Her *magnum opus*, the UN Declaration of Human Rights, is the prime exhibit: She listed all the wonderful, expensive services she thought people had a "right" to have others give them. Although she saw through communism, in her own way her goodness was as dangerous as the raw greed of others. And on a personal level, "perhaps in a way, because of her own strength, she had a need for people who were weak. I don't know. In a sense she tried to help people beyond their capacity to accept help," mused Morgenthau.[2004]

While Eleanor let herself be conned, James and the other siblings certainly raged against Elliott for his loss of the patrimony. James wrote that Eleanor provided most of the funds in the partnership with Elliott to purchase the remainder of the estate:

> In what I've called "The Rape of Hyde Park," Elliott sold his part to a Howard Johnson's and other commercial ventures that have turned it into a 42nd Street. The hilltop cottage father had built as his retreat was part of the property Elliott sold." … [later],

---

NYT, 12 OCT 51. The book *Whither Bound* was actually a pamphlet of an FDR speech dressed up as a book.

> "Mother willed her land to Elliott, who needing money, sold it, and for this I can't quite forgive him."[2005]

Both Elliott and James, who had dabbled in film directing, conceived the idea of making movies about their father. The productions were, of course, panegyrics. With other investors, James produced "*Freedom from Fear*," and Elliott, along with the theater entrepreneur Harry Brandt, cobbled together "*The Roosevelt Story*." It was an eighty-minute compilation of newsreels. Reportedly it "avoided controversial material and ends with a plan for international accord." [2006]

The film most associated with the family was, however "*Sunrise at Campobello*," which came out much later, in 1960 (following a much promoted play of the same name). It was another tearjerker about Franklin's struggle with paralysis, and its revenue provided a solid and unmissed opportunity for renewed squabbles between the siblings. James noted tartly that it was also factually inaccurate. For example, the Campobello retreat faced the sunset! Even more acidly, he said Franklin Jr. did a "dreadful job" negotiating the siblings' financial interest in the film.[2007]

These various media productions reflected not merely an attempt to cash in, but also the emergence of a personality cult centered on the late president. There were obviously many with an interest in perpetuating this view, while those who loathed FDR began, like old soldiers, to slowly fade away.

General Roosevelt now fancied getting into the hotel and restaurant business. He had ambitious plans drawn up for commercial development of sections of the Hyde Park area, including a 350-residence housing development complete with banks, sports arenas, gas stations and the sort. Most of these plans came to naught.[2008]

In 1947, Elliott did open the Val-Kill Inn, a 22-room hotel, with a 100-seat restaurant, catering to visitors to the already popular FDR Presidential Library. It was intended to take some of the products of the Roosevelt farm. The modest inn was a remodeled farmhouse, but Elliott soon began planning a much bigger hotel resort.[2009]

The resort project, like the planned super-farm, eventually petered out, but not before alienating a lot of people – family members as well as local creditors.

Many of Elliott's innumerable business ideas ended in a tangled knot of lawsuits. This one was no different. Already in September 1949, a local company and two individual contractors filed claims totaling $17,105 for unpaid work for the Val-Kill Company, Inc., and the Springwood Village, Inc. Elliott said that work would continue. But the subdivision plans eventually foundered, much to the delight of those who wanted to keep the estate as serene as possible.

Even the hotel-restaurant turned out to be a flop; and an ill-maintained one. By 1950, a delighted Walter Trohan was able to write his colleague Westbrook Pegler that there was trouble at the shrine:

> ...it seems visitors were using the rooms for purposes other than communing with the great spirit. They were and are indulging in sex without benefit of clergy. Seems that Elliott is only in favor of nookie when he gets it. Rank prejudism. I don't care who gets it.[2010]

Trohan noted this bit of titillation in passing while sending Pegler data he'd sniffed out on Lucy Mercer, FDR's most enduring love interest. It supplemented snippets about other FDR amours that Pegler had accumulated over the years.

The press corps was far better informed than it let on to the nation at the time.

THE F-11 FLIES HOME TO ROOST

All federal bureaucrats worth their salt know the drill when they are called to testify "up on the Hill." First, they have to watch with awe and canine submission as the politicians mounted above them huff and puff and deliver their pre-practiced sound bites for the cameras. Then they have to meekly, apologetically answer "questions" that are often staff-prepared verbal rapes flung at them by the senator or the representative trying to get his two seconds on radio or TV. Yessir, nossir, no excuse sir.

When Howard Hughes and Elliott Roosevelt showed up for their ritual disembowelment in 1947, something completely unexpected happened. The two famous rogues turned the table on their accusers, humiliated their persecutors, and made of the Senate War Investigating Committee (SWIC) a three-ring circus that spellbound the nation for weeks. Sex, lies, and hot cash (or "babes, booze, and brass") were the main ingredients.

In November 1946, Republicans took control of Congress in a sharp backlash against twelve years of increasingly totalitarian New Deal government. The new majority was steaming mad and bent on revenge. A standard way of showing who was boss was to haul in the less favorite members of the previous team for congressional investigation. We have seen how the Democrats did this in 1934, when, during the Air Mail Fiasco, they completely restructured American civil aviation on the trumped-up charges of "fraud and collusion" in the previous administration.

Many Republicans wanted to go all the way and indict the entire Roosevelt era. Pinning Pearl Harbor on the late president was and remains the holy grail of Roosevelt-bashing. Ever since 1941 numerous attempts have been made at that, but none convincing enough for most scholars.

Even if legally or morally justified, it is dangerous for a system to turn on its own history. The Soviet Union famously did so in 1956, and it crippled the USSR's legitimacy – such as it was – ever after. In the end, the American elites decided it was better to have Franklin D. Roosevelt canonized while his successors went about quietly dismantling the worst excesses of his regime.

Upon such reflection, the Congressional majority chose to go after the lowest-hanging fruit first. And that was bad news for General Elliott Roosevelt.

War profiteering was a hot issue after 1945. It seemed that everyone had a story of how industry, bureaucrats, military officers, and everyone else who could get their grubby little hands in the till had made out like bandits while the "little people" were dying, toiling, and saving to buy war bonds. That was partly true, as it always is; but there was plenty of blame to go around, as there usually is. Politics determines who gets singled out.

As the *enfant terrible* of the previous administration Elliott Roosevelt seemed a juicy target. So did one Howard R. Hughes, who had made big money and waded in licentious luxury while somehow not managing to build a single useable aircraft for the War Department. The two seemed a good place to start.

It didn't hurt that the new chairman of SWIC was Pan Am's "kept senator," Ralph Owen Brewster, who had a score to settle with Howard Hughes and his TWA. And for headlines, it helped that Mr. Hughes had barely survived a horrific crash into a Beverly Hills neighborhood – in that same airplane that was at the center of the scandal.

Hughes had two major contracts with the Pentagon. Both were disasters. He had (as a "hobby," snickered the Air Force), persisted in trying to build a fast warplane, first as a fighter, then a bomber, then a reconnaissance aircraft. The D-2 never flew well and its constant modification was a drag on the company and an embarrassment before the Air Force. It was destroyed in a suspicious fire in November 1944, but Hughes continued with a derivative, the F-11, for which he had so mysteriously gained an order for 101 back in October 1943.

USAAF Materiel Division at Wright Field prepared a secret case history of the F-11 in August 1946, shortly after the prototype's destruction. There was certain to be even more trouble, so better to be prepared with answers. From that highly detailed account we can track the airplane's sorry trajectory all the way to its final and literal impact. Along with the Senate testimony, it is the main source for this section.[2011]

The Hughes D-2 and its hangar burned on 11 November 1944 at its remote desert location. Some said it must have been hit by lightning in a freak electrical storm. Another employee thought a generator shorted out.[2012]

Whatever the cause, the sudden demise of the D-2 was extremely convenient for Mr. Hughes because Hughes Aircraft had spent much of 1944 engaged in a bitter dispute with the AAF over how much he should get paid for the D-2 development. Hughes said the D-2 and its projected versions had been the foundation for the F-11, so he should be reimbursed the $3.7 million he had spent on it. But Wright Field wanted nothing to do with the D-2.

The plain-spoken Brig. Gen. F.O. Carroll, chief of the Experimental Engineering Section, who had consistently recommended against doing business with Hughes, reached out in March 1944 with a searing memo:

> The Hughes Aircraft Company's contention that the D-2 is the prototype of the F-11 is ridiculous. We might just as well say the B-17 is the prototype of the B-29...The contention that the flying characteristics will be identical or even similar is too farfetched for further comment.[2013]

A compromise was to be decided by the end of 1944, but it required a five-man commission to visit Harper Dry Lake to evaluate the aircraft. Hughes, secretive as ever, did not want to facilitate this, although in September, the commission eventually did see the plane. At any rate, six days after the fire, the committee metaphorically chopped the D-2's ghost in half, in a Solomonic decision that yielded Hughes $1.9 million.[2014]

It is clear from the details that Hughes was being unreasonable on many accounts in this dispute – the D-2 was unquestionably a dead end. He had glibly asserted that he would cover all development costs if the aircraft turned out to be a failure; yet no sooner did he have a contract than he fought the Air Force for every last dollar. Apparently, he approached the war in general and the D-2 in specific as exercises in ego gratification.

At any rate, thereafter Hughes refused to have anything to do with this painful memory. Shortly after the fire, flying over Harper Dry Lake en route to Las Vegas, he reportedly stared stiffly and silently ahead.[2015]

The three years of the F-11's development were slow, painful, and constantly disputatious. Because of the unusual circumstances attending the original contract, Materiel Division was determined to offer Mr. Hughes no alibi for non-performance. Thus the AAF agreed to many ill-advised shortcuts, such as lowering the load factor (airframe G-limit), forgoing deicing equipment, and acquiescing to Hughes's disastrous choice of subcontractors.

In their own explicit terms, even though the Chief of the Air Forces and his operational staff continued to urge the Hughes contract forward on the highest priority, the procurement officers decided they were going to let Hughes "hang himself." This terminology would be of much later interest.

On 4 February 1944, Brig. Gen. Chidlaw advised Maj. Gen. Echols, his boss, that:

> ...the trouble we are encountering in getting this project under way should be brought to the attention of Gen. Giles [AAF Chief of Staff] to make certain that he knows we are doing our level best to get the project under way, but are faced with the inevitable delays we always encounter when attempting to deal with Mr. Hughes on any project.[2016]

Two weeks later, Lt. Col. Dichman from Wright Field visited the disorganized mess that was Hughes Aircraft Company in Culver City. He complained that:

> ...the main difficulty was the fact that Mr. Hughes, personally, wanted to make numerous detailed technical decisions. As Mr. Hughes had many other interests, he could not devote his full attention to this project which resulted in the development proceeding slowly. Mr. Hughes was asked to discuss his production plans but it developed that no definite production plans had been made. Mr. Dichman informed Mr. Hughes that if the project continued to lag he would recommend a cancellation.[2017]

On 10 August 1944, the AAF tried to plot the course ahead during a major conference attended by the stakeholders, including the Corps of Engineers. The discussion, which analyzed the F-11 in great detail, also revealed deep divisions:

> Col. Phillips [from Gen. Echols' office] stated that the AAF was most anxious to get this plane and no delay from changing the design would be tolerated and "that Mr. Hughes should be left more or less to 'hang himself' on the matter of the airplane and that the AAF should not get itself in such a position as to be the subject of criticism from anyone for having interfered with the project." Some of the points brought out in the conference were: (1) The fact that the F-11 would be superior to any other photo-reconnaissance airplane in existence; (2) OC&R representatives were most enthusiastic about the F-11 and believed they would rather fly it in combat than the F-12 because it was smaller, had higher strength factors and more visibility to the rear; (3) Col. Peterson, Eng. Div. (WF) thought that the XF-12 would fly before the XF-11 because of Republic's reputation as opposed to Hughes'. (This opinion was concurred in by Col. Phillips.)[2018]

The problems continued, but they were not all directly Hughes Aircraft's fault. The main subcontractor, Kaiser-Fleetwings, responsible for wings and empennage, underperformed badly. This was in part because of atrocious relations with HAC and a widely held belief that the F-11 would be cancelled anyway. More disappointingly, it was also because Fleetwings was simultaneously finishing the XBTK naval dive bomber of its own design. The BTK was similar to the AD-1 Skyraider and represented Henry Kaiser's reach for the sky after he had angrily split with Hughes over the giant HK-1 flying boat. Although the XBTK beat the F-11 into the air, it was itself cancelled after only five were built. It, too, had been a total waste.

The propeller plant, Hamilton Standard, could not get the F-11's extremely complex eight-bladed propeller assembly to work in time. Hamilton said it was because they couldn't get the engines from Pratt & Whitney. Then the blades that were received turned out to be defective and had to be replaced. Intermittent propeller malfunctions were experienced even before the first flight. Thus there was plenty to be worried about when Howard Hughes finally took the airplane up, two years behind schedule.

So whose fault was the debacle really? Legally, it was Hughes Aircraft Company's. HAC could not manage its chosen subcontractors any better than it could manage its own work. On the other hand, Hughes rightly complained that he couldn't get priority. Yet the final mismanagement would come directly at the hands of Howard Hughes.

As late as March 1945, AAF headquarters urgently pressed for the delivery of the F-11. A dubious officer recorded on the 31st of that month that "there has been such pressure brought to bear from very high places that the AAF in particular and the War Dept. in general, had no alternative … I don't believe that the War Dept. could cancel the contract if it wanted to." [2019]

Yet in March-April, the whole house of cards collapsed. In the meantime, victory in Europe was assured, air bases close to Japan were obtained, and President Truman took over in the White House. He had won his spurs as a ferocious battler against waste and abuse in war contracts. Many of FDR's friends found themselves suddenly without the influence to which they had become accustomed.

A devastating April report on the F-11 cited the following factors:

1. Photographic planes of comparative size and range costing about $223,000, or half the unit price of F-11, were in production.
2. It was doubtful whether the F-11 would be produced in time to be of material value in the war effort.
3. The amount of $70,247,667 for the F-11s was excessive in comparison to contracts for other similar planes.
4. Only $43,800,000 of the above contract was renegotiable; $18,000,000 was subcontracted to Fleetwings, who were requesting approval of an additional $6,000,000.
5. Lump sum basis contract, $13,000,000, provided for three XF-11s and was considered excessive.
6. Delays in production didn't justify an increase in contract fund advances.
7. The plant had been lax in cost control and accuracy because of scrambled facilities, labor usage, and other contract operations.
8. The F-11 contract could have been placed with a company which already had necessary facilities and labor.
9. Facilities at Culver City were not adequate for successful and economical production of 98 F-11s and parts.
10. Facilities for producing F-11 wings were available near Hughes plant, so placing the subcontract with Kaiser at a spot 3,000 miles away was unjustified; further, other commitments at Kaiser plant contributed to production delay at Hughes.[2020]

So, after a flurry of contract reviews, on 29 May 1945, Howard Hughes's ambition to build the fastest warplane in the world was formally reduced to three XF-11s, one of them for static tests only. The bleeding had stopped at about $22 million.[2021]

In new aircraft development, such disasters are hardly unknown. There have been costlier projects that did not even produce an airplane at the end. Usually, these debacles do not catch the public interest, even when they keep the courts busy for decades. This one was different. It involved famous men and infamous women. It was irresistible.

First, though, there was a near-death experience to captivate the nation.

The Accident

Who should first smell the blood in the water but columnist Westbrook Pegler? He kept detailed files of rumors involving the Roosevelts. On 1 March 1946, at Pegler's prodding, General Arnold was forced to begin defending the F-11 contract. He noted:

> Many many thousands of contracts were let for all conceivable types of equipment – experimental and production. Some proved to be failures; most were successful…My motives were guided purely and singly by desire to win the war in the shortest possible space of time.[2022]

But this failure was not yet complete. During April, hamstrung by constant propeller problems, Howard Hughes was at first limited to doing short hops on the Culver City runway. In the meantime, Pegler ripped into the War Department, which found it pointless to terminate the contract immediately; the money had already been spent. They might as well get both prototypes delivered.

On 7 July 1946, at 5:20 in the afternoon, Hughes finally took off in what was now officially the Army's airplane, XF-11 tail nr. 44-70155. He was supposed to carry out a detailed, line-by-line, 45-minute test program. Instead, he flew around doing his own thing, without making the agreed radio contact, and stayed up well over an hour.

Suddenly, the right aft propeller went into full reverse. It was a well-known problem previously experienced on the ground – a design flaw, in truth – but Hughes did not recognize it and seems to have thought it was related to the undercarriage. After a brief, desperate battle, at 6:35, he crashed into a Beverly Hills residential area. Sixty years later, the accident was dramatically but not completely accurately portrayed in the movie *The Aviator*, and the technical and contractual issues were of course hardly touched upon in that otherwise well-researched film.

Incredibly, Howard Hughes survived once again; but many think that his drug addiction arose from his difficult and painful recovery.

The USAAF was now further humiliated. In response to a headquarters inquiry, on 16 August Wright Field offered the following summary to General Carl Spaatz, the new commander of the Air Forces:

1. Contract called for Phase 1 of XF-11 flight testing to be conducted by the contractor. Because of his record, Hughes' request to personally make the first test had been granted; however, the initial test flight was supposed to have been limited to one hour.
2. The engine used in the XF-11 had passed military test, and there was no indication from the examined wreckage that the engine had failed.
3. Previous difficulties had occurred with the Hamilton Standard dual rotation reversible propellers on test stands and other airplanes, and the propellers had not passed a type test. Damaged XF-11 propellers were at Wright Field undergoing investigation.
4. Mr. Hughes started on a 45-minute flight, but remained in the air almost twice that time. He concentrated mainly on landing gear operation instead of following approved flight program. Cameras in the plane recorded flight information for 35 minutes. During last few minutes a drag developed on plane's right side, and Hughes did not have time to find the cause before the plane crashed.
5. It appeared that loss of hydraulic fluid caused failure of pitch change mechanism of right rear propeller. Mr. Hughes maintained full power of right engine and reduced that of left engine instead of trying to fly with right propeller windmilling without power.
6. It was Wright Field's understanding that the crash was attributed to pilot error.[2023]

Perhaps the Army Air Forces now regretted that it had not killed the two prototypes along with the production contract.

The Air Force's conclusions about the crash were much more damning than they might seem to a layman. Hughes had mishandled the testing, but he had also violated every multi-engine emergency procedure. Instead of pulling the power on the right engine, feathering the prop, cleaning up the plane, and immediately limping home, he had done the very opposite; even cycling the gear. But Hughes rightly pointed out that due to the peculiar design, he could not know that the problem was in the powertrain.

There was still one XF-11 left; this one, nr. 156, had conventional four-bladed propellers. Wright Field explicitly stated that "Hughes had been asked to name a pilot, *other than Howard Hughes*, to test the second plane. HAC was directed to conduct the first ten hours of flight testing at the Muroc Dry Lake testing facility."[2024]

There could not have been a more dramatic scene-setting for the Senate inquisition that would follow as soon as the Republicans took over Congress in the fall. The F-11 program had cost the taxpayers some $22 million, with nothing to show for it – except one crashed prototype and another completed aircraft, soon to be discarded.

The other big Hughes contract, the flying boat, was an even bigger waste. Over the following decades it gained greater fame, probably because this aircraft became an aeronautical zombie, kept flyable in Long Beach as long as Hughes was alive, but flown only once.

The industrialist Henry Kaiser had originally talked Hughes into a program to build the world's biggest flying boat, the HK-1 Hercules. Back then, there was real fear of losing the battle of the Atlantic to Germany, preventing sea transportation. However, the Hercules was "political" from the start, as both the Army and the Navy refused to order it. Even Colonel Roosevelt was sharply against the Hercules, purely because it took resources away from his F-11.

The problem with Henry Kaiser was that he had strong political connections, and a flair for publicity – much like Howard Hughes. But Kaiser had at least demonstrated the capability to turn out ships like cookies out of the oven. He thought a giant flying boat couldn't be that much harder.

Secretary of the Interior, J.A. Krug, had been head of the War Production Board.[2025] He testified that Kaiser "put the heat of Hell on everybody in Washington" to build the cargo plane. "Initially they told him that he couldn't have an airplane contract because he had no aircraft man. He lined up Hughes and came back and said that now he had an aircraft man. Then he got the contract." [2026]

Krug's Senate testimony was one of the more temperate dismissals of the Hercules seaplane. He was mainly interested in challenging the expense reports that listed his enjoyment of Hughes's party girls. However, FBI documents showed that Krug had been offered a job with Hughes, probably running TWA, after the war.[2027]

Henry Kaiser responded that, "I have never had in my entire history such a smear campaign attempted." Like Hughes, Kaiser thought that a "clever, mysterious kiss-off" had been given to the plane, and that "certain army generals were going to run me out of town." [2028]

The War Department had enough sense to cancel the HK-1 in 1943. This sent Howard Hughes into a panicked state, and through various ruses he managed to get the contract reinstated, although the military clearly had no more need of the airplane – particularly after 1946, when landplanes were supplanting seaplanes everywhere. Kaiser fell out with Hughes, and the latter continued the project as the H-4 Hercules, although now he had no clue how he was going to mass-produce the immense aircraft. Incidentally, the plane was the world's largest only in wing span; its mass was comparable to that of the first jetliners.

By the time the Senate hearings got under way in 1947, the giant flying boat was still unfinished and many doubted that it would, should, or even could fly. But its creator's ego would not rest until it did.

Pandemonium in the U.S. Senate

Thus, by early 1947, the Senate had a perfectly reasonable target for its investigations. It was well-rumored that Hughes had secured his contracts through unhealthy means. In particular, it was widely known that General Elliott Roosevelt had been the sinister force behind the scenes that had forced the Army Air Forces to order the F-11. Some went further. The FBI reported from Los Angeles that Elliott took $75,000 for the deal. But that, too, was only a rumor passed on. So there was plenty for the politicians to rip into.[i]

The resulting circus was by far the biggest news story of 1947.

Elliott hardly ever missed an opportunity to express his opinions to the media. Usually, his opinion was that the media treated him unfairly. The Hughes Aircraft hearings were no exception. On the day he began his Senate testimony on 4 August 1947, he gave the following statement to the more amenable Scripps-Howard newspaper chain:

> *This is Elliott Roosevelt's story told in an exclusive interview in his hotel room last night [4 AUG 47]. He talked for two hours, occasionally lighting a cigaret or sprawling his long legs out on the rug. He hadn't eaten anything since noon and his face showed fatigue, but you could tell it was something he'd wanted to get off his chest. And so, in the interest of giving every man the right to say his piece, here is Elliott's story:*
>
> I'd like to start off at the beginning – 1940. Let's get this record straight.
>
> I didn't specify whether I wanted to be an officer or a private. I didn't ask to be a captain. I just volunteered. When "I-want-to-be-a-Captain-Too" clubs sprang up all over the country, I submitted my resignation to the Army Air Forces, because I felt this talk against me was injurious to my father and to the AAF recruiting program. I told them I would volunteer as a private. That request was turned down. Immediately, I volunteered to go overseas. That request was accepted.
>
> Then there were stories that every one of the Roosevelt boys had plushie jobs. It was Senator Ferguson or Senator Brewster – I can't remember which – who said that all the Roosevelt boys had plushie jobs far from combat, with quick promotions.
>
> Then in 1944 I came back from Europe and brought this dog "Blaze" back in my aircraft with me. There was a full-fledged Senate investigation about that – and not a newspaper in the country published the results.

This was untrue. But Elliott wouldn't let go of the matter:

---

[i] This bribe was reported by the FBI Los Angeles field office in March 1947 and revealed during the Senate hearings, but the charge could not be substantiated and is regarded as false. It is not in Elliott's own FBI file. See Brown/Broeske: Howard Hughes. 228.

In the first place, I brought the dog back in a war-weary aircraft which was regarded as unsafe for service personnel and carried only its crew. At Presque Isle, Me., the dog was declared and put in a pound maintained there exactly for that purpose. I asked how I could get the dog to Washington, and they said, "Don't worry, we'll send the dog down with someone going in that direction."

That's what happened. Pilots were checking out every day on routine flights for flying time, carrying no passengers or war freight. So the dog got to the White House. I asked Bolling Field operations if they could take the dog to California, and they said they would put it on some operational aircraft that was going through.

Then a couple of weeks after I'd gone back to Europe, my sister called the airport, but she talked to an Air Transport Command officer instead of somebody at operations. It was completely the fault of this young officer, who thought he was being smart. He sent a car to the White House to pick up the dog and put him on a passenger plane to the West Coast.

When some Navy boy got bumped en route to California because of the dog, the uproar reached me way overseas. My outfit had three full-fledged inspections as a result. Peacetime inspections. They gave us such a thorough going over we didn't have time for our vital combat missions. We were doing K.P. all over the place.

The promotion affair came right after the "Blaze" thing. I will ask Senator Brewster to amplify his inference that Gen. Marshall turned it down twice because my record wasn't good enough to warrant a promotion.

Gen. Marshall told me about it himself. He said he did not want to submit it to my father because he felt it would embarrass him to send it to the Senate. I had requested Gen. Eisenhower, Gen. Spaatz, and Gen. Doolittle a number of times to please never put my name thru for promotion to general officer because it might embarrass my father, and I could do my work just as well as a colonel.

In spite of that, they did, and they explained that I rated it and they saw no reason why I should be penalized for being my father's son.

Exactly two months after my father's death I began to catch a terrific beating for financial transactions that took place before the war. The Treasury Department investigated me in the Fall of '45 for many months and gave me a completely clean bill of health. As a result of this investigation of my pre-war dealings, the Army Air Force did not choose to send me to the Pacific in spite of the fact that both Gen. Spaatz and Gen. Doolittle had requested it.

I requested relief from duty and got it on 15 August 1945.

Now here's a story that's never been told before. When I received that notice, I applied to the Royal Canadian Air Force for duty as a combat pilot. The only stipulation I made was that I be allowed to go immediately to a combat area with any rank they saw fit to give me.

I received notice that the RCAF did desire my services but they wanted to check first with the USAAF to make sure they had no further use for my services. Much to my surprise, I received a notice from the RCAF that they were sorry, but they had received word direct from the USAAF in Washington, admitting that it was true they were relieving me from active duty, but they hoped the RCAF would not commission me because it would be very embarrassing to them.

Of Elliott's histrionic outbursts, the quixotic threat to join the RCAF stood out. That slip actually revealed that he was turned down for further service in the Pacific, and thus that his military career had ended involuntarily. He had served bravely, but after his father's death the Air Force didn't want him anymore.

> In June 1946, I was asked to submit a request to the War Department as to whether I desired to retain a commission as brigadier general in the Reserves. I submitted my request to General Doolittle, head of the Air Forces Board which passed on all applications for Reserve commissions for general officers. He stated to me last Fall that his board had approved my application in routine fashion along with all others and it had been forwarded to the War Department for submission to the President and then to the Senate for confirmation.
>
> Announcement was made of all those approved. My name was not included. It was either knocked out by Secretary of War Patterson or by the Chief of Staff or by President Truman.
>
> This is a perfect example of the political stigma that has been placed on me because of the desire of certain political and business influences to smear me and what I stand for and beyond that, to smear the name of Roosevelt and ultimately the memory of Franklin Delano Roosevelt.[2029]

These were very serious charges, and next day the Senate subcommittee would tear into Elliott for it, charging him with stating that Truman, Eisenhower, and Secretary of War Patterson had terminated his Reserve career out of political cowardice. Senator Brewster said it was the first time he had heard their courage questioned in any way.[2030] To the newspaper, Elliott continued:

> No opportunity in this type of action is given for me to defend myself. I am quietly brushed out of the way. You'll never get the whole story of reconnaissance aviation. There are too many big shots covering up their record back here, and too many favored manufacturers whose production breakdowns have to be covered up.
>
> The major objection to Hughes and his wooden airplane was not that he manufactured wooden planes but that he wasn't one of the favored manufacturers. There are a lot of people trying to cover up the shortcomings of those manufacturers who were favored and shortcomings in the air force procurement division. Certain officers were not in favor of accepting any recommendations from the theaters in the way of changes because the changes might interfere with the prestige of the favored manufacturers or cost them more money.
>
> Aside from my initial contact with John Meyer and Hughes Aircraft – Meyer appeared to be more an errand boy or Grover Whalen[i] for Hughes – I never discussed Hughes business with Meyer because he was never sufficiently grounded in the business to be able to talk about aircraft.
>
> But Meyer moved in the same social circles as my wife-to-be and he moved in the same group of friends. He had known her since 1941 when she was under contract to Warner Bros. And he was in the publicity department. The fact that Mr. Meyer regarded me as a business acquaintance comes to me as a complete surprise. I find items charged to my entertainment which, as the record can exactly prove from his own testimony, does not necessarily represent entertainment of me at all. He charged his company with entertainment of me in New York City for some very fancy sums when, in fact, on those very dates I was in England, Luxembourg and Belgium on action combat missions.
>
> As far as I'm concerned, Mr. Meyer has revealed the fact that I am a business contact and not a social acquaintance as I regarded him. It rather amuses me that after I got completely out of the Army, Mr. Meyer and I were on several social gatherings where I picked up some of the checks and he picked up others. I wonder if he still lists me as a business contact. Maybe now all bills go to Hughes productions and I'm probably a potential actor.

---

[i] Grover Whalen was a foppish politician renowned for stuffy protocols and receptions.

> *Mr. Roosevelt said he would prove to the committee that Meyer only came to the White House once at his invitation – not twice as Meyer had claimed. "I asked him to come to my father's funeral," he said. "He paid for transportation of my wife and two sisters-in-law from the airport to the White House, and then charged it to business expenses. It's pretty low to say that was a business expense. It's downright ghoulish."* [Meyer testified on 2 August 1947 that he was twice invited to the White House after making friends with Elliott.] [2031]
>
> I am grateful to Senators Ferguson and Brewster for giving me the opportunity for a public hearing but at the same time I am under no illusions as to why they gave me that public hearing. I know this is a purely political inquiry and that they selected this very small contract from all the billions of dollars in contracts because they thought they could tie the name of Roosevelt into it and further partisan political aims and their own personal political ambitions.
>
> This is the follow-up of the Pearl Harbor campaign – which was a beautiful smear job – with no facts to back it up. They are trying to cover up for all of the isolationist votes which prevented this country from being prepared for the Jap attack on Pearl Harbor. The Republicans looking to '48 will try to divert attention from their war shortcomings.
>
> I would like to express my appreciation for the first opportunity that has ever been presented to me to state my side of these allegations and smear campaigns that have been circulated about me by public officials and the American press. This is the first newspaper that has been willing to listen to my story and print my side of the case.[2032]

That interview probably gave as clear a picture of Elliott's public persona as any. He was always totally innocent. Everyone was out to get him – and his family. He could explain everything if only he were allowed to speak. There was no fairness in the world for Elliott Roosevelt, or for Howard Hughes, or for Mr. Meyer and all their agents. It was all a vast right-wing conspiracy, or at least a plot by the favored manufacturers and their twisted officers trying to cover up their own dastardly malfeasance during the war.

As usual, there was just enough truth in some of his indignant protests – such as in the Blaze affair – that the Roosevelt wing of the Democratic Party could feel sympathetic. And the rumors and accusations against him were often so vicious that sensible people felt the need to back off.

A publicly broadcast Congressional hearing is a show trial. Its primary purpose is political theater, but that doesn't mean the truth won't come out. In this case, it mostly did, but all the attention was on the theater. There was extra meat for the masses: bribes, breasts, brass, and brew. The country was mesmerized.

The Senate War Investigating Committee (SWIC), technically the Special Committee to Investigate the National Defense Program, was an outgrowth of wartime efforts to make rampant war profiteering somewhat less rampant. Harry S. Truman originally chaired the outfit, and his success in going after unfair munitions contracts was a major factor in his replacing Henry Wallace on the 1944 ticket.[i]

As early as July 1942 Howard Hughes had been under suspicion, although nothing came of it then. SWIC was by no means dormant, though. Under Democratic leadership it spent the war years hunting down and exposing waste, fraud and abuse throughout the war industry.

Now a new team was in charge. SWIC was chaired by Senator R. Owen Brewster, a hard right Republican from Maine. He was already in a running and very public feud with Howard Hughes and Elliott Roosevelt. Considering his obvious conflict of interest,

---

[i] Truman wanted to go after the rumored Manhattan program, but Gen. Marshall asked him to back off.

he delegated the hearings to a subcommittee chaired by Senator Homer Ferguson (R-MI). However, that didn't extract Brewster from the battlefield – quite the contrary.

The hearings were held in the cavernous Senate Caucus Room, with well over a thousand people in attendance, and with all the clanking media paraphernalia of the time: newsreel cameras, forests of bulky microphones, Klieg lights, flash-bulb cameras. And this being 1947, almost everyone smoked. A reporter described it evocatively:

> In the high and ornate Senate Office Building caucus room sat and stood some 1,500 perspiring spectators. Outside stood lines of other hundreds. Over all played first two and then one blinding klieg light. The room rang with metallic bursts of voices from the amplifiers.[2033]

With this circus atmosphere it is not surprising that Elliott Roosevelt was able to evoke forbidden crowd applause, as well as spontaneous laughter, such as when he expressed his deep resentment at Mr. Meyer's insinuation that he drank $115 worth of liquor in one night.[2034]

Throughout early 1947, investigators had rummaged around in Hughes Aircraft Company's affairs. Howard knew he was being targeted, and so did Elliott. Indeed, Hughes had testified at a secret session in February and had at that time offered investigators access to HAC's archives. When they arrived there, they found, to the contrary, that HAC was not cooperating with the probe.

Conspiratorially, Hughes responded by engaging in private meetings off the record with Senator Brewster. The two were trying to reach an accommodation. Who was enticing whom, or attempting to entrap the other, would become a crucial issue later, but it is clear that some kind of crude trade was in the air during the spring. By summer, the rapprochement had failed, the investigation had developed its own inertia, and both sides girded for all-out battle.

Barely recovered from the crash that by all rules of probability should have killed him, Howard Hughes knew how to hold the public's attention. On 5 April 1947, he took up the second XF-11 for a one-hour flight from Culver City. The uneventful flight was covered massively by the media. Colonel Clarence Shoop, who had accompanied Elliott Roosevelt during the initial 1943 evaluation, was now a Hughes Aircraft test pilot who flew chase on Hughes in a Douglas A-20. Hughes's flight tests continued until November 1947, when the aircraft was handed over to the Air Force at Muroc Dry Lake, soon to be Edwards AFB.

In other words, during the SWIC "show-trial," Hughes was conducting an active flight test program with the remaining airplane of the type in dispute.[2035] Just before the hearings reconvened in November, he also tested the gigantic Hercules for the movie cameras, proving that it could fly, at least in ground effect. The media hoopla tended to obscure the investigators' assertion that both aircraft were a waste of money.

SWIC opened public hearings on 25 July 1947. It began by calling Johnny Meyer, already known as an extremely colorful rogue. He was an entertainer of business prospects, procurer of shapely girls, and general social handyman who had been responsible for the entertainment of military officers and other bureaucrats on behalf of HAC. It was noted with particular resentment that he had obtained six deferments from military service.[2036]

Another witness was retired Major General Oliver P. Echols, the man who had rejected Roosevelt's resignation in 1940, and who had fought furiously against his F-11 and his Constellation recommendations in 1943 and 1944.

As we saw, the Army Air Forces initially rejected the F-11, as it had the D-2, due to poor performance, wooden construction, suspect manufacturing capacity, and, it can safely be added, general contempt for HAC, which was considered a scattered rich man's hobby rather than a serious defense contractor. But General Arnold found himself inside a "Roosevelt sandwich" as both Elliott and FDR maintained the plane should be purchased, so he "against my better judgment" condescended to order 101 of the aircraft – two XF-11 prototypes, one static test article, and 98 production aircraft.[2037]

Arnold was now in poor health and was not called for the first series of hearings. But he had regrets. In San Francisco, near his retirement home, he issued a sort of apologia to the press:

> Hindsight is all very well, but at that time they wanted planes and wanted them fast…We were in a war. We needed the best equipment we could get in a hurry. We needed a fast photo reconnaissance plane like the British Mosquito. We tried to build the Mosquito here and we couldn't. We tried to build them in Canada and couldn't. We tried to get them from Europe and couldn't. The only plane we could get like it was Howard Hughes' XF-11 and that's why we bought it.[2038]

Arnold was clearly vexed at the matter, but interestingly, especially at the British. After the hearings, he wrote about his "mistake:"

> I thought it would be simple. We were giving the British, under lend-lease, and in other ways, thousands of airplanes, and it should have been an easy matter for them to turn a few hundred Mosquitoes over to us, thereby enabling us to get a high-altitude photo plane without going to all the trouble and expense of designing and building one of our own. – At first, we were told the British were going to build Mosquitoes in Canada; that we could get them from Canada. Later, we found out that plan was not going through. Then we were told we could have the drawings and build them ourselves. After our experience with the British Merlin engine (trying to change their metric drawings into our standard measurements) that was out of the question. When we tried to buy some Mosquitoes from the British, we were told they didn't have enough for their own use and therefore couldn't spare any. Consequently, I looked around in the United States to find an airplane with comparable characteristics. The only one which seemed to fit the bill was Howard Hughes' famous F-11. Our experts looked over this plane and its drawings to determine whether it would actually meet all our requirements, and reported it would. However, when the matter was turned over to our Materiel Command people, they all recommended against procurement of the F-11, their main reason being, I think, the fact that they did not believe we would get the planes in time to fight the war. I rather doubted it myself, but I also knew if we did not *try* to get some, we most certainly wouldn't get any. At that point it was the Hughes plane or nothing. So, much against my better judgment and against the advice of my staff I gave instructions to buy the famous F-11 airplane.[2039]

Arnold's anguished decision also coincided with the desires of the White House. But "you can never bring up the outside pressure in your defense afterwards," as Robert Lovett said to one of his officers.[2040]

Now the country finally learned that there had been a major battle behind the scenes to force the F-11 order through. At the time, the Air Force procurement hierarchy had predicted that the decision would later become the subject of congressional investigation. "Later" had arrived.

SWIC wasn't much interested in the merits of the F-11 anymore. The politicians wanted to expose the corrupted procedure by which the order had been secured by the Hughes Aircraft Company. The chairman, Judge Homer Ferguson (R-MI), exhibited a memorandum from Jerald W. McCoy to Colonel Leslie Peterson which aptly described Air Force thinking:

> The initial contract for the F-11 was promulgated prior to my assignment here. However, it is my understanding that there was such pressure brought to bear from very high places that the army air forces, in particular, [and] the war department, in general, had no alternative except to establish a special military characteristic, and upon the basis of that characteristic, accept a contract for the F-11.

As we have seen, Elliott Roosevelt badgered his father about the F-11 and complained to him about General Arnold's slowness in seeing its greatness. FDR had first prodded Arnold about the Hughes plane in 1942; in September 1943, the two Roosevelts together called Arnold to the White House and discussed the matter.

Testimony revealed that Harry Hopkins had intervened "several" times by calling General Meyers on the matter. But more significantly, Commerce Secretary Jesse Jones had also taken up the causes of both Hughes contracts. In the Senate, Howard Hughes described Houstonian Jesse Jones as one of his only two friends in Washington. The other, he maintained forlornly, was General Bennett Meyers – a man who would try to shake him down.[2041]

However, the initial hearings in early August first focused on Elliott Roosevelt's visit to the Hughes Aircraft Company (HAC) and his subsequent excesses on that company's ticket. The fun started when Johnny Meyer disclosed the details about the parties that had turned Colonel Roosevelt's head.

Meyer's Elliott account ran to $5,083. That was only a fraction of HAC's total entertainment budget of $169,000. Inconveniently, Hughes Aircraft had claimed these expenses on company tax returns, so the paper trail was clear. Elliott's entertainment was spread over three years: $2080 in 1943, $2304 in 1944, and $698 in 1945. This is significant because Colonel Roosevelt and his friends kept up the pressure for the F-11 and the Constellation until the spring of 1945. Elliott's recommendation dated from August 1943.

Oddly, the August 8-28 and September 17-18 entertainment for 1943 was less than half of the total amount. When Elliott came back from Europe in 1944, matters again heated up, culminating in his wedding at the Grand Canyon, for which Meyer paid some of the bills, and Hughes provided the aircraft – as well as the bride. As late as June 1945 there was further expensive socializing.

The Elliott account turned out to be a virtual travel guide to expensive night clubs in New York, Los Angeles, and Palm Springs. As a kind of inadvertent Yellow Pages of nightlife, the records showed how the rich and the profligate conducted business. Included were The Stork, El Morocco, Mocambo, Club 18, Club 21, Chasen's, Tail o' the Cock, Trioka Café, Copacabana, Monte Carlo, La Maze, Carlton, Statler, Ambassador Hotel (in LA), Waldorf Astoria (NY), the Mayflower (DC). There was Romanoff's in Beverly Hills; in Palm Springs, the Racquet Club, the Tennis Club, the Oasis.

But what really got people's attention were the girls. In 1943, numerous entries for girls, or "gifts for girls" were dutifully made. Later, Faye Emerson was the "gifted" entertainer, at least on Elliott's account.

The party continued with a thousand dollars of vouchers in New York City. There was a dinner for six at Club 21, with later stops at the Stork and el Morocco, costing $106.50. This raised eyebrows when it was noticed that the date, 20 August 1943, was the day Colonel Roosevelt finished his report on the Hughes reconnaissance aircraft – and they rose further because of an extra bill of $115 for "liquor for apartment."[2042]

However, Johnny Meyer denied that he had flown to New York specifically to entertain Roosevelt. He furthermore ruled it a "coincidence" that Faye Emerson was on the plane with him.

Then there was $200 in presents for girls. Why? "Because it was in the line of entertaining Elliott Roosevelt." And there was the $576.83 bill for putting Elliott up at the Beverly Hills Hotel. "I thought it would be a wedding present," said Meyer.[2043]

A leading newspaper, the *Pittsburgh Press*, gloated:

> On the night of Aug. 22, Mr. Meyer put out $163 for a dinner party at the Monte Carlo Club and $78 for dinner at Leon & Eddie's. Another item was $75 for "presents for two girls." More dinner parties followed on Aug. 23, 26, and 27th in New York and Washington. On the night of the 27th Mr. Meyer's vouchers listed $76 for dinner at the Statler Hotel in Washington and $50 for "girls at hotel (late)."
>
> Senator Ferguson pressed Mr. Meyer as to whether Elliott shared his Ritz-Tower apartment of "five bedrooms." Mr. Meyer was evasive. First he answered that "I don't know. He might have slept there a night." Pressed on the point, he answered "I would say so."
>
> Mr. Meyer defended his liquor expenditure as "not much." – "I might have been planning an extended stay…liquor was quite expensive," he said. Mr. Meyer agreed with Senator Pepper that "Col. Roosevelt didn't drink it all."
>
> …"Why were you charging $132 of nylon hose to aircraft production?" "Because she (Miss Emerson) had been very charming."
>
> "Well, then," Senator Ferguson asked of another item, "why did you give her $20 to go home if she was so very charming?"
>
> Spectators and committee members burst into laughter. Meyer bellowed, "that's very good – I'll concede that." Later he explained that he took Miss Emerson to the airport and she discovered that she had no money. "I finally consented to give her $20."
>
> Asked about a $50 payment on Aug. 23 to Chuck Farmer, press agent for the El Morocco Club, Mr. Meyer said: "I paid to have Mr. Farmer ask the photographer not to take a picture of Mr. Roosevelt. He didn't want it to appear."[2044]

And so it went all day; this is merely a sample. People were spellbound as they heard of the expensive fun, even down to the free air and railroad tickets that had been handed out. During the war, such travel required high priority. The Hughes team evidently had no trouble obtaining it.

Fat, bald, middle-aged Johnny Meyer's special talent was to procure such beauties as would take a hundred dollars to lounge in their swimsuits around the pool and coo at the military folks. It turned out that not only Col. Roosevelt, but many other high-ranking officers and bureaucrats were much valued guests of Mr. Hughes. There is no doubt that the Senate hearings triggered numerous uxorial inquisitions at home.

Meyer was asked what the girls were supposed to do for their $100. He said: "I don't know. Possibly just going to dinner and dancing." He said, "Officers did not like to go out and eat alone, especially if they had been overseas about a year." [2045]

The more gossipy papers, such as *Life*, were sprinkled with photos of nearly-naked Hughes girls. One, Marilyn Buferd, was the 1946 Miss America. Another, Martha Goldthwaite, complained her fiancée dropped her when he read what she was doing. Yet a third stunner, Judy Cook, became known as the "Wham Girl" because she riveted airplanes at night at Lockheed, but by day she made "wham," for which she appeared well qualified. She was subpoenaed because Meyer had billed $50 for her entertainment of the war procurement chief Julius Krug, but compared to the others she must have been shorted that evening. Hearing of the amounts, one government partaker asserted the girls hadn't been paid enough for what they did. [2046]

Other interesting names on the expense accounts included Colonel Eidson, who served on Elliott's reconnaissance aircraft survey while courting his commander's wife. Lt. Col. Johnny Hoover, Elliott's young protégé who had come back with him from England, was also well taken care of.[2047]

The colorful Col. James G. Hall had his own ledger with $3,732 of "entertainment" charged. Hall flew dangerous reconnaissance missions over Europe and became well known both at the front and in the Pentagon – but he was a "senior citizen" officer and should have known better. By the end of the war, he was in charge of procurement and was obviously targeted by Mr. Hughes and his handyman Meyer for this purpose.[2048]

Colonel Hall's expenses began in November 1943 and continued through October 1946, the approximate period of Hughes's F-11 contract. However, Hall called the amounts "fantastic and grossly exaggerated," and maintained that in no way did they affect his decisions. He said:

> I am no saint, and I have no apologies to make for accepting Mr. Hughes's hospitality. Nor can I deny the fact that I usually enjoyed myself. However, it is terribly humiliating and a shock to my ego to have Mr. Meyer testify that he gave young ladies presents to entertain me.[2049]

Jesse Jones was the highest ranking recipient of Hughes's largesse, although to a lesser degree than most. From 17 June to 16 July 1942, precisely the time when Hughes's press agent Russell Birdwell was trying every trick to get the President to favor the D-2, Birdwell charged Hughes Aircraft no less than $2,040 in cash expenses for his lobbying efforts, including everything from cigars to flowers. Most of it, over $1,300 was for "entertainment." However, Hughes contended that the record was fraudulently padded, and that Jesse Jones received no favors or gifts.[2050]

In Jones's case, it certainly wasn't necessary. He was a friend and ally. Jones believed Hughes was a genius, and he was a close personal friend of Hughes's right-hand man, Noah Dietrich.[2051] Henry Kaiser said that Jones told him, "You are safe in proceeding with Howard Hughes. I have known him since he was a boy – and I knew his able father before him – and I know of no more capable and reliable man than Howard Hughes."[2052]

Jones recommended Hughes's plane to President Roosevelt, sending him a gushing summary of the D-2's promised performance. Soon, on 7 July 1942, FDR forwarded Jones's information to General Arnold with the annotation: "What is there in this?"

Arnold responded to the president in two messages with a synopsis of the "plastic" plane's progress to date. He said the AAF was working on the issue and would order it if everything checked out as promised, and a "price agreeable" could be reached. His second memo, on the 17th, said that he had conferenced with Hughes and agreed to absorb the development costs if the plane was acceptable; otherwise Hughes would take the loss. He'd been told the plane would be ready for delivery in two months; in fact it would be a year before it even flew, and unacceptably so. But the point was that FDR had prodded Arnold to promise Hughes his favorable consideration.[2053]

At this early stage, there was nothing suspect *per se* in Arnold's response, nor in the president's question. *In toto*, however, Arnold was feeling the political heat.

Every defense contractor knows that wining and dining the customer is part of the game. Similarly, every defense official knows that this must be kept within the limits of rules, regulations, and decorum. Nowadays, usually the limits are set at the level of gift-trinkets and decent meals (but not alcohol). When both sides are mindful of the rules, they are able to conduct business in an amicable manner, knowing that the competition is acting in the same way.

The Hughes case was not like that. According to the Senate testimony, it was much, much worse. Yet Elliott Roosevelt managed to convey the impression, though assiduously refuted by the committee, that this was exactly the way all contractors did business during the war.

From the beginning, the subcommittee attempted to incriminate Elliott Roosevelt, since he seemed to be the most tainted player. Noah Dietrich, Hughes's able vice president and the secret behind his success, was the source of this widely suspected aspect of the case. As the *New York Times* reported:

> Mr. Hughes himself first brought forward the charge that Mr. Flanagan [chief investigator Francis D. Flanagan] had declared that the objective was to "get" Elliott Roosevelt. Saying that Mr. Dietrich stood ready to corroborate him, the industrialist asserted that Mr. Flanagan had made the remark last March when he arrived at the Hughes plant in California to begin his preliminary investigation in behalf of the committee.
>
> "Dietrich told me," Mr. Hughes went on, "that he said to Flanagan: 'You know that this investigation is inspired by political motives.' Flanagan replied: "We're out to get Elliott Roosevelt." Dietrich said, 'the trouble is you're shooting with a scattergun.' Flanagan replied, 'We want to shoot Roosevelt with a cannon.'
>
> Mr. Dietrich, a white-haired man much older than his rather deaf employer, Mr. Hughes, then took the stand. He told the subcommittee that he "liked" Mr. Flanagan and was "very sorry to put him in this position." He added with a smile that he himself, as a lifelong Republican, "was inclined to be sympathetic" with a thrust limited to Elliott Roosevelt.
>
> Directed to give his version of the conversation with Mr. Flanagan, Mr. Dietrich said: "I said to him that I didn't quite understand why these particular contracts were investigated; that I believed there was a political motive. I told him 'you are going to be disappointed and it will blow up in your face.'"
>
> "I thought that one of the motives was to discredit the Democratic Administration and the Roosevelt family and Elliott Roosevelt in particular. I said to Mr. Flanagan: 'I think you are shooting at Elliott Roosevelt with a shotgun and Mr. Hughes might get hurt in the process.' He told me, 'We are not using a shotgun; we are shooting at him with a cannon.' He may have said a rifle, or some other one-bullet weapon. What he was trying to convey was that it wasn't a scattergun they were using."

> Mr. Flanagan, whose face had reddened at this, then took the stand. He testified that he "made no mention of shooting, with a cannon or rifle or anything else," and added: "It was Mr. Dietrich who said we were after Roosevelt. I said we were not. I said that as far as I knew then the preliminary inquiry had indicated that $40 million of Government money went to the Hughes Tool Company, the parent of all Mr. Hughes's enterprises, and that no article had been produced during the war so far as we knew."[2054]

The Senate transcript shows a rather comical exchange of accusations and theories about whether a shotgun, a rifle, a cannon, or some "single-shot" device was intended for Mr. Roosevelt, and who had brought up this explosive language to begin with. It was symptomatic of a hearing that continuously tended to go off the deep end.[2055]

Shotgun or cannon, probably no one was in doubt that Elliott Roosevelt was the prime target, and thus the hearings were at least in part a political ploy. But it was also true that at the time of the investigation it was widely believed that Elliott had been not merely paid off with booze and babes, but also with a big pile of cold cash.

Thus, despite Howard Hughes's talent for portraying himself as a persecuted genius, the Senate had ample reason for nosing around in his affairs. The public, however, admired Hughes. A closer, dispassionate look at him and his business leaves little room for admiration. It is true that he became the richest man in the world, but genius (his, at least) had nothing to do with it.

Elliott Testifies

On 4 August 1947 Elliott Roosevelt finally appeared before the Senate subcommittee. The whole nation listened in, alerted that salacious details would be on the menu. Elliott cut a suave appearance with his thin new mustache, slicked back hair, and bow tie. In a bravura performance, he emulated his father's habit of tilting his head back, sucking on a cigarette and blowing smoke at his interlocutors, delivering soothing, smirking explanations.

> Mr. ROOSEVELT. It is perfectly true, if the facts are known, that wherever I go, whatever I do, whenever I appear in public, it is always in the newspapers; it is not in a news story, it is in a news column. I unfortunately have the type of personality that sometimes attracts a great deal of stories about me.[2056]

And, as was his "type of personality," he did not play defense with the Senators. He lashed out hard. He said that the proceedings were a plot by Messrs. Ferguson and Brewster to smear his father's name, one that had actually begun with the Pearl Harbor commission. In this vile errand, the Republicans were aided by "the Hearst and Patterson and McCormick press." [2057]

By labeling the hearings a political persecution he skirted culpability for his own deeds. He maintained that he had never spoken to his father about the F-11 (which, thanks to Ms. Suckley's diary, we know is not true). He said the girls were not procured for his sake, exactly. And at any rate, other defense contractors had done similar things. Why weren't the politicians going after them?

Chairman Ferguson sternly read Elliott Roosevelt the order on contractor relations, issued by General Arnold on 27 March 1942:

> The attention of all officers is directed to the grave responsibility which attaches to the AAF in the exercise of the stewardship, imposed by the existing emergency, over the expenditure of vast sums of public funds – a stewardship for which the AAF must be prepared at all times to render full account to the American people.
>
> In the proper discharge of this responsibility, a strict rule of personal conduct is enjoined upon each officer in his relations with individuals and firms having business dealings with the Government, to insure that relationships of a compromising character may be scrupulously avoided.
>
> Each officer will accordingly be governed by a full realization that acceptance by him of the most casual entertainment or insignificant gift, however innocently tendered, from one seeking consideration from the army air forces may tend to compromise both the AAF and himself as to seriously impair public confidence.[2058] [emphasis added]

That was clear and unambiguous language. Elliott smilingly asserted that he had followed this order and had done nothing wrong. Hard pressed, the closest thing he came to a *mea culpa* was the following statement:

> MR. ROOSEVELT. I, sir, will still maintain that whereas you may place a technical charge that I violated the directive of General Arnold, that in actual fact I probably violated that in several instances, because there were a number of presents given to my wife and myself from people who I am sure must have had something to do with Government contracts, but had been friends of either my wife or myself over a great many years.
>
> Senator PEPPER. But were not in payment of any contracting services?
>
> Mr. ROOSEVELT. I do not believe that any court of law in the land could ever state that because you accept a wedding gift, that that is any sort of evidence that you are using your influence in regard to a contract.[2059]

If all of the extravagance lavished upon him could not possibly be construed to have influenced his recommendations of Hughes-built aircraft, then what possibly could? For this Mr. Roosevelt had no answer.

He maintained his innocence when it was revealed that he had accepted a $1,000 personal loan from Mr. Meyer, and when he admitted that he had stayed at Mr. Meyer's hotel apartment during 20-23 August 1943, when he was writing his report on the F-11 evaluation to General Arnold.

He was not perturbed by the fact that Mr. Meyer and Mr. Jack Frye of TWA had paid for his fly-in wedding at the Grand Canyon, including providing the aircraft and the pilot. Then it was noted that Mr. Meyer's expense account was only a part of the "Elliott ledger," because Meyer had a credit line at some of the establishments in question, billable directly to Hughes Aircraft. Elliott retorted that, actually, the officers paid some costs themselves, and asserted that the dishonest Mr. Meyer had grossly inflated some of the expenses he had charged to the company. For example, he could prove that he was in Europe at the time of one of the "Roosevelt Party" entries.

The hearings bogged down in line-by-line, dollar-for-dollar scrutiny of Mr. Meyer's expense account; but that wasn't boring. A curious nation obtained an eye-opening education in the consumption habits of the rich, famous, and wanton. The fascination was heightened by the fresh memory of the lean and rationed years most Americans had just suffered through.

While Elliott contended that the high living was simply an expression of friendship, most of the committee was obviously not so impressed. Only Senator

Pepper of Florida consistently and laboriously defended the excesses, jumping in to help Elliott out whenever he hit a particularly rough spot.

Indeed, "Red Pepper" took further action. To promote Elliott's war record and justify his F-11 approval, he got ahold of one of his companions from the North African war, Maj. Gen. George C. McDonald. McDonald had written a summary of Elliott's operational situation as commander of NAPRW, and he made sure to alert his boss, General Spaatz. He noted:

> We could not during those hectic days of 1943 visualize that the European War would end as abruptly as it did, followed some months later by the capitulation of Japan. We had to go largely on the basis that it would be a long-term war both with Germany and Japan. Hence it was necessary to project our thoughts and try to interpret our requirements in the field of photographic requirements as well as other angles of the over-all Air Forces as far ahead as possible.[2060]

That was a sensible expression of the field's perspective. But the politicians were more interested in the hanky-panky at home.

However outrageous the extravagances tabulated, the General managed to land some blows of his own. He demonstrated fairly convincingly that Johnny Meyer had padded his accounts, and that he had attributed to Elliott Roosevelt a number of social functions with only a circumstantial Elliott connection. Evidently, Meyer had found that the hallowed name was a Sesame that opened up the company's treasury.

Mr. Meyer held that the Roosevelt label covered a number of people associated with the reconnaissance evaluation program, and need not necessarily apply to him personally. However, he said, the charges for a trip for Roosevelt and other officers to visit Mrs. Eleanor Roosevelt in Hyde Park for socializing were obviously a legitimate business entertainment expense, thus subject to tax deduction. So was paying for Ms. Faye Emerson's bets at the Agua Caliente race track.

Had Elliott Roosevelt really accepted a $75,000 bribe to recommend the F-11 aircraft? These reports, apparently originating from the War Department, were investigated by the FBI and could not be substantiated. However, Howard Hughes referred to the bribe obliquely when he stated that Mr. Flanagan, the Senate's investigator, had charged: "Look, we know there has been a $100,000 pay-off there to Elliott Roosevelt. What about it?" [2061] Likewise, senators of the SWIC kept circling back to the bribe issue, but without ever obtaining proof.[2062] The suspicion does, however, seem to justify the decision of the committee to inject the Roosevelt affair into the general war profiteering issue by the beginning of 1947.

Mr. Hughes was well-known to pay bribes to get his way, and Mr. Roosevelt was long famous for his shady financial transactions. But no evidence was ever brought forth, and it stands to reason that the Senate committee would have done so if possible.

Charles Higham, the venomous author of *Howard Hughes: The secret life*, states that it was no less than FBI director J. Edgar Hoover who tipped off the columnist Westbrook Pegler to the bribe. Others maintain that the War Department, worried about Hughes's out-of-control influence buying, had asked the FBI to investigate.[2063]

Higham treats the allegation as true without offering proof. He also maintains that Hughes attempted to pay off Senator Brewster with TWA stock, which may be a variant permutation of the informal Pan Am – TWA merger talks. Finally, he states that:

In early 1945, J. Edgar Hoover opened a major file on Hughes. Hughes and Meyer had hosted a party for visiting Russians; he was hoping, via Elliott Roosevelt, to make an across-the-board deal with Russia for his flying boat without the authorization of Henry Kaiser or General Hap Arnold.

Howard Hughes generated a monumental FBI file, two thousand pages in length. It was available to Senate researchers, and later to Hughes's numerous biographers. The FBI wired up Hughes's quarters and developed a thick and none too complimentary dossier on him. "Mr. Hughes has become a paranoid, vengeful, and emotionally disturbed man, whose mind has deteriorated to the point that he is capable of both suicide and murder," the FBI stated.[2064]

But when it came to wiretapping, the FBI was merely one at the party. The Brewster people bugged the Hughes Aircraft party's hotel rooms; when they found out, Hughes hired detectives who bugged the Brewster and Pan Am agents bugging him.[2065] But it may be that Hughes was the first to resort to such flagrantly illegal methods in general.

At the visible part of the vendetta, the hearings, the public wanted to hear about the girls. *Time* wrote:

> On the distaff side, the names read like theater marquees or the roll call at Hollywood's Central Casting. Actresses Lana Turner, Linda Darnell and Ava Gardner were said to be on the committee's list. A leggy, blonde ex-riveter named Judy Cook declared that she had been paid $100 to put on her swimming act in the Hughes pool for visiting dignitaries. Actress Myrna Dell and Lovelies Marilyn Buferd (Miss America '46) and Wendy Russell denied having been paid for their company. So did all the other girls.[2066]

The girls provided an opportunity for Elliott and Mr. Meyer to get into a sparring match that entertained the audience but left the chairman scrambling for order:

> Senator FERGUSON. What about the girls; the general wants to know about the girls.
>
> Mr. ROOSEVELT. Let us clear up my moral record.
>
> Sen. FERGUSON. Yes.
>
> Mr. MEYER. These could have been two girls that I had dinner with. If there were names down here, it might help clear up –
>
> Mr. ROOSEVELT. I asked the question, Can you state that this charge which you made against me of paying $50 to girls that were there late – that I was there? You told me before you were on the stand that you knew for a fact that I was not present, because I was staying at the White House, and I was not present.
>
> Sen. FERGUSON. Did you have a conversation with Mr. Meyer?
>
> Mr. ROOSEVELT. I challenged this, sir, when I ran into him in the hotel night before last.
>
> Sen. FERGUSON. What did he tell you?
>
> Mr. ROOSEVELT. Told me that was ridiculous.
>
> Mr. MEYER. He is not giving the question. He said, did I ever get a girl for him directly. I said there were always girls present, and you know there were always girls present.
>
> Mr. ROOSEVELT. Was I present?
>
> Mr. MEYER. We did not sit in the Jungle Room of the Statler Hotel alone.

Mr. ROOSEVELT. Was I present? Because the records of the White House on that night are available and it will show that I was not late at the Statler Hotel. I was at the White House.

Mr. MEYER. Maybe Eidson was with me at the Statler.

Mr. ROOSEVELT. Why should I be charged?

Mr. MEYER. Because that is my policy of putting the most important person's name down, which I have continually repeated.

Mr. ROOSEVELT. Most important person was not there.

Sen. FERGUSON. Senator Brewster, did you want to ask some questions?

The CHAIRMAN. If we may divert the course for a few moments.

Mr. MEYER. Are you talking to me or to the colonel?

The CHAIRMAN. General Roosevelt has properly termed it the "comedy relief" to the more serious aspects of this affair. I want to first express the committee's appreciation to Mr. Meyer for his testimony that he thinks this committee is unfamiliar with the procedures in New York night clubs which I think is probably correct.

Sen. PEPPER. Is that a virtue?

The CHAIRMAN. I do not know.

Sen. FERGUSON. The Senator from Florida won't admit that.

Sen. PEPPER. I doubt if the Senator from Maine has been altogether an abstainer.[2067]

On another occasion, when a wild party in New York had left its traces in some expensive "gifts to girls," the Abbott & Costello routine erupted again:

Mr. ROOSEVELT. Could I ask Mr. Meyer specifically, were any of these girls that he got paid and paid money to or that he gave presents to, was it for the purpose of getting in with me, and did any of those girls who were paid, were they procured for my entertainment?

… Mr. MEYER. I don't like the word "procured," because a girl who attends a party and is given a present is not necessarily "procured."

Mr. ROOSEVELT. Use any word you want, but were they for me?

Mr. MEYER. Is that correct? You can certainly give a girl a present and not make something bad out of it.

Senator PEPPER. Leaving that out, is there any intention on your part, the question is, to represent because you used the name of Colonel Roosevelt that the girls were designed for association with him?

Mr. MEYER. No; but I will say this, the colonel well knows that the girls were present.

Senator FERGUSON. Were they there to entertain all of the people?

Mr. MEYER. We were all together. I would say that the colonel was almost constantly in the company of Miss Emerson.

Mr. ROOSEVELT. Were any of these girls there specifically to entertain me? … You mean that their scintillating conversation was designed to influence me?

Mr. MEYER. That is hard to say, because you were quite busy with Miss Emerson.

Mr. ROOSEVELT. That is perfectly all right, but I might say, Mr. Meyer, that I resent very, very definitely, any effort on your part to implicate in any derogatory sense Miss Emerson's connection with me.

Mr. MEYER. Oh, that happens to be the last thing on my mind.

Senator FERGUSON. Did you answer the question?

Mr. MEYER. I said the girls were present with us.

… Mr. ROOSEVELT. But you have not specifically answered the question which I place, which was: "Did you get those girls specifically for me?"

Mr. MEYER. You cannot answer the question.

Mr. ROOSEVELT. Because you have said that I was with Miss Emerson, and how could you have been getting all of these additional girls, and what was I doing, lining them up, or something?

Mr. MEYER. There seems to be Squadron Leader Stevenson, Lt. Col. Polifka, and Eidson with us.

Mr. ROOSEVELT. And you are stating that those girls were there to entertain them?

Mr. MEYER. They sat around with us and had drinks with us and went to dinner with us, and the girls were probably not with anyone, they just danced with anybody who asked them to.

... Senator FERGUSON. Why did you have these other four officers up there, were they there because they came with the colonel?

Mr. MEYER. They were friends of the colonel.

... Mr. ROOSEVELT. Must I be my brother's keeper?

Mr. MEYER. I cannot answer that; I am not familiar with the Bible, if that is what it is.

Mr. ROOSEVELT. I am reminded of a very old Hebrew proverb with regard to the constant reference to Elliott Roosevelt on the books of the Hughes Co., placed in there by Mr. Meyer. It is a very short one, if you don't mind and I would like to depart from the general tenor of our conversation to read it:

He who digs a grave for another almost invariably falls into it.

Mr. MEYER. I think the colonel is questioning my veracity without reason.[2068]

It is easy to see why this comic-opera received a lot of attention, but it is just as obvious that the committee leadership was not able to control the protagonists, and that the serious matters at issue were being left to flounder in all the hilarity. Nonetheless, the testimony did bring out important technical and bureaucratic facts. That Roosevelt got away looking like he had won was due to his chutzpah, and to the lack of focused aggressiveness on the part of his interlocutors.

Elliott Roosevelt had been aware of his controversial position almost from the moment he went to Harper Dry Lake. For example, in a typical display of piqued bravado, in 1944 he complained to the boss. By his own account:

Mr. ROOSEVELT. There is one more, sir, that I think is of the utmost importance to this committee.

Some time in 1944 the charge was made by someone in Congress that appeared in the newspapers that I had used White House influence to secure the awarding of a contract to Howard Hughes for a photoreconnaissance plane...When I read this newspaper account, I sat down and wrote a longhand letter direct to General Arnold, and in that letter, I stated that I had read of a charge being made against me of using White House influence to secure the awarding of a contract to Howard Hughes.

I was so upset about that charge that I told General Arnold in the letter that I personally knew that he would stand up and back me up in my contention that I had never had any pressure brought to bear from the White House.

In addition to that, I stated in the letter that I felt that my usefulness to the AAF was impaired by these charges and that it would be far better if he were to agree to my being transferred to the paratroopers or to the OSS, for a combat assignment, immediately, in place of being in a position where any discredit would come to the AAF.

Senator FERGUSON. What was the general's reply?

Mr. ROOSEVELT. The general did not reply personally, because at that time, he was ill with heart trouble, and I received a letter from Gen. Barney Giles, his Chief of Staff, in which he stated ... that it was a completely ridiculous charge that I had ever used White

> House influence, that furthermore, I had nothing to do with the letting of that contract to the Hughes Aircraft Co., that it was let by a board of officers which he headed, and that they took full responsibility for all contracts and placed absolutely no responsibility on me for the award of that contract.[2069]

That was Elliott's take on the flap that ended with his promotion and wings. Elliott, indeed, had not let the contract; but it certainly would not have been let without his grandiose recommendation *and* his badgering of important people including his father.

Overall, General Roosevelt came off fairly well in the hearings, despite the scandalous backchatter. It was not only because of his aggressive and persuasive style, but because he was given ample chance to demonstrate how he had, in fact, aided the war effort. When it came to the eternal conflict between front-line warfighters and the bureaucrats of materiel and procurement, Elliott's self-defense rang clear and true even when veering into hyperbole:

> ...some officers in the Procurement Division were very, very unhappy with the fact that General Arnold called me back to reorganize the reconnaissance program, because – and I would like for you to get the records of the Procurement Division and see what happened between the time that I was called back and the new reorganization went in with regard to contracts that had to do with the reconnaissance program, and see how many contracts were cancelled which were proven to be absolutely useless.
>
> ...I made the recommendation to General Arnold that many, many thousands of contracts which came to my attention which came to well over $100,000,000, to the best of my memory, be canceled, as they were not producing anything of value for the war effort.
>
> ...Many contracts for the manufacture of equipment were canceled, and other contracts were increased, of materiel that could be used in the theaters. And I think that you can get testimony from every single theater, from reconnaissance officers and from air force commanders, that within six months a tremendous improvement took place in the situation of supplies arriving to enable us to do our job and that the entire war effort was speeded up, and I believe that even General Eisenhower, who is familiar enough to be able to testify on that matter, would agree.
>
> ...I got a number of photoreconnaissance aircraft which were great improvements as a result of recommendations that we made for other improvements that were to be made in addition to the possibility of Hughes' plane.
>
> ...We also secured a number of modifications, and speeded up and increased the range of the P-38, the F-5, and as a result of our recommendations, we who had been in the theater, that aircraft increased its range, from less than 700 miles to where we were flying missions of well over 2,400 miles, and it was on our recommendations and our insistence over, in many cases, the active opposition of Materiel Command officers, officers who never got into combat, and stayed in the country.
>
> ...and very frankly, we were lucky in having a wartime commander of the AAF that he backed us up on our requirements from the field, and forced it down the throats of these Wright Field officers, in so many thousands of instances.[2070]

Elliott Roosevelt used the hearings to get back at his enemy, Major General Echols. He complained that Echols had made insinuations about his integrity; then he went on to make his own about Echols. Did he know that Echols fought the F-11 contract?

> Mr. ROOSEVELT. Yes, and … he went ahead and kept putting the responsibility back to General Arnold for the procurement of this airplane in spite of the fact that it was the recommendation of flying officers who had been flying in the theaters, and then it is interesting to note that he would impugn by inference my integrity in this matter, and that I would make a recommendation that would hurt or would injure in any way the lives of my men in the active theater of combat, wherein I think that it might be interesting to note what is General Echols' present job, whom does he work for?
>
> Senator FERGUSON. Do you know?
>
> Mr. ROOSEVELT. Yes, sir. He works for the Association of American Aircraft Manufacturers as their president.
>
> Senator FERGUSON. Is that a criticism of Echols and his testimony?
>
> Mr. ROOSEVELT. I criticize General Echols' position, in the first place, that he should have tried to protect himself so much and have gone ahead, and his subordinate officers should have been so much against making an effort to get us an aircraft that would operate in theaters, and would meet our performance requirements, that they delayed in making the contract, and they enforced and forced through so many revisions, according to what Mr. Hughes told me at a later date wherein I said, "why didn't you get those airplanes to us like you promised them?" [2071]

Elliott, parroting Hughes's position, was implying that an established manufacturers' mafia was trying to prevent newcomers like Hughes breaking into the warplane market. Since his falling out with Robert Gross in 1934, he had never been very fond of Lockheed. It might have been a factor in his campaign against the P-38.

> Mr. ROOSEVELT. I am challenging the faith of General Echols in this matter in maintaining that the U.S. Government, which can manufacture thousands and hundred of thousands of airplanes and get them into the war theaters, that they should maintain that they could not manufacture a wooden airplane and that they did not believe that it would be suitable for the combat services which we people in the theaters, who had to fly the airplanes, maintained that they could do.[2072]

After turning the tables on General Echols and lamenting the corrupt relationship between defense contractors and retired officers, a helpful Elliott Roosevelt proceeded to suggest that "there should be a law" prohibiting such officers from accepting employment from the munitions industry; and further, that "if they were given sufficient expense accounts, and they had enough money in their pockets, there would never be any question" as to whether their judgments were swayed by contractor largesse.[2073]

That was quite a performance.

Hughes Testifies

Today, it is mostly the Senate dogfight between Howard Hughes and Senator Brewster that is remembered. Public opinion in general, and the movie "*The Aviator*" especially, pretend that Hughes was an innocent victim of a political set-up, and that he managed to demolish his accusers and cleanse his name – all culminating in the triumph of his long-derided Hercules lifting off majestically from the waters off Long Beach.

It is true that Hughes had the media's fawning attention – indeed he still does, judging by the immense literature he has caused to be written about himself, both in life and in death. But the opposing views have received scant sympathy, and that is a mistake.

Those who viewed *Aviator* received a warped image of the Senate proceedings. Notably, Mr. Hughes was one of many witnesses; his testimony was often flawed to the point of confusion and incoherence; Senator Brewster did not cross-examine Hughes; and the Hercules flying boat was only one bone of contention. And, the Hercules, despite its unscheduled hop, represented no triumph of aviation.

There had been intense speculation that Hughes was going to make a grand entrance by setting a trans-continental speed record in the XF-11 on his way to Washington. Columnist Jack Anderson thought this was a ploy; by leaking the story even though Hughes knew the plane wasn't ready, he could pretend that the Air Force had disapproved the attempt. Instead he flew in his personal B-23, and arrived in the capital amidst frenzied media attention.[i]

When Hughes finally deigned to show up at the Senate hearings, on the morning of Tuesday, 6 August, he was merely moving in for the kill at the end of a carefully laid ambush. He had been fighting a skirmish with Brewster through the media for months. He held himself to be the victim of a plot so vile, so infamous, that all else paled. Elliott Roosevelt had said that the hearings were held to smear FDR. Now Hughes maintained that the hearings were held to smear Elliott. But more than that, he, Hughes, was the victim of a demonic conspiracy of Hughes-haters in Congress and in the Air Forces.

At that time few people knew that Howard Hughes was insane. He was still able to collect himself for critical moments, and many consider his Senate testimony among his finest hours. Despite being paranoid, disheveled, megalomaniacal, and unrelentingly obnoxious, he still managed to come across as David slaying Goliath with the F-11 and the H-4 in lieu of a sling. Somehow, the underlying fact that he had grossly mismanaged the Air Force's contracts slipped the public's attention.

Hughes thought that Lockheed had stolen the P-38 design from his D-2. He said that some of his fired engineers went to work for Lockheed, and by strange coincidence, the P-38 then emerged, resembling his own design. However, the P-38 was designed in 1937 and flew in 1939, at a time when Hughes had only a "hobby shop" to Lockheed-Burbank's large plant, and the idea he submitted to the Air Corps in 1937 was not the D-2, but an earlier design that was never built.[2074]

Hughes also thought the Japanese had copied the Type 0 ("Zeke") from his Racer. That is absurd. The superficial similarities reflect a global convergence in fighter design of that era.[2075] Further, Hughes thought there was a vast conspiracy, the "Hate-Hughes Club" headed by General Echols, to destroy his prospects for delivering aircraft to the military – despite the fact that he was clearly unable to deliver on his grandiose promises.

About his troubles with the Army, Hughes testified:

> All I know is that I could not get to first base toward selling anything to the Army, although I had an outstanding record as a pilot and as a designer. I just pointed out I designed an airplane [H-1] which was considered the most efficient in the world and which was the fastest airplane in the world at that time other than some souped-up Snyder [Schneider] Cup trophy racer they had over in England, but for its horsepower and for the range and distance that the airplane would fly, it was a great deal faster than anything else in

[i] Anderson: Confessions, 70-71. The Douglas B-23 was modified bomber related to the DC-3.

> the world and I might say that without any limitation this airplane was faster than anything the Army or the Navy had in this country at that time.
>
> In other words, this first design I am talking about, the single-engine plane, which I designed, was faster than anything that the Army or Navy had in this country, and yet I could not sell it to them.
>
> It was also an excellent design in every other respect. I have reason to think that there was something vague [sic] when the Army would not buy that airplane.
>
> However, I just went back into my shell and, as I say, then when they turned down my two-engine interceptor design and gave Lockheed the contract for it when I felt Lockheed got the two-engine idea from some of my engineers, I felt I had gotten rough treatment, so I backed into my shell and decided to design and build from the ground up with my own money an entirely new airplane which would be so sensational in its performance that the Army would have to accept it.
>
> Now, I designed and built that airplane under closed doors, without even letting the Army in to see it. And I might also add that on one occasion General Arnold, the Chief of the Air Forces, came to California and of course I would not have gone to this extent had I known him, but I left orders that no one was being permitted in this plant…Now, Gen. Arnold came to the field and came to the factory and they would not let him in. And you can imagine that caused an explosion the like of which you have never heard, and that also did not enhance the feeling of the Army officers toward me and my company.[2076]

Then Hughes complained that he had been singled out for persecution. For example, he maintained, the F-11 competitor, the F-12 Rainbow, was actually a Pan American initiative – a twisted scheme to get the Air Force to subsidize Republic's and Pan Am's postwar airline business. And that plane had failed too, so why didn't they look into that? [2077] (In truth, a number of airlines sponsored the Rainbow.)

Later, he brought up other troubled, failed projects: the Consolidated C-99, the Lockheed Constitution transport, even the Northrop B-35 flying wing. The gigantic Constitution was, he said, another trick by Pan Am; they talked the Navy into funding it. As usual, his elaborate accusations sprang from a kernel of truth; but a kernel that seemed small or irrelevant to most informed observers. It was not news that money had been wasted during the war; the committee was trying to find outright corruption.[2078]

Most explosively of all, Hughes believed the Juan Trippe – Owen Brewster cabal had sicced the Senate upon him because he had refused to consent to a merger of TWA and Pan Am. This accusation, which he backed up in detail with names and places, hurt Brewster badly, precisely because it sounded eminently plausible.

It was revealed that Brewster and Hughes had gone around and around on this issue ever since the CAB route award to TWA in 1945. There is no question that there was some level of truth to the accusation; the real question is who was most to blame. Hughes eventually rejected the merger, and now he could, with considerable credibility, assert that Brewster had tried to trade TWA for quiet in the Senate.

When Howard Hughes began his public testimony, the audience came to life – it seems that this was the moment the nation had been waiting for. The half-deaf witness complained that the frenzy of picture-snapping made it difficult to hear and respond, so the chairman had to restore decorum. Even then, it was difficult for Hughes to follow the proceedings:

> Senator FERGUSON. Just one moment. I must have quiet in the room. I think the Chair and the committee have been as tolerant as they can be under the circumstances. We understand that this is a public business and that people are entitled to come here and to

hear the evidence, but we must have quiet and we want no remarks. The remarks from those in the audience were uncalled for…if he does not want pictures taken they will not be taken, and they have requested him about one light, and I think that he consented to the one light, is that correct, Mr. Hughes?

Mr. HUGHES. What is that?[2079]

It was obvious that the public had been primed for admiring Hughes, for his overall performance was not nearly as convincing as his initial offensive. By starting off with his attack on Brewster, he scored many points, but when he bogged down in the details later in the day, he came across as confused, even to the point of sometimes seeming to wind up in a "Who's on First" comedy. He got his dates wrong; he mixed up names; and he contradicted himself frequently. His memory seemed to be quite poor, especially when it suited his case. Worse, as the day wore on, he began arguing incessantly and obsessively about every last little detail, driving the Senate investigators to distraction and causing Senator Ferguson to burst out: "We are not going to make a farce out of this hearing." But in trying to give Hughes a fair chance, the committee allowed him to upstage it, and to get bogged down in the "He said – I said" morass of the Brewster – Hughes feud.[2080]

Yet surprisingly, Hughes was able to explain his case better than were many of Washington's veteran spinmeisters. The core of his counterattack came in this exchange:

I charge specifically that during luncheon at the Mayflower Hotel in the week beginning on February 10, 1947, in the suite of Senator Brewster, that the Senator told me in so many words that if I would agree to merge TWA with Pan American and would go along with his community airline bill there would be no further hearing in this matter.[2081]

Hughes said he had been willing to discuss a possible merger, but that Juan Trippe would not offer an equitable arrangement. He then decided to drop the matter. In truth, Hughes and Trippe had met in Palm Springs later and discussed the merger in detail. Hughes said that Jack Frye, on his way out as TWA chief, was vehemently opposed to the deal, which is understandable since Frye had built the airline. Trippe "knew as long as Frye was in there he did not have a chance." [2082]

Just about that time, Flanagan (Senate investigator) arrived in California and started getting very tough about the investigation. It was quite apparent to me that this was the application of the screws to me…After my refusal of Senator Brewster's proposition, Flanagan's course was entirely different. He began saying things such as he had information about a $100,000 payoff to Elliott Roosevelt.

I have been jealous of my reputation and there is no question that these threats of bad publicity were a very powerful weapon in my case. I was also pretty exhausted in fighting the political maneuvers of Juan Trippe in Washington. He came to California and we had some considerable discussion and I asked him what he would do about Senator Brewster.

He said Brewster was abroad but as soon as he returned he would ask him to hold up the investigation and also to try to delay hearings on the community air bill with the hope that we might get together on both matters.[2083]

Brewster immediately thereafter defended himself plaintively and reasonably persuasively. But there was no question that Hughes had gained the public's sympathy. Unfortunately it is not easy to determine exactly at which point business discussions became obviously odious, or whom to blame the most for the smell.

This was only the main thrust of Hughes's defamation of Brewster. Other highlights were the airline rides the senator had bummed both from TWA and Pan Am, the free vacations and business trips, and similar courtesies from the airline. This was of course a common *modus operandi* for politicians, but Hughes knew how to turn it against his accusers even as he had TWA engage in the same practice.

When Hughes returned next day, the hearings soon went off the rails again. Senator Ferguson, the chief inquisitor, and the testy witness argued incessantly on querulous and superfluous matters; it seemed that every time a matter of substance was approached, the two bogged down like a couple of snapping turtles.

Howard Hughes complained bitterly that he was singled out, and that the other companies were guilty of similar offenses. He brought in a list of sixty aircraft projects that had been initiated during the war, but did not result in operational aircraft. (Many of these were later successful.) In particular, he harped on the Republic Rainbow, which to him was Pan Am's airplane.[i]

His arguments were not incorrect; it takes a long time to design and produce a new aircraft, and while many are called, few are chosen. The problem was that this was not what the committee was investigating. It was trying to determine if Hughes had made extravagant, unkeepable promises, and whether unfair political pressure had been used to favor Hughes's two famous projects. SWIC was investigating whether bribery, corruption, or at the very least, unsavory business practices had been used by Hughes Aircraft. It is indicative of the poor control Ferguson and Brewster exercised that Hughes got away with his excuses, and managed to portray himself as the victim.

Johnny Meyer was a very elusive witness. Hughes had a tendency to send him to South America or other foreign countries when his testimony was needed. That was how Meyer obtained the nickname "Patagonia Johnny." It turned out that Meyer's sudden absence from the country would provide the embarrassed SWIC an excuse for halting the circus, or at least the first round of it.

On 8 August, the Hughes testimony ground to a halt in a dispute over whether Hughes would, could, or should produce Mr. Meyer for further interrogation.

Senator FERGUSON. Well, now, Mr. Hughes, I am asking you what your answer was.

Mr. HUGHES. I don't remember what it was.

Senator FERGUSON. We will not have this bickering back and forth. You are before this committee, and you are going to answer the question.

Mr. HUGHES. You asked me just now about a reply that I made. My answer is that I don't remember. Now, the man is taking everything down there. Why don't you ask him?

Senator FERGUSON. I will ask you again.

Mr. HUGHES. What?

Senator FERGUSON. Will you bring Mr. Meyer in at the 2 o'clock session?

Mr. HUGHES. No. I don't think I will.

Senator FERGUSON. Will you try to bring him in?

Mr. HUGHES. No. I don't think I will try.

Senator FERGUSON. All right. Counsel, will you have this delivered to the marshal?

Senator PEPPER. What is the paper?

Senator FERGUSON. You tell the marshal that we mean business on this subpoena. See that it is served at once. Mr. Dietrich. Mr. Dietrich. Mr. Dietrich. - I want the record to

---

[i] SBC Hearings, 1947, Part 40, 24360. C.R. Smith also had ordered the Rainbow.

> show that Mr. Flanagan had spoken to Mr. Meyer yesterday, and told him his presence was wanted at this hearing this morning, and Meyer promised to be here. - I would like to talk to Mr. Dietrich.
>
> Mr. SLACK. There he is, Senator.
>
> Senator FERGUSON. Mr. Dietrich, on the 4th of this month, you were served with a subpoena, duces tecum, to produce all the records, books of account, checkbooks, cancelled checks, and bank statements relating to the personal bank account of Howard Hughes, now in your possession. Up to date, they have not been given to the committee.
>
> Mr. DIETRICH. The committee has not asked for them, Senator.
>
> Senator FERGUSON. Well, you have a subpoena to bring them in.
>
> Mr. DIETRICH. All right. They would take a truck. Do you want the truck driven in here, or do you want them carried in?[2084]

And on and on they went. With this kind of circus it is no wonder SWIC decided to shut down the public hearings for the time being.

Hughes went back to California. Patagonia Johnny had disappeared again. The ports and airports were on notice to prevent his leaving the country.

It was a Set-up…

…a double set-up. For the public, it looked like Hughes had defeated Brewster, and that the Elliott Roosevelt – Johnny Meyer show had been mere sideshow levity. Many years afterwards the reason for this outcome was finally revealed. Using Brewster, Pan Am had meticulously set up the inquisition of Hughes and Roosevelt; but Brewster was double-crossed, and the trap he had set would end up destroying him.

Senator Brewster had found the Elliott connection while nosing around the new FDR Library looking for dirt on the Pearl Harbor case. But he was owned, body and soul, by Pan Am, and Juan Trippe was more interested in forcing Howard Hughes's TWA to the altar than in outing Elliott's orgies. That was why Brewster's "chosen instrument" bill had been written by Pan Am's lawyers; that was why Brewster had visited Hughes with the demand for a shotgun TWA-Pan Am merger while holding the threat of corruption hearings over his head.

Like many politicians, Brewster was accustomed to this way of doing business; it worked. He was totally unprepared for someone throwing rocks back. He should have been more careful. His palace was glass.

The influential columnist Drew Pearson was a left-wing Democrat who, for various reasons, warmed to General Roosevelt despite knowing of his excesses. More importantly for now, he despised Senator Brewster, and when Howard Hughes called him for help in dispatching his enemy, Pearson kissed his journalistic ethics goodbye and began plotting. This we know because Jack Anderson, who had just been hired by Pearson as an assistant, wrote about it in his memoirs. Pearson sent Anderson out to California to begin working out a strategy for handling the upcoming hearings. Anderson said Hughes was alert, intelligent, and receptive – in other words, he did not get the impression many others received at the time. Jack, who knew nothing of aircraft, also bought into Hughes's "persecuted genius" fantasy.

Jack Anderson was a tough political realist. He told Hughes that politicians were cowardly scum; they gloried in victimizing the defenseless, but they would run away if someone should unexpectedly fight back or retaliate. So his plan for Hughes was clear:

> …since he could never effectively defend his lobbying tactics or get far on his contract performance, and since any attempt to do so would only put him right where Brewster wanted him, his salvation lay in turning the hearing into a free-for-all that was to scare off the senators.
>
> And how was he to do that?
>
> By charging that he was a victim of a crooked cabal; by clamoring that the hearings were being rigged against him; by demanding fair, American procedures – like the right to cross-examine his accusers and call his own witnesses. An attack a day on Brewster and on un-American procedures – that was my formula.[2085]

Hughes had already had Brewster under surveillance, and the dirt he was able to feed to Drew Pearson enabled the columnist to prepare the ground for the effective counterstrike that came when Hughes finally showed up in Washington. And now we know why Hughes, instead of showing the expected deference, tore straight into Brewster and accused him of the vilest corruption. It was planned and promoted by the Pearson/Anderson team, and it succeeded spectacularly. Eventually, a weepy Brewster did run away to Maine and the committee did end its equally runaway inquiry.

Yet even that was not the end of the conspiracy. For some reason Pearson absolutely wanted Brewster destroyed politically. In 1950, he found out that Brewster had stealthily and illegally bugged and wiretapped Hughes, though ineffectively, and he trumpeted this sorry fact; apparently he was not concerned that Hughes had done the same in return, since Pearson got the take from that operation.

When Brewster was finally up for reelection in 1952, Pearson and Hughes again got together. Drew recruited an opposing candidate, and at the columnist's request, Hughes financed a campaign against Brewster that ended in the latter's defeat. Hughes was accustomed to buying politicians in either party; but this time he had the last laugh by defenestrating Brewster. Not that it was an undue exit, but the dark side of journalism, when revealed, was not pretty either.[2086]

Jack Anderson appeared to have been a bit troubled by it all. Brewster was far from the worst of the lot, and Jack thought his boss vindictive and politically motivated. Pearson's defense was significant:

> Once you catch one of these birds at anything, never worry about doing him an injustice by overplaying it. We'll never learn 10% of the evil they do. We can't subpoena their records or threaten witnesses with jail. We have to use what's lying around in the open, or only half hidden. So we always miss the worst of it.[2087]

There's some truth in that, but unfortunately, Pearson and Anderson were not equal-opportunity muckrakers. Their collusion with Hughes is usually overlooked in accounts of the famous hearings, but it is not only crucial to understanding the dynamics of them, but also as a reminder that you can't even trust journalists making a career of trusting no one.

Jack Anderson's detailed account is one of the best around – for good reason, since he was one of the architects of the showdown. Unfortunately, he was not interested in the technical truth and could not have recognized it if he had seen it. He focused on the glamor of the Hughes-Brewster gladiatorial combat and neglected the Elliott-Meyer cesspool. But it was the latter that illuminated the subversion of the procurement process, the failure of the contractor, and the politically driven waste of resources.

But there was more to come. Several other people unexpectedly had their careers destroyed by the Senate hearings.

Perhaps there wasn't much anyone could do to Elliott Roosevelt's reputation by now. He was who he was. Had his surname been different, he might have been court-martialed or indicted. His behavior was so egregious that it was inconceivable (at the time) that he would ever hold military or public office again. Add to this that his domestic troubles began to mount, that his pro-Soviet rants sounded sillier and tinnier, and there may just have been a general consensus that it would be pointless to go after him further.

Another general came out looking good. He was Oliver P. Echols, the Assistant Chief of Air Staff in charge of Materiel, Maintenance, and Distribution. He had had his run-ins with Elliott Roosevelt from the beginning. As early as 1942, Echols had said he would do no business with HAC because Hughes, obsessed with secrecy, had refused to allow the Air Corps to inspect his designs. To Hughes that meant Echols was a founding member of the "Hate Hughes Club."[2088]

Noah Dietrich was able to produce crucial evidence for the purported Hate-Hughes cabal. He said:

> His [Echols'] reply was that "so far as I am concerned, I will not do business with Howard Hughes, because I dislike him" ... he referred to two particular occasions which inspired his attitude. First, following Mr. Hughes' transcontinental record, he personally talked with Mr. Hughes; and, according to his statement, he made an arrangement with Mr. Hughes to have Mr. Hughes fly the ship into Wright Field, so that he and his staff could inspect it. For some reason that I have no knowledge about, that appointment was not kept.
>
> I do not know for what reason or whose fault, but he was quite incensed because he and his staff were awaiting the arrival of Mr. Hughes, who did not arrive with the plane.
>
> He said there was another incident that irritated him and aggravated him, which was that when the Air Corps had word of the D-2, while it was under construction, they phoned out and asked for permission to send someone out to inspect the plane. The consent was granted. He sent two officers with a staff of engineers. There was a Colonel Irwin, and I do not remember the other man; I think he was a major at that time. Upon arriving they contacted Mr. Hughes, and they were informed that because of the secret nature of the project he did not want a group of people inspecting the plane; that Colonel Irwin was welcome – either one of them – to look at the plane. He said "That was very embarrassing to me. I had sent a mission out there to inspect the plane."[2089]

Echols had alerted the committee to the F-11 fiasco, and he happily described how the technical advice from Wright Field had been overruled by Elliott's interference. Still, importantly, he found no actual fraud in the process. He did not then know what would crawl out from under the rocks in the second round of hearings in November.

Homer Ferguson, otherwise a capable jurist, twice lost control of the hearings; first when the Elliott – Johnny Meyer routine, likened to their comedic contemporaries Abbott & Costello, had the room erupting; secondly, when Howard Hughes tore into Senator Brewster and engaged in absurd, hilarious verbal sparring with the chairman.

Senator Brewster, humiliated, went home to Maine. Ferguson took a turn in the hospital.

The SWIC was looking for a face-saving way to end the matter. On 11 August Senator Ferguson suspended the hearings until further investigations could be made. The pretense was that Johnny Meyer could not be found any more, and Hughes refused to produce him. In reality, the SWIC needed a breather to bring things under control, and to pursue more loose ends uncovered during the proceedings.

Senate Hearings, Round Two

After new evidence had been gathered, the hearings resumed on 5 November 1947 and continued in public for over two weeks. Senator Brewster, whose political career had been gut-shot by Howard Hughes in August, did not play a role this time.

Senator Ferguson was still running the subcommittee, but a considerable part of the "inquisition" was verbalized by the committee's remarkably able chief counsel, William P. Rogers. Yes, he was that same Rogers who later served as President Nixon's Secretary of State. In this early venue, the young Navy veteran got into some fur-flying catfights with the odd characters he and Ferguson faced across the podium.

New and well-prepared artillery was leveled on Elliott Roosevelt. Meanwhile, Elliott had been busy promoting himself and the Progressive Citizens for America (PCA), the pro-communist group including former vice president Henry Wallace.[i]

Elliott also considered taking over as chairman of the American Veterans Committee, a sort of left-wing American Legion. That brought him – again – into conflict with brother Franklin Jr., who was ferociously trying to weed out the communists from the AVC. Elliott's candidacy collapsed, and so, soon after, did the AVC.[2090]

He was still a thorn in the side of both Congress and President Truman. The Roosevelt sons had infuriated Truman with their constant criticism and their much trumpeted preference for Eisenhower. Speaking before the NAACP, Elliott had the gall to denounce the president for not "once and for all" wiping out segregation and discrimination. Of course, it was Truman who integrated the armed forces and began the long struggle to enforce civil rights. Elliott's father had never shown any interest therein – nor had Elliott when he was a true Stetson-hatted Texan![2091]

When the Senate hearings resumed in November 1947, Elliott wasn't invited, although as usual he did get his opinion in. This time the Republican-led committee was determined to keep the hearings under control, and to remain focused on the serious matters at hand. Nonetheless, the show eventually closed on a note so dark and shocking that the entire nation recoiled.

While Elliott Roosevelt was not formally called to testify, many of the prior witnesses made repeat appearances, including "Patagonia Johnny" Meyer, whose disappearance purportedly had caused the suspension of the previous round in August.

Howard Hughes seized the chance, his last, to fiercely refute his critics. On 2 November, the man who had said that if the Hercules turned out to be a failure he'd leave the country and never come back concluded a series of taxi runs by lifting off and flying for over a minute in ground effect within the Long Beach harbor. Reportedly he said, "there you are, Brewster, you son-of-a-bitch." [2092]

---

[i] "Birds of a feather flock together," wrote Westbrook Pegler on the 1947 press clipping quoting Elliott at the PCA. Numerous left-wing luminaries were involved in this organization.

The Hercules was not ready for flight. In particular, the complex flight control system was not finished. It was ill-advised to take it aloft, especially as it had a number of non-essential people aboard. It appears that dumping a notch of flaps during a high-speed run caused it to levitate off the water, but it is pretty obvious that Hughes was pleased and considered the "flight" some sort of vindication.

It didn't hurt that the previous day, Hughes Aircraft had delivered the second XF-11 to Muroc Army Test Base.

Howard Hughes had the experience, knowledge, and stick-and-rudder competence of a great pilot. According to the Air Force, however, he did not have the judgment and professionalism they expected of an airman. Almost everyone can learn to fly, but not everyone can be trusted to follow the rules, and that's what counts in the system.

Miraculously, Hughes had survived his innumerable crashes. As we have seen, after his undisciplined handling of the first XF-11, the Air Force demanded someone else fly the second prototype. Major General Ira Eaker, now chief of the air staff, overrode this directive. Seven months later Eaker was a vice president of the Hughes Tool Company, which caused deep suspicion on the part of the Senate interrogators. But Eaker would be instrumental to the rehabilitation of the company.[2093]

Again, there was more to the story. General Bennett Meyers testified that Hughes had attempted to bribe him to ask his close friend Eaker to allow him to fly the second XF-11: "…he said, "After all, I thought you were working for me. All you have to do is pick up a telephone or go to see General Spaatz or General Eaker and get approval and overrule Wright Field on the matter." [2094]

General Eaker testified at his own request during the November hearings. He said he and General Spaatz agreed that Hughes should fly because he posted $5 million in security, and it might save an Air Force pilot's life. They both knew the F-11 was going nowhere. Indulgence was in order. Bribes were not discussed; but Eaker wisely had Spaatz come over to hear Hughes's spiel personally, thus protecting himself from any future accusations. Eaker testified that Hughes had come begging to his house on 16 September 1946:

> The decision to let Howard Hughes fly the F-11 was not made by me as has been inferred at these hearings. It was made by the commanding general. It was a wise decision since it not only guaranteed the Government against loss, but it saved an Army test pilot from assuming the risk of the early flights. Also, as Hughes had pointed out, he had spent several hours in testing the novel controls of the plane, had flown the first article, and it was much safer for him to fly it than it would have been for another pilot.[2095]

Although ultimately shocking, the hearings in November have been seen as anticlimactic compared to the August session, when a full-blown media circus developed around the matter. It is true that there was considerably more decorum and solemnity in November. But from an Air Force point of view, this round was far more consequential.

On 5 Nov 1947, the first witness to tear into Elliott Roosevelt was aeronautical engineer Ralph Graichen, who had headed the AAF Research and Engineering Division and would continue in important DOD posts in later years. Graichen ridiculed Elliott's judgment and charged that he had been the source of the political pressure exerted on the procurement process. In a Pentagon conference, Roosevelt had loudly claimed that the F-11 was the only capable reconnaissance aircraft available.[2096]

Senator Carl Hatch (D-NM) asked: "Is it pressure for an experienced officer to express an opinion?"

Graichen responded: "It is pressure when an officer says there is one contractor and one design which can accomplish a job in the face of the adverse opinion of the engineering organization of the Air Forces whose business it is to know these things."

Ferguson interjected that Graichen was not a pilot. Graichen sneered: "I readily agree to that, but it must be mentioned also, that neither is Colonel Roosevelt a pilot."

Graichen complained that Roosevelt was not qualified by "background, education, or experience" to give such an opinion. He said he could not recall another single instance where any one individual took it upon himself to overrule, or to use his influence to overrule, the recommendations of the technical group of the Air Force.[2097]

Senator Ferguson asked Graichen if Elliott was right that there was no other plane available to the job at the time. Graichen said: "I am afraid not. Most of us felt that to enter into a contract of that type at that late date with a contractor who had not demonstrated his ability to produce was not wise."

As a result, Graichen had left a sour note on the paperwork when Hughes's refund for D-2 development went through: "I'll be damned." [2098]

He was particularly incensed about the Duramold construction. He went into detail about how wooden planes had caused trouble by burning, rotting, or breaking. He presented a long, sorry list of the wooden prototypes the Air Corps evaluated and rejected – little asterisks of aviation history like the toy-like Bell XP-77.[2099]

Then he got to the Mosquito – praised to the skies by many, but not Graichen:

> The Mosquito airplane was thought quite well of, apparently, in England during the war...That is a completely wooden airplane. I believe it performed a number of missions fairly satisfactorily, although I believe that the records will show that the combat, or the battle, damage was very high, because of the characteristics of wood, whereas the flack hit will practically cause the section where it hit to disintegrate...
>
> We brought over a small number, I believe – some 13 of the Canadian-built Mosquitoes...for trial here. They were considered unsatisfactory by the Air Force, and as I recall, they were eventually sent down to NACA at Langley Field for going over to see what could be done, if anything, to make them satisfactory aircraft. They finally were given up as being unsatisfactory, and I believe they were eventually returned to Canada by some civilian pilots, and the reason, as I remember it, was that the ferry pilot who normally would do that refused to fly the airplanes back to Canada...They were considered dangerous from a structural point of view, and I guess they were afraid that they would fail in the air, probably.[2100]

This is a startling indictment of an aircraft that is usually considered one of the finest ever produced. But one can sympathize with the horror American engineers must have felt when they opened up an airframe made of balsawood, spruce, veneers, and various other woods, all glued and screwed together like a gigantic piece of fine furniture. This requires expert builders, and the new Canadian line simply hadn't gotten the kinks worked out.

Ferguson asked if the Mosquitoes were structurally unsound when tested at Langley Field. Graichen responded that complete tests had not been run, but in general "experiments with American-built wooden planes had ended in burning crashes from which pilots escaped by parachute, and the result of their tests was a finding that wooden planes were not satisfactory."

All this irked the Canadians. The RCAF protested vigorously while conceding that Mosquitoes were not as well suited to North American weather extremes as they were to England's temperate climate. But the *Montreal Gazette* got ahold of a "highly-decorated former RCAF pilot" who, disappointingly, corroborated the accusations:

> This pilot maintained that the British-built Mosquito was the finest and most versatile aircraft he ever flew in either operations or experimentally. The British "mossie" did everything asked of it, he said, and it was used for all kinds of work – bombing reconnaissance and low-level attacks. He maintained, however, that Canadian-built Mosquitos which arrived in England practically had to be rebuilt before they were fit for service. He mentioned particularly the ailerons, saying that new ones had to be installed, and that the Packard-built engines were replaced by Rolls-Royce Merlins.[2101]

Some Canadians thought the Americans just didn't know how to fly. One researcher quoted several Mossie pilots to the effect that the slight-finned, high-powered aircraft required a "commanding set of hands and feet" especially on the ground. And it is true that the Mosquito had a reputation as an angel in the air, a demon on the ground.[2102]

Ralph Graichen was pleased that the F-11 was changed from wood to aluminum, and conceded that it performed well when it was finally finished. He failed to mention that in static testing, the F-11 held up exceptionally well. But then the war had been over for two years.[2103]

Remarkably, Graichen also used the opportunity to refute Howard Hughes's accusations from August, line by line. It was particularly important for him, speaking undoubtedly on behalf of Wright Field technocrats, to show that Hughes had had the same chance as anyone else to compete in the P-38 selection, and he incidentally revealed that Hughes's 1937 design did not at all resemble Lockheed's – it was a conventional twin-engine concept.[2104]

He further charged:

> Mr. GRAICHEN. A great deal of effort was expended on the part of high-ranking officers within the Air Force to do business with Howard Hughes. I recall one particular instance in which General Echols spent an entire weekend out at Howard Hughes plant in an endeavor to enter into some kind of a logical agreement whereby we would employ Mr. Hughes' personnel and facilities, because they were certainly badly needed at that time…
>
> The result was as always happened. Mr. Hughes wanted to do business but he wanted to do it on his own terms, and in his own way, and he wanted to build an airplane that he thought the Air Forces needed.[2105]

Charles E. Wilson, former vice chairman of the War Production Board (WPB) said he had also opposed the F-11. It was "silly" to think that a new type of plane could be completed in time to win the war. He unsuccessfully urged the Air Forces to accept enhanced P-38s or the Northrop P-61 Black Widow.

Jesse Jones of the RFC was seen as the spider in the center of the Hughes faction's web. He had already testified that he had interested himself in Howard Hughes, whom he admired. He had indicated, however, that the final decision to overrule Mr. Wilson's aircraft experts had, in fact, come personally from President Roosevelt.[2106]

Later, Howard Hughes angrily contested Graichen's assertions. Referring to the "I'll be damned" note, and to both the Roosevelt and the following evaluation teams, he said:

> And what right does Mr. Graichen, sitting behind a desk in Wright Field – what right does he have to question the judgment of his own group of experts who were assigned by Wright Field to the job of making the decision? [2107]

Someone else was very unhappy with Mr. Graichen's admittedly rather supercilious testimony. That absent fellow was General Elliott Roosevelt. The next day, SWIC received a classical Elliott rejoinder by way of telegram. He restated his case for the Hughes F-11, and finished with a retaliatory strike:

> Unlike Mr. Graichen, I have no desire to cast aspersions on his qualifications as a reconnaissance aircraft engineer, but it is my humble opinion, that if the Procurement Division of the AAF had had, from the beginning, men who found out at first hand the needs of the combat units in the theater, that experience would have enabled the Procurement Division to better meet your needs in the theaters of operation. We were greatly hampered throughout the war in the various theaters of operation by the refusal of personnel such as Mr. Graichen to correct the mistakes which they were making in the procurement of equipment and supplies for units in action. Many thanks to you again for your expressed desire to see to it that I should not be false judged in the American press because of the dissemination of erroneous testimony such as people like Mr. Graichen has provided.[2108]

Again, Elliott had managed to slip in the last word; again, he had deflected attention from the real issue – unfair political pressure and influence-peddling – to his superior judgment as a combat pilot.

The Hughes Country Club

On the second day of second-round hearings, 6 November, Mr. Charles Perelle, who had been Hughes Aircraft Co. manager for about a year, seemingly testified both for and against his former employer. Hughes had brought in the well-regarded Perelle from Consolidated-Vultee when he needed adult supervision at HAC, and refused to provide it himself. When Hughes wouldn't stop his dilettantism, Perelle forced a confrontation that cost him his job.

Perelle's testimony, with its accompanying internal memoranda, is an invaluable source to what Hughes Aircraft was like in its infancy. He found payrolls padded with do-nothings, financial records in shambles, government relations the worst he'd ever seen, and a calculated contempt for "constituted authority" - except Mr. Hughes. On the F-11, he found "irresponsible engineering" and sloppy workmanship, as well as a culture of lying about the plane's progress.

Mr. Perelle offered a rather telling aside that would surely amuse former Hughes Aircraft employees:

> Sen. FERGUSON. Had you ever heard the expression, "The Hughes Country Club?"

> Mr. PERELLE. Oh, yes....Why, I think that was just one of the means of identifying, I believe, some of its activities...I previously stated there was considerable laxness from the standpoint of management, and as a result of that, it derived the nickname of the "Country Club."
>
> Sen. FERGUSON. Even among employees of the company?
>
> Mr. PERELLE. I believe Mr. Hughes once used that same expression to me prior to my going to work there. I mean there was nothing unusual about it. He recognized that it did have that reputation, and as he told me, he wanted me to do something about it.[2109]

Compared to most defense contractors, Hughes Aircraft did retain a reputation as a company lacking in discipline for decades to come. One wartime worker wrote to Westbrook Pegler:

> I call the Hughes Co. the rest home because for about 50% of the time I was there I sat on a stool and waited for a job and in the department where I worked about one half of the workers were idle one half of the time. A lot of the women employees bring their knitting and it is a common site to see a woman knitting during working hours.[2110]

Perelle said Hughes had secured the support of formerly hostile General Bennett Meyers, and that it was assumed that Meyers would have a high position in HAC after the war. That was when the noose began tightening around Meyers's neck. But Perelle also complained that HAC suffered from consistently low priorities in war materials and therefore had difficulty meeting schedule. He did not think the F-11 was a dog, and he thought it could have been finished earlier if the Air Force had pressed its priority.

Hughes fired Perelle on 19 December 1945 after fifteen months of work, but not until Perelle had fired Johnny Meyer, and secured for himself compensation of $330,000, including stock options. It may be recalled that Hughes paid HAC's manager throughout the Cold War, the exceptional Pat Hyland, $100,000 a year without ever giving him a raise; and that HAC was infamous for otherwise never offering stock options. So Perelle had some reason to grin during the hearings.[i]

The former manager wasn't the only one who thought HAC had received the short end of the stick. Major Richard Fabian was the Air Force's on-site representative during the F-11 period. It is customary, and wise, for the Defense Department to place a small team on-site with the contractor to keep an eye on things. Sometimes that local team begins sympathizing with the opposite side of the contract.

Fabian said Hughes had been given low priorities for supplies throughout the war, and that SWIC had been interested only in presenting the anti-Hughes side of the matter. He complained that the War Production Board had quietly undermined the F-11 with neglect and tardiness. His testimony suggests a common contract situation where a top-level decision, unsupported by lower echelons, can be insidiously sabotaged. Fabian said SWIC was being unfair and partisan in its pursuit of Hughes and Roosevelt.[2111]

Other officers were willing to stand up for the F-11. Later, Lt. Gen. Barney Giles, former chief of staff of the AAF, testified that the service's engineering officers had long resisted the Hughes contract, even after General Arnold's order to get on with it.

Giles thought that there was actually no favoritism behind the contract. He interpreted the matter as a struggle against innovation by the Wright Field officers. The

---

[i] Hyland, Pat: Call me Pat, details his career with HAC and his difficult relationship with Howard Hughes. Also see Marrett for Perelle details.

"ops guys," supported by Arnold, were demanding that the F-11 get a chance. This, of course, was the line expounded by Elliott Roosevelt, and in contrast with Mr. Graichen, Gen. Giles held him eminently qualified to make the judgment he did.

In the disputed matter of General Roosevelt's expertise, Giles was emphatic:

> Senator O'CONOR. In other words, are we to understand that his [Roosevelt's] superior officers, including others of the generals, did consult his judgment and experience as to the proper plane to procure?
>
> General GILES. Yes, sir. I would say that they did. Because he had a very responsible command in the combat zone. And I certainly know General Spaatz very well, and I will say this: That, unless Colonel Roosevelt had been efficient and working on the job, he would have been sent out of the theater.
>
> Senator O'CONOR. And was he sent out of the theater?
>
> General GILES. No, sir. Let me get this straight: He was not relieved and sent home; he was sent over on the photographic mission.
>
> Senator O'CONOR. That was for temporary duty?
>
> General GILES. Temporary duty; that is right.
>
> Senator O'CONOR. Now, General, in your opinion, was Colonel Roosevelt a qualified officer, a well qualified officer, for such a mission?
>
> General GILES. Yes, sir; I believe that he was well qualified. There has been some question raised about being in command of photographic units. I want to point out that a photographic airplane is not really a combat airplane. They have no weapons of any kind. They go over with no guns. They have to make the pictures and come back. And Roosevelt, I have been told – I didn't see him do it – did perform a number of missions himself, even though he had an eye deficiency, that was corrected with glasses.[2112]

The unequivocal support Elliott Roosevelt received from his operational superiors thus stood in sharp contrast with the ridicule he endured from others, in particular the procurement and materiel officers.

Giles's testimony mattered a lot. But it was also quite predictable. He had been among those operational types clamoring for the new aircraft early on – indeed, he testified he'd been with Colonel Roosevelt out in the desert, absorbing Hughes's spiel about the "already existing" but temporarily unflyable D-2.

Let Hughes Hang Himself!

Chairman Ferguson introduced the infamous August 1944 document from Major D.C. Riley to then Col. J.F. Phillips describing a conference about the F-11, stating:

> Colonel Phillips further stated that Hughes should be left more or less to hang himself on the matter of this airplane and that the AAF should not get itself in such a position as to be the subject of criticism from anyone for having interfered with this project.[2113]

Brigadier General Phillips was called and asked what he meant by Hughes hanging himself. He said:

> "I did not feel that we should insist on any major changes [in design] that might delay the plane. Let me put it this way: I thought that he [Hughes] was a little optimistic as to when he could produce a plane."[2114]
>
> Senator FERGUSON. …Wright Field and you people did not want to do a thing with that contract: it was "hands off" all along the line, because as you say "hang himself," that you did not expect it to be produced during the war. The Air Corps did not want to take the blame. They wanted to let it just where it was, in the hands of Hughes, and that is why you used this common expression "to let him hang himself."[2115]

General Phillips replied that it wasn't quite like that, but the feeling was left that it mostly was. Phillips admitted that he had "perhaps" mentioned that the contract had been let shortly after Colonel Roosevelt's trip back to the States, and that he was aware of President Roosevelt's letting his preferences be known to General Arnold.[2116]

First, Brig. Gen. Albert Browning testified that he had signed the F-11 contract only upon the direct, written order of Robert P. Patterson, then Undersecretary of War. He said that as Mr. Patterson's special representative, he had initiated about $100 billion worth of contracts and that the F-11 deal was the first and only one to require a directive from Patterson, who represented the political leadership.[2117]

Although it gathered little attention at the time, the most damning evidence of President Roosevelt's subversion of the regular procurement process was provided by Maj. Gen. Bennett Meyers. It was he who directly tied Elliott Roosevelt and Harry Hopkins, FDR's right-hand man, together:

> …about the time that Mr. Lovett had this discussion with me and was quite annoyed about the fact that we did not have a photoreconnaissance airplane, as I say, this was right after I came back from Africa, Harry Hopkins called me and asked me the same questions. I am not sure about this, but I believe that he sent for me and I went over to the White House…
>
> He thought…it was an outrage, that where had our Air Force been all of these years if we had not developed a photographic reconnaissance airplane and why did we not get busy and get one…
>
> It was obvious from the tenor of the conversation, though, that he had had discussions probably with Elliott Roosevelt, that it was so timed with the time Mr. Lovett was in a sense reprimanding the Air Force for not having developed this type of airplane, that there had been discussions at that level about this photoreconnaissance airplane…
>
> Now, certainly in my opinion, with President Roosevelt making such inquiry from General Arnold and Harry Hopkins making such an inquiry from me at about that time when this thing all seemed to get stirred up after Mr. Lovett got back from Africa, and subsequently Harry Hopkins talking to me again about it, it was quite certain in my mind that there was certainly outside – shall I call it interest? …
>
> Senator FERGUSON. Not long after that you had suggested, as Mr. Lovett had suggested, that there would be a congressional investigation about it?
>
> Mr. MEYERS. Yes, sir.[2118]

This is the clearest indicator of why General Arnold ordered his subordinates to buy the F-11. He had Harry Hopkins, Jesse Jones, Bob Lovett, and two Roosevelts breathing down his neck. To be sure, Arnold wrote: "I did not discuss the project with Mr. Harry Hopkins." [2119]

But Arnold knew the score. It would have been far more surprising if he had followed his own "better judgment" and thus incurred the wrath of a White House enthralled by the Hughes lobbying machine.

Lovett then got on Meyers's case and so the pressure was on. On 21 October 1943, Meyers and Lovett commiserated about the F-11 contract. Lovett said: "...this is one of those border-line cases that can be very embarrassing if we get into it; for example, Hughes has got very powerful friends here in Washington. " Meyers responded, "Yessir. Jesse Jones and the president and everyone else seems to be in this...[2120]

In a later conversation, Bennett Meyers said, "I am getting a lot of pressure from the Air Staff, why in hell I haven't ordered it. They think I am an obstructionist for not doing this but I swear it is full of dynamite." Lovett said, "Well, you can blame it on me. It is full of dynamite." He cautioned Meyers on details of the contract, adding "Then you will get a damn good case when and if Congress investigates this thing." And the clincher: "Benny, my own feeling is that I never like any of these projects that are gone into under outside pressure. You can never bring the outside pressure up in your defense."[2121]

The War Department recorded the telephone conversations between the two. The transcripts clearly indicate that the two knew they were dealing with a political hot potato and that they were being steamrollered.

A Genius in His Own Mind

Howard Hughes's extensive testimony in the November round of hearings received much less attention than his outbursts and accusations of the preceding August. Perhaps that is because this time he was comparatively lucid, reflective, and constructive. Of course, he had just come from the first flight of his wooden flying boat, which he viewed as some kind of vindication.

> Mr. HUGHES. ...The photo-reconnaissance group came to California, and saw the D-2 airplane, which was standing at Harper Lake, which was flying, and which was eminently successful, in my opinion. And the photo-reconnaissance group, plus Gen. Giles, plus Gen. Bennett Meyers, all said they thought it was a terrific airplane and just want they wanted.
>
> Then, thereafter, instead of my getting a contract to build the D-2, all I got was mañana, mañana, stall, stall, stall, and finally a contract to build an airplane under the jurisdiction of Wright Field; and Wright Field forced me to make so many changes that it turned out to be a whole new design. I had to build a whole new prototype from the ground up, which I couldn't possibly put into production during the war. But the D-2 I could have produced during the war.[2122]
>
> ...I would like to say right now that if the Army has any photo-reconnaissance aircraft that can outperform the XF-11 tomorrow or the next day or next week I will retire from designing and flying airplanes for the rest of my life, permanently.
>
> Now, I think the XF-11 has been as successful as any of the other experimental airplanes that I am familiar with; and certainly far more successful than the average. As to the other airplane, I do not attach any significance to the brief flight the other day, but I honestly believe it is going to fly; and I believe, if I succeed in designing, building, and flying an airplane which is twice as big as anything else in the world, that is something which does not justify the statement that you won't get a cotter key.[2123]

It was all an able but over-the-top celebration of his own aeronautical genius. He simply didn't know, or did not want to know, about the advances being made by others at the very same time – turbojets, supersonics, delta wings. He was not a visionary ahead of his time; he was a cantankerous hobbyist leapfrogged by a new science-based industry. In this respect, Howard Hughes was to aeronautics much as George Goddard was to rocketry. In both cases, admirers fiercely defended the jilted genius, even to this day. But the scientists and engineers saw through the matter and confined themselves to slightly patronizing praise.[2124]

Incidentally, Hughes did indeed retire from designing aircraft, though not yet from flying them. This threat, apparently intended to terrify, was a repeat of his assertion that he'd leave the country and never come back if his flying boat didn't fly.[2125] Interestingly, both aircraft did fly, if barely, and Hughes did later leave the country, never to come back alive – but that was for tax and insanity reasons.

SWIC gave Hughes the opportunity to launch into a long, detailed diatribe against other aircraft manufacturers. This soliloquy provides fascinating insight into the state of the immediate postwar industry. For example, Hughes thought there was a Douglas – American Airlines axis pushing the DC-4 and DC-6, just as there was a Pan-Am – Republic conspiracy to make the government pay for the F-12 Rainbow. In reality, it is hard to discern exactly where truth ran out and Hughes's paranoia picked up. In this particular rant he forgot that his own TWA and the Lockheed Constellation proponents were aggressively playing the very same game he denounced among his peers.[2126]

He also made fascinating technical revelations about his own Hercules. He knew it was overweight and that it had serious control problems. He admitted that it might never fly operationally. His defense was that, even as a pure research project, it was worth the money the government spent on it.[2127]

Hughes was unapologetic but understanding about the row over the "entertainment" of the officers. He thought he had initially been blackballed because he had been insufficiently solicitous of the Air Force's needs and in particular of its visiting officers. He took that to mean he should treat them in the Hollywood way, the one to which he was accustomed.

It wasn't an ideal way of doing business, but if that was how it was done, he'd do it. And he may well have been half right about that, at least at a time when the military was woefully lacking in its ability to police its own.

Hughes simply couldn't understand that there were legitimate issues with his planes and his plant. His lack of industry experience shone through when he talked about his immense aeronautical triumphs; he had little inkling of the cutting-edge work being done, more quietly and efficiently, at Lockheed, Douglas, Boeing, Republic, North American, and other successful shops. He did not have engineering superstars, a Kelly Johnson or an Ed Heinemann in his factory. The one highly-regarded administrator that he acquired, on the recommendation of General Bennett, was Vought's Charles Perelle, and he fired him for trying to fix the problems.

Nonetheless Hughes was able to make a remarkably lucid and persuasive case for his contracts. He said that the F-11 and the H-4 were minuscule contracts in the tidal wave of war business. Not only that, HAC had successfully produced a vast number of parts for other aircraft, this being in truth the company's major contribution to the war.

He argued that if President Roosevelt had indeed "overruled the normal procurement channels" in regards to the F-11, he had overruled these same channels to demand and get 100,000 aircraft a year, the "baby" escort carriers, and the atomic bomb:

> If President Roosevelt [and others] ... ordered these two airplanes, and ordered them without submitting to the suggestions or recommendations of the normal procurement bureaus, and if they made a mistake in the case of these two airplanes, let us say they did not make a mistake in these other instances I have just mentioned. Maybe President Roosevelt ...was entitled to make a few mistakes... The fact remains that President Roosevelt did lead this nation, and it did win the war.[2128]

Hughes had an important point. In all the squabbling over contract procedure, it tended to be forgotten that the president had the right to make his legitimate preferences stick, right or wrong. It was not the plane, but the sordid details of its procurement that the committee was justifiably investigating. In the other cases, such as the Manhattan Project, the president had only tardily gone along with the urgent requests of the British and the scientific community.

In the matter of the malignant corruption he had initiated, facilitated, or tolerated, Hughes thought himself quite the victim. When General Meyers demanded a $200,000 loan from him in order to purchase $10 million dollars of bonds on margin – leaving the risk to Hughes and the profit to Meyers – Hughes said there was no "evil intent" in the mind of Benny Meyers. He merely thought the deal could be "misinterpreted." Such naïveté was unconvincing from a man as unscrupulous as Hughes. The reality, supported by the evidence of the rest of his career, was that he was in business to win, and would use whatever means available to him.[2129]

God, aka Howard Hughes, speaks unto the Nations

Biographers have argued over when Howard Hughes went mad. By 1944 the stress of business, very strange relationships, social diseases, and frequent air crashes mounted. A clue to his condition can be seen in his epistle to the believers, offered via the *Washington Daily News* after he descended from Capitol Hill and addressed the faithful.

> The Texas flier talked eagerly, almost triumphantly. But he didn't gloat. He talked like a man who had just whipped one important opponent, and was still so angry he wanted to take on another. At the start of the interview he ordered a light rum and soda, but he left it untouched throughout his story.[2130]

Hughes told the credulous that he was an aeronautical god persecuted by evil losers:

> ...I've tried to get into the airplane business continually since 1932. I've done it alone. Every time I've ever tried to hook up with anybody else, it's just been a flop. I've done better by myself.
>
> Certainly TWA is independent compared to Pan American or some of the other companies. And my airplane company is small fry. I don't mean I tried to go into great mass production. I've tried to develop an advanced experimental laboratory, and to do that you've got to have some manufacturing.
>
> And I've just been blacked all down the road. I've had the rough end of it ever since I've been in this business. This entertaining which has been criticized so much wasn't

directed entirely at Elliott Roosevelt. I put Johnny Meyer in the position of public relations, and I let him work at it...During the war I didn't have any salesman whatsoever. I had Johnny Meyer as a public relations man, that is true, but the other companies had public relations men in addition to their salesmen...

When I started, there was a deep feeling of resentment toward me on the part of the Wright Field clique. I couldn't get any contracts – couldn't get my foot in the door.

The first ship I designed and built was the H-1 – a really outstanding airplane. It was judged the most efficient in the world. A lot better than anything the Army had. I had just broken the record over a 3-km course. Before I built that airplane, 314 mph was the record. I made 332 mph for 2500 miles.

No one had ever equaled speeds like that for even the shortest distance. That really was an airplane! If it hadn't been, the record wouldn't have stood for eight years. So anyway, it stands to reason that having built a ship like that and having flown around the world without a stop [!], I've had reason to get into the airplane business.

What have Bill Douglas, Glenn Martin, or Boeing done that I haven't done better?

I made a pinpoint flight around the world without even changing a spark plug. I was solely responsible for the Constellation airplane – designed it, financed it and everything.

With all that behind me, I certainly had a right to get my foot in the airplane business. What happened?....

What did I sell? $30 million worth. And I got such lousy priorities I couldn't deliver it.

I went off by myself, locked the door and built a bigger plane than the P-38 – a medium bomber faster than any pursuit ship in the world. They horsed around for one year before they gave me a contract. Then they changed it three times.

At the start of the war I had the D-2 flying – in the air – and in my mind it was better than any other airplane. But they wouldn't buy it. For one year they stalled around.

The point I'm making is, they say I'm the guy who got favoritism, while I got a bigger kicking around than anybody in the business. It stands to reason I should have got a better break. It doesn't seem logical that a guy with my record, Congressional Medal, every kind of trophy in existence, wasn't entitled to more than I got. The reason was that there was a distinct, violent hatred on the part of Wright Field toward me...

I hope this plane will fly [the Hercules]. Given a job to build a plane which has to be twice as big as anything is one thing. Being told it's got to be built out of wood is another. It's like fighting Joe Louis with one hand tied behind you.

If I had been a bungler in every other walk of life you might say it was my fault if I didn't get the breaks. That's our competitive system, our American system. Some guys fall by the wayside. That's all right.

But that hasn't been the case. I've been successful. I've made movies. I've rolled the 300,000 bucks I inherited into a fortune. I've got a wonderful plant in Houston – an example of what the new world ought to be coming to. We didn't have one strike in 20 years.

I think TWA has been pretty successful. I stretched it across the ocean. I brought out the Constellation. I've been successful at everything else, and I could have built airplanes if I'd had half a chance.

Now I'm going back to the coast and go to work. Some time this winter the cargo plane will be ready. I don't know whether or not I'll test-fly it. I want to reserve that decision until the time comes.

If it flops I said I might leave the country. I made that statement and I may do it. I'd feel so bad I might go down to South America and buy a ranch. Nobody in the world has ever built an airplane this size and no one knows whether it's going to fly. I didn't have to put $7,000,000 of my own money into it, but I felt it was a real step ahead in aviation. I didn't want to see it end up in the scrap heap.

Now, here is a question: If the Army granted the XF-11 contract against its wishes, then who is guilty of fraud? Surely Gen. Arnold would not have approved the purchase of

> the XF-11 unless he believed it was for the best interests of the Army. I don't think Gen. Arnold played politics, and I don't think he would let anybody pressure him into a deal.
>
> Now here is one more question: If the XF-11 was so undesirable, why wasn't the entire contract cancelled at the end of the war, when Elliott Roosevelt was no longer in a so-called position of influence? [2131]

The tirade showed that Howard Hughes's grip on reality was very tenuous indeed. Most of the 'facts' he advanced looked quite different to impartial experts. But America is a land of believers, and then as now, millions seemed perfectly happy to believe in Hughes's self-exaltation, and in the vast conspiracy he claimed had crucified him.

A thought experiment can be instructive here. Try to imagine Colonel Lindbergh holding forth like that.

Yet Elliott Roosevelt was still star-struck by his fellow Texan. It would be thirty years before he gained some perspective. He was then quoted saying, "Hughes is a completely perfect example of how a person like myself could be completely led down the garden path thinking, 'Boy, this is for real. He's so nice, so friendly and he wants to do all these nice things for me.'"

But that was far from Elliott's first perambulation along the garden path, and not by any means the last.

The Air Force Shamed

General Bennett Meyers's testimony directly implicated the White House in the irregular and tainted F-11 and H-4 contracts. One reason this did not inflame the press was that Meyers would now suffer about the greatest fall from grace of any American general officer since Benedict Arnold. This was the point where the wheels began to come off his testimony.

The committee – which already knew what was coming – began by needling Meyers on the thousands of dollars of lodging and entertainment HAC had spent on him. It was the same treatment Elliott Roosevelt had received. But as Meyers indignantly proclaimed his innocence, the senators zeroed in on the extensive financial discussions he had had with Mr. Hughes during the course of the war.

Howard Hughes visited General Meyers at home several times while Meyers handled the F-11 contract. During this time, either Hughes offered him a job – or Meyers demanded one from him. Hughes said Meyers "could write his own ticket" at HAC after the war. $50,000 a year was discussed, for which Meyers reportedly wanted an immediate advance. Meyers also said Hughes offered him Jack Frye's job as head of TWA after the war.[2132]

But Meyers had more immediate needs, first a $200,000 "loan" to jumpstart his favorite investments. He claimed he had similar arrangements with other contractors and was furious when Hughes refused the scheme. So, at least, said HAC's lawyer.

Meyers said all these shenanigans were actually proposed by Hughes and indignantly rejected by him – "you'll see me in hell first." He had many other outrageous claims against Hughes, whose "damnable lies" he denounced. However, virtually all his self-exculpatory statements were refuted by other witnesses.[2133]

Since either Meyers or Hughes was lying full-blast, the committee drilled tenaciously into the proposed job offers and the complex financial scams Meyers was involved in. But that was merely a warm-up.

Now, incredibly, Jane Russell's famous breasts suddenly protruded into the hearings. It turned out that Hughes had been desperate to get his risqué film "*The Outlaw*" released in theaters in New York City. Paranoid as ever, he thought Meyers, furious at having his financial schemes rejected, had put "the hex" on him in New York.

General Meyers was a friend of the mayor of New York City, William O'Dwyer, because then Brig. Gen. O'Dwyer had worked directly under him during the war. So now Hughes thought that Meyers was behind the banning of the film, and to top it off, he said Jack Frye claimed that Meyers had schemed against TWA in the awarding of airport concessions at Idlewild (later JFK) Airport.[2134]

Meyers, whose recollections were quite different, said he had gone to California in November 1946, invited by Hughes. He had flown there on TWA's new Constellation, and he was accompanied on the trip by no less than the ever-helpful Johnny Meyer. Hughes was cordial when he entertained the newly retired general over dinner:

> He said, "Well, you stopped the Outlaw picture." He said, "You stopped the TWA Idlewild contract."
>
> I asked him where he got those absurd things from, and I do not recall him telling me…I told him it was a fact that I had nothing to do with either the TWA-Idlewild contract nor anything to do with the Outlaw; as a matter of fact, that I had never heard of the Outlaw picture…and he said, "You are a good friend of O'Dwyer's… and I believe you can get the picture released… "If you will get that picture released, I will give you $100,000."[2135]

Reluctantly, Hughes mentioned that he had given the general a private showing of his film. Meyers was more explicit:

> So the next day, which was Sunday, was a very bad day. I know the air lines were not running [they were on strike], but Howard Hughes had his own airplane, and he and John Meyer and Sonja Henie and Richard Barthelmess and I got in his airplane with Howard at the controls and who did a magnificent job of flying through this bad weather back to Los Angeles; and we went up to the hotel and Howard took me over to a theater where his picture was being shown and introduced me to the manager of the theater and asked me to sit in there and watch that picture…[2136]

This is an interesting commentary on Hughes's often-questioned flying skills. The hop from Palm Springs to L.A. can be treacherous due to severe turbulence, high mountains, and thick fog. It seems that Hughes used his special executive B-23 for these runs; he owned several of the converted bombers at various times.

Hughes said he "might" also have flown Meyers in one of his private aircraft to meet the New York City mayor, who was visiting in the Coachella Valley. As a matter of fact, Meyers testified that he and Johnny Meyer used Hughes's aircraft and stayed at the Racquet Club in Palm Springs on Hughes's dime. Meyers then hunted down Mayor O'Dwyer in El Centro:

> I told O'Dwyer of the proposition. I put the cards right on the table and told him of Hughes's offer to me. O'Dwyer told me Hughes had tried every kind of method to get that picture shown in New York, and that it would be over his dead body if that picture was

shown before deletions. I said, "Well, Bill, if that's the way you feel about it, I'll drop the whole proposition." [2137]

On hearing this, Hughes asked Meyers to make one more try with O'Dwyer and to try to sway another New York official to approve the film. That fellow helpfully told the press that Meyers had said there was $100,000 in it, to share. He refused the bribe.[2138]

After that gambit failed, Hughes wanted Meyers to argue with the Catholic "Legion of Decency" and – no kidding – try to influence Francis, Cardinal Spellman, with the aid of a sizable "charitable" contribution.[2139]

Meyers finally declined to pursue the obviously hopeless cause. That hundred grand had slipped from his fingers, too. But as usual, Hughes won. The hysteria he masterfully instigated around Ms. Russell's breasts eventually made *The Outlaw* a hit.

The incident was only obliquely related to the reconnaissance contract; the sessions tended to careen off the true path. But it does tell us about the atmosphere of the times, how business was done, and the extreme value of knowing the right people. And now it got much, much worse for General Meyers.

The remainder of the hearings was devoted to increasingly shocking revelations about General Meyers's financial rackets. It turned out that some officers had at least partially known about his extensive stock holdings in the companies he negotiated with, about his shaking down contractors, and about his speculation in the markets. Reports of his high-stakes gambling didn't help. The Air Force already looked exceedingly bad when a memorandum was discovered stating that no further investigation should be made because it might make the Air Force look bad.[2140]

But that was still not the end of the slime trail.

On 19 November, a slight young man named B.H. Lamarre finally took the stand and swore to tell the truth after years of lying for General Meyers. Lamarre had been set up as the dummy president of an outfit called Aviation Electric Corporation of Dayton, Ohio, a business which served solely to funnel large sums of money for corrupt aircraft subcontracts to Benny Meyers. [2141] The company made over $140,000 for Meyers, while paying "President" Lamarre $50 a week. More precisely, Lamarre handed over 90% of "his" salary in cash to his secret "mentor," who then spent it on various luxuries.

Though shocking, the details of General Meyers's schemes are too complex to recount here. They exposed the general as more than a common scoundrel; he was a highly intelligent, calculating monster. The climax came when a cornered Benny Meyers revealed that poor Mr. Lamarre's pretty wife, Mildred, had for years actually been his mistress – with the "knowledge, approval, and acquiescence" of her husband. The entire Aviation Electric Co. had been not only a fraud, but a toy invented by Meyers to enrich himself and members of his family, and to humiliate and use Mr. Lamarre. And all this was merely one of the general's many "business interests."

It is likely that Mr. Lamarre spoke for most people present when he finished his testimony by: "It is my sincere hope that this committee will make General Meyers crawl out of this room on his belly like the snake that he is."[2142]

It is worth remembering that Meyers had been widely held to be one of the most effective general officers in the USAAF, in particular in connection with the B-29 program. It seems likely that the same qualities that secured his professional success also drove his sideline of psychopathic predation. The new Air Force took the revelations as a bitter lesson for the future.

The United States Air Force (USAF) had been created as a separate service only two months earlier, in September 1947. It is appalling that its birth should be accompanied by a major public scandal as sordid as that represented by the Hughes-Roosevelt hearings, concluding with the sickening denouement of General Meyers, the second highest Air Force procurement official.

The USAF was deeply shamed by the process. Despite ample warnings, the service had failed to investigate itself and to bring its criminals to justice during the war. SWIC had initially gone after Elliott Roosevelt, acting on reports he was bribed. But, as usual, nothing stuck to the teflon-coated Elliott; and Howard Hughes, although hardly blameless, turned the tables on the committee and came to be seen as the persecuted character he professed to be.

Instead, SWIC ended up exposing the demonic General Meyers, and some other characters unrelated to the Hughes case. The committee turned over its records to the Justice Department. On 19 December, Meyers was indicted, and on 15 May 1948 he was sentenced to five years in federal prison – a dramatic exit for the 52-year-old "go-getter" who had just retired on a disability pension and married a Hollywood actress.

If the committee had not pursued its first hunch about Elliott's bribe, would Meyers have gone free, and been forever after praised as one of the great heroes of the war? Very likely. The proceedings revealed a culture of corruption coexisting quietly with the substance of wartime service, sacrifice, and stoic suffering. Only a fool would suggest that most of the crookedness flourishing amidst the waste and chaos of the war eventually met up with justice.

The Air Force, and to some extent the entire military, instituted major changes to create a more accountable culture. This need became especially acute because simultaneously, a great national concern arose over Soviet agents submerged within the government. As a result, the military had to revamp and greatly tighten the now familiar security investigations. And in direct response to the Meyers scandal, the Air Force created a sort of internal FBI, the Office of Special Investigations.[2143] These actions helped to curb – but not end – the worst excesses uncovered by Congress.

Unfortunately, no such mechanism existed, then or now, to routinely and continuously verify the integrity of members of Congress. It is interesting that the best remembered outcome of the Hughes-Roosevelt hearings was the humiliation of Senator Brewster; yet in his mind he had merely done what he was hired for, namely serving the needs of his best contributors.

Even with these remedies, eternal vigilance obviously slipped occasionally from the Air Force's grasp. The military-industrial complex keeps some of the best minds in the country, and many probably know stealth in more ways than one. Periodically, raw scandals bubble to the surface, as with several cases involving Lockheed in the 1970s and Boeing in the 1990s. And this speaks only to the conscious corruption; the subtle, existential corruption that President Eisenhower warned about in his farewell address is apparently an unsolvable problem.

The Lament of the Father of the Air Force

The hearings concluded on 22 November 1947 with the solemn appearance of Henry H. Arnold, now five-star general of the Air Force, retired. Noting that he was the responsible wartime leader of men who served in the Army Air Forces, Hap said:

> I am here, because some of them, at least, begin to have an element of doubt as to their leaders; an element of doubt about what the Army Air Forces stood for, and I asked to come before your committee so that I could do what I could … to restore the confidence they had in their leaders, and in the arm of the service in which they served during the war…
>
> If, to our regret, we of the Air Force did not find a rotten apple in our barrel, we are grateful that others have done so.

General Arnold was clearly deeply dispirited with the revelations about Bennett Meyers in particular. He offered that there was no indication at the time but that Meyers was an exceptionally able officer, and he regretted that the danger signs, even an anonymous letter to the FBI detailing the crimes, had been ignored:

> … I think it unfair to attribute this decision to any desire to protect "brass hats" in view of the accompanying information as to the other agencies of Government involved and of the huge burden then being borne of transferring our air power from the European theater to the Pacific war …
>
> The evidence before you would indicate that a high-ranking officer has disgraced his uniform and his rank. He was able to do these things without detection by the military. The professional services of the United States, especially the Air Force, are subjected to bitter criticism for failure to detect the misconduct, for permitting the officer's retirement with honor after arduous service. I say to you that if we were at fault in not unearthing this misconduct, it should be noted that clever manipulators in other fields in many instances have successfully covered their wrongdoing.[2144]

Senator Ferguson acknowledged the heartfelt words of the ailing general, and volunteered sadly that politicians had scarcely been above blame during war. He noted that the committee had uncovered corruption and bribery by such men as Senator Theodore Bilbo, the vile racist from Mississippi, and even by Andrew May, the Kentucky representative who headed the House Military Affairs Committee.

After this last earnest testimony, Senator Ferguson closed down the Senate hearings and forwarded the results to the appropriate agencies, including Justice and the Bureau of Internal Revenue. What had started as a show trial against Elliott Roosevelt had ricocheted through the halls of the Pentagon, bounced off the defense contractors, and past many civilians. The entire Air Force looked shamed, but Howard Hughes seemed – at least to the public – to have come out a hero.

A jaded nation was not surprised by Elliott Roosevelt's antics. Ironically, Elliott himself was merely amused, and evidently took pleasure in likewise amusing the public. The show had been a bit reminiscent of the many furious accusations flung at his father during his time, and FDR's nonchalant responses. FDR didn't get angry; he got even. Elliott wasn't quite that professional. He acted out great fireworks of fulmination in response. But he was happy to stay out of jail.

Cross of Iron, or Duramold

Recent archival discoveries have renewed the attention given to President Eisenhower's famous "Cross of Iron" speech of 1953 and his warnings against the military-industrial complex in 1961. Ike warned against the unwarranted influence, whether sought or not, of a new cabal of industrialists and military officers. He might well have added to this undeclared conspiracy the think tanks, parts of academia, the foreign policy and the intelligence establishments, and assorted other paraphernalia of empire.

This self-interested and self-perpetuating complex didn't exist – at least not in America – before 1941. The Senate War Investigation Committee hearings of 1947 are a rare, detailed view into its emergence. It was natural for Eisenhower to worry about it, because he was forged in the era when the United States had a tiny military and selfrighteously professed a pacific and commercial outlook on the world.

Systemic explanations are seldom popular. Humans want to assign blame when a problem happens, and bureaucracies are no different. Politics further poisons the pot.

Yet programs usually fail due to systemic issues; blame is due most anywhere. In this particular case, the White House shouldn't have interfered; Arnold shouldn't have given in. Elliott should have offered his opinion, but not influenced the matter politically. Hughes should have performed better, and the Air Corps should have upped his priorities. The pilots should not have let themselves be bought by Hughes – although that is a lot to ask of wartime pilot carousers. Everyone should have been alert to indications of malfeasance, and should have reported them through channels for proper investigation. And the reports should have been acted upon.

There simply was enough slack in the interfaces that the whole thing spun out of control.

For all its good work especially under Senator Truman, the SWIC failed to focus on these systemic problems and instead allowed the proceedings to turn into a circus; and the politicians easily descended to posturing where corrective measures should have been sought. Although the worst outrages were outlawed (or at least better controlled) after 1947, the fundamental problem of the incestuous military-contractor relationship inevitably grew with the Cold War. There is no complete solution to it, any more than there is to the other self-seeking combinations led by government bureaucracies.

Eternal vigilance can only blunt the "unwarranted influence." While Eisenhower understood the distribution of blame, successors have not followed his lead; usually the contractors are blamed, whether in the media or among their government handlers. But in truth they do simply what they are told to do, and if they fail, the error belongs largely to their zealous overseers. The waste may be outrageous, as it was in the cases herein examined, but in the end the blame belongs to those who cut the checks: Congress. Blustering won't get you anything – except impress the dimmer voters.

Defense contracting is no more corrupt than other aspects of human organizational behavior, but it is corrupt in different ways. The intersection of business, military, and politics is a Petri dish for unsavory deals even when honest people fight continuously for the integrity of the process.

The orgies of "entertainment" provided by the contractors and bidders in the Hughes Aircraft case merely represented an extreme version of what was going on generally. Strict rules now limit this practice, but money, like water, always finds a way. The hiring of ex-officers by defense contractors is probably more corrosive of the game in the long run; but worse yet is the hiring of politicians, an untouchable vice.

Various regulatory fuses have been installed in an attempt to limit the "revolving door" problem. None works satisfactorily, because in the end the military-industrial complex is one beast.

The fact that officers consider themselves blameless and seldom break written rules does not absolve them of process bias. Professionals usually think themselves geniuses, and their opponents malicious or stupid, and it is a rare bureaucrat or soldier who is not convinced that he works for total idiots. Because people are perfectly capable of believing anything they want, they are also prone to believe what is most likely to benefit them personally. And a remarkable characteristic of government contracting is that personal affinities and animosities usually trump rational, dispassionate decisions. Officials may pretend to support abstract notions such as winning the war, but their decisions are likely to receive an assist from what matters to them personally – such as a grudge or a favor.

Elliott Roosevelt certainly was convinced that his fierce advocacy of the F-11 was as ethically pure as the driven snow. That he waded in de facto bribes during the process was to his mind entirely coincidental. His effusive, back-slapping personality was perfect for this way of operating.

Defense procurement requires not only a firewall around the deciders, but a process of scientific honesty and personal detachment. On paper, the system works that way, but with so much at stake, it is often undercut. When politicians get into the game, like rats into the granary, all bets are off – witness the decade-long farce that finally ended with the purchase of Boeing tankers in 2011.

The Hughes case also illustrated the Roosevelt administration's *modus operandi.* FDR often did business in a way more common to third world countries: loyalty to friends and family and personal allies, not to abstract ideas, rules and procedures; decisions made on the basis of who knows whom and who owes whom. It is well known that defense contractors throughout the world often operate this way; Americans are now actually handicapped because of laws against bribery, passed after a number of high-profile scandals involving foreign military purchases in the 1960s and 1970s.

The sordid irregularities of contracting often grab the public's attention, but they tend to obscure the inherent corruption of the system. Democracy is the allocation of resources through a constant boiling dogfight of pressure groups, rather than by the free market or by some untainted intellectual process. It is corruption institutionalized. In this more general view, the many foreign officials openly on the take are actually less corrupt than those in the United States, because they are honest about their thievery. It is ironic that the contractors, the officers, the bureaucrats, and the politicians often wallow in high admiration for each other's selfless service. Very rare is the man or woman, who – as Eisenhower did – could step back and ask: Is this the world we want? Do we really not know "what else to do?"

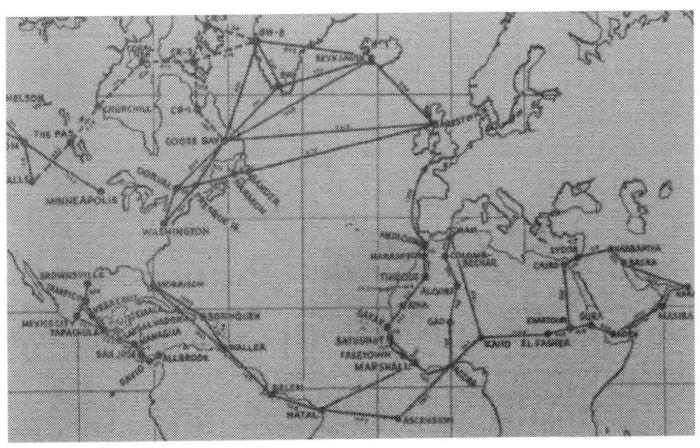

The ATC Atlantic route network, 1943. Pacific routes went to Australia and to the USSR.

V. UNCONTROLLED DESCENT (1950-1990)

Not all of Elliott Roosevelt's post-war activities ended in disaster, although even the successes incurred the wrath of many. He published under his name a number of important books about his father's administration; he produced radio and TV programs with Eleanor; and late in life he cranked out a tall stack of dreck – twenty-two short murder mysteries starring Eleanor Roosevelt as the detective, and including various villains who, if not fictional, had irritated the Roosevelts.

Elliott did not, however, get back to flying in more than an occasional way. Shortly before his death, Elliott said that he had first received a pilot's license in 1928 and quit flying in 1985.[2145] This requires some interpretation: a student license does allow limited solo flight, which he did engage in during his Gilpin Airlines days, and his civilian flight record was intermittent. FAA records show that in 1955, Elliott was first issued a private pilot's license. At one time in the 1950s he owned a Beechcraft Twin Bonanza, which he soon lost as he blew through his wife's inheritance. Despite a few attempts, he did not make any new mark on aviation, once his "life's work." [i]

During the mid-1950s, Elliott often flew Eleanor and other relatives back to the ranch in Colorado. During a scandal in 1961 (later detailed), it was reported that he jetted from Chicago to Washington D.C. for John F. Kennedy's inauguration, then flew back to Iowa from Chicago in his own plane to attend to business.[2146] Likewise, for one of his honeymoons, he flew a Cessna to Winthrop Rockefeller's hideaway ranch in Arkansas, and stayed there in immense luxury for a few days. Patricia recalled:

> Win-Rock was atop Patechek [Petit Jean] Mountain, about 15 minutes' flying time from Little Rock. It wasn't on the navigation charts. To find the place, you flew into the vicinity and searched for his private airfield. ...Win-Rock covered approximately 1,200 acres, surrounded by cast-iron fencing which, alone, cost about $500,000. The ranch had its own fire department with two engines, its own telephone exchange and directory, plus an elaborate security system with roving guards and police radio monitoring.[2147]

Bankrupt or not, Elliott (and his spouses) obviously still had excellent connections. Amusingly, Elliott's track twice crossed that of another well-known pilot, indeed of another Brigadier General. He was Arizona's Senator Barry Goldwater, who ran for president in 1964.

In the late 1950s, when he had spousal money, Elliott maintained a residence in Scottsdale, Arizona, a fashionable resort city where Goldwater also lived. Collier writes that Elliott had asked the real estate agent to find a place from which he could spit down on arch-Republican Barry Goldwater.[2148] The agent, who soon became nr. 5, remembered it quite differently:

> "I hope this is a high lot," he said, skirting a boulder.
> "Oh it is, Mr. Roosevelt, it's very high. You have to climb for miles."

---

[i] Prewar CAA licenses may have been issued to him, and military ratings can be converted to civilian licenses. Pilot certificates do not expire, but require current medical clearance and proficiency training. Even if a pilot does not meet medical criteria, in some cases restrictions or proof of demonstrated ability may substitute therefore. In a sense the regulations are merely intended to weed out the less determined.

"Good," he said, "I always wanted to build a house high enough so I could spit down on Barry Goldwater."

He gave me a small half-smile. At this point I didn't know whether to laugh or not to laugh, so I played it safe and merely simpered. I didn't know, of course, that Elliott was going through a period of agonizing insecurity. He was a man afraid to commit himself fully to a joke, lest the listener laugh at him instead of with him. I had no way of knowing, either, that Barry Goldwater was not only a friend but his locker mate at the Phoenix Country Club....

I stood beside him and stole a glance as he looked directly down on Goldwater's house, the first roof he could see. 'Ah," he said...and spat.[2149]

This passage suggests that Patricia was a better writer than her cowardly editors. In the published version, there is no spitting – just "and he stared down the mountain."[2150]

When Elliott came back to the United States "to die" in the 1980s, he again (eventually) settled back in Scottsdale, and resumed his friendship with the still healthy Senator Goldwater. The two obviously seem poles apart in their personal makeup, but at least they had a lot to talk about. Barry was a wartime ferry and transport pilot who was personally familiar with the route Elliott had blazed in the Arctic. And fortunately for Elliott, the Arizona senator was not one for grudges and sniping; more than most, he could appreciate Elliott's short but remarkable career as flak bait over Europe.

As the Eisenhower administration took hold and the New Deal faded in memory and effects, the second son of FDR still found himself sporadically in the limelight. Usually the news wasn't good. But at least this time the Republicans weren't spreading it; along with most of his siblings, Elliott publicly endorsed Republican candidates Eisenhower, Nixon, and Reagan. (Elliott did support Kennedy in 1960 and Johnson in 1968.)

Eisenhower was special: "I served under him for five years and I played bridge with him – we were very close friends – it would have been unthinkable not to vote for him – although my mother adored Adlai Stevenson." [2151]

Of course, the eminently pragmatic Ike could have run either as a Democrat or as a Republican, so there was no great ideological shift at stake. But Elliott's high regard for Ike would not survive Eisenhower's two terms.

Wife nr. 4: Minnewa Bell

Elliott met nr. 4 at home in Hyde Park. Rich, serially married, easy-living Minnewa Bell was a Roosevelt family friend who stayed over at Val-Kill in the late 1940s. Elliott said that "the John Roosevelts introduced us to each other and did nothing to discourage the interest developing between us when we were both susceptible to the attentions that a man can pay a woman, a woman return to a man." [2152]

She, of the wonderful Indian name, was an heiress to the fortune made by Alphonzo Bell, who had turned a California oil strike into the development of Bel-Air and other aristocratic enclaves. Her brother, Alphonzo Bell Jr., served honorably in Congress, overlapping some of the terms of James Roosevelt. Minnewa had a home in Beverly Hills and a ranch in Colorado, and a hefty trust fund.[2153]

By late 1950, Elliott rid himself of a number of loose women and lined up his sights on Minnewa.

On 23 December 1950, the *Chicago Tribune* reported:

> Dr. Rex L. Ross Jr., socially prominent Santa Monica physician, today accused his heiress wife of taking their 7 year old son and touring the country with Elliott Roosevelt. The names of the late President's son and Mrs. Minnewa Bell Ross, 39, often have been linked romantically in recent months…[2154]

"Perfectly ridiculous," sneered Elliott when he was found at Hyde Park.[2155]

Unfortunately, nobody could find Minnewa and her son.

During the time the two "allegedly" toured the country, Faye Emerson married musician and radio personality Lyle Henderson, known as "Skitch," in lovely Cuernavaca, Mexico.[2156] They were divorced in 1957 in lovely Acapulco, Mexico.

It seems Minnewa was a very good match for Elliott's tastes. She'd been married three times; she drank heavily and enjoyed *la dolce vita*; and she had tons of money. Eleanor Roosevelt liked Minnewa and was supportive of the two, even though nr. 3, Faye Emerson, remained in very good graces with her. Faye adored her mother-in-law and stayed close with her.

Eleanor and the White House staff thought highly of Faye and regretted her fate: "Around the White House, we all loved Faye Emerson. She never put on airs with the help and was very generous with all of us. We noticed that Faye tried to play down her glamour and be more like Eleanor Roosevelt." This maid thought Elliott resented Faye's qualities and especially the public attention she inadvertently stole from him.[2157]

The contrast with the successor was great. Minnewa was far more like Elliott: a rich inebriate, an irresponsible wastrel and serial monogamist. But she'd met her match.

Still, the willowy, vivacious 39-year-old Minnewa had a dramatic influence on her new husband. He lost some fifty pounds, getting thin for the first time since the war. Unfortunately, he also gradually lost – through successive sales – his patrimony.

Cancelling the President's Stamps

In October 1951, Elliott auctioned off FDR's famed library, full of valuable old books.[2158] Other items followed: the coin cabinet, a collection of book miniatures, a treasure of caricatures and sketches, silver, china, and glassware.[2159] Top Cottage was sold. The Campobello Island mansion went to Armand Hammer in the summer of 1952; it had been allowed to fall into ruin.[2160]

Perhaps saddest and most poignant was Elliott's sale of a unique painting. "*Tower of Katoubia Mosque*" was the only canvas Winston Churchill painted during the war. He composed it in Marrakech, after the Casablanca summit, and gave it to President Roosevelt. Elliott put it up through Hammer Galleries for $7,500. (It's probably worth more today.) [2161]

The famous FDR stamp collection was sold in 1946. It fetched an astonishing $211,000.[2162] The most valuable – and troubling – component of this sum came from initial trial runs and stamp die proofs dating back to 1896. The president, an avid philatelist, had asked Postmaster General James Farley, his former campaign strategist and patronage boss, to give him the American die proofs for his collection.

Jim Farley knew nothing of the harmless pastime, and saw no problem with paying face value for the imperforate first sheets of new issues and giving them to the president. He was soon educated. One of the sheets showed up on the market, with the seller demanding $20,000 for it. Before the scandal broke open, Farley told the Post Office to run off "a large number" of identical sheets, thus destroying their market value.[2163]

The stamp auction after FDR's death caused a riot in the philatelic world – to the extent philatelists ever riot – since the president had, post-mortem, converted public property to private gain.[2164]

Elliott himself said:

> The rarest of the stamps collected in the course of half a century fetched $250,000 at public auction. Other valuable items proved to be the engravers' die proofs of every U.S. issue since 1894, which sold for $52,955...the Roosevelt-haters fussed, as expected, over the inclusion of the die proofs in his estate, though the Bureau of Engraving and Printing had made similar gifts to every President to be accepted as personal property.[2165]

But philatelists said all this far exceeded any minor irregularities that had taken place before 1933. President Theodore Roosevelt had expressly forbidden the practice during his term; his cousin now had overridden the order.

The matter isn't quite as funny as it sounds. FDR was very attached to his stamp collection. James Roosevelt had heard that he was fiddling with it when Navy Secretary Frank Knox telephoned and told him the Japanese had bombed Pearl Harbor.[i] His other diversions – detective novels, poker games, etc. – were secondary to stamps. James said fussing over stamps was an important way for the president to unwind. But he was also well aware that the tiny government documents were a good investment, "and became quite proud of it." [2166]

On his first day in the White House, FDR had told Wilbur Carr of the State Department that they probably received a "good many interesting foreign stamps" over there, so maybe Carr could have them bundled up and sent over to him? [2167] This was merely the beginning; thereafter, foreign heads of state developed the custom of presenting complete, autographed stamp collections which FDR appropriated as his private property. In 1945, one such eminent Brazilian collection, signed by FDR and dictator Getulio Vargas, was stolen before it could be sold.[2168]

It helped that President Roosevelt specialized in South and Central American stamps, believing that other regions had been picked over. That was where the "Good Neighbor" policy began to show up in the stamp collection. The dictators of Haiti, Nicaragua, and the Dominican Republic donated valuable collections to FDR. Generalissimo Rafael Trujillo of the latter pushed that angle with premeditated relish; Anastasio Somoza of Nicaragua followed up.[2169]

The philatelic columnist Philip Ward wrote that by value, half of FDR's collection was obtained by raiding the Bureau of Engraving and Printing, but that did not include the rarities he received as gifts from foreign potentates. Such courtesy gifts are considered public property, but in FDR's case his heirs succeeding in monetizing them. Ward said it was a good thing the president didn't collect $1,000 bills or coinage. Philatelists generally held that those who purchased these stamps would not hold legal title to them. The controversy probably further inflated their market value! [2170]

The episode is interesting as another clue that President Roosevelt had trouble discerning where the public gave way to the private, and vice versa. In that sense it is of

---

[i] JR: My Parents, 266. FDR was looking at stamps and chatting aimlessly with Hopkins when the call came.

a piece with his coquettish attitude to the truth, his habitual skirting of the laws and the Constitution, and his tendency to rule by cronies rather than through the bureaucracy. Ironically, this easygoing attitude undoubtedly also increased his popular appeal.

It is for a judge to say whether either Elliott or his father broke the law in disposing of gifts of state. We can safely say, however, that FDR enriched his estate, for Elliott's gain in particular, by thus using his position; and that the ethical thing for Elliott to do would have been to donate the collection to the FDR Library, where it could have become a much-admired curiosum. Instead, Elliott soon scattered the riches far and wide.

The dismemberment of the estate proceeded apace. It was horrible to watch – even Minnewa said so. But as with the Hyde Park estate itself, some of this treasure has since been recovered, and is now kept at the museum-library complex.

If the selling of the patrimony was disconcerting, it was also odd. Unlike the Roosevelts, new friend Minnewa was very wealthy. She helped out, gladly at first. In Florida, Elliott decided that he needed a yacht, *Storm King II*, which of course needed a hired captain as well.[i] He also needed a hideaway in the Keys. The ever faster parade of get-rich-quick schemes began to crowd out all his normal activities in New York.

On 15 March 1951, Elliott married Minnewa Bell in a private ceremony in Miami Beach, four days after her Mexican divorce was approved in Florida. The state had a ninety-day waiting period; Minnewa had established residence there for the winter, thus enabling her to defeat the cuckolded Dr. Ross's attempts to stop the split-up. The honeymooners now went to Cuba's Varadero Beach for a short change of scenery.[2171]

The tabloids loved the tawdry story. Part of the attraction was that Minnewa – beautiful and charming as she was – matched her new husband in antics. Dr. Ross sicced detectives on the two, and led them on car chases in which son Rex hid on the floor of the car. The doctor got into a pulling-match with a group of nuns over seven-year-old Rexie at his parochial school. The fight over the property was protracted and expensive. Then her lawyer sued Minnewa for not paying him enough. After that, Minnewa's family sued her over her mishandling of the six-million dollar trust fund. Round and round it went, but the best was yet to come.

Eleanor Roosevelt and Minnewa hit it off, and there is no doubt from their letters that they loved and respected each other. The family said that at least Minnewa was "a lady" – some of the girls Elliott had drug back to Hyde Park lately weren't!

The two initially lived at Hyde Park's Top Cottage, but family relations soon deteriorated. Brother Johnny and his wife had been taken into Roosevelt Enterprises after his business failed back in California. He soon fell out with his benefactor.[2172]

There are as many versions of the family breakup as there are relatives, but Elliott's story was that John and Anne sniped at Minnewa. Elliott wrote that John and he, and especially John's wife Anne and Minnewa, were at each other's throats. Lash confirmed that the two couples fought like "Kilkenny Cats."[ii] Specifically, the new wife went ballistic at any reference to the old one, Faye Emerson.[2173] "She suspected a deliberate attempt to humiliate her, who had been their protégé."[2174]

It probably didn't help that Anne liked Faye and kept inviting her to the estate.[2175]

---

[i] "…Elliott, instead of saving money, had bought himself a boat and shipped it down to Florida; every nickel he got he just spent like water. That's the way they'd always done. He didn't save anything." OHI w. Minnewa Bell, 25, Eleanor OH project, FDR Lib.

[ii] Lash: A World, 386. Cats from Kilkenny were reputedly so vicious they fought until only tails remained.

Minnewa denied this later, but she understandably wanted out from under the Val-Kill extended family. The remarkable fact was that the entire scene would be replayed ten years later when Elliott showed up with nr. 5. Patricia ruefully remembered that in her first visit to Hyde Park, the others ganged up on her, glorying in digging at Elliott about his "good old days" and his adventures with women past:

> After two hours of more "good old days" conversation, some of it between Elliott and a woman he had met who had known him when, I succumbed to complete hysteria and burst out, sobbing, 'I don't have to stay here and listen to this.' My face puffed up from the emotional outburst as if I had mumps, in red splotches. [2176]

Another clue to "life among the Roosevelts" might be gleaned from this snippet:

> Later on, after everyone had had a few cocktails, Franklin Jr.'s mood changed. When Elliott was occupied elsewhere, he took Patty aside and said warmly, "We'll have to get together sometime." Not getting his drift, she asked him why. "Because you're the only sister-in-law I haven't had," he replied. [2177]

But Eleanor accentuated the positive: "Elliott & his wife came in this afternoon & all went smoothly. We were not alone but she was at ease & pleasant, he seems relaxed & affluent!"[2178]

In 1950-51, Eleanor was tiring of the radio program she produced with Elliott; she had a lot of irons in the fire, and was constantly traveling. It is disputed whether Eleanor excommunicated Elliott after he sold off the family "crown jewels" – Elliott totally denied that it fazed her at all.[2179]

Eleanor was depressed at the breakup of the "collective farm." She induced John to stay. The remaining 250 acres at Val-Kill was then valued at about $400,000, and Elliott and John were each given a half interest therein. Elliott said John paid "a nominal $10" on condition he and Anne would stay and look after Eleanor. The farm for which Elliott had had such grandiose dreams five years earlier was then leased out and later sold.[2180]

So the NBC contracts expired, the Eleanor-Elliott business partnership ended, and Elliott and Minnewa moved to Florida, where she had a *pied-a-terre* on Sunset Isle. In late 1951 they decided to build a house-and-pool at Vaca Key near Marathon, an hour out of Key West, following Elliott's own hand-drawn sketch. During the winter, the happy couple often anchored their yacht at a luxury hotel nearby in order to check on the construction.[2181]

It's a delightful place, but perhaps the quiet neighborhood wasn't exciting enough for the newlyweds. They never lived in it, but they did manage to skip out on taxes to Monroe County. The newlyweds were hit by a bill for $4,840 for back taxes and interest in July 1952. The 24-acre property with a mile of waterfront was sold in January 1953, bringing "close to $70,000." [2182]

Instead, they soon found the situation in nearby Habana highly interesting. In those days, the Cuban capital was a sort of Las Vegas without rules. American mobsters pretty much owned the city already; but they decided they wanted the island's government as well.

Feefty-Feefty, Señor Roosevelt!

Elliott was trading on his name for access to powerful Latin American connections almost to the day he died. But in 1952, he outdid himself and attempted to deal with "General" Fulgencio Batista, the sergeant-dictator who seized power (for the second time; the first was in 1933) in Cuba on 10 March. In fact, Elliott met with Batista on the day after the coup, eager to sell some new business ventures to him.[2183]

That wasn't their first meeting. Elliott had met the young dictator back when FDR was president.[i] And he had met the scheming Batista again just before he executed the *coup d'etat* that preempted the Cuban national elections in 1952.

Afterwards, Elliott Roosevelt assiduously misrepresented his involvement with Caribbean dictators. Unfortunately for him, his dealings were documented at the time by several sources in media and government.

Since January, Elliott had been working on a radio-TV deal with Cuban and American investors. Now he (and his manipulators) sensed an opportunity to cut a deal with "General" Batista to bring television to the island. The plan apparently involved laying a cable that would then provide programming in Habana. For this purpose, Elliott wanted to buy the RHC-Cadena Azul twelve-station network that stretched along the island. That was his flagship idea, but there were many others.

Another ambitious scheme was to take over Habana's infamous garbage and turn it into compost. This would require four fermentation plants with bacteria injection capability, producing good humus for tobacco growers, and at the same time save Habana from the foul smells often carried on uncooperative winds.[2184]

Either the garbage plan did not impress the dictator, or Elliott couldn't command the funds needed to pay him off. After a while, the contract instead went to a better-connected local businessman.[2185]

Yet another scheme had to do with pharmaceutical wholesaling. In this gambit, Elliott fronted for his younger brother John, and for the Donofrio brothers of Toledo, Ohio. It involved a troubled packaging company, McKay-Davis of Toledo.

There was something odd about the Roosevelt brothers' interest. John Roosevelt had become president of a cosmetics concern known as Lee Pharmacal. Through the politicized Office of Alien Property, it had taken over a confiscated German toiletries manufacturer.[2186] Now the Roosevelts and the Donofrios attempted to break into Cuban pharmaceuticals by forming the McKay-Davis Chemical Corporation of Cuba.[2187]

A few months after the coup, Luther Voltz of the *Miami Herald* reported that Elliott was also working on plans to assemble television sets, manufacture textiles, build an American-style supermarket, and construct a drive-in theater: "Elliott has talked of interesting "important" Cuban and United States investors in one or more of these projects. But now he is vacationing in Meeker, Colo., and the negotiations appear at a standstill." [2188]

The television project was the most notorious. According to Elliott's own account, in early 1952 he and his new wife moved to Marianao, a fashionable suburb of Habana. From an office in the Vedado section of downtown Habana, he tried to get back into the radio/TV business. Peter Collier had access to Elliott's old-age reminiscences and wrote:

---

[i] Batista visited the White House 11 NOV 38 and 8 DEC 42. (FDR Day-by-Day, FDR Lib)

> As front man for his investors, he finally had a summary conference with … Batista – "short, swarthy, and looking like a thug," in Elliott's later description – who spent one part of their meeting talking of his admiration for FDR and the other part demanding to be bought off with a half interest in the network. Elliott refused to grant him such a big cut and left Cuba immediately.[2189]

That version is certainly not true. Not even close.

Elliott's own, somewhat earlier, account of his liaison with Fulgencio Batista is a whitewash of the concerned, even alarmed newspaper accounts that circulated at the time. In his version, he absolves himself and indicts the dictator:

> It was my ambition to establish a wholesale pharmaceutical enterprise there, simultaneously representing a group of Americans who were looking to buy radio stations in the so-called Pearl of the Antilles as a step toward introducing television.[2190]

Elliott continued snidely:

> The two operations had been set up successfully, when Fulgencio Batista, the swarthy "Little Corporal" whom Father had treated with, seized control of the government as a dictator. What Father had said about him – "He's a bastard," gave me an idea of what to expect.
>
> All Batista's lieutenants started cutting themselves into every foreigner's business. The approach in my case came from Habana's brand new chief of police, who walked into the office one day with a message: "*He* wants to talk with you." I kept an appointment with Batista and heard immediately what he had in mind.
>
> "You should work with the chief as your partner," the Little Corporal grinned. "Fifty-fifty." [2191]

Generously, Elliott offered the thug to buy a 50% share of the business. That was not what Batista had in mind. He wanted half the profits, to start with; "after that, we shall want a more significant share."

Still according to his own account, Elliott backed out politely:

> Naturally, we parted with fulsome expressions of eternal goodwill. I went next to the investors in the radio-television project and recommended pulling out. One of them, a New Jersey restaurateur, elected nonetheless to stick to our original plan. Batista proceeded to pluck this *Yanqui* pigeon clean.[2192]

It certainly looked like Elliott was the instigator of the plans, but it later became clear that he, who had little money of his own, was only a "respectable" shill for some American investors with "interesting" backgrounds. The various proposed enterprises involving Elliott, his colorful new wife, and the dictator were well covered in the press at the time, since Elliott remained good copy. By now reporters could write about an *enfant terrible*, a *femme fatale*, and a *bête noire* all in some sort of *ménage-a-trois*. And it turned out that Batista and the Roosevelts were good friends.

The *New York Times* reported the television cable idea six days after the 1952 coup:

> Elliott Roosevelt said today that within 48 hours he would issue a public statement with respect to his plans for the purchase of the radio network RHC Cadena Azul and its

> expansion into the television field. Mr. Roosevelt said he was endeavoring to bring United States and Cuban capital together for the purpose of taking over RHC. The papers here had published the fact that Mr. Roosevelt saw Gen. Fulgencio Batista the first day the new Chief of State was in the Presidential palace after the revolt Monday. Mr. Roosevelt explained he wanted to find out if his associates and plans were acceptable to the new regime. He was accompanied by Bror G. Dahlberg, chairman of the Celotex Corporation. Mr. Roosevelt said he had taken a long lease on a house in Havana Country Club Park belonging to a niece of former President Ramon Grau San Martin.[i]

Bror Dahlberg was a remarkable companion. At one point, the State Department issued a protest after "…Dahlberg, the Chicago and Miami Beach capitalist, lost $140,000 in nine minutes in a phony game known as 'razzle-dazzle' in the Sans Souci nightclub in Habana." The Sans Souci, like most casinos, was run by the Mob-Batista syndicate.[2193]

The Cadena Azul network was snapped up by a man of the name Ben Marden "of the New York-New Jersey Mardens," who was reported to be "close" to Batista.[ii] The State Department confirmed this in a dispatch on 29 February 1952, days before the coup.[iii] Nevertheless, Ben Marden, who usually operated as a front for supergangster Meyer Lansky, was reported to be in the Cuban television deal along with partner Elliott Roosevelt. However, the American embassy in Habana was better informed than the papers. After the coup, the Habana attaché was able to report the sordid details:

> A few months ago, Gaspar PUMAREJO, who had sold his radio and television interests (Union Radio) conceived the idea of selling the RHC network to American interests. After agreeing with RHC's owner, Amado TRINIDAD, on a selling price of $1,500,000, out of which he was to receive a commission of $150,000, Pumarejo approached Ben Marden who appeared interested in the proposition. Before closing the deal, however, Marden declared that he would like to have the network appraised by an independent expert in order to determine whether it was worth $1,500,000. Mr. Elliott Roosevelt was engaged to make this survey.[2194]

So Marden, of the New Jersey mob, was using Elliott for assistance. But evidently there were many who wanted a cut:

> At this point, President PRIO, who was supposed to have been included in the deal, is reported to have balked at Marden's antecedents and refused to approve the plan which included the issuance of TV licenses to RHC at six cities in Cuba. It is more likely that he disapproved the proposal because his percentage was not large enough.

Now the smell of money ahead made Elliott woozy:

> When President Prio refused to allow Ben Marden to buy RHC, Elliott Roosevelt conceived the idea of buying it himself. The plan was approved by President Prio and Mr.

---

[i] NYT, 16 MAR 52. Bror Dahlberg, who moved to Cuba in '49, was a wealthy sugar-cane industrialist. He was a friend & business partner of swindler Wallace Groves (of whom more later) (TIME, 17 JAN 38, 6 MAR 39).

[ii] Miami Herald, 7 AUG 52. Ben Marden owned the famous Riviera night club in Fort Lee, New Jersey.

[iii] Austin, Kase: Bill Miller's Riviera, 38-9. See also the interesting observation: "American government policy toward Cuba was controlled by politicians in Washington who had close ties to the members of the national crime syndicate or to Meyer Lansky directly." (127)

> Roosevelt got a release from Ben Marden when he agreed not to present a bill for the cost of the survey, which was reported to be about $30,000. Mr. Roosevelt made an attempt to raise funds from Cuban and American interests but he was not successful and the March 10 change of Government brought his negotiations to an abrupt conclusion.

This last was mistaken. After the coup, Elliott tried to make his deal with Batista, but he was outmaneuvered:

> About this time, Edmund A. Chester of CBS came to Habana to interview his old friend, President Batista, for CBS. Apparently the purchase of RHC was discussed and for about a month Pumarejo and Chester worked together on the proposed sale which was to be financed by Ben Marden, possibly with President Batista receiving a percentage…With the financial backing of Ben Marden, Edmund Chester purchased all the shares of RHC from its sole owner, Amado Trinidad, for approximately $1,000,000.[2195]

Ed Chester was a prominent American journalist who functioned as a shill and apologist for Batista, even to the point of writing the hagiography *A Sergeant named Batista.*[2196] Here we can see that after the Cuban coup, whether it was ordered by the Mafia or not, word was out among enterprising Americans that there was loot to be had in Habana, and it was best to get in on the ground floor. But Elliott missed out; whether he was right that Marden was ripped off by Batista is harder to say.

Marianao, where the newlywed Roosevelts selected a home, was a wealthy suburb with a convenient airport. It was also the site of the famous mob-run Tropicana night club, and the preferred hang-out of top mobsters Santo Trafficante (Junior and Senior), and Meyer Lansky. The Trafficantes were widely acknowledged to control the underworld in both Florida (originally Tampa) and Cuba; Lansky was assumed to be the brains controlling the finances.

Later Senate investigation revealed that Elliott had, knowingly or not, worked with mafia kingpins in his Habana businesses. This would become clearer when Elliott's connection with the Miami Beach mafia surfaced publicly in 1973.

The U.S. Embassy in Habana was aware that something was badly amiss, and kept reporting on Elliott's activities during that spring. Finally, the legal attaché informed the FBI that Elliott had been spending considerable time looking for enterprises in which to invest, and that he was about to get in serious trouble: "Source expressed the opinion that ROOSEVELT will probably be taken if he continues this connection with [redacted] as he described [redacted] as a very sharp operator." The attaché went on to describe some other unrelated fraudulent activities.[2197]

In his memoirs, Elliott left Cuba in a huff after Batista tried to shake him down. In truth, quite the opposite happened. Elliott stayed and tried to develop one project after another under cover of his association with the dictator.

On 15 March, five days after the coup, UP had talked with Elliott and reported that he now intended to establish permanent residence in Habana:

> Roosevelt made the announcement last night after visiting Premier Gen. Fulgencio Batista. He said he already had ordered a house prepared for him in the fashionable suburb of Miramar. He said he felt "a great friendship" for Batista and had been in Habana during the Cuban general's coup last Monday.[2198]

Back in New York, Walter Winchell's finely tuned antenna-ears had also picked up a strange rumor. He wrote on the Thursday following the Monday coup that Elliott Roosevelt, Batista's pal, might "chief the Cuban Air Force." [2199]

The idea is so farfetched that it's odd how Winchell could have heard it, unless perhaps from Elliott's own fantasizing and boasting of his friendship with Batista.

But by far the most disturbing rumor was that the two generals, Elliott and Fulgencio, had somehow colluded in pulling off the Cuban coup itself.[2200]

Out came the standard Elliott denial form:

> It is ridiculous to state I had any connection or any prior knowledge of the coup d'etat in any manner, shape or form. I was the most surprised man in the world when it happened. With regard to previous meetings with the general the only time I saw him prior to the coup was last January when I went out on a Sunday to his country estate for luncheon at a social gathering. At no time was any political discussion carried on except the general assured the people at the luncheon he was certain of being elected.[2201]

It was probably inevitable that some would think the U.S. government had been involved in the coup. This suspicion was abetted by Elliott's presence and his meetings with Batista. But it is a safe assumption that the United States had no particular use for either of them; the White House didn't care much who was in charge there, since democratic government was quite an exception south of the border in any case. That does not mean, however, that lower-grade officials and businessmen of both the legal and illegal breeds might not have been left free to spin their webs in the shadows.

Although eventually no profits came from Elliott's friendship with Batista, there is good reason to puzzle over his activities in Cuba. The new *caudillo* had seized power to preempt an election he was almost certainly going to lose. Batista, it is generally agreed, was owned by Meyer Lansky of Miami and other American mafiosi, and while he had initially professed a great admiration for FDR and the New Deal, now his sole purpose in power seemed to be to enrich himself and his fellow *bandidos*.[i]

On that background, several caveats emerge. The first is that since Batista worked with the Mob, he was not likely to shake down Elliott entirely on his own. The second is that Elliott was a front for some characters whom Batista could reasonably view as fellow mobsters, and thus likely to speak his language. A third unharmonious note is that Elliott did not leave Cuba after meeting Batista, but proceeded with ever more grandiose plans.

A fuller account of Elliott's misfortunes on the island emerged when Luther Voltz of the *Miami Herald* got ahold of Thomas Donofrio, one of the collaborators on the schemes. Fully one year after the Batista coup, Voltz wrote about the scuttled plans:

> There aren't going to be any drive-in theatres, supermarkets in the American style or packaging of drugs or chemicals – at least temporarily. The pies in which the son of the late President had his thumb have exploded through heat generated by:
>
> 1. Strong Cuban labor opposition
> 2. Fear of smaller pharmaceutical laboratories that they would be driven to the wall by American competitors.
> 3. Impressions that Roosevelt was much too close to Strongman Fulgencio Batista.
> 4. Much too much talk.[2202]

---

[i] Russo: The Outfit, 279-284, believes the Lansky-Batista partnership actually dated back to the 1930s.

Donofrio told Voltz he had just closed the offices of the Donofrio-Roosevelt Industries in Habana. About Elliott, he said: "He's an easy fellow to meet – he's willing to talk to anybody. Why, anybody who wanted to sell telephones or something to the government might come to him and he'd say, Sure, he'd be happy to see that they met the right people."

Donofrio said that local opposition eventually scuttled their various schemes, although they had planned on investing at least a million dollars. The unions were especially wary of the pharmaceutical project, which they suspected would displace Cuban workers.

Perhaps Elliott got out before he was in too deep with these unsavory characters. Maybe he heeded the embassy's warning that he was swimming with sharks. However, this would not be Elliott's last involvement with the Toledo brothers of the honorable Sicilian name Donofrio.[2203]

During the time Elliott was working with Donofrio in Cuba, something "funny" was happening with the main Donofrio packaging company, known as McKay-Davis Corp., in Toledo. Elliott was persuaded to be an officer of McKay-Davis, and president of McKay-Davis Cuba. Brother John and the three Donofrio brothers served as vice presidents.[2204]

In U.S. district court in 1957, Thomas Donofrio provided testimony that he and his two brothers had contracted with Willys Motors to do military packaging, and then let some friends in on the scheme. The company was in court for overcharging on contracts to the tune of half a million dollars, and the investigation revealed further that:

> John E. Roosevelt, son of the late President, admitted having served as secretary and later president of the firm, according to a deposition. Mr. Roosevelt said he resigned Sept. 26, 1955, as president, but the firm's books still list him in this capacity…Another son of the late President, Elliott Roosevelt, served as vice president and a director and Efrain Miranda, served as treasurer…but both denied being officers of the company.
>
> An earlier suit for $220,052 in refunds from the company went unchallenged and resulted in a judgment in March, 1956. The U.S. marshal has been unable to find any assets of the firm and the judgment remains unsatisfied.[2205]

Clearly, the Roosevelt – Donofrio connection was not a one-off coincidence, and it would pop up again years later.

The inescapable inference is that Elliott attempted to relive his Tijuana glory days in Habana. The set-up was the same: a gangster government, an enormous Mob-run vice industry, millions of Americans ready to be fleeced after only an hour or two of travel. The casino owners made a big bet on Habana, but on 1 January 1959 they lost as epically as they had gambled. Fidel Castro didn't want any partners.

It is not clear whether Elliott knew Meyer Lansky at this time. The two were at least acquainted by the time he was in Florida politics in the 1960s, although Elliott denied a personal relationship; Lansky was generally unapproachable directly. By then, Fidel Castro had "involuntarily repatriated" Lansky to Miami Beach, the town of which Elliott was elected mayor in 1965. He had also unsubtly persuaded "General" Batista to leave Cuba, which Batista did along with a considerable fortune just as 1958 turned into 1959. The United States wouldn't have him, though. Portugal agreed to take him, but Batista still maintained business and family ties in the United States.

It is surely only coincidental that in 1960, newlywed Elliott and wife nr. 5, broke as often was the case, lived in Denver apartments owned by Batista; and merely ironic that both Elliott Roosevelt and Fulgencio Batista later retired to the Portuguese countryside, where they lived under the protection of Dr. Antonio Salazar and his successor, Dr. Marcelo Caetano.[2206] Batista died in Marbella, Spain, in 1973, the year Elliott got in hot water for an alleged role in a Mob hit.

The Roosevelt-Trujillo Axis

Elliott's adventures in Cuba place into perspective an attack he snuck in against a well-connected Democratic lawyer in New York City, namely his brother Franklin, Jr.:

> Until she [Eleanor] read newspaper disclosures that the Dominican Republic was among his clients, she had no idea that he was accepting fees from the like of its tyrant president, General Rafael Trujillo Molina. Franklin was free to represent whomever he chose, but she was appalled nonetheless that a Roosevelt would consort with a dictator.[2207]

In the Roosevelt family story, Trujillo pops up like a troll out of a box from time to time. As early as 1938, first son James Roosevelt accepted the hospitality of the Dominican dictator in the palace in Ciudad Trujillo, and was presented with the high honor of the Order of Duarte.[2208] Four years later, he was awarded the Dominican Order of Military Merit for his efforts to advance U.S.-Dominican relations.[2209] Eleanor, presumably not so easily impressed, visited with Trujillo on her Caribbean trip in 1934. The dictator himself visited the White House repeatedly.[2210]

FDR's grandson Curtis claims to remember that he attended a celebrated summit – "more intimate than a formal diplomatic reception" – of Trujillo and the president in the White House as late as September 1944.[2211] But there is no record of a meeting at that time. Trujillo's most publicized visit was in 1939; it caused controversy because the generalissimo was already known as the "worst of the worst," and Hugh Johnson, in his syndicated column, searingly indicted FDR's hypocrisy in supporting "the democracies" of Europe (over the gathering Danzig crisis) while coddling monsters in the Americas.[i]

But Trujillo, a Latin American Stalin who exulted in blood-baths, cunningly realized the importance of good connections in the United States. He paid well for the public relations people and lawyers who were willing to take his money. And this is where we meet, once again, Democratic kingpin Joseph Davies, the plutocrat President Roosevelt would use for his "missions to Moscow." (To be sure, influential Republicans were, over time, equally involved with praising and covering up for the Caribbean dictators: for example, Trujillo had purchased FDR's fierce enemy Repr. Hamilton Fish (R-NY) for a large sum in cold cash, and FDR knew it.)[2212]

Joe Davies early became the center of the Trujillo Lobby in the United States. In May 1933 he signed a four-year contract to serve as the dictator's lawyer and lobbyist. Numbers of rich people eyeing Dominican opportunities gathered around him. As he would in Moscow, Davies circumvented the State Department and dealt directly with the dictator and the president. He maintained the connection with Trujillo after the war,

---

[i] Hugh Johnson column, 10 JUL 39 in Washington Times-Herald. Johnson noticed that Poland was a dictatorship and Danzig 100% German. Of Trujillo, he said (mistakenly): "Of all the bloodstained terrorists that now encumber the earth, his record is the worst."

and as late as 1955, Davies sold his gigantic yacht, the *Sea Cloud II*, to the aging *caudillo,* who had become well acquainted with it over the years.[2213]

In the 1930s, Davies worked for Trujillo and against the United States, at least as represented by the State Department. That aggravation ended when FDR fetched him to be ambassador to Moscow. That would turn into a far bigger problem. At a large farewell dinner at D.C.'s Mayflower Hotel, Davies marked the transition with a toast to Roosevelt, Stalin, and Trujillo.[2214] You might say a new axis was celebrated there, albeit a lopsided one.

The Caribbean generalissimo also took care to hire other well-placed Americans. One of them was FDR's son, Franklin Jr., the former New York congressman. Drew Pearson was the first to notice that Franklin Jr. was working for Rafael Trujillo:

> Franklin D. Roosevelt Jr. has decided to give up his $60,000 contract as lobbyist of bloody dictator Trujillo of the Dominican Republic. Trujillo's latest reported involvement in the disappearance of Jerry Murphy, the pilot who reputedly spirited Columbia Professor Jesus de Galindez out of the U.S. was too much for young Roosevelt.[2215]

The murder of Galindez in New York and the disappearance of Murphy was a tough case to defend for Franklin Jr., representing Trujillo. But this was no arms-length business relationship; the two were friends.[2216] FDR Jr. fiercely defended the dictator against the American Department of Justice, saying – absurdly – that the "implication that perhaps there is some connection between the Dominican government and Dr. Galindez' disappearance is a vicious and unwarranted contradiction."[2217]

A year after the murders of Galindez and Murphy, FDR Jr. resigned as Trujillo's American agent. Apart from the maternal disapproval, the notoriety was unpleasant; his Madison Avenue law offices were picketed by demonstrators.[2218] The regime hired other well-connected American lawyers. However, the generalissimo himself was assassinated in 1961, leading to a period of civil unrest ending with the U.S. intervention in 1965.

In such profitable Caribbean ventures, Franklin had familiar company. If Elliott was Batista's boy, and Franklin Jr. Trujillo's, little brother John served Papa Doc Duvalier of Haiti. John Roosevelt represented Duvalier during the 1950s. Drew Pearson reported that John Roosevelt (who had joined Elliott's ventures in Habana) was paid $150,000 by Doctor Duvalier, and he attended Papa Doc's inauguration on 22 October 1957.[2219] By 1958, it was reported that Haiti "has retained the P.R. firm of Roosevelt, Summers, and Hamilton at a fee of $150,000 to act as its public relations consultant for one year."[2220]

Trujillo had many more American friends. Through a high-powered Washington lobbyist, I. Irving Davidson, the dictator worked with much of the American power-structure – legal and illegal, notably New Orleans-based Mob boss Carlos Marcello. Davidson also worked for the Nicaraguan and Haitian dictatorships. He lived "around the corner from, and socialized constantly with, J. Edgar Hoover, and like Marcello was a regular guest at El Charro, Clint Murchison's exclusive California hideaway."

Every time you think you are done with one of these types, he pops up again; but at least Trujillo was done in for good in 1961. Observers thought this was a reflection of Attorney General Robert Kennedy's determined moves against organized crime.[i]

Until then, these were very lucrative relationships, and along with the other Caribbean links highly influential in persuading the United States to turn a blind eye to atrocities abroad. According to Drew Pearson, the Haitian government also hired a number of high-placed Republican operatives to soften its image, tarnished then by the beating death of an American citizen by Port-au-Prince police. As Pearson wrote:

> When Duvalier was inaugurated, Eisenhower selected as his personal representatives for the ceremony, John Roosevelt, only Republican of the FDR family; Charles Willis, former White House assistant; and William Hassler, associated with Stone & Webster which operates the electric and light and power systems of Haiti. Hassler is also associated with the Haitian-American Sugar Company, which sells its sugar locally at 60% higher than world prices, due to high protective tariff. These three were sent as personal representatives of President Eisenhower, though they were actually bent on lining their own pocketbooks. And shortly after the inauguration, all three Eisenhower representatives ended up either on the Haitian President's payroll or profiting financially from the trip.[2221]

President Roosevelt had announced a policy of non-intervention during the Cuban unrest in 1933 that ended in Batista's first dictatorship, but this approach had an ugly side to it. A persistent and disturbing element of President Roosevelt's "good neighbor" policy was reflected in friendly and enabling relations with Batista, Trujillo, and Anastasio Somoza in Nicaragua.[ii] It is from this latter relationship that we have one of the most quoted FDR-isms: "He's a son-of-a-bitch, but he is our son-of-a-bitch." Although the remark may be apocryphal, Elliott himself quoted it.[iii]

Elliott remained true to the Cuban *ancien regime*, and in old age wrote:

> One of the great crimes of the century was committed when President John F. Kennedy authorized, then reneged on, the so-called Bay of Pigs fiasco. One would have thought our national policy was in the hands of some indecisive schoolboy rather than the most politically powerful figure on earth. At the time, the United States should have invoked and enforced the Monroe Doctrine. But instead we waffled, lied and acted like some guilt-ridden child caught with his hand in the cookie jar. It was a humiliating and immensely costly blunder.[2222]

Apparently Elliott had forgotten all about his fierce defense of Stalin. In his 1983 book, *the Conservators*, there is a deceptive silence about what he was advocating in 1945-52. By then, perhaps Elliott had simply spent too much time in Miami; or he had adopted the rhetoric of the Central American despots whose business and favors he

---

[i] Hersh, 257. RFK and his father had a conflict of interest over whether Trujillo should be kept. The story of the split was backed up by Arthur M. Schlesinger in *Robert Kennedy and his Times*. Trujillo's PR contract in the U.S. had been picked up Igor Cassini, a close friend and neighbor of Joe Kennedy.

[ii] The "good neighbor" policy, a reaction to the previous interventionist policy, was formulated and implemented by Herbert Hoover, but FDR got credit for it. A prime reason for toleration of bandit governments was that past experience suggested the alternative was either chaos and civil war, or costly U.S. military rule.

[iii] Cook, B.W.: Eleanor Roosevelt 2/173-4. If FDR said it, he may have first applied it to Anastasio Somoza. See Diederich, 21. Somoza got the grand tour of Hyde Park and the White House in first week of May 1939.

craved. Unlike the case with Stalin and some other unsavory allies, the Caribbean connection had personal and financial elements. And it would be grossly unfair to suggest that this unseemly coziness was limited to the Roosevelts, nor for that matter to Democrats.

These cunning dictators clearly understood that many important and powerful people in the United States were for sale. Trujillo took power in 1930, Batista and Somoza in 1933, and the FDR sons knew them of old. President Roosevelt accepted them as facts of diplomatic life. Perhaps he hid a twisted professional admiration for them, but it was for the sons to actually work for them.

The Kirschner Connection

Elliott well remembered the heyday of Habana: "bordellos, gambling casinos [sic] and abortion mills largely financed by United States gangland interests." [2223]

By 1958, the Mob-Batista syndicate ran eight large Habana casinos plus one on Varadero Beach and one in Matanzas. It seems that much of the tactical (i.e. dirty) work was done by Italian and Irish gangsters, with a smattering of chiseling American politicians; but financial command and control was clearly in Jewish "kosher-nostra" hands, and with Batista's *bandidos* getting a hefty cut.

From a Cuban standpoint it was a lucrative deal, since almost all the victims were willing Americans. It is interesting that on the eve of the revolution, Cuba was among the most prosperous countries in Latin America. Castro swiftly made it nearly the poorest, although he divided the misery much more evenly than the wealth had been back when Cuba was "the whorehouse of the Americas." [2224]

In 1958, construction began on what was intended to be the flagship of Habana's hotel-casinos: a flashy palace ambitiously named Monte Carlo de la Habana. With great hopes, the boys – presumably led by Meyer Lansky – chose an interesting fellow named Walter Kirschner to be director. Kirschner was one of the closest and most generous friends the Roosevelt family had.[2225]

Despite his being a "flamboyant" fellow, little is publicly known of Kirschner. Some said he was a live-in adviser to FDR for twelve years, but that is untrue. Instead, follow the money and ye shall find. Kirschner stayed over at the White House on 6 October 1944, and shortly after was revealed to have made a $4,000 contribution to the DNC – not, by any means, his only effort for the cause. He supported not only the Roosevelt family, but to some extent the Trumans and the Eisenhowers as well. That period matches Batista's control of Cuba.[2226]

Walter Kirschner was chairman of Grayson's Shops, Inc., a Hollywood-centered chain of women's apparel stores that once had numerous shops on both coasts. The company merged into Grayson-Robinsons, which became Robinsons-May. "He and his henchmen were a bunch of rascals on the brink of gangsterism," noted a historian of the suburban mall. "Kirschner was famous for his all-white suits, ten-gallon hat, and white convertibles full of 'lovely girls.'" [2227]

One thing about gangsters and their camp-followers: they make terrific travel guides. Miami Beach, Palm Springs. Las Vegas, Tucson. Del Charro in La Jolla; La Costa in Carlsbad. Acapulco Towers and Habana. The Bahamas and Beverly Hills. Perhaps this only reflected the wishes of most anyone who had made his money in

Cleveland and Toledo and New Jersey, except these types could afford the best in rest and relaxation.

Kirschner liked the Palm Springs area and owned a number of properties there. His main residence in the 1940s was a ranch in Indio. The Roosevelts were his guests. Local desert sources in the Coachella Valley have a similar recollection of the man:

> He always wore a big white felt western hat, white trousers, white boots, and a blue shirt. He was a large man and always deeply tanned. What an imposing figure he made! You know, Kirschner was a great Democrat and a very close friend of Roosevelt's and always travelled with him during campaigns. Kirschner built quite a few houses here…one of Kirschner's estates was bought by Al Capone's lawyer and was married to Capone's sister…I saw Eleanor and her friends, her sons and their wives. I remember seeing Elliott and his wife who was then Faye Emerson, the well-known TV personality at that time.[2228]

When President Truman left office, Kirschner wrote a check for $25,000 for his presidential library. So announced the outgoing Secretary of Labor, Maurice Tobin, who was then made a vice-president of Grayson-Robinsons.[2229] But Kirschner also had a close friendship with Dwight D. Eisenhower dating from at least 1948. An unwary president allowed this businessman to spend a minor fortune outfitting his ranch at Gettysburg. This was merely one of many valuable favors. "We are constantly in your debt for your kindly thoughtfulness in our behalf," wrote Ike. [2230]

Although Kirschner had ingratiated himself with FDR, here we are more interested in what he did for the children. Fortunately, a highly informative letter from him to John and Anna Boettiger survives in Eleanor's files. It turns out that Kirschner had first been deeply involved with James Roosevelt's business affairs. In fact, he thought Jimmy had been taken by his insurance partner, John Sargent, and he chastised him for being "a good diplomat and a good politician, but a very poor businessman." He said he'd talked extensively with Sargent:

> I took him back to the years when he started with Jimmy and how I came into the picture and gave all our insurance to Roosevelt and Sargent, and if I may refresh your memories, John Boettiger asked me to give our business to R&S. Since then I helped get one other big account for R&S and I could see no reason why John Sargent should take advantage of a man who spent five years in the Marines…[2231]

Kirschner was then working to get Jimmy into a number of new businesses, but he also "adopted" the other sons financially:

> Franklin is doing a fine job learning law in all the different departments and he is enjoying it very much. He started a week ago Monday and I saw him two or three times… we shall place John with Mr. Leland Good…John should have great advantages, as Mr. Good is a great merchandizer…We are starting John with $10,000 a year and the rest will be entirely up to him as far as bonuses and advancement are concerned.

No wonder Anna described Kirschner (in 1941) as "a very nice Jewish gentleman whose one big fault is over-generosity, and whose big passion in life is Father." Kirschner would slip John and Anna all kinds of gifts, even five fifty-dollar bills so the kids could decorate their rooms. (Anna wisely returned the money for more deserving people.) And like many other ulterior-motived friends, Kirschner made huge contributions to the Foundation for Infantile Paralysis.[2232]

Why would Kirschner want to put the Roosevelt family in his pocket? Apparently not for financial gain; in the end, it cost him dearly. Perhaps he was sincere when he said he thought President Roosevelt was the greatest president ever, and Eleanor the greatest woman that ever lived. Possibly there was another motive: Kirschner was a fierce partisan and supporter of the Jewish insurgency in Palestine.

In letters, Anna and Eleanor frequently tell how "W.K." helped out with loans when the going was tough. Anna's and Eleanor's correspondence file with Kirschner runs to many hundreds of pages. Eleanor wrote: "I like W.K. but he has certainly adopted the family. I hope none of the boys take favors without doing the equivalent in work. He seems to me a bit exotic & and I'd find easy intercourse difficult [sic]..."[2233]

To run the Hyde Park farm, Elliott and Eleanor got a Kirschner "loan."[2234] Anna had good reason to be thankful as well, for "W.K." would bankroll her doomed attempt to start a left-wing daily paper in Phoenix. After the war, Anna and her husband bought the *Arizona Times*, a weekly advertiser, and by 1948 they had lost $400,000 on the project. The Boettigers had 49% of the shares, Eleanor 2%, and Walter Kirschner the other 49%. Others Democratic luminaries were asked for help: Bernard Baruch ($25,000), Marshall Field ($50,000), Charles A. Ward ($50,000). Joseph E. Davies was another major investor; entrepreneurs Albert Trostel and Irving Geist likewise. Kirschner sank $159,000 into the venture. By late 1947, he was beginning to have second thoughts about underwriting losers. Home on the farm, Eleanor complained: "W.K. as usual makes me mad. He wouldn't accept a 2nd mortgage because I was not in it & I couldn't be because the land belongs to Elliott! He's all paid on interest & now he's taken the mortgage!"

The *Arizona Times* collapsed too. Finally infuriated, Kirschner got back $25,000 in 1948. Most investors received 1% on their money. [2235]

The Boettigers divorced. John killed himself. Elliott had to identify the corpse.[2236]

It would take a pit bull like Westbrook Pegler to sink his teeth into a related strange story and shake it. He found out that Milton Diamond was another director of Grayson-Robinsons. And Diamond, Poletti, & Hooker was the law firm for which Franklin D. Roosevelt, Jr., worked. For some reason the firm was also the legal counsel of Anna's *Arizona Times*. Oddly, when a marital spat broke out between Earl Miller, the bodyguard rumored (unfairly) to have been Eleanor's lover, and Miller's wife, somehow that high-powered law firm came to the rescue and settled the trifle quietly.

Why? "I have wracked my brain to the bone, but the answer eludes me, although sometimes I think it is almost within my grasp." This was eloquent Peglerian malice at its peak.[2237]

John Roosevelt, as we have seen, was often considered to be the "honest" Roosevelt. Jimmy said John was the least like his father and the one least close to him.[2238] Johnny was the kid who insisted on starting at the bottom and working his way up. He did, sort of. After his reluctant wartime tour in the Navy, John went to work for Grayson's in Los Angeles as an executive and merchandise manager. He then went into business for himself, failed, and went back to Hyde Park. By 1949, he was in cosmetics and pharmaceuticals. Until he got in with Jimmy Hoffa, managing the pension funds, his business life was unsettled. In 1952, he was involved with the Donofrios in Habana. Elliott said John was his entrée to the shady characters he worked with in Cuba. Was his connection with Kirschner the common link?

Some insiders reported that Elliott eventually turned over his horses to Kirschner in California.[2239] But the generosity apparently had limits, as Anna's disastrous venture in Arizona showed. By then, "W.K." was assiduously cultivating Truman and Ike.

If Kirschner got anything tangible in return for his extraordinary generosity to presidential families, it is not recorded. Some tycoons enjoy keeping presidents as pets, without seeking favors; and at any rate, most people regardless of politics would be happy to *legitimately* assist the chief executive. In turn, presidents must keep such relationships strictly proper, and most failed to do so.

At any rate, Fidel Castro ended Walter Kirschner's plans in Habana. Meyer Lansky is said to have left behind seven million dollars in cash there. We shall soon meet some of these very angry evictees again.[2240]

A new Ranch

For the newlyweds, between the sultry temptations of Cuba and the stark, lonely beauty of western Colorado, there was a raucous interlude in Minnewa's home town of Bel-Air, California. Her children told of mad, drunken parties going all night:

> They did heavy partying...Elliott entertained his friends with knowledgeable political monologues. Occasionally after a few drinks, he would climb up onto the coffee table and deliver a riotous parody of a stump speech. In the marathon, all-night sessions, Elliott was indefatigable, always the last person standing. [2241]

Retaining a bit of sense, Minnewa decided on a change of venue. Fortunately, she had an escape, inherited from her father. Thus in the 1950s, the couple settled on a gigantic ranch with an accompanying airstrip in remote and scenic Meeker, Colorado. It was named the Bar Bell Ranch, but Elliott imposed the new name "Rolling R." When they split, Minnewa restored the old name.[2242]

Minnewa later said she was trying to keep her husband from other women and to keep herself from "becoming as sunk as he was." She failed in both.

> He was a lost boy when I was married to him. I cried over him. Really, he made so many terrible mistakes businesswise. I cried over him when I was still in love with him. Really, I wouldn't say it was Mrs. Roosevelt's fault; I would say it was her inability to understand what a difficult thing it was for her sons to find a really good job with their name – and the *reputation* for great wealth...
>
> I just feel that Elliott was a lost child. He just couldn't get his feet to the ground. And he turned for love from woman to woman, and I believe (thinking out loud) that one of the main reasons that our marriage broke up was that I just had to criticize him. Because I didn't want just to feel as sunk as he was. What could I get him to do next? So I finally took him out to my family ranch in Colorado, and I started him on ranching. And that was the last thing. There was nothing else. That's when Elliott and I used to fight over the bills because they would come in and I didn't have a secretary then and I'd be sitting on the floor and have it seemed like thousands of bills. Here I was not even buying any clothes...Then the bankers came out and told me we were practically broke, and if I didn't stop giving Elliott all this money...Well actually I didn't...My money is in trust. He was taking it out of the bank. He got it through the trust department.
>
> It wasn't dishonest because evidently I signed that he could do it, but my father's will and trust deed says very definitely that it should not be invaded. In other words, the bank

> should not have loaned us a nickel. It was not Elliott that was really so much to blame; it was the bank's trust department. It was out of line. They were so impressed with Elliott that they gave him most all the money he wanted.[2243]

This was a remarkably tolerant view of her ex-husband. It would take him four years to run Minnewa's fortune and her giant ranch into the ground.[2244]

But Elliott was a great rancher, at first. Minnewa said, "He was wonderful at the Colorado ranch. Why, he just got in there and pitched in and hayed, and he even did the hay baling himself. There was nothing in hard work he was afraid of." [2245]

As one might expect, soon ranching wasn't enough. Elliott began chasing new mirages. Eleanor wrote, "his interests have branched out and he is in so many different things that I had to have the businesses explained to me." He tried oil wells and claimed to have made a "rather arid success" of them. The operation was described as a fifteen-well operation in Colorado's Julesburg Basin. He also had "a contract drilling service for uranium cores and shallow oil and gas wells." [2246]

Reportedly Elliott sank $200,000 into the oil and uranium ventures.[2247]

According to Elliott, his uranium leases were a "flop." He rather understated his involvement. From 1957 he was owner and director of Dalco Uranium. This company appears to have had a small claim in the Ambrosia Lake uranium district just north of the boomtown of Grants, New Mexico.[2248]

The timing makes it clear how Elliott went wrong. In the early 1950s, the West in general and Northwest New Mexico in specific experienced a frenzied uranium rush caused by the dawning atomic age. However, by 1958 the chain reaction of exploration, mining, and ore treatment and enrichment had played itself out. There was a glut of uranium oxide ore on the market, and the Atomic Energy Commission (AEC) had to refuse any more. Prices collapsed. So did the city of Grants. Nothing more was heard of Dalco Uranium, but there is still a hole with that name in the desert north of Grants.[2249]

By 1958, the "arid success" was apparently of such a nature that Elliott had to ask youngest brother John for a loan of $20,000 against security in his remaining Hyde Park share. Elliott would soon lose both.[2250]

On his 7,000 acre Rolling R ranch, Elliott's big dream now was to build a vast luxury resort for rich and influential people treasuring their privacy. It seemed a logical business to him, and obviously some have made a success of the idea elsewhere. But he could never get the funding together, and the project collapsed.

While Elliott was going through Minnewa's money, he flew a light aircraft (a Twin Bonanza) for ranching and business purposes. Later he would fly the new Cessna 310 Skynight.[2251]

The plane wasn't a simple indulgence. For his numerous businesses, it was an important tool. At that time, before Learjets and fractional ownerships, light piston twins were a tremendous improvement over rail and road, especially out West. That Elliott was a highly experienced multi-engine pilot clinched the deal. His first son Bill, successful in business, also became a pilot and helped out with the flying from time to time.

Mother Eleanor often came out to the ranch, and Elliott would pick her up in the Twin Bonanza in Denver. Flying a small twin under single-pilot IFR in the weather in the high Rockies is not for the faint of heart. Elliott evidently knew what he was doing. Eleanor was not worried. "She'd fall right off to sleep," said the children. [2252] Another time, when Eleanor visited the couple in Scottsdale, Elliott flew her down to Tucson to visit the Arizona Inn, where she visited again with the Greenway family. She spoke to a packed audience at the University auditorium.[2253]

Roosevelt held a private pilot certificate with single and multi-engine land ratings. Surprisingly, the instrument rating was not included. The FAA could not release further information about his airman certificates. Apparently Elliott had a hiatus in flying from the time he left the Air Corps until he got the civilian license in 1955.[2254]

Along with his brother Franklin Jr. and two passengers, Elliott was involved in a serious accident at Fort Scott airfield, Kansas, on 5 June 1957. The aircraft "failed to get enough speed on a soggy runway" and hit a soft spot during take-off. One wheel dug in. The plane careened off the runway, through a fence, and came to rest substantially damaged; a local pilot said to the tune of $10,000.[2255]

The brothers said they were bruised but had no serious injuries, so they continued on their cattle-buying trip the next day. It was the kind of accident that is not uncommon, seldom causes injuries, but is embarrassing and costly. Elliott was unfazed; he recalled his three "major" crackups during the war and said this wasn't even close.[2256]

Do you know who I am?

He got in more trouble on the road, a perennial issue for him. On 4 April 1959 in Scottsdale, where Minnewa was being treated, he was found passed out in his car along the side of the road, the ignition and headlights still on. The trooper, hauling him out for an arrest for drunk driving, recalled that the groggy Elliott kept protesting: "Do you know who I am?" [2257]

When the alcohol sample came out with a reading twice the legal limit, the case against Elliott seemed straightforward.

But again, there was more to it than this. Elliott retained a sharp lawyer, Richard Kleindienst, a former Republican state legislator. Hailing from Winslow, Kleindienst was long prominent in Arizona politics. Those of a certain age will recall that a dozen years later, as President Nixon's attorney general, he was one of the Watergate conspirators. German-speakers might also ponder that "Kleindienst" translates as "Little Favor."

Wife nr. 5, Patricia, wrote that the fiercely fought Elliott drunk-driving case became a legal landmark of how to beat the system.[2258] It is no secret that justice doesn't work quite the same for the well-connected, but evidently Elliott – and Kleindienst – pushed this principle to a new extreme worthy of legal attention nationwide.

> Roosevelt, under questioning by Defense Attorney Richard G. Kleindienst, said he arrived in nearby Phoenix the afternoon preceding his arrest. He had flown his light airplane from California after only four hours' sleep, he said, and was extremely tired.[2259]

He said he then had dinner – and "seven or eight" cocktails – with Jack O'Connor, a business associate from Grand Junction, Colorado, who then drove him downtown at 3 am. He said that when O'Connor went to check on his car, "I had moved over in the seat of my car, which was parked, and fell asleep over the steering wheel." He complained that he was roughly handled by the sheriff's deputies.

Scottsdale patrolmen Clyde Roosevelt Church [really] and Kenneth M. Pepper Jr. said they had to "hold him up on his feet," when they arrested him at 3 a.m. Deputy Marshal Pepper testified that Roosevelt had a "drunkometer" reading of 0.208.[2260]

The jury deliberated for only half an hour before declaring Elliott not guilty. "I'm very happy to have had an opportunity for a hearing in full court. I was confident that when the jurors heard the facts that a verdict of not guilty would be returned," said he and then shook hands with them all.

Unlike Elliott, the obviously very able Richard Kleindienst would go on to big things: Attorney General of the United States, and a conviction for trying to protect the Watergate burglars from justice. He would later be disbarred in Arizona for a role in a Teamsters-related swindle.[2261]

Apparently 1959 was a tough year for Elliott. That Christmas his new house partially burned after a party. Patricia had found the Roosevelts the $70,000 residence at 6601 North Palm Canyon after selling their previous Phoenix house for $85,000. The "eagle's nest" on Squaw Peak Mountain had a great view over Phoenix, but within a few months Elliott lost it, too.[2262] Both Minnewa and her mother-in-law loved that special house. Eleanor visited in January, when Elliott was still flying his plane:

> The house is built around a swimming pool and a gallery runs all the way around where she has hung the family portraits and many of their beautiful drawings. The colors she uses are sometimes daring, but somehow her house is restful and quite perfect. Her dining room has a view also out over a wide expanse, and you feel that so much of herself has gone into this house that you do not wonder she hates to leave it.[2263]

She soon would.

Given just how many irons he had in the fire, and how many of them burned him, it is startling that Elliott considered going into politics as well. However, it was a recurrent theme that the faster he was going downhill, the more numerous his schemes. In 1958, there was talk of him running for the Colorado state legislature in 1960 and then for governor in 1962. As chairman of the Democrats in Rio Blanco County, he was then using his plane to campaign for the Democrats. In 1960, he was expected to run for Democratic National Committeeman for Colorado.[2264] However, on 6 January he withdrew his candidacy, claiming the pressures of personal business.[2265]

He was not kidding. During 1960, Elliott finally ran out of Minnewa's modest fortune. She, too, was driven to drink in an increasingly serious way, and Elliott managed to gain access even to her personal trust fund.

Peter Collier remarked:

> Minnewa was in and out of the hospital. Finally Elliott put her in a sanatorium and authorized doctors to give her electroshock therapy. While she was undergoing this treatment, he tried to get a conservator-ship that would have allowed him to control all her assets. When she discovered what he was doing, it ended their relationship.[2266]

There were different perspectives on this sordid event. Elliott said that Minnewa had turned against him, and Minnewa conceded in her interview with the FDR Library that she had become quite critical; but it was hard when "your own husband cheats you" both sexually and financially.[2267]

Elliott declared that "Minnewa had gone through a harrowing nervous breakdown, calling for long spells in sanitariums. On medical advice, one of her family agreed that electrical shock should be part of the treatment, a traumatic experience for her which she attributed to my doing." [2268]

In those days, electroshock treatment was commonly prescribed for troubled individuals; but more to the point, family members also used the "therapy" to pacify those who might cause them trouble. That Minnewa, whose recklessness had alienated her own siblings, managed to extricate herself from Elliott's death grasp was actually remarkable. She kept one dear friend throughout, though: Elliott's mother.

The shocked Eleanor and Minnewa commiserated about Elliott. "If he is drinking, he is lost for he hasn't the strength to stop" wrote Eleanor in July 1960. She said she had thought Minnewa was strong enough to keep Elliott out of her money.[2269]

Wife nr. 5: Patricia Peabody

Minnewa filed for divorce in June 1960, but Elliott had been grooming a back-up for over a year. In November, he married Patricia Whitehead, née Peabody, a Seattle "socialite" and Phoenix real-estate agent who got modestly wealthy during the Arizona land frenzy of the late 1950s.

Patricia was an enthusiastic, bubbly firecracker with self-made money. She had shown up in Phoenix two years earlier with nothing but four kids and a husband who detested her, and had quickly become real estate lady of the year, and so she soon dropped the husband. Elliott targeted Patty a short while after hiring her to do his (and Minnewa's) numerous real estate turn-overs. Quite coincidentally, Patty was a pilot, although parental disapproval had prevented her from actually getting a certificate. As a youngster, she had soloed and took to buzzing her parents' house:

> One evening Mother complained at dinner: 'I really don't know what's happening these days. The planes keep coming over so low." As it turned out, she refused to sign the papers for my private pilot's license. Since both parents signatures were required, my flying training went down the drain." [2270]

Patty was a gutsy, energetic woman. Her sister said that she was a rebel all her life. Her feistiness may have suited her second husband more than her first. She was never afraid of speaking her mind, but her mind did not extend to serious matters. That conclusion can be safely drawn from her writings.[2271]

When Patricia escaped to Phoenix from rain-sodden Seattle, she heard some horror stories about a certain local resident. She wrote:

> In Phoenix, meanwhile, life may have taken some bizarre turns for Elliott Roosevelt, but it was never dull. Publicly he was regarded as something of a middle-aged rakehell who liked his liquor and whose men friends were, more often than not, carousers and philanderers. People gossiped that he had been banished from a country club after getting drunk and hurling chairs from the balcony. Paradise Country Club blackballed him on the vote of a single member, author [and fierce Republican] Clarence Buddington Kelland, whose only announced objection was that he did not wish to be in a club with a Roosevelt. After that, Barry and Bob Goldwater proposed him for membership in the Phoenix Country Club and Elliott was accepted unanimously.[2272]

Patricia was trying to sell Elliott's house. She thought Minnewa cold and hostile:

> She had an aloofness about her which could be turned on and off at will and directed at anyone. It was magnified, I think, by her incessant smoking, in quick, nervous puffs, and a curious habitual movement of the head and facial muscles, which gave her an air of impatience. I think these actually were early signs of her eventual emotional breakdown, which a friend of mine termed "acute Elliottitis." [2273]

Perhaps it is not absolutely necessary to insert another dog story here. But Patricia told one that was very characteristic of Elliott's exuberant lying, and the extent to which he would go to try to back it up. At dinner with friends one night:

> We danced, ate, drank. Elliott regaled them with stories of his life as the son of the President, and soon had the crowd laughing until tears streamed down their faces. Talk got around to dogs, and Mary Jane mentioned that she had always wanted a toy female white poodle. Elliott announced in lordly fashion that he had a kennel full of poodles. He would bring one around tomorrow morning. 'I'll be back here at nine-thirty.' [2274]

Unfortunately it was a lie. So the next morning, despite a monster hangover, Elliott found a place in Phoenix that sold poodle pups. He paid $125 for one. Patty was shocked to discover that it was, literally, his last $125. But the whelp was delivered on time.

By now, Elliott had been wiped out financially by a series of grandiose but scatterbrained projects, shady loans, his pawned inheritances from Franklin and Eleanor, and the divorce settlement with Minnewa – not counting a continued lifestyle of wanton excess. Patricia said that when they started married life, if it hadn't been for her funds, they wouldn't have had cigarette money.[2275]

Elliott estimated the size of the financial hole he was in at $600,000. He looked under every rock for a way out of it. He even asked his now arch-enemy, brother John, for a $10,000 loan, which surprisingly, he received with security in any property left at the Hyde Park estate. When Elliott couldn't pay it back, John screeched in triumph at finally having shut him out from the patrimony. Patricia remembered it this way:

> Five days before it became due, Johnny and his wife Anne dropped out of sight. Even Mrs. Roosevelt didn't know his whereabouts. We made repeated telephone calls to his home and sent letters by registered mail to no avail. The day after the note fell due, Johnny called it in, and assumed control of the Hyde Park property.[i]

The only member of the family who could reliably bring in money – about $150,000 a year – was mother Eleanor. Most of it went to charities, of which her offspring were the most persistent. The children were like vampires on her hard-won income from books, column, and speeches. As she was dying of old, untreated tuberculosis, Elliott, deep in bankruptcy, made his own sanctimonious case:

---

[i] PR, draft synopsis, 4, Drew Pearson collection, LBJ Lib. The incident is also described in PR, I Love a Roosevelt, 68. Patty was in friendly correspondence with Pearson. However, in her book she says it was a $20,000 loan against $225,000 security in Val-Kill property; the transaction enraged the officers of the bank Elliott owed. At that time Elliott owed over $600,000, but needed Johnny's loan for "living expenses."

> "There is nothing you can do to alleviate my situation. Don't feel sorry for me, because this is a great challenge. I think I can lick it, and if I do, it will make a great difference for the future of not only myself but all connected with or interested in me…I do hope that fate will give me a chance of seeing you in the not too distant future, as I do love you with all my heart. I know I'm terrible about writing or communicating, but when one is fighting with one's back to the wall, it is hard to write and wrong to share those difficulties."
>
> The reply came written in a hand so wavering as to be all but illegible. Seemingly, she said, the one way left for her to help her children was to die, so that we would share the inheritance. But she had been feeling better lately. Death, she regretted to say, was some distance away.[2276]

There would be little from the inheritance for Elliott. Years after, brother James got the following barb in, "In her last years, mother loaned or gave a lot of money to Elliott and Anna, who were deep in debt. She allowed Elliott to manage some of her money for a while, but she took a loss on that." [2277] He drove it in deeper with the aside, "If Patty thought they would be in line for any inheritance, she was wrong." Elliott had adopted Patty's four children, but only blood inherited in the Roosevelt family. This riled Patty so much she devoted a chapter of her book to the *per stirpes* – blood only – insult she and her brood had suffered. [2278]

When President Roosevelt died, James had been the executor, as it was the practice to leave this important role to the eldest son. Eleanor had enough sense to break this tradition. She was afraid to name Elliott a trustee, and she thought James had already done his duty for her husband. In other words, she wanted her youngest sons Franklin Jr. and John to serve in this role. They had shown a measure of financial responsibility.[2279]

The Biggest Little Bank Heist in Iowa

Minnewa Bell tersely described her former husband's business acumen in an interview in 1979: "Elliott, unfortunately, just had little business ability. He had imagination, but no real ability, particularly on details. He would be taken in by – well, he was taken in at Sheldon, Iowa, for instance, by a crook. You have never read about that? It was terrible, and sad." [2280]

It is one thing to have no business ability – hardly an unusual condition – but it is problematic if you are also going through your entire life sprouting one get-rich-quick scheme after another.

That particular unstable combination finally blew up nationwide in January 1961 just as a new Democratic president was taking office in Washington. It had an unlikely epicenter in rural Sheldon, Iowa. At the center of the explosion, not quite as unlikely, were Elliott Roosevelt and a little band of very bad people.

It is often hard to tell the swindlers from the swindled. In this case, all things considered, it does seem reasonable to believe Elliott's explanation (if not quite in these words): *I was an idiot.*[i]

---

[i] The following account is based mainly on Patricia Roosevelt's chapter on the Sheldon affair in I Love a Roosevelt, 117-32, and on extensive press coverage from January 1961.

A couple of years earlier, a convicted 35-year-old securities swindler by the name of Harold Kistner, Jr., moved to Sheldon from Nebraska, where he had become too well known for his comfort. He soon married a local girl and began a phenomenal business career that won the admiration of the entire town.

Kistner Senior, who moved to town with his son, had discovered a revolutionary new formula for an enzyme-based feed supplement for livestock and poultry. The feed produced fantastic results in the health and weight gain of its recipients. But the formula was a deeply held secret. Thus two new companies were created, Kistner Senior's Bio-Zyme, which produced the supplement; and Junior's Northern Biochemical Corporation (NBC), which mixed it in feed and marketed the miracle product to Midwestern farmers.

NBC had started with $8,000 and four employees. By late 1960, after only fourteen months of operation, the company had 150 employees, 27 company cars, and four twin-engine aircraft valued at $40,000 each. But the company was still expanding, and Mr. Kistner spent his time trying to drum up new capital for the miracle company.

Thus, in 1960, when Elliott Roosevelt was in deep trouble with the banks in Colorado, an executive of the North Denver Bank asked him to check out NBC and see what there was to the story. Since Elliott knew something about feeding cattle, this seemed like a good idea. It wasn't.

When the financially prostrate Elliott met with the young tycoon Kistner, each saw something to gain. Elliott walked out with an offer of a vice-presidency for marketing, $2,500 a month, and the use of a Cessna 310. And NBC now had a famous name to assist in "raising capital for expansion."

So, after an epic weather-plagued flight on 9 December, Elliott landed in Sheldon, Iowa, assembling the town notables to the music of high school marching bands and appropriately soaring rhetoric. Finally, things were looking up for the second son of the late president. Wasn't it about time?

Patricia said there were odd side tones to the howling, freezing winds of Sheldon. It seemed like some local people knew more than they could openly say. But Mr. Kistner was going gang-busters and Elliott had dollar signs in his eyes. Kistner and eight members of his family went on Christmas vacation in Honolulu. And he got lost when he was supposed to deliver a pitch for more money to a banker, leaving Elliott to hold up the flag. But Elliott was totally convinced that he had a miracle product on his hands.

He needed to check out in a company Cessna 310. Son Bill, an accomplished pilot, came to Denver to officiate. Patricia later wrote that Elliott protested that he had 13,500 hours in everything including P-38s. This is extraordinary, since only professional pilots with decades of service normally attain this level. More likely, either Patty or Elliott pulled the number out of the air. Also, every pilot knows that you have to check out in a new complex type no matter what your other experience.

At any rate, Patty wrote that Elliott promptly passed out from hypoxia when climbing past 10,000 feet, due to ill health. Bill radioed: "Pilot Roosevelt has blacked out. This is copilot William Roosevelt. I am taking the controls." This makes no sense, least of all for a Colorado mountain rancher. Whatever the nature of his trouble – and Patty said the aircraft was met by an ambulance – a recovered Elliott did pass the checkride later that day.[2281]

One month after Elliott took the NBC job, all hell broke loose. The FBI arrested one Bernice Geiger, 58, the accountant of Sheldon National Bank, for embezzling exactly $2,126,859.10 from the bank, which was owned by her father. "It's no use – the books won't balance," she confessed to a shocked bank examiner who thought he had found an accounting error.

About half the loot had been invested in NBC, whose president, Kistner, turned out to have a fraudulent business relationship with the bank and Mrs. Geiger, as well as a recent criminal record with the Securities and Exchange Commission. The bank went under; so did NBC, and the town of Sheldon was disgraced nationally as well as left with thousands of empty pockets.

It turned out that Ms. Geiger had been stealing for 35 years; indeed, she said when she was first hired in 1922, she found a $75,000 hole created by a previous light-fingered employee, and decided to keep the ruse going rather than inflict embarrassment on her father's bank. Apparently her impromptu arbitrage went well until she met Mr. Kistner, who persuaded her to invest about a million dollars in return for unregistered securities and other worthless paper.

The news broke just before John F. Kennedy's inauguration on 20 January. New friend Harold Kistner had been scheduled to attend, but he had to keep an appointment with the Sioux City jail instead. He joined Bernice there. As financial advisor for NBC, Elliott Roosevelt was called back immediately after the festivities in D.C. to try to untangle the mess. He was appointed NBC president *pro tem*, and immediately sat down with the FBI, the FDIC, and Arthur Andersen auditors, since that company had agreed to take the case *pro bono publico.*

The results were staggering. The team found that the company had not made "a dime in fourteen months." The finances had been a total fraud from beginning to end. NBC had prospered solely by the money Kistner had been able to scare up from "investors" – primarily Ms. Geiger.

This is where the unspoken "*I was an idiot*" observation inevitably comes to mind. Elliott Roosevelt remained convinced that he had a miracle product on his hands, and he pleaded with everyone to be given the opportunity to turn the company around and make it into the success he thought it should be. As his freezing, suffering new wife wrote when the debacle was still fresh:

> Even amid the disaster, Elliott's enthusiasm for the enzyme feed was undimmed. The results of the tests, he believed, were undeniable proof that here was a tremendously salable product. He hoped to buy the company out of bankruptcy and get it on its feet again. But, of course, this was impossible without the formula. The elder Kistner, who had developed it, sat on the secret and refused to budge…Not long after that, I went to Mrs. Harold E. Kistner, Sr., and tried to talk her into giving us the enzyme formula. By resuming operations, I argued, we could afford to get her son out of jail. She refused to discuss it.[2282]

They were the last believers. The nation watched in bemused fascination. "*Who else but Elliott,*" snarled the *Chicago Tribune.* [2283]

Mr. Kistner was finally located and convicted of stock fraud. Two other company officers were convicted of mail fraud and conspiracy. Kistner received eight years in jail. Mrs. Geiger got fifteen.[2284] The Cessnas were repossessed after some trouble with the local mechanics, who also had liens on them – they hid critical parts whenever the banks tried to snap up the planes. In the beginning of the clean-up, Elliott was allowed a small weekly salary, but after a couple of months of rough treatment by the receivers, there was nothing left of NBC.

Elliott appeared to have been personally innocent of any criminal act. Still, the association with what was, back in that staid age, reportedly one of the largest bank embezzlement cases ever, pushed a lot of old buttons. For Elliott, it wasn't the ideal way to start a new marriage; but in truth he was again lucky that he stayed out of jail.

Patricia said that during that horrific winter on the prairie, the Roosevelts soon felt the financially wrecked town's hostility mount against them. She mentioned that her Negro maid was especially singled out – the locals let it be known that no black folk, or apparently Roosevelts, were welcome there. By April 1961, Elliott washed his hands of the matter and went to Minneapolis for a job in touristic publishing and an attempt to run a travel club. He became executive director of Motor Travel Services, Inc., and though that gig lasted only a few months, he cleared a steep profit on his stock options.

Minnesota was no improvement over Sheldon climatically, but Elliott was able to work his connections better from there. The Democrats were back in the White House, and brother Franklin snared a junior cabinet post. Things were looking up for Elliott and Patty, though from where they had been everywhere was "up." Still, he soon soured on the travel club work and began scouting for something else to do.

Not that it is absolutely necessary to bring another dog into the picture, but after this debacle, the struggling Roosevelts again acquired a gigantic Great Dane:

> The neighbors were not fond of Marmaduke. He bayed at night. In the mornings, he liked to go around stealing milk cartons from their front porches, bringing them home in his giant jaws. After such forays our telephone clamored with angry complaints.[2285]

Not only that, but Elliott declared that a man who loves his dog sleeps with it, thus limiting his new (and far smaller) spouse to a corner of the bed.

This one (the dog) lasted four months before it was given up and flown across the country, escaping, and causing a major airport commotion. It appears that the media missed a great opportunity to resurrect *l'affaire Blaze*.

SECOND SHOT AT POLITICS

Exit Eleanor

Father Franklin had been the quintessential politician – so sharp that once in office, no man could remove him from it. Mother Eleanor was, in a curious and much admired way, above politics, although she left no doubt she was an Adlai Stevenson Democrat. In turn, her vicious but numerous enemies called her a nigger-loving communist, though that was before the lesbian rumors.[i]

The sons shared in the general admiration for their mother, and they had especially good reason to do so. When James was in France, building up the later so infamous

---

[i] "Nigger Lover, which is a term we often heard." C.R. Smith, OHI, Eleanor project, FDR Lib.

Investors Overseas (IOS) scam, he proposed that a new school for the expatriate children be named for Eleanor Roosevelt. It seemed like a sweet idea. Back came word from Paris: No, but you can name it the "Jeanne d'Arc School." General de Gaulle had never forgotten that FDR had ridiculed him, saying "he thinks he's Joan of Arc." [i]

Actually, Eleanor Roosevelt and Jeanne d'Arc did have quite a bit in common.

An era passed when Eleanor died. A giant figure in history, but a profoundly tragic one in person, she died of resurgent tuberculosis on 7 November 1962. All her adult life, she had been methodically fooled by Franklin and his family; she had been squished flat by her mother-in-law's domination; from the start she was tricked by her sons who used her as a living ATM. Her goodness knew no bounds, and her victimhood was assured.

Earl Miller, her attentive bodyguard, remembered many instances of Americans writing heartbreaking, sob-story letters to the first lady, getting a few dollars in return, only for police to tell Eleanor she'd been conned again. The Communists had done something similar to her in the 1930s in the political sense; by 1941 she was deeply wary of them.[2286]

Her lesbian friends at Val-Kill's Stone Cottage exploited her shamelessly; Elliott said that when he came back in 1945, they had to be bought off with a "large amount," which he wouldn't enumerate, before they could be made to move out.[2287] However, in *Mother R* (1977), he said: "Mother forked out something more than $30,000 for their 2/3 interest" – quite a sum to get rid of somebody. Elliott added that both he and Eleanor made themselves scarce until they were sure the two ladies had decamped.[2288]

By today's standards, it seems very likely that Eleanor suffered from clinical depression throughout her life, exacerbated almost to the terminal point by her discovery of Franklin's betrayal. At 78, desperately ill and tired of it all, Eleanor Roosevelt tried to will herself to die, fighting against every medical effort to prolong the agony. Yet even her demise was an occasion for family dispute.

> As the end approached, she made it clear that there were two family members who were not welcome in her room: "I do not want to see Elliott and I will not see Patty." When Anna passed her mother's wishes on to her brother, Elliott reacted by saying he would never speak to her again.[2289]

Anna claimed that version. There were, however, as many versions as there were Roosevelts. Minnewa Bell said it was all her successor's fault:

> She met Patty, and well, they just didn't get along. I think you'll find that none of the family liked Patty; what Patty has for Elliott is something that is his own personal business. Evidently she has something for him because he's stayed with her the longest of anybody. That's the way it is, but nobody likes her in the whole family, that I know of. But Mrs. Roosevelt never broke with Elliott. No, no. She probably would not let Patty in. Perhaps Elliott wouldn't go in – oh, I can't believe Elliott wasn't in there, didn't go to see her, or couldn't go to see her.[2290]

This is most emphatically not the account Patricia gave in 1967. We are indebted to her for a very detailed and highly unofficial account of the ex-First Lady's death.

---

[i] JR: My Parents, 205-6. IOC was in Switzerland but the school was proposed for Ferney Voltaire, France.

Patricia wrote in her draft memoir (not the published one) that the siblings fought like cats and dogs, although Eleanor herself was full of forgiveness while trying her damnedest to die as she lay defenseless in her New York apartment. Anna took charge and ordered the others around "like wooden soldiers." Anna's doctor husband, James Halsted, fought with Eleanor's long-time friend, Dr. David Gurewitsch over her treatment. She does not seem to have received good medical care: "aplastic anemia" was the best diagnosis the hospital could contrive. (Gurewitsch suspected the tuberculosis and at one time had her improving on antibiotics.)[2291]

Patricia wrote that Elliott couldn't be there all the time, for despite her best efforts, Eleanor took a long time about dying. Patty and Elliott were in Miami Beach when Franklin Jr. called them with the news. Then they went up to New York for the expected rounds of sorrow and regrets.[2292]

Nevertheless, emotional, Catholic Patricia was struck by the "seeming unconcern and lack of real mourning in the family. People were laughing and talking and appeared little concerned. Elliott was openly upset by this." [2293]

At least until the will was read. Then the siblings went for each other's throats again. "To my son Elliott what remains of Grandmother Hall's pink china and two silver serving trays…" The sons, except John, had squandered their monetary inheritances already.[2294]

Patricia made sure to get another dig in at the hated, "grasping" in-laws. She wrote to Drew Pearson:

> As Mrs. Roosevelt was lowered into her grave, Anna and Johnny ordered her cottage padlocked pending distribution of the estate, claiming they mistrusted the servants. By the time the actual distribution of personal effects was made, Anna and Johnny had the choice things cleaned out.[2295]

Patty did not mention something she had done to Eleanor on her death bed, but Joe Lash did. He wrote:

> When Trude saw her last week she was very depressed and somehow tied her illness together with Elliott and his new wife Patricia…She repeatedly said that she did not wish to go on living. Patty had called and said she and Elliott would need $1500 a month and it was up to the family to find it…Mrs. R turned over to the three other boys the job of getting Elliott out of his jam.[2296]

Those who find it hard to believe Patty's version might consider the testimony of the grandchildren, who were "frightened:"

> Tony Roosevelt: Remember the battles that apparently they had at her funeral?
>
> Lindsley: Oh, gosh. Well, I wasn't even going to mention that! <Laughter> All I said was that it went on until after her death. It was very, <u>very</u> bad. Very bad. But I think our generation is completely – we are not like they are.[2297]

Soon, though, Elliott would cash in on three books about Eleanor and her struggles – not counting the later fiction starring his mother as the spunky, clever detective. Eleanor died without the further indignity of knowing that forty years after her death she'd still be toiling for Elliott's estate as a detective in cheap novels.

Peter Collier described Eleanor's tragedy with eloquent brutality:

> ...when her own children wanted to cash in on the FDR heritage – one writer compared it to insects who hatch inside the corpse of a parent and eat their way out – she was powerless to stop it. It was something her husband had tacitly encouraged during his life by participating in their shady deals. Moreover, she had gotten in a position, as she admitted to friends, where she could not deny her children anything. She was particularly unable to say no to Elliott, the child who best understood her weaknesses and most adroitly played on her guilts and aspirations.[2298]

Shortly before she died, Eleanor had sent Elliott her $3,000 tax refund, pathetically regretting she could do only so much.[i]

Tropical Politics

Elliott had soured on the travel-club job during 1962, and business connections had persuaded him there were better opportunities in Miami, Florida, which was increasingly the gateway to Latin America. There, the new Alliance for Progress created great interest in securing U.S. loans for projects both public and private. As Patty said: "A shrewd and knowledgeable business consultant, based in Miami and working as an adviser and intermediary, could do quite well." [2299]

As 1963 dawned across Biscayne Bay, the Roosevelts settled into a ten-bedroom mansion on the waterfront. Martin Jones, who had been in the Eleanor-Elliott radio business, seems to have been instrumental in convincing Elliott that Miami was the perfect location for his new business selling access and influence. Elliott Roosevelt International was soon involved with projects in Latin America. For example, in October, the couple received a quasi-state-visit reception when meeting with Guillermo Valencia, president of Colombia. Since Elliott had no official title, he was operating on name recognition and bluster. Whether he did secure the loans he promised for infrastructure process was not clear to Patty when she wrote about the visit; she, a dog-fancier, was very preoccupied with the project of gifting the Colombian president with two rare Fox Hounds, a breed she had been discreetly told His Excellency wished to obtain from the United States. That turned into another major canine travel debacle; but we'll let that one alone.[2300]

In the meantime, John and Anne told Victor Hammer to auction off Eleanor's last belongings. Now it was for the Elliott Roosevelts to be appalled; Patty said she and Elliott bought $7,000 worth of them. If this seems an odd turnaround for a bankrupt man who "didn't have cigarette money" two years earlier, it is useful to remember that being broke didn't mean the same to the Roosevelts as it did to ordinary people. Elliott would always have speaking fees, book royalties, and various courtesy appointments to draw on. Thus the couple hired much help for their new house – even Eleanor's former servants, whom Patty, perhaps maliciously, said now felt unwelcome in Hyde Park and ill-treated by the rest of the family.[2301]

Elliott Roosevelt always seemed much better suited to the slippery world of politics than to the exacting one of aviation. It is no exaggeration to say that his reputation had preceded him, though, and there would be no real political breakthrough for him.

---

[i] ER: Mother R., 268; PR: I Love, 180. ER promised to make the gift "a loan."

Nonetheless, neither James, Elliott, nor Franklin Jr. could resist the siren song of politics. They would not be able to live up to their own ambitions. In a portrait of the "clumsy, irresponsible, likeable young hellion" Elliott, an analyst wrote as early as 1941:

> His older brother Jimmy was his father's favorite – suave, well-groomed, with a turn for public speaking and a taste for politics and the society of the well-born. His mother seems to have favored the intractable Elliott. 'He is the Roosevelts' problem child,' she said.[2302]

"Crown Prince" James was viewed with great suspicion by many political observers while his father was still alive. Jesse Jones went so far as to say that in June 1944, Jimmy was maneuvering in the shadows to become Assistant Secretary of the Navy, which had been the "Prince of Wales" posting for his father. Jones wrote that "if the President could be assured that his son James would be appointed" to this post, the president would not seek reelection.[2303] It is hard to know how much to make of this; it is hardly conceivable that Jimmy could have overcome the intense resistance, even among Democrats, that he had already stirred up.

James, despite a very checkered financial past, did serve as a Democratic congressman from California from 1955 to 1965. The well-reported sleaziness of his domestic situation somehow did not stop him from making brigadier general in the Marine Corps Reserves. Like Elliott, politically he switched his support as it suited him, although he remained a vocal Democrat.

Jimmy had no money of his own, but he attracted money for his campaigns. One of the biggest investors was a constituent whose business was still headquartered in Culver City. His name: Howard Hughes. James had met Howard during his Hollywood days, and now Hughes asked to meet him again. After a long mysterious night ride, Jimmy recalled, he was delivered to Howard, who asked how Elliott was doing, and after further polite conversation handed him $5,000. Hughes supported each of James Roosevelt's campaigns thereafter with the same amount.[2304]

That was legal, and maybe all there was to it. Tycoons usually try to cover both flanks. Howard Hughes was accustomed to paying large bribes to both parties. Noah Dietrich himself said he paid $100,000 to the Democratic National Committee to drop a criminal case against one of the Hughes companies. Many other transactions of similar character involving Hughes surfaced during the Watergate investigation.[2305]

Jimmy's career was punctuated by several upsets. Early on, Drew Pearson noted that "Jimmy probably made as many political enemies as it was possible for one human being to make." And later on, "Jimmy had got himself thoroughly disliked, politically and otherwise; had been blackballed by the prominent clubs, and was doing no one, particularly his family, any good." [2306]

Patty thought Jimmy "perhaps the least gullible" of the Roosevelts. Although he was considered far more stable than Elliott, his four marriages point to some of the same issues. His second divorce in 1954 revealed to all his industrial-scale philandering and uninhibited high-life. His wife Romelle's attempted blackmail and financial evisceration of him preoccupied the gossipers during much of 1954.[2307]

Significantly, the James-Romelle scandal had its roots during FDR's presidential tenure, and had been carefully suppressed at the time. The detailed, enumerated confession James had been forced to sign in 1945 was part of the blackmail. Jimmy borrowed $100,000 from his mother, then spent $75,000 to buy back the document from Romelle. She made a copy and kept the money. The mess left James financially and emotionally shattered, although he still managed to gain his central L.A. seat in Congress. It was said to be the one district where he could not possibly lose. [2308]

The blackmail letter was dated 27 February 1945. It named nine women. (Three more were named as co-defendants, meaning they still had affairs within the two-year statute of limitations.) Jimmy had been forced to write:

> I feel that I owe to you again to assert that during said period I have engaged in a course of conduct involving a succession of active adultery, disloyalty and deceptions which have caused you great and continuing mental and physical suffering. I also feel that I should again assert that prior to our marriage that I misrepresented my own character and my past life in an inexcusable manner.[i]

The family thought the debacle would be devastating to James; that not only would it cause him to drop his political campaign, but perhaps even to kill himself. That was why Eleanor sent Elliott out to talk sense to him. But Elliott found that while Jimmy was damaged, he was definitely not sorry:

> [Elliott]: "With your head bowed under the barrage of these frightful accusations, the only course open is for you to withdraw from public life." – Jimmy glared. "My head is *not* bowed, Elliott." He turned to his attorney, Sam Pecone. "Do you agree that the only thing for us to do is to fight this thing through and win?" Pecone nodded.[2309]

Elliott attended the press conference at which Jimmy returned fire on Romelle. Jimmy said he had had to sign to save his father the "horror" of further wartime burdens, and having been worn down by Romelle's "insatiable" demands for material things.[2310]

The court battle occupied the newspapers for weeks. The details, financial and otherwise, painted a truly revolting picture of Mr. Roosevelt, perhaps only slightly less so of his wife. The Roosevelt clan stuck together under this siege, but it must have been hell for the three young children.

Jimmy did win his seat in Congress. Romelle won only half of the $3,500 a month she had demanded. It had actually been she who tried to kill herself, per police records on 16 April 1948, leaving last words: "I'm too tired for any other course, waste no prayers on me but pray the children will not be like Jimmy or me." [2311]

Still, his marital excitements were not over by half. Told she was no longer needed, his third wife stabbed him eight times in the back – with his own Marine combat knife no less, yet failed to kill him. James said it might have had something to do with his work at the gigantic Swiss swindle, IOS, where kingpin Bernie Cornfeld made sure large numbers of desirable female bodies were always displayed and available.[2312]

James left the House in 1965 for a United Nations job. But amusingly, during the Democratic Convention in Atlantic City in August 1964, he pulled a nostalgic aviation stunt: to the joy of reporters and photographers, American Airlines flew him from Washington to the convention in its museum-piece Ford Trimotor. Just like Papa.[2313]

Franklin Junior, a lawyer and FIAT dealer, also had several medium-rank roles in Democratic politics. He served in the House of Representatives from New York City

---

[i] UPI/Star News, 30 JAN 54. There were actually two letters, same dates, and JR now disavowed them.

from 1949 to 1955. He married five times. The Democratic Party machinery turned against him, and his comeback efforts met with ever increasing failure.[2314]

Young Franklin was a disaster in Congress. James said he was lazy, unreliable and thought the job "beneath him," which fits with some of the accounts from his law practice. Franklin had one of the worst congressional attendance records ever, and House leader Sam Rayburn told James not to waste his time like his brother had done. In general, the Roosevelt kids were damaged goods in the Democratic Party after 1945, but at the urging of Joe Kennedy, Franklin Jr. did attach himself to young senator John F. Kennedy's campaign in 1960.[2315] Franklin's active campaigning in West Virginia is generally credited with securing that absolutely crucial state for JFK on 10 May 1960. This bought Franklin a post as Under-Secretary of Commerce, but he had expected better. However, old Joe didn't take chances, and according to Tip O'Neill (D-MA), he lubricated the critical people in West Virginia with cash before the vote.[2316]

Apparently Franklin did well selling FIATs (he was a friend of Gianni Agnelli), but his partner sued him for $9 million for "scheming" to swindle him out of the business.[2317] Despite this, his work for Trujillo, two tax fraud cases, and some accidents while driving with a suspended license, JFK appointed him to the subcabinet post in January 1963; he served for two years.[2318]

Family traits predominated. A reporter who covered one of Franklin's campaigns wrote that, "between speeches, Roosevelt, sitting in the front of the car, reached under the seat as the car pulled away and took frequent nips from a pint of whisky."[2319]

Politically and in other ways, kid brother John Aspinwall Roosevelt was the "traitor to his class." He went Republican early, never entered politics on his own behalf, and he only married twice. He also appeared to be generally successful in business, and avoided scandal if not always dubious involvements.

Whether supporting Democrats or Republicans, Elliott got along with none of his siblings. His sister Anna, who was active in Democratic causes, had been closer to Elliott initially. His later support for Eisenhower, Nixon, and Reagan alienated him from core Democratic operators.

Always eager to register his opinions, Elliott Roosevelt did make many political forays and maintained links with the Democratic establishment as well as the Kennedys. The Democratic convention in Los Angeles in 1960 was attended by three Roosevelt delegates pledged to John F. Kennedy: James, from California; Elliott, from Colorado; and Franklin Jr. from New York. But once again, all were not quite in line; Eleanor remained steadfastly loyal to the more cerebral Adlai Stevenson.[2320]

By the time Lyndon B. Johnson was elected president in 1964, the Roosevelt kids were suddenly out in the cold again. It hurt Elliott, who was now living in Miami and trying to scare up business with Latin American governments. He said he'd be happy to serve as an ambassador-at-large in the region. He mentioned that he had already flown 150,000 miles in sixteen months. Confirming LBJ's frequent assertion that President Roosevelt had been like a second father to him, he said "We three became great friends and I'd consider it a privilege to work for him." But Lyndon no longer found Elliott useful.[2321] It must have riled Elliott, who told his wife he had been responsible for starting LBJ's career – although he didn't mention receiving any payment for it.[2322]

Elliott, once again enmeshed in dubious deals, failed to gain political traction until he was elected National Democratic Committeeman from Florida in 1964. He handily beat all his opponents during the Democrats' primary election despite being viewed as an outsider by the political establishment.

Elliott was well-connected in Miami. One of his pals was the politician once known as "Red Pepper." Claude Pepper, now a Congressman, had switched to being a strong advocate for the senior set, which dominated Miami Beach. That particular constituency was one of the most demographically exceptional in the nation.

Patricia, writing to Drew Pearson, made some interesting observations about how Elliott was talked into running for office:

> In October of 1963, a group of affluent businessmen invited Elliott to lunch at the Miami Club and asked him to run for Democratic National Committeeman for Florida....they assured him the campaign wouldn't take any time or cost him a dime, they would line up all his workers, handle all the mailing, etc.[2323]

Patricia said this race cost $48,000. It seemed insane to spend that much for an unpaid post, but many tried and failed while Elliott succeeded. Clearly, there were other incentives than the salary.

There was a dark side to Elliott's victory. As Patricia reported, Elliott "somehow managed to nimbly avoid any public utterance" on the civil rights controversy of the time. This issue inflamed the public in 1964, especially in the South.[2324]

Even more disturbingly, Patricia noted:

> By coincidence, the night before we were to visit St. Augustine my cousin, Mrs. Endicott Peabody, mother of the Massachusetts governor, was jailed as a civil rights demonstrator. Elliott's sponsor ...pleaded, 'For God's sake, Patty, don't tell them your maiden name or who your relatives are. They'll run you out of town.' I kept it quiet.[2325]

Although this sounds like the vilest of cowardice, perhaps it isn't if the politician involved has no convictions to begin with.

The DNC position was normally rather irrelevant, but ambitious people could make something of it, considering that it entailed constant socializing with important people in Washington. Elliott stated that it was perfect for him, since he was already spending two or three days a week in D.C. The reason was that his occupation now was to aid Latin American businesses in "their dealings with financial agencies of the U.S. government and the World Bank."[2326] Elliott made numerous arrangements for Latin American businessmen to visit the United States, said Patricia, and invariably they came through Miami.[2327]

As the president of Elliott Roosevelt International, which he described variously as a management consulting, investing, or public relations venture, Elliott primarily sold his name. One report of his business operations quickly found its way to secret police chief J. Edgar Hoover.

Certain individuals whose names can still not be released were interested in opening a savings-and-loan association in the Miami area. For that they needed federal permission, which was hard to get – unless you talked with one Elliott Roosevelt, they had heard. Best to let the FBI report speak for itself:

> Dept. of Justice furnished information that [--], applicants for a charter from the Federal Home Loan Bank Board, were advised during a discussion of their application with [partner] and Elliott Roosevelt, that a favorable result on the application could be obtained

by paying $7,500 expenses to [partner] and Roosevelt. A contingency payment of $42,000 to these two individuals was also to be arranged. It was indicated part of this payment would go to [--], Member of FHLBB.[2328]

The report went on to provide details of a meeting in which Elliott demanded the non-refundable "expenses" and the balance of $42,500 to be placed in escrow pending approval of the application. He said that he knew "everyone" in Washington and implied, but did not openly state, that he could get the charter approved. He asked if the applicants had a corporate vehicle through which the funds could be funneled, offering to prepare papers to support the necessary fictitious justifications for the exchange.

> Both [---] and [---] stated that they became convinced that Roosevelt was more interested in the $7,500 fee for "expenses" than he was in the $42,500 and it was their opinion Roosevelt was running a little "deal" and trading on his name. They were of the opinion he would do nothing whatsoever for the group and they decided they would have nothing to do with him.[2329]

More dismayed than angry, the applicants consulted a lawyer, and through that channel the FBI was eventually notified. The investigation results were forwarded to the Department of Justice, which decided to take no further action.

The episode is unusual for having received the attention of law enforcement. Patricia wrote that she managed to abort a similar scheme when the two were living in Minneapolis: "A kingpin in Minnesota vice circles was in trouble with the Justice Department. Would Elliott use his influence in Washington to get him off the hook? There was money in it, perhaps $25,000 in cash." [2330]

She, not Elliott, threw out the "vice lord's emissary." But she couldn't forever watch the gate.

Influence-peddling was Elliott's ambition, but how much access did he really have? The bank incident occurred after he was elected to the DNC. Yet despite his efforts, the Democratic Party was still far from fond of him. During 1964, Elliott methodically ingratiated himself with the Jewish and Cuban communities in Miami, even leading tours to Israel. A more disturbing indication of how low he could stoop was his attack on his friend Barry Goldwater, who, that same fall, ran a doomed campaign for president:

> President Johnson as U.S. senator never belonged to a pro-Civil Rights organization, while Goldwater did; Johnson took no part in integration moves in Texas, while Goldwater integrated his department store. If I have the opportunity to tell the southern voters of this country the truth I will tell them of the dangers of a Goldwater administration and point out that a Johnson administration can be expected to be far more understanding of the point of view of all white southerners as he is one himself.[2331]

At least Eleanor Roosevelt, the Negroes' friend, would not have to read those lines.

The limits of patience were better seen in the national Democratic reaction to Elliott's noises from Florida. As the reader will recall, Elliott Roosevelt had been instrumental in jump-starting Lyndon Johnson's political career in 1937. Now Lyndon would not return his calls. The exceptionally well-informed columnist Drew Pearson nailed the matter down just before Election Day, on 30 October 1964:

In 1937, when a young Texan named Johnson wanted to get aboard the special train of President Franklin D. Roosevelt, en route through Texas from Aransas Pass, he phoned Elliott Roosevelt. "I'm running in a special election for Congress down here," the young Texan said, "and I need your help." If I can get aboard your father's train it will be a big boost."

Elliott got young Johnson aboard the Roosevelt train and he was elected to Congress...That began LBJ's real start in politics. Earlier, Elliott and Lyndon Johnson had become acquainted while speaking at a political rally in Texas in the 1932 election. Subsequently, Elliott introduced Lyndon to his father, who appointed the gangling young Texan National Youth Administrator for Texas.

"During the war," recalls Elliott, "I was home on leave when father was trying to decide what to do about some of the Congressmen who were on duty overseas, including Lyndon. 'You should bring him back here. He could be much more useful in Washington,' I advised."

"But now that he's President," mused Elliott, "I can't even get him on the phone." Elliott referred to the fact that when he was in Washington this month he had asked to see the President, but was told by one of the young blades around the White House, "Wait until after the election. We can't afford to antagonize George Smathers."[2332]

Senator Smathers's man had been defeated by Elliott in the DNC race and Smathers was still angry. Elliott was frozen out in internal Democratic politics and never was allowed to play on the national level. In November 1966, the White House ran an FBI check on Elliott, as is often done either to vet someone for further use, or to look for useful dirt. The FBI pointed out the bribe solicitation to the savings and loan, but stated that no further pertinent information was available.[2333]

Nonetheless, clues on the cover of a non-releasable file suggest Elliott's correspondence or telephone was under surveillance in 1963 in regard to "RUSSIA." No conclusions can be drawn from this; but unlike routine monitoring of foreign contacts, this effort had the attention of a collection of top FBI officers.[2334]

Very special Mayor of a very special Town

Locally, Elliott was more successful and much better connected. In June 1965, he was elected mayor of Miami Beach. He'd been a resident for only two years, making a living as a Latin American trade promoter in addition to his influence-peddling consultancy.

Patricia said that in November 1964, three extremely wealthy local Jewish businessmen came to Elliott and offered to manage and bankroll a run for mayor: "We've needed somebody like you for years, Elliott. You won't have to worry about a thing. It's in the bag. Big money behind you. We'll make all arrangements, etc., etc." [2335]

The man on the ballot usually doesn't matter as much as the men behind him. They can be hard to find, but Patty provided a good start in her published memoir, where she got carelessly specific:

> A group of about seven respected men were interested in finding the best possible candidate to run for mayor and the three expiring councilmen terms. Each was pledged to put up $3,000, providing a total fund of about $21,000 for the campaign.[2336]

At the time she wrote, she did not know that most of Elliott's "rich Jews" would soon be in jail. She mentioned Louis E. Wolfson, Max Orovitz, and Joseph Weintraub as the front men for several others. Vice-mayor and prominent builder Robert Turchin, attorney Murray Goodman (associated with local mob power-broker Ben Cohen), and Malvin Englander were among the early supporters.

Some of these names (though not Weintraub, who was a respected local banker) showed up in the *Miami Herald*'s exposure of mobsters secretly running Miami Beach.[2337] Wolfson, whom Patty declared "the spokesman," was then one of America's richest men. He is known to business history as the first corporate raider. He later served jail time for unregistered securities fraud. He claimed to have spent over one million dollars funding suitable political candidates nationwide. The high-profile Wolfson scandal drew many famous names into public scrutiny and eventually caused the resignation of Supreme Court Justice Abe Fortas, who had accepted a "life stipend" of an annual $20,000 from Wolfson.[i]

Max Orovitz was also later convicted on federal charges for illegal stock transactions involving Swiss banks. Orovitz had two identities; the visible one as a successful entrepreneur, philanthropist, and Israel-backer. The second *persona* shows up in innumerable accounts of the Mob's operations in Miami Beach, where he is usually seen as a Lansky lieutenant and a facilitator of money laundering and development of the Bahamian casinos. He was a bank director whom U.S. Attorney Robert Morgenthau accused "as having taken millions of dollars through the Bank of Miami Beach on behalf of Lansky." Along with Bebe Rebozo's Key Biscayne Bank, Orovitz's City National Bank financed some of Richard Nixon's peculiar real estate deals in the area.[ii]

Mal Englander, former vice mayor and attorney for a local mobster, was later indicted for bribery while he served on the city council.[2338] However, it is hard to tell who was Mob and who was merely going along to avoid trouble. But it is interesting that by the time Elliott showed up in Miami Beach, the Italians (beginning with Al Capone, who bought an estate on Palm Island) had ceded the leadership to the Jews. The Trafficantes were still prominent in close cooperation with the Lansky mob, though.

The Ben Cohen mentioned above was not the one we met as Tom Corcoran's compañero in FDR's "Gold Dust Twins." This Cohen was Teamsters union boss Jimmy Hoffa's former attorney and part of – if not leader of – the mob klavern that "allegedly" ran Miami Beach. Even before Elliott became mayor, locals noted:

> Cohen, who has been in courts in his own and well-known clients' defenses, lives on swank Dilido island and has numerous Beach financial interests. His posh Biscayne Bay home has an ultra-modern, white-marbled entertainment annex which seats 125 guests,

---

[i] NYT, 29 NOV 67, 9 AUG 68, 7 DEC 68, 5 MAY 69, 16 MAY 69. New Dealer Abe Fortas was a Corcoran crony and a White House insider. He and "the Cork," with the help of Hugo Black on the Supreme Court, had been instrumental in helping LBJ steal the 1948 Senate race in Texas. (The details are disputed.) (McKean, 204-5)

[ii] NYT, 15 FEB 70. Orovitz denied being an associate of Meyer Lansky's. (Palm Beach Post, 10 JUN 71). Summers, 112, 513n, draws on Justice Dept. memos to link Orovitz to Lansky and the Bahamas, along with other mob-affiliated Nixon-backers.

> where socially prominent persons such as Elliott Roosevelt, Mrs. Sailing Baruch, Dr. and Mrs. Fabien Sevitzky, and Dr. and Mrs. Arturo di-Filippi have visited.[i]

Obviously Cohen was a good one to know. So, it would turn out, was James Riddle Hoffa. His immense union pension fund was a glorious prize for mobsters across the nation. A huge source of kickbacks and naked theft, the various Teamsters pension funds paid for casinos, resorts, and other major construction throughout the country. For example, reminiscing on how thoroughly the Mob looted the city it built, a Las Vegas newspaper reported that "The Aladdin Theater for the Performing Arts was built at a cost of $60 million with the help of a Teamsters pension fund loan. 'Only $20 million actually went into the construction…'"[2339]

The incumbent mayor of Miami Beach, Melvin Richard, had been waging war against the Mafia since 1949 and was nationally known for outing and denouncing the thoroughly corrupt Florida power structure. A Senate report labeled him "a young councilman who had kept up an effective opposition to the machinations of the S&G syndicate, and who was largely responsible for revealing their members' close connections with the city government."[ii] Even Elliott's wife noticed that "As a council-man in 1951, he had taken a leading part in bringing the Kefauver investigating committee to Miami to help rid the city of syndicated gamblers and racketeers." [iii]

Reportedly, the Cohen brothers had offered Mayor Richard $200,000 a year to leave the Mob alone. As early as 1951, Richard said the syndicate offered him one fifth the annual local take.[2340] But he not only kept getting elected to the city council, in 1963 he was elected to one term as mayor. When Elliott defeated Richard two years later, the *Miami News* reminisced:

> Richard, who won a place on the council as a young crusader 14 years ago made a career of fighting Ben Cohen and the S&G syndicate. Cohen then was one of the real powers at the Beach and the syndicate, by Kefauver Committee estimates, was making $26.5 million a year in illegal bets. The syndicate went out of business for a number of reasons. One was that the local men who ran it were being muscled out by Chicago gangsters. But Richard's part in destroying the gambling empire was important enough to infuriate Ben Cohen and his brother, the late Sam Cohen, one of the syndicate partners.[2341]

Perhaps it is too simplistic to conclude from all this that the Mob decided to run Elliott for mayor. Miami Beach, a town of 70,000, had an odd mix of legitimate and illegal money. While the Jewish Mafia used the city to legitimize vice profits from Las Vegas, Cuba, and the Bahamas, obviously at some point the money lost its smell, and that seems to have been the case in most of Miami Beach. Many of Elliott's supporters were considered pillars of local society, as well as reliable supporters of Israel.

Melvin Richard won fame for having challenged, though not broken, the Mafia's hold on the town. That was a major reason the Cohen brothers and other syndicate members turned their attentions to Habana in the early 1950s. But their activities in

---

[i] Miami News, 28 JUN 63, 29 JUL 63. Cohen, indicted on tax charges, said Attorney General Robert Kennedy was "out to get him." He lost a Supreme Court appeal on 20 NOV 66 and got 18 months (Miami News, 21 NOV 66).

[ii] Senate, 1951, Report of Special Committee to Investigate Organized Crime, 36 (Kefauver comm.). S&G was the name commonly given to the early Mob outfit in Miami Beach.

[iii] PR: I Love, 329. The Kefauver committee in 1950-1 investigated organized crime. Kefauver had called Richard "magnificent" in his efforts to fight the Mob. (Miami News, 15 MAY 67)

Florida merely changed from bookmaking and gambling to money laundering and the conversion of ill-gotten gains to real-estate and other legitimate interests.

Although Richard was Jewish, Elliott's new friends were clearly disenchanted with the ruling local power structure. They had already done the groundwork and cleared the path for their preferred candidate. Elliott quickly succumbed to the flattery. But his brothers were incensed: James was running for mayor of Los Angeles (he lost to Sam Yorty), and Franklin Jr. was considering a run for New York City mayor (he didn't).[2342] They didn't appreciate the headline competition. "I enjoy seeing them squirm," Elliott told a newspaper.

Elliott did not run for mayor in order to capture a salary of $3,000 per year. As with the DNC job, the benefits were not reflected in regular paystubs. He said taking the office made him go broke, but "broke" was a one-acre bayfront mansion with 10 bedrooms and 10 bathrooms (attended by five servants), plus a 41-foot cabin cruiser to get away from all that.[2343]

During the incendiary campaign, Melvin Richard labeled Elliott a drunkard and a wastrel. Richard's advertisements alluded to his marriages: "Four out of five can't be wrong!"[2344]

Then Richard went too far. He knew that Drew Pearson and his understudy Jack Anderson, both muckraking columnists, maintained a hefty file on Elliott Roosevelt. So he wrote them and, basically, asked for dirt. He was outwitted by Elliott and Patricia, who were already friendly with the columnist. They forwarded Drew an amusing archival discovery. When Melvin Richard had been a student thirty years earlier, he had written in favor of leniency for the disturbed Calabrian, Joe Zangara, who had *reportedly* come within inches of shooting FDR in Miami in 1933, and was executed for his trouble.

Pearson triumphantly included that totally irrelevant tidbit in his column, snorting that having failed thirty years ago, now Richard seemed to be trying to assassinate the President's son instead![2345] It was a little reminiscent of Westbrook Pegler's ugly assertion that Zangara had killed the wrong man in Miami (he hit Antonin Cermak, the mayor of Chicago).[i]

That's politics. It is also more evidence of the deviousness of Drew Pearson, which we last encountered when he plotted with Howard Hughes in the Senate hearings of 1947. For some reason, he was especially enamored of Patricia Roosevelt and helped her publish her book. Perhaps this is why he stabbed Richard in the back; it cannot have been out of sympathy for the Mafia.

It was widely believed that Roosevelt won the election solely on the strength of his father's name. His campaign franked its envelopes with the newly issued Eleanor Roosevelt commemorative stamp, hoping that South Beach's Social Security set would take the hint.[2346] And the name again worked its magic. Elliott carried South Beach and its pensioners to victory.

Miami Beach might be the one place in the country where that was still possible. In the 1960s the town was reportedly 80% Jewish and majority elderly. Yet at the same time the town, and Dade County itself, were considered among the most corrupt places in the nation. It was not an easy place to run.

---

[i] Those who have actually investigated Zangara are emphatic that the killing of Cermak was a Mob hit caused by the new mayor's struggle to erase the Capone outfit. If so, FDR was not the target. See Russo, 94.

Elliott started off on a strong note. "His first 100 days have been a little like the first of his late father," wrote Drew Pearson. "Though the job pays only $3,000 a year, the new mayor has neglected his own business to put in nearly full time for the city. Just as busy planning and promoting for Miami Beach is his vivacious wife Pat, who usually sits in the front row at city council meetings." [2347] The new mayor's office was fortified with oversize portraits of Eleanor and Franklin, protectively looking over Elliott's shoulders as he worked at his desk.[2348]

Elliott Roosevelt was a good mayor, at least initially. He was applauded for his leadership abilities and his promotion of the town nationally. But it wasn't long before there was big trouble in the city council. Remarkably, circumstances conspired to make Elliott a crusader against corruption.

According to newspaper reports, it started with the city manager, dead drunk, crashing his car into a number of other vehicles. Responding police were told to falsify the records. The manager announced that his car had been stolen and he had taken the bus instead. It took a fierce battle to get him fired and the police disciplined. Patty said that an unexplained shooting incident at a party hosted by Roosevelt was intended to scare him off the case.[2349]

Mayor Roosevelt, having perhaps forgotten his own DUI case ten years earlier, presided over furious city council debates over the matter. He banged the gavel so hard the head flew off, but he got his way. Obviously, there was a new sheriff in town.[2350]

Then two other high-ranking town officials were exposed as taking bribes. Such news usually points to a top level power struggle. It seemed to Elliott that he was sitting on a powder keg, and he'd lit the fuse. Patricia informed her friend Drew Pearson:

> I do hope you will get a chance to read some of the articles we sent Jack [Anderson] and perhaps in a week or so you might even consider it worthwhile to send him down here for an on the spot story. It is definitely most fascinating, but unfortunate, as I feel Elliott is sitting on a keg of dynamite and in removing [the city manager] who for many years has been part of this arch of crime, it might bring the whole cornice tumbling around us. These are not small time people we are fighting and they will use every possible means to retaliate.[2351]

The new mayor's short tenure was a stormy one to say the least. His instincts in going up against an entrenched power structure were admirable, but they did not bring popularity. He wondered if he should even seek reelection; in December 1966 he caused a furor by stating publicly that "this city has lost millions and it's all done on graft and corruption." Many of his colleagues looked around and could see no corruption.[2352]

As usual, what "really" went on seldom made it into the light of day. But Haines Colbert, an indomitable *Miami News* sleuth, had a scoop on the front page when the purge of the city administration agitated the power structure:

> Miami Beach politics might have been even livelier today if the sons of FDR hadn't been taught it's impolite to punch the host. As it is, Elliott Roosevelt and some of the men who helped him become mayor won't be talking before Wednesday's appointment of a city manager and at least two department heads.
>
> Their partnership dissolved at a victory breakfast the morning after Roosevelt's election. The affair was private, but it produced rumors that almost every appointed official at the Beach was in danger of losing his job.

> Roosevelt told the Miami News he didn't know what he was getting into when he accepted an invitation to have breakfast at the home of one of his supporters, former Beach Councilman Wolfie Cohen. "Wolfie and a couple of the others started telling me we had to appoint a city manager immediately, and how it was imperative that we change police chiefs," Roosevelt said.
>
> "They were going right on down the list – telling me which department heads should be kept and which should be fired. I said, 'Let's stop all this conversation. I don't want to listen to you and I'm not going to commit myself. If you think I'm going to act on any of your recommendations before examining the qualifications of these people you're out of your minds.'
>
> Roosevelt said Cohen accused him of turning his back on his friends. "Wolfie finally got real mad and blew his stack at me," Roosevelt said. "He made it clear he thought he'd put me in office and could get me out.
>
> "I told him that if I weren't a guest in his house I'd take him outside and show him a thing or two." Roosevelt said he also was advised on the appointments by Ben Cohen, no relation to Wolfie, the former S&G gambling syndicate lawyer who is appealing a conviction for income tax evasion.[2353]

Maybe that's what Elliott alluded to years later, when he said he "ran straight into the power of the Mafia. I got sat on my can."

This explanation makes it clear that the "dark side" thought it had installed a string-puppet as mayor. Elliott was never anyone's reliable puppet; he was a loose cannon, and while he was easily excited by ambitious manipulators, those who lit the fuse could never be quite sure where the shot was going to land.

Elliott's term turned out to be characterized by high excitement and bitter confrontations as the local power structure fractured. But in one respect the jilted string-pullers were right; Elliott became a one-term mayor. He didn't have his father's gift for consulting and co-opting local political machines.

On 16 May 1967 the rematch came. In the mayoral election, Elliott came in first, but Richard only got third place. That forced Elliott into a run-off that enabled his enemies to coalesce against him.

Despite Elliott's best efforts, on 6 June 1967 he lost the run-off to a Jewish lawyer, Jay Dermer, after it was claimed Elliott's wife had made anti-Semitic utterances, and that he himself had been "soft on Arabs" in promoting the city abroad. The new mayor "had it over Roosevelt ethnically from the start. He campaigned in Yiddish and his Israeli wife campaigned for him in Hebrew." Perhaps it didn't hurt that the election was run while Israel was fighting for her survival in the Six-Day War.[2354]

James Roosevelt had also heard that Elliott and wife had somehow managed to join "the only country club in the community that excluded Jews." Since they always complained about the clubs that rejected them merely because they were Roosevelts, perhaps they were simply glad to get in.[2355]

Franklin and Eleanor had always been strongly associated with the Jewish lobby and FDR monopolized the Jewish vote. It's a bit odd, since he was known to make anti-Semitic remarks (as most did then), and was apparently only "politically" interested. But Eleanor had been a fervent and vocal supporter of the new Jewish state. What this had to do with Elliott was, again, the name. It had worked in 1965, but in 1967, the local voters were saying: "Vote for a Jew, don't vote for a goy." Dermer promised to restore dignity and decorum to the city government.[2356]

Mayor Elliott had been caught up in a tidal demographic transition. A generation earlier, Jews were discriminated against in Miami Beach, where some hotels allegedly sported "No Jews" signs. But after Jay Dermer took over, not only did they run the city, the Dermer dynasty (the son became mayor later) had a direct line of influence to the Israeli government.

A few years later, Elliott reflected: "From the standpoint of myself and my family and everyone else, it was a disastrous experiment but every experience gives you greater insight and knowledge." He said his "experiment" failed because he didn't have the gift to get across to people "the enormous potential they had to get the job done" with him at the helm.[2357]

Nevertheless, his two years as mayor very nearly set a record for endurance in terms of Elliott's employment. His next job, as executive director of the Miami Beach Tourist Development Authority (TDA) at the rate of $35,000 a year, lasted only eighteen months. He retired abruptly in March of 1971, asserting that he was tired of political games.[2358]

He claimed that "nobody can succeed in the atmosphere that exists on Miami Beach," given the infighting he had to endure. The city was trampled by "political and special interest groups bent on their own destruction."[2359] He also said there was a "witch hunt" to take his "scalp," and he was "tired of being involved in political controversy."[2360] As usual, that wasn't the whole story.

Sidelines and Lawsuits

Elliott's tenure had indeed been marked by ceaseless controversy. One row erupted when he promised to take the chairman of the TDA to court for smearing him. Damages asked would be in "the high six figures, perhaps even the millions." The chairman, flamboyant owner of the Fontainebleau Hotel Ben Novack, had said about Roosevelt: "I made a big mistake. I thought he'd be the right man. I felt he needed this job because he was in financial trouble." Elliott, the ingrate, thundered: "The result of these irrational remarks has greatly damaged financially my companies' activities and those of its affiliates and associates." This constellation of paper companies was then involved in obscure transactions from Panama, Grenada, and the Bahamas, to the United States.[2361]

Ben Novack was one of Patricia's "rich Jews" who had enticed Elliott to run for mayor. Hardly anyone doubted that he ran the famous hotel for the Mob. The complex and secret ways in which the "Minneapolis Combination," chiefly represented by Meyer Lansky, controlled the Fontainebleau and numerous other hotels were explored by the *Miami Herald* in a series of important exposés in January 1967.[2362]

Luis Kutner was a prominent attorney who corresponded with Elliott Roosevelt during this period. Kutner had been the cofounder of Amnesty International and was interested in using the Roosevelt name to promote some humanitarian ideas of his, including the intriguing notion of a "world habeas corpus" rule. But Elliott was instead interested in using Kutner for help with numerous business ideas that seemed to get run either to or from his shell companies in Miami and in the Caribbean.

It is now difficult to determine the legality of these schemes, none of which apparently amounted to much of anything, but many of the names would crop up again when Elliott testified in the Senate organized crime hearings in 1973. Kutner's correspondence suggests that Elliott wanted to off-load various obscure securities, but had trouble doing so through normal channels. Elliott was also involved with the promotion of a defunct restaurant chain, Bavarian Alpine Inns, which according to its prospectus should soon make him enormous amounts of money.

Elliott had started out as president of this outfit, but was then eased out. This fits the recurring pattern of light-shy entrepreneurs using his name for initial legitimacy. For his services as co-organizer and promoter, Elliott was given 19,000 shares and then an additional 46,666, valued by the company at an apparently entirely theoretical 3$ per share.[2363] Nothing more was heard of the company until Senate investigators asserted that Elliott had cleared "between $50,000 and $100,000" by the sale of his stock, which turned out to be "spurious." [2364]

Another company Elliott interested himself in, Powdered Metals Corporation, elicited this advice from Kutner: "immoral, unethical, and could very well be challenged in court…I say to you this is one we should pass with immediate vigor." [2365]

While all of this was going on, a Los Angeles publisher filed a $1.5 million dollar lawsuit against Elliott, who was then still mayor. Robert E. Petersen claimed that in September 1964, when he tried to buy the Pacific Plaza in Santa Monica, Elliott had promised to get him a $7.5 million loan from the Teamsters pension fund, and, 'for arranging the loan, Mr. Roosevelt was to receive $150,000 and a Mercedes Benz automobile.' [2366]

Despite his assurances of having an inside line on the Teamsters – then universally recognized as an arm of organized crime – Roosevelt could not deliver on the loan. But he would not return $75,000 he had been advanced as part of the brokerage fee. Thus the lawsuit. It was far from the only time the Roosevelt sons were mentioned in connection with the Teamsters, but the details are, not surprisingly, murky. In this connection, Roosevelt was reported as being assisted by an associate, Norman Tyrone, an odd fellow we shall meet again.[2367] The corporate defendants were Elliott Roosevelt International Bank & Trust, Ltd., and Elliott Roosevelt Inc. Financial Services.

In another complicated loan scheme, on 4 April 1965 Elliott was sued for $37,000 because he couldn't return a commission paid for another Teamster's Pension Fund loan commitment that failed to produce an actual loan. At that time Jimmy Hoffa was still in charge of the Teamsters Union, though he had been convicted of a number of crimes and was fighting to stay out of jail.

While still mayor, in February 1966 Elliott also borrowed $50,000 from Allied Leasing, resulting in a lawsuit when the promissory note went unpaid at its due date the next January. Clearly he was very hard up for money, and that helps explain the increasingly unsavory company he kept.[2368]

Like the Caribbean dictators, Jimmy Hoffa pops up repeatedly when the Roosevelt sons are watched. How close the relationship was is hard to gage, but both John and Elliott worked with Hoffa on several financial arrangements. Patricia thought that John was Hoffa's man:

> In his business dealings, too, Johnny did not always endear himself to his critics, particularly the press. As an executive for Bache & Co. in New York, he attended a convention of the Teamsters in Miami, and plugged for the reelection of Jimmy Hoffa as union president at a time when Bobby Kennedy was calling Hoffa a menace to the country. Bache & Co. had been advisers on investments made by the Teamsters Pension Fund.[2369]

So wrote Patty in 1966. The story fits Elliott's explanation for how he got involved with Hoffa. "I met them through my brother, John, who is investment counsel for the fund and I got the pension fund to lend Sottile's Canaveral Indian Groves $5 million. The commission was supposed to be 6% at first and my portion at first was supposed to be about $150,000. However, this was reduced to 3% by Teamster's policy…" [2370]

That was one of the loans the mayor of Miami Beach was sued over.[i]

In his autobiographical sketch, Elliott snipped that John had been paid off by Jimmy Hoffa for his active campaigning for Eisenhower and Nixon, and that's how Bache got to manage the Teamsters money. Bluntly, Elliott said, "It wasn't until Jimmy Hoffa offered to get him a position with Bache that John buckled under and became a Republican. Hoffa offered him control of a large part of the Teamsters' portfolio to ensure his defection." [2371]

At first that might sound like inter-fraternal sour grapes, but it turns out that John Roosevelt was indeed very tight with Hoffa. At the Teamster's convention in Miami Beach in July 1961, John offered a glowing endorsement of Hoffa:

> Mr. Chairman, Jimmy, I know you too well to call you Mr. Chairman…I have had the opportunity of working with Jimmy the last few years. I can tell you that at least from my side of the fence this has been a most satisfactory experience. I can only hope that in the years to come we will maintain that same close relationship; and I hope that…Jimmy will have more time to work for the affirmative side of your aims rather than to be under the continual harassment of certain agencies of the government.[ii]

James Roosevelt also sent greetings, regretting the persecution of Jimmy Hoffa.[2372]

That "continual harassment" was the long, groping, but feeble arm of the law. Nobody, least of all the FBI, had the slightest doubt that Jimmy Hoffa was one of the worst thugs ever to rise to national prominence. When John threw his support to Hoffa, Robert Kennedy, the attorney general, was finally about to get him locked up for good. Two years later Hoffa was first convicted on federal charges. He began serving a 13-year sentence in 1967, but was pardoned by President Nixon in 1971 in return for various considerations of disputed size.[2373] Nixon and Hoffa then resumed their pact of mutual admiration for fun and profit. Hoffa disappeared in July 1975.

In truth, John Roosevelt had been a Republican before his association with Hoffa. But in April 1957, he did declare for Nixon in '60, and in December that year his appointment with Bache was announced.[2374]

John was by far the most responsible brother, and association with the Mob is no proof of criminality. The constant circling of the Roosevelt brothers around Hoffa may simply reflect their finely-tuned nose for dirty money. The point, which many observers well noted at the time, was that the Roosevelts definitely did not have queasy stomachs.

A darker interpretation would be that the strong and enduring alliance between Hoffa, Nixon, and the Roosevelt kids simply was a reflection of Mafia control of the Nixon Administration. The links between Richard Nixon and the Mob are so pervasive,

---

[i] The Sicilian immigrant James Sottile, a South Florida banker, was one of the 50 wealthiest Americans when he died in 1964. The details of the Teamster loan Elliott tried to get Sottile Jr. are too cloudy to pursue here, but it seems Elliott wasn't paid in time to meet his obligation. (Charleston News & Courier, 18OCT64.)

[ii] NYT, 6 JUL 61; Victor Riesel column in the Hearst Press, 19 MAR 62, in Milwaukee Sentinel. Riesel wrote an influential labor issues column that exposed communist and mafia control of unions. In some respects Riesel was a successor to W. Pegler. In 1956, a Mob hit (sulphuric acid) blinded and disfigured him.

persistent and interlocking, extending from before his political debut in 1946 to after his dethronement, that no historian can ignore them; but their practical significance is a matter of opinion.[2375]

The meaning of all these peculiar schemes will become more obvious, if not less complex, when we get to the Senate investigation of securities fraud. But in the meantime, Elliott was still running the Miami Beach Tourist Development Agency, complaining bitterly that the controversy around it harmed his reputation and the profitability of his hardscrabble investment business.

In 1970, an independent audit of the TDA found serious problems, some of them related to expense accounts and payrolls. It said the authority would be in financial difficulty unless it was reformed.[2376]

In January, the city council had quietly appointed a special committee to investigate the TDA. Along with the audit, the council had heard reports of secret deals and financial malfeasance. Roosevelt was called to account. The local paper wrote:

> Roosevelt reacted like a wounded bear, telling TDA members the investigation was personal. He even threatened to call off a scheduled trip to London where he was later to open the TDA's first foreign office. It mattered little that the council committee, and the council, abandoned its investigation two weeks later without doing any investigating.
>
> Just a couple of weeks after that, TDA auditors reported that Roosevelt failed to account for $2,317 in cash advances made for travel expenses. There were no vouchers to support the expenditures, and Roosevelt hadn't returned the cash, the auditors said.
>
> Roosevelt said he had lost the vouchers, and for months had been trying to find them. Not having found them, Roosevelt paid back the money a few days after the audit was released….
>
> The authority talked of appointing a day-to-day financial manager to free Roosevelt for tourist promotion, which, they said, is "what he does best." [2377]

The mayor didn't think this was enough. And that's when Elliott Roosevelt resigned, on 9 March 1971. The scandal blew over, but it was the end of Roosevelt's public career.

Locals reportedly "heaved a sigh of relief." A TDA insider said: "He was a great front man, but nobody ever gave him a medal for being an administrator. At least not in this town." [2378]

The Roosevelts then abandoned the city, auctioned off their goods (including FDR memorabilia), and retired to a 29-acre ranch in rural Florida.[2379]

Political Tap-dancing

Where did Elliott Roosevelt stand politically? Despite his illustrious and frequently admired Democratic credentials, there is no discernible pattern – except possibly in the sense that he was the most easily influenced of all the Roosevelts, and went in whichever direction opportunity beckoned.[i]

---

[i] It is of interest that President Roosevelt began as a Republican when Uncle Ted was in office. He switched to the Democrats, explaining that since there were fewer of them in his area, he would stand out more. (Persico, 37, 43). Interestingly, he couldn't win his own rural Dutchess County even in landslides.

The accusations that he was a communist or a "comsymp" during the late 1940s are slightly amusing – neither he nor the other Roosevelts had the intellectual appetite for the finer points of dialectical materialism.[2380] It is likely that his fellow-traveling consisted of vague notions of "social justice" common among the well-to-do, as well as the flush of excitement of being singled out by Joseph Stalin as a dear son. That the roots weren't deep is attested by Elliott's strong advocacy for both Dwight D. Eisenhower and "Uncle Joe" during 1948-52. Elliott's admiration for Stalin took many years to wear off.

During his pre-war Hearst years, Elliott did not spout left-wing cant; on the contrary, he adopted some anti-New Deal rhetoric common in Texas at the time. His further political involvements were marked by extreme opportunism. He worked on business deals with Cuba's Batista, and went on to support the Portuguese dictatorship and white-ruled Rhodesia.

As a delegate or an honored guest, Elliott attended every Democratic convention from 1928 up to 1964 (except 1944). He tried to keep his links with the Democratic Party in spite of his repeated defections. As was the case with the other siblings, the Party was remarkably cool in return. There was a profound sense that the Roosevelt brothers were more liability than asset. The Party effectively blocked their political careers.

In sharp contrast with his mother, Elliott chose to support John F. Kennedy in 1960. So did James and Franklin Jr., who saw him as Joe's boy, as well as their type. In contrast, Eleanor never was comfortable with JFK, and she detested his scheming, manipulative – and Catholic – father. She could not forgive the Kennedy family's cozying up to Joe McCarthy, and besides, her political heart belonged to Adlai Stevenson. Jack said, ungraciously, that Eleanor could never get over that Joseph Kennedy's sons were far more successful than hers: 'She hated my father and she can't stand it that his children turned out so much better than theirs." [2381]

That was unfair. The Kennedy kids and the Roosevelt kids were very much alike: reckless, irresponsible, fun-loving, not quite as bright as their ambitions. But they differed in a crucial respect: the Kennedys had effortless, endless money, and they never were much interested in the further acquisition thereof.

In 1972, the once ultra-leftist Elliott Roosevelt had definitely lost his New Deal ardor. He made a splash by declaring for Nixon in the 1972 presidential election. Although he had by then moved out of the country, he found the opportunity to become involved with a Texas-led rebel outfit known as "Democrats for Nixon." Brother James, lifelong Democrat, also got involved with this insurgency, serving with the later so notorious CREEP (the Committee for the Reelection of the President).[2382]

At that time the Democrats still owned the South. But Southerners had never reconciled themselves to the new direction of "socialistic" policies that had been spearheaded by the New Deal, and even less with Yankee interference in race relations. Elliott's intervention on the Republican side was almost an inverted echo of the 1930s and his championing of Vice President Garner. Again, he stood with Texas.

This time the rebel Democrats were led by Texas governor John Connally, Lyndon Johnson's erstwhile aide. And the old-timers were still around: Connally was aided by a certain former Air Force general and prominent Texas Democrat – C.R. Smith.[2383]

This is a good point to revisit the fortunes of the Texas Cabal. With Elliott's exit from Texas in 1945, the cabal oriented itself around a triangle of Johnson-Connally, the oil barons, and the oil services company Halliburton, which acquired the construction company Brown & Root. That company had funded LBJ from the beginning and in turn received the necessary contracts for its rise to global prominence.

Sid Richardson, Elliott's former sugar daddy, provided an air force for Johnson's critical 1948 campaign. On his long hauls, Lyndon flew on Sid's surplus B-24 Liberator. The short hauls were handled by a Sikorsky S-51 and Bell-47s provided by Bell Helicopters, which decided to move to Fort Worth. C.R. Smith's American Airlines continued to be helpful; C.R. later became LBJ's Transportation Secretary.[2384]

Richardson died without immediate heirs and left only a pittance to his nephew Perry Bass. Aided by attorney John Connally, Bass was able to take over the eponymous foundation Uncle Sid had left his fortune to. The Bass Brothers would then become supreme sponsors of Republican political candidates, particularly during the two Bush administrations, themselves headed by Texas oil men.[2385]

With LBJ's help, John Connally was elected Texas governor. He survived the Dallas shooting and, as Nixon's Treasury Secretary, came to head Democrats for Nixon. Afterwards, Connally in turn saw to it that George H.W. Bush went to the political front.

The Texas Cabal had mutated from a Democratic to a Republican machine by the time of the second Nixon term. Connally himself shed his skin and reëmerged as a Republican. Roosevelt brothers James and Elliott followed, although they still pretended to be Democrats, and professed to venerate their father's reign.

Clearly, in both 1952 and 1972 the "East Coast" Democrats had irritated the moneyed and the powerful, especially in Texas; the results were as expected.[2386]

The Texas Oil – Republican Party coalition has long been well documented, although perhaps none has traced it all the way back to Elliott's escapade in March 1933. One (very hostile) recent chronicler of the cabal is Robert Bryce, who wrote *Cronies* in 2004. But the importance of the influence racket can probably easily be overstated. Like the rest of us, politicians work for those who pay them. That could be anyone – the defense lobby, Howard Hughes, the Mafia, the Israel lobby, or big labor unions like the Teamsters or the Teachers (NEA). Sometimes they even tend to cancel out.

The defection of the Roosevelt sons caused a commotion in 1972; especially so when Ford Roosevelt, Patricia's son adopted by Elliott, came forward to declare his father soft in the head:

> The last two times I saw my father, once in June shortly before he moved to Lisbon, and earlier this year in New York, he expressed a fear he had for the future of this country. It was not a fear founded on the chance of the election of Senator McGovern, but a fear of what Mr. Nixon would do if reelected. He felt if the President wins reelection this country would be in a severe economic depression within four years. My father would not say if he could support Senator McGovern, but he assured me he would never vote for Mr. Nixon. To me it is my father who is guilty of "fuzzy thinking" and I must apologize to Senator McGovern for my father's change of heart.[2387]

The Roosevelts always did have a fondness for taking their fights public.

The election of 1972 was nationally problematic because Richard Nixon was intensely mistrusted, whereas Senator McGovern represented the resurgence of the left wing triggered by the domestic tumult accompanying the Vietnam War. The Elliott Roosevelt of 1945 would surely have glowingly praised McGovern, a pacifist-leaning bomber pilot. The Elliott of 1972 was, however, working for the Portuguese dictatorship and defending colonial wars in Africa. Now he was for Nixon.

Obviously, a political icon's descendants have the right to pick their own political orientation. They just can't honestly capitalize on their names if they do so. The odious assumption that presidents sire princes and princesses, ready to take over where their parent left off, never fades completely even in the most democratic and egalitarian of societies. This left the Roosevelt kids with constant, inescapable public expectations, which they both exploited and resented.

Throughout their lives, James, Elliott, and Franklin Jr. tried to have it both ways. They claimed to be blue-blooded Democrats, demanding the recognition and political tailwinds this status suggested, but they flipped when it suited them. This left them with no credibility and no party backing when they attempted to pursue political careers.

With Elliott's unpredictable zig-zag political course it is perhaps not surprising that he wound up a Reagan supporter (although initially a skeptic). So did James Roosevelt. The brothers were flattered to have Ronald Reagan tell them that he had voted for their father four times.[2388] The crucial fact is, however, that Elliott chose his affiliations based on personal connection, or an instinctive liking, not on a deep-seated philosophical conviction. He was always vocal in his views, but they had no roots.[2389]

ELLIOTT AND THE MOB

In this chapter, the terms "alleged" and "allegedly" will, of necessity, get a real workout. Terrifying witness accounts will be quoted – some of them true, some of them not. The line between true and false cannot everywhere be pinned down with certainty. Apparently, even the U.S. Senate didn't want to know exactly where that line ran.

In September 1973 reports surfaced that – allegedly – Elliott Roosevelt and mafia business associates in Miami had ordered the assassination of the Bahamian prime minister, who had edged them out of a lucrative casino deal. We need to make clear right away that this accusation was almost certainly a deft confabulation of a conman who had briefly worked for Elliott; but that item was only a small piece of a very big and very ugly puzzle.

Mob sources said (with considerable exaggeration) that associates of Meyer Lansky had invested one million dollars in Premier Lynden Pindling's initial election in 1967 in order to grease the skids for a new casino in the Bahamas.[2390] When elected, Pindling reneged. So in 1968, the Mafia reportedly decided to bump him off. The investigation of the conspiracy was documented in the Senate hearings transcripts, which form the bedrock of this account.[2391] They make disturbing reading.

Pindling was a black nationalist (of disputed national origin) whose Progressive Liberal Party succeeded the local white regime that had ruled the crown colony for Britain. Despite Pindling's modest official salary, he soon became very rich. This did not faze Bahamian voters. Pindling said he had nothing to do with the Miami Beach crime syndicate, although probably nobody believed that.

Getting elected was only the beginning of Pindling's politico-criminal career. After the Bahamas became fully independent in 1973, he turned over parts of his archipelago for use by selected Colombian drug smugglers. This was well known and widely reported.[2392]

To see why Bahamians were not too worried about Pindling, and why Elliott Roosevelt wanted to do business with him, it is necessary to understand what preceded him.

How the Mafia bought the Bahamas

"The Mob" is a nebulous term, and "organized crime" can be quite misleading, at least the adjective. In the operations we are about to examine, it is hard to tell what's legal and what's not. In reviewing "Mob" activities, it is also often difficult to determine which are unethical, which is an entirely different question. Sometimes, though, it isn't hard at all. That's the nature of the beast.

The loss of Cuba was a severe setback to the Mob in general and boss Meyer Lansky in particular. The gangsters immediately began efforts to colonize the nearby Bahama Islands, still "nominally" a British crown colony. They already had a head start.

"Nominally," because imperial oversight had left a lot to be desired. The colony was in practice controlled by "the Bay Street Boys," white businessmen in Nassau organized into the United Bahamian Party. Their leader was Sir Stafford Sands, CBE, operating under legal cover as Minister of Finance and Tourism. In April 1963, after a number of discussions with organized crime figures – one of which was reportedly held at the Fontainebleau Hotel in Miami Beach in 1961 – Sands sold the first Bahamian casino monopoly to an outside cartel. Freeport on Grand Bahamas Island was given over to an enormous resort development anchored by the Lucayan Beach Hotel. Indeed, the name Freeport was aptly chosen, meaning free of taxes and free of pesky U.S. laws.

For this, Sands received checks totaling $1.8 million dollars merely in the period 1963-67. The important leaders in the Bahamian Executive Council, including the Symonette family, received smaller considerations. Sir Roland Symonette was premier from 1955 to 1967. Sir Roland was a former Prohibition rum runner whose family got to be among the richest in the world. Also, the United Bahamian Party was paid $10,000 a month by the casino.[2393] The resort company also agreed to pay the government $100,000 a year "with a provision that its books cannot be audited locally." [i]

All this became known in 1966-67, when a Royal Commission was sent to the colony to investigate. Sir Stafford testified, defiantly and truculently. Then the island native declared himself a non-resident and moved, with his fortune, to a pleasant retirement in Spain.

Many looked into this cesspool, including the *Wall Street Journal* and other newspapers. It was widely believed by those who examined the matter that Meyer Lansky in Miami Beach controlled the Bahamian operation, and that he and his lieutenants received the "skim" from the casinos. The principals denied this, and of

[i] *An informal history of the Bahamas* by Jim Baker, www. jabezcorner.com/Grand_Bahama/Informal4.html is an excellent detailed exposition of the otherwise scantly covered Mob-Bahamas-issue. It is supported by numerous published articles. The (known) payoff list to corrupt officials is listed there. Retr. 1 MAR 12.

course it has not been proved in a court of law. The casino partners were Canadian Louis Chesler and American Wallace Groves, long time mob-affiliated figures.[i] They did admit to having asked Lansky for expert advice in hiring and business operation. They certainly got it. That's how Dino Cellini and his brother Eddie got to run the Bahamian operation.[2394]

How the Mafia bought the Bahamas is worth a book of its own. One such book, *The Ugly Bahamian* by Allan Witwer, was due to be published in 1965. Witwer had been an employee of Stafford Sands and the casinos, so he knew exactly what he was talking about. Sir Stafford's friends bought up the two existing manuscripts for $53,000 and suppressed the book's publication.[2395]

Robert Morgenthau, the U.S. Attorney in New York (southern district), was engaged in a protracted fight with organized crime in America. He subpoenaed Witwer's notes, and thus detailed information about the matter became known to a few who cared to dig. This Morgenthau was the son of Henry, FDR's notoriously honest Treasury Secretary. He was widely regarded as the best in the business, and he was a constant scourge of rich criminals. For Morgenthau's troubles unraveling the tentacles of the Mafia and its connections with politicians, in 1969 Richard Nixon fired him and replaced him with a friend, Whitney Seymour. Incidentally, it was Seymour's law firm that bought up *The Ugly Bahamian* on behalf of Stafford Sands.[ii]

On that background, it suddenly doesn't seem so silly that Lynden Pindling ran on an anti-corruption platform in 1967. The colony's Negro voters thought the new prime minister was quite an improvement. From their point of view, it must be admitted, it was smart to keep the Mafia on board. After all, the great river of cash came from foreigners; it was its distribution on the islands that the voters preferred to modify. If shady characters skimmed off the top, it was a small price to pay for the huge economic boost the islands received. And shady or not, the "interests" did a phenomenal job running their islands, perhaps a far better job than the locals could have managed.

The Royal Commission report was released in 1967 and upset many. However, the Mob was not so easily dismissed. Lansky and others in Miami Beach were determined to control the government, regardless of its color. They also did not like competition. Another casino entrepreneur, Elliott Roosevelt's good friend Michael McLaney, helped finance Pindling's election in January 1967, but was then ejected from the islands after the victory. The damning conclusions of the Royal Commission, which denounced McLaney, were too high an obstacle for a continuing Pindling-McLaney operation. [iii]

During this period, the paradisical, tax-free islands less than an hour's flight from Florida were a haven for a lot of interesting characters, many of them with much money, and some of them with a great reluctance to return to the country in which they had made it. Even those still resident in Miami Beach were intensely interested in

---

[i] Groves was a lawyer and former stock promoter who had been imprisoned for an immense mail fraud, and turned ex-patriate after release; Chesler was a gambler and investor long associated with Lansky (Hersh, 123). He was also a friend of Senator John F. Kennedy and Mike McLaney (Hersh 123-4). Stafford Sands had represented Groves continuously since 1946, the same period in which he held an Assembly seat representing the Nassau business district (NYT, 7 JUL 67). Groves's early work with Sands and the first Bahamian casinos is described in Newton: Mr. Mob, 180. It seems that the 1961 Sands-Chesler alliance was the key decision behind the casinos.

[ii] Jack Anderson column, 28 NOV 69. See also editorial, NYT 16 AUG 69 and Marvin Miller: The Breaking of the President 1974. Miller says Witwer was told he would be killed if he published the book. Witwer later published his work in the Las Vegas Sun (1971), giving a detailed account of Lansky's control.

[iii] NYT, 20 APR 67. In Witwer's view, Lansky had changed his allegiance to Pindling, leaving McLaney out.

making money in the Bahamas, and in tapping into the great flow of cash, whatever its provenance. Some of the more famous names were Howard Hughes, who resided in the Bahamas from 1970 to 1976 (with interruptions elsewhere), and Bebe Rebozo, the owner of the Key Biscayne Bank and Richard Nixon's close friend and supporter. Nixon himself was fond of the Bahamas, casinos, and casino operators; he attended the opening of the Paradise Island Hotel and Casino at Nassau in January 1968.[2396] As early as 1951, Senator Nixon had been involved in a significant but partially suppressed gambling scandal in Habana.[i]

In that esteemed company, Elliott Roosevelt was merely a bit player. It was nonetheless a highly entertaining bit.

"Unprovable Allegations"

The allegations against Elliott Roosevelt came out of the blue during a Senate investigation of organized crime in South Florida. In a rather off-hand, parenthetical manner, one of the testifying crooks mentioned some minor dealings with Elliott Roosevelt, and then included the planned murder. To most people, the assassination plot seemed too far over the top even for Elliott, and he of course denied it furiously. He did admit, however, that he had hung with a very bad crowd in Miami Beach.

One of this unappetizing flock was Louis Pasquale Mastriana, a middle-aged career hoodlum specializing in securities fraud, loan sharking, and related scams. He was the origin of the Elliott lead, but he was only one of numerous witnesses who eventually incriminated him. The wire services reported the story on 18 September 1973.[2397] Jack Anderson, the muckraker who had taken over from Drew Pearson at the *Washington Post*, published the allegations in his column during September and October 1973, while Senate hearings were ongoing.[2398]

One irony of the sensational murder charge was that, being improbable and unprovable, it inadvertently let Elliott off the hook on his extensive and quite probably criminal involvement with securities swindles.

Investigators were aware of that peculiar problem at the time. They "expressed chagrin that [Senator Charles] Percy's questioning of Mastriana about the purported Pindling murder plan had obfuscated the original purpose of the hearings – the disclosure of international securities theft." [2399]

That tactical error opened the way for a characteristic, fulminating Elliott counteroffensive. From Portugal, Elliott told the *Washington Post* that the subcommittee "had been duped by 'a man who is absolutely crazy, a man who would never have been allowed to testify [after] even the most casual check of his background."

> I have never met Meyer Lansky. I have never had anything to do with Meyer Lansky or anything to do with gambling casinos, much less assassinations… This places a cloud over my name. I am damaged beyond repair, and I consider what is happening in the U.S. Senate to be the most un-American thing I have ever seen." [2400]

In September and October 1973, Elliott Roosevelt was called to testify about his dealings with the Mob before the Senate Permanent Subcommittee on Investigations.

---

[i] Summers, 124-7. It is likely that the tight Nixon-Rebozo alliance really dates from this unhappy episode.

This committee was known as the Jackson committee after chairman Henry "Scoop" Jackson. He was the long-serving Democratic senator from Washington – or Boeing, as it was often said. Jackson, although regretting the inadvertent way the allegations had surfaced, let it be known that there was more dirt to come.[2401]

Elliott swore to sue Senator Jackson, under whose watch the dubious charges had become public.[2402]

The committee was actually very interested in finding Elliott, who had just barely eluded their grasp when he flew to Lisbon from Miami. This was, however, a coincidence; Elliott had pledged to cooperate with the investigation. Apart from the Pindling hit, the committee wanted to ask him about some Swiss bank accounts, even if they had to go to Europe to get his version; this had to do with a separate investigation into the "Zürich International Investment Corporation," a fraudulent operation which the committee held up as a case study. It wasn't necessary; Elliott voluntarily came back to testify.[2403]

After the initial sensation, there was general agreement that Scoop Jackson was in the wrong, and that he had let an innocent man be maligned. There is no question that the committee stumbled out of the gate, but that doesn't mean that any and all charges investigated could be airily dismissed. As *Time* summarized:

> Both the virtues and defects of congressional investigating committees have lately been on display, thanks to Watergate, and last week there was some fresh evidence on the debit side – at least in form. The substance was still obscure...
>
> Obviously displeased that Mastriana's allegations were brought out prematurely by Percy, Jackson suspended further testimony until next week, when Roosevelt is scheduled to return to Washington and confront his accuser. It could be quite an encounter. Mastriana's police record includes arrest for gambling, grand larceny, forgery, aggravated assault and possession of the contents of stolen mail. Three years ago, he was declared mentally incompetent by a New Jersey court. "He's the greatest bull artist in the world," a Florida police official said of Mastriana last week.[2404]

Thus by letting Mastriana out in front with his lurid charges, the committee sabotaged its credibility in dealing with the far more substantive matters that were lurking in the details.

The Mob Accuses Elliott

Senate investigators wanted Elliott to account for his dealings with convicted swindlers Patsy Lepera, Harold Audsley, Allan Lefferdink, Mort Zimmerman, and perhaps most significantly, Paul and Clifford Noe, brothers who were world-renowned career confidence men. Someone editorialized that it was a line-up of characters "so complex and murky as to make the Watergate crew as easy to identify as the characters in 'Dick and Jane.' "[2405]

In addition, Elliott's dealings with Michael McLaney, the jilted casino entrepreneur who wanted Pindling shot, would be of Senate interest. McLaney had been twice convicted on tax and securities fraud, but there was much more to this truly extraordinary fellow than the rap sheet revealed.

McLaney was primarily a casino operator, although he had been involved in many business initiatives with other Mob figures. In late 1958, he had bought Habana's

Casino Nacional from Mo Dalitz, the gangster who created modern Las Vegas. With him were Carroll Rosenbloom and Lou Chesler, both long-time organized crime associates. McLaney lost nearly everything in the Cuban revolution, and was apparently driven half-mad with a need to get even with Castro.[2406]

This mattered because one of Mr. McLaney's best friends was the President of the United States. By many accounts, John F. Kennedy would frequently sit with his father Joe, McLaney, and other well-connected characters on the veranda of Joe's winter palace in Palm Beach, lamenting the loss of Cuba and contemplating ways to deal with Castro. McLaney didn't leave it at talk; in 1963 he and his brother were the masterminds of an armed invasion attempt that was unraveled before taking flight, although – surprise – no legal action was taken against the conspirators.[i]

Then he ran the only Haitian casino, in Port-au-Prince, and he tried hard to break into the Bahamian market. He was in fairly constant legal trouble.[2407] In the meantime, McLaney had somehow been involved with Meyer Lansky in the attempt to profit by the new Bahamian government. There are conflicting reports over whether the two were still working together, or whether Lansky was trying to ease out McLaney. At any rate, this sharp, suave, well-connected fellow understood the need to keep people in his debt.

Perhaps this is why McLaney willingly indulged Elliott Roosevelt from time to time. But it is unlikely that he, or the Mob in general, saw much more in Elliott than at best a marginally useful tool and, more likely, a potential troublemaker. In contrast, most likely the Mob regarded James Roosevelt as a professional, someone you could do business with for the long run. Jimmy was, after all, the "foster son" of old Joe Kennedy, and he had the run of the hacienda when he was in Palm Beach.

Elliott Roosevelt fiercely asserted that while he had had business dealings with organized crime figures, he had not himself committed any offense. All indications to the contrary were "vicious lies." Specifically, he denied having offered $100,000 to assassinate Pindling. The accuser, Mastriana, said he had received an initial down payment of $10,800 from Elliott and McLaney.

Roosevelt acknowledged this was largely true, but that the money was for another purpose having to do with a domestic shakedown. Specifically, Elliott asserted the money was a "finder's fee" for forcing a loan out of a Newark, NJ labor union.[2408] As the evidence developed, however, Mastriana had fooled him with the promise of easy money, and Elliott never saw either the loan or the ten grand again.

Another convicted swindler, Patsy Lepera, also told the Senate committee that Roosevelt had received stolen securities for resale from the Mob, something Roosevelt denied any knowledge of.[2409]

Lepera charmingly introduced himself to the committee as "a veteran of many years in the stolen securities racket." And, "I was the best in the country." [2410]

> One of my roles was to serve as a middle man between organized crime syndicates and reputable as well as crooked brokerages, banks, lending institutions, CPAs, and attorneys. I was also a link to the underworld for prominent and seemingly reputable people…And I worked with some famous people who used their good names to gain the

---

[i] Hersh, 125-6, 277. "McLaney was polished enough to expose to the kids. Throughout the fifties he visited the Palm Beach mansion. 'I had drinks at the home…I liked the President very much. I thought Bobby was a mess…'"

> confidence of financial institutions in stolen securities transactions. One of the prominent persons I worked with was Elliott Roosevelt.

Specifically, Lepera said Roosevelt sold $440,000 in stolen securities for him on three occasions in 1969 and 1970. Elliott knew they were stolen because Lepera told him. He said "He was just one guy with a famous name who needed money and was willing to use that name to get it." As Lepera added, "99% of these people that you do business with are drowning and they are looking to survive." [2411]

Lepera said it was a hassle dealing with Elliott, but he did deliver on his promises:

> Roosevelt delivered to me $110,000 in $100 bills across the street from the Doral Hotel in Miami Beach. In fact, he had the money in the same attaché case that I had given him with the securities. I believe that Roosevelt got rid of these securities through a contact at the Bank of Nova Scotia in the Bahamas because I had to give him money for his expenses to the island and his return to the States.
>
> A short time later, I again met with Roosevelt and he asked me if I could supply him with more stolen securities. I got the impression that he was desperate and really needed ready cash. We agreed that there would be a 50-50 split…

Lepera proceeded to describe in detail the alleged criminal transactions, focusing on Elliott's seemingly endless need for cash.[2412]

Lepera was also involved with Roosevelt in a coin and medallion minting scheme. It seemed Elliott thought money could very literally be made off the Roosevelt name by minting such trifles in the memory of the Roosevelts and selling them to collectors. Elliott did not deny his attempt to work with Lepera on this project, which failed. But Elliott added:

> …I was going to sell a medallion of Democratic Presidents to the Democratic National Committee as a means of raising money to cover their huge debt, and I went to see Mr. Strauss [Robert Strauss, Democratic leader] who at that time was the Finance Committee chairman. He will bear out the fact that I brought Mr. Lepera into his office. I might say, sir, that shortly thereafter, within a few days, we found out what Mr. Lepera's record had been before, and I lived in absolute fear of the fact that all of these organizations would find out the same thing I did.[2413]

This business, one of the innumerable short-lived companies Roosevelt was president of, was known as Mint Sales International. Elliott was supposed to be paid $25,000 a year, though he said he never saw that money. The Franklin and Eleanor coins were only to be the beginning. Elliott planned to market the medallion minting business to Central American countries as a way of raising revenue:

> Panama is a country that has done this for several years very successfully. I asked him for an advance of $1,500 to pay us to get the original letters out to these countries, mostly smaller countries without their own mints, to be able to solicit their business. He never made the loan.[2414]

Lepera was uncomfortable working with Elliott. "We were in Saks Fifth Avenue and he starts signing autographs for people right on top of a briefcase full of stolen securities. And I says, Elliott what are you doing? Let's get out of here."[2415] Soon Lepera wiggled out of dealing with him. He justified it thus:

> Mr. LEPERA. I felt, Senator, that he needed an awful lot of money all the time, fast, and I felt like he was going to bust me out. I felt like, here I am, a guy that came from Second Street, and I have a record, and if anything happens to me he is going to throw me to the wolves and he is going to get a medal for finding me. I just felt as though I was on bad ground and everybody that I was doing business with, that was connected in the Miami area, was telling me that I was doing business with the wrong guy.[2416]

That does sound plausible. Even the dark side found Elliott to be dangerously unpredictable. But Elliott called the entire thing a "vile and dastardly hoax." The surviving documentation could all be explained to apply to perfectly legitimate transactions, he claimed.[2417]

Other Mob figures came forward to claim ties with Mr. Roosevelt. One was Clifford Noe. The Noe Brothers, Clifford and Paul, were the aristocracy of swindlers. They had made their jail-punctuated careers conning people out of millions worldwide. To the FBI, they were collectively "Dr. Noe," an epic and perennial enemy. Both brothers recorded extremely detailed accounts of financial dealings of head-splitting complexity, but largely hinging on fake, stolen, or dubious securities.

To illustrate Elliott Roosevelt's *modus operandi* in connection with the Noe gang, a bank official provided the following account. He said Elliott and his son and "Doctor" Noe entered his office:

> By way of introduction, Mr. Roosevelt stated that he had known Dr. Noe's father and Dr. Noe's uncle, and he further stated that both of these gentlemen had been very active in the Democratic Party and stated further that one had been a governor of Louisiana and the other a governor of Oklahoma.

Elliott, who had only known Noe for a short time, had actually asked him if he was related to the Noe who had once been Louisiana governor. (No Noe ever governed Oklahoma.) Noe responded, as he said he always did, by saying that he'd never met a Noe he wasn't related to. Later he testified: "I did not correct anything [Elliott said to the banker] as I knew Roosevelt was aware of the true facts and assumed he often slightly twisted things to put connections…back to President Roosevelt's time."

For this introduction, whose purpose was to fence worthless securities with the bank, Noe paid Elliott $1,400, which was substantiated by records.[2418]

The Noes could testify about these matters because both of them were then in prison, Clifford in England and Paul in Texas. This episode was merely one highlight of the Noe-Elliott link. It was reported that the Noes first met Elliott in 1968 when he was a director of a Miami-based firm, Comutrix Corporation:

> Paul Noe says he and his brother supplied some phony Tennessee land deeds, which Comutrix listed at great value in its financial statement. In return…they received Comutrix stock, which …they marketed illegally with the help of a lawyer recommended by Mr. Roosevelt.
>
> Reports issued by Comutrix at the time show Mr. Roosevelt as a director, and contain a $2 million financial statement including not only the phony land deeds but also stock in a phony industrial firm and notes from a phony religious charity. Comutrix stock was sold nationally over the counter at from $8 to $10 a share, and management used the shares to acquire legitimate small businesses around the country. The businesses became insolvent

> and Comutrix itself was nearing collapse about the time Dr. Noe came to Mr. Roosevelt – who was no longer a director of Comutrix – for his banking introduction.[2419]

Florida court cases show Comutrix was a swindle operating from 1967 to 1970.[2420]

Elliott's role in these transactions was to function as a go-between, an ambassador between the underworld and the legal financial universe. He had a leg planted firmly in both of these. He had the name recognition and the contacts as a former mayor. It is clear from the testimony that he knew what he was doing, that he desperately needed the money, and that he tried to cover his tracks by various means.

The criminals testified that Elliott made his money mostly as a chiseler, someone who demanded fees and commissions, loans and assistance with his own numerous projects. Elliott, however, maintained that he was the one who had been duped, defrauded, and smeared by these unsavory characters, notably the "true psycho," Mr. Mastriana.

Mastriana provided an interesting account of how he had been set up with Elliott:

> When I was released from Trenton State Prison, a fellow by the name of Dennis Carey, who was the Essex County boss, the Democratic chairman for Essex County – I knew him very well through one of the Democratic chairmen up in the Bronx, Edward Flynn – I went in to see Mr. Carey about a problem I was having trying to get back to Miami. He interceded with Pete Rodino for me, and Rodino got ahold of Congressman Fascell, and in the interim Mr. Carey said to me, "When you get down to Miami, look up Elliott Roosevelt.[2421]

The names Mastriana mentioned were very big in Democratic politics, but they were not associated with criminality. Presumably their staffs were only doing a favor for a local boss. What was more interesting is that according to Elliott, Mastriana showed up with an introduction from brother Franklin Jr., who had a New Jersey automobile dealership and remained plugged in with the local Democratic machine.[2422]

"Elliott was framed" became the official narrative after the Jackson committee declined to refer the charges, which, considering the sources, could not have held up in court. Closer examination of the Senate testimony, however, reveals far more than was publicly reported. An excerpt from the Senate hearings read:

> Mr. MASTRIANA. For example, when I was associated with Elliott Roosevelt we took down a place for about $15,000 on Biscayne Boulevard.
>
> Senator GURNEY. How were you associated with Elliott Roosevelt?
>
> Mr. MASTRIANA. Elliott would represent one side and I would represent the other.
>
> …Senator GURNEY. Was he mayor at that time?
>
> Mr. MASTRIANA. No, I believe he had just lost the election.
>
> Senator GURNEY. Describe the nature of these business arrangements.
>
> Mr. MASTRIANA. For example, if there was a strike in an area and they wanted the strike broken up, they would get ahold of Elliott; Elliott would call me in and I would break up the strike.[2423]

Mastriana said he broke strikes by breaking legs: "I don't talk too much. If I talk too much I am wasting my time." Furthermore:

> Mr. MASTRIANA. The transaction involving Mr. Procacci – I believe I brought to Mr. Roosevelt's office about $150,000 worth of stolen securities, which he attempted to unload.[i]
>
> Senator PERCY. Which he attempted to what?
>
> Mr. MASTRIANA. To borrow money on them, unload them for us. He didn't meet with any success, so he returned them to me.
>
> Senator PERCY. Did he have any knowledge of the nature of those securities?
>
> Mr. MASTRIANA. Yes, he did, sir.[2424]

Mastriana had been given a job by Elliott Roosevelt, in order to do "labor consulting." That was true, said Elliott, for Mastriana had connections with the labor unions. But if Mastriana was right that he was accustomed to shaking down unions, he seemed to have dreamt up Elliott's involvement. At least Elliott strenuously protested that he was, in fact, the unions' best friend.

At that point in the testimony, the alleged assassination plot came up:

> Mr. MASTRIANA: Roosevelt knew Mantell.[ii] As a matter of fact, when Roosevelt went broke, Mantell sold his boat. They were very close and on occasion the three of us sat down together and had lunch.
>
> Senator PERCY. Would you tell us who Mike McLaney is?
>
> Mr. MASTRIANA. He used to work for Meyer Lansky. He had a place over in Nassau. Mr. Pindling, the Prime Minister, was supposed to give him a gambling license. I understand they come up with $1 million in cash. Right after the election, when he was elected Prime Minister, he threw McLaney out of the islands.
>
> Senator PERCY. Is he a business partner of Mr. Elliott Roosevelt?
>
> Mr. MASTRIANA. Who?
>
> Senator PERCY. Mr. Mike McLaney?
>
> Mr. MASTRIANA. He represents organized crime. He is a gambler. He used to run a casino.
>
> Senator PERCY. Do you know of any direct relationship? Can you describe from your own personal knowledge any direct relationship between him and Elliott Roosevelt?
>
> Mr. MASTRIANA. Well, he got a check from him for $2,500 and gave it to me in McLaney's house.
>
> ...Senator PERCY. What can you tell us about the planned assassination attempt of the Governor of the Bahamas, Lynden Pindling?
>
> Mr. MASTRIANA. They came to me and they wanted him dead, they wanted him killed...offered $100,000 to whack him, to kill him. They give me $10,000 front money, $7,500 in cash and a check for $2,500....McLaney had come up with part of the money to Roosevelt. They had brought the contract to Roosevelt and they brought it to me.[2425]

This sorry hoodlum further revealed that during some of his work with Roosevelt he had worn a wire on behalf of the postal authorities, who were interested in pursuing mail fraud charges against Elliott. The tape was reviewed in regard to the Pindling job, but it was inconclusive due to a poor quality recording. The Bahamian job was determined to be impractical:

---

[i] Procacci and Mastriani were, among others, federally indicted in a gigantic case of mail theft of securities in 1970. (AP, 14 JUL 70, Sarasota Journal: *Bullet silences stock theft figure*)

[ii] Dominic Mantell, "previously identified in hearings before this subcommittee in 1963, as an organized crime figure from the Buffalo, NY area, as a prime mover in the Zürich International Investment Corp." (Hearings, 130) Mastriana said Mantell was next to Santo Trafficante Jr. in Florida's underworld.

> Mr. MASTRIANA. Well, you have a problem over in Nassau. It is not a healthy situation. 90% of the population is Negro, and they think the world of him. So if somebody wants to commit the assassination, as you put it, he would probably be turned in. There is no way you can get off the island.[2426]

All this plotting occurred in the period 1968 through 1970. The documentary exhibits showed that Elliott employed Louis Mastriana on 21 May 1968, and it was about that time that the Bahamian job allegedly was to be carried out. Elliott's secretary swore that McLaney and Elliott did much business and discussed the Bahamian casino deal in the office, although she did not know of any contract on Pindling.

It is likely that Mastriana had overheard his mafia comrades talk about the efforts to assassinate Fidel Castro, an endeavor once discreetly encouraged by the U.S. government. Lansky and Trafficante certainly were willing to try this, and the million-dollar contract on Fidel was widely rumored. It wasn't so hard to extrapolate a fancy tale about bumping off Pindling as well.

After the alleged hit failed, McLaney carried on with his business interests and Roosevelt went on to his ranch. Pindling proceeded to rent an island, Norman's Cay, to Colombian drug lord Carlos Lehder. Mastriana received temporary immunity for his testimony and lived in taxpayer-funded comfort for a while. His lurid accusations had obviously served him well – for a while – but was there any truth in them at all?

I'm Not a Crook! (but some of my best friends are)

Elliott Roosevelt flew from Lisbon to Miami on 29 September 1973. He first testified to the Senate subcommittee on 3 October.[2427] He received a surprisingly friendly, even deferential welcome from the panel, considering the sheer volume and diversity of the allegations. Members praised his "distinguished family." Senator Charles Percy gushed that his lifelong Republican mother switched party to vote for FDR. On several occasions the committee emphasized that witnesses could be prosecuted for perjury. Elliott was dutifully advised of this, too.[2428]

When Elliott spoke, he categorically denied any actual criminal activity – but he did not deny the provable facts, which were supported by canceled checks, receipts, plane tickets, and tape recordings. There was even an autographed photo from Elliott to Louis Mastriana: "To my friend and associate, Louis Mastriana, with the fond hope that your association with my company will prove more rewarding to you and your family in years to come." [2429]

Mr. Mastriana had again submitted a detailed affidavit in which he described his criminal dealings with Mr. Roosevelt and others, and on the last page he came to the 1968 Pindling assassination plan. He said:

> I have been asked to provide more details on the contract on Lyndon Pindling which I referred to in my previous testimony. Very early in my association with Elliott Roosevelt, Dominic Mantell called me and wanted to sit and talk with me regarding a business transaction.[i] I met with Mr. Mantell in Scotty's Coffee House in Miami Beach and we then

[i] Mastriana said that Mantell "is the Florida business rep. of the Stefano Magaddino organized crime family, Bufallo, NY… also represents the interests of the Carlo Gambino family, NY and the Angelo Bruno family,

took a ride in his Cadillac. His son-in-law was driving; his name is Anthony Celeste. At this point, Dominic told me that Meyer Lansky had given one Mike McLaney one million dollars and Mr. McLaney was to turn this money over to the Prime Minister of Nassau [sic], Lyndon O. Pindling, for a gambling license. This had transpired but the Prime Minister Pindling had failed to deliver the license upon his election. Dom at that time asked me if I would accept the contract on Pindling, and I said if the price was right I would. Dom told me to contract Mr. Roosevelt and also at that time, I would meet a Mr. McLaney who was very good people and he was associated with Mr. Lansky. The next day I met Elliott and Mr. McLaney and was asked if I would take a contract on Lyndon O. Pindling, and I said I would if the price was right. I was asked what I wanted, and I said $10,000 in advance and $100,000 when the hit was completed. This was agreed upon and I was told to pick up the money in Elliott's office. When I went to his office he had only $7500 in cash and I told him that this was not the deal discussed. I do not know where he got this money from. We then got into Elliott's car and went to Mr. McLaney's home on Venetian Causeway. At McLaney's house, Mr. Roosevelt got a check from McLaney made payable to Mr. Roosevelt and McLaney told him to cash it and give me the balance of the money. Instead of cashing the check himself (Elliott) he endorsed it over to me and I deposited it in my bank and proceeded to make arrangements to fulfill the contract.

I was told upon my arrival in Nassau to contact Mr. Dino Cellini, and he would render any possible assistance as needed. [i]

I journeyed to the Bahamas and contacted Mr. Cellini who assisted me with a car and driver in a tour of the island. I stayed at the Britannia Beach Hotel in Nassau. However, because of the peculiarity of the situation in that I could not quickly leave the island after the assassination was completed, I left the Bahamas and returned to Miami. I called Mantell up and gave him the reasons why I was unable to fulfill the obligation and at that time I was informed that Pindling made frequent trips to Florida and stayed at the DuPont Plaza Hotel in Miami. I made a survey of the grounds around the DuPont Plaza Hotel and found that it could be done under certain conditions. At a subsequent later date, it was attempted but due to circumstances it was never completed. The $10,000 was never returned to either Mr. McLaney or Mr. Roosevelt.[2430]

Even from an accomplished liar this was pretty strong stuff. It turned out that much of the story checked out, but not the clincher. McLaney had indeed helped Mr. Pindling win the election in expectation of a casino concession in the Bahamas. He had established offices in Nassau, ingratiated himself with leading party officials, and had submitted a plan for taking over gambling in the islands.

And Mr. Pindling had indeed reneged on the deal because of legal warnings. A British commission checked out the American gambler for the Bahamian government. It regarded "Mr. McLaney as a thoroughly dangerous person who is likely to do nothing but harm to the Bahamas." [2431]

McLaney, the casino-boss who worked with Lansky and the Kennedys, was a dear friend of Elliott's, and a frequent source of money for him. He was furious at Pindling, and he and his cohorts did discuss what to do about the matter. When the story first broke, McLaney confirmed that he had engineered Pindling's election on the promise

---

Philad." The subcommittee identified the "Mantell-Shinwell Group" as a major international securities fraud ring. Ernest Shinwell was the son of Britain's Baron Shinwell and lent credibility to the racket via the phony "Bank of Sark."

[i] Dino Cellini was a Bahamas-based casino boss associated with Lansky, and also with Robert Vesco and the IOS swindle. The Cellini brothers were not in direct charge in Nassau by this time; they apparently ran operations from Miami.

that Pindling would "run the bad guys out of gambling and have the government operate it:"

> …he would operate gambling for the government. McLaney would operate all the casinos for the government and then get half of the profits he said Pindling had promised. "He didn't keep his commitment with me," McLaney said, and did not hire foreign assistants and he allowed the same people to run gambling operations." [2432]

McLaney had been doublecrossed, probably by the Cellini-Lansky operation; Dino Cellini had been McLaney's guy in running the Nacional in Habana, but where his loyalty lay now was cloudy. From an investigatory viewpoint, there definitely was motive. But that was where the trail began fading out.[2433]

Angry and hurt, Elliott Roosevelt further testified:

> At this point, gentlemen, I desire to state that I am convinced that Mastriana and Lepera have perjured themselves before this subcommittee and have perpetrated a hoax upon the subcommittee to the point that they should be prosecuted to the fullest extent of the law…I sincerely believe that at the close of this inquiry I shall stand before the world completely acquitted of all the vicious lies…[2434]

Then Roosevelt, claiming poverty, complained that he was out thousands of dollars for his defense whereas his accusers were living "the life of Riley" on the taxpayer's dime. He regretted that he could not provide all the records asked for, because:

> Unfortunately, when I moved to Portugal, I had over two tons of records in the loft of my barn. If I had taken them over to Portugal I would have been taxed too much. Furthermore, to put them into storage would have cost me too much, because, as I say, I wasn't very wealthy. So those were all destroyed, burned, right out on the farm.[2435]

At this point historians are allowed to keel over screaming. Whatever was lost, it is a fact that Elliott's papers are the only ones (from the Roosevelt siblings) not available at the FDR Presidential Library. However, in this case at least, Elliott was primarily referring to his destruction of correspondence and financial records that might have incriminated him.

The Senate wanted to know, how did the son of FDR, General Elliott Roosevelt, come to be associated with this Miami Beach freak show?

> Miami Beach is known throughout the world as a place where many undesirable people gather. In fact, when I was mayor, they ran a newspaper investigation to find out the influence of the underworld, continuing influence in Miami Beach of the underworld, on the government of Miami Beach.
>
> A *Miami Herald* reporter came to me and had an interview and he asked me the direct question. He said, "Does the underworld," only he called it the Mafia – "control Miami Beach?"
>
> My answer was, "Hell, no. They own it."[2436]

That esteemed newspaper, in an important series of exposés of the Mafia in South Florida, commented: "He is far more accurate than he realizes."[2437] Or did he? The Senate investigation confirmed that Elliott was well-acquainted with numerous high-profile mobsters – that they used him, and he them.

Evidently Elliott knew what he was getting into.

> When I retired, or was defeated for reelection, I tried to rebuild my business, which suffered greatly in the time that I was mayor. I must say that I had a very, very difficult time in rebuilding. But a tremendous number of freaks and strange characters came through my office. I tried to run checks on them…
>
> One of the people that introduced me to S. Mort Zimmerman was a man called Thomas Donofrio, from Toledo, Ohio. [He] had been a very close friend of my brother John, and had done a great deal of business with him. I at one time had worked for Donofrio in trying to set up a pharmaceutical operation down in Cuba before the advent of the present Mr. Castro…[2438]

Elliott's connections from the Batista days were still warm.

The Capital National Bank Swindle

By now Donofrio was involved in some complex Florida banking transactions, referred to as the Capital National Bank (CNB) "situation." Elliott's secretary provided sworn testimony that "Mr. Donofrio was closely associated with Mr. Roosevelt in a number of business ventures which I cannot describe." In fact Donofrio rented office space in Roosevelt's office suite.[2439]

The secretary gave the names of a rogue's gallery of well-known mobsters, racketeers, con men and thieves who did regular business with her boss. The Capital National Bank appears to have been a flagship operation, but there were many other more or less concurrent scams active from 1968 to 1971.[i]

One of these professional hoodlums took credit for introducing Elliott to one Allan Lefferdink, "and subsequently Roosevelt acted as a broker in introducing Lefferdink to S. Mort Zimmerman in a transaction involving the purchase of the Capital National Bank of Miami by Lefferdink." [2440] The main reason for Elliott's eager compliance and assistance was his indebtedness.

Elliott, who had been appointed as bank director, told the subcommittee he had bowed out after a couple of months, having become suspicious. That, however, did not end his work with the main characters. Roosevelt was supposed to obtain an $87,000 fee for his assistance in "offshore bank transactions," but he said he only got a few tiny payments of that amount.[2441]

Something else bothered Elliott. It was that, "I must add that another reason for my feeling that I could not properly serve on that bank was that I did obtain a loan with collateral of horses in the amount of $45,000 from that bank…"[2442]

Yet Elliott continued his tight association with these and other organized crime figures. He said he was "willing to go into almost anything that would bring revenue in because I was having a hard time feeding my family." [2443]

As usual, what Elliott said did not quite match what others discovered. The Capital National Bank turned out to be an international swindle in which Mr. Roosevelt had been enlisted to play an important role. The bank had been acquired by Mort Zimmerman, a Texas wheeler-dealer. Because it was federally chartered, the bank had access to international business and carried a certain prestige upon which Mr.

---

[i] The Miami National Bank case was a different operation headed by Jimmy Hoffa and his mob friends.

Zimmerman could capitalize. That status also meant that the U.S. Comptroller of the Currency's office was trying to get the bank sold and into more reputable hands before the wheels came off entirely. Unfortunately, the new purchaser would turn out to be the Bermuda-based confidence artist Allan Lefferdink. And who set up the transfer?

Elliott Roosevelt, of course. A star mafia witness, Philip M. Wilson, told the committee that Elliott and a top securities swindler, Harold Audsley, together bought CNB from Zimmerman in order for it to be turned over to Lefferdink. The purpose was to use the Miami bank for clearing transactions of the latter's phony off-shore banks.[2444]

Elliott and Harold Audsley flew to Bermuda to sell Capital National. The bank's apparently honest vice president later said that Elliott had some $80,000 in overdue loans to the bank, against security in some family keepsakes: Roosevelt portraits. Presumably in addition to the horses.

> What the comptroller found at CNB was a jumble of bad loans made to friends and associates of Zimmerman and of his general counsel, Eugene Tannenbaum. Infante, the executive vice president of the bank, was charged with cleaning out the bad loans. But no sooner had he made progress than new bad loans would appear on the bank.[2445]

Attorney Tannenbaum went to prison for theft, embezzlement, false bank entries, reports and transactions in February 1972. Zimmerman, who had long known Robert Vesco, had a number of other felonious adventures. Columnist Jack Anderson linked him to Republican fund raiser Frederick Cheney LaRue, the "Watergate bag-man," in an FBI investigation ordered shut down by the Nixon regime.[i]

Roosevelt had no choice but to confirm most of the incontrovertible evidence already collected about CNB. He said:

> It is perfectly true that Mr. Lefferdink shortly thereafter came to the U.S., and I did take him to Dallas, TX, at the request of Mr. Donofrio, to introduce him to Mr. J. Mort Zimmerman for the purpose of buying that bank. It is true that Mr. Donofrio had arranged with Mr. Zimmerman for a finder's fee in the event of the sale of the bank. The agreement, as I remember, was drawn by Mr. Donofrio, in which he spelled out what each person was to receive from the sale of the bank, which involved several million dollars. It is perfectly true that Mr. Mort Zimmerman does not have a very favorable reputation, and it certainly has turned out later that Mr. Lefferdink has not got a very favorable reputation.

---

[i] Jack Anderson column, 9 JAN 74, in Palm Beach Post. Zimmerman seems to have led an exciting life. He began as a weapons engineer in Texas, was linked to Robert Vesco as early as 1968, and then got involved with a very large number of ephemeral companies in frequent legal trouble. Elliott was introduced to Z. by Donofrio via John R. Jack Anderson wrote that Z. was also connected with Lloyd Sahley in a scheme to funnel dirty money to the Republicans, specifically through Watergate conspirator Fred LaRue. That was apparently why Att. Gnl. Mitchell fired the FBI agent, Higgins, who found this out. Sahley was a serial swindler reputed to have worked with Carlos Marcello, New Orleans mafia boss. LaRue was a Mississippi oil fortune heir, a close friend of Mitchell's who quietly handled the money flows for the RNC. He worked with Bebe Rebozo and his bank to effect these transfers. Judge Sirica sentenced him to 1-3 years in return for cooperation. As it happened, LaRue's father was Sid Richardson's cousin. (Anderson's column is well worth reading. Excerpt: *The summary that Higgins allegedly was ordered to destroy and its supporting documents describes in detail how wealthy Republicans planned to loot a bank. One of the alleged principals was Lloyd Sahley, a far-traveling entrepreneur who headed the bankrupted Midwestern Securities Corp. The documents claim that Sahley was linked through securities holdings with S. Mort Zimmerman, a felon who allegedly has dealt in stolen securities with the Mafia. He also was a business associate of Nixon fund-raiser Fred LaRue.* See also NYT, 14 JUL 74, 24 DEC 75, 28 JUN 73, 11 MAY 74; and local Florida papers for Z.'s many scams.)

> I, at that time, had no way of being able to know that these men were anything but honorable men.[2446]

Lefferdink took over the bank, and from 1969-71 used it to loot overseas investors. Lefferdink's various shell companies ranged from Guernsey, Brussels and Amsterdam to the Bahamas, Panama, and the Cayman Islands. He was convicted in April 1976 of 15 counts of mail and wire fraud, and conspiracy. The federal government had to bring in the largest-ever number of foreign witnesses to testify.[2447]

At that time, Elliott ran an "investment consulting firm" known as Elliott Roosevelt International. This outfit listed assets of $137,000, of which $87,000 was the commission to be paid on the sale of CNB:

> The sale transferred the bank from the control of S. Mort Zimmerman, who would later plead guilty of fraud involving a related insurance company, to the control of a cloudy offshore fund run by Allen J. Lefferdink, who had played a role in some big-money swindles overseas.[2448]

Lefferdink was finally introduced to the public in a book in 1975 as "one of the truly great conmen of our times, who has bilked the public out of tens of millions of dollars, yet never spent a day in prison."[i] Although centered on Miami, Lefferdink ran his swindles via Bermuda and Europe and from his peripatetic yacht.

The Swiss Connection

While Elliott was in Miami hustling up cash in various convoluted ways, his brother James lived in luxury in a villa overlooking Lake Geneva, Switzerland, where he was the president of a unit of Investors Overseas Services (IOS).

At that time Switzerland's bank secrecy laws were still fully intact, and dirty money easily found its way into Geneva and Zürich, as well as into closer little paradises like the Bahamas, Bermuda, and Panama. There helpful shell companies and crooked banks could be quickly set up. That was why the subcommittee had been interested in questioning Elliott about the "Zürich International" bank fraud. He had allegedly been involved with offshore mutual funds used to bilk Americans out of their savings.

IOS, which James Roosevelt lent his name to, was an incredibly successful investment company that sold shares in American mutual funds to overseas investors. By the time James got in, it was already a $440 million company. By operating through a number of overseas shell companies, it was able to circumvent American and other national laws. The brain behind IOS was Bernard Cornfeld, a former social worker who was now suddenly famous for not only his "financial genius," but also for world-class sybaritic living.

IOS eventually collapsed in an orgy of theft orchestrated by the famous fugitive swindler Robert Vesco. Vesco had tried to cover his back by paying $200,000 to CREEP, the Committee to Reelect the President, and he was never caught by the U.S. government (it didn't try too hard). Vesco also hired Donald Nixon, the president's

---

[i] NYT, 6 JUL 75. The book was Dirty Money, by Thurston Clarke and John H. Tigue, Jr., 1975. In March 1975, a Miami grand jury charged Lefferdink with 18 counts of mail fraud, conspiracy, use of telephone to defraud, etc. (NYT, 22 MAR 75)

troubled nephew. Donald and his father of the same name were associates of Howard Hughes.[2449]

James said the crushing burden of supporting several greedy ex-wives induced him to take the Geneva job, despite numerous warning signs – but what he "personally" did was not crooked. Because he was then a U.S. representative to the United Nations, many observers denounced his acceptance of an IOS post in August 1966, especially since the investment company was under intense investigation by the SEC. The government knew already that IOS was big trouble brewing.[2450] Nevertheless, James ditched the UN job and went to work for IOS full-time.[2451]

The brief account James made of the Investors Overseas job is evasive and does not reflect what was reported at the time. It turned out that James was indebted to Bernie Cornfeld, the IOS mastermind. Apparently his financial needs induced him to go all the way with something he already knew was criminal. He even stuck it out as Robert Vesco edged out Cornfeld in IOS and took off with the remaining loot. He said afterwards, "When I saw that they were interested in their own fortunes, not the company's, I left entirely."[2452]

Contrition was not a family trait, but in his later writing, Jimmy occasionally professed to feel pangs of it.

Unfortunately, the public record, again, is sharply at variance. James Roosevelt was among 41 IOS executives accused by the SEC of stealing at least $224 million. The complaint charged that Mr. Roosevelt "chose to acquiesce in defendant Vesco's fraudulent plans and failed to discharge properly his responsibilities as director." It said his independence was impaired by a loan of $150,000 he had obtained through Mr. Vesco from the Bahamas Commonwealth Bank.[2453] That, however, was a small sum compared to Jimmy's total take from IOS.

James worked on this epic, colossal swindle with the crème-de-la-crème of global scammers from August 1966 until its collapse. The company had been in the searchlights of the SEC from the start. The Swiss authorities finally issued an arrest warrant for James Roosevelt in February 1973, but by then he had moved back to the California coast.[2454]

This is where the connection with Elliott, then in Miami and up to his eyeballs in mobsters, becomes of acute interest. Many of the criminal financial transactions associated with IOS went through the Bahamas. IOS invested heavily in casino resorts. Jimmy had long-standing connections with the top leaders of organized crime and apparently was instrumental in linking IOS with American mobsters.[2455] In time, space, and personal connections, Elliott's and Jimmy's financial machinations show numerous common data points. One of the shared IOS-Lansky agents was Swiss-born Sylvain Ferdman, used as a courier. Another common data point was Dino Cellini, the gangster who ran casinos for Meyer Lansky. He oversaw the Mob in the Bahamas, and it was Dino whom Louis Mastriana said he contacted to carry out the hit on Prime Minister Pindling. Cellini was also associated with laundering the cash stolen from IOS. It was widely thought that the new casino resort the Cellini brothers operated on Paradise Island near Nassau was funded by that money.[2456]

All in all, the islands were a pleasant refuge and a reasonably safe headquarters for international criminals. With the IOS loot, Robert Vesco went into drug-smuggling with Carlos Lehder, paying off the government as necessary. James, however, got out of IOS and opened an investment business in Corona del Mar, California.[2457] He was allowed off the hook by the SEC, and evidently the Swiss charges were never pursued. Jimmy stuck with Richard Nixon until the very end – not Watergate, but death.[2458] The two remained personal friends even in disgrace.[i]

Jimmy sued the *Sunday Telegraph* for libel in 1975, it having reported his involvement in the IOS story as recounted above. He lost, and had to pay an estimated $56,000 court costs.[2459]

Via Donald Nixon, the Bahamas connection ties into the Watergate scandal. The Nixons and their friend Bebe Rebozo in Key Biscayne were looking for "unofficial" ways of funding the president's reelection. Cash contributions from Hughes, who hid on a floor of a luxury hotel in the Bahamian capital from 1970 to 1972, were much appreciated; one who kept count said Nixon received "at least $505,000 that is known."[ii] Many thought that the Watergate burglary was ordered because the president's lieutenants were concerned that the Democrats had evidence of the extensive dealings between the Nixon family, Howard Hughes, Robert Vesco, and the Mafia. If so, they failed to some extent, for the contours of the matter became known in the course of unraveling Watergate; but that happened after the Jackson Committee washed its hands of the Roosevelt situation in late 1973.[2460]

We do know that in 1973, Robert Vesco retreated to Costa Rica, where he was soon reported to have made some powerful friends:

> Young Donald Nixon, 27, flies regularly on Vesco's private Boeing 707, outfitted with sauna bath, discotheque, and a communications system so sophisticated that Donald once said it makes his uncle's Air Force One look like a Piper Cub. Vesco also has had business dealings with the President's brothers, F. Donald Nixon, 57, and Edward C. Nixon, 42, and he lent $150,000 to James Roosevelt when FDR's eldest son was on the IOS's board of directors. Another loan, of $200,000, went to Bahamas President Lynden O. Pindling… Vesco lent $2.15 million at 7% interest to a firm owned by President of Costa Rica Jose Figueres.[2461]

It is thought-provoking that in and around 1970, the two eldest sons of President Roosevelt were both deeply mired in enormous international swindles. The other two brothers had peripheral roles in the network, providing contacts, introductions, and occasional business partnerships. All of them walked off scot-free.

Despite the recency and the curious overlap of his troubles, James Roosevelt was not called to testify to the Senate subcommittee in Elliott's case. It's a shame, for it could have been very interesting.[2462]

Wriggling off the Hook

As for the accusations of Mr. Mastriana, Elliott Roosevelt presented himself as a victim of a demonic hoax perpetrated by that pathetic con artist. He said it took him 45 days to discover that all the business opportunities Mastriana brought to him were

---

[i] LAT, 29 MAR 76. Nixon sent JR to Vienna to represent the U.S. at the Austrian president's funeral in 1974. Whether the Swiss considered this a premeditated slap was not recorded. The SEC chairman was later indicted for impeding the Vesco case (1975), after Vesco was let go by the Swiss after high-level US intervention (1973).

[ii] After the Bahamas, Hughes fled to Managua, Nicaragua, where a proud Anastasio Somoza welcomed him in person (a rare treat by that time). (Barlett/Steele, Empire.) Amount to RN: Russo, 349.

fraudulent. He lost $10,000 to him, though most was not his own money; when he called the FBI they said "You might as well kiss it goodbye." [2463]

Roosevelt was correct in labeling Mastriana a pathological liar. It is far more plausible that Elliott was a gullible victim of the mob than a Mafia kingpin. Yet there is a common saying, "You can't cheat an honest man." The point is that if Elliott had been on the straight and narrow, not hunting for easy riches with shady characters, he would not have been taken in.

Looking back, he offered a strange admission to a reporter:

> Roosevelt recalls an "infinite number" of people offering him positions while his parents were alive. "All they were really doing is conning you and getting close to the decision-makers. It's almost impossible to differentiate between the honest ones and those conning you."
>
> Despite this, Roosevelt said, "I still bite." [2464]

Still, the big story was the Pindling job. How did Elliott explain the existence of the down-payment check?

> Mr. McLaney, on several different occasions when I needed money at a particular time for a particular purpose, when I didn't have it in my account, did advance me funds, all of which I repaid, and he can testify to that, and at this time Mastriana needed the money that minute. So when I obtained the check from Mr. McLaney I just endorsed it over to Mastriana right then and there…[2465]

This matches what McLaney told the *Miami News* the day after the story came out. He said he'd lent Elliott $2,500 to $5,000 on "four or five occasions." But he never asked what for (he said), and he always eventually got the money back.[2466]

Mastriana, Elliott said, needed the money to obtain a loan on a labor union in New Jersey, not to kill anybody: "I went to Mr. McLaney and asked him if I could borrow for a few days $2,500 to get a commitment for funds which would be invested by me by a union…the net result was that Mastriana was in such a tremendous hurry to get his money that rather than even depositing it and then drawing a check to Mastriana, I just endorsed the check over to Mastriana for him to go and do his part." [2467]

The Senate subcommittee was relieved to hear that, believing that Mastriana had conned Elliott. Senator Edward Gurney (R-FL) even volunteered that, "The purpose of this hearing, of course, is to permit you to clear your good name." Next year, Gurney would be up on bribery charges himself.[i]

Elliott admitted to being aware of McLaney's dispute with Pindling. But his involvement with him was of a different nature – one he had some experience with. The casino boss wanted Elliott to be an airline president!

> Mr. ROOSEVELT. I have had a relationship with Mr. McLaney over many, many years. He is one of the finest people to have as a friend that I have ever enjoyed. He may have had his difficulties from time to time, and he may be, as alleged that he is, in fact, a gambler. I think he fully acknowledges that he has been in the casino operation business.
>
> But as far as my relations with him, they were purely social. From time to time I did have occasion to borrow money from him when he said he had a few dollars, and I repaid

---

[i] Ibid, 375. Two trials found Gurney not guilty of taking bribes, conspiracy, and lying. (NYT, 24 JUL 74).

him, as he will be prepared to testify. As far as I am concerned, I can say nothing against Mr. McLaney.

As far as I am concerned, I can state that at no time did I have anything to do with Mr. McLaney's business in the Bahamas, nor with his efforts to get the casino license. I know for a fact that at that time he told me he was very upset over what he thought Mr. Pindling did to him in reneging on a previous commitment.... He told me he was extremely upset, because he had helped quite considerably, as I think the record bears out, in helping Mr. Pindling on his election campaign.

I have had one business transaction in the whole time that I have known Mr. McLaney, and that was to assist him in the purchase of an airplane. I have been a pilot for a great many years, dating back to before World War II, and he wanted me to examine an airplane that he wanted to buy to use between Miami and Haiti for the purpose of bringing customers down, tourists down, to Haiti as is a practice followed by various hotels and casinos in Las Vegas from various parts of the country.

This is a DC-3 aircraft. I went out, I examined the aircraft, I made a recommendation to him as to how much it would cost. I agreed to temporarily serve as president of the company that he was setting up to operate it under because he wanted somebody knowledgeable to get the aircraft in flying condition, to operate for not only the tourist trade but also for freight purposes between Miami and Haiti.

I only was president for a few days at that time because I got some publicity stating that I was going in the airline business and I wanted no misunderstanding.[2468]

There is no indication Elliott Roosevelt was still flying at this time. It is interesting though, that barring the unfavorable publicity, he might have continued in an outfit that sounds pretty close to a "Casino Airlines." The business was incorporated as Air Transport Corporation. It never operated.[2469]

It turned out that McLaney's assistance to Mr. Pindling had consisted of a helicopter, a single-engine Cessna, and a DC-3. (Another time he said there had been two DC-3s, two helicopters, and two boats given to the campaign.)[2470] The expectation was that McLaney would receive concessions of equivalent value if Pindling won. He did win, but a British inquiry concluded that McLaney was so dangerous that the Prime Minister should have nothing to do with him. So Pindling did not approve the casino – but he did eventually repay McLaney $60,000.[2471]

After being declared *persona non grata* in the Bahamas, McLaney had some choice words for the guy he had installed as prime minister. As early as 1969 he had publicly said that Pindling's government was "run on dictatorship and by manipulation for the benefit of a few." Except him. And he screeched that he'd pay $10,000 to anyone who could prove he, McLaney, was really associated with the Mob.[2472]

Elliott Roosevelt admitted that he had indeed met with Prime Minister Pindling. To promote some business ideas, he met with George Thompson, Pindling's law partner in Nassau. This was in connection with another scheme Elliott was promoting. It involved the building of a tomato canning factory in the islands. Like most of his projects, it went nowhere.[2473] But that wasn't all: "I met him on a couple of other occasions. One was when he opened the casino at Lucaya [Freeport], I believe."[2474] Elliott said he had no gambling interests himself, although he was well aware of McLaney's.

I knew him all the way through while I was the mayor of Miami Beach. As a matter of fact, on one occasion he did ask me for a character reference. At that time it was in relationship to his efforts to get a gambling casino license from the Government of the Bahamas.[2475]

And that's where we finally get to the elusive Meyer Lansky, widely acknowledged to be the brains behind the underworld's operations in the entire region. The senators asked Elliott about him.

> Mr. ROOSEVELT. Not only did it not show that [relationship], but I even asked Mr. McLaney on occasion about what his relationship could be with Mr. Lansky or any of Mr. Lansky's associates. He invariably answered to me that he did not know Mr. Lansky, that he had never done business with him, and that as far as he was concerned Mr. Lansky was responsible for him not getting the gambling casino license in the Bahamas…I have never seen Mr. Lansky. I don't even know what he looks like…I swear under oath that I have never done any business with Mr. Lansky.[2476]

Despite his close association with McLaney, and his knowledge of the fury McLaney had for Mr. Pindling, Elliott swore that "at no time did I ever hear or hear anybody discuss an assassination plot on the life of Mr. Pindling."

Norman Tyrone had been named as an Elliott associate in some of the lawsuits against him. Now he showed up again. Under intense questioning, Elliott admitted that he had sent Tyrone to the Bahamas to set up a corporation, which, he said, never did any business. Tyrone had also been involved in the Bavarian Inns situation. It appears that Tyrone used Elliott for legitimacy in rigged business initiatives. In that connection, the senators wanted to know if Elliott knew anything about a number of named persons and corporate entities. It was apparent that the committee was privy to information about Elliott's activities which it was not willing to reveal publicly. Thus he was able to claim that he had no recollection of the entities mentioned.

Another character Elliott worked with was Sam Kay. Kay had, among many other things, been involved in a Mob scheme to market now worthless Cuban pesos at face value.[2477] Kay was a peculiar old fellow, known as "Miami Beach's mystery financial wizard." Local reporters wrote:

> At one time or another, Kay has been involved with most of the mobsters, fronting for them, guiding them through the corporate and financial maze. 'They are no good. Their word is no good,'…I could tell you lots of stories," Kay says with a smile. "But my life insurance isn't paid up." Kay doesn't want to talk about Meyer Lansky, although he says Lansky is 'making lots of money. He's gotten involved in the Bahamas gambling now. He's a big man on the Beach, but it wouldn't do anybody any good to go into that." [i]

Elliott went to Kay when he needed money:

> Mr. ROOSEVELT. Sam Kaye is probably the biggest shylock on Miami Beach and occasionally we would go…when we were looking for funds – I know of one occasion I was so hard up and I needed $500. My wife gave me her most valuable ring to go and

---

[i] Miami Herald, 29 JAN 67: Mob Money: Silent Host in Beach Hotels, in FBI file. Mastriana said Sam Kay represented most of the money from Detroit and Cleveland and would pick up hotels and motels in Florida for those interests. Of course Dom Mantell was there to make sure he didn't step out of line. (Hearings 147)

> pawn. Sam Kaye sent us to a jewelry store on Lincoln Road where I got $500 on about a $5,000 ring…I paid 10% interest a week for that…
>
> Mr. Kaye did, on occasion, say that he would like to look at some of our investment packages because he did trade in real estate in the south Florida area. I think we may very easily have taken some properties that we knew about, income properties, to him, none of which did we do any business on.
>
> I might also add that when I was trying to raise money, I had a 25-foot fishing boat that had cost me quite a lot of money and finally Kaye through one of his people, Mr. Mantell, I believe his name was, Dominic Mantell, brought a man over who bought the boat from me for $8,000.[2478]

"Mantell, I believe his name was." Everyone in organized crime knew Dominic Mantell; he was the driving force in the Mantell-Shinwell operation, a multinational racket making millions on fake and stolen securities. The Jackson committee only briefly touched on this operation. When other investigators delved into it, they came across the names of very powerful people in the United States, Europe, the Caribbean, and, surprisingly, the Vatican. One of the few writers who have looked into this hole asserted that Nixon's people – Kleindienst specifically – shut down any further investigation.[i]

On that background, Mantell's selling Elliott Roosevelt's boat seemed like a trivial favor for a rather pathetic, peripheral figure. The Jackson subcommittee had accidentally lifted the veil a crack over far greater things.

You can't Cheat an Honest Man

Bedrock of Anglo-American jurisprudence is the principle that the accused must be assumed innocent until proven guilty. Sometimes, however, the "assumed" is forgotten in favor of the delusion that the guilty are in fact innocent until a verdict is rendered. The investigation of Elliott Roosevelt's mafia connections was cut short, and we are therefore left with a cloud of probabilities.

Mr. Mastriana, a deranged con-man, certainly heard of Mr. McLaney's wish to get back at Pindling. Most likely, by cleverly adding this overheard background to the checks he had already received from Elliott, he concocted an assassination story that would get him a few more "paid federal holidays."

Mr. Lepera's testimony is far harder to dismiss. He was under a Mob death sentence, subject to secret witness resettlement, and was singing like a bird about every last thing he'd ever done for the dark side. Of that, Elliott's alleged illegal transactions constituted merely one percent or so. They were trivial entries in Lepera's catalog of misdeeds. Most of Lepera's stories checked out; but there was sufficient ambiguity in the evidence of Elliott's transactions to leave the committee with loose ends.

Perhaps there was no fire – just a billowing cloud of thick smoke, and more heat than normal people could stand. What good would it do anyone to determine that Elliott Roosevelt, whose family still was of at least symbolic prominence in the Democratic Party, was a crook? He said he did nothing actually illegal, and if he did, it was hard if not impossible to prove.

---

[i] Hammer: The Vatican Connection, 1982, investigated the Mantell-Shinwell operation without being able to determine its full cast and extent. The Senate hearings elicited testimony that described some details of it.

Furthermore, this long after the war, few people remembered Elliott and his once famous shenanigans. Probably fewer still cared. To young people, he was by now a curiosity, a genetic residual of vaguely glorious days a generation ago. In 1973, mentioning the Roosevelts no longer caused shouting, spitting, and fistfights.

Like it or not, justice is political. The laws are political by definition; their application is often political in practice. To send someone to jail, somebody has to have an interest therein; if enough people have an interest to the contrary, the wheels of justice may just grind to a halt.

Because Senator Jackson had found and contacted Elliott through his brother Franklin Jr., Elliott thought that it was Franklin who was out to destroy him. Franklin evidently said "Well I hope they bury him." [2479] Elliott said Franklin was paying him back for his controversial book about his parents by implicating him in the swindles. It did not help Franklin's case that it was he who had first sent Mr. Mastriana, the "pathological liar" down to Elliott to offer his assistance.[2480]

The plan had been to pursue the matter with further hearings towards the end of 1973. In fact, it was noted that "the subcommittee staff is upset over the derailment of its plans for a series of hearings about securities swindles. They hadn't intended for the unsubstantiated murder allegations against Mr. Roosevelt to get a public hearing…"[2481]

It was not to be. In December, the Senate Permanent Subcommittee on Investigations declined to pursue the fraud leads, and a final report was issued in June 1974. Senator Jackson said investigators could not corroborate the charges against Elliott Roosevelt, and they had failed to disclose any illegal transaction in which he had been involved.[2482]

Patsy Lepera had testified that such transactions would leave no paper trail.

Senator Jackson decided not to proceed because the evidence was unlikely to hold up in court. He must also have considered that, in the midst of the Watergate scandal, few would have been eager to drag an icon of American history through the mud. In 1973, there was no Senator Brewster with an axe to grind; no journalistic stalkers with elephant memories like Westbrook Pegler or Walter Trohan.

In addition, pursuing the matter could be acutely inconvenient both at home and abroad. It would drag down the Bahamas' first prime minister, who was a hero in the newly independent nation. It would destroy the reputation (or what remained thereof) of Sir Stafford Sands, the finance minister who was the architect of the resurgent economy of the Bahamas, and many of his thieving cohorts. Would Haiti, Mr. McLaney's operating location, get involved, or pre-Castro Cuba? Among the high and mighty at home, whose names might turn up?

One such name was Robert Vesco's. He was living as a fugitive in the Bahamas and other small countries without extradition treaties. Vesco had close ties to Richard Nixon, and researchers have spent considerable effort trying to map his worldwide financial mycelium. Had the U.S. pursued him for real, it would have drawn in, probably not Elliott, but James Roosevelt, who worked with Vesco in the IOS swindle in Switzerland. Numerous high-ranking Europeans would get stained with him.

If Vesco had turned up, so would certainly Bebe Rebozo, president of the Key Biscayne Bank. Rebozo, according to the FBI "a non-member associate of organized crime," funneled illegal campaign contributions and "discount" real estate to his close friend Richard Nixon. Elliott Roosevelt admitted to dealing with Rebozo in some cases where he fronted for mob figures. Rebozo had gained riches while staying close to Florida's playboy Senator George Smathers – literally, as they were neighbors in

Biscayne. Nixon was helped to move into the same neighborhood, purchasing the "Florida White House" from Smathers. The other rich Nixon crony, Robert Abplanalp, who secured the mansion in San Clemente known as the Western White House, also had a house in Biscayne – and an island hideaway in the Bahamas.[2483]

John Connally visited with Bebe, Abplanalp and Nixon on that island. He remembered:

> Bebe had been a close friend of Lyndon Johnson and John Kennedy before him [RN]. I knew him through those same years, and he has never used his Presidential ties for any personal gain. He never divulged to anyone the secrets entrusted to him, and some were intimate indeed. What Bebe saw, he kept to himself.

Connally was impressed; friends like that, especially of the multimillionaire kind, are most useful.[2484]

Rebozo's bank was a suspected pipeline for mafia money from Bahamian casinos. Bebe was, much like Elliott Roosevelt, a sort of ambassador between the underworld and the visible world. Nixon, Rebozo, and the mobsters were all involved in complex Florida real estate deals. That Nixon was the Mafia's president is probably an exaggeration; but he helped those who helped him.[2485]

Rebozo was also a friend of another rich fugitive who could turn up, Howard Hughes. He too was in exile in the Bahamas, having convinced the local government he was worth sheltering despite American tax charges against him. Hughes worked with Rebozo to support Nixon with briefcases full of cash. And Hughes had been interested in purchasing a casino in Nassau himself during that same period, thus competing with the Mob as he had done in Las Vegas. The deal did not go through.

For Senate investigators, slogging through these fuming lava fields must have been a dispiriting task. There was a lot going on in 1973-74, and most of it wasn't pretty. After a prolonged death struggle, Richard Nixon resigned in August 1974, and an exhausted nation left many leads on, or under, the table. It was over; move on. Then pardon the president and declare the long national nightmare over.

And Elliott Roosevelt skated again, at least the fifth time Congress gave up on him.

In his own mind, he had been absolutely and irrefutably exonerated. He was furiously bitter at the media for nosing around in the matter. Senator Jackson's cautious conclusion that the committee hadn't found enough evidence for judicial referral seemed to mean to Elliott that he was the most unfairly persecuted innocent in the history of the world. "It caused me to have a heart attack," he said.[2486]

Follow the Money

There are a couple of persistent problems writing about the Mafia. One could be called the "Frank Sinatra syndrome." You may do business with mobsters, your friends may be mobsters, and you may eagerly take their favors and happily return them, but all that doesn't make you a mobster. "Association" is not a crime. You have to be proved beyond a reasonable doubt to actually have committed crimes. That's hard enough even with the true bad guys.

The second problem might be called the "Joe Kennedy syndrome." Even someone who is undeniably a thoroughly dishonest schemer, seemingly in cahoots with every gangster on the globe, may well spend most of his time doing honest work and may in many respects bequeath the world an estimable legacy. Organized crime is a spectrum.

This makes it difficult to determine whether the undeniably strong association between mobsters and the Roosevelt sons was somehow essential or merely circumstantial.

Some believe that the link between organized crime and the Roosevelts (as well as many subsequent presidents of either party) began with Prohibition. We can, however, definitely discern an early mob link to James Roosevelt. It seems to have begun with Joe Kennedy, migrating over Joe Schenck and Sidney Korshak to many of the hallowed names of organized crime.[i]

From time to time, the kid brothers followed in Jimmy's footsteps, but they did not fill them. Elliott's gangster buddies did not trust him, and he was usually more swindlee than swindler in the schemes he pursued. Jimmy was the professional. He died on a "high note;" i.e. a low but unprosecuted note. Elliott died begging the government for relief.

J. Edgar Hoover left the Mafia alone. He had been hired to protect the system, and he realized that organized crime was an integral part of the system. To fight it would have been, well, *subversive.*

Today, the Mafia is a pale shadow of its former bloody self. There are two explanations for that. The first is that after J. Edgar Hoover and Richard Nixon were out of the way, federal law enforcement gradually became serious about eliminating the great crime families. Few would deny this.

The other explanation, more fundamental, is simply that the Mafia won. Almost all its work has been legalized: alcohol, gambling, loan-sharking, even financial schemes of head-splitting complexity that effectively cover for astronomical-scale looting. The Mob's bread-and-butter, the numbers rackets, are now run by the states, with far worse odds. Only illegal drugs can now support massive organized crime per sé; and most of that has been outsourced abroad. Finally, the purchase of politicians is now seen as a routine and integral part of democracy.

By that interpretation, the overlap between politics and organized moneymen of ill repute has not disappeared; it has been normalized.

Perhaps it is time for political scientists to devise a Turing test for governments: if it is not possible to detect any difference in behavior between organized crime and organized government, then how can one claim they are different? At the very least it is really hard to tell where one ends and the other begins.

On that background it is not so surprising that the Roosevelt kids were involved with gangsters. Of course the Mayor of Miami Beach had to be cognizant of, and duly respectful of, the overwhelming influence of the Mafia. To suggest that James did not see through the IOS swindle, or any of the others he was associated with in his life, is absurd. As for Franklin Jr. and John, the associations were clearly more circumstantial. They had always been more careful.

After the debacles of the early 1970s, Elliott – and Jimmy – lay low for a few years. At least as far as the public knew.

---

[i] Russo: Supermob, leaves that impression in his richly documented exposé.

I NEVER MET A DICTATOR I DIDN'T LIKE

It is not recorded whether Elliott Roosevelt's emigration to Portugal in June 1972 had anything to do with his connections with Florida mobsters, or with a need to make distance with them. The Senate investigation of his financial affairs did not take place until September and October of 1973.

When Elliott and Patty moved to Portugal, they had "a ton of money." Their finances had turned around suddenly and dramatically. The reason apparently was the purportedly sensational tell-all book about his parents, *An Untold Story,* which Elliott was about to have published.

Both before and after Elliott came back to testify before the Senate in September 1973, he had a number of odd adventures in Portugal, then still a semi-fascist state. The Roosevelts did not make the news in the United States on that account, but they certainly did exercise the State Department.

Why Portugal? Elliott had suggested Central America, where he had connections, but Patty was not too keen on the banana republics her husband had tried to do business with in Miami. She, influenced by *Fodor's*, thought Portugal would be nifty. It was warm, beautiful, and cheap – kind of like the California coast, but with civilized people. The Portuguese, lagging well behind the rest of Europe, retained a reputation for being delightful and generous.[2487]

It was quite an improvement for the ex-mayor and his wife. Around 1970 Elliott and Patty were broke and desperately hustling for money. In 1971, Elliott had abruptly left his job as executive director of the Miami Beach Tourist Authority. He made clear that this was the end of his public career. He also had to resume his occasional auctioning of his and Patty's belongings – including Rooseveltiana.[2488]

Elliott and Patty had temporarily moved to a ranch south of Miami. Again, Elliott kept Arabian horses. Wags suggested that now he'd lost the Jewish vote for sure.[2489]

The reporter Jim Bishop caught up with them and noted:

> We talked across the fence, Elliott Roosevelt on the inside teaching manners to a white Arabian stallion. The ranch is on a Kelly-green billiard table called Goulds, Florida. His wife, Patti, plump and quick of mind and tongue, was in a stable watching a new-born colt breathe rapidly.[2490]

How did the Roosevelts go from penury to buying a large estate in sunny Portugal? For one thing, the couple sold or auctioned off a number of possessions and memorabilia before leaving the country. Another answer lies in Elliott's bestselling new book, which certainly netted him in the hundreds of thousands. It was later leaked that *An Untold Story* "went to Dell paperback for half a million dollars" after being published by Putnam. The book caused a row and a family explosion in March 1973 when prepublicity and excerpts in *Ladies Home Journal* ripped open some old wounds.[2491]

An Untold Story infuriated a great number of people because of its honesty. For the first time one of the Roosevelts dropped the pretense, repudiated the hagiographers, and plainly listed FDR's affairs and Eleanor's marital boycott. The image presented was one of real people with real problems and faults. If anything, for courage in truth-telling the book should have gotten its author applause. Not that the book was an academic work – it had the light, gossipy Elliott stamp all over it. Almost as if he'd written it himself.

"Literary Matricide," *Time* spat.[2492]

Perhaps the problem was that opinioneers seldom pause to actually read the works they get puffed up about. Everyone focused on one sentence of Elliott's: the one about Eleanor and Franklin never again living as "husband and wife" – presumably acceptable doublespeak for "they did not have sex." This was surely the truth; the rest of the book wasn't about that, but who cared? This "hook" did serve to sell the book.

FDR's dalliances were actually perfectly well-known from the outset by the savvy and connected, but in those pre-Clintonian days the public wasn't deemed worthy of knowing such things. That sham ran parallel to the principal deception, the systematic concealment of FDR's paraplegia and then his physical unraveling in 1944-5.

The Hebrew admonition "Thou shalt honor thy father and mother" was much bandied about by critics. But Elliott had reached the stage where he thought he would now honor his parents by telling the truth about them, and stop spouting the by then virtually solidified Roosevelt mythology.

Amazingly, one ancient Congressman who lashed out in rage was no less than Hamilton Fish of New York, FDR's stubborn arch-enemy during the neutrality debate. He still called FDR a Fabian socialist and a sell-out to Stalin. But he couldn't handle seeing a son reveal his parents' bedroom secrets. "No son has ever before placed such a contemptible stigma on his parents." Fish, who loathed and fiercely fought the late president's policies, nevertheless recommended that Elliott be horsewhipped.[2493]

Others who flew into a rage were Elliott's siblings, who, of course, knew full well what their brother was talking about. They issued a joint declaration: "We, four of the five children of Franklin and Eleanor Roosevelt, are deeply aware of their lifetime dedication to help people in this country and in all lands…painful as it is, we therefore feel we must disassociate ourselves completely from this book." [2494]

To columnist Jack Anderson, the brothers let it be known just how many times each of them had bailed Elliott out of his crackpot investment schemes:

> "I have bailed Elliott out of one business deal after another. I've just written it all off," said Franklin. "Elliott has borrowed money from every member of the family, including his own children, and has made little effort to pay it back," said James.[2495]

A few years later, James submitted some choice comments to the FDR Library's oral history program. He noted that:

> There were many, many instances where something would have happened in my brother Elliott's life where she [Eleanor] was called upon to do something for him or for his family that she would never let on the rest of the family that she had done it or was going to do it or even how she felt about it…I know she would occasionally send him money if he appealed to her and told her he was so hard up that he couldn't eat for the next week or something.[2496]

James instructed the Library that his more incendiary statements about his brother not be revealed until Elliott was safely dead. He commented on kid Elliott's "deep" problems and then said:

> …when he used to have family gatherings it nearly always ended up with Franklin and John and myself having a bitter argument with Elliott. And I would say that probably Franklin and John and I were closer overall through the years than with Elliott because we

kept in more natural contact, not through any great effort on our part, just in natural contact. It just happened that way.[2497]

That was 1979. James noted that the siblings were unable to find Elliott at the time.

The enmity renewed by the book would have consequences, when, during the ensuing Mafia scandal, Elliott perceived his brothers as being behind the allegations against him. Safe in Portugal, he didn't need their money for a while. He was busy with a whole new crop of unusual entrepreneurial initiatives.

The verdant countryside west of Lisbon, holding the charming medieval towns of Estoril, Cascais, Sintra and many others, has long been a preferred retreat for wealthy foreigners in need of peace and quiet. Coincidentally, Estoril was the retirement home for Fulgencio Batista, and Dino Cellini operated the world-famous casino there after he was run out of Cuba and the Bahamas.

Elliott purchased the 170-acre Quinta dos Cedros, and began to farm once again. Sidelines included cattle, fruits and vegetables, and a "big chicken operation for eggs and broilers." But the flagship hobby was to raise Arabian horses. All his life raising horses was his joy; but not theirs. Horses – and dogs – unfortunate enough to wind up with Elliott faced an uncertain future. Finally, though, the retired American couple had some peace and some money.[2498] "We are mad about Portugal and are going to live there forever. We have 26 horses and servants coming out of our ears."[2499]

It would be nice to end with: *and they lived happily ever after*. Yet Elliott hadn't been in Portugal long before he got himself into serious diplomatic, legal and financial troubles.

In August 1968, Portugal's frugal, sensible, and competent dictator, the aging economist Dr. Antonio de Oliveira Salazar, suffered a debilitating stroke that landed him in an iron lung. The forty-year old dictatorship passed to his dour associate, Prime Minister Marcelo Caetano, a stern but highly regarded law professor. However, dictators, no matter how humble, were then rapidly going out of style. The authoritarian *Estado Novo* in a "multicontinental Portugal" that Salazar and Caetano had seen as the absolute bedrock of the ancient nation was elsewhere regarded as an ossified, anachronistic colonial empire.

Thus, in 1972, Portugal's rulers had very few friends. Elliott Roosevelt and a few other rogues were among them.

The Caetano regime could use the famous name Roosevelt for many purposes: to promote tourism and business, to lobby with the American government, and to generally legitimize itself. In turn, Elliott could use his new country's government for financial assistance as well as help in promoting himself as an important international diplomat.

At first, his "lobbying" was touristic in character. Also, he dabbled in promoting Portuguese wines. He established a real-estate company to supplement the ranch. But Elliott didn't limit himself to non-controversial items. True to habit, he soon fell in with a shady crowd.

The first indication that something was amiss came when Elliott announced to the press that he was resigning as an officer of Commerce International Inc., a Portuguese trading firm that sold weapons to small countries around the world. He quit that gig in December 1972, claiming he hadn't been paid for his work.[2500] The *Miami Herald* heard that Elliott had been president of the shadowy outfit, which had tried to "exploit" his name to "maximize profits in the world's arms market." Now who, in 1972, would be interested in purchasing weapons through Portugal? Curiously, Elliott later claimed that it wasn't *Fodor's* that had sent him to Portugal: "I was working for a trading corporation and this was a very central spot from which to travel and be able to have some time at home…but I now do not work for that firm."[2501]

Now we know a lot more about the trouble Elliott got into, because a large archive of State Department correspondence has been recently declassified. This casts the son of the late president into a peculiar and troubled light.

> BEGIN CONFIDENTIAL:
>
> FOR YOUR INFORMATION, ROOSEVELT HAS A HISTORY OF QUESTIONABLE DEALINGS HERE IN PORTUGAL. GOP'S [Government of Portugal] SUSPICION CONCERNING CURRENCY TRANSFER IS NOT WHOLLY UNFOUNDED. THE TAX CLAIM IS GETTING WIDE PRESS PUBLICITY HERE IN PORTUGAL, AND NEWSPAPER ACCOUNTS ARE RECITING OLD STORIES OF ROOSEVELT'S BEING QUESTIONED BY CONGRESS CONCERNING AN ASSASSINATION PLOT AGAINST BAHAMIAM PRIME MINISTER PINDLING TWO YEARS AGO AND HIS ASSOCIATION WITH A REAL ESTATE FIRM IN PORTUGAL CALLED TORRALTA IN WHICH THE GOVERNMENT HAS HAD TO INTERVENE BECAUSE OF FINANCIAL AND CURRENCY IRREGULARITIES. ROOSEVELT HAS ALSO BEEN VERY CLOSE WITH THE REPRESENTATIVES OF RHODESIA IN LISBON AND ONCE INVOLVED THE EMBASSY IN A VERY EMBARRASSING SITUATION ON ACCOUNT OF IT. END CONFIDENTIAL [2502]

So wrote Frank Carlucci, American ambassador in Lisbon, in a warning to the embassy in London on 14 February 1975. The Roosevelts were then busy evacuating themselves and their property from strife-torn Portugal to the relative safety of England.

Carlucci was no second-rater. He was a top operative who was sent to troubled places to keep the Soviets out. In 1975, that place was Lisbon. In 1987, Carlucci, a long-time associate of Donald Rumsfeld, replaced Caspar Weinberger as Secretary of Defense.

For the Roosevelts, a lot had happened during their two years of exile. On 25 April 1974, the Carnation Revolution overthrew the fifty-year dictatorship and replaced it with an unstable and ill-defined faction of young Army officers known as the MFA (*Movimiento das Forças Armadas*). This movement was not nearly so keen on having Elliott Roosevelt around. In the gathering Portuguese chaos, which initially tended towards communism, the Roosevelts were not comfortable with the surroundings anymore.

The ex-New Dealer, who had so ferociously railed against European imperialism in his earlier days, had oddly enough found Portuguese imperialism very much to his liking. This we know because he held forth in an interview with a leading daily, *Diario de Noticias*, published prominently on 21 September 1973.

The American embassy reported that Roosevelt had said he believed "certain powerful interests" in the United States were out to get him. They were using the Bahamas-Mastriana connection for this purpose. Now why would anyone want to do that? Because, he said, he had publicly expressed displeasure with U.S. policy toward Portugal and Rhodesia in letters to President Nixon, Dr. Kissinger, and the *New York Times* and other newspapers.

That was an unusual defense, because three months earlier he had actually written a ringing defense of President Nixon, whose Watergate hole was getting deeper by each day. As late as just prior to Nixon's resignation, Elliott railed against the investigation:

"We're just playing into the hands of the Communist nations."[2503] He said Nixon's offenses were nothing compared to the past:

> As an American living abroad, the most frequent comment I hear is that "America is destroying itself in the eyes of the world"...Europeans express no surprise that the chief of Government should have organized spying and bugging activities against foreign embassies. They say this is standard operating procedure for all governments. When it comes to suspected domestic saboteurs or government opposition, they believe us to be extraordinarily naïve. They have observed the character assassinations over the years in American political campaigns.
>
> ...Why does our leadership and our press seem intent on self-immolation for suddenly discovered moral beliefs when it has all been a way of life in our system since the start? ...When we destroy the President's image, we destroy our country's and our own people's image.[2504]

He did have a point here; it was his father who had let loose J. Edgar Hoover from inconvenient legal constraints. It is also true, however, that the point of view he now recited was that of Marcelo Caetano and his regime. So, on the eve of going to Washington to defend himself before the Senate subcommittee on organized crime, he apparently thought someone was out to get him, and he let the Portuguese know this, as well as how wrong U.S. policy in Africa was:

> It is his belief "that the best steps to achieve the well-being of the African peoples have been and are being taken by the Portuguese and that U.S. foreign policy should support...those who do something for their people, like Portugal, and, in a certain way...like Rhodesia, which follows Portugal's example.
>
> I think Portugal's cause is one which merits our support because Portugal is right and is acting intelligently."
>
> He added: "Now this is contrary to some aspects of U.S. foreign policy and, above all, to the interests of many powerful groups. It is possible that these interest groups think that the U.S. public or the U.S. government might listen to and agree with my views. Thus the solution would be to discredit me by means of a great scandal like this."
>
> Roosevelt also complained that U.S. Embassy in Lisbon, ever since his arrival in Portugal, has "criticized" him for his personal relationship with Col. Knox, Rhodesia's representative in Lisbon. He did not, however, imply the Embassy was a part to the "attacks" on him.
>
> After again denying "the ridiculous accusations" against him, he thanked the Portuguese people for their friendship and expressed the hope he could live the rest of his life in Portugal, "doing what I can for Portugal, trying to convince America that some aspects of its foreign policy with respect to Portugal have not been correct."[2505]

An earful like that must have had the American embassy on its toes. The Logan Act prohibits American citizens from conducting foreign policy with other nations on a "*franc tireur*" basis. It seems that the son of President Roosevelt was working for a foreign dictator and actively campaigning against American foreign policy – once again!

In those eventful days, Rhodesia, now called Zimbabwe, was often in the news, and not in a nice way. In 1965, Ian Smith, on behalf of white settlers, had unilaterally declared independence from the United Kingdom in what was then Southern Rhodesia. (Northern Rhodesia became Zambia.) Britain declared the race-based Smith government illegal and subjected it to an embargo and trade boycott that made its survival highly precarious.

For obvious reasons, Rhodesia found friends in Portugal and South Africa. With Mozambique bordering it, Rhodesia was able to survive as long as Lisbon permitted supplies to filter in via the ports in Beira and Lourenço Marques. Unsurprisingly, the black majority did not approve of this situation. The result was a bloody insurgency which further strained Rhodesia's relations with the world.

It turned out that Elliott's ideas were influenced by a friend he had in the nearly non-existent Rhodesian diplomatic corps. Since Rhodesia was a pariah state, it had only a "representative," Colonel Knox, attending to liaison with the Portuguese government in Lisbon. To diplomats from other countries, including the United States, Colonel Knox was therefore a diplomatic leper who needed to be circled at a great distance.

On 23 July 1973, the American embassy sent a rather upset cable concerning a party Mr. Roosevelt had held two days earlier for a visiting Floridian delegation at his ranch:

> BUFFET RECEPTION INCLUDED SOME 70 GUESTS AMONG WHOM WAS REPRESENTATIVE OF RHODESIA TO PORTUGAL COLONEL KNOX AND WIFE. KNOX KEPT INVISIBLY LOW PROFILE IN SEPARATE GARDEN UNTIL ARRIVAL TWO BUSLOADS FLORIDIANS ENABLED HIM TO MINGLE IN CROWD. MID-WAY THROUGH EVENING ROOSEVELT LAUNCHED SERIES OF TOASTS DURING WHICH COMMISSIONER CONNER [Florida] PRESENTED TOKENS OF ESTEEM TO FORMER PORTUGUESE AMBASSADOR TO US VASCO GARIN AND TO CHARGE POST [U.S. chargé d'affaires].
>
> ROOSEVELT THEN CALLED ON KNOX TO STEP FORWARD WHO WAS SIMILARLY HONORED AND REFERRED TO BY CONNER AS "RHODESIAN AMBASSADOR." KNOX IN THANKING CONNER DELIVERED AGGRESSIVE, WELL-TUNED SPEECH IN WHICH HE (1) THANKED HOST AND CONNER FOR THEIR KINDNESSES WHICH HE WOULD REPORT BY TELEGRAM TO PRIME MINISTER IAN SMITH (2) EXPRESSED KNOWLEDGE OF FLORIDA GROUPS PREVIOUS TOURS IN AFRICA AND HOPED MEMBERS NOT ALREADY FAMILIAR WITH RHODESIA WOULD INCLUDE IT IN FUTURE TRAVEL (3) DECLARED THAT "WITH ALL DUE RESPECT TO THE AMERICAN CHARGE D'AFFAIRES, AMERICA HAS NO FINER AMBASSADOR TO PORTUGAL THAN ELLIOTT ROOSEVELT" (4) REITERATED INVITATION TO FLORIDIANS TO VISIT RHODESIA TO SEE FIRSTHAND "THAT WE ARE NOT THE BLACK COUNTRY WE ARE MADE OUT TO BE."
>
> CHEERING APPLAUSE FOLLOWED LAST COMMENT. CHARGE ABANDONED PARTY AT ONCE.[2506]

Diplomatically, this is about as bad as it gets when a rogue citizen tries to conduct his own foreign policy. Roosevelt had just "recognized" the illegal regime in Rhodesia; he had appointed Colonel Knox "ambassador" which was a higher dignity than even Portugal accorded him; and he had given Colonel Knox the chance to glory in equal diplomatic status with other attendants, encouraging him to pursue relations with American officials from the various states.

On the date of the cable, Chargé Post called Roosevelt and read him the riot act. Post reported that Roosevelt was apparently close friends with the Rhodesian representative, and he said that Roosevelt's professed ignorance of the diplomatic *faux pas* "stretches the imagination." Yet, "his explanation and apology seemed entirely sincere."

They always did.

General Roosevelt maintained his close liaison with Colonel Knox. This became extremely important when the Carnation Revolution set off a rapid and chaotic decolonization that ended with Mozambique's independence under the continuing threat of an insurgency supported by Rhodesia and South Africa.

Colonel Knox then attempted to set up a back-channel link to the American State Department using his new friend Elliott Roosevelt. In response, the political section chief secretly met with Knox at Elliott's ranch. The American was limited to reporting Knox's views, which he did in a secret cable on 25 May 1974. At that time the interim Portuguese president, the aging, monocled Stalingrad-veteran General Antonio de Spinola, was trying to hold on to the colonies, but it was clear that his left-leaning coup government was about to cut them loose.

The Rhodesian concern was the standard Pretoria-Salisbury jeremiad about the Soviet Union attempting to take over strategically located South Africa and its wealth of minerals. An independent Mozambique and Angola would threaten the survival of the white-ruled regimes, and a Soviet-controlled southern Africa could be catastrophic to the survival of the West. Knox did have a point: at Soviet behest, Cuban troops soon intervened in Angola and fought a protracted war with South Africa.

The Americans could do little with Elliott's leprous connections. Whether this back-channel was used for anything is doubtful, since both protagonists soon had to leave the country. But next year, when Roosevelt was evacuating himself and Patty from Lisbon, and the Portuguese situation deteriorated into a struggle between the Communists and the Moderates (which the moderates eventually won), Elliott was again approached for back-channel work.

This time it was the Portuguese who called. Otelo Saraiva de Carvalho, a fairly enigmatic leader of the revolution and at the time Prime Minister, sought to establish a channel through London, bypassing the American embassy in Lisbon. For some reason he thought Roosevelt might be helpful. At this time, 9 April 1975, Carvalho presented himself as a socialist who was trying to prevent a Communist take-over.

To say that conditions were murky in Portugal in 1975 would be an understatement, and it is still not entirely clear who was up to what. Carvalho's feeler might have been a ruse. At any rate, the Americans probably had better ways of communicating with the requisite leaders than anything Mr. Roosevelt could help with in London.

For nineteen months, Portugal hung in the balance. On 25 November 1975 the situation was settled when a reputedly Communist coup attempt was throttled by the intervention of General Antonio Ramalho Eanes, who proceeded to secure Portugal as a Western parliamentary democracy.

At that time, Elliott Roosevelt was done with Portugal. But it had not been easy to get out. He had to sell Quinta dos Cedros at a loss, but his business ventures incurred the wrath of the local tax authorities. The suspicion that he was smuggling currency or other valuables was the reason that he and Patty were detained and strip-searched on 8 February 1975, while attempting to fly to London. Patty, especially, was very upset. She later complained, "The Communists took all of our material goods, absconded with our horses and the quinta – that's Portuguese for farm."[2507]

The American embassies in London and Lisbon again got involved in sorting out the mess. That was because Elliott was not done unraveling his businesses in Portugal. He needed assistance in traveling back to Lisbon without the risk of further detention. The embassy, although it found the Portuguese suspicions "not entirely unfounded," did its consular duty and assisted its problematic citizen.

After checking with the Portuguese government, the American embassy concluded that Roosevelt was suspected of both currency concealment and tax avoidance. "Since claim arises out of ordinary business dealings and is not arbitrary or discriminatory, embassy has no standing to intervene on Roosevelt's behalf."

This was the cable that detailed Elliott's shady and embarrassing history in Portugal. It refuted Elliott's contention that the socialists were out to get him. The embassy left him to his own legal resources, but promised consular assistance.

> ELLIOTT ROOSEVELT AND SON DAVID WERE MET AT AIRPORT BY EMBASSY OFFICER WHEN HE RETURNED TO PORTUGAL ON FEBRUARY 16. THEY PASSED THROUGH BOTH IMMIGRATION AND CUSTOMS INSPECTION WITHOUT INCIDENT. – OCCASIONAL ARTICLES ON TAX PROBLEMS CONTINUE TO APPEAR IN LOCAL PRESS, BUT NOTHING INFLAMMATORY. – WE APPRECIATE ASSISTANCE RENDERED BY AMEMBASSY LONDON IN THIS MATTER. – CARLUCCI.

That wasn't the end of it. On 10 April the Roosevelts again left for London, and were strip-searched. "Mrs. Roosevelt strongly objected to the search." [2508]

And then the ranch in Portugal joined the long cavalcade of residences the Roosevelts had called home. Patty would later count 35 residencies in 20 years.[2509]

Last Days

In ill health, General Roosevelt spent his last fifteen years seemingly looking for a place to die. He lasted only a few years in England's soggy climate despite the comfortable digs at Harold MacMillan's old country home. He told James, shortly after having infuriated him with his books, that he was on his last legs: "Elliott called to tell me he'd had open-heart surgery and been given a pacemaker. Later, the first pacemaker failed and a new one had to be implanted." [2510]

That operation nearly killed him. Then he said he developed cancer of the colon and had a colostomy in England in 1977. The cancer did not immediately recur, but Elliott decided he'd rather die in America. Off he and Patty went to her old hometown of Seattle (Bellevue, to be specific). Elliott sold commercial real estate. He lectured. He invested and lost. He hounded the Veterans Administration with disability claims. He lasted seven years there.[2511]

Weatherwise Seattle was scant improvement over England. Palm Springs was; he moved to affluent, nearby Indian Wells during his last years, still dabbling in investments.[i] Collier cited him as getting involved in a venture to build a world-class race track in Palm Springs. That failed. He also said he now had no contact with his brothers, saying "I'll never forgive what they did to me until my dying day." [2512]

---

[i] Although Palm Springs is considered the main city, Elliott actually resided in Palm Desert and Indian Wells, the richest enclaves of the Coachella Valley.

It is not obvious why Elliott should feel that way, but perhaps the high profile James continued to hold in old age had something to do with it. After the tight escape from the law in Switzerland, Jimmy settled in Corona del Mar, and then Newport Beach, as a business consultant; he entertained some very prominent people there, including ex-president Nixon, for whom he remained a fierce apologist.[2513] By October 1975, Nixon dared to come out in public, at the Teamster-funded La Costa Country Club, which was to gangsters roughly what the Vatican is to Catholics. At his golf game, Nixon was accompanied by high Teamster officials then out of jail, and by Tony Provenzano, the Genovese capo and convicted murderer.[i]

By 1982, it would have been fair to assume that the scandals were over for James. Just then, a big and particularly rancid one erupted.

That year there was great uncertainty over the future of Social Security, at least until the Greenspan commission fashioned the compromise that gave the program another few decades of life. Aging folks wondered whether they would ever see a check, and who better to reassure them than James Roosevelt, the son of the program's creator? Off went Jimmy with a non-profit organization that mass-mailed a scare-mongering fund-raiser to anxious oldsters.

For only ten dollars, they could send for a computer printout of their registered earnings and projected payments. (Such reports are free from the government.) Also, James implied that he would be launching a program to reinsure people's pensions, so that if Social Security should fail, they would still receive something. For only a very low premium, he said.

Jimmy's "National Committee to Preserve Social Security" direct-mailed an official-looking appeal to 400,000 people. The letter, from a "National Administrative Office" with a return address on D.C.'s Pennsylvania Avenue that turned out to be a video store mail-drop, said that "this free service is available only to those joining the National Committee." The letter:

> ...promises to send members a gold-embossed plastic membership card and a newsletter, then concludes, "The National Committee to Preserve Social Security is negotiating with Lloyds of London for a very low-cost group insurance policy to cover members against the loss of Social Security benefits."[2514]

On 11 February 1983, the Social Security Administration asked the Postmaster General to consider mail fraud charges against Roosevelt's group, which then consisted of James Roosevelt, a lawyer named Wewer, and an answering service. Ten days later, after a national uproar, Jimmy offered refunds to those who had applied for his service while denying the charges of unethical, misleading, and unscrupulous conduct. No charges were laid, and the lobby group continued on its controversial ways; critics said it raised money for the sole purpose of collecting more money. This scam – "geriatric terrorism" – caused revulsion even among the hardened cynics of Capitol Hill. In June 1986, further enraged protests against the lobby group's "scare tactics" and "dishonest," "fast-buck" operations came from Congressmen shocked that such things went on.[ii]

---

[i] NYT, 10 OCT 75. Provenzano went to jail in 1978 for murder of a Teamsters official (NYT, 15 JUN 78). He was a close associate of Jimmy Hoffa and is often thought to have been behind Hoffa's demise.

[ii] NYT, 22 FEB 83; 2 JUN 86; Collier, 480. Detailed exposés of this scam by Don Meiklejohn (21 MAY 84, Ocala Star-Banner) and Christopher Connell (AP, 17 MAY 87, Pittsburgh Press). DM wrote that it took in "almost $6 million in about 18 months." In 1986, the operation took in $30 million and Senator Jay

Jimmy was 79 when he was hauled before Congress again. When denounced before the House Ways and Means Committee in March 1987, he threw back his head, jutted his jaw, and flashed his best FDR "You can't touch me" smile. He made good money – reportedly $60,000 a year – off the direct-mail scheme, and despite the denunciations he skated from this one, too. As late as 1989, the committee was hauled before Congress; the hearings provided details of the Roosevelt operation's origin, the people involved, and the group's finances, which even then showed only a tiny fraction going into actual advocacy.[2515]

Unrepentant as ever, Jimmy outlived Elliott by one year, dying on 13 August 1991.

In contrast, Elliott seemed to be making the most honest living in many years. Towards the end, Elliott enlisted old political connections to make an end run around the Veterans Administration. It turned out that the VA had denied him supplementary disability benefits, having been unable to find any documentary evidence supporting any claims of wartime injury. This is not in itself remarkable, since thousands of veterans spend their dotage trying to come up with creative reasons why their mounting infirmities are caused by some event in the service half a century ago. The VA has a difficult task since the sympathy is almost automatically with the suffering hero.

But very few veterans have the option of getting Congress to consider a bill for their personal relief. In March 1986, both House and Senate introduced private bills "for the relief of Elliott Roosevelt." And who should introduce House Bill 4361 but good old "Red Pepper," the now octogenarian Claude Pepper of Florida? Old New Dealers have to stick together. Senator Hatfield of Oregon, who had badgered the VA and the military records offices on Elliott's behalf, introduced the Senate version.[2516]

Specifically, Elliott's allegation was that his cancer was service-related. The legislation attempted to force the VA to award him the maximum benefit, then about $1,000 a month, which "he needs desperately." [2517]

It is ironic that Congress wasn't yet done investigating Elliott Roosevelt. But both that bill and the retry bill next year perished in committee after VA testimony was solicited. Even responding to inquiries after Elliott's death, the NPRC could find no evidence anywhere of wartime injuries, much less the Purple Hearts of the obituaries.

Down in the Coachella Valley, Elliott should have been doing pretty well, especially with royalties from the murder mysteries he lent his name to. As late as 1989 he still lectured aboard cruise ships for fare and free food.

Patty served as somewhat of a moderating influence. In 1985 she scored a major victory for herself and the Pope when she remarried Elliott within the Catholic Church – she considered her previous official ceremony way short of legitimate. This became possible because all four of Elliott's earlier wives had died, so by some inscrutable Catholic logic he was now allowed to remarry. A little crowd of twelve attended the wedding in the couple's home. "The happy couple knelt on Eleanor Roosevelt's footstool," noted the gossip columnist; his mother was still supporting him! [2518]

Obviously Patty was instrumental in claiming her husband as a Catholic in his old age, amusing as it may sound, or shocking as it would have been to his super-WASP parents. Worse yet, he became a Republican.[2519]

Religion is hardly the first attribute one associates with the Roosevelts. Only Eleanor seems to have had some serious, childhood-inculcated concern about it. But

---

Rockefeller called it "a fund-raising scam that degrades the Roosevelt name" (10 MAR 87, LAT). The NCPSS&M continued in operation and may now be legitimate.

FDR and Elliott approached it like they did all social opportunities. They enthusiastically embraced Episcopalian ritual and folderol, as exemplified by their leading in singing rousing hymns at the Atlantic summit.[2520] But later, Elliott's behavior got him dropped from the social register, then a formidable indicator of caste, and then kicked out as a vestryman of the Hyde Park Church (St. James's).[2521]

An interesting capsule of President Roosevelt's attitude to religion was provided in the following reputed exchange triggered by Eleanor's fretting over the children's beliefs:

> "[They] should go to church and learn what we did. It could do them no harm." – "But are you sure you believe in everything you learned?" – "I really never thought about it…I think it is just as well not to think about things like that too much."[2522]

With his unfailing instinct, Franklin had seen through "belief" and resolved to use it as effectively as possible. Eleanor was left to wonder about "truth." Still, Elliott's dying a papist could have raised eyebrows in his vast family.

There is a clipping in Minnewa Bell's papers annotated "How Terrible!" Patricia had told a newspaper that she and Elliott knelt by the casket of mother Eleanor, and Elliott "slipped his rosary beads beneath the floral blanket." "Later, someone found the beads and threw them away." Patricia lamented that although a Catholic priest was allowed inside, he was not permitted to offer any blessing. But other reports say the priest, who knew Eleanor, declined an inappropriate imposition.[2523]

In 1989, for medical reasons, the couple moved back to Scottsdale outside Phoenix, where Patty had made her small fortune in real estate thirty years earlier. Elliott was in sharply declining health and wanted to be close to the Mayo Clinic in that fashionable town. Now Elliott made it his last goal to outlive James, the other siblings having already died off in reverse birth order. He failed by a whisker. Having just turned 80, Elliott Roosevelt died in Scottsdale on 27 October 1990 of congestive heart failure.[2524]

Though almost always broke, it is fair to say he lived a rich life.

A GREAT MYSTERY: ROOSEVELT THE WRITER

Elliott Roosevelt attained greater fame and success as a writer than for anything else he did in life. But an immense mystery surrounds this seventy-year long writing career. Even Eleanor Roosevelt, the super-sleuth, might have trouble with the case – although she did have some clues.

Had she been alive, Eleanor would surely have noticed a peculiar fact that many others overlooked: her son Elliott kept writing long after he was dead. He published from the grave for over ten years.

She might then have recalled that Elliott's first, best-selling work *As He Saw It* was only partially Elliott's own work. She, Eleanor, had a strong hand in its completion. So did many others.

One equally renowned detective who took an interest in this whodunit was J. Edgar Hoover, Director, FBI. On 30 April 1947, his staff wrote:

> You will recall advice was recently received from the Boston Office that a highly confidential source had advised them that Elliott Roosevelt's book *As I Saw It*, was ghost-written for phraseology and readability by one David Miller, whose services was secured by the publishing company, and that David Miller was a Communist. The New York Office was instructed to attempt to identify David Miller.
>
> The New York Office was unable to identify this man through record sources so was authorized to make extremely discreet inquiries....They feel, however, that eventually they will learn the identity of whoever worked on Elliott Roosevelt's book through three highly confidential contacts in the publishing field who are trying, through their own sources, to find this out for the New York Field Office.
>
> It is a well known fact of course that whenever a ghost writer is used on such a book, the publishing company uses every device to keep his identity and the fact that such a writer was used a secret. Such a person is usually employed by the publishing company through one of the executives who pays him personally so that no record appears in the company's books.[2525]

The results of the FBI's "extremely discreet" inquiries were not released. Nonetheless we are indebted to the G-men for that tart summary of publishing practices. Not that Hoover wasn't well aware of that from his own writing efforts. Perhaps the publishers would counter that, since reviewers often don't read the books they review, and readers often don't read the books they buy, it's a lot to ask that authors should actually write the books they flog.

Dubious of Elliott's writing prowess, many critics assumed a ghostwriter was involved. He lashed back:

> I certainly don't mind Jimmy's, Franklin's, or Johnny's resentment toward my book. I did not even become angry when I was accused of having a ghost writer. I think that the man who made this accusation is entitled to state his opinion. I wrote the book from my records and diary and it was approved by Mother and by political experts. It has been published in 17 languages and was a bestseller in the United States and Europe.[2526]

There are some serious problems with Elliott's story. To start off, there was no diary; Elliott said he had lost it.[2527] But then who "really" wrote the book?

Despite the furious denials of Elliott and his retinue, today it is possible to answer the Whodunit question with some confidence. That first book was a collaborative effort involving a number of people, and of course the publisher, Duell, Sloan, & Pierce, would have employed an editor, communistic or not.

Nonetheless, Elliott's first book has a distinctive style that impregnated all his work. Elliott could write quite well; it is his absence of reflection, organization and depth that ought to be the reader's complaint. When Elliott said he wrote *As He Saw It*, he meant that it was his idea and he approved the words. That's fair.

Those poor sods who have to bang out the words all by their lonesome may well consider Elliott Roosevelt a fraud as a writer. His best books were written by James Brough, a professional writer of British origin. His sick, twisted murder novels were written by William Harrington, a hack once described as a drinker with a writing problem. Apparently, the posthumous books were entirely the work of Harrington.[2528]

The multi-volume editions of Franklin D. Roosevelt's correspondence were mainly the work of Joseph Lash's industrious editing, as well as of other assistants.

To such complaints, Eleanor protested:

> Any insinuation that Mr. Lash has the power to withhold any information from the public is completely incorrect. The last volumes, covering the period from 1928 to my husband's death in 1945, are now in process of compilation and annotation and they will be the responsibility – as far as the determination of what is to be included or excluded – solely of Elliott Roosevelt, as editor.[2529]

The columns and radio scripts Elliott produced by the bushel in the 1930s also mostly had professional writers behind them. For example, one hack noted in requesting information from the FBI that he had prepared two scripts for Elliott but he didn't know which one Elliott was going to use. On the other hand many of his later efforts, such as some columns and the book *the Conservators*, were so vacuous and plodding that they must have been mainly his own work.[2530]

What is truth? Elliott struggled with that difficult question all his life. The rest of us, duped or not, should bear in mind that the "truthiness" of the contents is far more important than whose name is on the cover, and it is on that criterion that the work should be judged. In that sense, Elliott was responsible for his work, whether he wrote it or not, and he got clobbered for it accordingly.

Writing is a breeze when you have help

After Elliott Roosevelt eloped to Los Angeles in 1933, he wrote a silly little magazine article, which, with his customary magnanimity, he forwarded to mother Eleanor. It is still found in her files.[i]

In it, he wrote airily about how difficult it was to be a son of politicians and public persons, and of how foolish party politics really was. The tone was literate but impulsive and fatuous. Veering off into various directions, Elliott offered some remarkably uninformed ideas about world trade. Reflecting on Arizona's economic collapse due to the crash in the price of copper, he thought trade barriers were the solution, at least until the rest of the world saw the light and raised their salaries to American levels.

Granted, he was only 22. But he wrote more like a precocious twelve-year old. He was good with words, but not with the thoughts behind them.

Writing style is much like fingerprints. You see this same happy, shallow kid in the breezy murder mysteries he cranked out during his seventies. Still, in between, he had to write about serious matters.

Elliott Roosevelt's book *"As He Saw It"* (1946) about FDR's wartime summits is considered an important source to the transition from the German war to the Soviet one. This is not because of any astute political analysis, nor even accuracy – to fit Elliott's novelistic style, he made up quotes as he went along – but simply because he was there and reported (approximately) what he saw and heard. Eleanor and other

---

[i] "Rambling Thoughts of a Donkey on his Journeys" manuscript, with note to Dearest Mama dated 29-12: "Here is a rough copy (uncorrected) of an article appearing in a new magazine on the coast – thought you might be interested in my literary efforts in political fields," in Roosevelt family papers donated by the children, ER 1933-45, FDR Lib

political advisers went over the book, he admitted. Certainly, the book's ideological orientation, well to the left of FDR himself, is that which the world associated with Eleanor Roosevelt; but it was actually to the left of her, too.

"Have you ever considered writing a book," Elliott said his mother asked him one day.

"Frankly, no. I've never tried to."

"I think you might want to. A firsthand account of what you saw and heard at the conferences could be *invaluable*, if you could find the time to do it."

"I can give it a try," Elliott said. That winter, encouraged by her and others at every step of the way, he began the job of producing a book which, when it was published, would turn out to be even more controversial than Blaze's flight to California.[2531]

Elliott confirmed later that Eleanor "approved every line." Even then, Eleanor's foreword was cautiously distancing; she admitted that others might have witnessed the same events and come to different conclusions. At that particular time, she was moving away from the communists while her son was moving towards them.

As He Saw It came out in October 1946. Elliott said he had to do some rewriting after Churchill's Fulton speech, often seen as the first definition of the Cold War. That ought to raise suspicion. What was there to rewrite? Obviously, he and Eleanor took strong exception to Churchill's stand, and that may be why much of the book reads like it was written by *Daily Worker* hacks.[2532]

Although *As He Saw It* sold extremely well, the book was much ridiculed. Elliott's infantile admiration for Stalin (and his contempt for Britain) did not play well after 1945. For a taste of his viewpoints, we can point to the assertion that it was "insane" not to share the A-bomb secret with the Soviet Union. And, he noted, when it was clear that the "secret" had been involuntarily shared, it was actually never a "secret" at all! [2533]

Again, Elliott had a point, if a dull one. There was nothing secret about the A-bomb principle; it had been discussed publicly before the war. It's just that people thought it would take thousands of years to produce enough fissile material for even one device; and the Soviet bomb was almost entirely a result of espionage. To Elliott, the bomb was a secret during the war; but, interestingly, James heard about it from his father, who let him know (at the fourth inauguration) that he had a weapon that would make an invasion of Japan unnecessary.[2534] This was a serious lapse of security. Truman didn't find out about the bomb until he got the job to drop it.[i]

Moscow was enthusiastic about Elliott's book. *Pravda* wrote that Elliott, true to his father, had written it to try to correct the recent reverses in US-Soviet relations:

> Among these events, he speaks of drastic departure from Franklin Roosevelt's course in foreign policy which typifies U.S. foreign policy today, the ill-famed Churchill speech in Fulton, and accumulation of atomic bombs by the U.S. All the signs of a resurgence of the power policy pursued by the recklessly greedy imperialists are present, he writes. – Elliott Roosevelt believes that the present American course in foreign policy, toward unrestrained imperialist expansion, runs counter to the interests of peace and is fraught with danger for the national interests of the American people. This represents a complete departure from and a fundamental revision of the course of the late President....As different from Churchill, thoroughly permeated with class hatred of the Soviet Union, Roosevelt fully

---

[i] Truman, I/419. Truman heard something about a secret weapon from FDR in November 1944. See Curtis Roosevelt: Too Close to the Sun, 251-2.

realized that the Soviet Union represents a tremendous force in international relations and a powerful factor for peace. [2535]

In the West, critics were more troubled. *As He Saw It* instantly became a serious headache for historians, and it remains so to this day. A young Arthur Schlesinger Jr. wrote in *The Nation* that Elliott's work had to be approached with great caution until corroborating material became available. Henry Steele Commager, speaking probable for most professionals, reviewed it in the *New York Times* and found it deeply flawed. He doubted very much the veracity of the soliloquys Elliott put in his father's mouth. He was especially puzzled by the intense anti-British line, which seemed well beyond what other records could support. Still, he had to appreciate the fact of the book's existence, because there was – in 1946 – little else to go by, and many of the summit participants were already dead. Others would die before leaving their records. Not so Churchill, though; he pronounced Elliott's book "rubbish." [2536]

The fury of columnists gained more attention than the skepticism of professional historians. The deepest wounds were inflicted by Joseph and Stewart Alsop's influential column. Not only were the Alsops cousins of Eleanor, they also consulted with those family members who were carrying daggers behind their backs. Because of its informed accusations, it is necessary to quote the Alsop column at length:

> The former close associates of President Roosevelt are now angrily determined that Elliott Roosevelt must stop peddling fragments of his father's memory as communist propaganda souvenirs. Few could admire Elliott Roosevelt's behavior while his father lived. But this business of turning a dubious penny by putting "Daily Worker" fire-cracker mottoes into the mouth of the great and helpless dead is just too ghoulish to be borne with patience.
>
> Young Roosevelt's latest exploit has been to explain his views on foreign policy – or rather the views that have been carefully implanted in him – at a party given by a member of the Moscow embassy staff. In a mixed gathering of Soviet officials and Americans, he endorsed the Soviet claim to the Dardanelles; declared that American foreign policy was purely imperialistic in motive, and even asserted that American participation in the United Nations was only another aspect of this "imperialism."
>
> Under the circumstances, it is time to point out the contrast between Elliott Roosevelt and the other Roosevelts. Mrs. Roosevelt is incomparably better qualified to speak for the president. Now a greater figure among American progressives than all the Henry Wallaces and other so-called Roosevelt heirs rolled into one, she is as strongly anti-communist as her second son is the contrary. And so are James Roosevelt and Franklin Roosevelt, jr., both of whom have already embarked on serious political careers.
>
> In the New York campaign, Elliott Roosevelt was content to serve as the empty sounding board to the local party-liners, basking in their easy applause. Franklin Roosevelt, jr., on the other hand, very carefully avoided any such involvement, and is now one of the leaders of the important fight against communist infiltration of the American Veteran's committee. As for Mrs. Roosevelt, she has powerfully aided the Union for Democratic Action, chief anti-communist progressive organization, in its plans for a meeting in Washington of American non-communist progressive leaders. The meeting is to be held on Jan. 4, and will hammer out an American non-communist Left program, with emphasis on the "non-communist." Along with many other persons of national stature, both Mrs. Roosevelt and Franklin Roosevelt, jr., will participate actively. There is reason to hope that the result will be a turning point in the story of American progressivism.[2537]

The Alsops were wrong in playing up a supposed breach in political line between mother and son. But it is clear that they had been given dirt by one or more brothers. About the infamous *As He Saw It*, they continued:

> In itself, the history of the book is interesting. As originally written, it was too incompetently organized for publication. It will of course be denied; yet it is now known that the manuscript was returned for revision, and that Elliott Roosevelt somehow acquired a smart party-liner, reputedly of the Hollywood contingents, as his ghost-writer. It was the ghost who brought every paragraph into exact accord with the Communist party line, and gave to the whole its slick, soap-opera, B-picture style.
>
> The volume resulting from this collaboration was then submitted, for serialization, to a well-known national weekly. According to a well authenticated report, this first editor to whom the book was offered requested Elliott Roosevelt to substantiate his facts by producing the diary he claims to have kept. Young Roosevelt replied, according to the same report, that his valuable document was now unfortunately missing. Thus the serial rights were in the end sold to "*Look*," the picture paper, for $25,000.[2538]

In other words, the anti-communist commentariat had declared Elliott a fraud. Not only the FBI believed the book had been put together by a communist hack writer. What is significant is not merely the incipient red-baiting or the playing up of a family schism, but also that this particular time witnessed the fragmentation of the American left – and for that matter, the worldwide left –into Moscow and anti-Moscow factions.

Still, Elliott's writing, what of it there was, showed that the Roosevelt genes were very much active; he had a glib, slippery, fast-talking and confident style, and he always asserted his innocence in the face of the outrageous unfairness of his accusers. On the other hand, a fair evaluation of his voluminous writings suggests that the epithets "shallow" and "silly" were at least sometimes exaggerated. While he was not a conscientious and thorough writer (and certainly not an academic), by the standards of politicians he seemed fairly intelligent and even oddly honest. It wasn't his natural instinct to hedge and weasel. As a friend recalled, he did everything with full enthusiasm and completely without cynicism.[2539]

Elliott Roosevelt was no fool; he wrote for money. This also limited him. He was more inclined to write exposés and argumentative pieces than careful recollections and analyses. For example, we are missing the much needed memoir of his wartime service. Instead we have the maligned tell-all book about Franklin's and Eleanor's disastrous marriage, as well as a stack of fluffy fiction.

When *An Untold Story* came out in 1973, it caused a "limited" sensation. After thirty years, the truth about the Roosevelts was mainly of academic interest. A Rooseveltologist, Kenneth Davis, wrote a damning review of the book in the *New York Times*. Because he was very familiar with the literature, he recognized that most of the events described had been rewritten from other sources and references.

That shouldn't be surprising, though. Even Churchill didn't write his monumental history from memory; he consulted his archives. Likewise we shouldn't read Elliott for a totally independent story, but rather for his interpretation and additions or subtractions relative to the main body.

More worrisome was Davis's complaints about Elliott's authorship. Davis said he knew that Elliott had mainly left his name on the four-volume *FDR: His Personal Letters*, for which he had received an advance of $10,000.[2540] While this important work was well received due to the competent team behind it, within the family the fur flew over

Elliott's monetary reward. Virtually every time one of the siblings hit the publishing jackpot, a great chorus of caterwauling arose from aggrieved brothers, and in the case of *Letters*, even sister Anna bitterly complained to her mother. She thought she had somehow been cheated, at least a bit.[2541]

Family letters suggest that Elliott did his part and, because of expenses, did not make a killing on the FDR volumes. But apparently no sibling trusted him.[2542]

Eleanor's radical friend Joseph Lash had actually done much of the editorial work. The modest Lash, however, made certain to mention that invaluable academic assistance had been provided by a promising Bard College student, James Rosenau, whom later generations of international affairs specialists would recognize as one of the biggest names in the field of political science.[2543] In addition, for security reasons the Truman administration limited what material could be published.[2544]

About *Untold Story*, Kenneth Davis continued:

> All of which, joined to one's knowledge of how the book was written and of Elliott's past performances, leads one to expect here a totally bad book. It isn't quite that bad. James Brough did the actual writing – Elliott's contribution was largely confined to tape-recorded talk, plus a review of the manuscript – and he has done a better than average journalistic job over-all... [2545]

Such faint praise was actually a cover for the real problem: the FDR hagiographers were threatened by Elliott's rough and all-too-human portrait of his parents – especially that of Saint Eleanor. As Davis said of Eleanor's purported acceptance of Franklin's mistresses:

> It is wholly incredible if we accept as true the callous, vulgar, simplistic one drawn of her by her second-eldest son, whose animosity toward her, whose wish to tarnish her reputation as a great and good woman (from what motive one can only guess), is evident in almost every line.[2546]

An Untold Story doesn't actually read like that at all. It is much more balanced in its assessment. But "balance" depends on the bias you come with. Elliott said in his oral history interview that he immensely admired his mother, "the most gallant person that ever lived, but you have to be truthful." [2547]

Conversely he complained that Joe Lash's famous hagiographies of Eleanor were completely mistaken, and that Joe was "mesmerized" all his life with Eleanor, which does seem to be true, even if you doubt the intelligence reports that they were lovers. And Elliott made it clear that the president hated Joe and wanted nothing to do with him; but he did not then know the reason why.[i]

The book's narrative was continued with *A Rendezvous with Destiny*, which covered the FDR presidency, but was very much in the same style. It added little to historical knowledge, being mostly a rewrite of already published events.

The family agreed to denounce Elliott when *Untold Story* came out. The *auto-da-fé* was led by Franklin Jr. This helped the book's sales further.

---

[i] Ibid. Army Counterintelligence, quoted in Lash's *Love, Eleanor*, stated that Lash had an affair with Eleanor, and that a furious FDR sent him to the Pacific front to be killed when he was told. Eleanor then visited Lash during her tour of the Pacific. Pegler found out about the story, and after 1945 it was known by many, but not published.

The row wasn't discouraging for Elliott, quite the contrary. Needing money, he tried to fan the flames with two more books about his mother. *Mother R: Eleanor Roosevelt's Untold Story* came out in 1977. It was, once more, written "with" Brough. It is quite readable, informative, and interesting, although the distinct novelistic style with invented conversations still dominates. Elliott did slip in a few knife-jobs – against his brothers and aunt Alice (who usually did the stabbing and thus was fair game).[2548]

In 1984, Elliott tried to shake the money-tree once more, writing, this time without acknowledged help, *Eleanor Roosevelt, with Love: A Centenary Remembrance*. The book was ostensibly written for young people, recognizing the human interest that still applied to Eleanor's both tortured and triumphant life. It was very brief and pretty awful – there are a few interesting vignettes, but mostly Elliott was recycling what he'd read, or already written.

These Eleanor volumes were further regurgitations of well-known and some less well-known events in Eleanor's life. They were not as controversial, perhaps because the less uplifting elements of the Roosevelt era were now common knowledge.

The feud among the brothers had always tended to overflow into the newspapers. Now it spilled over into the book business. Brother James issued *My Parents, a Different View*, in 1976. It was an excellent book (written with Bill Libby), and shows a more reflective mind at work. Still, the siblings weren't really fighting over facts; they conceded their father's affairs, and Jimmy added some for his mother. One cannot help but think the sibling rivalry and resentment were either staged, or a result of publicity-envy.

Jimmy was trying to take the wind out of Elliott's sails, but the difference between the pictures presented weren't nearly as big as it was assumed or pretended. Probably, historians grew tired of the spat; the consummation (or not) of various affairs wasn't after all as important as the Great Depression and World War II. About these, the Roosevelt children had surprisingly little to add.

At any rate, shortly after the book war, Elliott told James that he had to have open-heart surgery to get a pacemaker implanted, which then failed and had to be replaced. Elliott said he moved to England because authors there don't have to pay taxes on books published elsewhere. He and Patty rented "a lovely estate in Gloucester, owned by former Prime Minister MacMillan."[2549]

That was in 1975; Harold MacMillan was still alive, and one source said the Gloucestershire house, which Elliott rented for $375 a month, belonged to son Maurice MacMillan, a minor member of the Heath cabinet.[2550] Harold had been diplomatically prominent in North Africa during the war, but whether he was friends with Elliott is not clear.

In the 1980s, Elliott's last decade, his writing degenerated into a vast *oeuvre* of murder mysteries. They can be attributed to his constant need for cash, but since most of these books were issued in a metered fashion for years after his death, coming up with the ideas must have been a source of enjoyment in his declining years as well. The actual books were increasingly if not completely written by the aforementioned Mr. Harrington. When *Murder on Hobcaw Barony* (Bernard Baruch's estate) came out, the Baruch Foundation noted that Harrington had called and "asked a lot of questions about the estate and said he was writing a book." Harrington wrote that Bernie drank, the foundation said; but he never was called "Bernie" and he never drank, and you'd think Elliott knew that.[2551]

Still it was quite a coup for Elliott to be able to make his mother pay the bills even into the next century. But when Harrington shot himself in 2000, the books stopped.

The Conservators (1983) was Elliott's only serious attempt to write something that wasn't an obvious cashing-in on his name. It expressed "an ordinary citizen's thoughts," but was grandiosely dedicated to the "President of the United States." It also contained a sophomoric 14-point program for world peace and global government, which, Elliott cautioned, was not to be confused with President Wilson's agenda.

The Conservators was published with the literary assistance of a friend, Richard Sawyer. Elliott lets on: "I must say that without Dick's friendship and prodigious efforts, this book would surely have failed."[2552]

It did anyway. The book is mind-numbingly tedious, full of platitudes and half-baked populist excretions, and clearly very much Elliott's work. It ponderously proceeds from Prologue, over Introduction, to Preface, followed by the first chapter, Apathy. The second, Fatalism, ends with the stirring profundity: "It is time to begin thinking!"

Throughout, the author blesses readers with unremarkable opinions of numerous unconnected things, interleaved with almost endless recapitulations of history's headlines. Reading it one senses an average thoughtful but entirely unoriginal intellect, free of any coherent philosophy or consistent approach.

It is doubtful that anyone ever read all four hundred pages. But the turkey occasionally pops a golden egg, and in this book that happens when Elliott drops some personal recollections of world leaders. After all he knew many of them. The book is also remarkable for tracking Elliott's opinion of all and sundry, yet seldom revealing any connection with the positions he had held in the past.

The long, disingenuous book failed to explain Elliott's love and admiration for Joe Stalin, or his attempts to sabotage Truman's foreign policy. He denounced Truman's decision to drop the atomic bombs on Japan – apparently overlooking that he had been engaged in a similar business in Germany. But oddly, he now thought Truman should have taken military action against Stalin over the Berlin blockade!

He made clear that he couldn't stand that little man Truman, and that he admired his successor Eisenhower immensely. He thought John F. Kennedy "an indecisive schoolboy" who committed "one of the great crimes of the century" by not supporting the Bay of Pigs insurgents decisively. "I was filled with chagrin that two of my brothers and I had backed his nomination at the Democratic convention."[2553]

In 1983, he thought his erstwhile buddy Lyndon B. Johnson was corrupt and even "crazy." "I'm sorry I ever introduced him to my father," he wrote to a friend in 1967. He had admired and vocally supported Nixon, but now he recognized his criminal side, and the fact that he was also "crazy."[2554] Ford and Carter were "inept," but Reagan, to whom the book was dedicated, was OK. After all, he had been a Roosevelt Democrat – perhaps he would still listen to one!

This god-awful book gained little attention. It could be published because of the author's name, but that couldn't make people read it. Elliott said it appealed to the "delving mind." "It was a think book that involved a lot of research and took me two years to write." As the *Los Angeles Times* noted:

> There appears to have been an insufficiency of delving minds, and Roosevelt says wryly that a friend told him it was the greatest book to cure insomnia he'd ever found. "I had to do something livelier," Roosevelt admits. He considered romance novels but his wife pointed out that his track record in that area was not terrific.[2555]

With his connections and social skills, Roosevelt would have been easily able to support himself had he not gone through his own and other people's wealth at breakneck speed. The adoring fifth wife, Patricia Peabody, held out until the end, despite being perpetually broke and reportedly living in 35 different residences during the last twenty years of Elliott's life.[2556]

With the aid of a writer, in 1967 Patricia produced a book about her husband. Published during Elliott's term as mayor of Miami Beach, "*I Love a Roosevelt*" was met with derision and atrocious reviews. It seemed to confirm the impression that the Roosevelts preferred their womenfolk clueless and fawning.

In truth, *I Love a Roosevelt* is excellent on its own terms. There are no astute foreign policy insights or profound judgments on politics. But if you endure the endless descriptions of what rich and famous people wore, and what they had for dinner, and what liquor they preferred, and who they knew and gossiped about, the book provides another sideways view into history – a corrective perspective on what these sorts of people thought and did. It's not like Patty was the first to write Roosevelt gossip.

One gets the impression that the Roosevelts and their circle constitute a kind of super-connected hyper-social subspecies of humanity – that they constantly consulted a vast relational database in their heads of like persons, who owed or were owed favors, who might someday be useful. Missing from this circus is any hint of political, ideological, or philosophical conviction; it's all about who's for whom. Perhaps this trait is endemic among politicians, but it helps explain the ease with which Elliott could serve both Stalin and Hearst, Batista and Eleanor, the Jews and southern rednecks. In that family, only Eleanor seemed to possess the nobler faculties; but, being naïve and warm-hearted, she was the one truly tragic Roosevelt, doomed to be used, by her husband, by her children, and by the nation itself.

I Love a Roosevelt ends on a truly terrifying note. Patricia had become friendly with the famous pseudo-psychic, Jeane Dixon, who cunningly predicted that a Roosevelt would soon rise to national prominence. The other siblings having failed in their political careers, starry-eyed Patricia assumed that her husband would become president. He himself might have been deluded enough to think so, but he was defeated for mayor next year and soon found himself back in the familiar miasma of debt, shady dealings, and relentless controversy.[2557]

It's not surprising that Patty listened to Dixon, but that her husband did too.

Elliott Roosevelt did make an attempt to produce an autobiography, collaborating with Arizona historian Dean Smith to hammer out a manuscript. It has not been released, but Peter Collier, who wrote "*The Roosevelts*" had access to the text, and he noted that Elliott made up stories with himself as the hero, which is definitely supported by this investigation. (About the same time, Elliott submitted a number of such untruths about his wartime service to the book about the Soviet alliance, *Remembering War*.) Collier interviewed Elliott shortly before his death. He quoted from the manuscript numerous times to illustrate Elliott's own point of view.[2558]

There is no need to go over the mystery novels; these mass-produced packets of literary chewing gum seem to have an immense readership, but they are not helpful for truth seekers. For authentic color, Elliott and his writer did sprinkle references to real events within them. The novels tend to have many aviation and mafia asides, and the reader may well muse that their dubious validity may reflect the same tendency to conflate fact and fiction that is found in other works by the same author.

VI. CONCLUSION

The innocent neophyte who first attempts to conquer the vast and still growing mountain of Roosevelt books soon reaches the "Ohmigod" point. This happens when it dawns that the covers don't always match the pages; sometimes, that what's in the words is not what's between the lines. Slowly, regardless of politics, the reassuring myth of FDR the Hero who saved America and the world fades away; competing for its place emerges the faint shadow of a Mephistophelian monster; a spectre whose jutting jaw and toothy grin increasingly terrifies instead of providing comfort.[i]

Sooner or later, most of Franklin's closest collaborators also reached the Ohmigod point. They left, and some of them didn't keep the peace. Some, like Harry Truman, in retrospect also saw a monster: "The coldest man I ever met." Past the cloak of charm, "inside he's as cold as ice," gasped Harold Ickes. "He was the greatest salesman that ever lived," said C.R. Smith. This interpretation might be called the "human hologram" theory of FDR: the face who could "be all things to all people," but had no substance; you could never get behind the floating Cheshire grin. The apparition glowed brightly to secure the adoration of the masses, but was there anything in it to grab hold of?[2559]

Virtually all Rooseveltologists, haters and defenders alike, share in one observation: FDR was the most inscrutable, incomprehensible of all American presidents. No one knew him. So admitted even those closest to him. If he was indeed a "hollow man" there was nothing to know; he was a hall of mirrors, shapeshifting at will, the politician perfected, a fantasm that fed off and continually sought to recreate the limitless worship his mother gushed upon him after his first breath.

The study of FDR's children runs into no such supernatural terrors. Their flaws are hard and fast, blatant to everyone who digs in the archives. You can even feel sorry for them; something you never do for FDR, cripple or not. Their nefarious but grandiose ambitions fell so flat the kids were run out of town again and again. After Dad died, most never could get a grip for long. You feel compelled to protest that when properly harnessed, the sons' energy and enthusiasm did accomplish things of great value. You have the sense, as did Elliott's wives, of children in grown men's bodies.

No man is just one thing. Adolf Hitler was nice to dogs, but that is not what he is remembered for. President Roosevelt was many things, many of them contradictory. But his sons, Elliott in particular, were so many things at once and in succession that it is mind-boggling that they could cohabit within the same person. Elliott Roosevelt lived the experiences of a thousand or more regular folks.

The assessment of an individual reflects the values of the observer. From the standpoint of the Roosevelt-haters, Elliott Roosevelt could be described by a number of monikers, many of them starting with S – shyster, scoundrel, sociopath. From the perspective of his superiors in the military he was a very competent officer with a quite extraordinary visibility and an unmatchable index of personal connections. Yet his subordinates often viewed him with hostility and suspicion.

---

[i] This historiographical sleight of hand was detectable early, especially among FDR's erstwhile disciples like Farley, Ickes, and Jones. This discordant duality has only increased with the years; see recent books like *Franklin and Lucy, FDR's Deadly Secret, Franklin and Winston, The Defining Moment.* Even FDR's sons, especially James, were often two-faced in their accounts. This phenomenon is largely independent of political views.

From his mother Eleanor's viewpoint he was a misunderstood, troubled kid. She blamed herself for his problems. By reflex, she blamed herself for most anything. His father, however, hid a twisted admiration for Elliott. One keen observer stated that FDR was actually fascinated by his most scandal-prone son and drawn to the amorality in his character.[2560]

There is no getting around genetics here. The other siblings were variations on the same theme.

It is obvious that Elliott Roosevelt had distilled within him many of his father's signature traits: a vigorous optimism, slippery charm, confident mendacity, unscrupled ambition, energetic physicality, perhaps most of all the innate ability to navigate the world through the deft manipulation of a vast store of friends and connections, favors and obligations. But in Franklin Delano Roosevelt, these traits stayed just within the bounds of usefulness. By his own limitless confidence, he was able to gain the confidence of most of the nation and much of the world. "The chameleon on plaid," as Herbert Hoover called him, won the war and shaped half the world in America's image. When he died, millions cried.[2561]

In Elliott's case, these two-faced characteristics edged over the line. His father had sent the federal budget into the stratosphere, but his son reserved profligacy for himself. The president was famously economical with the truth, but not with the public purse. Elliott went a step further. He could spout obvious lies with indignant conviction, and he went straight for other people's money without troubling with the middleman of government.

Both father and son were inveterate experimenters. Those who called FDR a socialist missed the curious *ad hoc* nature of the New Deal: the sense that if this doesn't stick to the wall, we'll just throw something else at it. In that, he was continuing on a grander scale his own dilettantism in business. Elliott followed the same course with business, politics, even marriages.

The Roosevelts, father and son, had an approach to the world that could, for lack of a better word, be called "busybodyism" – the instinctive belief that the world would be much better if only "I" got to run it, coupled with a lack of self-doubt, caution, respect for boundaries, contrition and reflection, all the constraints that usually limit and often cripple actors in the public sphere. They operated on intuition, not reason. It made for a sharp contrast with FDR's predecessor, the cerebral, humorless engineer Herbert Hoover.

For this reason, it should be no surprise that Elliott jumped untroubled from one standpoint to another, from one presidential candidate to another. His father had sat in his bed in the morning, airily decreeing that, today, let's make the price of gold 34 dollars (or whatever caught his fancy). His son denounced Churchill for imperialism and then endorsed Stalin's empire, and ended with defending Ian Smith's Rhodesia. It made sense to him, that day.[i]

Sexually, Franklin messed around without shame, but maintained the veneer of propriety as a sop to the masses. His sons dispensed with the latter, indulging in a steady supply of new women with triumphant publicity. The father liked to drink and smoke, sending him to an early grave; son Elliott was a functioning alcoholic and chain-smoker, but he lived to old age.

---

[i] Jones, Jesse: 50 Billion Dollars, 248: "Jess, you and Henry [Morgenthau] drop by my bedroom tomorrow morning and we'll fix the price of gold."

In business, Franklin had been inept but always game for a new, usually questionable, venture. Elliott was catastrophically adventurous, zig-zagging unpredictably within the twilit no-man's-land between hard con jobs and the barely legal. The president enjoyed danger, but Elliott was addicted to it. It worked for him in the war, but in peace it made him self-destruct.

As he saw it, Elliott Roosevelt was a dashing war hero and lover of glamorous women, a "big man" thwarted in his ambitions by the enemies of Roosevelt and the purge of socialists and communists after FDR's death.[i] He was courageous, intelligent, compassionate, peace-loving, visionary. He nobly offered his unsolicited and often incoherent advice to presidents all the way up to Reagan. He and his enemies agreed that he was larger than life, but not in the same ways.

Our pigeon-holing instinct exhorts us to make a choice. But there is no reason why Elliott couldn't be all these various things at once, or at least all of them in some interleaved progression. Chance and circumstance happen to them all, and often determine which side flourishes.

There is no discernible pattern of fairness in the attacks on Elliott Roosevelt; in politics, the stiletto goes in wherever it finds an unguarded spot. This investigation should make it clear that there was no error or direct favoritism in his rise in the Air Force. His name inevitably opened doors for him, but if shameless profiteering on it is the complaint, that smears his daring and useful wartime service. The flak certainly showed no preference. It was pure dumb luck that Elliott came back alive, when so many others, like friend Joe Kennedy Jr., did not.

Elliott Roosevelt did play a peripheral role in the development of prewar aviation. Though he gained prominence as a booster, his achievements – fortunately – fell far short of his grandiose schemes.

During the war, he did undeniably important work in the effort to locate landing fields, chart remote areas, and introduce effective aerial reconnaissance. He was a keen observer and chronicler of the summits, albeit one of far more controversy than consequence. If he had not lived, all of these things would have been done, perhaps equally well, by others. His importance was not nearly as great as he would have liked it to be, but during the rest of his life he traded off of those twelve years during which chance had made him the aide and confidant of the President of the United States.

In today's Air Force, this debt-ridden, alcoholic philanderer and college refusenik would never even have come close to a security clearance, much less a commission. The same, ironically, might pass for many presidents of the United States. In 1945, when his father died and the friends of the USSR were methodically purged, Elliott lost his greatest asset. His last claim to influence was his Moscow mission and his radio and television work promoting his mother. But from about 1950 his life was a dreadful procession of failed marriages, businesses, residences, and projects. At last he found some success as a mass producer of silly murder mysteries, trading to his dying day off his name and his White House memories.

Still, in history, there are the actual facts, and then there is the narrative produced in order to serve our needs – or more precisely, the needs of the system to which the observer adheres. This is why we cannot separate Elliott's story from Franklin D. Roosevelt's. That is where the battle lines have been drawn up for two generations.

---

[i] His unpublished manuscript constantly referred to his need to be a "big man." Collier, passim.

In 2010, a survey of presidential scholars showed that FDR was the single most highly rated U.S. president.[2562] This ranking remains high even after necessary correction for liberal bias. Considering the rankings of other presidents, it is likely that such esteem actually attaches to whomever was in charge when monumental events transpired. The "great ones" were those who produced a lot of history, and talked a lot about it – reverse Coolidges.

For example, it is thought-provoking that a man as solid and decent as Hoover should have been so far eclipsed by a successor as glib and devious as Roosevelt, largely due to the vicissitudes of war and depression. Yet, in that position, the ability to appear great may be far more important than actually being so.

At the time of the Depression, few if any people understood what was going on – even today, despite the autopsy Milton Friedman produced, there is great dispute about the details. Thus any action to heal the economy was hit-and-miss. Few economists deny that FDR exacerbated the Depression, but it is by no means clear that others would have done better. It is not possible for serious legal scholars to condone FDR's disregard of the Constitution, particularly during the war. That is hardly a unique presidential distinction, however.

After the fall of the USSR, we have also learned that the Soviet Union had decisively penetrated the Roosevelt administration, and that from July 1941 to April 1945, Joseph Stalin largely controlled U.S. policy in Europe. And, if that doesn't give pause, we must realize that until Harry Truman became vice president, the United States was one heartbeat away from becoming a vague simile of a Soviet republic, led by the likes of Wallace, Hopkins, Eleanor Roosevelt, Joe Lash, Alger Hiss, and untold others, most of whom were swept aside after 1945. Surely a startling indicator of this is that General Elliott Roosevelt, the man who thought it was "insane" not to share the Bomb with his friend Stalin, might have ended up as head of Air Force reconnaissance.

If it is right that we should speak no ill of the dead – and it surely isn't – then at least we can justifiably thank Elliott for writing several historically important books, all of which cast light on Franklin D. Roosevelt's career and legacy. They may be unreliable and novelistic in tone, but they are there, and he was there, and we need all the help we can get. Ironically, Elliott became one of the most useful sources for those who shine the light, and not necessarily a kind one, on this mythic period. He deserves our profound gratitude if not always our admiration.

Even his Air Force status as a reconnaissance guru has been left oddly unpraised. That is unfair, and due all remedy. Elliott Roosevelt was a strong voice for the recognition of aerial reconnaissance as a cornerstone of national security. He lived to see the immense reach of his creation.

VII. ILLUSTRATIONS

Photographs are courtesy of the Franklin D. Roosevelt Presidential Library and Museum, Hyde Park, New York, unless individually annotated otherwise.

Father and Son aboard the SS Aquitania, 11 MAY 31. – Age 14 (right)
With FDR at Hyde Park, 1940 (below)

Nr.1, Betty Donner, 1932. Did her cat just die or did she have a premonition? Below, Isabella Greenway, Eleanor, and Elliott pose in front of the American Airlines Ford Trimotor in which Eleanor left Tucson for D.C. June 1933. *Historic Images*

Unbelievable but true. Love fest between columnist Westbrook Pegler and Eleanor Roosevelt, 1938, before they became mortal enemies.

With Elliott Roosevelt, son of the president, and his wife watching the takeoff, 10 Martin bombers left Washington on an army training flight to Alaska. The first stop was at Dayton, Ohio, and the flight continued from there in short hops. The Roosevelts are shown above with Col. H. H. Arnold, the flight leader, in front of one of the bombers, and below are the ships as they left Bolling field. Today the bombing planes took off from Minneapolis with Winnipeg as their next stop.
(Associated Press Photo.)

The Air Corps's Alaskan mapping expedition attracted much attention; here Ruth and Elliott bid Hap Arnold adieu at Bolling Field. *Clipping, The Day, 20 July 1934.*

Oddly vampiric photo of ER, 1 Oct. 1930, "at the time he gave up college to go into advertising."

ER and Ruth Googins, year unknown – aboard his favorite airline, 1937 – broadcasting for Texas State Network.

Elliott's Gilpin Airlines flew the Bach Trimotor between L.A. and Tijuana's Agua Caliente racetrack and resort. *Greenway collection / Arizona Historical Society.*

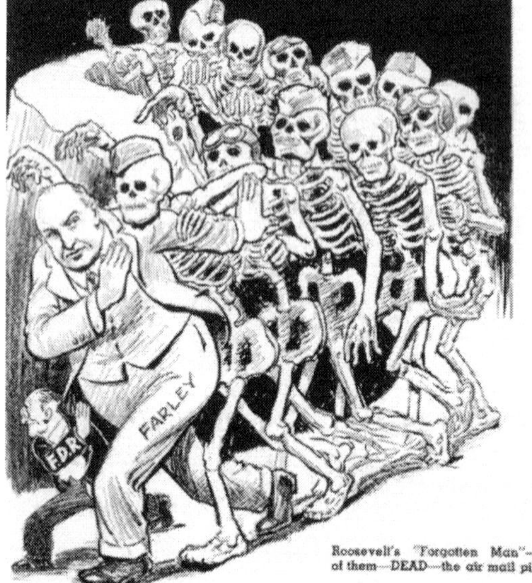

Frank Tichenor's damning article in *Aero Digest*, October 1936, broke open the conspiracy to take over the airlines. *Aero Digest* – Four brothers at war; Elliott was in the Air Corps, Jimmy was in the Marines; sailors Frankie and Johnny, bottom. Incidentally, John wanted to register as a conscientious objector, but he had his mind changed for him rather abruptly.

Ridiculed by the Republicans, October 1940.

WASHINGTON, SEPTEMBER 24th

"Elliott Roosevelt, second son of the President, was commissioned this afternoon as a captain in the specialists reserve of the army, and was immediately assigned to active duty with the Air Corps Procurement Division at Wright Field, Dayton, Ohio. Because of his age he would have been subject to the draft, October 16.

Captain Roosevelt, who has had no military training and rather limited experience in aviation, will report for duty on October 1. . . . Elliott, who was 30 years old

WASHINGTON, SEPTEMBER 24th

"Selective service officials stated that a draftee able to walk fifteen to twenty miles, after dus ing, with fifty pounds on his back." No m accepted for limited service. Conscripts mu qualified to serve in ANY branch of the a

More "I wanna be a captain too" cartoons.

Play games and war is not all hell. And everyone smokes.

At the Broadmoor Golf Course with Ruth, Colorado Springs, August 1942. The cane is for the aftereffects of knee surgery. – Nr. 3 was Faye Emerson, pushed by Howard Hughes.

Col. Roosevelt briefs General Eisenhower. "Print received 13 August 1943 from 1st Motion Picture Unit." *U.S. Gov.*

Holding up the president at the Atlantic Summit, 24 August 1941.
With Mother Eleanor at RAF Steeple Morden, 29 October 1942.*(below)*

That's Franklin Jr., USN, left. W.C. is the "tram conductor." – Odd man out in Teheran *(right)*.
At Casablanca, Elliott, Harry Hopkins Jr., Frankie Jr., George Durno, and the P. *(below)*

Durno was a close friend of FDR, long-time INS (Hearst) White House correspondent, and now a "captain, too," ferry division, ATC. He served as press secretary at Casalanca. FDR specifically demanded him for the task. FDR once gave an Iron Cross to a reporter who he thought had criticized Durno.

When Eleanor visited Britain, she also met with volunteer U.S. women pilots used by the RAF to ferry aircraft. Probably 26 Oct 1942. It rained that day too.

FDR stamp ceremony at U.S. Post Office, Hyde Park, 25 July 1945, E.R. still in uniform. Experimenting with film and cameras shortly after move to Algiers, 1942. Major Powers right, Captain Richie left *(below)*. *AFHRA*

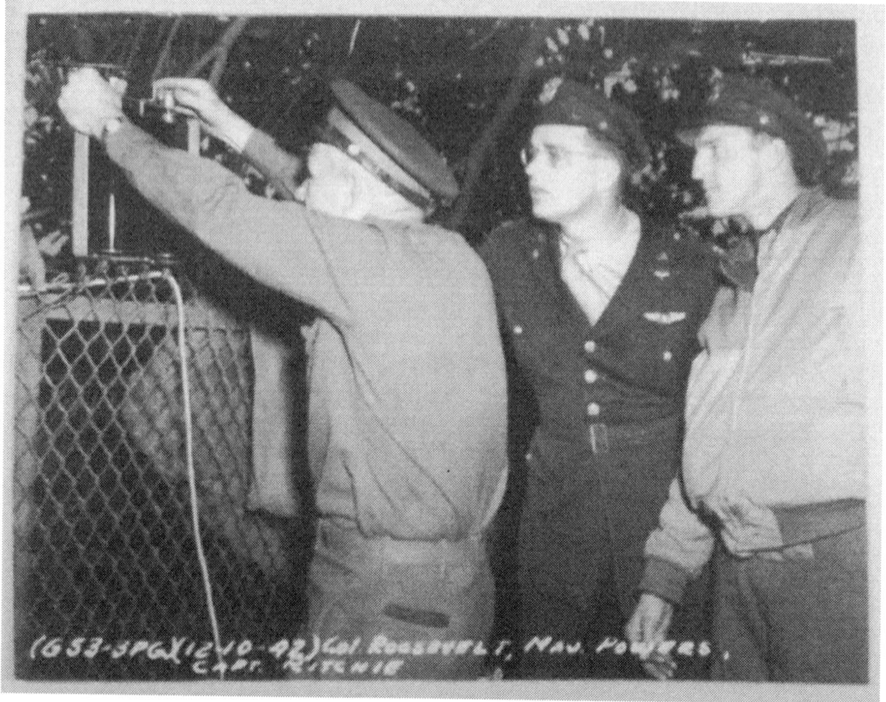

P-38 recon version, North Africa (below), and its unusual cockpit (right). Note roll-up windows and offset control column. *AFHRA*

F-8 "Spook" Mosquito flown by Elliott. From the unit scrapbooks. *AFHRA*

B-17F "I got Spurs" with crew, North Africa. Elliott flew early missions in this (Nov. 1942). *AFHRA* – This 15th Photographic Mapping Squadron plane was later photographed with the "GOT" lined out and renamed "I HAD Spurs."

The original NAPRW photo lists Lt. Col. William Pottinger (right), Col. Minton Kaye (left), Elliott with cigarette. North African visit, 1943. Despite appearances, even then Kaye and ER did not get along. Next year, Elliott destroyed Kaye's career with a letter home. *AFHRA*

General Patton signs Elliott's short snorter at Casablanca.

The Yak-9s were no help when the Germans erased the American base at Poltava. *USAAF*

An early unarmed B-24A of the type Elliott used in Greenland and the North Atlantic. Note the enormous flags, screaming "I am neutral!" *USAF.*

ER used one of the early blistered B-17Bs, 39 built, for Operation RUSTY in 1942. His was featherweighted, extreme altitude being its only defense. No information could be found on the secret *Blue Goose*, all-blue without insignia, written off in North Africa, 1942. *USAF.*

Elliott installed a photolab in a war-prize Potez 540 in Algiers. One of the strangest aircraft in the USAAF, it was flown by willing French pilots. *Avionslegendaires.net.*

Briefing a mission under the wing of a P-38, April 1943. Pilot Joseph David with cigarette next to the drop tank. Notice the cold-weather gear. 5th PRS commander Glen J. McClernon (later Brig. Gen.) to the right. Col. Roosevelt wears only his DFC. – One of Elliott's Mossies, below. *Internet, nc.*

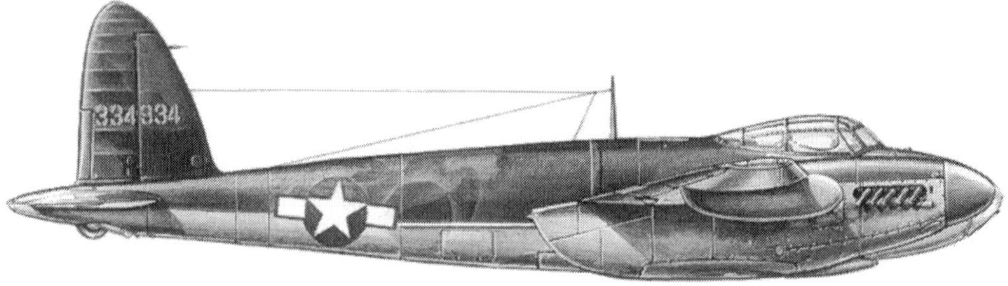

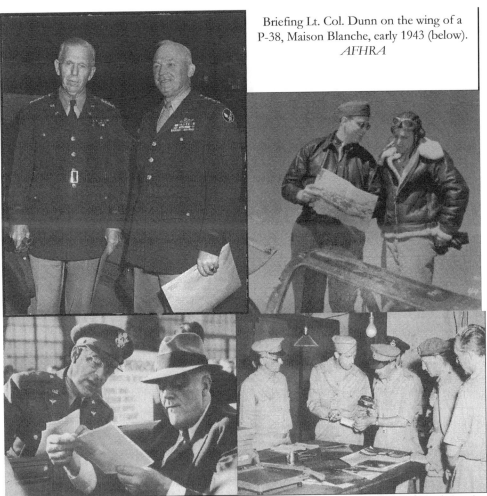

Briefing Lt. Col. Dunn on the wing of a P-38, Maison Blanche, early 1943 (below). *AFHRA*

(Top) George C. Marshall and Henry "Hap" Arnold. *National Archives* – Col. Goddard showing the president air photos of home, at Wright Field, Oct. 1940 – In the photoshop: Elliott, w. cigarette, briefing the British, Gen. Spaatz left.– *USAAF.*

High living in Italy. Christmas Dinner, San Severo, Dec. 43. Uniforms of many nations.

"Dear Pop: This shows you what a silly grin your son wears when he hears he's been promoted. This is the aircraft that takes me there and back."– Late model F-5, Jan 1945.

The first Hughes XF-11 displays its characteristic contrarotating propellers that would cause its demise. Notice the extremely narrow fuselage pod. Hughes's Constellation is in the background at Culver City. *AAHS.*

(Below, middle): Elliott first tried to sell Lockheed Electra bombers to Stalin in 1934, but made himself so obnoxious that the Soviets threatened to complain to his father. He was better received ten years later in Moscow. This is the first military version, an XC-35. *USAF.*

Elliott, Faye, Anna at the president's funeral. *US gov.* – Blaze wasn't invited. *(news clip)*

Leaving New York 2 Nov. 1946 on American Overseas; Arriving Moscow 17 Dec. 1946 on Soviet DC-3. The couple traveled widely in Europe and the USSR in the interim.

"Fellow Travelers" Henry Wallace, Harlow Shapley, Jo Davidson, and ER denounced U.S. foreign policy and argued for internationalization of the Dardanelles, Suez and Panama, to an overflow crowd of 19,000+, Madison Square Garden, 31 March 1947. – In Moscow Candy Factory, 1946, celebrated guests of the All-Soviet Society for Cultural Relations with Foreign Countries (VOKS).

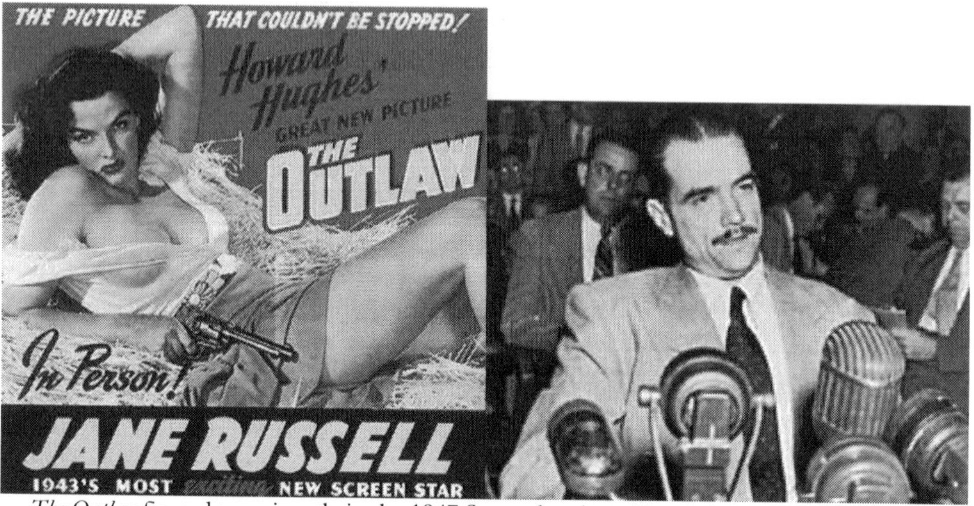

The Outlaw figured prominently in the 1947 Senate hearings; Howard Hughes tried to bribe influential Air Force officers to get it released. The film made Jane Russell famous, though not for acting. *Public Miniature Poster.*

H. Hughes bought a whole squadron of surplus B-23s, and made his triumphant Aug. 1947 trip to Washington in one. *USAF*

Senate Caucus Room. Ferguson left, Elliott right. (Right) With Johnny Meyer and the bills

The New Elliott with bow tie, mustache, and glasses but the old denials. 4 & 5 Aug 47.

Meeting with Sen. Homer Ferguson before the Senate inquisition. --- Right: The General selling Christmas trees in New York.

A Tucson newspaper snapped ER, Eleanor, and Minnewa in front of the Twin Bonanza named for the "Rolling R Ranch." - *Below*: Friends again in old age. Henry "Scoop" Jackson greets Patty and Elliott Roosevelt, Jan. 1982. Nine years earlier, Scoop was their inquisitor; this time, he is their senator, helping celebrate the FDR birth centennial.

Kept Waiting For Ride

Mrs. Franklin D. Roosevelt had quite a day in Tucson yesterday. Flown to Tucson by her son, Elliott, in his private plane, she found that no transportation was available at the airport to get her into town. However, an airport guard saw her plight and arranged transportation for her to the Arizona Inn, where she rested up for her talk at the Sunday Evening Forum. Elliott, who was accompanied by his wife, got back into his plane and flew back to Phoenix after seeing his mother was taken care of. (Jack Sheaffer photo)

Above: University of Washington Libraries, Special Collections, HMJ0718

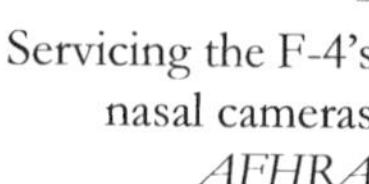

Servicing the F-4's nasal cameras
AFHRA

Assist. Secr. of the Navy F. D. Roosevelt after his first flight in Pauillac, France, 14 Aug. 1918.
FDR's first flight in a dirigible, Paimboeuf, France, 17 Aug. 1918.

Eleanor posing with an Eastern Air Transport Curtiss Condor, probably late Nov. 1932

Reportage on Miami Beach's new mayor. Mom and Dad keep watch. The job paid $57.69 a week, said the paper. "The bucks stop here?" *Newsclip at FDR Lib., dated 8 May 1966*

VIII. SOURCES AND METHODS

Elliott Roosevelt is largely forgotten today, but he left a trail like a tornado in the nation's archives and libraries.

U.S. Air Force records are the chief source to Elliott Roosevelt's activities during his military service. There is an immense amount of unpublished but highly relevant detail in these archives, chiefly at the Air Force Historical Research Agency (AFHRA) at Maxwell AFB, Alabama – especially in regards to Operations TORCH, FRANTIC and APHRODITE, and the Hughes F-11 controversy.

The National Archives and Records Administration (NARA) and the National Personnel Records Center (NPRC) round out the military material, and include some exceptionally enlightening oral history interviews. Most of General Roosevelt's military records apparently perished in the 1973 file at St. Louis, but a summary survives in the National Archives. Importantly, his discharge document was found; it includes promotions, dates, postings, medals and other details.

Congressional records provide excruciatingly detailed evidence for those Elliott scandals that reached the attention of House and Senate committees, extending from 1934 to 1973. So do the related agency investigations, especially the tax bureau files.

As it does for all Rooseveltiana, the Franklin D. Roosevelt Presidential Library and Museum in Hyde Park, New York, offers detailed corroboration for many events, chiefly through preserved letters and records. Unfortunately, Elliott Roosevelt is the only one of FDR's children whose personal papers are not preserved at the Library. Papers that should have been saved may have been among the material Elliott discarded or sold when he was broke and could not afford to move them. Much, however, can be triangulated from the letters and records of his family.

Elliott and his siblings, as well as their mother and her associates, wrote profusely about their lives. Even considering that the memoirist's primary objective is to place himself in a pleasant and exculpatory light, the Roosevelts' books are amazing for their errors of omission, commission, and contortion. On the other hand, since the secondary objective is often to speak ill of others, many of Elliott's friends and relatives were only too eager to fill in the gaps by their own writings.

The other presidential libraries also provide important material, because Elliott remained intermittently in the limelight over the course of ten administrations. Furthermore, he was once a friend of General Eisenhower, and served with many of the general officers whose papers have been preserved. He also was closely connected with launching Lyndon B. Johnson's political career.

The Eisenhower Library has, in addition to Ike's material pertaining to Elliott Roosevelt, the papers of General Lauris Norstad, under whom Elliott served. The Hoover Library has the papers of Westbrook Pegler, Elliott's syndicated columnist nemesis. Pegler left two big boxes, full of shocking allegations, specifically on Elliott; he also kept poison files on the other family members. The Johnson Library contains the extensive file that Drew Pearson, a less ill-tempered reporter, maintained on Elliott. The Truman Library has a smaller amount of material. The Hoover Institution at Stanford

University unexpectedly provided important material, chiefly in the General Frederick Anderson collection.

Official sources must always be approached with the utmost caution. They reflect a carefully managed, even sanitized truth. For example, secret or truly incriminating data – i.e., the researcher's paydirt – often disappears before it gets archived (sometimes after). Elliott published his father's correspondence in four large volumes; but they contain only preferred excerpts of the entire corpus. Likewise, the truth about FDR's unusual marriage only slowly became publicly known, but for this we can in large part thank Elliott Roosevelt. (Not that many did.)

The Isabella Greenway collection at the Arizona Historical Society turned out to be especially helpful in illuminating the years 1933-34. Rep. Greenway was deeply involved in the famous Air Mail Fiasco, in which Elliott played a so far unacknowledged role.

The newspapers, both pro and con Franklin Roosevelt, followed Elliott like bloodhounds. An immense amount of scandalous material was published, enabling archive trolls to plot the man's progress and setbacks year for year. In particular, the *Chicago Tribune* and certain syndicated columnists published thorough research on Elliott that remains invaluable. Only towards the end of his life, when most journalists had no personal memory of his career, did the press take a certain curious or reverential stance towards Elliott and his siblings. The availability of Google News Archives allowed wire service reports, often published in minor newspapers, to be consulted. The archives of Elliott's "local" papers, the *New York Times*, the *Los Angeles Times*, and the *Dallas Morning News* were of the utmost help.

Elliott himself produced vast stacks of written and broadcast material, most of which was eminently inconsequential as well as redundant. His best writing was always outsourced. Occasionally his columns do provide insights into his thinking on aviation matters, and after 1945 his books and articles dealt with the overall political situation. Though his memory was always suspect, and even clearly mendacious in old age, his words were valuable when he recounted events he participated in.

Elliott Roosevelt's descendants were not consulted directly for this work. They are unfortunately not likely to be pleased with the secrets it has uncovered, especially in regard to Elliott's persistent collaboration with organized crime. Family members usually have little insight into the more technical details of the matters discussed, although they are full of opinions about family relations. For these, however, the Roosevelt Library, oral history interviews, and published works already provide an overwhelming amount of data. For example, Elliott's children were interviewed by the library staff, as were many of his wives and acquaintances.

For reasons that should be painfully obvious, the FBI maintained a thick file on Elliott Roosevelt. So did Other Government Agencies (OGAs), among which the State Department agreed to release a number of highly interesting cables. Under the Freedom of Information Act (FOIA), the FBI released 82 out of 96 pages for this work. They are of crucial importance in detailing Elliott's extensive criminal associations, some of which did touch the president. Still, not everything could be released, and the files of his friends suggest that most of what the FBI had on Elliott did not get into his file. All researchers know that FOIA is a double-edged sword, and so should readers.

Some FBI records about Elliott relating to the Soviet Union could unfortunately not be released. If military intelligence investigated Elliott, there is no record of this causing him any trouble despite his strident pro-Soviet stance. Soviet files, although likely to be very relevant, have not been located, but some TASS (Soviet news agency) material about Elliott was kept by the FBI.

Congress has investigated few people more thoroughly, or more repeatedly, than Elliott Roosevelt. The transcripts of his various congressional testimonies, as well as records of interrogation by tax authorities survive and provide details of his financial affairs. Yet everything Elliott said should be double-checked with the testimony of others. Much of this is in the Congressional Record; other transcripts were found in the Pegler, Nye, and McCracken papers at the Hoover Presidential Library.

Quotations

This book quotes primary sources at length. This enables the reader to better assess the veracity and relevance of the information. Since much material is shockingly controversial, and often reflects hearsay and personal testimony, it seems prudent in these cases to avoid the historian's customary summarizing and paraphrasing.

For that reason, casual readers may find the detail excessive. However, those who need to know what really happened, be they historians or lay persons, should be gratified that the raw data is here. For example, much misinformation and mythology attaches to the first flight of the Hughes XF-11. Here you will find the government's report on the crash. Likewise, the FBI's investigation of Elliott's shakedown schemes, which were aided by his father, is quoted at length; otherwise the reader might not believe it!

Chronology

From the age of majority almost to his death sixty years later, Elliott Roosevelt skated from one scandal to another. Sometimes they had long fuses, causing them to detonate publicly several years after the deed. This was certainly the case for Elliott's collaboration with Howard Hughes. The details revealed by the Senate Hearings of 1947 transfixed the nation, but most of the fun had happened in 1943.

The Hartford loan scandal, which had the potential to take President Roosevelt to the brink of impeachment, bracketed Elliott's wartime service. The damage was done in 1939-40, but the story did not break openly until just after FDR's death.

In these cases it has been necessary to describe the initial involvement in regular chronological order, yet wait to reveal details of the investigations until they became public much later. Otherwise the national reaction to them would not make any sense.

This unintentionally suspenseful aspect may cause a sense of foreboding, but it also necessitates a certain amount of explanatory backtracking when "the second shoe" finally drops. This device is intended as a reminder rather than as duplication.

"Follow the Money"

Deep Throat's advice to the Watergate sleuths remains unchallenged. This book spends a lot of time in the middle of the Venn diagram, at the intersection of politics, business, and organized crime. The common language of these domains is money. By tracking its flow, it is often possible to determine what was "really" going on.

Elliott Roosevelt followed this advice in a much more literal way. His problem was that he couldn't hold onto the fortunes he obtained. Throughout his career, the nation held an extraordinary interest in his (and his siblings') extravagant finances; therefore this book constantly references dollar amounts. Alas, the dollar is a vanishing yardstick, thanks, ironically, in no small part to President Franklin D. Roosevelt.

Elliott's career began just before Roosevelt closed the banks and devalued the dollar. In time the link between Federal Reserve notes and gold was severed entirely. Thus, to sense the true value of the numerous dollar amounts referred to, we have to apply a correction factor.

The cost of first-class postage is as good an indicator as any; in 1932 it was two cents. As a rule of thumb, we can reasonably multiply pre-war amounts by twenty, and post-war amounts by ten. Thus, the $5,000 bribe Elliott reportedly took to endorse Lyndon Johnson in 1937 was worth almost $100,000, and the $20 million contract for the Hughes F-11 would have been more than $200 million today.

The effect of increasing wealth and population sometimes necessitates a logarithmmic mindset. When President Roosevelt took office, the federal budget was about $5 billion, and the nation's GNP was $56 billion. In 2011, federal spending stands at $3.8 trillion out of a GDP of $15 trillion. This perspectivizes, for example, the $58,000 Lockheed Electra bombers that Elliott tried to sell to Joseph Stalin. An aircraft of similar capability today would cost several million. But a modern combat aircraft of equal interest to today's dictators would run over a hundred million, about two thousand times as much.

Elliott would have been ecstatic.

Notations and Abbreviations

Dates, numbers, agencies and the like have been shortened where reasonable, even in quotes. Volume, chapter and page may be shortened to XX/xx/xx form. Major works consulted are abbreviated. For obvious reasons, in this work ER = Elliott Roosevelt, while Eleanor Roosevelt is referred to as "Eleanor" where appropriate. JR = James (brother), and PR = Patricia (wife nr. 5).

- AAHS: American Aviation Historical Society
- AFHRA: Air Force Historical Research Agency
- AHS: Arizona Historical Society
- Anderson/HI: Hoover Institution at Stanford Univ., Gen. Fred Anderson Collection
- BIR: Bureau of Internal Revenue
- ChigTrib: Archives of the Chicago Tribune, the leading anti-Roosevelt newspaper.
- CongRec: Congressional Record
- DallasMN: Archives of the Dallas Morning News, one of ER's "local" papers, 1933-45
- DDE Lib: Dwight D. Eisenhower Presidential Library and Museum
- ESCOMHIST: Eastern Command, AAF secret history of op. FRANTIC, end 1944.
- FBI: Federal Bureau of Investigations, ER File obtained under FOIA
- FDR Lib: Franklin D. Roosevelt Presidential Library and Museum

- FOIA: Freedom of Information Act; used with FAA, FBI, State Department.
- FRUS: Foreign Relations of the United States, official State Dept. series.
- Greenway/AHS: Isabella Greenway collection, Arizona Historical Society, Tucson.
- HH Lib: Herbert Hoover Presidential Library and Museum
- HST Lib: Harry S. Truman Presidential Library and Museum
- KIA/MIA: Killed in Action/ Missing in Action
- LAT: Archives of the Los Angeles Times
- LBJ Lib: Lyndon B. Johnson Presidential Library and Museum
- LOC: Library of Congress
- NPRC: National Personnel Records Center
- NADHIST: History, North Atlantic Division, Air Transport Command, 2 vols. with supplements and photographic material, AFHRA
- NAPRWHIST: History, North African Photogr. Recon. Wing w. rel. material, AFHRA
- NYT: Archives of the New York Times
- OHI: Oral History Interview
- Pearson/LBJ: Drew Pearson collection at LBJ Lib
- Pegler/HH: Westbrook Pegler collection at HH Lib
- PPF: President's Personal File; PSF: President's Secretary's File
- PRU: Photographic Reconnaissance Unit
- RAF, RCAF, SAAF: British, Canadian, South African Air Force
- SBC Hearings: Senate Subcommittee on Investig. of the National Defense Prog., 1947
- USAAC/F: United States Army Air Corps (to 1941), Air Forces (1941-47)
- USCG: United States Coast Guard

Warranty

The author apologizes for all errors in this work. They are all his fault, even those of editing, formatting, and style. The delicacy and frequent ambiguity of the subject matter, especially when dealing with criminal allegations, increases the risk of errors. Sources often conflict. Often, stories have been tracked down only to find them wrong, or quite divergent from accepted truth. Some loose ends inescapably remain.

People should never believe anything they read. This applies here as well, but all efforts have been made to find the original sources, to cross-check information, and to attribute unverifiable information accurately.

Criticism is welcome and appreciated. Please bring corrections and omissions to the attention of the author via the contact information on the title page. Corrections and additions add to our historical knowledge.

About the Author

Tucson resident Chris Hansen is a retired engineer for Hughes Aircraft and the FAA, a flight instructor, and a former resident of some of Elliott Roosevelt's Arctic bases. His career touched many issues discussed herein. Startled when he came across Elliott's *As He Saw It*, he could not leave well enough alone and began unraveling the thread of Elliott's life. Innumerable "omigods" later, this book is the result.

IX. APPENDIX

IN HIS OWN WORDS

In 1966-67, Brigadier General George Goddard produced a series of oral history interviews with Air Force luminaries before their recollections dimmed irretrievably. One of them was with Goddard's good friend and collaborator, Elliott Roosevelt.

Read this with great caution. Goddard's transcript is somewhat chopped out – thus some lacunae and repetitions. Many of Elliott's numbers are wrong, and his judgments are often at variance with those expressed by others or even with his own at the time of the events. Also, Goddard - the Air Force's photographic expert - was eager to assert the excellence of his own work, and Roosevelt clearly wanted to support him therein.

TAPE #8 – Elliott Roosevelt – Nov 6, 1966

[USAF Oral History Program, AFHRA K239.0512-1024]

ER: I was assigned to Wright Field when I went onto active duty, then I got transferred out of procurement there. I applied to go on foreign duty and was assigned to a mission that went to Africa. We were there to do the reconnaissance of the North African coast and then move on to Cairo and the Middle East and the mapping of the route to China for the airlift that went clear from the United States to Brazil, across Africa and the Middle East to India and then across into China. This was a long way to carry your supplies in those days, but it hadn't even been mapped back in 1940, so in '41 [actually spring 1942] we went on that mission in two stripped-down B-17's out of Langley Field. On the south side of the Sahara Desert we took the time to re-map and provide new maps of the North African coast from Dakar over to Alexandria. We flew those missions with one B-17, the other one was lost on a flight from Puerto Rico to Trinidad and they never did find the plane or the crew during the entire remainder of the war. [added in pencil: The theory was that they overflew into the mountains of Venezuela]

In the course of our work, as you know, we flew practically every kind of airplane there was. The photographic Mosquito was used during the period in England to drop our counter-intelligence people behind the lines. We used to fly in at night and drop them at low altitude and go up directly over the target of drop and wait until we heard them tune their radio in. As soon as we knew they were safe we'd return to our base.

We went over with the 3rd Reconnaissance Group, which was the first one to go over to the European theatre. We had sent several squadrons to the Pacific; Pop Polifka took one of the first squadrons over to the Pacific. Later he returned to the States after Guadalcanal and joined my outfit as deputy commander of the 90th wing down in the Mediterranean. Pop was a very colorful guy – he wasn't the most reverent fellow with regard to brass that ever lived. He didn't like General MacArthur very much, that's why he transferred out of that theatre as early as he possibly could. He was the pilot who flew MacArthur up from Australia and over the battlefields at Guadalcanal. He was there on the bombardment and he also watched the paratroop dropping. But Polifka was rude to him and I think MacArthur was very glad to get rid of Pop. Anyway, Pop came over to our group in Africa, and he succeeded me as commander of the 90th wing. He was one of the best pilots I have ever seen. He knew more about the technique of taking low-altitude pictures, particularly, and especially obliques. He was very good on coastal work and things of that nature. Some of the best pictures that came out of World War II were pictures that Pop took. He would go in at the assigned altitude of 28,000 to 30,000 feet and take his pictures, then he'd go down and get some low-altitude dicing pictures. Often his pictures brought out all kinds of things you couldn't pick out otherwise – things that were camouflaged from overhead came right out on his obliques.

They tell the story about Pop, that he went up on a mission and was supposed to have caused an enemy aircraft to spin in by his having maneuvered him around as well as the fighter who was on his tail and got the fellow so mixed up he spun out.

Actually, the most terrific stories in my outfit are told about Leon Gray. He was my deputy commander of the 325th Reconnaissance Wing in England. He had most of the Mosquito operations and the P-51 operations that were used. Also, as you know, after the Germans got their jet aircraft into operation we had to have two piston-driven fighter aircraft to fly cover for us. We used them in this way, not as protection, but as spotters. They'd lie back about two or three miles and about 5,000 feet above us and watch for the fellows come in on our tail.

We had one low-altitude mission we had to fly in Yugoslavia and we had ordered Polifka specifically not to fly that mission. So he promised us faithfully – after all he was the deputy wing commander and was only supposed to go in on certain missions, due to his value. He ignored the order, at the last minute he told the fellow to go on back to his bunk and he'd take the mission. This was a mission to try to identify the headquarters of Tito in this valley in preparation to our going in to drop some people to be of assistance to Tito and also some extremely valuable supplies and messages. Polifka filled out the forms with the other fellow's name and then he took over the mission, which, as you know, made him liable for court-martial. We overlooked it, though. He flew 130-odd missions in the European theatre and he had some 35 missions in the Asiatic theatre. He was one of the most highly decorated reconnaissance officers – he and Leon Gray and Johnny Hoover. Leon Gray flew 146 missions in the European theatre and Johnny Hoover flew 144. Johnny Hoover came to me as a boy of 18 – a 2nd Lieutenant replacement pilot in North Africa – and Leon Gray came to me as a man who had been court martialed in the Air Transport Command and was given the choice of accepting a very severe punishment or of going on combat duty. He thought he was going onto the fighters and bombers, but instead he found himself, much to his disgust, flying reconnaissance. He came to love reconnaissance when he found that it really wasn't very sissified and when he found that we had a higher rate loss than any other outfit flying in World War II. He became an outstanding reconnaissance pilot and added a great deal to the techniques of reconnaissance. He did some of the best work of the war in night photography. He was probably one of the most difficult young men to keep disciplined that I've ever known in my life. As you know, he stayed in the Air Force after World War II, but he never got beyond a full Colonel, which he was when he came out of World War II.

GG: A couple of months before we got into the war, Gen. Arnold called me into his office and said, "You get on over to the RAF and study their operation because their equipment is far superior to ours, and the Corps of Engineers are complaining because we don't have any mapping equipment." You didn't find much trouble with our cameras in your mapping work, did you?

ER: George, if you really want to know, our camera equipment was far superior to theirs and our mountings in our ships were superior, as well. Where we were handicapped in World War II was in the quality of the aircraft … The photographic version of the P-38 was a stripped-down version of the P-38 fighter. It was designed to fly at speeds of 400 mph and higher, because we took out all the armour plating and we had nothing but the cameras in place of the armament. In spite of that we lost 93 out of 96 pilots in North Africa in the first six weeks after the invasion of North Africa purely and simply through the failure of the aircraft. The P-38 – or the F-4, as it was known then – used to throw rods in those Allison engines every time we went over 17,000 feet. When we tried flying the missions under that altitude we were sitting ducks. So you either went above 17,000 feet and lost your power or went under that and lost your plane.

Our camera equipment was far superior – in fact, you can talk to anyone today who was in the RAF over there during World War II and they'll tell you they swiped almost every technique we had for aerial photography for the RAF. The RAF had better aircraft. Their techniques weren't as good as ours – they learned from us. The proof of the pudding lay in the fact that the entire RAF reconnaissance – the interpreters, all their physical plants on the ground, plus all their combat units for flying the photography – were put under the command of the U.S. reconnaissance forces. We flew all the way through the European part of the war with a combined recon. outfit that included South African, Australian, free French, one Polish outfit, all the RAF outfits, the Canadian outfits, in addition to ours, and they were all under United States control. This doesn't point to the fact that they were ahead of us. We built the largest photographic processing unit for tactical and strategic reconnaissance in World War II, which you'll remember, at High [Wycombe] which turned out in any photographic laboratory in history. We turned out an average of a little better than 13 million prints a day when we reached our peak operation.

GG: I always remember visiting your [English] operation. There was a petition as you came in the front door. I hear a Sergeant say one day, "You know, whoever developed that waterproof paper ought to really get promoted." That waterproof paper came about through the assignment I had, from 1927 to '29. We used to make prints and put them on cheesecloth racks in the morning and they were just as wet at night as when we first put them on. We had to resort to alcohol. So when I went back to the States I decided I was going to work on waterproof paper. By the time the war started we had waterproof paper and it was perfected.

ER: George, do you remember when you perfected the infra-red film? You brought that over just about the time that we were trying to detect the installations of the V-2. We flew the first missions that proved this absolutely detected those camouflaged areas and we were able to pinpoint those things for the bomber command. That was back in 1944.

ER: You know, some of the personnel stories they tell are rather nice. They tell one about Leon Gray flying over Rome. You know we had to do a very intensive photographing job over Rome because we had orders not to bomb any of the Roman Catholic holy places in Rome so it was a pretty hard job to pinpoint your bombing raids so meticulously. Gray was on a run over the target area and these two Italian fighters came at him from either side. He stayed right on course, figuring they'd have trouble if he pulled up at the last minute. He waited until the tracers were coming in on him and he pulled his nose up and went into a vertical climb. The two planes crashed into each other and both went down.

Then you know the stories they tell about Warburton, who was a wing commander in the RAF. He was the recon squadron commander at Malta when it was under siege. He had the last operational airplane – a Spitfire that was a photographic plane so it didn't have any guns. He would fly over the German air force bases in the south end of Sicily and get them to scramble and chase him back toward Malta. He'd wait until they were just off the coast of Malta, let them come in and try to shoot him down and then he'd take evasive action. They said he used to put on these shows every three or four days for the inhabitants of Malta to make them feel better because they were undergoing bombardment every night. Thousands of people would watch from the cliffs while he had these aerial dog fights with these ME-109's. They do claim that on one occasion he flew so close to the tail of one of these ME-109's that he used his prop to carve up the tail and caused it to crash. There's another story that he maneuvered one German pilot so close to sea level that when he pulled out the German couldn't and went into the sea. He was supposed to have kept the morale of the siege of Malta up. He's one of the classic examples of a recon. pilot who flew many hundreds of missions – he flew about 80 missions during the Battle of Britain and about 100 down in North Africa and Italy. He was lost on a mission with Johnny Hoover. He flew over a combat mission on a target in southern Germany and then they were to go on and land in Italy. They were flying south over Switzerland to Italy, they were both flying F-5's. He and Johnny were talking on the inter-com and they got over Lake Como. Warburton said, "I think I'll go on down, you stay on course, Johnny, and I'll catch up with you." That was the last thing ever heard from wing commander Warburton. We don't think he was shot down because he was over Switzerland. Our theory is that he may have been a little war-weary and he may have parachuted down and let his plane crash into a mountain, and he may have left the war at about that time.

GG: What's that story they tell about Johnny Hoover at that [ ]?

ER: This came at the close of the European fighting, right after V-D Day. [presumably V-E Day] Johnny learned the news of the end of the fighting and he wanted to celebrate. He flew over this hospital where there was a nurse that he was kind of sweet on and he wanted to get her attention to let her know the war was over. He was flying a Mosquito – you know those Mosquitos, they were made of plywood. He knicked one of these big brick chimneys and it caused him to crash. He walked away from a completely wrecked plane. They court-martialed him – this was about two weeks after my father's death – and my first job was to get character witnesses. They had a prosecutor assigned for Johnny who had just come over from the Pentagon and they really threw the book at him. They were going to strip him of all his wartime decorations – he had something like five DFCs, 30 Air Medals, the Distinguished Service Cross. And they were going to fine him for the cost of the airplane he'd wrecked. So I got these character witnesses and I got depositions from General Eisenhower, General Spaatz, and General Doolittle testified at his trial. He was fined $2,000 and allowed to pay that off over the next two years out of his pay.

GG: You remember you were having some trouble flying up the [air], because they were forcing you up – how high did they force you to go?

ER: The highest we flew with the F-5's was about 38,000 feet - we did fly as high with the Mosquito as 42,000 feet. With the Spitfire and the P-51's we flew up to 39,000 feet and, of course, with most of the night photography we did we never got up more than 10-12,000, because with those flares in order to get any kind of good definition to our pictures we very rarely went over that. In fact, our favorite altitude on night missions was between 6-8,000 feet. Considering that we were using planes that weren't designed to fly at these altitudes, we did a lot of high-altitude flying.

GG: On our missions we always had to fly full throttle most of the time while pilots on bombing runs only used full power when they were over the target. Few people realize the extra work on those engines.

ER: Of course you know that during the last year and a half in the ETO the Luftwaffe gave double credit for every recon plane shot down. My recollection is that we lost 24...% of pilots per month. Of course, these weren't all lost in combat. We lost a great many through being shot at, being crippled, through the weather situation – particularly flying out of England, I don't remember coming back into England on anything but GCA [ground controlled approach].

[The following paragraph is out of sequence and doesn't match ER's style. It may have been Goddard's own composition]

George, one of the important things you did for our activity was when you had some of the newly developed infra-red camouflage detection film sent over to us in England from your photographic laboratory at Wright Field in Dayton. I understand you and Kodak worked on this development for a long time and it was very timely received in England to help us locate the well camouflaged sites in Northern France and the low countries. It was those wonderful pictures that broke down the German camouflage. The pictures showed all the natural vegetation – the growing grass, bushes and trees – in a red color. All the artificial German green painted fishnets, canvas covers and the withered branches of trees were shown up in the pictures in a blue color. We discovered many V-1 rocket sites in such pictures, but the real find was the important underground German V-1 manufacturing and loading plant 90 miles or so NE of Paris. At the entrance to this mammoth underground plant the Germans had constructed a large railroad yard and it was cleverly covered completely with enormous green-painted fishnets and fake bushes and trees. When the aerial picture was made it clearly showed a great big fan-shaped area in blue color with the surrounding natural grass and tree vegetation with its natural chlorophyll in a red color.

Hundreds of pictures had been made with ordinary film of this suspected area but they did not disclose the V-1 installation with its natural vegetation and its fake vegetation. I think Kodak and your laboratory made a great contribution with this important development.

Col. Leon Gray, my deputy commander of the 325th reconnaissance wing in England, had most of the Mosquito aircraft and the P-51 operations. After the Germans started using their highly efficient jet aircraft "the world's first military jets in operation," we had to have two piston-driven fighter aircraft accompany our photographic airplane. They were not required actually for protection, but as spotters. They would lie back about two or three miles and about 5,000 feet above us and watch for the German 262 jets to come in on our tail. They worked out real well for the reconnaissance pilot would be forewarned over the radio and immediately make a sharp turn. The high speed jets couldn't make such sharp turns. They had to go six or seven miles to make the turn to get lined up again to attack the recce plane. The first operative jets did not carry much fuel and the number of times they could attack was limited. However, they did get several of our planes for they always knew the important targets we would be photographing and they were generally follow-ups to a bombing, taking the evaluation pictures.

One of the things I think was an interesting development in North Africa – you know, when we had the F-4's the boys felt they were flying in a death trap. If the airplane was crippled, you had to ride it down, because you couldn't bail out of that airplane without getting caught on that twin-boom tail – that aileron [sic] would cut you in two. That is, until we got this one kid – a second lieutenant. He was shot up by an ME-109, to the east of the German lines, and he lost both engines. He eased the nose up and stepped out on the wing and dove over the leading edge of the wing – between the wing and the windmilling prop – he dropped and opened his chute. He was rescued by some Arabs – he'd been shot pretty bad and had a lot of shrapnel – but they brought him back through the German lines on a burro and delivered him to the Allies. I interviewed him in a field hospital about six hours later. He told me about this and I jumped twice using this same technique and it saved countless lives. You know a P-38 with no power is no fun to land.

All reconnaissance in the European theatre was under my command – under the 325th wing.

GG: It was pretty well integrated, wasn't it?

ER: Completely integrated – we integrated completely at the integration level. We also integrated to a fair extent down at High Wycombe in the production – taking the film and putting out the prints. We had a number of RAF units that were integrated right in with our ground units. We ran a 24-hour operation, so we had three eight-hour shifts. There were between 500 and 600 men who were assigned to each shift, so we had a pretty good-sized operation going.

Of course, you remember when we went up doing all that recon work in Labrador, Baffin Island and Greenland and Iceland back in 1940 [summer 1941]. We were up there with a joint Army-Navy-Air Force mission to find those airfields up there – and in those days flying in the Arctic was a little bit different than it is today. The navigation was a little touchy, because the instruments were highly unreliable. We flew up in that area from November of '40 until September of '41. We operated out of Newfoundland. We were about three days ahead of the RCAF in the discovery of the Goose Bay air base, which became a U.S. air base because we were in there first. [the exact opposite is true] That November – one year and a few days more after we had discovered the site – they were flying airplanes directly across the Atlantic. [GB was found in July 41 and supported aircraft movements in Nov. 1941] But there, again, our reconnaissance cameras were of the utmost importance – it was through the pictures we took that we were able to determine the type of equipment required for not only our air bases, but the weather stations that we put up all through that area.

Upon the completion of this work I was assigned to the mapping and charting of the strip maps of the North African coasts, through Cairo, the Middle East, on to India and China. …

There is one point that I've always felt had been a little bit obscured. People have always wondered why it was that we weren't aware, prior to the Battle of the Bulge, that the Germans were carrying out this big build-up in November of '44. For the record, I'd just like to say that you can go back through the records of all the tactical air commands throughout the entire theatre and you will find they had the information fully ten days before the attack. The only thing is, for three days prior to the attack they had a very heavy ground fog over the entire area. And for two days after the attack, both our tactical and strategic recon units were very severely hampered in carrying out any recon. at all in the immediate area of the attack. The truth … is that the failure lies with the intel. officers who received this information at the various headquarters, who did not believe it.

GG: Were you in on the photography of Peenemünde?

ER: Oh yes sir, I was in full charge of that.

GG: Who made those first pictures over there?

ER: These were all the U.S. and RAF units that flew those. We flew about 50-50 as to the number of units that were flown over Peenemünde.

I place the entire credit for winning the war on the job that was done at Peenemünde – they were that close to turning the tide, with the combination of their production of their V-2's, V-1's and atomic warheads.

Certainly today everyone recognizes that reconnaissance is, by far, the most important feature of all of the winning of the war and only through recon. are we going to be able to contain the developments for destructive purposes of the hydrogen and atomic bombs of the future.

[Goddard provides a second outtake of Elliott Roosevelt's interview elsewhere. It is apparently provided to support Goddard's side in his feud with an Air Corps rival]

ER: Maybe I'd just better recount the time I started with you back at Wright Field in 1940. Father was running for president for the third time and I had the honor to be Captain [blank]. I got so much mail out there that the other officers couldn't get their mail, particularly those whose names started with the letter R. I got 30,000 letters in six weeks from people who were either derogatory or praising me for being in the Air Force and having a commission. To make a long story short, I applied to go on foreign duty and was assigned to a mission that went to Africa. We were there to do the reconnaissance of the north African coast and then we were to move on to Cairo and into the Middle East and the mapping of the route to China for the airlift that went from the United States to Brazil, across Africa and across the Middle East into India and then, on the airlift, into China.

***

GG: Well you know, I couldn't talk to Kaye [Minton Kaye] about things, he wouldn't listen, he didn't want me to make an impression on Arnold. You know we wrote that letter back – we got him tossed out. [added in pencil: Kaye was Colonel Nemesis in Overview [Goddard's book]]

ER: Yes, we got him tossed out.

GG: And then he went to Burma, and I also found out that he would have been made a Brigadier General if he'd stayed in that office two weeks longer.

ER: That's right. You know he retired to Colorado Springs a year or so after World War II. He joined one of these organizations out there and he was very bitter about me all the time – he must have felt about the same about you – but he had no kind words to say about me.

GG: I remember you told me one time, when I first met you, I asked you how you ever got into the photo business, you said, "Well, you know, Minton Kaye got me in for the politics in the thing, and I think I'm going to show him some politics now," and you sat down and wrote that letter to your father.

ER: That's right.

GG: It was one of the finest things you ever did.

ER: Well we've gone a long way and we've certainly proved one thing, which was that photography was a very important element of that whole World War II action in the European theatre and, from everything I've been able to learn, although I wasn't personally involved in the Asiatic theatre, I would say that, at the end of the war at least, it played a very strategic part in bringing the war to a close.

*** END OF FILE ***

Asst. Chief of Air Staff, Intelligence - Interview with Col. Elliott Roosevelt – 27 July 1943

[In the last week of July 1943, Roosevelt returned to Washington to consult on reconnaissance projects. On 27 July, according to Stephen Early's papers, he spoke to officers in the Air Room at the War Department. The following testimony of the same day, found in Air Force files, may be a transcript of that debriefing interview, summarizing reconnaissance in the North African campaign. It is particularly illuminating since it contradicts some of the assertions in the Doolittle interview. Mr. Early was told that Elliott did a swell job, but he was told to do no more interviews "and is not to go on the air." AFHRA file 142.052, supported by Stephen T. Early papers, FDR Lib.]

ER: The story of our operations in North Africa is very largely the story of Combat Photo Reconnaissance in its entirety, from the standpoint of the USAAF. Up until the time we went on foreign duty only one flight of one squadron had previously seen active duty. That was the squadron in Australia commanded by Lt. Colonel Polifka.

The operation of the 3rd PG, from the start when it received most of its training in the U.K. prior to proceeding to North Africa, was conceived purely as servicing the needs of bombardment, both for target information, and bomb damage assessment. After arrival in North Africa we proceeded with that work almost exclusively until January, when we were called upon to take up in large measure the intelligence picture for the Navy to keep them posted on the movements of all Axis shipping in the Mediterranean.

The theatre we are called upon to cover is very largely shown by this map: From Gibraltar to Corfu, and on a line from Corfu down to Tripoli and inland 100 miles along the Eastern Adriatic. In the area to the north of the Mediterranean we are supposed to take care of everything up to the 40th parallel. In certain instances we have been cooperating with, and crossing zones of responsibility with the PRUs in the U.K. The work, as carried on by us, was consolidated very early in the game with the work of the RAF, and a consolidated photographic reconnaissance wing was formed, consisting of the British photographic recon. and American photographic recon. in the theatre. We were equipped with P-38's, Spitfires, and an occasional Mosquito.

From March on we operated also in support of the ground forces, and it is notable here that the fact that the fact that our operations in support of the ground forces were limited, was largely due to the fact that the USAAF and the RAF had failed to realize a long while ago the part that photographic reconnaissance plays in support of the ground forces. Our operations were very much restricted because of a lack of aircraft to get the job done on the scale which the ground forces required. The only other use of photographic reconnaissance by ground forces on the part of the Allies was the use made by the 8th Army of an RAF squadron, and they were able to operate very successfully with a flight that was fed into them by this squadron because they operated on a very narrow front. When the Tunisian campaign settled down, as it did, on a rather large front, the coverage demanded was far too great for the resources at hand. The U.S. Army operating in Tunisia did not receive proper photographic reconnaissance support mainly because of the lack of realization of the difference between Tac/R (tactical reconnaissance), or observation, and photo reconnaissance.

Since returning to Washington I have found plans on foot which call for large numbers of squadrons for tactical air forces, both Tac/R and photographic reconnaissance, and I feel that it must be borne in mind that each theatre will have a different type of operation, and therefore, that too great a rigidity of organization on reconnaissance aviation is a bad thing. We have found that the pictures which are taken by our Tac/R or observation type aircraft are taken to check on a visual observation. They are pictures which are not stereoscopic pairs and which no trained photo interpreter can use for detailed study; we cannot get anything more out of them than the average person can get from a photograph.

Photo-recon pictures are high altitude vertical pictures, and the information gained by them for the ground armies is information about movement of enemy troops, enemy communications lines, location of mine fields, location of artillery positions, and other intelligence information that plays a great and vital part in an offensive.

From observations of our whole operations over the period of the last eight months, I would say that we failed to go in properly prepared for the job which we had to do. We were never provided with sufficient aircraft to do the job, the proper type of cameras, and sufficient photographic production equipment and supplies; in addition, we do not have in the U.S. Photo Wing more than a very small handful of photo interpreters.

In photographic reconnaissance there are three divisions: The flying end, the processing of pictures, and the interpreting of those pictures; no one is any good without the others. We never had an organization that was properly balanced at any time; the RAF and the British Army supplied practically all photo interpretation in the theatre.

The work carried on by photographic reconnaissance is divided into different categories, - ground, air, and naval support, as well as other needs which are occasioned by the fact that while you are carrying on intelligence work for an operation, you must carry on intelligence work for the planning staffs for the next operations. Thus, during the Tunisian Campaign, we were providing for the planning staffs on the Pantelleria operation and the Sicilian operation. While the Sicilian Campaign is going on, other projects are being planned.

In order to carry on all that work, it takes a very highly centralized organization in order to avoid duplication. For instance – the Ground Forces, the Planning Staff, the Navy, the Tactical Air Force, and the Strategic Striking Group would all like aircraft specifically assigned to carry out their particular requests. If that occurs, the difficulties as to areas that are to be covered are multitudinous for there is no theatre that is so widespread that its activities are unrelated geographically. In addition, the problem of producing the number of desired pictures calls for a tremendous duplication of photographic equipment when there is no centralized control. It might be of interest to you to know that in the month of July in our one plant at La Marsa we produced over 400,000 prints for the Ground Forces, Air Forces, and the Navy. That represents 12½% of the tactical amount which was requested, which are considered legitimate requests. There were requests for over 10½ million pictures during the month of July which we cut down rather considerably. I tell you that only to point out that if each unit operates separately with its own separate flying unit and production unit, we would probably produce in the theatre in the neighborhood of 20 million prints every month.

I think it should be recognized that reconnaissance aviation as such is just as definitely a branch of our offensive weapon in the air as our fighters and bombers. The bomber is of practically no value unless it has the latest information on the target which it is striking. Also I recall one occasion in particular in Tunisia, when an Army Ground Force commander said, "I should not move from this position until I have pictures of what lies in front of us." He got them. That is the attitude of more and more ground commanders, and we must recognize the fact that that support must be given to them.

The Ground commanders would like to be able to distribute pictures as they did in the case of landings in Sicily, when they provided pictures of the particular area at which they were landing to every company commander. That is a huge number of photographs – but it pays dividends, and is a worthwhile request.

I might point to the Pantelleria operation as one of particular interest where we took photographs which provided approximately 94% of all the intelligence with regard to Pantelleria. [The tiny Italian island was bombed to surrender] The complete operation was planned on the basis of those photographs. During the operations we were able to save a tremendous amount in bombs dropped on the targets by continuous photographing throughout the daylight hours, thereby being able to quickly advise the Strategic Air Force and the Tactical Air Force as to what targets had been knocked out.

Ground study of Pantelleria completely proved all of the photographic interpretations that had been done during the show. This was one target where the experts were able to go in afterwards to compare the photographic interpretation reports of the bombing with the actual damage on the ground. They were shown to have been completely accurate in all their reports.

Missions such as those against Rome and operations against all major points would have been absolutely impossible without photographic reconnaissance; and all of the concentration of sea power on the landings in Sicily would have been impossible without photographic reconnaissance because a very large proportion of the striking fleet would have had to have been used to shadow and watch the Italian fleet during the operations. Admiral Cunningham in the Mediterranean has indicated by figures just what photographic reconnaissance meant to him, and I can state definitely that he feels that it is worth a great many warships to have PR in an area such as the Mediterranean.

Mr. McCloy: What is your most satisfactory photographic plane? What kind is the most useful?

A: The two that are the most satisfactory are the F-5A, which is a version of the P-38 and the Spitfire 11. For long-range work at 2,000 miles or so we prefer the Mosquito.

Q: What is your normal photographing altitude?

A: Between 27,000 and 30,000 feet.

Q: Were you called upon for any mapping? How was it accomplished?

A: There has been some talk that the engineers [Corps of Eng.] have very stiff requirements, and that we can't meet them. That is not correct. We can meet the engineers' requirements and do perfectly satisfactory work for them; we are doing it; it is just a matter of understanding each other, and I see no reason why that cannot be done.

Q: Are they doing that with F-5's or Mosquitos?

A: They are doing it at the present time with F-5's.

Q: Are the engineers satisfied?

A: The engineers will tell you exactly what I will tell you – that it isn't the best. In certain areas where they want a map the Mosquito couldn't live – only the F-5 could live in it. The photography taken isn't the best that could be taken; it isn't as good as it would be here in the U.S. – but they are using it and managing to get quite a lot of good results from it. We had done a complete mapping job of Sardinia purely for tactical purposes and not for mapping purposes. They utilized 80% of the photography that had been flown and we had to re-fly only 20%.

Q: What kind of interception did you get of planes up to 30,000 feet?

A: It all depends on the area. During the Tunisian campaign the places where we had the most interception were Tunis and Bizerte. They were the most heavily defended areas we have ever run across. The boys flying out of Malta ran into quite heavy interception at various points on Sicily, but we have never run into very serious interception in Sardinia, Corsica, or Northern Italy. At the present time our hottest interception is around the Naples area, where there is a large concentration of patrolling aircraft. Our losses in the first nine months of operations there were 3% on combat missions flown.

Q: Is the Mosquito more vulnerable, or [does] its speed counteract its lack of armament?

A: We have never had the new model Mosquito. The only ones I have any familiarity with are the Mosquito 4's which are not as fast as the Spitfire, nor as fast as the F-5A. The Mosquito is not as maneuverable as either of these aircraft; its main advantage is its internally contained fuel supply which enables it to cover wide areas, such as around Venice and up into the Balkans. Our need for the Mosquito is for long-range reconnaissance beyond the safe range of our present Spits and F-5A's.

Q: Was there any night photographic reconnaissance accomplished?

A: Yes. We conducted the first night photo reconnaissance conducted by USAAF in the European theatre. We started it in the Sicilian Campaign and it was highly successful. As a matter of fact we only did it during the last ten days before I left. I flew three night missions over Sicily on pin pointing of road junctions and watching the movement of troops at night against the 7th Army. Those missions have proved very successful. We used B-25's on them.

Q: What altitude were those?

A: All of our photography on that was done from 12,000 feet.

Q: Colonel, you mentioned shortcomings in aerial camera equipment. Would you run through the major defects?

A: We had very serious disadvantages with heating American camera equipment – we have never had a satisfactory heater. We had a large number of defective lenses, and a great deal of shutter trouble. With the cameras we had, 9% of our missions flown, which otherwise were successful were unsuccessful due to camera failure. The RAF in the same time, with approximately the same number of missions flown had less than 1/10 of one percent of their missions failures because of cameras. The most heartbreaking thing a man can possibly do is to finish a mission, having flown it successfully, and find he has nothing on the film at all.

Q: During the Sicilian campaign what liaison [did] ground forces [maintain] with your HQ?

A: During the Sicilian campaign the ground forces had liaison officers stationed at our headquarters and they had ground courier service which they maintained between ground HQ and our HQ; we maintained air courier service with their advanced headquarters. Our photo. recon. wing flies an average of over 4,000 miles a day on courier missions delivering prints and photo interpretation reports to the various interested headquarters. The time element is most important and there is no satisfactory service of communications which is maintained by anyone else. Therefore the reconnaissance unit operating in a theatre must maintain its own air courier service. As a matter of fact, I maintain 32 aircraft which do nothing but fly courier missions.

Q: What is the comparative practical range of the Spitfire, the Mosquito, and the F-5A?

A: The practical range using the Spitfire 11 and the F-5A is approximately the same – between 600 and 650 miles radius. The Mosquito 4 has operated up to 1,000 miles radius.

Q: What recommendations would you make with respect to training photo interpreters?

A: Photo interpreters should be trained in a central school where the basic training program is the same for military and air interpreters; then they need very short periods of training for their specialties. At [present] there is an inter-service school in the Middle East maintained jointly by the British Army and RAF. They are willing to train up to 60 American interpreters per month. We have a school in England maintained by the 8th AF under the command of Major Sterling which could train a very much larger group of men, but we have evidently failed to make use of their training courses because I have seen very few graduates who have come from either the U.S. or England. We have found on the whole that the graduates turned out by English schools are thoroughly satisfactory, even though they had no operational experience prior to joining us.

Q: How was the enemy ack ack in the Sicilian campaign?

A: The interesting thing in the Sicilian campaign was that there was practically no opposition whatsoever. There were instances when we were fired on by our own ground forces, and the British and our own Navies. This suggests the need for more training in aircraft recognition.

*** END OF FILE ***

U.S. Navy Interview with Elliott Roosevelt

DECLASSIFIED – AFHRA HI-SU-RE
<u>U.S. CONFIDENTIAL</u>
<u>BRITISH SECRET</u>

NAVAER Interview of
COLONEL ELLIOTT ROOSEVELT, AAF
Commanding Officer, Photo Reconnaissance Wing, North African Air Forces
in the Bureau of Aeronautics
30 July 1943

[After Colonel Roosevelt had made his debrief with the Air Staff, he gave the Navy its cut three days later. This interview is more detailed and technical. Relevant excerpts are provided below.]

ORGANIZATION

The Photo Recon. Wing in North Africa is a combined operation of the RAF, the USAAF, the French Air Force, and the South African Air Force. There are four squadrons of U.S. aircraft, two squadrons of RAF aircraft, one squadron of French aircraft, and one South African squadron.

The work we have done since last November in North Africa has been for three principal agencies: the Air Force, the Ground Force, and the Navy. In addition to those three main classifications, the work is broken down into operational requirements for the Headquarters (HQ) of the Air Force on overall general intelligence, for the Tactical Air Force, and for the Strategic Air Force. The operation for the Ground Forces has been divided into the operations for the Allied Force HQ on general reconnaissance requirements, the operations on behalf of the armies in the field, and the operations on behalf of the planning staffs. In addition to these requirements for air and ground, we were further charged with producing the Intelligence information required in the Mediterranean and the area from Gibraltar to the eastern part of the Adriatic (from Corfu on a line directly down to Tripoli), and all of the information on the position of Axis shipping in the harbors and at sea for the Navy.

NAVAL REQUIREMENTS

The naval requirements during the Tunisian campaign were to cover the major ports of southern France three times per week; the ports along western Italy three times per week; the ports on the Adriatic once per week; and the ports in Sicily every day. In addition, until the fall of Tripoli, we had to cover the ports in Tunisia as far as Tripoli every day. As a general over-all requirement, we have always been required to photograph every vessel passed over going to or from a reconnaissance mission. And inasmuch as most of our flying was over water, it was very rare that we did not photograph three or more vessels while on a single flight. As we proceeded in the Tunisian campaign, activity in covering the ports in southern Italy increased. There was also continuous pressure for coverage of the Tunisian ports of Tunis, Bizerte, Sousse, Sfax, and Gabes. During the closing weeks of the Tunisian campaign those ports were photographed twice per day.

In the Sicilian campaign we were required to photograph every day all ports in the entire area for which we were responsible, and twice a day the major ports where the Italian Fleet was located: Spezia, Leghorn, and Genoa, as well as all the ports in Sicily and southern Italy. Cagliari, which is in southern Sardinia, had become less active because of heavy bombardment and had not been used very much. The coverage of most of the Sardinian ports was once per day. Corsica's few ports were rather easy to cover once per day on the regular missions. But even the smaller ports that lay in between the larger shipping centers, where there was little opportunity for any large vessels to enter and which could be used only by coast craft, had to be photographed at least once per week. Ports in southern Italy which could be used in reinforcing Sicily were watched very carefully and were covered as often as once per day.

BuAer Comment: The U.S. Naval Forces, not having photographic reconnaissance of its own during the preparatory period or during the assault against Sicily, were dependent upon the RAF and AAF for photographic coverage of the areas concerned. The interpretation of these photographs and preparation of strategic and tactical maps, annotated and gridded mosaics, beach and terrain studies, land fall perspective sketches and written reports were made by the Photographic Interpretation Unit, Commander Amphibious Force, Atlantic Fleet and the Photographic Interpretation Unit, ComNavNAW.

The interpretation of the Sicilian beaches and terrain inland to 5-10 miles … has been verified by land observers since landing and found to be about 100% correct in every detail of military consequence….

OPERATIONS FOR THE AIR FORCE

The operations for the Air Force were as follows: We were required to photograph all airdromes in the entire area up to the 40th parallel in Europe and to 100 miles east of the eastern shore of the Adriatic, including all of airdromes in Italy, Sicily, Sardinia, Corsica, and when the Axis were in North Africa, all Axis airdromes in North Africa. Once per week we were required within a four-hour period to photograph all airdromes within four hours of each other, in order to get a reading on the exact location of the Axis airpower at a given time. The interesting part of all this airdrome coverage is that the Axis strength as shown from aerial photographs never varied more than 6% from the Intelligence information available from all other sources on the true strength of the Axis air force. That differential of approximately 6% can be explained by the fact that certainly there were aircraft in the air at the time we flew over, because we were photographing usually during the best daylight hours. Airdrome and harbor coverage, industrial area coverage, communications lines coverage, were all made for the Strategic Air Force to secure target information for bombing raids.

BOMB FALL PLOTS

During bombing raids there are in each bombardment squadron at least two to three aircraft equipped with cameras for taking strike photographs. These are immediately sent to the PRW for evaluation. Bombfall plots, showing exactly how the runs occurred in relation to the target, and exactly where the bombs fell, are made for the education of bombardiers and pilots. During the five-month period in which this work with bombfall plots has been going on the bombardment score has improved as much as 70% in some of the outfits of the Strategic Air Force.

PHOTOGRAPHS AFTER A RAID

As soon as possible after each air raid, as a general rule from two to four hours afterwards, we were required to photograph the target. From these photographs bomb damage assessments were made, to determine whether the target had to be hit again, and if so, when. In the instance of a railroad yard, the assessors would arrive at a date when there would probably be sufficient progress towards repair to have it again become operative.

SUPPORTING THE GROUND FORCE

The Tactical Air Force requires very much the same type of reconnaissance. As they are operating directly in support of the Ground Force, however, the work is of much shorter range. The same units which support the ground troops and provide their photography as a general rule carry out the reconnaissance required by the Tactical Air Force.

The units supporting the Ground Forces represent the largest effort we make. These units are required to cover completely the entire area in front of an army, every day, to a depth of approximately 150 miles. Frequent reconnaissance missions are run, in addition, for the purpose of keeping the ground commanders advised as to the movement of all enemy troops, personnel, and equipment behind the front lines.

The location of mine fields is done mainly by photo reconnaissance. The location of artillery emplacements is done by photo recon.. Even though a mine has been camouflaged so successfully that it cannot be detected on approaching it on the ground, it is clearly evident to a good photo interpreter on photographs taken from 27,000 to 30,000 feet with proper focal length cameras.

WORK FOR PLANNING STAFFS

The staff which planned the Sicilian operation, known as Force 141, began work in January of this year, when we started flying missions for them. I was asked this morning to make an estimate of how many missions we flew in preparation for the Sicilian operation, and I estimated the number to be approximately 500. We completely mapped the entire 12,000 square miles of Sicily; a mosaic mentioning 19 ½ feet by 12 ½ feet was produced to the scale of 1:50,000. This work was extremely difficult of accomplishment, because all last winter and spring the main strength of the Axis air force was located in Sicily. Of the 500 missions I would estimate that not more than 1/10 were accomplished without enemy aircraft interception. Areas such as Palermo and Trapani, moreover, and the larger airdromes were very heavily defended by flak installations; by the use of box-type barrages they were accurate with their anti-aircraft fire up to approximately 36,000 feet. The work done for planning staffs is carried on concurrently with work for operational units. All such work done on the invasion of Sicily was performed during the operations on the Tunisian front.

SETTING UP PHOTO RECONNAISSANCE

We were handicapped because the RAF and our Air Force completely failed to realize the part photo reconnaissance plays in support of a ground force or in carrying out an operation of the size of that in North Africa. We were sent there with inadequate equipment. We started with two squadrons and a flight of a third squadron. The flight of the third squadron was equipped with B-17 aircraft. Somebody on the staff in Washington had read amazing stories about how the B-17 airplane knocked down more fighters than any other; so it was thought a single B-17 could be sent out to do photo reconnaissance. We had to find out what happens to a B-17 when it's out by itself on a mission; it was a very sad experience. We had inferior aircraft to the 109's and 190's, and we had a very high rate of loss, our loss in the first three months averaging 30% per month. Our operations have improved, and over a nine-month period we have built up a highly skilled group of pilots who know their business. In the Sicily operation we didn't lose a single aircraft. It is, of course, true that in the conduct of the Sicily operation we were fortunate in not having any air opposition whatsoever. In fact, it was quite a pleasure to fly over Sicily during the invasion because all the Axis aircraft had been driven back at least 200 miles from their former operational bases; it was a great contrast to previous operations during the Tunisian campaign when Sicily was the hot spot to fly over.

The aids for photo recon. pilots are few and far between whenever they operate more than 150 miles from friendly territory. Within the 150-mile area of Malta over Sicily we were greatly aided by Malta's combination radar and RDF control, which kept us advised of enemy aircraft in our vicinity, so that we weren't continually operating with a swivel neck. It was the only thing that made it possible for us to live up there. But beyond the effective range of the radar … we were on our own, and operated completely by eyesight to prevent interception.

The Intelligence information regarding targets for briefing pilots was very scanty until our pictures were interpreted. When we first hit North Africa and went on missions over Bizerte and Tunis, we didn't know how much anti-aircraft there was; we didn't know how many airplanes there were, or where the airdromes were; we didn't know what we were running into. But as soon as we had made a sufficient number of photo recon missions over the area, we were able to supply ourselves and all other aviation in that area with complete information as to flak installations and the position of enemy aircraft from day to day.

ENEMY OPPOSTION

The enemy, as a general rule, depend on their radar equipment to notify them that we were coming over; and they endeavor to get fighters up to intercept us. We can fool them to a certain extent on their radio-controlled anti-aircraft, by changing altitude and coming in on the target; but the box-type barrage, which operated usually 1,000 feet above us to 1,000 feet below us, made it possible for them to force us to fly through anti-aircraft fire. That situation necessitated very often more than the usual number of two to three runs, because the aircraft would be thrown around so much by the bursts that the vertical pictures would not come out.

OPERATIONS

The picture of how we operate is rather simple. It's divided into three divisions – the flying end, the processing end, and the interpretation end. No one of these is any good without the other. There are in the United States Army very few trained photo interpreters. We depend to a large extent on the British Army for military interpreters and on the RAF for general interpretation – shipping, airdrome, etc. – and for industrial interpretation. As a matter of fact, we have in North Africa right now twelve qualified interpreters as against several hundred British interpreters. We control all interpreters in our Wing organization and they are assigned by us to the various headquarters – to Army HQs, Seventh and Eighth Armies in the case of the Sicilian campaign; to each corps HQs participating in the operations and to each division. As a division is taken out of action, the interpreters are taken away from it and are placed with the next division occupying the area. The interpreters do not remain at the division or corps or army HQs; they are assigned to work for a division, or for a corps or for an army; but they work with our field unit supporting the particular operation. The film is flown to an airport and taken immediately to our field plant for processing. Two wet prints are taken off, and the interpreters go to work immediately on the part which is of concern to the HQs for which they're working. They get their interpretation report out, hand it to the Army liaison officer, who has his own courier service, to deliver it to his HQs.

In addition to reports on these pictures, it is often necessary for us to produce a large number of prints which are used by the artillery in stereoscopic pairs for directing their fire, and for other purposes. The ground forces also use a large number of mosaics, as map substitutes, and many enlargements. We produced in the month of July a little over 400,000 contact prints, slightly over 50,000 negatives, about 2,800 mosaics, and about 14,000 enlargements. Those figures probably don't mean very much, but they represent actually 12½ % of what were considered legitimate requests from the three main forces operating in the theatre. We have 1800 men in the Wing, including 12 RAF WAAF officers, in order to fill the requirement of the theatre, based on demands, we need approximately 4,000 men.

QUESTIONS

Q: [How long is required] to train a pilot to become a good flyer for photo recon missions?

A: A photo reconnaissance pilot must embody all the training that goes into a bombardment pilot and a bombardier without the use of a bombsight, because in making a photographic run over a target almost the same technique is employed as in making a bombing run over a target. He must also have complete training as a fighter pilot and must be extremely proficient in the use of evasive tactics. Since he does not have any guns of any kind on his aircraft, the only skill he isn't required to have that fighter and bombardment pilots must have is proficiency in firing a gun. He has to know when to press the button to start his cameras operating. At the time the photographic run is made, at 30,000 feet, the pin point area to be covered is about 1 ½ inches wide to the eyes.

Q: What are the shortcomings of the U.S. photo interpreters, both the Army and the Navy? What do you consider the qualifications for photo interpreters?

A: …the ability accurately to obtain all the desired information on a photograph for which the mission was run. I'll give you a very good example. I had an American-trained Army photo interpreter in the early days of the Tunisian campaign who had been through interpretation school in the United States. He received a photograph of a certain road in Tunisia. On that road there was what looked like a long train of vehicles, and he said it was an armored column moving toward a certain frontal area. That information was phoned in to Army HQs, and a division was started that night to meet this armored column which was on the move. Well, about 6 o'clock that night a British RAF interpreter got hold of that print and said, "Hey, there's something wrong here! That is a column of camels – a camel caravan." The word was flashed up to Army

HQs, but by that time the division was on its way and had been moving uselessly against a non-existent enemy for a period of 7½ hours. That's what I mean by a competent photo interpreter; he must be able to tell exactly what is in the picture; and unless one has had extremely careful schooling, he is apt to say things and express opinions which are not actually true. The photo interpreter who is properly trained never makes a claim unless he is positive. What is needed for photo interpretation training is to take a leaf out of the book of the RAF training course at Medmenham in England, or the training course which has been set up in the Middle East, which is an inter-Service school, British Army and RAF, and you'll find a good interpretation school. As far as the American Navy interpreters are concerned, I don't know, because I've never seen an American Navy interpreter in North Africa; I've never seen any Royal Navy interpreters.

Q: Do you think our faults are due to lack of experience on the part of the United States interpreters – or is there some other catch?

A: I think our program over here has been very poor. The course may be all right. I got an interpreter from the United States here not long ago who for nine months from the time he got out of school until I got hold of him hadn't interpreted a single picture… He was no longer competent – that is one business which you must stay at day after day to remain proficient. He'd been a mess officer; he'd been through replacement school in Oran, and they'd assigned him as a mess officer to some squadron; he hadn't been interpreting, which he had been trained to do, for nine months. So he was of no value to me until I'd put him through a six-week training course.

Q: Did you find you had sufficient basic information on naval subjects to give your naval photo interpreters the basic stuff they needed?

A: Our photo interpreters, as I said, for the most part, as far as naval information was concerned were comprised of RAF personnel. Those 12 women officers in the RAF are some of the best experts on naval information there are. They came from Medmenham, and they had a background of three years of work on Axis shipping. Their work is absolutely accurate.

STRIKE PHOTOGRAPHS; NIGHT PHOTOGRAPHY; EQUIPMENT

A: Strike photographs are made by one of the waist gunners in the bombardment aircraft who leaves his gun during the bombing run and operates the cameras. These provide a strip of pictures that cover the entire length of the bombing run. He turns the camera off at the end of the bombing run when the bomb bay doors are finally closed. That camera is usually located in the after part of the ship in the camera well.

Q: Has there been any employment of night photography?

A: Yes. We operated on night photography for the first time in the Sicilian campaign. I flew the first three missions over there with B-25's and the first target we were given by the 7th Army HQ, General Patton's HQ, was the harbor of Termini, to the east of Palermo, which was suspected by the Tactical Air Force of being used as a reinforcement port at night with small boats. It was definitely determined through the use of night photography that the harbor was not used for that purpose. We were also required to photograph major road junctions, such as the junction at Enna where the main roads crossing Sicily converge – … in order to observe the movement at night of enemy transports.

Q: Did you find it necessary to use camera heat?

A: Camera heat is essential; it is one of the respects in which American equipment falls down. We have no adequate heating system in our type aircraft to serve our cameras, and also we have a very inadequate heating system for our pilots. Our pilot efficiency was very much lowered because of the extreme cold in which we had to operate.

Q: What temperature were you getting?

A: Minus thirty, minus forty.

Q: You did not have camera heat then, is that right?

A: We did not have camera heat. We had a heating system, but it was inadequate and actually all that camera heat turned on full on those cameras did was to raise it from the outside temperature, -30, -40, to maybe -25 to -35.

Q: No film breakage?

A: We have had film breakage, yes. About 9% of all our American missions, which were otherwise successfully flown, were unsuccessful because of camera failure. And on the same number of missions with the RAF equipment, the RAF had less than 1/10 of 1% failures on account of their cameras.

LANDING BEACH RECONNAISSANCE

Q: Any special missions for landing beach reconnaissance?

A: Yes, sir. All of the beach areas were flown vertically... the Western and Eastern Task Force landing areas were vertically flown for the three weeks previous to the actual assault, and there was not a day when they weren't flown twice. And we flew oblique runs from approximately 100 to 150 feet of not only those areas but of numerous other beach areas, in order to provide deception as to just where we were going. The oblique missions are known in our jargon as "dicing" missions, and are not the nicest kind of job. In the Pantelleria show, we were required, the day before the task force was due to show off, to go in and photograph the jetties and the harbor from within the harbor at 150 feet off the water. That was requirement of the Navy's.

SKETCHES

A: Drawing sketches? Sketches are not a requirement of ours. When the use of the photograph stopped, our responsibility stopped. The sketches are provided by Intelligence agencies. We do the model making, or a certain amount of it. The models for the Sicilian campaign were made, half over here in Washington and half in London. We did a few ourselves down there, but very few. Most of ours were done for the paratroopers.

UPKEEP PERSONNEL

Q: Were the camera upkeep personnel the same as those that operated the camera?

A: No. You see, a pilot operates his own cameras in the F-5A or P-38 type, and in the Mosquito the navigator operates the cameras. The only times people responsible for the upkeep of the cameras actually fly are in the use of the B-25's on night missions, and then we have enlisted photographers to operate the cameras.

Q: That might account for the great difference then between the results because in the Solomons and in Alaska, the same people are operating the cameras as do the upkeep. They're operating without heat and they're having good results, consistent results, with the American cameras. That's where that heat – you said they raised about 5 or 10 degrees...

A: That is, in large part, a fault of the aircraft heating system, the amount of heat you can pull off your generators.

PRIORITIES

Q: You spoke of these requests for certain coverage from various headquarters, and said you could cover only about 12% of those – who reconciled these requests?

A: The requests were reconciled by a priorities board which consisted of representative of the Army, the Navy, and the Air Force. That Board passed on all the requests that came in, and determined the priority of the jobs to be done.

Q: Were the officers who did the interpretation for ground forces primarily those who had had ground force experience previously – that is, infantry or artillery officers?

A: ... Yes. For the most part they are officers who are familiar with certain specialties. The officers who specialize on artillery emplacements are former artillery officers. Although they all have a wide general background which is applicable to all photo interpretation, the military interpreters are for the most part drawn from the Army officers in the field units.

*** END OF INTERVIEW ***

COL. ROOSEVELT'S RECOMMENDATION OF THE F-11

EXHIBIT Nr. 2500: INVESTIGATION OF THE NAT. DEFENSE PROGRAM
20 AUGUST 1943
MEMORANDUM FOR THE COMMANDING GENERAL, ARMY AIR FORCES

Subject: Report on inspection trip re reconnaissance aviation.

1. Personnel making the inspection trip were as follows: Col. Elliott Roosevelt, Lt. Col. Karl L. Polifka, Lt. Col. Harry T. Eidson, Maj. W.R. Boyd III, Squadron Leader D.W. Stevenson [sic, sb. Steventon]
2. Itinerary: Departed Washington 6-8-43, arriving Wright Field 6-8-43. Departed Wright Field 8-8-43, arriving Burbank, Calif., 8-8-43. Departed Burbank 11-8-43, arriving Harper's Lake 11-8-43. Departed Harper's Lake 11-8-43, arriving Burbank 11-8-43. Departed Burbank 12-8-43, arriving Dallas, Tex., 13-8-43. Departed Dallas 16-8-43, arriving Colorado Springs 16-8-43. Departed Colorado Springs 16-8-43, arriving Dallas 16-8-43. Departed Dallas 17-8-43, arriving Washington 17-8-43.
3. While at Wright Field, Matériel Division was visited as well as the Air Service Command at Patterson Field. Matériel Division, Photographic Laboratory Section (department 59), was visited and all projects undergoing development there were examined in detail. Conferences were held with Col. H. K. Baisley, chief of the section, and his assistant, Lieutenant General Powers. It was found that the greatest difficulty confronting this section was the lack of directives outlining what was actually needed most in the theaters. Many directives had been received which were conflicting and which had given rise to a great amount of confusion when compared to the reports brought back from the theaters by qualified officer personnel. The procurement program for cameras was found to be completely out of line with requirements. No procurement program was in effect for the A-4 trailer group, which was designed after receiving specifications from experienced theater personnel. No procurement program was in effect for automatic printing and processing equipment which has been developed and which is vitally needed in the theaters. The 36-inch focal-length camera has been consistently ignored in spite of continuous reports from the European and North African theaters that this is the ideal focal length camera for reconnaissance photography. No aircraft are available at Wright Field assigned to the Photographic Laboratory Section which would enable them to make experimental mountings of cameras in these aircraft as requested by the theaters.
4. Following discovery of this information at the Photographic Laboratory Section, a visit was paid to General Frank, commanding general, Air Service Command, and to Col. James F. Early. It developed after conversations with the Air Service Command, as well as with the Photographic Laboratory Section, that both organizations are greatly handicapped, due to a lack of clear directives as to just exactly what equipment is desired and when. Furthermore, the Air Service Command is greatly handicapped by a lack of competent photographic officers to deal with the highly specialized photographic problems. Most of the men handling the procurement program in the Air Service Command and the distribution of the equipment and supplies have no understanding of their problems. As an example, there is the way in which the procurement of R-5 intervalometers has been held up for a period of months by a man in the contract section over a small technicality without any regard to the fact that these intervalometers are vitally and urgently needed in the theaters by the photo-reconnaissance units.
5. Another example of wastage that is going on in the procurement of materiel for reconnaissance aviation is on the question of procurement of film and paper. Approximately 10 times more paper than film is actually consumed, and yet there is a

procurement program in effect at the present time which is seriously straining the resources of this country for film. The quantities of film on procurement is almost equal to the procurement of paper. It is a fact that at the present time there is in storage in Australia a 5-year supply of film based on the present rate of consumption times 3.

6. All of these problems can be traced directly to the lack of organizational responsibility centered in one man in Headquarters, Army Air Forces, Washington, D.C.
7. Following the visit to Wright Field and the Air Service Command, a visit was made to the Lockheed Aircraft Co. at Burbank, Calif. Examination was made of the records of the company with regard to past difficulties encountered in the delivery of F-4 and F-5 type aircraft. Conferences were held with various executives of the company, as well as the Air Force representative at the factory. In addition, an examination was made of the XP-58 for the purpose of determining whether the aircraft could be redesigned for photo-reconnaissance purposes. The net result of these conferences and the examination of the various types of aircraft was as follows: A large number of conflicting directives have been received by the company during the past year, and the procurement program for photographic-reconnaissance-type aircraft has changed so often that, as a result, the company has been greatly handicapped in turning out any aircraft on schedule. As an example, the factory at the present time has no commitment on any program for next year. Another example is the fact that the factory has been required to install all the plumbing for automatic pilots and yet the Air Force has never had any automatic pilots to install in the aircraft, nor were automatic pilots necessary. To this day the Lockheed factory does not know what a standard photographic aircraft should contain in the way of camera mountings, camera openings, and other technical specifications which could very well have been standardized many, many months ago.
8. The XP-58 could not be redesigned as a photographic aircraft without a 60-percent basic redesign of the aircraft involving the entire wing sections and center nacelle. The XP-58 listed performance figures, as the aircraft is now constituted, would not provide a sufficient improvement over improved versions of the F-5A and F-5B to warrant a procurement program on this aircraft. Furthermore, the Lockheed people estimate that it would take 18 months to produce a prototype photographic aircraft of this design and that it would be well over 2 years before they could start production.
9. Another aircraft which was examined at this factory was a two-place T-38 aircraft with two pilots' cockpits in tandem. This aircraft was regarded by the inspection party as a very desirable aircraft for photo reconnaissance if it would be procured within a reasonable length of time. The Lockheed Co. officials stated that the first one of this type would not be able to be produced for at least 18 months, inasmuch as no engineering had as yet been done on the basic design. Therefore, this aircraft was also ruled out of consideration.
10. The inspection party then proceeded to the Hughes Aircraft Co. at Culver City, where a conference was held with company executives, including Mr. Howard Hughes. Discussion was had regarding the possibility of developing D-5 type aircraft into a photo-reconnaissance ship which would mean certain specifications as to performance and delivery dates. From the factory the party then proceeded to Harper's Lake, where the first aircraft of this type has been undergoing tests. This aircraft is known as the D-2, and, while it is basically the same aircraft, it is at the present time undergoing changes in the wing and a new NACA-design wing is being installed on the aircraft.
11. Conclusions reached by the inspection party regarding the D-5 aircraft and the Hughes Aircraft Co. were as follows: It is highly necessary that a super-priority program be instituted immediately similar to the B-29 program in order to insure that 1 year from now the Army Air Forces will have a photographic-reconnaissance aircraft which will have the range, speed, altitude, and performance to procure target information and provide bomb-damage information for aircraft of the B-29 type. It is further necessary that a development program be instituted immediately looking to the future to insure

that photo reconnaissance will always have an aircraft in production which has a better performance than any fighter or bomber aircraft in existence in the world. With this in mind, it is felt that a designer, such as Howard Hughes, in the aircraft field should be immediately contracted with to concern himself with nothing but this development program. The reason that Howard Hughes as a designer would be an extremely fortuitous choice is the fact that he is primarily a designer of racing aircraft and long-range aircraft and has interested himself in these two fields for the past decade. In addition, Mr. Hughes has expressed himself as being particularly anxious to work on this type of aircraft design to the exclusion of all others. He has spent 5 years and $5,000,000 in designing and engineering of the D-5 airplane. Estimated data on the D-5 is attached as Exhibit A.

12. Mr. Hughes expressed himself as being willing to accept a contract for a number of photographic reconnaissance aircraft of the D-5 type, the exercising of the contract by the Government being contingent upon the D-5 living up to minimum performance figures and required delivery dates. In the event that the aircraft does not live up to specifications, he would then be willing to bear all costs in connection therewith. In the event that delivery dates were not met, he would be willing to include in the contract penalty clauses. Development costs would be spread over the first contract of production aircraft. The manufacturer feels that he has sufficient facilities if relieved of all other contractual obligations for Vultee trainer parts. He can produce the first complete photo-reconnaissance aircraft for flight testing in 5 months with factory and U.S. Army tests taking the 7 months before the first production aircraft is produced in 12 months from date of contract. Production will be at the rate of 2 per day in 18 months. This, of course, does not allow for Wright Field static and accelerated tests to be run before delivery of the first contract production aircraft but manufacturer agrees to assume full financial responsibility for aircraft to meet all Wright Field requirements included in the contract.
13. It is urgently recommended that a project be immediately instituted for procurement of this aircraft for photo-reconnaissance purposes inasmuch as it represents the only possible improvement in sight for photographic reconnaissance over the present F-5 type series. It is further recommended that in order to avoid needless complications and slow-downs which will result from normal channels handling of the development of this airplane, a competent officer be given complete responsibility and authority for seeing that this program proceeds without delay. Inasmuch as all the risk in connection with this contract will lie with the contractor and not with the contractee, it seems that the USAAF would be well justified in proceeding in an unorthodox fashion, particularly in view of the urgency of the situation as it pertains to reconnaissance aviation.
14. Following the visit to the Hughes Aircraft factory and testing grounds, a visit was paid to the Lockheed modification center at Dallas, Tex. Here again, after conferences with the manager and after examination of the records, it becomes evident that due to a continuous stream of conflicting directives regarding modifications to be made on photographic aircraft, this center has been unable to do a competent and workmanlike job on photographic aircraft. The fault in no way lies with the modification center but is just another instance of incompetent army officer personnel contradicting themselves continuously and preventing photo reconnaissance aircraft from being prepared for the theaters on time and as required by the theaters. It is quite evident that a few experienced photo-reconnaissance officers have endeavored to straighten this situation out but they have not had sufficient authority and they have been overruled continuously in their efforts by personnel with no experience whatsoever.
15. An example of the incompetent modification of reconnaissance aircraft is the fact that shortly 100 P-38-J's are to be modified at the modification depot of Northwest Airlines at St. Paul, Minn. The reason given for having these aircraft modified at this new depot,

which is without any experience in modifications of this kind, is the statement that the Dallas modification center is so full of other projects that it will not be able to handle any other airplanes for the next 5 months. Investigation by this inspection party shows that the Dallas modification is practically without any work at all at the present time and very little work in sight during the next several months. In fact, the manager has stated time and time again that he could handle all of the photographic aircraft modifications without affecting any of the remainder of his program. Upon questioning as to what part of his facilities would be employed if he were required to modify 150 F-5 type aircraft per month, he replied, "Not more than 35%," if he could get a clear-cut directive on a standard modification for the aircraft. At the present time he has no standard modification directive of any nature for any photographic airplane.

16. Proceeding from the Dallas modification center, the inspection party proceeded to Colorado Springs, Peterson Field, where all photographic-reconnaissance training is in progress. An interview was had with Colonel Rich and Colonel Tipton, commanding officer and executive of the post, who stated that they are in charge of the training program. Colonel Rich stated that he personally did not know anything about cameras and practically nothing about photo-reconnaissance as it pertains to combat theaters. In fact, he stated that he did not know one type of camera from another. The morale at the field is at a low ebb. The training program is practically non-existent. Colonel Rich complained that this was due to the fact that he had no training directive of any nature. There are 8,000 men located at this training center, all presumably either in training or training photo-reconnaissance personnel. There were a total of 102 aircraft on the field, only 28 of which were P-38 and 7 were F-4. There were practically no cameras of the type used most frequently in combat theaters on the field. No altitude flight training was taking place. In short, all of the things necessary to make a training program that will meet the requirements of the theaters were conspicuous by their absence. The commanding officer was queried as to how many officers of his command had had combat experience and he stated not more than two in his command had had combat experience. Actually this inspection party knows that there are seven pilots with combat experience assigned to that base.
17. After the visit to Colorado Springs, the inspection party returned to Washington, D.C.
18. The following specific recommendations are made:
    (a) That a head of the newly constituted Reconnaissance Division be immediately appointed who has had combat theater experience and who knows photo-reconnaissance and also tactical reconnaissance as it is applied in a theater of operations. This officer must have the respect of and the complete backing of the Air Staff in Washington, D.C.
    (b) A procurement program on a special project basis must be immediately instituted under the direction of a qualified officer with sufficient authority and the responsibility to see that a new reconnaissance aircraft is produced within the next year to replace the F-5.
    (c) A standardized program of procurement must be immediately instituted for F-5 aircraft to cover the next year and a half and the factory and the modification depot must be given clear-cut directives which will not be changed except upon direct request of the theaters. The directives must be clear-cut and specific enough to enable the factory to tool up and the modification center to plan on a regular schedule of deliveries which should be lived up to and can be depended upon by the theaters.
    (d) The Chief of the Reconnaissance Division of O.C. and R. must immediately institute a clear-cut training directive to the Third Air Force for the training of tactical reconnaissance pilots, photo reconnaissance pilots, and a complete ground training program for all reconnaissance units. These directives must be based on the experience of personnel who have been in active combat theaters.

(e) A complete restudy of procurement program for cameras and photographic supplies and equipment should be prepared by competent officer personnel within the next two weeks and should be favorably acted upon and instituted by directive from the Reconnaissance Division of O.C. and R. and that directive should not be deviated from by the Matériel Division or the Air Service Command.

(f) The personnel to head the different branches and sections of the Reconnaissance Division of O.C. and R. should be selected from personnel experienced in combat theaters and they should be ordered to report for duty regardless of their indispensability to the theater. Personnel likewise should be drawn from the combat theaters to head, direct, and carry out the training of reconnaissance aviation personnel at Colorado Springs. Undoubtedly every air theater commander, if queried as to availability of any personnel required for this program, will come back and state that the personnel cannot be spared. It should be pointed out that they must be spared if the air theater commander desires to have any reconnaissance aviation in his theater 6 months from today. Competent personnel in this field are practically nonexistent; therefore it is necessary to take that personnel which has been developed in the theaters in order to build up a sound program in this country so that the theaters will have any reconnaissance aviation which is capable of performing its mission. That situation does not exist today.

ELLIOTT ROOSEVELT,
Colonel, Air Corps.

HOW THE HUGHES XF-11 CRASHED

From the USAAF incident reported, reproduced in Senate Hearings, Part 40, p.24505:

The flight of the XF-11 originated at the field of Hughes Aircraft Company, Culver City, California, at approximately 1720 hours after 1:55 of high speed taxi tests. The verbal account of the flight by the pilot discloses that take-off was normal, and that immediately after becoming airborne the landing gear was retracted. (The operation of the landing gear retraction mechanism was not called for on the first flight of the Flight Test Schedule. The pilot stated, however, that it was his intention prior to the flight to definitely operate the landing gear to determine its status.) After waiting a normal time interval for complete gear retraction, the pilot noticed the landing gear warning light was still red, indicating to him that complete retraction had not been accomplished. After gaining some altitude the gear was operated several times but the light continued to indicate that the gear was not completely retracted. He then discovered that by pushing sharply forward on the control wheel as the gear retracted, the light would go out and he assumed the gear was up and locked. The pilot stated that he still was not too well satisfied with the gear operation and made two more operations, each completed by exerting sharp forward pressure on the control wheel. After completion of the last retraction, the pilot stated that he decided it would be advisable to have a visual check made to determine that the nose gear had rotated to its proper position before an attempt to land was made. The pilot further stated that he decided to fly low across his home field with the gear extended and then come back over the field to see if any of the spectators gave any indication that anything was wrong. A descent was started, and upon reaching 2,000 feet, the pilot saw a company owned A-20 climbing after take-off from the field. The pilot desired that the A-20 observe the gear and tried to fly close with the A-20 during the climb back to 2,000 feet. Observation could not be obtained because the A-20 stayed inside of the left turn, above and to the rear, and too far from the XF-11 for such observation. Seeing that it was not possible to contact occupants of the A-20 visually, the pilot attempted to establish contact through some tower. When questioned by the Board if an attempt was made to contact the A-20 or anyone else on "C" channel, he replied that he did not, and had no reason to since the "B" channel was available. (It must be noted that HQ AMC, by authority of the FCC, had assigned a "C" channel frequency of 150 megacycles to the Hughes Company for use in the flight test program of the XF-11. A ground control setup had been made at Hughes field operating on this assigned frequency. The ground control was checked off with the radio in the XF-11 several hours before the flight, and both were found to be operating satisfactorily.) It could not be established that a radio check was made immediately prior to take-off. The Los Angeles Municipal tower responded to the XF-11 "B" channel call to "any tower" in which the pilot said he was having gear trouble and wanted to contact the A-20. During the answer of the L.A. tower operator to the effect that it might take some time to contact the A-20, the pilot said he first experienced what he thought was a strong force somewhere on the right side of the aircraft. Not wanting to be occupied on the radio during trouble, he acknowledged the reply shortly, and made no further attempt at radio contact with anyone before the crash. At this time the pilot said he was approximately two to three miles east of Hughes field, heading north at approximately 5,000 feet. According to the pilot of the A-20, it was about this point that he broke away to the left and proceeded to descend and land. He said that he did not observe that the XF-11 was in any unusual position or any difficulty. The L.A. tower operator observed the A-20 on its approach to Hughes field at 1840.

The pilot of the XF-11 described the drag force as very strong, causing the aircraft to turn to the right and lose altitude. He allowed the aircraft to turn to the right until it was headed almost due east, then he stopped the turn and began a 180° turn to the left. He loosened his safety belt and moved about the cabin, holding the airplane as best he could with his left hand, and looked out every possible place through the canopy to see if he could locate any cause for the drag. He could not see any reason for the drag and returned to the seat, but was too busy to refasten his safety belt. He stated that the drag got progressively worse from the time trouble was first encountered until the crash. After returning to his seat power was increased to fifty or more inches of mercury and 2,800 RPM on both engines with no apparent effect. He then lowered power to about the original setting; applied full throttle to the right engine at about 2,200 RPM with no apparent effect. This was followed by reduction of throttle on the right engine, also with no apparent effect. When asked by the Board if at any time he pulled off power on both engines simultaneously, he replied that he did not. The pilot considered bailing out once at about 2,500 feet, but decided against it because he thought he might be able to correct the situation, and too, he might be too low by that time to get out. The drag had now become so great it was necessary to hold full left rudder and full left aileron to hold the aircraft approximately level. Holding full left aileron brought the spoilers on the left wing to their full "up" position. The aircraft was controllable in direction, but there was no control over the rapid loss of altitude. He still did not know what was causing the trouble, but was still trying to determine what the cause could be. By this time he realized that he was very low (eye witness estimates from 300 to 800 feet and heading approximately northwest, tail low, and continuing to lose altitude). Realizing that if he was to locate the trouble it must be soon, and thinking that it might possibly be a landing gear door or some other underside surface torn loose and turned broadside to the wind, he decided to drop the landing gear, which, if it were a torn door, might knock the door off and stop the drag force. By the time the gear was down he realized that the gear door was not the trouble, and that a crash was imminent. He planted his feet high on the instrument panel and attempted to flare the aircraft into the roof of the house directly ahead (800 North Linden Drive). The pilot estimated that elapsed time from first indication of drag trouble to crash was approximately three minutes. Crash occurred at 1842. Eye witnesses at the latter part of the flight immediately prior to the crash observed the airplane traveling approximately northwest, tail down and to the right, and nose left. At an estimated altitude of 350 to 800 feet the aircraft was observed to attempt a medium bank to the left and then straighten. A few seconds later a violent bank to the left was made, so violent that when viewed from the ground the aircraft was seen in plan form from the rear, then again straightened, heading in a northwest direction. At this time the main landing gear was observed to be down. Although the aircraft was observed to be in a climbing attitude a steady loss of altitude was apparent.

It was in this attitude, with the right wing low, that the aircraft first struck the house at 800 North Linden Drive. The right landing gear and engine penetrated the roof. The initial impact caused the aircraft to yaw severely to the right. The right wing tip striking the neighboring house at 802 North Linden Drive added to the severity of the yaw. With the aircraft travelling sideways, the next contact was made by the left side of the cockpit with a power line pole, breaking the pilot's canopy, and the remainder of the right wing with the roof of the garage at 802 North Linden Drive. From this point the aircraft continued on, striking the ground across the alley from 802 North Linden Drive, then bounced and skidded sideways, the left wing penetrating the rear of the house at 808 Whittier Drive and finally coming to rest between the houses at 808 and 810 North Whittier Drive, with the remainder of the left wing and left tail boom against the rear of the house at 808 North Whittier. Fire broke out immediately, destroying the house and its contents and a large portion of the aircraft.

The right engine was sheared from its mounts and came to rest nose down between the house, the cockpit, and the right firewall. The left engine was sheared from its mounts and thrown against the front corner of the house and came to rest on the front lawn 60 feet from the cockpit.

The right landing gear was broken off and came to rest against the trees at the tip of the remaining portion of the right wing, while the left landing gear was broken off and came to rest in the kitchen of the house at 808 Whittier.

CONCLUSION

1. The Board is of the opinion that there was a functional failure of the right hand engine's rear propeller resulting from a loss of oil through the seal of the rear component shaft, and to the nose section of the engine, with the result that the blade angle of the rear component was less in degrees than that of the front component. The pilot, at the time the propeller difficulties were encountered, was preoccupied with the possibility that the drag then being experienced was due to the landing gear difficulties previously encountered during this flight.
2. Further, several indirect causes contributing to the accident were a result of technique employed by the pilot in operating the aircraft and in following the procedure as outlined in the flight test program.
   a. The pilot did not utilize the special radio frequency and facilities that were provided.
   b. The pilot was acquainted with the normal operating procedures for this propeller but was not sufficiently acquainted with its emergency operating procedures.
   c. The pilot retracted the landing gear immediately after take-off which action the Board feels was incompatible with the flight test program, inasmuch as the flight authorization extended for approximately 45 minutes, and the flight-test program specified that the maneuvers were to be conducted with gear down. It was not until the second flight that operation of the gear was specified.
   d. The pilot did not give proper attention to the possibility of an emergency landing during the period when sufficient altitude and directional control were available. The Board has determined that the propeller trouble occurred at an altitude of 5,000 feet, two or more miles northwest of Hughes' airport heading approximately north. The aircraft turned to a heading of east and then began a slow descent, turning back toward the west and passing within three miles of the west end of Hughes' airport at a heading of northwest, and at approximately 2,500 feet.
   e. The pilot failed to analyze or evaluate the possibility of failure in the right hand power section. The Board believes that the pilot conducted an extensive visual check for structural failure, but that he did not reduce power on both engines simultaneously in order to distinguish between structural and/or power failure.
   f. Further, the Board feels that there was poor coordination by the principals concerned, i.e. Hughes Aircraft Company employees, Air Materiel Command, Mr. Howard R. Hughes, and Hamilton Standard Service representatives, which resulted in a lack of single centralized control over the entire flight program.
   g. The Board is of the opinion that this accident was avoidable after propeller trouble was experienced.

AS OTHERS SAW IT

Several oral history interviews were conducted with officers who worked with Elliott Roosevelt. Relevant excerpts follow below. [USAF OHI Program, AFHRA K239.0512]

Jimmy Crabb: "He was a drunk"

Major Jarred "Jimmy" Crabb, who later rose to Brigadier General, commanded the 21st Reconnaissance Squadron in Newfoundland and the US air base there. He was Elliott Roosevelt's first operational boss. He was definitely not impressed:

...

Crabb: So I went to Miami as an engineering officer in a squadron and I think the 14th was the one I took to Newfoundland [it was the 21st].

Question: Again, our records are fragmented, but I have you down as commander of Gander, in May'41.

Crabb: I was commander of that squadron. That was the 14th. And went to Gander.

Q: What was their function? Anti-sub work?

Crabb: Anti-sub work. You see, we were not in the war then, and there was a lot of worry about us – getting us in the war if we did things that were wrong.

A lot of what we did was to get the base set up, to get it functioning, and get it able to do a job if we needed it. We did a lot of patrolling. We didn't actually do any sub work, but we were told to watch for them. We went up there actually as anti-sub patrols. We weren't in the war, so we were on foreign territory. So you had to be very cautious in what you did.

We had a full squadron, and our job was to keep them flying over this water up there, colder than hell. The whole area was colder than hell.

Q: Was this visual reconnaissance, sir, or did you have airborne radar?

Crabb: It was strictly visual reconnaissance.

Q: What were you flying, sir? What kind of aircraft?

Crabb: B-18s. I found that the B-18 was not the airplane for that job. The B-18 wouldn't stay aloft much on one engine. If it got down a little on gas it would stay on, but it took a four-engine airplane and long range to do any good up there. I recommended and they did send B-17s up there.

Q: Were you the first American unit that went into Gander? That's why you were the base commander? What special problems did you have in setting up in foreign territory, sir?

Crabb: Well, we went up there, and the hangars were just being finished. They had dirt floors. I remember one hangar – we had a pile of equipment that must have been 40 feet high, and we had to sort it all out, chicken wire was all around, that was all the protection there, and a lot of thievery and so forth. And mud, you wore boots all the time to keep out of the mud.

I think one of the worst things was the conditions we had to live in: quarters were bad, they hadn't been finished yet.

Q: Those were new quarters then.

Crabb: Yes. And the conditions under which we worked were pretty bad. However, it wasn't too bad considering that we were starting a new base, and you moved in before it was ready.

There was a narrow road that came up there – a railroad. And lots of things got lost. There was an infantry outfit at St. John's which was on our supply line, and they had first chance at everything.

Q: This was a US infantry outfit.

Crabb: Yes. So a lot of things were short-circuited.

Q: How did you get along with the Canadians? Were the Canadian air forces there?

Crabb: They were there. They had a group captain in charge of 'em. I guess I was a lieutenant colonel, I don't know. But anyhow they were a tremendous help to us, because they were flying anti-sub patrols, but it was obvious that they were doing anti-sub patrol, I mean they could say it. We were doing anti-sub patrol but we couldn't say so. I remember that the Intelligence officer of the Air Force came up there once. I forget his name right now.

. . .

Crabb: … Anyhow he came up here and I talked to him. I said, "We got a weather report from Bluie West One, but we don't know where Bluie West One is." He said, "Well, if you haven't been told where it is, I can't tell you." So there we were. It was up there on Greenland and we needed it badly and they wouldn't let us have it.

Q: Did you informally perhaps get together with the Canadians to learn about their anti-sub tactics? And if you had any contacts, did you have arrangements to report this to anyone for action, sir?

Crabb: The only thing we could do, we could report it, and primarily our way of reporting it would be through the Canadians because you could put almost anything through them, because they were our friends and they'd take it and say not how they got it.

But we didn't have much of a channel.

Q: Nothing established.

Crabb: No. Not while I was there. You see I was only there three or four months.

Q: When they sent you up, what did your orders say would be your objective? To train, or…

Crabb: They told me I was going to Newfoundland, and to get the base started. I had very limited orders. I went up on the boat with the ground echelon, and we lived on that for a few days, until we could get lined up to go out to Gander, and we went up to Gander as soon as we got the train loaded, but it was a bad situation there. Newfoundland isn't good to start with, and we had very limited accommodations, at least while I was there.

Q: Your contacts with the Canadian group captain then and anything you got – I understand these were pretty much informal, is that right, sir?

Crabb: Yes.

. . .

Q: What was your expectation at the time, sire, and those perhaps of your contemporaries? Did you expect us to be in the war soon, or what was your feeling?

Crabb: Yes, I did expect it. Privately I think I did expect to get in the war. But I'll admit that I was a bit surprised when my squadron commander came in and said they bombed Warsaw, and that made it feel more and more likely that we were getting into it, then the Athenia was sunk, and then I think almost everybody felt like we were in it. We were then on anti-sub patrol in Florida.

Q: Were you there with the Atlantic Charter with FDR? Were you on a ship or something? There's something in there [about that].

Crabb: I was up in Newfoundland with Roosevelt. You know that he caused me more trouble than any other one man I ever served with.

Q: How's that, sir? When you say Roosevelt, you are talking about the President's son?

Crabb: Elliott Roosevelt. He was a drunk.

Q: Oh!

Crabb: He was a drunk, and it was just sort of a political assignment that he had to survey a route to Europe for airplanes to go through.

Q: This was when you were there with the 14th, is that right, sir?

Crabb: Yes.

Q: Oh, I see. He was attached to you for this purpose?

Crabb: He was attached to me for Rating – well actually I didn't officially know what he was doing. He was working with the Navy. I remember I went down to see them – they were in Argentia Bay and I flew down there in an amphibian and got ashore and went into the ship and talked to the Admiral about Elliott being such a drunkard: he wasn't much good to me; he wasn't much good to the United States either, as far as I was concerned.

Q: When you left Newfoundland, sir, where did you go? What were you orders out of there? Did you go back to Florida?

Crabb: I went back to MacDill [Florida].

...

John Dixon – "I don't know any stories that would bear printing"

Captain, later General John Dixon was one of Elliott Roosevelt's squadron commanders in England. Unusually, he went through Canadian flying school and entered the war with the RAF. He was shot down and became a P.O.W. [Tape #58, 16 SEP 67]

...

GG: Do you know any good stories about Elliott?

JD: I don't know any stories about Elliott that would bear printing. I do know that one of my boys shot one of his dogs – Blaze's brother. It was at night, we were having an invasion scare and the kid shot the dog. I remember vividly that that was very hard to explain.

...

GG: How did you get involved, you said Elliott Roosevelt tried to court martial you ...

JD: Oh yes, we were wrong, no question about it. It didn't have anything to do with flying. A fellow named Nesselrode – he had another squadron – George Nesselrode. He and I wanted to go to a nurses' dance. In order to go to a nurses' dance you had to have some transportation. I had a jeep so we promptly drove the jeep to the nurses' dance. The trouble was, that wasn't the purpose for which the jeep was given us. I guess nothing ever would have happened if a wheel hadn't come off the jeep. When we called in to report that we had a damaged jeep we were also reporting that we had it where it didn't belong. In addition we had non-rated ground commanders who were like the Deputy Group Commander – they used to call them Group Exec, I guess. The one we had was Colonel Gwenn. I was a captain and, of course, we were always feuding with Colonel Gwenn because he wanted the morning report made out correctly and he wanted saluting on the base and what we wanted to do was fly. I called him up when the wheel came off the jeep and complained about the condition of the motor pool. That's all it took. George and I were accused of having wrongfully appropriated for our own purposes one U.S. Government vehicle which was damaged.

We were tried and convicted. Matter of fact, in one week I had a letter from the people who ran the duplicating machine at 8th AF headquarters. They called this particular week "Dixon's week" because I was court martialed, promoted and decorated all within a five-day period. They said they'd never run so many orders on one guy in their whole lives. I was court martialed on Monday, promoted on Wednesday and decorated on Friday. That was about '44.

GG: How was Elliott involved?

JD: He was the commander.

GG: He liked to have a good time himself.

GD: Oh yes, but at the time there was a drive on officers driving cars because you could be sued personally. I could have had a driver very easily just by asking for one. The trouble was, when we got to the dance, Nesselrode knew what to do, I knew what to do, and we knew what to do with the jeep – but we sure wouldn't have known what to do with the driver....

They put all the Spitfires into one squadron, the 14th PR Squadron, and I started out flying in that squadron as a first lieutenant and wound up commanding it several years later. In fact, I was shot down when I was commanding [it]. That was the 7th Group which belonged to Elliott's outfit. We had 12 Spitfires, six P-38's and eventually we got some P-51's to fly our own escort.

GG: Did you get any Mosquitos?

JD: No, [they] were at Watton, where Leon Gray was, and they were flying night mostly.

GG: Do you have any real good stories that … happened before you were shot down?

JD: I remember being amazed when I started flying with the British. They had taken all the armor plate out of the Spitfires. The wings, you know, were full of gas; there weren't any guns on them, of course. They took the armor plate out; they even took the radios out to get another thousand feet or so. They had supercharged Rolls Royce Merlin engines and we were flying them at 40,000 feet with demand oxygen system, no pressurization and no heat, and you could see through the floorboards right down to the ground.

GG: Did you fly any of those long range missions over Peenemünde and places like that?

JD: Yes, and to Berlin and to Leipzig. As a matter of fact, I finished my first tour going to Stettin, which is north of and beyond Berlin. If we had anything like a 75- or 80-knot wind we just could not make it, so we'd go about halfway and if we knew exactly where we were and if all the timing was working out we'd keep going and if it wasn't we'd turn around and come back.

Late in the war we got a "slipper tank," which was like a plastic tank that the British made which fit under the bottom of the airplane – not in the conventional sense of a gas tank, this was aerodynamically shaped like the airplane. I'll never forget, this thing gave you another hour. Sixty imperial gallons is what it held and the airplane used a gallon a minute….

GG: Did the Germans ever try to intercept you over there?

JD: Oh yes, they couldn't get to 40,000 but you could look down and see them trying. They were trying the early version of the pop-up. They'd fly along and then pull it up and squeeze a couple of shots off at you. Unless you got down below that, though, they weren't going to get you.

GG: You think they got up to about 35,000?

JD: Oh yes, they were visible at least beneath you. I think they could have gotten to forty if they'd been smart enough to get out and fly up there and wait for you instead of trying to get you as you went by. I think the 109 could have gotten up there, certainly.

The jets could get up there and did, but the early ones weren't very good airplanes and didn't have very good gunnery systems. We had a couple of people intercepted and I was intercepted over Munich, which is where they were flying them from. We don't think we ever lost anybody to them, but two or three people saw them….

JD: The British had a lot of Australians with them, of course. What they'd do is detach you from the Australian AF or from the Canadian AF and put you on duty with the RAF. They did it … quite freely and it never seemed to make any difference – you got your money just the same, you wore your own uniform, but you were in another organization. The Australians are pretty wild people, quite like Americans as a matter of fact. The stories they tell were not really believable.

You know the expression "dicing" was one they used and they still say a thing is "dicey." We used to think it came from Dyce, in Aberdeen, which is where the PRU OTU [Operational Training Unit] was, but they used it to describe low level. A dicing mission was a low level reconnaissance mission and they flew a lot of them. People would come back with clotheslines, trees, all sorts of things stuck in the scoop of the Spitfire. The allegation they had in a mess in a frame was a pair of ladies pants and it was alleged that it had been brought back by an Australian.

The British were very good at PRU, and they were good at it before we got very good at it. Those two 35-inch cameras they had were pretty good cameras.

GG: Did you ever have trouble with our cameras?

JD: Not to speak of. We didn't have a 35-inch focal length.

GG: Ours was forty, wasn't it?

JD: Well we didn't have forties early in the war. You couldn't get a P-38 – no matter what the Lockheed and Allison people tell you – … to fly above 35,000 feet for any great length of time. The turbos let go on them, we finally put armor plate on the turbos in the back to keep the pieces from flying out and hitting us, but you just couldn't keep those engines going in thin air.

That Spitfire was built for thin air. It had a supercharger on it that kicked in about 18,000 feet and you could fly that thing all day at 40,000 feet.

GG: You weren't in the African thing, were you?

JD: No, I never got down there. I spent the whole time, from the time I transferred to the time I was shot down, right at Mount Farm. During that period we also operated some droop-snoots – we had some P-38's with a radar observer.

GG: That was up at Langford Lodge. [Belfast]

JD: That's right, I went up there and flew 15 missions up there – we were searching for the V-2's. We thought at the time that they were radio guided.

GG: Did you get involved in the landing in Normandy, did they use any of your airplanes?

JD: Yes, we flew beachhead reconnaissance; we flew reconnaissance behind the line. Before the landings we took the airplanes and went out and flew the railroad lines, particularly in Holland. I think that we were doing was keeping track of German divisions. You'd go out and get on the track at 25,000 or 30,000 feet and fly down the track as far as you could till you ran out of film, then turn around and come back. We did this day after day after day. We did the normal recon., of course, then the TAC Air came in and we turned around and went back to strategic recon. again.

GG: Didn't have much trouble with your processing, did you?

GD: Oh no, we had a real fine photo lab, better than the British had, as a matter of fact – and they had a damn good one. They had real fine P.I. though, because they had people who had been doing it for so long – Constance Babington Smith among them – they probable knew every house in Germany.

...

Jimmy Doolittle – "He was absolutely fearless"

Lt. Gen. James Doolittle, USAR, became the highest ranking reserve officer in the Army. He led the 12th AF during the chaotic first days of TORCH. Elliott Roosevelt had a high opinion of him because he, as a reservist, cared about "getting things done" and not so much about protocol. Doolittle returned the high regard. [taped 20 July 1967]

...

GG: When did you first meet Elliott Roosevelt?

JD: Elliott Roosevelt had the photo reconnaissance squadron in North Africa, and did a splendid job. Then he came to England and had the photo reconnaissance group there and again, did a splendid job. My only worry with Elliott was that he was absolutely fearless and I had a tremendous worry that he would be killed and I would have to explain to the President why I let him do some of the things he did. He flew a great many very difficult missions. Finally, I almost broke his heart by taking him off flying. [passage is almost identical to Doolittle's autobio., p.400]

GG: Did they do any night photography in Africa?

JD: Let me say this, George. You can get much better information on the day to day operations of the reconnaissance squadrons from the people who actually commanded them, rather than from the senior commanders who commanded the whole Air Force. But I will say this, in North Africa, in Italy and in England, where I had, first, the 12th, then the 15th, then the 8th Air Force, the photo recon. missions were essential – they were of inestimable value. Because they permitted us to look for specific targets, to analyze those targets and determine whether or not they should be bombed promptly or permitted to go a while longer. For instance, if you saw a target that was just being built up, you did not want to bomb it until they had spent considerable time building it up and then you took it out. The recon flights permitted us to select targets, determine the best time to attack and then, of course, the post-strike recon flights permitted us to find out how much damage was done, whether the target should be hit again. I would say that photographic recon increased the effectiveness of our bombing operations many times.

GG: I made a recording of George C. MacDonald, up in Philadelphia, the other day, and he was telling me how he'd receive these pictures in intelligence, take them up to [RAF] Medmenham, which was the interpretation center, where they'd make these studies. Then they'd go up to [RAF] Alconbury and send some of these Germans who had lived in these various cities over there and they'd go and substantiate the things they were seeing in these pictures. You weren't involved in any of that, were you?

JD: Only very indirectly. [They] did a fine job, and the British were superb at photo-interpretation, although, … toward the end of the war some of our people became very fine at that work. I remember one little British girl that was uniquely competent – she wrote a book.

Of course, what you've got to realize, and what nobody realizes better than you, is that photo-interpretation is very much like playing a violin – you can have the best pictures in the world, just as you can have a Stradivarius violin, and unless people are properly trained they cannot get out of those pictures what is in them, any more than a chap could pick up a fine violin and play without proper training, So, you have, first, the requirement of a good camera, good technique in using the camera in order to bring back useful photographs – and, of course, the enemy makes this as difficult as possible, with camouflage and other means of interference – but the final analysis of how good the work you do is how good your photo-interpreters are.

GG: You used some radar photography too, toward the end of the war, didn't you?

JD: Yes, of course we did a great deal of radar photography before the invasion, in order to get some information on what was going on along the coast. Very frequently, the day you wanted to get pictures the fog was in and you couldn't get them, so radar photography permitted us to obtain information regardless of weather, and this was very helpful.

GG: Elliott had his photographic headquarters out at High Wycombe, didn't he?

JD: Near there, yes. We had our 8th AF HQ in girls' college called Wycombe Abbey, at High Wycombe. This was a fine headquarters, we had what we called our "mole-hole," the communications center, and nearby, Elliott Roosevelt had his photographic organization where he and his people did a really first-class job. Of course, the information was passed on to our intelligence officer, then in a daily meeting the information obtained from aerial photography was analyzed and our operations then determined what to do with the information we had received.

GG: I think we've overlooked one very important detail, and that is about the type of aircraft that were used for aerial photography. The P-38 did a wonderful job for you over there.

JD: It did, and, of course, the Mosquito, with the same idea, did an excellent job for the British – but that didn't come until later.

One of our P-38's we sent to Russia – that was when we were allowed to have three fields in Russia. When our ground crews first arrived [to set] up the fields, getting our supplies lined up, getting the bombs and fuel, they were met by the Russians and treated royally. When our first fliers arrived, they also were treated royally by the Russians. But, very quickly, the Russians began to be disturbed by our people being there. For instance, our people would bring in a copy of the *Saturday Evening Post*, and the Russians would look through and see the advertisements – all the wonderful things you could get in America. Well, they had been told that America was about ready to fold, that it was being kept in the war simply because of the good fighting of the Russians, and the Russian propaganda began to fold up because people saw what was going on in America. This, of course, was anathema to the Russian leaders. So, they immediately issued an order that there would be no fraternizing of the Russians with our people. So these people who had been tremendously friendly suddenly became distant and would have nothing to do with our boys.

We went on with our bombing missions and did our work. Then it seemed expedient to the Russians that they should get rid of us – although Stalin had agreed to let us have these three fields and operate from Russia. From then on they began to suffer indignities on our people until we recalled them and abandoned the flying fields.

GG: But that was a great help to you, being able to have people go across…

JD: This was the 8th AF flying from England to Russia, and the 15th did the same thing under Nate Twining, flying from Italy, they would bomb and then go to Russia and come back… – so we were getting two missions out of just a little more than what would have been just one. That made it real easy for your fighters and reconnaissance, as well, because instead of going into the absolute maximum penetration depth and not having much time there, you could spend all the time you wanted, go a little further, land in Russia and come back.

Johnny Hoover –

Hoover flew many important missions for Elliott Roosevelt. [Tape #37, Feb. 1955] …

GG: When did you enter the service?

JH: I was commissioned and graduated from flying school in 1942. I trained as a fighter pilot and went to North Africa, about February 1943, as a P-38 fighter pilot. It was at that time that I got into reconnaissance.

GG: How did you move from fighters to reconnaissance?

JH: Well, we happened to be sitting in a replacement depot down in Oujda [Morocco]…. Captain Ted Erb (sp?) came down wanting volunteers [from the P-38 pilots to go into recon]. That's when I got into it and did my training up at Algiers, at Maison Blanche.

GG: Who was the Air Force General in charge of all the activities over there?

JH: General Eaker was the overall theatre commander. As I recall, we flew about three training missions out of Maison Blanche.

GG: When did Roosevelt take command of the unit?

JH: I joined this unit – the 3rd Photo Group – in about March, 1943. To my recollection, Elliott came in around July of '43. [false].

GG: Did you have any unusual experiences …, up to the point when Roosevelt took over?

JH: Well, Leon Gray, group operations officer, Dick Berner (sp?) and myself all came in about the same time and, I think, between the three of us we were perhaps more responsible than anyone else for taking the range of the P-38, or the F-5, from about a 300-mile radius to about a 700-mile radius. Not only did we extend range, but we increased target coverage.

GG: Operating out of Algeria, what were some of the targets you had to cover?

JH: Southern France, northern Italy, Sardinia and Corsica.

GG: None of those were night missions, were they?

JH: Not while we were in Algiers. It was not until we got up into La Marsa near Tunis, when we got the B-25s and started flying the night missions with the M-46 flash bombs. We almost blew up a couple of B-25s trying to get the fusing so that detonation would occur at the proper altitude to assure maximum illumination, and so on. It was strictly through a hit-or-miss operation and, I think, it was finally a British fuse which we settled on.

GG: Were the pictures pretty good?

JH: They were quite good – they were useful for the purpose. We were covering the northern side of the front line in southern Italy, roads and railroads coming into the front line. Of course, the visual reports were about as useful as the actual photographs.

GG: Did you get any pictures around Naples and Rome?

JH: Well, at that time we weren't going up quite that far?

GG: Who was this RAF man Roosevelt [said] was always doing something spectacular?

JH: That was probably Wing Commander Warburton. He was a fantastic character. He used to do things like dressing up as an American Lt. Col. – this was when he had a unit at Malta

– and he'd fly over to visit us and coordinate with us on targets when were at La Marsa. One day, something was wrong with his airplane, so Colonel Dunn gave him a P-38 to fly back to Malta. He aborted the take-off, the belly skidded off the runway, he came back in and said that one wouldn't make it to Malta, so we gave him another one and off he went to Malta. While people were asking who was in the burning airplane out there, I replied that he was already on his way to Malta.

I don't know what happened to him. He was missing on a mission on which he was flying a P-38 from England to Italy with a flight of four Mustangs – P-51s – escorting him as far as Switzerland. He was last seen by the escorts over Lake Constance [Bodensee] – at which point the plan was that the escort would leave him and he would proceed over the Alps into Italy. That was the last ever seen or heard of him.

GG: Well, when did Elliott Roosevelt start flying?

JH: My first knowledge of his flying was when I was transferred from the Italian theatre up to England – about February of 1944. I was ordered into Elliott's wing there at High Wycombe.

GG: Where were the airplanes based in England?

JH: At that time all the recce effort was located at Mt. Farm. About six months later we were operating out of a base at Chalgrove.

GG: I remember Elliott asked me to fly up with him in this twin-engine wooden Cessna to Northern Ireland, I hadn't realized that he knew how to fly. I recall that on the way back I was riding back with the mechanic and I looked out and saw all this oil streaming out the left side of the plane. I went up and told Elliott he was having trouble with that left engine and suggested we land at the Isle of Man. He said we weren't losing that much power and thought we could make it, that he had an appointment back in London and had to get there. We didn't even have any life preservers in that plane, so I went up and told him, "Listen, I am the command pilot, you guys can go on, but I want to land at the Isle of Man." He then cocked it around and landed, and I think it was on the way to the hangar that something else came out of that engine. So he suggested that we get a B-17 over from Watton, which we did. Some young kid – 19, 20 years of age, came in on that downhill runway with a hell of a lot of speed and when he saw he was going to go over the seawall he ground-looped it and it ran out into the mud. I remember the wheels settled down so far you could walk right off the surface of the mud onto the wing of the plane….

GG: How did the Russians treat you?

JH: Well, first they tried to shoot me down. I'm sure I was a little off course because when I left Poland I ran into this front, so all I could do was fly by instruments until I could get out of it. I had dropped down to about 10,000 feet for better orientation and I was jumped by four Yaks. I did what I was briefed to do – lowered the landing gear and rocked the wings, the sign that I was friendly. I thought everything was alright until I looked in the mirror and saw these tracers coming at me and a black puff from that 20mm cannon in the nose. When I saw that I pushed everything to the firewall and got away. I think what confused them was that this was only a week or two after the invasion and we had these black and white stripes painted on the fuselage and on the wings. They were D-day invasion markings for easy identification of friendly forces.

There was a Russian General Primnov (sp?) who wanted to see me as soon as I got into Poltava. He seemed quite perturbed over the whole thing, but I took off the next morning and never knew what happened, if any, to the pilots who had done the shooting.

GG: About how long a mission was it from England to Poltava?

JH: It was about 6 ½ hours. …

GG: What was your opinion of our cameras? Six months before we got into the war, Minton Kaye stated to General Arnold that we had such lousy cameras they wouldn't even put them into an airplane. That they were considered very poor, unreliable and nothing compared to the British cameras. [Arnold sent me to England to investigate]. Did you have any failures with the cameras?

JH: No, in fact, that's something with which we had less problems than anything else.

GG: Did you use the K-18, long-focal-length – made a 9*18 picture?

JH: Yes. The interpreters, of course, were always looking for good detail and good scale. North Africa is where we started dropping the altitude to give the interpreters better scale – the difference between a picture taken with a 36-inch focal length at 30,000-35,000 feet and one taken at about 22,000 is tremendous from an interpreter's point of view.

GG: … on a long mission, you had a great interest in seeing those films developed, didn't you? You went in, watched them developed, and followed right through the interpreter stage.

JH: We would do that, particularly, to be sure we got the target. … we extended the range of the P-38 from 300 miles to about 700. Along with this we increased target coverage from about three or four to 45 or 50 separate targets on one mission. If you wanted to cover that many targets it required reducing the number of exposures to only as many as you felt you needed.

GG: The lab boys were pretty satisfied with the developing equipment too, weren't they – they didn't have too many troubles?

JH: No, not particularly. There was a little difficulty at High Wycombe getting everything set, but once we got going we were doing a good percentage of our work for 9th AF over in France, particularly when General Patton started moving. The front kept moving so fast that neither the 9th AF or our effort, either one, could keep up with the movement of the front lines. We had to take to photographing roads in advance of wherever we thought Patton would be going.

GG: Who was running that 9th AF? Hall?

JH: Hall was running the 7th Group (7 PRG) in England, initially – part of the 8th AF. George Peck had the 10th Recce Wing in 9th AF.

GG: Did you ever see boys develop pictures in those little tents?

JH: Yes, we used them in North Africa. I might mention, too, that we checked out and trained this French reconnaissance squadron. One of their pilots was St. Exupery (sp?), who's written several books on aviation. Captain Gavuelle (sp?) was the commander of the group.

I remember I refueled at Corsica one time on a mission that covered the B-17s that bombed Genoa. I had a fuel pump problem on one engine which made it impossible, above 15,000 feet, to use two, so I went ahead and used one. I covered the bomb damage and, coming out of Genoa they were still firing flack at me. I could see the bursts were falling short, so I'd fly back and forth and when the bursts got a little closer I'd move out a little further – just watch them creep out and keep out of their range. Then I saw what looked like a battleship coming into the port of Genoa. I had almost two full drop tanks of fuel left – as you know, we never had any guns – and I just wondered what two full drop tanks would do to the battleship, so I peeled off and went down. The P-38 had an electrical release button to drop both tanks at once, so I came in at the battleship, pressed the button, pulled up and saw one tank drop short – I'd released a little early. I circled around and came in a second time, which was a mistake. They were ready and the tracers coming back looked like snowflakes. I came around just above the water and out the other side – but I never went back up to see if it had hit, although I don't know how it could have missed. With all that firing at me, though, there was never a scratch on the airplane.

…

George C. Mcdonald:

Major General MacDonald was an intelligence officer who worked closely with photo-recon units. He was also involved with the insertion of agents into Europe, a secret activity of Roosevelt's 325th PRW.

…

GM: My job was in plans and operations of the USAF, while also serving as AF attaché and assigned diplomatic status, so we could have more freedom in our contacts with foreign nations.

General Spaatz received word that Elliott Roosevelt was looking for a job and he had the nucleus of an Air Force in aerial photography. Spaatz sent me out to take a look at the outfit and make a recommendation on its future status. I looked it over and was disappointed at the low intelligence area these fellows had. I recommended to Spaatz that they be immediately pulled out of England and sent to N. Africa. Little did I realize what a headache I was promoting for myself.

Spaatz directed me, in addition to my other duties, to work on that project. I was going to go to Africa with the outfit and remain with them to help them in any way that I could. Everything seemed to work all right, progressively. Gradually, the mistakes of ignorance were corrected as we got more training and experience.

At that time Elliott Roosevelt was not a pilot, he was an observer, and a good one, and a good organizer. As time permitted, he got in some flight training, using some of the pilots from the photographic unit.

GG: He learned to fly in one of those wooden twin-engine Cessnas. [UC-78 / AT-17]

GM: Elliott made a fine job of anything he attempted.

GG: Did you know he was having trouble with Minton Kay (sp?)? ["Col. Nemesis"]

GM: That resulted in Minton Kay being transferred elsewhere.

GG: When did you get to be a B.G.? Were you in England?

GM: I was stationed in England, but on temporary assignment for these duties in North Africa. My job then was intelligence for the Air Force and General Eisenhower and his command.

GG: Did you work with the RAF?

GM: Yes, a lot of the coaching we got was from the RAF, both in improvements in equipment and training …as time went on, that personnel became the stars of aerial photography. A lot of them got knocked down by the Germans, but in the end their efforts were rewarded by the intelligence of which I kept close track. We tried to work as far ahead as possible in getting photography of all the worthwhile proposed targets for bombing. In France, Italy, Denmark, Sweden, and a few other places. By that time we were beginning to get B-17's stripped for aerial photography, and that worked beautifully, because the Germans could not quite catch them.

GG: What was the date, was this in Africa?

GM: The initial operations were in North Africa – with the stripped B-17's. We increased the size of the laboratory and flying personnel. General Lanham had made a trip through by that time, and with General Spaatz and General Eaker, we outlined the shortcomings of our U.S. effort in aerial photography, with recommendations as to what should be done. The equipment and laboratory space we put on trucks for mobility, which later gave us trouble. As we moved into North Africa the Army proceeded to steal every photographic truck they could. They threw the photographic equipment out as junk while they used those van-type vehicles for personal offices and sleeping quarters. When I got wind of that I got hold of Elliott Roosevelt and told him what we were up against. I knew the route the Army was taking in North Africa, so I put up a road-block and put Elliott in charge of it, with orders to stop every truck coming through and search their papers and if any of these van-type vehicles that were found were to be confiscated right there. --- When I got that job we started with five men. By the time the war was almost over it was up to 20,000 men – 10,000 in North Africa and 10,000 in England.

GG: When I talked to Elliott he told me we integrated all the nationalities, they were all under his organization.

GM: We assigned everyone we could get our hands on. There was a language barrier between the foreigners and our people, but as we got liaison established between those people and ourselves, we got some of them assigned, as part of their duty to the combination USAF and RAF, and that turned out to be a good move – with one exception. I wondered where the Russians were getting photography of the identical objects that we had. I instituted an investigation of it and found that these fellows – the French, principally, were selling their photographic products to the French and the French were selling them to the Germans. [sic!]

GG: In other words, the Russians would fly over and take the pictures, they'd sell them to the French and the French would sell them to the Germans.

GM: That's right. It was difficult as could be cleaning house on that. We took some of the German prisoners of war and questioned them as to how they thought the war would end. They were almost unanimous in saying they thought the Germans would be defeated. Those that said that, of course, were apple-polishing. We got a list of those people and sorted them out until we had a satisfactory nucleus for our purposes. We wanted to put them in these laboratories to find out who was receiving these stolen photographs.

GG: How were these flights carried out in reconnaissance where you had to go so deep into Germany you had to go on and land at other places beyond that country?

GM: Intelligence had been making a continuous study. I had 35 men just working on the intricacies of that, plotting the landing fields and radio help, food supplies and rest camp for the fellows. They all wanted to go to Italy – they'd never been to Italy. I had been to Europe several times during peacetime. From my observations I could tell we were following a smug line in the Air Force of not sending our personnel on leave. Whereas, the RAF had been sending their people to Europe on bicycle tours, so they would see what was a good target. They were given lectures explaining what constituted a good target. There were electrical installations, oil facilities, storage warehouses for aircraft, cannon, tanks – anything and everything that could be of destructive use to the enemy....

GM: We had to know it, but we also had to use various means other than photography. Among those were newspaper clippings from Germany where they advertised for more personnel with experience in electronics, cameras, missiles. It finally ended up with Peenemünde and we landed some of our sleuths.

GG: You dropped them out of those night airplanes by parachute. If you took one of these Germans over and dropped him at Peenemünde, how long would it take him to get back to the U.K. – how did he get his report back?

GM: We had lines of communication installed with a code that changed every few days, as we found out that the Germans were getting some of the real stuff and interpreting it to suit their purposes. Greater emphasis was put on the coding. The British had a wonderful organization near King's Landing – each piece of equipment cost about $10,000 – for the purpose of interpreting and acquiring the codes the British were using.

GG: But how did the people you dropped at Peenemünde get their reports back – by radio?

GM: We did it by every means possible – by radio, by the man personally coming back again. OSS – the Baker Street Gang of Intelligence, as it was called – would pick up these fellows at an interception point and bring them back to England, and sometimes they were interpreted on the Continent, after landing, which was a great help to intelligence. These fellows were members of the RAF and USAF and were men of extremely high caliber. They fluently spoke the language of the country in which they were dropped. On a couple of trips I flew over to Southern France to talk to some of these fellows, I was not too certain they were not dreaming some of this stuff up to make a good story.

I made friends with one fellow who spoke fluent English, Italian, and French. One of his main jobs was to locate radar and radio installations, of the Germans. He not only found them, but sabotaged some of them.

GG: What part did you play in the Normandy invasion?

Some of the equipment and the results were created by General George Goddard, which is important because his photography penetrated the water to almost any reasonable depth, so that the Navy and the landing crews knew exactly where the water was shallow and where it was most favorable for their landings. George Goddard, to my mind, deserves a world of credit and a commendation from the President, and a proper decoration in keeping with what he accomplished. [sic!]

Barney Giles:

Lt. Gen. Barney Giles was Chief of Staff, Air Forces during the later stages of the war. He publicly took the Roosevelt-Hughes side in the F-11 controversy. [20 June 1966]

...

BG: During the last World War, when I was in Air Force headquarters as the Air Staff, we kept getting reports from General Spaatz – all over North Africa at first, later over England – that the photographic airplane he was using was very unsatisfactory. We had equipped some P-38 airplanes with a single pilot trying to fly the plane and make the pictures. Then he equipped some B-17's, taking them out of his bomber force trying to equip some kind of reconnaissance airplane to make the pictures getting the results of the bombing he was doing over Ploesti and cross the Alps into Germany and Austria, but everything was unsatisfactory. He said the camera equipment was okay, but the airplane was no good, and he wanted to know what we could do about furnishing him a better airplane. We asked Elliott Roosevelt, who was working with him at the time, to come into Washington, and I had a conference with Elliott and some of the other boys at Wright Field about the photographic airplane that would take pictures to do the job.

It seemed that Howard Hughes had an airplane with more promise than anything we had in the Service at that time, so we flew out to the West Coast where we met Hughes. We went out to a dry lake bed where he was operating this particular airplane – a two-engine job, similar to the P-38's. I didn't fly the plane, due to a flat tire, but I was very anxious to have it flown. I had a couple of test boys from Dayton go out and they spent a week flying this airplane around, demonstrating that it could be a good photographic airplane. So, I immediately had General Echols put an order in to buy 100 of these airplanes, giving it very high priority, and having the photographic equipment installed, to be furnished, especially, to the European theatre at that time. Well, of course, the war came rapidly to a conclusion and we never did get any of these airplanes actually into operation at the front, but I'm sure it would have turned out to be a good airplane.

Of course, this deal we had with Hughes got into politics – we had the investigation of Mr. Brewster and a few of the other people who had Howard Hughes in and accused the administration of favoring Hughes in contracts, especially the flying boat he was building. During this investigation they wanted to know what Hughes was paying me as to ordering the airplane – they assumed someone in the Air Force was taking a rake-off to buy this particular equipment. It was proven beyond any question of a doubt that this airplane was bought on its merit; politics had nothing whatever to do with it.

Leon Gray:

Lt. Col. Leon Gray was Operations Officer of the 3rd Photo Group from July 1943 to September 1943, and C.O. of the 5th Photo Group from September 1943 to February 1944. On 12 May 1944, Col. Gray delivered the following lecture on night photography and "dicing" to a class of Ground Liaison Officers at Will Rogers Field, Oklahoma. [AFHRA Archives on the 3rd PRG (GP-PHOTO-3-SU-PE)]:

LG: Along with night flights, the one phase of photography that I got most interested in was low altitude work. My last ten or twelve missions were all "dicing" or low altitude missions. I imagine you've heard all about PR – high altitude from the other fellows, and I thought you would be interested in "dicing" missions. "Dicing" missions are used to help the landing of the task forces. Before a task organization makes a beach landing, they have the advantage of having these low altitude flights, taken from a P-38, 60 degrees angle horizontal – 400 feet – which gives the task force the exact location of their objective. What they do with a picture like this is first check the strip to find the best place to have the tanks go in.

Our organizations did the flights that supported General Patton when he leap-frogged and landed back of the enemy on the north coast of Sicily. We did the low altitude flights for the Salerno and Anzio Beachhead. With all these ops, General Patton and General Clark were very well pleased. They take the pictures and make a mosaic. In the front end of each landing craft the pilot of the barge had the picture of the territory he is to approach. They drive the landing barges to the right spot. That is the most important part of low altitude photography. These are the pictures taken for the Anzio beachhead. All these pictures were taken between 200 and 500 feet.

In North Africa, we did more in developing the range in a P-38 than in any other theater. Our range was 700 miles. We pick up between 19-30 pinpoints from the time we go out. I was assigned to night photography July and August 1943 – in support of the Sicily invasion. Night photography has its limitations. Navigation at night is the hardest part of night photography – that is to get over the right object. We were limited to 20 pictures because we carried 20 flash bombs.

[with the] Army in Italy, they were having trouble locating concealed ammunition dumps because Jerry would not transport ammunition out of these dumps in the day time. He did all his work at night. Night photography tried to pick up these dumps at night. It presented a problem as we did not know where to work. We knew they had to transport it in some way so they had to be within a short radius of the railroad. We then started taking pictures up and down these railroad strips and started picking up the dumps. We finally found out that they did most of it after sunset and by 10:00 at night. So we started going out these hours and found the road and followed up the convoy in the direction they were coming and once in a while would pick up an ammunition dump. We picked up five dumps – and I think three dumps were destroyed just before we left.

The only other phase of low-altitude flying which we were called on to do was when the weather was so bad the overcast conditions lasted for days and days – and they wanted to know if a bridge had been blown out.

During the winter months in the Italian Campaign there would be weeks at a time we would not be able to get over a certain port to keep track of their water transportation. So once in a while we [had to] take low altitude pictures of a port to find out if they were bringing anything in or out.

[Photo interpreters] with us were mostly British. They knew their job and were interested in their work. Without the proper cooperation between the ground and air force, you might as well stay at home yourself. We have no way of knowing what the ground force wants unless we work together. We did not want them to tell us how to run our job and we didn't tell them how to run their job. The ordinary conversation between us was something like this: "We need some pictures of Cassino. We can't get them from high altitude so want your suggestion as to how to get them any other way."

My last two months over there (Dec. 1943 and Jan. 1944) was in low altitude and night photography, so I probably don't know the latest in the high altitude work. In night photography, we use a B-25 airplane with 20 flash bombs and two cameras – the two cameras set to give 30% side light. Taken at 12,000 feet, we would cover an area two miles long and approximately 4½ miles wide, using it to discover road communications and field communications. We used it in support of the 5th Army. Night photo has its limitations, for instance in a B-25 we could only go a radius of 500 miles. We became very proficient in that and were getting 98% pictures and about 85-90% of the target. We had all of Italy mapped; had a mosaic of most of Italy. ....

Edgar Cohen – Oral History Interview, Library of Congress, 5/1/2002.

Captain Edgar M. Cohen participated in Project RUSTY, the mapping of North Africa.

... After training I was sent to Washington, D.C., and I joined the 1st Mapping Group, which was an aerial photo organization, and I learned their ways of doing things... At Lowry Field the photo school is very interesting because it showed us how photography was used to make maps. We learned to use aerial cameras and aerial equipment, which is entirely different...

Did they have good equipment?

Oh, excellent, yes. The very best. And after I learned that... -- it was in February of '42 I was sent on a mission to Africa and our purpose was to photograph the landing areas for the invasion in November 1942... General Eisenhower needed maps and we made the maps.

... We flew home on the Clipper, not the whole way. We just flew across the Atlantic on the clipper. ...And we stayed a week in Brazil on the way back waiting for transportation back to the U.S. and we flew back to Washington... after a few days.

Did you have a base near to Africa that you landed at before you made the photographic trip or was it right from Washington to Africa to take the photographs?

No.... I went by boat from Washington to -- ... Lagos, Nigeria on a boat... It took a month.

Wow. Were there other photographers with you?

Yes. It was a small expedition, about 20 men, and some of us went by boat, which was quite an interesting trip.

Was the whole boat filled with military personnel?

No. There were diving experts going to Mashava [Massawa], which is on the Red Sea, a port there that was clogged with ships. Before the Italians pulled out there they blew up a lot of ships in the harbor, you know, just to make it rough for anybody who came back, the British and the Americans. And there were steelworkers. There were some other military....

What kind of plane did you fly in to take your pictures?

We had an old Fortress... It was a four-engine aircraft, but it wasn't a new one. They couldn't spare anything new in those days, and we had one -- just one airplane. It was painted blue and had no identification... because we were flying in an area where you might meet anyone.

Was it difficult to get good pictures from a plane that wasn't that smooth?

Oh, the airplane was smooth enough.... The airplane was fine, and we were there during the good season. You know, in the tropics you have the rainy season... So we were there at the right time...We were there four months. We came back in May. May 21.

Were there other places that you photographed?

No. On this mission we just -- we just photographed within the limits of Africa, from the west -- from the west coast over to Egypt.... We got around pretty well... [After that] We came back and we worked in the -- in the lab in Washington. We had a photo lab there where we processed films from other missions and the maps were made by engineers after they got our pictures.... We did set up a lab in Africa and we processed -- we processed the film and printed one set of proofs, sent the film home on one plane and the prints on another.

Oh, okay. Was your -- plane in danger at all when you were flying over to photograph...?

Well, there was always -- something that could occur.... Fortunately, I had no trouble....

Wow. And going back to the mission that you had in Africa taking the pictures for the maps, it was a secret mission; right?

Top.

Top secret. And how many people were with you, about?

Oh, altogether there weren't more than twenty.

Okay. And you had a very famous person with you. Who was that?

Elliott Roosevelt, the President's son, was our navigator. The navigator in this instance figured out where we would start taking a strip of photos and, of course, he directed the flight. Our colonel, the leader of the mission, was Colonel Cullen, C-u-l-l-e-n. He did some of the flying, piloting, and some of the planning too, but I think Elliott did most of the laying out of directions and directing what we should shoot.

He had a very important job, then, taking care of it?

Oh, yeah, great.

And even the son of the President wasn't able to stay out of dangerous situations?

No. No, I think he was everywhere. He had been on other trips that were just as exciting. We used a three-camera system. One camera shot a vertical picture and the other two cameras were on the side and made what we call oblique angle photographs, and from those the engineers could make their maps. They could figure distances and elevations and the landscaping. ...

Okay. At the time - this was in February of 1942 - airplanes and ships and all kinds of equipment were very scarce and they sent us -- they sent some of us on a small ship from New York. And we talked about the crew. They were going all over Africa. At that time there were submarines all along the coast. Off Florida you could see submarines -- German submarines. We went to Florida by way of the intracoastal waterway and we weren't in the ocean until there. Then we crossed the South Atlantic on this small boat without a convoy. It had a couple small guns on it, but they were no protection. And we crossed the South Atlantic. We slept in our life belts.

... We had some submarine alarms. People thought they saw conning towers of submarines on the way over.

Well, what happened when you had a submarine alarm? Would bells go off or people yell or what happened?

Well, they couldn't do anything. What could they do? They couldn't do anything. We had two small guns, and I guess they manned those, but that was about all.

After you left the coast, did you see any submarines?

No. We had some alarms -- false alarms, and we had one big cruiser pull up to us but, thank goodness, it was one of our ships, because it had a big American flag on it. They came to identify us, because we had no markings on the ship. [They were very suspicious of us]... And that's about the only excitement that we had on the whole way across. We stopped at Lagos, Nigeria and we flew from there to the west coast across, which would be our base. [Accra]

But when you left there you didn't take a boat back; you flew back?

Yes, we flew back. Elliott was with us. He got a Clipper. He managed a Clipper.

[Why would they] send you over by a boat that would take a month, rather than by plane?

That's all there were. There was nothing else... available. They were still trying to salvage Pearl Harbor and repair it and get it ready, and salvage the ships, and it was just too busy a time to get good equipment.

X. NOTES

A. POSITIONS HELD (23 Sep. 1910 – 27 Oct. 1990)

Teenage Cowhand and Math Tutor
Competitive Rodeo contestant
Football player, "semi-pro"
Advertising agent
Advertisement Bureau owner
Airline manager or president (episodic)
Aviation editor (1933-34)
Aircraft salesman (1934 etc.)
Radio Station Manager (1935)
Broadcasting Network owner (1936-40)
Radio commentator (1936-40, 1945-1950s)
Columnist (1934 and sporadically thereafter)
Lobbyist (fairly continuous)
Air Race Promoter (1936, Texas)
University Trustee (Texas A & M)
Democratic Convention Delegate
Horse Breeder (episodic)
Dog Breeder (episodic)
Vestryman, Episcopalian Church
Freemason, suspended
Air Force Officer, Captain to Brig. General
Arctic Explorer (1941)
Pilot (Private, Single and Multi-engine Land)
Navigator (1941-45)
Reconnaissance Expert (1943-45)
Photographer (wartime)
Diplomat, amateur (episodic)
Author of Memoirs
Mystery Novel author (1984 – 2000)
Christmas tree salesman (1947-48)
Television Producer (1946-50s)
Democratic National Committeeman
Farmer (Hyde Park)
Rancher (several attempts, Texas, Colo.)
Historian (several works)
Editor (of FDR letters; 1946 et s.)
Spokesman for dictators (Stalin; Batista; Caetano; Ian Smith; to varying and disputed extents)
Compost Entrepreneur (several)
Liquid Fertilizer Promoter (1984)
Livestock Food consultant (1960, IA)
Uranium Miner (1950s)
Wildcat Oil Driller and Investor (episodic)
Hotelier and Restaurateur (1947)
Television Entrepreneur (1950s, Cuba)
Publishing Co. administrator (1961, Minneapolis)
Automobile Club Director (1961)
Greeter (1964, Miami Beach)
Mayor (1965-67, Miami Beach)
Tourist Agency Head (1970-71, Miami Bch)
University Lecturer
Cruise Ship Lecturer (several tours)
Tour Guide (Israel)
Bank President (episodic)
Investment Advisor
Management Consultant
Public Relations Consultant
Arms Trader (1934, 1972)
Race Track promoter
Real Estate Investor (episodic)
Real Estate Agent and Promoter (several)

B. ROOSEVELT SIBLINGS

- **Anna Eleanor Roosevelt**, 3 May 1906 - 1 Dec 1975; married Curtis Bean Dall in 1926 (div. 30 Jul 1934); Clarence John Boettiger 18 Jan 1935 (div. 1949); Dr. James Addison Halsted (1952) .
- **James Roosevelt**, 23 Dec 1907 - 13 Aug 1991; married Betsey Cushing (1930-40); Romelle Schneider (1941-55); Gladys Owens (1956-69); Mary Lena Winskill (1969).
- **Franklin Delano Roosevelt, Jr.**, 18 Mar 1909 - 7 Nov. 1909.
- **Elliott Roosevelt**, 23 Sep 1910 - 27 Oct 1990; marriages and descendants below.
- **Franklin Delano Roosevelt**, Jr., 17 Aug 1914 - 17 Aug 1988; married Ethel du Pont (1937-49); Suzanne Perrin (1949); Felicia Schiff Warburg Sarnoff (1970); Patricia Luisa Oakes (1977); Linda McKay Stevenson Weicker (1984).
- **John Aspinwall Roosevelt**, 13 Mar 1916 - 27 Apr 1981; married Anne Lindsay Clark (1938-65); Irene Boyd (1965).

C. MARRIAGES and DESCENDANTS

- **Elizabeth (Betty) Browning Donner**, 16 Jan 1932 – 17 Jul 1933. (died 1980). Son: William Donner R.
- **Ruth Josephine Googins**, 22 Jul 1933 – Mar 1944. (died 1974). Daughter: Ruth Chandler R. Sons: Elliott (Tony) R., David Boynton R.
- **Faye Emerson**, 3 Dec 1944 – 17 Jan 1950. (died 1983)
- **Minnewa Bell Gray Burnside Ross,** 15 Mar 1951 – 1960. (died 1983)
- **Patricia Peabody Whitehead**, 3 Nov 1960. (died 1996). Three sons and one daughter adopted by Elliott Roosevelt. One son died in infancy.

D. MILITARY SERVICE, Brig. Gen. Elliott Roosevelt, O-396475

Assigned:

21st Reconnaissance Squadron (Heavy), Gander Lake, Newfoundland. April – Sep 1941. (This unit flew the B-18 Bolo, B-17 Fortress, OA-8, OA-9, and OA-10. It was redesignated 411th Bombardment Squadron in April 1942.)

6th Recon. Squadron (Medium), Muroc Bombing and Gunnery Range, California: Dec 1941. (Flew the B-18 and the LB-30 Liberator on anti-submarine patrol. Redesignated 396th Bomb. Sq. in April 1942.)

2nd Recon. Squadron (Heavy), Muroc and Hammer Field (Fresno), California: Jan – Feb 1941. (Flew the B-18, LB-30, B-17, and B-24 on anti-submarine patrol. Redesignated 392nd Bomb Sq. in April 1942.)

1st Mapping Group, Bolling Field, D.C., Special Reconnaissance Mission to Africa: March – June 1942

Commanded:

3rd Photographic Reconnaissance and Mapping Group, RAF Membury, RAF Steeple Morden, England, and Oran/La Sénia, Algiers/Maison Blanche, Tunis/La Marsa: 11 July 1942 – 13 Aug 1942 and 30 Sep 1942 – Mar 1943.
5th, 12th, 13th, 14th, 15th Reconnaissance Squadrons

Northwest African Photographic Reconnaissance Wing (NAPRW), Maison Blanche, Algeria and La Marsa, Tunisia: Feb 1943 – Sep 1943
3rd Photographic Reconnaissance Group Group
5th Photographic Reconnaissance Group, La Marsa, Tun. and San Severo, It.
15th, 21st, 22nd, 23rd, 24th Reconnaissance Squadrons
RAF 682 Squadron
SAAF 60 Squadron
Free French II/33 (two escadrilles in II Escadron, 33 Escadre).

90th Photographic Wing, Reconnaissance, La Marsa, 22 Nov 1943; San Severo, Italy: 14 Dec 1943 – 25 Jan 1944
3rd Recon Group, 5th Recon Group

8th Photographic Reconnaissance Wing (Provisional): Jan 1944 – Aug 1944

325th Photographic Wing (Reconnaissance), RAF High Wycombe, England: Aug 1944 – Apr 1945
7th Photographic Group (Recon.), RAF Mount Farm
13th, 14th, 22nd, 27th Reconnaissance Squadrons
25th Bombardment Group (Recon), RAF Watton
652 Bomb Squadron (Heavy) (B-17, B-24),
653 BS (Light) (Mosq.),
654 BS (Special) (B-25, B-26, Mosq.)

Per: Air Force Combat Units of World War II – Groups, Wings, Office of AF History, D.C., 1983 and Combat Squadrons of the Air Force – World War II. HQ USAF, Maurer, 1982.

E. BOOKS ATTRIBUTED TO ELLIOTT ROOSEVELT

Mr. Roosevelt was credited with a very large *oeuvre* of books, magazine articles, newspaper columns, radio and television scripts, extensive media interviews, and miscellaneous writings.

There is dispute over how much of this substantial production can be attributed solely to him. In most cases, however, Elliott provided at least the ideas, the plots, the gist and tone, and the final approval.

1946: As He Saw It.
1950: FDR: His Personal Letters, Vol I-IV. Ed. Elliott R. (with Joseph Lash and others.)
1973: An Untold Story: The Roosevelts of Hyde Park. (with James Brough.)
1975: A Rendezvous with Destiny: The Roosevelts of the White House. (w. James Brough.)
1977: Mother R: Eleanor Roosevelt's Untold Story
1983: The Conservators. Arbor House, New York
1984: Eleanor Roosevelt, with Love: A Centenary Remembrance.

1984: Murder and the First Lady
1985: The Hyde Park Murder
1986: Murder at Hobcaw Barony
1987: The White House Pantry Murder
1988: Murder at the Palace
1989: Murder in the Rose Garden
1989: Murder in the Oval Office
1990: Murder in the Blue Room
(Elliott Roosevelt died in 1990. Residual work was published in following years.)
1991: A First Class Murder
1991: Murder in the Red Room
1991: The President's Man
1992: Murder in the West Wing
1993: Murder in the East Room
1993: New Deal for Death
1994: A Royal Murder
1995: Murder in the Executive Mansion
1996: Murder in the Chateau
1997: Murder at Midnight
1998: Murder in the Map Room.
1999: Murder in Georgetown
2000: Murder in the Lincoln Bedroom
2001: Murder at the President's Door (by William Harrington)

Elliott Roosevelt completed a novel based on the life of U.S. naval hero John Paul Jones. It had been begun by his father in 1923, but it was apparently not publishable. Elliott, Minnewa, and Anna worked on it in the early 1950s. He said it was finished but never submitted to a publisher.[2563]

In his declining years, Elliott attempted an autobiography with Professor Dean Smith of Arizona State University. It was never published.

BIBLIOGRAPHY

Abbazia, Patrick. *Mr. Roosevelt's Navy.* Annapolis: Naval Institute Press, 1975.

Air Ministry, United Kingdom. *Atlantic Bridge: The official account of RAF Transport Command's Ocean Ferry.* London: His Majesty's Stationery Office, 1945.

Alter, Jonathan. *The Defining Moment: FDR's 100 Days and the Triumph of Hope.* New York: Simon & Schuster, 2006.

Ancker, Paul E. *Narsarsuaq Air Base.* DIAS Denmark, 1995.

Anderson, Jack. *Confessions of a Muckraker.* New York: Random House, 1979.

Armstrong, Anne. *Unconditional Surrender: The Impact of the Casablanca Policy upon WW2.* City: Rutgers Univ. Press, 1961.

Arnold, Henry. *Global Mission.* New York: Harper & Row, 1949.

Arnold, Henry w. John W. Huston. *American Air Power Comes of Age.* Honolulu: University Press of the Pacific, 1998.

Asbell, Bernard. *Mother & Daughter: The Letters of Eleanor and Anna Roosevelt.* New York: Fromm International Pub., 1988.

Austin, Tom, and Kase, Ron. *Bill Miller's Riviera: America's Showplace in Fort Lee, NJ.* Charleston, SC: The History Press, 2011.

Barlett, Donald (w. James Steele). *Howard Hughes: His Life and Madness.* New York: W.W. Norton, 1979.

Barlett, Donald, and Steele, James. *Empire: The Life, Legend and Madness of Howard Hughes.* New York: Norton, 1979.

Baruch, Bernard. *The Public Years.* New York: Holt Rinehart & Winston, 1960.

Bennett, Donald C. T. *Pathfinder: A War Autobiography.* London: Sphere, 1972.

Berg, A. Scott. *Lindbergh.* New York: Berkley / Penguin Putnam, 1998.

Beschloss, Michael. *Kennedy and Roosevelt.* New York: Norton, 1980.

Bishop, Jim. *FDR's Last Year.* New York: William Morrow, 1974.

Block, Alan. *Masters of Paradise.* Transaction Publishers: New Brunswick, NJ, 1991.

Bowman, Martin. *Mosquito Photoreconnaissance Squadrons of World War 2.* London: Osprey (13), 1999.

Boyd, Alexander. *The Soviet Air Force Since 1918.* New York: Stein & Day, 1977.

Brands, H. W. *T.R.: The Last Romantic.* New York: Basic Books, 1997.

Bridle, Paul (ed.). *Documents on Relations between Canada and Newfoundland.* Ottawa: Dept. of External Affairs, 1974.

Broeske, Pat (w. Peter Harry Brown). *Howard Hughes: The Untold Story.* New York: Dutton div. of Penguin, 1996.

Brugioni, Dino. *Eyes in the Sky.* Annapolis: Naval Institute Press, 2010.

Bryce, Robert. *Cronies: Oil, the Bushes, and the Rise of Texas.* Cambridge, MA: Perseus, 2004.

Burns, James McGregor. *Roosevelt, the Soldier of Freedom.* New York: Smithmark, 1970.

Burrough, Bryan. *The Big Rich: The Rise and Fall of the Biggest Texas Oil Fortunes.* New York: Penguin, 2009.

Carlson, William S. *Lifelines Through the Arctic.* New York: Duell Sloan Pierce, 1962.

Caro, Robert. *The Years of Lyndon Johnson, Means of Ascent.* New York: Knopf, 1990.

—. *The Years of Lyndon Johnson, The Path to Power.* New York: Vintage/Random, 1983.

Carr, W.C. *Checkmate in the North.* Toronto: MacMillan, 1944.

Chandler, Alfred D. *The Papers of Dwight David Eisenhower III: The War Years.* Baltimore: The Johns Hopkins Press, 1970.

Chaney, Lindsay and Cieply, Michael. *The Hearsts: Family and Empire, The Later Years.* New York: Simon & Schuster, 1981.

Chester, Edmund. *A Sergeant named Batista.* N.Y.: Holt, 1954.

Christie, Carl. *Ocean Bridge.* Toronto: University of Toronto Press, 1995.

Churchill, Winston. *The Second World War, 1-6.* London, Boston: Houghton Mifflin, 1950.

Clarke, Thurston and Tigue, John. *Dirty Money: Swiss Banks, the Mafia, Money Laundering and White Collar Crime.* New York: Simon and Schuster, 1975.

Collier, Peter (w. David Horowitz). *The Roosevelts: An American Saga.* New York: Simon & Schuster, 1994.

Connally, John. *In History's Shadow.* New York: Hyperion, 1993.

Cook, Blanche Wiesen. *Eleanor Roosevelt.* New York: Penguin, 1992.

Corell, John T. "The Air Mail Fiasco." *Air Force Magazine*, March 2008.

Cronkite, Walter. *A Reporter's Life.* New York: Random House, 1997.

Dallek, Robert. *Lone Star Rising: Lyndon Johnson and his Times 1908-60.* New York: Oxford, 1991.

Daniels, Jonathan. *White House Witness.* Garden City, NY: Doubleday, 1975.

Danish Ministry of Foreign Relations. *Groenland under den Kolde Krig.* Copenhagen: Dansk Udenrigspolitisk Institut (DUPI), 1999.

Davis, Kenneth. *The Hero: Charles A. Lindbergh and the American Dream.* Garden City NY: Doubleday, 1959.

D'Este, Carlo. *Eisenhower- A Soldier's Life.* New York: Henry Holt & Co., 2002.

Diederich, Bernard. *Somoza and the legacy of U.S. involvement in Central America.* New York: E.P. Dutton, 1981.

Doolittle, James H., with Carroll Glines. *I could never be so lucky again.* New York: Bantam Doubleday Dell, 1991.

Dudgeon, AVM A.G. *Hidden Victory: The Battle of Habbaniya.* Stroud, Glos.: Tempus, 2000.

Duffy, James. *Lindbergh v. Roosevelt.* Washington DC: Regnery, 2010.

Dzuiban, Col. Stanley (ed.). *U.S. Army in World War II: Military Relations between the United States and Canada.* Washington D.C.: Office of the Chief of Military History, U.S. Army, 1959.

Eisenhower, Dwight David. *Crusade in Europe.* London: William Heinemann, Ltd, 1948.

English, T.J. *Havana Nocturne: How the Mob Owned Cuba.* New York: William Morrow, 2008.

Eno, Robert. "Crystal Two: The Origin of Iqaluit." *Arctic, Vol.56, No.1*, 2003: 63-67.

Eubank, Keith. *Summit at Teheran.* New York: William Morrow & Co, 1985.

Farer, Tom (ed). *Transnational Crime in the Americas.* New York: Routledge, 1999.

Farley, James w. Walter Trohan. *The Roosevelt Years.* New York: McGraw-Hill, 1948.

Ferrell, Robert (ed.). *The Eisenhower Diaries.* New York: Norton, 1981.

Flynn, John. *Country Squire in the White House.* New York: Doubleday Doran & Co, 1940.

—. *The Roosevelt Myth.* New York: Devin-Adair Co., 1948.

Forbes, Alexander. *Quest for a Northern Air Route.* Cambridge, MA: Harvard University Press, 1953.

Foulois, Benjamin w. Carroll Glines. *From the Wright Brothers to the Astronauts.* New York: McGraw Hill, 1968.

Gentry, Curt. *J. Edgar Hoover: The Man and the Secrets.* New York: W.W. Norton, 1991.

Glines, Carroll. *Bernt Balchen.* Washington D.C.: Smithsonian, 1999.

—. *The First Flight Around the World.* Missoula: Pictorial Histories Publishing Company, 2000.

Goodwin, D.K. *No Ordinary Time.* New York: Simon & Schuster, 1994.

Grierson, John. *Challenge to the Poles.* London: G.T. Foulis & Co., 1964.

Hack, Richard. *Howard Hughes: The Private Diaries, Memos and Letters.* Beverly Hills, CA: New Millennium Press, 2001.

Hagerty, Edward J. *The Air Force Office of Special Investigations, 1948-2000.* DC: AFOSI History Office, 2008.

Halsell, Grace. *In Their Shoes.* Fort Worth: Texas Christian University Press, 1996.

Hammer, Richard. *The Vatican Connection.* New York: Henry Holt & Co., 1982.

Hardwick, Jeffrey M. & Victor Gruen. *Mall Maker: Victor Gruen, architect of an American dream.* Philadelphia: University of Pennsylvania, 2004.

Harriman, Averell (w. Elie Abel). *Special Envoy to Churchill and Stalin.* New York: Random House, 1975.

Havas, Laslo. *Hitler's Plot to Kill the Big Three.* New York: Cowles, 1969.

Helman, Grover. *Aerial Photography: The Story of Aerial Mapping and Reconnaissance.* New York: MacMillan (Air Force Academy Series), 1972.

Hersh, Burton. *Bobby and J. Edgar.* New York: Carroll & Graff, 2007.

Higham, Charles. *Howard Hughes: The Secret Life.* New York: Putnam, 1993.

Hobbs, William H. *Exploring about the North Pole of the Winds.* London: G.P. Putnam & Sons, 1930.

Hooton, E.R. *Eagle in Flames.* London: Arms and Armor Press, 1999.

Hyland, L.A. "Pat". *Call Me Pat.* Virginia Beach, VA: The Donning Co., 1993.

Ickes, Harold. *The Secret Diary of Harold L. Ickes I-III.* New York: Simon & Schuster, 1953.

Infield, Glenn. *Unarmed and Unafraid.* London: MacMillan, 1960.

Irving, David. *The Mare's Nest.* Windsor: Electronic Edition, Parforce Ltd./Focal Point Publications, 2001.

Isserman, Ferdinand. *A Rabbi with the American Red Cross.* New York: Whittier Books, 1958.

Jackson, Robert. *The Red Falcons: The Soviet Air Force in Action 1919-69.* London: Clifton, 1970.

Jones, Jesse. *Fifty Billion Dollars.* New York: McMillan, 1951.

Josephson, Emanuel. *The Strange Death of Franklin D. Roosevelt.* City: Chedney, 1948.

Kane, Robert. *Air Transportation (14th Ed.).* Dubuque: Kendall Hunt, 2003.

Karlson, Gunnar. *The History of Iceland.* London: Hurst, 2000.

Katz, Robert. *The Battle for Rome.* New York: Simon & Schuster, 2003.

Kean, Patricia Fussell. *Eyes of the Eighth.* Sun City, AZ: CAVU Publishers, 1996.

Kern, Gary. "How Uncle Joe bugged FDR." *Studies in Intelligence,* 2003: 47:1.

Kessler, Ronald. *The Sins of the Father: Joseph P. Kennedy.* New York: Warner, 1997.

Keyssar, Helene and Pozner, Vladimir. *Remembering War: A U.S.-Soviet Dialogue.* New York: Oxford University Press, 1990.

Kimball, Warren. *Churchill and Roosevelt.* Princeton, NJ: Princeton University Press, 1984.

Knutsen, Will C. *Arctic Sun on my Path.* Guilford, CT: The Lyons Press, 2005.

Koskoff, David. *Joseph P. Kennedy: A Life and Times.* New York: Prentice Hall, 1974.

Kreis, John (ed.). *Piercing the Fog.* Washington D.C.: Air Force History and Museums Program, Bolling AFB, 1996.

La Farge, Oliver. *The Eagle in the Egg.* Boston: Houghton Mifflin, 1949.

Larrabee, Eric. *Commander-in-Chief: Franklin Delano Roosevelt, his Lieutenants, and their War.* Annapolis: Naval Institute Press, 1987.

Lash, Joseph. *A World of Love: Eleanor Roosevelt and Her Friends II (1943-1962).* New York: Doubleday, 1984.

—. *Eleanor and Franklin.* New York: Norton, 1971.

—. *Love, Eleanor: Eleanor Roosevelt and Her Friends.* New York: Doubleday, 1982.

Lawrence, Harry. *Aviation and the Role of Government.* Dubuque: Kendall/Hunt, 2004.

Leaf, Edward. *Above all Unseen: The RAF's Photographic Reconnaissance Units 1939-45.* England: Patrick Stephens Ltd, 1997.

Lidegaard, Bo. *I Kongens Navn (In the Name of the King).* Samleren: Copenhagen, 2005.

Linden, F. Robert van der. *The Post Office and the Birth of the Commercial Aviation Industry.* Lexington: University Press of Kentucky, 2002.

Lomazov, Steven (w. Eric Fettman). *FDR's Deadly Secret.* New York: Public Affairs/ Perseus, 2009.

Loomis, William Raymond. *Fighting Firsts.* New York: Vantage Press, 1958.

MacMillan, Harold. *The Blast of War.* New York: Harper and Row, n.d.

Marrett, George. *Howard Hughes, Aviator.* Annapolis MD: Naval Institute Press, 2004.

Maurer, Maurer. *Air Force Combat Units of World War II.* Washington, D.C.: Office of Air Force History, 1983.

Mayle, Paul. *Eureka Summit: Agreement in Principle and the Big Three at Teheran.* Cranbury, NJ: Ass. Univ. Presses, Inc, 1987.

McKean, David. *Influence Peddler: Thomas Corcoran.* Hanover, NH: Steerforth Press, 2004.
McNulty, Thomas. *Errol Flynn: the Life and Career.* Jefferson, NC: McFarland & Co., 2004.
Meacham, Jon. *Franklin and Winston.* New York: Random House , 2004.
Miller, Kristie. *Isabella Greenway.* Tucson, AZ: University of Arizona Press, 2004.
Miller, Marvin. *The Breaking of the President 1974.* Covina: Classic Productions, 1975.
Miller, McGinnis (eds.). *A Volume of Friendship: The Letters of Eleanor Roosevelt and Isabella Greenway.* Tucson: Arizona Historical Society, 2009.
Miller, Merle. *Plain Speaking: An Oral Biography of Harry S. Truman.* New York: Berkley Publishing, 1973.
Morgan, Ted. *FDR.* New York: Touchstone/Simon&Schuster, 1985.
—. *Reds: McCarthyism in 20th Century America.* New York: Random House, 2004.
Newton, Michael. *Mr. Mob: The Life and Crimes of Moe Dalitz.* Jefferson, NC: McFarland & Co., 2009.
Okrent, Daniel. *Last Call: The Rise and Fall of Prohibition.* New York City: Scribner/Simon&Schuster, 2010.
Olsen, Jack. *Aphrodite: Desperate Mission.* New York: Ibooks, 1970.
Parks, Lillian Rogers. *The Roosevelts: A Family in Turmoil.* Englewood Cliffs, NJ: Prentice-Hall, 1981.
Perling, Joseph. *President's Sons: The Prestige of Name in a Democracy.* New York: Books for Libraries Press 1971, 1947.
Perry, Mark. *Partners in Command.* New York: Penguin, 2007.
Persico, Joseph. *Franklin & Lucy.* New York: Random House, 2008.
Porter, Darwin. *Howard Hughes: Hell's Angel.* New York: Blood Moon , 2005.
Reilly, Michael. *Reilly of the White House.* New York: Simon & Schuster, 1947.
Reynolds, Quentin. *The Curtain Rises.* New York: Random House, 1944.
Roorda, Eric. *The Dictator Next Door: The good neighbor policy and the Trujillo regime.* Durham, NC: Duke University Press, 1998.
Roosevelt, Curtis. *Too Close to the Sun.* New York: Public Affairs, 2008.
Roosevelt, Eleanor. *On My Own.* New York: Harper & Bros., 1958.
—. *This I Remember.* New York: Harper & Bros, 1949.
Roosevelt, Elliott (editor w. Joseph Lash). *FDR: His Personal Letters, Vol. I-IV.* New York: Duell Sloan Pierce, 1950.
Roosevelt, Elliott (w. James Brough). *The Roosevelts of Hyde Park: An Untold Story.* New York: Putnam, 1973.
—. *The Roosevelts of the White House: A Rendezvous with Destiny.* New York: Putnam, 1975.
Roosevelt, Elliott. *As He Saw It.* New York: Duell Sloan Pierce, 1946.
—. *Eleanor Roosevelt, with Love.* New York: Lodestar Books, 1984.
—. *Mother R: Eleanor Roosevelt's Untold Story.* New York: Putnam, 1977.
—. *The Conservators.* New York: Arbor House, 1983.
Roosevelt, James (w. Bill Libby). *My Parents: A Differing View.* Chicago: Playboy Press, 1976.
Roosevelt, James (w. Sidney Shalett). *Affectionately, FDR.* New York: Avon Hearst, 1959.
Rumbold, Richard. *The Winged Life.* New York: David MacKay, 1955.
Russo, Gus. *Supermob.* New York: Bloomsbury, 2006.
—. *The Outfit.* New York: Bloomsbury, 2001.
Saint-Exupéry, Antoine de. *Wartime Writings 1939-44.* New York: Harcourt Brace Jovanovich, 1986.
Schiff, Stacy. *Saint-Exupéry: A Biography.* New York: Holt, 2006.
Searls, Hank. *Young Joe, the Forgotten Kennedy.* New York: Ballantine, 1969.
Serling, Robert. *Eagle: The Story of American Airlines.* New York: St. Martin's Press, 1985.
Sherwood, Robert. *Roosevelt and Hopkins: An Intimate History.* New York, 1948.
Shiner, J. *Foulois and the USAAC 1931-35.* Washington D.C.: Office of Air Force History, 1983.

Smith, Constance Babington. *Air Spy (orig. Evidence in Camera).* Falls Church, VA: American Society for Photogrammetry Foundation, 1957, reprint 1986.

Smith, Gary Scott. *Faith and the Presidency.* New York: Oxford Univ. Press, 2006.

Smith, Jean Edward. *FDR.* New York: Random House, 2008.

Smith, Richard Norton. *The Colonel: The Life and Legend of Robert R. McCormick.* Evanston, IL: Northwestern University Press, 2003.

Stanley, Roy M., II. *World War II Photo Intelligence.* New York: Charles Scribner's Sons, 1981.

Steinberg, Alfred. *Mrs. R.: The Life of Eleanor Roosevelt.* New York: Putnam, 1958.

Streitmatter, Rodger. *Empty Without You: The Intimate Letters of Eleanor Roosevelt and Lorena Hickok.* Da Capo, 1998.

Summers, Anthony. *The Arrogance of Power: The Secret World of Richard Nixon.* New York: Penguin Putnam Inc., 2000.

Summersby, Kay. *Eisenhower was my Boss.* New York: Prentice-Hill, 1948.

Taylor, John W.R. *Combat Aircraft of the World.* London: George Rainbird Ltd, 1969.

Thomas, Morley. *Metmen in Wartime: Meteorology in Canada 1939-45.* Toronto: ECW, 2001.

Thompson, J. Steve, w. Peter C. Smith. *Air Combat Manoeuvres.* Hersham, Surrey: Ian Allan, 2008.

Thompson, Robert L. "Bob". *Flying in Coffin Corner.* Tucson: Whitewing Press, 1995.

Toland, John. *Infamy.* New York: Doubleday, 1982.

Tolstoy, Nikolai. *Stalin's Secret War.* New York: Holt, Rinehart, and Winston, 1982.

Tregaskis, Richard. *Invasion Diary.* New York: Random House, 1944.

Truman, Harry. *Memoirs.* Doubleday: Garden City, NJ, 1956.

Tully, Grace. *FDR was my Boss.* New York: Scribner, 1949.

U.S. *Pilot's Manual for Lockheed P-38 Lightning.* Appleton WI: Aviation Publications (reprint), 1945 (orig.).

Vanderwood, Paul. *Satan's Playground.* Durham and London: Duke University Press, 2010.

Vidal, Gore. *Point to Point Navigation.* New York: Vintage E-books, 2007.

Waller, John. *The Unseen War in Europe.* New York: Random House, 1996.

Ward, Geoffrey. *Closest Companion: The Unknown Story of the Intimate Friendship between Franklin Roosevelt and Margaret Suckley.* New York: Simon & Schuster, 1995.

Weiner, Ed. *Let's go to Press: A Biography of Walter Winchell.* New York: Putnam, 1955.

Willoughby, Malcolm. *The U.S. Coast Guard in WW2.* Annapolis, MD: United States Naval Institute, 1957.

ARCHIVES, JOURNALS AND UNPUBLISHED SOURCES

Air Force Historical Research Agency (AFHRA), Maxwell AFB, Alabama.
National Archives (NARA), College Park, Md.
National Personnel Records Administration (NPRC), St. Louis, MO.

Federal Bureau of Investigation (FOIA File).
Federal Aviation Administration (Publicly releasable information only).

Herbert Hoover Presidential Library and Museum, West Branch, Iowa.
Franklin D. Roosevelt Presidential Library and Museum, Hyde Park, New York.
Harry Truman Presidential Library and Museum, Independence, Missouri.
Dwight D. Eisenhower Presidential Library and Museum, Abilene, Kansas.
John F. Kennedy Presidential Library and Museum, Boston, Mass.
Lyndon B. Johnson Presidential Library and Museum, Johnson City, Texas.

Hoover Institution, Gen. Frederick Anderson Papers. Palo Alto, California.

Arizona Historical Society, Isabella Greenway Collection. Tucson, Arizona.

Congressional Record, and Reports of Subcommittees, as annotated.
Foreign Relations of the United States (FRUS)
Canadian Foreign Relations (Ottawa)

Archives of the *New York Times, Chicago Tribune, Los Angeles Times, Arizona Daily Star, Fort Worth Star-Telegram, Dallas Morning News,* TIME Magazine online archive, LIFE Magazine archive, Google News Archive. Other newspapers and periodicals as listed in end/footnotes.

SEEING THE ENEMY: *Army Air Force aerial reconnaissance support to U.S. Army operations in the Mediterranean in World War II* : A thesis presented to the Faculty of the U.S. Army Command and General Staff College by David W. Dengler, Major, USAF, University of Nebraska, Lincoln, Nebraska, 1998 Fort Leavenworth, Kansas 2009

BDA: *Anglo-American Air Intelligence, Bomb Damage Assessment, and The Bombing Campaigns Against Germany, 1914-45.* Dissertation by Robert S. Ehlers, Jr. Ohio State University 2005

Administrative History of The Ferrying Command, 29 May 1941 – 30 Jun 1942. Army Air Forces Historical Studies Nr. 33, Asst. Chief of Air Staff Intelligence, Historical Division, June 1945.

U.S. ARMY IN WORLD WAR II, THE CORPS OF ENGINEERS, 1958

U.S. ARMY AIR FORCES IN WW II, Vol I, PLANS AND EARLY OPERATIONS

AIR FORCE COMBAT UNITS OF WORLD WAR II, Office of Air Force History, D.C., 1983.

COMBAT SQUADRONS OF THE AIR FORCE – WORLD WAR II. Maurer, Office of AF History, HQ USAF, 1982

Journal of Meteorology, Vol 2 Nr 3, September 1945, p 135.

The Roosevelt Administration, David Ben Gurion, and the Failure to Bomb Auschwitz: A Mystery Solved. Rafael Medoff. The David S. Wyman Inst. for Holocaust Studies, retrvd. 2 Feb 2011.

USAF Oral History Program, AFHRA Maxwell AFB, call nr. K239.0512 (several tapes and transcripts of interviews with ranking officers)

CASE HISTORY OF HUGHES D-2, D-5, F-11 PROJECT. SECRET. Compiled by Historical Section, Intelligence, Air Materiel Command, Wright Field, August 1946.

Report of the Special Committee on Investigation of the Munitions Industry, U.S. Senate 74th Congress, 2nd Session, 24 February, 1936

General Henry H. Arnold file at AFHRA, including; Communications on Mosquito acquisition; Communications on establishment of bases in Greenland and Iceland; Reports of Survey, Labrador and Baffin Island, Captain Elliott Roosevelt. Introduction letter in Arnold file; Report on Crystal Force Expedition, with preliminary mention of Bluie West 8 and Bluie East 2. Issued aboard M/S *Cormorant,* 11 Nov 1941, by Lieut. Cdr. C. J. Hubbard; Report on Project RUSTY, by Col. Cullen. 22 May 1942.

Historical Data Concerning U.S. Photographic Reconnaissance in World War II. Prepared by USAF Historical Division, Research Studies Institute, Maxwell AFB, Alabama. March 1957

AIR FORCE SPECIAL HISTORICAL STUDY: Tracing of Organizational Structures, Weather Reconnaissance Squadrons, End of WW II to Present. 13 February 1959 - PREPARED FOR: Office of Safety, Headquarters AWS, PREPARED BY: Historical Division, AWSIS

INDEX

ENDNOTES

[1] New York Times (NYT), 19 SEP 40
[2] Lash: Love, Eleanor, 334
[3] Elliott Roosevelt: As He Saw It, 7-9
[4] NYT, 24 SEP 40; Kentucky New Era, 27 SEP 40 had photo of ER taking oath.
[5] Ernest Lindley column in Dallas Morning News (DallasMN), 7 OCT 40
[6] Peter Collier: The Roosevelts, 349-50; Chicago Tribune (ChigTrib), 20 JUN 48
[7] Persico: Franklin & Lucy, 271-2
[8] James Roosevelt: My Parents, 200
[9] E.R. testimony, p215, Hartford Loan File, E. R. Box, Pegler Collection, HH Lib
[10] ER, As He Saw It, 9
[11] Henry "Hap" Arnold: Global Mission, 17
[12] Wire, ER to FDR, 18 APR 34, President's Personal File (PPF) 8559, Franklin D. Roosevelt Presidential Library, Hyde Park, New York (FDR Lib)
[13] Arnold: American Air Power Comes of Age: see Maj. Gen. John W. Huston's introductory chapter for Arnold's standing with the White House 1935-45.
[14] ER: As He Saw It, 9
[15] Sheila Graham column (Hollywood in Person), in DallasMN, 1 JUN 45
[16] ER: As He Saw It, 10
[17] Collier: 377, quoting from Elliott's memoir; FDR Appts. Day-to-Day, FDR Lib.
[18] James Roosevelt (JR): Affectionately FDR, 266-7
[19] JR: Affectionately, 258
[20] NYT, 24 SEP 40
[21] Congressional Record (CongRec), 1947, Part 40, 23976
[22] ER: As He Saw It, 13
[23] Arnold: Global Mission, 213
[24] NYT, 13 OCT 40
[25] NYT, 28 SEP 40; ChigTrib, 28 SEP 40
[26] NYT, 17 OCT 40
[27] NYT, 6 OCT 40
[28] Hugh Johnson column, 17 SEP 40, in Pittsburgh Press
[29] Hugh Johnson column reprinted in CongRec, 25 SEP 40, 12622
[30] NYT, 26 SEP 40
[31] Eleanor Roosevelt: This I Remember, 219; CongRec, 1940, 13319
[32] The FDR tapes were transcribed and then partly published in American Heritage, FEB/MAR1982, 19-20.
[33] Eleanor Roosevelt: This I Remember, 90
[34] NYT, 13 OCT 40; Eleanor's My Day columns, 2 FEB 37 and 9 MAR 37
[35] NYT, 24 SEP 40
[36] CongRec, 8 OCT 40, added by Francis Harter (R-NY), poem by Guy E. Bradley.
[37] NYT, 10 OCT 40, 13 OCT 40; also AP, 10 OCT 40

38 ER: As He Saw It, 13; NYT, 15 OCT 40; ChigTrib, 15OCT40
39 NYT, 13 OCT 40; George Goddard, Overview, 270
40 ER: As He Saw It, 14
41 ER: A Rendez-vous with Destiny, 274
42 NYT, 15 OCT 40; AP, 15 OCT 40 in St. Petersburg Times
43 TIME, 21 OCT 40; UP, 16 OCT 40 in St. Petersburg Times
44 Lash: Love, Eleanor, 317
45 Eleanor: This I Remember, 219.
46 Earnest Lindley column in DallasMN, 7 OCT 40
47 Federal Aviation Administration, response to inquiry, information released 2011
48 Lee Morris in Free Speeches, 22 OCT 40 in the Evening Independent
49 Letter, Gen. Giles to Gen. Spaatz, 21 JAN 45, LOC/Spaatz/1-20
50 E. R. discharge sheet of 1945, National Personel Records Center (NPRC)
51 UP, 14 OCT 40, in St. Petersburg Times, 15 OCT 40
52 ER: A Rendezvous with Destiny, 275
53 TIME, 28 OCT 40
54 ER: As He Saw It, 14; also Personnel Record found in ER file, President's Personal File (PPF), FDR Lib
55 ER: A Rendezvous with Destiny, 253
56 PPF, Memo reg. ER, 30 MAY 41, FDR Lib
57 Personnel Record found in ER file, PPF, FDR Lib; various letters in ER, Broadcast file, Pegler/HH Lib
58 NYT, 13 OCT 40
59 Goddard: Overview, 270-271
60 Goddard: Overview, 304
61 ER: As He Saw It, 9
62 Miller/McGinnis: A Volume of Friendship, 26
63 JR: My Parents, 11-12; Collier, the Roosevelts, 87
64 Brands: T.R., 259
65 OHI, ER about Eleanor, p31, Acc #80-6, FDR Lib. By Emily Williams, 20 JUN 79.
66 Persico: Franklin & Lucy, 26
67 Unattributed radio script "As They Saw Him," 24, Minnewa Bell papers, FDR Lib
68 JR: My Parents, 57
69 JR: My Parents, 293
70 OHI, JR, Eleanor Project, 26-7, FDR Lib.
71 Roosevelt, Curtis: Too Close to the Sun, 22
72 D.K. Goodwin: No Ordinary Time, 179, quoting JR.
73 JR: My Parents, 25.
74 JR: My Parents, 29
75 OHI with ER about Eleanor, 6, FDR Lib.
76 ER Testimony, 48, Hartford loan file, ER box, Pegler/HH Lib
77 Roosevelt, Curtis: Too Close to the Sun, 28
78 Unattributed radio script "As They Saw Him," 13, Minnewa Bell papers, FDR Lib
79 Elliott told this story in the Saturday Evening Post: FDR as we remember Him, 10 APR 65.
80 D.K. Goodwin: No Ordinary Time, 245
81 JR: My Parents, 217, makes this point explicitly.
82 Patricia Roosevelt (PR): I Love a Roosevelt, 63
83 JR: My Parents, 123
84 Steinberg: Mrs. R, 82
85 OHI with ER on Eleanor, 14, FDR Lib
86 ER: An Untold Story, 230
87 ER: An Untold Story, 228; NYT, 21 JUL 32 and associated NYT coverage. Flynn, 38-40, has an interesting contemporary summary of banking-political corruption in New York during Roosevelt's term.
88 ER: An Untold Story, 232
89 NYT, 26 FEB 22; 11 MAR 22; 10 FEB 23; 12 FEB 23; 25 FEB 23; 4 MAR 23
90 ER: Murder in the Rose Garden, 3.

[91] ER: An Untold Story, 232. FDR thought he had been "in the Navy" on account of his cabinet post.
[92] Letter ER to FDR, ER correspondence, PPF, FDR Lib
[93] Poughkeepsie Journal, 5 AUG 84
[94] JR: My Parents, 67
[95] Prescott (AZ) Evening Courier, 2 JUL 28
[96] JR: Affectionately 150-2; letter ER to FDR, 1928, FDR Lib
[97] www.dmairfield.org/people/vanzandt_jp/index.htm, retrieved 8 APR 11
[98] ER: FDR: His Personal Letters I, 158
[99] ChigTrib, 20 JUN 48
[100] Eleanor R.: This I Remember, 17
[101] JR: Affectionately, 180
[102] Morgan: FDR, 285
[103] Asbell: Mother & Daughter, 46
[104] Eleanor: This I Remember, 56
[105] Ibid.
[106] Steinberg: Mrs. R, 166
[107] Collier: The Roosevelts, 370
[108] Steinberg: Mrs. R, 167-8
[109] Collier: the Roosevelts, 370
[110] JR: My Parents, 300
[111] NYT, 19 SEP 31; 8 OCT 31
[112] ER: Rendezvous, 36
[113] *Aero Digest*, AUG 34, 24
[114] Letter, anonymous to Pegler, ER Box, Pegler/HH Lib
[115] Ibid.
[116] Collier: The Roosevelts, 370
[117] Morgan: FDR, 459
[118] NYT, 8 OCT 31; Collier 370
[119] NYT, 31 OCT 31
[120] Time Magazine (TIME), 04 APR 34
[121] Eleanor: This I Remember, 82
[122] OHI, Minnewa Bell interview, 5, FDR Lib; shoes: Collier, 371.
[123] Cook: Eleanor Roosevelt, 94
[124] Collier, 371
[125] ER, This I Remember, 82
[126] Lash: Love Eleanor, 138
[127] Lillian Helms: A Family in Turmoil, 3.
[128] NYT, 9 MAR 33
[129] Eleanor: This I Remember, 82
[130] NYT, 10 MAR 33
[131] Dallas Morning News (DallasMN), 12 MAR 33
[132] ER: An Untold Story, 294
[133] Collier: the Roosevelts, 368
[134] Collier the Roosevelts, 370
[135] OHI with Minnewa Bell, 14, Eleanor OH project, FDR Lib
[136] Steinberg: Mrs. R., 169
[137] John told this story in the Saturday Evening Post: FDR as we remember Him, 1965.
[138] Steinberg: Mrs. R., 88-9
[139] ER: Eleanor Roosevelt with Love, 120-1
[140] Collier, 368; LAT, 1 MAR 90.
[141] ER told the story with variations. Collier, 368-9; NY Journal American, 27 NOV 65.
[142] ER: Rendezvous, 37
[143] Lash: Love Eleanor, 153
[144] ER: Rendezvous, 37-8
[145] Morgan, 459
[146] Fort Worth Star-Telegram, 10 MAR 33. This, Amon Carter's newspaper, covered Elliott's visit in detail.

147 AP, 11 MAR 33, in the Spokesman-Review
148 Fort Worth Star-Telegram coverage
149 ER: Rendez-vous, 38
150 DallasMN, 12 MAR 33
151 DallasMN, 12 MAR 33; AP, 11 MAR 33, in the Youngstown Vindicator
152 Collier, 367, quoting from Elliott memoir.
153 ER: Rendez-vous, 38
154 LAT, 9 JUN 33; TIME, 31 JUL 33. (ref. Wellesley College for the elite's daughters, outside Boston.)
155 UP, 22 JUL 33, in the Milwaukee Journal.
156 RG Testimony; also ER Testimony 81, Hartford file, ER box, Pegler/HH Lib
157 ER: Rendez-vous, 38; NYT, 13 MAR 33
158 ER: Rendezvous, 38
159 Arizona Daily Star, 14 MAR 33
160 Stephens County Sun, 24 MAR 33, has posed photograph taken at El Paso. Erlich photo in FDR Lib.
161 Arizona Daily Star, 14 MAR 33
162 Fort Worth Star-Telegram, 14 MAR 33
163 Letter ER to "Ma," 13 MAR 33, R. family papers donated by the children, FDR Lib
164 Letter, ER to "Ma," R. family papers donated by the children, FDR Lib
165 INS, 7 MAR 33, in the Telegraph-Herald and Times-Journal (Dubuque, IA)
166 Arizona Daily Star, 16 MAR 33
167 Lubbock Avalanche, quoted in opinion roundup in DallasMN, 31 MAR 33.
168 NYT, 16 MAR 33; 19 MAR 33
169 ER: Rendezvous, 38-9
170 OHI with C.R. Smith, Eleanor project, FDR Lib
171 Arnold: Global Mission, 295
172 Eleanor: My Day column, 3 JUL 46
173 Patricia R.: I love a Roosevelt, 263
174 Serling: Eagle, 166
175 Halsell: In their Shoes, 46
176 Reilly: Reilly, 59-60
177 www.cartermuseum.org/about/amon-carter-bio, retrieved 26 JUL 11
178 Jesse Jones's actions and attitudes are well recorded in his tart memoir, Fifty Million Dollars (1951).
179 Miller/McGinnis: Eleanor and Isabella: A Volume of Friendship, 214
180 Cook: Eleanor Roosevelt, 323
181 Arizona Daily Star, 21 MAR 33
182 Ibid
183 Telegram, ER to Eleanor, 22 MAR 33, Family papers donated by the children, FDR Lib; also Miller/McGinnis, 228
184 ER correspondence, Greenway collection, AHS
185 AP report in Lewiston Morning Tribune, 1 APR 33
186 Letter, Greenway agents to Motz, 15 MAY 33, IHS file, Greenway Collection, AHS
187 IHS file, Greenway Collection, AHS
188 ER correspondence, Greenway Collection, AHS
189 Aero Digest, AUG 34, 24
190 Ibid
191 AP report in St. Joseph Gazette, 4 JUN 33
192 Gilpin Airlines file, Greenway Collection, AHS
193 The Aeroplane, April 2006, 59-60
194 www.dmairfield.org/people/gilpin_cw/index.htm, retrieved 4 OCT 10
195 Miller, Isabella Greenway, 163-4
196 MS1019, AZ Hist Soc; Miller, 193. A great article on Pickwick Airways is in AAHS Journal, Winter 2009.
197 www.dmairfield.org/Collections/Gilpin%20Collection/index.html, retr. 27 JUL 11
198 AP, Meriden Record, 16 JUL 32; UP, Pittsburgh Press, 14 JUL 32
199 www.dmairfield.org/Collections/Gilpin%20Collection/Obituary/index.html,retr.27JUL11,has clippings.

[200] Gilpin Airlines file, Greenway collection, AHS
[201] Eleanor to Isabella, 2 JUN 33, ER corresp. Greenway collection, AHS; see A Volume of Friendship, 229
[202] UP, Berkeley Daily Gazette, 12 MAY 33
[203] Morgan, 459, gives no source for this.
[204] Interview with ER in Parade Magazine, 10 OCT 82
[205] NYT, 12 MAY 33
[206] NEA/Erskine Johnson in Spokane Daily Chronicle, 8 JUN 33
[207] LAT, 12 MAY 33
[208] Jones: Fifty Billion Dollars, 303
[209] Letter ER to DP, 8 JUL 36, ER file, Drew Pearson collection, LBJ Lib
[210] NYT, 27 NOV 32
[211] NYT, 16 MAR 33; Serling, 68
[212] TIME, 23 APR 34
[213] Drew Pearson column (Washington Merry Go Round) in Pittsburgh Press, 14 JUL 36
[214] Letter ER to Pearson, 8 JUL 36, ER file, Drew Pearson collection, LBJ Lib
[215] Letter "American in Pittsburgh" to Pegler, 14 JUN 45, Misc. file, ER box, Pegler/HH Lib
[216] AP, Berkeley Daily Gazette, 12 MAY 33
[217] LAT, 25 MAY 33
[218] Vanderwood: Satan's Playground, passim
[219] Vanderwood: Satan, 300
[220] Vanderwood: Satan, 322-3
[221] Miller: Isabella Greenway, 180
[222] LAT, 25 MAY 33
[223] LAT, 6 JUN 33
[224] TIME, 19 JUN 33
[225] AP, Pittsburgh Post-Gazette, 10 JUN 33
[226] NYT, 10 JUN 33
[227] AP, the Telegraph-Herald, 9 JUN 33; AP, Pittsburgh Post-Gazette, 10 JUN 33
[228] Arizona Daily Star, 6 JUN 33
[229] ER: Rendez-vous, 66; LAT, 6 JUN 33
[230] Carl Miller to Pearson, 4 SEP, ER file, Drew Pearson collection, LBJ Lib
[231] DallasMN, 5 JUN 33, 9 JUN 33
[232] OHI with C.R. Smith, Eleanor project, FDR Lib
[233] Letter, Eleanor to Anna, 5 AUG 37, in Asbell: Mother and Daughter, 88
[234] LAT, 6 JUN 33
[235] Miller/McGinnis: A Volume of Friendship, 229; AP, Miami News, 6 JUN 33
[236] Arizona Daily Star, 7 JUN 33
[237] LAT, 7 JUN 33
[238] LAT, 8 JUN 33
[239] LAT, 9 JUN 33
[240] Arizona Daily Star, 8 JUN 33
[241] LAT, 9 JUN 33; NYT, 9 JUN 33
[242] LAT, 9 JUN 33
[243] Lash: Love Eleanor, 155
[244] Lash: Love Eleanor, 156
[245] AP, the Telegraph Herald, 9 JUN 33
[246] LAT, 5 AUG 33
[247] AP in Lewiston Morning Tribune, 17 MAY 33
[248] NEA/New York, 10 JUN 33 in the Southeast Missourian
[249] ibid
[250] NYT, 9 JUN 33
[251] www.onlinenevada.org/samuel_platt, retr. 27 JUL 11
[252] AP in Pittsburgh Post-Gazette, 10 JUN 33
[253] ER: Rendez-vous, 55-7
[254] Collier, 376
[255] Parks: A Family in Turmoil, 142

256 NYT 14 JUL 33; JR: My Parents, 310
257 Lash Eleanor Roosevelt, 164.
258 LAT, 18 JUL 33
259 NYT, 27 OCT 40
260 NYT, 17 JUL 33
261 DallasMN, 18 JUL 33
262 DallasMN, 10 JUN 33
263 DallasMN, 21 JUL 33
264 DallasMN, 22 JUL 33
265 NYT, 23 JUL 33
266 ER, Rendezvous, 101
267 The Telegraph Herald, 11 AUG 33
268 Asbell, 75
269 Streitmatter: Empty Without You, 102-3
270 Letter, Anna to Eleanor, 19 JUN 39, quoted in Morgan, 461
271 NYT, 19 JUL 33
272 Gilpin Airlines Records, Greenway Collection, AHS
273 LAT, 18 JUL 33, 30 JUL 33
274 Aero Digest, AUG 34, 24; MS1019 Box 1, Greenway collection, AHS; LAT, 17 DEC 33
275 IHS file, Greenway collection, AHS
276 NYT, 19 JUL 33; 23 JUL 33
277 DallasMN, 25 JUL 33, 29 JUL 33
278 DallasMN, 5 AUG 33
279 LAT, 5 AUG 33; NYT, 5 AUG 33
280 Rochester Evening Journal, 19 SEP 33
281 Clip from Washington Herald, 14 AUG 33, ER file, Pearson/LBJ
282 McLarren to Pegler, 5 SEP 45, Misc. file, ER box, Pegler/HH Lib
283 Lash: Love, Eleanor, 163
284 Letter Middleton to Pegler, 2 DEC 45, Stratton file, ER box, Pegler/HH Lib
285 ER file, 1933, PPF 4, FDR Lib; also NYT, 14 NOV 33, 22 NOV 33
286 NYT, 28 NOV 33
287 Pegler column, 9 SEP 49, in the Milwaukee Sentinel
288 NYT, 13 SEP 39; Kessler, 104.
289 Morgan, 465-6.
290 Russo: Supermob, 147; Hersh: Bobby and J. Edgar, 32, 191. Also described in Tim Adler: Hollywood and the Mob. For Schenck's role in Agua Caliente, see Vanderwood: Satan's Playground, 231-3.
291 See for ex. Kessler: Sins, 104-6, Russo:, 93, 100, et passim; 140 for Schenck's control of politicians.
292 LAT, 23 SEP 33
293 Letter, Middleton to Pegler, 2 DEC 45, Stratton file, ER box, Pegler/HH Lib
294 Miller/McGinnis: A Volume of Friendship, 231
295 Senate, Brewster Committee Hearings ("SBC Hearings"), 1947, Part 40, 23974
296 Cook: Eleanor Roosevelt, 2/98-9
297 NYT, 27 AUG 33
298 Aero Digest, AUG 34, 24
299 Keyssar: Remembering War, 176
300 ER column, Rochester Evening Journal, 28 AUG 33
301 ER column, Washington Herald, 31 AUG 33
302 Serling, 110
303 Serling, 91
304 Telegram 30 MAR 34, ER, PPF, FDR Lib
305 NYT, 2 APR 34
306 NYT, 4 APR 34; JR: Affectionately, 227
307 JR: My Parents, 217
308 Note, ER, PPF, FDR Lib

[309] NYT, 4 APR 34
[310] ER: Rendez-vous, 101
[311] JR: Affectionately, 227
[312] Ibid
[313] Ibid
[314] Aero Digest, AUG 34, 22-4
[315] Ibid
[316] Paul Mallon, News Behind the News, in the Reading Eagle, 29JUN34
[317] FDR Appts Day-by-Day, FDR Lib
[318] ER: Rendez-vous, 102
[319] ChigTrib, 20 JUN 48
[320] Flynn: the Roosevelt Myth, 242
[321] ER Testimony, 8, Hartford Loan file, ER box, Pegler/HH Lib
[322] TIME, 20 SEP 37
[323] TIME, 10 JAN 38
[324] Cook: Eleanor Roosevelt, II/482
[325] NYT, 2 JAN 38, 12 OCT 38, 15 APR 39
[326] ER: An Untold Story, 306-7
[327] Lawrence: Aviation and the Role of Government, surveys well the evolution of the aviation bureaucracy.
[328] NYT, 11 JAN 34, 26 JAN 34
[329] TIME, 18 DEC 33
[330] NYT, 28 FEB 33
[331] NYT, 1 OCT 33; see also the motion picture "Amelia."
[332] Letter, Putnam to Basil O'Connor and the President, 19 MAY 33, PPF, FDR Lib
[333] NYT, 21 APR 33
[334] Cook: Eleanor Roosevelt, I/363-4, II/ 50
[335] Eleanor: My Day, 20 JUL 40
[336] Universal, 27 JUL 33, in the Milwaukee Sentinel
[337] Notes, ER file, Drew Pearson collection, LBJ Lib
[338] Serling: Eagle, for the early history of AVCO, American Airways and Airlines.
[339] Notes, ER files, Drew Pearson collection, LBJ Lib
[340] Ibid
[341] JR: My Parents, 185
[342] NYT, 14 JAN 34
[343] Shiner: Foulois, 125-42
[344] Duffy: Lindbergh vs. Roosevelt, 15; see also Aero Digest, OCT 36
[345] UP/Pittsburgh Press, 5 MAR 34, lists the stock trades and short positions.
[346] Smith, Richard Norton: The Colonel, 346-7; also ChigTrib 9 OCT 36; FDR Day-by-Day, FDR Lib.
[347] Corell, John: The Air Mail Fiasco, Air Force Magazine, March 2008
[348] NYT, 5 SEP 31, 30 AUG 31, 4 MAR 32; see also Ludington case in McCracken collection, HH Lib.
[349] NYT, 3 JUN 30
[350] Serling, 63-73; provides one of the best summaries of the origins of the Air Mail fiasco.
[351] Public letter, PM Farley to Sen Black, p7, 14 FEB 34, Aviation file, Repr. Greenway collection, AHS
[352] Shiner: Foulois, 125
[353] Farley, chapter 6, esp. 46-47
[354] Farley, 46-7
[355] Davis, Kenneth: The Hero Charles A. Lindbergh and the American Dream, 291
[356] Public Letter, Farley to Black, 14 FEB 34, Aviation file, Greenway/AHS
[357] Davis: Hero, 293-4
[358] Public letter, Robbins to Farley, 15 FEB 34, Aviation file, Greenway/ AHS
[359] Kane: Air Transportation, 104-6
[360] Ibid, 107
[361] Ibid, 107-8. Similar numbers were quoted in LAT editorial, 21 FEB 34.
[362] Duffy: Lindbergh vs. Roosevelt, 42
[363] Kane:Air Transportation, 109
[364] Shiner: Foulois, 127

365 Ibid, 131
366 Shiner: Foulois, 140
367 Corell: Air Mail Fiasco, Air Force Magazine, MAR 2008
368 Wire, ER to FDR, ER correspondence, FDR Lib
369 Wire, FDR to ER, ER correspondence, FDR Lib
370 Wire, ER to McIntyre, 19 MAR 34, PPF, FDR Lib
371 Greenway response to Carter, 20 APR 34, in Correspondence, Aviation file, Greenway/AHS.
372 Hearst columnist James T. Williams in New York, 27 FEB 34, Aviation File, Greenway/ AHS
373 Foulois, 258; NYT, 25 FEB 34
374 Carl Vinson memorandum, 18 APR 34, PPF, FDR Lib
375 Davis: Hero, 335
376 Shiner: Foulois, 148
377 Glines: Foulois, passim
378 Foulois, 254-6. Quotes are from chapter "The truth about the Air Mail Fiasco," in his autobiography.
379 Duffy: Lindbergh vs. Roosevelt, 33-5
380 Manchester: American Caesar. Quoted therein by Bonner Fellers, McArthur's aide.
381 Duffy: Lindbergh vs. Roosevelt, 16-7
382 Davis: Hero, 336
383 Duffy, op. cit., 17-18
384 Berg, A. Scott: Lindbergh, 295
385 Foulois: From the Wright Bros. to the Astronauts, 241; NYT, 10 APR 34
386 LAT, 20 FEB 34
387 ER: Rendez-Vous, 102
388 CongRec, Senate, 14 MAR 34, 4500, quoting from ER in Washington Herald
389 ER: Rendez-vous, 101-2
390 CongRec, Senate, 30 MAR 34, 7635
391 CongRec, Senate, 30 MAR 34, 7636
392 Shiner: Foulois, 148
393 Lawrence: Aviation and the Role of Government, for bureaucratic evolution of aviation.
394 Duffy: *Lindbergh vs. Roosevelt*, 110-11. Discussion in Larrabee, 227-8. Records of the try are at AFHRC.
395 Aero Digest, OCT 36, 24
396 NYT, 15 JUN 34
397 Drew Pearson column, 14 JUL 36, in Pittsburgh Press; story supported by DP notes, LBJ Lib.
398 Aero Digest, AUG 34, 22
399 Aero Digest, AUG 34, 53
400 CongRec, 25 MAR 35, 4384; also NYT 26 MAR 35
401 CongRec, 25 MAR 35, 1935
402 Baltimore Sun, 26 MAR 35
403 CongRec, 25 MAR 35, 4404
404 CongRec, 25 MAR 35, 4388
405 Morgan, 462
406 Alva Johnston: Jimmy's Got It!, Saturday Evening Post, 2 JUL 38
407 Saturday Evening Post, 18 MAY 1940
408 Hersh: Bobby and J. Edgar, 56
409 ChigTrib, 4 DEC 34; NYT, 30 DEC 34; TIME, 31 JUL 33
410 Letter, Greenwood to Pegler, 17 DEC 42, Misc. file, ER box, Pegler/HH Lib
411 Letter, Greenwood to Pegler, 30 NOV 45, Misc. file, ER box, Pegler/HH Lib
412 Letter, Eggel to Pegler, 21 APR 54, JR file, Pegler/HH Lib
413 Letter, Willis to Pegler, 11 JUL 45, Misc file, ER box, Pegler/HH Lib
414 Spokane Daily Chronicle, 11 DEC 34; NYT, 17 DEC 34; Rochester Evening Journal, 17 DEC 34
415 Boyd: The Soviet Air Force, 38-39
416 NYT, 22 NOV 34
417 Frank Tichenor in *Aero Digest,* OCT36; ChigTrib 6OCT36; Pittsburgh Press, 7OCT36; TIME, 19OCT36
418 ChigTrib, 12 OCT 36

[419] ibid
[420] ibid
[421] ibid
[422] ChigTrib, 6 OCT 36
[423] Aero Digest, OCT 36; ChigTrib, 27 OCT 36
[424] Fokker Deal, Nye Collection, HH Lib; also clips, New York Sun, 7 OCT 36, McCracken papers, HH Lib
[425] TIME, 19 OCT 36
[426] ChigTrib, 8 OCT 36
[427] Report, Special Comm. on Investig. of the Munitions Industry, Senate 74th Congr./2nd Sess., 24FEB36
[428] LAT, 8 OCT 36
[429] Memo on Nye, ER file, Drew Pearson collection, LBJ Lib
[430] TIME, 19 OCT 36
[431] ChigTrib, 6 OCT 36
[432] Fokker deal, Nye collection, HH Lib
[433] ChigTrib, 7 OCT 36; UP, 7 OCT 36, Lewiston Daily Sun; AP, 7 OCT 36, Miami News
[434] TIME, 19 OCT 36
[435] AP, 7 OCT 36, Miami News
[436] ChigTrib, 7 OCT 36; AP, 7 OCT 36, Miami News
[437] New York Daily Sun, 7 OCT 36
[438] ChigTrib, 7 OCT 36
[439] Deposition by Fokker, clipping in McCracken papers, HH Lib
[440] TIME, 19 OCT 36
[441] NYT, 7 OCT 36
[442] UP, 7 OCT 36, Berkeley Daily Gazette
[443] TIME, 19 OCT 36
[444] Baruch: The Public Years, 267
[445] TIME, 19 OCT 36
[446] Pittsburgh Press, 7 OCT 36
[447] TIME, 19 OCT 36
[448] Memo on Nye, ER file, Drew Pearson collection, LBJ Lib
[449] Fokker deal, Gerald Nye collection, HH Lib
[450] Morgan, 457
[451] Frank Tichenor: *And --- Roosevelt and Farley Charged "Fraud and Collusion"!!* in Aero Digest, OCT 36
[452] Aero Digest, OCT 36, 23
[453] ChigTrib, 9 OCT 36
[454] ChigTrib, 10 OCT 36
[455] Harry Carr in LAT, 7DEC 34. For conspiracy around FDR's illness, see Lomazov: FDR's Deadly Secret.
[456] Smith, R. N.: The Colonel, 346
[457] Smith, R. N, 347-8
[458] Columnist Paul Mallon discussed Gardner's role in a June 1934 column (Reading Eagle, 29 JUN34).
[459] Aero Digest, OCT 36, 18
[460] Ibid
[461] Aero Digest, OCT 36, 21
[462] Jones, 237-44
[463] Aero Digest, OCT 36, 22
[464] NYT, 10 MAR 34
[465] Aero Digest, OCT 36, 23
[466] Aero Digest, OCT 36, 23
[467] Ickes, I/160
[468] Aviation file, Greenway/ AHS
[469] Telegram, Greenway to ER, 7 APR 34, Aviation File, Greenway/ AHS
[470] Telegram, CR to Greenway, same loc.
[471] Telegram, AC to Farley, cc Greenway, same loc.
[472] Aero Digest, OCT 36, 23
[473] Fokker deal, Nye collection, HH Lib
[474] Serling, 74

475 Berg, A. S.: Lindbergh, 205
476 Lawrence, 107
477 Lawrence, 131
478 Arnold: Global Mission, 145
479 NYT, 26 MAR 35
480 Goddard: Overview, 227
481 NYT, 21 JUL 34
482 NYT, 1 AUG 34, 2 AUG 34, 3 AUG 34
483 NYT, 29 JUN 35. See the documentary *Under a Jarvis Moon* by Noelle Kahanu, JAN 2010.
484 NYT, 9 DEC 33; FDR Day-by-Day, FDR Lib.
485 Letter, Pegler to Maj. Gen. Patrick Hurley, 25 AUG 47, Elliott file, Pegler Papers, HH Lib
486 NYT, 6 DEC 35
487 NYT, 7, 14, 15 MAR 33, 13 MAY 33; Kessler: The Sins of the Father, 56.
488 Ickes, 262
489 Ickes, I/353
490 NYT, 6 DEC 35
491 NYT, 6 DEC 35
492 NYT, 6 DEC 35
493 Carlisle Bergeron, Washington Post, 17 DEC 35
494 NYT, 26 MAR 35
495 Column, (assumed to be Pegler's draft), ER box, Pegler/HH. Following excerpts therefrom.
496 ibid
497 NYT, 5 OCT 35
498 NYT, 5 SEP 35
499 Herbert Corey in *the American Mercury*, 161, in the Pearson collection, LBJ Lib.
500 ChigTrib, 9 JUL 45. Other more parenthetical references to this transaction exist.
501 ER Testimony, 92, Hartford Loan file, ER box, Pegler/HH Lib
502 www.cityofbenbrook.com/flestorage, city history pages, accessed 7JUN11
503 Memo for Mr. McIntyre, PPF-4, FDR Lib
504 PR: I Love a Roosevelt, 143
505 Clipping, ER file, PPF, FDR Lib
506 PR: I Love a Roosevelt, 144
507 LAT, 27 JAN 35
508 LAT, 27 JAN 35
509 DallasMN, 03 APR 35, 04 APR 35
510 DallasMN, 18 AUG 35; NYT, 18 AUG 35
511 NYT, 18 AUG 35, Clip from UP/Dallas, 13 SEP 35, in Pearson collection, LBJ Lib
512 Drew Pearson column, 15 JUL 36; in DP collection, LBJ Lib.
513 AP, 6 SEP 35, in Spokane Daily Chronicle
514 DallasMN, 14 SEP 35
515 DallasMN, 11 DEC 36
516 DallasMN, 11 JUL 38
517 Letter, Anonymous to Pegler, 13 JUN 45, Hartford Loan File, ER box, Pegler/HH Lib
518 NYT, 17 JUL 35
519 NYT, 27 OCT 35
520 DallasMN, 8 JUN 35
521 DallasMN, 16 JUN 35
522 DallasMN, 23 JUN 35
523 NYT, 16 JUN 35
524 NYT, 22 JUN 35
525 Dallas MN, 15 JUL 35
526 NYT, 17 JUL 35
527 Serling, 233
528 Buck biography at library.tcu.edu/spcoll/finding%20aid_files/Buck%20-%20MS13.pdf, retr. 22 JUN 11.

[529] Serling, 283
[530] Lewiston Daily Sun, 16 JUL 35
[531] DallasMN, 5 SEP 35
[532] Drew Pearson / Robert Allen column, 12 SEP 35, in the Spokane Daily Chronicle.
[533] DallasMN, 04 OCT 35
[534] DallasMN, 12 APR 36, 12 NOV 39, et a.
[535] DallasMN, 6 SEP 35
[536] DallasMN, 01 OCT 35; ChigTrib, 8 JUL 45
[537] www.dfwradioarchives.com, retr. 29 JUL 11
[538] DallasMN, 12 JUN 37, 18 JUN 37
[539] DallasMN, 13 APR 45
[540] Coverage in Dallas News, 13 to 15 June 1936.
[541] DallasMN, 15 OCT 38, 18 FEB 39
[542] St. Joseph Gazette, 12 JUL 38
[543] GNS news service report, 5 JUL 45, in the Newburgh News
[544] DallasMN, 14 JUL 38; 1 DEC 38
[545] DallasMN, 30 APR 37
[546] DallasMN, 28 DEC 89
[547] Connally: In History's Shadow, 139, 143
[548] Clip from Corpus Christi Times, 11 MAY 37, ER box, Pegler/HH Lib
[549] NYT, 12 MAY 37, 14 MAY 37; Eleanor, My Day, 30 JUN 37.
[550] Criminal case No. 7354 summary, in ER box, Pegler/HH Lib
[551] Hot Oil, numerous reports in ER box, Pegler/HH Lib, incl. Nat. Petr. News, 19MAY37; Letter, Barger to Pegler, 7DEC45
[552] Memo, Mooers to Lindeman of the Seattle Post-Intelligencer, 17 DEC 45, Hot Oil, ER Box, Pegler/HH
[553] NYT, 9 MAR 37
[554] Drew Pearson column, St. Petersburg Times, 17 APR 45
[555] Burrough, Bryan: The Big Rich, 140-2.
[556] Letter from informer to Pegler, Oil, ER box, Pegler/HH Lib
[557] ChigTrib, 10 NOV 45
[558] Walter Trohan, ChigTrib, 11 NOV 45
[559] Burrough, 147-8
[560] FDR Appointments Day-to-Day, FDR Lib
[561] Connally, 143
[562] Tamm to Hoover, 8 OCT 45, FBI FOIA file on ER
[563] ER Testimony, 10 JUL 45, 84, in Hartford Loan file, ER box, Pegler/HH Lib
[564] Walter Trohan, ChigTrib, 10 NOV 45
[565] Jones, 293-303
[566] Burrough, 143-4
[567] ER Testimony, Pegler/HH Lib
[568] Morgan, 459
[569] See discussion of the allowance in Bryce: Cronies, 46-50 et passim.
[570] Burrough, 143-4
[571] NYT, 22 NOV 35; Ickes: Secret Diary, I/472-3; NYT 4 DEC 35
[572] ER: Rendez-vous, 112
[573] Ibid, 133
[574] Caro: Johnson, *The Path to Power*, 636-7, for the Texas money machine and the switch from ER to LBJ.
[575] ER: Rendez-vous, 102
[576] Gentry: J. Edgar Hoover, 225-8
[577] DallasMN, 11 APR 37
[578] Polk and Nell Shelton Oral History Interview (OHI), 2 MAR 68, by Paul Bolton, at LBJ Lib
[579] ER: the Conservators, 265-6
[580] DallasMN, 11 APR 37
[581] McKean: Peddling Influence, 121
[582] Peddling Influence, a recent analysis of Corcoran's reign, is an excellent source to his machinations.
[583] Dallek, 202 et passim.

584 Robert A. Caro: The Years of Lyndon Johnson, Means of Ascent, 81
585 ChigTrib, 8 JUL45
586 DallasMN, 7 MAR 36, 22 OCT 37
587 ChigTrib, 8 JUL45. The amounts quoted differ somewhat by source.
588 Ibid
589 NYT, 15 MAR 36, 6 MAY 36
590 Letter ER to John, 8 FEB 37, ER file, Boettiger Papers, FDR Lib
591 ER Testimony to US Treasury, 79, Hartford Loan file, ER box, Pegler/HH Lib
592 ER file, PPF-4, FDR Lib
593 Letter, Eleanor to Anna, 21 MAR 37, in Asbell, 80
594 Ickes, I/632
595 Ickes, I/692
596 TIME, 20 SEP 37; DallasMN 3 AUG 37, 6 JUL 37, 22 OCT 37
597 NYT, 18 AUG 38
598 ChigTrib, 8 JUL 45
599 ER Testimony, 3, 10 JUL 45, Hartford Loan file, ER box, Pegler/HH Lib
600 ChigTrib, 8 JUL 45
601 Herald-Journal, 30 OCT 40
602 Flynn, Country Squire, 111; supported by ER Testimony, 78, Hartford Loan file, ER box, Pegler/HH
603 TIME, 20 SEP 37
604 NYT, 10 OCT 40
605 ChigTrib, 8 JUL 45
606 TIME, 12 JUN 38; NYT 15 APR 39
607 Editorial, Pittsburgh Press, 8 JUN 37
608 CongRec, Appendix, 14 OCT 40, 6318-9
609 Unattributed letter to Pegler, 17 MAY 48, Radio file, ER box, Pegler/HH Lib
610 Office Memo, 2 OCT 45, Radio file, ER box, Pegler/HH Lib
611 ER Testimony, 10, Hartford Loan file, ER box, Pegle/HH Lib
612 Pegler column, 19 JUL 45, in Toledo Blade
613 Signed letter to Pegler, 26 JUN 45, Radio file, ER box, Pegler/HH Lib
614 Pegler column, 4 AUG 45, in Deseret News
615 Adams Testimony, 2, 23 JUL 45, Hartford file, ER box, Pegler/HH Lib
616 Reported in various forms. JR: Affectionately, 216; Collier, 376; Lash: E&F, 493
617 Herbert Corey in the American Mercury, 161, clip in Drew Pearson collection, LBJ Lib
618 Ibid
619 Curtis Roosevelt, 50
620 ChigTrib, 8 JUL 45
621 Herbert Corey in the American Mercury, 161, clip in Pearson/LBJ Lib
622 UP, 21 MAR 39, in Telegraph-Herald
623 NYT, 4 JUN 39
624 Ickes, III/600-1, 606.
625 Ickes, III/618
626 Curtis Roosevelt, 268
627 DallasMN, 7 MAR 39
628 Charles Hurd in NYT, 23 APR 39
629 Clipping in Boettiger papers, from UP report 25 MAR 39.
630 Letter, JB to ER, 29 MAR 39, in Boettiger papers, FDR Lib.
631 ChigTrib, 29 OCT 39; NYT, 6 SEP 39
632 NYT, 8 MAR 39
633 NYT, 16 MAR 36
634 Robert Caro: The Johnson Years: Means of Ascent: Chapter 6.
635 Dallek, 248-51, and passim, for summaries of LBJ's manipulation of the FCC.
636 AP/NYT, 8 MAR 39; INS/Palm Beach Post, 8 MAR 39.
637 Herbert Corey in the American Mercury, 161, clip in Drew Pearson collection, LBJ Lib

638 CongRec, Appendix, 28 JUN 39, 2930
639 DallasMN, 30 DEC 38
640 LAT, 9 SEP 40
641 DallasMN, 15 NOV 36
642 LAT, 10 APR 40
643 DallasMN, 17 JAN 39
644 JR: My Parents, 174
645 JR: My Parents, 163
646 JR: My Parents, 174
647 DallasMN, 19 JUL 40
648 Farley: The Roosevelt Years, 300
649 Farley, 360
650 Jones: 50 Billion $, 292-3
651 ER: Eleanor Roosevelt with Love, 74
652 NYT, 11 SEP 40
653 Connally: 141
654 DallasMN, 11 SEP 40
655 NYT, 25 OCT 39; TIME, 25 MAR 40.
656 LAT, 25 AUG 39
657 Windsor (Ont.) Daily Star, 30 OCT 39
658 Morgan, 460
659 NYT, 24 JUL 39
660 NYT, 27 NOV 39
661 Boettiger to ER, 27 MAR 39, ER file, Boettiger papers, FDR Lib
662 Memo to Hoover, 4 JUL 45, FBI file (FOIA) on ER.
663 AP, 10 JAN 40, in DallasMN; ChigTrib 6 JAN 40
664 Adams Testimony, 21, Hartford Loan file, ER box, Pegler/HH Lib
665 DallasMN, 4 DEC 39, 3 FEB 40
666 TIME, 13 NOV 39
667 NYT, 31 DEC 39; ChigTrib, 6 JAN 40; Schenectady Gazette, 6 JAN 40; NYT, 20 AUG 41
668 Advertising Age, 16 JUL 45, Radio file, ER box, Pegler/HH Lib
669 ibid
670 Adams Testimony, Hartford Loan file, ER box, Pegler/HH Lib
671 Ibid
672 Advertising Age, 16 JUL 45, clip in Broadcast file, ER box, Pegler/HH Lib
673 Washington Times-Herald, 29 AUG 45
674 JR: My Parents, 222
675 ER: Mother R, 222; Collier 460
676 Minority Report, Hartford Loan Investig., House Ways & Means Committee, 1OCT45. Estimates differ.
677 CongRec Appendix, 14 OCT 40, 6318
678 TIME, 25 JUN 45, 8 OCT 45; also Caruthers Ewing memo, 17 (Hartford case) in Pegler/HH Lib
679 Robert Caro: The Johnson Years: Means of Ascent: Chapter 6.
680 "preferential treatment" : Josephson: The strange death, 201-2. Supported by details following.
681 Sarasota Herald-Tribune, 25 MAR 44
682 Pegler column, 7 JAN 46, in the Milwaukee Sentinel; Pegler column, 3 MAY 46, in the Toledo Blade.
683 ibid
684 DallasMN, 21 JAN 39
685 ER: the Conservators, 66-7
686 Flynn: The Roosevelt Myth, 242
687 The News, 22 MAY, clipping in ER box, Pegler/HH Lib
688 DallasMN, 23 May 44
689 ibid
690 ER correspondence, Steven Early papers, FDR Lib
691 ibid
692 Pegler column, stamped 2 OCT 45, W. Times Herald, clipping in Pegler/HH Lib
693 Drew Pearson column, 21 JUN 45, clipping in Pegler/HH Lib

694 NYT, 13 OCT 45
695 NYT, 13 OCT 45; notes, ER file, Pearson/LBJ Lib
696 ChigTrib, 8 JUL 45
697 Walter Trohan in ChigTrib, 10 NOV 45
698 AP, 17 JUN 42, in Spokane Daily Chronicle
699 ChigTrib, 6 JUL 45; NYT, 20 AUG 41
700 AP, 14 JUN 45; Pegler column clipping from W. Times-Herald, 2 JUL 45, in Pegler ER files/HH Lib
701 Flynn: Country Squire, 109-10
702 Eleanor: This I Remember, 15-6
703 ER: Love Eleanor, 317
704 Congressional Record, 25 SEP 40, 12622
705 ER Testimony to US Treasury, 60, Hartford Loan File, ER box, Pegler/HH Lib
706 Senate Special Comm. to Investigate the Nat. Def. Prg. (Brewster Cm. Hearings), 1947, Part 40, 23976
707 Memo, Stimson to FDR, 8 APR 41, War Dept. file, PSF, FDR Lib
708 U.S.Army in WW2, Special Studies, Military Relations betw. the U.S. & Canada, Ch. 7, Eastern Ops., 190
709 Ibid, Chapter 4, Joint Defense Planning, 97-8
710 Eleanor: This I Remember, 225
711 Karlsson: The History of Iceland, 313-8
712 Glines: Bernt Balchen, 135
713 This is covered in great detail in both FRUS (Foreign Relations of the U.S.) and the Canadian equivalent, with quite different perspectives.
714 Lidegaard: *I Kongens Navn*, 152, et passim. "Minister" Kauffmann did not have formal Ambassador rank.
715 DUPI: Greenland, passim
716 U.S. Army in WW2, Special Studies, Mil. Relations btw the U.S. & Canada, Ch. 7, Eastern Ops., 164
717 Abbazia: Mr. Roosevelt's Navy, 186
718 Willoughby: The USCG in WW2, 98-100.
719 The Army Air Forces in World War II, Volume 1, 155; also Metmen in Wartime, 99
720 Ibid, 156
721 ER: As He Saw It, 47
722 Ickes, III/527
723 Abbazia, 185
724 Ibid, 179-80
725 Atlantic Bridge (Air Ministry, 1945)
726 ER: As He Saw It, 15
727 Glines: Bernt Balchen, 135
728 USAF Hist. Study 33: Admin. History of the Ferrying Cmd, 2-10, AFHRA; also Christie: Ocean Bridge
729 Administrative History of the Ferrying Command, 43-44, AFHRA
730 Ibid, 8-9
731 La Farge: The Eagle in the Egg
732 Senate, Brewster Committee Hearings, 1947, Part 40, 24038
733 ER: As He Saw It, 18
734 Discharge Document, ER, National Personnel Records Center; Giles to Spaatz, 21JAN45 (LOC/Spaatz)
735 JR: My Parents, 269
736 Service Record, President's Private File, FDR Lib; ER Wartime Service file, Pegler/HH Lib
737 ER Testimony, 49, Hartford Loan File, ER Box, Pegler/HH Lib
738 AFHRA biography of Dixon; accounting referred to in letter, Pegler to Lehner, 19 AUG 47, Pegler/HH
739 PR: I Love a Roosevelt, 151; NYT Obituary, ER, OCT 1990; NPRC discharge document for ER.
740 Oral History Interview (OHI) with General James Doolittle, AFHRA
741 ER Senate Testimony, Brewster Committee, 1947; also Pittsburgh Press, 5 AUG 47
742 Elliott's accidents are documented piecemeal in numerous places. Air Force Unit Histories, AFHRA; Pittsburgh Press, 10 MAR 44; Reading Eagle, 17 MAY 43; Miami News, 6 JUN 43.
743 Ibid; also Walter Winchell column, 6 SEP 43
744 NYT, 18 DEC 42; TIME, 28 DEC 42
745 TIME, 3 JUL 44

[746] AAF in WWII, 318, quotes Report, Captain E.R., 21st Recon. Sq. to TAG, 8 SEP 41; Memo for Col. Olds from Captain J.H.Rothrock, 6 SEP 41. Also referenced in History, North Atlantic Division, Air Transport Command, AFHRA.
[747] ER: As He Saw It, 15
[748] Christie: Ocean Bridge, 127, quotes several British and Canadian documents for the Ottawa meeting; NYT, 06JUN41, 07JUN41. -- [Report, Min. of Nat Def for Air, Mission to the UK (30-6-41 to 24-7-41) Note of meeting at Air Ministry 10-7-41; CAS to Undersec of state for ext affairs, 18-6-41; Bridle, Documents, 347]
[749] ER: Rendez-vous, 282
[750] ER: Rendez-vous, 398
[751] NYT, 2 MAY 41
[752] NYT, 14 MAY 41; FDR Appts Day-by-Day, FDR Lib
[753] Eleanor: This I Remember, 225
[754] Eleanor, My Day, 19 NOV 41, gwu.edu Eleanor papers.
[755] FBI FOIA file on ER, report 23 JUN 41
[756] ChigTrib, 26 JUL 41; also military reports on ER's movements in PPF, FDR Lib; FDR Day-to-Day.
[757] Letter, Eleanor to Anna, 22 JUN 41, in Asbell, 133
[758] ChigTrib, 26 JUL 41
[759] Reilly, 118
[760] National Archives, 201 file on ER
[761] Ibid
[762] ChigTrib, 06 JUN 41; NYT, 06 JUN 41
[763] FDR Appts. Day-to-Day, FDR Lib
[764] Arnold: Global Mission, 213
[765] Senate, Brewster Committee Hearings, 1947, Part A, 23977
[766] Grierson, 646-55
[767] Berg, 355-6
[768] Hobbs: Exploring about the North Pole of the Winds.
[769] *Journal of Meteorology*, Vol 2, Nr. 3, SEP 45, 135
[770] Christie: Ocean Bridge, 49-57
[771] Arnold: Global Mission, 215; also Arnold: War Diary for 1941
[772] President's speech as brought by AP, in the Portsmouth Times, 28 MAY 41.
[773] History of the North Atlantic Div., Air Transport Command, AFHRA; OHI with Gen. Crabb, AFHRA.
[774] Later Maj. Gen. Lacey. (see USAF e-biogr.). Was accompnd by USCG Lt. W. D. Shields, who also flew.
[775] R.A. Logan, "Notes on Greenland" manuscript in ATC History, AFRHA
[776] Bennett: Pathfinder, 116-7
[777] Atlantic Bridge
[778] Ancker, 22-3
[779] Carlson, Lifelines, 55
[780] OHI with MG Crabb, AFHRA
[781] Forbes, Alexander: Quest for a Northern Air Route, 1-2.
[782] NYT, 6 and 7 JUN 41; ChigTrib, 9 JUN 41. See also Ottawa conferences in Christie, Ocean Bridge.
[783] Christie, 362, references resulting report on *Construction of staging aerodromes in Grenland-Iceland ferrying route.*
[784] ER OHI, AFHRA
[785] Of the Dominion Geodetic Survey Branch
[786] Carr: Checkmate in the North, 79-85
[787] Carr, 80
[788] Admin. Hist. of the U.S. Atlantic Fleet in WW II, Volume II, Cmdr Task Force 24, 50-51
[789] Forbes, Alexander: Quest for a Northern Air Route, 4-8
[790] Carr, 52
[791] Christie, 129
[792] Arnold: Global, 318-9
[793] NADHIST, 21, 90-1, AFRHA.
[794] Arnold: Global, 330, 451
[795] See Carr for a participant's account of the building of Goose Bay; Christie for a historian's account.
[796] Carr, 84

797 Carr, 95
798 Memo, 8 JUL 41, PPF, FDR Lib
799 Forbes, 8-17
800 Forbes, 16
801 Forbes, 17
802 Report of the Expedition, AFHRA
803 Forbes, 66, 77
804 Christie, 132-3
805 Letter, Major Bert Hassell to CG NAW, 20 FEB 43, in NADHIST, AFHRA.
806 Memo to Deputy Chief of Air Staff, GHQ, U.S. Army, 27AUG41, Major Edward P. Curtis. In Arnold file, AFHRA
807 Report on building the Crystal Stations, AFHRA
808 Report on building the Crystal Stations, AFHRA
809 Christie, 132-3
810 Hobbs: Exploring. Also Carlson, 52
811 Glines, 133-49; uscg.mil/history/webcutters/Cayuga1932.asp, 27 FEB 11. New spelling: Kangerlussuak
812 Memo, FDR to SecState, SecWar, SecNavy, 18 APR 41, PSF, War Dept., FDR Lib.
813 Abbazia, 178.
814 Abbazia, 179
815 Admin. Hist. of the U.S. Atlantic Fleet in WW II, Volume II, Cmdr Task Force 24, 37 et passim
816 U.S. Army in WW2, Special Studies, 190 Guarding the U.S. and its Outposts, Chapter XVIII, 493
817 NADHIST, AFRHA
818 NYT, 20 AUG 41, 23 AUG 41, 28 AUG 41, 31 AUG 41, 8 SEP 41.
819 Eleanor, My Day, 9 SEP 41
820 Memo to Arnold, 10 SEP 41, Arnold file, AFHRA.
821 Memo Gen. George to Gen. Arnold, Arnold file, AFHRA
822 Glines, 135. The report is no longer in the Balchen papers, if it were.
823 NADHIST, AFHRA
824 Carlson, 56, 60
825 Carlson, 56
826 NADHIST, 31, AFHRA
827 NADHIST, AFHRA; USCG cutter Comanche log.
828 8th Wea Sq History, BE-2 monthly weather histories, AFHRA
829 BE-2 Monthly Reports, AFHRA
830 Forbes, 32
831 NADHIST, AFHRA
832 Carlson, 60
833 Eleanor: This I Remember, 225
834 Forbes, 15
835 Ward: Closest Companion, 185
836 Eleanor, My Day, 30 SEP 42, GWU Eleanor Project.
837 Knutsen: Arctic Sun on my Path, 224-6
838 NADHIST, Crimson Project monograph, AFHRA
839 Arnold: Diary, 223
840 Knutsen: Arctic Sun on my Path, 195
841 NADHIST, Crimson monograph, 1, AFHRA
842 Thomas: Metmen in Wartime, 107-8
843 NADHIST, 192 et passim, AFHRA
844 ER: As He Saw It, 16
845 JR: MY Parents, 258-65, details the adventures James had as a secret ambassador.
846 Churchill and Roosevelt: The Complete Correspondence, 207, C-99X. Also see R-45X, C-95X, C-96X.
847 Arnold: Diary: American Air Power comes of Age, 220
848 Churchill: *The Grand Alliance*, My meeting with Roosevelt, The Atlantic Charter, provides the PM's view.
849 Churchill: WW2 abridged, 490-3

[850] ER: As He Saw It, 16
[851] ER: Rendez-vous, 291
[852] Arnold: Diary: American Air Power comes of Age, 220
[853] Churchill: The Grand Alliance, 364
[854] Arnold Diary: American Air Power comes of Age, 220
[855] Arnold: Global Mission, 250
[856] OHI with Brig. Gen. Crabb, AFHRA
[857] ER: As He Saw It, 40, 57
[858] ER: Rendez-vous, 306
[859] Collier, 440
[860] ER: As He Saw It, 26
[861] ER: Rendez-vous, 293
[862] Arnold: Diary, American Air Power comes of Age (Vol. 1), 231
[863] LIFE, 25 AUG 41; NYT, 16 AUG 41
[864] ER: As He Saw It, 44
[865] ER: As He Saw It, 45
[866] Ward: Closest Companion, 142
[867] ER: As He Saw It, 57; NYT, 20 AUG 41, 27 AUG 41; DallasMN, 20 AUG 41
[868] NYT, 25 AUG 41
[869] Wireless Report to the Miami News, 30 AUG 41
[870] Ibid
[871] Based also on UP, AP repts, 21AUG, 26AUG, 30AUG41; NYT, 31AUG41; Eleanor, My Day, 11SEP41
[872] Senate, Brewster Committee Hearings, 1947, Part 40, 23977
[873] ER Personnel Summary found in PPF, FDR Lib
[874] ER: As He Saw It, 47; NYT, 12 SEP 41
[875] ER: Conservators, 229
[876] Letter, Eleanor to Anna, 7 DEC 41, in Asbell, 139
[877] Eleanor: This I Remember, 236; FDR Appts. Day-to-Day, FDR Lib; Eleanor, My Day, 10 DEC 41.
[878] Southeast Missourian, 23 DEC 41, w.photograph; AP reports quoted Harmon, 21 DEC 41.
[879] NYT, 17 DEC 41; AFHRA records; Personnel record in PPF, FDR Lib
[880] Senate, Brewster Committee Hearings, 1947, Part 40, 23869
[881] ER Testimony, Hartford Loan File, ER box, Pegler/HH Lib
[882] USAAF Combat Chronology, DEC 41 to JAN 42
[883] NYT, 27 FEB 42; also NPRC discharge summary for ER, 1945; Secret Service records for ER 1942
[884] ER: As He Saw It, 51
[885] Arnold: Global, 214
[886] Lash: Love, Eleanor, 376
[887] ER: Conservators, 230
[888] Ibid
[889] Letter DDE to Boettiger, Pre-Presidential Papers, 211, DDE Lib
[890] ER: Rendez-vous, 311
[891] Christie, 150-1
[892] Arnold: Global, 214
[893] FDR Appts. Day-to-Day, FDR Lib
[894] ER: As He Saw It, 55
[895] Goddard, 326; Maurer: Air Force Combat Units of World War II, 24
[896] Maurer
[897] ER discharge summary, 1945, NPRC; FDR Appts Day-to-Day, FDR Lib
[898] NYT, 11 MAR 42
[899] Christie, 161
[900] LAT, 3 MAY 42
[901] Raymond Clapper column, 9 MAY 42, in the Pitsburgh Press
[902] OHI with Edgar Cohen, National Archives
[903] UP reports, 3 MAY 42, 18 MAY 42
[904] Goddard: Overview, 304-5
[905] Air Force Serial Number Utility by Joe Baugher, Internet version.

906 www.nationalmuseum.af.mil/factsheets/factsheet.asp?id=2449; MACR (Missing Air Crew Reports).
907 Kean: Eyes of the Eighth, 4
908 Memo dd. to Arnold, Arnold file, AFHRA
909 Arnold: Global, 214, 288, 431; La Farge: Eagle in the Egg, 215.
910 ER PersRec, PPF, FDR Lib; UP, 27 DEC 42; NYT 28 DEC 42
911 Collier, 403
912 Eleanor, My Day, Toledo Blade, 8 MAY 42; TIME, 18 MAY 42; FDR Appts Day-to-Day.
913 Letters, Eleanor to Anna, 7, 11 MAY 42, in Asbell 143-145.
914 Report on Rusty Project, 22 May 1942, Arnold file, AFHRA
915 Ibid
916 Memo to Arnold, Subject Protection of Ferry Route, Northwest Africa, 30APR42, Arnold file, AFHRA
917 FDR Appts. Day-to-Day, FDR Lib
918 Air Route Guide Africa, Dir. Of Intel. Svcs., A-2 Div. Air Staff, HQ AAF, Washington, APR 42, in AFHRA ATC collection.
919 Report so named, AFHRA ATC collection
920 LAT, 20 APR 43
921 ER: As He Saw It, 65
922 LAT, 20 APR 43
923 ChigTrib, 6 JUN 43
924 TIME, 24 AUG 42
925 Miami News, 6 JUN 43
926 OHI with Edgar Cohen, National Archives
927 NYT, 16 APR 42
928 C.L. Sulzberger in NYT, 29 MAR 42
929 NYT, 21 OCT 40
930 ER: As He Saw It, 56; ChigTrib, 26 JAN 45; Lash: Love, Eleanor, 395
931 DallasMN, 13 JUN 42
932 Maurer: Units.
933 Secret Service Records pert. to protection of ER, 1942, FDR Lib.
934 DallasMN, 01 OCT 42; FDR Appts. Day-to-Day, FDR Lib
935 ER: As He Saw It, 57
936 Ibid
937 Letter FDR to Ruth G.R., 8 OCT 42, ER Vertical File, FDR Lib
938 ER: This I Remember, 276
939 Lash: Eleanor and Franklin, 660
940 Lash: Love, Eleanor, 411; ER: As He Saw It, 58-9
941 ER: Eleanor Roosevelt with Love, 86
942 ER: As He Saw It, 59; Parade Magazine, 10 OCT 82
943 History, Northwest Africa Photographic Reconnaissance Wing (NAPRWHIST), AFHRA
944 Butcher: My Three Years with Eisenhower, 140
945 Robert S. Ehlers, Jr.: BDA: ANGLO-AMERICAN AIR INTELLIGENCE, BOMB DAMAGE ASSESSMENT, AND THE BOMBING CAMPAIGNS AGAINST GERMANY, 1914-45. Dissertation, Ohio State University 2005, 228
946 Ehlers, 163-4
947 Ehlers, 14
948 Thompson: Flying in Coffin Corner, 317; many other examples.
949 Perry: Partners in Command, 150
950 Letter, Butcher to Carter, 19 APR 43, Corr. File 1942, Butcher collection, DDE Lib
951 Numerous letters, Corr 42, Butcher collection, DDE Lib
952 Letter, Carter to Butcher, Corr 42, Butcher collection, DDE Lib
953 AC to HB, inc. copy of letter from Jr to Sr, 20 MAR 43, Corr 42, Butcher collection, DDE Lib
954 USAF Historical Study nr. 114, p.120, AFHRA
955 Infield: Unarmed and Unafraid, 73
956 Thompson: Coffin Corner, 65-69

[957] ER: As He Saw It, 91
[958] Loomis: Fighting Firsts, 15
[959] NAPRWHIST, AFHRA
[960] Ibid
[961] Short History of Life of the Squadron, 12th PRS to 3rd PRG, 28 MAY 43, Group history, AFHRA
[962] Daily Intelligence Summaries, Norstad collection, DDE Lib
[963] Maurer: Units, and Operational History of NAPRW (NAPRWHIST), WG-90-HI, AFHRA
[964] NAPRWHIST
[965] Babington Smith, 159-160; Doolittle, 332; FDR Appts Day-by-Day, FDR Lib.
[966] Infield: Unarmed and Unafraid, 68
[967] Dengler, D: Seeing the Enemy, 72; NAPRWHIST
[968] Letter about recovery of the B-17s to Algiers, in ATC History, AFHRA
[969] Operational Difficulties and Problems, NAPRWHIST, AFHRA
[970] NAPRWHIST, AFRHA; Dengler, 72
[971] Senate, Brewster Committee Hearings, 1947, PART 40, 23978-9
[972] ER: The Conservators, 143; ER: Murder at the Palace, 26
[973] Letter, McDonald to Norstad, 8 AUG 47, Norstad file, DDE Lib
[974] Dengler, 60
[975] NAPRWHIST
[976] 3rd PRG History Files, AFHRA.
[977] Senate, Brewster Committee Hearings, 1947, PART 40, 23980
[978] ER: Mother R., 54
[979] Arnold: Global, 261
[980] Memo, McDonald to Norstad, 8 AUG 47, Norstad File, DDE Lib
[981] ER: Mother R, 54
[982] Memo, Humbrecht to ER, 12 JUL 43, NAPRW, AFHRA
[983] Humbrecht to ER, 19 APR 43, NAPRW, AFHRA
[984] Bodendieck to ER, 12 JUL 43, NAPRW, AFHRA
[985] Ibid
[986] Daily Intelligence Summaries, May and June 1943, Norstad collection, DDE
[987] USAF Historical Study nr. 114: The 12th Air Force in the North African Winter Campaign, AFHRA
[988] Letter, ER to Spaatz, 5 OCT 42, in 3rd PRG History, NAPRW
[989] Lt. Col. Eldridge to Col. MacDonald, A-2, 8 SEP 43, 12th AF, AFHRA. Eldridge was ER's chief of staff.
[990] Starck: Allied Photo Reconnaissance in World War II, 67
[991] Memo "Photographic Aviation" by Minton Kaye, late 1943, in AFHRA files.
[992] Letter, ER to Eleanor, 1 JUN 43, E. corr., FDR Lib
[993] See report of 20 AUG 43, Appendix.
[994] Letter, Lt. Col. Frank Dunn to ER, 17 JUL 43, in NAPRW files, AFHRA
[995] Connally, 88; MAPRW photo book in ER Vertical File, FDR Lib., by Capt Roger Larson, 12 DEC 42.
[996] Thompson, J. Steve with Peter C. Smith: *Air combat manoeuvres*, 240. Hersham (Surrey), Ian Allan, 2008
[997] Infield: Unarmed and Unafraid, 87
[998] Infield: Unarmed and Unafraid, 76
[999] D.K. Goodwin: No Ordinary Time, 471-3
[1000] Anna to Boettiger, 11 NOV 43, op. cit. 471
[1001] Curtis Roosevelt, 282-3
[1002] ER: As He Saw It, 96
[1003] Meacham, Jon: Franklin and Winston, 237
[1004] Babington Smith, 154-5
[1005] ER: As He Saw It, 60
[1006] ER: As He Saw It, 62
[1007] ER: Rendez-vous, 324
[1008] Arnold: Global, 389
[1009] Ward: Closest Companion, 198; Reilly, 146
[1010] ER: FDR Letters, 1393
[1011] Arnold: Global 391
[1012] ER: As He Saw It, 63

1013 Ward: Closest Companion, 198
1014 ER: As He Saw It, 68
1015 Harriman: Special Envoy, 187
1016 Interview in Miami News, 22 MAR 71
1017 ER: As He Saw It, 71
1018 Churchill, IV/682
1019 ER: As He Saw It, 76
1020 ER: As He Saw It, 117
1021 ER: Rendez-vous, 333
1022 Churchill, IV/685
1023 Ibid, 684
1024 Sherwood: Roosevelt and Hopkins, 696; contains an examination of the term's origin
1025 Churchill, IV, 687
1026 Anne Armstrong: "Unconditional Surrender: The Impact of the Casablanca Policy upon WW II." Rutgers Univ. Press 1961; also see discussion in Harriman, 189-90.
1027 Harriman: Special Envoy, 188
1028 Churchill, IV/688-691 discusses "U.S." at length.
1029 ER: As He Saw It, 184.
1030 ER: As He Saw It, 104
1031 Waller, 250-2
1032 ER: As He Saw it, 98
1033 ER: As He Saw It, 81
1034 Senate, Brewster Committee Hearings, 1947, PART 40, 23891
1035 Arnold: Global, 394
1036 Reilly, 158
1037 ER: As He Saw It, 120
1038 Reilly, 159
1039 MacMillan: The Blast of War, 201
1040 ER: Mother R, 237
1041 ER: As He Saw It, 109-111
1042 FRUS, Casablanca, 531-2
1043 ER to Eleanor, 28 FEB 43, quoted in D.K. Goodwin, 405.
1044 JR: My Parents, 268 and preface, x.
1045 ER: As He Saw It, 84; DallasMN, 6 MAR 43
1046 NYT, 15 JAN 43
1047 JR: Affectionately, 276; My Parents, 268
1048 ER: FDR Letters, II/1408-9
1049 NYT, 6 MAR 43
1050 ER: FDR Letters, II/1407-8
1051 Early/ER file, FDR Lib
1052 DallasMN, 5 MAR 43
1053 Winchell column, 12 MAY 43, in Milwaukee Sentinel
1054 Ed Weiner: Let's go to Press: A biography of Walter Winchell, 164, 186-7, and xiv.
1055 NAPRWHIST, report dated 14 OCT 1943, AFHRA. Unit histories are default source for this section.
1056 St.-Exupéry, 124, 146
1057 Stanley, 204
1058 Babington Smith: Air Spy, describes Cotton's efforts.
1059 Malayney: F-8 in AAF Service, AAHS Journal, Spring 2007
1060 Historical Data Concerning NAPRW, Part 6, AFHRA
1061 Senate, Brewster Committee Hearings, 1947, PART 40, 23978
1062 Bowman: Mosquito PR, 39
1063 Malayney: F-8 in AAF Service, AAHS Journal, Spring 2007
1064 Bowman, 37; Malayney (AAHS Journal, Spring 2007); Setchell Jr. Internet posting; and Toronto Aerospace Museum collection on the de Havilland Canada Mosquito.

[1065] Malayney, (AAHS Journal, Spring 2007)
[1066] Senate, Brewster Committee Hearings, 1947, PART 40, 24035
[1067] McDonald to Norstad, Norstad file, 8AUG47, DDE Lib
[1068] Taylor, J.W.R: Combat Aircraft of the World (1969)
[1069] Memo to Arnold, Arnold files, AFHRA
[1070] Senate, Brewster Committee Hearings, 1947, PART 43, 26238
[1071] Malayney: F-8 in AAF Service, AAHS Journal, Spring 2007
[1072] Bowman: Mosquito PR Squadrons of WW II, 38-62; for a summary of PR Mosquitoes in U.S. service.
[1073] Signal, Portal (?) to Arnold, 11 APR 43, Arnold file, AFHRA
[1074] ACM Christopher Courtney (chief RAF Supply) to Arnold, 6JUL43, Arnold file
[1075] RAF to War Dept. 15JUL43, Arnold file
[1076] Larrabee: C-in-C FDR, 32
[1077] Chapter XIX: An Old Mission Expands: Mapping and Engineer Strategic Intelligence, pp. 438-463 of The U.S. Army in World War II – The Corps of Engineers, 1958
[1078] Goddard, 247
[1079] Ehlers, 161-2
[1080] Ehlers, 228
[1081] Malayney: F-8 in AAF Service, AAHS Journal, Spring 2007
[1082] Isserman, 208-210
[1083] TIME, 2 AUG 43; UP, in Pittsburgh Press, 25 JUL 43
[1084] Leonard Lyons column, in DallasMN 7 NOV 43. Refers to William L. White article in Readers Digest, condensed from "They fight with Cameras" in American Mercury, NOV 43, 537-42.
[1085] American Mercury, NOV 43, 537
[1086] American Mercury, NOV 43, 542
[1087] FDR Appts. Day-to-Day, FDR Lib
[1088] 5th PRW History, AFHRA
[1089] Daily squadron notes, 5th PRS, 26 NOV 43, AFHRA
[1090] UP, 23 DEC 43, in San Jose News
[1091] Infield: Unarmed and Unafraid, 80-1
[1092] Schiff: St.Exupéry, 207
[1093] St.-Exupéry: Wartime Writings, 137-8
[1094] Rumbold: The Winged Life, 201
[1095] Schiff, 411
[1096] Schiff, 412
[1097] FDR Appts Day-by-Day, FDR Lib
[1098] LAT, 25 JUL 43
[1099] Reynolds: The Curtain Rises, 191
[1100] Katz: The Battle for Rome, 12 etc. has discussion of the disputed casualties and the subsequent events.
[1101] Stanley, ch. 5. This book is the bible for technical information on WW2 photographic reconnaissance. Also, see P-38 Pilot's Manual for camera installation and operation.
[1102] The details are excellently covered in Chapter XIX: An Old Mission Expands: Mapping and Engineer Strategic Intelligence, pp. 438-463 of The U.S. Army in World War II – The Corps of Engineers, 1958
[1103] NYT, 26 MAY 45; Minton Kaye file, report quoting Spaatz commendation to Roosevelt, AFHRA.
[1104] 5th PRG History files, AFHRA
[1105] Infield: Unarmed and Unafraid, 73-4
[1106] Tregaskis: Invasion Diary, 5-6
[1107] ER: As He Saw It, 130-1
[1108] Letter, NAPRW, 29 JUL 43, NAPRWHIST, AFHRA
[1109] Arnold: Global 490
[1110] 3rd PRG History notes, AFHRA
[1111] 3 PRG files, AFHRA
[1112] 3 PRG files, AFHRA
[1113] Narrative in 3rd PRG History, AFHRA.
[1114] Thompson: Coffin corner, 157-64
[1115] Peter S. Rask collection, Trailer case, AFHRA
[1116] ibid

1117 Thompson: Coffin Corner, 157
1118 Ibid, 164
1119 Thompson, 31-2
1120 NYT, 14 FEB 33; TIME, 26 MAR 35
1121 AP, 23 JUL 41, Baltimore Sun
1122 DallasMN, 08 NOV 35
1123 Thompson, 32
1124 JR: My Parents, 182-3; also many other examples in this book and JR: Affectionately, FDR.
1125 Letter, Weaver to FDR, Elliott correspondence, PPF, FDR Lib
1126 Lash: Eleanor and Franklin, 661
1127 For examples see Perry: Partners in Command, 146, 152, 168, 174, 180
1128 Doolittle: I could never, 330
1129 Leonard Slater in San Diego Magazine, FEB 76
1130 Summersby: Eisenhower, 23
1131 George Hall Papers, OHI with Mattie Pinette, 66-67, George Hall Papers, DDE Lib
1132 Collier, 414
1133 D'Este, Carlo: A Soldier's Life, 389
1134 Collier, 415
1135 Senate, Brewster Committee Hearings, 1947, PART 40, 23981
1136 ER to Grace Tully, 6 JAN 43, Grace Tully Archive, FDR Lib.; FDR Appts Day-to-Day, FDR Lib.
1137 Tully: FDR was by Boss, 124-5
1138 Collier, 415
1139 Leonard Slater in San Diego Magazine, FEB 76.
1140 DallasMN, 24 JUN 44; Air Force Accident summaries. A standard internet obituary for Eidson claimed the sabotage. See also Malayney, F-8 in USAAF Service, AAHS Journal, Spring 2007.
1141 Leonard Slater in San Diego Magazine, FEB 76
1142 AP, 23 JUN 44, in DallasMN, 24 JUN 44
1143 ER: Mother R, 58; Letter, ER to Eleanor, 13 MAR 44, E. corresp. FDR Lib.
1144 TIME, 27 MAR 44; DallasMN, 19 APR 44
1145 DallasMN, 18 JUL 44
1146 D'Este, 318-9
1147 D'Este, 464; Summersby: Eisenhower was my boss, 102-3
1148 Senate, Brewster Committee Hearings, 1947, PART 40 23081-2
1149 ER: As He Saw It, 125, 128
1150 Senate, Brewster Committee Hearings, 1947, PART 40, 23083-4
1151 Ibid
1152 AFHRA F-11 Case History, 1; SBC Hearings, 1947, PART 40, 23807
1153 SBC Hearings, 1947, PART 40, 23819
1154 SBC Hearings, 1947, PART 40, 24448
1155 Hyland, Lawrence: Call me Pat, 202
1156 SBC Hearings, 1947, PART 40, 23811
1157 SBC Hearings, 1947, PART 40, 23843
1158 Case History
1159 Senate, Brewster Committee Hearings, 1947, PART 40, 23820
1160 SBC Hearings, 1947, PART 40, 24495
1161 SBC Hearings, 1947, PART 40, 24483
1162 SBC Hearings, 1947, PART 40, 23086
1163 SBC Hearings, 1947, PART 40, 23968-9
1164 SBC Hearings, 1947, PART 40, 23989
1165 DallasMN, 14 AUG 43
1166 DallasMN, 17 MAR 44
1167 Marrett: Howard Hughes Aviator, 56, 82
1168 SBC Hearings, 1947, PART 40, 23990
1169 SBC Hearings, 1947, PART 40, 23990

[1170] SBC Hearings, 1947, PART 40, 23991
[1171] SBC Hearings, 1947, PART 43, 26583
[1172] SBC Hearings, 1947, PART 43, 26587
[1173] NYT, 06 AUG 47
[1174] FDR Appts. Day-to-Day, FDR Lib
[1175] SBC Hearings, 1947, PART 40, 23825
[1176] SBC Hearings, 1947, PART 40, 23829
[1177] Ward: Closest Companion, 239-40
[1178] SBC Hearings, 1947, PART 43, 26472, 26478
[1179] Walter Winchell column, 01 OCT 43, Morgan County News
[1180] SBC Hearings, 1947, PART 43, 26368, 26378, e.a.
[1181] SBC Hearings, 1947, PART 40, 24396
[1182] SBC Hearings, 1947, PART 40, 23831; NYT, 2 AUG 47
[1183] SBC Hearings, 1947, PART 43, 26343
[1184] SBC Hearings, 1947, PART 40, 23834
[1185] SBC Hearings, 1947, PART 43, 26364, 27212
[1186] SBC Hearings, 1947, PART 40, 23815, 24069; found in President's. Secretary File, Arnold/82, FDR Lib.
[1187] Letter, Birdwell to Marvin MacIntyre, 11 JUL 42, OF3321, Howard Hughes, FDR Lib.
[1188] SBC Hearings, 1947, PART 43, 26375
[1189] NYT, 9 SEP 43
[1190] SBC Hearings, 1947, PART 40
[1191] SBC Hearings, 1947, PART 40, 24267
[1192] SBC Hearings, 1947, PART 43, 26238
[1193] SBC Hearings, 1947, PART 40, 24080, 24081
[1194] SBC Hearings, 1947, PART 43, 26589
[1195] SBC Hearings, 1947, PART 43, 26580
[1196] Arnold: Global, 378; FDR Appts Day-by-Day
[1197] Goddard: Overview, 360
[1198] Hack, Richard: Hughes, 146-7
[1199] Leonard Slater in San Diego Magazine, JAN 76.
[1200] Leonard Slater in San Diego Magazine, JAN 76.
[1201] Collier, 415
[1202] Entertainment Weekly, 11 MAR 11
[1203] LAT, 10 MAR 2004
[1204] Russell, Jane: My Path and Detours
[1205] Higham: Howard Hughes, 104
[1206] Higham, discussion of sources.
[1207] Leonard Slater in San Diego Magazine, JAN 76
[1208] ibid
[1209] An interesting account of Meyer is in McNulty: Errol Flynn, 163-4.
[1210] NYT, 03 AUG 47
[1211] Winchell column, 7 SEP 43, in St. Petersburg Times
[1212] Leonard Slater in San Diego Magazine, JAN 76
[1213] Ward: Closest Companion, 240
[1214] Connally, 81
[1215] Connally, 82, 88; ER jumps, see ER interview in appendix.
[1216] ER: the Conservators, 202
[1217] Serling: Eagle, 40-1
[1218] JE Smith, 710 n117; Hans Baur (pilot) autobiography for Hitler's election campaign.
[1219] ER: Untold Story, 232
[1220] NYT, 14 APR 19
[1221] FDR Diary, 14 AUG 18. In FDR Lib.
[1222] FDR Diary, 17 AUG 18. In FDR Lib.
[1223] NYT, 3 JUL 32
[1224] FDR Library exhibits show photograph of the Pauillac flight; www.history.navy.mil/ download/ ww1-10.pdf retr 15 MAR 11; Aircraft identified in Taylor, Combat Aircraft of the World, 468

1225 ER: As He Saw It, 65
1226 Roosevelt, F.D.: England's Air Force and Ours, article in U.S. Air Service, reprinted NYT, 29 JUN 19.
1227 Letter, ER to Eleanor, 23 MAY 43, reprinted in Eleanor: This I Remember, 288
1228 Letter, ER to Eleanor, 1 JUN 43, E. corr. FDR Lib
1229 Doolittle: I could never, 400
1230 Letter, ER to Eleanor, 29 MAY 43, E. Corresp. FDR Lib
1231 ChigTrib, 17 MAY 43
1232 NYT, 5 AUG 43
1233 Reading Eagle, 17 MAY 43
1234 Letter, ER to Eleanor, 23 MAY 43, reprinted in Eleanor: This I Remember, 288
1235 Keyssar: Remembering War, 176-7
1236 UP report from Switzerland, 22 NOV 43, in Spokane Daily News; Asbell, 172.
1237 See Appendix.
1238 From a narrative, "Frontiersmen of the Air," in the NAPRW History, AFHRA. Also recounted in Fort Worth Star-Telegram, 18 APR 43, clip in PPF, FDR Lib. This was Amon Carter's newspaper.
1239 Loomis: Fighting Firsts, 23-24
1240 NYT, 28 MAY 42
1241 Lash: Love, Eleanor, 395
1242 ChigTrib, 26 JAN 45
1243 CongRec, 5 MAR 43, 1618
1244 ER: FDR Letters, 1396
1245 ER: As He Saw It, 132; Rendez-vous, 346
1246 ER: Rendez-vous, 347
1247 ER: As He Saw It, 134
1248 ER: Rendez-vous, 347
1249 ER: As He Saw It, 135
1250 Reilly, M.: Reilly of the White House, 168-169
1251 Letter, FDR to Eleanor, 21 NOV 43, in ER: FDR, His Personal Letters, II/1469-70
1252 ER: Rendez-vous, 347
1253 ER: As He Saw It, 139
1254 ER: As He Saw It, 146
1255 ER: As He Saw It, 143-51
1256 ER: As He Saw It, 154
1257 ER: As He Saw It, 153
1258 D'Este, 164; ER: As He Saw It, 167
1259 Summersby, 99-105
1260 Leonard Lyons column, in DallasMN 02 JAN 44
1261 ER: As He Saw It, 168
1262 Dudgeon: Hidden Victory, passim
1263 Eubank: Summit at T., 116
1264 FRUS, 460 (President's Log)
1265 ER: Rendez-vous 350; As He Saw It, 168
1266 ER: As He Saw It, 172
1267 Kern, G.: How Uncle Joe bugged FDR, Studies in Intelligence (CIA), Vol. 47:1, 2003
1268 Reilly, 175
1269 Havas: Hitler's plot to kill the Big Three, 218 etc.
1270 Tolstoy, N.: Stalin's Secret War, 57
1271 Mayle, Paul: Eureka Summit, 52
1272 Montefiore: Stalin, 463
1273 Meacham, 253
1274 Mayle, 133
1275 ER: Rendez-vous, 389
1276 ER: As He Saw It, 179
1277 ER: As He Saw It, 186-7

[1278] ER: As He Saw It, 190-1
[1279] Mayle, 96
[1280] ER: Rendez-vous, 358
[1281] Churchill: WW II, Closing the Ring: V/XX/330
[1282] Montefiore: Stalin, 470
[1283] Eubank, 72 quoting Eden's memoirs.
[1284] Meacham: Franklin and Winston, 316
[1285] Eubank, 318
[1286] Meacham, 259
[1287] Eubank, 310
[1288] ER: As He Saw It, 195
[1289] Mayle, 97
[1290] Persico, 8
[1291] Jesse Jones, 287
[1292] ER: The Conservators, 113
[1293] ER: As He Saw It, 192
[1294] NYT, 25 NOV 49; Eleanor, My Day, 30 MAR 59
[1295] ER: Mother R, 173
[1296] ER in Papers of Robert D. Graff, Transcripts of Interviews, Draft TV Scripts, Scene 100B, FDR Lib.
[1297] Ferell: DDE, Diaries, 104-5
[1298] ER: As He Saw It, 212
[1299] DDE: Crusade, 227
[1300] ER: Rendez-vous, 363-4
[1301] ER: Rendez-vous, 364-5
[1302] ER: the Conservators, 234
[1303] ER: As He Saw It, 209
[1304] ER: As He Saw It, 210
[1305] ER: As He Saw It, 212
[1306] ER: FDR His Personal Letters, 1471
[1307] Anna to John Boettiger, 27 DEC 43, quoted in D.K.Goodwin, 480
[1308] ER: As He Saw It, 215
[1309] ER Personnel Record in Elliott file, PPF, FDR Lib.
[1310] Brugioni: Eyes in the Sky, passim.
[1311] Kreis: Piercing the Fog, examines relations between U.S. and British reconnaissance commands.
[1312] CIA: Center for the Study of Intelligence, Studies in Intelligence, Vol. 49, Nr. 3, 41 (2005)
[1313] ER: As He Saw It, 215-6
[1314] 325th PRW History, AFHRA (main source for this chapter) has the founding order for 8th PRW.
[1315] Unit History, WG-325-HI, AFHRA
[1316] Kreis, 82
[1317] Bowman: Mosquito PR units of WW 2, passim
[1318] Signal, Portal (?) to Arnold, 11 APR 43, Arnold file, AFHRA
[1319] Malayney: F-8 in USAAF Service, AAHS Historical Journal, Spring 2007.
[1320] Kreis, 89-90
[1321] GP-25-HI (BOMB) History, and associated reports, correspondence, and photographs, AFRHA
[1322] Maurer: Air Force Combat Units
[1323] Bowman, 39
[1324] Operational detail is from 25th Bomb Group History, AFHRA, except as stated.
[1325] 652 PRS History, November 1944, AFHRA, and accompanying records.
[1326] Unit History, WG-325-HI, AFHRA
[1327] Kreis, 90
[1328] OHI with General Doolittle, AFHRA
[1329] LAT, 10 MAR 44
[1330] Foreign Aircraft Landings in Ireland 1939-46 by D. Burke, at www.csn.ul.ie/~dan/. htm retr. 20JUL11
[1331] ER wartime service, ER box, Pegler/HH Lib
[1332] Stanley, 153
[1333] Goddard: Overview, 319

1334 Goddard, 321
1335 Goddard, 321-3
1336 Goddard, 320-3
1337 Goddard, 324-5
1338 OHI with Gen. Doolittle, AFHRA
1339 ER file, PPF, FDR Lib
1340 Bowman, 39
1341 MICFILM 28102, Arnold File, AFHRA
1342 Arnold: Global, 492 et passim
1343 Arnold: Global, 479
1344 Air & Space Magazine, March 2001. The USSR built 845 copies.
1345 SBC Hearings, PART 40, 24322
1346 Marrett: Howard Hughes, has details of Shoop's career at Hughes Aircraft.
1347 www.nationalmuseum.af.mil/ exhibits/ presidential/ index.asp, retr. 23NOV10
1348 MICFILM 28102, Arnold file, AFHRA
1349 Goddard, 277-80
1350 The professional details (not the personal ones) of the mapping controversy are excellently covered in Chapter XIX: An Old Mission Expands: Mapping and Engineer Strategic Intelligence, pp. 438-463 of The U.S. Army in World War II – The Corps of Engineers, 1958
1351 Ibid, 447
1352 Goddard, 314-7
1353 Goddard, 311-2
1354 Mapping and Engineer Strategic Intelligence, (op. cit.), 451
1355 Ibid, 453
1356 Ibid
1357 Goddard, 326
1358 OHI with ER, conducted by Goddard, in AFHRA OHI files.
1359 FBI file on ER, report 8 MAR 44, FBI FOIA file.
1360 Arnold: Global, 493-4
1361 History of Eastern Command, USSTAF in Europe, 13 Dec 1944, AFHRA (ESCOMHIST, chaps. 1-14)
1362 ESCOMHIST, 1/1
1363 ESCOMHIST, 1/12 , 10/11
1364 Arnold: Global, 471
1365 ESCOMHIST, 1/6-7
1366 Deane: Strange Alliance, 3
1367 ESCOMHIST, 1/7
1368 Deane, 20
1369 Deane, 23
1370 Harriman, 254
1371 Deane, 16-21
1372 Deane, 45; Mayle, 133; ESCOMHIST 2/1,2,13
1373 ER: As He Saw It, 206
1374 Mayle, 85
1375 Arnold: Global, 467
1376 Mayle, 133
1377 FRUS, US-USSR Relations, 1943, 593
1378 ESCOMHIST, 2/13
1379 Keyssar: Remembering War, 181
1380 Infield: The Poltava Affair, speculated thus on Stalin's motives, passim.
1381 Record of conversation, Anderson w. Col. Hickam, 26 APR 44, Frantic file, Anderson Collection, HHI
1382 Harriman: Special Envoy, 296
1383 ESCOMHIST, 2/13
1384 Office diary, box 2, 17FEB 44, Gen. Anderson collection, Hoover Inst., Stanford Un. (Anderson/HHI)
1385 ER: As He Saw It, 216. SHAEF: Supreme HQ Allied Expeditionary Forces.

[1386] ESCOMHIST, 2/11
[1387] Daily Progress Report for General Hugh J. Knerr, message 4 February, Frantic 522.115, AFHRA
[1388] Office diary, box 2, 17 FEB 44, 8 FEB 44, Anderson/HHI
[1389] Record of meeting, 8 FEB 44, Spaatz presiding, Frantic file, Anderson Collection, HHI
[1390] Directive, Spaatz to Cullen, 8 FEB 44, Frantic file, Anderson Collection, HHI
[1391] Chronology, Frantic file, Anderson Collection, HHI
[1392] ESCOMHIST, 11/56; Deane also gave an interesting account of his failed efforts to bypass his handler.
[1393] ESCOMHIST, 2/11, 3/33, 9/42, 10/27; Chronology, Frantic file, Anderson Collection, HHI
[1394] Infield: Poltava, 36; ESCOMHIST, 11
[1395] Infield: Poltava, 40
[1396] Deane, 110
[1397] Letter, Cullen to Deane, 12 MAY 44, Frantic file, Anderson Collection, HHI
[1398] ER: As He Saw It, 216
[1399] Keyssar: Remembering War, 178-9
[1400] ESCOMHIST, 3/5
[1401] ESCOMHIST, 7/11
[1402] ESCOMHIST, 11/53
[1403] Deane, 108
[1404] Diary of Major General Alfred A. Kessler, Frantic file 522.059 1-3, AFHRA
[1405] ESCOMHIST, 11/35
[1406] ESCOMHIST, 2/12; Infield, 41-2
[1407] Infield, 42
[1408] Frantic file, reports on meetings, Anderson/HI. Several reports dated 11 MAY 44.
[1409] Keyssar: Remembering War, 177-8
[1410] Irving, David: The Mare's Nest, 278
[1411] Irving, 281-2, 288-9; ESCOMHIST 5/23-24 details Air Force participation in this mission.
[1412] Radio, Anderson to Spaatz, 12 MAY 44, Frantic file, Anderson/HHI
[1413] Letter, Anderson to Spaatz, 21 MAY 44, Frantic file, Anderson/HHI
[1414] Memo to Col. Weicker, 13 MAY 44, Frantic file, Anderson/HHI
[1415] Letter, Deane to Gen. Evstigneev (liaison), 13 MAY 44, Frantic file, Anderson/HHI
[1416] ESCOMHIST, 3/17
[1417] NYT, 25 MAY 44
[1418] Radio, Deane to Eaker, Arnold, Harriman, 16 MAY 44, Frantic file, Anderson/HHI
[1419] ESCOMHIST, 2/12; Infield, 49
[1420] ESCOMHIST, 3/36
[1421] ESCOMHIST, 2/4
[1422] Butcher, 547
[1423] TIME, 12 JUN 44
[1424] For an insightful discussion, see David Mayers: The Ambassadors, Oxford, New York, 1995.
[1425] Kessler diary, Frantic file, AFHRA
[1426] ESCOMHIST, 9/17, 11/36
[1427] ESCOMHIST, 4/16
[1428] Teletype Messages, Frantic file, Anderson/HI
[1429] Memo, Briefing Information for Combat Crews, F.J. Sutterlin, 17 JUN 44, Frantic file, Anderson/HHI
[1430] Radio, Deane to Spaatz, 31 MAY 44, Frantic file, Anderson/HI
[1431] ESCOMHIST, 4/25
[1432] Kean: Eyes, 133
[1433] Infield, 111
[1434] ESCOMHIST, 4/28
[1435] Kean, 138
[1436] La Farge: Eagle, 187-8
[1437] Infield, 55, 111
[1438] Keyssar: Remembering War, 178
[1439] Bishop: FDR's Last Year, 259
[1440] Infield, 92; Boyd, 217; Montefiore, 536, 539
[1441] Infield, 89, 107

1442 Eleanor: On My Own, 68
1443 ESCOMHIST; Keen, Eyes, 146
1444 ESCOMHIST, 5/6
1445 ESCOMHIST, 5/8, 9
1446 Col. Archie Old, Jr., (Task Force Commander) Report on shuttle mission to Russia to Commanding General, 3rd Bomb Div., 6 JUL 44, Frantic operation, Anderson/HHI
1447 Infield, 109, 125
1448 ESCOMHIST, 5/10, Infield 139
1449 Old, Report on shuttle mission, 3
1450 ESCOMHIST, 6/11
1451 ESCOMHIST, 6/12
1452 ESCOMHIST, 6/12
1453 Olds: Report, 8 (op.cit.)
1454 Radio, Deane to Arnold, 25 JUN 44, Frantic file, Anderson/HHI
1455 Olds, Report, Appendix
1456 ESCOMHIST, 6/11
1457 ESCOMHIST, 6/15
1458 Infield, 127
1459 Infield, 148
1460 Deane, 122
1461 Jackson, 142-3
1462 Infield, 226; ESCOMHIST passim
1463 ESCOMHIST, 10/16
1464 Montefiore, 536-9
1465 ESCOMHIST 6/28, 27
1466 NYT, 4 OCT 44, 12 OCT 44
1467 ESCOMHIST, 5/40-2
1468 Arnold: Global, 524-5
1469 Chronology of operations from ESCOMHIST.
1470 Deane, 123
1471 Keyssar: Remembering War, 179
1472 Ibid
1473 Martin Gilbert, Could Britain have done more to stop the horrors of Auschwitz, The Sunday Times, 27 JAN 05; Dino Brugioni, The Holocaust Revisited: A Retrospective Analysis of the A-B exterm. complex, Washington D.C., 1979. Brugioni, Military Intelligence, IX/1, JAN 83, 50-55 has a convincing professional analysis of the recon. issue; Stanley, 340-351, provides a technical discussion with imagery.
1474 History, 325th PRW, 1945, AFHRA. Brugioni also emphasizes this point.
1475 Medoff, Rafael: The Roosevelt Administration, David Ben Gurion, and the Failure to Bomb Auschwitz: A Mystery Solved, 13
1476 Harriman, 340 et passim
1477 Deane, 90 and 98
1478 Deane, 99
1479 Arnold: Global, 387
1480 Report on Status of Morale in the Eastern Command, 5 OCT 44, Frantic file 522.115-1, AFHRA
1481 ESCOMHIST, 7 passim
1482 Kean, 208
1483 Infield, 223-5
1484 Letter, Gousev to Spaatz, 22 MAY 44, Frantic file, Anderson/HHI
1485 Doolittle, 411, 485
1486 Deane, 320
1487 Butcher, 546-7
1488 ESCOMHIST, 4/17, 7/30
1489 ESCOMHIST, 4/17
1490 ESCOMHIST, 5/8,9

[1491] Brugioni: Eyes in the Sky, 55
[1492] ESCOMHIST, 10/33
[1493] Letter, ER to Eleanor, 14 SEP 45, Eleanor correspondence w. ER, FDR Lib.
[1494] Senate, Brewster Comm. Hearings, 1947, PART 40, 23935; ER Testim., Hartford Loan File, Pegler/HH
[1495] 325th PRW History, WI-325-HI, AFHRA
[1496] Goddard: Overview, 360
[1497] Kean, 260; also, web.ukonline.co.uk/lait/site/index.htm, retr. 21 Dec 10; the need to urge the jet program ahead was expressed only one week earlier, in Giles to Spaatz, 21 JAN 45 (LOC/Spaatz/I-20).
[1498] Irving: The Mare's Nest, 54
[1499] Irving, 312
[1500] Starck: Allied Photoreconnaissance, 77; Leaf: Above all Unseen, 99
[1501] Operation CROSSBOW is well covered in standard works, inc. the official *The USAAF in World War II.*
[1502] Arnold: Global, 499
[1503] Irving, 245, 313
[1504] Leaf, 102
[1505] Irving, 250
[1506] Arnold: Global, 497-9
[1507] Final Report, Aphrodite Project, intro., AFHRA
[1508] Olsen: Aphrodite, 46, 308
[1509] NYT, 25 OCT 45; Look, 27 FEB 62
[1510] Unit History, August, 25th Bomb Group, AFHRA
[1511] Joe Baugher's database of U.S. military aircraft serial numbers (Internet version, 2011).
[1512] Searls, 243
[1513] Searls, 245-6
[1514] Teletyped tasking order, Mission folder, Aphrodite box, AFHRA
[1515] Report, Office of the Operations Officer, Station 140 (RAF Winfarthing), to 3rd Bomb Division, 14 AUG 1944, Captain John M. Sande signing. AFHRA.
[1516] Andrew Wilson, reprinted in the Youngstown Vindicator, 23 NOV 72
[1517] Searls, 263
[1518] Olsen: Aphrodite, Desperate Mission, 252
[1519] Olsen, passim
[1520] This report is also in the Air Force file on APHRODITE. The Navy referred to it publicly in 1945.
[1521] Aphrodite Final Report, AFHRA
[1522] Olsen, 239-40
[1523] Searls, 250
[1524] 8th AAFCCU history for AUG 44, 25-GP-HI (Recon), AFHRA
[1525] Bowman, 47
[1526] Telegram to AWW, cipher, Top Secret, 17 AUG 44, AFHRA Aphrodite project box.
[1527] Mr. Mick Muttitt from Blythburg reported this on April 1995 on the Internet (see Norfolk and Suffolk Aviation Museum web site). He knew aircraft recognition, and the event made a big impression on the kid.
[1528] Final Report, Aphrodite Project, 8, AFHRA
[1529] Olsen, 231 et passim
[1530] NYT, 15 AUG 44, 17 AUG 44
[1531] NYT, 25 OCT 45; AP / Spartanburg Herald-Journal, 25 OCT 45. UP / Newburgh News, same.
[1532] NYT, 25 OCT 45
[1533] NYT, 23 NOV 63; also Bob Considine column on Kennedys, INS, 10 MAY 57, in St Petersburg Times.
[1534] Beschloss: Kennedy & Roosevelt, 257; Olsen, 316-7; FDR Appts Day-to-Day, FDR Lib
[1535] Corbis Images (former Bettman Archive)
[1536] Beschloss, 106
[1537] Kessler: The Sins of the Father, 137 etc., examined the Joe-Jimmy relationship in detail.
[1538] Beschloss, ch. 4, for a neutral account of the beginning alliance; Kessler, chapter 8, for anything but.
[1539] Alva Johnston in Saturday Evening Post, 2 JUL 38
[1540] ibid
[1541] Follow-up in Saturday Evening Post, 18 MAY 40
[1542] Kessler, Beschloss describe the J-J relationship. Beschloss, 292, Notes.
[1543] ER: Rendez-vous, 55

1544 Beschloss, 82-3; also see Okrent, 366-71 for the JR-JK trip.
1545 Kessler: The Sins of the Father, 107
1546 Final Report, Aphrodite Project, 9
1547 Olsen, 308-9
1548 ER Interview, Boston Herald, 10NOV86. Original claim was in Bild am Sonntag (Germany) 9 NOV 86.
1549 NYT, 15 AUG 44
1550 Beschloss, 262
1551 ER: An Untold Story, 315
1552 Koskoff, David: Joseph P. Kennedy, A Life and Times, 504; Beschloss: Kennedy and Roosevelt, 113
1553 www.oocities.com/mark_willey/fdr.html retrieved 23 JUL 11
1554 Final Report, Aphrodite P., 81; Keen, Eyes, 239.
1555 Letter, ER to Eleanor, 30 OCT 44, Eleanor correspondence w. ER, FDR Lib
1556 Leonard Lyons column, 3 DEC 44, in the Miami News; FDR Appts Day-by-Day, FDR Lib
1557 TIME, 4 DEC 44
1558 Miami News, 22 NOV 44.
1559 Leonard Slater in San Diego Magazine, FEB 76
1560 Ibid
1561 AP, 28 JUL 47, in the Baltimore Sun
1562 San Diego Magazine, Vol. 78, JAN 76
1563 Westbrook Pegler column, 1 DEC 44, in LAT
1564 Secret Service records pert. to protection of ER, FDR Lib
1565 INS reportage, 4 DEC 44, in the Milwaukee Sentinel; also San Diego Magazine, FEB 76
1566 NYT, 4 DEC 44
1567 San Diego Magazine, Vol. 78, JAN 76
1568 ER: Mother R., 58
1569 John Rosenfield: The Passing Show column, In DallasMN, 01 APR 45
1570 A Sedona local historian, Randall Reynolds, has covered the Fryes' hosting of the honeymoon at www.sedonalegendhelenfrye.com, retr. 27 AUG 11
1571 Leonard Slater in San Diego Magazine, FEB 76
1572 Senate, Brewster Committee Hearings, 1947, Part 40, 24052
1573 SBC Hearings, 1947, Part 40, 24053
1574 SBC Hearings, 1947, Part 40, 24630-1; the appendix reproduced a large number of bills associated with the entertainment of Mr. Roosevelt.
1575 SBC Hearings, 1947, Part 40, 24063
1576 Drew Pearson, Lewiston Daily Sun, 2 JUN 50; J. Alsop, Toledo Blade, 18 OCT 51. For more snippets on the Alien Properties corruption, see Drew Pearson column (Washington Merry Go Round, 30 MAY 58.
1577 Alsop column, 30 JAN 52, in Lewiston Morning Tribune
1578 Russo: Supermob, 106, 110.
1579 Drew Pearson column, 23 FEB 55, in Greensburg Daily Tribune
1580 Arizona Daily Star, Tucson, 4 FEB 59
1581 NYT, 15 SEP 55. STOL: Short Take-Off and Landing.
1582 Randall Reynolds discussed the Hughes meeting at www.sedonalegendhelenfrye.com, r. 27 AUG 11
1583 Arizona Daily Star, Tucson, 4 FEB 59
1584 www.sedonalegendhelenfrye.com, retr. 27 AUG 11
1585 NYT, 18 APR 44
1586 Kean, 157; FDR Appointments Day-to-Day, FDR Lib
1587 SBC Hearings, 1947, PART 40 appendix
1588 Eleanor My Day Column, 4 JAN 45, at FDR Lib collection
1589 Letter, ER to Eleanor, 17 OCT 44, Eleanor correspondence w. ER, FDR Lib
1590 Letter, ER to Eleanor, 30 OCT 44, Eleanor correspondence w. ER, FDR Lib
1591 SBC Hearings, 1947, PART A, 24020-1
1592 Kean: Eyes, 157
1593 ChigTrib, 18 JAN 45.
1594 See Dixon interview, Appendix.

1595 Marrett: HH Aviator, 232
1596 Letter, Rotchford to Pegler, 22 AUG 46, ER military file, Pegler/HH
1597 www.bullmastiff.us/index.php, retr. 29 AUG 11
1598 NYT, 11 AUG 45
1599 ER: Mother R., 58
1600 Curtis Roosevelt, 268-9
1601 Parks: A Family in Turmoil, 52.
1602 ER: Mother R., 58
1603 NYT, 10 FEB 45
1604 AP, 18 JAN 45, in The Norwalk Hour
1605 NYT, 26 JAN 45
1606 NYT, 11 FEB 45
1607 Serling, 166
1608 Letter, DP to officers, ER file, Drew Pearson collection, LBJ Lib
1609 NYT, 30 JAN 45
1610 JR: My Parents, 65
1611 Curtis Roosevelt, 32
1612 NYT, 20 JAN 45
1613 NYT, 24 JAN 45
1614 NYT, 10 FEB 45
1615 UP, 11 FEB 45, in the Sunday Morning Star
1616 ER: As He Saw It, 230
1617 UP, 1 DEC 45, in Pittsburgh Post-Gazette
1618 ER: Mother R., 70-71; child attack, letter Eleanor to Anna, 5 DEC 45, in Asbell, 200
1619 Kessler, 271
1620 Letter, HB to Steve Early, 11 JUN 43, and numerous subsequent letters to/from Early, Emanuel, Smith, Carter, and others, Butcher correspondence, DDE Lib
1621 Letter, ER to Eleanor, 23 OCT 44, Eleanor correspondence w. ER, FDR Lib
1622 Letter, FDR to ER, 3 MAR 45, in ER: FDR Letters, 2/1572
1623 Letter, Eleanor to Anna, 9 MAY 45, in Asbell, 188
1624 ChigTrib, 26 JAN 45
1625 CongRec, Senate, 12 FEB 45, 1052; NYT, 30 JAN 45, 13 FEB 45; TIME, 5 FEB 45. FDR kept a copy of the CongRec page, yeas and nays highlighted, in the family file. FDR Lib.
1626 Drew Pearson column, 2 FEB 45, in DallasMN
1627 Drew Pearson column, 4 JUN 44, in St. Petersburg Times
1628 Ward: Closest Companion, 390
1629 ER: As He Saw It, 229
1630 ER: As He Saw It, 230
1631 Senate, Brewster Committee Hearings, 1947, Part 40, 24008
1632 NYT, 13 FEB 45
1633 See footnote to "Rusty Secrecy" section
1634 Arnold: American Air Power Comes of Age (Diary Vol II), 42
1635 Letter, Arnold to Spaatz, 15 JAN 45, LOC/Spaatz, 1-20
1636 Letter, Giles to Spaatz, 21 JAN 45, LOC/Spaatz, 1-20
1637 Letter, Spaatz to Arnold, 29 JAN 45, LOC/Spaatz/1-20.
1638 Senate, Brewster Committee Hearings, 1947, Part 40, 24009
1639 JR: My Parents, 223
1640 OHI with C.R. Smith, Eleanor project, FDR Lib
1641 ibid
1642 ER Wartime Service file, ER box, Pegler/HH
1643 Memorandum based on informant assertions in Pegler's ER wartime file, HH Lib
1644 Letter, Beach to Wesson, 16 OCT 47, ER Wartime, ER box, Pegler/HH
1645 Ward: Closest Companion, 390 (diary for 22JAN); Letter, Giles to Spaatz, 21JAN45, LOC/Spaatz, 1-20
1646 NYT, 25 MAR 45; OHI with Doolittle, AFHRA
1647 Keen: Eyes, 284
1648 Keen: Eyes, 288-9

1649 Letter, ER to Eleanor, 2 MAR 45, Eleanor correspondence with ER, FDR Lib
1650 Quoted in Pegler column, 17 AUG 46, New York Herald American
1651 Keen: Eyes, 204-5; Chaney, Cieply: The Hearsts: Family and Empire, the later years, 124-5
1652 Letter, Rotchford to Pegler, 22 AUG 46, ER wartime file, Pegler/HH Lib
1653 NPRC discharge document for ER; also Pittsburgh Press, 5 AUG 47
1654 ER Personnel Record, ER file, PPF, FDR Lib
1655 ibid
1656 Ward: Closest Companion, 198
1657 Patricia R: I Love a Roosevelt, 151
1658 American Mercury, NOV 43, 542
1659 ER Certificate of Service, ER file, NPRC; ER Testimony, Hartford Loan file, ER box, Pegler/HH Lib
1660 ER file at NPRC, retr. 15 DEC2010, Req # 1-9190795309
1661 ER: As He Saw It, 56
1662 CongRec, 5 MAR 43, 1618
1663 Maurer, AF Units; Letter, Col. Rockwell to Pegler, 29 OCT 47, Pegler/HH; NPRC personnel records.
1664 This section is based on the transcript of Eldridge's court-martial, JAN 44, NPRC.
1665 Eldridge's Court-Martial testimony.
1666 Lt. Ludwick Zupancic maintained this in his Pegler correspondence.
1667 Court-martial file on Lt. Col. Eldridge, 1943-44, 176 pages, NPRC.
1668 Letter, Eldridge to Pegler, ER wartime file, Pegler/HH Lib
1669 Letter, Zupancic to Pegler, ER wartime file, Pegler /HH Lib
1670 NAPRW History items, AFRHA
1671 Letter, Best to Pegler, 24 AUG 47, ER wartime file, Pegler collection, HH Lib
1672 NAPRWHIST, AFHRA
1673 From an unsigned sheet titled "Stories about Elliott told by Members of his Old Photoreconnaissance Outfit," ER wartime file, Pegler collection, HH Lib
1674 Porter: Howard Hughes Hell's Angel, 396-402; NYT, 10 DEC 42
1675 Babington Smith: Air Spy, 156
1676 ER: As He Saw It, 226
1677 Babington Smith, 255-6
1678 Radio Script "As They Saw Him," 25, Minnewa Bell papers, FDR Lib
1679 ER: Rendez-vous, 410
1680 Bishop: FDR's Last Year, 592-9, 604.
1681 ER: Rendez-vous, 411
1682 Bishop, 592-9; "early morning": Churchill: WW2, VII/412
1683 Presumably meaning SHAEF, Supreme Headquarters Allied Expeditionary Force, then in Versailles.
1684 ER file, Robert D. Graff collection, TV scripts, 122-3, FDR Lib. Slight variations of the text exist.
1685 ER: Eleanor Roosevelt with Love, 100
1686 Baruch, 353; ER file, Minnewa Bell interview 25, FDR Lib; Letter DD to FDR, 19 JUN 44, PSF
1687 Baruch, 355
1688 ER: Eleanor Roosevelt with Love, 100-1
1689 Eleanor: This I Remember, 344-5
1690 Truman: Memoirs, I/36
1691 Miller: Plain Speaking.
1692 Memo, HQ USSTAF to Commanding General 8th AF, 18 APR 45
1693 ER: Mother R., 40
1694 NYT, 31 JUL 45
1695 NYT, 1 AUG 45
1696 ChigTrib, 30 JUL 45
1697 Memo, Gen. William E. Hall to Gen. Anderson, 30 JUL 45, Anderson collection, Hoover Institution
1698 Memo, War Dept (Lt. Col. Davenport) to Gen. Vaughan, ER file, White House Confidential File, War Dept. (1 of 5), Truman correspondence, HST Lib
1699 Ibid
1700 DallasMN, 31 JUL 45

1701 DallasMN, 1 AUG 45
1702 Pittsburgh Press, 14 AUG 45
1703 Miami News, 16 AUG 45
1704 ER, Mother R., 54-55
1705 Collier, 436; ChigTrib, 30 JUL 45
1706 Interview with ER in Spokane Chronicle, 9 FEB 82
1707 Drew Pearson column, 19 FEB 47, in the Free-Lance Star
1708 Berg: Lindbergh, 487-8
1709 Clippings from Poughkeepsie New Yorker, 28 JUN 46, in Pegler/HH; and numerous other newspaper quotations; ChigTrib 18 JUL 48, 17 DEC 49, 18 DEC 49, 25 DEC 49.
1710 NYT, 6 DEC 41
1711 NYT, 13 OCT 40
1712 ChigTrib, 2 MAR 46
1713 FCC Hearings 1945, II/98, 106
1714 FCC Hearings 1945, II/110-1
1715 JR: My Parents, 177, 247
1716 The transcripts are at the Truman Library.
1717 McKean: Peddling Influence, 180-6.
1718 Washington Times-Herald, 15 JUN 45
1719 ChigTrib, 2 MAR 46
1720 Alva Johnston in Saturday Evening Post, 13 OCT 45
1721 NYT, 10 FEB 44
1722 House FCC Hearings, 1945, III/387
1723 NYT, 9 FEB 44
1724 McKean, ch. 12
1725 NYT, 25 NOV 1944
1726 Alva Johnston in Saturday Evening Post, 13 OCT 45
1727 FCC Hearings, 1945, Final Report 44.
1728 New York to Moscow Message 786, 1JUN44. On the pub. NSA website (The Venona Story / Benson)
1729 ChigTrib, 2 MAR 46
1730 FCC Hearings, 1945, Roberts testimony, III.
1731 FCC Hearings, 1945, III/388-9
1732 Alva Johnston in the Saturday Evening Post, 13 OCT 45.
1733 NYT, 23 NOV 44; details in FCC Hearings 1945, I/89-90.
1734 NYT, 17 FEB 44
1735 NYT, 26 FEB 44
1736 Daniels: White House Witness, 168
1737 Alva Johnston in the Saturday Evening Post, 13 OCT 45
1738 See editorial, Toledo Blade, 1 DEC 44 for the political meaning of the Littell case.
1739 NYT, 27 FEB 44
1740 NYT, 29 NOV 44
1741 NYT, 29 NOV 44; Washington Times-Herald, 29 JUN 45, in Pegler / HH Lib
1742 Washington Times-Herald, 29 JUN 1945, investigative reporting by W.P. Flythe. Found in Pegler/HH.
1743 Alva Johnston in Saturday Evening Post, 13 OCT 45.
1744 McKean, 187; Alva Johnston, op cit.
1745 Alva Johnston in Saturday Evening Post, 13 OCT 45.
1746 NYT, 15 DEC 44
1747 NYT, 4 JAN 44
1748 FCC Hearings, 1945, Final Report, 48
1749 FCC Hearings, 1945, Final Report, 58
1750 AP, 29 NOV 44 in the Spartanburg Herald
1751 NYT, 23 NOV 44
1752 FCC Hearings, 1945, Part 5, 4819-23.
1753 Letter, Ewing to Julia Pegler, 21 JUN 45, Hartford file, Pegler/HH Lib
1754 ChigTrib, 2 MAR 46; NYT 2 MAR 46
1755 ChigTrib, 8 OCT 49

1756 McKean, 188-9.
1757 Pegler column, Washington Times-Herald, 12 JUN 45
1758 Pegler column, Rome News-Tribune, 29 MAR 55
1759 LAT, 2 AUG 45
1760 NYT, 1 AUG 45
1761 Adams Testimony, 12, 23 JUL 45, Hartford Loan file, ER box, Pegler/HH Lib
1762 NYT, 16 OCT 51. The notes and associated correspondence is reproduced in Jesse Jones's memoir.
1763 Unattributed letter about "Uncle Jessie" to WP, 17 MAY 48, Broadcast file, ER box, Pegler/HH Lib
1764 NYT, 4 JUN 41
1765 NYT, 14 JUN 41
1766 Jones, 293-4
1767 Drew Pearson column in DallasMN, 23 JUL 45
1768 NYT, 16 OCT 51
1769 ChigTrib, 16 OCT 51
1770 ER Testimony, 61, 111, Hartford Loan File, ER box, Pegler/HH Lib
1771 Jones, 294
1772 ER Testimony, 127-45 et passim, Hartford Loan File, ER box, Pegler/HH Lib
1773 Ewing Testimony, 19, 11 JUL 45, Hartford Loan File, ER box, Pegler/HH Lib
1774 Jones, 295
1775 Jones, 296
1776 Jones, 300
1777 UP, DallasMN, 25 SEP 45
1778 Jones, 302-3
1779 Flynn, John T.: The Roosevelt Myth, 273
1780 Jones, 300
1781 News Clipping dated 16 JAN 46, Hartford Loan File, ER box, Pegler/HH Lib
1782 Farley: The Roosevelt Years, 169
1783 Roeser Testimony to Bureau of Internal Revenue, 5 SEP 45, in Hartford File, ER box, Pegler/HH
1784 UP, 11 JUL 45, in Pittsburgh Post-Gazette
1785 Pegler column, 27 DEC 46, clipping in the Pegler Vertical File, Miscellaneous/Columns, FDR Lib.
1786 Letter, G.W. to Pegler, 14 NOV 45, Broadcast file, ER box, Pegler/HH
1787 Clip, 27 AUG 45, Schenectady Gazette, UP; column 28 SEP 45 ER/B. file, Pegler/HH; UP, 27 SEP 45, in Pittsburgh Press quotes Daily Variety (show-business mag.) that ER's stock was now worth $1.5 million.
1788 Ewing testimony, 8; also Pegler column, 19 JUL 45, in Toledo Blade
1789 W.P. Flythe Sr., in Washington-Times Herald, 4 JUL 45; & the testimonies of several principals to BIR.
1790 Adams testimony, 1, 23 JUL 45, ER/Broadcast file, Pegler/HH Lib
1791 AP report in DallasMN, 22 SEP 45
1792 U.S. House of Representatives, 79th Congress, 1st Session, Report Nr. 1033: Reporting the Matter of the Loan of John A. Hartford to Elliott Roosevelt, 1 OCT 45, pp 1-9 contains the minority report quoted here.
1793 ibid
1794 Ewing testimony, 17, ER/Broadcast file, Pegler/HH Lib
1795 ER testimony, 194, ER/Broadcast file, Pegler/HH Lib
1796 Letter, Tucker to Pegler, 23 JUL 45, ER/Broadcast file, Pegler/ HH Lib
1797 Minority Report, House Investigation of the Hartford Loan issue, 1945.
1798 Hartford Affidavit, ER/Broadcast file, Pegler/HH Lib; also in Congressional Record, with elisions
1799 Ibid, 7
1800 Ewing testimony, 5-6, ER/Broadcast file, Pegler/HH Lib
1801 Hartford testimony, ER/Broadcast file, Pegler/HH Lib
1802 ER testimony, 23, ER/Broadcast file, Pegler/HH Lib
1803 Memo, Ewing, 31 MAR 39, ER/Broadcast file, Pegler/HH Lib
1804 ER testimony, 23, ER/Broadcast file, Pegler/HH Lib
1805 Hartford testimony, 29 JUL 45, ER/Broadcast file, Pegler/HH; also Minority Report, 1 OCT 45
1806 Ewing testimony, 18, ER/Broadcast file, Pegler/HH Lib
1807 Hartford testimony, ER/Broadcast file, Pegler/HH Lib

[1808] ibid
[1809] Quoted in Congressional Record, 6079, 4 OCT 40.
[1810] TIME, 10 OCT 38
[1811] Letter, Pegler to FDR, 18 JUL 34, PPF 1403, FDR Lib
[1812] Pegler column, 26 AUG 47, in Reading Eagle.
[1813] Pegler columns, 1 APR 60, 14 OCT 60, in Park City Daily News. AVCO: one of the forebears of American Airlines.
[1814] JR: My Parents, 189
[1815] Seattle Times, 01 NOV 90
[1816] JR: Affectionately, 213
[1817] Account in Seattle Times, 01 NOV 90, by Emmett Watson
[1818] OHI with ER on Eleanor, 35-6, FDR Lib; Pegler column, 24 AUG 54, in Sarasota Herald Tribune discusses tax targeting in detail; JR also confirms tax story in My Parents, 190.
[1819] Lomazov: FDR's Deadly Secret; Josephson: The Strange Death of F.D.R.
[1820] Report to DFBI, 4 JUL 45, ER FBI File (FOIA); the following excerpts are from that file unless stated.
[1821] NYT, 18 DEC 38; Pegler column 6 JUL 45, in the Evening Independent
[1822] NYT, 14 MAY 41
[1823] ChigTrib, 18 JUL 45
[1824] Kantor testimony, A-147, ER/Broad. file, Pegler/HH; letter, Eleanor to Anna, 10SEP41, in Asbell, 137
[1825] Quote was encountered but source could not be verified in time for publication.
[1826] Steinberg, 170
[1827] Morgan: FDR, 446
[1828] Steinberg, 224
[1829] Jones, 266
[1830] NYT, 16 OCT 51
[1831] FBI file quote; NYT 26 NOV 41; Kantor testimony, ER/Broadcast file, Pegler/HH
[1832] Letter, Oswald Villard to Pegler, quoting the financial columnist John F. Sinclair, 14 JUN 1945
[1833] Corresp. Landon–Pegler, and numerous other letters, JAN47, ER/Comm.Enterprises.Misc, Pegler/HH
[1834] Kantor testimony, F-150, 94, ER/Broadcast file, Pegler/HH
[1835] Ewing testimony, 15, ER/Broadcast file, Pegler/HH
[1836] Kantor testimony, 110, 24 JUL 45, ER/Broadcast file, Pegler/HH
[1837] Ewing testimony per telephone, 3-4, 20 AUG 45, ER/Broadcast file, Pegler/HH
[1838] Kantor testimony, ER/Broadcast file, Pegler/HH
[1839] Kantor testimony, B-128, ER/Broadcast file, Pegler/HH
[1840] ibid
[1841] Ibid, C-166-8
[1842] Ibid, C-17, 177
[1843] Ibid, D-132
[1844] Ibid. Murphy made numerous visits to the White House during this episode.
[1845] Ibid, D-199
[1846] Kantor testimony, A-63, ER/Hartford Loan file, Pegler/HH
[1847] Kantor testimony, A-80-5, ER/Hartford Loan file, Pegler/HH
[1848] Pegler column, 9 AUG 46, New York Journal American touches on Hall-Segal relation.
[1849] NYT, 18 DEC 47
[1850] Memo, JEH to subordinates, 4 JUL 45, in ER FBI file, FOIA request
[1851] Arizona Daily Star, 25 JUN 69
[1852] Buckley in the New Yorker, 1 MAR 04
[1853] Kantor testimony, D-4, ER/Hartford file, Pegler/HH
[1854] Ibid, D-6
[1855] Ibid, D-7
[1856] ER testimony, U.S. Treasury, 45, 1945, ER/Hartford file, Pegler/HH
[1857] Ibid, 46
[1858] Letter, Eleanor to Anna, 17 JUL 39, in Asbell, 109
[1859] LAT, 21 AUG 45
[1860] LAT, 27 JUL 45
[1861] LAT, 26 NOV 45

1862 Pegler attempted to find out who Stratton really was and collected several letters of hearsay about him.
1863 The Blood Horse, 16 JUN 45
1864 LAT, 26 NOV 45
1865 Wire, Pegler to Flaherty of LA Examiner, ER/Stratton, Pegler/HH
1866 Pegler column, 9 JUN 58, in Sarasota Herald Tribune
1867 ibid
1868 ibid
1869 ibid
1870 Greenville, SC Newspaper clipping in Minnewa Bell papers, FDR Lib, and other local press coverage.
1871 NYT, 6 JUL 45
1872 Discussed by columnist Marquis Childs, 10 JUL 45, in the Miami News.
1873 Lawrence: Air Transportation, 207
1874 NYT, 6 JUL 45
1875 Clipping of Joseph Heart article, Chicago Tribune, 6 JUL 45, in ER/Misc, Pegler/HH
1876 Daniels: White House Witness, 185, 240-1
1877 NYT, 31 JUL 45
1878 ibid
1879 ChigTrib, 12 JUL 45
1880 Barlett: Empire, 216
1881 FBI file on Howard Hughes, public, report late 1945.
1882 FBI file on Howard Hughes, public, report 5 MAY 45
1883 Ibid, 19 MAY 45
1884 FBI file on Hughes / Meyer, public.
1885 Barlett: Empire, 146
1886 Ray Tucker column in DallasMN, 17 FEB 54
1887 Editorial, DallasMN, 18 FEB 54
1888 Vidal, Gore: Point to Point Navigation, Ch. 12/1
1889 Senate, Brewster Committee Hearings, 1947, Part 40, 24071
1890 NYT, 31 JAN 46
1891 NYT, 20 SEP 46
1892 NYT, 10 DEC 46
1893 NYT, 28 SEP 46
1894 Letter, Zahnto to Pegler, 6 NOV 47, ER/Misc, Pegler/HH
1895 ER: the Conservators, 216
1896 ER: Mother R., 42
1897 NYT, 17 MAY 45
1898 Eleanor to HST, 14 MAY 45, Truman Lib
1899 Gentry: Hoover, 366
1900 Meacham: Franklin & Winston, xv
1901 Eleanor column, 22 JUN 45, My Day, FDR Lib
1902 Joseph Starobin in the Daily Worker, 13 JUN 45; Adam Lapin, ibid, 26 JUN 45
1903 LAT, 19 APR 47
1904 NYT, 27 MAR 48; 4 APR 48
1905 ER: As He Saw It, 247-8
1906 Telegram, Moscow Embassy to Sec. State, 21 AUG 46, Dept of State, released under FOIA.
1907 ER: Mother R., 103
1908 NYT, 20 OCT 46, 1 NOV 46
1909 NYT, 13 NOV 46
1910 Collier, 441
1911 AP, 2 NOV 46, in Spokane Daily Chronicle
1912 Look, 4 SEP 47
1913 Newsweek, 27 NOV 46; NYT, 2 DEC 46
1914 Cable, Stockholm Legation to Sec. State, 5 NOV 46, per State Dept. FOPA.
1915 Truman: Memoirs, I/552

[1916] Telegram, Moscow embassy to Sec. State, 29 MAR 47, per Dept. State FOIA
[1917] FBI file on ER, 2 APR 47, FOIA
[1918] ChigTrib, 1 DEC 46
[1919] Extensive coverage by Walter Cronkite, UP Moscow correspondent, 30NOV46, clipping from "World" in Kohlberg papers, HHI; NYT, 29 NOV 47, 2 DEC 46; Editorial, San Jose Evening News, 2 DEC 46
[1920] ChigTrib, 7 DEC 46
[1921] Leonard Slater in San Diego Magazine, FEB 76
[1922] OHI with Sue Sarafian Jehl, DDE Lib
[1923] Leonard Lyons column, 5 DEC 44, in Miami News
[1924] OHI with Mattie Pinette, 66-7, George Hall Papers, DDE Lib
[1925] Henry J. Taylor, Scripps-Howard News Service, 6 DEC 46
[1926] Walter Cronkite, UP Staff Correspondent, 30NOV46, clipping from "World" in Kohlberg papers, HHI.
[1927] NYT, 2 DEC 46
[1928] Telegram, Moscow Embassy to Sec. State, 29 NOV 46, per State Dept. FOIA
[1929] Cronkite: A Reporter's Life, 148
[1930] Eubank: Summit at Teheran, III/A Second Mission to Moscow
[1931] Cronkite: A reporter's life, 147-8
[1932] UP, DallasMN, 27 DEC 46
[1933] DallasMN, 01 DEC 46
[1934] DallasMN, 27 DEC 46
[1935] FDR's Son Turns Table on "Smear" Guys, Daily Worker, 12 FEB 47
[1936] ibid
[1937] UP, New York (8 FEB 47), in Pittsburgh Press, 8 FEB 47
[1938] Telegram, Warsaw embassy to Sec. State, 15 DEC 46, per State Dept. FOIA
[1939] Radio Script "As They Saw Him," 14, In Minnewa Bell papers on ER, FDR Lib
[1940] Look, 4 FEB 47; also reported in advance in the press.
[1941] ER: Eleanor Roosevelt with Love, 100
[1942] Keyssar: Remembering War, 229
[1943] Collier, 442
[1944] AP Interview with ER, 7 FEB 86, in Houston Chronicle
[1945] Montefiore, 638
[1946] AP Interview with ER, 7 FEB 86, in Houston Chronicle.
[1947] ER: As He Saw It, 220
[1948] Lomazov, FDR's Deadly Secret, 73, 195-8, et passim.
[1949] Collier, 442; Arnold: Global 466. The young exiled Stalin had traveled in Europe, including London.
[1950] Keyssar: Remembering War, 178
[1951] Look, 4 FEB 47
[1952] ER: Mother R., 107
[1953] NYT, 24 DEC 46
[1954] ER: Mother R., 107-8
[1955] Look, 18 FEB 47
[1956] ER file, 6 JAN 50, 12 JAN 50, FBI, FOIA
[1957] Leonard Lyons column in Pittsburgh Post Gazette, 19JAN50; LL column in Miami News, 29 MAR 50.
[1958] ER: Eleanor Roosevelt with Love, 119
[1959] ER: Mother R, 177
[1960] ER: Mother R., 55
[1961] OHI with Henry Morgenthau III, 2-6, FDR Lib.
[1962] Asbell, 263
[1963] ER: Eleanor Roosevelt with Love, 113
[1964] The publishing dispute and Elliott's timely intervention also detailed in Lash, A World of Love, 298-9.
[1965] Collier, 455
[1966] ER: Mother R., 153
[1967] NYT, 9 APR 48
[1968] Minnewa Bell papers, radio script "As They Saw Him," 5, FDR Lib
[1969] Eleanor: On My Own, 8
[1970] Minnewa Bell papers, radio script, 5, FDR Lib

1971 NYT, 18 DEC 47
1972 ER: Mother R., 199
1973 NYT, 24 DEC 48
1974 NYT, 9 APR 48
1975 ChigTrib, 28 DEC 48
1976 ChigTrib, 28 DEC 48
1977 Washington Times-Herald, 13 SEP 49
1978 FBI file on ER, New York office memo, 29 DEC 48, FOIA
1979 JR: My Parents, 311
1980 Collier, 453
1981 ER: Mother R., 103; Collier, 441
1982 Lash: A World of Love, 387; PR: I Love, 97-9; AP/Mary Campbell in Gettysburg Times, 10 AUG 84
1983 Miami News, 8 FEB 47; LAT, 8 FEB 47
1984 Lash: A World of Love, 387
1985 ER: Mother R., 221
1986 OHI with ER on Eleanor, 28-9, FDR Lib.
1987 Drew Pearson column, 6FEB54 for James's harrowing marriage and successful congressional campaign.
1988 ER: Mother R., 167
1989 UP, 18 FEB 50, in Oxnard Press-Courier; also see LIFE, "The truth about the Stork," 4 FEB 47
1990 New York Sunday Herald, 7 SEP 52
1991 New York Sunday Herald, 12 OCT 58
1992 New York Sunday Herald, 7 SEP 52
1993 UP/St. Joseph News-Press, 21 APR 50
1994 New York Sunday Herald, 12 OCT 58
1995 Washington Daily News, 21 JUN 50; Washington Post, 4 JUL 50
1996 Minnewa Bell papers; FDR Mem. Fnd. Series I IV.A.4 ER, FDR Lib
1997 UPI, The Bulletin, 10 MAR 83
1998 JR: My Parents, 311
1999 OHI with Minnewa Bell, on Eleanor, 22, FDR Lib
2000 NYT, 17 JUN 51, 18 JUN 51;
2001 Collier, 458
2002 OHI with ER on Eleanor, 31, FDR Lib; Interview in New York Post Mag., 1 APR 74.
2003 OHI with Henry Morgenthau III, 31, FDR Lib
2004 OHI, Henry Morgenthau III, 33.
2005 JR: My Parents, 46, 293
2006 NYT, 4 MAY 47
2007 JR: My Parents, 55, 313
2008 Details of Elliott's grandiose plans for Hyde Park businesses are preserved in Pegler/HH Elliott files.
2009 TIME, 19 APR 48
2010 Letter, Trohan to Pegler, 25 MAY 50, in Pegler/HH
2011 Case History [F-11 HIST] of the Hughes F-11, Wright Field Materiel Division, 1946, AFHRA. Details unless otherwise cited are from it.
2012 Marrett, 61
2013 Senate, Brewster Committee Hearings, 1947, Part 40, 24497-8
2014 SBC Hearings, 1947, Part 43, 26413
2015 Marrett, 61
2016 F-11 HIST
2017 F-11 HIST
2018 SBC Hearings, 1947, Part 40, 23860; also in F-11 HIST
2019 SBC Hearings, 1947, Part 40, 23861
2020 F-11 HIST
2021 SBC Hearings, 1947, Part 43, 26332
2022 F-11 HIST
2023 F-11 HIST

[2024] F-11 HIST
[2025] AP, 24 JUL 47, in Reading Eagle
[2026] Ibid; also SBC Hearings, 1947, Part A, 23638-9. Here Kaiser defended his "Heat of Hell" remark.
[2027] FBI file on Johnny Meyers/Howard Hughes, public, report dated 24 OCT 1945
[2028] AP, 29 JUL 47, in the Telegraph; Senate, Brewster Committee Hearings, 1947, Part A, 23580 and 23642
[2029] Published under Elliott Roosevelt's byline, 5AUG47. Scripps-Howard Service, here in Pittsburgh Press.
[2030] Senate, Brewster Committee Hearings, 1947, Part 40, 24058
[2031] SBC Hearings, 1947, PART 43, 23907. He meant one trip was for FDR's funeral.
[2032] Scripps-Howard interview continued.
[2033] NYT, 7 AUG 47
[2034] Following details are drawn from the Congressional Record hearing transcripts unless otherwise noted.
[2035] Marrett, 83-7
[2036] NYT, 03 AUG 47
[2037] Arnold: Global, 378
[2038] AP, 2 AUG 47, in St. Petersburg Times
[2039] Arnold: Global, 377-8
[2040] SBC Hearings, 1947, PART 43, 26374-5
[2041] SBC Hearings, 1947, PART 43, 26742
[2042] UP, 2 AUG 47, in Milwaukee Journal
[2043] SBC Hearings, 1947, PART 40, 24061-2 (JM) and 24051 (ER)
[2044] UP, 3 AUG 47, in Pittsburgh Press
[2045] UP, 26 JUL 47, in Windsor Daily Star
[2046] LIFE, 4 AUG 47
[2047] The expense reports and supporting bills were added in the appendix of the Senate hearings transcript.
[2048] NYT, 7 AUG 47
[2049] NYT, 12 AUG 47
[2050] SBC Hearings, 1947, PART 40, 24262-4
[2051] SBC Hearings, 1947, PART 43, 23700
[2052] SBC Hearings, 1947, PART 43, 24439
[2053] SBC Hearings, 1947, PART 43, 24445-6; the Jones-Arnold-FDR exchange is in PSF, Arnold/82.
[2054] NYT, 08 AUG 47
[2055] SBC Hearings, 1947, PART 40, 24227
[2056] SBC Hearings, 1947, PART 40, 24045
[2057] SBC Hearings, 1947, PART 40, 24057; also NYT, 6 AUG 47
[2058] SBC Hearings, 1947, PART 40, 24001-2
[2059] SBC Hearings, 1947, PART 40, 24055; also NYT, 06 AUG 47
[2060] Letter, McDonald to Norstad, 8 AUG 47, Norstad collection, DDE Lib
[2061] SBC Hearings, 1947, Part 40, 24121
[2062] SBC Hearings, 1947, Part 40, 24233
[2063] Higham, 115
[2064] Broeske/Brown: Howard Hughes, 278, quotes FBI file 62-1476-4.
[2065] Broeske/Brown, 231-232, details the orgy of competitive wiretapping.
[2066] TIME, 4 AUG 47
[2067] SBC Hearings, 1947, Part 40, 24026
[2068] SBC Hearings, 1947, Part 40, 24017-19
[2069] SBC Hearings, 1947, Part 40, 24067
[2070] SBC Hearings, 1947, Part 40, 24072-5
[2071] SBC Hearings, 1947, Part 40, 24036-7
[2072] SBC Hearings, 1947, Part 40, 24038
[2073] SBC Hearings, 1947, Part 40, 24041
[2074] SBC Hearings, 1947, Part 40, 24367
[2075] SBC Hearings, 1947, Part 40, 24366
[2076] SBC Hearings, 1947, Part 40, 24369-70
[2077] SBC Hearings, 1947, Part 40, 25245, Part 43, 26533
[2078] SBC Hearings, 1947, Part 43, 26526-7
[2079] SBC Hearings, 1947, Part 40, 24116

2080 SBC Hearings, 1947, Part 40, 24251
2081 SBC Hearings, 1947, Part 40, 24119; NYT 7 AUG 47 differs slightly.
2082 SBC Hearings, 1947, Part 40, 24184
2083 NYT, 7 AUG 47
2084 SBC Hearings, 1947, Part 40, 24278
2085 Anderson: Confessions, 59-60. Chptr describes in great detail Hughes-Pearson plot against Brewster.
2086 ibid
2087 Anderson, 96
2088 NYT, 9 AUG 47
2089 Senate, Brewster Committee Hearings, 1947, Part 40, 24268-9
2090 NYT, 22 JUN 47; Lash, A World of Love, 234
2091 The Evening Star, 19 APR 48
2092 Marrett, 94
2093 Senate, Brewster Committee Hearings, 1947, Part 43, 26516-7, 26652
2094 SBC Hearings, 1947, Part 43, 26653
2095 SBC Hearings, 1947, Part 43, 26791-2
2096 SBC Hearings, 1947, Part 43, 26233
2097 Senate, Brewster Committee Hearings, 1947, Part 43, 26234-41
2098 SBC Hearings, 1947, Part 43, 26218
2099 SBC Hearings, 1947, Part 43, 26237-8
2100 SBC Hearings, 1947, Part 43, 26238
2101 Montreal Gazette, 7 NOV 47
2102 Malayney, AAHS Journal, Spring 2007
2103 Fred Othman in the Pittsburgh Press, 6 NOV 47
2104 SBC Hearings, 1947, Part 43, 26230
2105 SBC Hearings, 1947, Part 43, 26231-2
2106 NYT, 6 NOV 47
2107 SBC Hearings, 1947, Part 43, 26522
2108 SBC Hearings, 1947, Part 43, 26670-1
2109 Senate, Brewster Committee Hearings, 1947, Part 43, 26272-3
2110 Letter, Wagner to Pegler, 17 DEC 52, ER/Hughes file, Pegler/HH Lib
2111 SBC Hearings, 1947, Part 43, 24446
2112 SBC Hearings, 1947, Part 43, 26589
2113 F-11 HIST; discussed in various parts of the SWIC Hearings.
2114 Senate, Brewster Committee Hearings, 1947, Part 43, 26321
2115 SBC Hearings, 1947, Part 43, 26320
2116 SBC Hearings, 1947, Part 43, 26319, 26330, et passim
2117 SBC Hearings, 1947, Part 43, 26353
2118 SBC Hearings, 1947, Part 43, 26378-80
2119 Letter, Arnold to Pegler, 1 MAR 46, ER/Hughes file, Pegler/HH
2120 SBC Hearings, 1947, Part 43, 26368
2121 SBC Hearings, 1947, Part 43, 26374-5
2122 SBC Hearings, 1947, Part 43, 26488-9
2123 SBC Hearings, 1947, Part 43, 26579
2124 The Robert H. Goddard case has been ably told in Clary, Robert: Rocket Man, Hyperion N.Y. 2003.
2125 SBC Hearings, 1947, Part 43, 26579
2126 SBC Hearings, 1947, Part 43, 26537 et passim
2127 SBC Hearings, 1947, Part 43, 26527 et passim
2128 SBC Hearings, 1947, Part 43, 26580
2129 SBC Hearings, 1947, Part 43, 26498
2130 Washington Daily News, 12 AUG 47, clipping in ER/Hughes, Pegler/HH Lib
2131 Washington Daily News, 12 AUG 47
2132 SBC Hearings, 1947, Part 43, 26603
2133 SBC Hearings, 1947, Part 43, 26392-3, 26600

[2134] SBC Hearings, 1947, Part 43, 26508, 26554 et passim
[2135] SBC Hearings, 1947, Part 43, 26392-3, 26600, 26605-6
[2136] SBC Hearings, 1947, Part 43, 26392-3, 26600, 26608
[2137] SBC Hearings, 1947, Part 43, 26607, edited
[2138] SBC Hearings, 1947, Part 43, 26644
[2139] SBC Hearings, 1947, Part 43, 26609, 26505
[2140] SBC Hearings, 1947, Part 43, 26708, 26731
[2141] SBC Hearings, 1947, Part 43, 26880, 26976, et passim
[2142] SBC Hearings, 1947, Part 43, 27143
[2143] *The Air Force Office of Special Investigations*, 1948-2000, by Col. Edward J. Hagerty, OSI History Office, contains an inside discussion of the Bennett Meyers debacle (Chapter 1).
[2144] SBC Hearings, 1947, Part 43, 27145-8
[2145] ER Interview, LAT, 01 MAR 90
[2146] ChigTrib, 23 JAN 61; PR, I Love a Roosevelt, 91-6, 119-25
[2147] PR: I Love a Roosevelt, 92-3
[2148] Collier, 465
[2149] Draft of "I Love a Roosevelt," by PR, 2/14, ER file, in Drew Pearson collection, LBJ Lib
[2150] PR: I Love a Roosevelt, 23
[2151] Special Interview, 25 MAY 80 in the Bend (OR) Bulletin
[2152] ER: Mother R., 181
[2153] OHI with Minnewa Bell, 3, ER on Hyde Park, FDR Lib
[2154] ChigTrib, 23 DEC 50
[2155] NYT, 23 DEC 50
[2156] NYT, 13 DEC 50
[2157] Parks: Family in Turmoil, 143
[2158] NYT, 12 OCT 51
[2159] NYT, 18 OCT 51
[2160] NYT, 10 JUL 52
[2161] NYT, 28 OCT 53, in "About New York" by Meyer Berger. Larrabee: Commander-in-Chief, 651, discusses the painting, but his year of sale must be wrong.
[2162] The publicly reported total varied from $211,000 to $275,000.
[2163] Flynn: the Roosevelt Myth, 275
[2164] NYT, 16 JAN 46, 3 APR 46
[2165] ER: Mother R., 52
[2166] JR on Eleanor, OHI, 10, FDR Lib
[2167] Alter: The Defining Moment, 226-7
[2168] LAT, 25 JUL 25, clipping in ER/files, Pegler/HH Lib
[2169] Roorda: The Dictator Next Door, 121; Diederich: Somoza, 21
[2170] Mekeel's Weekly Stamp News, 459, 24 DEC 45; in FDR/Stamp Collection, Pegler/HH Lib
[2171] Miami Sunday News, 15 MAR 51
[2172] ER: Mother R., 158
[2173] Pittsburgh Press, 13 MAR 51; ER, Mother R., 201
[2174] ER: Mother R, 200
[2175] Collier, 457
[2176] PR draft synopsis, 5, in Drew Pearson collection, LBJ Lib.
[2177] Collier, 466
[2178] Letter, Eleanor to Anna, 15 JAN 61, in Asbell, 347
[2179] OHI with Minnewa Bell, on Eleanor, 9, FDR Lib; Collier, 457
[2180] ER: Mother R., 203
[2181] ChigTrib, 30 JAN 52
[2182] Miami News, 8 MAR, 2 DEC 51; M. Herald, 11 JUL 52; NYT, 28 JAN 53; AP/Herald Trib., 27JAN 53.
[2183] NYT, 16 MAR 52
[2184] NYT, 13 JUN 52
[2185] Miami Herald, 7 AUG 52; NYT 14 NOV 54
[2186] NYT, 29 OCT 51
[2187] NYT, 28 APR 52, 2 SEP 52

2188 Miami Herald, 7 AUG 52
2189 Collier, 462
2190 ER: Mother R., 204
2191 ibid
2192 Ibid, 205
2193 Edwin Lahey in exposé of Cuban casinos, 8 JAN 58, in the Youngstown Vindicator/ Chic. Daily News.
2194 Confidential Security Information, 16 MAY 1952, AMEMBASSY, HABANA to Dept. of State
2195 Confidential Security Information, 16 MAY 1952, AMEMBASSY, HABANA to Dept. of State
2196 Edmund Chester: A Sergeant named Batista, 1954, Holt. Discussion in Havana Post, 22 APR 52.
2197 FBI file on ER, 30 JUN 52
2198 UPI, 15 MAR 52, in Reading Eagle
2199 Walter Winchell, 14 MAR 52, Daytona Beach Morning Journal
2200 NYT, 18 MAR 52
2201 ibid
2202 Voltz in Pittsburgh Press, 13 MAR 53
2203 ibid
2204 Toledo Blade, 22 APR 52
2205 Toledo Blade, 18 DEC 57
2206 PR: I Love A Roosevelt, 88
2207 ER: Mother R., 243
2208 Drew Pearson column, 8 MAR 38; Roorda, 121
2209 NYT, 21 DEC 42
2210 FDR Appointments Day-to-Day, FDR Lib
2211 Curtis Roosevelt Dall: Too Close to the Sun, 249-50
2212 PPF/6012, Trujillo file, FDR Lib; also numerous published accounts of Fish's corruption.
2213 Roorda, 111 et passim.
2214 Roorda, 197
2215 Drew Pearson column, 28 FEB 57, in St. Joseph Gazette
2216 NYT, 30 MAY 56, 12 SEP 56; 22 JUL 57
2217 NYT, 22 MAY 56
2218 NYT, 19 MAR 57
2219 NYT, 23 OCT 57, 28 JAN 58; Drew Pearson column, 30 MAY 58, in the Tuscaloosa News
2220 Drew Pearson column, 28 JAN 58, 28 MAR 58
2221 Drew Pearson column, 30 AUG 59
2222 ER: The Conservators, 91
2223 ER: The Conservators, 249
2224 Examples, Edwin Lahey's Cuban exposé, 8JAN58, in the Youngstown Vindicator/Chicago Daily News.
2225 English: Havana Nocturne, 289-291
2226 FDR Appts Day-by-Day, FDR Lib; NYT 29 OCT 44.
2227 Hardwick: Mall Maker, 49
2228 1966 manuscript, *President F.D.R.'s Shangri-La in Indio, CA, Fact or Fiction?* By P.S. Frederick of Indio. Monograph of Coachella Valley resident reminiscences. Describes "The Old Tower Ranch." Retr. 7 FEB12.
2229 Drew Pearson column, 25 JAN 53, in Herald-Journal.
2230 DDE: The Papers of, NATO and the campaign of 1952, 294, and many other references to WK-DDE.
2231 Letter, WK to John & Anna Boettiger, 17 DEC 45, Boettiger Papers, FDR Lib.
2232 Kirschner correspondence, Boettiger file, FDR Lib.
2233 Letter, Eleanor to Anna, 20 DEC 45, in Asbell, 202
2234 Letter, Eleanor to Anna, 28 JUL 47, in Asbell, 227
2235 Pegler column, 1 APR 49; Letter, Eleanor to Anna, 19 SEP 47, in Asbell, 229.
2236 Asbell, 278
2237 Pegler column, 21 FEB 50, 1 APR 50, Reading Eagle
2238 JR: My Parents, 306
2239 San Diego Magazine, Vol. 78, NOV 75
2240 Newton: Mr. Mob, 179; other sources vary on how much Lansky lost.

2241 Collier, 462
2242 Clipping, Minnewa Bell papers, FDR Lib
2243 OHI with Minnewa Bell, 29-30, FDR Lib
2244 Collier, 462
2245 OHI with Minnewa Bell on ER, 15, FDR Lib
2246 Eleanor, My Day, 27 AUG 57; Washington Reporter, 31 OCT 58
2247 Collier, 463
2248 ER: Mother R., 262
2249 UPI/Washington Reporter, 31 OCT 58
2250 Collier, 463
2251 PR: I Love A Roosevelt, 69; Collier, 463
2252 OHI with Tony Lindsley (grandchild) on Eleanor, FDR Lib
2253 Eleanor, My Day, 13 FEB 58
2254 FAA letter to author, 5 APR 11
2255 AP, 6 JUN 57, in Pittsburgh Post-Gazette
2256 NYT, 6 JUN 57
2257 UPI, 10 JUN 59, in St. Joseph Gazette
2258 PR: I Love A Roosevelt, 40
2259 UPI, 10 JUN 59, in St. Joseph Gazette
2260 UPI, 10 JUN 59, in Eugene Register Guard
2261 Russo, 469; NYT, 24 APR 82
2262 PR: I Love a R., 21, 23, 38; Scottsdale Progress, 1959.
2263 Eleanor, My Day, 13 JAN 60.
2264 UPI, 31 OCT 58, in Washington Reporter
2265 AP, 7 JAN 60, in the Spokesman-Review
2266 Collier, 464
2267 OHI with Minnewa Bell on ER, FDR Lib
2268 ER: Mother R., 254-5
2269 Letter, Eleanor to MB, Minnewa Bell papers, 89, FDR Lib; also OHI with MB on ER, 72-3
2270 PR draft manuscript, 1/9, Drew Pearson file, LBJ Lib
2271 Seattle Times obituary, 6 APR 96
2272 PR: I Love a Roosevelt, 42
2273 PR draft manuscript, 2/9, Drew Pearson file, LBJ Lib
2274 PR: I Love a Roosevelt, 49-50
2275 PR: I Love a Roosevelt, 71
2276 ER: Mother R., 266
2277 JR: My Parents, 294
2278 JR: My Parents, 310
2279 JR: My Parents, 294-5
2280 OHI with Minnewa Bell on ER, 13, FDR Lib
2281 PR: I Love, 119
2282 PR: I Love a Roosevelt, 128
2283 ChigTrib, 22 JAN 61
2284 Convictions detailed in UPI/Pittsburgh Post-Gazette, 29APR61; NYT reps. 26, 31 JAN 61, 30 APR 61.
2285 PR: I Love, 139-147, chronicles this dog disaster.
2286 Lash: Love, Eleanor, 120
2287 OHI with ER on Eleanor, 5, FDR Lib
2288 ER: Mother R., 61
2289 Collier, 469
2290 Minnewa Bell OHI, 100, FDR Lib
2291 PR draft manuscript, 11, Drew Pearson file, LBJ Lib
2292 PR: I Love a Roosevelt, 212
2293 PR draft manuscript, 11, Drew Pearson file, LBJ Lib
2294 PR: I Love a Roosevelt, 215-6
2295 PR draft manuscript, synopsis, 6, Drew Pearson file, LBJ Lib
2296 Lash: A World of Love, 553

2297 OHI with Chandler R. (Lindsley)/Elliott (Tony)R. Jr., Eleanor OH project, FDR Lib
2298 Collier, 436
2299 PR: I Love, 240
2300 PR: I Love, 253
2301 PR: I Love, 249
2302 Herbert Corey in the American Mercury, 161, ER file, Drew Pearson collection, LBJ Lib
2303 Jones, 289
2304 JR: My Parents 339
2305 Barlett/Steele: Empire, 220
2306 Drew Pearson column, 17 JUN 1936, St. Petersburg Times
2307 PR: I Love, 230; NYT, 2 FEB 54, 3 FEB 54
2308 ER: Mother R., 220; James gently summarized his catastrophic marriage to Romelle, My Parents, 318-9.
2309 ER: Mother R., 224
2310 UP/Pittsburgh Press and NYT, 2 FEB 54
2311 INS/Miami News, 4 FEB 54
2312 Collier, 478; JR: My Parents: 319; NYT, 17, 22 MAY 69.
2313 DallasMN, 24 AUG 64
2314 Collier, 478
2315 JR: My Parents, 314, 333
2316 Kessler, 376
2317 NYT, 14 JUN 58
2318 NYT, 15 MAR 63
2319 David Murray in Chicago Sun Times, 7 OCT 73
2320 ER: Eleanor Roosevelt with Love, 149
2321 HTNS, Hy Gardner, 6 FEB 64, in The Sumter Daily Item
2322 PR: I Love, 225
2323 PR manuscript, ER file, Drew Pearson collection, LBJ Lib
2324 ibid
2325 ibid
2326 Palm Beach Post, 4 APR 64
2327 Collier, 479; PR draft manuscript 11/8, in ER file, Drew Pearson collection, LBJ Lib
2328 FBI FOIA file on ER, report, 28 JUL 64
2329 ibid
2330 PR: I Love A Roosevelt, 134
2331 Elliott was quoted speaking at the DNC meeting in Tallahassee. AP / in Ocala Star Banner, 23 AUG 64
2332 Drew Pearson column, LAT, 30 OCT 64
2333 FBI FOIA file on ER
2334 ibid
2335 PR manuscript in ER file, Drew Pearson collection, LBJ Lib
2336 PR: I Love, 327-8
2337 Several articles in the Miami Herald, 29-30 JAN 1967, saved in FBI file.
2338 NYT, 19 MAY 69
2339 Las Vegas Review-Journal, 14 JAN 2012
2340 Collier, 1951, Vol 127/1, 12. The origins of Mafia control of Florida are in Kefauver Comm. Report.
2341 Miami News, 12 JUN 65
2342 PR: I Love, 331
2343 Interview by Paul Coates, NY Journal American, 27 NOV 65
2344 ER file, Drew Pearson collection, LBJ Lib
2345 Miami Beach Times, 28 MAY 65
2346 TIME, 11 JUN 65
2347 Drew Pearson column, 3 AUG 65, in the Free-Lance Star
2348 Clipping dated 8 MAY 66, ER Vertical File, FDR Lib
2349 PR: I Love, 350
2350 Miami News, 20 JAN 66

[2351] Letter, PR to DP, 8 NOV 68 (65?), ER file, Drew Pearson collection, LBJ Lib
[2352] Miami News, 16 DEC 66
[2353] Miami News, 12 JUN 65
[2354] Miami News, 14 MAY 71, 17 MAY 67
[2355] JR: My Parents, 309
[2356] Drew Pearson column, 3 JUN 67, in the Press Courier; Miami News, 7 JUN 67
[2357] Miami News, 22 MAR 71
[2358] AP, 4 MAY 71, in Sarasota Herald-Tribune
[2359] Sarasota Journal, 10 MAR 71
[2360] Miami News, 11 MAR 71
[2361] Ian Glass in The Miami News, 17 NOV 69
[2362] Miami Herald, 30 JAN 67: Fontainebleau: Mob Money's Beach Prize. In FBI file.
[2363] Prospect, 1968, ER file, in Kutner collection, HHI Lib
[2364] Senate Organized Crime Hearings, 1973, Part 3, 20 SEP, 3, 4 OCT 73, 422 e.a.
[2365] Letter, Kutner to ER, 24 JAN 68, in Kutner collection, HHI Lib
[2366] NYT, 26 JUL 66
[2367] St. Petersburg Times, 27 JUL 66
[2368] Miami News, 3 AUG 67
[2369] PR: I Love, 379-80
[2370] Miami News, 5 APR 66
[2371] Collier, 463; see also note to page 462.
[2372] Riesel column, 10 MAR 77, in the Rome News-Tribune
[2373] Hersh, 272; Russo, Ch. 17. Summers, 398-99, discusses the logistics of the pay-offs to Nixon.
[2374] NYT, 27 APR 57, 2 DEC 57
[2375] Anthony Summers: The Arrogance of Power, is one of the more detailed expositions of this link.
[2376] Miami News, 11 FEB 71
[2377] Miami News, 11 MAR 71
[2378] NYT, 9 JAN 72
[2379] Palm Beach Post, 4 MAY 71
[2380] ER's FBI file is full of such accusations from "patriotic" Americans. So was Truman's correspondence.
[2381] Beschloss, 263
[2382] NYT, 31 AUG 72; Palm Beach Post, 22 AUG 72
[2383] NYT, 1 OCT 72: "Rustling the strays from the D[emocratic] Ranch"
[2384] Bryce: Cronies, Chapter V
[2385] Connally, 148-152
[2386] ChigTrib, 17 FEB 52
[2387] Letter from Ford Roosevelt, NYT, 22 OCT 72
[2388] Dick Shaw in the Bangor Daily News, 3 AUG 84
[2389] ER: the Conservators, 292-3; UPI, 10 OCT 84, the Telegraph Herald
[2390] NYT, 19 SEP 73
[2391] Senate, Permanent Subcommittee on Investigations (Jackson Committee) Hearings, 1973.
[2392] NBC Evening News 12MAY88, Vanderbilt TVNews Archive, retr. 18 MAR 11; background in Farer, Transnational Crime in the Americas.
[2393] NYT, 27 AUG 67.
[2394] NYT, 2 SEP 67. Also Marvin Miller: The Breaking of the President 1974; and Newton, 226.
[2395] NYT, 26 AUG 67 for Sand's testimony, flight, and the book buy.
[2396] Barlett/Steele: Empire, 498-9; NYT, 7 JAN 68
[2397] AP, 19 SEP 73, Daytona Beach Sunday-News-Journal
[2398] UP, 19 SEP 73, Toledo Blade William Claiborne, special from the Washington Post, in Chicago Sun Times, 20 SEP 73; Anderson column, 2 OCT 73, 4 OCT 73.
[2399] William Claiborne, special from the Washington Post, in Chicago Sun Times, 20 SEP 73
[2400] ibid
[2401] NYT, 21 SEP 73
[2402] NYT, 20 SEP 73
[2403] Miami News, 27 SEP 73; Hearings, 194.
[2404] TIME, 1 OCT 73

2405 David Murray in Chicago Sun-Times, 7 OCT 73
2406 Newton, 178-9
2407 NYT, 5 OCT 73; Miami News, 23 MAY 71
2408 Senate, Jackson Committee Hearings, 1973, 327, 337-9
2409 Ibid, 390
2410 Ibid, 402
2411 Ibid, 390, 414
2412 Ibid, 391
2413 Ibid, 377
2414 Ibid, 381-2
2415 Washington Star News, 4 OCT 73
2416 Ibid, 407
2417 Ibid, 419
2418 Wall Street Journal, 18 OCT 73, carried an extensive report on the Noe-Roosevelt connection.
2419 Wall Street Journal, 18 OCT 73
2420 307 So.2d 883 (1974) No. 74-1214, Dist. Court of Appeal, FL 3rd District, 31 DEC 74.
2421 Senate, Jackson Committee Hearings, 189
2422 Senate, Jackson Committee Hearings, 362
2423 Senate, Jackson Committee Hearings, 1973, 390, 178-9
2424 Senate, Jackson Committee Hearings, 1973, 188
2425 Senate, Jackson Committee Hearings, 1973, 188-90
2426 Senate, Jackson Committee Hearings, 1973, 191
2427 NYT, 4 OCT 73
2428 Senate, Jackson Committee Hearings, 1973, 353-5, 362
2429 Senate, Jackson Committee Hearings, 1973, 193
2430 Senate, Jackson Committee Hearings, 1973, 328
2431 Senate, Jackson Committee Hearings, 1973, 333
2432 Miami News, 20 SEP 73
2433 Newton: Mr. Mob, 226
2434 Senate, Jackson Committee Hearings, 355
2435 Senate, Jackson Committee Hearings, 1973, 356
2436 Senate, Jackson Committee Hearings, 1973, 358
2437 Miami Herald, 29 JAN 67: Mob Money, in FBI file.
2438 Senate, Jackson Committee Hearings, 1973, 359
2439 Senate, Jackson Committee Hearings, 1973, 334
2440 Senate, Jackson Committee Hearings, 340
2441 Senate, Jackson Committee Hearings, 1973, 359-61
2442 Senate, Jackson Committee Hearings, 1973, 373
2443 Senate, Jackson Committee Hearings, 1973, 361
2444 Senate, Jackson Committee Hearings, 1973, 255
2445 John F. Berry of the Washington Post provided this account (28 APR 76, Watertown Daily Times).
2446 Senate, Jackson Committee Hearings, 1973, 360-1
2447 Senate, Jackson Committee Hearings, 1973
2448 Wall Street Journal, 18 OCT 73
2449 NYT, 11 MAY 73
2450 NYT, 9 AUG 66, 10 AUG 66
2451 NYT, 15 DEC 66
2452 JR: My Parents, 356
2453 NYT, 28 NOV 72
2454 NYT, 14 AUG 66, 10 FEB 73, 19 MAY 73, 27 SEP 73
2455 Russo, 346-347, 350.
2456 The IOS-Lansky link and the Bahamas operation is explored in Alan Block: Masters of Paradise, 1991.
2457 For a summary see for example Tom J. Farer (ed), Transnational crime in the Americas.
2458 NYT, 22 JUL 74

[2459] AP, 8 JUL 75, in Reading Eagle.
[2460] For example, Jane Denison/UPI, 19 JAN 74, Pittsburgh Press, part of a series of articles on the subject.
[2461] Article on Vesco by Ralph Blumenfeld and Josh Friedman of N.Y. Post, 17 JUN 73, Boca Raton News.
[2462] Collier, 478; Miami News, 22 MAR 71.
[2463] Senate, Jackson Comm. Hearings, 1973, 365. No record of Mastriana case in Elliott's released FBI file.
[2464] Miami News, 22 MAR 71
[2465] Senate, Jackson Committee Hearings, 1973, 374
[2466] Miami News, 20 SEP 73
[2467] Senate, Jackson Committee Hearings, 1973, 380.
[2468] Ibid, 379-80
[2469] Ibid, 432
[2470] Ibid, 446
[2471] Ibid, 352
[2472] Washington Afro-American, 28 JAN69
[2473] Senate, Jackson Committee Hearings, 1973, 420
[2474] Ibid, 427
[2475] ibid
[2476] Ibid, 428
[2477] Pittsburgh Press, 7 FEB 65
[2478] Senate, Jackson Committee Hearings, 1973, 386.
[2479] Jack Anderson column, 3 OCT 73, in Washington Star-News
[2480] Senate, Jackson Committee Hearings, 1973, 368
[2481] Wall Street Journal, 18 OCT 73
[2482] NYT, 12 DEC 73
[2483] Summers: *The Arrogance of Power*, Ch. 11, and notes, provide details of the Nixon-Rebozo relationship.
[2484] Connally, 258
[2485] Many have examined this relationship. Summers, *The Arrogance of Power*, details the Nixon-Mafia axis.
[2486] Interview in New York Post Mag., 1 APR 74
[2487] Collier, 479
[2488] Miami News, 22 MAR 71
[2489] Palm Beach Post, 4 MAY 71
[2490] Jim Bishop, 25 FEB 72, in the Beaver Country Times
[2491] Earl Wilson in the Sarasota Herald, 12 MAR 73
[2492] TIME, 23 APR 73
[2493] Letter, Hamilton Fish to editor, 25 APR 73, Evening News
[2494] NYT, 19 MAR 73
[2495] Jack Anderson column, 4 OCT 73, in the Spokane Daily Chronicle
[2496] JR on Eleanor, OHI, 1979, FDR Lib
[2497] JR on Eleanor, OHI, 1979, FDR Lib, 28
[2498] New York Post Mag., 1 APR 74
[2499] Washington Star News, 3 OCT 73
[2500] LAT, 29 DEC 72
[2501] New York Post Mag., 1 APR 74; Miami Herald quoted by AP 28 DEC 72.
[2502] Dept. of State, Cables decoded 2005, National Archives
[2503] New York Post Mag., 1 APR 74
[2504] 13 JUN 73 letter to NYT, publ. 27 JUN 73.
[2505] State Dept. cable, 21 SEP 73, National Archives
[2506] State Dept. cable, 23 JUL 1973, National Archives
[2507] NYT, 28 OCT 90.
[2508] Dept of State Cable, 19 FEB 75, National Archives
[2509] Collier, 480
[2510] JR: My Parents, 312
[2511] Seattle Times, 1 NOV 90; Parade Magazine, 10 OCT 82.
[2512] Collier, 480
[2513] Numerous accounts of JR-Nixon closeness. e.g. Miami Herald, 10JUN83; LAT, 29 MAR 76, 23MAY78.
[2514] AP, 12 FEB 83, in Palm Beach Post

2515 Hearing, the Subcomm. on Social Sec. and Family Policy of the Comm. on Finance, Senate, 20NOV 89.
2516 Congressional Record, 11 MAR 86, 4313; 11 JUN 86, 13372; 1987; Chicago Sun-Times, 17 MAR 86
2517 Chicago Sun Times, 17 MAR 86
2518 Palm Beach Daily News, 3 JAN 86
2519 Collier, 480
2520 ER: As He Saw It, 31-2
2521 UP, 2 DEC 45, in DallasMN, 3 DEC 45
2522 Gary Scott Smith: Faith and the Presidency, 194
2523 Clipping of an AP (New York) report in Minnewa Bell papers, FDR Lib.
2524 Arizona Daily Star, 28 OCT 90
2525 Memo, Mumford to Ladd, 30 APR 47, FBI file on ER.
2526 Radio Script "As They Saw Him," 8, in Minnewa Bell papers, FDR Lib
2527 Collier, 440
2528 mentioned in *The Ghost of Miss Truman* by Jon Breen, The Weekly Standard, 18 NOV 2002
2529 Eleanor, My Day, 25 NOV 49, gwu.edu Eleanor papers.
2530 ER FOIA FBI File
2531 ER: Mother R., 58, paraphrased for context.
2532 ER: Mother R., 82
2533 ER: As He Saw It, 247-52
2534 JR: My Parents, 169-70
2535 ER FBI file, Foreign Radio Broadcast, 10JUL47
2536 *The Nation*, 2 NOV 46; NYT, 6 OCT 46; Churchill, Memoirs of WW II, The Hinge of Fate, 680. "Rubbish" reported in American press NOV 50.
2537 Alsop column, 4 DEC 46, in the Miami News
2538 ibid
2539 Collier, 437
2540 Collier, 440
2541 Lash: A World of Love, 236-7; letter, Anna to Eleanor, 21 JUL 47, in Asbell, 225-6.
2542 Asbell, 225
2543 Lash: A World of Love, 237
2544 ER: Mother R., 113
2545 NYT, 20 MAY 73
2546 ibid
2547 OHI with ER on Eleanor, 8, FDR Lib
2548 Alice Roosevelt Longworth, President TR's daughter. (ER: Mother R, 44)
2549 JR: My Parents, 312
2550 The Spokesman-Review, Personality Parade, 19 JUL 75
2551 AP Charleston, 13 JUL 86, in the Rock Hill Herald.
2552 ER: the Conservators, prologue
2553 ER: the Conservators, 91, 260
2554 ER: the Conservators, 271; "I'm sorry" letter Weel to Curator, in ER Vertical File, FDR Lib.
2555 C. Champlin in LAT, 01 MAR 90
2556 Collier, 480
2557 PR: I Love a Roosevelt, 384, 387
2558 Collier, passim; Keyssar: Remembering War
2559 OHI with C.R. Smith, Eleanor project, FDR Lib
2560 Collier, 343
2561 The presidents: A reference history. H.F. Graff, 429
2562 Siena College Research Institute Survey; .siena.edu/sri/research, retr. 13 JAN 11
2562 ER, Mother R., 203

37013865R00462

Made in the USA
Lexington, KY
13 November 2014